Advanced Accounting

Fourteenth Edition

Joe B. Hoyle

Associate Professor of Accounting
Robins Teaching Fellow
Robins School of Business
University of Richmond

Thomas F. Schaefer

KPMG Professor of Accountancy
Mendoza College of Business
University of Notre Dame

Timothy S. Doupnik

Distinguished Professor Emeritus of Accounting
Darla Moore School of Business
University of South Carolina

ADVANCED ACCOUNTING, FOURTEENTH EDITION

Published by McGraw-Hill Education, 2 Penn Plaza, New York, NY 10121.

This book is printed on acid-free paper.

1 2 3 4 5 6 7 8 9 LWI 24 23 22 21 20

ISBN 978-1-260-24782-4 (bound edition)
MHID 1-260-24782-1 (bound edition)
ISBN 978-1-260-72644-2 (loose-leaf edition)
MHID 1-260-72644-4 (loose-leaf edition)

Managing Director: *Tim Vertovec*
Director: *Rebecca Olson*
Product Development Manager: *Michele Janicek*
Product Developers: *Danielle McLimore and Christina Sanders*
Director of Digital Content: *Kevin Moran*
Marketing Manager: *Zach Rudin*
Program Manager: *Marianne Musni*
Content Project Managers: *Erika Jordan, Brian Nacik, and Karen Jozefowicz*
Buyer: *Susan K. Culbertson*
Design: *Egzon Shaqiri*
Content Licensing Specialist: *Gina Oberbroeckling*
Cover Image: *Tokarchuk Andrii/Shutterstock*
Compositor: *SPi Global*

Library of Congress Cataloging-in-Publication Data

Names: Hoyle, Joe Ben, author. | Schaefer, Thomas F., author. | Doupnik, Timothy S., author.
Title: Advanced accounting / Joe B. Hoyle, Associate Professor of Accounting, Robins School of Business, University of Richmond, Thomas F. Schaefer, KPMG Professor of Accountancy, Mendoza College of Business, University of Notre Dame, Timothy S. Doupnik, Distinguished Professor Emeritus of Accounting, Darla Moore School of Business, University of South Carolina.
Description: Fourteenth Edition. | New York : McGraw-Hill Education, 2020. | Revised edition of the authors' Advanced accounting, 2016.
Identifiers: LCCN 2019036373 | ISBN 9781260247824 (hardcover) | ISBN 9781260726435 (ebook)
Subjects: LCSH: Accounting.
Classification: LCC HF5636 .H69 2020 | DDC 657/.046—dc23
LC record available at https://lccn.loc.gov/2019036373

mheducation.com/highered

To our families

The real purpose of books is to trap the mind into doing its own thinking.

—Christopher Morley

About the Authors

Joe B. Hoyle, *University of Richmond*

Joe B. Hoyle is associate professor of accounting at the Robins School of Business at the University of Richmond. He is also a Robins Teaching Fellow. In 2015, he was the first recipient of the J. Michael and Mary Anne Cook Prize for undergraduate teaching. The Cook Prize is awarded by the American Accounting Association and "is the foremost recognition of an individual who consistently demonstrates the attributes of a superior teacher in the discipline of accounting." In 2019, former students raised money to create an Accounting Teaching Fellowship, which will be renamed the "Joe Hoyle Accounting Teaching Fellowship" on his eventual retirement." He has authored a book of essays titled *Tips and Thoughts on Improving the Teaching Process in College,* which is available at https://facultystaff.richmond.edu/~jhoyle/documents/book-teaching-x.doc.pdf. His blog, *Teaching—Getting the Most from Your Students,* at http://joehoyle-teaching.blogspot.com/ was named the Accounting Education Innovation of the Year for 2013 by the American Accounting Association.

Thomas F. Schaefer, *University of Notre Dame*

Thomas F. Schaefer is the KPMG Professor of Accounting at the University of Notre Dame. He has written a number of articles for scholarly journals such as the *Accounting Review, Journal of Accounting Research, Journal of Accounting & Economics, Accounting Horizons,* and others. His primary teaching and research interests are in financial accounting and reporting. Tom is a past president of the American Accounting Association's Accounting Program Leadership Group. He received the 2007 Joseph A. Silvoso Faculty Merit Award from the Federation of Schools of Accountancy and the 2013 Notre Dame Master of Science in Accountancy Dincolo Outstanding Professor Award.

Timothy S. Doupnik, *University of South Carolina*

Timothy S. Doupnik is distinguished professor emeritus of accounting at the University of South Carolina. His primary teaching interests are in financial and international accounting. Tim has published extensively in the area of international accounting in journals such as the *Accounting Review; Accounting, Organizations, and Society; Abacus; International Journal of Accounting;* and *Journal of International Business Studies.* Tim is a past president of the American Accounting Association's (AAA) International Accounting Section and a recipient of the section's Outstanding International Accounting Educator Award. He is a coauthor of the paper that received the AAA's Notable Contribution to the Auditing Literature Award in 2019.

Advanced Accounting 14e Stays Current

Overall—this edition of the text provides relevant and up-to-date accounting standards references to the Financial Accounting Standards Board (FASB) *Accounting Standards Codification*® (ASC).

Chapter Changes for *Advanced Accounting,* 14th Edition:

Chapter 1

- Added a new section on business motivations for making equity method investments emphasizing economic benefits of significant influence.
- Updated real-world references, with a new reference when an equity method investment is reduced to zero.

Chapter 2

- Three new business combinations are discussed in terms of motivations to combine Amazon–Whole Foods, Salesforce.com–MuleSoft, and Tesla–Grohmann.
- Updated real-world references.
- Added a Discussion Question addressing situations where an acquired entity is not a business.
- Added new end-of-chapter problems and three new cases.

Chapter 3

- Updated material on goodwill impairment to reflect ASU updates for ASC Topic 350, *Intangibles—Goodwill and Other.*
- Updated real-world references.
- Revised and expanded section on accounting for contingent consideration in periods subsequent to acquisition.
- Revised and added new end-of-chapter problems and cases.

Chapter 4

- Introduced a table showing recent noncontrolling interest reported values by business entities.
- Updated real-world references.
- Revised and added new end-of-chapter problems and cases.
- Provided additional ASC citations on valuing noncontrolling interests and control premiums.
- Revised the section covering control premiums to provide additional focus on goodwill implications.

Chapter 5

- Streamlined and clarified the coverage for intra-entity gross profits in inventory and implications of the parent's investment accounting methods.
- Revised and added new end-of-chapter problems and cases.

Chapter 6

- Updated real-world references.
- Revised and clarified the section on accounting for variable interest entities including additional ASC citations. Revised the consolidation examples for variable interest entities (acquisition date and post-acquisition) by incorporating a management fee paid by the variable interest entity to the primary beneficiary.
- Revised several end-of-chapter problems.
- Revised examples and end-of-chapter problems for changes in federal corporate income tax rates from the *Tax Cut and Jobs Act* enacted in December 2017.

Chapter 7

- Revised and updated coverage of income taxes for business combinations for changes from the *Tax Cut and Jobs Act.*
- Updated real-world references.
- Revised/updated several end-of chapter problems and cases to align with new tax regulations.

Chapter 8

- Updated references to actual company practices and excerpts from annual reports.

- Changed the real-world companies used to demonstrate disclosure of geographic information in "Entitywide Information" and the seasonal nature of operations in "Interim Reporting."
- Added an annual report excerpt related to the determination and aggregation of reportable segments.
- Added a paragraph on the recent SEC requirement to include a reconciliation of changes in stockholders' equity in an interim report.
- Decreased the scope of the requirements in the two research cases at the end of the chapter.

Chapter 9

- Updated the chapter to reflect *Accounting Standards Update* (ASU) No. 2017-12, "Derivatives and Hedging (Topic 815): Targeted Improvements to Accounting for Hedging Activities," which amends ASC Topic 815, Derivatives and Hedging.

  This ASU requires an entity to present the income effect of the hedging instrument in the same income statement line item in which the income effect of the hedged item is reported. If an entity excludes certain portions of a hedging instrument's change in fair value from the assessment of hedge effectiveness (a so-called excluded component), the ASU permits an entity to recognize the initial value of the excluded component in net income using (1) changes in the fair value of the excluded component or (2) a systematic and rational method (such as straight-line) over the life of the hedging instrument. Further, the ASU requires the income effect of an excluded component to be recognized in the same income statement line item in which the income effect of the hedged item is reported.
- Introduced the concept of forward points in describing foreign currency forward contracts.
- Added a timeline in "Hedges of Foreign Exchange Risk" to illustrate how the various hedges differ in terms of timing.
- Added a subsection to the discussion on "Hedge Effectiveness" to cover issues relating to the "Exclusion of Components from Hedge Effectiveness Assessment."
- Changed the hedge examples to exclude the forward points on a forward contract and the time value of an option from the assessment of hedge effectiveness whenever possible. In allocating the excluded components to net income, the examples consistently use a straight-line amortization approach for forward points on a forward contract and the change in fair value approach for the time value of an option.
- Changed the name of the fictitious company in the hedge examples to Eximco and the example currency to British pounds to signal that examples have been changed.
- Deleted reference to the effective interest method for allocating forward points to net income, as well as the comparison of the effective interest versus straight line methods of allocation.
- Revised the hedges examples, for simplicity, to ignore discounting to present value in determining the fair value of forward contracts and firm commitments.
- Changed the journal entries in the hedge examples so that all gains and losses related to foreign currency denominated assets and liabilities, firm commitments, forward contracts, and options are recognized in a single income statement line item titled "Foreign Exchange Gains and Losses."
- Changed the journal entries in the hedge examples so that those entries that are ultimately reflected in accumulated other comprehensive income are first debited or credited to an "Other Comprehensive Income (OCI)" account rather than to "Accumulated Other Comprehensive Income (AOCI)."
- Revised the facts and instructions in most of the end-of-chapter problems dealing with hedges to be consistent with changes made in the chapter. Also, changed company names in revised problems to signal that these problems have been changed.
- Updated real-world references including examples of company practices, excerpts from annual reports, and foreign exchange rates.

Chapter 10

- Updated information about countries currently meeting the definition of highly inflationary economy.
- Changed the hypothetical exchange rates used in the Swissco example ("The Translation Process Illustrated") to be more consistent with the current U.S. dollar/Swiss franc exchange rate. Changed the hypothetical exchange rates and U.S. dollar amounts in Exhibits 10.4–10.9 accordingly.
- Expanded the discussion related to hedging balance sheet exposure and added a numerical example demonstrating the accounting related to a hedge of a net investment.

- Updated real-world references including examples of company practices and excerpts from annual reports.
- Changed the foreign currency in several end-of-chapter problems to eliminate the use of nonexistent currency names.
- Revised the facts in an end-of-chapter problem related to a hedge of a net investment.
- Changed one of the companies included in the requirements for the second research case at the end of the chapter.

Chapter 11

- Updated real-world references including excerpts from annual reports.
- Introduced the nomenclature "IFRS Standards" now used by the IASB when referring to its standards.
- Updated exhibits listing IFRS Standards and countries' use of IFRS Standards.
- Updated information on the use of full IFRS and *IFRS for SMEs.*
- Updated CPA exam coverage of IFRS based upon the AICPA's 2018 CPA exam blueprints.
- Updated the discussion and exhibit related to differences between IFRS and U.S. GAAP.
- Deleted the section related to gain on sale and leaseback from the comprehensive illustration.
- Added a question to the end-of-chapter material.
- Deleted end-of-chapter problems related to gain on sale and leaseback.
- Revised the end-of-chapter second analysis case to replace the requirement related to gain on sale and leaseback with convertible bonds.
- Replaced the end-of-chapter research case related to "Reconciliation to U.S. GAAP" with a case focusing on "Differences between IFRS and U.S. GAAP."

Chapter 12

- Added new section on *SEC Content in the FASB's Accounting Standards Codification® (ASC).*
- Added new section on *SEC and PCAOB Fees and Budgets.*
- Added discussion of Regulation FD (Fair Disclosure) and its effect on disclosures in Form 8-K.
- Added discussion of expanded reporting requirements requiring greater use of real-time disclosures for material changes in their financial condition or operations between periodic 10-K and 10-Q filings on Form 8-K, which were enacted as rules to implement the Sarbanes–Oxley Act.
- Updated SEC data on filing fees.
- Updated web references as necessary.

Chapter 13

- Revised references to include companies that have recently experienced bankruptcy such as Sears Holdings, Nine West, Claire's, Bon-Ton, Brookstone, and Rockport.

Chapter 14

- Revised and updated coverage of the tax implications of partnership for changes from the *Tax Cut and Jobs Act.*
- Updated real-world references.
- Updated several end-of-chapter problems.

Chapter 15

- Added two learning objectives related to (1) preparing a statement of partnership liquidation and (2) calculating safe payments.
- Made "Partnership Liquidation Procedures," "Statement of Partnership Liquidation," and "Deficit Capital Balances" major headings.
- Moved the "Two Partners with Deficit Capital Balances" example to the "Deficit Capital Balances" section.
- Renamed "Statement of Liquidation" as "Statement of Partnership Liquidation."
- Reorganized "Safe Payments to Partners" as a major section with a new, related learning objective.
- Deleted the subsection on "Insolvent Partnership."
- Relabeled the section on "Installment Liquidations" as "Preliminary Distribution of Partnership Assets."
- Made "Predistribution Plan" a major heading.
- Deleted an end-of-chapter question related to the Uniform Partnership Act and revised a question related to safe payments.

- Revised requirements in several end-of-chapter problems to require preparation either of a statement of partnership liquidation, proposed schedule of liquidation, or predistribution plan.
- Replaced a multi-part problem with a problem requiring preparation of a proposed schedule of liquidation.
- Deleted the Research Case.
- Replaced the previous Analysis Case with a new case.
- Replaced the previous Communication Case with two new cases.

Chapter 16

- Updated numerous references to the financial statements of a wide variety of state and local governments such as the City of Portland, the City of Phoenix, the City of Greensboro, and the City of Las Vegas.
- Discussed the ongoing evolution of U.S. GAAP to highlight GASB's release of two Preliminary Views documents, *Financial Reporting Model Improvements* and *Recognition of Elements of Financial Statements* that could eventually create significant changes in state and local government accounting.

Chapter 17

- Provided coverage of new pronouncement: *GASB Statement No. 87,* "Leases," including comparison with *FASB Accounting Standards Update No. 2016-02,* "Leases." The two authoritative groups take significantly different approaches to the reporting of lease contracts.
- Rearranged chapter coverage to increase emphasis on the reporting of defined benefit pension plans to highlight the risk of such large government obligations.
- Updated references to the financial statements of state and local governments such as the City of Los Angeles, the City of Chicago, the City of Orlando, the City of Cincinnati, and the City of Boston.

Chapter 18

- Rewrote significant sections of the chapter as a result of *Accounting Standards Update 2016-14, Presentation of Financial Statements for Not-for-Profit Entities,* (released in August 2016) and *Accounting Standards Update 2018-08, Clarifying the Scope and the Accounting Guidance for Contributions Received and Contributions Made* (released in June 2018).
- Described new reporting rules that require a not-for-profit (NFP) entity to classify its net asset total as either with donor restrictions or without donor restrictions.
- Examined the difference between an exchange transaction and a contribution based on *Accounting Standards Update 2014-09, Revenues from Contracts with Customers.*
- Identified conditional contributions and discussed the reporting of conditional contributions versus unconditional contributions.
- Explained other new NFP reporting changes such as for the statement of cash flows as well as the disclosure of functional expenses and the entity's expected method of handling liquidity issues.

Chapter 19

- Updated tax code references, numbers, and statistics.
- Included coverage of the Tax Cuts and Jobs Act of 2017.
- Revised web links in footnote references as appropriate.
- Revised end-of-chapter material reflecting changes from the chapter.

Students Solve the Accounting Puzzle

The approach used by Hoyle, Schaefer, and Doupnik allows students to think critically about accounting, just as they will in their careers and as they prepare for the CPA exam. Read on to understand how students will succeed as accounting majors and as future CPAs by using *Advanced Accounting, 14e.*

Thinking Critically

With this text, students gain a well-balanced appreciation of the accounting profession. As *Hoyle 14e* introduces them to the field's many aspects, it often focuses on past controversies and present resolutions. The text shows the development of financial reporting as a product of intense and considered debate that continues today and will in the future.

Readability

The writing style of the 13 previous editions has been highly praised. **Students easily comprehend** chapter concepts because of the conversational tone used throughout the book. The authors have made every effort to ensure that the writing style remains engaging, lively, and consistent.

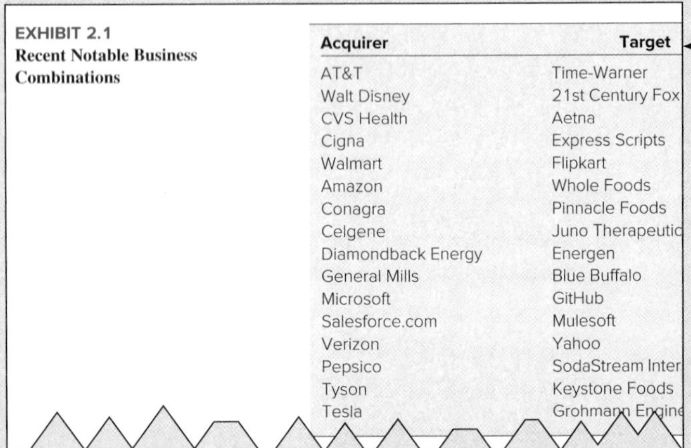

EXHIBIT 2.1
Recent Notable Business Combinations

Acquirer	Target
AT&T	Time-Warner
Walt Disney	21st Century Fox
CVS Health	Aetna
Cigna	Express Scripts
Walmart	Flipkart
Amazon	Whole Foods
Conagra	Pinnacle Foods
Celgene	Juno Therapeutic
Diamondback Energy	Energen
General Mills	Blue Buffalo
Microsoft	GitHub
Salesforce.com	Mulesoft
Verizon	Yahoo
Pepsico	SodaStream Inter
Tyson	Keystone Foods
Tesla	Grohmann Engine

Real-World Examples

Students are better able to relate what they learn to what they will encounter in the business world after reading these frequent examples. Quotations, articles, and illustrations from *Forbes,* the *Wall Street Journal, Time,* and *Bloomberg BusinessWeek* are incorporated throughout the text. Data have been pulled from business, not-for-profit, and government financial statements as well as official pronouncements.

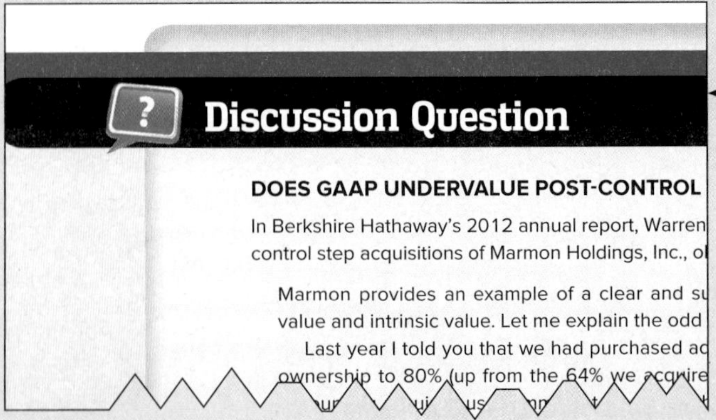

Discussion Question

DOES GAAP UNDERVALUE POST-CONTROL

In Berkshire Hathaway's 2012 annual report, Warren
control step acquisitions of Marmon Holdings, Inc., o

Marmon provides an example of a clear and s
value and intrinsic value. Let me explain the odd
Last year I told you that we had purchased ac
ownership to 80% (up from the 64% we acquire

Discussion Questions

This feature **facilitates student understanding** of the underlying accounting principles at work in particular reporting situations. Similar to minicases, these questions help explain the issues at hand in practical terms. Many times, these cases are designed to demonstrate to students why a topic is problematic and worth considering.

with 14th Edition Features

McGraw-Hill has partnered with Roger CPA Review (Powered by UWorld), a global leader in CPA Exam preparation, to provide students a smooth transition from the accounting classroom to successful completion of the CPA Exam. While many aspiring accountants wait until they have completed their academic studies to begin preparing for the CPA Exam, research shows that those who become familiar with exam content earlier in the process have a stronger chance of successfully passing the CPA Exam. Accordingly, students using these McGraw-Hill materials will have access to Roger CPA Review multiple choice questions supported by explanations written by CPAs focused on exam preparation. McGraw-Hill and Roger CPA Review are dedicated to supporting every accounting student along their journey, ultimately helping them achieve career success in the accounting profession. For more information about the full Roger CPA Review program, exam requirements, and exam content, visit www.rogercpareview.com.

End-of-Chapter Materials

As in previous editions, the end-of-chapter material remains a strength of the text. The sheer number of questions, problems, and Internet assignments test and, therefore, **expand the students' knowledge** of chapter concepts.

Excel Spreadsheet Assignments extend specific problems and are located on the 14th edition Instructor Resources page, with template versions that can be provided to students for assignments. An Excel icon appears next to those problems that have corresponding spreadsheet assignments.

"Develop Your Skills" asks questions that address the four skills students need to master to pass the CPA exam: Research, Analysis, Spreadsheet, and Communication. An icon indicates when these skills are tested.

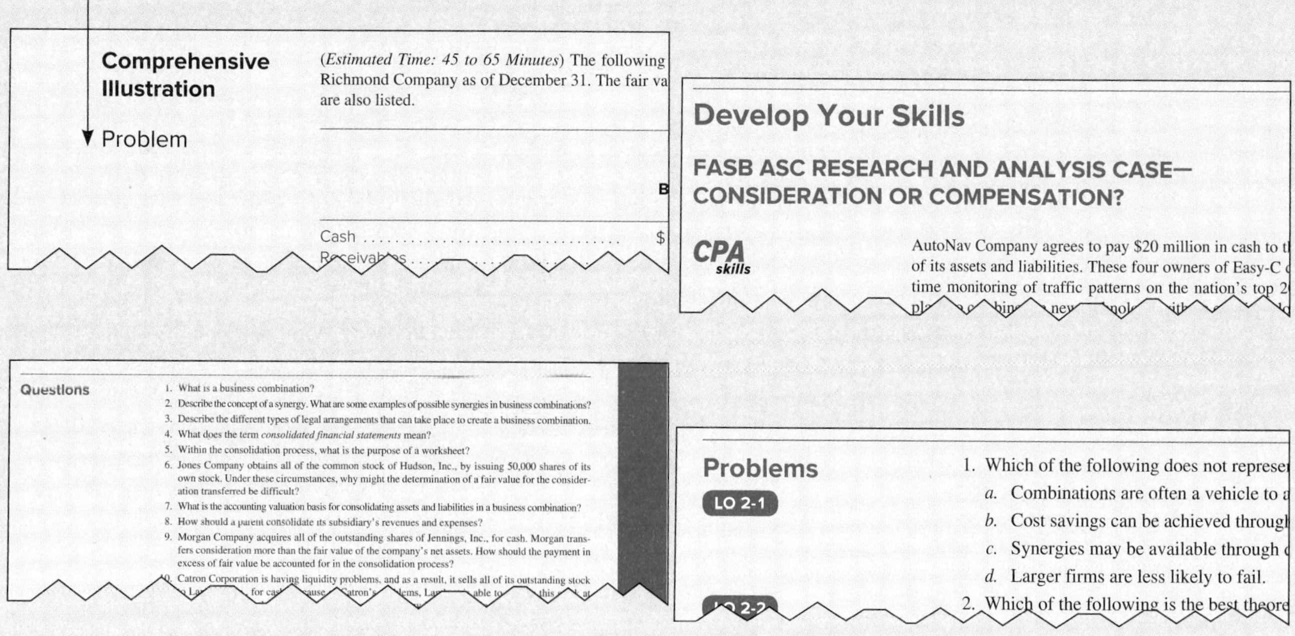

The 14th edition of *Advanced Accounting* has a full Connect package, with the following features available for instructors and students.

- **SmartBook®** is the market-leading adaptive study resource that is proven to strengthen memory recall, increase retention, and boost grades. SmartBook 2.0 identifies and closes knowledge gaps through a continually adapting reading and questioning experience that helps students master the key concepts in the chapter. SmartBook 2.0 is the latest version of SmartBook, with key updates to: improve accessibility, provide mobile functionality, allow a more granular level of content selection, and provide the ability to assign Recharge activities.
- The **End-of-Chapter Content** in Connect provides a robust offering of review and question material designed to aid and assess the student's retention of chapter content. The End-of-Chapter content is composed of both static and algorithmic versions of the problems in each chapter, which are designed to challenge students using McGraw-Hill Education's state-of-the-art online homework technology. Connect helps students learn more efficiently by providing feedback and practice material when and where they need it. Connect grades homework automatically, and students benefit from the immediate feedback that they receive, particularly on any questions they may have missed.

Example of Connect End-of-Chapter Problem

Prepare a consolidated balance sheet for Pratt and Spider as of December 31, 2021.

PRATT COMPANY AND SUBSIDIARY Consolidated Balance Sheet December 31, 2021			
Assets		**Liabilities and Owners' Equity**	
Cash			
Total assets		Total liabilities and equities	

- The **Test Bank** for each chapter has been updated for the 14th edition to stay current with new and revised chapter material, with all questions available for assignment through Connect. Instructors can also create tests and quizzes with Test Builder, a cloud-based tool available within Connect that formats tests for printing or for administering within an LMS.
- The **Instructor and Student Resources** have been updated for the 14th edition and are available in the Connect Instructor Resources page. Available resources include Instructor and Solutions Manuals, PowerPoint presentations, Test Bank files, Excel templates, and Chapter Check Figures. All applicable Student Resources will be available in a convenient file that can be distributed to students for classes either directly, through Connect, or via courseware.

Acknowledgments

We could not produce a textbook of the quality and scope of *Advanced Accounting* without the help of a great number of people. Special thanks go to the following:

- Tom Stober of the University of Notre Dame for his contribution to Chapter 12 and Stacie Hughes of Athens State University for her contributions to Chapter 19 and corresponding Solutions Manual files.
- Gregory Schaefer for his Chapter 2 descriptions of recent business combinations.
- Ilene Leopold Persoff of Long Island University (LIU Post) for her work on detailed reviews of the 12th edition and 13th edition manuscript, solutions manuals, and test bank files for accuracy. Ilene's subject matter knowledge, detail-oriented nature, and quality of work were instrumental in ensuring that this edition stayed accurate, relevant, and of tremendous quality.

Additionally, we would like to thank John Abernathy of Kennesaw State University, for updating and revising the PowerPoint presentations; Jack Terry of ComSource Associates for updating the Excel Template Exercises for students to use as they work the select end-of-chapter material; Stacie Hughes of Athens State University for checking the text and Solutions Manual for accuracy and for updating the test bank; Mark McCarthy of East Carolina University and Beth Kobylarz of Accuracy Counts for checking the text, Solutions Manual, and test bank for accuracy; Angela Sandberg for checking the end-of-chapter material and the test bank for accuracy; and Barbara Gershman of Northern Virginia Community College for checking the PowerPoints.

We also want to thank the many people who completed questionnaires and reviewed the book. Our sincerest thanks to them all:

Subash Adhikari
University of South Dakota

Kevin Cabe
Indiana Wesleyan University

Shuoyuan He
Tulane University

Stacie Hughes
Athens State University

Lisa Ludlum
Western Illinois University

Sehan Kim
University of Houston-Clear Lake

Daniel Neely
University of Wisconsin-Milwaukee

Peggy O'Kelly
Northeastern University

Andrea Still
Indiana University

Inho Suk
SUNY-Buffalo

Sung Wook Yoon
California State University, Northridge

We also pass along a word of thanks to all the people at McGraw-Hill Education who participated in the creation of this edition. In particular, Erika Jordan, Content Project Manager; Sue Culbertson, Buyer; Egzon Shaqiri, Designer; Christina Sanders, Senior Core Product Developer; Danielle McLimore, Assessment Product Developer; Becky Olson, Director; Tim Vertovec, Managing Director; Brian Nacik, Lead Assessment Content Project Manager; and Zach Rudin, Marketing Manager, all contributed significantly to the project, and we appreciate their efforts.

FOR INSTRUCTORS

You're in the driver's seat.

Want to build your own course? No problem. Prefer to use our turnkey, prebuilt course? Easy. Want to make changes throughout the semester? Sure. And you'll save time with Connect's auto-grading too.

65%

Less Time Grading

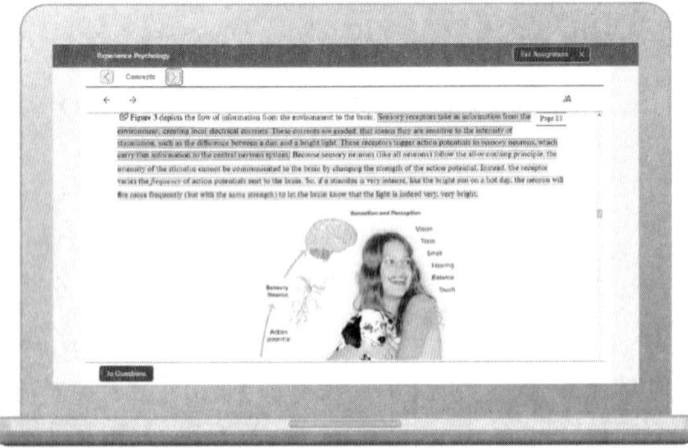

Laptop: McGraw-Hill; Woman/dog: George Doyle/Getty Images

They'll thank you for it.

Adaptive study resources like SmartBook® 2.0 help your students be better prepared in less time. You can transform your class time from dull definitions to dynamic debates. Find out more about the powerful personalized learning experience available in SmartBook 2.0 at **www.mheducation.com/highered/connect/smartbook**

Make it simple, make it affordable.

Connect makes it easy with seamless integration using any of the major Learning Management Systems—Blackboard®, Canvas, and D2L, among others—to let you organize your course in one convenient location. Give your students access to digital materials at a discount with our inclusive access program. Ask your McGraw-Hill representative for more information.

Padlock: Jobalou/Getty Images

Solutions for your challenges.

A product isn't a solution. Real solutions are affordable, reliable, and come with training and ongoing support when you need it and how you want it. Our Customer Experience Group can also help you troubleshoot tech problems—although Connect's 99% uptime means you might not need to call them. See for yourself at **status.mheducation.com**

Checkmark: Jobalou/Getty Images

FOR STUDENTS

Effective, efficient studying.

Connect helps you be more productive with your study time and get better grades using tools like SmartBook 2.0, which highlights key concepts and creates a personalized study plan. Connect sets you up for success, so you walk into class with confidence and walk out with better grades.

Study anytime, anywhere.

Download the free ReadAnywhere app and access your online eBook or SmartBook 2.0 assignments when it's convenient, even if you're offline. And since the app automatically syncs with your eBook and SmartBook 2.0 assignments in Connect, all of your work is available every time you open it. Find out more at **www.mheducation.com/readanywhere**

"I really liked this app—it made it easy to study when you don't have your text-book in front of you."

- Jordan Cunningham, Eastern Washington University

Calendar: owattaphotos/Getty Images

No surprises.

The Connect Calendar and Reports tools keep you on track with the work you need to get done and your assignment scores. Life gets busy; Connect tools help you keep learning through it all.

Learning for everyone.

McGraw-Hill works directly with Accessibility Services Departments and faculty to meet the learning needs of all students. Please contact your Accessibility Services office and ask them to email accessibility@mheducation.com, or visit **www.mheducation.com/about/accessibility** for more information.

Top: Jenner Images/Getty Images, Left: Hero Images/Getty Images, Right: Hero Images/Getty Images

Brief Contents

Contents

Chapter Ten
Translation of Foreign Currency Financial Statements 479

Chapter Eleven
Worldwide Accounting Diversity and International Standards 539

Chapter Twelve
Financial Reporting and the Securities and Exchange Commission 593

Chapter Thirteen
Accounting for Legal Reorganizations and Liquidations 619

Chapter Fourteen
Partnerships: Formation and Operation 669

Chapter Fifteen
Partnerships: Termination and Liquidation 707

Chapter Sixteen
Accounting for State and Local Governments (Part 1) 739

chapter **1**

The Equity Method of Accounting for Investments

The first several chapters of this text present the accounting and reporting for investment activities of businesses. The focus is on investments when one firm possesses either significant influence or control over another through ownership of voting shares. When one firm owns enough voting shares to be able to affect the decisions of another, accounting for the investment can become challenging and complex. The source of such complexities typically stems from the fact that transactions among the firms affiliated through ownership cannot be considered independent, arm's-length transactions. As in many matters relating to financial reporting, we look to transactions with *outside parties* to provide a basis for accounting valuation. When firms are affiliated through a common set of owners, measurements that recognize the relationships among the firms help provide objectivity in financial reporting.

Learning Objectives

After studying this chapter, you should be able to:

LO 1-1 Describe motivations for a firm to gain significant influence over another firm.

LO 1-2 Describe in general the various methods of accounting for an investment in equity shares of another company.

LO 1-3 Identify the sole criterion for applying the equity method of accounting and know the guidelines to assess whether the criterion is met.

LO 1-4 Describe the financial reporting for equity method investments and prepare basic equity method journal entries for an investor.

LO 1-5 Allocate the cost of an equity method investment and compute amortization expense to match revenues recognized from the investment to the excess of investor cost over investee book value.

LO 1-6 Understand the financial reporting consequences for:

- a. A change to the equity method.
- b. Investee's other comprehensive income.
- c. Investee losses.
- d. Sales of equity method investments.

LO 1-7 Describe the rationale and computations to defer the investor's share of gross profits on intra-entity inventory sales until the goods are either consumed by the owner or sold to outside parties.

LO 1-8 Explain the rationale and reporting implications of fair-value accounting for investments otherwise accounted for by the equity method.

Why Do Business Firms Invest in the Equity Shares of Other Business Firms?

We frequently see businesses buying equity shares (e.g., common stock) of other businesses. To understand the accounting for equity share acquisitions, it's helpful to understand two fundamental motivations for such investments. First, firms may temporarily invest in another firm's equity shares simply to earn a return on otherwise idle cash. Companies such as Microsoft, Google, and Starbucks each have large amounts of short-term investments in marketable equity securities that can produce both dividend income and share value appreciation.

Second, in sufficient quantity, equity shares can provide a powerful business tool to investors. Equity share ownership typically provides voting privileges to elect members to a firm's board of directors. Boards of directors are the highest authority in the management of a corporation. They make strategic decisions regarding how the firm will conduct its business. Boards set company policies and hire (and fire) management. Thus, the ability to vote for directors can be a powerful tool to influence the decisions of an investee corporation. Consequently, many firms will buy sufficient voting shares to enable the election of their representatives to another firm's board of directors. The range of ownership may result in the ability to influence the investee through the election of a single director all the way to complete control.

By exercising their voting rights over the investee, an investor firm can wield power over the strategic direction of the investee in ways that align with its own operating and financial interests. For example, an investee may be considering inventory purchase or sale contracts with several

LO 1-1

Describe motivations for a firm to gain significant influence over another firm.

outside firms. An investor firm, through its designated members on the investee board of directors, possesses the power to influence the selection of the outside firm—including the investor firm itself. Other examples abound, including cooperation between the investor and investee on research, technology, product development, licensing, advertising, distribution, market expansion, etc. Thus, we see businesses acquiring the equity shares of other businesses throughout the economy.

The Reporting of Investments in Corporate Equity Securities

In its 2018 annual report, The Coca-Cola Company describes its 28 percent investment in Coca-Cola FEMSA, a Mexican bottling company with operations throughout much of Latin America. The Coca-Cola Company uses the equity method to account for several of its bottling company investments, including Coca-Cola FEMSA. The annual report states,

> We use the equity method to account for investments in companies, if our investment provides us with the ability to exercise significant influence over operating and financial policies of the investee. Our consolidated net income includes our Company's proportionate share of the net income or loss of these companies.
>
> Our judgment regarding the level of influence over each equity method investment includes considering key factors such as our ownership interest, representation on the board of directors, participation in policy-making decisions and material intercompany transactions.

Such information is hardly unusual in the business world; corporate investors frequently acquire ownership shares of both domestic and foreign businesses. These investments can range from the purchase of a few shares to the acquisition of 100 percent control. Although purchases of corporate equity securities (such as the ones made by Coca-Cola) are not uncommon, they pose a considerable number of financial reporting issues because a close relationship has been established without the investor gaining actual control. These issues are currently addressed by the *equity method.* This chapter deals with accounting for stock investments that fall under the application of this method.

LO 1-2

Describe in general the various methods of accounting for an investment in equity shares of another company.

Generally accepted accounting principles (GAAP) recognize four different approaches to the financial reporting of investments in corporate equity securities:

1. Fair-value method.
2. Cost method for equity securities without readily determinable fair values.
3. Consolidation of financial statements.
4. Equity method.

The financial statement reporting for a particular investment depends primarily on the degree of influence that the investor (stockholder) has over the investee, a factor most often indicated by the relative size of ownership.[1] Because voting power typically accompanies ownership of equity shares, influence increases with the relative size of ownership. The resulting influence can be very little, a significant amount, or, in some cases, complete control.

Fair-Value Method

In many instances, an investor possesses only a small percentage of an investee company's outstanding stock, perhaps only a few shares. Because of the limited level of ownership, the investor cannot expect to significantly affect the investee's operations or decision making. These shares are bought in anticipation of cash dividends or appreciation of stock market values. Such investments are recorded at cost and periodically adjusted to fair value according to the Financial Accounting Standards Board (FASB) *Accounting Standards Codification®* (ASC) Topic 321, "Investments—Equity Securities."

[1] The relative size of ownership is most often the key factor in assessing one company's degree of influence over another. However, as discussed later in this chapter, other factors (e.g., contractual relationships between firms) can also provide influence or control over firms regardless of the percentage of shares owned.

Fair value is defined by the ASC (Master Glossary) as the "price that would be received to sell an asset or paid to transfer a liability in an orderly transaction between market participants at the measurement date." For most investments in equity securities, quoted stock market prices represent fair values.

Because a full coverage of limited ownership investments in equity securities is presented in intermediate accounting textbooks, only the following basic principles are noted here:

- Initial investments in equity securities are recorded at cost and subsequently adjusted to fair value if fair value is readily determinable (typically by reference to market value); otherwise, the investment remains at cost.
- Changes in the fair values of equity securities during a reporting period are recognized as income.[2]
- Dividends declared on the equity securities are recognized as income.

The preceding procedures are followed for equity security investments (with readily determinable fair values) when the owner possesses neither significant influence nor control.

Cost Method (Investments in Equity Securities without Readily Determinable Fair Values)

When the fair value of an investment in equity securities is not readily determinable, and the investment provides neither significant influence nor control, the investment may be measured at cost. Such investments sometimes can be found in ownership shares of firms that are not publicly traded or experience only infrequent trades.

Investments in equity securities that employ the cost method often continue to be reported at their original cost over time.[3] Income from cost method equity investments usually consists of the investor's share of dividends declared by the investee. However, despite its emphasis on cost measurements, GAAP allows for two fair value assessments that may affect cost method amounts reported on the balance sheet and the income statement.

- First, cost method equity investments periodically must be assessed for impairment to determine if the fair value of the investment is less than its carrying amount. The ASC allows a qualitative assessment to determine if impairment is likely.[4] Because the fair value of a cost method equity investment is not readily available (by definition), if impairment is deemed likely, an entity must estimate a fair value for the investment to measure the amount (if any) of the impairment loss.
- Second, ASC (321-10-35-2) allows for recognition of "observable price changes in orderly transactions for the identical or a similar investment of the same issuer." Any unrealized holding gains (or losses) from these observable price changes are included in earnings with a corresponding adjustment to the investment account. So even if equity shares are only infrequently traded (and thus fair value is not readily determinable), such trades can provide a basis for financial statement recognition under the cost method for equity investments.

Consolidation of Financial Statements

Many corporate investors acquire enough shares to gain actual control over an investee's operations. In financial accounting, such control may be achieved when a stockholder

[2] ASC 320, *Investments—Debt and Equity Securities,* requires equity investments (except those accounted for under the equity method of accounting or those that result in consolidation of the investee) to be measured at fair value with changes in fair value recognized in net income, unless fair values are not readily determinable. Thus, the previous available-for-sale category with fair value changes recorded in other comprehensive income is no longer available.

[3] Dividends received in excess of earnings subsequent to the date of investment are considered returns of the investment and are recorded as reductions of cost of the investment.

[4] Impairment indicators include assessments of earnings performance, economic environment, going-concern ability, etc. If the qualitative assessment does not indicate impairment, no further testing is required. If an equity security without a readily determinable fair value is impaired, the investor recognizes the difference between the investment's fair value and carrying amount as an impairment loss in net income (ASC 321-10-35-3).

accumulates more than 50 percent of an organization's outstanding voting stock. At that point, rather than simply influencing the investee's decisions, the investor often can direct the entire decision-making process. A review of the financial statements of America's largest organizations indicates that legal control of one or more subsidiary companies is an almost universal practice. PepsiCo, Inc., as just one example, holds a majority interest in the voting stock of literally hundreds of corporations.

Investor control over an investee presents a special accounting challenge. Normally, when a majority of voting stock is held, the investor–investee relationship is so closely connected that the two corporations are viewed as a single entity for reporting purposes.[5] Consequently, an entirely different set of accounting procedures is applicable. Control generally requires the consolidation of the accounting information produced by the individual companies. Thus, a single set of financial statements is created for external reporting purposes with all assets, liabilities, revenues, and expenses brought together. The various procedures applied within this consolidation process are examined in subsequent chapters of this textbook.

The FASB ASC Section 810-10-05 on variable interest entities expands the use of consolidated financial statements to include entities that are financially controlled through special contractual arrangements rather than through voting stock interests. Prior to the accounting requirements for variable interest entities, many firms (e.g., Enron) avoided consolidation of entities that they owned little or no voting stock in but otherwise controlled through special contracts. These entities were frequently referred to as special purpose entities (SPEs) and provided vehicles for some firms to keep large amounts of assets and liabilities off their consolidated financial statements. Accounting for these entities is discussed in Chapters 2 and 6.

Equity Method

Another investment relationship is appropriately accounted for using the equity method. In many investments, although control is not achieved, the degree of ownership indicates the ability of the investor to exercise *significant influence* over the investee. If an investor holds between 20 and 50 percent of the voting stock of the investee, significant influence is normally assumed and the equity method is applied. Recall Coca-Cola's 28 percent investment in Coca-Cola FEMSA's voting stock. Through its ownership, Coca-Cola can undoubtedly influence Coca-Cola FEMSA's decisions and operations.

To provide objective reporting for investments with significant influence, FASB ASC Topic 323, "Investments—Equity Method and Joint Ventures," describes the use of the equity method. The equity method employs the accrual basis for recognizing the investor's share of investee income. Accordingly, the investor recognizes income as it is earned by the investee. As noted in FASB ASC (para. 323-10-05-5), because of its significant influence over the investee, the investor

> has a degree of responsibility for the return on its investment and it is appropriate to include in the results of operations of the investor its share of earnings or losses of the investee.

Furthermore, under the equity method, the investor records its share of investee dividends declared as a decrease in the investment account, not as income.

In today's business world, many corporations hold significant ownership interests in other companies without having actual control. The Coca-Cola Company, for example, owns between 20 and 50 percent of several bottling companies, both domestic and international. Many other investments represent joint ventures in which two or more companies form a new enterprise to carry out a specified operating purpose. For example, Ford Motor Company and Sollers formed FordSollers, a passenger and commercial vehicle manufacturing, import, and distribution company in Russia. Each partner owns 50 percent of the joint venture. For each of these investments, the investors do not possess absolute control because they hold less than a majority of the voting stock. Thus, the preparation of consolidated financial statements is inappropriate. However, the large percentage of ownership indicates that each investor possesses some ability to affect the investee's decision-making process.

[5] As discussed in Chapter 2, ownership of a majority voting interest in an investee does not always lead to consolidated financial statements.

Discussion Question

DID THE COST METHOD INVITE EARNINGS MANIPULATION?

Prior to GAAP for equity method investments, firms used the cost method to account for their unconsolidated investments in common stock regardless of the presence of significant influence. Under the cost method, when the investee declares a dividend, the investor records "dividend income." The investment account typically remains at its original cost—hence the term *cost method.*

Many firms' compensation plans reward managers based on reported annual income. How might the use of the cost method of accounting for significant influence investments have resulted in unintended wealth transfers from owners to managers? Do the equity or fair-value methods provide similar incentives?

Finally, as discussed at the end of this chapter, firms may elect a fair-value option in their financial reporting for certain financial assets and financial liabilities. Among the qualifying financial assets for fair-value reporting are significant influence investments otherwise accounted for by the equity method.

Application of the Equity Method

An understanding of the equity method is best gained by initially examining the FASB's treatment of two questions:

1. What factors indicate when the equity method should be used for an investment in another entity's ownership securities?
2. How should the investor report this investment, and the income generated by it, to reflect the relationship between the two entities?

LO 1-3

Identify the sole criterion for applying the equity method of accounting and guidance in assessing whether the criterion is met.

Criteria for Utilizing the Equity Method

The rationale underlying the equity method is that an investor begins to gain the ability to influence the decision-making process of an investee as the level of ownership rises. According to FASB ASC Topic 323 on equity method investments, achieving this "ability to exercise significant influence over operating and financial policies of an investee even though the investor holds 50 percent or less of the common stock" is the sole criterion for requiring application of the equity method (FASB ASC [para. 323-10-15-3]).

Clearly, a term such as *the ability to exercise significant influence* is nebulous and subject to a variety of judgments and interpretations in practice. At what point does the acquisition of one additional share of stock give an owner the ability to exercise significant influence? This decision becomes even more difficult in that only the *ability* to exercise significant influence need be present. There is no requirement that any actual influence must ever be applied.

FASB ASC Topic 323 provides guidance to the accountant by listing several conditions that indicate the presence of this degree of influence:

- Investor representation on the board of directors of the investee.
- Investor participation in the policy-making process of the investee.
- Material intra-entity transactions.

- Interchange of managerial personnel.
- Technological dependency.
- Extent of ownership by the investor in relation to the size and concentration of other ownership interests in the investee.

No single one of these guides should be used exclusively in assessing the applicability of the equity method. Instead, all are evaluated together to determine the presence or absence of the sole criterion: the ability to exercise significant influence over the investee.

These guidelines alone do not eliminate the leeway available to each investor when deciding whether the use of the equity method is appropriate. To provide a degree of consistency in applying this standard, the FASB provides a general ownership test: *If an investor holds between 20 and 50 percent of the voting stock of the investee, significant influence is normally assumed, and the equity method is applied.*

> An investment (direct or indirect) of 20 percent or more of the voting stock of an investee shall lead to a presumption that in the absence of predominant evidence to the contrary an investor has the ability to exercise significant influence over an investee. Conversely, an investment of less than 20 percent of the voting stock of an investee shall lead to a presumption that an investor does not have the ability to exercise significant influence unless such ability can be demonstrated.[6]

Limitations of Equity Method Applicability

At first, the 20 to 50 percent rule may appear to be an arbitrarily chosen boundary range established merely to provide a consistent method of reporting for investments. However, the essential criterion is still the ability to significantly influence (but not control) the investee, rather than 20 to 50 percent ownership. If the absence of this ability is proven (or control exists), the equity method should not be applied, regardless of the percentage of shares held.

For example, the equity method is not appropriate for investments that demonstrate any of the following characteristics, regardless of the investor's degree of ownership:[7]

- An agreement exists between investor and investee by which the investor surrenders significant rights as a shareholder.
- A concentration of ownership operates the investee without regard for the views of the investor.
- The investor attempts but fails to obtain representation on the investee's board of directors.

In each of these situations, because the investor is unable to exercise significant influence over its investee, the equity method is not applied.

Alternatively, if an entity can exercise *control* over its investee, regardless of its ownership level, consolidation (rather than the equity method) is appropriate. FASB ASC (para. 810-10-05-8) limits the use of the equity method by expanding the definition of a controlling financial interest and addresses situations in which financial control exists absent majority ownership interest. In these situations, control is achieved through contractual and other arrangements called *variable interests.*

To illustrate, one firm may create a separate legal entity in which it holds less than 50 percent of the voting interests but nonetheless controls that entity through governance document provisions and/or contracts that specify decision-making power and the distribution of profits and losses. Entities controlled in this fashion are typically designated as *variable interest entities,* and their sponsoring firm may be required to include them in consolidated financial reports despite the fact that ownership is less than 50 percent. For example, the Walt Disney Company reclassified several former equity method investees as variable interest entities and now consolidates these investments.[8]

[6] FASB ASC (para. 323-10-15-8).

[7] FASB ASC (para. 323-10-15-10). This paragraph deals specifically with limits to using the equity method for investments in which the owner holds 20 to 50 percent of the outstanding shares.

[8] Chapters 2 and 6 provide further discussions of variable interest entities.

Extensions of Equity Method Applicability

For some investments that either fall short of or exceed 20 to 50 percent ownership, the equity method is nonetheless appropriately used for financial reporting. As an example, The Coca-Cola Company owns a 19 percent investment in Monster Beverage Corporation. Coca-Cola notes in its recent financial statements that "Based on our equity ownership percentage, the significance that our expanded distribution and coordination agreements have on Monster's operations, and our representation on Monster's Board of Directors, the Company is accounting for its interest in Monster as an equity method investment."

Conditions can also exist where the equity method is appropriate despite a majority ownership interest. In some instances, rights granted to noncontrolling shareholders restrict the powers of the majority shareholder. Such rights may include approval over compensation, hiring, termination, and other critical operating and capital spending decisions of an entity. If the noncontrolling rights are so restrictive as to call into question whether control rests with the majority owner, the equity method is employed for financial reporting rather than consolidation. For example, prior to its acquisition of BellSouth, AT&T Inc., stated in its financial reports, "we account for our 60 percent economic investment in Cingular under the equity method of accounting because we share control equally with our 40 percent partner BellSouth."

To summarize, the following table indicates the method of accounting that is typically applicable to various stock investments:

Criterion	Normal Ownership Level	Applicable Accounting Method
Inability to significantly influence	Less than 20%	Fair value or cost method
Ability to significantly influence	20%–50%	Equity method or fair value
Control through voting interests	More than 50%	Consolidated financial statements
Control through variable interests (governance documents, contracts)	Primary beneficiary status (no ownership required)	Consolidated financial statements

LO 1-4

Describe the financial reporting for equity method investments and prepare basic equity method journal entries for an investor.

Accounting for an Investment—The Equity Method

Now that the criteria leading to the application of the equity method have been identified, a review of its reporting procedures is appropriate. Knowledge of this accounting process is especially important to users of the investor's financial statements because the equity method affects both the timing of income recognition and the carrying amount of the investment account.

In applying the equity method, the accounting objective is to report the investment and investment income to reflect the close relationship between the investor and investee. After recording the cost of the acquisition, two equity method entries periodically record the investment's impact:

1. The investor's investment account *increases as the investee recognizes and reports income*. Also, the investor recognizes investment income using the accrual method—that is, in the same period as reported by the investee in its financial statements. If an investee reports income of $100,000, a 30 percent owner should immediately increase its own income by $30,000. This earnings accrual reflects the essence of the equity method by emphasizing the connection between the two companies; as the owners' equity of the investee increases through the earnings process, the investment account also increases. Although the investor initially records the acquisition at cost, upward adjustments in the asset balance are recorded as soon as the investee makes a profit. The investor reduces the investment account if the investee reports a loss.

2. The investor decreases its investment account for its share of investee cash dividends. When the investee declares a cash dividend, its owners' equity decreases. The investor mirrors this change by recording a reduction in the carrying amount of the investment rather than recognizing the dividend as revenue. Furthermore, because the investor recognizes income when the investee recognizes it, double counting would occur if the investor also recorded its share of subsequent investee dividends as revenue. Importantly, a cash dividend declaration is not an appropriate point for income recognition. As stated in FASB ASC (para. 323-10-35-4),

> Under the equity method, an investor shall recognize its share of the earnings or losses of an investee in the periods for which they are reported by the investee in its financial statements rather than in the period in which an investee declares a dividend.

Because the investor can influence their timing, investee dividends cannot objectively measure income generated from the investment.

Application of Equity Method	
Investee Event	**Investor Accounting**
Income is recognized.	Proportionate share of income is recognized.
Dividends are declared.	Investor's share of investee dividends reduce the investment account.

Application of the equity method thus causes the investment account on the investor's balance sheet to vary directly with changes in the investee's equity.

In contrast, the fair-value method reports investments at fair value if it is readily determinable. Also, income is recognized both from changes in fair value and upon receipt of dividends. Consequently, financial reports can vary depending on whether the equity method or fair-value method is appropriate.

To illustrate, assume that Big Company owns a 20 percent interest in Little Company purchased on January 1, 2020, for $210,000. Little then reports net income of $200,000, $300,000, and $400,000, respectively, in the next three years while declaring dividends of $50,000, $100,000, and $200,000. The fair values of Big's investment in Little, as determined by market prices, were $245,000, $282,000, and $325,000 at the end of 2020, 2021, and 2022, respectively.

Exhibit 1.1 compares the accounting for Big's investment in Little across the two methods. The fair-value method carries the investment at its market values, presumed to be readily available in this example. Income is recognized both through changes in Little's fair value and as Little declares dividends.

In contrast, under the equity method, Big recognizes income as it is recorded by Little. As shown in Exhibit 1.1, Big recognizes $180,000 in income over the three years, and the

EXHIBIT 1.1 Comparison of Fair-Value Method (ASC 321) and Equity Method (ASC 323)

			Accounting by Big Company When Influence Is Not Significant (fair-value method)			Accounting by Big Company When Influence Is Significant (equity method)	
Year	**Income of Little Company**	**Dividends Declared by Little Company**	**Dividend Income**	**Fair-Value Change to Income**	**Carrying Amount of Investment**	**Equity in Investee Income***	**Carrying Amount of Investment†**
2020	$200,000	$ 50,000	$10,000	$ 35,000	$245,000	$ 40,000	$240,000
2021	300,000	100,000	20,000	37,000	282,000	60,000	280,000
2022	400,000	200,000	40,000	43,000	325,000	80,000	320,000
Total income recognized			$70,000	$115,000		$180,000	

*Equity in investee income is 20 percent of the current year income reported by Little Company.

†The carrying amount of an investment under the equity method is the original cost plus income recognized less dividends. For 2020, as an example, the $240,000 reported balance is the $210,000 cost plus $40,000 equity income less $10,000 in dividends.

carrying amount of the investment is adjusted upward to $320,000. Dividends from Little are not an appropriate measure of income because of the assumed significant influence over the investee. Big's ability to influence Little's decisions applies to the timing of dividend distributions. Therefore, dividends from Little do not objectively measure Big's income from its investment in Little. As Little records income, however, under the equity method Big recognizes its share (20 percent) of the income and increases the investment account. Thus, the equity method reflects the accrual model: The investor recognizes income as it is recognized by the investee, not when the investee declares a cash dividend.

Exhibit 1.1 shows that the carrying amount of the investment fluctuates each year under the equity method. This recording parallels the changes occurring in the net asset figures reported by the investee. If the owners' equity of the investee rises through income, an increase is made in the investment account; decreases such as losses and dividends cause reductions to be recorded. Thus, the equity method conveys information that describes the relationship created by the investor's ability to significantly influence the investee.

Equity Method Accounting Procedures

Once guidelines for the application of the equity method have been established, the mechanical process necessary for recording basic transactions is straightforward. The investor accrues its percentage of the earnings reported by the investee each period. Investee dividend declarations reduce the investment balance to reflect the decrease in the investee's book value.[9]

Referring again to the information presented in Exhibit 1.1, Little Company reported a net income of $200,000 during 2020 and declared and paid cash dividends of $50,000. These figures indicate that Little's net assets have increased by $150,000 during the year. Therefore, in its financial records, Big Company records the following journal entries to apply the equity method:

	Debit	Credit
Investment in Little Company	40,000	
Equity in Investee Income		40,000
To accrue earnings of a 20 percent owned investee ($200,000 × 20%)		
Dividend Receivable	10,000	
Investment in Little Company		10,000
To record a dividend declaration by Little Company ($50,000 × 20%)		
Cash	10,000	
Dividend Receivable		10,000
To record collection of the cash dividend.		

In the first entry, Big accrues income based on the investee's reported earnings. The second entry reflects the dividend declaration and the related reduction in Little's net assets followed then by the cash collection. The $30,000 net increment recorded here in Big's investment account ($40,000 – $10,000) represents 20 percent of the $150,000 increase in Little's book value that occurred during the year.

LO 1-5

Allocate the cost of an equity method investment and compute amortization expense to match revenues recognized from the investment to the excess of investor cost over investee book value.

Excess of Investment Cost over Book Value Acquired

After the basic concepts and procedures of the equity method are mastered, more complex accounting issues can be introduced. Surely one of the most common problems encountered in applying the equity method occurs when the investment cost exceeds the proportionate book value of the investee company.[10]

[9] In this text, the terms *book value* and *carrying amount* are used synonymously. Each refers to either an account balance, an amount appearing in a financial statement, or the amount of net assets (stockholders' equity) of a business entity.

[10] Although encountered less frequently, investments can be purchased at a cost that is less than the underlying book value of the investee. Accounting for this possibility is explored in later chapters.

Discussion Question

DOES THE EQUITY METHOD REALLY APPLY HERE?

Abraham, Inc., a New Jersey corporation, operates 57 bakeries throughout the northeastern section of the United States. In the past, its founder, James Abraham, owned all the company's outstanding common stock. However, during the early part of this year, the corporation suffered a severe cash flow problem brought on by rapid expansion. To avoid bankruptcy, Abraham sought additional investment capital from a friend, Dennis Bostitch, who owns Highland Laboratories. Subsequently, Highland paid $700,000 cash to Abraham, Inc., to acquire enough newly issued shares of common stock for a one-third ownership interest.

At the end of this year, the accountants for Highland Laboratories are discussing the proper method of reporting this investment. One argues for maintaining the asset at its original cost: "This purchase is no more than a loan to bail out the bakeries. Mr. Abraham will continue to run the organization with little or no attention paid to us. After all, what does anyone in our company know about baking bread? I would be surprised if Abraham does not reacquire these shares as soon as the bakery business is profitable again."

One of the other accountants disagrees, stating that the equity method is appropriate. "I realize that our company is not capable of running a bakery. However, the official rules state that we must have only the *ability* to exert significant influence. With one-third of the common stock in our possession, we certainly have that ability. Whether we use it or not, this ability means that we are required to apply the equity method."

How should Highland Laboratories account for its investment in Abraham, Inc.?

Unless the investor acquires its ownership at the time of the investee's conception, paying an amount equal to book value is rare. A number of possible reasons exist for a difference between the book value of a company and its fair value as reflected by the price of its stock. A company's fair value at any time is based on a multitude of factors such as company profitability, the introduction of a new product, expected dividend payments, projected operating results, and general economic conditions. Furthermore, stock prices are based, at least partially, on the perceived worth of a company's net assets, amounts that often vary dramatically from underlying book values. Many asset and liability accounts shown on a balance sheet tend to measure historical costs rather than current value. In addition, these reported figures are affected by the specific accounting methods adopted by a company. Inventory costing methods such as LIFO and FIFO, for example, obviously lead to different book values as does each of the acceptable depreciation methods.

If an investment is acquired at a price in excess of the investee's book value, logical reasons should explain the additional cost incurred by the investor. The source of the excess of cost over book value is important. Income recognition requires matching the income generated from the investment with its cost. Excess costs allocated to fixed assets will likely be expensed over longer periods than costs allocated to inventory. In applying the equity method, the cause of such an excess payment can be divided into two general categories:

1. Specifically identifiable investee assets and liabilities can have fair values that differ from their present book values. The excess payment can be identified directly with individual accounts such as inventory, equipment, franchise rights, and so on.
2. The investor may pay an extra amount because it expects future benefits to accrue from the investment. Such benefits could be anticipated as the result of factors such as the estimated profitability of the investee or the expected relationship between the two companies. When

the additional payment cannot be attributed to any specifically identifiable investee asset or liability, the investor recognizes an intangible asset called *goodwill*. For example, eBay Inc. once disclosed in its annual report that goodwill related to its equity method investments was approximately $27.4 million.

As an illustration, assume that Grande Company is negotiating the acquisition of 30 percent of the outstanding shares of Chico Company. Chico's balance sheet reports assets of $500,000 and liabilities of $300,000 for a net book value of $200,000. After investigation, Grande determines that Chico's equipment is undervalued in the company's financial records by $60,000. One of its patents is also undervalued, but only by $40,000. By adding these valuation adjustments to Chico's book value, Grande arrives at an estimated $300,000 worth for the company's net assets. Based on this computation, Grande offers $90,000 for a 30 percent share of the investee's outstanding stock.

Book value of Chico Company [assets minus liabilities (or stockholders' equity)]	$200,000
Undervaluation of equipment	60,000
Undervaluation of patent	40,000
Value of net assets	$300,000
Percentage acquired	30%
Purchase price	$ 90,000

Although Grande's purchase price is in excess of the proportionate share of Chico's book value, this additional amount can be attributed to two specific accounts: Equipment and Patents. No part of the extra payment is traceable to any other projected future benefit. Thus, the cost of Grande's investment is allocated as follows:

Payment by investor		$90,000
Percentage of book value acquired ($200,000 × 30%)		60,000
Payment in excess of book value		30,000
Excess payment identified with specific assets:		
Equipment ($60,000 undervaluation × 30%)	$18,000	
Patent ($40,000 undervaluation × 30%)	12,000	30,000
Excess payment not identified with specific assets—goodwill		$ -0-

Of the $30,000 excess payment made by the investor, $18,000 is assigned to the equipment whereas $12,000 is traced to a patent and its undervaluation. No amount of the purchase price is allocated to goodwill.

To take this example one step further, assume that Chico's owners reject Grande's proposed $90,000 price. They believe that the value of the company as a going concern is higher than the fair value of its net assets. Because the management of Grande believes that valuable synergies will be created through this purchase, the bid price is raised to $125,000 and accepted. This new acquisition price is allocated as follows:

Payment by investor		$125,000
Percentage of book value acquired ($200,000 × 30%)		60,000
Payment in excess of book value		65,000
Excess payment identified with specific assets:		
Equipment ($60,000 undervaluation × 30%)	$18,000	
Patent ($40,000 undervaluation × 30%)	12,000	30,000
Excess payment not identified with specific assets—goodwill		$ 35,000

As this example indicates, *any extra payment that cannot be attributed to a specific asset or liability is assigned to the intangible asset goodwill.* Although the actual purchase price can be computed by a number of different techniques or simply result from negotiations, goodwill is always the excess amount not allocated to identifiable asset or liability accounts.

Under the equity method, the investor enters total cost in a single investment account regardless of the allocation of any excess purchase price. If all parties accept Grande's bid of $125,000, the acquisition is initially recorded at that amount despite the internal assignments made to equipment, patents, and goodwill. The entire $125,000 was paid to acquire this investment, and it is recorded as such.

The Amortization Process

In the preceding transaction, the extra payment over Grande's book value was made for specific identifiable assets (equipment and patents), and goodwill. Even though the actual dollar amounts are recorded within the investment account, a definite historical cost can be attributed to these assets. With a cost to the investor as well as a specified life, the payment relating to each asset (except land, goodwill, and other indefinite life intangibles) should be amortized over an appropriate time period.[11] However, certain intangibles such as goodwill are considered to have indefinite lives and thus are not subject to amortization.[12]

Goodwill associated with equity method investments, for the most part, is measured in the same manner as goodwill arising from a business combination (see Chapters 2 through 7). One difference is that goodwill arising from a business combination is subject to annual impairment reviews, whereas goodwill implicit in equity method investments is not. Equity method investments are tested in their entirety for permanent declines in value.[13]

To show the amortization process for definite-lived assets, we continue with our Grande and Chico example. Assume that the equipment has a 10-year remaining life, the patent a 5-year life, and the goodwill an indefinite life. If the straight-line method is used with no salvage value, *the investor's cost* should be amortized initially as follows:[14]

Account	Cost Assigned	Remaining Useful Life	Annual Amortization
Equipment	$18,000	10 years	$1,800
Patent	12,000	5 years	2,400
Goodwill	35,000	Indefinite	–0–
Annual expense (for five years until patent cost is completely amortized)			$4,200

In recording this annual expense, Grande reduces the investment balance in the same way it would amortize the cost of any other asset that had a limited life. Therefore, at the end of the first year of holding the investment, the investor records the following journal entry under the equity method:

	Debit	Credit
Equity in Investee Income	4,200	
Investment in Chico Company		4,200
To record amortization of excess payment allocated to equipment and patent.		

[11] A 2015 FASB *Proposed Accounting Standards Update,* "Simplifying the Equity Method of Accounting," recommended the elimination of the identification and amortization of excess cost over acquired investee book value. However, at a December 2015 meeting, the FASB did not affirm the proposed elimination of current accounting treatment for the excess cost over acquired investee book value and directed its staff to research additional alternatives for improving the equity method.

[12] Other intangibles (such as certain licenses, trademarks, etc.) also can be considered to have indefinite lives and thus are not amortized unless and until their lives are determined to be limited. Further discussion of intangibles with indefinite lives appears in Chapter 3.

[13] Because equity method goodwill is not separable from the related investment, goodwill should not be separately tested for impairment. See also FASB ASC (para. 350-20-35-59).

[14] Unless otherwise stated, all amortization computations are based on the straight-line method with no salvage value.

Because this amortization relates to investee assets, the investor does not establish a specific expense account. Instead, as in the previous entry, the expense is recognized by decreasing the the investor's equity income accruing from the investee company.

To illustrate this entire process, assume that Tall Company purchases 20 percent of Short Company for $200,000. Tall can exercise significant influence over the investee; thus, the equity method is appropriately applied. The acquisition is made on January 1, 2020, when Short holds net assets with a book value of $700,000. Tall believes that the investee's building (10-year remaining life) is undervalued within the financial records by $80,000 and equipment with a 5-year remaining life is undervalued by $120,000. Any goodwill established by this purchase is considered to have an indefinite life. During 2020, Short reports a net income of $150,000 and at year-end declares a cash dividend of $60,000.

Tall's three basic journal entries for 2020 pose little problem:

January 1, 2020		
Investment in Short Company	200,000	
Cash		200,000
To record acquisition of 20 percent of the outstanding shares of Short Company.		

December 31, 2020		
Investment in Short Company	30,000	
Equity in Investee Income		30,000
To accrue 20 percent of the 2020 reported earnings of investee ($150,000 × 20%).		
Dividend Receivable	12,000	
Investment in Short Company		12,000
To record a dividend declaration by Short Company ($60,000 × 20%).		

An allocation of Tall's $200,000 purchase price must be made to determine whether an additional adjusting entry is necessary to recognize annual amortization associated with the extra payment:

Payment by investor		$200,000
Percentage of 1/1/20 book value ($700,000 × 20%)		140,000
Payment in excess of book value		60,000
Excess payment identified with specific assets:		
Building ($80,000 × 20%)	$16,000	
Equipment ($120,000 × 20%)	24,000	40,000
Excess payment not identified with specific assets—goodwill		$ 20,000

As can be seen, $16,000 of the purchase price is assigned to a building and $24,000 to equipment, with the remaining $20,000 attributed to goodwill. For each asset with a definite useful life, periodic amortization is required.

Asset	**Attributed Cost**	**Remaining Useful Life**	**Annual Amortization**
Building	$16,000	10 years	$1,600
Equipment	24,000	5 years	4,800
Goodwill	20,000	Indefinite	–0–
Total for 2020			$6,400

At the end of 2020, Tall must also record the following adjustment in connection with these cost allocations:

Equity in Investee Income	6,400	
Investment in Short Company		6,400
To record 2020 amortization of excess payment allocated to building ($1,600) and equipment ($4,800).		

Although these entries are shown separately here for better explanation, Tall would probably net the income accrual for the year ($30,000) and the amortization ($6,400) to create a single entry increasing the investment and recognizing equity income of $23,600. Thus, the first-year return on Tall Company's beginning investment balance (defined as equity earnings/beginning investment balance) is equal to 11.80 percent ($23,600/$200,000).

International Accounting Standard 28—Investments in Associates

The International Accounting Standards Board (IASB), similar to the FASB, recognizes the need to take into account the significant influence that can occur when one firm holds a certain amount of voting shares of another. The IASB defines significant influence as the power to participate in the financial and operating policy decisions of the investee, but it is not control or joint control over those policies. The following describes the basics of the equity method in International Accounting Standard (IAS) 28:[15]

> If an investor holds, directly or indirectly (e.g., through subsidiaries), 20 percent or more of the voting power of the investee, it is presumed that the investor has significant influence, unless it can be clearly demonstrated that this is not the case. Conversely, if the investor holds, directly or indirectly (e.g., through subsidiaries), less than 20 per cent of the voting power of the investee, it is presumed that the investor does not have significant influence, unless such influence can be clearly demonstrated. A substantial or majority ownership by another investor does not necessarily preclude an investor from having significant influence.
>
> Under the equity method, the investment in an associate is initially recognised at cost and the carrying amount is increased or decreased to recognise the investor's share of the profit or loss of the investee after the date of acquisition. The investor's share of the profit or loss of the investee is recognised in the investor's profit or loss. Distributions received from an investee reduce the carrying amount of the investment.

As seen from the above excerpt from IAS 28, the equity method concepts and applications described are virtually identical to those prescribed by the FASB ASC. Nonetheless, some differences do exist. First, as described later in this chapter, the FASB allows a fair-value reporting option for investments that otherwise are accounted for under the equity method. IAS 28, however, does not provide for a fair-value reporting option. Second, if the investee employs accounting policies that differ from those of the investor, IAS 28 requires the financial statements of the investee to be adjusted to reflect the investor's accounting policies for the purpose of applying the equity method. U.S. GAAP does not have a similar conformity requirement.

Equity Method—Additional Issues

The previous sections on equity income accruals and excess cost amortizations provide the basics for applying the equity method. However, several other non-routine issues can arise during the life of an equity method investment. More specifically, special procedures are required in accounting for each of the following:

1. Reporting a change to the equity method.
2. Reporting investee income from sources other than continuing operations.
3. Reporting investee losses.
4. Reporting the sale of an equity investment.

[15] International Accounting Standards Board, IAS 28, "Investments in Associates," Technical Summary, www.iasb.org.

LO 1-6a

Understand the financial reporting consequences for a change to the equity method.

Reporting a Change to the Equity Method

In many instances, an investor's ability to significantly influence an investee is not achieved through a single stock acquisition. The investor could possess only a minor ownership for some years before purchasing enough additional shares to require conversion to the equity method. Before the investor achieves significant influence, any investment should be reported by either the fair-value method or, if the investment fair value is not readily determinable, the cost method. After the investment reaches the point at which the equity method becomes applicable, a technical question arises about the appropriate means of changing from one method to the other.[16]

FASB ASC (para. 323-10-35-33) addresses the issue of how to account for an investment in the common stock of an investee that, through additional stock acquisition or other means (e.g., increased degree of influence, reduction of investee's outstanding stock, etc.) becomes qualified for use of the equity method.

> If an investment qualifies for use of the equity method . . . , the investor shall add the cost of acquiring the additional interest in the investee (if any) to the current basis of the investor's previously held interest and adopt the equity method of accounting as of the date the investment becomes qualified for equity method accounting.

Thus, the FASB requires a prospective approach by requiring that the cost of any new share acquired simply be added to the current investment carrying amount. By mandating prospective treatment, the FASB avoids the complexity of restating prior period amounts.[17]

To illustrate, assume that on January 1, 2020, Alpha Company exchanges $84,000 for a 10 percent ownership in Bailey Company. At the time of the transaction, officials of Alpha do not believe that their company gained the ability to exert significant influence over Bailey. Alpha properly accounts for the investment using the fair-value method and recognizes in net income its 10 percent ownership share of changes in Bailey's fair value. The fair and book values of Bailey's common stock appear in the following table:

Date	Fair Value	Book Value
January 1, 2020	$840,000	$670,000
December 31, 2020	890,000	715,000

At the end of 2020, Alpha recognizes the increase in its 10 percent share of Bailey's fair value and increases its investment account to $89,000. Because the fair-value method is used to account for the investment, Bailey's $670,000 book value balance at January 1, 2020 does not affect Alpha's accounting.

Then on January 1, 2021, Alpha purchases an additional 30 percent of Bailey's outstanding voting stock for $267,000 and achieves the ability to significantly influence the investee's decision making. Alpha will now apply the equity method to account for its investment in Bailey. To bring about the prospective change to the equity method, Alpha prepares the following journal entry on January 1, 2021:

	Debit	Credit
Investment in Bailey Company	267,000	
Cash		267,000
To record an additional 30 percent investment in Bailey Company.		

On January 1, 2021, Bailey's carrying amounts for its assets and liabilities equaled their fair values except for a patent, which was undervalued by $175,000 and had a 10-year remaining useful life.

[16] A switch to the equity method also can be required if the investee purchases a portion of its own shares as treasury stock. This transaction can increase the investor's percentage of outstanding stock.

[17] Prior to 2017, the FASB required a retrospective adjustment to an investor's previous ownership shares upon achieving significant influence over an investee.

To determine the proper amount of excess fair-value amortization required in applying the equity method, Alpha prepares an investment allocation schedule. The fair value of Alpha's total (40 percent) investment serves as the valuation basis for the allocation schedule as of January 1, 2021, the date Alpha achieves the ability to exercise significant influence over Bailey. The following is the January 1, 2021 investment allocation schedule:

Investment Fair Value Allocation Schedule
Investment in Bailey Company
January 1, 2021

Current fair value of initial 10 percent ownership of Bailey	$ 89,000
Payment for additional 30 percent investment in Bailey	267,000
Total fair value of 40 percent investment in Bailey	$356,000
Alpha's share of Bailey's book value (40% × $715,000)	286,000
Investment fair value in excess of Bailey's book value	$ 70,000
Excess fair value attributable to Bailey's patent (40% × $175,000)	$ 70,000
	-0-

We next assume that Bailey reports net income of $130,000 and declares and pays a $50,000 dividend at the end of 2021. Accordingly, Alpha applies the equity method and records the following three journal entries at the end of 2021:

	Debit	Credit
Investment in Bailey Company	45,000	
Equity in Investee Income		45,000
To accrue 40 percent of the year 2021 income reported by Bailey Company ($130,000 × 40%) – $7,000 excess patent amortization (10-year remaining life).		
Dividend Receivable	20,000	
Investment in Bailey Company		20,000
To record the 2021 dividend declaration by Bailey Company ($50,000 × 40%).		
Cash	20,000	
Dividend Receivable		20,000
To record collection of the cash dividend.		

LO 1-6b

Understand the financial reporting consequences for investee's other comprehensive income.

Reporting Investee's Other Comprehensive Income and Irregular Items

In many cases, reported net income and dividends sufficiently capture changes in an investee's owners' equity. By recording its share of investee income and dividends, an investor company typically ensures its investment account reflects its share of the underlying investee equity. However, when an investee company's activities require recognition of other comprehensive income (OCI), its owners' equity (and net assets) will reflect changes not captured in its reported net income.[18]

Equity method accounting requires that the investor record its share of investee OCI, which then is included in its balance sheet as Accumulated Other Comprehensive Income (AOCI). As noted by The Coca-Cola Company in its 2018 annual 10-K report,

> AOCI attributable to shareowners of The Coca-Cola Company is separately presented on our consolidated balance sheets as a component of The Coca-Cola Company's shareowners' equity, which also includes our proportionate share of equity method investees' AOCI.

Included in AOCI are items such as accumulated derivative net gains and losses, foreign currency translation adjustments, and certain pension adjustments.

[18] OCI is defined as revenues, expenses, gains, and losses that under generally accepted accounting principles are included in comprehensive income but excluded from net income. OCI is accumulated and reported in stockholders' equity.

To examine this issue, assume that Charles Company applies the equity method in accounting for its 30 percent investment in the voting stock of Norris Company. No excess amortization resulted from this investment. In 2020, Norris reports net income of $500,000. Norris also reports $80,000 in OCI from pension and other postretirement adjustments. Charles Company accrues earnings of $150,000 based on 30 percent of the $500,000 net figure. However, for proper financial reporting, Charles must recognize an increase in its Investment in Norris account for its 30 percent share of its investee's OCI. This treatment is intended, once again, to mirror the close relationship between the two companies.

The journal entry by Charles Company to record its equity interest in the income and OCI of Norris follows:

Investment in Norris Company	174,000	
Equity in Investee Income		150,000
Other Comprehensive Income of Investee		24,000
To accrue the investee's operating income and other comprehensive income from equity investment.		

OCI thus represents a source of change in investee company net assets that is recognized under the equity method. In the preceding example, Charles Company includes $24,000 of other comprehensive income in its balance sheet AOCI total.

Other equity method recognition issues arise for irregular items traditionally included within net income. For example, an investee may report income (loss) from discontinued operations as components of its current net income. In such cases, the equity method requires the investor to record and report its share of these items in recognizing equity earnings of the investee.

LO 1-6c

Understand the financial reporting consequences for investee losses.

Reporting Investee Losses

Although most of the previous illustrations are based on the recording of profits, accounting for losses incurred by the investee is handled in a similar manner. The investor recognizes the appropriate percentage of each loss and reduces the carrying amount of the investment account. Even though these procedures are consistent with the concept of the equity method, they fail to take into account all possible loss situations.

Impairments of Equity Method Investments

Investments can suffer permanent losses in fair value that are not evident through equity method accounting. Such declines can be caused by the loss of major customers, changes in economic conditions, loss of a significant patent or other legal right, damage to the company's reputation, and the like. Permanent reductions in fair value resulting from such adverse events might not be reported immediately by the investor through the normal equity entries discussed previously. The FASB ASC (para. 323-10-35-32) provides the following guidance:

> A loss in value of an investment which is other than a temporary decline shall be recognized. Evidence of a loss in value might include, but would not necessarily be limited to, absence of an ability to recover the carrying amount of the investment or inability of the investee to sustain an earnings capacity that would justify the carrying amount of the investment.

Thus, when a permanent decline in an equity method investment's value occurs, the investor must recognize an impairment loss and reduce the asset to fair value.

However, this loss must be permanent before such recognition becomes necessary. Under the equity method, a temporary drop in the fair value of an investment is simply ignored.

Navistar International Corporation, a manufacturer of trucks and buses, for example, noted the following in its 2018 annual report:

> We assess the potential impairment of our equity method investments and determine fair value based on valuation methodologies, as appropriate, including the present value of estimated future cash flows, estimates of sales proceeds, and market multiples. If an investment is determined to be impaired and the decline in value is other than temporary, we record an appropriate write-down.

Investment Reduced to Zero

Through the recognition of reported losses as well as any permanent drops in fair value, the investment account can eventually be reduced to a zero balance. This condition is most likely to occur if the investee has suffered extreme losses or if the original purchase was made at a low, bargain price. Regardless of the reason, the carrying amount of the investment account is sometimes eliminated in total.

When an investment account is reduced to zero, the investor should discontinue using the equity method rather than establish a negative balance. The investment retains a zero balance until subsequent investee profits eliminate all unrecognized losses. Once the original cost of the investment has been eliminated, no additional losses can accrue to the investor (since the entire cost has been written off).

For example, Switch, Inc., a technology infrastructure company, explains in its 2018 annual 10-K report that

> The Company discontinues applying the equity method of accounting when the investment is reduced to zero. If the investee subsequently reports net income or other comprehensive income, the Company resumes applying the equity method of accounting only after its share of unrecognized net income and other comprehensive income, respectively, equals the share of losses not recognized during the period the equity method of accounting was suspended.

LO 1-6d

Understand the financial reporting consequences for sales of equity method investments.

Reporting the Sale of an Equity Investment

At any time, the investor can choose to sell part or all of its holdings in the investee company. If a sale occurs, the equity method continues to be applied until the transaction date, thus establishing an appropriate carrying amount for the investment. The investor then reduces this balance by the percentage of shares sold.

As an example, assume that Top Company owns 40 percent of the 100,000 outstanding shares of Bottom Company, an investment accounted for by the equity method. Any excess investment cost over Top's share of Bottom's book value is considered goodwill. Although these 40,000 shares were acquired some years ago for $200,000, application of the equity method has increased the asset balance to $320,000 as of January 1, 2021. On July 1, 2021, Top elects to sell 10,000 of these shares (one-fourth of its investment) for $110,000 in cash, thereby reducing ownership in Bottom from 40 percent to 30 percent. Bottom Company reports net income of $70,000 during the first six months of 2021 and declares and pays cash dividends of $30,000.

Top, as the investor, initially makes the following journal entries on July 1, 2021, to accrue the proper income and establish the correct investment balance:

Account	Debit	Credit
Investment in Bottom Company	28,000	
Equity in Investee Income		28,000
To accrue equity income for first six months of 2021 ($70,000 × 40%).		
Dividend Receivable	12,000	
Investment in Bottom Company		12,000
To record a cash dividend declaration by Bottom Company ($30,000 × 40%).		
Cash	12,000	
Dividend Receivable		12,000
To record collection of the cash dividend.		

These two entries increase the carrying amount of Top's investment by $16,000, creating a balance of $336,000 as of July 1, 2021. The sale of one-fourth of these shares can then be recorded as follows:

Account	Debit	Credit
Cash	110,000	
Investment in Bottom Company		84,000
Gain on Sale of Investment		26,000
To record sale of one-fourth of investment in Bottom Company (¼ × $336,000 = $84,000).		

After the sale is completed, Top continues to apply the equity method to this investment based on 30 percent ownership rather than 40 percent. However, if the sale had been of sufficient magnitude to cause Top to lose its ability to exercise significant influence over Bottom, the equity method would cease to be applicable. For example, if Top Company's holdings were reduced from 40 percent to 15 percent, the equity method might no longer be appropriate after the sale. The remaining shares held by the investor are reported according to the fair-value method with the remaining book value becoming the new *cost* figure for the investment rather than the amount originally paid.

If an investor is required to change from the equity method to the fair-value method, no retrospective adjustment is made. As previously demonstrated, a change to the equity method is also treated prospectively.

LO 1-7

Describe the rationale and computations to defer gross profits on intra-entity inventory sales until the goods are either consumed by the owner or sold to outside parties.

Deferral of Intra-Entity Gross Profits in Inventory[19]

Many equity acquisitions establish ties between companies to facilitate the direct purchase and sale of inventory items. For example, The Coca-Cola Company recently disclosed net sales in excess of $14.1 billion to its equity method investees. The significant influence relationship between an investor and investee in many ways creates its own entity that works to achieve business objectives. Thus, we use the term *intra-entity* to describe sales between an investor and its equity method investee.

Intra-entity sales require special accounting to ensure proper timing for profit recognition. A fundamental accounting concept is that an entity cannot recognize profits through activities with itself. For example, when an investor company sells inventory to its 40 percent-owned investee at a profit, 40 percent of this sale effectively is with itself. Consequently, the investor company delays 40 percent of the gross profit recognition until the inventory is sold to an independent party or is consumed.[20]

Thus, in the presence of significant influence, the amount of profit deferred is limited to the investor's ownership share of the investee. In applying the equity method, the investor therefore defers only its share of the profit from intra-entity sales until the buyer's ultimate disposition of the goods. When the inventory is eventually consumed within operations or resold to an unrelated party, the investor recognizes the remaining gross profit. Accounting for both the profit deferral and subsequent recognition takes place through adjustments to the "Equity in Investee Income" and "Investment" accounts.

Intra-entity inventory sales are identified as either *downstream* or *upstream. Downstream sales* refer to the investor's sale of an item to the investee. Conversely, an *upstream sale* describes one that the investee makes to the investor (see Exhibit 1.2). *Although the direction of intra-entity sales does not affect reported equity method balances for investments when significant influence exists, it has definite consequences when financial control requires the consolidation of financial statements, as discussed in Chapter 5.* Therefore, these two types of intra-entity sales are examined separately even at this introductory stage.

EXHIBIT 1.2
Downstream and Upstream Sales

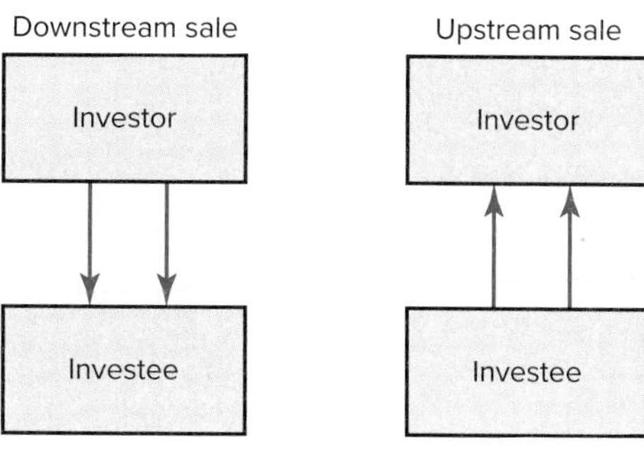

[19] Intra-entity transfers can involve the sale of items other than inventory. The intra-entity transfer of depreciable fixed assets and land is discussed in a later chapter.

[20] When inventory is consumed—for example, in a manufacturing process—sales of the resulting production are assumed to generate revenues from outside, unrelated parties.

Downstream Sales of Inventory

Assume that Major Company owns a 40 percent share of Minor Company and accounts for this investment through the equity method. In 2021, Major sells inventory to Minor at a price of $50,000. This figure includes a gross profit of 30 percent, or $15,000. By the end of 2021, Minor has sold $40,000 of these goods to outside parties while retaining $10,000 in inventory for sale during the subsequent year.

The investor has made downstream sales to the investee. In applying the equity method, recognition of the related profit must be delayed until the buyer disposes of these goods. Although total intra-entity inventory sales amounted to $50,000 in 2021, $40,000 of this merchandise has already been resold to outsiders, thereby justifying the normal reporting of profits. For the $10,000 still in the investee's inventory, the investor delays gross profit recognition. In computing equity income, the investor's portion of the intra-entity profit must be deferred until Minor disposes of the goods.

The gross profit on the original intra-entity sale was 30 percent of the sale price; therefore, Major's profit associated with these remaining items is $3,000 ($10,000 × 30%). *However, because only 40 percent of the investee's stock is held, just $1,200 ($3,000 × 40%) of this profit is deferred.* Major's ownership percentage reflects the intra-entity portion of the profit. The total $3,000 gross profit within the ending inventory balance is not the amount deferred. Rather, 40 percent of that gross profit is viewed as the currently deferred figure.

Remaining Ending Inventory	Gross Profit Percentage	Gross Profit in Ending Inventory	Investor Ownership Percentage	Deferred Intra-Entity Gross Profit
$10,000	30%	$3,000	40%	$1,200

After calculating the appropriate deferral, the investor decreases current equity income by $1,200 to reflect the deferred portion of the intra-entity profit. This procedure temporarily removes this portion of the profit from the investor's books in 2021 until the investee disposes of the inventory in 2022. Major accomplishes the actual deferral through the following year-end journal entry:

Intra-Entity Gross Profit Deferral		
Equity in Investee Income	1,200	
Investment in Minor Company		1,200
To defer gross profit on sale of inventory to Minor Company.		

In the subsequent year, when this inventory is eventually consumed by Minor or sold to unrelated parties, the deferral is no longer needed. Because a sale to an outside party has now occurred, Major should recognize the $1,200. By merely reversing the preceding deferral entry, the accountant succeeds in moving the investor's profit into the appropriate time period. Recognition shifts from the year of inventory transfer to the year in which the sale to customers outside of the affiliated entity takes place.

Subsequent Recognition of Intra-Entity Gross Profit		
Investment in Minor Company	1,200	
Equity in Investee Income		1,200
To recognize income on intra-entity sale that now can be recognized after sales to outsiders.		

Upstream Sales of Inventory

Unlike consolidated financial statements (see Chapter 5), the equity method reports upstream sales of inventory in the same manner as downstream sales. Hence, the investor's share of gross profits remaining in ending inventory is deferred until the items are used or sold to unrelated parties. To illustrate, assume that Major Company once again owns 40 percent of Minor Company. During the current year, Minor sells merchandise costing $40,000 to Major for $60,000. At the end of the fiscal period, Major still retains $15,000 of these goods. Minor reports net income of $120,000 for the year.

To reflect the basic accrual of the investee's earnings, Major records the following journal entry at the end of this year:

Income Accrual		
Investment in Minor Company	48,000	
Equity in Investee Income		48,000
To accrue income from 40 percent owned investee ($120,000 × 40%).		

The amount of the deferred intra-entity gross profit remaining at year-end is computed using the 33⅓ gross profit percentage of the sales price ($20,000/$60,000):

Remaining Ending Inventory	Gross Profit Percentage	Gross Profit in Ending Inventory	Investor Ownership Percentage	Deferred Intra-Entity Gross Profit
$15,000	33⅓%	$5,000	40%	$2,000

Based on this calculation, a second entry is required of the investor at year-end. Once again, a deferral of the gross profit created by the intra-entity sale is necessary for proper timing of income recognition. *Under the equity method for investments with significant influence, the direction of the sale between the investor and investee (upstream or downstream) has no effect on the final amounts reported in the financial statements.*

Intra-Entity Gross Profit Deferral		
Equity in Investee Income	2,000	
Investment in Minor Company		2,000
To defer recognition of intra-entity gross profit until inventory is used or sold to unrelated parties.		

After the adjustment, Major, the investor, reports earnings from this equity investment of $46,000 ($48,000 – $2,000). The income accrual is reduced because the investor defers its portion of the intra-entity gross profit. In an upstream sale, the investor's own inventory account contains the deferred gross profit. The previous entry, though, defers recognition of this profit by decreasing Major's investment account rather than the inventory balance. An alternative treatment would be the direct reduction of the investor's inventory balance as a means of accounting for this deferred amount. Although this alternative is acceptable, decreasing the investment account remains the traditional approach for deferring gross profits, even for upstream sales.

When the investor eventually consumes or sells the $15,000 in merchandise, the preceding journal entry is reversed as shown below. In this way, the effects of the inventory transfer are reported in the proper accounting period when sales to an outside party allow the recognition of the previously deferred intra-entity gross profit via the Equity in Investee Income account.

Subsequent Recognition of Intra-Entity Gross Profit		
Investment in Minor Company	2,000	
Equity in Investee Income		2,000
To recognize income on intra-entity sale that now can be recognized after sales to outsiders.		

Whether upstream or downstream, the investor's sales and purchases are still reported as if the transactions were conducted with outside parties. Only the investor's share of the gross profit is deferred, and that amount is adjusted solely through the equity income account. Furthermore, because the companies are not consolidated, the investee's reported balances are not altered at all to reflect the nature of these sales/purchases. Obviously, readers of the financial statements need to be made aware of the inclusion of these amounts in the income statement. Thus, reporting companies must disclose certain information about related-party transactions. These disclosures include the nature of the relationship, a description of the transactions, the dollar amounts of the transactions, and amounts due to or from any related parties at year-end.

Financial Reporting Effects and Equity Method Criticisms

Equity Method Reporting Effects

It is important to realize that business decisions, including equity investments, typically involve the assessment of a wide range of consequences. For example, managers frequently are very interested in how financial statements report the effects of their decisions. This attention to financial reporting effects of business decisions arises because measurements of financial performance often affect the following:

- The firm's ability to raise capital.
- Managerial compensation.
- The ability to meet debt covenants and future interest rates.
- Managers' reputations.

Managers are also keenly aware that measures of earnings per share can strongly affect investors' perceptions of the underlying value of their firms' publicly traded stock. Consequently, prior to making investment decisions, firms will study and assess the prospective effects of applying the equity method on the income reported in financial statements. Additionally, such analyses of prospective reported income effects can influence firms regarding the degree of influence they wish to have, or even on the decision of whether to invest. For example, managers could have a required projected rate of return on an initial investment. In such cases, an analysis of projected income will be made to assist in setting an offer price.

For example, Investmor Co. is examining a potential 25 percent equity investment in Marco, Inc., that will provide a significant level of influence. Marco projects an annual income of $300,000 for the near future. Marco's book value is $450,000, and it has an unrecorded newly developed technology appraised at $200,000 with an estimated useful life of 10 years. In considering offer prices for the 25 percent investment in Marco, Investmor projects equity earnings as follows:

Projected income (25% × $300,000)	$75,000
Excess unpatented technology amortization [(25% × 200,000) ÷ 10 years]	(5,000)
Annual expected equity in Marco earnings	$70,000

Investmor's required first-year rate of return (before tax) on these types of investments is 20 percent. Therefore, to meet the first-year rate of return requirement involves a maximum price of $350,000 ($70,000 ÷ 20% = $350,000). If the shares are publicly traded (leaving the firm a "price taker"), such income projections can assist the company in making a recommendation to wait for share prices to move to make the investment attractive.

Criticisms of the Equity Method

Over the past several decades, thousands of business firms have accounted for their investments using the equity method. Recently, however, the equity method has come under criticism for the following:

- Emphasizing the 20–50 percent of voting stock in determining significant influence versus control.
- Allowing off-balance-sheet financing.
- Potentially biasing performance ratios.

The guidelines for the equity method suggest that a 20–50 percent ownership of voting shares indicates significant influence that falls short of control. But can one firm exert "control" over another firm absent an interest of more than 50 percent? Clearly, if one firm controls another, consolidation is the appropriate financial reporting technique. However, over the years, firms have learned ways to control other firms despite owning less than 50 percent of voting shares. For example, contracts across companies can limit one firm's ability to act without permission of the other. Such contractual control can be seen in debt arrangements, long-term sales and purchase agreements, and agreements concerning board membership. As a result, control is exerted through a variety of contractual arrangements. For financial reporting purposes, however, if ownership is 50 percent or less, a firm can argue that control technically does not exist.

In contrast to consolidated financial reports, when applying the equity method, the investee's assets and liabilities are not combined with the investor's amounts. Instead, the investor's balance sheet reports a single amount for the investment, and the income statement reports a single amount for its equity in the earnings of the investee. If consolidated, the assets, liabilities, revenues, and expenses of the investee are combined and reported in the body of the investor's financial statements.

Thus, for those companies wishing to actively manage their reported balance sheet numbers, the equity method provides an effective means. By keeping its ownership of voting shares less than 50 percent, a company can technically meet the rules for applying the equity method for its investments and at the same time report investee assets and liabilities "off balance sheet." As a result, relative to consolidation, a firm employing the equity method will report smaller values for assets and liabilities. Consequently, higher rates of return for its assets and sales, as well as lower debt-to-equity ratios, could result.

On the surface, it appears that firms can avoid balance sheet disclosure of debts by maintaining investments at less than 50 percent ownership. However, the equity method requires summarized information as to assets, liabilities, and results of operations of the investees to be presented in the notes or in separate statements. Therefore, supplementary information could be available under the equity method that would not be separately identified in consolidation. Nonetheless, some companies have contractual provisions (e.g., debt covenants, managerial compensation agreements) based on ratios in the main body of the financial statements. Meeting the provisions of such contracts could provide managers strong incentives to maintain technical eligibility to use the equity method rather than full consolidation.

LO 1-8

Explain the rationale and reporting implications of fair-value accounting for investments otherwise accounted for by the equity method.

Fair-Value Reporting for Equity Method Investments

Financial reporting standards allow a fair-value option under which an entity may irrevocably elect fair value as the initial and subsequent measurement attribute for certain financial assets and financial liabilities. Under the fair-value option, changes in the fair value of the elected financial items are included in earnings. Among the many financial assets available for the fair-value option were investments otherwise accounted for under the equity method.

For example, Citigroup has reported at fair value certain of its investments that previously were reported using the equity method. In its 2018 annual report, Citigroup noted that "certain investments in non-marketable equity securities and certain investments that would otherwise have been accounted for using the equity method are carried at fair value, since the Company has elected to apply fair-value accounting. Changes in fair value of such investments are recorded in earnings." Many other firms, however, have been reluctant to elect the fair-value option for their equity method investments.

Firms using fair-value accounting simply report the investment's fair value as an asset and changes in fair value as earnings. As such, firms neither compute excess cost amortizations nor adjust earnings for intra-entity profits. Dividends from an investee are included in earnings under the fair-value option. Because dividends typically reduce an investment's fair value, an increase in earnings from investee dividends would be offset by a decrease in earnings from the decline in an investment's fair value.

To illustrate, on January 1, 2020, Westwind Co. pays $722,000 in exchange for 40,000 common shares of Armco, Inc., which has 100,000 common shares outstanding, the majority of which continue to trade on the New York Stock Exchange. During the next two years, Armco reports the following information:

Year	Net Income	Cash Dividends	Common Shares Total Fair Value at December 31
2020	$158,000	$25,000	$1,900,000
2021	125,000	25,000	1,870,000

Westwind elects to use fair-value accounting and accordingly makes the following journal entries for its investment in Armco over the next two years.

Investment in Armco, Inc.	722,000	
Cash		722,000
To record Westwind's initial 40 percent investment in Armco, Inc.		
Cash	10,000	
Dividend Income*		10,000
To recognize 2020 dividends received (40%) as Investment income.		
Investment in Armco, Inc.	38,000	
Investment Income		38,000
To recognize Westwind's 40 percent of the 2020 change in Armco's fair value [($1,900,000 × 40%) – $722,000].		
Cash	10,000	
Dividend Income*		10,000
To recognize 2021 dividends received (40%) as investment income.		
Investment Loss	12,000	
Investment in Armco, Inc.		12,000
To recognize Westwind's 40 percent of the 2021 change in Armco's fair value [40% × ($1,870,000 – $1,900,000)].		

*This example assumes dividend declaration and payment occur at the same time.

In its December 31, 2021, balance sheet, Westwind thus reports its Investment in Armco account at $748,000, equal to 40 percent of Armco's total fair value (or $722,000 initial cost adjusted for 2020–2021 fair value changes of $38,000 less $12,000).

In addition to the increasing emphasis on fair values in financial reporting, the fair-value option also was motivated by a perceived need for consistency across various balance sheet items. In particular, the fair-value option is designed to limit volatility in earnings that occurs when some financial items are measured using cost-based attributes and others at fair value.

As FASB ASC (para. 825-10-10-1) observes, the objective of the fair-value option is

> to improve financial reporting by providing entities with the opportunity to mitigate volatility in reported earnings caused by measuring related assets and liabilities differently without having to apply complex hedge accounting provisions.

Thus, the fair-value option is designed to match asset valuation with fair-value reporting requirements for many liabilities.

Summary

1. The equity method of accounting for an investment reflects the close relationship that could exist between an investor and an investee. More specifically, this approach is available when the owner achieves the ability to apply significant influence to the investee's operating and financial decisions. Significant influence is presumed to exist at the 20 to 50 percent ownership level. However, the accountant must evaluate each situation, regardless of the percentage of ownership, to determine whether this ability is actually present.
2. To mirror the relationship between the companies, the equity method requires the investor to accrue income when the investee reports it in its financial statements. In recording this profit or loss, the investor separately reports items such as other comprehensive income and discontinued operations, to highlight their special nature. Dividend declarations decrease the owners' equity of the investee company; therefore, the investor reduces the investment account for its share of investee dividends.
3. When acquiring capital stock, an investor often pays an amount that exceeds the investee company's underlying book value. For accounting purposes, such excess payments must be either identified with specific assets and liabilities (such as land or buildings) or allocated to an intangible asset referred to as *goodwill*. The investor then amortizes each assigned cost (except for any amount attributed to land, goodwill, or other indefinite life assets) over the expected useful lives of the assets and liabilities. This amortization affects the amount of equity income recognized by the investor.
4. If the investor sells the entire investment or any portion of it, the equity method is applied until the date of disposal. A gain or loss is computed based on the adjusted book value at that time. Remaining shares are accounted for by means of either the equity method or the fair-value method, depending on the investor's subsequent ability to significantly influence the investee.
5. Inventory (or other assets) can be transferred between investor and investee. Because of the relationship between the two companies, the equity income accrual should be reduced to defer the portion of any gross profit included on these intra-entity sales until the items are either sold to outsiders or consumed. Thus, the amount of intra-entity gross profit in ending inventory decreases the amount of equity income recognized by the investor in the current period although this effect is subsequently reversed.
6. Firms may elect to report significant influence investments at fair value with changes in fair value as earnings. Under the fair-value option, firms simply report the investment's fair value as an asset and changes in fair value as earnings.

Comprehensive Illustration

(*Estimated Time: 30 to 50 Minutes*) Every chapter in this textbook concludes with an illustration designed to assist students in tying together the essential elements of the material presented. After a careful reading of each chapter, attempt to work through the comprehensive problem. Then review the solution that follows the problem, noting the handling of each significant accounting issue.

Problem

Part A

On January 1, 2019, Red Hawk Company pays $70,000 for a 10 percent interest in Wolf Company's common stock. Because market quotes for Wolf's stock are readily available on a continuing basis, the investment account has been appropriately maintained at fair value.

On January 1, 2020, Red Hawk acquires an additional 20 percent of Wolf Company for $176,000. This second purchase provides Red Hawk the ability to exert significant influence over Wolf, and Red Hawk will now apply the equity method. At the time of this transaction, Wolf had a January 1, 2020 book value of $650,000 although Wolf's equipment with a four-year remaining life was undervalued by $80,000 relative to its fair value.

During these two years, Wolf reported the following operational results (cash dividends are declared and paid in July each year):

Year	Net Income	Cash Dividends	Fair Value at January 1
2019	$210,000	$110,000	$700,000
2020	270,000	110,000	880,000

Required

a. What income did Red Hawk originally report for 2019 in connection with this investment?

b. On comparative financial statements for 2019 and 2020, what figures should Red Hawk report in connection with this investment?

Part B (Continuation of Part A)

In 2021, Wolf Company reports $400,000 in income and $60,000 in other comprehensive income from foreign currency translation adjustments. The company declares and pays a $120,000 cash dividend. During this fiscal year, Red Hawk sells inventory costing $80,000 to Wolf for $100,000. Wolf continues to hold 50 percent of this merchandise at the end of 2021. Red Hawk maintains 30 percent ownership of Wolf throughout the period.

Required

Prepare all necessary journal entries for Red Hawk for the year 2021.

Solution

Part A

a. Red Hawk Company accounts for its investment in Wolf Company at fair value during 2019. Because Red Hawk held only 10 percent of the outstanding shares, significant influence apparently was absent. Because stock quotes were readily available, the investment was periodically updated to fair value. Therefore, the investor recorded both dividends and changes in fair value in its 2019 financial statements as follows:

Dividend income (10% × $110,000)	$11,000
Increase in fair value [10% × ($880,000 – 700,000)]	18,000
Total income recognized from investment in Wolf in 2019	$29,000

b. Changes to the equity method are accounted for prospectively. Therefore, in comparative statements, Red Hawk's 2019 income from its investment in Wolf is $29,000, as reflected in the fair value method shown in (*a*).

Red Hawk's 2020 financial statements will reflect the equity method as a result of the January 1, 2020, share purchase that resulted in significant influence. To determine the 2020 equity method income, Red Hawk first evaluates its combined investments in Wolf to assess whether either goodwill or incremental asset values need to be reflected within the equity method procedures.

Fair Value Allocation of 30 Percent Ownership of Wolf Company on January 1, 2020

Fair value of initial 10 percent purchase	$ 88,000
Payment for 20 percent investment at January 1, 2020	176,000
Fair value of 30 percent ownership	264,000
Book value acquired ($650,000 × 30%)	195,000
Fair value in excess of book value	69,000
Excess fair value identified with specific assets:	
Equipment ($80,000 × 30%)	24,000
Excess fair value not identified with specific assets—goodwill	$ 45,000

In allocating Wolf's January 1, 2020, fair value, $24,000 of the payment is attributable to the undervalued equipment with $45,000 assigned to goodwill. Because the equipment now has only a four-year remaining life, annual amortization of $6,000 is appropriate ($24,000/4).

Financial Reporting—2020

Equity in Investee Income (income statement)	
Income reported by Wolf	$270,000
Red Hawk's ownership	30%
Red Hawk's share of Wolf's reported income	$ 81,000
Less: Amortization expense:	
Equipment ($24,000/4 years)	(6,000)
Equity in investee income—2020	$ 75,000
Investment in Wolf (balance sheet)	
Fair value—1/1/20 (above)	$264,000
Equity in investee income (above)	75,000
Less: Investee dividends ($110,000 × 30%)	(33,000)
Investment in Wolf—12/31/20	$306,000

Part B

In July 2021 Wolf declares and pays a $36,000 cash dividend to Red Hawk (30% × $120,000). According to the equity method, this dividend reduces the carrying amount of the investment account:

Dividend Receivable	36,000	
Investment in Wolf Company		36,000
To record the 2021 cash dividend declaration by Wolf Company.		
Cash	36,000	
Dividend Receivable		36,000
To record collection of the cash dividend.		

Red Hawk records no other journal entries in connection with this investment until the end of 2021. At that time, the annual accrual of income as well as the adjustment to record amortization is made (see Part A for computation of expense). The investee's net income is reported separately from its other comprehensive income.

Investment in Wolf Company	138,000	
Equity in Investee Income		120,000
Investee Other Comprehensive Income		18,000
To recognize reported income of investee based on a 30 percent ownership level of $400,000 net income and $60,000 other comprehensive income.		
Equity in Investee Income	6,000	
Investment in Wolf Company		6,000
To record annual amortization on excess payment made in relation to equipment ($24,000/4 years).		

Red Hawk needs to make only one other equity entry during 2021. Intra-entity sales have occurred, and Wolf continues to hold a portion of the inventory. Therefore, the investor's share of gross profit must be deferred. The gross profit rate from the sale was 20 percent ($20,000/$100,000). Because the investee still possesses $50,000 of this merchandise, the related gross profit is $10,000 ($50,000 × 20%). However, Red Hawk owns only 30 percent of Wolf's outstanding stock; thus, the intra-entity gross profit in inventory at year-end is $3,000 ($10,000 × 30%). That amount must be deferred until Wolf either consumes the inventory or sells it to unrelated parties.

Equity in Investee Company	3,000	
Investment in Wolf Company		3,000
To defer the investor's share of intra-entity gross profit in ending inventory.		

Questions

1. What advantages does a company achieve when it possesses significant influence over another company through voting stock ownership?
2. A company acquires a rather large investment in another corporation. What criteria determine whether the investor should apply the equity method of accounting to this investment?
3. What accounting treatments are appropriate for investments in equity securities without readily determinable fair values?
4. What indicates an investor's ability to significantly influence the decision-making process of an investee?
5. Why does the equity method record dividends from an investee as a reduction in the investment account, not as dividend income?
6. Jones Company owns a 25 percent interest in shares of Sandridge Company common stock. Under what circumstances might Jones decide that the equity method would not be appropriate to account for this investment?
7. Smith, Inc., has maintained an ownership interest in Watts Corporation for a number of years. This investment has been accounted for using the equity method. What transactions or events create changes in the Investment in Watts Corporation account as recorded by Smith?

8. Although the equity method is a generally accepted accounting principle (GAAP), recognition of equity income has been criticized. What theoretical problems can opponents of the equity method identify? What managerial incentives exist that could influence a firm's percentage ownership interest in another firm?
9. Because of the acquisition of additional investee shares, an investor will now change from the fair-value method to the equity method. Which procedures are applied to accomplish this accounting change?
10. Riggins Company accounts for its investment in Bostic Company using the equity method. During the past fiscal year, Bostic reported other comprehensive income from translation adjustments related to its foreign investments. How would this other comprehensive income affect the investor's financial records?
11. During the current year, Davis Company's common stock suffers a permanent drop in market value. In the past, Davis has made a significant portion of its sales to one customer. This buyer recently announced its decision to make no further purchases from Davis Company, an action that led to the loss of market value. Hawkins, Inc., owns 35 percent of the outstanding shares of Davis, an investment that is recorded according to the equity method. How would the loss in value affect this investor's financial reporting?
12. Wilson Company acquired 40 percent of Andrews Company at a bargain price because of losses expected to result from Andrews's failure in marketing several new products. Wilson paid only $100,000, although Andrews's corresponding book value was much higher. In the first year after acquisition, Andrews lost $300,000. In applying the equity method, how should Wilson account for this loss?
13. In a stock acquisition accounted for by the equity method, a portion of the purchase price often is attributed to goodwill or to specific assets or liabilities. How are these amounts determined at acquisition? How are these amounts accounted for in subsequent periods?
14. Princeton Company holds a 40 percent interest in shares of Yale Company common stock. On June 19 of the current year, Princeton sells part of this investment. What accounting should Princeton make on June 19? What accounting will Princeton make for the remainder of the current year?
15. What is the difference between downstream and upstream sales? How does this difference affect application of the equity method?
16. How is the investor's share of gross profit on intra-entity sales calculated? Under the equity method, how does the deferral of gross profit affect the recognition of equity income?
17. How are intra-entity transfers reported in an investee's separate financial statements if the investor is using the equity method?
18. What is the fair-value option for reporting equity method investments? How do the equity method and fair-value accounting differ in recognizing income from an investee?

Problems

LO 1-4

1. When an investor uses the equity method to account for investments in common stock, the investor's share of cash dividends from the investee should be recorded as
   a. A deduction from the investor's share of the investee's profits.
   b. Dividend income.
   c. A deduction from the stockholders' equity account, Dividends to Stockholders.
   d. A deduction from the investment account.
   (AICPA adapted)

LO 1-2

2. The equity method tends to be most appropriate if
   a. An investment represents 50 percent or more of the voting stock of an investee.
   b. An investment enables the investor to influence the operating and financial decisions of the investee.
   c. Majority ownership of the investee is concentrated among a small group of shareholders who operate the investee without regard to the views of the investor.
   d. The investor is unable to obtain representation on the investee's board of directors.

LO 1-6a

3. Hawkins Company has owned 10 percent of Larker, Inc., for the past several years. This ownership did not allow Hawkins to have significant influence over Larker. Recently, Hawkins acquired an additional 30 percent of Larker and now will use the equity method. How will the investor report change?
   a. A cumulative effect of an accounting change is shown in the current income statement.
   b. A retrospective adjustment is made to restate all prior years presented using the equity method.
   c. No change is recorded; the equity method is used from the date of the new acquisition.
   d. Hawkins will report the change as a component of accumulated other comprehensive income.

LO 1-8

4. Under fair-value accounting for an equity investment, which of the following affects the income the investor recognizes from its ownership of the investee?
   a. The investee's reported income adjusted for excess cost over book value amortizations.
   b. Changes in the fair value of the investor's ownership shares of the investee.
   c. Intra-entity profits from upstream sales.
   d. Other comprehensive income reported by the investee.

LO 1-6c

5. When an equity method investment account is reduced to a zero balance
   a. The investor should establish a negative investment account balance for any future losses reported by the investee.
   b. The investor should discontinue using the equity method until the investee begins paying dividends.
   c. Future losses are reported as unusual items in the investor's income statement.
   d. The investment retains a zero balance until subsequent investee profits eliminate all unrecognized losses.

LO 1-4

6. On January 1, Belleville Company paid $2,295,000 to acquire 90,000 shares of O'Fallon's voting common stock, which represents a 30 percent investment. No allocations to goodwill or other specific accounts were made. Significant influence over O'Fallon is achieved by this acquisition, and so Belleville applies the equity method. O'Fallon declared a $1 per share dividend during the year and reported net income of $750,000. What is the balance in the Investment in O'Fallon account found in Belleville's financial records as of December 31?
   a. $2,295,000
   b. $2,430,000
   c. $2,520,000
   d. $2,610,000

LO 1-4, 1-5

7. In January 2020, Domingo, Inc., acquired 20 percent of the outstanding common stock of Martes, Inc., for $700,000. This investment gave Domingo the ability to exercise significant influence over Martes, whose balance sheet on that date showed total assets of $3,900,000 with liabilities of $900,000. Any excess of cost over book value of the investment was attributed to a patent having a remaining useful life of 10 years.

   In 2020, Martes reported net income of $170,000. In 2021, Martes reported net income of $210,000. Dividends of $70,000 were declared in each of these two years. What is the equity method balance of Domingo's Investment in Martes, Inc., at December 31, 2021?
   a. $728,000
   b. $748,000
   c. $756,000
   d. $776,000

LO 1-4, 1-5

8. Franklin purchases 40 percent of Johnson Company on January 1 for $500,000. Although Franklin did not use it, this acquisition gave Franklin the ability to apply significant influence to Johnson's operating and financing policies. Johnson reports assets on that date of $1,400,000 with liabilities of $500,000. One building with a seven-year remaining life is undervalued on Johnson's books by $140,000. Also, Johnson's book value for its trademark (10-year remaining life) is undervalued by $210,000. During the year, Johnson reports net income of $90,000 while declaring dividends of $30,000. What is the Investment in Johnson Company balance (equity method) in Franklin's financial records as of December 31?
   a. $504,000
   b. $507,600
   c. $513,900
   d. $516,000

LO 1-4, 1-5

9. Evan Company reports net income of $140,000 each year and declares an annual cash dividend of $50,000. The company holds net assets of $1,200,000 on January 1, 2020. On that date, Shalina purchases 40 percent of Evan's outstanding common stock for $600,000, which gives it the ability to significantly influence Evan. At the purchase date, the excess of Shalina's cost over its proportionate share of Evan's book value was assigned to goodwill. On December 31, 2022, what is the Investment in Evan Company balance (equity method) in Shalina's financial records?
   a. $600,000
   b. $660,000
   c. $690,000
   d. $708,000

LO 1-7

10. Perez, Inc., applies the equity method for its 25 percent investment in Senior, Inc. During 2021, Perez sold goods with a 40 percent gross profit to Senior, which sold all of these goods in 2021. How should Perez report the effect of the intra-entity sale on its 2021 income statement?
    a. Sales and cost of goods sold should be reduced by the amount of intra-entity sales.
    b. Sales and cost of goods sold should be reduced by 25 percent of the amount of intra-entity sales.
    c. Investment income should be reduced by 25 percent of the gross profit on the amount of intra-entity sales.
    d. No adjustment is necessary.

LO 1-7

11. Jubilee, Inc., owns 35 percent of JPW Company and applies the equity method. During the current year, Jubilee buys inventory costing $60,000 and then sells it to JPW for $75,000. At the end of the year, JPW still holds only $30,000 of merchandise. What amount of gross profit must Jubilee defer in reporting this investment using the equity method?
    a. $2,100
    b. $2,625
    c. $6,000
    d. $10,500

LO 1-4, 1-5, 1-7

12. Alex, Inc., buys 40 percent of Steinbart Company on January 1, 2020, for $530,000. The equity method of accounting is to be used. Steinbart's net assets on that date were $1.2 million. Any excess of cost over book value is attributable to a trade name with a 20-year remaining life. Steinbart immediately begins supplying inventory to Alex as follows:

Year	Cost to Steinbart	Transfer Price	Amount Held by Alex at Year-End (at transfer price)
2020	$70,000	$100,000	$25,000
2021	96,000	150,000	45,000

Inventory held at the end of one year by Alex is sold at the beginning of the next.

Steinbart reports net income of $80,000 in 2020 and $110,000 in 2021 and declares $30,000 in dividends each year. What is the equity income in Steinbart to be reported by Alex in 2021?
    a. $34,050
    b. $38,020
    c. $46,230
    d. $51,450

LO 1-4, 1-5

13. On January 3, 2021, Matteson Corporation acquired 40 percent of the outstanding common stock of O'Toole Company for $1,160,000. This acquisition gave Matteson the ability to exercise significant influence over the investee. The book value of the acquired shares was $820,000. Any excess cost over the underlying book value was assigned to a copyright that was undervalued on its balance sheet. This copyright has a remaining useful life of 10 years. For the year ended December 31, 2021, O'Toole reported net income of $260,000 and declared cash dividends of $50,000. On December 31, 2021, what should Matteson report as its investment in O'Toole under the equity method?

LO 1-4

14. On January 1, 2021, Fisher Corporation paid $2,290,000 for 35 percent of the outstanding voting stock of Steel, Inc., and appropriately applied the equity method for its investment. Any excess of cost over Steel's book value was attributed to goodwill. During 2021, Steel reports $720,000 in net income and a $100,000 other comprehensive income loss. Steel also declares and pays $20,000 in dividends.
    a. What amount should Fisher report as its Investment in Steel on its December 31, 2021, balance sheet?
    b. What amount should Fisher report as Equity in Earnings of Steel on its 2021 income statement?

LO 1-4, 1-5

15. On January 1, 2020, Ridge Road Company acquired 20 percent of the voting shares of Sauk Trail, Inc., for $2,700,000 in cash. Both companies provide commercial Internet support services but serve markets in different industries. Ridge Road made the investment to gain access to Sauk Trail's board of directors and thus facilitate future cooperative agreements between the two firms. Ridge Road quickly obtained several seats on Sauk Trail's board, which gave it the ability to significantly influence Sauk Trail's operating and investing activities.

The January 1, 2020, carrying amounts and corresponding fair values for Sauk Trail's assets and liabilities follow:

	Carrying Amount	Fair Value
Cash and Receivables	$ 110,000	$ 110,000
Computing Equipment	5,000,000	5,700,000
Patented Technology	100,000	4,000,000
Trademark	150,000	2,000,000
Liabilities	(185,000)	(185,000)

Also, as of January 1, 2020, Sauk Trail's computing equipment had a seven-year remaining estimated useful life. The patented technology was estimated to have a three-year remaining useful life. The trademark's useful life was considered indefinite. Ridge Road attributed to goodwill any unidentified excess cost.

During the next two years, Sauk Trail reported the following net income and dividends:

	Net Income	Dividends Declared
2020	$1,800,000	$150,000
2021	1,985,000	160,000

a. How much of Ridge Road's $2,700,000 payment for Sauk Trail is attributable to goodwill?

b. What amount should Ridge Road report for its equity in Sauk Trail's earnings on its income statements for 2020 and 2021?

c. What amount should Ridge Road report for its investment in Sauk Trail on its balance sheets at the end of 2020 and 2021?

LO 1-4, 1-5, 1-8

16. On January 1, 2020, Alison, Inc., paid $60,000 for a 40 percent interest in Holister Corporation's common stock. This investee had assets with a book value of $200,000 and liabilities of $75,000. A patent held by Holister having a $5,000 book value was actually worth $20,000. This patent had a six-year remaining life. Any further excess cost associated with this acquisition was attributed to goodwill. During 2020, Holister earned income of $30,000 and declared and paid dividends of $10,000. In 2021, it had income of $50,000 and dividends of $15,000. During 2021, the fair value of Allison's investment in Holister had risen from $68,000 to $75,000.

    a. Assuming Alison uses the equity method, what balance should appear in the Investment in Holister account as of December 31, 2021?

    b. Assuming Alison uses fair-value accounting, what income from the investment in Holister should be reported for 2021?

LO 1-4, 1-7

17. On January 1, 2021, Alamar Corporation acquired a 40 percent interest in Burks, Inc., for $210,000. On that date, Burks's balance sheet disclosed net assets with both a fair and book value of $360,000. During 2021, Burks reported net income of $80,000 and declared and paid cash dividends of $25,000. Alamar sold inventory costing $30,000 to Burks during 2021 for $40,000. Burks used all of this merchandise in its operations during 2021. Prepare all of Alamar's 2021 journal entries to apply the equity method to this investment.

LO 1-2, 1-3, 1-4, 1-5, 1-6a

18. Milani, Inc., acquired 10 percent of Seida Corporation on January 1, 2020, for $190,000 and appropriately accounted for the investment using the fair-value method. On January 1, 2021, Milani purchased an additional 30 percent of Seida for $600,000 which resulted in significant influence over Seida. On that date, the fair value of Seida's common stock was $2,000,000 in total. Seida's January 1, 2021, book value equaled $1,850,000, although land was undervalued by $120,000. Any additional excess fair value over Seida's book value was attributable to a trademark with an eight-year remaining life. During 2021, Seida reported income of $300,000 and declared and paid dividends of $110,000. Prepare the 2021 journal entries for Milani related to its investment in Seida.

LO 1-7

19. Camille, Inc., sold $120,000 in inventory to Eckerle Company during 2020 for $200,000. Eckerle resold $85,000 of this merchandise in 2020 with the remainder to be disposed of during 2021. Assuming that Camille owns 30 percent of Eckerle and applies the equity method, what journal entry is recorded at the end of 2020 to defer the intra-entity gross profit?

LO 1-4, 1-5, 1-7

20. BuyCo, Inc., holds 25 percent of the outstanding shares of Marqueen Company and appropriately applies the equity method of accounting. Excess cost amortization (related to a patent) associated

with this investment amounts to $10,000 per year. For 2020, Marqueen reported earnings of $100,000 and declares cash dividends of $30,000. During that year, Marqueen acquired inventory for $50,000, which it then sold to BuyCo for $80,000. At the end of 2020, BuyCo continued to hold merchandise with a transfer price of $32,000.

a. What Equity in Investee Income should BuyCo report for 2020?

b. How will the intra-entity transfer affect BuyCo's reporting in 2021?

c. If BuyCo had sold the inventory to Marqueen, how would the answers to (*a*) and (*b*) have changed?

LO 1-2, 1-3, 1-4, 1-5, 1-6a

21. On January 1, 2019, Halstead, Inc., purchased 75,000 shares of Sedgwick Company common stock for $1,480,000, giving Halstead 25 percent ownership and the ability to apply significant influence over Sedgwick. Any excess of cost over book value acquired was attributed solely to goodwill.

Sedgwick reports net income and dividends as follows. These amounts are assumed to have occurred evenly throughout these years. Dividends are declared and paid in the same period.

	Net Income	Annual Cash Dividends (paid quarterly)
2019	$340,000	$120,000
2020	480,000	140,000
2021	600,000	160,000

On July 1, 2021, Halstead sells 12,000 shares of this investment for $25 per share, thus reducing its interest from 25 to 21 percent, but maintaining its significant influence.

Determine the amounts that would appear on Halstead's 2021 income statement relating to its ownership and partial sale of its investment in Sedgwick's common stock.

LO 1-2, 1-3, 1-4, 1-5, 1-6d

22. Echo, Inc., purchased 10 percent of ProForm Corporation on January 1, 2020, for $345,000 and accounted for the investment using the fair-value method. Echo acquires an additional 15 percent of ProForm on January 1, 2021, for $580,000. The equity method of accounting is now appropriate for this investment. No intra-entity sales have occurred.

a. How does Echo initially determine the income to be reported in 2020 in connection with its ownership of ProForm?

b. What factors should have influenced Echo in its decision to apply the equity method in 2021?

c. What factors could have prevented Echo from adopting the equity method after this second purchase?

d. What is the objective of the equity method of accounting?

e. What criticisms have been leveled at the equity method?

f. In comparative statements for 2020 and 2021, how would Echo determine the income to be reported in 2020 in connection with its ownership of ProForm? Why is this accounting appropriate?

g. How is the allocation of Echo's acquisition made?

h. If ProForm declares a cash dividend, what impact does it have on Echo's financial records under the equity method? Why is this accounting appropriate?

i. On financial statements for 2021, what amounts are included in Echo's Investment in ProForm account? What amounts are included in Echo's Equity in Income of ProForm account?

LO 1-4, 1-7

23. Parrot Corporation holds a 42 percent ownership of Sunrise, Inc., and applies the equity method to account for its investment. Parrot assigned the entire original excess purchase price over book value to goodwill. During 2020, the two companies made intra-entity inventory transfers. A portion of this merchandise was not resold until 2021. During 2021, additional transfers were made.

a. What is the difference between upstream transfers and downstream transfers?

b. How does the direction of an intra-entity transfer (upstream versus downstream) affect the application of the equity method?

c. How is the intra-entity gross profit deferral computed in applying the equity method?

d. How should Parrot compute the amount of equity income to be recognized in 2020? What entry is made to record this income?

e. How should Parrot compute the amount of equity income to be recognized in 2021?

f. If none of the transferred inventory had remained at the end of 2020, how would these transfers have affected the application of the equity method?

g. How do these intra-entity transfers affect Sunrise's financial reporting?

LO 1-2, 1-6d

24. Several years ago, Einstein, Inc., bought 40 percent of the outstanding voting stock of Brooks Company. The equity method is appropriately applied. On August 1 of the current year, Einstein sold a portion of these shares.

a. How does Einstein compute the book value of this investment on August 1 to determine its gain or loss on the sale?

b. How should Einstein account for this investment after August 1?

c. If Einstein retains only a 2 percent interest in Brooks so that it holds virtually no influence over Brooks, what figures appear in the investor's income statement for the current year?

d. If Einstein retains only a 2 percent interest in Brooks so that virtually no influence is held, does the investor have to retroactively adjust any previously reported figures?

LO 1-4, 1-5, 1-7

25. Matthew, Inc., owns 30 percent of the outstanding stock of Lindman Company and has the ability to significantly influence the investee's operations and decision making. On January 1, 2021, the balance in the Investment in Lindman account is $335,000. Amortization associated with this acquisition is $9,000 per year. In 2021, Lindman earns an income of $90,000 and declares cash dividends of $30,000. Previously, in 2020, Lindman had sold inventory costing $24,000 to Matthew for $40,000. Matthew consumed all but 25 percent of this merchandise during 2020 and used the rest during 2021. Lindman sold additional inventory costing $28,000 to Matthew for $50,000 in 2021. Matthew did not consume 40 percent of these 2021 purchases from Lindman until 2022.

a. What amount of equity method income would Matthew recognize in 2021 from its ownership interest in Lindman?

b. What is the equity method balance in the Investment in Lindman account at the end of 2021?

LO 1-2, 1-4, 1-5

26. On December 31, 2019, Akron, Inc., purchased 5 percent of Zip Company's common shares on the open market in exchange for $16,000. On December 31, 2020, Akron, Inc., acquires an additional 25 percent of Zip Company's outstanding common stock for $95,000. During the next two years, the following information is available for Zip Company:

	Income	Dividends Declared	Common Stock Fair Value (12/31)
2019			$320,000
2020	$75,000	$ 7,000	380,000
2021	88,000	15,000	480,000

At December 31, 2020, Zip reports a net book value of $290,000. Akron attributed any excess of its 30 percent share of Zip's fair over book value to its share of Zip's franchise agreements. The franchise agreements had a remaining life of 10 years at December 31, 2020.

a. Assume Akron applies the equity method to its Investment in Zip account:

1. What amount of equity income should Akron report for 2021?
2. On Akron's December 31, 2021, balance sheet, what amount is reported for the Investment in Zip account?

b. Assume Akron uses fair-value accounting for its Investment in Zip account:

1. What amount of income from its investment in Zip should Akron report for 2021?
2. On Akron's December 31, 2021, balance sheet, what amount is reported for the Investment in Zip account?

LO 1-4, 1-5, 1-6d, 1-7

27. Belden, Inc., acquires 30 percent of the outstanding voting shares of Sheffield, Inc., on January 1, 2020, for $312,000, which gives Belden the ability to significantly influence Sheffield. Sheffield has a net book value of $800,000 at January 1, 2020. Sheffield's asset and liability accounts showed carrying amounts considered equal to fair values, except for a copyright whose value accounted for Belden's excess cost over book value in its 30 percent purchase. The copyright had a remaining life of 16 years at January 1, 2020. No goodwill resulted from Belden's share purchase.

Sheffield reported net income of $180,000 in 2020 and $230,000 of net income during 2021. Dividends of $70,000 and $80,000 are declared and paid in 2020 and 2021, respectively. Belden uses the equity method.

a. On its 2021 comparative income statements, how much income would Belden report for 2020 and 2021 in connection with the company's investment in Sheffield?

b. If Belden sells its entire investment in Sheffield on January 1, 2022, for $400,000 cash, what is the impact on Belden's income?

c. Assume that Belden sells inventory to Sheffield during 2020 and 2021 as follows:

Year	Cost to Belden	Price to Sheffield	Year-End Balance (at transfer price)
2020	$30,000	$50,000	$20,000 (sold in following year)
2021	33,000	60,000	40,000 (sold in following year)

What amount of equity income should Belden recognize for the year 2021?

LO 1-4, 1-5, 1-6b, 1-7

28. Harper, Inc., acquires 40 percent of the outstanding voting stock of Kinman Company on January 1, 2020, for $210,000 in cash. The book value of Kinman's net assets on that date was $400,000, although one of the company's buildings, with a $60,000 carrying amount, was actually worth $100,000. This building had a 10-year remaining life. Kinman owned a royalty agreement with a 20-year remaining life that was undervalued by $85,000.

Kinman sold inventory with an original cost of $60,000 to Harper during 2020 at a price of $90,000. Harper still held $15,000 (transfer price) of this amount in inventory as of December 31, 2020. These goods are to be sold to outside parties during 2021.

Kinman reported a $40,000 net loss and a $20,000 other comprehensive loss for 2020. The company still manages to declare and pay a $10,000 cash dividend during the year.

During 2021, Kinman reported a $40,000 net income and declared and paid a cash dividend of $12,000. It made additional inventory sales of $80,000 to Harper during the period. The original cost of the merchandise was $50,000. All but 30 percent of this inventory had been resold to outside parties by the end of the 2021 fiscal year.

Prepare all journal entries for Harper for 2020 and 2021 in connection with this investment. Assume that the equity method is applied.

LO 1-4, 1-5, 1-6b, 1-7

29. On January 1, 2021, Pine Company owns 40 percent (40,000 shares) of Seacrest, Inc., which it purchased several years ago for $182,000. Since the date of acquisition, the equity method has been properly applied, and the carrying amount of the investment account as of January 1, 2021, is $293,600. Excess patent cost amortization of $12,000 is still being recognized each year. During 2021, Seacrest reports net income of $342,000 and a $120,000 other comprehensive loss, both incurred uniformly throughout the year. No dividends were declared during the year. Pine sold 8,000 shares of Seacrest on August 1, 2021, for $93,000 in cash. However, Pine retains the ability to significantly influence the investee.

During the last quarter of 2020, Pine sold $50,000 in inventory (which it had originally purchased for only $30,000) to Seacrest. At the end of that fiscal year, Seacrest's inventory retained $10,000 (at sales price) of this merchandise, which was subsequently sold in the first quarter of 2021.

On Pine's financial statements for the year ended December 31, 2021, what income effects would be reported from its ownership in Seacrest?

LO 1-4, 1-5, 1-7

30. On July 1, 2019, Killearn Company acquired 88,000 of the outstanding shares of Shaun Company for $13 per share. This acquisition gave Killearn a 25 percent ownership of Shaun and allowed Killearn to significantly influence the investee's decisions.

As of July 1, 2019, the investee had assets with a book value of $3 million and liabilities of $74,400. At the time, Shaun held equipment appraised at $364,000 more than book value; it was considered to have a seven-year remaining life with no salvage value. Shaun also held a copyright with a five-year remaining life on its books that was undervalued by $972,000. Any remaining excess cost was attributable to goodwill. Depreciation and amortization are computed using the straight-line method. Killearn applies the equity method for its investment in Shaun.

Shaun's policy is to declare and pay a $1 per share cash dividend every April 1 and October 1. Shaun's income, earned evenly throughout each year, was $598,000 in 2019, $639,600 in 2020, and $692,400 in 2021.

In addition, Killearn sold inventory costing $91,200 to Shaun for $152,000 during 2020. Shaun resold $92,000 of this inventory during 2020 and the remaining $60,000 during 2021.

a. Determine the equity income to be recognized by Killearn during each of these years.

b. Compute Killearn's investment in Shaun Company's balance as of December 31, 2021.

LO 1-2, 1-3, 1-4, 1-5, 1-6d

31. On January 1, 2020, Fisher Corporation purchased 40 percent (80,000 shares) of the common stock of Bowden, Inc., for $982,000 in cash and began to use the equity method for the investment. The price paid represented a $60,000 payment in excess of the book value of Fisher's share of Bowden's underlying net assets. Fisher was willing to make this extra payment because of a recently developed patent held by Bowden with a 15-year remaining life. All other assets were considered appropriately valued on Bowden's books.

    Bowden declares and pays a $100,000 cash dividend to its stockholders each year on September 15. Bowden reported net income of $400,000 in 2020 and $380,000 in 2021. Each income figure was earned evenly throughout its respective years.

    On July 1, 2021, Fisher sold 10 percent (20,000 shares) of Bowden's outstanding shares for $330,000 in cash. Although it sold this interest, Fisher maintained the ability to significantly influence Bowden's decision-making process.

    Prepare the journal entries for Fisher for the years of 2020 and 2021.

LO 1-4, 1-5, 1-7

32. On January 1, 2020, Stream Company acquired 30 percent of the outstanding voting shares of Q-Video, Inc., for $770,000. Q-Video manufactures specialty cables for computer monitors. On that date, Q-Video reported assets and liabilities with book values of $1.9 million and $700,000, respectively. A customer list compiled by Q-Video had an appraised value of $300,000, although it was not recorded on its books. The expected remaining life of the customer list was five years with straight-line amortization deemed appropriate. Any remaining excess cost was not identifiable with any particular asset and thus was considered goodwill.

    Q-Video generated net income of $250,000 in 2020 and a net loss of $100,000 in 2021. In each of these two years, Q-Video declared and paid a cash dividend of $15,000 to its stockholders.

    During 2020, Q-Video sold inventory that had an original cost of $100,000 to Stream for $160,000. Of this balance, $80,000 was resold to outsiders during 2020, and the remainder was sold during 2021. In 2021, Q-Video sold inventory to Stream for $175,000. This inventory had cost only $140,000. Stream resold $100,000 of the inventory during 2021 and the rest during 2022.

    For 2020 and then for 2021, compute the amount that Stream should report as income from its investment in Q-Video in its external financial statements under the equity method.

Develop Your Skills

DATA ANALYSIS CASE 1

CPA skills

On January 1, 2021, Acme Co. is considering purchasing a 40 percent ownership interest in PHC Co., a privately held enterprise, for $700,000. PHC predicts its profit will be $185,000 in 2021, projects a 10 percent annual increase in profits in each of the next four years, and expects to pay a steady annual dividend of $30,000 for the foreseeable future. Because PHC has on its books a patent that is undervalued by $375,000, Acme realizes that it will have an additional amortization expense of $15,000 per year over the next 10 years—the patent's estimated remaining useful life. All of PHC's other assets and liabilities have book values that approximate market values. Acme uses the equity method for its investment in PHC.

Required

1. Using an Excel spreadsheet, set the following values in cells:
    - Acme's cost of investment in PHC.
    - Percentage acquired.
    - First-year PHC reported income.
    - Projected growth rate in income.
    - PHC annual dividends.
    - Annual excess patent amortization.
2. Referring to the values in (1), prepare the following schedules using columns for the years 2021 through 2025.
    - Acme's equity in PHC earnings with rows showing these:
        - Acme's share of PHC reported income.
        - Amortization expense.
        - Acme's equity in PHC earnings.

- Acme's Investment in PHC balance with rows showing the following:
    - Beginning balance.
    - Equity earnings.
    - Dividends.
    - Ending balance.
- Return on beginning investment balance = Equity earnings/Beginning investment balance in each year.

3. Given the preceding values, compute the average of the projected returns on beginning investment balances for the first five years of Acme's investment in PHC. What is the maximum Acme can pay for PHC if it wishes to earn at least a 10 percent average return on beginning investment balance? (*Hint:* Under Excel's Data tab, select What-If Analysis, and the Goal Seek capability to produce a 10 percent average return on beginning investment balance by changing the cell that contains Acme's cost of investment in PHC. Excel's Solver should produce an exact answer while Goal Seek should produce a close approximation. You may need to first add in the Solver capability in Excel under File>Options>Add-ins.)

DATA ANALYSIS CASE 2

On January 1, Intergen, Inc., invests $200,000 for a 40 percent interest in Ryan, a new joint venture with two other partners, each investing $150,000 for 30 percent interest. Intergen plans to sell all of its production to Ryan, which will resell the inventory to retail outlets. The equity partners agree that Ryan will buy inventory only from Intergen. Also, Intergen plans to use the equity method for financial reporting.

During the year, Intergen expects to incur costs of $850,000 to produce goods with a final retail market value of $1,200,000. Ryan projects that, during this year, it will resell three-fourths of these goods for $900,000. It should sell the remainder in the following year.

The equity partners plan a meeting to set the price Intergen will charge Ryan for its production. One partner suggests a transfer price of $1,025,000 but is unsure whether it will result in an equitable return across the equity holders. Importantly, Intergen agrees that its total rate of return (including its own operations and its investment in Ryan) should be equal to that of the other investors' return on their investments in Ryan. All agree that Intergen's value including its investment in Ryan is $1,000,000.

Required

1. Create an Excel spreadsheet analysis showing the following:
    - Projected income statements for Intergen and Ryan. Formulate the statements to do the following:
        - Link Ryan's cost of goods sold to Intergen's sales (use a starting value of $1,025,000 for Intergen's sales).
        - Link Intergen's equity in Ryan's earnings to Ryan's net income (adjusted for Intergen's gross profit rate × Ryan's ending inventory × 40 percent ownership percentage).
        - Be able to change Intergen's sales and see the effects throughout the income statements of Ryan and Intergen. Note that the cost of goods sold for Intergen is fixed.
    - The rate of return for the two 30 percent equity partners on their investment in Ryan.
    - The total rate of return for Intergen based on its $1,000,000 value.
2. What transfer price will provide an equal rate of return for each of the investors in the first year of operation? (*Hint:* Under Excel's Data tab, select What-If Analysis and then the Goal Seek capability to produce a zero difference in rates of return across the equity partners by changing the cell that contains Intergen's sales. Excel's Solver add-in will work as well.)

RESEARCH AND DISCUSSION CASE

Access a recent copy of The Coca-Cola Company's SEC 10-K filing at www.coca-cola.com and address the following:

1. What companies does Coca-Cola describe as significant equity method investments? How do these investments help Coca-Cola?
2. What criteria does Coca-Cola use in choosing to apply the equity method for these investments?

3. How does Coca-Cola describe its application of the equity method?
4. What amount of equity income did Coca-Cola report?
5. Coca-Cola discloses the fair values of its publicly traded bottlers accounted for as equity method investments. List the carrying amounts and fair values for these equity method investments that have publicly traded data. Discuss the relevance of each of these two values.

RESEARCH AND ANALYSIS CASE—IMPAIRMENT

CPA skills

Wolf Pack Transport Co. has a 25 percent equity investment in Maggie Valley Depot (MVD), Inc., which owns and operates a warehousing facility used for the collection and redistribution of various consumer goods. Wolf Pack paid $1,685,000 for its 25 percent interest in MVD several years ago, including a $300,000 allocation for goodwill as the only excess cost over book value acquired. Wolf Pack Transport has since appropriately applied the equity method to account for the investment. In its most recent balance sheet, because of recognized profits in excess of dividends since the acquisition, Wolf Pack reported a $2,350,000 amount for its Investment in Maggie Valley Depot, Inc., account.

However, competition in the transit warehousing industry has increased in the past 12 months. In the same area as the MVD facility, a competitor company opened two additional warehouses that are much more conveniently located near a major interstate highway. MVD's revenues declined 30 percent as customers shifted their business to the competitor's facilities and the prices for warehouse services declined. The market value of Wolf Pack's stock ownership in MVD fell to $1,700,000 from a high last year of $2,500,000. MVD's management is currently debating ways to respond to these events but has yet to formulate a firm plan.

Required

1. What guidance does the FASB ASC provide for equity method investment losses in value?
2. Should Wolf Pack recognize the decline in the value of its holdings in MVD in its current year financial statements?
3. Should Wolf Pack test for impairment of the value it had initially assigned to goodwill?

RESEARCH CASE—NONCONTROLLING SHAREHOLDER RIGHTS

CPA skills

Consolidated financial reporting is appropriate when one entity has a controlling financial interest in another entity. The usual condition for a controlling financial interest is ownership of a majority voting interest. But in some circumstances, control does not rest with the majority owner—especially when noncontrolling owners are contractually provided with approval or veto rights that can restrict the actions of the majority owner. In these cases, the majority owner employs the equity method rather than consolidation.

Required

Address the following by searching the FASB ASC Topic 810 on consolidation.

1. What are protective noncontrolling rights?
2. What are substantive participating noncontrolling rights?
3. What noncontrolling rights overcome the presumption that all majority-owned investees should be consolidated?
4. Zee Company buys 60 percent of the voting stock of Bee Company with the remaining 40 percent noncontrolling interest held by Bee's former owners, who negotiated the following noncontrolling rights:
   - Any new debt above $1,000,000 must be approved by the 40 percent noncontrolling shareholders.
   - Any dividends or other cash distributions to owners in excess of customary historical amounts must be approved by the 40 percent noncontrolling shareholders.

   According to the FASB ASC, what are the issues in determining whether Zee should consolidate Bee or report its investment in Bee under the equity method?

chapter 2

Consolidation of Financial Information

Financial statements published and distributed to owners, creditors, and other interested parties appear to report the operations and financial position of a single company. In reality, these statements frequently represent a number of separate organizations tied together through common control (a *business combination*). When financial statements represent more than one corporation, we refer to them as *consolidated financial statements.*

Consolidated financial statements are typical in today's business world. Most major organizations, and many smaller ones, hold control over an array of organizations. For example, from 2000 to 2018, Cisco Systems, Inc., reported more than 100 business acquisitions that now are consolidated in its financial reports. PepsiCo, Inc., as another example, annually consolidates data from a multitude of companies into a single set of financial statements. By gaining control over these companies (often known as *subsidiaries*)—which include Frito-Lay, Naked Juice, Quaker Oats, South Beach Beverage, and Tropicana Products—PepsiCo (the *parent*) forms a single business combination and single reporting entity.

The consolidation of financial information as exemplified by Cisco Systems and PepsiCo is one of the most complex procedures in all of accounting. Comprehending this process completely requires understanding the theoretical logic that underlies the creation of a business combination. Furthermore, a variety of procedural steps must be mastered to ensure that proper accounting is achieved for this single reporting entity. The following coverage introduces both of these aspects of the consolidation process.

The FASB *Accounting Standards Codification*® (ASC) contains the current accounting standards for business combinations under the following topics:

- "Business Combinations" (Topic 805).
- "Consolidation" (Topic 810).

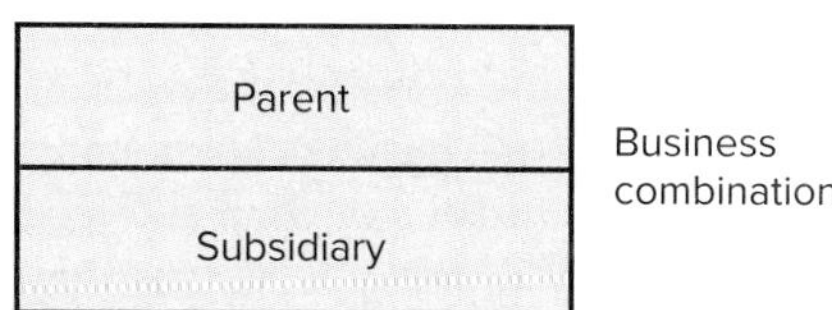

The ASC "Business Combinations" topic provides guidance on the accounting and reporting for business combinations using the *acquisition method.* The acquisition method embraces a *fair-value* measurement attribute. Adoption of this attribute reflects the FASB's increasing emphasis on fair value for measuring and assessing business activity. In the past, financial reporting standards embraced the cost principle to measure and report the

Learning Objectives

After studying this chapter, you should be able to:

LO 2-1	Discuss the motives for business combinations.
LO 2-2	Recognize when consolidation of financial information into a single set of statements is necessary.
LO 2-3	Define the term *business combination* and differentiate across various forms of business combinations.
LO 2-4	Describe the valuation principles of the acquisition method.
LO 2-5	Determine the fair value of the consideration transferred for an acquisition, and allocate that fair value to specific assets acquired (including goodwill) and liabilities assumed or to a gain on bargain purchase.
LO 2-6	Prepare an acquiring firm's journal entry to record a. a business combination when dissolution takes place. b. the various related costs involved in a business combination. c. a business combination when the acquired firm retains its separate existence.
LO 2-7	Prepare a worksheet to consolidate the financial statements of two companies that form a business combination in the absence of dissolution.
LO 2-8	Describe the accounting treatment for the various intangible assets often acquired in a business combination.
LO 2-9	Appendix 2A: Identify the general characteristics of the legacy purchase and pooling of interest methods of accounting for past business combinations. Understand the effects that persist today in financial statements from the use of these legacy methods.
LO 2-10	Appendix 2B: Explain the rationale and procedures underlying a subsidiary's election to adopt pushdown accounting.

financial effects of business combinations. This fundamental change from a cost-based to a fair-value model has transformed the way we account for and report business combinations in our society.

The ASC "Consolidation" topic provides guidance on circumstances that require a firm to prepare consolidated financial reports and various other related reporting issues. Basically, consolidated financial reports must be prepared whenever one firm has a controlling financial interest in another. Although ownership of a majority voting interest is the usual condition for a controlling financial interest, the power to control may also exist with a lesser percentage of ownership through governance contracts, leases, or agreement with other stockholders.[1]

In this chapter, we first present expansion through corporate takeovers and present an overview of the consolidation process. Then we present the specifics of the acquisition method of accounting for business combinations where the acquirer obtains complete ownership of another firm. Later, beginning in Chapter 4, we introduce coverage of acquisitions with less than complete ownership.

Financial reporting for business combinations has experienced many changes over the past decade. Prior to the acquisition method requirement, accounting standards allowed either the purchase method or the earlier pooling of interests method of accounting for business combinations. Neither of these methods is now permitted for reporting the formation of new business combinations. However, because of the prospective application of the acquisition method beginning in 2009, legacy effects of these methods remain in many of today's financial statements. Therefore, an appendix to this chapter provides a review of the purchase method and pooling of interests method.

LO 2-1

Discuss the motives for business combinations.

Expansion through Corporate Takeovers

Reasons for Firms to Combine

A frequent economic phenomenon is the combining of two or more businesses into a single entity under common management and control. During recent decades, the United States and the rest of the world have experienced an enormous number of corporate mergers and takeovers, transactions in which one company gains control over another. According to Dealogic, the volume of mergers and acquisitions globally in 2018 exceeded $3.35 trillion, its highest level since 2015. Of these deals, more than $1.74 trillion involved a U.S. firm. As indicated by Exhibit 2.1, the magnitude of recent combinations continues to be large.

As with any other economic activity, business combinations can be part of an overall managerial strategy to maximize shareholder value. Shareholders—the owners of the firm—hire managers to direct resources so that the firm's value grows over time. In this way, owners receive a return on their investment. Successful firms receive substantial benefits through enhanced share value. Importantly, the managers of successful firms also receive substantial benefits in salaries, especially if their compensation contracts are partly based on stock market performance of the firm's shares.

If the goal of business activity is to maximize the firm's value, in what ways do business combinations help achieve that goal? Clearly, the business community is moving rapidly toward business combinations as a strategy for growth and competitiveness. Size and scale are obviously becoming critical as firms compete in today's markets. Importantly, valuable synergies often accompany business combinations.

If large firms can be more efficient in delivering goods and services, they gain a competitive advantage and become more profitable for the owners. Increases in scale can produce larger profits from enhanced sales volume despite smaller (more competitive) profit margins. When two firms integrate successive stages of production and distribution of products, coordinating

[1] We discuss entities controlled through contractual means (known as variable interest entities) in Chapter 6.

EXHIBIT 2.1
Recent Notable Business Combinations

Acquirer	Target	Deal Value
AT&T	Time-Warner	$79.4B
Walt Disney	21st Century Fox	$71.3B
CVS Health	Aetna	$69.0B
Cigna	Express Scripts	$52.0B
Walmart	Flipkart	$16.0B
Amazon	Whole Foods	$13.7B
Conagra	Pinnacle Foods	$10.9B
Celgene	Juno Therapeutics	$ 9.0B
Diamondback Energy	Energen	$ 8.4B
General Mills	Blue Buffalo	$ 8.0B
Microsoft	GitHub	$ 7.5B
Salesforce.com	Mulesoft	$ 6.5B
Verizon	Yahoo	$ 4.7B
Pepsico	SodaStream International	$ 3.2B
Tyson	Keystone Foods	$ 2.2B
Tesla	Grohmann Engineering	$109M

raw material purchases, manufacturing, and delivery, substantial savings can result. As an example, Oracle's acquisition of Sun Microsystems creates synergies by enabling Oracle to integrate its software product lines with Sun's hardware specifications. The acquisition further allows Oracle to offer complete systems made of chips, computers, storage devices, and software with an aim toward increased efficiency and quality.[2] Other cost savings resulting from elimination of redundant processes, such as data processing and marketing, can make a single entity more profitable than the separate parent and subsidiary had been in the past. Such synergies often accompany business combinations.

Although no two business combinations are exactly alike, many share one or more of the following characteristics that potentially enhance profitability:

- Vertical integration of one firm's output and another firm's distribution or further processing.
- Cost savings through elimination of duplicate facilities and staff.
- Quick entry for new and existing products into domestic and foreign markets.
- Economies of scale allowing greater efficiency and negotiating power.
- The ability to access financing at more attractive rates. As firm size increases, negotiating power with financial institutions can increase also.
- Diversification of business risk.

Business combinations also occur because many firms seek the continuous expansion of their organizations, often into diversified areas. Acquiring control over a vast network of different businesses has been a strategy utilized by a number of companies (sometimes known as *conglomerates*) for decades. Entry into new industries is immediately available to the parent without having to construct facilities, develop products, train management, or create market recognition. Many corporations have successfully employed this strategy to produce huge, highly profitable organizations. Unfortunately, others discovered that the task of managing a widely diverse group of businesses can be a costly learning experience. Even combinations that are designed to take advantage of operating synergies and cost savings will fail if the integration is not managed carefully.

Overall, the primary motivations for many business combinations can be traced to an increasingly competitive environment. Three recent business combinations provide interesting examples of distinct motivations to combine: Amazon and Whole Foods Market, Salesforce .com and MuleSoft, and Tesla and Grohmann Engineering. Each is discussed briefly in turn.

[2] Ben Worthen, Cari Tuna, and Justin Scheck, "Companies More Prone to Go 'Vertical,'" *The Wall Street Journal*, November 30, 2009.

Amazon and Whole Foods Market

On August 28, 2017, Amazon acquired Whole Foods Market, an upscale grocery store chain. As stated in its 2017 annual 10-K report, Amazon paid a total of $13.7 billion in what was its largest acquisition to date. According to the acquisition agreement, Whole Foods Market will continue as a wholly owned subsidiary of Amazon. The acquisition represents a move by Amazon into the traditional brick-and-mortar grocery business with over 430 grocery stores in high-end markets. Given Amazon's technology expertise and distribution advantages in delivering good to consumers' homes, the acquisition will likely seek to expand its e-commerce offerings to food.

Many analysts weighed in on why Amazon, primarily an online retailer, would buy a business that operates almost entirely in physical outlets. As tweeted by Dennis Berman, a *Wall Street Journal* financial editor, "Amazon did not just buy Whole Foods grocery stores. It bought 431 upper-income, prime-location distribution nodes for everything it does." By acquiring Whole Foods's physical outlets, Amazon now has many more effective fulfillment centers to expand its product delivery set—especially the Prime Now service, which promises to deliver certain products within an hour or less. Moreover, adding Whole Foods may give Amazon a competitive edge in grocery distribution against Google Express, Instacart, Peapod, and FreshDirect.[3]

Of the total $13.7 billion purchase consideration for Whole Foods Market, Amazon recognized more than $9 billion in goodwill. According to Amazon's 2017 10-K, the goodwill value "is primarily related to expected improvements in technology performance and functionality, as well as sales growth from future product and service offerings and new customers." As is common in many recent acquisitions, much of the purchase price for Whole Foods Market was attributed to other intangibles. Amazon reported an additional $2.3 billion in intangible assets (beyond goodwill) including marketing-related and contract-based intangible assets.

Salesforce.com and MuleSoft

On May 18, 2018, Salesforce.com, a cloud-based software company specializing in online customer relationship management, acquired MuleSoft, Inc., for $6.5 billion in a cash-and-stock deal. The acquisition was Salesforce's largest among more than 50 of its other acquisitions since 2006. MuleSoft provides a cloud platform for integrating and connecting applications, data, and devices. As observed by Marc Benioff, CEO of Salesforce, "Together, Salesforce and MuleSoft will enable customers to connect all of the information throughout their enterprise across all public and private clouds and data sources."[4] The acquisition reflects business demand for cloud computing applications beyond the website to enable faster customer decisions based on connected customer experiences with the supplier.

MuleSoft's ability to help their clients utilize data in their legacy information technology systems was a key motivation for Salesforce's acquisition. As Salesforce COO Keith Block noted, "Being able to coordinate and unlock and integrate all this data is so important. Over time all of these organizations' legacy systems will be moving to the cloud. But it has taken years to build up these systems and I don't think we can underestimate how much legacy is still out there." MuleSoft's application programming interface will allow Salesforce to help customers to unlock and use prospects and sales data across their disparate systems.[5]

Intangible assets represented the majority of the value paid for MuleSoft. According to Salesforce's October 31, 2018, 10-Q report, included in the $6.5 billion purchase price was a $4.8 billion allocation to goodwill. Clearly, Salesforce expects substantial synergies with MuleSoft's application programming interface enabling clients to connect across various data sources. Other intangibles, such as developed technology and customer relationships, accounted for more than $1.3 billion in Salesforce's fair-value allocation schedule for the MuleSoft acquisition.

[3] Lisa Eadicicco, "5 Reasons Why Amazon Bought Whole Foods," *Time,* June 16 , 2017.

[4] MuleSoft press release, "Salesforce Signs Definitive Merger Agreement to Acquire MuleSoft," March 20, 2018.

[5] Angus Loten, "Salesforce Says MuleSoft Deal Will Help Companies Unlock Data," *The Wall Street Journal,* March 28, 2018.

Tesla and Grohmann Engineering

On January 3, 2017, Tesla, Inc., completed an acquisition of Grohmann Engineering, a designer and manufacturer of automated manufacturing systems for batteries and fuel cells in Prum, Germany, for $109 million in cash. According to Tesla, the acquisition will help in the design of its production facilities: "Combined with our California and Michigan engineering facilities, as well as other locations to follow, we believe the result will yield exponential improvements in the speed and quality of production, while substantially reducing the capital expenditures required per vehicle."[6] Thus, the prospect of cost synergies was a large factor in Tesla's decision to acquire Grohmann.

At the time of the acquisition, Tesla was looking to rapidly expand production. Following the acquisition, Grohmann manufacturing systems is expected to contribute to not only highly automated factories, but also production of lithium-ion battery packs that power its vehicles.[7] More recently available data show that Tesla has been able to raise its battery pack production to 6,000 per week and is expected to expand that number to 8,000 using Grohmann technology.[8]

As with so many business combinations, Tesla's 10-K revealed a large allocation of its consideration transferred in the Grohmann acquisition to goodwill and other intangible assets. Tesla recognized over $40 million of goodwill in the acquisition citing "the expected synergies from potential modernization opportunities and from integrating Grohmann's technology into our automotive business as well as the acquired talent." Other intangible assets acquired were allocated more than $21 million and included developed technology, software, customer relations, and the Grohmann trade name.

LO 2-2

Recognize when consolidation of financial information into a single set of statements is necessary.

Business Combinations, Control, and Consolidated Financial Reporting

The consolidation of financial information into a single set of statements becomes necessary when the business combination of two or more companies creates a single economic entity. As stated in FASB ASC (810-10-10-1): "There is a presumption that consolidated financial statements are more meaningful than separate financial statements and that they are usually necessary for a fair presentation when one of the entities in the consolidated group directly or indirectly has a controlling financial interest in the other entities."

Thus, in producing financial statements for external distribution, the reporting entity transcends the boundaries of incorporation to encompass (i.e., consolidate) all companies for which control is present. Even though the various companies may retain their legal identities as separate corporations, the resulting information is more meaningful to outside parties when consolidated into a single set of financial statements.

To explain the process of preparing consolidated financial statements for a business combination, we address three questions:

1. How is a business combination formed?
2. What constitutes a controlling financial interest?
3. How is the consolidation process carried out?

LO 2-3

Define the term *business combination* and differentiate across various forms of business combinations.

Business Combinations—Creating a Single Economic Entity

A business combination refers to a transaction or other event in which an acquirer obtains control over one or more businesses.

Business combinations are formed by a wide variety of transactions or events with various formats. For example, each of the following is identified as a business combination although

[6] Press release, *Formation of Tesla Advanced Automation Germany,* The Tesla Team, November 8, 2016.

[7] Alan Ohnsman, "Tesla Buying Germany's Grohmann Engineering to Automate, Accelerate Production," *Forbes,* November 8, 2016.

[8] Kyle Field, "Tesla Bringing 3 New 'Grohmann Machines' Online to Reach 8,000 Battery Packs/Week," *Clean Technica,* September 13, 2018.

it differs widely in legal form. In every case, two or more enterprises are united into a single economic entity so that consolidated financial statements are required.

1. One company obtains the assets, and often the liabilities, of another company in exchange for cash, other assets, liabilities, stock, or a combination of these. The second organization normally dissolves itself as a legal corporation. Thus, only the acquiring company remains in existence, having absorbed the acquired net assets directly into its own operations. Any business combination in which only one of the original companies continues to exist is referred to in legal terms as a *statutory merger.*

2. One company obtains all of the capital stock of another in exchange for cash, other assets, liabilities, stock, or a combination of these. After gaining control, the acquiring company can decide to transfer all assets and liabilities to its own financial records with the second company being dissolved as a separate corporation.[9] The business combination is, once again, a statutory merger because only one of the companies maintains legal existence. This statutory merger, however, is achieved by obtaining equity securities rather than by buying the target company's assets. Because stock is obtained, the acquiring company must gain 100 percent control of all shares before legally dissolving the subsidiary.

3. Two or more companies transfer either their assets or their capital stock to a newly formed corporation. Both original companies are dissolved, leaving only the new organization in existence. A business combination effected in this manner is a *statutory consolidation.* The use here of the term *consolidation* should not be confused with the accounting meaning of that same word. In accounting, *consolidation* refers to the mechanical process of bringing together the financial records of two or more organizations to form a single set of statements. A statutory consolidation denotes a specific type of business combination that has united two or more existing companies under the ownership of a newly created company.

4. One company achieves legal control over another by acquiring a majority of voting stock. *Although control is present, no dissolution takes place; each company remains in existence as an incorporated operation.* Whole Foods Market, as an example, continues to retain its legal status as a limited liability company after being acquired by Amazon. Separate incorporation is frequently preferred to take full advantage of any intangible benefits accruing to the acquired company as a going concern. Better utilization of such factors as licenses, trade names, employee loyalty, and the company's reputation can be possible when the subsidiary maintains its own legal identity. Moreover, maintaining an independent information system for a subsidiary often enhances its market value for an eventual sale or initial public offering as a stand-alone entity.

Because the asset and liability account balances are not physically combined as in statutory mergers and consolidations, each company continues to maintain an independent accounting system. To reflect the combination, the acquiring company enters the takeover transaction into its own records by establishing a single investment asset account. However, the newly acquired subsidiary omits any recording of this event; its stock is simply transferred to the parent from the subsidiary's shareholders. Thus, the subsidiary's financial records are not directly affected by a takeover.

5. A final vehicle for control of another business entity does not involve a majority voting stock interest or direct ownership of assets. Control of a variable interest entity (VIE) by design often does not rest with its equity holders. Instead, control is exercised through contractual arrangements with a sponsoring firm that, although it technically may not own the VIE, becomes its "primary beneficiary" with rights to its residual profits. These contracts can take the form of leases, participation rights, guarantees, or other interests. Past use of VIEs was criticized because these structures provided sponsoring firms with off-balance sheet financing and sometimes questionable profits on sales to their VIEs. Prior to 2004, many sponsoring entities of VIEs did not technically meet the definition of a controlling financial interest (i.e., majority voting stock ownership) and thus did not consolidate their VIEs.

[9] Although the acquired company has been legally dissolved, it frequently continues to operate as a separate division within the surviving company's organization.

EXHIBIT 2.2
Business Combinations

Type of Combination	Action of Acquiring Company	Action of Acquired Company
Statutory merger through asset acquisition.	Acquires assets and often liabilities.	Dissolves and goes out of business.
Statutory merger through capital stock acquisition.	Acquires all stock and then transfers assets and liabilities to its own books.	Dissolves as a separate corporation, often remaining as a division of the acquiring company.
Statutory consolidation through capital stock or asset acquisition.	Newly created entity receives assets or capital stock of original companies.	Original companies may dissolve while remaining as separate divisions of newly created company.
Acquisition of more than 50 percent of the voting stock.	Acquires stock that is recorded as an investment; controls decision making of acquired company.	Remains in existence as legal corporation, although now a subsidiary of the acquiring company.
Control through ownership of variable interests (see Chapter 6). Risks and rewards often flow to a sponsoring firm that may or may not hold equity shares.	Establishes contractual control over a variable interest entity to engage in a specific activity.	Remains in existence as a separate legal entity—often a trust or partnership.

Current GAAP, however, expands the notion of control and thus requires consolidation of VIEs by their primary beneficiary.

As you can see, business combinations are created in many distinct forms. The specific format is a critical factor in the subsequent consolidation of financial information. Exhibit 2.2 provides an overview of the various combinations.

Control—An Elusive Quality

The definition of control is central to determining when two or more entities become one economic entity and therefore one reporting entity. Control of one firm by another is most often achieved through the acquisition of voting shares. The ASC (810-10-15-8) describes control as follows:

> The usual condition for a controlling financial interest is ownership of a majority voting interest, and, therefore, as a general rule ownership by one reporting entity, directly or indirectly, of more than 50 percent of the outstanding voting shares of another entity is a condition pointing toward consolidation.

By exercising majority voting power, one firm can literally dictate the financing and operating activities of another firm. Accordingly, U.S. GAAP traditionally has pointed to a majority voting share ownership as a controlling financial interest that requires consolidation.

Notably, the power to control may also exist with less than 50 percent of the outstanding shares of another entity. The ASC (810-10-15-8) goes on to observe that

> The power to control may also exist with a lesser percentage of ownership, for example, by contract, lease, agreement with other stockholders, or by court decree.

Therefore, despite possessing less than 50 percent of the subsidiary's voting stock, one ownership group can enter into contractual arrangement with other ownership groups that provide control.

Alternatively, majority ownership does not always indicate an exclusive ability for one entity to exercise control over another. According to the FASB ASC Glossary, control can also be defined as

> The direct or indirect ability to determine the direction of management and policies through ownership, contract, or otherwise.

This description recognizes the complex profit-sharing agreements that sometimes accompany economic resource sharing. To reduce their risk, several parties may participate in directing the activities of another entity. For example, a parent with majority ownership may grant certain decision rights to noncontrolling shareholders in exchange for economic support. Such noncontrolling participation rights may be powerful enough to prevent the majority owners from controlling the entity.

As the complexity of ownership arrangements increases, defining when one firm controls another remains a continuing challenge for financial reporting standard setters. Nonetheless, the primary way U.S. firms exercise control remains through the acquisition of a majority of another firm's voting shares. Consequently, in this text, we largely focus on control relationships established through voting interests. In Chapter 6, however, we expand our coverage to include the consolidation of firms where control is exercised through variable interests.

Consolidation of Financial Information

When one company gains control over another, a business combination is established. Financial data gathered from the individual companies are then brought together to form a single set of consolidated statements. Although this process can be complicated, the objectives of a consolidation are straightforward—to report the financial position, results of operations, and cash flows for the combined entity. As a part of this process, reciprocal accounts and intra-entity transactions must be adjusted or eliminated to ensure that all reported balances truly represent the single entity.

Applicable consolidation procedures vary significantly depending on the legal format employed in creating a business combination. *For a statutory merger or a statutory consolidation, when the acquired company (or companies) is (are) legally dissolved, only one accounting consolidation ever occurs.* On the date of the combination, the surviving company simply records the various account balances from each of the dissolving companies. Because the accounts are brought together permanently in this manner, no further consolidation procedures are necessary. After the balances have been transferred to the survivor, the financial records of the acquired companies are closed out as part of the dissolution.

Conversely, in a combination when all companies retain incorporation, a different set of consolidation procedures is appropriate. Because the companies preserve their legal identities, each continues to maintain its own independent accounting records. *Thus, no permanent consolidation of the account balances is ever made. Rather, the consolidation process must be carried out anew each time the reporting entity prepares financial statements for external reporting purposes.*

When separate recordkeeping is maintained, the accountant faces a unique problem: The financial information must be brought together periodically without disturbing the accounting systems of the individual companies. Because these consolidations are produced outside the financial records, worksheets traditionally are used to expedite the process. Worksheets are a part of neither company's accounting records nor the resulting financial statements. Instead, they are an efficient structure for organizing and adjusting the information used to prepare externally reported consolidated statements.

Consequently, the legal characteristics of a business combination have a significant impact on the approach taken to the consolidation process:

What is to be consolidated?

- If dissolution takes place, appropriate account balances are physically consolidated in the surviving company's financial records.
- If separate incorporation is maintained, only the financial statement information (not the actual records) is consolidated.

When does the consolidation take place?

- If dissolution takes place, a permanent consolidation occurs at the date of the combination.
- If separate incorporation is maintained, the consolidation process is carried out at regular intervals whenever financial statements are to be prepared.

How are the accounting records affected?

- If dissolution takes place, the surviving company's accounts are adjusted to include appropriate balances of the dissolved company. The dissolved company's records are closed out.
- If separate incorporation is maintained, each company continues to retain its own records. Using worksheets facilitates the periodic consolidation process without disturbing the individual accounting systems.

LO 2-4

Describe the valuation principles of the acquisition method.

Financial Reporting for Business Combinations

The Acquisition Method

Regardless of whether the acquired firm maintains its separate incorporation or dissolution takes place, current standards require the acquisition method to account for business combinations.[10] Applying the acquisition method involves recognizing and measuring

- The consideration transferred for the acquired business and any noncontrolling interest.
- The separately identified assets acquired and liabilities assumed.
- Goodwill, or a gain from a bargain purchase.

Fair value is the measurement attribute used to recognize these and other aspects of a business combination. Therefore, prior to examining specific applications of the acquisition method, we present a brief discussion of the fair-value concept as applied to business combinations.

Consideration Transferred for the Acquired Business

The fair value of the consideration transferred to acquire a business from its former owners is the starting point in valuing and recording a business combination. In describing the acquisition method, the FASB ASC states:

> The consideration transferred in a business combination shall be measured at fair value, which shall be calculated as the sum of the acquisition-date fair values of the assets transferred by the acquirer, the liabilities incurred by the acquirer to former owners of the acquiree, and the equity interests issued by the acquirer. (ASC 805-30-30-7)

The acquisition method thus embraces the fair value of the consideration transferred in measuring the acquirer's interest in the acquired business.[11] Fair value is defined as the price that would be received to sell an asset or paid to transfer a liability in an orderly transaction between market participants at the measurement date. Thus, market values are often the best source of evidence of the fair value of consideration transferred in a business combination. Items of consideration transferred can include cash, securities (either stocks or debt), and other property or obligations.

Contingent Consideration: An Additional Element of Consideration Transferred

Contingent consideration, when present in a business combination, is an additional element of consideration transferred. Contingent consideration can be useful in negotiations when two parties disagree with each other's estimates of future cash flows for the target firm or when valuation uncertainty is high.[12] Acquisition agreements often contain provisions to pay

[10] To qualify for the acquisition method, an acquired entity must first meet the definition of a *business*. According to ASC 805, a business must include an input and a substantive process that together significantly contribute to the ability to create output. Thus, if only a single asset (or group of similar assets) is acquired, the assets do not represent a business.

[11] An occasional exception occurs in a bargain purchase in which the fair value of the net assets acquired serves as the valuation basis for the acquired firm. Other exceptions include situations in which control is achieved without a transfer of consideration, or determination of the fair value of the consideration transferred is less reliable than other measures of the business fair value.

[12] Cain, Denis, and Denis, "Earnouts: A Study of Financial Contracting in Acquisition Agreements," *Journal of Accounting and Economics* 51 (2011), 151–170.

former owners (typically cash or additional shares of the acquirer's stock) upon achievement of specified future performance measures. Such agreements are frequently referred to as *earnouts*.

Contingent consideration frequently involves potential cash payments to the acquired firm's former owners and accordingly are recorded at acquisition-date fair value on the records of the acquiring firm. For example, when Albertsons Companies acquired DineInFresh, Inc., a provider of meal kit services, included in its consideration transferred was contingent consideration. As part of the agreement, the sellers of DineInFresh are able to earn additional contingent consideration of up to $125.0 million if certain revenue targets are met over the three years following the acquisition. Because the achievement of the revenue targets was uncertain, Albertsons estimated the fair value of the contingent consideration at $60.1 million at the acquisition date.[13] The acquisition method treats contingent consideration obligations as a negotiated component of the fair value of the consideration transferred. Albertsons estimates the fair value of contingent future payments using probability assessments based on circumstances existing on the acquisition date and accordingly recorded a $60.1 million contingent liability.

Regardless of the elements that constitute the consideration transferred, the parent's financial statements must now incorporate its newly acquired ownership interest in a controlled entity. In Chapters 2 and 3, we focus exclusively on combinations that result in complete ownership by the acquirer (i.e., no noncontrolling interest in the acquired firm). As described in Chapter 4, in a less-than-100-percent acquisition, the noncontrolling interest also is measured initially at its fair value. Then, the combined fair values of the parent's consideration transferred and the noncontrolling interest comprise the valuation basis for the acquired firm in consolidated financial reports.

Assets Acquired and Liabilities Assumed

A fundamental principle of the acquisition method is that an acquirer must identify the assets acquired and the liabilities assumed in the business combination. Further, once these have been identified, the acquirer measures the assets acquired and the liabilities assumed at their acquisition-date fair values, with only a few exceptions.[14] As demonstrated in subsequent examples, the principle of recognizing and measuring assets acquired and liabilities assumed at fair value applies across all business combinations.

Fair value, as defined by GAAP, is the price that would be received from selling an asset or paid for transferring a liability in an orderly transaction between market participants at the measurement date. However, determining the acquisition-date fair values of the individual assets acquired and liabilities assumed can prove challenging.[15] The ASC (820-10-35-28) points to three sets of valuation techniques typically employed: the market approach, the income approach, and the cost approach.

Market Approach

The market approach estimates fair values using other market transactions involving similar assets or liabilities. In a business combination, assets acquired such as marketable securities and some tangible assets may have established markets that can provide comparable market values for estimating fair values. Similarly, the fair values of many liabilities assumed can be determined by reference to market trades for similar debt instruments.

Income Approach

The income approach relies on multi-period estimates of future cash flows projected to be generated by an asset. These projected cash flows are then discounted at a required rate of

[13] Albertsons Companies, Inc., Annual Report Form 10-K, February 24, 2018.

[14] Exceptions to the fair-value measurement principle include deferred taxes, certain employee benefits, indemnification assets, reacquired rights, share-based awards, and assets held for sale.

[15] Identifying and measuring the acquired firm's financial statement items can take some time. ASC (805-10-25-14) allows an acquirer to adjust the provisional amounts recognized for a business combination up to a year after the acquisition date.

return that reflects the time value of money and the risk associated with realizing the future estimated cash flows. The multi-period income approach is often useful for obtaining fair-value estimates of intangible assets and acquired in-process research and development.

Cost Approach

The cost approach estimates fair values by reference to the current cost of replacing an asset with another of comparable economic utility. Used assets can present a particular valuation challenge if active markets only exist for newer versions of the asset. Thus, the cost to replace a particular asset reflects both its estimated replacement cost and the effects of obsolescence. In this sense, obsolescence is meant to capture economic declines in value including both technological obsolescence and physical deterioration. The cost approach is widely used to estimate fair values for many tangible assets acquired in business combinations such as property, plant, and equipment.

Goodwill, and Gains on Bargain Purchases

In a business combination, the parent must account for both the consideration transferred and the individual amounts of the identified assets acquired and liabilities assumed at their acquisition-date fair values. However, in many cases, the respective collective amounts of these two values will differ. Current GAAP accounting for the difference requires one of two outcomes—in one, the acquirer recognizes an asset (goodwill); in the other, a gain.

When the consideration transferred exceeds the acquisition-date net amount of the identified assets acquired and the liabilities assumed, the acquirer recognizes the asset goodwill for the excess.[16] Goodwill is defined as an asset representing the future economic benefits arising in a business combination that are not individually identified and separately recognized. Goodwill often embodies the expected synergies that the acquirer expects to achieve through control of the acquired firm's assets. Goodwill may also capture non-recognized intangibles of the acquired firm such as employee expertise.

Conversely, if the collective fair value of the net identified assets acquired and liabilities assumed exceeds the consideration transferred, the acquirer recognizes a "gain on bargain purchase." In such cases, the fair value of the net assets acquired replaces the consideration transferred as the valuation basis for the acquired firm. Bargain purchases can result from business divestitures forced by regulatory agencies or other types of distress sales. Before recognizing a gain on bargain purchase, however, the acquirer must reassess whether it has correctly identified and measured all of the acquired assets and liabilities. Illustrations and further discussions of goodwill and of bargain purchase gains follow in the next section.

LO 2-5

Determine the total fair value of the consideration transferred for an acquisition, and allocate that fair value to specific subsidiary assets acquired (including goodwill) and liabilities assumed or to a gain on bargain purchase.

Procedures for Consolidating Financial Information

To demonstrate an application of the acquisition method, assume BigNet Company specializes in communications equipment and business software that provide web-based applications for retail companies. BigNet seeks to expand its operations and plans to acquire Smallport on December 31. Smallport Company owns computers, telecommunications equipment, and software that customize website billing and ordering systems for their customers. BigNet hopes to expand Smallport's customer contracts, utilize its recently developed software, and create other synergies by combining with Smallport.

Exhibit 2.3 lists the December 31 account balances for both BigNet and Smallport. In addition, the estimated fair values of Smallport's assets and liabilities are shown. Although Smallport's computers and equipment have a $400,000 book value, their current fair value is $600,000. Smallport's software has only a $100,000 value on its books; the internal development costs were primarily expensed. The software's observable fair value, however, is $1,200,000. Similarly, although not reflected in its financial records, Smallport has several

[16] Assuming a 100 percent acquisition. For combinations with less than complete ownership, goodwill is computed as the excess of the consideration transferred plus the acquisition-date fair value of the noncontrolling interest over the collective fair values of the net identified assets acquired and liabilities assumed.

EXHIBIT 2.3 Basic Consolidation Information

	BigNet Company	Smallport Company	
	Book Values December 31	Book Values December 31	Fair Values December 31
Current assets	$ 1,100,000	$ 300,000	$ 300,000
Computers and equipment (net)	1,300,000	400,000	600,000
Capitalized software (net)	500,000	100,000	1,200,000
Customer contracts	–0–	–0–	700,000
Notes payable	(300,000)	(200,000)	(250,000)
Net assets	**$ 2,600,000**	**$ 600,000**	**$2,550,000**
Common stock—$10 par value	$ (1,600,000)		
Common stock—$5 par value		$ (100,000)	
Additional paid-in capital	(40,000)	(20,000)	
Retained earnings, 1/1	(870,000)	(370,000)	
Dividends declared	110,000	10,000	
Revenues	(1,000,000)	(500,000)	
Expenses	800,000	380,000	
Owners' equity 12/31	**$(2,600,000)**	**$(600,000)**	
Retained earnings, 12/31	(960,000)*	(480,000)*	

*Retained earnings balance after closing out revenues, expenses, and dividends.
Note: Parentheses indicate a credit balance.

large ongoing customer contracts. BigNet estimates the fair value of the customer contracts at $700,000. Smallport also has a $200,000 note payable incurred to help finance the software development. Because interest rates are currently low, this liability (incurred at a higher rate of interest) has a present value of $250,000.

Smallport's net assets (total assets less total liabilities) have a book value of $600,000 but a fair value of $2,550,000. Fair values for only the assets and liabilities are appraised here; the capital stock, retained earnings, dividend, revenue, and expense accounts represent historical measurements rather than any type of future values. Although these equity and income accounts can give some indication of the organization's overall worth, they are not property and thus not transferred in the combination.

Legal as well as accounting distinctions divide business combinations into several separate categories. To facilitate the introduction of consolidation accounting, we present the various procedures utilized in this process according to the following sequence:

1. Acquisition method when dissolution takes place.
2. Acquisition method when separate incorporation is maintained.

Acquisition Method When Dissolution Takes Place

When the acquired firm's legal status is dissolved in a business combination, the continuing firm takes direct ownership of the former firm's assets and assumes its liabilities. Thus, the continuing firm will prepare a journal entry to record

- The fair value of the consideration transferred by the acquiring firm to the former owners of the acquiree, and
- The identified assets acquired and liabilities assumed at their individual fair values.

However, the entry to record the combination further depends on the relation between the consideration transferred and the net amount of the fair values assigned to the identified assets acquired and liabilities assumed. Therefore, we initially provide three illustrations that demonstrate the procedures to record a business combination, each with different amounts of consideration transferred relative to the acquired asset and liability fair values. Each example assumes a merger takes place, and, therefore, the acquired firm is dissolved. In each situation, the consideration transferred is compared to the fair value of the net identifiable assets acquired and liabilities assumed to determine if goodwill or a bargain purchase gain should be recorded.

Consideration Transferred Equals Net Fair Values of Identified Assets Acquired and Liabilities Assumed

Assume that after negotiations with the owners of Smallport, BigNet agrees to pay cash of $550,000 and to issue 20,000 previously unissued shares of its $10 par value common stock (currently selling for $100 per share) for all of Smallport's assets and liabilities. Following the acquisition, Smallport then dissolves itself as a legal entity. The consideration transferred from BigNet to Smallport is computed as follows and, in this case, exactly equals the collective fair values of Smallport's assets less liabilities:

Cash payment	$ 550,000
Common stock issued by BigNet ($100 × 20,000 shares)	2,000,000
Total consideration transferred	$2,550,000
Fair value of Smallport's net identifiable assets	$2,550,000

The $2,550,000 fair value of the consideration transferred by BigNet represents the fair value of the acquired Smallport business and serves as the basis for recording the combination in total.

BigNet also must record all of Smallport's identified assets and liabilities at their ***individual*** fair values. These two valuations present no difficulties because BigNet's consideration transferred exactly equals the $2,550,000 collective net fair values of the individual assets and liabilities acquired as shown in Exhibit 2.3.

Because Smallport Company will be dissolved, BigNet (the surviving company) enters a journal entry in its financial records to record the combination. BigNet has directly acquired the assets and assumed the liabilities of Smallport. Under the acquisition method, BigNet records Smallport's assets and liabilities at fair value ignoring original book values. Revenue, expense, dividend, and equity accounts cannot be transferred to a parent and are not included in recording the business combination.

LO 2-6a

Prepare the journal entry to consolidate the accounts of a subsidiary if dissolution takes place.

Acquisition Method: Consideration Transferred Equals Net Identified Asset Fair Values—Subsidiary Dissolved

BigNet Company's Financial Records—December 31		
Current Assets	300,000	
Computers and Equipment	600,000	
Capitalized Software	1,200,000	
Customer Contracts	700,000	
Notes Payable		250,000
Cash (paid by BigNet)		550,000
Common Stock (20,000 shares issued by BigNet at $10 par value)		200,000
Additional Paid-In Capital		1,800,000
To record acquisition of Smallport Company. Assets acquired and liabilities assumed are recorded at fair value.		

BigNet's financial records now show $1,900,000 in the Computers and Equipment account ($1,300,000 former balance + $600,000 acquired), $1,700,000 in Capitalized Software ($500,000 + $1,200,000), and so forth. Note that the customer contracts, despite being unrecorded on Smallport's books, are nonetheless identified and recognized on BigNet's financial records as part of the assets acquired in the combination. These items have been added into BigNet's balances (see Exhibit 2.3) at their fair values. Conversely, BigNet's revenue balance continues to report the company's own $1,000,000 with expenses remaining at $800,000 and dividends of $110,000. Under the acquisition method, only the subsidiary's revenues, expenses, dividends, and equity transactions that occur subsequent to the takeover affect the business combination.

Consideration Transferred Exceeds Net Amount of Fair Values of Identified Assets Acquired and Liabilities Assumed

In this next illustration, BigNet transfers to the owners of Smallport consideration of $1,000,000 in cash plus 20,000 shares of common stock with a fair value of $100 per share in exchange for ownership of the company. The consideration transferred from BigNet to Smallport is now computed as follows and results in an excess amount exchanged over the fair value of the net assets acquired:

Cash payment	$1,000,000
Common stock issued by BigNet ($100 × 20,000 shares)	2,000,000
Total consideration transferred	$3,000,000
Fair value of Smallport's net identifiable assets	$2,550,000
Goodwill	$ 450,000

As presented in the preceding calculation, when the consideration transferred in an acquisition exceeds total net fair value of the identified assets and liabilities, the excess ($450,000 in this case) is allocated to an unidentifiable asset known as goodwill.[17] Unlike other assets, we consider goodwill as unidentifiable because we presume it emerges from several other assets acting together to produce an expectation of enhanced profitability. Goodwill essentially captures all sources of profitability beyond what can be expected from simply summing the fair values of the acquired firm's assets and liabilities.

The resulting consideration paid is $450,000 more than the $2,550,000 fair value of Smallport's net identifiable assets and is assigned to the unidentifiable asset Goodwill.

Several factors may have affected BigNet's $3,000,000 acquisition offer. First, BigNet may expect its assets to act in concert with those of Smallport, thus creating synergies that will produce profits beyond the total expected for the separate companies. In our earlier examples, Facebook, WestRock, and AT&T all clearly anticipated substantial synergies from their acquisitions. Other factors such as Smallport's history of profitability, its reputation, the quality of its personnel, and the current economic condition of the industry in which it operates may also affect the acquisition offer. In general, if a target company is projected to generate unusually high profits relative to its asset base, acquirers frequently are willing to pay a premium price.

Acquisition Method: Consideration Transferred Exceeds Net Identified Asset Fair Values—Subsidiary Dissolved

Returning to BigNet's $3,000,000 consideration, $450,000 is in excess of the fair value of Smallport's net assets. Thus, goodwill of that amount is entered into BigNet's accounting system along with the fair value of each individual asset and liability. BigNet makes the following journal entry at the date of acquisition:

BigNet Company's Financial Records—December 31		
Current Assets	300,000	
Computers and Equipment	600,000	
Capitalized Software	1,200,000	
Customer Contracts	700,000	
Goodwill	450,000	
Notes Payable		250,000
Cash (paid by BigNet)		1,000,000
Common Stock (20,000 shares issued by BigNet at $10 par value)		200,000
Additional Paid-In Capital		1,800,000
To record acquisition of Smallport Company. Assets acquired and liabilities assumed are recorded at individual fair values with excess fair value attributed to goodwill.		

[17] In business combinations, such excess payments are not unusual and can be quite large. When Oracle acquired PeopleSoft, it initially assigned $4.5 billion of its $11 billion purchase price to the fair value of the acquired identified net assets. It assigned the remaining $6.5 billion to goodwill.

Prepare the journal entry to consolidate the accounts of a subsidiary if dissolution takes place.

Once again, BigNet's financial records now show $1,900,000 in the Computers and Equipment account ($1,300,000 former balance + $600,000 acquired), $1,700,000 in Capitalized Software ($500,000 + $1,200,000), and so forth. As the only change, BigNet records goodwill of $450,000 for the excess consideration paid over the net identified asset fair values.[18]

Bargain Purchase—Consideration Transferred Is Less Than Net Amount of Fair Values of Identified Assets Acquired and Liabilities Assumed

Occasionally, the fair value of the consideration transferred by the acquirer is less than the fair value received in an acquisition. Such bargain purchases typically are considered anomalous. Businesses generally do not sell assets or businesses at prices below their fair values. Nonetheless, bargain purchases do occur—most often in forced or distressed sales.

For example, Akoustic Technology's acquisition of STC-MEMS, a semiconductor wafer manufacturing business, resulted in a $6.3 million "bargain purchase" gain. As Akoustic reported in their 2017 10-K annual report:

> The Company accounted for the STC-MEMS Business acquisition as the purchase of a business under GAAP under the acquisition method of accounting, as specified in ASC 805 Business Combinations, and the assets and liabilities acquired were recorded as of the acquisition date, at their respective fair values and consolidated with those of the Company. The fair value of the net assets acquired was approximately $6.3 million. The excess of the aggregate fair value of the net tangible and intangible assets over the consideration paid has been treated as a gain on bargain purchase in accordance with ASC 805.

This gain treatment is consistent with the view that the acquiring firm is immediately better off by the amount that the fair value acquired in the business combination exceeds the consideration transferred.

To demonstrate accounting for a bargain purchase, our third illustration begins with BigNet transferring consideration of $2,000,000 to the owners of Smallport in exchange for their business. BigNet conveys no cash and issues 20,000 shares of $10 par common stock that has a $100 per share fair value. The consideration transferred from BigNet to Smallport is now computed as follows and results in a gain on bargain purchase:

Cash payment	$ -0-
Common stock issued by BigNet ($100 × 20,000 shares)	2,000,000
Total consideration transferred	$2,000,000
Fair value of Smallport's identifiable net assets	$2,550,000
Gain on bargain purchase	$ 550,000

In accounting for this acquisition, at least two competing fair values are present. First, the $2,000,000 consideration transferred for Smallport represents a negotiated transaction value for the business. Second, the net amount of fair values individually assigned to the identified assets acquired and liabilities assumed produces $2,550,000. Additionally, based on expected synergies with Smallport, BigNet's management may believe that the fair value of the business exceeds the net asset fair value. Nonetheless, because the consideration transferred is less than the net asset fair value, a bargain purchase has occurred.

The acquisition method records the identified assets acquired and liabilities assumed at their individual fair values. In a bargain purchase situation, this net asset fair value effectively replaces the consideration transferred as the acquired firm's valuation basis for financial reporting. The consideration transferred serves as the acquired firm's valuation basis only if the consideration equals or exceeds the net amount of fair values for the assets acquired and liabilities assumed (as in the first two examples). In this case, however, the $2,000,000 consideration paid is less than the $2,550,000 net asset fair value, indicating a bargain purchase. Thus, the $2,550,000 net asset fair value serves as the valuation basis for the combination.

[18] As discussed in Chapter 3, the assets and liabilities (including goodwill) acquired in a business combination are assigned to reporting units of the combined entity. A reporting unit is simply a line of business (often a segment) in which an acquired asset or liability will be employed. The objective of assigning acquired assets and liabilities to reporting units is to facilitate periodic goodwill impairment testing.

A $550,000 *gain on bargain purchase* results because the $2,550,000 recorded value is accompanied by a payment of only $2,000,000. The acquirer recognizes this gain on its income statement in the period the acquisition takes place.

Acquisition Method: Consideration Transferred Is Less Than Net Identified Asset Fair Values—Subsidiary Dissolved

BigNet Company's Financial Records—December 31		
Current Assets	300,000	
Computers and Equipment	600,000	
Capitalized Software	1,200,000	
Customer Contracts	700,000	
Notes Payable		250,000
Common Stock (20,000 shares issued by BigNet at $10 par value)		200,000
Additional Paid-In Capital		1,800,000
Gain on Bargain Purchase		550,000
To record acquisition of Smallport Company. Assets acquired and liabilities assumed are each recorded at fair value. Excess net asset fair value is attributed to a gain on bargain purchase.		

LO 2-6a

Prepare the journal entry to consolidate the accounts of a subsidiary if dissolution takes place.

A consequence of implementing a fair-value concept to acquisition accounting is the recognition of an unrealized gain on the bargain purchase. A criticism of the gain recognition is that the acquirer recognizes profit from a buying activity that occurs prior to traditional accrual measures of earned income (i.e., selling activity). Nonetheless, an exception to the general rule of recording business acquisitions at fair value of the consideration transferred occurs in the rare circumstance of a bargain purchase. Thus, in a bargain purchase, the fair values of the assets received and all liabilities assumed in a business combination are considered more relevant for asset valuation than the consideration transferred.

Summary: Acquisition Method When Dissolution Takes Place

When the acquired firm is dissolved in a business combination, the acquiring firm prepares a journal entry to record the combination on its books. The fair value of the consideration transferred by the acquiring firm provides the starting point for recording the acquisition. With few exceptions, the separately identified assets acquired and liabilities assumed are recorded at their individual fair values. Goodwill is recognized if the fair value of the consideration transferred exceeds the net identified asset fair value. If the net identified asset fair value of the business acquired exceeds the consideration transferred, a gain on a bargain purchase is recognized and reported in current income of the combined entity. Exhibit 2.4 summarizes possible allocations using the acquisition method.

Related Costs of Business Combinations

LO 2-6b

Prepare the journal entry to record the various related costs involved in a business combination.

Three additional categories of costs typically accompany business combinations, regardless of whether dissolution takes place. First, firms often engage attorneys, accountants, investment bankers, and other professionals for combination-related services. The acquisition

EXHIBIT 2.4
Consolidation Values—The Acquisition Method

Consolidation Values	Acquisition Accounting
Consideration transferred equals the fair values of net identified assets acquired.	Identified assets acquired and liabilities assumed are recorded at their fair values.
Consideration transferred is greater than the fair values of net identified assets acquired.	Identified assets acquired and liabilities assumed are recorded at their fair values. The excess consideration transferred over the net identified asset fair value is recorded as goodwill.
Bargain purchase—consideration transferred is less than the fair values of net identified assets acquired. The total of the individual fair values of the net identified assets acquired effectively becomes the acquired business fair value.	Identified assets acquired and liabilities assumed are recorded at their fair values. The excess amount of net identified asset fair value over the consideration transferred is recorded as a gain on bargain purchase.

EXHIBIT 2.5
Acquisition Method—Accounting for Costs Frequently Associated with Business Combinations

Types of Combination Costs	Acquisition Accounting
Direct combination costs (e.g., accounting, legal, investment banking, appraisal fees, etc.)	Expense as incurred
Indirect combination costs (e.g., internal costs such as allocated secretarial or managerial time)	Expense as incurred
Amounts incurred to register and issue securities	Reduce the value assigned to the fair value of the securities issued (typically a debit to additional paid-in capital)

method does not consider such expenditures as part of the fair value received by the acquirer. Therefore, professional service fees are expensed in the period incurred. The second category concerns an acquiring firm's internal costs. Examples include secretarial and management time allocated to the acquisition activity. Such indirect costs are reported as current-year expenses, too. Finally, amounts incurred to register and issue securities in connection with a business combination simply reduce the otherwise determinable fair value of those securities. Exhibit 2.5 summarizes the three categories of related payments that accompany a business combination and their respective accounting treatments.

To illustrate the accounting treatment of these costs that frequently accompany business combinations, assume the following in connection with BigNet's acquisition of Smallport.

- BigNet pays an additional $100,000 in accounting and attorney fees.
- Internal secretarial and administrative costs of $75,000 are indirectly attributable to BigNet's combination with Smallport.
- Costs to register and issue BigNet's securities issued in the combination total $20,000.

Following the acquisition method, regardless of whether dissolution occurs or separate incorporation is maintained, BigNet would record these transactions as follows:

BigNet Company's Financial Records		
Professional Services Expense	100,000	
Cash		100,000
To record as expenses of the current period any direct combination costs.		
Salaries and Administrative Expenses	75,000	
Accounts Payable (or Cash)		75,000
To record as expenses of the current period any indirect combination costs.		
Additional Paid-In Capital	20,000	
Cash		20,000
To record costs to register and issue stock in connection with the Smallport acquisition.		

The Acquisition Method When Separate Incorporation Is Maintained

When each company retains separate incorporation in a business combination, many aspects of the consolidation process are identical to those demonstrated in the previous section. Fair value, for example, remains the basis for initially consolidating the subsidiary's assets and liabilities. Also, the acquiring firm records a journal entry on its books reflecting the investment and the consideration transferred in the combination.

However, several significant differences are evident in combinations in which each company remains a legally incorporated separate entity. Most noticeably, the consolidation of the financial information is only simulated; the acquiring company does not physically record the acquired assets and liabilities. *Because dissolution does not occur, each company maintains independent record keeping.* To facilitate the preparation of consolidated financial statements, a worksheet and consolidation entries are employed using data gathered from these separate companies.

A worksheet provides the structure for generating financial reports for the single economic entity. An integral part of this process employs consolidation worksheet entries that either adjust or eliminate various account balances of the parent and subsidiary. These adjustments and eliminations are entered on the worksheet to produce consolidated statements as if the financial records had been physically combined. *Because no actual union occurs, neither company ever records consolidation worksheet entries in its journals.* Instead, these adjustments and eliminations appear solely on the worksheet to derive consolidated balances for financial reporting purposes.

Example (Includes Stock Issue, Related Combination Costs, and Contingent Consideration)

To illustrate the worksheet mechanics, we again use the Exhibit 2.3 example of BigNet and Smallport. We also include combination costs and contingent consideration. Assume that BigNet acquires Smallport Company on December 31 by issuing 26,000 shares of $10 par value common stock valued at $100 per share (or $2,600,000 in total). BigNet pays fees of $40,000 to a third party for its assistance in arranging the transaction.

Then, to settle a difference of opinion regarding Smallport's fair value, BigNet promises to pay an additional $83,200 to the former owners if Smallport's earnings exceed $300,000 during the next annual period. BigNet estimates a 25 percent probability that the $83,200 contingent payment will be required. A discount rate of 4 percent (to represent the time value of money) yields an expected present value of $20,000 for the contingent liability ($83,200 × 25% × 0.961538). The fair-value approach of the acquisition method views such contingent payments as part of the consideration transferred. According to this view, contingencies have value to those who receive the consideration and represent measurable obligations of the acquirer.[19] Therefore, the fair value of the consideration transferred in this example consists of the following two elements:

Fair value of securities issued by BigNet	$2,600,000
Fair value of contingent performance liability	20,000
Total fair value of consideration transferred	$2,620,000

To facilitate a possible future spin-off, BigNet maintains Smallport as a separate corporation with its independent accounting information system intact. Therefore, whenever financial statements for the combined entity are prepared, BigNet utilizes a worksheet in simulating the consolidation of these two companies.

LO 2-6c

Prepare the journal entry to record a business combination when the acquired firm retains its separate existence.

Although the assets and liabilities are not transferred, BigNet must still record the consideration provided to Smallport's owners. When the subsidiary remains separate, the parent establishes an investment account that initially reflects the acquired firm's acquisition-date fair value. Because Smallport maintains its separate identity, BigNet prepares the following journal entries on its books to record the business combination.

LO 2-7

Prepare a worksheet to consolidate the accounts of two companies that form a business combination in the absence of dissolution.

Acquisition Method—Subsidiary Is Not Dissolved

BigNet Company's Financial Records—December 31		
Investment in Smallport Company (consideration transferred)	2,620,000	
Contingent Performance Liability		20,000
Common Stock (26,000 shares issued by BigNet at $10 par value)		260,000
Additional Paid-In Capital (value of shares in excess of par value)		2,340,000
To record acquisition of Smallport Company, which maintains its separate legal identity.		
Professional Services Expense	40,000	
Cash (paid for third-party fees)		40,000
To record combination costs.		

As Exhibit 2.6 demonstrates, a worksheet can be prepared on the date of acquisition to arrive at consolidated totals for this combination. The entire process consists of six steps.

[19] The ASC (805-30-35-1) notes several reasons for contingent consideration including meeting an earnings target, reaching a specified share price, or reaching a milestone on a research and development project.

EXHIBIT 2.6 Acquisition Method—Date of Acquisition

Accounts	BigNet	Smallport	Consolidation Entries Debits	Consolidation Entries Credits	Consolidated Totals
Income Statement					
Revenues	(1,000,000)				(1,000,000)
Expenses	840,000*				840,000
Net income	(160,000)				(160,000)
Statement of Retained Earnings					
Retained earnings, 1/1	(870,000)				(870,000)
Net income (above)	(160,000)*				(160,000)
Dividends declared	110,000				110,000
Retained earnings, 12/31	(920,000)				(920,000)
Balance Sheet					
Current assets	1,060,000*	300,000			1,360,000
Investment in Smallport Company	2,620,000*	–0–		(S) 600,000 (A) 2,020,000	–0–
Computers and equipment	1,300,000	400,000	(A) 200,000		1,900,000
Capitalized software	500,000	100,000	(A) 1,100,000		1,700,000
Customer contracts	–0–	–0–	(A) 700,000		700,000
Goodwill	–0–	–0–	(A) 70,000		70,000
Total assets	5,480,000	800,000			5,730,000
Notes payable	(300,000)	(200,000)		(A) 50,000	(550,000)
Contingent performance liability	(20,000)*				(20,000)
Common stock	(1,860,000)*	(100,000)	(S) 100,000		(1,860,000)
Additional paid-in capital	(2,380,000)*	(20,000)	(S) 20,000		(2,380,000)
Retained earnings, 12/31 (above)	(920,000)	(480,000)	(S) 480,000		(920,000)
Total liabilities and equities	(5,480,000)	(800,000)	2,670,000	2,670,000	(5,730,000)

Note: Parentheses indicate a credit balance.

*Balances have been adjusted for consideration transferred and payment of direct acquisition costs. Also note follow-through effects to net income and retained earnings from the expensing of the direct acquisition costs.

(S) Elimination of Smallport's stockholders' equity accounts as of December 31 and book value portion of the investment account.

(A) Allocation of BigNet's consideration fair value in excess of book value.

Step 1

Prior to constructing a worksheet, the parent prepares a formal allocation of the acquisition-date fair value similar to the equity method procedures presented in Chapter 1.[20] Thus, the following schedule is appropriate for BigNet's acquisition of Smallport:

Acquisition-Date Fair-Value Allocation Schedule		
Fair value of consideration transferred by BigNet		$2,620,000
Book value of Smallport (see Exhibit 2.3)		600,000
Excess of fair value over book value		$2,020,000
Allocations made to specific accounts based on acquisition-date fair and book value differences (see Exhibit 2.3):		
Computers and equipment ($600,000 – $400,000)	$ 200,000	
Capitalized software ($1,200,000 – $100,000)	1,100,000	
Customer contracts ($700,000 – 0)	700,000	
Notes payable ($250,000 – $200,000)	(50,000)	1,950,000
Excess fair value not identified with specific items—Goodwill		$ 70,000

[20] This allocation procedure is helpful but not critical if dissolution occurs. The asset and liability accounts are simply added directly into the parent's books at their acquisition-date fair value with any excess assigned to goodwill, as shown in the previous sections of this chapter.

Note that this schedule initially subtracts Smallport's acquisition-date book value. The resulting $2,020,000 difference represents the total amount needed on the Exhibit 2.6 worksheet to adjust Smallport's individual assets and liabilities from book value to fair value (and to recognize goodwill). Next, the schedule shows how this $2,020,000 total is allocated to adjust each individual item to fair value. The fair-value allocation schedule thus effectively serves as a convenient supporting schedule for the Exhibit 2.6 worksheet and is routinely prepared for every consolidation.

No part of the $2,020,000 excess fair value is attributed to the current assets because their book values equal their fair values. The Notes Payable account shows a negative allocation because the debt's present value exceeds its book value. An increase in debt decreases the fair value of the company's net assets.

Step 2

The consolidation process begins with preparing the first two columns of the worksheet (see Exhibit 2.6) containing the separate companies' acquisition-date book value financial figures (see Exhibit 2.3). BigNet's accounts have been adjusted for the journal entries recorded earlier for the investment and the combination costs. As another preliminary step, Smallport's revenue, expense, and dividend accounts have been closed into its Retained Earnings account. The subsidiary's operations prior to the December 31 takeover have no direct bearing on the operating results of the business combination. These activities occurred before Smallport was acquired; thus, the new owner should not include any precombination subsidiary revenues or expenses in the consolidated statements.

Step 3

Consolidation Entry S eliminates Smallport's stockholders' equity accounts (S is a reference to beginning subsidiary stockholders' equity) as follows:

Consolidation Entry S

Common Stock (Smallport Company)	100,000	
Additional Paid-In Capital (Smallport Company)	20,000	
Retained Earnings (Smallport Company)	480,000	
Investment in Smallport Company		600,000

Consolidation Entry S is a worksheet entry and accordingly does not affect the financial records of either company. The subsidiary balances (Common Stock, Additional Paid-In Capital, and Retained Earnings) represent ownership interests that are now held by the parent—thus, they are not represented as equity in the parent's consolidated balance sheet. Moreover, by removing these account balances on the worksheet, only Smallport's assets and liabilities remain to be combined with the parent company figures.

Consolidation Entry S also removes the $600,000 component of the parent's Investment in Smallport Company account balance that equates to the book value of the subsidiary's net assets. For external reporting purposes, BigNet should include each of Smallport's assets and liabilities rather than a single investment balance. In effect, this portion of the parent's Investment in Smallport Company account balance is eliminated and replaced by the specific subsidiary assets and liabilities that are already listed in the second column of the worksheet.

Step 4

Consolidation Entry A removes the $2,020,000 excess payment in the Investment in Smallport Company and assigns it to the specific accounts indicated by the fair-value allocation schedule as follows:

Consolidation Entry A

Computers and Equipment	200,000	
Capitalized Software	1,100,000	
Customer Contracts	700,000	
Goodwill	70,000	
Note Payable		50,000
Investment in Smallport Company		2,020,000

Consequently, Computers and Equipment is increased by $200,000 to agree with Smallport's fair value: $1,100,000 is attributed to Capitalized Software, $700,000 to Customer Contracts, and $50,000 to Notes Payable. The unidentified excess of $70,000 is allocated to Goodwill. This entry for the consolidation worksheet is labeled Entry A to indicate that it represents the allocations made in connection with Smallport's acquisition-date fair value.

Consolidation Entry A also completes the Investment in Smallport Company account balance elimination on the worksheet. The investment remains on BigNet's books, but it does not appear on the consolidated balance sheet. Instead the investment account is replaced on the worksheet with Smallport's actual assets and liabilities as shown in Step 5.

Step 5

All accounts are extended into the Consolidated Totals column. For accounts such as Current Assets, this process simply adds Smallport and BigNet book values. However, when applicable, this extension also includes any allocations to establish the acquisition-date fair values of Smallport's assets and liabilities. Computers and Equipment, for example, is increased by $200,000. By increasing the subsidiary's book value to fair value, the reported balances are the same as in the previous examples when dissolution occurred. The use of a worksheet does not alter the consolidated figures but only the method of deriving those numbers.

Step 6

We subtract consolidated expenses from revenues to arrive at a $160,000 net income. Note that because this is an acquisition-date worksheet, we consolidate no amounts for Smallport's revenues and expenses. Having just been acquired, Smallport has not yet earned any income for BigNet owners. Consolidated revenues, expenses, and net income are identical to BigNet's balances. Subsequent to acquisition, of course, Smallport's revenue and expense accounts will be consolidated with BigNet's (coverage of this topic begins in Chapter 3).

Worksheet Mechanics

In general, totals (such as net income and ending retained earnings) are not directly consolidated across on the worksheet. Rather, the components (such as revenues and expenses) are extended across and then combined vertically to derive the appropriate figure. Net income is then carried down on the worksheet to the statement of retained earnings and used (along with beginning retained earnings and dividends) to compute the December 31 retained earnings balance. In the same manner, ending retained earnings of $920,000 is entered into the balance sheet to arrive at total liabilities and equities of $5,730,000, a number that reconciles with the total of consolidated assets.

Although it remains on BigNet's books, the Investment in Smallport account is eliminated entirely in consolidation. On the worksheet, the investment account is effectively replaced with the acquisition-date fair values of Smallport's assets and liabilities along with goodwill created by the combination.

The balances in the final column of Exhibit 2.6 are used to prepare consolidated financial statements for the business combination of BigNet Company and Smallport Company. The worksheet entries serve as a catalyst to bring together the two independent sets of financial information. The actual accounting records of both BigNet and Smallport remain unaltered by this consolidation process.

Bargain Purchase of a Separately Incorporated Subsidiary

Finally, although not addressed directly by the preceding example, bargain purchase gains can also occur in acquisitions of separately incorporated subsidiaries. If the consideration transferred is less than the fair value of a newly acquired subsidiary's identifiable net assets, then the parent records a bargain purchase gain on its books as part of the investment journal entry. The bargain purchase gain then appears on the the consolidated income statement for the reporting period that contains the acquisition date.

LO 2-8

Describe the accounting treatment for the various intangible assets often acquired in a business combination.

Acquisition-Date Fair-Value Allocations—Additional Issues

Intangibles

An important element of acquisition accounting is the acquirer's recognition and measurement of the assets acquired and liabilities assumed in the combination. In particular, the advent of the information age brings new measurement challenges for a host of intangible assets that provide value in generating future cash flows. Intangible assets often comprise the largest proportion of an acquired firm. For example, when AT&T acquired AT&T Broadband, it allocated approximately $19 billion of the $52 billion purchase price to franchise costs. These franchise costs form an intangible asset representing the value attributed to agreements with local authorities that allow access to homes.

Intangible assets include both current and noncurrent assets (not including financial instruments) that lack physical substance. In determining whether to recognize an intangible asset in a business combination, two specific criteria are essential.

1. Does the intangible asset arise from contractual or other legal rights?
2. Is the intangible asset capable of being sold or otherwise separated from the acquired enterprise?

Intangibles arising from contractual or legal rights are commonplace in business combinations. Often identified among the assets acquired are trademarks, patents, copyrights, franchise agreements, and a number of other intangibles that derive their value from governmental protection (or other contractual agreements) that allow a firm exclusive use of the asset. Most intangible assets recognized in business combinations meet the contractual-legal criterion.

Also seen in business combinations are intangible assets meeting the separability criterion. An acquired intangible asset is recognized if it is capable of being separated or divided from the acquiree and sold, transferred, licensed, rented, or exchanged individually or together with a related contract, identifiable asset, or liability. The acquirer is not required to have the intention to sell, license, or otherwise exchange the intangible in order to meet the separability criterion. For example, an acquiree may have developed internally a valuable customer list or other noncontractual customer relationships. Although the value of these items may not have arisen from a specific legal right, they nonetheless convey benefits to the acquirer that may be separable through sale, license, or exchange.

Exhibit 2.7 provides an extensive listing of intangible assets with indications of whether they typically meet the contractual-legal or separability criteria.

The FASB (Exposure Draft, *Business Combinations and Intangible Assets,* para. 271) recognized the inherent difficulties in estimating the separate fair values of many intangibles and stated that

> difficulties may arise in assigning the acquisition cost to individual intangible assets acquired in a basket purchase such as a business combination. Measuring some of those assets is less difficult than measuring other assets, particularly if they are exchangeable and traded regularly in the marketplace. . . . Nonetheless, even those assets that cannot be measured on that basis may have more cash flow streams directly or indirectly associated with them than can be used as the basis for measuring them. While the resulting measures may lack the precision of other measures, they provide information that is more representationally faithful than would be the case if those assets were simply subsumed into goodwill on the grounds of measurement difficulties.

EXHIBIT 2.7 Illustrative Examples of Intangible Assets That Meet the Criteria for Recognition Separately from Goodwill (FASB ASC paragraphs 805-20-55-11 through 45)

The following are examples of intangible assets that meet the criteria for recognition as an asset apart from goodwill. The following illustrative list is not intended to be all-inclusive; thus, an acquired intangible asset could meet the recognition criteria of this statement but not be included on that list. Assets designated by the symbol (c) are those that would generally be recognized separately from goodwill because they meet the contractual-legal criterion. Assets designated by the symbol (s) do not arise from contractual or other legal rights but should nonetheless be recognized separately from goodwill because they meet the separability criterion. The determination of whether a specific acquired intangible asset meets the criteria in this statement for recognition apart from goodwill should be based on the facts and circumstances of each individual business combination.*

Marketing-Related Intangible Assets

1. Trademarks, trade names.[c]
2. Service marks, collective marks, certification marks.[c]
3. Trade dress (unique color, shape, or package design).[c]
4. Newspaper mastheads.[c]
5. Internet domain names.[c]
6. Noncompetition agreements.[c]

Customer-Related Intangible Assets

1. Customer lists.[s]
2. Order or production backlog.[c]
3. Customer contracts and related customer relationships.[c]
4. Noncontractual customer relationships.[s]

Artistic-Related Intangible Assets

1. Plays, operas, and ballets.[c]
2. Books, magazines, newspapers, and other literary works.[c]
3. Musical works such as compositions, song lyrics, and advertising jingles.[c]
4. Pictures and photographs.[c]
5. Video and audiovisual material, including motion pictures, music videos, and television programs.[c]

Contract-Based Intangible Assets

1. Licensing, royalty, standstill agreements.[c]
2. Advertising, construction, management, service, or supply contracts.[c]
3. Lease agreements.[c]
4. Construction permits.[c]
5. Franchise agreements.[c]
6. Operating and broadcast rights.[c]
7. Use rights such as landing, drilling, water, air, mineral, timber cutting, and route authorities.[c]
8. Servicing contracts such as mortgage servicing contracts.[c]
9. Employment contracts.[c]

Technology-Based Intangible Assets

1. Patented technology.[c]
2. Computer software and mask works.[c]
3. Unpatented technology.[s]
4. Databases, including title plants.[s]
5. Trade secrets, including secret formulas, processes, and recipes.[c]

*The intangible assets designated by the symbol (c) also could meet the separability criterion. However, separability is not a necessary condition for an asset to meet the contractual-legal criterion.

Undoubtedly, as our knowledge economy continues its rapid growth, asset allocations to items such as those identified in Exhibit 2.7 are expected to be frequent.

Preexisting Goodwill on Acquired Firm's Books

In our examples of business combinations so far, the assets acquired and liabilities assumed have all been specifically identifiable (e.g., current assets, capitalized software, computers and equipment, customer contracts, and notes payable). However, in many cases, an acquired firm has an unidentifiable asset (i.e., goodwill recorded on its books in connection with a previous business combination of its own). A question arises as to the parent's treatment of this pre-existing goodwill on the newly acquired subsidiary's books.

By its very nature, such pre-existing goodwill is not considered identifiable by the parent. Therefore, in calculating the new goodwill acquired in the combination, the new owner simply excludes the carrying amount of any pre-existing goodwill from the subsidiary's acquisition-date net assets. In a merger situation, the acquiring firm simply records any new goodwill (along with the identifiable assets and liabilities acquired) and ignores the acquired firm's pre-existing goodwill.

In the case of an acquisition where the subsidiary continues its separate legal existence, the pre-existing subsidiary goodwill must be eliminated on the consolidated worksheet. The parent company effectively reallocates any pre-existing subsidiary goodwill via a credit in consolidation worksheet Entry A. This worksheet credit to the subsidiary's goodwill balance is then offset by worksheet entries to identifiable assets and liabilities, followed by a debit to the new goodwill from the combination.

For example, assume Pride Company acquires Stone Company for cash consideration and will maintain Stone as a wholly owned subsidiary. Stone has previously recognized $5,000 goodwill on its books. Also assume that Stone has a trademark undervalued by $4,000 on its books and Pride will recognize new goodwill of $3,000 from the acquisition. Consolidation worksheet entry A would then be prepared as follows:

Consolidation Entry A		
Goodwill (new)	3,000	
Trademark	4,000	
Goodwill (previous subsidiary amount)		5,000
Investment in Stone		2,000

Note that the subsidiary's precombination goodwill balance is eliminated in consolidation Entry A in formulating an acquisition-date consolidated balance sheet. The logic is that the parent's consideration transferred is first allocated to the subsidiary's identifiable assets and liabilities. Only if an excess amount remains after recognizing the fair values of the net identified assets is any goodwill recognized. Thus, in all business combinations, only goodwill reflected in the current acquisition is brought forward in the consolidated entity's financial reports.

Acquired In-Process Research and Development

The negotiations for a business combination begin with the identification of the tangible and intangible assets acquired and liabilities assumed by the acquirer. The fair values of the acquired individual assets and liabilities then provide the basis for financial statement valuations. Many firms—especially those in pharmaceutical and high-tech industries—have allocated significant portions of acquired businesses to in-process research and development (IPR&D).

Current accounting standards require that acquired IPR&D be measured at acquisition-date fair value and recognized in consolidated financial statements as an asset. However, this was not always the case. Past standards required immediate expense treatment for acquired IPR&D. Nonetheless, arguments about the future economic benefits of IPR&D ultimately persuaded the FASB to require asset recognition. For example, in commenting on the nature of IPR&D as an asset, Pfizer in an October 28, 2005, comment letter to the FASB observed that

> board members know that companies frame business strategies around IPR&D, negotiate for it, pay for it, fair value it, and nurture it and they view those seemingly rational actions as inconsistent with the notion that IPR&D has no probable future economic benefit.

Asset recognition for acquired IPR&D is now standard even though benefits must be estimated and may be uncertain. To illustrate, when ARCA Biopharma acquired a significant in-process research and development asset through a merger with Nuvelo, Inc., it disclosed the following in its financial statements:

> A valuation firm was engaged to assist ARCA in determining the estimated fair values of these (IPR&D) assets as of the acquisition date. Discounted cash flow models are typically used in these valuations, and the models require the use of significant estimates and assumptions including but not limited to:
>
> - Projecting regulatory approvals.
> - Estimating future cash flows from product sales resulting from completed products and in-process projects.
> - Developing appropriate discount rates and probability rates by project.

The IPR&D asset is initially considered an indefinite-lived intangible asset and is not subject to amortization. IPR&D is then tested for impairment annually or more frequently if events or changes in circumstances indicate that the asset might be impaired.

Recognizing acquired IPR&D as an asset is clearly consistent with the FASB's fair-value approach to acquisition accounting. Similar to costs that result in goodwill and other internally generated intangibles (e.g., customer lists, trade names, etc.), IPR&D costs are expensed as incurred in ongoing business activities. However, a business combination is considered a significant recognition event for which all fair values transferred in the transaction should be fully accounted for, including any values assigned to IPR&D. Moreover, because the acquirer paid for the IPR&D, an expectation of future economic benefit is assumed, and, therefore, the amount is recognized as an asset.

To illustrate further, assume that ClearTone Company pays $2,300,000 in cash for all assets and liabilities of Newave, Inc., in a merger transaction. ClearTone manufactures components for cell phones. The primary motivation for the acquisition is a particularly attractive research and development project under way at Newave that will extend a cell phone's battery life by up to 50 percent. ClearTone hopes to combine the new technology with its manufacturing process and projects a resulting substantial revenue increase. ClearTone is optimistic that Newave will finish the project in the next two years. At the acquisition date, ClearTone prepares the following schedule that recognizes the items of value it expects to receive from the Newave acquisition:

Consideration transferred		$2,300,000
Receivables	$ 55,000	
Patents	220,000	
In-process research and development	1,900,000	
Accounts payable	(175,000)	
Fair value of identified net assets acquired		2,000,000
Goodwill		$ 300,000

ClearTone records the transaction as follows:

Receivables	55,000	
Patents	220,000	
Research and Development Asset	1,900,000	
Goodwill	300,000	
Accounts Payable		175,000
Cash		2,300,000

Research and development expenditures incurred subsequent to the date of acquisition will continue to be expensed. Acquired IPR&D assets initially should be considered indefinite-lived until the project is completed or abandoned. As with other indefinite-lived intangible assets, an acquired IPR&D asset is tested for impairment and is not amortized until its useful life is determined to be no longer indefinite.

Convergence between U.S. and International Accounting Standards

The FASB ASC Topics "Business Combinations" (805) and "Consolidation" (810) represent outcomes of a joint project between the FASB and the International Accounting Standards Board (IASB). The primary objective of the project was stated as follows:

> to develop a single high-quality standard for business combinations that can be used for both domestic and cross-border financial reporting. The goal is to develop a standard that includes a common set of principles and related guidance that produces decision-useful information and minimizes exceptions to those principles. The standard should improve the completeness, relevance, and comparability of financial information about business combinations . . . [21]

The IASB subsequently issued International Financial Reporting Standard 3 (*IFRS 3*) Revised (effective July 2009), which along with FASB ASC Topics 805, "Business Combinations," and 810, "Consolidation," effectively converged the accounting for business combinations internationally. The two standards are identical in most important aspects of accounting for business combinations although differences can result in noncontrolling interest valuation and some other limited applications.[22] The joint project on business combinations represents one of the first successful implementations of the agreement between the two standard-setting groups to coordinate efforts on future work with the goal of developing high-quality comparable standards for both domestic and cross-border financial accounting.

[21] FASB Project Updates: Business Combinations: Applying the Acquisition Method—Joint Project of the IASB and FASB: October 25, 2007.

[22] Chapter 4 of this text provides further discussion of noncontrolling interest accounting differences across U.S. GAAP and IFRS. Other differences are presented in chapters where the applicable topics are covered.

Discussion Question

WHAT IF AN ACQUIRED ENTITY IS NOT A BUSINESS?

To qualify for the acquisition method (ASC 805), the acquired entity must meet the definition of a *business.* Otherwise the transaction is accounted for as an *asset acquisition.*

When substantially all of the fair value of gross assets acquired is concentrated in a single asset (or a group of similar assets), the assets acquired would not represent a business. To be considered a business, an acquisition must include an input and a substantive process that together significantly contribute to the ability to create outputs.

Asset acquisitions are measured and reported based on cost and reflect the following:

- No goodwill (or gain on bargain purchase)—excess consideration transferred is reallocated to identifiable assets based on relative fair values.
- Transaction costs (expensed in a business combination but capitalized in an asset acquisition).
- In-process research and development (capitalized in a business combination but expensed in an asset acquisition).
- Contingent consideration (recognized at fair value on the acquisition date in a business combination but generally recognized when resolved in an asset acquisition).

For example, when Celgene Corporation acquired all of the outstanding shares of Impact Biomedicines, Inc., in 2018, the acquisition was reported in Celgene's 10-Q as follows:

> The acquisition of Impact was concentrated in one single identifiable asset and thus, for accounting purposes, we have concluded that the acquired assets do not meet the accounting definition of a business. The initial payment was allocated primarily to fedratinib [a cancer therapy], resulting in a $1.1 billion research and development asset acquisition expense . . .

Because Impact was not considered a business, Celgene expensed the acquired research and development cost in the acquisition period. Also, Celgene did not recognize in its financial statements the fair values of the contingent consideration elements at the acquisition date.

What potential accounting complexities (and costs) does a company avoid when it acquires another company that does not qualify as a business?

Summary

1. Consolidation of financial information is required for external reporting purposes when one organization gains control of another, thus forming a single economic entity. In many combinations, all but one of the companies is dissolved as a separate legal corporation. Therefore, the consolidation process is carried out fully at the date of acquisition to bring together all accounts into a single set of financial records. In other combinations, the companies retain their identities as separate enterprises and continue to maintain their own separate accounting systems. For these cases, consolidation is a periodic process necessary whenever the parent produces external financial statements. This periodic procedure is frequently accomplished through the use of a worksheet and consolidation entries.
2. Current financial reporting standards require the acquisition method in accounting for business combinations. Under the acquisition method, the fair value of the consideration transferred provides the starting point for valuing the acquired firm. The fair value of the consideration transferred by the acquirer includes the fair value of any contingent consideration. The acquired company assets and liabilities are consolidated at their individual acquisition-date fair values. Direct combination costs are expensed as incurred because they are not part of the acquired business fair value. Also, the fair value of all acquired in-process research and development is recognized as an asset in business combinations and is subject to subsequent impairment reviews.

3. If the consideration transferred for an acquired firm exceeds the total fair value of the acquired firm's net assets, the residual amount is recognized in the consolidated financial statements as goodwill, an intangible asset. When a bargain purchase occurs, individual assets and liabilities acquired continue to be recorded at their fair values, and a gain on bargain purchase is recognized.
4. Particular attention should be given to the recognition of intangible assets in business combinations. An intangible asset must be recognized in an acquiring firm's financial statements if the asset arises from a legal or contractual right (e.g., trademarks, copyrights, artistic materials, royalty agreements). If the intangible asset does not represent a legal or contractual right, the intangible will still be recognized if it is capable of being separated from the firm (e.g., customer lists, noncontractual customer relationships, unpatented technology).

Comprehensive Illustration

Problem

(Estimated Time: 45 to 65 Minutes) The following are the account balances of Miller Company and Richmond Company as of December 31. The fair values of Richmond Company's assets and liabilities are also listed.

	Miller Company Book Values 12/31	Richmond Company Book Values 12/31	Richmond Company Fair Values 12/31
Cash	$ 600,000	$ 200,000	$ 200,000
Receivables	900,000	300,000	290,000
Inventory	1,100,000	600,000	820,000
Buildings and equipment (net)	9,000,000	800,000	900,000
Unpatented technology	–0–	–0–	500,000
In-process research and development	–0–	–0–	100,000
Accounts payable	(400,000)	(200,000)	(200,000)
Notes payable	(3,400,000)	(1,100,000)	(1,100,000)
Totals	$ 7,800,000	$ 600,000	$1,510,000
Common stock—$20 par value	$ (2,000,000)		
Common stock—$5 par value		$ (220,000)	
Additional paid-in capital	(900,000)	(100,000)	
Retained earnings, 1/1	(2,300,000)	(130,000)	
Revenues	(6,000,000)	(900,000)	
Expenses	3,400,000	750,000	
Totals	$ (7,800,000)	$ (600,000)	

Note: Parentheses indicate a credit balance.

Additional Information (not reflected in the preceding figures)

- On December 31, Miller issues 50,000 shares of its $20 par value common stock for all of the outstanding shares of Richmond Company.
- As part of the acquisition agreement, Miller agrees to pay the former owners of Richmond $250,000 if certain profit projections are realized over the next three years. Miller calculates the acquisition-date fair value of this contingency at $100,000.
- In creating this combination, Miller pays $10,000 in stock issue costs and $20,000 in accounting and legal fees.

Required

a. Miller's stock has a fair value of $32 per share. Using the acquisition method:

1. Prepare the necessary journal entries if Miller dissolves Richmond so it is no longer a separate legal entity.
2. Assume instead that Richmond will retain separate legal incorporation and maintain its own accounting systems. Prepare a worksheet to consolidate the accounts of the two companies.

b. If Miller's stock has a fair value of $26 per share, describe how the consolidated balances would differ from the results in requirement (*a*).

Solution

a. 1. In a business combination, the accountant first determines the total fair value of the consideration transferred. Because Miller's stock is valued at $32 per share, the 50,000 issued shares are worth $1,600,000 in total. Included in the consideration transferred is the $100,000 acquisition-date fair value of the contingent performance obligation.

This $1,700,000 total fair value is compared to the $1,510,000 fair value of Richmond's assets and liabilities (including the fair value of IPR&D). Miller recognizes the $190,000 excess fair value ($1,700,000 – $1,510,000) as goodwill. Because dissolution occurs, Miller records on its books the individual fair values of Richmond's identifiable assets and liabilities with the excess recorded as goodwill.

The $10,000 stock issue cost reduces Additional Paid-In Capital. The $20,000 direct combination costs (accounting and legal fees) are expensed when incurred.

Miller Company's Financial Records—December 31

Cash	200,000	
Receivables	290,000	
Inventory	820,000	
Buildings and Equipment	900,000	
Unpatented Technology	500,000	
Research and Development Asset	100,000	
Goodwill	190,000	
Accounts Payable		200,000
Notes Payable		1,100,000
Contingent Performance Obligation		100,000
Common Stock (Miller) (par value)		1,000,000
Additional Paid-In Capital (fair value in excess of par value)		600,000
To record acquisition of Richmond Company.		
Professional Services Expense	20,000	
Cash (paid for combination costs)		20,000
To record legal and accounting fees related to the combination.		
Additional Paid-In Capital	10,000	
Cash (stock issuance costs)		10,000
To record payment of stock issuance costs.		

2. Under this scenario, the acquisition fair value is equal to that computed in part (*a*1).

50,000 shares of stock at $32.00 each	$1,600,000
Contingent performance obligation	100,000
Acquisition-date fair value of consideration transferred	$1,700,000

Because the subsidiary is maintaining separate incorporation, Miller establishes an investment account to reflect the $1,700,000 acquisition consideration:

Miller's Financial Records—December 31

Investment in Richmond Company	1,700,000	
Contingent Performance Obligation		100,000
Common Stock (Miller) (par value)		1,000,000
Additional Paid-In Capital (fair value in excess of par value)		600,000
To record investment in Richmond Company.		
Professional Services Expense	20,000	
Cash (paid for combination costs)		20,000
To record legal and accounting fees related to the combination.		
Additional Paid-In Capital	10,000	
Cash (stock issuance costs)		10,000
To record payment of stock issuance costs.		

Because Richmond maintains separate incorporation and its own accounting system, Miller prepares a worksheet for consolidation. To prepare the worksheet, Miller first allocates Richmond's fair value to assets acquired and liabilities assumed based on their individual fair values:

Fair value of consideration transferred by Miller	$1,700,000
Book value of Richmond	600,000
Excess fair value over book value	$1,100,000

Allocations are made to specific accounts based on differences in fair values and book values:

Receivables ($290,000 – $300,000)	$ (10,000)	
Inventory ($820,000 – $600,000)	220,000	
Buildings and equipment ($900,000 – $800,000)	100,000	
Unpatented technology ($500,000 – 0)	500,000	
In-process research and development	100,000	910,000
Goodwill		$190,000

The following steps produce the consolidated financial statements total in Exhibit 2.8:

Exhibit 2.8 Comprehensive Illustration—Solution—Acquisition Method

MILLER COMPANY AND RICHMOND COMPANY
Consolidation Worksheet
For Period Ending December 31

Accounts	Miller Company	Richmond Company	Consolidation Entries Debit	Consolidation Entries Credit	Consolidated Totals
Income Statement					
Revenues	(6,000,000)				(6,000,000)
Expenses	3,420,000*				3,420,000*
Net income	(2,580,000)				(2,580,000)
Statement of Retained Earnings					
Retained earnings, 1/1	(2,300,000)				(2,300,000)
Net income (above)	(2,580,000)				(2,580,000)
Retained earnings, 12/31	(4,880,000)				(4,880,000)
Balance Sheet					
Cash	570,000*	200,000			770,000
Receivables	900,000	300,000		(A) 10,000	1,190,000
Inventory	1,100,000	600,000	(A) 220,000		1,920,000
Investment in Richmond Company	1,700,000*	–0–		(A) 1,100,000 (S) 600,000	–0–
Buildings and equipment (net)	9,000,000	800,000	(A) 100,000		9,900,000
Goodwill	–0–	–0–	(A) 190,000		190,000
Unpatented technology	–0–	–0–	(A) 500,000		500,000
Research and development asset	–0–	–0–	(A) 100,000		100,000
Total assets	13,270,000	1,900,000			14,570,000
Accounts payable	(400,000)	(200,000)			(600,000)
Notes payable	(3,400,000)	(1,100,000)			(4,500,000)
Contingent performance obligation	(100,000)*	–0–			(100,000)
Common stock	(3,000,000)*	(220,000)	(S) 220,000		(3,000,000)
Additional paid-in capital	(1,490,000)*	(100,000)	(S) 100,000		(1,490,000)
Retained earnings, 12/31 (above)	(4,880,000)*	(280,000)†	(S) 280,000		(4,880,000)
Total liabilities and equities	(13,270,000)	(1,900,000)	1,710,000	1,710,000	(14,570,000)

Note: Parentheses indicate a credit balance.
*Balances have been adjusted for issuance of stock, payment of combination expenses, and recognition of contingent performance obligation.
†Beginning retained earnings plus revenues minus expenses.

- Miller's balances have been updated on this worksheet to include the effects of both the newly issued shares of stock, the recognition of the contingent performance liability, and the combination expenses.
- Richmond's revenue and expense accounts have been closed to Retained Earnings. The acquisition method consolidates only postacquisition revenues and expenses.
- Worksheet Entry S eliminates the $600,000 book value component of the Investment in Richmond Company account along with the subsidiary's stockholders' equity accounts.

  Entry A adjusts all of Richmond's assets and liabilities to fair value based on the allocations determined earlier.

b. If the fair value of Miller's stock is $26.00 per share, then the fair value of the consideration transferred in the Richmond acquisition is recomputed as follows:

Fair value of shares issued ($26 × 50,000 shares)	$1,300,000
Fair value of contingent consideration	100,000
Total consideration transferred at fair value	$1,400,000

Because the consideration transferred is $110,000 less than the $1,510,000 fair value of the net assets received in the acquisition, a bargain purchase has occurred. In this situation, Miller continues to recognize each of the separately identified assets acquired and liabilities assumed at their fair values. Resulting differences in the consolidated balances relative to the requirement (*a*) solution are as follows:

- The $110,000 excess fair value recognized over the consideration transferred is recognized as a "gain on bargain purchase."
- Consolidated net income increases by the $110,000 gain to $2,690,000.
- No goodwill is recognized.
- Miller's additional paid-in capital decreases by $300,000 to $1,190,000.
- Consolidated retained earnings increase by the $110,000 gain to $4,990,000.

Also, because of the bargain purchase, the "Investment in Richmond Company" account balance on Miller's separate financial statements shows the $1,510,000 fair value of the net identified assets received. This valuation measure is an exception to the general rule of using the consideration transferred to provide the valuation basis for the acquired firm.

Appendix A

LO 2-9

Identify the general characteristics of the legacy purchase and pooling of interest methods of accounting for past business combinations. Understand the effects that persist today in financial statements from the use of these legacy methods.

Legacy Methods of Accounting for Business Combinations

The acquisition method provides the accounting for business combinations occurring in 2009 and thereafter. However, for decades, business combinations were accounted for using either the **purchase** or **pooling of interests** method. From 2002 through 2008, the purchase method was used exclusively for business combinations. Prior to 2002, financial reporting standards allowed two alternatives: the purchase method and the pooling of interests method. Because the FASB required prospective application of the acquisition method for 2009 and beyond, the purchase and pooling of interests methods continue to provide the basis for financial reporting for pre-2009 business combinations and thus will remain relevant for many years. Literally tens of thousands of past business combinations will continue to be reported in future statements under one of these legacy methods.

The following sections describe the purchase and pooling of interests methods along with comparisons to the acquisition method.

The Purchase Method: An Application of the Cost Principle

A basic principle of the purchase method was to record a business combination at the cost to the new owners. For example, several years ago MGM Grand, Inc., acquired Mirage Resorts, Inc., for approximately $6.4 billion. This purchase price continued to serve as the valuation basis for Mirage Resorts' assets and liabilities in the preparation of MGM Grand's consolidated financial statements.

Several elements of the purchase method reflect a strict application of the cost principle. The following items represent examples of how the cost-based purchase method differs from the fair-value–based acquisition method.

- Acquisition date allocations (including bargain purchases).
- Direct combination costs.
- Contingent consideration.
- In-process research and development.

We next briefly discuss the accounting treatment for these items across the current and previous financial reporting regimes.

Purchase-Date Cost Allocations (Including Bargain Purchases)

In pre-2009 business combinations, the application of the cost principle often was complicated because literally hundreds of separate assets and liabilities were acquired. Accordingly, for asset valuation and future income determination, firms needed a basis to allocate the total cost among the various assets and liabilities received in the bargained exchange. Similar to the acquisition method, the purchase method based its cost allocations on the combination-date fair values of the acquired assets and liabilities. Also closely related to the acquisition method procedures, any excess of cost over the sum of the net identified asset fair values was attributed to goodwill.

But the purchase method stands in marked contrast to the acquisition method in bargain purchase situations. Under the purchase method, a bargain purchase occurred when the sum of the individual fair values of the acquired net assets exceeded the purchase cost. To record a bargain purchase at cost, however, the purchase method required that certain long-term assets be recorded at amounts below their assessed fair values.

For example, assume Adams Co. paid $520,000 for Brook Co. in 2008. Brook has the following assets with appraised fair values:

Accounts receivable	$ 15,000
Land	200,000
Building	400,000
Accounts payable	(5,000)
Total net fair value	$610,000

However, to record the combination at its $520,000 cost, Adams cannot use all of the fair values. The purchase method solution was to require that Adams reduce the valuation assigned to the acquired long-term assets (land and building) proportionately by $90,000 ($610,000 – $520,000). The total fair value of the long-term assets, in this case $600,000, provided the basis for allocating the reduction. Thus, Adams would reduce the acquired land by (2/6 × $90,000) = $30,000 and the building by (4/6 × $90,000) = $60,000. Adams's journal entry to record the combination using the purchase method would then be as follows:

Accounts Receivable	15,000	
Land ($200,000 – $30,000)	170,000	
Building ($400,000 – $60,000)	340,000	
Accounts Payable		5,000
Cash		520,000

Note that current assets and liabilities did not share in the proportionate reduction to cost. Long-term assets were subject to the reduction because their fair-value estimates were considered less reliable than current items and liabilities. Finally, in rare situations, firms recognized an extraordinary gain on a purchase, but only in the very unusual case that the long-term assets were reduced to a zero valuation.

In contrast, the acquisition method embraces the fair-value concept and discards the consideration transferred as a valuation basis for the business acquired in a bargain purchase. Instead, the acquirer measures and recognizes the fair values of each of the assets acquired and liabilities assumed at the date of combination, regardless of the consideration transferred in the transaction. As a result, (1) no assets are recorded at amounts below their assessed fair values, as is the case with bargain purchases accounted for by the purchase method, and (2) a gain on bargain purchase is recognized at the acquisition date.

Direct Combination Costs

Almost all business combinations employ professional services to assist in various phases of the transaction. Examples include target identification, due diligence regarding the value of an acquisition, financing, tax planning, and preparation of formal legal documents. Prior to 2009, under the purchase method, the investment cost basis included direct combination costs. In contrast, the acquisition method considers these costs as payments for services received, not part of the fair value exchanged for the business. Thus, under the acquisition method, direct combination costs are expensed as incurred.

Contingent Consideration

Often business combination negotiations result in agreements to provide additional payments to former owners if they meet specified future performance measures. The purchase method accounted for such contingent consideration obligations as postcombination adjustments to the purchase cost (or stockholders' equity if the contingency involved the parent's equity share value) upon resolution of the contingency. The acquisition method treats contingent consideration obligations as a negotiated component of the fair value of the consideration transferred, consistent with the fair-value measurement attribute.

In-Process Research and Development (IPR&D)

Prior to 2009, financial reporting standards required the immediate expensing of acquired IPR&D if the project had not yet reached technological feasibility and the assets had no future alternative uses. Expensing acquired IPR&D was consistent with the accounting treatment for a firm's ongoing research and development costs.

The acquisition method, however, requires tangible and intangible assets acquired in a business combination to be used in a particular research and development activity, including those that may have no alternative future use, to be recognized and measured at fair value at the acquisition date. These capitalized research and development costs are reported as intangible assets with indefinite lives subject to periodic impairment reviews. Moreover, because the acquirer identified and paid for the IPR&D, the acquisition method assumes an expectation of future economic benefit and therefore recognizes an asset.

The Pooling of Interests Method: Continuity of Previous Ownership

Historically, former owners of separate firms would agree to combine for their mutual benefit and continue as owners of a combined firm. It was asserted that the assets and liabilities of the former firms were never really bought or sold; former owners merely exchanged ownership shares to become joint owners of the combined firm. Combinations characterized by exchange of voting shares and continuation of previous ownership became known as pooling of interests. Rather than an exchange transaction with one ownership group replacing another, a pooling of interests was characterized by a continuity of ownership interests before and after the business combination. Prior to its elimination, this method was applied to a significant number of business combinations.[23] To reflect the continuity of ownership, two important steps characterized the pooling of interests method:

1. The book values of the assets and liabilities of both companies became the book values reported by the combined entity.
2. The revenue and expense accounts were combined retrospectively as well as prospectively. The idea of continuity of ownership gave support for the recognition of income accruing to the owners both before and after the combination.

Therefore, in a pooling, reported income was typically higher than under the contemporaneous purchase accounting. Under pooling, not only did the firms retrospectively combine incomes, but also the smaller asset bases resulted in smaller depreciation and amortization expenses. Because net income reported in financial statements often is used in a variety of contracts, including managerial compensation, managers considered the pooling method an attractive alternative to purchase accounting.

Prior to 2002, accounting and reporting standards allowed both the purchase and the pooling of interest methods for business combinations. However, standard setters established strict criteria for use of the pooling method. The criteria were designed to prevent managers from engaging in purchase transactions and then reporting them as poolings of interests. Business combinations that failed to meet the pooling criteria had to be accounted for by the purchase method.

These criteria had two overriding objectives. First, to ensure the complete fusion of the two organizations, one company had to obtain substantially all (90 percent or more) of the voting stock of the other. The second general objective of these criteria was to prevent purchase combinations from being disguised as poolings. Past experience had shown that combination transactions were frequently manipulated so that they would qualify for pooling of interests treatment (usually to increase reported earnings). However, subsequent events, often involving cash being paid or received by the parties, revealed the true nature of the combination: One company was purchasing the other in a bargained exchange. A number of qualifying criteria for pooling of interests treatment were designed to stop this practice.

[23] Past prominent business combinations accounted for by the pooling of interests method include Exxon-Mobil, Pfizer-Warner Lambert, Yahoo!-Broadcast.com, and Pepsi-Quaker Oats, among thousands of others.

EXHIBIT 2.9
Precombination Information for Baker Company

January 1	Book Values	Fair Values
Current assets	$ 30,000	$ 30,000
Internet domain name	160,000	300,000
Licensing agreements	–0–	500,000
In-process research and development	–0–	200,000
Notes payable	(25,000)	(25,000)
Total net assets	$165,000	$1,005,000

Note: Parentheses indicate a credit balance.

Comparisons across the Pooling of Interests, Purchase, and Acquisition Methods

To illustrate some of the differences across the purchase, pooling of interests, and acquisition methods, assume that on January 1, Archer Inc. acquired Baker Company in exchange for 10,000 shares of its $1.00 par common stock having a fair value of $1,200,000 in a transaction structured as a merger. In connection with the acquisition, Archer paid $25,000 in legal and accounting fees. Also, Archer agreed to pay the former owners additional cash consideration contingent upon the completion of Baker's existing contracts at specified profit margins. The current fair value of the contingent obligation was estimated to be $150,000. Exhibit 2.9 provides Baker's combination-date book values and fair values.

Purchase Method Applied

Archer's valuation basis for its purchase of Baker is computed and allocated as follows:

Fair value of shares issued		$1,200,000
Direct combination costs (legal and accounting fees)		25,000
Cost of the Baker purchase		$1,225,000
Cost allocation:		
Current assets	$30,000	
Internet domain name	300,000	
Licensing agreements	500,000	
Research and development expense	200,000	
Notes payable	(25,000)	
Total net fair value of items acquired		1,005,000
Goodwill		$ 220,000

Note the following characteristics of the purchase method from the above schedule.

- The valuation basis is cost and includes direct combination costs but excludes the contingent consideration.
- The cost is allocated to the assets acquired and liabilities assumed based on their individual fair values (unless a bargain purchase occurs and then the long-term items may be recorded as amounts less than their fair values).
- Goodwill is the excess of cost over the fair values of the net assets purchased.
- Acquired in-process research and development is expensed immediately at the purchase date.

Pooling of Interests Method Applied

Because a purchase sale was deemed not to occur, the pooling method relied on previously recorded values reflecting a continuation of previous ownership. Thus, the following asset would be recorded by Archer in a business combination accounted for as a pooling of interests.

	Values Assigned
Current assets	$ 30,000
Internet domain name	160,000
Licensing agreements	–0–
In-process research and development	–0–
Notes payable	(25,000)
Total value assigned within the combination	$165,000

Note the following characteristics of the pooling of interests method from the preceding schedule.

- Because a pooling of interests was predicated on a continuity of ownership, the accounting incorporated a continuation of previous book values and ignored fair values exchanged in a business combination.
- Previously unrecognized (typically internally developed) intangibles continue to be reported at a zero-value postcombination.
- Because the pooling of interests method values an acquired firm at its previously recorded book value, no new amount for goodwill was ever recorded in a pooling.

Acquisition Method Applied

According to the acquisition method, Archer's valuation basis for its acquisition of Baker is computed as follows:

Fair value of shares issued		$1,200,000
Fair value of contingent performance obligation		150,000
Total consideration transferred for the Baker acquisition		$1,350,000
Cost allocation:		
Current assets	$ 30,000	
Internet domain name	300,000	
Licensing agreements	500,000	
Research and development asset	200,000	
Notes payable	(25,000)	
Total net fair value of items acquired		1,005,000
Goodwill		$ 345,000

Note the following characteristics of the acquisition method from the preceding schedule.

- The valuation basis is fair value of consideration transferred and includes the contingent consideration but excludes direct combination costs.
- The assets acquired and liabilities assumed are recorded at their individual fair values.
- Goodwill is the excess of the consideration transferred over the fair values of the net assets acquired.
- Acquired in-process research and development is recognized as an asset.
- Professional service fees to help accomplish the acquisition are expensed.

The following table compares the amounts from Baker that Archer would include in its combination-date consolidated financial statements under the pooling of interests method, the purchase method, and the acquisition method.

Values Incorporated in Archer's Consolidated Balance Sheet Resulting from the Baker Transaction

	Pooling of Interests Method	Purchase Method	Acquisition Method
Current assets	$ 30,000	$ 30,000	$ 30,000
Internet domain name	160,000	300,000	300,000
Licensing agreements	–0–	500,000	500,000
In-process research and development asset*	–0–	–0–	200,000
Goodwill	–0–	220,000	345,000
Notes payable	(25,000)	(25,000)	(25,000)
Contingent performance obligation	–0–	–0–	(150,000)
Total net assets recognized by Archer	$165,000	$1,025,000	$1,200,000

*Acquired in-process research and development was expensed under the purchase method and not recognized at all under the pooling of interests method.

Several comparisons should be noted across these methods of accounting for business combinations:

- In consolidating Baker's assets and liabilities, the purchase and acquisition methods record fair values. In contrast, the pooling method uses previous book values and ignores fair values. Consequently, although a fair value of $1,350,000 is exchanged, only a net value of $165,000 (assets less liabilities) is reported in the pooling.
- The pooling method, as reflected in the preceding example, typically shows smaller asset values and consequently lowers future depreciation and amortization expenses. Thus, higher future net income was usually reported under the pooling method compared to similar situations that employed the purchase method.
- Under pooling, financial ratios such as Net Income/Total Assets were dramatically inflated. Not only was this ratio's denominator understated through failure to recognize internally developed assets acquired (and fair values in general), but the numerator was overstated through smaller depreciation and amortization expenses.
- Although not shown, the pooling method retrospectively combined the acquired firm's revenues, expenses, dividends, and retained earnings. The purchase and acquisition methods incorporate only postcombination values for these operational items. Also all costs of the combination (direct and indirect acquisition costs and stock issue costs) were expensed in the period of combination under the pooling of interests method.
- Finally, with adoption of the acquisition method, the FASB has moved clearly in the direction of increased management accountability for the fair values of all assets acquired and liabilities assumed in a business combination.

Appendix B

Pushdown Accounting

In the analysis of business combinations to this point, discussion has focused on (1) the recording of the combination by the parent company and (2) required consolidation procedures. An additional reporting issue, however, arises concerning the separate postacquisition financial statements of subsidiary companies.

This issue has become especially significant in recent years because of business acquisitions by private-equity firms. An organization, for example, might acquire a company, work to improve its business model, and subsequently offer the shares back to the public in hopes of making a large profit. What valuation basis should be used in reporting the subsidiary's financial statements that accompany the initial public offering? In other situations, a subsidiary company may need to provide its own separate financial statements in connection with a new public debt issue. Should the subsidiary's financial statements utilize the new basis of accounting that the parent company established in the acquisition or continue its financial statement carrying amounts established prior to the acquisition?

To illustrate, assume that Strand Company owns one asset: a production machine with a carrying amount of $200,000 but a fair value of $900,000. Parker Corporation pays exactly $900,000 in cash to acquire Strand. Consolidation offers no real problem here: The machine will be reported by the business combination at $900,000.

However, if Strand continues to issue separate financial statements (for example, to its creditors or potential stockholders), should the machine be reported at $200,000 or $900,000? If adjusted, should the $700,000 increase be reported as a gain by the subsidiary or as an addition to contributed capital? Should depreciation be based on $200,000 or $900,000? If the subsidiary is to be viewed as a new entity with a new basis for its assets and liabilities, should Retained Earnings be returned to zero? If the parent acquires only 51 percent of Strand, does that change the answers to the previous questions?

Proponents of pushdown accounting argue that a change in ownership creates a new basis for subsidiary assets and liabilities. An unadjusted balance ($200,000 in the preceding illustration) is a cost figure applicable to previous stockholders. That amount is no longer relevant information. Rather, according to this argument, the fair value at the date control of the company changes is now relevant, a figure best reflected by the consideration transferred to acquire the subsidiary. Balance sheet accounts should be reported at the asset's acquisition-date fair value. ($900,000 in the illustration) rather than the cost incurred by the previous owners of the company. Moreover, the subsidiary can now recognize any previously unrecognized intangible assets as valued by its new owner concurrently with the acquisition.

External Reporting Option for Pushdown Accounting

To address the valuation issues for a subsidiary's separately issued financial statements, the FASB issued Accounting Standards Update (ASU) No. 2014-17, *Business Combinations: Pushdown Accounting* in November 2014. The ASU does not require pushdown accounting, but instead provides an option to apply pushdown accounting following a business combination in which the acquirer obtains control of an acquired entity and the acquired entity maintains separate incorporation. A newly acquired entity (e.g., subsidiary firm) may elect the option to apply pushdown accounting in the reporting period immediately following the acquisition.[24] Alternatively, a newly acquired company may simply choose to continue using its previous accounting valuations in separately issued financial statements.

When an acquired entity elects to apply pushdown accounting, it reflects in its financial statements the valuations for the individual assets and liabilities used by the parent in allocating the consideration transferred in the acquisition. Thus, the parent's acquisition-date valuations for its newly acquired subsidiary are "pushed down" to the subsidiary's financial statements.

As discussed next, the FASB (ASC 805-50-30) provides particular guidance for three accounting issues: goodwill, bargain purchase gains, and acquisition-related liabilities. We then discuss other accounting issues including acquisition-date retained earnings and other owners' equity effects.

Goodwill

When an entity elects pushdown accounting, any goodwill recognized in the combination is reported in the acquired entity's separate financial statements.

Bargain Purchase Gains

An exception to pushdown accounting's general rule of using the parent's valuations for the subsidiary's separate financial statement occurs for bargain purchases. Recall that when the fair values assigned to the subsidiary's collective net assets exceed the parent's consideration transferred, the parent recognizes a bargain purchase gain on its income statement. In this case, however, pushdown accounting requires that the acquired entity not recognize the gain in its income statement, but instead as an adjustment to its additional paid-in capital. The reflection of the bargain purchase gain in additional paid-in capital prevents income recognition by both the acquirer and the acquiree for the same event.

Acquisition-Related Liabilities

When acquisition-related liabilities arise, pushdown accounting recognizes only the debt that the acquired firm must recognize under other generally accepted accounting principles. Thus, if an acquired firm is either jointly or severally liable for repayment of the debt, such debt is pushed down to its separate financial statements, possibly including debt incurred by the acquirer.

Acquisition-Date Subsidiary Retained Earnings

After recognizing the new basis for its assets and liabilities, the acquired firm must then report the effects of the acquisition in its owners' equity section. Because pushdown accounting treats the acquired firm as a new reporting entity, the acquired firm reports zero acquisition-date retained earnings. The elimination of acquisition-date subsidiary retained earnings is consistent with consolidated financial reporting.

Additional Paid-In Capital from Pushdown Accounting

The overall effect of the combined pushdown accounting adjustments to the previous carrying amounts of the subsidiary's assets and liabilities then is reported as an adjustment to the subsidiary's additional paid-in capital attributable to the common shareholders. For example, a subsidiary may report "Additional paid-in capital from pushdown accounting" in its separate balance sheet. The total effect in the additional paid-in capital from pushdown accounting results from both the elimination of acquisition-date retained earnings and the revaluation of the acquired firm's assets and liabilities to the parent's basis.

[24] The acquired entity can also elect to apply pushdown accounting in periods subsequent to the acquisition, but must report the election as a retrospective change in accounting principle (ASC Topic 250, Accounting Changes and Error Corrections). Once made, the decision to apply pushdown accounting to a specific change-in-control event is irrevocable.

EXHIBIT 2.10
Pushdown Accounting—Date of Acquisition

Smallport Company Balance Sheet at January 1	
Current assets	$ 300,000
Computers and equipment	600,000
Capitalized software	1,200,000
Customer contracts	700,000
Goodwill	70,000
Total assets	$ 2,870,000
Liabilities	$ (250,000)
Common stock	(100,000)
Additional paid-in capital excess over par	(20,000)
Additional paid-in capital from pushdown accounting	(2,500,000)
Retained earnings, 1/1	–0–
Total liabilities and equities	$ 2,870,000

Example: Pushdown Accounting

To illustrate an application of pushdown accounting, we use the Exhibit 2.3 BigNet and Smallport Company example presented previously in this chapter. If Smallport Company applies pushdown accounting, its acquisition-date separately reported balance sheet would appear as presented in Exhibit 2.10.

Note that the values for each asset and liability in Smallport's separate balance sheet are identical to those reported in BigNet's consolidated acquisition-date balance sheet.

Internal Reporting

Pushdown accounting has several advantages for internal reporting. For example, it simplifies the consolidation process. If the subsidiary enters the acquisition-date fair value allocations into its records, worksheet Entry A (to recognize the allocations originating from the fair-value adjustments) is not needed. Amortizations of the excess fair value allocation (see Chapter 3) would be incorporated in subsequent periods as well.

Despite some simplifications to the consolidation process, pushdown accounting does not address the many issues in preparing consolidated financial statements that appear in subsequent chapters of this text. Therefore, it remains to be seen how many acquired companies will choose to elect pushdown accounting. For newly acquired subsidiaries that expect to issue new debt or eventually undergo an initial public offering, fair values may provide investors with a better understanding of the company.

In summary, pushdown accounting provides a newly acquired subsidiary the option to revalue its assets and liabilities to acquisition-date fair values in its separately reported financial statements. This valuation option may be useful when the parent expects to offer the subsidiary shares to the public following a period of planned improvements. Other benefits from pushdown accounting may arise when the subsidiary plans to issue debt and needs its separate financial statements to incorporate acquisition-date fair values and previously unrecognized intangibles in their standalone financial reports.

Questions

1. What is a business combination?
2. Describe the concept of a synergy. What are some examples of possible synergies in business combinations?
3. Describe the different types of legal arrangements that can take place to create a business combination.
4. What does the term *consolidated financial statements* mean?
5. Within the consolidation process, what is the purpose of a worksheet?
6. Jones Company obtains all of the common stock of Hudson, Inc., by issuing 50,000 shares of its own stock. Under these circumstances, why might the determination of a fair value for the consideration transferred be difficult?
7. What is the accounting valuation basis for consolidating assets and liabilities in a business combination?
8. How should a parent consolidate its subsidiary's revenues and expenses?
9. Morgan Company acquires all of the outstanding shares of Jennings, Inc., for cash. Morgan transfers consideration more than the fair value of the company's net assets. How should the payment in excess of fair value be accounted for in the consolidation process?
10. Catron Corporation is having liquidity problems, and as a result, it sells all of its outstanding stock to Lambert, Inc., for cash. Because of Catron's problems, Lambert is able to acquire this stock at less than the fair value of the company's net assets. How is this reduction in price accounted for within the consolidation process?

11. Sloane, Inc., issues 25,000 shares of its own common stock in exchange for all of the outstanding shares of Benjamin Company. Benjamin will remain a separately incorporated operation. How does Sloane record the issuance of these shares?
12. To obtain all of the stock of Molly, Inc., Harrison Corporation issued its own common stock. Harrison had to pay $98,000 to lawyers, accountants, and a stock brokerage firm in connection with services rendered during the creation of this business combination. In addition, Harrison paid $56,000 in costs associated with the stock issuance. How will these two costs be recorded?

Problems

LO 2-1

1. Which of the following does not represent a primary motivation for business combinations?
   a. Combinations are often a vehicle to accelerate growth and competitiveness.
   b. Cost savings can be achieved through elimination of duplicate facilities and staff.
   c. Synergies may be available through quick entry for new and existing products into markets.
   d. Larger firms are less likely to fail.

LO 2-2

2. Which of the following is the best theoretical justification for consolidated financial statements?
   a. In form, the companies are one entity; in substance, they are separate.
   b. In form, the companies are separate; in substance, they are one entity.
   c. In form and substance, the companies are one entity.
   d. In form and substance, the companies are separate. (AICPA)

LO 2-3

3. What is a statutory merger?
   a. A merger approved by the Securities and Exchange Commission
   b. An acquisition involving the purchase of both stock and assets
   c. A takeover completed within one year of the initial tender offer
   d. A business combination in which only one company continues to exist as a legal entity

LO 2-4

4. What is goodwill?
   a. An intangible asset representing the excess of consideration transferred over the collective fair values of the net identifiable assets acquired in a business combination
   b. An expense that an acquiring firm recognizes for the excess of consideration transferred over the collective fair values of the net identifiable assets acquired in a business combination
   c. A concept representing synergies resulting from a business combination but not recognized for financial reporting purposes
   d. An internally developed intangible asset that is recognized on a business firm's balance sheet as the business generates profits in excess of a normal rate of return on its identifiable net assets

LO 2-4

5. FASB ASC 805, "Business Combinations," provides principles for allocating the fair value of an acquired business. When the collective fair values of the separately identified assets acquired and liabilities assumed exceed the fair value of the consideration transferred, the difference should be
   a. Recognized as an ordinary gain from a bargain purchase.
   b. Treated as negative goodwill to be amortized over the period benefited, not to exceed 40 years.
   c. Treated as goodwill and tested for impairment on an annual basis.
   d. Applied pro rata to reduce, but not below zero, the amounts initially assigned to specific noncurrent assets of the acquired firm.

LO 2-8

6. What is the appropriate accounting treatment for the value assigned to in-process research and development acquired in a business combination?
   a. Expense upon acquisition.
   b. Capitalize as an asset.
   c. Expense if there is no alternative use for the assets used in the research and development and technological feasibility has yet to be reached.
   d. Expense until future economic benefits become certain and then capitalize as an asset.

LO 2-8

7. Consolidated financial statements are typically prepared when one company has
   a. Accounted for its investment in another company by the equity method.
   b. Dividend income from another company.
   c. Significant influence over the operating and financial policies of another company.
   d. Control over another company.

LO 2-4

8. When does gain recognition accompany a business combination?
   a. When a bargain purchase occurs.
   b. In a combination created in the middle of a fiscal year.

c. In an acquisition when the value of all assets and liabilities cannot be determined.

d. When the amount of a bargain purchase exceeds the value of the applicable noncurrent assets (other than certain exceptions) held by the acquired company.

LO 2-6b

9. According to the acquisition method of accounting for business combinations, costs paid to attorneys and accountants for services in arranging a merger should be

a. Capitalized as part of the overall fair value acquired in the merger.

b. Recorded as an expense in the period the merger takes place.

c. Included in recognized goodwill.

d. Written off over a five-year maximum useful life.

LO 2-4

10. When negotiating a business acquisition, buyers sometimes agree to pay extra amounts to sellers in the future if performance metrics are achieved over specified time horizons. How should buyers account for such contingent consideration in recording an acquisition?

a. The amount ultimately paid under the contingent consideration agreement is added to goodwill when and if the performance metrics are met.

b. The fair value of the contingent consideration is expensed immediately at acquisition date.

c. The fair value of the contingent consideration is included in the overall fair value of the consideration transferred, and a liability or additional owners' equity is recognized.

d. The fair value of the contingent consideration is recorded as a reduction of the otherwise determinable fair value of the acquired firm.

LO 2-5

11. An acquired firm's financial records sometimes show goodwill from previous business combinations. How does a parent company account for the preexisting goodwill of its newly acquired subsidiary?

a. The parent tests the preexisting goodwill for impairment before recording the goodwill as part of the acquisition.

b. The parent includes the preexisting goodwill as an identified intangible asset acquired.

c. The parent ignores preexisting subsidiary goodwill and allocates the subsidiary's fair value among the separately identifiable assets acquired and liabilities assumed.

d. Preexisting goodwill is excluded from the identifiable assets acquired unless the subsidiary can demonstrate its continuing value.

LO 2-5

12. On June 1, Cline Co. paid $800,000 cash for all of the issued and outstanding common stock of Renn Corp. The carrying amounts for Renn's assets and liabilities on June 1 follow:

Cash	$150,000
Accounts receivable	180,000
Capitalized software costs	320,000
Goodwill	100,000
Liabilities	(130,000)
Net assets	$620,000

On June 1, Renn's accounts receivable had a fair value of $140,000. Additionally, Renn's in-process research and development was estimated to have a fair value of $200,000. All other items were stated at their fair values. On Cline's June 1 consolidated balance sheet, how much is reported for goodwill?

a. $320,000

b. $120,000

c. $80,000

d. $20,000

Problems 13 and 14 relate to the following:

On May 1, Donovan Company reported the following account balances:

Current assets	$ 90,000
Buildings & equipment (net)	220,000
Total assets	$310,000
Liabilities	$ 60,000
Common stock	150,000
Retained earnings	100,000
Total liabilities and equities	$310,000

On May 1, Beasley paid $400,000 in stock (fair value) for all of the assets and liabilities of Donovan, which will cease to exist as a separate entity. In connection with the merger, Beasley incurred $15,000 in accounts payable for legal and accounting fees.

Beasley also agreed to pay $75,000 to the former owners of Donovan contingent on meeting certain revenue goals during the following year. Beasley estimated the present value of its probability adjusted expected payment for the contingency at $20,000. In determining its offer, Beasley noted the following:

- Donovan holds a building with a fair value $30,000 more than its book value.
- Donovan has developed unpatented technology appraised at $25,000, although is it not recorded in its financial records.
- Donovan has a research and development activity in process with an appraised fair value of $45,000. The project has not yet reached technological feasibility.
- Book values for Donovan's current assets and liabilities approximate fair values.

LO 2-4, 2-5

13. What should Beasley record as total liabilities incurred or assumed in connection with the Donovan merger?
    a. $15,000
    b. $75,000
    c. $95,000
    d. $150,000

LO 2-5, 2-8

14. How much should Beasley record as total assets acquired in the Donovan merger?
    a. $400,000
    b. $420,000
    c. $410,000
    d. $480,000

LO 2-5

15. Prior to being united in a business combination, Atkins, Inc., and Waterson Corporation had the following stockholders' equity figures:

	Atkins	Waterson
Common stock ($1 par value)	$180,000	$ 45,000
Additional paid-in capital	90,000	20,000
Retained earnings	300,000	110,000

Atkins issues 51,000 new shares of its common stock valued at $3 per share for all of the outstanding stock of Waterson. Immediately afterward, what are consolidated Additional Paid-In Capital and Retained Earnings, respectively?
    a. $104,000 and $300,000
    b. $110,000 and $410,000
    c. $192,000 and $300,000
    d. $212,000 and $410,000

Problems 16 through 19 are based on the following information:

On July 1, TruData Company issues 10,000 shares of its common stock with a $5 par value and a $40 fair value in exchange for all of Webstat Company's outstanding voting shares. Webstat's precombination book and fair values are shown along with book values for TruData's accounts as follows.

	TruData Book Values	Webstat Book Values	Webstat Fair Values
Revenues (1/1 to 7/1)	$(250,000)	$(130,000)	
Expenses (1/1 to 7/1)	170,000	80,000	
Retained earnings, 1/1	(130,000)	(150,000)	
Cash and receivables	140,000	60,000	$ 60,000
Inventory	190,000	145,000	175,000
Patented technology (net)	230,000	180,000	200,000
Land	400,000	200,000	225,000
Buildings and equipment (net)	100,000	75,000	75,000
Liabilities	(540,000)	(360,000)	(350,000)
Common stock	(300,000)	(70,000)	
Additional paid-in capital	(10,000)	(30,000)	

LO 2-5

16. On its acquisition-date consolidated balance sheet, what amount should TruData report as goodwill?
   a. –0–
   b. $15,000
   c. $35,000
   d. $100,000

LO 2-5

17. On its acquisition-date consolidated balance sheet, what amount should TruData report as patented technology (net)?
   a. $200,000
   b. $230,000
   c. $410,000
   d. $430,000

LO 2-5, 2-7

18. On its acquisition-date consolidated balance sheet, what amount should TruData report as common stock?
   a. $70,000
   b. $300,000
   c. $350,000
   d. $370,000

LO 2-5, 2-7

19. On its acquisition-date consolidated balance sheet, what amount should TruData report as retained earnings as of July 1?
   a. $130,000
   b. $210,000
   c. $260,000
   d. $510,000

Problems 20 and 21 are based on the following information. The separate condensed balance sheets of Patrick Corporation and its wholly-owned subsidiary, Sean Corporation, are as follows:

BALANCE SHEETS
December 31, 2020

	Patrick	Sean
Cash	$ 80,000	$ 60,000
Accounts receivable (net)	140,000	25,000
Inventories	90,000	50,000
Plant and equipment (net)	625,000	280,000
Investment in Sean	460,000	
Total assets	$1,395,000	$415,000
Accounts payable	$ 160,000	$ 95,000
Long-term debt	110,000	30,000
Common stock ($10 par)	340,000	50,000
Additional paid-in capital		10,000
Retained earnings	785,000	230,000
Total liabilities and shareholders' equity	$1,395,000	$415,000

Additional Information:

- On December 31, 2020, Patrick acquired 100 percent of Sean's voting stock in exchange for $460,000.
- At the acquisition date, the fair values of Sean's assets and liabilities equaled their carrying amounts, respectively, except that the fair value of certain items in Sean's inventory were $25,000 more than their carrying amounts.

LO 2-4, 2-5

20. In the December 31, 2020, consolidated balance sheet of Patrick and its subsidiary, what amount of total assets should be reported?
   a. $1,375,000
   b. $1,395,000
   c. $1,520,000
   d. $1,980,000

LO 2-4, 2-5

21. In the December 31, 2020, consolidated balance sheet of Patrick and its subsidiary, what amount of total stockholders' equity should be reported?
    a. $1,100,000
    b. $1,125,000
    c. $1,150,000
    d. $1,355,000

LO 2-8

22. Prycal Co. merges with InterBuy, Inc., and acquires several different categories of intangible assets including trademarks, a customer list, copyrights on artistic materials, agreements to receive royalties on leased intellectual property, and unpatented technology.
    a. Describe the criteria for determining whether an intangible asset acquired in a business combination should be separately recognized apart from goodwill.
    b. For each of the acquired intangibles listed, identify which recognition criteria (separability and contractual-legal) may or may not apply in recognizing the intangible on the acquiring firm's financial statements.

LO 2-6a, 2-6b

23. The following book and fair values were available for Westmont Company as of March 1.

	Book Value	Fair Value
Inventory	$ 630,000	$600,000
Land	750,000	990,000
Buildings	1,700,000	2,000,000
Customer relationships	–0–	800,000
Accounts payable	(80,000)	(80,000)
Common stock	(2,000,000)	
Additional paid-in capital	(500,000)	
Retained earnings, 1/1	(360,000)	
Revenues	(420,000)	
Expenses	280,000	

Arturo Company pays $4,000,000 cash and issues 20,000 shares of its $2 par value common stock (fair value of $50 per share) for all of Westmont's common stock in a merger, after which Westmont will cease to exist as a separate entity. Stock issue costs amount to $25,000, and Arturo pays $42,000 for legal fees to complete the transaction. Prepare Arturo's journal entries to record its acquisition of Westmont.

LO 2-6a, 2-6b, 2-8

24. Use the same facts as in Problem 23, but assume instead that Arturo pays cash of $4,200,000 to acquire Westmont. No stock is issued. Prepare Arturo's journal entries to record its acquisition of Westmont.

LO 2-4, 2-5, 2-6a, 2-6b, 2-6c

25. Following are preacquisition financial balances for Padre Company and Sol Company as of December 31. Also included are fair values for Sol Company accounts.

	Padre Company	Sol Company	
	Book Values 12/31	Book Values 12/31	Fair Values 12/31
Cash	$ 400,000	$ 120,000	$ 120,000
Receivables	220,000	300,000	300,000
Inventory	410,000	210,000	260,000
Land	600,000	130,000	110,000
Building and equipment (net)	600,000	270,000	330,000
Franchise agreements	220,000	190,000	220,000
Accounts payable	(300,000)	(120,000)	(120,000)
Accrued expenses	(90,000)	(30,000)	(30,000)
Long-term liabilities	(900,000)	(510,000)	(510,000)
Common stock—$20 par value	(660,000)		
Common stock—$5 par value		(210,000)	
Additional paid-in capital	(70,000)	(90,000)	
Retained earnings, 1/1	(390,000)	(240,000)	
Revenues	(960,000)	(330,000)	
Expenses	920,000	310,000	

Note: Parentheses indicate a credit balance.

On December 31, Padre acquires Sol's outstanding stock by paying $360,000 in cash and issuing 10,000 shares of its own common stock with a fair value of $40 per share. Padre paid legal and accounting fees of $20,000 as well as $5,000 in stock issuance costs.

Determine the value that would be shown in Padre's consolidated financial statements for each of the accounts listed

Accounts	
Inventory	Revenues
Land	Additional paid-in capital
Buildings and equipment	Expenses
Franchise agreements	Retained earnings, 1/1
Goodwill	Retained earnings, 12/31

LO 2-5, 2-6a, 2-6b, 2-8

26. On May 1, Soriano Co. reported the following account balances along with their estimated fair values:

	Carrying Amount	Fair Value
Receivables	$ 90,000	$ 90,000
Inventory	75,000	75,000
Copyrights	125,000	480,000
Patented technology	825,000	700,000
Total assets	$1,115,000	$1,345,000
Current liabilities	$ 160,000	$ 160,000
Long-term liabilities	645,000	635,000
Common stock	100,000	
Retained earnings	210,000	
Total liabilities and equities	$1,115,000	

On that day, Zambrano paid cash to acquire all of the assets and liabilities of Soriano, which will cease to exist as a separate entity. To facilitate the merger, Zambrano also paid $100,000 to an investment banking firm.

The following information was also available:

- Zambrano further agreed to pay an extra $70,000 to the former owners of Soriano only if they meet certain revenue goals during the next two years. Zambrano estimated the present value of its probability adjusted expected payment for this contingency at $35,000.
- Soriano has a research and development project in process with an appraised value of $200,000. However, the project has not yet reached technological feasibility, and the project's assets have no alternative future use.

Prepare Zambrano's journal entries to record the Soriano acquisition assuming its initial cash payment to the former owners was

a. $700,000.

b. $800,000.

LO 2-4, 2-5, 2-6b, 2-7

27. On June 30, 2020, Wisconsin, Inc., issued $300,000 in debt and 15,000 new shares of its $10 par value stock to Badger Company owners in exchange for all of the outstanding shares of that company. Wisconsin shares had a fair value of $40 per share. Prior to the combination, the financial statements for Wisconsin and Badger for the six-month period ending June 30, 2020, were as follows (credit balances in parentheses):

	Wisconsin	Badger
Revenues	$ (900,000)	$ (300,000)
Expenses	660,000	200,000
Net income	$ (240,000)	$ (100,000)
Retained earnings, 1/1	$ (800,000)	$ (200,000)
Net income	(240,000)	(100,000)
Dividends declared	90,000	–0–
Retained earnings, 6/30	$ (950,000)	$ (300,000)

(continued)

(continued)

	Wisconsin	Badger
Cash	$ 80,000	$ 110,000
Receivables and inventory	400,000	170,000
Patented technology (net)	900,000	300,000
Equipment (net)	700,000	600,000
Total assets	$ 2,080,000	$ 1,180,000
Liabilities	$ (500,000)	$ (410,000)
Common stock	(360,000)	(200,000)
Additional paid-in capital	(270,000)	(270,000)
Retained earnings	(950,000)	(300,000)
Total liabilities and equities	$(2,080,000)	$(1,180,000)

Wisconsin also paid $30,000 to a broker for arranging the transaction. In addition, Wisconsin paid $40,000 in stock issuance costs. Badger's equipment was actually worth $700,000, but its patented technology was valued at only $280,000.

What are the consolidated balances for the following accounts?

a. Net income
b. Retained earnings, 1/1/20
c. Patented technology
d. Goodwill
e. Liabilities
f. Common stock
g. Additional paid-in capital

LO 2-4, 2-7

28. On January 1, 2021, Casey Corporation exchanged $3,300,000 cash for 100 percent of the outstanding voting stock of Kennedy Corporation. Casey plans to maintain Kennedy as a wholly owned subsidiary with separate legal status and accounting information systems.

At the acquisition date, Casey prepared the following fair-value allocation schedule:

Fair value of Kennedy (consideration transferred)		$3,300,000
Carrying amount acquired		2,600,000
Excess fair value		$ 700,000
to buildings (undervalued)	$ 382,000	
to licensing agreements (overvalued)	(108,000)	274,000
to goodwill (indefinite life)		$ 426,000

Immediately after closing the transaction, Casey and Kennedy prepared the following postacquisition balance sheets from their separate financial records (credit balances in parentheses).

Accounts	Casey	Kennedy
Cash	$ 457,000	$ 172,500
Accounts receivable	1,655,000	347,000
Inventory	1,310,000	263,500
Investment in Kennedy	3,300,000	–0–
Buildings (net)	6,315,000	2,090,000
Licensing agreements	–0–	3,070,000
Goodwill	347,000	–0–
Total assets	$ 13,384,000	$5,943,000
Accounts payable	$ (394,000)	$ (393,000)
Long-term debt	(3,990,000)	(2,950,000)
Common stock	(3,000,000)	(1,000,000)
Additional paid-in capital	–0–	(500,000)
Retained earnings	(6,000,000)	(1,100,000)
Total liabilities and equities	$(13,384,000)	$(5,943,000)

Prepare an acquisition-date consolidated balance sheet for Casey Corporation and its subsidiary Kennedy Corporation.

LO 2-4, 2-5, 2-6b, 2-6c, 2-7

29. On January 1, 2021, Marshall Company acquired 100 percent of the outstanding common stock of Tucker Company. To acquire these shares, Marshall issued $200,000 in long-term liabilities and 20,000 shares of common stock having a par value of $1 per share but a fair value of $10 per share. Marshall paid $30,000 to accountants, lawyers, and brokers for assistance in the acquisition and another $12,000 in connection with stock issuance costs.

Prior to these transactions, the balance sheets for the two companies were as follows:

	Marshall Company Book Value	Tucker Company Book Value
Cash	$ 60,000	$ 20,000
Receivables	270,000	90,000
Inventory	360,000	140,000
Land	200,000	180,000
Buildings (net)	420,000	220,000
Equipment (net)	160,000	50,000
Accounts payable	(150,000)	(40,000)
Long-term liabilities	(430,000)	(200,000)
Common stock—$1 par value	(110,000)	
Common stock—$20 par value		(120,000)
Additional paid-in capital	(360,000)	–0–
Retained earnings, 1/1/21	(420,000)	(340,000)

Note: Parentheses indicate a credit balance.

In Marshall's appraisal of Tucker, it deemed three accounts to be undervalued on the subsidiary's books: Inventory by $5,000, Land by $20,000, and Buildings by $30,000. Marshall plans to maintain Tucker's separate legal identity and to operate Tucker as a wholly owned subsidiary.

a. Determine the amounts that Marshall Company would report in its postacquisition balance sheet. In preparing the postacquisition balance sheet, any required adjustments to income accounts from the acquisition should be closed to Marshall's retained earnings. Other accounts will also need to be added or adjusted to reflect the journal entries Marshall prepared in recording the acquisition.

b. To verify the answers found in part (*a*), prepare a worksheet to consolidate the balance sheets of these two companies as of January 1, 2021.

LO 2-4, 2-5, 2-7, 2-8

30. Pratt Company acquired all of the outstanding shares of Spider, Inc., on December 31, 2021, for $495,000 cash. Pratt will operate Spider as a wholly owned subsidiary with a separate legal and accounting identity. Although many of Spider's book values approximate fair values, several of its accounts have fair values that differ from book values. In addition, Spider has internally developed assets that remain unrecorded on its books. In deriving the acquisition price, Pratt assessed Spider's fair and book value differences as follows:

	Book Values	Fair Values
Computer software	$ 20,000	$ 70,000
Equipment	40,000	30,000
Client contracts	–0–	100,000
In-process research and development	–0–	40,000
Notes payable	(60,000)	(65,000)

At December 31, 2021, the following financial information is available for consolidation (credit balances in parentheses):

	Pratt	Spider
Cash	$ 36,000	$ 18,000
Receivables	116,000	52,000
Inventory	140,000	90,000
Investment in Spider	495,000	–0–
Computer software	210,000	20,000

(continued)

(continued)

	Pratt	Spider
Buildings (net)	595,000	130,000
Equipment (net)	308,000	40,000
Client contracts	–0–	–0–
Goodwill	–0–	–0–
Total assets	$ 1,900,000	$ 350,000
Accounts payable	$ (88,000)	$ (25,000)
Notes payable	(510,000)	(60,000)
Common stock	(380,000)	(100,000)
Additional paid-in capital	(170,000)	(25,000)
Retained earnings	(752,000)	(140,000)
Total liabilities and equities	$(1,900,000)	$(350,000)

Prepare a consolidated balance sheet for Pratt and Spider as of December 31, 2021.

LO 2-4, 2-5, 2-6a

31. Allerton Company acquires all of Deluxe Company's assets and liabilities for cash on January 1, 2021, and subsequently formally dissolves Deluxe. At the acquisition date, the following book and fair values were available for the Deluxe Company accounts:

	Book Values	Fair Values
Current assets	$ 60,000	$ 60,000
Building	90,000	50,000
Land	10,000	20,000
Trademark	–0–	30,000
Goodwill	15,000	?
Liabilities	(40,000)	(40,000)
Common stock	(100,000)	
Retained earnings	(35,000)	

Prepare Allerton's entry to record its acquisition of Deluxe in its accounting records assuming the following cash exchange amounts:

a. $145,000.

b. $110,000.

LO 2-4, 2-5, 2-6a, 2-6b

32. On June 30, 2021, Streeter Company reported the following account balances:

Receivables	$ 83,900	Current liabilities	$ (12,900)
Inventory	70,250	Long-term liabilities	(54,250)
Buildings (net)	78,900	Common stock	(90,000)
Equipment (net)	24,100	Retained earnings	(100,000)
Total assets	$257,150	Total liabilities and equities	$(257,150)

On June 30, 2021, Princeton Company paid $310,800 cash for all assets and liabilities of Streeter, which will cease to exist as a separate entity. In connection with the acquisition, Princeton paid $15,100 in legal fees. Princeton also agreed to pay $55,600 to the former owners of Streeter contingent on meeting certain revenue goals during 2022. Princeton estimated the present value of its probability adjusted expected payment for the contingency at $17,900.

In determining its offer, Princeton noted the following pertaining to Streeter:

- It holds a building with a fair value $43,100 more than its book value.
- It has developed a customer list appraised at $25,200, although it is not recorded in its financial records.
- It has research and development activity in process with an appraised fair value of $36,400. However, the project has not yet reached technological feasibility, and the assets used in the activity have no alternative future use.
- Book values for the receivables, inventory, equipment, and liabilities approximate fair values.

Prepare Princeton's accounting entries to record the combination with Streeter.

LO 2-4, 2-5, 2-8, 2-6b

33. SafeData Corporation has the following account balances and respective fair values on June 30:

	Book Values	Fair Values
Receivables	$ 80,000	$ 80,000
Patented technology	100,000	700,000
Customer relationships	–0–	500,000
In-process research and development	–0–	300,000
Liabilities	(400,000)	(400,000)
Common stock	(100,000)	
Additional paid-in capital	(300,000)	
Retained earnings deficit, 1/1	700,000	
Revenues	(300,000)	
Expenses	220,000	

Privacy First, Inc., obtained all of the outstanding shares of SafeData on June 30 by issuing 20,000 shares of common stock having a $1 par value but a $75 fair value. Privacy First incurred $10,000 in stock issuance costs and paid $75,000 to an investment banking firm for its assistance in arranging the combination. In negotiating the final terms of the deal, Privacy First also agrees to pay $100,000 to SafeData's former owners if it achieves certain revenue goals in the next two years. Privacy First estimates the probability adjusted present value of this contingent performance obligation at $30,000.

a. What is the fair value of the consideration transferred in this combination?

b. How should the stock issuance costs appear in Privacy First's postcombination financial statements?

c. How should Privacy First account for the fee paid to the investment bank?

d. How does the issuance of these shares affect the stockholders' equity accounts of Privacy First, the parent?

e. How is the fair value of the consideration transferred in the combination allocated among the assets acquired and the liabilities assumed?

f. What is the effect of SafeData's revenues and expenses on consolidated totals? Why?

g. What is the effect of SafeData's Common Stock and Additional Paid-In Capital balances on consolidated totals?

h. If Privacy First's stock had been worth only $50 per share rather than $75, how would the consolidation of SafeData's assets and liabilities have been affected?

LO 2-4, 2-5, 2-6a, 2-6b, 2-6c

LO 2-7, 2-8

34. On January 1, NewTune Company exchanges 15,000 shares of its common stock for all of the outstanding shares of On-the-Go, Inc. Each of NewTune's shares has a $4 par value and a $50 fair value. The fair value of the stock exchanged in the acquisition was considered equal to On-the-Go's fair value. NewTune also paid $25,000 in stock registration and issuance costs in connection with the merger. Several of On-the-Go's accounts' fair values differ from their book values on this date (credit balances in parentheses):

	Book Values	Fair Values
Receivables	$65,000	$ 63,000
Trademarks	95,000	225,000
Record music catalog	60,000	180,000
In-process research and development	–0–	200,000
Notes payable	(50,000)	(45,000)

Precombination book values for the two companies are as follows:

	NewTune	On-the-Go
Cash	$ 60,000	$ 29,000
Receivables	150,000	65,000
Trademarks	400,000	95,000
Record music catalog	840,000	60,000
Equipment (net)	320,000	105,000
Totals	$ 1,770,000	$ 354,000

(continued)

(continued)

	NewTune	On-the-Go
Accounts payable	$ (110,000)	$ (34,000)
Notes payable	(370,000)	(50,000)
Common stock	(400,000)	(50,000)
Additional paid-in capital	(30,000)	(30,000)
Retained earnings	(860,000)	(190,000)
Totals	$(1,770,000)	$(354,000)

a. Assume that this combination is a statutory merger so that On-the-Go's accounts will be transferred to the records of NewTune. On-the-Go will be dissolved and will no longer exist as a legal entity. Prepare a postcombination balance sheet for NewTune as of the acquisition date.

b. Assume that no dissolution takes place in connection with this combination. Rather, both companies retain their separate legal identities. Prepare a worksheet to consolidate the two companies as of the combination date.

c. How do the balance sheet accounts compare across parts (*a*) and (*b*)?

LO 2-4, 2-5, 2-6b, 2-6c, 2-7

35. On December 31, Pacifica, Inc., acquired 100 percent of the voting stock of Seguros Company. Pacifica will maintain Seguros as a wholly owned subsidiary with its own legal and accounting identity. The consideration transferred to the owner of Seguros included 50,000 newly issued Pacifica common shares ($20 market value, $5 par value) and an agreement to pay an additional $130,000 cash if Seguros meets certain project completion goals by December 31 of the following year. Pacifica estimates a 50 percent probability that Seguros will be successful in meeting these goals and uses a 4 percent discount rate to represent the time value of money.

Immediately prior to the acquisition, the following data for both firms were available:

	Pacifica	Seguros Book Values	Seguros Fair Values
Revenues	$(1,200,000)		
Expenses	875,000		
Net income	$ (325,000)		
Retained earnings, 1/1	$ (950,000)		
Net income	(325,000)		
Dividends declared	90,000		
Retained earnings, 12/31	$(1,185,000)		
Cash	$ 110,000	$ 85,000	$ 85,000
Receivables and inventory	750,000	190,000	180,000
Property, plant, and equipment	1,400,000	450,000	600,000
Trademarks	300,000	160,000	200,000
Total assets	$ 2,560,000	$ 885,000	
Liabilities	$ (500,000)	$ (180,000)	$ (180,000)
Common stock	(400,000)	(200,000)	
Additional paid-in capital	(475,000)	(70,000)	
Retained earnings	(1,185,000)	(435,000)	
Total liabilities and equities	$(2,560,000)	$ (885,000)	

In addition, Pacifica assessed a research and development project under way at Seguros to have a fair value of $100,000. Although not yet recorded on its books, Pacifica paid legal fees of $15,000 in connection with the acquisition and $9,000 in stock issue costs.

Prepare the following:

a. Pacifica's entries to account for the consideration transferred to the former owners of Seguros, the direct combination costs, and the stock issue and registration costs. (Use a 0.961538 present value factor where applicable.)

b. A postacquisition column of accounts for Pacifica.

c. A worksheet to produce a consolidated balance sheet as of the acquisition date.

LO 2-4, 2-7, 2-8

36. On January 1, 2021, James Corporation exchanged $3,050,000 cash for 100 percent of the outstanding voting stock of Johnson Corporation. James plans to maintain Johnson as a wholly owned subsidiary with separate legal status and accounting information systems.

At the acquisition date, James prepared the following fair-value allocation schedule:

Consideration transferred for Johnson Corporation		$3,050,000
Johnson's carrying amount	$2,300,000	
Less: Johnson's pre-existing goodwill	(75,000)	
Identifiable net assets carrying amount		2,225,000
Excess consideration transferred over carrying amount of identifiable net assets		$ 825,000
to Johnson's patents (undervalued)		800,000
to new goodwill from Johnson acquisition (indefinite life)		$ 25,000

Immediately after closing the transaction, James and Johnson prepared the following postacquisition balance sheets from their separate financial records.

Accounts	James	Johnson
Cash	$ 245,000	$ 110,000
Accounts receivable	1,830,000	360,000
Inventory	3,500,000	280,000
Investment in Johnson	3,050,000	–0–
Patents	7,000,000	1,000,000
Trademarks	–0–	3,200,000
Goodwill	150,000	75,000
Total assets	$ 15,775,000	$ 5,025,000
Accounts payable	$ (100,000)	$ (515,000)
Long-term debt	(4,300,000)	(2,210,000)
Common stock	(5,000,000)	(1,000,000)
Additional paid-in capital	–0–	(200,000)
Retained earnings	(6,375,000)	(1,100,000)
Total liabilities and equities	$(15,775,000)	$(5,025,000)

Prepare an acquisition-date consolidated balance sheet for James Corporation and its subsidiary Johnson Corporation.

Appendix 2A Problems

LO 2-9

37. In a pre-2009 business combination, Acme Company acquired all of Brem Company's assets and liabilities for cash. After the combination, Acme formally dissolved Brem. At the acquisition date, the following book and fair values were available for the Brem Company accounts:

	Book Values	Fair Values
Current assets	$ 80,000	$ 80,000
Equipment	120,000	180,000
Trademark	–0–	320,000
Liabilities	(55,000)	(55,000)
Common stock	(100,000)	
Retained earnings	(45,000)	

In addition, Acme paid an investment bank $25,000 cash for assistance in arranging the combination.

a. Using the legacy purchase method for pre-2009 business combinations, prepare Acme's entry to record its acquisition of Brem in its accounting records assuming the following cash amounts were paid to the former owners of Brem:

1. $610,000.
2. $425,000.

b. How would these journal entries change if the acquisition occurred post-2009 and therefore Acme applied the acquisition method?

LO 2-9

38. On February 1, Piscina Corporation completed a combination with Swimwear Company. At that date, Swimwear's account balances were as follows:

	Book Values	Fair Values
Inventory	$ 600,000	$ 650,000
Land	450,000	750,000
Buildings	900,000	1,000,000
Unpatented technology	–0–	1,500,000
Common stock ($10 par value)	(750,000)	
Retained earnings, 1/1	(1,100,000)	
Revenues	(600,000)	
Expenses	500,000	

Piscina issued 30,000 shares of its common stock with a par value of $25 and a fair value of $150 per share to the owners of Swimwear for all of their Swimwear shares. Upon completion of the combination, Swimwear Company was formally dissolved.

Prior to 2002, business combinations were accounted for using either purchase or pooling of interests accounting. The two methods often produced substantially different financial statement effects. For this scenario,

a. What are the respective consolidated values for Swimwear's assets under the pooling method and the purchase method?

b. Under each of the following methods, how would Piscina account for Swimwear's current year, but prior to acquisition, revenues and expenses?

- Pooling of interests method.
- Purchase method.

c. Explain the alternative impact of pooling versus purchase accounting on performance ratios such as return on assets and earnings per share in periods subsequent to the combination.

Appendix 2B Problems

LO 2-10

39. What is pushdown accounting?

a. A requirement that a subsidiary must use the same accounting principles as a parent company.

b. Inventory transfers made from a parent company to a subsidiary.

c. A subsidiary's recording of the fair-value allocations as well as subsequent amortization.

d. The adjustments required for consolidation when a parent has applied the equity method of accounting for internal reporting purposes.

LO 2-10

40. On May 1, Burns Corporation acquired 100 percent of the outstanding ownership shares of Quigley Corporation in exchange for $710,000 cash. At the acquisition date, Quigley's book and fair values were as follows:

	Book Values	Fair Values
Cash	$ 95,000	$ 95,000
Receivables	200,000	200,000
Inventory	210,000	260,000
Land	130,000	110,000
Building and equipment (net)	270,000	330,000
Patented technology	–0–	220,000
Total assets	$905,000	$1,215,000
Accounts payable	$120,000	$ 120,000
Long-term liabilities	510,000	510,000
Common stock ($5 par value)	210,000	
Additional paid-in capital	90,000	
Retained earnings	(25,000)	
Total liabilities and stockholders equity	$905,000	

Burns directs Quigley to seek additional financing for expansion through a new long-term debt issue. Consequently, Quigley will issue a set of financial statements separate from that of its new parent to support its request for debt and accompanying regulatory filings. Quigley elects to apply pushdown accounting in order to show recent fair valuations for its assets.

Prepare a separate acquisition-date balance sheet for Quigley Corporation using pushdown accounting.

Develop Your Skills

FASB ASC RESEARCH AND ANALYSIS CASE—CONSIDERATION OR COMPENSATION?

CPA skills

AutoNav Company agrees to pay $20 million in cash to the four former owners of Easy-C, Inc., for all of its assets and liabilities. These four owners of Easy-C developed and patented a technology for real-time monitoring of traffic patterns on the nation's top 200 frequently congested highways. AutoNav plans to combine the new technology with its existing global positioning systems and projects a resulting substantial revenue increase.

As part of the acquisition contract, AutoNav also agrees to pay additional amounts to the former owners upon achievement of certain financial goals. AutoNav will pay $8 million to the four former owners of Easy-C if revenues from the combined system exceed $100 million over the next three years. AutoNav estimates this contingent payment to have a probability adjusted present value of $4 million.

The four former owners have also been offered employment contracts with AutoNav to help with system integration and performance enhancement issues. The employment contracts are silent as to service periods, have nominal salaries similar to those of equivalent employees, and specify a profit-sharing component over the next three years (if the employees remain with the company) that AutoNav estimates to have a current fair value of $2 million. The four former owners of Easy-C say they will stay on as employees of AutoNav for at least three years to help achieve the desired financial goals.

Should AutoNav account for the contingent payments promised to the former owners of Easy-C as consideration transferred in the acquisition or as compensation expense to employees?

ASC RESEARCH CASE—DEFENSIVE INTANGIBLE ASSET

ComWire Company manufactures wireless transponders for satellite applications. ComWire has recently acquired Martin Company, which is primarily known for its software communications development but also manufactures a specialty transponder under the trade name "M-Tech" that competes with one of ComWire's products. ComWire will now discontinue M-Tech and projects that its own product line will see a market share increase. Nonetheless, ComWire's management will maintain the rights to the M-Tech trade name as a defensive intangible asset to prevent its use by competitors, despite the fact that its highest and best use would be to sell the trade name. ComWire estimates that the trade name has an internal value of $1.5 million but, if sold, would yield $2 million.

Answer the following with supporting citations from the FASB ASC:

a. How does the FASB ASC Glossary define a defensive intangible asset?

b. According to ASC Topic 805, "Business Combinations," what is the measurement principle that an acquirer should follow in recording identifiable assets acquired in a business combination?

c. According to ASC Topic 820, "Fair Value Measurement," what value premise (in-use or in-exchange) should ComWire assign to the M-Tech trade name in its consolidated financial statements?

d. According to ASC Topic 350, "General Intangibles Other Than Goodwill," how should ComWire determine the estimated useful life of its defensive intangible asset?

RESEARCH CASE—HERSHEY'S ACQUISITION OF AMPLIFY SNACK BRANDS

On January 31, 2018, The Hershey Company acquired Amplify Snack Brands, Inc., its largest business acquisition to date. Access Hershey's 2018 financial statements and media reports near the time of the acquisition, and answer the following questions.

1. Why did Hershey acquire Amplify Snack Brands?
2. How did Hershey account for Amplify's cash acquired in the business combination?
3. What amount of goodwill did Hershey recognize in the combination? Prepare a schedule that computes the goodwill recognized in the acquisition as the difference between the consideration transferred for Amplify and the fair values of the individually identified assets and liabilities acquired.
4. How did Hershey determine the fair values of Amplify's assets?
5. What were the acquisition-related costs Hershey incurred regarding the combination, and how were these costs accounted for?
6. How did Hershey report the Amplify acquisition in its statement of cash flows?

RESEARCH CASE—MICROCHIP'S ACQUISITION OF MICROSEMI

On May 29, 2018, Microchip Technology Incorporated acquired all of the outstanding stock of Microsemi Corporation in exchange for $8.19 billion in cash to the stockholders of Microsemi. Referring to Microchip's March 31, 2019 financial statements and any media coverage, answer the following questions regarding the Microsemi acquisition.

1. Why did Microchip acquire Microsemi?
2. What accounting method was used, and for what amount, to record the acquisition?
3. What amount did Microchip include in precombination service compensation (for acquisition-related equity awards) in the total consideration transferred? What support is provided for this treatment in the *Accounting Standards Codification*® (see ASC 805-30-30, paragraphs 9-13)?
4. What allocations did Microchip make to the assets acquired and liabilities assumed in the acquisition? Provide a calculation showing how Microchip determined the amount allocated to goodwill.
5. How will Microchip account for the core technology and the in-process research and development acquired in the Microsemi combination?

RESEARCH CASE—KROGER'S ACQUISITION OF HOME CHEF

On June 22, 2018, Kroger, Inc., acquired the assets and liabilities of Home Chef, a privately owned company based in Chicago, Illinois, in exchange for $197 million in cash (net of 30 million cash acquired) and contingent consideration. Referring to Kroger's 2018 financial statements, answer the following questions regarding the Home Chef acquisition.

1. Why did Kroger acquire Home Chef?
2. Provide a schedule showing Kroger's allocations of the consideration transferred to Home Chef's identifiable assets acquired and liabilities assumed with the remainder going to goodwill.
3. What is the maximum potential contingent payout (i.e., earnout) to the former owners of Home Chef? What were the factors that entered into the determination of the acquisition-date fair value of the contingent consideration?

chapter 3

Consolidations—Subsequent to the Date of Acquisition

In 1996, Berkshire Hathaway Inc., acquired all of the outstanding stock of Geico, Inc., an insurance company. Although this transaction involved well-known companies, it was not unique; mergers and acquisitions have long been common in the business world.

Berkshire Hathaway's current financial statements indicate that Geico is still a component of this economic entity. However, Geico, Inc., continues as a separate legally incorporated concern long after its acquisition. As discussed in Chapter 2, a parent will often maintain separate legal status for a subsidiary corporation to better utilize its inherent value as a going concern.

For external reporting purposes, maintenance of incorporation creates an ongoing challenge for the accountant. In each subsequent period, consolidation must be simulated anew through the use of a worksheet and consolidation entries. Thus, for many years, the financial data for Berkshire Hathaway and Geico (along with dozens of other subsidiaries) have been brought together periodically to provide figures for the financial statements that represent this business combination.

As also discussed in Chapter 2, the acquisition method governs the way we initially record a business combination. In periods subsequent to acquisition, the fair-value bases (established at the acquisition date) for subsidiary assets acquired and liabilities assumed will be amortized (or tested for possible impairment) for proper income recognition. Additionally, some combinations require accounting for the eventual disposition of contingent consideration, which is typically resolved with the passage of time.

In the next several sections of this chapter, we present the procedures to prepare consolidated financial statements in the years subsequent to acquisition. We start by analyzing the relation between the parent's internal accounting method for its subsidiary investment and the adjustments required in consolidation. We also examine the specific procedures for amortizing the acquisition-date fair-value adjustments to the subsidiary's assets and liabilities. We then cover testing for goodwill impairment and postacquisition accounting for contingent consideration. Finally, an appendix presents the alternative goodwill model available as a reporting option for private companies.

Learning Objectives

After studying this chapter, you should be able to:

LO 3-1 Recognize the complexities in preparing consolidated financial reports that emerge from the passage of time.

LO 3-2 Identify and describe the various methods available to a parent company in order to maintain its Investment in Subsidiary account in its internal records.

LO 3-3 Prepare consolidated financial statements subsequent to acquisition when the parent has applied in its internal records:
a. The equity method.
b. The initial value method.
c. The partial equity method.

LO 3-4 Understand that a parent's internal accounting method for its subsidiary investments has no effect on the resulting consolidated financial statements.

LO 3-5 Discuss the rationale for the goodwill impairment testing approach.

LO 3-6 Describe the procedures for conducting a goodwill impairment test.

LO 3-7 Describe the rationale and procedures for impairment testing for intangible assets other than goodwill.

LO 3-8 Understand the accounting and reporting for contingent consideration subsequent to a business acquisition.

LO 3-9 Appendix: Describe the alternative accounting treatments for goodwill and other intangible assets available for business combinations by private companies.

LO 3-1

Recognize the complexities in preparing consolidated financial reports that emerge from the passage of time.

Consolidation—The Effects Created by the Passage of Time

In Chapter 2, consolidation accounting is analyzed at the date that a combination is created. The present chapter carries this process one step further by examining the consolidation procedures that must be followed in subsequent periods whenever separate incorporation of the subsidiary is maintained.

Despite complexities created by the passage of time, the basic objective of all consolidations remains the same: to combine asset, liability, revenue, expense, and equity accounts of a parent and its subsidiaries. From a mechanical perspective, a worksheet and consolidation entries continue to provide structure for the production of a single set of financial statements for the combined business entity.

Consolidated Net Income Determination

Subsequent to an acquisition, the parent company must report consolidated net income. Consolidated income determination involves first combining the separately recorded revenues and expenses of the parent with those of the subsidiary on a consolidated worksheet. Because of separate recordkeeping systems, however, the subsidiary's expenses typically are based on their original book values and not the acquisition-date values the parent must recognize. Consequently, adjustments are made that reflect the amortization of the excess of the parent's consideration transferred over the subsidiary book value. Additionally, the effects of any intra-entity transactions are removed.

The Parent's Choice of Investment Accounting

The time factor introduces other complications into the consolidation process as well. For internal recordkeeping purposes, the parent must select and apply an accounting method to monitor the relationship between the two companies. The investment balance recorded by the parent varies over time as a result of the method chosen, as does the income subsequently recognized. These differences affect the periodic consolidation process but not the figures to be reported by the combined entity. Regardless of the amount, the parent's investment account is eliminated (brought to a zero balance) on the worksheet so that the subsidiary's actual assets and liabilities can be consolidated. Likewise, the income figure accrued by the parent is removed each period so that the subsidiary's revenues and expenses can be included when creating an income statement for the combined business entity.

LO 3-2

Identify and describe the various methods available to a parent company in order to maintain its investment in subsidiary account in its internal records.

Investment Accounting by the Acquiring Company

For a parent company's external financial reporting, consolidation of a subsidiary becomes necessary whenever control exists. For internal recordkeeping, though, the parent has a choice for monitoring the activities of its subsidiaries. Although several variations occur in practice, three methods have emerged as the most prominent: the equity method, the initial value method,[1] and the partial equity method.

At the acquisition date, each investment accounting method (equity, initial value, and partial equity) begins with an identical value recorded in an investment account. Typically the fair value of the consideration transferred by the parent will serve as the recorded valuation basis on the parent's books.[2] Subsequent to the acquisition date, however, the three methods produce different amounts on the parent company's accounting records for the following:

- Investment in subsidiary
- Income recognized from the subsidiary's activities
- Retained earnings

[1] The initial value method is sometimes referred to as the cost method.

[2] In the unusual case of a bargain purchase, the valuation basis for the investment account is the fair value of the net amount of the assets acquired and liabilities assumed.

Importantly, the selection of a particular method does not affect the totals ultimately reported for the combined companies. Nonetheless, the parent's choice of an internal accounting method does lead to distinct procedures for consolidating financial information from the separate organizations.

Internal Investment Accounting Alternatives—The Equity Method, Initial Value Method, and Partial Equity Method

The internal reporting philosophy of the acquiring company often determines the accounting method choice for its subsidiary investment. Depending on the measures a company uses to assess the ongoing performances of its subsidiaries, parent companies may choose their own preferred internal reporting method. Regardless of this choice, however, the investment balance will be eliminated in preparing consolidated financial statements for external reporting.

The Equity Method

The equity method embraces full accrual accounting in maintaining the parent's investment in subsidiary account and related income over time. Under the equity method, the parent company accrues its share of subsidiary income in the same period when the subsidiary earns it. To match the additional fair values recorded in the combination against income, amortization expense stemming from the acquisition-date excess fair-value allocations is recognized through periodic adjusting entries. Unrealized gross profits on intra-entity transactions are deferred; subsidiary dividends serve to reduce the investment account balance. As discussed in Chapter 1, the equity method creates a parallel between the parent's investment accounts and changes in the underlying equity of the acquired company.[3]

When the parent has complete ownership, equity method earnings from the subsidiary, combined with the parent's other income sources, create a total income figure reflective of the entire combined business entity. Consequently, the equity method often is referred to as a single-line consolidation. The equity method is especially popular in companies where management periodically (e.g., monthly or quarterly) measures each subsidiary's profitability using accrual-based income figures.

The Initial Value Method

Under the initial value method, the investment balance remains on the parent's financial records at the initial fair value assigned at the acquisition date. In contrast to the equity method, the initial value method does not recognize income as it its earned by the subsidiary. Instead, the parent recognizes dividend income from its share of any subsidiary dividends when declared. Because little time typically elapses between dividend declaration and cash distribution, the initial value method frequently reflects the cash basis for income recognition.

A parent might select the initial value method because it does not require an accrual-based income measure of subsidiary performance. For example, the parent may wish to assess subsidiary performance on its ability to generate cash flows, on revenues generated, or some other non-income basis. Also, some firms may find the initial value method's ease of application attractive. Because the investment account is eliminated in consolidation, and the actual subsidiary revenues and expenses are eventually combined, firms may avoid the complexity of the equity method unless they need the specific information provided by the equity income measure for internal decision making.

The Partial Equity Method

A third method available to the acquiring company is a partial application of the equity method. Similar to the equity method, the parent company accrues its share of subsidiary income in the same period when the subsidiary earns it. Also, like the equity method, subsidiary dividends declared reduce the investment balance. However, no other equity adjustments

[3] In Chapter 1, the equity method was introduced in connection with the external reporting of investments in which the owner held the ability to apply significant influence over the investee (usually by possessing 20 to 50 percent of the company's voting stock). Here, the equity method is utilized for the internal reporting of the parent for investments in which control is maintained. Although the accounting procedures are similar, the reason for using the equity method is different.

Discussion Question

HOW DOES A COMPANY REALLY DECIDE WHICH INVESTMENT METHOD TO APPLY?

Pilgrim Products, Inc., buys a controlling interest in the common stock of Crestwood Corporation. Shortly after the acquisition, a meeting of Pilgrim's accounting department is convened to discuss the internal reporting procedures required by the ownership of this subsidiary. Each member of the staff has a definite opinion as to whether the equity method, initial value method, or partial equity method should be adopted. To resolve this issue, Pilgrim's chief financial officer outlines several of her concerns about the decision.

> I already understand how each method works. I know the general advantages and disadvantages of all three. I realize, for example, that the equity method provides more detailed information whereas the initial value method is much easier to apply. What I need to know are the factors specific to our situation that should be considered in deciding which method to adopt. I must make a recommendation to the president on this matter, and he will want firm reasons for my favoring a particular approach. I don't want us to select a method and then find out in six months that the information is not adequate for our needs or that the cost of adapting our system to monitor Crestwood outweighs the benefits derived from the data.

What are the factors that Pilgrim's officials should evaluate when making this decision?

(e.g., amortizations or deferrals of unrealized gross profits) are recorded. Thus, in many cases, net income figures as computed from the parent's accounting records approximate consolidated totals but without the effort associated with a full application of the equity method.

Moreover, some parent companies rely on internally designed performance measures (rather than GAAP net income) to evaluate subsidiary management or to make resource allocation decisions. For such companies, a full equity method application may be unnecessary for internal purposes. In these cases, the partial equity method, although only approximating the GAAP net income measure, may be sufficient for decision making.

Summary of Internal Investment Accounting Methods

Exhibit 3.1 summarizes the three internal accounting techniques. Importantly, the method the acquiring company adopts affects only its separate financial records and has no impact on the subsidiary's balances. Regardless of the parent's choice of internally accounting for its

EXHIBIT 3.1 Internal Reporting of Investment Accounts by Acquiring Company

Method	Investment Account	Income Account	Advantages
Equity	Continually adjusted to reflect current owner's equity of acquired company.	Income accrued as earned; amortizations and other adjustments are recognized.	Acquiring company totals give a true representation of consolidation figures.
Initial value	Remains at acquisition-date value assigned.	Dividends declared recorded as Dividend Income.	It is easy to apply; it often reflects cash flows from the subsidiary.
Partial equity	Adjusted only for accrued income and dividends declared by the acquired company.	Income accrued as earned; no other adjustments recognized.	It usually gives balances approximating consolidation figures, but it is easier to apply than equity method.

subsidiary, the particular method selected (i.e., initial value, equity, or partial equity) has no effect on the amounts ultimately reported on consolidated financial statements to external users.

Because specific worksheet procedures differ depending on the investment method utilized by the parent, the consolidation process subsequent to the date of combination will be introduced twice. First, we review consolidations in which the acquiring company uses the equity method. Then we redevelop all procedures when the investment is recorded by one of the alternative methods.

LO 3-3a

Prepare consolidated financial statements subsequent to acquisition when the parent has applied **the equity method** in its internal records.

Subsequent Consolidation—Investment Recorded by the Equity Method

Acquisition Made during the Current Year

As a basis for this illustration, assume that Parrot Company obtains all of the outstanding common stock of Sun Company on January 1, 2020. Parrot acquires this stock for $800,000 in cash.

The book values as well as the appraised fair values of Sun's accounts follow:

	Book Values 1/1/20	Fair Values 1/1/20	Difference
Current assets	$ 320,000	$320,000	$ –0–
Trademarks (indefinite life)	200,000	220,000	+ 20,000
Patented technology (10-year remaining life)	320,000	450,000	+130,000
Equipment (5-year remaining life)	180,000	150,000	(30,000)
Liabilities	(420,000)	(420,000)	–0–
Net book value	$ 600,000	$720,000	$ 120,000
Common stock—$40 par value	$(200,000)		
Additional paid-in capital	(20,000)		
Retained earnings, 1/1/20	(380,000)		

Parrot considers the economic life of Sun's trademarks as extending beyond the foreseeable future and thus having an indefinite life. Such assets are not amortized but are subject to periodic impairment testing.[4] For the definite lived assets acquired in the combination (patented technology and equipment), we assume that straight-line amortization and depreciation with no salvage value is appropriate.[5]

Parrot paid $800,000 cash to acquire Sun Company, clear evidence of the fair value of the consideration transferred. This $800,000 consideration transferred becomes the acquisition-date subsidiary valuation basis for consolidated reporting purposes. As shown in Exhibit 3.2, after recognizing Sun's overall $600,000 book value, Parrot makes individual allocations totaling $200,000 to adjust Sun's accounts from their book values to their acquisition-date collective $800,000 net fair value. Because the total net fair value of Sun's *identifiable* assets and liabilities was only $720,000, Parrot recognizes *goodwill* of $80,000 for consolidation purposes.

Note that the Exhibit 3.2 adjustments to patented technology and equipment represent valuations associated with a definite life. As discussed in Chapter 1, under the equity method Parrot must amortize each allocation over its expected life. The expense recognition necessitated by this fair-value allocation is calculated in Exhibit 3.3.

Two aspects of this amortization schedule warrant further explanation. First, we use the term *amortization* in a generic sense to include both the amortization of definite-lived intangibles and depreciation of tangible assets. Second, the acquisition-date fair value of Sun's equipment is $30,000 *less* than its book value. Therefore, instead of attributing an additional

[4] In other cases, trademarks can have a definite life and thus would be subject to regular amortization.

[5] Unless otherwise stated, all amortization and depreciation expense computations in this textbook are based on the straight-line method with no salvage value.

EXHIBIT 3.2
Excess Fair-Value Allocation

PARROT COMPANY 100 Percent Acquisition of Sun Company Allocation of Acquisition-Date Subsidiary Fair Value January 1, 2020		
Sun Company fair value (consideration transferred by Parrot Company)		$800,000
Book value of Sun Company:		
Common stock	$200,000	
Additional paid-in capital	20,000	
Retained earnings, 1/1/20	380,000	(600,000)
Excess of fair value over book value		200,000
Allocation to specific accounts based on fair values:		
Trademarks	$ 20,000	
Patented technology	130,000	
Equipment (overvalued)	(30,000)	120,000
Excess fair value not identified with specific accounts—goodwill		$ 80,000

EXHIBIT 3.3
Annual Excess Amortization

PARROT COMPANY
100 Percent Acquisition of Sun Company
Excess Amortization Schedule—Allocation of Acquisition-Date Fair Values

Account	Allocation	Remaining Useful Life	Annual Excess Amortizations
Trademarks	$ 20,000	Indefinite	$ –0–
Patented technology	130,000	10 years	13,000
Equipment	(30,000)	5 years	(6,000)
Goodwill	80,000	Indefinite	–0–
			$ 7,000*

*Total excess amortizations will be $7,000 annually for five years until the equipment allocation is fully removed. At the end of each asset's life, future amortizations will change.

amount to this asset, the $30,000 allocation actually reflects a fair-value reduction. As such, the amortization shown in Exhibit 3.3 relating to Equipment is not an additional expense but instead is an expense reduction.

Having determined the allocation of the acquisition-date fair value in the previous example as well as the associated amortization, the parent's separate recordkeeping for its first year of Sun Company ownership can be constructed. Assume that Sun earns income of $100,000 during the year, declares a $40,000 cash dividend on August 1, and pays the dividend on August 8.

In this first illustration, Parrot has adopted the equity method. Apparently, this company believes that the information derived from using the equity method is useful in its evaluation of Sun.

Application of the Equity Method

	Parrot's Financial Records		
1/1/20	Investment in Sun Company	800,000	
	Cash		800,000
	To record the acquisition of Sun Company.		
8/1/20	Dividend Receivable	40,000	
	Investment in Sun Company		40,000
	To record cash dividend declaration from subsidiary.		
8/8/20	Cash	40,000	
	Dividend Receivable		40,000
	To record receipt of the subsidiary cash dividend.		

(continued)

(continued)

	Parrot's Financial Records		
12/31/20	Investment in Sun Company	100,000	
	Equity in Subsidiary Earnings		100,000
	To accrue income earned by 100 percent owned subsidiary.		
12/31/20	Equity in Subsidiary Earnings	7,000	
	Investment in Sun Company		7,000
	To recognize amortizations on allocations made in acquisition of subsidiary (see Exhibit 3.3).		

Parrot's application of the equity method, as shown in this series of entries, causes the Investment in Sun Company account balance to rise from \$800,000 to \$853,000 (\$800,000 − \$40,000 + \$100,000 − \$7,000). During the same period, the parent recognizes a \$93,000 equity income figure (the \$100,000 earnings accrual less the \$7,000 excess amortization expenses).

The consolidation procedures for Parrot and Sun one year after the date of acquisition are illustrated next. For this purpose, Exhibit 3.4 presents the separate 2020 financial statements for these two companies. Parrot recorded both investment-related accounts (the \$853,000 asset balance and the \$93,000 income accrual) based on applying the equity method.

EXHIBIT 3.4
Separate Records—Equity Method Applied

PARROT COMPANY AND SUN COMPANY
Financial Statements
For Year Ending December 31, 2020

	Parrot Company	Sun Company
Income Statement		
Revenues	\$(1,500,000)	\$ (400,000)
Cost of goods sold	700,000	232,000
Amortization expense	120,000	32,000
Depreciation expense	80,000	36,000
Equity in subsidiary earnings	(93,000)	–0–
Net income	\$ (693,000)	\$ (100,000)
Statement of Retained Earnings		
Retained earnings, 1/1/20	\$ (840,000)	\$ (380,000)
Net income (above)	(693,000)	(100,000)
Dividends declared*	120,000	40,000
Retained earnings, 12/31/20	\$(1,413,000)	\$ (440,000)
Balance Sheet		
Current assets	\$ 1,040,000	\$ 400,000
Investment in Sun Company (at equity)	853,000	–0–
Trademarks	600,000	200,000
Patented technology	370,000	288,000
Equipment (net)	250,000	220,000
Total assets	\$ 3,113,000	\$ 1,108,000
Liabilities	\$ (980,000)	\$ (448,000)
Common stock	(600,000)	(200,000)
Additional paid-in capital	(120,000)	(20,000)
Retained earnings, 12/31/20 (above)	(1,413,000)	(440,000)
Total liabilities and equity	\$(3,113,000)	\$(1,108,000)

Note: Parentheses indicate a credit balance.

*Dividends declared, whether currently paid or not, provide the appropriate amount to include in a statement of retained earnings. To help keep the number of worksheet rows (i.e., dividends payable and receivable) at a minimum, throughout this text we assume that dividends are declared and paid in the same period.

Determination of Consolidated Totals

Before becoming immersed in the mechanical aspects of a consolidation, the objective of this process should be understood. As indicated in Chapter 2, in the preparation of consolidated financial reports, the subsidiary's revenue, expense, asset, and liability accounts are added to the parent company balances. Within this procedure, several important guidelines must be followed:

- Sun's assets and liabilities are adjusted to reflect their their acquisition-date fair-value allocations.
- Because of the passage of time, the income effects (e.g., amortizations) of these allocations must also be recognized within the consolidation process.
- Any reciprocal or intra-entity[6] accounts must be offset. If, for example, one of the companies owes money to the other, the receivable and the payable balances have no connection with an outside party. Thus, when the companies are viewed as a single consolidated entity, the receivable and the payable represent intra-entity balances that should be eliminated for external reporting purposes.

The consolidation of the two sets of financial information in Exhibit 3.4 is a relatively uncomplicated task and can even be carried out without the use of a worksheet. Understanding the origin of each reported figure is the first step in gaining a knowledge of this process.

- *Revenues* = \$1,900,000. The revenues of the parent and the subsidiary are added together.
- *Cost of goods sold* = \$932,000. The cost of goods sold of the parent and subsidiary are added together.
- *Amortization expense* = \$165,000. The balances of the parent and of the subsidiary are combined along with the \$13,000 additional amortization from the recognition of the excess fair value over book value attributed to the subsidiary's patented technology, as shown in Exhibit 3.3.
- *Depreciation expense* = \$110,000. The depreciation expenses of the parent and subsidiary are added together along with the \$6,000 reduction in equipment depreciation, as indicated in Exhibit 3.3.
- *Equity in subsidiary earnings* = –0–. The investment income recorded by the parent is eliminated and replaced by adding across the subsidiary's revenues and expenses to the consolidated totals.
- *Net income* = \$693,000. Consolidated revenues less consolidated expenses.
- *Retained earnings, 1/1/20* = \$840,000. The parent figure only. This acquisition-date parent's balance has yet to be affected by any equity method adjustments.
- *Dividends declared* = \$120,000. The parent company balance only because the subsidiary's dividends are attributable intra-entity to the parent, not to an outside party.
- *Retained earnings, 12/31/20* = \$1,413,000. Consolidated retained earnings as of the beginning of the year plus consolidated net income less consolidated dividends declared.
- *Current assets* = \$1,440,000. The parent's book value plus the subsidiary's book value.
- *Investment in Sun Company* = –0–. The asset recorded by the parent is eliminated and replaced by adding the subsidiary's assets and liabilities across to the consolidated totals.
- *Trademarks* = \$820,000. The parent's book value plus the subsidiary's book value plus the \$20,000 acquisition-date fair-value allocation. Note that the trademark has an indefinite life and therefore is not amortized.
- *Patented technology* = \$775,000. The parent's book value plus the subsidiary's book value plus the \$130,000 acquisition-date fair-value allocation less current year amortization of \$13,000.

[6] The FASB *Accounting Standards Codification*® (ASC) uses the term *intra-entity* to describe transfers of assets across business entities affiliated though common stock ownership or other control mechanisms. The phrase indicates that although such transfers occur across separate legal entities, they are nonetheless made within a commonly controlled entity. Prior to the use of the term intra-entity, such amounts were routinely referred to as intercompany balances.

- *Equipment* = $446,000. The parent's book value plus the subsidiary's book value less the $30,000 fair-value reduction allocation plus the current-year expense reduction of $6,000.
- *Goodwill* = $80,000. The residual allocation shown in Exhibit 3.2. Note that goodwill is considered to have an indefinite life and thus is not amortized.
- *Total assets* = $3,561,000. A vertical summation of consolidated assets.
- *Liabilities* = $1,428,000. The parent's book value plus the subsidiary's book value.
- *Common stock* = $600,000. The parent's book value. Subsidiary shares owned by the parent are treated as if they are no longer outstanding.
- *Additional paid-in capital* = $120,000. The parent's book value. Subsidiary shares owned by the parent are treated as if they are no longer outstanding.
- *Retained earnings, 12/31/20* = $1,413,000. Computed previously.
- *Total liabilities and equities* = $3,561,000. A vertical summation of consolidated liabilities and equities.

Consolidation Worksheet

Although the consolidated figures to be reported can be computed as just shown, accountants normally prefer to use a worksheet. A worksheet provides an organized structure for this process, a benefit that becomes especially important in consolidating complex combinations.

For Parrot and Sun, only five consolidation entries are needed to arrive at the same figures previously derived for this business combination. As discussed in Chapter 2, *worksheet entries are the catalyst for developing totals to be reported by the entity but are not physically recorded in the individual account balances of either company.*

Consolidation Entry S

Common Stock (Sun Company)	200,000	
Additional Paid-In Capital (Sun Company)	20,000	
Retained Earnings, 1/1/20 (Sun Company)	380,000	
Investment in Sun Company		600,000

As shown in Exhibit 3.2, Parrot's $800,000 Investment account balance at January 1, 2020, reflects two components: (1) a $600,000 amount equal to Sun's book value and (2) a $200,000 figure attributed to the acquisition-date difference between the book value and fair value of Sun's assets and liabilities (with a residual allocation made to goodwill). Entry **S** removes the $600,000 component of the Investment in Sun Company account, which is then replaced by adding the *book values* of each subsidiary asset and liability across to the consolidated figures. A second worksheet entry (Entry **A**) eliminates the remaining $200,000 portion of the January 1, 2020 Investment in Sun account and replaces it with the specific acquisition-date excess fair over book value allocations along with any goodwill. Importantly, worksheet entries **S** and **A** are part of the sequence of worksheet adjustments that bring the investment account to zero.

Entry **S** also removes Sun's stockholders' equity accounts as of the beginning of the year. Because consolidated statements are prepared for the parent company owners, the subsidiary equity accounts are not relevant to the business combination and should be eliminated for consolidation purposes. The elimination is made through this entry because the equity accounts and the $600,000 component of the investment account represent reciprocal balances: Both provide a measure of Sun's book value as of January 1, 2020.

Before moving to the next consolidation entry, a clarification point should be made. In actual practice, worksheet entries are usually identified numerically. However, as in the previous chapter, the label "Entry **S**" used in this example refers to the elimination of Sun's beginning **S**tockholders' Equity. As a reminder of the purpose being served, all worksheet entries are identified in a similar fashion. Thus, throughout this textbook, "Entry **S**" always refers to the removal of the subsidiary's beginning stockholders' equity balances for the year against the book value portion of the investment account.

Consolidation Entry A

Trademarks	20,000	
Patented Technology	130,000	
Goodwill	80,000	
Equipment		30,000
Investment in Sun Company		200,000

Consolidation Entry **A** adjusts the subsidiary balances from their book values to acquisition-date fair values (see Exhibit 3.2) and includes goodwill created by the acquisition. This entry is labeled "Entry **A**" to indicate that it represents the **A**llocations made in connection with the excess of the subsidiary's fair values over its book values. Sun's accounts are adjusted collectively by the $200,000 excess of Sun's $800,000 acquisition-date fair value over its $600,000 book value.

Consolidation Entry I

Equity in Subsidiary Earnings	93,000	
Investment in Sun Company		93,000

"Entry **I**" (for **I**ncome) removes from the worksheet the subsidiary income recognized by Parrot during the year. For reporting purposes, we must add the subsidiary's individual revenue and expense accounts (and the current excess amortization expenses) to the parent's respective amounts to arrive at consolidated totals. Worksheet entry **I** thus effectively removes the one-line Equity in Subsidiary Earnings, which is then replaced with the addition of the subsidiary's separate revenues and expenses (already listed on the worksheet in the subsidiary's balances). The $93,000 figure eliminated here represents the $100,000 income accrual recognized by Parrot, reduced by the $7,000 in excess amortizations. Observe that the entry originally recorded by the parent is simply reversed on the worksheet to remove its impact.

Consolidation Entry D

Investment in Sun Company	40,000	
Dividends Declared		40,000

The dividends declared by the subsidiary during the year also must be eliminated from the consolidated totals. The entire $40,000 dividend goes to the parent, which from the viewpoint of the consolidated entity is simply an intra-entity transfer. The dividend declaration did not affect any outside party. Therefore, "Entry **D**" (for **D**ividends) is designed to offset the impact of this transaction by removing the subsidiary's Dividends Declared account. Because the equity method has been applied, Parrot originally recorded these dividends as a decrease in the Investment in Sun Company account. To eliminate the impact of this reduction, the investment account is increased.

Consolidation Entry E

Amortization Expense	13,000	
Equipment	6,000	
Patented Technology		13,000
Depreciation Expense		6,000

This final worksheet entry recognizes the current year's excess amortization expenses relating to the adjustments of Sun's assets to acquisition-date fair values. Because the equity method amortization was eliminated within Entry **I**, "Entry **E**" (for **E**xpense) now enters on the worksheet the current-year expense attributed to each of the specific account allocations (see Exhibit 3.3). Note that we adjust depreciation expense for the tangible asset *equipment* and we adjust amortization expense for the intangible asset *patented technology*. As mentioned earlier, we refer to the adjustments to all expenses resulting from excess acquisition-date fair-value allocations collectively as *excess amortization expenses.*

Thus, the worksheet entries necessary for consolidation when the parent has applied the equity method are as follows:

Entry S—Eliminates the subsidiary's stockholders' equity accounts as of the beginning of the current year along with the equivalent book value component within the parent's investment account.

Entry A—Recognizes the unamortized allocations as of the beginning of the current year associated with the original adjustments to fair value.

Entry I—Eliminates the impact of intra-entity subsidiary income accrued by the parent.

Entry D—Eliminates the impact of intra-entity subsidiary dividends.

Entry E—Recognizes excess amortization expenses for the current period on the allocations from the original adjustments to fair value.

Exhibit 3.5 provides a complete presentation of the December 31, 2020, consolidation worksheet for Parrot Company and Sun Company. The series of entries just described brings together the separate financial statements of these two organizations. Note that the consolidated totals are the same as those computed previously for this combination.

Observe that Parrot separately reports net income of $693,000 as well as ending retained earnings of $1,413,000, figures that are identical to the totals generated for the consolidated entity. However, subsidiary income earned after the date of acquisition is to be *added* to that of the parent. Thus, a question arises in this example as to why the parent company figures alone equal the consolidated balances of both operations.

In reality, Sun's income for this period is contained in both Parrot's reported balances and the consolidated totals. Through the application of the equity method, the current-year earnings of the subsidiary have already been accrued by Parrot along with the appropriate amortization expense. *The parent's Equity in Subsidiary Earnings account is, therefore, an accurate representation of Sun's effect on consolidated net income.* If the equity method is employed properly, the worksheet process simply replaces this single $93,000 balance with the specific revenue and expense accounts that it represents. *Consequently, when the parent employs the equity method, its net income and retained earnings mirror consolidated totals.*

Consolidation Subsequent to Year of Acquisition—Equity Method

In many ways, every consolidation of Parrot and Sun prepared after the date of acquisition incorporates the same basic procedures outlined in the previous section. However, the continual financial evolution undergone by the companies prohibits an exact repetition of the consolidation entries demonstrated in Exhibit 3.5.

As a basis for analyzing the procedural changes necessitated by the passage of time, assume that Parrot Company continues to hold its ownership of Sun Company as of December 31, 2023. This date was selected at random; any date subsequent to 2020 would serve equally well to illustrate this process. As an additional factor, assume that Sun now has a $40,000 liability that is payable to Parrot.

For this consolidation, assume that the January 1, 2023, Sun Company's Retained Earnings balance has risen to $600,000. Because that account had a reported total of only $380,000 on January 1, 2020, Sun's book value apparently has increased by $220,000 during the 2020–2022 period. Although knowledge of individual operating figures in the past is not required, Sun's reported totals help to clarify the consolidation procedures.

EXHIBIT 3.5 Consolidation Worksheet—Equity Method Applied

PARROT COMPANY AND SUN COMPANY
Consolidation Worksheet
For Year Ending December 31, 2020

Investment: Equity Method

Accounts	Parrot Company	Sun Company	Consolidation Entries Debit	Consolidation Entries Credit	Consolidated Totals
Income Statement					
Revenues	(1,500,000)	(400,000)			(1,900,000)
Cost of goods sold	700,000	232,000			932,000
Amortization expense	120,000	32,000	(E) 13,000		165,000
Depreciation expense	80,000	36,000		(E) 6,000	110,000
Equity in subsidiary earnings	(93,000)	–0–	(I) 93,000		–0–
Net income	(693,000)	(100,000)			(693,000)
Statement of Retained Earnings					
Retained earnings, 1/1/20	(840,000)	(380,000)	(S) 380,000		(840,000)
Net income (above)	(693,000)	(100,000)			(693,000)
Dividends declared	120,000	40,000		(D) 40,000	120,000
Retained earnings, 12/31/20	(1,413,000)	(440,000)			(1,413,000)
Balance Sheet					
Current assets	1,040,000	400,000			1,440,000
Investment in Sun Company	853,000	–0–	(D) 40,000	(S) 600,000 (A) 200,000 (I) 93,000	–0–
Trademarks	600,000	200,000	(A) 20,000		820,000
Patented technology	370,000	288,000	(A) 130,000	(E) 13,000	775,000
Equipment (net)	250,000	220,000	(E) 6,000	(A) 30,000	446,000
Goodwill	–0–	–0–	(A) 80,000		80,000
Total assets	3,113,000	1,108,000			3,561,000
Liabilities	(980,000)	(448,000)			(1,428,000)
Common stock	(600,000)	(200,000)	(S) 200,000		(600,000)
Additional paid-in capital	(120,000)	(20,000)	(S) 20,000		(120,000)
Retained earnings, 12/31/20 (above)	(1,413,000)	(440,000)			(1,413,000)
Total liabilities and equities	(3,113,000)	(1,108,000)	982,000	982,000	(3,561,000)

Note: Parentheses indicate a credit balance.
Consolidation entries:
(S) Elimination of Sun's stockholders' equity January 1 balances and the book value portion of the investment account.
(A) Allocation of Sun's acquisition-date excess fair values over book values.
(I) Elimination of parent's equity in subsidiary earnings accrual.
(D) Elimination of intra-entity dividends.
(E) Recognition of current year excess fair-value amortization and depreciation expenses.

Year	Sun Company Net Income	Dividends Declared	Increase in Book Value	Ending Retained Earnings
2020	$100,000	$ 40,000	$ 60,000	$440,000
2021	140,000	50,000	90,000	530,000
2022	90,000	20,000	70,000	600,000
	$330,000	$110,000	$220,000	

For 2023, the current year, we assume that Sun reports net income of $160,000 and declares and pays cash dividends of $70,000. Because it applies the equity method, Parrot recognizes earnings of $160,000. Furthermore, as shown in Exhibit 3.3, amortization expense of $7,000 applies to 2023 and must also be recorded by the parent. Consequently, Parrot reports an Equity in Subsidiary Earnings balance for the year of $153,000 ($160,000 – $7,000).

Although this income figure can be reconstructed with little difficulty, the current balance in the Investment in Sun Company account is more complicated. Over the years, the initial $800,000 acquisition price has been subjected to adjustments for

1. The annual accrual of Sun's income.
2. The receipt of dividends from Sun.
3. The recognition of annual excess amortization expenses.

Exhibit 3.6 analyzes these changes and shows the components of the Investment in Sun Company account balance as of December 31, 2023.

Following the construction of the Investment in Sun Company account, the consolidation worksheet developed in Exhibit 3.7 should be easier to understand. Current figures for both companies appear in the first two columns. The parent's investment balance and equity income accrual as well as Sun's income and stockholders' equity accounts correspond to the information given previously. Worksheet entries (lettered to agree with the previous illustration) are then utilized to consolidate all balances.

Several steps are necessary to arrive at these reported totals. The subsidiary's assets, liabilities, revenues, and expenses are added to those same accounts of the parent. The unamortized portion of the original acquisition-date fair-value allocations are included along with current excess amortization expenses. The investment and equity income balances are both eliminated as are the subsidiary's stockholders' equity accounts. Intra-entity dividends are removed as are the existing receivable and payable balances between the two companies.

Consolidation Entry S

Once again, this first consolidation entry offsets reciprocal amounts representing the subsidiary's book value as of the beginning of the current year. Sun's January 1, 2023, stockholders' equity accounts are eliminated against the book value portion of the parent's investment account. Here, though, the amount eliminated is $820,000 rather than the $600,000 shown in Exhibit 3.5 for 2020. Both balances have changed during the 2020–2022 period. Sun's

EXHIBIT 3.6
Investment Account under Equity Method

PARROT COMPANY
Investment in Sun Company Account
As of December 31, 2023
Equity Method Applied

Fair value of consideration transferred at date of acquisition		$ 800,000
Entries recorded in prior years:		
Accrual of Sun Company's income		
2020	$100,000	
2021	140,000	
2022	90,000	330,000
Sun Company—Dividends declared		
2020	$ (40,000)	
2021	(50,000)	
2022	(20,000)	(110,000)
Excess amortization expenses		
2020	$ (7,000)	
2021	(7,000)	
2022	(7,000)	(21,000)
Entries recorded in current year—2023		
Accrual of Sun Company's income	$160,000	
Sun Company—Dividends declared	(70,000)	
Excess amortization expenses	(7,000)	83,000
Investment in Sun Company, 12/31/23		$1,082,000

EXHIBIT 3.7 Consolidation Worksheet Subsequent to Year of Acquisition—Equity Method Applied

PARROT COMPANY AND SUN COMPANY
Consolidation Worksheet
For Year Ending December 31, 2023

Investment: Equity Method

Accounts	Parrot Company	Sun Company	Consolidation Entries Debit	Consolidation Entries Credit	Consolidation Totals
Income Statement					
Revenues	(2,100,000)	(600,000)			(2,700,000)
Cost of goods sold	1,000,000	380,000			1,380,000
Amortization expense	200,000	20,000	(E) 13,000		233,000
Depreciation expense	100,000	40,000		(E) 6,000	134,000
Equity in subsidiary earnings	(153,000)	–0–	(I) 153,000		–0–
Net income	(953,000)	(160,000)			(953,000)
Statement of Retained Earnings					
Retained earnings, 1/1/23	(2,044,000)	(600,000)	(S) 600,000		(2,044,000)
Net income (above)	(953,000)	(160,000)			(953,000)
Dividends declared	420,000	70,000		(D) 70,000	420,000
Retained earnings, 12/31/23	(2,577,000)	(690,000)			(2,577,000)
Balance Sheet					
Current assets	1,705,000	500,000		(P) 40,000	2,165,000
Investment in Sun Company	1,082,000	–0–	(D) 70,000	(S) 820,000	–0–
				(A) 179,000	
				(I) 153,000	
Trademarks	600,000	240,000	(A) 20,000		860,000
Patented technology	540,000	420,000	(A) 91,000	(E) 13,000	1,038,000
Equipment (net)	420,000	210,000	(E) 6,000	(A) 12,000	624,000
Goodwill	–0–	–0–	(A) 80,000		80,000
Total assets	4,347,000	1,370,000			4,767,000
Liabilities	(1,050,000)	(460,000)	(P) 40,000		(1,470,000)
Common stock	(600,000)	(200,000)	(S) 200,000		(600,000)
Additional paid-in capital	(120,000)	(20,000)	(S) 20,000		(120,000)
Retained earnings, 12/31/23 (above)	(2,577,000)	(690,000)			(2,577,000)
Total liabilities and equities	(4,347,000)	(1,370,000)	1,293,000	1,293,000	(4,767,000)

Note: Parentheses indicate a credit balance.
Consolidation entries:
(S) Elimination of Sun's stockholders' equity January 1 balances and the book value portion of the investment account.
(A) Allocation of Sun's acquisition-date excess fair values over book values, unamortized balance as of beginning of year.
(I) Elimination of parent's equity in subsidiary earnings accrual.
(D) Elimination of intra-entity dividends.
(E) Recognition of current-year excess fair-value amortization and depreciation expenses.
(P) Elimination of intra-entity receivable/payable.

operations caused a $220,000 increase in retained earnings. Parrot's application of the equity method created a parallel effect on its Investment in Sun Company account (the income accrual of $330,000 less dividends collected of $110,000).

Although Sun's Retained Earnings balance is removed in this entry, the income this company earned since the acquisition date is still included in the consolidated figures. Parrot accrues these profits annually through application of the equity method. Thus, elimination of the subsidiary's entire Retained Earnings is necessary; a portion was earned prior to the acquisition, and the remainder has already been recorded by the parent.

Entry **S** removes these balances as of the first day of 2023 rather than at the end of the year. The consolidation process is made a bit simpler by segregating the effect of preceding operations from the transactions of the current year. Thus, *all worksheet entries relate specifically to either the previous years (**S** and **A**) or the current period (**I, D, E,** and **P**).*

Consolidation Entry A

In the initial consolidation (2020), fair-value allocations amounting to $200,000 were entered, but these balances have now undergone three years of amortization. As computed in Exhibit 3.8, expenses for these prior years totaled $21,000, leaving a balance of $179,000. Allocation of this amount to the individual accounts is also determined in Exhibit 3.8 and reflected in worksheet Entry **A.** As with Entry **S,** these balances are calculated as of January 1, 2023, and replaced by current-year expenses as shown in Entry **E.**

Consolidation Entry I

As before, this entry eliminates the equity income recorded currently by Parrot ($153,000) in connection with its ownership of Sun. The subsidiary's revenue and expense accounts are left intact so they can be included in the consolidated figures.

Consolidation Entry D

This worksheet entry offsets the $70,000 intra-entity dividends (from Sun to Parrot) during the current period.

Consolidation Entry E

Excess amortization expenses relating to acquisition-date fair-value adjustments are individually recorded for the current period.

Before progressing to the final worksheet entry, note the close similarity of these entries with the five entries incorporated in the 2020 consolidation (Exhibit 3.5). Except for the numerical changes created by the passage of time, the entries are identical.

Consolidation Entry P

This last entry (labeled "Entry **P**" because it eliminates an intra-entity **P**ayable) introduces a new element to the consolidation process. As noted earlier, intra-entity reciprocal accounts do not relate to outside parties. Therefore, Sun's $40,000 payable and Parrot's $40,000 receivable must be removed on the worksheet because the companies are being reported as a single entity.

In reviewing Exhibit 3.7, note several aspects of the consolidation process:

- The stockholders' equity accounts of the subsidiary are removed.
- The Investment in Sun Company and the Equity in Subsidiary Earnings are both removed.
- The parent's Retained Earnings balance is not adjusted. Because the parent applies the equity method, this account should be correct.
- The acquisition-date fair-value adjustments to the subsidiary's assets are recognized but only after adjustment for prior periods' annual excess amortization expenses.
- Intra-entity balances such as dividends and receivables/payables are offset.

EXHIBIT 3.8
Excess Amortizations Relating to Individual Accounts as of January 1, 2023

		Annual Excess Amortizations			
Accounts	**Original Allocation**	**2020**	**2021**	**2022**	**Balance 1/1/23**
Trademarks	$ 20,000	$ –0–	$ –0–	$ –0–	$ 20,000
Patented technology	130,000	13,000	13,000	13,000	91,000
Equipment	(30,000)	(6,000)	(6,000)	(6,000)	(12,000)
Goodwill	80,000	–0–	–0–	–0–	80,000
	$200,000	$ 7,000	$ 7,000	$ 7,000	$179,000
			$21,000		

Subsequent Consolidations—Investment Recorded Using Initial Value or Partial Equity Method

As discussed at the beginning of this chapter, the parent company may opt to use the initial value method or the partial equity method for internal recordkeeping for its subsidiary investment rather than the equity method. Application of either alternative changes the balances recorded by the parent over time and, thus, the procedures followed in preparing consolidation worksheets. *Nonetheless, the parent's choice of either the initial value method or the partial equity method does not affect any of the final consolidated figures to be reported.*

As demonstrated in the previous section, when a company utilizes the equity method, the consolidated worksheet eliminates all reciprocal accounts, assigns unamortized fair-value allocations to specific accounts, and records amortization expense for the current year. Application of either the initial value method or the partial equity method has no effect on these basic worksheet processes. For this reason, many of the consolidation entries remain the same regardless of the parent's investment accounting method.

In reality, just three of the parent's accounts actually vary because of the method applied:

- The investment in subsidiary account.
- The income recognized from the subsidiary.
- The parent's retained earnings (in periods after the initial year of the combination).

Only the differences found in these balances of the parent affect the consolidation process. Thus, any time after the acquisition date, accounting for these three balances is of special importance.

Acquisition Made during the Current Year

To illustrate the modifications required by the adoption of an alternative investment accounting method, the consolidation of Parrot and Sun as of December 31, 2020, is reconstructed. Only one differing factor is introduced: the method by which Parrot accounts for its investment. Exhibit 3.9 presents the 2020 consolidation based on Parrot's use of the **initial value method.** Exhibit 3.10 demonstrates this same process assuming that the parent applied the **partial equity method.** Each consolidation entry on these worksheets is labeled to correspond with the 2020 consolidation in which the parent used the equity method (Exhibit 3.5). Differences with the equity method (both for the parent company records and the consolidation entries) are highlighted on each of the worksheets.

LO 3-3b

Prepare consolidated financial statements subsequent to acquisition when the parent has applied **the initial value method** in its internal records.

Initial Value Method Applied—2020 Consolidation

Although the initial value method theoretically stands in marked contrast to the equity method, few reporting differences actually exist. In the year of acquisition, Parrot's income and investment accounts relating to the subsidiary are the only accounts affected.

Under the initial value method, income recognition in 2020 is limited to the $40,000 dividend received by the parent; no equity income accrual is made. At the same time, the investment account retains its $800,000 initial value. Unlike the equity method, no adjustments are recorded in the parent's investment account in connection with the current-year operations, subsidiary dividends, or amortization of any fair-value allocations.

After the composition of the dividend income and investment accounts has been established, worksheet entries can be used to produce the consolidated figures found in Exhibit 3.9 as of December 31, 2020.

Consolidation Entry S

As with the previous Entry **S** in Exhibit 3.5, the $600,000 component of the investment account is eliminated against the beginning stockholders' equity account of the subsidiary. Both are equivalent to Sun's net assets at January 1, 2020, and are, therefore, reciprocal balances that must be offset. This entry is not affected by the accounting method in use.

EXHIBIT 3.9 Consolidation Worksheet—Initial Value Method Applied

PARROT COMPANY AND SUN COMPANY
Consolidation Worksheet
For Year Ending December 31, 2020

Investment: Initial Value Method

Accounts	Parrot Company	Sun Company	Consolidation Entries Debit	Consolidation Entries Credit	Consolidation Totals
Income Statement					
Revenues	(1,500,000)	(400,000)			(1,900,000)
Cost of goods sold	700,000	232,000			932,000
Amortization expense	120,000	32,000	(E) 13,000		165,000
Depreciation expense	80,000	36,000		(E) 6,000	110,000
Dividend income	(40,000)*	–0–	(I) 40,000*		–0–
Net income	(640,000)	(100,000)			(693,000)
Statement of Retained Earnings					
Retained earnings, 1/1/20	(840,000)	(380,000)	(S) 380,000		(840,000)
Net income (above)	(640,000)	(100,000)			(693,000)
Dividends declared	120,000	40,000		(I) 40,000*	120,000
Retained earnings, 12/31/20	(1,360,000)	(440,000)			(1,413,000)
Balance Sheet					
Current assets	1,040,000	400,000			1,440,000
Investment in Sun Company	800,000*	–0–		(S) 600,000 (A) 200,000	–0–
Trademarks	600,000	200,000	(A) 20,000		820,000
Patented technology	370,000	288,000	(A) 130,000	(E) 13,000	775,000
Equipment (net)	250,000	220,000	(E) 6,000	(A) 30,000	446,000
Goodwill	–0–	–0–	(A) 80,000		80,000
Total assets	3,060,000	1,108,000			3,561,000
Liabilities	(980,000)	(448,000)			(1,428,000)
Common stock	(600,000)	(200,000)	(S) 200,000		(600,000)
Additional paid-in capital	(120,000)	(20,000)	(S) 20,000		(120,000)
Retained earnings, 12/31/20 (above)	(1,360,000)	(440,000)			(1,413,000)
Total liabilities and equities	(3,060,000)	(1,108,000)	889,000	889,000	(3,561,000)

Note: Parentheses indicate a credit balance.
*Boxed items highlight differences with consolidation in Exhibit 3.5.
Consolidation entries:
(S) Elimination of Sun's stockholders' equity January 1 balances and the book value portion of the investment account.
(A) Allocation of Sun's acquisition-date excess fair values over book values.
(I) Elimination of intra-entity dividend income and dividends declared by Sun.
(E) Recognition of current-year excess fair-value amortization and depreciation expenses.
Note: Consolidation entry (D) is unnecessary when the parent applies the initial value method. Entry (I) eliminates intra-entity dividend effects.

Consolidation Entry A

Sun's $200,000 excess acquisition-date fair value over book value is allocated to Sun's assets and liabilities based on their fair values at the date of acquisition. The $80,000 residual is attributed to goodwill. This procedure is identical to the corresponding entry in Exhibit 3.5 in which the equity method was applied.

Consolidation Entry I

Under the initial value method, the parent records dividends declared by the subsidiary as income. Entry **I** removes this Dividend Income account along with Sun's Dividends Declared. From a consolidated perspective, these two $40,000 balances represent an intra-entity transfer that had no financial impact outside of the entity. In contrast to the equity method, Parrot has not accrued subsidiary income, nor has amortization been recorded; thus, no further income elimination is needed.

EXHIBIT 3.10 Consolidation Worksheet—Partial Equity Method Applied

PARROT COMPANY AND SUN COMPANY
Consolidation Worksheet
For Year Ending December 31, 2020

Investment: Partial Equity Method

Accounts	Parrot Company	Sun Company	Consolidation Entries Debit	Consolidation Entries Credit	Consolidation Totals
Income Statement					
Revenues	(1,500,000)	(400,000)			(1,900,000)
Cost of goods sold	700,000	232,000			932,000
Amortization expense	120,000	32,000	(E) 13,000		165,000
Depreciation expense	80,000	36,000		(E) 6,000	110,000
Equity in subsidiary earnings	(100,000)*	–0–	(I) 100,000*		–0–
Net income	(700,000)	(100,000)			(693,000)
Statement of Retained Earnings					
Retained earnings, 1/1/20	(840,000)	(380,000)	(S) 380,000		(840,000)
Net income (above)	(700,000)	(100,000)			(693,000)
Dividends declared	120,000	40,000		(D) 40,000	120,000
Retained earnings, 12/31/20	(1,420,000)	(440,000)			(1,413,000)
Balance Sheet					
Current assets	1,040,000	400,000			1,440,000
Investment in Sun Company	860,000*	–0–	(D) 40,000	(S) 600,000 (A) 200,000 (I) 100,000*	–0–
Trademarks	600,000	200,000	(A) 20,000		820,000
Patented technology	370,000	288,000	(A) 130,000	(E) 13,000	775,000
Equipment (net)	250,000	220,000	(E) 6,000	(A) 30,000	446,000
Goodwill	–0–	–0–	(A) 80,000		80,000
Total assets	3,120,000	1,108,000			3,561,000
Liabilities	(980,000)	(448,000)			(1,428,000)
Common stock	(600,000)	(200,000)	(S) 200,000		(600,000)
Additional paid-in capital	(120,000)	(20,000)	(S) 20,000		(120,000)
Retained earnings, 12/31/20 (above)	(1,420,000)	(440,000)			(1,413,000)
Total liabilities and equities	(3,120,000)	(1,108,000)	989,000	989,000	(3,561,000)

Note: Parentheses indicate a credit balance.
*Boxed items highlight differences with consolidation in Exhibit 3.5.
Consolidation entries:
(S) Elimination of Sun's stockholders' equity January 1 balances and the book value portion of the investment account.
(A) Allocation of Sun's acquisition-date excess fair values over book values.
(I) Elimination of parent's equity in subsidiary earnings accrual.
(D) Elimination of intra-entity dividends.
(E) Recognition of current-year excess fair-value amortization and depreciation expenses.

	Debit	Credit
Dividend Income	40,000	
Dividends Declared		40,000
To eliminate intra-entity income.		

Consolidation Entry D

When the initial value method is applied, the parent records intra-entity dividends as income. Because these dividends were already removed from the consolidated totals by Entry **I,** no separate Entry **D** is required.

Consolidation Entry E

Regardless of the parent's method of accounting for its subsidiary investment, the reporting entity must recognize excess amortizations for the current year in connection with the original fair-value allocations. Thus, Entry **E** serves to bring the current-year expenses into the consolidated financial statements.

Consequently, using the initial value method rather than the equity method changes only Entries **I** and **D** in the year of acquisition. Despite the change in methods, reported figures are still derived by (1) eliminating all reciprocals, (2) allocating the excess portion of the acquisition-date fair values, and (3) recording amortizations on these allocations. As indicated previously, the consolidated totals appearing in Exhibit 3.9 are identical to the figures produced previously in Exhibit 3.5. Although the income and the investment accounts on the parent company's separate statements vary, the consolidated balances are not affected.

One significant difference between the initial value method and equity method does exist: The parent's separate statements do not reflect consolidated income totals when the initial value method is used. Because equity adjustments (such as excess amortizations) are not recorded, neither Parrot's reported net income of $640,000 nor its retained earnings of $1,360,000 provide an accurate portrayal of consolidated figures.

LO 3-3c

Prepare consolidated financial statements subsequent to acquisition when the parent has applied **the partial equity method** in its internal records.

Partial Equity Method Applied—2020 Consolidation

Exhibit 3.10 presents a worksheet to consolidate Parrot and Sun for 2020 (the year of acquisition) based on the assumption that Parrot applied the partial equity method in accounting for its subsidiary investment. Again, the only changes from previous examples are found in (1) the parent's separate records for this investment and its related income and (2) worksheet Entries **I** and **D.**

As discussed earlier, under the partial equity approach, the parent's recordkeeping is limited to two periodic journal entries: the annual accrual of subsidiary income and the recognition of dividends. Hence, within the parent's records, only a few differences exist when the partial equity method is applied rather than the initial value method. Exhibit 3.11 shows the journal entries recorded by Parrot in connection with Sun's 2020 operations to illustrate both of these approaches to accounting for the parent's subsidiary investment.

As seen in Exhibit 3.11, by applying the partial equity method, the investment account on the parent's pre-consolidation balance sheet rises to $860,000 by the end of 2020. This total is composed of the original $800,000 acquisition-date fair value for Sun adjusted for the $100,000 income recognition and the $40,000 cash dividend. The same $100,000 equity income figure appears within the parent's separate pre-consolidation income statement. These two balances are appropriately found in Parrot's records in Exhibit 3.10.

Because of differences in income recognition and the effects of subsidiary dividends when the parent employs the partial equity method, Entries **I** and **D** again differ on the worksheet. The $100,000 partial equity method income is eliminated (Entry **I**) by reversing the parent's entry. Removing this accrual allows the individual revenue and expense accounts of the subsidiary to be reported without double-counting. The $40,000 intra-entity dividend must also be removed (Entry **D**). The Dividends Declared account is simply brought to zero on the worksheet. However, note that Entry **D** increases the Investment in Sun balance. As part of

EXHIBIT 3.11 Comparisons of Parrot Company Journal Entries Across Initial Value and Partial Equity Methods

Parrot Company Books Initial Value Method 2020			Parrot Company Books Partial Equity Method 2020		
Dividend Receivable	40,000		Dividend Receivable	40,000	
Dividend Income		40,000	Investment in Sun Company		40,000
Subsidiary dividends declared.			Subsidiary dividends declared.		
Cash	40,000		Cash	40,000	
Dividend Receivable		40,000	Dividend Receivable		40,000
To record the receipt of the cash dividend.			To record the receipt of the cash dividend.		
			Investment in Sun Company	100,000	
			Equity in Subsidiary Earnings		100,000
			Accrual of subsidiary income.		

the investment elimination sequence, this increase offsets the reduction in the Investment in Sun account recorded when the parent recognized the subsidiary dividend. All other consolidation entries (Entries **S, A,** and **E**) are the same for all three methods.

LO 3-4

Understand that a parent's internal accounting method for its subsidiary investments has no effect on the resulting consolidated financial statements.

Comparisons across Internal Investment Methods

Consolidated financial worksheets have now been completed when the parent uses the equity, initial value, and partial equity methods. At this point, it is instructive to compare the final consolidated balances in Exhibits 3.5, 3.9, and 3.10. Note the identical final consolidated column balances across the three internal methods of investment accounting. Thus, the parent's internal investment method choice has no effect on the resulting consolidated financial statements.

Consolidation Subsequent to Year of Acquisition—Initial Value and Partial Equity Methods

By again incorporating the December 31, 2023, financial data for Parrot and Sun (presented in Exhibit 3.7), consolidation procedures for the initial value method and the partial equity method are examined for years subsequent to the date of acquisition. *In both cases, establishment of an appropriate beginning retained earnings figure becomes a significant goal of the consolidation.*

Conversion of the Parent's Retained Earnings to a Full-Accrual (Equity) Basis

Consolidated financial statements require a *full accrual-based measurement of both income and retained earnings.* The initial value method, however, recognizes income when the subsidiary declares a dividend, thus ignoring when the underlying income was earned. The partial equity method only partially accrues subsidiary income. Thus, neither provides a full accrual-based measure of the subsidiary activities on the parent's income. As a result, over time the parent's retained earnings account fails to show a full accrual-based amount. Therefore, new worksheet adjustments are required to convert the parent's beginning-of-the-year retained earnings balance to a full-accrual basis. These adjustments are made to *beginning-of-the-year retained earnings* because current-year earnings are readily converted to full-accrual basis by simply combining current-year revenue and expenses. The resulting current-year combined income figure is then added to the adjusted beginning-of-the-year retained earnings to arrive at a full-accrual ending retained earnings balance.

This concern was not faced previously when the equity method was adopted. Under that approach, the parent's Retained Earnings account balance already reflects a full-accrual basis so that no adjustment is necessary. In the earlier illustration, the $330,000 income accrual for the 2020–2022 period as well as the $21,000 amortization expense was recognized by the parent in applying the equity method (see Exhibit 3.6). Having been recorded in this manner, these two balances form a permanent part of Parrot's retained earnings and are included automatically in the consolidated total. Consequently, if the equity method is applied, the process is simplified; no worksheet entries are needed to adjust the parent's Retained Earnings account to record subsidiary operations or amortization for past years.

Conversely, if a method other than the equity method is used, a worksheet change must be made to the parent's beginning Retained Earnings account (in every subsequent year) to equate this balance with a full-accrual amount. To quantify this adjustment, the parent's recognized income for these past three years under each method is first determined (Exhibit 3.12). For consolidation purposes, the beginning Retained Earnings account must then be increased or decreased to create the same effect as the equity method.

EXHIBIT 3.12
Retained Earnings Differences

PARROT COMPANY AND SUN COMPANY
Previous Years—2020–2022

	Equity Method	Initial Value Method	Partial Equity Method
Equity accrual	$330,000	$ –0–	$330,000
Dividend income	–0–	110,000	–0–
Excess amortization expenses	(21,000)	–0–	–0–
Increase in parent's retained earnings	$309,000	$110,000	$330,000

Initial Value Method Applied—Subsequent Consolidation

As shown in Exhibit 3.12, if Parrot applied the initial value method during the 2020–2022 period, it recognizes $199,000 less income than under the equity method ($309,000 – $110,000). Two items cause this difference. First, Parrot has not accrued the $220,000 increase in the subsidiary's book value across the periods prior to the current year. Although the $110,000 in dividends was recorded as income, the parent never recognized the remainder of the $330,000 earned by the subsidiary.[7] Second, no accounting has been made of the $21,000 excess amortization expenses. Thus, the parent's beginning Retained Earnings account is $199,000 ($220,000 – $21,000) below the appropriate consolidated total and must be adjusted.[8]

To simulate the equity method so that the parent's beginning Retained Earnings account reflects a full-accrual basis, this $199,000 increase is recorded through a worksheet entry. The initial value method figures reported by the parent effectively are converted into equity method balances.

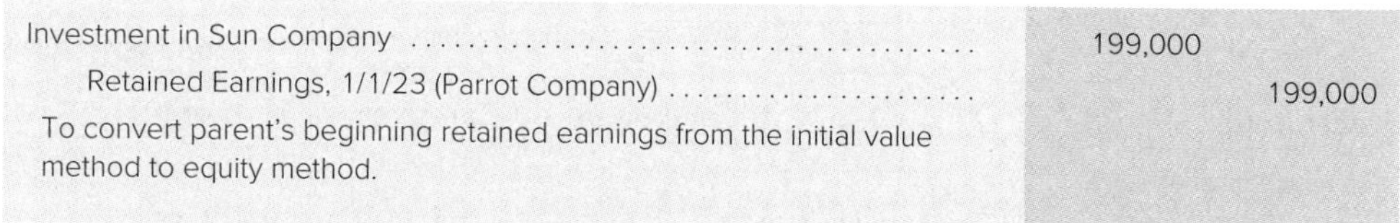

Investment in Sun Company	199,000	
Retained Earnings, 1/1/23 (Parrot Company)		199,000
To convert parent's beginning retained earnings from the initial value method to equity method.		

This adjustment is labeled Entry ***C**. The *C* refers to the **c**onversion being made to equity method (full-accrual) totals. The asterisk indicates that this equity simulation relates solely to transactions of prior periods. Thus, *Entry *C should be recorded before the other worksheet entries to align the beginning balances for the year.*

Exhibit 3.13 provides a complete presentation of the consolidation of Parrot and Sun as of December 31, 2023, based on the parent's application of the initial value method. After Entry ***C** has been recorded on the worksheet, the remainder of this consolidation follows the same pattern as previous examples. Sun's stockholders' equity accounts are eliminated (Entry **S**) while the allocations stemming from the $800,000 initial fair value are recorded (Entry **A**) at their unamortized balances as of January 1, 2023 (see Exhibit 3.8). Intra-entity dividend income is removed (Entry **I**), and current-year excess amortization expenses are recognized (Entry **E**). To complete this process, the intra-entity receivable and payable of $40,000 are offset (Entry **P**).

In retrospect, the only new element introduced here is the adjustment of the parent's beginning Retained Earnings. For a consolidation produced after the initial year of acquisition, an Entry ***C** is required if the parent has not applied the equity method.

Partial Equity Method Applied—Subsequent Consolidation

Exhibit 3.14 demonstrates the worksheet consolidation of Parrot and Sun as of December 31, 2023, when the investment accounts have been recorded by the parent using the partial equity method. This approach accrues subsidiary income each year but records no other equity adjustments. Therefore, as of December 31, 2023, Parrot's Investment in Sun Company account has a balance of $1,110,000:

[7] Two different calculations are available for determining the $220,000 in nonrecorded income for prior years. (1) subsidiary income less dividends declared and (2) the change in the subsidiary's book value as of the first day of the current year. The second method works only if the subsidiary has had no other equity transactions such as the issuance of new stock or the purchase of treasury shares. Unless otherwise stated, the assumption is made that no such transactions have occurred.

[8] Because neither the income in excess of dividends nor excess amortization is recorded by the parent under the initial value method, its beginning Retained Earnings account is $199,000 less than the $2,044,000 reported under the equity method (Exhibit 3.7). Thus, a $1,845,000 balance is shown in Exhibit 3.12 ($2,044,000 less $199,000). Conversely, if the partial equity method had been applied, Parrot's absence of amortization would cause the Retained Earnings account to be $21,000 higher than the figure derived by the equity method. For this reason, Exhibit 3.13 shows the parent with a beginning Retained Earnings account of $2,065,000 rather than $2,044,000.

Fair value of consideration transferred for Sun Company 1/1/20		$ 800,000
Sun Company's 2020–2022 increase in book value:		
Accrual of Sun Company's income	$330,000	
Sun Company's dividends	(110,000)	220,000
Sun Company's 2023 operations:		
Accrual of Sun Company's income	$160,000	
Sun Company's dividends	(70,000)	90,000
Investment in Sun Company, 12/31/23 (Partial equity method)		$1,110,000

EXHIBIT 3.13 Consolidation Worksheet Subsequent to Year of Acquisition—Initial Value Method Applied

PARROT COMPANY AND SUN COMPANY
Consolidation Worksheet
For Year Ending December 31, 2023

Investment: Initial Value Method

Accounts	Parrot Company	Sun Company	Consolidation Entries Debit	Consolidation Entries Credit	Consolidation Totals
Income Statement					
Revenues	(2,100,000)	(600,000)			(2,700,000)
Cost of goods sold	1,000,000	380,000			1,380,000
Amortization expense	200,000	20,000	(E) 13,000		233,000
Depreciation expense	100,000	40,000		(E) 6,000	134,000
Dividend income	(70,000)*	–0–	(I) 70,000*		–0–
Net income	(870,000)	(160,000)			(953,000)
Statement of Retained Earnings					
Retained earnings, 1/1/23					
Parrot Company	(1,845,000)[†]*			(*C) 199,000*	(2,044,000)
Sun Company		(600,000)	(S) 600,000		–0–
Net income (above)	(870,000)	(160,000)			(953,000)
Dividends declared	420,000	70,000		(I) 70,000*	420,000
Retained earnings, 12/31/23	(2,295,000)	(690,000)			(2,577,000)
Balance Sheet					
Current assets	1,705,000	500,000		(P) 40,000	2,165,000
Investment in Sun Company	800,000*	–0–	(*C) 199,000	(S) 820,000 (A) 179,000	–0–
Trademarks	600,000	240,000	(A) 20,000		860,000
Patented technology	540,000	420,000	(A) 91,000	(E) 13,000	1,038,000
Equipment (net)	420,000	210,000	(E) 6,000	(A) 12,000	624,000
Goodwill	–0–	–0–	(A) 80,000		80,000
Total assets	4,065,000	1,370,000			4,767,000
Liabilities	(1,050,000)	(460,000)	(P) 40,000		(1,470,000)
Common stock	(600,000)	(200,000)	(S) 200,000		(600,000)
Additional paid-in capital	(120,000)	(20,000)	(S) 20,000		(120,000)
Retained earnings, 12/31/23 (above)	(2,295,000)	(690,000)			(2,577,000)
Total liabilities and equities	(4,065,000)	(1,370,000)	1,339,000	1,339,000	(4,767,000)

Note: Parentheses indicate a credit balance.
*Boxed items highlight differences with consolidation in Exhibit 3.7.
[†]See footnote 8.
Consolidation entries:
(*C) To convert parent's beginning retained earnings to full accrual basis.
(S) Elimination of Sun's stockholders' equity January 1 balances and the book value portion of investment account.
(A) Allocation of Sun's excess acquisition-date fair value over book value, unamortized balance as of beginning of year.
(I) Elimination of intra-entity dividend income and dividends declared by Sun.
(E) Recognition of current-year excess fair-value amortization and depreciation expenses.
(P) Elimination of intra-entity receivable/payable.
Note: Consolidation entry (D) is not needed when the parent applies the initial value method because entry (I) eliminates the intra-entity dividend effects.

EXHIBIT 3.14 Consolidation Worksheet Subsequent to Year of Acquisition—Partial Equity Method Applied

PARROT COMPANY AND SUN COMPANY
Consolidation Worksheet
For Year Ending December 31, 2023

Investment: Partial Equity Method

Accounts	Parrot Company	Sun Company	Consolidation Entries Debit	Consolidation Entries Credit	Consolidation Totals
Income Statement					
Revenues	(2,100,000)	(600,000)			(2,700,000)
Cost of goods sold	1,000,000	380,000			1,380,000
Amortization expense	200,000	20,000	(E) 13,000		233,000
Depreciation expense	100,000	40,000		(E) 6,000	134,000
Equity in subsidiary earnings	(160,000)*	–0–	(I) 160,000*		–0–
Net income	(960,000)	(160,000)			(953,000)
Statement of Retained Earnings					
Retained earnings, 1/1/23					
Parrot Company	(2,065,000)[†]*		(*C) 21,000*		(2,044,000)
Sun Company		(600,000)	(S) 600,000		–0–
Net income (above)	(960,000)	(160,000)			(953,000)
Dividends declared	420,000	70,000		(D) 70,000*	420,000
Retained earnings, 12/31/23	(2,605,000)	(690,000)			(2,577,000)
Balance Sheet					
Current assets	1,705,000	500,000		(P) 40,000	2,165,000
Investment in Sun Company	1,110,000*	–0–	(D) 70,000	(*C) 21,000*	–0–
				(S) 820,000	
				(A) 179,000	
				(I) 160,000*	
Trademarks	600,000	240,000	(A) 20,000		860,000
Patented technology	540,000	420,000	(A) 91,000	(E) 13,000	1,038,000
Equipment (net)	420,000	210,000	(E) 6,000	(A) 12,000	624,000
Goodwill	–0–	–0–	(A) 80,000		80,000
Total assets	4,375,000	1,370,000			4,767,000
Liabilities	(1,050,000)	(460,000)	(P) 40,000		(1,470,000)
Common stock	(600,000)	(200,000)	(S) 200,000		(600,000)
Additional paid-in capital	(120,000)	(20,000)	(S) 20,000		(120,000)
Retained earnings, 12/31/23 (above)	(2,605,000)	(690,000)			(2,577,000)
Total liabilities and equities	(4,375,000)	(1,370,000)	1,321,000	1,321,000	(4,767,000)

Note: Parentheses indicate a credit balance.
*Boxed items highlight differences with consolidation in Exhibit 3.7.
[†]See footnote 8.
Consolidation entries:
(*C) To convert parent's beginning retained earnings to full accrual basis.
(S) Elimination of Sun's stockholders' equity January 1 balances and the book value portion of investment account.
(A) Allocation of Sun's excess acquisition-date fair over book value, unamortized balance as of beginning of year.
(I) Elimination of parent's equity in subsidiary earnings accrual.
(D) Elimination of intra-entity dividends.
(E) Recognition of current-year excess fair-value amortization and depreciation expenses.
(P) Elimination of intra-entity receivable/payable.

As indicated here and in Exhibit 3.12, Parrot has recognized the yearly equity income accrual but not amortization. When the parent employs the partial equity method, the parent's beginning Retained Earnings account must be adjusted to include this expense. Therefore, Entry ***C** provides the three-year $21,000 amortization total to simulate the equity method and, hence, consolidated totals.

Discussion Question

In consolidation worksheet entry *C, we adjust the parent's *beginning of the year* retained earnings to a full accrual basis. Why don't we adjust to the parent's *end of the year* retained earnings balance using consolidation worksheet entry *C?

Clearly, in a consolidated balance sheet, we wish to report the parent's end-of-period consolidated retained earnings at its full-accrual GAAP basis. To accomplish this goal, we utilize the following separate individual components of end-of-period retained earnings available on the worksheet.

Beginning-of-the year balance (after *C adjustment if parent does not employ equity method)
+ Net income (parent's share of consolidated net income adjusted to full accrual by combining revenues and expenses—including excess acquisition-date fair value amortizations)
– Dividends (parent's dividends)
= End of the year balance

The worksheet provides for the computation of current year full-accrual consolidated net income via the income statement section. Dividends are already provided in the retained earnings section of the consolidated worksheet. The only component of the ending balance of retained earnings that requires a special adjustment (*C) is the beginning balance.

How does the consolidation worksheet entry *C differ when the parent uses the initial value method versus the partial equity method? Why is no *C adjustment needed when consolidated statements are prepared for the first fiscal year-end after the business combination?

*Consolidation Entry *C*

Retained Earnings, 1/1/23 (Parrot Company)	21,000	
Investment in Sun Company		21,000
To convert parent's beginning Retained Earnings from partial equity method to equity method by including excess amortizations.		

By recording Entry ***C** on the worksheet, all of the subsidiary's operational results for the 2020–2022 period are included in the consolidation. As shown in Exhibit 3.14, the remainder of the worksheet entries follow the same basic pattern as that illustrated previously for the year of acquisition (Exhibit 3.10).

Summary of Worksheet Procedures

Having three investment methods available to the parent means that three sets of entries must be understood to arrive at reported figures appropriate for a business combination. The process can initially seem to be a confusing overlap of procedures. However, at this point in the coverage, only three worksheet entries actually are affected by the choice of either the equity method, partial equity method, or initial value method: Entries ***C, I,** and **D.** Furthermore, accountants should never get so involved with a worksheet and its entries that they lose sight of the balances that this process is designed to calculate. Exhibit 3.15 provides a summary of the final consolidated totals and how they are calculated. These figures are never affected by the parent's choice of an accounting method.

After the appropriate balance for each account is understood, worksheet entries assist the accountant in deriving these figures. To help clarify the consolidation process required under each of the three accounting methods, Exhibit 3.16 describes the purpose of each worksheet entry: first during the year of acquisition and second for any period following the year of acquisition.

EXHIBIT 3.15
Consolidated Totals Subsequent to Acquisition*

Current revenues	Parent revenues are included. Subsidiary revenues are included but only for the period since the acquisition.
Current expenses	Parent expenses are included. Subsidiary expenses are included but only for the period since the acquisition. Amortization expenses of the excess fair-value allocations are included by recognition on the worksheet.
Investment (or dividend) income	Income recognized by parent is eliminated and effectively replaced by the subsidiary's revenues and expenses.
Retained earnings, beginning balance	Parent balance is included. The change in the subsidiary balance since acquisition is included either as a regular accrual by the parent or through a worksheet entry to increase parent balance. Past amortization expenses of the excess fair-value allocations are included either as a part of parent balance or through a worksheet entry.
Assets and liabilities	Parent balances are included. Subsidiary balances are included after adjusting for acquisition-date fair values less amortization to beginning of current period. Intra-entity receivable/payable balances are eliminated.
Goodwill Investment in subsidiary	Original fair-value allocation is included unless reduced by impairment. Asset account recorded by parent is eliminated on the worksheet so that the balance is not included in consolidated figures.
Capital stock and additional paid-in capital	Parent balances only are included although they will have been adjusted at acquisition date if stock was issued.

*The next few chapters discuss the necessity of altering some of these balances for consolidation purposes. Thus, this table is not definitive but is included only to provide a basic overview of the consolidation process as it has been described to this point.

EXHIBIT 3.16 Consolidation Worksheet Entries

Equity Method Applied		Initial Value Method Applied	Partial Equity Method Applied
Any Time during Year of Acquisition			
Entry **S**	Beginning stockholders' equity of subsidiary is eliminated against book value portion of investment account.	Same as equity method.	Same as equity method.
Entry **A**	Excess fair value is allocated to assets and liabilities based on difference in book values and fair values; residual is assigned to goodwill.	Same as equity method.	Same as equity method.
Entry **I**	Equity income accrual (including amortization expense) is eliminated.	Dividend income is eliminated.	Equity income accrual is eliminated.
Entry **D**	Intra-entity dividends declared by subsidiary are eliminated.	No entry—intra-entity dividends are eliminated in Entry **I.**	Same as equity method.
Entry **E**	Current-year excess amortization expenses of fair-value allocations are recorded.	Same as equity method.	Same as equity method.
Entry **P**	Intra-entity payable/receivable balances are offset.	Same as equity method.	Same as equity method.

(continued)

EXHIBIT 3.16 (continued)

Equity Method Applied		Initial Value Method Applied	Partial Equity Method Applied
Any Time Following Year of Acquisition			
Entry ***C**	No entry—equity income for prior years has already been recognized along with amortization expenses.	Increase in subsidiary's book value during prior years and excess amortization expenses are recognized (conversion is made to equity method).	Excess amortization expenses for prior years are recognized (conversion is made to equity method).
Entry **S**	Same as initial year.	Same as initial year.	Same as initial year.
Entry **A**	Unamortized excess fair value at beginning of year is allocated to specific accounts and to goodwill.	Same as equity method.	Same as equity method.
Entry **I**	Same as initial year.	Same as initial year.	Same as initial year.
Entry **D**	Same as initial year.	Same as initial year.	Same as initial year.
Entry **E**	Same as initial year.	Same as initial year.	Same as initial year.
Entry **P**	Same as initial year.	Same as initial year.	Same as initial year.

Excess Fair Value Attributable to Subsidiary Long-Term Debt: Postacquisition Procedures

In the previous consolidation examples for Parrot and Sun Company, the acquisition-date excess fair values were attributed solely to long-term assets. Similarly, however, the acquisition-date fair value of subsidiary long-term debt may also differ from its carrying amount. Although the long-term debt adjustment to fair value is relatively straightforward, the adjustments to interest expense in periods subsequent to acquisition require additional analysis.

In subsequent periods, the acquisition-date fair value adjustment to long-term debt is amortized to interest expense over the remaining life of the debt. When the acquisition-date fair value of subsidiary long-term debt exceeds its carrying amount on the subsidiary's books, the parent increases the value of the debt reported on its consolidated balance sheet (and vice versa). Consequently, when the parent reflects the increased value of the subsidiary's long-term debt valuation, it must reduce interest expense recognized on the consolidated income statement over the debt's remaining life. When the long-term debt valuation is decreased, interest expense increases.

Exhibit 3.17 summarizes the worksheet effects when acquisition-date long-term debt's carrying amount differs from its fair value.

At first glance, it may seem counterintuitive that when long-term debt is ***increased,*** interest expense is ***decreased.*** Certainly for plant assets like equipment, when we increase their carrying amounts to acquisition-date fair values on the worksheet, we increase the related depreciation expense. Why do we seem to do the opposite for long-term liabilities?

The answer can be seen in the fact that even though the acquisition-date fair value of the subsidiary's long-term debt exceeds its carrying amount, the acquisition does not affect the

EXHIBIT 3.17 Long-Term Debt: Consolidation Worksheet Adjustments

Long-Term Debt Valuation at Acquisition Date	Worksheet Adjustment to Long-Term Debt	Worksheet Adjustment to Interest Expense
Fair value > Carrying amount	Increase long-term debt to adjust to fair value (less previous periods interest amortization)	Debit Long-Term Debt and credit Interest Expense
Fair value < Carrying amount	Decrease long-term debt to adjust to fair value (less previous periods interest amortization)	Debit Interest Expense and credit Long-Term Debt

EXHIBIT 3.18 Acquisition-Date Long-Term Debt Valuation

	Long-Term Debt January 1, 2020	Long-Term Debt Maturity Value January 1, 2025
Fair value	$105,000	$100,000
Carrying amount	100,000	100,000

subsidiary's contractual obligation for repaying the debt. The ultimate amount of debt to be repaid at maturity remains the same. For example, assume Pax Company acquires Sax Company on January 1, 2020. Exhibit 3.18 provides information about Sax Company's long-term debt.

By acquiring Sax, Pax has taken on (and effectively borrowed) $105,000 of fair-value debt but will only have to pay back $100,000 at the debt's maturity date. As shown in Exhibit 3.19, the additional $5,000 excess fair over book value (that will not be repaid) is recognized as a reduction in overall interest expense, similar to amortizing a bond premium. Therefore, when consolidated statements are prepared, interest expense is reduced over the life of the long-term debt.

To complete this example, we assume the sole acquisition-date excess fair-value adjustment made by Pax Company is to long-term debt, and straight-line amortization is used for the interest adjustments.

Finally, the carrying amount of a subsidiary's long-term debt may exceed its fair value. In that case, a consolidation entry is required to decrease the long-term debt reported in the consolidated balance sheet. Then, in periods subsequent to acquisition, worksheet entries are also needed to increase the amount of interest expense to be recognized in the consolidated income statement.

Goodwill Impairment

LO 3-5

Discuss the rationale for the goodwill impairment testing approach.

FASB ASC Topic 350, "Intangibles—Goodwill and Other," provides accounting standards for determining, measuring, and reporting goodwill impairment losses. Because goodwill is considered to have an indefinite life, an impairment approach is used rather than amortization. The FASB reasoned that although goodwill can decrease over time, it does not do so in the "rational and systematic" manner that periodic amortization suggests. Only upon recognition of an impairment loss (or partial sale of a subsidiary) will goodwill decline from one period

EXHIBIT 3.19 Worksheet Adjustments for Excess Acquisition-Date Fair Value Attributable to Subsidiary Long-Term Debt

December 31, 2020, Consolidation Worksheet		
Consolidation Entry A		
Investment in Sax Company	5,000	
Long-term debt		5,000
To adjust the subsidiary's long-term debt to acquisition-date fair value.		
Consolidation Entry E		
Long-term debt	1,000	
Interest expense		1,000
To recognize the reduction in current-year interest expense.		
December 31, 2021, Consolidation Worksheet		
Consolidation Entry A		
Investment in Sax Company	4,000	
Long-term debt		4,000
To adjust the subsidiary's long-term debt to unamortized balance as of the beginning of the year ($5,000 – $1,000 from year 2020).		
Consolidation Entry E		
Long-term debt	1,000	
Interest expense		1,000
To recognize the reduction in current-year interest expense.		

EXHIBIT 3.20
Recent Goodwill Impairments

Company	Impairment
General Electric	$ 22.0 billion
Heinz-Kraft	7.3 billion
CVS Health	6.1 billion
Verizon	4.6 billion
Frontier Communications	2.7 billion
Community Health Systems	1.4 billion
Discovery, Inc.	1.3 billion
Lowes	952.0 million
GameStop	557.3 million
Accto	235.1 million
Starbucks	69.3 million

to the next. Goodwill impairment losses are reported as operating items in the consolidated income statement.

The notion of an indefinite life allows many firms to report over time the original amount of goodwill recognized in a business combination. However, goodwill can become impaired, requiring loss recognition and a reduction in the amount reported in the consolidated balance sheet. Evidence shows that goodwill impairment losses can be substantial. Exhibit 3.20 provides examples of some recent goodwill impairment losses. Unlike amortization, which periodically reduces asset values, impairment must first be revealed before a write-down is justified. Accounting standards therefore require periodic tests for goodwill impairment.

Goodwill impairment tests are performed at the reporting unit level within a combined entity. As discussed next, all assets acquired (including goodwill) and liabilities assumed in a business combination must be assigned to *reporting units* within a consolidated enterprise. The goodwill residing in each reporting unit is then separately subjected to periodic impairment reviews. Current financial reporting standards require, at a minimum, an annual assessment for potential goodwill impairment.

Because impairment testing procedures can be costly, the FASB provides firms the option to first conduct a *qualitative* analysis to assess whether further testing procedures are appropriate. If circumstances indicate a potential decline in the fair value of a reporting unit below its carrying amount, then a further test determines the existence of goodwill impairment. Our coverage of goodwill impairment addresses the following:

- The assignment of acquired goodwill to reporting units.
- The option to conduct an annual qualitative test for potential goodwill impairment.
- The goodwill impairment testing procedure.
- Comparison with international accounting standards.

Assigning Goodwill to Reporting Units

Combined companies typically organize themselves into separate *units* along distinct operating lines. Each individual operating unit has responsibility for managing its assets and liabilities to earn profits for the combined entity. These operating units report information about their earnings activities to top management to support decision making. Such operating units are known as *reporting units.*

Following a business combination, the identifiable assets and liabilities acquired are assigned to the firm's reporting units based on where they will be employed. Any amount assigned to goodwill also is assigned to reporting units expected to benefit from the synergies of the combination. Thus, any individual reporting unit where goodwill resides is the appropriate level for goodwill impairment testing.

In practice, firms often assign goodwill to reporting units either at the level of a reporting segment—as described in ASC Topic 280, "Segment Reporting"—or at a lower level within a segment of a combined enterprise. Reporting units may thus include the following:

- A component of an operating segment at a level below that operating segment. Segment management should review and assess performance at this level. Also, the component should be a business in which discrete financial information is available and should differ economically from other components of the operating segment.

- The segments of an enterprise.
- The entire enterprise.

For example, AT&T, Inc. is a provider of communications and digital entertainment services. In its recent annual report, AT&T identified its principal operating segments (or one level below them) as reporting units:

> Goodwill is tested by comparing the book value of each reporting unit, deemed to be our principal operating segments or one level below them (Business Solutions, Entertainment Group, Consumer Mobility, and Mexico Wireless, Brazil and PanAmericana in the International segment), to the fair value using both discounted cash flow as well as market multiple approaches.

Thus, all goodwill impairment testing is performed at the reporting unit level, rather than collectively at the combined entity level. Separate testing of goodwill within individual reporting units also prevents the masking of goodwill impairment in one reporting unit with contemporaneous increases in the value of goodwill in other reporting units.

LO 3-6

Describe the procedures for conducting a goodwill impairment test.

Qualitative Assessment Option

Because goodwill impairment tests require firms to calculate fair values for their reporting units each year, such a comprehensive measurement exercise can be costly. To help reduce costs, FASB ASC Topic 305 allows an entity the option to first assess qualitative factors to determine whether more rigorous testing for goodwill impairment is needed.[9] The qualitative approach assesses the *likelihood* that a reporting unit's fair value is less than its carrying amount. The more-likely-than-not threshold is defined as having a likelihood of more than 50 percent.

In assessing whether a reporting unit's fair value exceeds its carrying amount, a firm must examine all relevant facts and circumstances, including

- Macroeconomic conditions such as a deterioration in general economic conditions, limitations on accessing capital, fluctuations in foreign exchange rates, or other developments in equity and credit markets.
- Industry and market considerations such as a deterioration in the environment in which an entity operates, an increased competitive environment, a decline (both absolute and relative to its peers) in market-dependent multiples or metrics, a change in the market for an entity's products or services, or a regulatory or political development.
- Cost factors such as increases in raw materials, labor, or other costs that have a negative effect on earnings.
- Overall financial performance such as negative or declining cash flows or a decline in actual or planned revenue or earnings.
- Other relevant entity-specific events such as changes in management, key personnel, strategy, or customers; contemplation of bankruptcy; or litigation.
- Events affecting a reporting unit such as a change in the carrying amount of its net assets, a more-likely-than-not expectation of selling or disposing all or a portion of a reporting unit, the testing for recoverability of a significant asset group within a reporting unit, or recognition of a goodwill impairment loss in the financial statements of a subsidiary that is a component of a reporting unit.
- If applicable, a sustained decrease (both absolute and relative to its peers) in share price. (FASB ASC, para. 350-20-35-3C)

The underlying rationale for comparing a reporting unit's fair value and carrying amount is as follows. If a reporting unit's fair value is deemed greater than its carrying amount, then its collective net assets are maintaining their value. It then can be argued that a decline in

[9] An entity, on the basis of its discretion, may bypass the qualitative assessment for any reporting unit in any period and proceed directly to performing the quantitative impairment test. An entity may resume performing the qualitative assessment in any subsequent period (FASB ASC, para. 350-20-35-3B).

any particular asset (i.e., goodwill) within the reporting unit is also unlikely, and no further impairment tests are necessary. On the other hand, if the relevant facts and circumstances listed earlier suggest that a reporting unit's fair value is likely less than its carrying amount, then a quantitative test for goodwill impairment is appropriate. Nonetheless, a qualitative assessment of a sufficient fair value for a reporting unit circumvents further goodwill impairment testing.

The FASB ASC (para. 350-20-35-28) requires an entity to assess its goodwill for impairment annually for each of its reporting units where goodwill resides. Moreover, more frequent impairment assessment is required if events or circumstances change that make it more likely than not that a reporting unit's fair value has fallen below its carrying amount.

Testing Goodwill for Impairment

In contrast to the qualitative assessment, goodwill impairment measurement relies on quantitative fair-value measures for reporting units as a whole as compared to their individually respective carrying amounts. If, after performing the qualitative assessment described earlier, an entity concludes that it is more likely than not that the fair value of a reporting unit is less than its carrying amount, then the entity is required to proceed to quantitative goodwill impairment testing.

Goodwill Impairment Test: Is the Carrying Amount of a Reporting Unit More Than Its Fair Value?

For impairment testing, the consolidated entity calculates fair values for each of its reporting units with allocated goodwill. Each reporting unit's fair value is then compared with its carrying amount (*including goodwill*)[10]. If an individual reporting unit's fair value exceeds its carrying amount, its goodwill is not considered impaired—goodwill remains at its current carrying amount. Alternatively, if the fair value of a reporting unit has fallen below its carrying amount, then goodwill impairment is measured as the excess of the carrying amount over the fair value of the reporting unit, and a loss is recognized. The impairment loss equals the excess of the carrying amount of the reporting unit goodwill over its fair value. However, the impairment loss is limited to the carrying amount of goodwill.[11]

Illustration—Accounting and Reporting for a Goodwill Impairment Loss

To illustrate the testing procedures for goodwill impairment, assume that on January 1, 2020, investors form Newcall Corporation to consolidate the telecommunications operations of DSM, Inc., and VisionTalk Company in a deal valued at $2.2 billion. Newcall organizes each former firm as an operating segment. Additionally, DSM comprises two divisions—DSM Wired and DSM Wireless—that, along with VisionTalk, are treated as independent reporting units for internal performance evaluation and management reviews. Newcall recognizes $215 million as goodwill at the merger date and allocates this entire amount to its reporting units as follows:

Newcall's Reporting Units	Goodwill Assigned at Acquisition Date
DSM Wired	$ 22,000,000
DSM Wireless	155,000,000
VisionTalk	38,000,000

[10] A reporting unit's carrying amount simply consists of the net sum of the values of the assets and liabilities assigned to that reporting unit. When an acquired subsidiary is designated in its entirety as a reporting unit, and the parent employs the equity method, then the parent's investment in subsidiary account reflects that reporting unit's carrying amount.

[11] Prior to 2020, goodwill impairment standards relied on comparisons across goodwill's implied value and its carrying amount (known as Step 2 of the legacy ASC 350). The goodwill implied value computation required fair value determinations for each reporting unit's assets and liabilities and thus was considered costly. The new standard (ASU 2017-04) shown in this text simplifies goodwill impairment testing and is effective for fiscal years beginning after December 15, 2019, for public business entities with early adoption permitted.

In December 2020, Newcall performs a qualitative analysis for each of its three reporting units to assess potential goodwill impairment. Accordingly, Newcall examines the relevant events and circumstances that may affect the fair values of its reporting units. The analysis reveals that the fair value of each reporting unit likely exceeds its carrying amount—except for DSM Wireless, which has had difficulty realizing expected cost-saving synergies with VisionTalk.

Because the DSM Wireless reporting unit has failed the qualitative assessment for goodwill impairment, Newcall must now proceed to the quantitative goodwill impairment test. Consequently, Newcall computes the following December 31, 2020, amounts for its DSM Wireless reporting unit:

December 31, 2020	Fair Value	Carrying Amount
DSM Wireless reporting unit as a whole	$650,000,000	$720,000,000*

* Reporting unit's assets (including goodwill) – liabilities.

Then, to measure any goodwill impairment, Newcall compares the fair value of the DSM Wireless reporting unit to its carrying amount as follows:

DSM Wireless December 31, 2020, carrying amount before impairment	$720,000,000
DSM Wireless December 31, 2020, fair value	650,000,000
Goodwill impairment loss	$ 70,000,000

Thus, Newcall reports a $70,000,000 goodwill impairment loss as a separate line item in the operating section of its consolidated income statement. As of December 31, 2020, Newcall reports $85,000,000 of goodwill ($155,000,000 less $70,000,000 goodwill impairment loss) for its DSM Wireless reporting unit. Additional disclosures are required describing (1) the facts and circumstances leading to the impairment and (2) the method of determining the fair value of the associated reporting unit (e.g., market prices, comparable business, present value technique, etc.). The reported amounts for the other assets and liabilities of DSM Wireless remain the same and are not changed based on the goodwill testing procedure.

The only exception to the previously mentioned impairment measurement occurs when the initially computed goodwill impairment loss exceeds the carrying amount of goodwill. In the Newcall example, the DSM reporting unit's goodwill carrying amount of $155,000,000 is sufficient to absorb the $70,000,000 impairment. However, if the reporting unit's goodwill carrying amount was less than $70,000,000, the goodwill impairment loss would be limited to the lower carrying amount. Thus, the impairment loss cannot exceed the carrying amount of any particular reporting unit's goodwill.

Comparisons with International Accounting Standards

International Financial Reporting Standards (IFRS) and U.S. GAAP both require goodwill recognition in a business combination when the fair value of the consideration transferred exceeds the net fair values of the assets acquired and liabilities assumed. Subsequent to acquisition, both IFRS and U.S. GAAP require an assessment for goodwill impairment at least annually, and more frequently in the presence of indicators of possible impairment. Also, for both sets of standards, goodwill impairments, once recognized, are not recoverable. However, differences exist across the two sets of standards in the way goodwill impairment is tested for and recognized. In particular, goodwill allocation, impairment testing, and determination of the impairment loss differ across the two reporting regimes as discussed next.

Goodwill Allocation

- *U.S. GAAP.* Goodwill acquired in a business combination is allocated to reporting units expected to benefit from the goodwill. Reporting units are operating segments or a business component one level below an operating segment.

- *IFRS.* International Accounting Standard *(IAS) 36* requires goodwill acquired in a business combination to be allocated to cash-generating units (CGU) or groups of CGUs that are expected to benefit from the synergies of the business combination. CGUs represent the lowest level within the entity at which the goodwill is monitored for internal management purposes and are not to be larger than an operating segment as determined in accordance with *IFRS 8,* "Operating Segments."

Impairment Testing

- *U.S. GAAP.* Firms have the option to perform a qualitative assessment to evaluate possible goodwill impairment based on a greater than 50 percent likelihood that a reporting unit's fair value is less than its carrying amount. If such a likelihood exists, then a reporting unit's total fair value is compared to its carrying amount. If the carrying amount exceeds fair value, a goodwill impairment loss is recognized for the difference, limited to the carrying amount of goodwill assigned to the reporting unit.
- *IFRS.* No similar qualitative assessment option for goodwill impairment (as in U.S. GAAP) exists under IFRS. Instead, a one-step approach compares the carrying amount (including goodwill) and *recoverable amounts* of each cash-generating unit where goodwill resides. The recoverable amount is the higher of fair value less cost to sell and value in use[12] of the cash-generating unit. If the carrying amount exceeds the recoverable amount of the cash-generating unit, then goodwill (and possibly other assets of the cash-generating unit) is considered impaired.

Determination of the Impairment Loss

- *U.S. GAAP.* Goodwill impairment is computed as the excess of a reporting unit's carrying amount over its fair value. Goodwill impairment is limited to its carrying amount for each reporting unit.
- *IFRS.* Any excess carrying amount over recoverable amount for a cash-generating unit is first assigned to reduce goodwill. If goodwill is reduced to zero, then the other assets of the cash-generating unit are reduced pro rata based on the carrying amounts of the cash-generating unit's assets.

LO 3-7

Describe the rationale and procedures for impairment testing for intangible assets other than goodwill.

Amortization and Impairment of Other Intangibles

As discussed in Chapter 2, the acquisition method governs how we initially consolidate the assets acquired and liabilities assumed in a business combination. Subsequent to acquisition, income determination becomes a regular part of the consolidation process. The fair-value bases (established at the acquisition date) for definite-lived subsidiary assets acquired and liabilities assumed will be amortized over their remaining lives for income recognition. For indefinite-lived assets (e.g., goodwill, certain other intangibles), an impairment model is used to assess whether asset write-downs are appropriate.

Current accounting standards suggest categories of intangible assets for possible recognition when one business acquires another. Examples include noncompetition agreements, customer lists, patents, subscriber lists, databases, trademarks, lease agreements, licenses, and many others. All identified intangible assets should be amortized over their economic useful life unless such life is considered *indefinite.* The term *indefinite life* is defined as a life that extends beyond the foreseeable future. A recognized intangible asset with an indefinite life should not be amortized unless and until its life is determined to be finite. Importantly, *indefinite* does not mean "infinite." Also, the useful life of an intangible asset should not be considered indefinite because a precise finite life is not known.

For intangible assets with finite lives, the amortization method should reflect the pattern of decline in the economic usefulness of the asset. If no such pattern is apparent, the straight-line

[12] IFRS defines value in use as the present value of future cash flows expected to be derived from an asset or a cash-generating unit.

method of amortization should be used. The amount to be amortized should be the value assigned to the intangible asset less any residual value. In most cases, the residual value is presumed to be zero. However, that presumption can be overcome if the acquiring enterprise has a commitment from a third party to purchase the intangible at the end of its useful life or an observable market exists for the intangible asset.

The length of the amortization period for identifiable intangibles (i.e., those not included in goodwill) depends primarily on the assumed economic life of the asset. Factors that should be considered in determining the useful life of an intangible asset include

- Legal, regulatory, or contractual provisions.
- The effects of obsolescence, demand, competition, industry stability, rate of technological change, and expected changes in distribution channels.
- The enterprise's expected use of the intangible asset.
- The level of maintenance expenditure required to obtain the asset's expected future benefits.

Any recognized intangible assets considered to possess indefinite lives are not amortized but instead are assessed for impairment on an annual basis.[13] Similar to goodwill impairment assessment, an entity has the option to first perform qualitative assessments for its indefinite-lived intangibles to see if further quantitative tests are necessary. According to the FASB ASC (350-30-65-3), if an entity elects to perform a qualitative assessment, it examines events and circumstances to determine whether it is more likely than not (that is, a likelihood of more than 50 percent) that an indefinite-lived intangible asset is impaired. Qualitative factors include costs of using the intangible, legal and regulatory factors, industry and market considerations, and other. If the qualitative assessment indicates impairment is unlikely, no additional tests are needed.

If the qualitative assessment indicates that impairment is likely, the entity then must perform a quantitative test to determine if a loss has occurred. To test an indefinite-lived intangible asset for impairment, its carrying amount is compared to its fair value. If the fair value is less than the carrying amount, then the intangible asset is considered impaired and an impairment loss is recognized. The asset's carrying amount is reduced accordingly for the excess of its carrying amount over its fair value.

LO 3-8

Understand the accounting and reporting for contingent consideration subsequent to a business acquisition.

Contingent Consideration—Postcombination

As introduced in Chapter 2, contingency agreements frequently accompany business combinations. In many cases, the target firm asks for consideration based on projections of its future performance. The acquiring firm, however, may not share the projections and, thus, may be unwilling to pay now for uncertain future performance. To close the deal, future contingent payment agreements from the acquirer to the former owners of the target, also known as "earnouts," are common. Such contingent payments may be in the form of cash or the acquirer's equity shares—with each form requiring separate accounting in periods subsequent to a business combination.

Accounting for Contingent Consideration in Periods Subsequent to a Business Combination

To illustrate the accounting for contingent consideration, assume that ClearView, Inc., acquires 100 percent of the voting stock of Optima Company on January 1, 2020, in exchange for the following:

- $850,000 market value of 10,000 shares of its $1 par common stock.
- A contingent payment of $35,000 cash if Optima's 2020 cash flow from operations exceeds $70,000.
- A contingent issuance of 1,000 shares of ClearView common stock if Optima's 2020 net income exceeds $100,000.

[13] An entity has an unconditional option to bypass the qualitative assessment for any indefinite-lived intangible asset in any period and proceed directly to performing the quantitative impairment test.

Under the acquisition method, each of the three elements of consideration represents a portion of the negotiated fair value of Optima and therefore must be included in the recorded value entered on ClearView's accounting records. For the cash contingency, ClearView estimates that there is a 75 percent chance that the $35,000 payment will be required. For the stock contingency, ClearView estimates a 21 percent probability that Optima will meet the $100,000 net income target. In the event of the contingent stock issue, ClearView and Optima agree that the 1,000 shares would have a likely $85,000 total future value. ClearView employs an interest rate of 5 percent to incorporate the time value of money.

To determine the fair values of the contingent consideration, ClearView computes the probability-adjusted present value of the expected payments as follows:

- *Cash contingency fair value* = $35,000 × 75% × [1/(1 + .05)] = $25,000
- *Stock contingency fair value* = $85,000 × 21% × [1/(1 + .05)] = $17,000

ClearView then records in its accounting records the acquisition of Optima as follows:

Investment in Optima	892,000	
Common Stock ($1 par)		10,000
Additional Paid-in Capital		840,000
Contingent Performance Obligation		25,000
Additional Paid-in Capital—Contingent Equity Outstanding		17,000
To record acquisition of Optima at fair value of consideration transferred including performance contingencies.		

ClearView, on its acquisition-date consolidated balance sheet, will report the contingent performance obligation under liabilities and the contingent stock payment as a component of stockholders' equity. Subsequent to acquisition, however, the accounting for contingent consideration differs depending on it balance sheet classification as a liability or equity. In each accounting period subsequent to acquisition,

- An obligation for contingent consideration classified as a **liability** is remeasured to current fair value. An increase (decrease) in the fair value of the contingent consideration obligation is recognized in each period's net income as a revaluation loss (gain).
- An obligation for contingent consideration classified as **equity** is not subsequently remeasured to fair value, consistent with other equity issues (e.g., common stock).

To continue the preceding example, assume that by the end of 2020 Optima exceeds the cash flow from operations threshold of $70,000, thus requiring an additional payment of $35,000 from ClearView. Also, Optima's 2020 net income was $117,000, triggering the payment of an additional 1,000 shares of ClearView common stock to the former owners of Optima. Clearview's recording of these events is as follows:

Clear View's Journal Entries—Both Year-End Cash and Stock Contingency Thresholds Are Met		
Loss from Revaluation of Contingent Performance Obligation	10,000	
Contingent Performance Obligation		10,000
To remeasure the contingent performance obligation to fair value.		
Contingent Performance Obligation	35,000	
Cash		35,000
To record cash payment required by original Optima acquisition contingency agreement.		
Additional Paid-in Capital—Contingent Equity Outstanding	17,000	
Common Stock ($1 par)		1,000
Additional Paid-in Capital		16,000
To record contingent stock issue required by original Optima acquisition contingency agreement.		

The loss from revaluation of the contingent performance obligation is reported in Clear-View's consolidated income statement as a component of ordinary income. Regarding the additional required stock issue, note that ClearView's total paid-in capital (Common Stock plus APIC) remains unchanged from the total $867,000 recorded at the acquisition date. Contingent equity is not adjusted to fair value over time but remains at its originally recorded amount.

Alternatively, if Optima failed to meet either the $70,000 operating cash flow threshold or the $100,000 net income threshold, Clear View would record the following adjustments to its records:

Clear View's Journal Entries—Neither Year-End Cash and Stock Contingency Thresholds Are Met		
Contingent Performance Obligation	25,000	
Gain from Revaluation of Contingent Performance Obligation		25,000
To record Optima's failure to meet performance threshold and remeasure the contingent performance obligation to zero.		
Additional Paid-in Capital—Contingent Equity Outstanding	17,000	
Additional Paid-In Capital—Contingent Equity Forfeited		17,000
To reclassify contingent stock issue as APIC—contingent equity forfeited. Optima did not meet performance threshold to qualify for additional stock issue.		

The preceding illustrations demonstrate that the initial fair value assigned to the acquired firm continues as the acquisition-date valuation for the business combination, regardless of whether the contingency thresholds are met or not.

Summary

1. The procedures used to consolidate financial information generated by the separate companies in a business combination are affected by both the passage of time and the method applied by the parent in accounting for the subsidiary. Thus, no single consolidation process that is applicable to all business combinations can be described.
2. The parent might elect to utilize the equity method to account for a subsidiary. As discussed in Chapter 1, the parent accrues income when earned by the subsidiary. The parent records dividend declarations by the subsidiary as reductions in the investment account. The effects of excess fair-value amortizations or any intra-entity transactions also are reflected within the parent's financial records. The equity method provides the parent with accurate information concerning the subsidiary's impact on consolidated totals; however, it is usually somewhat complicated to apply.
3. The initial value method and the partial equity method are two alternatives to the equity method. The initial value method recognizes only the subsidiary's dividends as income while the asset balance remains at the acquisition-date fair value. This approach is simple and typically reflects cash flows between the two companies. Under the partial equity method, the parent accrues the subsidiary's income as earned but does not record adjustments that might be required by excess fair-value amortizations or intra-entity transfers. The partial equity method is easier to apply than the equity method, and, in many cases, the parent's income is a reasonable approximation of the consolidated total.
4. For a consolidation in any subsequent period, all reciprocal balances must be eliminated. Thus, the subsidiary's equity accounts, the parent's investment balance, intra-entity income, dividends, and liabilities are removed. In addition, the remaining unamortized portions of the fair-value allocations are recognized along with excess amortization expenses for the period. If the equity method has not been applied, the parent's beginning Retained Earnings account also must be adjusted for any previous income or excess amortizations that have not yet been recorded.
5. For each subsidiary acquisition, the parent must assign the acquired assets and liabilities (including goodwill) to individual reporting units of the combined entity. The reporting units should be at operating segment level or lower and serve as the basis for future assessments of fair value. Any value assigned to goodwill is not amortized but instead is tested annually for impairment. Firms have the option to perform a qualitative assessment to evaluate whether a reporting unit's fair value more likely than not exceeds its carrying amount. If the assessment shows excess fair value over carrying amount for the reporting unit, a firm can forgo further testing. Otherwise, if a reporting unit fails the qualitative test, the reporting unit's fair value is compared to its carrying amount. If the reporting unit's carrying amount exceeds its fair value, then a goodwill impairment loss is measured as the excess of a reporting unit's carrying amount over its fair value. A goodwill impairment loss is reported as an operating item in the consolidated income statement.

6. Subsequent to a business combination, any newly recognized subsidiary identifiable intangible assets (i.e., other than goodwill) considered to possess indefinite lives are not amortized but instead are assessed for impairment on an annual basis. Similar to goodwill impairment assessment, an entity has the option to first perform qualitative assessments for its indefinite-lived intangibles to see if further quantitative tests are necessary. For intangible assets with finite lives, amortization expense is recognized over the intangible asset's useful life. The amortization method should reflect the pattern of decline in the economic usefulness of the asset. If no such pattern is apparent, the straight-line method of amortization should be used.
7. The acquisition-date fair value assigned to a subsidiary can be based, at least in part, on the fair value of any contingent consideration. For contingent obligations that meet the definition of a liability, the obligation is adjusted for changes in fair value over time with corresponding recognition of gains or losses from the revaluation. For contingent obligations classified as equity, no remeasurement to fair value takes place. In either case, the initial value recognized in the combination does not change, regardless of whether the contingency is eventually paid or not.

Comprehensive Illustration

Problem

(*Estimated Time: 40 to 65 Minutes*) On January 1, 2019, Top Company acquired all of Bottom Company's outstanding common stock for $842,000 in cash. As of that date, one of Bottom's buildings with a 12-year remaining life was undervalued on its financial records by $72,000. Equipment with a 10-year remaining life was undervalued, but only by $10,000. The book values of all of Bottom's other assets and liabilities were equal to their fair values at that time except for an unrecorded licensing agreement with an assessed value of $40,000 and a 20-year remaining useful life. Bottom's book value at the acquisition date was $720,000.

During 2019, Bottom reported net income of $100,000 and declared $30,000 in dividends. Earnings were $120,000 in 2020 with $20,000 in dividends declared by the subsidiary. As of December 31, 2021, the companies reported the following selected balances, which include all revenues and expenses for the year:

	Top Company December 31, 2021		Bottom Company December 31, 2021	
	Debit	**Credit**	**Debit**	**Credit**
Buildings	$1,540,000		$460,000	
Cash and receivables	50,000		90,000	
Common stock		$ 900,000		$400,000
Dividends declared	70,000		10,000	
Equipment	280,000		200,000	
Cost of goods sold	500,000		120,000	
Depreciation expense	100,000		60,000	
Inventory	280,000		260,000	
Land	330,000		250,000	
Liabilities		480,000		260,000
Retained earnings, 1/1/21		1,360,000		490,000
Revenues		900,000		300,000

Required

a. If Top applies the equity method, what is its investment account balance as of December 31, 2021?

b. If Top applies the initial value method, what is its investment account balance as of December 31, 2021?

c. Regardless of the accounting method in use by Top, what are the consolidated totals as of December 31, 2021, for each of the following accounts?

Buildings	Revenues
Equipment	Net Income
Land	Investment in Bottom
Depreciation Expense	Dividends Declared
Amortization Expense	Cost of Goods Sold

d. Prepare the worksheet entries required on December 31, 2021, to consolidate the financial records of these two companies. Assume that Top applied the equity method to its investment account.

e. How would the worksheet entries in requirement *(d)* be altered if Top has used the initial value method?

Solution

a. To determine the investment balances under the equity method, four items must be determined: the initial value assigned, the income accrual, dividends, and amortization of excess acquisition-date fair value over book value. Although the first three are indicated in the problem, amortizations must be calculated separately.

An allocation of Bottom's acquisition-date fair values as well as the related amortization expense follows.

Fair value of consideration transferred by Top Company . .	$842,000
Book value of Bottom Company, 1/1/19	(720,000)
Excess fair value over book value	$122,000

Adjustments to specific accounts based on fair values:

		Remaining Life (years)	Annual Amortization
Buildings	$ 72,000	12	$6,000
Equipment	10,000	10	1,000
Licensing agreement	40,000	20	2,000
Totals	$122,000		$9,000

Thus, if Top adopts the equity method to account for this subsidiary, the Investment in Bottom account shows a December 31, 2021, balance of $1,095,000, computed as follows:

Initial value (fair value of consideration transferred by Top)		$ 842,000
Bottom Company's 2019–2020 increase in book value (income less dividends)		170,000
Excess amortizations for 2019–2020 ($9,000 per year for two years)		(18,000)
Current year recognition (2021):		
Equity income accrual (Bottom's revenues less its expenses) . . .	$120,000	
Excess amortization expenses	(9,000)	
Dividends from Bottom	(10,000)	101,000
Investment in Bottom Company, 12/31/21		$ 1,095,000

The $120,000 income accrual and the $9,000 excess amortization expenses indicate that an Equity in Subsidiary Earnings balance of $111,000 appears in Top's income statement for the current period.

b. If Top Company applies the initial value method, the Investment in Bottom Company account permanently retains its original $842,000 balance, and the parent recognizes only the intra-entity dividend of $10,000 as income in 2021.

c.
- The consolidated Buildings account as of December 31, 2021, has a balance of $2,054,000. Although the two book value figures total only $2 million, a $72,000 allocation was made to this account based on fair value at the date of acquisition. Because this amount is being depreciated at the rate of $6,000 per year, the original allocation will have been reduced by $18,000 by the end of 2021, leaving only a $54,000 increase.
- On December 31, 2021, the consolidated Equipment account amounts to $487,000. The book values found in the financial records of Top and Bottom provide a total of $480,000. Once again, the allocation ($10,000) established by the acquisition-date fair value must be included in the consolidated balance after being adjusted for three years of depreciation ($1,000 × 3 years, or $3,000).
- Land has a consolidated total of $580,000. Because the book value and fair value of Bottom's land were in agreement at the date of acquisition, no additional allocation was made to this account. Thus, the book values are simply added together to derive a consolidated figure.
- *Cost of goods sold* = $620,000. The cost of goods sold of the parent and subsidiary are added together.
- *Depreciation expense* = $167,000. The depreciation expenses of the parent and subsidiary are added together along with the $6,000 additional building depreciation and the $1,000 additional equipment depreciation as presented in the fair-value allocation schedule.

- *Amortization expense* = $2,000. An additional expense of $2,000 is recognized from the amortization of the licensing agreement acquired in the business combination.
- The Revenues account appears as $1.2 million in the consolidated income statement. None of the worksheet entries in this example affects the individual balances of either company. Consolidation results merely from the addition of the two book values.
- Net income for this business combination is $411,000: consolidated expenses of $789,000 subtracted from revenues of $1.2 million.
- The parent's Investment in Bottom account is removed entirely on the worksheet so that no balance is reported. For consolidation purposes, this account is always eliminated so that the individual assets and liabilities of the subsidiary can be included.
- Dividends declared for the consolidated entity should be reported as $70,000, the amount Top distributed. Because Bottom's dividends are entirely intra-entity, they are deleted in arriving at consolidated figures.

d. Consolidation Entries Assuming Equity Method Used by Parent

Entry S

Common Stock (Bottom Company)	400,000	
Retained Earnings, 1/1/21 (Bottom Company)	490,000	
Investment in Bottom Company		890,000

Elimination of subsidiary's beginning stockholders' equity accounts against book value portion of investment account.

Entry A

Buildings	60,000	
Equipment	8,000	
Licensing Agreement	36,000	
Investment in Bottom Company		104,000

To recognize fair-value allocations to the subsidiary's assets in excess of book value. Balances represent original allocations less two years of amortization for the 2019–2020 period.

Entry I

Equity in Subsidiary Earnings	111,000	
Investment in Bottom Company		111,000

To eliminate parent's equity income accrual, balance is computed in requirement (*a*).

Entry D

Investment in Bottom	10,000	
Dividends Declared		10,000

To eliminate intra-entity dividends from the subsidiary to the parent (and recorded as a reduction in the investment account because the equity method is in use).

Entry E

Depreciation Expense	7,000	
Amortization Expense	2,000	
Equipment		1,000
Buildings		6,000
Licensing Agreement		2,000

To recognize excess fair-value depreciation and amortization for 2021.

e. If Top utilizes the initial value method rather than the equity method, three changes are required in the development of consolidation entries:

(1) An Entry *C is required to update the parent's beginning Retained Earnings account as if the equity method had been applied. Both an income accrual as well as excess amortizations for the prior two years must be recognized because these balances were not recorded by the parent.

Entry *C

Investment in Bottom Company	152,000	
Retained Earnings, 1/1/21(Top Company)		152,000
To convert to the equity method by accruing the net effect of the subsidiary's operations (income less dividends) for the prior two years ($170,000) along with excess amortization expenses ($18,000) for this same period.		

(2) An alteration is needed in Entry **I** because, under the initial value method, only dividends are recorded by the parent as income.

Entry I

Dividend Income	10,000	
Dividends Declared		10,000
To eliminate intra-entity dividends recorded by parent as income.		

(3) Finally, because the intra-entity dividends have been eliminated in Entry **I,** no separate Entry **D** is needed.

Appendix: Private Company Accounting for Business Combinations

LO 3-9

Describe the alternative accounting treatments for goodwill and other intangible assets available for business combinations by private companies.

External Reporting Option for Private Company Goodwill Accounting

In January 2014, the Financial Accounting Standards Board (FASB) approved an *Accounting Standards Update* (ASU 2014-02) to Topic 350, "Intangibles—Goodwill and Other, on Accounting for Goodwill." This ASU emerged as a consensus of the FASB's Private Company Council (PCC) and gives private companies an option to apply a simplified alternative to the more complex goodwill accounting model required of public companies. As discussed this appendix, the new standard allows a private company both to amortize goodwill and to apply a simplified impairment test at either the reporting unit or entity level.

The private company standards apply only to businesses that do not meet the definition of a public business entity or a not-for-profit entity. In general, a business is a public entity if the Securities and Exchange Commission (or a foreign or other domestic regulatory agency) requires the business to furnish financial statements (ASU 2013-12). In this textbook, our focus is squarely on public business entities. Nonetheless, the goodwill accounting option for private companies provides an interesting alternative that the FASB may someday consider for public entities as well.[14]

The new standard allows a private company to elect to amortize goodwill over a 10-year period.[15] The amortization process effectively treats goodwill as a definite-lived intangible asset. This approach, of course, stands in marked contrast to the goodwill accounting for public companies, which treats goodwill as an indefinite-lived asset, prohibits amortization, and requires annual impairment testing for goodwill. In justifying the differential treatment for private companies, the FASB reasoned that, based on research by the PCC, goodwill impairment tests provided

> limited decision-useful information because most users of private company financial statement generally disregard goodwill and goodwill impairment losses in their analysis of a private company's financial condition and operating performance. (ASU 2014-02, Summary)

Equally important, the PCC expressed concerns about the cost and complexity of goodwill impairment tests, especially for private companies. The cost and complexity arise in large part from the efforts required in determining fair values for a company's reporting units and their identifiable assets and liabilities.

In many cases, goodwill amortization will replace the need to periodically assess and, when deemed necessary, write-down goodwill through the recognition of impairment losses. Private companies who elect the alternative goodwill accounting, however, will still be required to test goodwill balances for impairment in some circumstances, although a simplified approach is employed.

[14] In November 2014, the FASB directed its staff to extend its research on goodwill amortization to public companies, focusing on the most appropriate useful life if goodwill were amortized and simplifying the goodwill impairment test

[15] A less-than-10-year amortization period is available if it can be shown to be appropriate (ASC 350-20-35-63).

The goodwill impairment process is simplified in two respects for private companies. First, if a triggering event occurs (i.e., any event or change in circumstances that may have caused the fair value of the acquired entity—or the reporting unit—to fall below its carrying amount), then the unamortized balance of goodwill must be assessed for impairment.[16] However, to save costs and streamline the process, there is no requirement (as exists for public companies) to remeasure each of the entity's (or reporting unit's) separate assets and liabilities at current fair values to compute a residual implied value for goodwill. The measurement of the goodwill impairment loss simply equals the excess (if any) of the fair value of the acquired entity (or reporting unit) over its total carrying amount. The amount of the impairment loss, however, is limited to the remaining unamortized balance in the goodwill account.

Unlike public companies, a private company also has the option to designate and test goodwill for impairment either at the entity level or the reporting unit level—a policy election made at the adoption of the alternative goodwill method. Thus, the accounting for goodwill impairment is simplified by both the ability to assess goodwill at the entity level and the use of a single-step test that compares the fair value of the entity to its carrying amount. Similar to public companies, a private company may skip the qualitative assessment. Unlike public companies, a private company can then go directly to a single-step quantitative impairment test.

External Reporting Option for Private Company Accounting for Other Intangible Assets in a Business Combination

In addition to the private company separate guidance for goodwill, in December 2014, the FASB issued ASU 2014-18, "Accounting for Identifiable Intangible Assets in a Business Combination (a consensus of the Private Company Council)," an amendment of Business Combinations (Topic 805). The new standard allows private companies an option to simplify their accounting by recognizing fewer intangible assets in future business combinations. Private companies can now elect to (1) limit the customer-related intangibles it recognizes separately to those capable of being sold or licensed independently from the other assets of the business, and (2) avoid separate recognition of noncompetition agreements.

By limiting the separate recognition of customer-related intangibles (e.g., customer lists, customer relationships, commodity supply contracts, etc.) and noncompetition agreements, the value of these intangible assets is effectively subsumed into goodwill. As with other private company financial reporting options, the FASB cites cost/benefit considerations.

> By providing an accounting alternative, this Update reduces the cost and complexity associated with the measurement of certain identifiable intangible assets without significantly diminishing decision-useful information to users of private company financial statements (ASU 2014-18, Summary).

A private company may elect this alternative only if it also elects the private company goodwill accounting alternative, which includes goodwill amortization—thus ensuring that any non-recognized intangibles subsumed into goodwill are also subject to amortization. Companies that choose the goodwill accounting alternative, however, are not required to elect the intangible assets accounting alternative.

Questions

1. CCES Corporation acquires a controlling interest in Schmaling, Inc. CCES may utilize any one of three methods to internally account for this investment. Describe each of these methods, and indicate their advantages and disadvantages.
2. Maguire Company obtains 100 percent control over Williams Company. Several years after the takeover, consolidated financial statements are being produced. For each of the following accounts, briefly describe the values that should be included in consolidated totals.
   a. Equipment.
   b. Investment in Williams Company.
   c. Dividends Declared.
   d. Goodwill.
   e. Revenues.
   f. Expenses.
   g. Common Stock.
   h. Net Income.
3. When a parent company uses the equity method to account for an investment in a subsidiary, why do both the parent's Net Income and Retained Earnings account balances agree with the consolidated totals?

[16] Distinct from public company requirements, no annual assessment for goodwill impairment is required for private companies.

4. When a parent company uses the equity method to account for investment in a subsidiary, the amortization expense entry recorded during the year is eliminated on a consolidation worksheet as a component of Entry **I.** What is the necessity of removing this amortization?
5. When a parent company applies the initial value method or the partial equity method to an investment, a worksheet adjustment must be made to the parent's beginning Retained Earnings account (Entry ***C**) in every period after the year of acquisition. What is the necessity for this entry? Why is no similar entry found when the parent utilizes the equity method?
6. Several years ago, Jenkins Company acquired a controlling interest in Lambert Company. Lambert recently borrowed $100,000 from Jenkins. In consolidating the financial records of these two companies, how will this debt be handled?
7. Benns adopts the equity method for its 100 percent investment in Waters. At the end of six years, Benns reports an investment in Waters of $920,000. What figures constitute this balance?
8. One company acquired another in a transaction in which $100,000 of the acquisition price is assigned to goodwill. Several years later, a worksheet is being produced to consolidate these two companies. How is the reported value of the goodwill determined at this date?
9. When should a parent consider recognizing an impairment loss for goodwill associated with a subsidiary? How should the loss be reported in the financial statements?
10. Reimers Company acquires Rollins Corporation on January 1, 2020. As part of the agreement, the parent states that an additional $100,000 cash payment to the former owners of Rollins will be made in 2021, if Rollins achieves certain income thresholds during the first two years following the acquisition. How should Reimers account for this contingency in its 2020 consolidated financial statements?

Problems

LO 3-2

1. A company acquires a subsidiary and will prepare consolidated financial statements for external reporting purposes. For internal reporting purposes, the company has decided to apply the initial value method. Why might the company have made this decision?
   a. It is a relatively easy method to apply.
   b. Operating results appearing on the parent's financial records reflect consolidated totals.
   c. GAAP now requires the use of this particular method for internal reporting purposes.
   d. Consolidation is not required when the parent uses the initial value method.

LO 3-2

2. A company acquires a subsidiary and will prepare consolidated financial statements for external reporting purposes. For internal reporting purposes, the company has decided to apply the equity method. Why might the company have made this decision?
   a. It is a relatively easy method to apply.
   b. Operating results appearing on the parent's financial records reflect consolidated totals.
   c. GAAP now requires the use of this particular method for internal reporting purposes.
   d. Consolidation is not required when the parent uses the equity method.

LO 3-4

3. On January 1, 2021, Jay Company acquired all the outstanding ownership shares of Zee Company. In assessing Zee's acquisition-date fair values, Jay concluded that the carrying value of Zee's long-term debt (eight-year remaining life) was less than its fair value by $20,000. At December 31, 2021, Zee Company's accounts show interest expense of $12,000 and long-term debt of $250,000. What amounts of interest expense and long-term debt should appear on the December 31, 2021, consolidated financial statements of Jay and its subsidiary Zee?

	Interest expense	*Long-term debt*
a.	$14,500	$270,000
b.	$14,500	$267,500
c.	$9,500	$270,000
d.	$9,500	$267,500

LO 3-5

4. When should a consolidated entity recognize a goodwill impairment loss?
   a. When the fair value of a reporting unit exceeds its respective carrying amount
   b. Whenever the entity's fair value declines significantly
   c. When the fair value of a reporting unit with goodwill falls below its carrying amount
   d. Annually on a systematic and rational basis

LO 3-1

5. Paar Corporation bought 100 percent of Kimmel, Inc., on January 1, 2018. On that date, Paar's equipment (10-year remaining life) has a book value of $420,000 but a fair value of $520,000. Kimmel has equipment (10-year remaining life) with a book value of $272,000 but a fair value of $400,000. Paar uses the equity method to record its investment in Kimmel. On December 31, 2020, Paar has equipment with a book value of $294,000 but a fair value of $445,200. Kimmel has equipment with a book value of $190,400 but a fair value of $357,000. What is the consolidated balance for the Equipment account as of December 31, 2020?
   a. $574,000
   b. $802,200
   c. $612,600
   d. $484,400

LO 3-4

6. How would the answer to problem (5) change if the parent had applied the initial value method rather than the equity method?
   a. No effect: The method the parent uses is for internal reporting purposes only and has no impact on consolidated totals.
   b. The consolidated Equipment account would have a higher reported balance.
   c. The consolidated Equipment account would have a lower reported balance.
   d. The balance in the consolidated Equipment account cannot be determined for the initial value method using the information given.

LO 3-5

7. Goodwill recognized in a business combination must be allocated across a firm's identified reporting units. For a consolidated entity with multiple reporting units, when is goodwill considered to be impaired?
   a. When any individual reporting unit's carrying amount exceeds its fair value
   b. When any individual reporting unit's fair value exceeds its carrying amount
   c. When the sum of the carrying amounts of all reporting units within a business combination exceeds the sum of their respective fair values
   d. When the sum of the fair values of all reporting units within a business combination exceeds the sum of their respective carrying amounts

LO 3-7

8. If no legal, regulatory, contractual, competitive, economic, or other factors limit the life of an intangible asset, the asset's assigned value is allocated to expense over which of the following?
   a. 20 years
   b. 20 years with an annual impairment review
   c. Infinitely
   d. Indefinitely (no amortization) with an annual impairment review until its life becomes finite

LO 3-7

9. Camille, Inc., bought all outstanding shares of Jordan Corporation on January 1, 2019, for $700,000 in cash. This portion of the consideration transferred results in a fair-value allocation of $35,000 to equipment and goodwill of $88,000. At the acquisition date, Camille also agrees to pay Jordan's previous owners an additional $110,000 on January 1, 2021, if Jordan earns a 10 percent return on the fair value of its assets in 2019 and 2020. Jordan's profits exceed this threshold in both years. Which of the following is true?
   a. The additional $110,000 payment is reported as an adjustment to the beginning balance of consolidated retained earnings.
   b. The fair value of the expected contingent payment increases goodwill at the acquisition date.
   c. Consolidated goodwill as of January 1, 2021, increases by $110,000.
   d. The $110,000 is recorded as a revaluation gain in 2021.

Problems 10, 11, and 12 relate to the following:
On January 1, 2019, Phoenix Co. acquired 100 percent of the outstanding voting shares of Sedona Inc. for $600,000 cash. At January 1, 2019, Sedona's net assets had a total carrying amount of $420,000. Equipment (eight-year remaining life) was undervalued on Sedona's financial records by $80,000. Any remaining excess fair over book value was attributed to a customer list developed by Sedona (four-year remaining life), but not recorded on its books. Phoenix applies the equity method to account for its investment in Sedona. Each year since the acquisition, Sedona has declared a $20,000 dividend. Sedona recorded net income of $70,000 in 2019 and $80,000 in 2020.

Selected account balances from the two companies' individual records were as follows:

	Phoenix	Sedona
2021 Revenues	$498,000	$285,000
2021 Expenses	350,000	195,000
2021 Income from Sedona	55,000	
Retained earnings 12/31/21	250,000	175,000

LO 3-3a

10. What is consolidated net income for Phoenix and Sedona for 2021?
    a. $148,000
    b. $203,000
    c. $228,000
    d. $238,000

LO 3-3a

11. What is Phoenix's consolidated retained earnings balance at December 31, 2021?
    a. $250,000
    b. $290,000
    c. $330,000
    d. $360,000

LO 3-3a

12. On its December 31, 2021, consolidated balance sheet, what amount should Phoenix report for Sedona's customer list?
    a. $10,000
    b. $20,000
    c. $25,000
    d. $50,000

LO 3-7

13. SK Corporation acquired Neptune, Inc., on January 1, 2020, by issuing 125,000 shares of common stock with a $5 per share par value and a $30 market value. This transaction resulted in recognizing $95,000 of goodwill. SK also agreed to compensate Neptune's former owners with an additional 20,000 shares of SK's common stock if Neptune's 2020 cash flow from operations exceeds $600,000. On February 1, 2021, SK issues the additional 20,000 shares to Neptune's former owners to honor the contingent consideration agreement. Which of the following is true?
    a. The fair value of the number of shares issued for the contingency increases the Goodwill account on February 1, 2021.
    b. The parent's additional paid-in capital from the contingent equity recorded at the acquisition date is reclassified as a regular common stock issue on February 1, 2021.
    c. All of the subsidiary's asset and liability accounts must be revalued for consolidation purposes based on their fair values as of February 1, 2021.
    d. The additional shares are assumed to have been issued on January 1, 2020, so that a retrospective adjustment is required.

LO 3-3, 3-4

14. Herbert, Inc., acquired all of Rambis Company's outstanding stock on January 1, 2020, for $574,000 in cash. Annual excess amortization of $12,000 results from this transaction. On the date of the takeover, Herbert reported retained earnings of $400,000, and Rambis reported a $200,000 balance. Herbert reported internal net income of $40,000 in 2020 and $50,000 in 2021 and declared $10,000 in dividends each year. Rambis reported net income of $20,000 in 2020 and $30,000 in 2021 and declared $5,000 in dividends each year.
    a. Assume that Herbert's internal net income figures do not include any income from the subsidiary.
        - If the parent uses the equity method, what is the amount reported as consolidated retained earnings on December 31, 2021?
        - Would the amount of consolidated retained earnings change if the parent had applied either the initial value or partial equity method for internal accounting purposes?
    b. Under each of the following situations, what is the Investment in Rambis account balance on Herbert's books on January 1, 2021?
        - The parent uses the equity method.
        - The parent uses the partial equity method.
        - The parent uses the initial value method.

c. Under each of the following situations, what is Entry *C on a 2021 consolidation worksheet?

- The parent uses the equity method.
- The parent uses the partial equity method.
- The parent uses the initial value method.

LO 3-3, 3-4

15. Haynes, Inc., obtained 100 percent of Turner Company's common stock on January 1, 2020, by issuing 9,000 shares of $10 par value common stock. Haynes's shares had a $15 per share fair value. On that date, Turner reported a net book value of $100,000. However, its equipment (with a five-year remaining life) was undervalued by $5,000 in the company's accounting records. Also, Turner had developed a customer list with an assessed value of $30,000, although no value had been recorded on Turner's books. The customer list had an estimated remaining useful life of 10 years.

The following balances come from the individual accounting records of these two companies as of December 31, 2020:

	Haynes	Turner
Revenues	$(600,000)	$(230,000)
Expenses	440,000	120,000
Investment income	Not given	–0–
Dividends declared	80,000	50,000

The following balances come from the individual accounting records of these two companies as of December 31, 2021:

	Haynes	Turner
Revenues	$(700,000)	$(280,000)
Expenses	460,000	150,000
Investment income	Not given	–0–
Dividends declared	90,000	40,000
Equipment	500,000	300,000

a. What balance does Haynes's Investment in Turner account show on December 31, 2021, when the equity method is applied?

b. What is the consolidated net income for the year ending December 31, 2021?

c. What is the consolidated equipment balance as of December 31, 2021? How would this answer be affected by the investment method applied by the parent?

d. If Haynes has applied the initial value method to account for its investment, what adjustment is needed to the beginning of the Retained Earnings account on a December 31, 2021, consolidation worksheet? How would this answer change if the partial equity method had been in use? How would this answer change if the equity method had been in use?

LO 3-6

16. Alfonso Inc. acquired 100 percent of the voting shares of BelAire Company on January 1, 2020. In exchange, Alfonso paid $198,000 in cash and issued 100,000 shares of its own $1 par value common stock. On this date, Alfonso's stock had a fair value of $15 per share. The combination is a statutory merger with BelAire subsequently dissolved as a legal corporation. BelAire's assets and liabilities are assigned to a new reporting unit.

The following shows fair values for the BelAire reporting unit for January 1, 2020 along with respective carrying amounts on December 31, 2021.

BelAire Reporting Unit	Fair Values 1/1/20	Carrying Amounts 12/31/21
Cash	$ 65,000	$ 40,000
Receivables	203,000	235,000
Inventory	275,000	250,000
Patents	531,000	550,000
Customer relationships	580,000	450,000

(continued)

(continued)

BelAire Reporting Unit	Fair Values 1/1/20	Carrying Amounts 12/31/21
Equipment (net)	215,000	335,000
Goodwill	?	400,000
Accounts payable	(111,000)	(275,000)
Long-term liabilities	(460,000)	(425,000)

a. Prepare Alfonso's journal entry to record the assets acquired and the liabilities assumed in the BelAire merger on January 1, 2020.

b. On December 31, 2021, Alfonso opts to forgo any goodwill impairment qualitative assessment and estimates that the total fair value of the entire BelAire reporting unit is $1,325,000. What amount of goodwill impairment, if any, should Alfonso recognize on its 2021 income statement?

LO 3-6

17. Alomar Co., a consolidated enterprise, conducted an impairment review for each of its reporting units. In its qualitative assessment, one particular reporting unit, Sellers, emerged as a candidate for possible goodwill impairment. Sellers had recognized net assets with carrying amounts totaling $1,094, including goodwill of $755. Seller's reporting unit fair value is assessed at $1,028 and includes two internally developed unrecognized intangible assets (a patent and a customer list with fair values of $199 and $56, respectively). The following table summarizes current financial information for the Sellers reporting unit:

	Carrying Amounts	Fair Values
Tangible assets, net	$ 84	$137
Recognized intangible assets, net	255	326
Goodwill	755	?
Unrecognized intangible assets	–0–	255

a. Determine the amount of any goodwill impairment for Alomar's Sellers reporting unit.

b. After recognition of any goodwill impairment loss, what are the reported carrying amounts for the following assets of Alomar's reporting unit Sellers?

- Tangible assets, net
- Goodwill
- Patent
- Customer list

LO 3-6

18. Purchase Company recently acquired several businesses and recognized goodwill in each acquisition. Purchase has allocated the resulting goodwill to its three reporting units: RU-1, RU-2, and RU-3. Purchase opts to skip the qualitative assessment and therefore performs a quantitative goodwill impairment review annually.

In its current-year assessment of goodwill, Purchase provides the following individual asset and liability carrying amounts for each of its reporting units:

	Carrying Amounts		
	RU-1	RU-2	RU-3
Tangible assets	$180,000	$200,000	$140,000
Trademark	170,000		
Customer list	90,000		
Unpatented technology		170,000	
Licenses		90,000	
Copyrights			50,000
Goodwill	120,000	150,000	90,000
Liabilities	(30,000)		

The total fair values for each reporting unit (including goodwill) are $510,000 for RU-1, $580,000 for RU-2, and $560,000 for RU-3. To date, Purchase has reported no goodwill impairments.

How much goodwill impairment should Purchase report this year for each of its reporting units?

Problems 19 through 21 should be viewed as independent situations. They are based on the following data:

Chapman Company obtains 100 percent of Abernethy Company's stock on January 1, 2020. As of that date, Abernethy has the following trial balance:

	Debit	Credit
Accounts payable		$ 50,000
Accounts receivable	$ 40,000	
Additional paid-in capital		50,000
Buildings (net) (4-year remaining life)	120,000	
Cash and short-term investments	60,000	
Common stock		250,000
Equipment (net) (5-year remaining life)	200,000	
Inventory	90,000	
Land	80,000	
Long-term liabilities (mature 12/31/23)		150,000
Retained earnings, 1/1/20		100,000
Supplies	10,000	
Totals	$600,000	$600,000

During 2020, Abernethy reported net income of $80,000 while declaring and paying dividends of $10,000. During 2021, Abernethy reported net income of $110,000 while declaring and paying dividends of $30,000.

LO 3-3a

19. Assume that Chapman Company acquired Abernethy's common stock for $490,000 in cash. As of January 1, 2020, Abernethy's land had a fair value of $90,000, its buildings were valued at $160,000, and its equipment was appraised at $180,000. Chapman uses the equity method for this investment. Prepare consolidation worksheet entries for December 31, 2020, and December 31, 2021.

LO 3-3b

20. Assume that Chapman Company acquired Abernethy's common stock for $500,000 in cash. Assume that the equipment and long-term liabilities had fair values of $220,000 and $120,000, respectively, on the acquisition date. Chapman uses the initial value method to account for its investment. Prepare consolidation worksheet entries for December 31, 2020, and December 31, 2021.

LO 3-3c

21. Assume that Chapman Company acquired Abernethy's common stock by paying $520,000 in cash. All of Abernethy's accounts are estimated to have a fair value approximately equal to present book values. Chapman uses the partial equity method to account for its investment. Prepare the consolidation worksheet entries for December 31, 2020, and December 31, 2021.

LO 3-3a, 3-3b, 3-4

22. Adams, Inc., acquires Clay Corporation on January 1, 2020, in exchange for $510,000 cash. Immediately after the acquisition, the two companies have the following account balances. Clay's equipment (with a five-year remaining life) is actually worth $440,000. Credit balances are indicated by parentheses.

	Adams	Clay
Current assets	$ 300,000	$ 220,000
Investment in Clay	510,000	–0–
Equipment	600,000	390,000
Liabilities	(200,000)	(160,000)
Common stock	(350,000)	(150,000)
Retained earnings, 1/1/20	(860,000)	(300,000)

In 2020, Clay earns a net income of $55,000 and declares and pays a $5,000 cash dividend. In 2020, Adams reports net income from its own operations (exclusive of any income from Clay) of $125,000 and declares no dividends. At the end of 2021, selected account balances for the two companies are as follows:

	Adams	Clay
Revenues	$(400,000)	$(240,000)
Expenses	290,000	180,000
Investment income	Not given	–0–
Retained earnings, 1/1/21	Not given	(350,000)

(continued)

(continued)

	Adams	Clay
Dividends declared. . . .	–0–	8,000
Common stock	(350,000)	(150,000)
Current assets	580,000	262,000
Investment in Clay. . . .	Not given	–0–
Equipment	520,000	420,000
Liabilities. . . .	(152,000)	(130,000)

a. What are the December 31, 2021, Investment Income and Investment in Clay account balances assuming Adams uses the
- Equity method.
- Initial value method.

b. How does the parent's internal investment accounting method choice affect the amount reported for expenses in its December 31, 2021, consolidated income statement?

c. How does the parent's internal investment accounting method choice affect the amount reported for equipment in its December 31, 2021, consolidated balance sheet?

d. What is Adams's January 1, 2021, Retained Earnings account balance assuming Adams accounts for its investment in Clay using the
- Equity value method.
- Initial value method.

e. What worksheet adjustment to Adams's January 1, 2021, Retained Earnings account balance is required if Adams accounts for its investment in Clay using the initial value method?

f. Prepare the worksheet entry to eliminate Clay's stockholders' equity.

g. What is consolidated net income for 2021?

LO 3-1, 3-4

23. The following are selected account balances from Penske Company and Stanza Corporation as of December 31, 2021:

	Penske	Stanza
Revenues	$(700,000)	$(400,000)
Cost of goods sold	250,000	100,000
Depreciation expense	150,000	200,000
Investment income	Not given	–0–
Dividends declared. . . .	80,000	60,000
Retained earnings, 1/1/21. . . .	(600,000)	(200,000)
Current assets	400,000	500,000
Copyrights	900,000	400,000
Royalty agreements	600,000	1,000,000
Investment in Stanza	Not given	–0–
Liabilities. . . .	(500,000)	(1,380,000)
Common stock	(600,000) ($20 par)	(200,000) ($10 par)
Additional paid-in capital. . . .	(150,000)	(80,000)

On January 1, 2021, Penske acquired all of Stanza's outstanding stock for $680,000 fair value in cash and common stock. Penske also paid $10,000 in stock issuance costs. At the date of acquisition, copyrights (with a six-year remaining life) have a $440,000 book value but a fair value of $560,000.

a. As of December 31, 2021, what is the consolidated copyrights balance?

b. For the year ending December 31, 2021, what is consolidated net income?

c. As of December 31, 2021, what is the consolidated retained earnings balance?

d. As of December 31, 2021, what is the consolidated balance to be reported for goodwill?

LO 3-2, 3-3, 3-4

24. Foxx Corporation acquired all of Greenburg Company's outstanding stock on January 1, 2019, for $600,000 cash. Greenburg's accounting records showed net assets on that date of $470,000, although equipment with a 10-year remaining life was undervalued on the records by $90,000. Any recognized goodwill is considered to have an indefinite life.

Greenburg reports net income in 2019 of $90,000 and $100,000 in 2020. The subsidiary declared dividends of $20,000 in each of these two years.

Account balances for the year ending December 31, 2021, follow. Credit balances are indicated by parentheses.

	Foxx	Greenburg
Revenues	$ (800,000)	$ (600,000)
Cost of goods sold	100,000	150,000
Depreciation expense	300,000	350,000
Investment income	(20,000)	–0–
Net income	$ (420,000)	$ (100,000)
Retained earnings, 1/1/21	$(1,100,000)	$ (320,000)
Net income	(420,000)	(100,000)
Dividends declared	120,000	20,000
Retained earnings, 12/31/21	$(1,400,000)	$ (400,000)
Current assets	$ 300,000	$ 100,000
Investment in subsidiary	600,000	–0–
Equipment (net)	900,000	600,000
Buildings (net)	800,000	400,000
Land	600,000	100,000
Total assets	$ 3,200,000	$ 1,200,000
Liabilities	$ (900,000)	$ (500,000)
Common stock	(900,000)	(300,000)
Retained earnings	(1,400,000)	(400,000)
Total liabilities and equity	$(3,200,000)	$(1,200,000)

a. Determine the December 31, 2021, consolidated balance for each of the following accounts:

Depreciation Expense	Buildings
Dividends Declared	Goodwill
Revenues	Common Stock
Equipment	

b. How does the parent's choice of an accounting method for its investment affect the balances computed in requirement (*a*)?

c. Which method of accounting for this subsidiary is the parent actually using for internal reporting purposes?

d. If the parent company had used a different method of accounting for this investment, how could that method have been identified?

e. What would be Foxx's balance for retained earnings as of January 1, 2021, if each of the following methods had been in use?

- Initial value method
- Partial equity method
- Equity method

LO 3-1, 3-3a, 3-4

25. Allison Corporation acquired all of the outstanding voting stock of Mathias, Inc., on January 1, 2020, in exchange for $5,875,000 in cash. Allison intends to maintain Mathias as a wholly owned subsidiary. Both companies have December 31 fiscal year-ends. At the acquisition date, Mathias's stockholders' equity was $2,000,000 including retained earnings of $1,500,000.

At the acquisition date, Allison prepared the following fair-value allocation schedule for its newly acquired subsidiary:

Consideration transferred		$5,875,000
Mathias stockholders' equity		2,000,000
Excess fair over book value		$3,875,000
to unpatented technology (8-year remaining life)	$ 800,000	
to patents (10-year remaining life)	2,500,000	
to increase long-term debt (undervalued, 5-year remaining life)	(100,000)	3,200,000
Goodwill		$ 675,000

Postacquisition, Allison employs the equity method to account for its investment in Mathias. During the two years following the business combination, Mathias reports the following income and dividends:

	Income	Dividends
2020	$480,000	$25,000
2021	960,000	50,000

No asset impairments have occurred since the acquisition date.

Individual financial statements for each company as of December 31, 2021, follow. Parentheses indicate credit balances. Dividends declared were paid in the same period.

Income Statement	**Allison**	**Mathias**
Sales	(6,400,000)	(3,900,000)
Cost of goods sold	4,500,000	2,500,000
Depreciation expense	875,000	277,000
Amortization expense	430,000	103,000
Interest expense	55,000	60,000
Equity earnings in Mathias	(630,000)	–0–
Net income	(1,170,000)	(960,000)
Statement of Retained Earnings		
Retained earnings 1/1	(5,340,000)	(1,955,000)
Net income (above)	(1,170,000)	(960,000)
Dividends declared	560,000	50,000
Retained earnings 12/31	(5,950,000)	(2,865,000)
Balance Sheet		
Cash	75,000	143,000
Accounts receivable	950,000	225,000
Inventories	1,700,000	785,000
Investment in Mathias	6,580,000	–0–
Equipment (net)	3,700,000	2,052,000
Patents	95,000	–0–
Unpatented technology	2,125,000	1,450,000
Goodwill	425,000	–0–
Total assets	15,650,000	4,655,000
Accounts payable	(500,000)	(90,000)
Long-term debt	(1,000,000)	(1,200,000)
Common stock	(8,200,000)	(500,000)
Retained earnings 12/31	(5,950,000)	(2,865,000)
Total liabilities and equity	(15,650,000)	(4,655,000)

Required:

a. Show how Allison determined its December 31, 2021, Investment in Mathias balance.

b. Prepare a worksheet to determine the consolidated values to be reported on Allison's financial statements.

LO 3-1, 3-3a

26. On January 3, 2019, Persoff Corporation acquired all of the outstanding voting stock of Sea Cliff, Inc., in exchange for $6,000,000 in cash. Persoff elected to exercise control over Sea Cliff as a wholly owned subsidiary with an independent accounting system. Both companies have December 31 fiscal year-ends. At the acquisition date, Sea Cliff's stockholders' equity was $2,500,000 including retained earnings of $1,700,000.

Persoff pursued the acquisition, in part, to utilize Sea Cliff's technology and computer software. These items had fair values that differed from their values on Sea Cliff's books as follows:

Asset	Book Value	Fair Value	Remaining Useful Life
Patented technology	$140,000	$2,240,000	7 years
Computer software	$ 60,000	$1,260,000	12 years

Sea Cliff's remaining identifiable assets and liabilities had acquisition-date book values that closely approximated fair values. Since acquisition, no assets have been impaired. During the next three years, Sea Cliff reported the following income and dividends:

	Net Income	Dividends
2019	$900,000	$150,000
2020	940,000	150,000
2021	975,000	150,000

December 31, 2021, financial statements for each company follow. Parentheses indicate credit balances. Dividends declared were paid in the same period.

Income Statement	Persoff	Sea Cliff
Revenues	$ (2,720,000)	$(2,250,000)
Cost of goods sold	1,350,000	870,000
Depreciation expense	275,000	380,000
Amortization expense	370,000	25,000
Equity earnings in Sea Cliff	(575,000)	–0–
Net income	$ (1,300,000)	$ (975,000)
Statement of Retained Earnings		
Retained earnings 1/1	$ (7,470,000)	$(3,240,000)
Net income (above)	(1,300,000)	(975,000)
Dividends declared	600,000	150,000
Retained earnings 12/31	$ (8,170,000)	$(4,065,000)
Balance Sheet		
Current assets	$ 490,000	$ 375,000
Investment in Sea Cliff	7,165,000	–0–
Computer software	300,000	45,000
Patented technology	800,000	80,000
Goodwill	100,000	–0–
Equipment	1,835,000	4,500,000
Total assets	$ 10,690,000	$ 5,000,000
Liabilities	$ (520,000)	$ (135,000)
Common stock	(2,000,000)	(800,000)
Retained earnings 12/31	(8,170,000)	(4,065,000)
Total liabilities and equity	$(10,690,000)	$(5,000,000)

a. Construct Persoff's acquisition-date fair-value allocation schedule for its investment in Sea Cliff.

b. Show how Persoff determined its Equity earnings in Sea Cliff balance for the year ended December 31, 2021.

c. Show how Persoff determined its December 31, 2021, Investment in Sea Cliff balance.

d. Prepare a worksheet to determine the consolidated values to be reported on Persoff's financial statements.

LO 3-1, 3-3a

27. On January 1, 2020, Prestige Corporation acquired 100 percent of the voting stock of Stylene Corporation in exchange for $2,030,000 in cash and securities. On the acquisition date, Stylene had the following balance sheet:

Cash	$ 23,000	Accounts payable	$1,050,000
Accounts receivable	97,000		
Inventory	140,000		
Equipment (net)	1,490,000	Common stock	800,000
Trademarks	850,000	Retained earnings	750,000
	$2,600,000		$2,600,000

At the acquisition date, the book values of Stylene's assets and liabilities were generally equivalent to their fair values except for the following assets:

Asset	Book Value	Fair Value	Remaining Useful Life
Equipment	$1,490,000	$1,610,000	8 years
Customer lists	–0–	160,000	4 years
Trademarks	850,000	900,000	Indefinite

During the next two years, Stylene has the following income and dividends in its own separately prepared financial reports to its parent.

	Net Income	Dividends
2020	$175,000	$25,000
2021	375,000	45,000

Dividends are declared and paid in the same period. The December 31, 2021, separate financial statements for each company follow. Parentheses indicate credit balances.

Income Statement	Prestige	Stylene
Revenues	$ (4,200,000)	$(2,200,000)
Cost of goods sold	2,300,000	1,550,000
Depreciation expense	495,000	275,000
Amortization expense	105,000	–0–
Equity earnings in Stylene	(320,000)	–0–
Net income	$ (1,620,000)	$ (375,000)
Statement of Retained Earnings		
Retained earnings 1/1	$ (2,900,000)	$ (900,000)
Net income (above)	(1,620,000)	(375,000)
Dividends declared	150,000	45,000
Retained earnings 12/31	$ (4,370,000)	$(1,230,000)
Balance Sheet		
Cash	$ 430,000	$ 35,000
Accounts receivable	693,000	75,000
Inventory	890,000	420,000
Investment in Stylene	2,400,000	–0–
Equipment	6,000,000	1,400,000
Customer lists	115,000	–0–
Trademarks	2,500,000	850,000
Goodwill	172,000	–0–
Total assets	$ 13,200,000	$ 2,780,000
Accounts payable	$ (330,000)	$ (750,000)
Common stock	(8,500,000)	(800,000)
Retained earnings 12/31	(4,370,000)	(1,230,000)
Total liabilities and equity	$(13,200,000)	$(2,780,000)

a. Prepare Prestige's acquisition-date fair-value allocation schedule for its investment in Stylene.

b. Show how Prestige determined its December 31, 2021, Investment in Stylene balance.

c. Prepare a worksheet to determine the balances for Prestige's December 31, 2021, consolidated financial statements.

LO 3-1, 3-3a

28. Patrick Corporation acquired 100 percent of O'Brien Company's outstanding common stock on January 1 for $550,000 in cash. O'Brien reported net assets with a carrying amount of $350,000 at that time. Some of O'Brien's assets either were unrecorded (having been internally developed) or had fair values that differed from book values as follows:

	Book Values	Fair Values
Trademarks (indefinite life)	$ 60,000	$160,000
Customer relationships (5-year remaining life)	–0–	75,000
Equipment (10-year remaining life)	342,000	312,000

Any goodwill is considered to have an indefinite life with no impairment charges during the year.

The following are financial statements at the end of the first year for these two companies prepared from their separately maintained accounting systems. O'Brien declared and paid dividends in the same period. Credit balances are indicated by parentheses.

	Patrick	O'Brien
Revenues	$(1,125,000)	$(520,000)
Cost of goods sold	300,000	228,000
Depreciation expense	75,000	70,000
Amortization expense	25,000	–0–
Income from O'Brien	(210,000)	–0–
Net Income	$ (935,000)	$(222,000)
Retained earnings 1/1	$ (700,000)	$(250,000)
Net Income	(935,000)	(222,000)
Dividends declared	142,000	80,000
Retained earnings 12/31	$(1,493,000)	$(392,000)
Cash	$ 185,000	$ 105,000
Receivables	225,000	56,000
Inventory	175,000	135,000
Investment in O'Brien	680,000	–0–
Trademarks	474,000	60,000
Customer relationships	–0–	–0–
Equipment (net)	925,000	272,000
Goodwill	–0–	–0–
Total assets	$ 2,664,000	$ 628,000
Liabilities	$ (771,000)	$(136,000)
Common stock	(400,000)	(100,000)
Retained earnings 12/31	(1,493,000)	(392,000)
Total liabilities and equity	$(2,664,000)	$(628,000)

a. Show how Patrick computed the $210,000 Income of O'Brien balance. Discuss how you determined which accounting method Patrick uses for its investment in O'Brien.

b. Without preparing a worksheet or consolidation entries, determine and explain the totals to be reported for this business combination for the year ending December 31.

c. Verify the totals determined in part (*b*) by producing a consolidation worksheet for Patrick and O'Brien for the year ending December 31.

LO 3-1, 3-3a, 3-3b, 3-4

29. Following are separate financial statements of Michael Company and Aaron Company as of December 31, 2021 (credit balances indicated by parentheses). Michael acquired all of Aaron's outstanding voting stock on January 1, 2017, by issuing 20,000 shares of its own $1 par common stock. On the acquisition date, Michael Company's stock actively traded at $23.50 per share.

	Michael Company 12/31/21	Aaron Company 12/31/21
Revenues	$ (610,000)	$ (370,000)
Cost of goods sold	270,000	140,000
Amortization expense	115,000	80,000
Dividend income	(5,000)	–0–
Net income	$ (230,000)	$ (150,000)
Retained earnings, 1/1/21	$ (880,000)	$ (490,000)
Net income (above)	(230,000)	(150,000)
Dividends declared	90,000	5,000
Retained earnings, 12/31/21	$(1,020,000)	$ (635,000)
Cash	$ 110,000	$ 15,000
Receivables	380,000	220,000
Inventory	560,000	280,000
Investment in Aaron Company	470,000	–0–
Copyrights	460,000	340,000
Royalty agreements	920,000	380,000
Total assets	$ 2,900,000	$ 1,235,000
Liabilities	$ (780,000)	$ (470,000)
Preferred stock	(300,000)	–0–
Common stock	(500,000)	(100,000)
Additional paid-in capital	(300,000)	(30,000)
Retained earnings, 12/31/21	(1,020,000)	(635,000)
Total liabilities and equity	$(2,900,000)	$(1,235,000)

On the date of acquisition, Aaron reported retained earnings of $230,000 and a total book value of $360,000. At that time, its royalty agreements were undervalued by $60,000. This intangible was assumed to have a six-year remaining life with no residual value. Additionally, Aaron owned a trademark with a fair value of $50,000 and a 10-year remaining life that was not reflected on its books. Aaron declared and paid dividends in the same period.

a. Using the preceding information, prepare a consolidation worksheet for these two companies as of December 31, 2021.

b. Instead of the initial value method, assume now that Michael applies the equity method to its Investment in Aaron account. What account balances would the parent's individual financial statements then show for the Equity in Subsidiary Earnings, Retained Earnings, and Investment in Aaron accounts?

c. Assuming that Michael applied the equity method to this investment, how would the consolidation entries differ on a December 31, 2021, worksheet?

d. Assuming that Michael applied the equity method to this investment, how would the December 31, 2021, reported consolidated balances differ?

LO 3-1, 3-3, 3-6

30. Giant acquired all of Small's common stock on January 1, 2017, in exchange for cash of $770,000. On that day, Small reported common stock of $170,000 and retained earnings of $400,000. At the acquisition date, $90,000 of the fair-value price was attributed to undervalued land while $50,000 was assigned to undervalued equipment having a 10-year remaining life. The $60,000 unallocated portion of the acquisition-date excess fair value over book value was viewed as goodwill. Over the next few years, Giant applied the equity method to the recording of this investment.

The following are individual financial statements for the year ending December 31, 2021. On that date, Small owes Giant $10,000. Small declared and paid dividends in the same period. Credits are indicated by parentheses.

a. How was the $135,000 Equity in Income of Small balance computed?

b. Without preparing a worksheet or consolidation entries, determine and explain the totals to be reported by this business combination for the year ending December 31, 2021.

c. Verify the amounts determined in part (*b*) by producing a consolidation worksheet for Giant and Small for the year ending December 31, 2021.

d. If Giant determined that the entire amount of goodwill from its investment in Small was impaired in 2021, how would the parent's accounts reflect the impairment loss? How would the worksheet process change? What impact does an impairment loss have on consolidated financial statements?

	Giant	Small
Revenues	$(1,175,000)	$ (360,000)
Cost of goods sold	550,000	90,000
Depreciation expense	172,000	130,000
Equity in income of Small	(135,000)	–0–
Net income	$ (588,000)	$ (140,000)
Retained earnings, 1/1/21	$(1,417,000)	$ (620,000)
Net income (above)	(588,000)	(140,000)
Dividends declared	310,000	110,000
Retained earnings, 12/31/21	$(1,695,000)	$ (650,000)
Current assets	$ 398,000	$ 318,000
Investment in Small	995,000	–0–
Land	440,000	165,000
Buildings (net)	304,000	419,000
Equipment (net)	648,000	286,000
Goodwill	–0–	–0–
Total assets	$ 2,785,000	$ 1,188,000
Liabilities	$ (840,000)	$ (368,000)
Common stock	(250,000)	(170,000)
Retained earnings (above)	(1,695,000)	(650,000)
Total liabilities and equity	$(2,785,000)	$ (1,188,000)

LO 3-1, 3-3a, 3-3b, 3-4

31. On January 1, 2020, Pinnacle Corporation exchanged $3,200,000 cash for 100 percent of the outstanding voting stock of Strata Corporation. On the acquisition date, Strata had the following balance sheet:

Cash	$ 122,000	Accounts payable	$ 375,000
Accounts receivable	283,000	Long-term debt	2,655,000
Inventory	350,000	Common stock	1,500,000
Buildings (net)	1,875,000	Retained earnings	1,100,000
Licensing agreements	3,000,000		$5,630,000
	$5,630,000		

Pinnacle prepared the following fair-value allocation:

Fair value of Strata (consideration transferred)		$3,200,000
Carrying amount acquired		2,600,000
Excess fair value		600,000
to buildings (undervalued)	$300,000	
to licensing agreements (overvalued)	(100,000)	200,000
to goodwill (indefinite life)		$ 400,000

At the acquisition date, Strata's buildings had a 10-year remaining life and its licensing agreements were due to expire in five years. On December 31, 2021, Strata's accounts payable included an $85,000 current liability owed to Pinnacle. Strata Corporation continues its separate legal existence as a wholly owned subsidiary of Pinnacle with independent accounting records. Pinnacle employs the initial value method in its internal accounting for its investment in Strata.

The separate financial statements for the two companies for the year ending December 31, 2021, follow. Credit balances are indicated by parentheses.

	Pinnacle	Strata
Sales	$ (7,000,000)	$(3,000,000)
Cost of goods sold	4,650,000	1,700,000
Interest expense	255,000	160,000
Depreciation expense	585,000	350,000
Amortization expense		600,000
Dividend income	(50,000)	
Net income	$ (1,560,000)	$ (190,000)
Retained earnings 1/1/21	$ (5,000,000)	$(1,350,000)
Net income	(1,560,000)	(190,000)
Dividends declared	560,000	50,000
Retained earnings 12/31/21	$ (6,000,000)	$(1,490,000)
Cash	$ 433,000	$ 165,000
Accounts receivable	1,210,000	200,000
Inventory	1,235,000	1,500,000
Investment in Strata	3,200,000	
Buildings (net)	5,572,000	2,040,000
Licensing agreements		1,800,000
Goodwill	350,000	
Total assets	$ 12,000,000	$ 5,705,000
Accounts payable	$ (300,000)	$ (715,000)
Long-term debt	(2,700,000)	(2,000,000)
Common stock	(3,000,000)	(1,500,000)
Retained earnings 12/31/21	(6,000,000)	(1,490,000)
Total liabilities and OE	$(12,000,000)	$(5,705,000)

a. Prepare a worksheet to consolidate the financial information for these two companies.

b. Compute the following amounts that would appear on Pinnacle's 2021 separate (nonconsolidated) financial records if Pinnacle's investment accounting was based on the equity method.

- Subsidiary income.
- Retained earnings, 1/1/21.
- Investment in Strata.

c. What effect does the parent's internal investment accounting method have on its consolidated financial statements?

LO 3-1, 3-3, 3-4

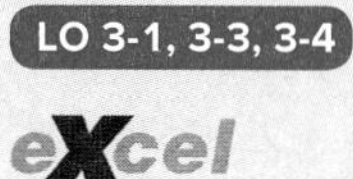

32. The following are selected accounts and balances for Mergaronite Company and Hill, Inc., as of December 31, 2021. Several of Mergaronite's accounts have been omitted. Credit balances are indicated by parentheses. Dividends were declared and paid in the same period.

	Mergaronite	Hill
Revenues	$(600,000)	$(250,000)
Cost of goods sold	280,000	100,000
Depreciation expense	120,000	50,000
Investment income	Not given	NA
Retained earnings, 1/1/21	(900,000)	(600,000)
Dividends declared	130,000	40,000
Current assets	200,000	690,000
Land	300,000	90,000
Buildings (net)	500,000	140,000
Equipment (net)	200,000	250,000
Liabilities	(400,000)	(310,000)
Common stock	(300,000)	(40,000)
Additional paid-in capital	(50,000)	(160,000)

Assume that Mergaronite acquired Hill on January 1, 2017, by issuing 7,000 shares of common stock having a par value of $10 per share but a fair value of $100 each. On January 1, 2017, Hill's land was undervalued by $20,000, its buildings were overvalued by $30,000, and equipment was undervalued by $60,000. The buildings had a 10-year remaining life; the equipment had a 5-year remaining life. A customer list with an appraised value of $100,000 was developed internally by Hill and was estimated to have a 20-year remaining useful life.

a. Determine and explain the December 31, 2021, consolidated totals for the following accounts:

Revenues	Amortization Expense	Customer List
Cost of Goods Sold	Buildings	Common Stock
Depreciation Expense	Equipment	Additional Paid-In Capital

b. In requirement (*a*), why can the consolidated totals be determined without knowing which method the parent used to account for the subsidiary?

c. If the parent uses the equity method, what consolidation entries would be used on a 2021 worksheet?

LO 3-3, 3-4, 3-6

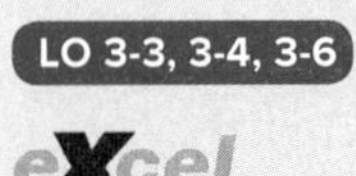

33. On January 1, 2021, Brooks Corporation exchanged $1,183,000 fair-value consideration for all of the outstanding voting stock of Chandler, Inc. At the acquisition date, Chandler had a book value equal to $1,105,000. Chandler's individual assets and liabilities had fair values equal to their respective book values except for the patented technology account, which was undervalued by $204,000 with an estimated remaining life of six years. The Chandler acquisition was Brooks's only business combination for the year.

In case expected synergies did not materialize, Brooks Corporation wished to prepare for a potential future spin-off of Chandler, Inc. Therefore, Brooks had Chandler maintain its separate incorporation and independent accounting information system as elements of continuing value.

On December 31, 2021, each company submitted the following financial statements for consolidation. Dividends were declared and paid in the same period. Parentheses indicated credit balances.

	Brooks Corp.	Chandler Inc.
Income Statement		
Revenues	$ (640,000)	$ (587,000)
Cost of goods sold	255,000	203,000
Gain on bargain purchase	(126,000)	–0–
Depreciation and amortization	150,000	151,000
Equity earnings from Chandler	(199,000)	–0–
Net income	$ (560,000)	$ (233,000)
Statement of Retained Earnings		
Retained earnings, 1/1	$(1,835,000)	$ (805,000)
Net income (above)	(560,000)	(233,000)
Dividends declared	100,000	40,000
Retained earnings, 12/31	$(2,295,000)	$ (998,000)
Balance Sheet		
Current assets	$ 343,000	$ 432,000
Investment in Chandler	1,468,000	–0–
Trademarks	134,000	221,000
Patented technology	395,000	410,000
Equipment	693,000	341,000
Total assets	$ 3,033,000	$ 1,404,000
Liabilities	$ (203,000)	$ (106,000)
Common stock	(535,000)	(300,000)
Retained earnings, 12/31	(2,295,000)	(998,000)
Total liabilities and equity	$(3,033,000)	$(1,404,000)

a. Show how Brooks determined the following account balances:

- Gain on bargain purchase.
- Earnings from Chandler.
- Investment in Chandler.

b. Prepare a December 31, 2021, consolidated worksheet for Brooks and Chandler.

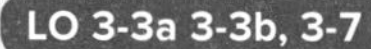

34. Branson paid $465,000 cash for all of the outstanding common stock of Wolfpack, Inc., on January 1, 2020. On that date, the subsidiary had a book value of $340,000 (common stock of $200,000 and retained earnings of $140,000), although various unrecorded royalty agreements (10-year remaining life) were assessed at a $100,000 fair value. Any remaining excess fair value was considered goodwill.

In negotiating the acquisition price, Branson also promised to pay Wolfpack's former owners an additional $50,000 if Wolfpack's income exceeded $120,000 total over the first two years after the acquisition. At the acquisition date, Branson estimated the probability-adjusted present value of this contingent consideration at $35,000. On December 31, 2020, based on Wolfpack's earnings to date, Branson increased the value of the contingency to $40,000.

During the subsequent two years, Wolfpack reported the following amounts for income and dividends:

	Net Income	Dividends Declared
2020	$65,000	$25,000
2021	75,000	35,000

In keeping with the original acquisition agreement, on December 31, 2021, Branson paid the additional $50,000 performance fee to Wolfpack's previous owners.

Prepare each of the following:

a. Branson's entry to record the acquisition of the shares of its Wolfpack subsidiary.

b. Branson's entries at the end of 2020 and 2021 to adjust its contingent performance obligation for changes in fair value and the December 31, 2021, payment.

c. Consolidation worksheet entries as of December 31, 2021, assuming that Branson has applied the equity method.

d. Consolidation worksheet entries as of December 31, 2021, assuming that Branson has applied the initial value method.

LO 3-3, 3-8

35. Allen Company acquired 100 percent of Bradford Company's voting stock on January 1, 2017, by issuing 10,000 shares of its $10 par value common stock (having a fair value of $14 per share). As of that date, Bradford had stockholders' equity totaling $105,000. Land shown on Bradford's accounting records was undervalued by $10,000. Equipment (with a five-year remaining life) was undervalued by $5,000. A secret formula developed by Bradford was appraised at $20,000 with an estimated life of 20 years.

The following are the separate financial statements for the two companies for the year ending December 31, 2021. There were no intra-entity payables on that date. Credit balances are indicated by parentheses.

	Allen Company	Bradford Company
Revenues	$ (485,000)	$(190,000)
Cost of goods sold	160,000	70,000
Depreciation expense	130,000	52,000
Subsidiary earnings	(66,000)	–0–
Net income	$ (261,000)	$ (68,000)
Retained earnings, 1/1/21	$ (659,000)	$ (98,000)
Net income (above)	(261,000)	(68,000)
Dividends declared	175,500	40,000
Retained earnings, 12/31/21	$ (744,500)	$(126,000)
Current assets	$ 268,000	$ 75,000
Investment in Bradford Company	216,000	–0–
Land	427,500	58,000
Buildings and equipment (net)	713,000	161,000
Total assets	$ 1,624,500	$ 294,000
Current liabilities	$ (190,000)	$(103,000)
Common stock	(600,000)	(60,000)
Additional paid-in capital	(90,000)	(5,000)
Retained earnings, 12/31/21	(744,500)	(126,000)
Total liabilities and equity	$(1,624,500)	$(294,000)

a. Explain how Allen derived the $66,000 balance in the Subsidiary Earnings account.

b. Prepare a worksheet to consolidate the financial information for these two companies.

36. Tyler Company acquired all of Jasmine Company's outstanding stock on January 1, 2019, for $206,000 in cash. Jasmine had a book value of only $140,000 on that date. However, equipment (having an eight-year remaining life) was undervalued by $54,400 on Jasmine's financial records. A building with a 20-year remaining life was overvalued by $10,000. Subsequent to the acquisition, Jasmine reported the following:

	Net Income	Dividends Declared
2019	$50,000	$10,000
2020	60,000	40,000
2021	30,000	20,000

In accounting for this investment, Tyler has used the equity method. Selected accounts taken from the financial records of these two companies as of December 31, 2021, follow:

	Tyler Company	Jasmine Company
Revenues—operating	$(310,000)	$(104,000)
Expenses	198,000	74,000
Equipment (net)	320,000	50,000
Buildings (net)	220,000	68,000
Common stock	(290,000)	(50,000)
Retained earnings, 12/31/21	(410,000)	(160,000)

Determine and explain the following account balances as of December 31, 2021:

a. Investment in Jasmine Company (on Tyler's individual financial records).

b. Equity in Subsidiary Earnings (on Tyler's individual financial records).

c. Consolidated Net Income.

d. Consolidated Equipment (net).

e. Consolidated Buildings (net).

f. Consolidated Goodwill (net).

g. Consolidated Common Stock.

h. Consolidated Retained Earnings, 12/31/21.

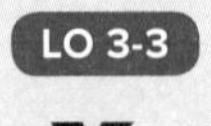

37. On January 1, 2020, Procise Corporation acquired 100 percent of the outstanding voting stock of GaugeRite Corporation for $1,980,000 cash. On the acquisition date, GaugeRite had the following balance sheet:

Cash	$ 14,000	Accounts payable	$ 120,000
Accounts receivable	100,000	Long-term debt	930,000
Land	700,000	Common stock	1,000,000
Equipment (net)	1,886,000	Retained earnings	650,000
	$2,700,000		$2,700,000

At the acquisition date, the following allocation was prepared:

Fair value of consideration transferred		$1,980,000
Book value acquired		1,650,000
Excess fair value over book value		330,000
To in-process research and development	$44,000	
To equipment (8-year remaining life)	56,000	100,000
To goodwill (indefinite life)		$ 230,000

Although at acquisition date Procise had expected $44,000 in future benefits from GaugeRite's in-process research and development project, by the end of 2020 it was apparent that the research project was a failure with no future economic benefits.

On December 31, 2021, Procise and GaugeRite submitted the following trial balances for consolidation. There were no intra-entity payables on that date.

	Procise	GaugeRite
Sales	$ (3,500,000)	$(1,000,000)
Cost of goods sold	1,600,000	630,000
Depreciation expense	350,000	130,000
Other operating expenses	190,000	30,000
Subsidiary income	(203,000)	–0–
Net income	$ (1,563,000)	$ (210,000)
Retained earnings 1/1/21	$ (3,000,000)	$ (800,000)
Net income	(1,563,000)	(210,000)
Dividends declared	200,000	25,000
Retained earnings 12/31/21	$ (4,363,000)	$ (985,000)
Cash	$ 228,000	$ 50,000
Accounts receivable	840,000	155,000
Inventory	900,000	580,000
Investment in GaugeRite	2,257,000	–0–
Land	3,500,000	700,000
Equipment (net)	4,785,000	1,700,000
Goodwill	290,000	–0–
Total assets	$ 12,800,000	$ 3,185,000
Accounts payable	$ (193,000)	$ (400,000)
Long-term debt	(3,094,000)	(800,000)
Common stock	(5,150,000)	(1,000,000)
Retained earnings 12/31/21	(4,363,000)	(985,000)
Total liabilities and equities	$(12,800,000)	$(3,185,000)

a. Show how Procise derived its December 31, 2021, Investment in GaugeRite account balance.

b. Explain the treatment of the acquired in-process research and development.

c. Prepare a consolidated worksheet for Procise and GaugeRite as of December 31, 2021.

LO 3-4, 3-6

38. On January 1, Palisades, Inc., acquired 100 percent of Sherwood Company's common stock for a fair value of $120,000,000 in cash and stock. The carrying amounts of Sherwood's assets and liabilities equaled their fair values except for its equipment, which was undervalued by $500,000 and had a 10-year remaining life.

Palisades specializes in media distribution and viewed its acquisition of Sherwood as a strategic move into content ownership and creation. Palisades expected both cost and revenue synergies from controlling Sherwood's artistic content (a large library of classic movies) and its sports programming specialty video operation. Accordingly, Palisades allocated all of Sherwood's assets and liabilities (including all $50,000,000 of goodwill recognized in the acquisition) to a newly formed operating segment appropriately designated as a reporting unit.

However, Sherwood's assets have taken longer than anticipated to produce the expected synergies with Palisades's operations. Accordingly, Palisades reviewed events and circumstances and concluded that Sherwood's fair value was likely less than its carrying amount. At year-end, Palisades assessed the Sherwood reporting unit's fair value to $110,000,000.

At December 31, Palisades and Sherwood submitted the following balances for consolidation. There were no intra-entity payables on that date. Also, Palisades had not yet recorded any goodwill impairment.

	Palisades, Inc.	Sherwood Co.
Revenues	$(18,570,000)	$(12,000,000)
Operating expenses	10,350,000	11,800,000
Equity in Sherwood's earnings	(150,000)	
Dividends declared	300,000	80,000
Retained earnings, 1/1	(52,000,000)	(2,000,000)

(continued)

(continued)

	Palisades, Inc.	Sherwood Co.
Cash	175,000	109,000
Receivables (net)	210,000	897,000
Investment in Sherwood	120,070,000	
Broadcast licenses	350,000	14,014,000
Movie library	365,000	45,000,000
Equipment (net)	131,000,000	17,500,000
Current liabilities	(185,000)	(650,000)
Long-term debt	(21,915,000)	(7,250,000)
Common stock	(170,000,000)	(67,500,000)

a. What is the relevant test to determine whether goodwill is impaired?

b. How did Palisades determine Sherwood's December 31 carrying amount of $120,070,000?

c. At what amount should Palisades record an impairment loss for its Sherwood reporting unit for the year?

d. What is consolidated net income for the year?

e. What is the December 31 consolidated balance for goodwill?

f. Prepare a consolidated worksheet for Palisades and Sherwood (Palisades's trial balance should first be adjusted for any appropriate impairment loss).

Appendix Problems

LO 3-8

39. Briefly discuss the cost savings that may result from a private company electing to amortize goodwill as opposed to annual impairment testing.

LO 3-8

40. Angela Corporation (a private company) acquired all of the outstanding voting stock of Eddy Tech, Inc., on January 1, 2021, in exchange for $9,000,000 in cash. At the acquisition date, Eddy Tech's stockholders' equity was $7,200,000 including retained earnings of $3,000,000.

At the acquisition date, Angela prepared the following fair value allocation schedule for its newly acquired subsidiary:

Consideration transferred		$9,000,000
Eddy's stockholder's equity		7,200,000
Excess fair over book value		$1,800,000
to patented technology (5-year remaining life)	$150,000	
to trade names (indefinite remaining life)	500,000	
to equipment (8-year remaining life)	50,000	700,000
Goodwill		$1,100,000

At the end of 2021, Angela and Eddy Tech report the following amounts from their individually maintained account balances, before consideration of their parent–subsidiary relationship. Parentheses indicate a credit balance.

	Angela	EddyTech
Sales	$(7,850,000)	$(2,400,000)
Cost of goods sold	4,200,000	1,300,000
Depreciation expense	425,000	48,000
Amortization expense	250,000	12,000
Other operating expenses	75,000	53,750
Net income	$(2,900,000)	$ (986,250)

Required:

Prepare a 2021 consolidated income statement for Angela and its subsidiary Eddy Tech. Assume that Angela, as a private company, elects to amortize goodwill over a 10-year period.

Develop Your Skills

RESEARCH CASE

Jonas Tech Corporation recently acquired Innovation Plus Company. The combined firm consists of three related businesses that will serve as reporting units. In connection with the acquisition, Jonas requests your help with the following asset valuation and allocation issues. Support your answers with references to FASB ASC as appropriate.

Jonas recognizes several identifiable intangibles from its acquisition of Innovation Plus. It expresses the desire to have these intangible assets written down to zero in the acquisition period.

The price Jonas paid for Innovation Plus indicates that it paid a large amount for goodwill. However, Jonas worries that any future goodwill impairment may send the wrong signal to its investors about the wisdom of the Innovation Plus acquisition. Jonas thus wishes to allocate the combined goodwill of all of its reporting units to one account called *Enterprise Goodwill*. In this way, Jonas hopes to minimize the possibility of goodwill impairment because a decline in goodwill in one business unit could be offset by an increase in the value of goodwill in another business unit.

Required

1. Advise Jonas on the acceptability of its suggested immediate write-off of its identifiable intangibles.
2. Indicate the relevant factors to consider in allocating the value assigned to identifiable intangibles acquired in a business combination to expense over time.
3. Advise Jonas on the acceptability of its suggested treatment of goodwill.
4. Indicate the relevant factors to consider in allocating goodwill across an enterprise's business units.

CVS HEALTH IMPAIRMENT ANALYSIS CASE

In 2018, CVS Health Corporation reported a $6.1 billion charge for the impairment of goodwill in one of its reporting units (segments) in its 10-K annual report. Referring to CVS Health's 2018 financial statements and any other information from the media, address the following:

1. CVS Health's segments serve as its reporting units for assessing goodwill for potential impairments. Which segment suffered a 2018 impairment? Describe the revenue model for this segment.
2. What were the underlying business reasons that required CVS Health to record a goodwill impairment in 2018?
3. How did CVS Health reflect the 2018 goodwill impairment in its income statement and cash flow statement?
4. Describe in your own words the goodwill impairment testing steps performed by CVS Health in 2018 and the consequent loss measurement.

FASB ASC AND IASB RESEARCH CASE

A vice president for operations at Poncho Platforms asks for your help on a financial reporting issue concerning goodwill. Two years ago, the company suffered a goodwill impairment loss for its Chip Integration reporting unit. Since that time, however, the Chip Integration unit has recovered nicely and its current cash flows (and projected cash flows) are at an all-time high. The vice president now asks whether the goodwill loss can be reversed given the reversal of fortunes for the Chip Integration reporting unit.

1. Is impairment of goodwill reversible under U.S. GAAP? How about under IFRS? (Refer to FASB Topic 350, "Intangibles—Goodwill and Other," and *IAS 36,* "Impairment of Assets.")
2. Are goodwill impairment testing procedures the same under IFRS and U.S. GAAP? If not, how is goodwill tested for impairment under IFRS? (Refer to *IAS 36,* "Impairment of Assets.")

EXCEL CASE 1

On January 1, 2020, Innovus, Inc., acquired 100 percent of the common stock of ChipTech Company for $670,000 in cash and other fair-value consideration. ChipTech's fair value was allocated among its net assets as follows:

Fair value of consideration transferred for ChipTech		$670,000
Book value of ChipTech:		
Common stock and Additional Paid-In Capital (APIC)	$130,000	
Retained earnings	370,000	500,000
Excess fair value over book value to		170,000
Trademark (10-year remaining life)	$ 40,000	
Existing technology (5-year remaining life)	80,000	120,000
Goodwill		$ 50,000

The December 31, 2021, trial balances for the parent and subsidiary follow (there were no intra-entity payables on that date):

	Innovus	ChipTech
Revenues	$ (990,000)	$(210,000)
Cost of goods sold	500,000	90,000
Depreciation expense	100,000	5,000
Amortization expense	55,000	18,000
Dividend income	(40,000)	–0–
Net income	$ (375,000)	$ (97,000)
Retained earnings 1/1/21	$(1,555,000)	$(450,000)
Net income	(375,000)	(97,000)
Dividends declared	250,000	40,000
Retained earnings 12/31/21	$(1,680,000)	$(507,000)
Current assets	$ 960,000	$ 355,000
Investment in ChipTech	670,000	
Equipment (net)	765,000	225,000
Trademark	235,000	100,000
Existing technology	–0–	45,000
Goodwill	450,000	–0–
Total assets	$ 3,080,000	$ 725,000
Liabilities	$ (780,000)	(88,000)
Common stock	(500,000)	(100,000)
Additional paid-in capital	(120,000)	(30,000)
Retained earnings 12/31/21	(1,680,000)	(507,000)
Total liabilities and equity	$(3,080,000)	$(725,000)

Required

a. Using Excel, compute consolidated balances for Innovus and ChipTech. Either use a worksheet approach or compute the balances directly.

b. Prepare a second spreadsheet that shows a 2021 impairment loss for the entire amount of goodwill from the ChipTech acquisition.

EXCEL CASE 2

On January 1, 2020, Hi-Speed.com acquired 100 percent of the common stock of Wi-Free Co. for cash of $730,000. The consideration transferred was allocated among Wi-Free's net assets as follows:

Wi-Free fair value (cash paid by Hi-Speed)		$730,000
Book value of Wi-Free:		
Common stock and additional paid-in capital (APIC)	$ 130,000	
Retained earnings	370,000	500,000
Excess fair value over book value to		230,000
In-process R&D	$ 75,000	
Computer software (overvalued)	(30,000)	
Internet domain name	120,000	165,000
Goodwill		$ 65,000

At the acquisition date, the computer software had a 4-year remaining life, and the Internet domain name was estimated to have a 10-year remaining life. By the end of 2020, it became clear that the acquired in-process research and development would yield no economic benefits and Hi-Speed.com recognized an impairment loss. At December 31, 2021, Wi-Free's accounts payable included a $30,000 amount owed to Hi-Speed.

The December 31, 2021, trial balances for the parent and subsidiary follow:

	Hi-Speed.com	Wi-Free Co.
Revenues	$(1,100,000)	$(325,000)
Cost of goods sold	625,000	122,000
Depreciation expense	140,000	12,000
Amortization expense	50,000	11,000
Equity in subsidiary earnings	(175,500)	–0–
Net income	$ (460,500)	$(180,000)
Retained earnings 1/1/21	$(1,552,500)	$(450,000)
Net income	(460,500)	(180,000)
Dividends declared	250,000	50,000
Retained earnings 12/31/21	$(1,763,000)	$(580,000)
Current assets	$ 1,034,000	$ 345,000
Investment in Wi-Free	856,000	–0–
Equipment (net)	713,000	305,000
Computer software	650,000	130,000
Internet domain name	–0–	100,000
Goodwill	–0–	–0–
Total assets	$ 3,253,000	$ 880,000
Liabilities	$ (870,000)	$(170,000)
Common stock	(500,000)	(110,000)
Additional paid-in capital	(120,000)	(20,000)
Retained earnings 12/31/21	(1,763,000)	(580,000)
Total liabilities and equity	$(3,253,000)	$(880,000)

Required

a. Using Excel, prepare calculations showing how Hi-Speed derived the $856,000 amount for its investment in Wi-Free.

b. Using Excel, compute consolidated balances for Hi-Speed and Wi-Free. Either use a worksheet approach or compute the balances directly.

Excel Spreadsheet Project

Alternative Investment Methods, Goodwill Impairment, and Consolidated Financial Statements

In this project, you are to provide an analysis of alternative accounting methods for controlling interest investments and subsequent effects on consolidated reporting using Excel. Modeling in Excel helps you quickly assess the impact of alternative accounting methods on consolidated financial reporting, and helps you develop a better understanding of accounting for combined reporting entities

Consolidated Worksheet Preparation

You will be creating and entering formulas to complete four worksheets. The first objective is to demonstrate the effect of different methods of accounting for the investments (equity, initial value, and partial equity) on the parent company's trial balance and on the consolidated worksheet subsequent to acquisition. The second objective is to show the effect on consolidated balances and key financial ratios of recognizing a goodwill impairment loss.

The project requires preparation of the following four separate worksheets:

a. Consolidated information worksheet (follows).
b. Equity method consolidation worksheet.
c. Initial value method consolidation worksheet.
d. Partial equity method consolidation worksheet.

In formulating your solution, each worksheet should link directly to the first worksheet. Also, feel free to create supplemental schedules to enhance the capabilities of your worksheet.

Project Scenario

Pecos Company acquired 100 percent of Suaro's outstanding stock for $1,450,000 cash on January 1, 2020, when Suaro had the following balance sheet:

Assets		Liabilities and Equity	
Cash	$ 37,000	Liabilities	$(422,000)
Receivables	82,000		
Inventory	149,000	Common stock	(350,000)
Land	90,000	Retained earnings	(126,000)
Equipment (net)	225,000		
Software	315,000		
Total assets	$898,000	Total liabilities and equity	$(898,000)

At the acquisition date, the fair values of each identifiable asset and liability that differed from book value were as follows:

Land	$ 80,000	
Brand name	60,000	(indefinite life—unrecognized on Suaro's books)
Software	415,000	(2-year estimated remaining useful life)
In-process R&D	300,000	

Additional Information

- Although at acquisition date Pecos expected future benefits from Suaro's in-process research and development (R&D), by the end of 2020 it became clear that the research project was a failure with no future economic benefits.
- During 2020, Suaro earns $75,000 and pays no dividends.
- Selected amounts from Pecos's and Suaro's separate financial statements at December 31, 2021, are presented in the consolidated information worksheet. All consolidated worksheets are to be prepared as of December 31, 2021, two years subsequent to acquisition.
- Pecos's January 1, 2021, Retained Earnings balance—before any effect from Suaro's 2020 income—is $(930,000) (credit balance).
- Pecos has 500,000 common shares outstanding for EPS calculations and reported $2,943,100 for consolidated assets at the beginning of the period.

The following is the consolidated information worksheet.

	A	B	C	D
1	**December 31, 2021, trial balances**			
2				
3		**Pecos**	**Suaro**	
4	Revenues	$(1,052,000)	$(427,000)	
5	Operating expenses	821,000	262,000	
6	Goodwill impairment loss	?		
7	Income of Suaro	?		
8	Net income	?	$(165,000)	
9				
10	Retained earnings—Pecos 1/1/21	?		
11	Retained earnings—Suaro 1/1/21		(201,000)	
12	Net income (above)	?	(165,000)	
13	Dividends declared	200,000	35,000	
14	Retained earnings 12/31/21	?	$(331,000)	
15				
16	Cash	195,000	95,000	
17	Receivables	247,000	143,000	
18	Inventory	415,000	197,000	
19	Investment in Suaro	?		
20				
21				
22				
23	Land	341,000	85,000	
24	Equipment (net)	240,100	100,000	
25	Software		312,000	
26	Other intangibles	145,000		
27	Goodwill			
28	Total assets	?	$ 932,000	
29				
30	Liabilities	(1,537,100)	(251,000)	
31	Common stock	(500,000)	(350,000)	
32	Retained earnings (above)	?	(331,000)	
33	Total liabilities and equity	?	$(932,000)	
34				
35	Fair-value allocation schedule			
36	Price paid	1,450,000		
37	Book value	476,000		
38	Excess initial value	974,000	Amortizations	
39	to land	(10,000)	2020	2021
40	to brand name	60,000	?	?

(continued)

(continued)

	A	B	C	D
41	to software	100,000	?	?
42	to IPR&D	300,000	?	?
43	to goodwill	524,000	?	?
44				
45	Suaro's RE changes	Income	Dividends	
46	2020	75,000	0	
47	2021	165,000	35,000	

Project Requirements

Complete the four worksheets as follows:

1. Input the consolidated information worksheet provided and complete the fair-value allocation schedule by computing the excess amortizations for 2020 and 2021.
2. Using separate worksheets, prepare Pecos's trial balances for each of the indicated accounting methods (equity, initial value, and partial equity). Use only formulas for the Investment in Suaro, the Income of Suaro, and Retained Earnings accounts.
3. Using references to other cells only (either from the consolidated information worksheet or from the separate method sheets), prepare for each of the three consolidation worksheets:
   - Adjustments and eliminations.
   - Consolidated balances.
4. Calculate and present the effects of a 2021 total goodwill impairment loss on the following ratios for the consolidated entity:
   - Earnings per share (EPS).
   - Return on assets.
   - Return on equity.
   - Debt to equity.

   Your worksheets should have the capability to adjust immediately for the possibility that all acquisition goodwill can be considered impaired in 2021.
5. **Prepare a report that describes and discusses the following worksheet results:**
   a. The effects of alternative investment accounting methods on the parent's trial balances and the final consolidation figures.
   b. The relation between consolidated retained earnings and the parent's retained earnings under each of the three (equity, initial value, partial equity) investment accounting methods.
   c. The effect on EPS, return on assets, return on equity, and debt-to-equity ratios of the recognition that all acquisition-related goodwill is considered impaired in 2021.

chapter 4

Consolidated Financial Statements and Outside Ownership

Walmart Inc. (Walmart), in its 2018 consolidated financial statements, includes the accounts of the company and all of its subsidiaries in which a controlling interest is maintained. For those consolidated subsidiaries where Walmart's ownership is less than 100 percent, the outside stockholders' interests are shown as *noncontrolling interests* in the stockholders' equity section of its consolidated balance sheet. On its consolidated income statement, Walmart also allocates a share of the consolidated net income to the noncontrolling interest.

A number of reasons exist for one company to hold less than 100 percent ownership of a subsidiary. The parent might not have had sufficient resources available to obtain all of the outstanding stock. As a second possibility, a few subsidiary stockholders may elect to retain their ownership, perhaps in hope of getting a better price at a later date.

Lack of total ownership is frequently encountered with foreign subsidiaries. The laws of some countries prohibit outsiders from maintaining complete control of domestic business enterprises. In other areas of the world, a parent can seek to establish better relations with a subsidiary's employees, customers, and local government by maintaining some percentage of native ownership.

LO 4-1

Understand that business combinations can occur with less than complete ownership.

Regardless of the reason for owning less than 100 percent, the parent consolidates the financial data of every subsidiary when control is present. As discussed in Chapter 2, *complete ownership is not a prerequisite for consolidation.* A single economic entity is formed whenever one company is able to control the decision-making process of another.

Although most parent companies own 100 percent of their subsidiaries, a significant number, such as Walmart, establish control with a lesser amount of stock. The remaining outside owners are collectively referred to as *a noncontrolling interest,* which replaces the traditional term *minority interest.*[1] The presence of these other stockholders poses a number of reporting questions for the accountant. Whenever less than 100 percent of a subsidiary's voting stock is held, how should the subsidiary's accounts be valued within consolidated financial statements? How should the presence of these additional owners be acknowledged?

[1] The term *minority interest* had been used almost universally to identify the presence of other outside owners. However, current GAAP refers to these outside owners as the noncontrolling interest. Because this term is more descriptive, it is used throughout this textbook.

Learning Objectives

After studying this chapter, you should be able to:

- LO 4-1 Understand that business combinations can occur with less than complete ownership.
- LO 4-2 Describe the concepts and valuation principles underlying the acquisition method of accounting for the noncontrolling interest.
- LO 4-3 Allocate goodwill acquired in a business combination across the controlling and noncontrolling interests.
- LO 4-4 Demonstrate the computation and allocation of consolidated net income in the presence of a noncontrolling interest.
- LO 4-5 Identify and calculate the four noncontrolling interest figures that must be included within the consolidation process and prepare a consolidation worksheet in the presence of a noncontrolling interest.
- LO 4-6 Identify appropriate placements for the components of the noncontrolling interest in consolidated financial statements.
- LO 4-7 Determine the effect on consolidated financial statements of a control premium paid by the parent.
- LO 4-8 Understand the impact on consolidated financial statements of a midyear acquisition.
- LO 4-9 Understand the impact on consolidated financial statements when a step acquisition has taken place.
- LO 4-10 Record the sale of a subsidiary (or a portion of its shares).

LO 4-2

Describe the concepts and valuation principles underlying the acquisition method of accounting for the noncontrolling interest.

Consolidated Financial Reporting in the Presence of a Noncontrolling Interest

Noncontrolling Interest Defined

The authoritative accounting literature defines a noncontrolling interest as follows:

> The ownership interests in the subsidiary that are held by owners other than the parent is a noncontrolling interest. The noncontrolling interest in a subsidiary is part of the equity of the consolidated group. (FASB ASC 810-10-45-15)

When a parent company acquires a controlling ownership interest with less than 100 percent of a subsidiary's voting shares, it must account for the noncontrolling shareholders' interest in its consolidated financial statements. The noncontrolling interest represents an additional set of owners who have legal claim to the subsidiary's net assets. Examples of companies with noncontrolling interests include the following:

Company	Recent Noncontrolling Interest Value
AT&T	$ 9.8 billion
Walmart	7.4 billion
Exxon Mobil	6.8 billion
Walt Disney	4.0 billion
General Motors	3.9 billion
Coca-Cola	1.9 billion
Verizon	1.6 billion
Chevron	1.2 billion
AT&T	1.1 billion
Costco	304 million
Merck	233 million

Exhibit 4.1 provides a framework for introducing several fundamental challenges in accounting and reporting for a noncontrolling interest. The issues focus on how the parent, in its consolidated financial statements, should

- Recognize the subsidiary's assets and liabilities.
- Assign values to the subsidiary's assets and liabilities.
- Value and disclose the presence of the other owners as the noncontrolling interest.

The acquisition method's solution to these challenges involves both the *economic unit concept* and the *fair value* measurement attribute. First, the economic unit concept views the parent and subsidiary companies as a single economic unit for financial reporting purposes. Thus, a controlled company must always be consolidated as a whole regardless of the parent's level of ownership. As shown in Exhibit 4.1, when a parent controls a subsidiary through a 70 percent ownership, the parent must consolidate 100 percent of the subsidiary's (and the parent's) assets and liabilities in order to reflect the single economic unit. The consolidated balance sheet then provides an owners' equity amount for the noncontrolling owners' interest—a recognition that the parent does not own 100 percent of the subsidiary's assets and liabilities.

EXHIBIT 4.1
Noncontrolling Interest—Date of Acquisition

PARENT AND 70% OWNED SUBSIDIARY COMPANIES
Consolidated Balance Sheet
Date of Acquisition

Parent's assets (100%)	Parent's liabilities (100%)
Subsidiary's assets (100%)	**Subsidiary's liabilities (100%)**
	Parent company owners' equity
	• 100% of parent's net assets
	• **70% of subsidiary's net assets**
	Noncontrolling owners' interest
	• **30% of subsidiary net assets**

The acquisition method also captures the subsidiary's acquisition-date fair values as the relevant measurement attribute for reporting the financial effects of the business combination—including the noncontrolling interest. Fair values also provide for managerial accountability to investors and creditors for assessing the success or failure of the combination. In contrast, the parent's assets and liabilities remain at their previous carrying amounts.

Control and Accountability

In acquiring a controlling interest, a parent company becomes responsible for managing all the subsidiary's assets and liabilities even though it may own only a partial interest. If a parent can control the business activities of its subsidiary, it directly follows that the parent is accountable to its investors and creditors for all of the subsidiary's assets, liabilities, and profits. To provide a complete picture of the acquired subsidiary requires fair-value measurements for both the subsidiary as a whole and its individual assets and liabilities. Thus, for business combinations involving less-than-100 percent ownership, the acquirer recognizes and measures the following at the acquisition date:

- All subsidiary identifiable assets and liabilities at their full fair values.[2]
- Noncontrolling interest at fair value.
- Goodwill or a gain from a bargain purchase.

In concluding that consolidated statements involving a noncontrolling interest should initially show all of the subsidiary's assets and liabilities at their full fair values, the 2005 FASB exposure draft Business Combinations (para. B23.a.) observed:

> The acquirer obtains control of the acquiree at the acquisition date and, therefore, becomes responsible and accountable for all of the acquiree's assets, liabilities, and activities, regardless of the percentage of its ownership in the investee.
>
> . . . an important purpose of financial statements is to provide users with relevant and reliable information about the performance of the entity and the resources under its control. That applies regardless of the extent of the ownership interest a parent holds in a particular subsidiary. The Boards concluded that measurement at fair value enables users to better assess the cash generating abilities of the identifiable net assets acquired in the business combination and the accountability of management for the resources entrusted to it.

To summarize, even though a company acquires less than 100 percent of another firm, financial reporting standards require the parent to include 100 percent of the assets acquired and liabilities assumed. At the acquisition date, the parent measures at fair value both the subsidiary as a whole and its identifiable assets and liabilities. Also, the parent recognizes the noncontrolling interest at its acquisition-date fair value. However, as discussed next, measuring the fair value of the noncontrolling interest presents some special challenges.

Subsidiary Acquisition-Date Fair Value in the Presence of a Noncontrolling Interest

When a parent company acquires a less-than-100 percent controlling interest in another firm, the acquisition method requires a determination of the acquisition-date fair value of the acquired firm for consolidated financial reporting. The total acquired firm fair value in the presence of a partial acquisition is the sum of the following two components at the acquisition date:

- The fair value of the controlling interest.
- The fair value of the noncontrolling interest.

The sum of these two components serves as the starting point for the parent in valuing and reporting the subsidiary acquisition. If the sum exceeds the collective fair values of the identifiable net assets acquired and liabilities assumed, then goodwill is recognized. Conversely, if the collective fair values of the identifiable net assets acquired and liabilities assumed exceed the total fair value, the acquirer recognizes a gain on bargain purchase.

Measurement of the acquisition-date **controlling interest** fair value remains straightforward in the vast majority of cases—the consideration transferred by the parent typically

[2] As noted in Chapter 2, exceptions to the fair-value measurement principle include deferred taxes, certain employee benefits, indemnification assets, reacquired rights, share-based awards, and assets held for sale.

Discussion Question

The FASB received numerous comment letters during its deliberations prior to adopting the current financial accounting standards on business combinations. Many of these letters addressed the FASB's proposed (and ultimately accepted) use of the economic unit concept as a valuation basis for less-than-100-percent acquisitions. A sampling of these letters includes the following observations:

Bob Laux, Microsoft: Microsoft agrees with the Board that the principles underlying standards should strive to reflect the underlying economics of transactions and events. However, we do not believe the Board's conclusion that recognizing the entire economic value of the acquiree, regardless of the ownership interest in the acquiree at the acquisition date, reflects the underlying economics.

Patricia A. Little, Ford Motor Company: We agree that recognizing 100 percent of the fair value of the acquiree is appropriate. We believe that this is crucial in erasing anomalies which were created when only the incremental ownership acquired was fair valued and the minority interest was reflected at its carryover basis.

Sharilyn Gasaway, Alltel Corporation: One of the underlying principles . . . is that the acquirer should measure and recognize the fair value of the acquiree as a whole. If 100 percent of the ownership interests are acquired, measuring and recognizing 100 percent of the fair value is both appropriate and informative. However, if less than 100 percent of the ownership interests are acquired, recognizing the fair value of 100 percent of the business acquired is not representative of the value actually acquired. In the instance in which certain minority owners retain their ownership interest, recognizing the fair value of the minority interest does not provide sufficient benefit to financial statement users to justify the additional cost incurred to calculate that fair value.

Pricewaterhouse Coopers: We agree that the noncontrolling interest should be recorded at its fair value when it is initially recorded in the consolidated financial statements. As such, when control is obtained in a single step, the acquirer would record 100 percent of the fair value of the assets acquired (including goodwill) and liabilities assumed.

Loretta Cangialosi, Pfizer: While we understand the motivation of the FASB to account for all elements of the acquisition transaction at fair value, we are deeply concerned about the practice issues that will result. The heavy reliance on expected value techniques, use of the hypothetical market participants, the lack of observable markets, and the obligation to affix values to "possible" and even "remote" scenarios, among other requirements, will all conspire to create a standard that will likely prove to be nonoperational, unauditable, representationally unfaithful, abuse-prone, costly, and of limited (and perhaps negative) shareholder value.

Do you think the FASB made the correct decision in requiring consolidated financial statements to recognize all of the subsidiary's assets and liabilities at fair value regardless of the percentage ownership acquired by the parent?

provides the best evidence of fair value of the acquirer's interest. However, there is no parallel consideration transferred available to value the **noncontrolling interest** at the acquisition date. Therefore, the parent must employ other valuation techniques to estimate the fair value of the noncontrolling interest at the acquisition date. Often, a parent can rely on readily available market trading activity to provide a fair valuation for its subsidiary's noncontrolling interest. As seen in FASB ASC 805-20-30-7, the acquisition method

> requires the acquirer to measure a noncontrolling interest in the acquiree at its fair value at the acquisition date. An acquirer sometimes will be able to measure the acquisition-date fair value of a noncontrolling interest on the basis of a quoted price in an active market for the equity shares (that is, those not held by the acquirer).

However, in the absence of fair value evidence based on market trades, firms must turn to less objective measures of noncontrolling interest fair value. FASB ASC 805-20-30-7 goes on to say that

> In other situations, however, a quoted price in an active market for the equity shares will not be available. In those situations, the acquirer would measure the fair value of the noncontrolling interest using another valuation technique.

For acquired firms that are not actively traded (e.g., private companies), noncontrolling interest fair value measurements are frequently determined using significant inputs not observable in a market.[3] In such cases, valuation models based on subsidiary discounted cash flows or residual income projections may be employed to estimate the acquisition-date fair value of the noncontrolling interest.

For example, in 2018 Walmart Inc. acquired 77 percent of FlipKart, an Indian e-commerce company for $16 billion. Walmart measured the acquisition-date fair value of the 23 percent noncontrolling interest at $4.9 billion. As noted in Walmart's third quarter 2018 10-Q report, The $4.9 billion noncontrolling interest measurement was determined using a projected income approach.

Control Premiums, Noncontrolling Interest Valuation, and Goodwill

Acquirers frequently pay a premium price per share to garner sufficient shares to ensure a controlling interest. Then, once enough shares are acquired to obtain control (and the percentage ownership desired), the remaining (noncontrolling interest) shares no longer provide the added benefit of transferring control to the new owner and, therefore, may sell at a price less than the shares that yielded control.

For example, when Expedia, Inc., acquired its 63 percent controlling interest in Trivago, the fair value of the noncontrolling interest excluded any control premium. In discussing the Trivago acquisition, Expedia's annual report noted

> The fair value of the 37% noncontrolling interest was estimated to be $344 million at the time of acquisition based on the fair value per share, excluding the control premium. The control premium was derived directly based on the additional consideration paid to certain shareholders in order to obtain control. The additional consideration was determined to be the best estimate to represent the control premium as it was a premium paid only to the controlling shareholders.

Control premiums are properly included in the fair value of the controlling interest, but as the Expedia–Trivago combination demonstrates, they sometimes do not affect the fair values of the remaining subsidiary shares. Therefore, separate independent valuations for the controlling and noncontrolling interests are often needed for measuring the total fair value of the subsidiary.

One important accounting and reporting effect of a control premium involves the goodwill acquired in the acquisition. When a parent company pays a control premium, the additional consideration transferred typically increases goodwill. However, because the noncontrolling interest shareholders did not pay a control premium, the incremental amount of goodwill is attributable to the parent.

To properly report ownership equity in consolidated financial statements, acquisition-date goodwill should be apportioned across the controlling and noncontrolling interests. As presented in the following section, the amount of goodwill attributable to the parent and noncontrolling interest depends on whether the parent has paid a control premium in the acquisition. If no control premium was paid, goodwill is allocated in proportion to the ownership percentages of the parent and noncontrolling interests. However, when a control premium is paid, the goodwill is allocated disproportionately to the parent, reflecting the extra price paid to extract synergies from the acquired firm.

LO 4-3

Allocate goodwill acquired in a business combination across the controlling and noncontrolling interests.

Goodwill Allocation across Ownership Interests—Parent Pays No Control Premium

In some situations, the parent pays no control premium for an acquired firm. Such cases may include the acquisition of firms in distress or firms for which a sale to an acquirer presents an attractive option for current shareholders to maintain their value going forward. To illustrate,

[3] Such determinations represent a level 3 fair value measurement in the fair value hierarchy as defined in ASC Topic 820, Fair Value Measurement.

assume Portage, Inc., pays $70 per share for 9,000 shares of Stone, Inc., representing a 90 percent equity interest. Also assume that the remaining 1,000 noncontrolling interest shares continue to trade at $70. The total fair value of Stone is then estimated at $700,000 as follows:

Fair value of controlling interest ($70 × 9,000 shares)	$630,000
Fair value of noncontrolling interest ($70 × 1,000 shares)	70,000
Acquisition-date fair value of Stone, Inc.	$700,000

At the acquisition date, Portage assessed the total fair value of Stone's identifiable net assets at $600,000. Therefore, we compute goodwill as the excess of the acquisition-date fair value of the firm as a whole over the sum of the fair values of the identifiable net assets as follows:

Acquisition-date fair value of Stone, Inc.	$700,000
Fair value of Stone's identifiable net assets	600,000
Goodwill	$100,000

We then allocate goodwill across the controlling and noncontrolling interest based on the excess of their respective acquisition-date fair values and their proportionate share of the subsidiary's identifiable net assets as follows:

	90% Controlling Interest	10% Noncontrolling Interest	Total
Acquisition-date fair value of Stone, Inc. . . .	$630,000	$70,000	$700,000
Relative fair value of Stone's identifiable net assets (90% and 10%).	540,000	60,000	600,000
Goodwill	$ 90,000	$10,000	$100,000

Note that in this case, because the price per share paid by the parent equals the noncontrolling interest per share fair value, goodwill is recognized proportionately across the two ownership groups.

Goodwill Allocation across Ownership Interests—Parent Pays a Control Premium

In many situations, acquirers must bid up the price beyond current trading values to induce sufficient numbers of shareholder to sell. The incremental amount paid in a business combination above the preacquisition subsidiary value is referred to as a **control premium.** As observed in ASC 805-20-30-8,

> The fair values of the acquirer's interest in the acquiree and the noncontrolling interest on a per-share basis might differ. The main difference is likely to be the inclusion of a control premium in the per-share fair value of the acquirer's interest in the acquiree.

Such control premiums affect acquisition-date valuation and goodwill allocation across the controlling and noncontrolling interests. To illustrate, we now assume that Portage pays a control premium to acquire Stone. Although Stone's shares were trading at $70 per share, Portage ended up paying $675,000 (an average of $75 per share) to acquire 90 percent of the outstanding shares.[4] Thus, Portage paid a $45,000 control premium for its acquisition of 90 percent of Stone as follows:

Amount paid by Portage, Inc., for 90% of Stone, Inc. shares	$675,000
Preacquisition trading value of 90% Stone, Inc. shares	630,000
Control premium	$ 45,000

During the weeks following the acquisition, the 10 percent noncontrolling interest in Stone, Inc., continues to trade in a $69-to-$71 range.

In this case, the $75 average per share price paid by Portage ($675,000 ÷ 9,000 shares) does not appear representative of the fair value of all the shares of Stone, Inc. The fact that

[4] A more detailed analysis of the effect of a control premium on consolidated financial reporting is presented later in this chapter.

the noncontrolling interest shares continued to trade around $70 per share indicates a $70,000 fair value for the 1,000 shares not owned by Portage. Therefore, the noncontrolling interest valuation is best evidenced by the $70,000 traded fair value for 1,000 of Stone's shares, not the price paid by Portage.

The 9,000 shares acquired by Portage, though, have a fair value of $675,000 and incorporate the additional value Portage expects to extract with Stone beyond the per share preacquisition price. Thus, the fair value of Stone is measured as the sum of the respective fair values of the controlling and noncontrolling interests as follows:

Fair value of controlling interest ($75 × 9,000 shares)	$675,000
Fair value of noncontrolling interest ($70 × 1,000 shares)	70,000
Acquisition-date fair value of Stone, Inc.	$745,000

Next, we allocate the goodwill acquired in the Stone acquisition across the controlling and noncontrolling interests as follows:

	Controlling Interest	Noncontrolling Interest	Total
Acquisition-date fair value of Stone, Inc.	$675,000	$70,000	$745,000
Relative fair value of Stone's identifiable net assets (90% and 10% of $600,000)	540,000	60,000	600,000
Goodwill	$135,000	$10,000	$145,000

Observe in the schedule that the parent first allocates goodwill to its controlling interest for the excess of the fair value of the parent's equity interest over its share of the fair value of the identifiable net assets. In a similar fashion, the acquisition-date fair value of the noncontrolling interest is compared to its share of the fair value of the identifiable net assets. As a result, the previous goodwill allocation (~93 percent to the controlling interest and ~7 percent to the noncontrolling interest) is disproportionate to the 90 percent and 10 percent relative ownership interests.

Comparing the current case (control premium paid) with the previous case (no control premium paid) provides insight into the resulting goodwill allocation.

	No Control Premium	Control Premium	Difference
Price paid by Portage	$630,000	$675,000	+$45,000
Goodwill allocated to Portage	$ 90,000	$135,000	+$45,000

As seen in the preceding schedule, the entire incremental $45,000 paid by Portage as a control premium results in an extra $45,000 goodwill allocation to Portage. None of the incremental payment resulted in additional goodwill allocation to the noncontrolling interest, which remains at $10,000 in both cases.

In the unlikely event that the noncontrolling interest's proportionate share of the subsidiary's net asset fair values exceeds its total fair value, such an excess would serve to reduce the goodwill recognized by the parent and no goodwill would be allocated to the noncontrolling interest. Finally, if the total fair value of the acquired firm is less than the collective sum of its identifiable net assets, a *bargain purchase* occurs. In such rare combinations, the parent recognizes the entire gain on bargain purchase in current income. In no case is any amount of the gain allocated to the noncontrolling interest.

LO 4-4

Demonstrate the computation and allocation of consolidated net income in the presence of a noncontrolling interest.

Allocating Consolidated Net Income to the Parent and Noncontrolling Interest

Consolidated net income measures the results of operations for the combined entity. Reflecting the economic unit concept, consolidated net income includes 100 percent of the parent's net income and 100 percent of the subsidiary's net income, adjusted for excess acquisition-date fair value over book value amortizations. Once consolidated net income is determined, it is then allocated to the parent company and the noncontrolling interests. Because the noncontrolling interests' ownership pertains only to the subsidiary, their share of consolidated net income is limited to a share of the subsidiary's net income adjusted for acquisition-date excess fair-value amortizations.[5]

To illustrate, again assume that Portage acquires 90 percent of Stone, Inc. Further assume that current-year consolidated net income equals $108,000, including $10,000 of annual acquisition-date excess fair-value amortization. If Stone reports revenues of $280,000 and expenses of $160,000 based on its internal book values, then the noncontrolling interest share of Stone's income can be computed as follows:

Noncontrolling Interest in Subsidiary Stone Company Net Income	
Stone revenues	$280,000
Stone expenses	160,000
Stone net income	$120,000
Excess acquisition-date fair-value amortization	10,000
Stone net income adjusted for excess amortization	$110,000
Noncontrolling interest percentage	10%
Noncontrolling interest share of adjusted subsidiary net income	$ 11,000

The $11,000 noncontrolling interest share of adjusted subsidiary net income is equivalent to the noncontrolling interest share of consolidated net income. This figure is then simply subtracted from the combined entity's consolidated net income to derive the parent's interest in consolidated net income. Thus, the allocation is presented in Portage's consolidated financial statements as follows:

Consolidated Net Income Allocation	
Consolidated net income	$108,000
Less: Net income attributable to noncontrolling interest	11,000
Net income attributable to parent (controlling interest)	$ 97,000

Note that the noncontrolling shareholders' portion of consolidated net income is limited to their 10 percent share of the adjusted *subsidiary* income. These shareholders own a 10 percent interest in the subsidiary company but no ownership in the parent firm.[6]

LO 4-5

Identify and calculate the four noncontrolling interest figures that must be included within the consolidation process, and prepare a consolidation worksheet in the presence of a noncontrolling interest.

Partial Ownership Consolidations (Acquisition Method)

Having reviewed the basic concepts of accounting for a noncontrolling interest, we now concentrate on the mechanical aspects of the consolidation process when an outside ownership is present. Specifically, we examine consolidations for time periods subsequent to the date of acquisition to analyze the full range of accounting complexities created by a noncontrolling interest. This discussion centers on the acquisition method as required under generally accepted accounting principles.

The acquisition method focuses initially on incorporating in the consolidated financial statements 100 percent of the subsidiary's assets and liabilities at their acquisition-date fair values. Note that subsequent to acquisition, changes in current fair values for assets and liabilities are not recognized.[7] Instead, the subsidiary assets acquired and liabilities assumed are

[5] Adjusting the subsidiary net income for the excess fair-value amortizations recognizes that the noncontrolling interest represents equity in the subsidiary's net assets as remeasured to fair values on the acquisition date.

[6] In this text, we assume that the relative ownership percentages of the parent and noncontrolling interest represent an appropriate basis for allocating adjusted subsidiary net income across ownership groups.

[7] Exceptions common to all firms (whether subject to consolidation or not) include recognizing changing fair values for marketable equity securities and other financial instruments.

reflected in future consolidated financial statements using their acquisition-date fair values net of subsequent excess fair value amortizations (or possibly reduced for impairment).

The presence of a noncontrolling interest does not dramatically alter the consolidation procedures presented in Chapter 3. The unamortized balance of the acquisition-date fair-value allocation must still be computed and included within the consolidated totals. Excess fair-value amortization expenses of these allocations are recognized each year as appropriate. Reciprocal balances are eliminated. Beyond these basic steps, the measurement and recognition of four noncontrolling interest balances add a new dimension to the process of consolidating financial information. The parent company must determine and then enter each of these figures when constructing a worksheet:

- Noncontrolling interest in the subsidiary as of the beginning of the current year.
- Net income attributable to the noncontrolling interest.
- Subsidiary dividends attributable to the noncontrolling interest.
- Noncontrolling interest as of the end of the year (found by combining the three preceding balances).

We next illustrate the effects of a less-than-100-percent acquisition on the preparation of consolidated financial statements when no control premium was paid by the parent. Then, we provide an example characterized by an acquisition control premium.

Illustration—Partial Acquisition with No Control Premium

To illustrate, assume that King Company acquires 80 percent of Pawn Company's 100,000 outstanding voting shares on January 1, 2020, for $9.75 per share or a total of $780,000 cash consideration. Further assume that the 20 percent noncontrolling interest shares traded both before and after the acquisition date at an average of $9.75 per share. The total fair value of Pawn to be used initially in consolidation is

Consideration transferred by King ($9.75 × 80,000 shares)	$780,000
Noncontrolling interest fair value ($9.75 × 20,000 shares)	195,000
Pawn's acquisition-date fair value	$975,000

Thus King did not pay a control premium to acquire its share of Pawn—both sets of shares have identical per share fair values.

Exhibit 4.2 presents the book value of Pawn's accounts as well as the fair value of each asset and liability on the acquisition date. Pawn's total fair value is attributed to Pawn's assets and liabilities as shown in Exhibit 4.3. Annual amortization relating to these allocations also is included in this schedule. Although expense figures are computed for only the initial years, some amount of amortization is recognized in each of the 20 years following the acquisition (the life assumed for the patented technology).

EXHIBIT 4.2
Subsidiary Accounts—Date of Acquisition

PAWN COMPANY
Account Balances
January 1, 2020

	Book Value	Fair Value	Difference
Current assets	$ 440,000	$440,000	$ –0–
Trademarks (indefinite life)	260,000	320,000	60,000
Patented technology (20-year remaining life) . . .	480,000	600,000	120,000
Equipment (10-year remaining life)	110,000	100,000	(10,000)
Long-term liabilities (8 years to maturity)	(550,000)	(510,000)	40,000
Net assets	$ 740,000	$950,000	$210,000
Common stock	$(230,000)		
Retained earnings, 1/1/20	(510,000)		

Note: Parentheses indicate a credit balance.

EXHIBIT 4.3 Excess Fair-Value Allocations

KING COMPANY AND 80% OWNED SUBSIDIARY PAWN COMPANY
Fair-Value Allocation and Amortization
January 1, 2020

	Allocation	Remaining Life (years)	Annual Excess Amortizations
Pawn's acquisition-date fair value (100%)	$975,000		
Pawn's acquisition-date book value (100%)	(740,000)		
Fair value in excess of book value	$235,000		
Adjustments (100%) to			
Trademarks	$ 60,000	indefinite	$ -0-
Patented technology	120,000	20	6,000
Equipment	(10,000)	10	(1,000)
Long-term liabilities (8 years to maturity)	40,000	8	5,000
Goodwill	$ 25,000	indefinite	$ -0-
Annual amortizations of excess fair value over book value (initial years)			$ 10,000

Goodwill Allocation to the Controlling and Noncontrolling Interests

	Controlling Interest	Noncontrolling Interest	Total
Fair value at acquisition date	$780,000	$195,000	$975,000
Relative fair value of Pawn's identifiable net assets (80% and 20%)	760,000	190,000	950,000
Goodwill	$ 20,000	$ 5,000	$ 25,000

Exhibit 4.3 shows first that all identifiable assets acquired and liabilities assumed are adjusted to their full individual fair values at the acquisition date. The noncontrolling interest will share proportionately in these fair-value adjustments. Exhibit 4.3 also shows that any excess fair value not attributable to Pawn's identifiable net assets is assigned to goodwill. Because the controlling and noncontrolling interests' acquisition-date fair values are identical at $9.75 per share, the resulting goodwill is allocated proportionately across these ownership interests.

Consolidated financial statements will be produced for the year ending December 31, 2021. This date is arbitrary. Any time period subsequent to 2020 could serve to demonstrate the applicable consolidation procedures. Having already calculated the acquisition-date fair-value allocations and related amortization, the accountant can construct a consolidation of these two companies along the lines demonstrated in Chapter 3. Only the presence of the 20 percent noncontrolling interest alters this process.

To complete the information needed for this combination, assume that Pawn Company reports the following changes in retained earnings since King's acquisition:

Current year (2021)	
Net income	$90,000
Less: Dividends declared	(50,000)
Increase in retained earnings	$40,000
Prior years (only 2020 in this illustration):	
Increase in retained earnings	$70,000

Assuming that King Company applies the equity method, the Investment in Pawn Company account as of December 31, 2021, can be constructed as shown in Exhibit 4.4. Note that the $852,000 balance is computed based on applying King's 80 percent ownership to Pawn's income (less amortization) and dividends. Although 100 percent of the

EXHIBIT 4.4
Equity Method Investment Balance

KING COMPANY
Investment in Pawn Company
Equity Method
December 31, 2021

Acquisition price for 80% interest		$780,000
Prior year (2020):		
Increase in retained earnings (80% × $70,000)	$56,000	
Excess amortization expenses (80% × $10,000) (Exhibit 4.3)	(8,000)	48,000
Current year (2021):		
Income accrual (80% × $90,000)	72,000	
Excess amortization expense (80% × $10,000) (Exhibit 4.3)	(8,000)	
Equity in subsidiary earnings	64,000*	
Dividends from Pawn (80% × $50,000)	(40,000)	24,000
Balance, 12/31/21		$852,000

*This figure appears in King's 2021 income statement. See Exhibit 4.5.

EXHIBIT 4.5
Separate Financial Records

KING COMPANY AND PAWN COMPANY
Separate Financial Statements
For December 31, 2021, and the Year Then Ended

	King	Pawn
Revenues	$ (910,000)	$ (430,000)
Cost of goods sold	344,000	200,000
Depreciation expense	60,000	20,000
Amortization expense	100,000	75,000
Interest expense	70,000	45,000
Equity in subsidiary earnings (see Exhibit 4.4)	(64,000)	–0–
Net income	$ (400,000)	$ (90,000)
Retained earnings, 1/1/21	$ (860,000)	$ (580,000)
Net income (above)	(400,000)	(90,000)
Dividends declared	60,000	50,000
Retained earnings, 12/31/21	$(1,200,000)	$ (620,000)
Current assets	$ 726,000	$ 445,000
Trademarks	304,000	295,000
Patented technology	880,000	540,000
Equipment (net)	390,000	160,000
Investment in Pawn Company (see Exhibit 4.4)	852,000	–0–
Total assets	$ 3,152,000	$ 1,440,000
Long-term liabilities	$(1,082,000)	$ (590,000)
Common stock	(870,000)	(230,000)
Retained earnings, 12/31/21	(1,200,000)	(620,000)
Total liabilities and equities	$(3,152,000)	$(1,440,000)

Note: Parentheses indicate a credit balance.

subsidiary's assets, liabilities, revenues, and expenses will be combined in consolidation, the internal accounting for King's investment in Pawn is based on its 80 percent ownership. This technique facilitates worksheet adjustments that allocate various amounts to the noncontrolling interest. Exhibit 4.5 presents the separate financial statements for these two companies as of December 31, 2021, and the year then ended, based on the information provided.

Consolidated Totals

Although the inclusion of a 20 percent outside ownership complicates the consolidation process, the 2021 totals to be reported by this business combination can nonetheless be determined without the use of a worksheet:

- *Revenues* = \$1,340,000. The revenues of the parent and the subsidiary are added together. The acquisition method includes the subsidiary's revenues in total although King owns only 80 percent of the stock.
- *Cost of Goods Sold* = \$544,000. The parent and subsidiary balances are added together.
- *Depreciation Expense* = \$79,000. The parent and subsidiary balances are added together along with the \$1,000 reduction in equipment depreciation as indicated in Exhibit 4.3.
- *Amortization Expense* = \$181,000. The parent and subsidiary balances are added together along with the \$6,000 additional patented technology amortization expense as indicated in Exhibit 4.3.
- *Interest Expense* = \$120,000. The parent and subsidiary balances are added along with an additional \$5,000. Exhibit 4.3 shows Pawn's long-term debt reduced by \$40,000 to fair value. Because the maturity value remains constant, the \$40,000 represents a discount amortized to interest expense over the remaining eight-year life of the debt.
- *Equity in Subsidiary Earnings* = –0–. The parent's investment income is replaced with the subsidiary's separate revenues and expenses, which are then included in the consolidated totals.
- *Consolidated Net Income* = \$416,000. The consolidated entity's total earnings before allocation to the controlling and noncontrolling ownership interests.
- *Net Income Attributable to Noncontrolling Interest* = \$16,000. The outside owners are assigned 20 percent of Pawn's reported net income of \$90,000 less \$10,000 total excess fair-value amortization. The acquisition method shows this amount as an allocation of consolidated net income.
- *Net Income Attributable to King Company (Controlling Interest)* = \$400,000. The acquisition method shows this amount as an allocation of consolidated net income.
- *Retained Earnings, 1/1* = \$860,000. The parent company figure equals the consolidated total because the equity method was applied. If the initial value method or the partial equity method had been used, the parent's balance would require adjustment to include any unrecorded figures.
- *Dividends Declared* = \$60,000. Only the parent company balance is reported. Eighty percent of the subsidiary's dividends are distributable to the parent and are thus eliminated. The remaining distribution goes to the outside owners and serves to reduce the noncontrolling interest balance.
- *Retained Earnings,* 12/31 = \$1,200,000. The balance is found by adding the controlling interest's share of consolidated net income to the beginning consolidated retained earnings balance and then subtracting the parent's dividends. Because the equity method is utilized, the parent company figure reflects the total for the business combination.
- *Current Assets* = \$1,171,000. The parent's and subsidiary's balances are added.
- *Trademarks* = \$659,000. The parent's balance is added to the subsidiary's balance plus the \$60,000 allocation of the acquisition-date fair value (see Exhibit 4.3).
- *Patented Technology* = \$1,528,000. The parent's balance is added to the subsidiary's balance plus the \$120,000 excess fair-value allocation less two years' excess amortizations of \$6,000 per year (see Exhibit 4.3).
- *Equipment* = \$542,000. The parent's balance is added to the subsidiary's balance less the \$10,000 acquisition-date fair-value reduction plus two years' expense reductions of \$1,000 per year (see Exhibit 4.3).
- *Investment in Pawn Company* = –0–. The balance reported by the parent is eliminated so that the subsidiary's assets and liabilities can be included in the consolidated totals.
- *Goodwill* = \$25,000. The total goodwill allocation shown in Exhibit 4.3 is reported.

- *Total Assets* = $3,925,000. This balance is a summation of the consolidated assets.
- *Long-Term Liabilities* = $1,642,000. The parent's balance is added to the subsidiary's balance less the $40,000 acquisition-date fair-value allocation net of two years' amortizations of $5,000 per year (see Exhibit 4.3).
- *Noncontrolling Interest in Subsidiary* = $213,000. The outside ownership is 20 percent of the subsidiary's year-end book value adjusted for any unamortized excess fair value attributed to the noncontrolling interest:

Noncontrolling interest in Pawn at 1/1/21	
20% of $810,000 beginning book value—common stock plus 1/1/21 retained earnings	$162,000
20% of unamortized excess fair-value allocations as of 1/1	45,000
Noncontrolling interest in Pawn 1/1/21	$207,000
Net income attributable to noncontrolling interest (see page 168)	16,000
Dividends distributable to noncontrolling interest (20% of $50,000 total)	(10,000)
Noncontrolling interest in Pawn at 12/31/21	$213,000

- *Common Stock* = $870,000. Only the parent's balance is reported.
- *Retained Earnings, 12/31* = $1,200,000, as shown in Exhibit 4.5.
- *Total Liabilities and Equities* = $3,925,000. This total is a summation of consolidated liabilities, noncontrolling interest, and equities.

Alternative Calculation of Noncontrolling Interest at December 31, 2021

The acquisition method requires that the noncontrolling interest in the subsidiary's net assets be measured at fair value at the date of acquisition. Subsequent to acquisition, however, the noncontrolling interest value is adjusted for its share of subsidiary net income, excess fair-value amortizations, and dividends. The following schedule demonstrates how the noncontrolling interest's acquisition-date fair value is adjusted to show the ending consolidated balance sheet amount.

Fair value of 20% noncontrolling interest in Pawn at acquisition date		$195,000
20% of $70,000 change in Pawn's 2020 retained earnings	14,000	
20% of excess fair-value amortizations	(2,000)	12,000
2021 net income allocation [20% × ($90,000 − $10,000)]		16,000
2021 dividends (20% × $50,000)		(10,000)
Noncontrolling interest in Pawn at December 31, 2021		$213,000

As can be seen in the schedule, the fair-value principle applies only to the initial noncontrolling interest valuation.

Worksheet Process—Acquisition Method

The consolidated totals for King and Pawn also can be determined by means of a worksheet as shown in Exhibit 4.6. Comparing this example with Exhibit 3.7 in Chapter 3 indicates that the presence of a noncontrolling interest does not create a significant number of changes in the consolidation procedures.

The worksheet still includes elimination of the subsidiary's stockholders' equity accounts (Entry **S**) although, as explained next, this entry is expanded to record the beginning noncontrolling interest for the year. The second worksheet entry (Entry **A**) recognizes the excess acquisition-date fair-value allocations at January 1 after one year of amortization with an additional adjustment to the beginning noncontrolling interest. Intra-entity income and dividends are removed also (Entries **I** and **D**) while current-year excess amortization expenses are recognized (Entry **E**). The differences from the Chapter 3 illustrations relate exclusively to

EXHIBIT 4.6 Noncontrolling Interest (No Control Premium) Illustrated

KING COMPANY AND PAWN COMPANY
Consolidation Worksheet
For Year Ending December 31, 2021

Investment: Equity Method — *Ownership: 80%*

Accounts	King Company*	Pawn Company*	Consolidation Entries Debit	Consolidation Entries Credit	Noncontrolling Interest	Consolidated Totals
Revenues	(910,000)	(430,000)				(1,340,000)
Cost of goods sold	344,000	200,000				544,000
Depreciation expense	60,000	20,000		(E) 1,000		79,000
Amortization expense	100,000	75,000	(E) 6,000			181,000
Interest expense	70,000	45,000	(E) 5,000			120,000
Equity in Pawn's earnings (see Exhibit 4.4)	(64,000)	–0–	(I) 64,000			–0–
Separate company net income	(400,000)	(90,000)				
Consolidated net income						(416,000)
Net income attributable to noncontrolling interest					(16,000)	16,000
Net income attributable to King Company						(400,000)
Retained earnings, 1/1	(860,000)	(580,000)	(S) 580,000			(860,000)
Net income (above)	(400,000)	(90,000)				(400,000)
Dividends declared	60,000	50,000		(D) 40,000	10,000	60,000
Retained earnings, 12/31	(1,200,000)	(620,000)				(1,200,000)
Current assets	726,000	445,000				1,171,000
Trademarks	304,000	295,000	(A) 60,000			659,000
Patented technology	880,000	540,000	(A) 114,000	(E) 6,000		1,528,000
Equipment (net)	390,000	160,000	(E) 1,000	(A) 9,000		542,000
Investment in Pawn Company (see Exhibit 4.4)	852,000	–0–	(D) 40,000	(S) 648,000 (A) 180,000 (I) 64,000		–0–
Goodwill	–0–	–0–	(A) 25,000			25,000
Total assets	3,152,000	1,440,000				3,925,000
Long-term liabilities	(1,082,000)	(590,000)	(A) 35,000	(E) 5,000		(1,642,000)
Common stock	(870,000)	(230,000)	(S) 230,000			(870,000)
Noncontrolling interest in Pawn, 1/1				(S) 162,000 (A) 45,000	(207,000)	
Noncontrolling interest in Pawn, 12/31					(213,000)	(213,000)
Retained earnings, 12/31	(1,200,000)	(620,000)				(1,200,000)
Total liabilities and equities	(3,152,000)	(1,440,000)	1,160,000	1,160,000		(3,925,000)

*See Exhibit 4.5.
Note: Parentheses indicate a credit balance.
Consolidation entries:
(S) Elimination of subsidiary's stockholders' equity along with recognition of January 1 noncontrolling interest.
(A) Allocation of subsidiary total fair value in excess of book value, unamortized balances as of January 1.
(I) Elimination of intra-entity income (equity accrual less amortization expenses).
(D) Elimination of intra-entity dividends.
(E) Recognition of amortization expenses of fair-value allocations.

the recognition of the three components of the noncontrolling interest. In addition, *a separate Noncontrolling Interest column is added to the worksheet to accumulate these components to form the year-end figure to be reported on the consolidated balance sheet.*

Noncontrolling Interest—Beginning of Year Under the acquisition method, the noncontrolling interest shares proportionately in the fair values of the subsidiary's identifiable net assets as adjusted for excess fair-value amortizations. On the consolidated worksheet, this total net fair value is represented by two components:

1. Pawn's stockholders' equity accounts (common stock and beginning retained earnings) indicate a January 1, 2021, book value of $810,000.
2. January 1, 2021, acquisition-date fair-value net of previous year's amortizations (in this case, 2020 only).

Therefore, the January 1, 2021, balance of the 20 percent outside ownership is computed as follows:

20% × $810,000 subsidiary book value at 1/1/21	$162,000
20% × $225,000* unamortized excess fair-value allocation at 1/1/21	45,000
Noncontrolling interest in Pawn at 1/1/21	$207,000
*Acquisition-date excess fair over book value (Exhibit 4.3)	$235,000
Less: 2020 excess fair over book value amortization	(10,000)
Unamortized excess fair over book value amount at 1/1/21	$225,000

The $207,000 noncontrolling interest balance at 1/1/21 is recognized on the worksheet through Entry **S** ($162,000) and Entry **A** ($45,000):

Consolidation Entry S

Common Stock (Pawn)	230,000	
Retained Earnings, 1/1/21 (Pawn)	580,000	
Investment in Pawn Company (80%)		648,000
Noncontrolling Interest in Pawn Company, 1/1/21 (20%)		162,000

To eliminate beginning stockholders' equity accounts of subsidiary along with book value portion of investment (equal to 80 percent ownership). Noncontrolling interest of 20 percent is also recognized.

Consolidation Entry A

Trademarks	60,000	
Patented Technology	114,000	
Liabilities	35,000	
Goodwill	25,000	
Equipment		9,000
Investment in Pawn Company (80%)		180,000
Noncontrolling Interest in Pawn Company, 1/1/21 (20%)		45,000

To recognize unamortized excess fair value as of January 1, 2021, to Pawn's assets acquired and liabilities assumed in the combination. Also to allocate the unamortized fair value to the noncontrolling interest. Goodwill is attributable proportionately to controlling and noncontrolling interests.

The total $207,000 balance assigned here to the outside owners at the beginning of the year is extended to the Noncontrolling Interest worksheet column (see Exhibit 4.6).

To complete the required worksheet adjustments, Entries **I, D,** and **E** are prepared as follows:

Consolidation Entry I

Equity in Pawn's Earnings	64,000	
Investment in Pawn Company		64,000

To eliminate intra-entity income accrual comprising subsidiary income less excess acquisition-date fair-value amortizations.

Consolidation Entry D

Investment in Pawn Company	40,000	
Dividends Declared		40,000
To eliminate intra-entity dividends.		

Consolidation Entry E

Amortization Expense	6,000	
Interest Expense	5,000	
Equipment (net)	1,000	
Depreciation Expense		1,000
Patented Technology		6,000
Long-Term Liabilities		5,000
To recognize current year excess fair-value amortizations.		

Noncontrolling Interest—Share of Current Year Consolidated Net Income Exhibit 4.6 shows the noncontrolling interest's share of current year earnings is $16,000. The amount is based on the subsidiary's $90,000 net income (Pawn Company column) less excess acquisition-date fair-value amortizations. Thus, King assigns $16,000 to the outside owners computed as follows:

Net Income Attributable to Noncontrolling Interest	
Pawn Company net income	$90,000
Excess acquisition-date fair-value amortization	10,000
Net income adjusted for excess amortizations	$80,000
Noncontrolling interest percentage	20%
Net income attributable to noncontrolling interest in Pawn	$16,000

In effect, 100 percent of each subsidiary revenue and expense account (including excess acquisition-date fair-value amortizations) is consolidated with an accompanying 20 percent allocation to the noncontrolling interest. The 80 percent net effect corresponds to King's ownership.

Because $16,000 of consolidated net income accrues to the noncontrolling interest, this amount is added to the $207,000 beginning balance assigned (in Entries **S** and **A**) to these outside owners. The noncontrolling interest increases because the subsidiary generated a profit during the period.

Although we could record this allocation through an additional worksheet entry, the $16,000 is usually shown, as in Exhibit 4.6, by means of a columnar adjustment. The current-year accrual is simultaneously entered in the Income Statement section of the consolidated column as an allocation of consolidated net income and in the Noncontrolling Interest column as an increase. This procedure assigns a portion of the combined earnings to the outside owners rather than to the parent company owners.

Noncontrolling Interest—Dividends The $40,000 dividend to the parent company is eliminated routinely through Entry **D,** but the remainder of Pawn's dividend went to the noncontrolling interest. The impact of the dividend (20 percent of the subsidiary's total) distributable to the other owners must be acknowledged. As shown in Exhibit 4.6, this remaining $10,000 is extended directly into the Noncontrolling Interest column on the worksheet as a reduction. It represents the decrease in the underlying claim of the outside ownership that resulted from the subsidiary's dividend declaration.

Noncontrolling Interest—End of Year The ending assignment for these other owners is calculated by a summation of

Noncontrolling interest in Pawn beginning of year—credit balance	$207,000
Net income attributable to noncontrolling interest	16,000
Less: Dividends to the outside owners	(10,000)
Noncontrolling interest in Pawn end of year—credit balance	$213,000

The Noncontrolling Interest column on the worksheet in Exhibit 4.6 accumulates these figures. The $213,000 total is then transferred to the balance sheet, where it appears in the consolidated financial statements.

LO 4-6

Identify appropriate placements for the components of the noncontrolling interest in consolidated financial statements.

Consolidated Financial Statements

Having successfully consolidated the information for King and Pawn, the resulting financial statements for these two companies are produced in Exhibit 4.7. These figures are taken from the consolidation worksheet.

Exhibit 4.7 shows the consolidated income statement first. Consolidated net income is computed at the combined entity level as $416,000 and then allocated to the noncontrolling and controlling interests. The statement of changes in owners' equity provides details of the

EXHIBIT 4.7
Consolidated Statements with Noncontrolling Interest—Acquisition Method

KING COMPANY AND PAWN COMPANY
Consolidated Financial Statements
Income Statement
Year Ended December 31, 2021

Revenues	$1,340,000
Cost of goods sold	(544,000)
Depreciation expense	(79,000)
Amortization expense	(181,000)
Interest expense	(120,000)
Consolidated net income	$ 416,000
To noncontrolling interest	16,000
To King Company (controlling interest)	$ 400,000

Statement of Changes in Owners' Equity
Year Ended December 31, 2021

	King Company Owners		
	Retained Earnings	**Common Stock**	**Noncontrolling Interest**
Balance, January 1	$ 860,000	$870,000	$207,000
Net income	400,000		16,000
Less: Dividends	(60,000)		(10,000)
Balance, December 31	$1,200,000	$870,000	$213,000

Balance Sheet
At December 31, 2021

Assets	
Current assets	$1,171,000
Trademarks	659,000
Patented technology	1,528,000
Equipment (net)	542,000
Goodwill	25,000
Total assets	$3,925,000
Liabilities	
Long-term liabilities	$1,642,000
Owners' Equity	
Common stock—King Company	870,000
Noncontrolling interest in Pawn	213,000
Retained earnings	1,200,000
Total liabilities and owners' equity	$3,925,000

ownership changes for the year for both the controlling and noncontrolling interest shareholders. Finally, note the placement of the noncontrolling interest in the subsidiary's equity squarely in the consolidated owners' equity section.[8]

LO 4-7

Determine the effect on consolidated financial statements of a control premium paid by the parent.

Illustration—Partial Acquisition with Control Premium

To illustrate the valuation implications for an acquisition involving a control premium, again assume that King Company acquires 80 percent of Pawn Company's 100,000 outstanding voting shares on January 1, 2020. We also again assume that Pawn's shares traded before the acquisition date at an average of $9.75 per share. In this scenario, however, we assume that to acquire sufficient shares to gain control King pays a total of $880,000 cash consideration (an average price of $11 per share) for its 80 percent interest. King thus pays a $100,000 control premium to acquire Pawn ($880,000 less $9.75 × 80,000 shares). King anticipates that synergies with Pawn will create additional value for King's shareholders. Following the acquisition, the remaining 20 percent noncontrolling interest shares continue to trade at $9.75.

The total fair value of Pawn to be used initially in consolidation is thus computed as follows:

Consideration transferred by King ($11.00 × 80,000 shares)	$ 880,000
Noncontrolling interest fair value ($9.75 × 20,000 shares)	195,000
Pawn's total fair value at January 1, 2020	$1,075,000

In keeping with the acquisition method's requirement that identifiable assets acquired and liabilities assumed be adjusted to fair value, King allocates Pawn's total fair value as follows:

Fair value of Pawn at January 1, 2020		$1,075,000
Book value of Pawn at January 1, 2020		(740,000)
Fair value in excess of book value		$ 335,000
Adjustments to		
Trademarks	$ 60,000	
Patented technology	120,000	
Equipment	(10,000)	
Long-term liabilities	40,000	210,000
Goodwill		$ 125,000

Compared to the previous illustration with no control premium, note that the *identifiable* assets acquired and liabilities assumed are again adjusted to their full individual fair values at the acquisition date. Only the amount designated as goodwill is changed. Goodwill recognized is now $125,000—a $100,000 increase from $25,000 in the original fair-value allocation example as shown in Exhibit 4.3. In this case, King allocates $120,000 of the $125,000 total goodwill amount to its own interest as follows:

	Controlling Interest	Noncontrolling Interest	Total
Fair value at acquisition date	$880,000	$195,000	$1,075,000
Relative fair value of Pawn's identifiable net assets (80% and 20%)	760,000	190,000	950,000
Goodwill	$120,000	$ 5,000	$ 125,000

The initial acquisition-date fair value of $195,000 for the noncontrolling interest includes only a $5,000 goodwill allocation from the combination. Because the parent paid proportionately more for its share than the noncontrolling interest fair value, it receives a disproportionate amount of the combination goodwill.

[8] If appropriate, each component of other comprehensive income is allocated to the controlling and noncontrolling interests. The statement of changes in owners' equity would also provide an allocation of accumulated other comprehensive income elements across the controlling and noncontrolling interests.

Next we separate the familiar consolidated worksheet entry **A** into two components labeled **A1** and **A2.** The **A1** worksheet entry allocates the excess acquisition-date fair value to the *identifiable* assets acquired and liabilities assumed (trademarks, patented technology, equipment, and liabilities). Note that the relative ownership percentages of the parent and noncontrolling interest (80 percent and 20 percent) provide the basis for allocating the net $200,000 adjustment to the parent's Investment account ($160,000) and the January 1, 2021, balance of the noncontrolling interest ($40,000).

Next, consolidated worksheet entry **A2** provides the recognition and allocation of the goodwill balance taking into account the differing per share prices of the parent's consideration transferred and the noncontrolling interest fair value. Note that the presence of a control premium affects primarily the parents' shares, and, thus, goodwill is disproportionately (relative to the ownership percentages) allocated to the controlling and noncontrolling interests. Exhibit 4.8 shows the consolidated worksheet for this extension to the King and Pawn example.

Consolidation Entry A1 (see page 171 for excess fair value allocations)

Trademarks	60,000	
Patented Technology	114,000	
Liabilities	35,000	
Equipment		9,000
Investment in Pawn Company (80%)		160,000
Noncontrolling Interest in Pawn 1/1/21 (20%)		40,000

Consolidation Entry A2

Goodwill	125,000	
Investment in Pawn Company		120,000
Noncontrolling Interest in Pawn 1/1/21		5,000

The worksheet calculates the December 31, 2021, noncontrolling balance as follows:

Pawn January 1, 2021: 20% book value	$162,000
January 1, 2021: 20% excess fair-value allocation for Pawn's identifiable net assets ($200,000 × 20%) + $5,000 goodwill allocation	45,000
Noncontrolling interest at January 1, 2021	$207,000
2021 consolidated net income allocation	16,000
Noncontrolling interest share of Pawn dividends	(10,000)
Noncontrolling interest in Pawn, December 31, 2021	$213,000

Note that the $45,000 January 1 excess fair-value allocation to the noncontrolling interest includes the noncontrolling interest's full share of the *identifiable* assets acquired and liabilities assumed in the combination but only $5,000 for goodwill. Because King Company paid a $100,000 control premium (80,000 shares × $1.25), the additional $100,000 is allocated entirely to the controlling interest.

By comparing Exhibits 4.6 and 4.8, we can assess the effect of the separate acquisition-date valuations for the controlling and noncontrolling interests. As seen in the differences across Exhibits 4.6 and 4.8 calculated next, the presence of King's control premium affects the goodwill component in the consolidated financial statements and little else.

	Exhibit 4.6	Exhibit 4.8	Difference
On King's Separate Financial Statements			
Current assets	$ 726,000	$ 626,000	−$100,000
Investment in Pawn	852,000	952,000	+ 100,000
On the Consolidated Balances			
Current assets	1,171,000	1,071,000	− 100,000
Goodwill	25,000	125,000	+ 100,000

EXHIBIT 4.8 Noncontrolling Interest (Control Premium) Illustrated

KING COMPANY AND PAWN COMPANY
Consolidation Worksheet
For Year Ending December 31, 2021

Investment: Equity Method | *Ownership: 80%*

Accounts	King Company	Pawn Company	Consolidation Entries Debit	Consolidation Entries Credit	Noncontrolling Interest	Consolidated Totals
Revenues	(910,000)	(430,000)				(1,340,000)
Cost of goods sold	344,000	200,000				544,000
Depreciation expense	60,000	20,000		(E) 1,000		79,000
Amortization expense	100,000	75,000	(E) 6,000			181,000
Interest expense	70,000	45,000	(E) 5,000			120,000
Equity in Pawn's earnings	(64,000)	–0–	(I) 64,000			–0–
Separate company net income	(400,000)	(90,000)				
Consolidated net income						(416,000)
Net income attributable to noncontrolling interest					(16,000)	16,000
Net income attributable to King Company						(400,000)
Retained earnings, 1/1	(860,000)	(580,000)	(S) 580,000			(860,000)
Net income (above)	(400,000)	(90,000)				(400,000)
Dividends declared	60,000	50,000		(D) 40,000	10,000	60,000
Retained earnings, 12/31	(1,200,000)	(620,000)				(1,200,000)
Current assets	626,000	445,000				1,071,000
Trademarks	304,000	295,000	(A1) 60,000			659,000
Patented technology	880,000	540,000	(A1) 114,000	(E) 6,000		1,528,000
Equipment (net)	390,000	160,000	(E) 1,000	(A1) 9,000		542,000
Investment in Pawn Company	952,000	–0–	(D) 40,000	(S) 648,000 (A1) 160,000 (A2) 120,000 (I) 64,000		–0–
Goodwill	–0–	–0–	(A2) 125,000			125,000
Total assets	3,152,000	1,440,000				3,925,000
Long-term liabilities	(1,082,000)	(590,000)	(A1) 35,000	(E) 5,000		(1,642,000)
Common stock	(870,000)	(230,000)	(S) 230,000			(870,000)
Noncontrolling interest in Pawn 1/1				(S) 162,000 (A1) 40,000 (A2) 5,000	(207,000)	
Noncontrolling interest in Pawn 12/31					(213,000)	(213,000)
Retained earnings, 12/31	(1,200,000)	(620,000)				(1,200,000)
Total liabilities and equities	(3,152,000)	(1,440,000)	1,260,000	1,260,000		(3,925,000)

Note: Parentheses indicate a credit balance.
Consolidation entries:
(S) Elimination of subsidiary's stockholders' equity along with recognition of January 1 noncontrolling interest.
(A1) Allocation of subsidiary identifiable net asset fair value in excess of book value, unamortized balances as of January 1.
(A2) Allocation of goodwill to parent and noncontrolling interest.
(I) Elimination of intra-entity income (equity accrual less amortization expenses).
(D) Elimination of intra-entity dividends.
(E) Recognition of amortization expenses of fair-value allocations.

Because King paid an additional $100,000 for its 80 percent interest in Pawn, the initial value assigned to the Investment account increases, and current assets (i.e., additional cash paid for the acquisition) decrease by $100,000. The extra $100,000 then simply increases goodwill on the consolidated balance sheet. Note that the noncontrolling interest amount remains unchanged at $213,000 across Exhibits 4.6 and 4.8, consistent with the fact that its acquisition-date fair value was left unchanged at $195,000.

Effects Created by Alternative Investment Methods

In the King and Pawn illustrations, the parent uses the equity method and bases all worksheet entries on that approach. As discussed in Chapter 3, had King incorporated the initial value method or the partial equity method, a few specific changes in the consolidation process would be required although the reported figures would be identical.

Initial Value Method

The initial value method ignores two accrual-based adjustments. First, the parent recognizes dividend income rather than an equity income accrual. Thus, the parent does not accrue the percentage of the subsidiary's net income earned in past years in excess of dividends (the increase in subsidiary retained earnings). Second, the parent does not record amortization expense under the initial value method and therefore must include it in the consolidation process if proper totals are to be achieved. Because neither of these figures is recognized in applying the initial value method, an Entry ***C** is added to the worksheet to convert the previously recorded balances to the equity method. The parent's beginning Retained Earnings is affected by this adjustment as well as the Investment in Subsidiary account. The exact amount is computed as follows.

*Conversion to Equity Method from Initial Value Method (Entry *C)*

Combine:

1. The increase (since acquisition) in the subsidiary's retained earnings during past years (net income less dividends) times the parent's ownership percentage, and
2. The parent's percentage of total amortization expense for these same past years.

The parent's use of the initial value method requires an additional procedural change. Under this method, the parent recognizes income when its subsidiary declares a dividend. Entry (**I**) removes both intra-entity dividend income and subsidiary dividends to the parent. Thus, when the initial value method is used, Entry **D** is unnecessary.

Partial Equity Method

Again, an Entry ***C** is needed to convert the parent's retained earnings as of January 1 to the equity method. In this case, however, only the amortization expense for the prior years must be included. Recall that under the partial equity method, although the parent accrues its share of reported subsidiary income, it does not recognize any acquisition-date excess fair value amortization expenses.

LO 4-8

Understand the impact on consolidated financial statements of a midyear acquisition.

Revenue and Expense Reporting for Midyear Acquisitions

In virtually all of our previous examples, the parent gains control of the subsidiary on the first day of the fiscal year. How is the consolidation process affected if an acquisition occurs on a midyear (any other than the first day of the fiscal year) date?

When a company gains control at a midyear date, a few obvious changes are needed. The new parent must compute the subsidiary's book value as of that date to determine excess total fair value over book value allocations (e.g., intangibles). Excess amortization expenses as well as any equity accrual and dividend distributions are recognized for a period of less than a year. Finally, because only net income earned by the subsidiary after the acquisition date accrues to the new owners, it is appropriate to include only postacquisition revenues and expenses in consolidated totals.

Consolidating Postacquisition Subsidiary Revenue and Expenses

Following a midyear acquisition, a parent company excludes current-year subsidiary revenue and expense amounts that have accrued prior to the acquisition date from its consolidated totals. For example, when Comcast acquired AT&T Broadband, its December 31 year-end income statement included AT&T Broadband revenues and expenses only subsequent to the acquisition date. Comcast reported $8.1 billion in revenues that year. However, in a pro forma schedule, Comcast noted that had it included AT&T Broadband's revenues from January 1, total revenue for the year would have been $16.8 billion. However, because the $8.7 billion additional revenue ($16.8 billion – $8.1 billion) was not earned by Comcast owners, Comcast excluded this preacquisition revenue from its consolidated total.

To further illustrate the complexities of accounting for a midyear acquisition, assume that Tyler Company acquires 90 percent of Steven Company on July 1, 2021, for $900,000 and prepares the following fair-value allocation schedule:

Steven Company fair value, 7/1/21		$1,000,000
Steven Company book value, 7/1/21		
Common stock	$600,000	
Retained earnings, 7/1/21	200,000	800,000
Excess fair value over book value		$ 200,000
Adjust trademark to fair value (4-year remaining life)		200,000
Goodwill		$ –0–

The affiliates report the following 2021 income statement amounts from their own separate operations:

	Tyler	Steven
Revenues	$450,000	$300,000
Expenses	325,000	150,000
Dividends (declared quarterly)	100,000	20,000

Assuming that all revenues and expenses occurred evenly throughout the year, the December 31, 2021, consolidated income statement appears as follows:

TYLER COMPANY
Consolidated Income Statement
For the Year Ended December 31, 2021

Revenues	$600,000
Expenses	425,000
Consolidated net income	$175,000
To noncontrolling interest	5,000
To Tyler Company (controlling interest)	$170,000

The consolidated income statement components are computed as follows:

- *Revenues* = $600,000. Combined balances of $750,000 less $150,000 (½ of Steven's revenues).
- *Expenses* = $425,000. Combined balances of $475,000 less $75,000 (½ of Steven's expenses) plus $25,000 excess amortization ($200,000 ÷ 4 years × ½ year).
- *Net Income Attributable to Noncontrolling Interest* = $5,000. 10% × ($150,000 Steven's income – $50,000 excess amortization) × ½ year.

In this example, preacquisition subsidiary revenue and expense accounts are eliminated from the consolidated totals. Note also that by excluding 100 percent of the preacquisition income accounts from consolidation, the noncontrolling interest is viewed as coming into being as of the parent's acquisition date.[9]

[9] Current practice provides comparability across fiscal years through pro forma disclosures of various categories of revenue and expense as if the combination had occurred at the beginning of the reporting period. With the advent of modern information systems, separate cutoffs for revenues and expenses are readily available.

A midyear acquisition requires additional adjustments when preparing consolidation worksheets. The balances the subsidiary submits for consolidation typically include results for its entire fiscal period. Thus, in the December 31 financial statements, the book value of the firm acquired on a midyear date is reflected by a January 1 retained earnings balance plus revenues, expenses, and dividends from the beginning of the year to the acquisition date. To effectively eliminate subsidiary book value as of the acquisition date, Consolidation Entry **S** includes these items in addition to the other usual elements of book value (i.e., stock accounts). To illustrate, assuming that both affiliates submit fiscal year financial statements for consolidation, Tyler would make the following 2021 consolidation worksheet entry:

Consolidation Worksheet Entry S

Common Stock—Steven	600,000	
Retained Earnings—Steven (1/1/21)*	135,000	
Revenues	150,000	
Dividends Declared—Steven		10,000
Expenses		75,000
Noncontrolling Interest (7/1/21)		80,000
Investment in Steven		720,000

*To arrive at Steven's January 1 retained earning balance, we use the July 1 balance of $200,000 less income from the first six months of $75,000 (1/2 of $150,000 annual Steven income) plus $10,000 dividends declared.

Through Entry **S,** preacquisition subsidiary revenues, expenses, and dividends are effectively

- Included as part of the subsidiary book value elimination in the year of acquisition.
- Included as components of the beginning value of the noncontrolling interest.
- Excluded from the consolidated income statement and statement of retained earnings.

Acquisition Following an Equity Method Investment

In many cases, a parent company owns a noncontrolling equity interest in a firm prior to obtaining control. In such cases, as the preceding example demonstrates, the parent consolidates the postacquisition revenues and expenses of its new subsidiary. Because the parent owned an equity investment in the subsidiary prior to the control date, however, the parent reports on its income statement the "equity in earnings of the investee" that accrued up to the date control was obtained. In this case, in the year of acquisition, the consolidated income statement reports both combined revenues and expenses (postacquisition) of the subsidiary and equity method income (preacquisition).

In subsequent years, the need to separate pre- and postacquisition amounts is limited to ensuring that excess amortizations correctly reflect the midyear acquisition date. Finally, if the parent employs the initial value method of accounting for the investment in subsidiary on its books, the conversion to the equity method must also reflect only postacquisition amounts.

LO 4-9

Understand the impact on consolidated financial statements when a step acquisition has taken place.

Step Acquisitions

When Starbucks increased its percentage of ownership in its East China joint venture from 50 percent to 100 percent, it began consolidating its investment in East China. Prior to the acquisition of control through majority ownership, Starbucks accounted for its investment in East China using the equity method of accounting.

In all previous consolidation illustrations, control over a subsidiary was assumed to have been achieved through a single transaction. Obviously, Starbucks's takeover of East China shows that a combination can also result from a series of stock purchases. These step acquisitions further complicate the consolidation process. The financial information of the separate companies must still be brought together, but varying amounts of consideration have been transferred to former owners at several different dates. How do the initial acquisitions affect this process?

Control Achieved in Steps—Acquisition Method

A **step acquisition** occurs when control is achieved in a series of equity acquisitions, as opposed to a single transaction. As with all business combinations, the acquisition method measures the acquired firm (including the noncontrolling interest) at fair value at the date control is obtained. The acquisition of a controlling interest is considered an important economic, and therefore measurement, event. Consequently, the parent utilizes a single uniform valuation basis for all subsidiary assets acquired and liabilities assumed—fair value at the date control is obtained.

If the parent previously held a noncontrolling interest in the acquired firm, the parent remeasures that interest to fair value and recognizes a gain or loss. For example, when eBay increased its equity ownership from 10 percent to 93 percent, it obtained control over GittiGidiyor, a Turkish online marketplace. To measure the subsidiary's acquisition-date fair value, eBay revalued its previously held 10 percent equity interest to fair value and recognized a $17 million gain. As a result, eBay increased its investment account for both the cash paid for the newly acquired shares and the increase in the fair value of its previously owned shares in GittiGidiyor.

If after obtaining control, the parent increases its ownership interest in the subsidiary, no further remeasurement takes place. The parent simply accounts for the additional subsidiary shares acquired as an equity transaction—consistent with any transactions with other owners, as opposed to outsiders. Next we present an example of consolidated reporting when the parent obtains a controlling interest in a series of steps. Then we present an example of a parent's post-control acquisition of its subsidiary's shares.

Example: Step Acquisition Resulting in Control—Acquisition Method

To illustrate, assume that Arch Company obtains control of Zion Company through two cash acquisitions. The details of each acquisition are provided in Exhibit 4.9. Assuming that Arch has gained the ability to significantly influence Zion's decision-making process, the first investment, for external reporting purposes, is accounted for by means of the equity method as discussed in Chapter 1. Thus, Arch must determine any allocations and amortization associated with its purchase price (see Exhibit 4.10). A customer base with a 22-year estimated remaining life represented the initial excess payment.

Application of the equity method requires the accrual of investee income by the parent while any dividends from the investee are recorded as a decrease in the Investment account. Arch must also reduce both the income and asset balances in recognition of the annual $2,000 amortization indicated in Exhibit 4.10. Following the information provided in Exhibits 4.9 and 4.10, over the next two years, Arch Company's Investment in Zion account grows to $190,000:

Price paid for 30% investment in Zion—1/1/19	$164,000
Accrual of 2019 equity income ($60,000 × 30%)	18,000
Share of dividends 2019 ($20,000 × 30%)	(6,000)
Amortization for 2019	(2,000)
Accrual of 2020 equity income ($80,000 × 30%)	24,000
Share of dividends 2020 ($20,000 × 30%)	(6,000)
Amortization for 2020	(2,000)
Investment in Zion—1/1/21	$190,000

EXHIBIT 4.9
Consolidation Information for a Step Acquisition

ARCH COMPANY'S ACQUISITIONS OF ZION COMPANY SHARES

	Consideration Transferred	Percentage Acquired	Zion Company (100%) Book Value	Zion Company (100%) Fair Value
January 1, 2019	$164,000	30%	$400,000	$546,667
January 1, 2021	350,000	50	500,000	700,000

Zion Company's Income and Dividends for 2019–2021

	Income	Dividends
2019	$ 60,000	$ 20,000
2020	80,000	20,000
2021	100,000	20,000

EXHIBIT 4.10
Allocation of First Noncontrolling Acquisition

ARCH COMPANY AND ZION COMPANY Fair Value Allocation and Amortization January 1, 2019	
Fair value of consideration transferred	$164,000
Book value equivalent of Arch's ownership ($400,000 × 30%)	(120,000)
Customer base	$ 44,000
Assumed remaining life	22 years
Annual amortization expense	$ 2,000

On January 1, 2021, Arch's ownership is increased to 80 percent by the purchase of another 50 percent of Zion Company's outstanding common stock for $350,000. Although the equity method can still be utilized for internal reporting, this second acquisition necessitates the preparation of consolidated financial statements beginning in 2021. Arch now controls Zion; the two companies are viewed as a single economic entity for external reporting purposes.

Once Arch gains control over Zion on January 1, 2021, the acquisition method focuses exclusively on control-date fair values and considers any previous amounts recorded by the acquirer as irrelevant for future valuations. Thus, in a step acquisition, all previous values for the investment prior to the date control is obtained are remeasured to fair value on the date control is obtained.

We add the assumption that the $350,000 consideration transferred by Arch in its second acquisition of Zion represents the best available evidence for measuring the fair value of Zion Company at January 1, 2021. Therefore, an estimated fair value of $700,000 ($350,000 ÷ 50%) is assigned to Zion Company as of January 1, 2021, and provides the valuation basis for the assets acquired, the liabilities assumed, and the 20 percent noncontrolling interest. Exhibit 4.11 shows Arch's allocation of Zion's $700,000 acquisition-date fair value, first to the ownership interests and then to Zion's assets.

Note that the acquisition method views a multiple-step acquisition as essentially the same as a single-step acquisition. In the Arch Company and Zion Company example, once control is evident, the only relevant values in consolidating the accounts of Zion are fair values at January 1, 2021. A new basis of accountability arises for Zion Company on that single date because obtaining control of another firm is considered a significant remeasurement event.

EXHIBIT 4.11
Allocation of Acquisition-Date Fair Value

ARCH COMPANY AND ZION COMPANY Zion Fair Value at Date Control Is Obtained January 1, 2021	
Fair value of Arch's 50% equity acquisition	$350,000
Fair value of 30% equity already owned by Arch	210,000
Fair value of 20% noncontrolling interest	140,000
Total fair value assigned to Zion Company	$700,000
Excess Fair over Book Value Allocation and Amortization January 1, 2021	
Zion Company fair value	$700,000
Zion Company book value	(500,000)
Customer base	$200,000
Assumed remaining life	20 years
Annual amortization expense	$ 10,000

Previously owned noncontrolling blocks of stock are consequently revalued to fair value on the date control is obtained.

In revaluing a previous stock ownership in the acquired firm, the acquirer recognizes any resulting gain or loss in income. Therefore, on January 1, 2021, Arch increases the Investment in Zion account to $210,000 (30% × $700,000 fair value) and records the revaluation gain as follows:

Investment in Zion	20,000	
Gain on Revaluation of Zion		20,000

Fair value of Arch's 30% investment in Zion at 1/1/21 (30% × $700,000)	$210,000
Book value of Arch's 30% investment in Zion at 1/1/21	190,000
Gain on revaluation of Zion to fair value	$ 20,000

Worksheet Consolidation for a Step Acquisition (Acquisition Method)

To continue the example, the amount in Arch Company's 80 percent Investment in Zion account is updated for 2021:

Investment in Zion (after revaluation on 1/1/21)	$210,000
January 1, 2021—Second acquisition price paid	350,000
Equity income accrual—2021 (80% × $100,000)	80,000
Amortization of customer base (80% × $10,000)	(8,000)
Share of Zion dividends—2021 (80% × $20,000)	(16,000)
Investment in Zion—12/31/21	$616,000

The worksheet for consolidating Arch Company and Zion Company is shown in Exhibit 4.12. Observe that

- The consolidation worksheet entries are essentially the same as if Arch had acquired its entire 80 percent ownership on January 1, 2021.
- The noncontrolling interest is allocated 20 percent of the excess fair-value allocation from the customer base.
- The noncontrolling interest is allocated 20 percent of Zion's 2021 income less its share of the excess amortization attributable to the customer base.
- The gain on revaluation of Arch's initial investment in Zion is recognized as income of the current period.

Example: Step Acquisition Resulting after Control Is Obtained

The previous example demonstrates a step acquisition with control achieved with the most recent purchase. Post-control acquisitions by a parent of a subsidiary's stock, however, often continue as well. Recall that the acquisition method measures an acquired firm at its fair value on the date control is obtained.

A parent's subsequent subsidiary stock acquisitions do not affect these initially recognized fair values. For example, when Walmart increased its ownership in Walmart Chile from 75 percent to 100 percent, it did not change the valuation bases of Walmart Chile's assets. The acquisition of the 25 percent noncontrolling interest was treated as an equity transaction with a corresponding adjustment to additional paid-in capital. As the Walmart example shows, once the subsidiary's valuation basis is established as of the date control is obtained, as long as control is maintained, this valuation basis remains the same. Any further purchases (or sales) of the subsidiary's stock are treated as equity transactions.

EXHIBIT 4.12 Step Acquisition Illustrated

ARCH COMPANY AND ZION COMPANY
Consolidation Worksheet
For Year Ending December 31, 2021

Investment: Equity Method | *Ownership: 80%*

Accounts	Arch Company	Zion Company	Consolidation Entries Debit	Consolidation Entries Credit	Noncontrolling Interest	Consolidated Totals
Income Statement						
Revenues	(600,000)	(260,000)				(860,000)
Expenses	425,000	160,000	(E) 10,000			595,000
Equity in subsidiary earnings	(72,000)	–0–	(I) 72,000			–0–
Gain on revaluation of Zion	(20,000)	–0–				(20,000)
Separate company net income	(267,000)	(100,000)				
Consolidated net income						(285,000)
Net income attributable to noncontrolling interest					(18,000)	18,000
Net income attributable to Arch Company						(267,000)
Statement of Retained Earnings						
Retained earnings, 1/1						
Arch Company	(758,000)					(758,000)
Zion Company		(230,000)	(S) 230,000			
Net income (above)	(267,000)	(100,000)				(267,000)
Dividends declared	125,000	20,000		(D) 16,000	4,000	125,000
Retained earnings, 12/31	(900,000)	(310,000)				(900,000)
Balance Sheet						
Current assets	509,000	280,000				789,000
Land	205,000	90,000				295,000
Buildings (net)	646,000	310,000				956,000
Investment in Zion Company	616,000	–0–	(D) 16,000	(A) 160,000 (S) 400,000 (I) 72,000		–0–
Customer base	–0–	–0–	(A) 200,000	(E) 10,000		190,000
Total assets	1,976,000	680,000				2,230,000
Liabilities	(461,000)	(100,000)				(561,000)
Noncontrolling interest in Zion Company, 1/1	–0–	–0–		(S) 100,000 (A) 40,000	(140,000)	
Noncontrolling interest in Zion Company, 12/31	–0–	–0–			(154,000)	(154,000)
Common stock	(355,000)	(200,000)	(S) 200,000			(355,000)
Additional paid-in capital	(260,000)	(70,000)	(S) 70,000			(260,000)
Retained earnings, 12/31 (above)	(900,000)	(310,000)				(900,000)
Total liabilities and equities	(1,976,000)	(680,000)	798,000	798,000		(2,230,000)

Note: Parentheses indicate a credit balance.
Consolidation entries:
(S) Elimination of subsidiary's stockholders' equity along with recognition of 1/1 noncontrolling interest.
(A) Allocation of subsidiary total fair value in excess of book value, unamortized balances as of 1/1.
(I) Elimination of intra-entity income (equity accrual less amortization expenses).
(D) Elimination of intra-entity dividends.
(E) Recognition of amortization expenses on fair-value allocations.

To illustrate a post-control step acquisition, assume that on January 1, 2020, Amanda Co. obtains 70 percent of Schallman, Inc., for \$350,000 cash. We also assume that the \$350,000 consideration paid represents the best available evidence for measuring the fair value of the noncontrolling interest. Therefore, Schallman Company's total fair value is assessed at \$500,000 (\$350,000 ÷ 70%). Because Schallman's net assets' book values equal their collective fair values of \$400,000, Amanda recognizes goodwill of \$100,000. Then, on

Discussion Question

DOES GAAP UNDERVALUE POST-CONTROL STOCK ACQUISITIONS?

In Berkshire Hathaway's 2012 annual report, Warren Buffett, in discussing the company's post-control step acquisitions of Marmon Holdings, Inc., observed the following:

> Marmon provides an example of a clear and substantial gap existing between book value and intrinsic value. Let me explain the odd origin of this differential.
>
> Last year I told you that we had purchased additional shares in Marmon, raising our ownership to 80% (up from the 64% we acquired in 2008). I also told you that GAAP accounting required us to immediately record the 2011 purchase on our books at far less than what we paid. I've now had a year to think about this weird accounting rule, but I've yet to find an explanation that makes any sense—nor can Charlie or Marc Hamburg, our CFO, come up with one. My confusion increases when I am told that if we hadn't already owned 64%, the 16% we purchased in 2011 would have been entered on our books at our cost.
>
> In 2012 (and in early 2013, retroactive to year end 2012) we acquired an additional 10% of Marmon and the same bizarre accounting treatment was required. The $700 million write-off we immediately incurred had no effect on earnings but did reduce book value and, therefore, 2012's gain in net worth.
>
> The cost of our recent 10% purchase implies a $12.6 billion value for the 90% of Marmon we now own. Our balance-sheet carrying value for the 90%, however, is $8 billion. Charlie and I believe our current purchase represents excellent value. If we are correct, our Marmon holding is worth at least $4.6 billion more than its carrying value.

How would you explain the accounting valuations for the post-control step acquisitions to the Berkshire Hathaway executives? Do you agree or disagree with the GAAP treatment of reporting additional investments in subsidiaries when control has previously been established?

January 1, 2021, when Schallman's book value has increased to $420,000, Amanda buys another 20 percent of Schallman for $95,000, bringing its total ownership to 90 percent. Under the acquisition method, the valuation basis for the subsidiary's net assets was established on January 1, 2020, the date Amanda obtained control. Subsequent transactions in the subsidiary's stock (purchases or sales) are now viewed as transactions in the combined entity's own stock. Therefore, when Amanda acquires additional shares post-control, it recognizes the difference between the fair value of the consideration transferred and the underlying subsidiary valuation as an adjustment to Additional Paid-In Capital.

The difference between the $95,000 price and the underlying consolidated subsidiary value is computed as follows:

1/1/21 price paid for 20% interest		$95,000
Noncontrolling interest (NCI) acquired:		
Book value (20% of $420,000)	$84,000	
Goodwill (20% of $100,000)	20,000	
Noncontrolling interest book value (20%) 1/1/21		104,000
Additional paid-in capital from 20% NCI acquisition		$ 9,000

Amanda then prepares the following journal entry to record the acquisition of the 20 percent noncontrolling interest:

Investment in Schallman	104,000	
Cash		95,000
Additional Paid-In Capital		9,000

By purchasing 20 percent of Schallman for $95,000, the consolidated entity's owners have acquired a portion of their own firm at a price $9,000 less than consolidated book value. From a worksheet perspective, the $104,000 increase in the investment account simply replaces the 20 percent allocation to the noncontrolling interest. Note that the $95,000 exchanged for the 20 percent interest in Schallman's net assets does not affect consolidated asset valuation. The basis for the reported values in the consolidated financial statements was established on the date control was obtained.

LO 4-10

Record the sale of a subsidiary (or a portion of its shares).

Parent Company Sales of Subsidiary Stock—Acquisition Method

Frequently, a parent company will sell a portion or all of the shares it owns of a subsidiary. For example, when General Electric Company reported the sale of its NBC Universal business, it noted in its financial statements:

> We transferred the assets of the NBCU business and Comcast transferred certain of its assets to a newly formed entity, NBC Universal LLC (NBCU LLC). In connection with the transaction, we received $6,197 million in cash from Comcast and a 49% interest in NBCU LLC. Comcast holds the remaining 51% interest in NBCU LLC. We will account for our investment in NBCU LLC under the equity method. As a result of the transaction, we expect to recognize a small after-tax gain.

Importantly, the accounting effect from selling subsidiary shares depends on whether the parent continues to maintain control after the sale. If the sale of the parent's ownership interest results in the loss of control of a subsidiary as in the GE example, it recognizes any resulting gain or loss in consolidated net income.

If the parent sells some subsidiary shares but retains control, it recognizes no gains or losses on the sale. Under the acquisition method, as long as control remains with the parent, transactions in the stock of the subsidiary are considered to be transactions in the equity of the consolidated entity. Because such transactions are considered to occur with owners, the parent records any difference between proceeds of the sale and carrying amount as additional paid-in capital.

Sale of Subsidiary Shares with Control Maintained

To illustrate, assume Adams Company owns 100 percent of Smith Company's 25,000 voting shares and appropriately carries the investment on its books at January 1, 2021, at $750,000 using the equity method. Assuming Adams sells 5,000 shares to outside interests for $165,000 on January 1, 2021, the transaction is recorded as follows:

Cash	165,000	
Investment in Smith		150,000
Additional Paid-In Capital from Noncontrolling Interest Transaction		15,000
To record sale of 5,000 Smith shares to noncontrolling interest with excess of sale proceeds over carrying amount attributed to additional paid-in capital.		

The $15,000 "gain" on sale of the subsidiary shares is not recognized in income, but is reported as an increase in owners' equity. This equity treatment for the "gain" is consistent with the economic unit notion that as long as control is maintained, payments received from owners of the firm are considered contributions of capital. The ownership group of the consolidated entity specifically includes the noncontrolling interest. Therefore, the preceding treatment of sales to an ownership group is consistent with accounting for other stock transactions with owners (e.g., treasury stock transactions).

Sale of Subsidiary Shares with Control Lost

The loss of control of a subsidiary is a remeasurement event that can result in gain or loss recognition. The gain or loss is computed as the difference between the sale proceeds and the carrying amount of the shares sold. Using the Adams and Smith example, assume now that instead of selling 5,000 shares, Adams sells 20,000 of its shares in Smith to outside interests on January 1, 2021, and keeps the remaining 5,000 shares. Assuming sale proceeds of $675,000, we record the transaction as follows:

	Debit	Credit
Cash	675,000	
Investment in Smith		600,000
Gain on Sale of Smith Investment		75,000
To record sale of 20,000 Smith shares, resulting in the loss of control over Smith Company.		

If the former parent retains any of its former subsidiary's shares, the retained investment should be remeasured to fair value on the date control is lost. Any resulting gain or loss from this remeasurement should be recognized in the parent's net income.

In our Adams and Smith example, Adams still retains 5,000 shares of Smith Company (25,000 original investment less 20,000 shares sold). Assuming further that the $675,000 sale price for the 20,000 shares sold represents a reasonable value for the remaining shares of $33.75, Adams's shares now have a fair value of $168,750 ($33.75 × 5,000 shares). Adams would thus record the revaluation of its retained 5,000 shares of Smith as follows:

	Debit	Credit
Investment in Smith	18,750	
Gain on Revaluation of Retained Smith Shares to Fair Value		18,750
To record the revaluation of Smith shares to a $33.75 per share fair value from their previous equity method January 1, 2021, carrying amount of $30.00 per share.		

The preceding revaluation of retained shares reflects the view that the loss of control of a subsidiary is a significant economic event that changes the fundamental relationship between the former parent and subsidiary. Also, the fair value of the retained investment provides the users of the parent's financial statements with more relevant information about the investment.

Cost-Flow Assumptions

If it sells less than an entire investment, the parent must select an appropriate cost-flow assumption when it has made more than one purchase. In the sale of securities, the use of specific identification based on serial numbers is acceptable, although averaging or FIFO assumptions often are applied. Use of the averaging method is especially appealing because all shares are truly identical, creating little justification for identifying different cost figures with individual shares.

Accounting for Shares That Remain

If Adams sells only a portion of the investment, it also must determine the proper method of accounting for the shares that remain. Three possible scenarios are described as follows:

1. Adams could have so drastically reduced its interest that the parent no longer controls the subsidiary or even has the ability to significantly influence its decision making. For example, assume that Adams's ownership drops from 80 to 5 percent. In the current period prior to the sale, the 80 percent investment is reported by means of the equity method with the market-value method used for the 5 percent that remains thereafter. Consolidated financial statements are no longer applicable.
2. Adams could still apply significant influence over Smith's operations although it no longer maintains control. A drop in the level of ownership from 80 to 30 percent normally meets this condition. In this case, the parent utilizes the equity method for the entire year. Application is based on 80 percent until the time of sale and then on 30 percent for the remainder of the year. Again, consolidated statements cease to be appropriate because control has been lost.
3. The decrease in ownership could be relatively small so that the parent continues to maintain control over the subsidiary even after the sale. Adams's reduction of its ownership in Smith from 80 to 60 percent is an example of this situation. After the disposal, consolidated financial statements are still required, but the process is based on the *end-of-year ownership percentage.* Because only the retained shares (60 percent in this case) are consolidated, the parent must separately recognize any current-year income accruing to it from its terminated interest. Thus, Adams shows earnings on this portion of the investment (a 20 percent interest in Smith for the time during the year that it is held) in the consolidated income statement as a single-line item computed by means of the equity method.

Comparisons with International Accounting Standards

As observed in previous chapters of this text, the accounting and reporting standards for business combinations between U.S. and international standards have largely converged with FASB ASC Topic 805 and *IFRS 3R,*—each of which carries the title "Business Combinations"—and ASC Topic 810: Consolidation. Each set of standards requires the acquisition method and embraces a fair-value model for the assets acquired and liabilities assumed in a business combination. Both sets of standards treat exchanges between the parent and the noncontrolling interest as equity transactions, unless control is lost. However, the accounting for the noncontrolling interest can diverge across the two reporting regimes.

- *U.S. GAAP.* In reporting the noncontrolling interest in consolidated financial statements, U.S. GAAP requires a fair-value measurement attribute, consistent with the overall valuation principles for business combinations. Thus, acquisition-date fair value provides a basis for reporting the noncontrolling interest, which is adjusted for its share of subsidiary income and dividends subsequent to acquisition.
- *IFRS.* In contrast, *IFRS 3R* allows an option for reporting the noncontrolling interest for each business combination. Under IFRS, the noncontrolling interest may be measured either at its acquisition-date fair value, which can include goodwill, or at a proportionate share of the acquiree's identifiable net asset fair value, which excludes goodwill. The IFRS proportionate-share option effectively assumes that any goodwill created through the business combination applies solely to the controlling interest.

Summary

1. A parent company need not acquire 100 percent of a subsidiary's stock to form a business combination. Only control over the decision-making process is necessary, a level that has historically been achieved by obtaining a majority of the voting shares. Ownership of any subsidiary stock that is retained by outside unrelated parties is collectively referred to as a noncontrolling interest.
2. A consolidation takes on an added degree of complexity when a noncontrolling interest is present. The noncontrolling interest represents a group of subsidiary owners, and their equity is recognized by the parent in its consolidated financial statements.
3. The valuation principle for the noncontrolling interest is acquisition-date fair value. The fair value of the noncontrolling interest is added to the consideration transferred by the parent to determine the acquisition-date fair value of the subsidiary. This fair value is then allocated to the subsidiary's assets acquired and liabilities assumed based on their individual fair values. At the acquisition date, each of the subsidiary's assets and liabilities is included in consolidation at its individual fair value regardless of the degree of parent ownership. Any remaining excess fair value beyond the total assigned to the identifiable net assets is recognized as goodwill.
4. The fair value of the noncontrolling interest is adjusted over time for subsidiary income (less excess fair-value amortization) and subsidiary dividends.
5. Consolidated goodwill is allocated across the controlling and noncontrolling interests based on the excess of their respective acquisition-date fair values less their percentage share of the identifiable subsidiary net asset fair value. The goodwill allocation, therefore, does not necessarily correspond proportionately to the ownership interest of the parent and the noncontrolling interest.
6. Four noncontrolling interest figures appear in the annual consolidation process. First, a beginning-of-the-year balance in the book value of the subsidiary's net assets is recognized on the worksheet (through Entry **S**) followed by the noncontrolling interest's share of the unamortized excess acquisition-date fair values of the subsidiary's assets and liabilities (including a separate amount for goodwill if appropriate). Next, the noncontrolling interest share of the subsidiary's net income for the period (recorded by a columnar entry) is recognized. Subsidiary dividends to these unrelated owners are entered as a reduction of the noncontrolling interest. The final balance for the year is found as a summation of the Noncontrolling Interest column and is presented on the consolidated balance sheet, within the Stockholders' Equity section.
7. When a midyear business acquisition occurs, consolidated revenues and expenses should not include the subsidiary's current year preacquisition revenues and expenses. Only postacquisition subsidiary revenues and expenses are consolidated.
8. A parent can obtain control of a subsidiary by means of several separate purchases occurring over time, a process often referred to as a step acquisition. Once control is achieved, the acquisition method requires that the parent adjust to fair value all prior investments in the acquired firm and recognize any gain or loss. The fair values of these prior investments, along with the consideration transferred in the current investment that gave the parent control and the noncontrolling interest fair value, all constitute the total fair value of the acquired company.
9. When a parent sells some of its ownership shares of a subsidiary, it must establish an appropriate investment account balance to ensure an accurate accounting. If the equity method has not been used, the parent's investment balance is adjusted to recognize any income or amortization previously omitted. The resulting balance is then compared to the amount received for the stock to arrive at either an adjustment to additional paid-in capital (control maintained) or a gain or loss (control lost). Any shares still held will subsequently be reported through either consolidation, the equity method, or the fair-value method, depending on the influence retained by the parent.

Comprehensive Illustration

Problem

(Estimated Time: 60 to 75 Minutes) On January 1, 2017, Father Company acquired an 80 percent interest in Sun Company for $425,000. The acquisition-date fair value of the 20 percent noncontrolling interest's ownership shares was $102,500. Also as of that date, Sun reported total stockholders' equity of $400,000: $100,000 in common stock and $300,000 in retained earnings. In setting the acquisition price, Father appraised four accounts at values different from the balances reported within Sun's financial records.

Buildings (8-year remaining life)	Undervalued by $20,000
Land	Undervalued by $50,000
Equipment (5-year remaining life)	Undervalued by $12,500
Royalty agreement (20-year remaining life)	Not recorded, valued at $30,000

As of December 31, 2021, the trial balances of these two companies are as follows:

	Father Company	Sun Company
Debits		
Current assets	$ 605,000	$ 280,000
Investment in Sun Company	425,000	–0–
Land	200,000	300,000
Buildings (net)	640,000	290,000
Equipment (net)	380,000	160,000
Expenses	550,000	190,000
Dividends declared	90,000	20,000
Total debits	$2,890,000	$1,240,000
Credits		
Liabilities	$ 910,000	$ 300,000
Common stock	480,000	100,000
Retained earnings, 1/1/21	704,000	480,000
Revenues	780,000	360,000
Dividend income	16,000	–0–
Total credits	$2,890,000	$1,240,000

Included in these figures is a $20,000 payable that Sun owes to the parent company. No goodwill impairments have occurred since the Sun Company acquisition.

Required

a. Determine consolidated totals for Father Company and Sun Company for the year 2021.

b. Prepare worksheet entries to consolidate the trial balances of Father Company and Sun Company for the year 2021.

c. Assume instead that the acquisition-date fair value of the noncontrolling interest was $104,500. What balances in the December 31, 2021, consolidated statements would change?

Solution

a. The consolidation of Father Company and Sun Company begins with the allocation of the subsidiary's acquisition-date fair value as shown in Exhibit 4.13. Because this consolidation is taking place after several years, the unamortized balances for the various allocations at the beginning of the current year also should be determined (see Exhibit 4.14).

Next, the parent's method of accounting for its subsidiary should be ascertained. The continuing presence of the original $425,000 acquisition price in the investment account indicates that Father is applying the initial value method. This same determination can be made from the Dividend Income account, which equals 80 percent of the subsidiary's dividends. Thus, Father's accounting records have ignored the increase in Sun's book value as well as the excess amortization expenses for the prior periods of ownership. These amounts have to be added to the parent's January 1, 2021, Retained Earnings account to arrive at the proper consolidated balance.

During the 2017–2020 period of ownership, Sun's Retained Earnings account increased by $180,000 ($480,000 – $300,000). Father's 80 percent interest necessitates an accrual of $144,000 ($180,000 × 80%) for these years. In addition, the acquisition-date fair-value allocations require the recognition of $20,800 in excess amortization expenses for this same period ($6,500 × 80% × 4 years). Thus, a net increase of $123,200 ($144,000 – $20,800) is needed to adjust the parent's beginning retained earnings balance to reflect the equity method.

Once the adjustment from the initial value method to the equity method is determined, the consolidated figures for 2021 can be calculated:

Current Assets = $865,000. The parent's book value is added to the subsidiary's book value. The $20,000 intra-entity balance is eliminated.

Investment in Sun Company = –0–. The intra-entity ownership is eliminated so that the subsidiary's specific assets and liabilities can be consolidated.

Land = $550,000. The parent's book value is added to the subsidiary's book value plus the $50,000 excess fair-value allocation (see Exhibit 4.13).

EXHIBIT 4.13
Excess Fair-Value Allocations

FATHER COMPANY AND SUN COMPANY
Acquisition-Date Fair-Value Allocation and Amortization
2017–2020

	Allocation	Remaining Life (years)	Annual Excess Amortization
Acquisition-date fair value	$527,500		
Sun book value (100%)	400,000		
Excess fair value	127,500		
Allocation to specific subsidiary accounts based on fair value:			
Buildings	$ 20,000	8	$ 2,500
Land	50,000	indefinite	–0–
Equipment	12,500	5	2,500
Royalty agreement	30,000	20	1,500
Goodwill	$ 15,000		
Annual excess amortization expenses			$ 6,500

Goodwill Allocation to the Controlling and Noncontrolling Interests

	Controlling Interest	Noncontrolling Interest	Total
Acquisition-date fair value	$425,000	$102,500	$527,500
Relative fair value of Sun's identifiable net assets (80% and 20%)	410,000	102,500	512,500
Goodwill	$ 15,000	$ –0–	$ 15,000

EXHIBIT 4.14
Excess Fair-Value Allocation Balances

FATHER COMPANY AND SUN COMPANY
Unamortized Excess Fair- over Book-Value Allocation
January 1, 2021, Balances

Account	Excess Original Allocation	Excess Amortization 2017–2020	Balance 1/1/21
Buildings	$ 20,000	$10,000	$ 10,000
Land	50,000	–0–	50,000
Equipment	12,500	10,000	2,500
Royalty agreement	30,000	6,000	24,000
Goodwill	15,000	–0–	15,000
Total	$127,500	$26,000	$101,500

Buildings (net) = $937,500. The parent's book value is added to the subsidiary's book value plus the $20,000 fair-value allocation (see Exhibit 4.14) and less five years of amortization (2017 through 2021).

Equipment (net) = $540,000. The parent's book value is added to the subsidiary's book value. The $12,500 fair-value allocation has been completely amortized after five years.

Royalty Agreement = $22,500. The original residual allocation from the acquisition-date fair value is recognized after taking into account five years of amortization (see Exhibit 4.13).

Goodwill = $15,000. Original acquisition-date value assigned.

Liabilities = $1,190,000. The parent's book value is added to the subsidiary's book value. The $20,000 intra-entity balance is eliminated.

Revenues = $1,140,000. The parent's book value is added to the subsidiary's book value.

Expenses = $746,500. The parent's book value is added to the subsidiary's book value plus current-year amortization expenses on the fair-value allocations (see Exhibit 4.13).

Consolidated Net Income = $393,500. The combined total of consolidated revenues and expenses.

Net Income Attributable to Noncontrolling Interest = \$32,700. The outside owners are assigned a 20 percent share of the subsidiary's net income less excess fair-value amortizations: 20% × (\$170,000 – \$6,500).

Net Income Attributable to Father Company = \$360,800. Consolidated net income less the amount allocated to the noncontrolling interest.

Common Stock = \$480,000. Only the parent company's balance is reported.

Retained Earnings, 1/1/21 = \$827,200. Only the parent company's balance after a \$123,200 increase to convert from the initial value method to the equity method.

Dividends Declared = \$90,000. Only parent company dividends are consolidated. Subsidiary dividends distributable to the parent are eliminated; the remainder reduce the Noncontrolling Interest balance.

Retained Earnings 12/31/21 = \$1,098,000. The parent's adjusted beginning balance of \$827,200, plus \$360,800 net income to the controlling interest, less \$90,000 dividends declared by Father Company.

Dividend Income = –0–. The intra-entity dividend declarations are eliminated.

Noncontrolling Interest in Subsidiary, 12/31/21 = \$162,000.

NCI in Sun's 1/1/21 book value (20% × \$580,000)	\$ 116,000
NCI in unamortized excess fair-value allocations (20% × \$86,500)	17,300
January 1, 2021, NCI in Sun's fair value	133,300
NCI in Sun's net income [20% × (\$360,000 – 196,500)]	32,700
NCI dividend share (20% × \$20,000)	(4,000)
Noncontrolling interest in Sun Company, December 31, 2021	\$ 162,000

b. Six worksheet entries are necessary to produce a consolidation worksheet for Father Company and Sun Company.

Entry *C

Investment in Sun Company	123,200	
Retained Earnings, 1/1/21 (parent)		123,200

This increment is required to adjust the parent's Retained Earnings from the initial value method to the equity method.
The amount is \$144,000 (80% of the \$180,000 increase in the subsidiary's book value during previous years) less \$20,800 in excess amortization over this same 4-year period (\$6,500 × 80% × 4 years).

Entry S

Common Stock (subsidiary)	100,000	
Retained Earnings, 1/1/21 (subsidiary)	480,000	
Investment in Sun Company (80%)		464,000
Noncontrolling Interest in Sun Company (20%)		116,000

To eliminate beginning stockholders' equity accounts of the subsidiary and recognize the beginning balance book value attributed to the outside owners (20%).

Entry A1 and A2 Combined

Buildings	10,000	
Land	50,000	
Equipment	2,500	
Royalty Agreement	24,000	
Goodwill	15,000	
Investment in Sun Company		84,200
Noncontrolling Interest in Sun Company		17,300

To recognize unamortized excess fair- over book-value allocations as of the first day of the current year (see Exhibit 4.14). All goodwill is attributable to the controlling interest.

Entry I

Dividend Income	16,000	
Dividends Declared		16,000

To eliminate intra-entity dividend declarations recorded by parent (using the initial value method) as income.

Entry E

Depreciation Expense	5,000	
Amortization Expense	1,500	
Buildings		2,500
Equipment		2,500
Royalty Agreement		1,500

To recognize excess amortization expenses for the current year (see Exhibit 4.13).

Entry P

Liabilities	20,000	
Current Assets		20,000

To eliminate the intra-entity receivable and payable.

c. If the acquisition-date fair value of the noncontrolling interest were $104,500, then Sun's fair value would increase by $2,000 to $529,500 and goodwill would increase by the same $2,000 to $17,000. The entire $2,000 increase in goodwill would be allocated to the noncontrolling interest as follows:

	Controlling Interest	Noncontrolling Interest	Total
Acquisition-date fair value	$425,000	$104,500	$529,500
Relative fair value of Sun's identifiable net assets (80% and 20%)	410,000	102,500	512,500
Goodwill	$ 15,000	$ 2,000	$ 17,000

Therefore, the consolidated balance sheet would show goodwill at $17,000 (instead of $15,000), and the noncontrolling interest in Sun Company balance would show $164,000 (instead of $162,000).

Questions

1. What does the term *noncontrolling interest* mean?
2. Atwater Company acquires 80 percent of the outstanding voting stock of Belwood Company. On that date, Belwood possesses a building with a $160,000 book value but a $220,000 fair value. At what value would this building be consolidated?
3. What is a control premium and how does it affect consolidated financial statements?
4. Where should the noncontrolling interest's claims be reported in a set of consolidated financial statements?
5. How is the noncontrolling interest in a subsidiary company calculated as of the end of a reporting period?
6. December 31 consolidated financial statements are being prepared for Allsports Company and its new subsidiary acquired on July 1 of the current year. Should Allsports adjust its consolidated balances for the preacquisition subsidiary revenues and expenses?
7. Tree, Inc., has held a 10 percent interest in the stock of Limb Company for several years. Because of the level of ownership, this investment has been accounted for using the fair-value method. At the beginning of the current year, Tree acquires an additional 70 percent interest, which provides the company with control over Limb. In preparing consolidated financial statements for this business combination, how does Tree account for the previous 10 percent ownership interest?
8. Duke Corporation owns a 70 percent equity interest in Salem Company, a subsidiary corporation. During the current year, a portion of this stock is sold to an outside party. Before recording this transaction, Duke adjusts the book value of its investment account. What is the purpose of this adjustment?
9. In question (8), how would the parent record the sales transaction?
10. In question (8), how would Duke account for the remainder of its investment subsequent to the sale of this partial interest?

Problems

LO 4-1

1. What is a basic premise of the acquisition method regarding accounting for a noncontrolling interest?
   a. Consolidated financial statements should be primarily for the benefit of the parent company's stockholders.
   b. Consolidated financial statements should be produced only if both the parent and the subsidiary are in the same basic industry.
   c. A subsidiary is an indivisible part of a business combination and should be included in its entirety regardless of the degree of ownership.
   d. Consolidated financial statements should not report a noncontrolling interest balance because these outside owners do not hold stock in the parent company.

LO 4-2

2. Mittelstaedt, Inc., buys 60 percent of the outstanding stock of Sherry, Inc. Sherry owns a piece of land that cost $212,000 but had a fair value of $549,000 at the acquisition date. What value should be attributed to this land in a consolidated balance sheet at the date of takeover?
   a. $549,000
   b. $337,000
   c. $127,200
   d. $421,800

LO 4-2

3. Jordan, Inc., holds 75 percent of the outstanding stock of Paxson Corporation. Paxson currently owes Jordan $400,000 for inventory acquired over the past few months. In preparing consolidated financial statements, what amount of this debt should be eliminated?
   a. –0–
   b. $100,000
   c. $300,000
   d. $400,000

LO 4-2

4. On January 1, 2020, Grand Haven, Inc., reports net assets of $760,000 although equipment (with a four-year remaining life) having a book value of $440,000 is worth $500,000 and an unrecorded patent is valued at $45,000. Van Buren Corporation pays $692,000 on that date to acquire an 80 percent equity ownership in Grand Haven. If the patent has a remaining life of nine years, at what amount should the patent be reported on Van Buren's consolidated balance sheet at December 31, 2021?
   a. $28,000
   b. $35,000
   c. $36,000
   d. $40,000

LO 4-6

5. The noncontrolling interest represents an outside ownership in a subsidiary that is not attributable to the parent company. Where in the consolidated balance sheet is this outside ownership interest recognized?
   a. In the liability section.
   b. In a mezzanine section between liabilities and owners' equity.
   c. In the owners' equity section.
   d. The noncontrolling interest is not recognized in the consolidated balance sheet.

LO 4-4

6. On January 1, 2020, Chamberlain Corporation pays $388,000 for a 60 percent ownership in Neville. Annual excess fair-value amortization of $15,000 results from the acquisition. On December 31, 2021, Neville reports revenues of $400,000 and expenses of $300,000 and Chamberlain reports revenues of $700,000 and expenses of $400,000. The parent figures contain no income from the subsidiary. What is consolidated net income attributable to Chamberlain Corporation?
   a. $385,000
   b. $351,000
   c. $366,000
   d. $400,000

Problems 7 and 8 relate to the following:

On January 1, 2019, Pride Corporation purchased 90 percent of the outstanding voting shares of Star, Inc., for $540,000 cash. The acquisition-date fair value of the noncontrolling interest was $60,000. At January 1, 2019, Star's net assets had a total carrying amount of $420,000. Equipment (eight-year remaining life) was undervalued on Star's financial records by $80,000. Any remaining excess fair value over book value was attributed to a customer list developed by Star (four-year remaining life), but not recorded on its books. Star recorded net income of $70,000 in 2019 and $80,000 in 2020. Each year since the acquisition, Star has declared a $20,000 dividend. At January 1, 2021, Pride's retained earnings show a $250,000 balance.

Selected account balances for the two companies from their separate operations were as follows:

	Pride	Star
2021 Revenues	$498,000	$285,000
2021 Expenses	350,000	195,000

LO 4-4

7. What is consolidated net income for 2021?
   a. $194,000
   b. $197,500
   c. $203,000
   d. $238,000

LO 4-4

8. Assuming that Pride, in its internal records, accounts for its investment in Star using the equity method, what amount of retained earnings would Pride report on its January 1, 2021, consolidated balance sheet?
   a. $250,000
   b. $286,000
   c. $315,000
   d. $360,000

LO 4-8

9. James Company acquired 85 percent of Mark-Right Company on April 1. On its December 31 consolidated income statement, how should James account for Mark-Right's revenues and expenses that occurred before April 1?
   a. Include 100 percent of Mark-Right's revenues and expenses and deduct the preacquisition portion as noncontrolling interest in net income.
   b. Exclude 100 percent of the preacquisition revenues and 100 percent of the preacquisition expenses from their respective consolidated totals.
   c. Exclude 15 percent of the preacquisition revenues and 15 percent of the preacquisition expenses from consolidated expenses.
   d. Deduct 15 percent of the net combined revenues and expenses relating to the preacquisition period from consolidated net income.

LO 4-9

10. Amie, Inc., has 100,000 shares of $2 par value stock outstanding. Prairie Corporation acquired 30,000 of Amie's shares on January 1, 2018, for $120,000 when Amie's net assets had a total fair value of $350,000. On July 1, 2021, Prairie bought an additional 60,000 shares of Amie from a single stockholder for $6 per share. Although Amie's shares were selling in the $5 range around July 1, 2021, Prairie forecasted that obtaining control of Amie would produce significant revenue synergies to justify the premium price paid. If Amie's identifiable net assets had a fair value of $500,000 at July 1, 2021, how much goodwill should Prairie report in its postcombination consolidated balance sheet?
    a. $60,000
    b. $90,000
    c. $100,000
    d. $-0-

LO 4-9

11. A parent buys 32 percent of a subsidiary in one year and then buys an additional 40 percent in the next year. In a step acquisition of this type, the original 32 percent acquisition should be
    a. Maintained at its initial value.
    b. Adjusted to its equity method balance at the date of the second acquisition.
    c. Adjusted to fair value at the date of the second acquisition with any resulting gain or loss recognized.
    d. Adjusted to fair value at the date of the second acquisition with a resulting adjustment to additional paid-in capital.

LO 4-4, 4-8

12. On April 1, Pujols, Inc., exchanges $430,000 for 70 percent of the outstanding stock of Ramirez Corporation. The remaining 30 percent of the outstanding shares continued to trade at a collective fair value of $165,000. Ramirez's identifiable assets and liabilities each had book values that

equaled their fair values on April 1 for a net total of $500,000. During the remainder of the year, Ramirez generates revenues of $600,000 and expenses of $360,000 and declared no dividends. On a December 31 consolidated balance sheet, what amount should be reported as noncontrolling interest?

a. $219,000
b. $237,000
c. $234,000
d. $250,500

LO 4-10

13. McKinley, Inc., owns 100 percent of Jackson Company's 45,000 voting shares. On June 30, McKinley's internal accounting records show a $192,000 equity method balance for its investment in Jackson. McKinley sells 15,000 of its Jackson shares on the open market for $80,000 on June 30. How should McKinley record the excess of the sale proceeds over its carrying amount for the shares?

a. Reduce goodwill by $64,000.
b. Recognize a gain on sale for $16,000.
c. Increase its additional paid-in capital by $16,000.
d. Recognize a revaluation gain on its remaining shares of $48,000.

Use the following information for Problems 14 through 16:

On January 1, 2020, French Company acquired 60 percent of K-Tech Company for $300,000 when K-Tech's book value was $400,000. The fair value of the newly comprised 40 percent noncontrolling interest was assessed at $200,000. At the acquisition date, K-Tech's trademark (10-year remaining life) was undervalued in its financial records by $60,000. Also, patented technology (5-year remaining life) was undervalued by $40,000.

In 2020, K-Tech reports $30,000 net income and declares no dividends. At the end of 2021, the two companies report the following figures (stockholders' equity accounts have been omitted):

	French Company Carrying Amounts	K-Tech Company Carrying Amounts	K-Tech Company Fair Values
Current assets	$ 620,000	$ 300,000	$ 320,000
Trademarks	260,000	200,000	280,000
Patented technology	410,000	150,000	190,000
Liabilities	(390,000)	(120,000)	(120,000)
Revenues	(900,000)	(400,000)	
Expenses	500,000	300,000	
Investment income	Not given		

LO 4-2

14. What is the 2021 consolidated net income before allocation to the controlling and noncontrolling interests?

a. $400,000
b. $486,000
c. $491,600
d. $500,000

LO 4-4, 4-5

15. In 2021, assuming K-Tech has declared no dividends, what are the noncontrolling interest's share of the subsidiary's income and the ending balance of the noncontrolling interest in the subsidiary?

a. $26,000 and $230,000
b. $28,800 and $252,000
c. $34,400 and $240,800
d. $40,000 and $252,000

LO 4-2

16. What amount is reported for trademarks in the 2021 consolidated balance sheet?

a. $508,000
b. $514,000
c. $520,000
d. $540,000

Use the following information for Problems 17 through 21:

On January 1, Park Corporation and Strand Corporation had condensed balance sheets as follows:

	Park	Strand
Current assets	$ 70,000	$20,000
Noncurrent assets	90,000	40,000
Total assets	$160,000	$60,000
Current liabilities	$ 30,000	$10,000
Long-term debt	50,000	–0–
Stockholders' equity	80,000	50,000
Total liabilities and equities	$160,000	$60,000

On January 2, Park borrowed $60,000 and used the proceeds to obtain 80 percent of the outstanding common shares of Strand. The acquisition price was considered proportionate to Strand's total fair value. The $60,000 debt is payable in 10 equal annual principal payments, plus interest, beginning December 31. The excess fair value of the investment over the underlying book value of the acquired net assets is allocated to inventory (60 percent) and to goodwill (40 percent). On a consolidated balance sheet as of January 2, what should be the amount for each of the following?

LO 4-2

17. Current assets:
    a. $105,000
    b. $102,000
    c. $100,000
    d. $90,000

LO 4-2

18. Noncurrent assets:
    a. $130,000
    b. $134,000
    c. $138,000
    d. $140,000

LO 4-2

19. Current liabilities:
    a. $50,000
    b. $46,000
    c. $40,000
    d. $30,000

LO 4-2

20. Noncurrent liabilities:
    a. $110,000
    b. $104,000
    c. $90,000
    d. $50,000

LO 4-2

21. Stockholders' equity:
    a. $80,000
    b. $90,000
    c. $95,000
    d. $130,000

    (AICPA adapted)

LO 4-3, 4-4, 4-5

22. On January 1, 2021, Ackerman Company acquires 80% of Seidel Company for $1,712,000 in cash consideration. The remaining 20 percent noncontrolling interest shares had an acquisition-date estimated fair value of $428,000. Seidel's acquisition-date total book value was $1,700,000.

    The fair value of Seidel's recorded assets and liabilities equaled their carrying amounts. However, Seidel had two unrecorded assets—a trademark with an indefinite life and estimated fair value of $245,000 and several customer relationships estimated to be worth $180,000 with four-year remaining lives. Any remaining acquisition-date fair value in the Seidel acquisition was considered goodwill.

    During 2021, Seidel reported $172,000 net income and declared and paid dividends totaling $50,000. Also in 2021, Ackerman reported $350,000 net income, but neither declared nor paid dividends.

a. What amount should Ackerman assign to the 20 percent noncontrolling interest of Seidel at the acquisition date?

b. How much of 2021 consolidated net income should be allocated to the noncontrolling interest?

c. What amount of 2021 dividends should be allocated to the noncontrolling interest?

d. What amount of noncontrolling interest should appear in the owners' equity section of Ackerman's consolidated balance sheet at December 31, 2021?

LO 4-4, 4-5

23. On January 1, 2020, Harrison, Inc., acquired 90 percent of Starr Company in exchange for $1,125,000 fair-value consideration. The total fair value of Starr Company was assessed at $1,200,000. Harrison computed annual excess fair-value amortization of $8,000 based on the difference between Starr's total fair value and its underlying book value. The subsidiary reported net income of $70,000 in 2020 and $90,000 in 2021 with dividend declarations of $30,000 each year. Apart from its investment in Starr, Harrison had net income of $220,000 in 2020 and $260,000 in 2021.

a. What is the consolidated net income in each of these two years?

b. What is the balance of the noncontrolling interest in Starr at December 31, 2021?

LO 4-2, 4-4, 4-5

24. On January 1, 2021, Johnsonville Enterprises, Inc., acquired 80 percent of Stayer Company's outstanding common shares in exchange for $3,000,000 cash. The price paid for the 80 percent ownership interest was proportionately representative of the fair value of all of Stayer's shares.

At acquisition date, Stayer's books showed assets of $4,200,000 and liabilities of $1,600,000. The recorded assets and liabilities had fair values equal to their individual book values except that a building (10-year remaining life) with book value of $195,000 had an appraised fair value of $345,000. Stayer's books showed a $175,500 carrying amount for this building at the end of 2021.

Also, at acquisition date Stayer possessed unrecorded technology processes (zero book value) with an estimated fair value of $1,000,000 and a 20-year remaining life. For 2021, Johnsonville reported net income of $650,000 (before recognition of Stayer's income), and Stayer separately reported earnings of $350,000. During 2021, Johnsonville declared dividends of $85,000 and Stayer declared $50,000 in dividends.

Compute the amounts that Johnsonville Enterprises should report in its December 31, 2021, consolidated financial statements for the following items:

a. Stayer's building (net of accumulated depreciation).

b. Stayer's technology processes (net of accumulated amortization).

c. Net income attributable to the noncontrolling interest.

d. Net income attributable to controlling interest.

e. Noncontrolling interest in Stayer.

LO 4-4, 4-5, 4-7

25. On January 1, Patterson Corporation acquired 80 percent of the 100,000 outstanding voting shares of Soriano, Inc., in exchange for $31.25 per share cash. The remaining 20 percent of Soriano's shares continued to trade for $30 both before and after Patterson's acquisition.

At January 1, Soriano's book and fair values were as follows:

	Book Values	Fair Values	Remaining Life
Current assets	$ 80,000	$ 80,000	
Buildings and equipment	1,250,000	1,000,000	5 years
Trademarks	700,000	900,000	10 years
Patented technology	940,000	2,000,000	4 years
	$2,970,000		
Current liabilities	$ 180,000	$ 180,000	
Long-term notes payable	1,500,000	1,500,000	
Common stock	50,000		
Additional paid-in capital	500,000		
Retained earnings	740,000		
	$2,970,000		

In addition, Patterson assigned a $600,000 value to certain unpatented technologies recently developed by Soriano. These technologies were estimated to have a three-year remaining life.

During the year, Soriano declared a $30,000 dividend for its shareholders. The companies reported the following revenues and expenses from their separate operations for the year ending December 31.

	Patterson	Soriano
Revenues	$3,000,000	$1,400,000
Expenses	1,750,000	600,000

a. What amount should Patterson recognize as the total value of the acquisition in its January 1 consolidated balance sheet?

b. What valuation principle should Patterson use to report each of Soriano's identifiable assets and liabilities in its January 1 consolidated balance sheet?

c. For years subsequent to acquisition, how will Soriano's identifiable assets and liabilities be valued in Patterson's consolidated financial statements?

d. How much goodwill resulted from Patterson's acquisition of Soriano?

e. What is the consolidated net income for the year and what amounts are allocated to the controlling and noncontrolling interests?

f. What is the noncontrolling interest amount reported in the December 31 consolidated balance sheet?

g. Assume instead that, based on its share prices, Soriano's January 1 total fair value was assessed at $2,250,000. How would the reported amounts for Soriano's net assets change on Patterson's acquisition-date consolidated balance sheet?

LO 4-9

26. On January 1, 2020, Palka, Inc., acquired 70 percent of the outstanding shares of Sellinger Company for $1,141,000 in cash. The price paid was proportionate to Sellinger's total fair value, although at the acquisition date, Sellinger had a total book value of $1,380,000. All assets acquired and liabilities assumed had fair values equal to book values except for a patent (six-year remaining life) that was undervalued on Sellinger's accounting records by $240,000. On January 1, 2021, Palka acquired an additional 25 percent common stock equity interest in Sellinger Company for $415,000 in cash. On its internal records, Palka uses the equity method to account for its shares of Sellinger.

During the two years following the acquisition, Sellinger reported the following net income and dividends:

	2020	2021
Net income	$340,000	$440,000
Dividends declared	150,000	180,000

a. Show Palka's journal entry to record its January 1, 2021, acquisition of an additional 25 percent ownership of Sellinger Company shares.

b. Prepare a schedule showing Palka's December 31, 2021, equity method balance for its Investment in Sellinger account.

LO 4-2, 4-7, 4-8

27. Parker, Inc., acquires 70 percent of Sawyer Company for $420,000. The remaining 30 percent of Sawyer's outstanding shares continue to trade at a collective value of $174,000. On the acquisition date, Sawyer has the following accounts:

	Book Value	Fair Value
Current assets	$ 210,000	$210,000
Land.	170,000	180,000
Buildings.	300,000	330,000
Liabilities.	(280,000)	(280,000)

The buildings have a 10-year remaining life. In addition, Sawyer holds a patent worth $140,000 that has a five-year remaining life but is not recorded on its financial records. At the end of the year, the two companies report the following balances:

	Parker	Sawyer
Revenues	$(900,000)	$(600,000)
Expenses	600,000	400,000

a. Assume that the acquisition took place on January 1. What figures would appear in a consolidated income statement for this year?

b. Assume that the acquisition took place on April 1. Sawyer's revenues and expenses occurred uniformly throughout the year. What amounts would appear in a consolidated income statement for this year?

LO 4-2, 4-4, 4-5

28. On January 1, Beckman, Inc., acquires 60 percent of the outstanding stock of Calvin for $36,000. Calvin Co. has one recorded asset, a specialized production machine with a book value of $10,000 and no liabilities. The fair value of the machine is $50,000, and the remaining useful life is estimated to be 10 years. Any remaining excess fair value is attributable to an unrecorded process trade secret with an estimated future life of four years. Calvin's total acquisition-date fair value is $60,000.

At the end of the year, Calvin reports the following in its financial statements:

Revenues	$50,000	Machine	$ 9,000	Common stock	$10,000
Expenses	20,000	Other assets	26,000	Retained earnings	25,000
Net income	$30,000	Total assets	$35,000	Total equity	$35,000
Dividends declared	$ 5,000				

Determine the amounts that Beckman should report in its year-end consolidated financial statements for noncontrolling interest in subsidiary income, noncontrolling interest, Calvin's machine (net of accumulated depreciation), and the process trade secret.

LO 4-1, 4-5, 4-6

29. Plaza, Inc., acquires 80 percent of the outstanding common stock of Stanford Corporation on January 1, 2021, in exchange for $900,000 cash. At the acquisition date, Stanford's total fair value, including the noncontrolling interest, was assessed at $1,125,000. Also at the acquisition date, Stanford's book value was $690,000.

Several individual items on Stanford's financial records had fair values that differed from their book values as follows:

	Book Value	Fair Value
Trade names (indefinite life)	$360,000	$383,000
Property and equipment (net, 8-year remaining life)	290,000	330,000
Patent (14-year remaining life)	132,000	272,000

For internal reporting purposes, Plaza, Inc., employs the equity method to account for this investment. The following account balances are for the year ending December 31, 2021, for both companies.

	Plaza	Stanford
Revenues	$(1,400,000)	$ (825,000)
Cost of goods sold	774,000	395,750
Depreciation expense	328,000	36,250
Amortization expense	–0–	28,000
Equity in income of Stanford	(280,000)	–0–
Net income	$ (578,000)	$ (365,000)
Retained earnings, 1/1/21	$(1,275,000)	$ (530,000)
Net income	(578,000)	(365,000)
Dividends declared	300,000	50,000
Retained earnings, 12/31/21	$(1,553,000)	$ (845,000)
Current assets	$ 860,000	$ 432,250
Investment in Stanford	1,140,000	–0–
Trade names	240,000	360,000
Property and equipment (net)	1,030,000	253,750
Patents	–0–	104,000
Total assets	$ 3,270,000	$ 1,150,000
Accounts payable	$ (142,000)	$ (145,000)
Common stock	(300,000)	(120,000)
Additional paid-in capital	(1,275,000)	(40,000)
Retained earnings (above)	(1,553,000)	(845,000)
Total liabilities and equities	$(3,270,000)	$(1,150,000)

At year-end, there were no intra-entity receivables or payables.

Prepare a worksheet to consolidate the financial statements of Plaza, Inc., and its subsidiary Stanford.

LO 4-3, 4-5, 4-7

30. On January 1, 2019, Parflex Corporation exchanged $344,000 cash for 90 percent of Eagle Corporation's outstanding voting stock. Eagle's acquisition date balance sheet follows:

Cash and receivables	$ 15,000	Liabilities	$ 76,000
Inventory	35,000	Common stock	150,000
Property and equipment (net)	350,000	Retained earnings	174,000
	$400,000		$400,000

On January 1, 2019, Parflex prepared the following fair-value allocation schedule:

Consideration transferred by Parflex	$344,000
10% noncontrolling interest fair value	36,000
Fair value of Eagle	380,000
Book value of Eagle	324,000
Excess fair over book value	56,000
to equipment (undervalued, remaining life of 9 years)	18,000
to goodwill (indefinite life)	$ 38,000

The companies' financial statements for the year ending December 31, 2021, follow:

	Parflex	Eagle
Sales	$ (862,000)	$(366,000)
Cost of goods sold	515,000	209,000
Depreciation expense	191,200	67,000
Equity in Eagle's earnings	(79,200)	–0–
Separate company net income	$ (235,000)	$ (90,000)
Retained earnings 1/1	$ (500,000)	$(278,000)
Net income	(235,000)	(90,000)
Dividends declared	130,000	27,000
Retained earnings 12/31	$ (605,000)	$(341,000)
Cash and receivables	$ 135,000	$ 82,000
Inventory	255,000	136,000
Investment in Eagle	488,900	–0–
Property and equipment (net)	964,000	328,000
Total assets	$ 1,842,900	$ 546,000
Liabilities	$ (722,900)	(55,000)
Common stock—Parflex	(515,000)	–0–
Common stock—Eagle	–0–	(150,000)
Retained earnings 12/31	(605,000)	(341,000)
Total liabilities and owners' equity	$(1,842,900)	$(546,000)

At year-end, there were no intra-entity receivables or payables.

a. Compute the goodwill allocation to the controlling and noncontrolling interest.

b. Show how Parflex determined its "Investment in Eagle" account balance.

c. Determine the amounts that should appear on Parflex's December 31, 2021, consolidated statement of financial position and its 2018 consolidated income statement.

LO 4-3, 4-5, 4-7

31. On January 1, 2020, Holland Corporation paid $8 per share to a group of Zeeland Corporation shareholders to acquire 60,000 shares of Zeeland's outstanding voting stock, representing a 60 percent ownership interest. The remaining 40,000 shares of Zeeland continued to trade in the market close to its recent average of $6.50 per share both before and after the acquisition by Holland. Zeeland's acquisition date balance sheet follows:

Current assets	$ 14,000	Liabilities	$212,000
Property and equipment (net)	268,000	Common stock	100,000
Patents	190,000	Retained earnings	160,000
	$472,000		$472,000

On January 1, 2020, Holland assessed the carrying amount of Zeeland's equipment (5-year remaining life) to be undervalued by $55,000. Holland also determined that Zeeland possessed unrecorded patents (10-year remaining life) worth $285,000. Zeeland's acquisition-date fair values for its current assets and liabilities were equal to their carrying amounts. Any remaining excess of Zeeland's acquisition-date fair value over its book value was attributed to goodwill.

The companies' financial statements for the year ending December 31, 2021, follow:

	Holland	Zeeland
Sales	$ (640,500)	$(428,500)
Cost of goods sold	325,000	200,000
Depreciation expense	80,000	34,000
Amortization expense	14,000	21,000
Other operating expenses	52,000	63,500
Equity in Zeeland earnings	(42,300)	–0–
Separate company net income	$ (211,800)	$(110,000)
Retained earnings 1/1	$ (820,200)	$(296,500)
Net income	(211,800)	(110,000)
Dividends declared	50,000	30,000
Retained earnings 12/31	$ (982,000)	$(376,500)
Current assets	$ 125,000	$ 81,500
Investment in Zeeland	562,500	–0–
Property and equipment (net)	837,000	259,000
Patents	149,000	147,500
Total assets	$ 1,673,500	$ 488,000
Liabilities	$ (371,500)	$ (11,500)
Common stock—Holland	(320,000)	–0–
Common stock—Zeeland	–0–	(100,000)
Retained earnings 12/31	(982,000)	(376,500)
Total liabilities and owners equity	$(1,673,500)	$(488,000)

At year-end, there were no intra-entity receivables or payables.

a. Compute the amount of goodwill recognized in Holland's acquisition of Zeeland and the allocation of goodwill to the controlling and noncontrolling interest.

b. Show how Holland determined its December 31, 2021, Investment in Zeeland account balance.

c. Prepare a worksheet to determine the amounts that should appear on Holland's December 31, 2021, consolidated financial statements.

LO 4-8, 4-9

32. On January 1, 2021, Morey, Inc., exchanged $178,000 for 25 percent of Amsterdam Corporation. Morey appropriately applied the equity method to this investment. At January 1, the book values of Amsterdam's assets and liabilities approximated their fair values.

On June 30, 2021, Morey paid $560,000 for an additional 70 percent of Amsterdam, thus increasing its overall ownership to 95 percent. The price paid for the 70 percent acquisition was proportionate to Amsterdam's total fair value. At June 30, the carrying amounts of Amsterdam's assets and liabilities approximated their fair values. Any remaining excess fair value was attributed to goodwill.

Amsterdam reports the following amounts at December 31, 2021 (credit balances shown in parentheses):

Revenues	$ (210,000)
Expenses	140,000
Retained earnings, January 1	(200,000)
Dividends declared, October 1	20,000
Common stock	(500,000)

Amsterdam's revenue and expenses were distributed evenly throughout the year, and no changes in Amsterdam's stock have occurred.

Using the acquisition method, compute the following:

a. The acquisition-date fair value of Amsterdam to be included in Morey's June 30 consolidated financial statements.

b. The revaluation gain (or loss) reported by Morey for its 25 percent investment in Amsterdam on June 30.

c. The amount of goodwill recognized by Morey on its December 31 balance sheet (assume no impairments have been recognized).

d. The noncontrolling interest amount reported by Morey on its

- June 30 consolidated balance sheet.
- December 31 consolidated balance sheet.

LO 4-10

33. Posada Company acquired 7,000 of the 10,000 outstanding shares of Sabathia Company on January 1, 2019, for $840,000. The subsidiary's total fair value was assessed at $1,200,000 although its book value on that date was $1,130,000. The $70,000 fair value in excess of Sabathia's book value was assigned to a patent with a five-year remaining life.

    On January 1, 2021, Posada reported a $1,085,000 equity method balance in the Investment in Sabathia Company account. On October 1, 2021, Posada sells 1,000 shares of the investment for $191,000. During 2021, Sabathia reported net income of $120,000 and declared dividends of $40,000. These amounts are assumed to have occurred evenly throughout the year.

    a. How should Posada report the 2021 income that accrued to the 1,000 shares prior to their sale?

    b. What is the effect on Posada's financial statements from this sale of 1,000 shares?

    c. How should Posada report in its financial statements the 6,000 shares of Sabathia it continues to hold?

LO 4-5

34. On January 1, 2019, Telconnect acquires 70 percent of Bandmor for $490,000 cash. The remaining 30 percent of Bandmor's shares continued to trade at a total value of $210,000. The new subsidiary reported common stock of $300,000 on that date, with retained earnings of $180,000. A patent was undervalued in the company's financial records by $30,000. This patent had a five-year remaining life. Goodwill of $190,000 was recognized and allocated proportionately to the controlling and noncontrolling interests. Bandmor earns net income and declares cash dividends as follows:

Year	Net Income	Dividends
2019	$ 75,000	$39,000
2020	96,000	44,000
2021	110,000	60,000

    On December 31, 2021, Telconnect owes $22,000 to Bandmor.

    a. If Telconnect has applied the equity method, what consolidation entries are needed as of December 31, 2021?

    b. If Telconnect has applied the initial value method, what Entry *C is needed for a 2021 consolidation?

    c. If Telconnect has applied the partial equity method, what Entry *C is needed for a 2021 consolidation?

    d. What noncontrolling interest balances will appear in consolidated financial statements for 2021?

LO 4-2, 4-3, 4-5

35. Miller Company acquired an 80 percent interest in Taylor Company on January 1, 2019. Miller paid $664,000 in cash to the owners of Taylor to acquire these shares. In addition, the remaining 20 percent of Taylor shares continued to trade at a total value of $166,000 both before and after Miller's acquisition.

    On January 1, 2019, Taylor reported a book value of $600,000 (Common Stock = $300,000; Additional Paid-In Capital = $90,000; Retained Earnings = $210,000). Several of Taylor's buildings that had a remaining life of 20 years were undervalued by a total of $80,000.

    During the next three years, Taylor reports income and declares dividends as follows:

Year	Net Income	Dividends
2019	$ 70,000	$10,000
2020	90,000	15,000
2021	100,000	20,000

    Determine the appropriate answers for each of the following questions:

    a. What amount of excess depreciation expense should be recognized in the consolidated financial statements for the initial years following this acquisition?

b. If a consolidated balance sheet is prepared as of January 1, 2019, what amount of goodwill should be recognized?

c. If a consolidation worksheet is prepared as of January 1, 2019, what Entry S and Entry A should be included?

d. On the separate financial records of the parent company, what amount of investment income would be reported for 2019 under each of the following accounting methods?

- The equity method.
- The partial equity method.
- The initial value method.

e. On the parent company's separate financial records, what would be the December 31, 2021, balance for the Investment in Taylor Company account under each of the following accounting methods?

- The equity method.
- The partial equity method.
- The initial value method.

f. As of December 31, 2020, Miller's Buildings account on its separate records has a balance of $800,000 and Taylor has a similar account with a $300,000 balance. What is the consolidated balance for the Buildings account?

g. What is the balance of consolidated goodwill as of December 31, 2021?

h. Assume that the parent company has been applying the equity method to this investment. On December 31, 2021, the separate financial statements for the two companies present the following information:

	Miller Company	Taylor Company
Common stock	$500,000	$300,000
Additional paid-in capital	280,000	90,000
Retained earnings, 12/31/21	620,000	425,000

What will be the consolidated balance of each of these accounts?

LO 4-1, 4-8

36. The following are several account balances taken from the records of Karson and Reilly as of December 31, 2021. A few asset accounts have been omitted here. All revenues, expenses, and dividend declarations occurred evenly throughout the year. Annual tests have indicated no goodwill impairment.

	Karson	Reilly
Sales	$ (800,000)	$(500,000)
Cost of goods sold	400,000	280,000
Operating expenses	200,000	100,000
Investment income	not given	–0–
Retained earnings, 1/1	(1,400,000)	(700,000)
Dividends declared	80,000	20,000
Trademarks	600,000	200,000
Royalty agreements	700,000	300,000
Licensing agreements	400,000	400,000
Liabilities	(500,000)	(200,000)
Common stock ($10 par value)	(400,000)	(100,000)
Additional paid-in capital	(500,000)	(600,000)

On July 1, 2021, Karson acquired 80 percent of Reilly for $1,330,000 cash consideration. In addition, Karson agreed to pay additional cash to the former owners of Reilly if certain performance measures are achieved after three years. Karson assessed a $30,000 fair value for the contingent performance obligation as of the acquisition date and as of December 31, 2021.

On July 1, 2021, Reilly's assets and liabilities had book values equal to their fair value except for some trademarks (with five-year remaining lives) that were undervalued by $150,000. Karson estimated Reilly's total fair value at $1,700,000 on July 1, 2021.

For the following items, what balances would be reported on Karson's December 31, 2021, consolidated financial statements?

Sales	Consolidated Net Income
Expenses	Retained Earnings, 1/1
Noncontrolling Interest in Subsidiary's Net Income	Trademarks
	Goodwill

LO 4-5

37. Nascent, Inc., acquires 60 percent of Sea-Breeze Corporation for $414,000 cash on January 1, 2018. The remaining 40 percent of the Sea-Breeze shares traded near a total value of $276,000 both before and after the acquisition date. On January 1, 2018, Sea-Breeze had the following assets and liabilities:

	Book Value	Fair Value
Current assets	$ 150,000	$ 150,000
Land	200,000	200,000
Buildings (net) (6-year remaining life)	300,000	360,000
Equipment (net) (4-year remaining life)	300,000	280,000
Patent (10-year remaining life)	–0–	100,000
Liabilities	(400,000)	(400,000)

The companies' financial statements for the year ending December 31, 2021, follow:

	Nascent	Sea-Breeze
Revenues	$ (600,000)	$ (300,000)
Operating expenses	410,000	210,000
Investment income	(42,000)	–0–
Net income	$ (232,000)	$ (90,000)
Retained earnings, 1/1/21	$ (700,000)	$ (300,000)
Net income	(232,000)	(90,000)
Dividends declared	92,000	70,000
Retained earnings, 12/31/21	$ (840,000)	$ (320,000)
Current assets	$ 330,000	$ 100,000
Land	220,000	200,000
Buildings (net)	700,000	200,000
Equipment (net)	400,000	500,000
Investment in Sea-Breeze	414,000	–0–
Total assets	$ 2,064,000	$ 1,000,000
Liabilities	$ (500,000)	$ (200,000)
Common stock	(724,000)	(480,000)
Retained earnings, 12/31/21	(840,000)	(320,000)
Total liabilities and equities	$(2,064,000)	$(1,000,000)

Answer the following questions:

a. What account balances reveal that the parent has applied the initial value method?

b. What is the annual excess amortization initially recognized in connection with this acquisition?

c. If the parent had applied the equity method, what investment income would the parent have recorded in 2021?

d. What amount should the parent report as retained earnings in its January 1, 2021, consolidated balance sheet?

e. What is consolidated net income for 2021, and what amounts are attributable to the controlling and noncontrolling interests?

f. Within consolidated statements at January 1, 2021, what balance is included for the subsidiary's Buildings account?

g. What is the consolidated Buildings reported balance as of December 31, 2021?

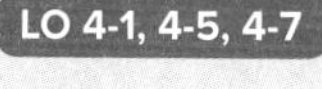

38. On January 1, 2020, Paloma Corporation exchanged $1,710,000 cash for 90 percent of the outstanding voting stock of San Marco Company. The consideration transferred by Paloma provided a reasonable basis for assessing the total January 1, 2020, fair value of San Marco Company. At the acquisition date, San Marco reported the following owners' equity amounts in its balance sheet:

Common stock	$400,000
Additional paid-in capital	60,000
Retained earnings	265,000

In determining its acquisition offer, Paloma noted that the values for San Marco's recorded assets and liabilities approximated their fair values. Paloma also observed that San Marco had developed internally a customer base with an assessed fair value of $800,000 that was not reflected on San Marco's books. Paloma expected both cost and revenue synergies from the combination.

At the acquisition date, Paloma prepared the following fair-value allocation schedule:

Fair value of San Marco Company	$1,900,000
Book value of San Marco Company	725,000
Excess fair value	1,175,000
to customer base (10-year remaining life)	800,000
to goodwill	$ 375,000

At December 31, 2021, the two companies report the following balances:

	Paloma	San Marco
Revenues	$(1,843,000)	$ (675,000)
Cost of goods sold	1,100,000	322,000
Depreciation expense	125,000	120,000
Amortization expense	275,000	11,000
Interest expense	27,500	7,000
Equity in income of San Marco	(121,500)	–0–
Net income	$ (437,000)	$ (215,000)
Retained earnings, 1/1	$(2,625,000)	$ (395,000)
Net income	(437,000)	(215,000)
Dividends declared	350,000	25,000
Retained earnings, 12/31	$(2,712,000)	$ (585,000)
Current assets	$ 1,204,000	$ 430,000
Investment in San Marco	1,854,000	–0–
Buildings and equipment	931,000	863,000
Copyrights	950,000	107,000
Total assets	$ 4,939,000	$ 1,400,000
Accounts payable	$ (485,000)	$ (200,000)
Notes payable	(542,000)	(155,000)
Common stock	(900,000)	(400,000)
Additional paid-in capital	(300,000)	(60,000)
Retained earnings, 12/31	(2,712,000)	(585,000)
Total liabilities and equities	$(4,939,000)	$(1,400,000)

At year-end, there were no intra-entity receivables or payables.

a. Determine the consolidated balances for this business combination as of December 31, 2021.

b. If instead the noncontrolling interest's acquisition-date fair value is assessed at $167,500, what changes would be evident in the consolidated statements?

LO 4-5, 4-6, 4-7

39. The Holtz Corporation acquired 80 percent of the 100,000 outstanding voting shares of Devine, Inc., for $7.20 per share on January 1, 2020. The remaining 20 percent of Devine's shares also traded actively at $7.20 per share before and after Holtz's acquisition. An appraisal made on that date determined that all book values appropriately reflected the fair values of Devine's underlying accounts except that a building with a five-year future life was undervalued by $85,500 and a fully amortized

trademark with an estimated 10-year remaining life had a $64,000 fair value. At the acquisition date, Devine reported common stock of $100,000 and a retained earnings balance of $226,500.

Following are the separate financial statements for the year ending December 31, 2021:

	Holtz Corporation	Devine, Inc.
Sales	$ (641,000)	$(399,000)
Cost of goods sold	198,000	176,000
Operating expenses	273,000	126,000
Dividend income	(16,000)	–0–
Net income	$ (186,000)	$ (97,000)
Retained earnings, 1/1/21	$ (762,000)	$(296,500)
Net income (above)	(186,000)	(97,000)
Dividends declared	70,000	20,000
Retained earnings, 12/31/21	$ (878,000)	$(373,500)
Current assets	$ 121,000	$ 120,500
Investment in Devine, Inc.	576,000	–0–
Buildings and equipment (net)	887,000	335,000
Trademarks	149,000	236,000
Total assets	$ 1,733,000	$ 691,500
Liabilities	$ (535,000)	$(218,000)
Common stock	(320,000)	(100,000)
Retained earnings, 12/31/21 (above)	(878,000)	(373,500)
Total liabilities and equities	$(1,733,000)	$(691,500)

At year-end, there were no intra-entity receivables or payables.

a. Prepare a worksheet to consolidate these two companies as of December 31, 2021.

b. Prepare a 2021 consolidated income statement for Holtz and Devine.

c. If instead the noncontrolling interest shares of Devine had traded for $4.76 surrounding Holtz's acquisition date, what is the impact on goodwill?

LO 4-1, 4-5, 4-6

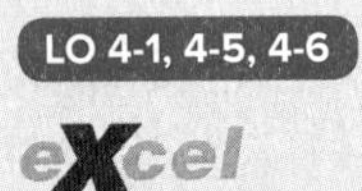

40. Padre, Inc., buys 80 percent of the outstanding common stock of Sierra Corporation on January 1, 2021, for $802,720 cash. At the acquisition date, Sierra's total fair value, including the noncontrolling interest, was assessed at $1,003,400 although Sierra's book value was only $690,000. Also, several individual items on Sierra's financial records had fair values that differed from their book values as follows:

	Book Value	Fair Value
Land	$ 65,000	$ 290,000
Buildings and equipment (10-year remaining life)	287,000	263,000
Copyright (20-year remaining life)	122,000	216,000
Notes payable (due in 8 years)	(176,000)	(157,600)

For internal reporting purposes, Padre, Inc., employs the equity method to account for this investment. The following account balances are for the year ending December 31, 2021, for both companies.

	Padre	Sierra
Revenues	$(1,394,980)	$ (684,900)
Cost of goods sold	774,000	432,000
Depreciation expense	274,000	11,600
Amortization expense	0	6,100
Interest expense	52,100	9,200
Equity in income of Sierra	(177,120)	–0–
Net income	$ (472,000)	$ (226,000)

(continued)

(continued)

	Padre	Sierra
Retained earnings, 1/1/21	$(1,275,000)	$ (530,000)
Net income	(472,000)	(226,000)
Dividends declared	260,000	65,000
Retained earnings, 12/31/21	$(1,487,000)	$ (691,000)
Current assets	$ 856,160	$ 764,700
Investment in Sierra	927,840	–0–
Land	360,000	65,000
Buildings and equipment (net)	909,000	275,400
Copyright	–0–	115,900
Total assets	$ 3,053,000	$ 1,221,000
Accounts payable	$ (275,000)	$ (194,000)
Notes payable	(541,000)	(176,000)
Common stock	(300,000)	(100,000)
Additional paid-in capital	(450,000)	(60,000)
Retained earnings (above)	(1,487,000)	(691,000)
Total liabilities and equities	$(3,053,000)	$(1,221,000)

At year-end, there were no intra-entity receivables or payables.

Prepare a worksheet to consolidate the financial statements of these two companies.

LO 4-1, 4-5

41. Adams Corporation acquired 90 percent of the outstanding voting shares of Barstow, Inc., on December 31, 2019. Adams paid a total of $603,000 in cash for these shares. The 10 percent noncontrolling interest shares traded on a daily basis at fair value of $67,000 both before and after Adams's acquisition. On December 31, 2019, Barstow had the following account balances:

	Book Value	Fair Value
Current assets	$ 160,000	$160,000
Land	120,000	150,000
Buildings (10-year remaining life)	220,000	200,000
Equipment (5-year remaining life)	160,000	200,000
Patents (10-year remaining life)	–0–	50,000
Notes payable (due in 5 years)	(200,000)	(180,000)
Common stock	(180,000)	
Retained earnings, 12/31/19	(280,000)	

December 31, 2021, adjusted trial balances for the two companies follow:

	Adams Corporation	Barstow, Inc.
Debits		
Current assets	$ 610,000	$ 250,000
Land	380,000	150,000
Buildings	490,000	250,000
Equipment	873,000	150,000
Investment in Barstow, Inc.	702,000	–0–
Cost of goods sold	480,000	90,000
Depreciation expense	100,000	55,000
Interest expense	40,000	15,000
Dividends declared	110,000	70,000
Total debits	$3,785,000	$1,030,000
Credits		
Notes payable	$ 860,000	$ 230,000
Common stock	510,000	180,000
Retained earnings, 1/1/21	1,367,000	340,000
Revenues	940,000	280,000
Investment income	108,000	–0–
Total credits	$3,785,000	$1,030,000

At year-end, there were no intra-entity receivables or payables.

a. Prepare schedules for acquisition-date fair-value allocations and amortizations for Adams's investment in Barstow.

b. Determine Adams's method of accounting for its investment in Barstow. Support your answer with a numerical explanation.

c. Without using a worksheet or consolidation entries, determine the balances to be reported as of December 31, 2021, for this business combination.

d. To verify the figures determined in requirement (*c*), prepare a consolidation worksheet for Adams Corporation and Barstow, Inc., as of December 31, 2021.

LO 4-1, 4-4, 4-8

42. Following are the individual financial statements for Gibson and Davis for the year ending December 31, 2021:

	Gibson	Davis
Sales	$ (600,000)	$ (300,000)
Cost of goods sold	300,000	140,000
Operating expenses	174,000	60,000
Dividend income	(24,000)	–0–
Net income	$ (150,000)	$ (100,000)
Retained earnings, 1/1/21	$ (700,000)	$ (400,000)
Net income	(150,0000)	(100,000)
Dividends declared	80,000	40,000
Retained earnings, 12/31/21	$ (770,000)	$ (460,000)
Cash and receivables	$ 248,000	$ 100,000
Inventory	500,000	190,000
Investment in Davis	528,000	–0–
Buildings (net)	524,000	600,000
Equipment (net)	400,000	400,000
Total assets	$ 2,200,000	$ 1,290,000
Liabilities	(800,000)	(490,000)
Common stock	(630,000)	(340,000)
Retained earnings, 12/31/21	(770,000)	(460,000)
Total liabilities and stockholders' equity	$(2,200,000)	$(1,290,000)

Gibson acquired 60 percent of Davis on April 1, 2021, for $528,000. On that date, equipment owned by Davis (with a five-year remaining life) was overvalued by $30,000. Also on that date, the fair value of the 40 percent noncontrolling interest was $352,000. Davis earned income evenly during the year but declared the $40,000 dividend on November 1, 2021.

a. Prepare a consolidated income statement for the year ending December 31, 2021.

b. Determine the consolidated balance for each of the following accounts as of December 31, 2021:

Goodwill	Buildings (net)
Equipment (net)	Dividends Declared
Common Stock	

LO 4-2, 4-3, 4-6, 4-7, 4-8

43. On July 1, 2021, Truman Company acquired a 70 percent interest in Atlanta Company in exchange for consideration of $720,000 in cash and equity securities. The remaining 30 percent of Atlanta's shares traded closely near an average price that totaled $290,000 both before and after Truman's acquisition.

In reviewing its acquisition, Truman assigned a $100,000 fair value to a patent recently developed by Atlanta, even though it was not recorded within the financial records of the subsidiary. This patent is anticipated to have a remaining life of five years.

The following financial information is available for these two companies for 2021. In addition, the subsidiary's income was earned uniformly throughout the year. The subsidiary declared dividends quarterly.

	Truman	Atlanta
Revenues	$ (670,000)	$ (400,000)
Operating expenses	402,000	280,000
Income of subsidiary	(35,000)	–0–
Net income	$ (303,000)	$ (120,000)
Retained earnings, 1/1/21	$ (823,000)	$ (500,000)
Net income (above)	(303,000)	(120,000)
Dividends declared	145,000	80,000
Retained earnings, 12/31/21	$ (981,000)	$ (540,000)
Current assets	$ 481,000	$ 390,000
Investment in Atlanta	727,000	–0–
Land	388,000	200,000
Buildings	701,000	630,000
Total assets	$ 2,297,000	$ 1,220,000
Liabilities	$ (816,000)	$ (360,000)
Common stock	(95,000)	(300,000)
Additional paid-in capital	(405,000)	(20,000)
Retained earnings, 12/31/21	(981,000)	(540,000)
Total liabilities and stockholders' equity	$(2,297,000)	$(1,220,000)

Answer each of the following:

a. How did Truman allocate Atlanta's acquisition-date fair value to the various assets acquired and liabilities assumed in the combination?

b. How did Truman allocate the goodwill from the acquisition across the controlling and noncontrolling interests?

c. How did Truman derive the Investment in Atlanta account balance at the end of 2021?

d. Prepare a worksheet to consolidate the financial statements of these two companies as of December 31, 2021. At year-end, there were no intra-entity receivables or payables.

LO 4-9

44. On January 1, 2020, Allan Company bought a 15 percent interest in Sysinger Company. The acquisition price of $184,500 reflected an assessment that all of Sysinger's accounts were fairly valued within the company's accounting records. During 2020, Sysinger reported net income of $100,000 and declared cash dividends of $30,000. Allan possessed the ability to significantly influence Sysinger's operations and, therefore, accounted for this investment using the equity method.

On January 1, 2021, Allan acquired an additional 80 percent interest in Sysinger and provided the following fair-value assessments of Sysinger's ownership components:

Consideration transferred by Allan for 80% interest	$1,400,000
Fair value of Allan's 15% previous ownership	262,500
Noncontrolling interest's 5% fair value	87,500
Total acquisition-date fair value for Sysinger Company	$1,750,000

Also, as of January 1, 2021, Allan assessed a $400,000 value to an unrecorded customer contract recently negotiated by Sysinger. The customer contract is anticipated to have a remaining life of four years. Sysinger's other assets and liabilities were judged to have fair values equal to their book values. Allan elects to continue applying the equity method to this investment for internal reporting purposes.

At December 31, 2021, the following financial information is available for consolidation:

	Allan Company	Sysinger Company
Revenues	$ (931,000)	$ (380,000)
Operating expenses	615,000	230,000
Equity earnings of Sysinger	(47,500)	–0–
Gain on revaluation of Investment in Sysinger to fair value	(67,500)	–0–
Net income	$ 431,000	$ 150,000

(continued)

(continued)

	Allan Company	Sysinger Company
Retained earnings, January 1	$ (965,000)	$ (600,000)
Net income	(431,000)	(150,000)
Dividends declared	140,000	40,000
Retained earnings, December 31	$(1,256,000)	$ (710,000)
Current assets	$ 288,000	$ 540,000
Investment in Sysinger (equity method)	1,672,000	–0–
Property, plant, and equipment	826,000	590,000
Patented technology	850,000	370,000
Customer contract	–0–	–0–
Total assets	$ 3,636,000	$ 1,500,000
Liabilities	$(1,300,000)	$ (90,000)
Common stock	(900,000)	(500,000)
Additional paid-in capital	(180,000)	(200,000)
Retained earnings, December 31	(1,256,000)	(710,000)
Total liabilities and equities	$(3,636,000)	$(1,500,000)

a. How should Allan allocate Sysinger's total acquisition-date fair value (January 1, 2021) to the assets acquired and liabilities assumed for consolidation purposes?

b. Show how the following amounts on Allan's pre-consolidation 2021 statements were derived:
- Equity in earnings of Sysinger
- Gain on revaluation of Investment in Sysinger to fair value
- Investment in Sysinger

c. Prepare a worksheet to consolidate the financial statements of these two companies as of December 31, 2021.

At year-end, there were no intra-entity receivables or payables.

LO 4-9

45. On January 1, 2020, Bretz, Inc., acquired 60 percent of the outstanding shares of Keane Company for $573,000 in cash. The price paid was proportionate to Keane's total fair value although at the date of acquisition, Keane had a total book value of $810,000. All assets acquired and liabilities assumed had fair values equal to book values except for a copyright (six-year remaining life) that was undervalued in Keane's accounting records by $120,000. During 2020, Keane reported net income of $150,000 and declared cash dividends of $80,000. On January 1, 2021, Bretz bought an additional 30 percent interest in Keane for $300,000.

The following financial information is for these two companies for 2018. Keane issued no additional capital stock during either 2020 or 2021. Also, at year-end, there were no intra-entity receivables or payables.

	Bretz, Inc.	Keane Company
Revenues	$ (402,000)	$ (300,000)
Operating expenses	200,000	120,000
Equity in Keane earnings	(144,000)	–0–
Net income	$ (346,000)	$ (180,000)
Retained earnings, 1/1	$ (797,000)	$ (500,000)
Net income (above)	(346,000)	(180,000)
Dividends declared	143,000	60,000
Retained earnings, 12/31	$(1,000,000)	$ (620,000)
Current assets	$ 224,000	$ 190,000
Investment in Keane Company	994,500	–0–
Trademarks	106,000	600,000
Copyrights	210,000	300,000
Equipment (net)	380,000	110,000
Total assets	$ 1,914,500	$ 1,200,000

(continued)

(continued)

	Bretz, Inc.	Keane Company
Liabilities	$ (453,000)	$ (200,000)
Common stock	(400,000)	(300,000)
Additional paid-in capital	(60,000)	(80,000)
Additional paid-in capital—step acquisition	(1,500)	–0–
Retained earnings, 12/31	(1,000,000)	(620,000)
Total liabilities and equities	$(1,914,500)	$(1,200,000)

a. Show the journal entry Bretz made to record its January 1, 2021, acquisition of an additional 30 percent of Keane Company shares.

b. Prepare a schedule showing how Bretz determined the Investment in Keane Company balance as of December 31, 2021.

c. Prepare a consolidated worksheet for Bretz, Inc., and Keane Company for December 31, 2021.

Develop Your Skills

ACCOUNTING THEORY RESEARCH CASE

CPA skills

The FASB ASC paragraph 810-10-45-16 states: "The noncontrolling interest shall be reported in the consolidated statement of financial position within equity, separately from the parent's equity. That amount shall be clearly identified and labeled, for example, as noncontrolling interest in subsidiaries."

However, prior to issuing this current reporting requirement, the FASB considered several alternative display formats for the noncontrolling interest. Access the precodification standard, *SFAS 160,* "Noncontrolling Interest in Consolidated Financial Statements," at www.fasb.org to answer the following:

1. What alternative financial statement display formats did the FASB consider for the noncontrolling interest?
2. What criteria did the FASB use to evaluate the desirability of each alternative?
3. In what specific ways did FASB *Concept Statement 6* affect the FASB's evaluation of these alternatives?

RESEARCH CASE: CELGENE'S STEP ACQUISITION OF JUNO THERAPEUTICS

Prior to 2018, Celgene Corporation, a biopharmaceutical company (with specialities in oncology, inflammation, and immunology) had owned a 9.6 percent equity interest in Juno Therapeutics Inc. (Juno). Juno is a scientific and manufacturing company specializing in the development of cancer therapies. On March 6, 2018, Celgene acquired the remaining 90.4 percent of Juno, resulting in Juno becoming a wholly owned subsidiary of Celgene.

Access Celgene's 2018 10-K annual report, and answer the following:

1. What amounts and components did Celgene identify to determine the total consideration for the acquisition of Juno?
2. How did Celgene allocate the acquisition-date fair value of Juno among the assets acquired and liabilities assumed? What was the largest asset recognized in the Juno acquisition, and how was its fair value determined.
3. Upon acquisition of its controlling interest on March 6, 2018, how did Celgene account for the change in fair value of its original 9.6 percent ownership interest in Juno? How was this amount reported in the consolidated financial statements?
4. How did Celgene account for the precombination equity compensation provided by Juno's employees? How did Celgene account for the postcombination equity compensation provided by Juno's employees?

RESEARCH CASE: COSTCO'S NONCONTROLLING INTERESTS

Costco Wholesale Corporation owns and operates membership warehouses in the United States, Canada, United Kingdom, Mexico, Japan, Korea, Australia, Spain, France, and Iceland. Costco also engages in retail operations through a majority-owned subsidiary in Taiwan. The outside equity interests (not owned by Costco) in the Taiwanese subsidiary are presented as noncontrolling interests in Costco's consolidated financial statements.

Access Costco's 2018 10-K annual report, and answer the following:

1. How does Costco present the noncontrolling interest in the following financial statements?
   - Consolidated Balance Sheet
   - Consolidated Income Statement
   - Consolidated Statement of Other Comprehensive Income
   - Consolidated Statement of Cash Flows
2. Explain how Costco's presentations of the noncontrolling interest reflect the acquisition method for consolidated financial reporting as a single economic entity.

BARDEEN ELECTRIC: FASB ASC AND IFRS RESEARCH CASE

On October 18, 2020, Armstrong Auto Corporation ("Armstrong") announced its plan to acquire 80 percent of the outstanding 500,000 shares of Bardeen Electric Corporation's ("Bardeen") common stock in a business combination following regulatory approval. Armstrong will account for the transaction in accordance with ASC 805, "Business Combinations."

On December 1, 2020, Armstrong purchased an 80 percent controlling interest in Bardeen's outstanding voting shares. On this date, Armstrong paid $40 million in cash and issued one million shares of Armstrong common stock to the selling shareholders of Bardeen. Armstrong's share price was $26 on the announcement date and $24 on the acquisition date.

Bardeen's remaining 100,000 shares of common stock had been purchased for $3,000,000 by a small number of original investors. These shares have never been actively traded. Using other valuation techniques (comparable firms, discounted cash flow analysis, etc.), Armstrong estimated the acquisition-date fair value of Bardeen's noncontrolling shares at $16,500,000.

The parties agreed that Armstrong would issue to the selling shareholders an additional one million shares contingent upon the achievement of certain performance goals during the first 24 months following the acquisition. The acquisition-date fair value of the contingent stock issue was estimated at $8 million.

Bardeen has a research and development (R&D) project underway to develop a superconductive electrical/magnetic application. Total costs incurred to date on the project equal $4,400,000. However, Armstrong estimates that the technology has a fair value of $11 million. Armstrong considers this R&D as in-process because it has not yet reached technological feasibility and additional R&D is needed to bring the project to completion. No assets have been recorded in Bardeen's financial records for the R&D costs to date.

Bardeen's other assets and liabilities (at fair value) include the following:

Cash	$ 425,000
Accounts receivable	788,000
Land	3,487,000
Building	16,300,000
Machinery	39,000,000
Patents	7,000,000
Accounts payable	(1,500,000)

Neither the receivables nor payables involve Armstrong.

Answer the following questions citing relevant support from the ASC and IFRS.

1. What is the total consideration transferred by Armstrong to acquire its 80 percent controlling interest in Bardeen?
2. What values should Armstrong assign to identifiable intangible assets as part of the acquisition accounting?
3. What is the acquisition-date value assigned to the 20 percent noncontrolling interest? What are the potential noncontrolling interest valuation alternatives available under IFRS?
4. Under U.S. GAAP, what amount should Armstrong recognize as goodwill from the Bardeen acquisition? What alternative goodwill valuations are allowed under IFRS?

chapter 5

Consolidated Financial Statements—Intra-Entity Asset Transactions

Learning Objectives

After studying this chapter, you should be able to:

- **LO 5-1** Understand why intra-entity asset transfers create accounting effects within the financial records of affiliated companies that must be eliminated or adjusted in preparing consolidated financial statements.
- **LO 5-2** Demonstrate the consolidation procedures to eliminate intra-entity sales and purchases balances.
- **LO 5-3** Explain why consolidated entities defer intra-entity gross profit in ending inventory and the consolidation procedures required to subsequently recognize profits.
- **LO 5-4** Understand that the consolidation process for inventory transfers is designed to defer the intra-entity gross profit remaining in ending inventory from the year of transfer into the year of disposal or consumption.
- **LO 5-5** Explain the difference between upstream and downstream intra-entity transfers and how each affects the computation of noncontrolling interest balances.
- **LO 5-6** Prepare the consolidation entry to defer any gain created by an intra-entity transfer of land from the accounting records of the year of transfer and subsequent years.
- **LO 5-7** Prepare the consolidation entries to remove the effects of upstream and downstream intra-entity fixed asset transfers across affiliated entities.

Chapter 1 analyzed the deferral and subsequent recognition of gross profits created by inventory transfers between two affiliated companies in connection with equity method accounting. The central theme of that discussion is that intra-entity[1] profits cannot be recognized until the goods are ultimately sold to an unrelated party or consumed in the production process. This same accounting logic applies to transactions between companies within a business combination. Such sales within a single economic entity create neither profits nor losses. In reference to this issue, FASB ASC 810-10-45-1 states,

> As consolidated financial statements are based on the assumption that they represent the financial position and operating results of a single economic entity, such statements shall not include gain or loss on transactions among the entities in the consolidated group. Accordingly, any intra-entity profit or loss on assets remaining within the consolidated group shall be eliminated; the concept usually applied for this purpose is gross profit or loss.

The elimination of the accounting effects created by intra-entity transfers is one of the most significant problems encountered in the consolidation process. Such transfers are especially common in companies organized as a vertically integrated chain of organizations. For example, after acquiring its bottling companies, PepsiCo noted,

> we acquired PBG and PAS to create a more fully integrated supply chain and go-to-market business model, improving the effectiveness and efficiency of the distribution of our brands and enhancing our revenue growth.

[1] The FASB *Accounting Standards Codification*® (ASC) uses the term *intra-entity* to describe transfers of assets across entities affiliated through common ownership or other control mechanisms. The term indicates that although such transfers occur across separate legal entities, they are nonetheless made within a consolidated entity. In addition to the term *intra-entity,* such transfers are routinely referred to as *intercompany.*

Entities such as PepsiCo can reduce their costs and increase revenues by developing affiliations in which one operation furnishes products to another.

Intra-entity asset transactions take several forms. In particular, inventory transfers are especially prevalent. However, the sale of land and depreciable assets also can occur between the parties within a combination. This chapter examines the consolidation procedures for each of these different types of intra-entity asset transfers.[2]

Intra-Entity Inventory Transfers

LO 5-1

Understand why intra-entity asset transfers create accounting effects within the financial records of affiliated companies that must be eliminated or adjusted in preparing consolidated financial statements.

As previous chapters discussed, companies that make up a business combination frequently retain their legal identities as separate operating centers and maintain their own recordkeeping. Thus, inventory sales between these companies trigger the independent accounting systems of both parties. The seller duly records revenue, and the buyer simultaneously enters the purchase into its accounts. For internal reporting purposes, recording an inventory transfer as a sale/purchase provides vital data to help measure the operational efficiency of each enterprise.[3]

Despite the internal information benefits of accounting for the transaction in this manner, from a consolidated perspective, neither a sale nor a purchase has occurred. *An intra-entity transfer is merely the internal movement of inventory, an event that creates no net change in the financial position of the business combination taken as a whole.* Thus, in producing consolidated financial statements, the recorded effects of these transfers are eliminated so that consolidated statements reflect only transactions (and thus profits) with outside parties. Worksheet entries serve this purpose; they adapt the financial information reported by the separate companies to the perspective of the consolidated enterprise. The entire impact of the intra-entity transfer must be identified and then removed. Deleting the effects of the actual transfer is described here first.

The Sales and Purchases Accounts

LO 5-2

Demonstrate the consolidation procedures to eliminate intra-entity sales and purchases balances.

To account for related companies as a single economic entity requires eliminating all intra-entity sales/purchases balances. For example, if Arlington Company makes an $80,000 inventory sale to Zirkin Company, an affiliated party within a business combination, both parties record the transfer in their internal records as a normal sale/purchase. The following consolidation worksheet entry is then necessary to remove the resulting balances from the externally reported figures. Cost of Goods Sold is reduced here under the assumption that the Purchases account usually is closed out prior to the consolidation process.

Consolidation Entry TI		
Sales	80,000	
Cost of Goods Sold (purchases component)		80,000
To eliminate effects of intra-entity transfer of inventory. (Labeled ***TI*** in reference to the transferred inventory.)		

In the preparation of consolidated financial statements, the preceding elimination must be made for all intra-entity inventory transfers. The total recorded (intra-entity) sales figure is deleted regardless of whether the transfer was downstream (from parent to subsidiary) or

[2] In practice, the terms *intra-entity transaction* and *intra-entity transfer* are used interchangeably. Some argue that the use of the term *transaction* should be reserved for activities with entities outside the condolidated group.

[3] For all intra-entity transfers, the two parties involved view the events from different perspectives. Thus, the transfer is both a sale and a purchase, often creating both a receivable and a payable. To indicate the dual nature of such transfers, these accounts are indicated within this text as sales/purchases, receivables/payables, and so on.

upstream (from subsidiary to parent). Furthermore, any gross profit included in the transfer price does not affect this sales/purchases elimination. Because the entire amount of the transfer occurred between related parties, the total effect must be removed in preparing the consolidated statements.

Intra-Entity Gross Profit—Year of Transfer (Year 1)

Removal of the sale/purchase is often just the first in a series of consolidation entries necessitated by inventory transfers. Despite the previous elimination, gross profits in ending inventory created by such sales can still exist in the accounting records at year-end. These profits initially result when the merchandise is priced at more than historical cost. Actual transfer prices are established in several ways, including the normal sales price of the inventory, sales price less a specified discount, or at a predetermined markup above cost. For example, in past financial statements, Ford Motor Company explained that

> intercompany sales among geographic areas consist primarily of vehicles, parts, and components manufactured by the company and various subsidiaries and sold to different entities within the consolidated group; transfer prices for these transactions are established by agreement between the affected entities.

Regardless of the method used for this pricing decision, gross profits that remain in inventory at year-end as a result of intra-entity sales during the period must be removed in arriving at consolidated figures.

LO 5-3

Explain why consolidated entities defer intra-entity gross profit in ending inventory and the consolidation procedures required subsequently to recognize profits.

All Inventory Remains at Year-End

In the preceding illustration, assume that Arlington acquired or produced this inventory at a cost of $50,000 and then sold it to Zirkin, an affiliated party, at the indicated $80,000 price. From a consolidated perspective, the inventory still has a historical cost of only $50,000. However, Zirkin's records now reflect the inventory at the $80,000 transfer price. In addition, because of the markup, Arlington's records show a $30,000 gross profit from this intra-entity sale. However, because the transaction did not occur with an outside party, recognition of this profit is not appropriate for the combination as a whole.

Thus, although the Consolidation Entry **TI** shown earlier eliminated the sale/purchase figures, the $30,000 inflation created by the transfer price still exists in two areas of the individual statements:

- Ending inventory remains overstated by $30,000.
- Gross profit is artificially overstated by this same amount.

Correcting the ending inventory requires only reducing the asset. However, correcting gross profit requires a careful analysis of the effect of the intra-entity transfer on the Cost of Goods Sold account.

	Cost of Goods Sold Computation
	Beginning Inventory
+	Purchases
=	Goods Available
–	Ending Inventory
=	**Cost of Goods Sold**

Note that the ending inventory total serves as a negative component within the Cost of Goods Sold computation; it represents the *cost* of inventory that was not sold. Thus, the $30,000 *overstatement* of Inventory *understates* Cost of Goods Sold. *Despite Entry **TI**, the inflated ending inventory figure causes Cost of Goods Sold to be too low and, thus, profits to be too high by $30,000.* For consolidation purposes, we increase Cost of Goods Sold by this amount through a worksheet adjustment that effectively removes the gross profit from consolidated net income.

Discussion Question

EARNINGS MANAGEMENT

Enron Corporation's 2001 third-quarter 10-Q report disclosed the following activities with LJM2, a nonconsolidated special purpose entity (SPE) that was formed by Enron:

> In June 2000, LJM2 purchased dark fiber optic cable from Enron for a purchase price of $100 million. LJM2 paid Enron $30 million in cash and the balance in an interest-bearing note for $70 million. Enron recognized $67 million in pretax earnings in 2000 related to the asset sale. Pursuant to a marketing agreement with LJM2, Enron was compensated for marketing the fiber to others and providing operation and maintenance services to LJM2 with respect to the fiber. LJM2 sold a portion of the fiber to industry participants for $40 million, which resulted in Enron recognizing agency fee revenue of $20.3 million.

As investigations later discovered, Enron controlled LJM2 in many ways.

The FASB ASC now requires the consolidation of SPEs (as variable interest entities) that are essentially controlled by their primary beneficiary.

By selling goods to SPEs that it controlled but did not consolidate, did Enron overstate its earnings? What effect does consolidation have on the financial reporting for transactions between a firm and its controlled entities?

Consequently, if all of the transferred inventory is retained by the business combination at the end of the year, the following worksheet entry also must be included to eliminate the effects of the seller's gross profit that remains within the buyer's ending inventory:

Consolidation Entry G—Year of Transfer (Year 1)		
All Inventory Remains		
Cost of Goods Sold (ending inventory component)	30,000	
Inventory (balance sheet account)		30,000
To remove gross profit in ending inventory created by intra-entity sales.		

This entry (labeled **G** for gross profit) reduces the consolidated Inventory account to its original $50,000 historical cost. Furthermore, increasing Cost of Goods Sold by $30,000 effectively removes the intra-entity amount from recognized gross profit. Thus, this worksheet entry resolves both reporting problems created by the transfer price markup.

Only a Portion of Inventory Remains

Obviously, a company does not buy inventory to hold it for an indefinite time. It either uses the acquired items within the company's operations or resells them to unrelated, outside parties. Intra-entity profits ultimately are recognized by subsequently consuming or reselling these goods. Therefore, only the transferred inventory still held at year-end continues to be recorded in the separate statements at a value more than the historical cost. For this reason, *the ending inventory intra-entity gross profit elimination (Entry **G**) is based not on total intra-entity sales but only on the amount of transferred merchandise retained within the business at the end of the year.*

To illustrate, assume that Arlington transferred inventory costing $50,000 to Zirkin, a related company, for $80,000, thus recording a gross profit of $30,000. Assume further that by year-end, Zirkin has resold \$60,000 of these goods to unrelated parties but retains the other \$20,000 (for resale in the following year). From the viewpoint of the consolidated company, it has now completed the revenue recognition process on the \$60,000 portion of the intra-entity sale and need not make an adjustment for consolidation purposes.

Nonetheless, any gross profit recorded in connection with the \$20,000 in merchandise that remains is still a component within Zirkin's Inventory account. Because the gross profit rate was 37½ percent (\$30,000 gross profit/\$80,000 transfer price), this retained inventory is stated at a value \$7,500 more than its original cost (\$20,000 × 37½%). The required reduction (Entry **G**) is not the entire \$30,000 shown previously but only the \$7,500 intra-entity gross profit that remains in ending inventory.

Consolidation Entry G—Year of Transfer (Year 1) **25% of Inventory Remains (replaces previous entry)**		
Cost of Goods Sold (ending inventory component)	7,500	
Inventory		7,500
To defer the intra-entity gross profit in ending inventory in year of transfer.		

Intra-Entity Gross Profit—Year Following Transfer (Year 2)

LO 5-4

Understand that the consolidation process for inventory transfers is designed to defer the intra-entity gross profit in ending inventory from the year of transfer into the year of disposal or consumption.

Whenever intra-entity profit is present in ending inventory, one further consolidation entry is eventually required. Although Entry **G** removes the gross profit from the *consolidated* inventory balances in the year of transfer, the \$7,500 overstatement remains within the separate financial records of the buyer and seller. The effects of this deferred gross profit are carried into their beginning balances in the subsequent year. Hence, a worksheet adjustment is necessary in the period following the transfer. For consolidation purposes, the ending inventory portion of intra-entity gross profit must be adjusted in two successive years (from ending inventory in the year of transfer and from beginning inventory of the next period).

Referring again to Arlington's sale of inventory to Zirkin, the \$7,500 intra-entity gross profit is still in Zirkin's Inventory account at the start of the subsequent year. Once again, the overstatement is removed within the consolidation process but this time from the beginning inventory balance (which appears in the financial statements only as a positive component of cost of goods sold). This consolidation worksheet entry is labeled ***G.** The asterisk indicates that a previous-year transfer created the intra-entity gross profits.

Consolidation Entry *G—Year Following Transfer (Year 2)		
Retained Earnings (beginning balance of seller)	7,500	
Cost of Goods Sold (beginning inventory component)		7,500
To remove from retained earnings the gross profit in beginning inventory and to currently recognize the profit through a reduction in cost of goods sold.		

Reducing Cost of Goods Sold (beginning inventory) through Entry ***G** increases the gross profit reported for this second year. For consolidation purposes, the gross profit on the transfer is recognized in the period in which the items are actually sold to outside parties. As shown in the following diagram, Entry **G** initially deferred the \$7,500 intra-entity gross profit in the year of transfer. Entry ***G** now increases consolidated net income (by decreasing cost of goods sold) to reflect the sales activity with outside parties in the current year.

In Entry ***G,** removal of the \$7,500 from beginning inventory (within Cost of Goods Sold) appropriately increases current net income and should not pose a significant conceptual problem. However, the rationale for decreasing the seller's beginning Retained Earnings deserves further explanation. This reduction removes the intra-entity gross profit in ending inventory (recognized by the seller in the year of transfer) so that the profit is reported in the period when a sale to an outside party takes place. Despite the consolidation entries in

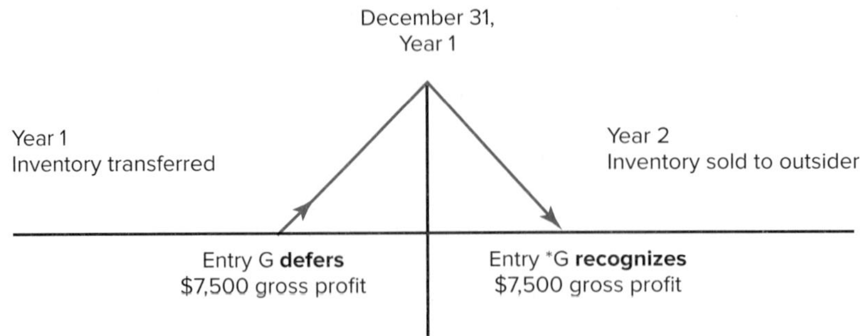

Year 1, the $7,500 gross profit remained on this company's separate books and was closed to Retained Earnings at the end of the period. Recall that consolidation entries are never posted to the individual affiliate's books. Therefore, from a consolidated view, the buyer's Cost of Goods Sold (through the beginning inventory component) and the seller's Retained Earnings accounts as of the beginning of Year 2 contain the intra-entity profit and must both be reduced in Entry ***G.**[4]

Intra-Entity Beginning Inventory Profit Adjustment—Downstream Sales When Parent Uses Equity Method

The worksheet eliminations for intra-entity sales/purchases (Entry **TI**) and intra-entity gross profit in ending inventory (Entry **G**) are both standard, regardless of the circumstances of the consolidation. In contrast, for one specific situation, the consolidation entry to recognize intra-entity beginning inventory gross profit differs from the Entry ***G** just presented. If (1) the original transfer is downstream (intra-entity sales made by the parent), and (2) the parent applies the equity method for internal accounting purposes, then the **Investment in Subsidiary** account replaces the parent's beginning Retained Earnings in Consolidation Entry ***G** as follows:

Consolidation Entry *G—Year Following Transfer (Year 2) (replaces previous Entry *G for downstream transfers when the equity method is used)		
Investment in Subsidiary	7,500	
Cost of Goods Sold (beginning inventory component)		7,500
To recognize previously deferred intra-entity downstream inventory gross profit as part of current-year net income when the parent uses the equity method.		

Why debit the Investment in Subsidiary (and not the parent's beginning Retained Earnings) account in this situation? When the parent uses the equity method in its internal records, it recognizes beginning inventory gross profits on its books (and defers intra-entity ending inventory gross profits) as part of its equity income accruals. Therefore, both the parent's net income and retained earnings appropriately reflect consolidated balances and require no adjustment.

At year-end, using the equity method, the parent increases its Investment in Subsidiary account for beginning inventory intra-entity gross profits. These same intra-entity profits were recorded as decreases to the Investment account in the prior year. Consolidation Entry **I,** however, removes the current-year equity income accruals from the Investment in Subsidiary account as part of the investment elimination sequence. With the equity income accrual removed, the beginning inventory intra-entity profit reappears as a credit to the Investment in Subsidiary account's beginning-of-the-year balance.

[4] For upstream intra-entity profit in beginning inventory, the subsidiary's retained earnings remain overstated and must be adjusted through Consolidation Entry ***G.**

Following our example, Consolidation Entry *G is thus needed to transfer the original $7,500 Year 1 Investment in Subsidiary account credit to a Year 2 earnings credit (through Cost of Goods Sold). Consolidation Entry *G also ensures that the Investment in Subsidiary account is brought to a zero balance on the worksheet.[5]

To summarize, for **intra-entity beginning inventory profits resulting from downstream transfers when the parent applies the equity method:**

- The parent's beginning retained earnings reflect the consolidated balance from application of the equity method and need no adjustment.
- The parent's Investment in Subsidiary account as of the beginning of Year 2 contains a credit from the deferral of Year 1 intra-entity downstream profits.
- Worksheet Entry ***G** debits the Investment account and credits Cost of Goods Sold, effectively recognizing the profit in the year of sale to outsiders.

Finally, various markup percentages determine the dollar values for intra-entity profit deferrals. Exhibit 5.1 shows formulas for both the gross profit rate and markup on cost and the relationship between the two.

LO 5-5

Explain the difference between upstream and downstream intra-entity transfers and how each affects the computation of noncontrolling interest balances.

Intra-Entity Gross Profit—Effect on Noncontrolling Interest

The worksheet entries just described appropriately account for the effects of intra-entity inventory transfers on business combinations. However, one question remains: What impact do these procedures have on the measurement of a noncontrolling interest? In regard to this issue, paragraph 810-10-45-18 of the FASB ASC states,

> The amount of intra-entity profit or loss to be eliminated in accordance with paragraph 810-10-45-1 is not affected by the existence of a noncontrolling interest. The complete elimination of the intra-entity income or loss is consistent with the underlying assumption that consolidated financial statements represent the financial position and operating results of a single economic entity. The elimination of the intra-entity income or loss may be allocated between the parent and noncontrolling interests.

EXHIBIT 5.1
Relationship between Gross Profit Rate and Markup on Cost

In determining appropriate amounts of intra-entity profits for deferral and subsequent recognition in consolidated financial reports, two alternative—but mathematically related—profit percentages are often seen. Recalling that Gross Profit = Sales − Cost of Goods Sold, then

$$\textbf{Gross profit rate } (GPR) = \frac{\text{Gross profit}}{\text{Sales}} = \frac{MC}{1 + MC}$$

$$\textbf{Markup on cost } (MC) = \frac{\text{Gross profit}}{\text{Cost of goods sold}} = \frac{GPR}{1 - GPR}$$

Example:		
	Sales (transfer price)	$1,000
	Cost of goods sold	800
	Gross profit	$ 200

Here the $GPR = \$200 \div \$1{,}000 = 20\%$, and the $MC = \$200 \div \$800 = 25\%$. In most intra-entity purchases and sales, the sales (transfer) price is known, and, therefore, the *GPR* is the simplest percentage to use to determine the amount of intra-entity profit.

$$\text{Intra-entity profit} = \text{Transfer price} \times GPR$$

Instead, if the markup on cost is available, it readily converts to a *GPR* by the preceding formula. In this case, $0.25 \div 1.25 = 20\%$.

[5] An acceptable alternative to recognizing intra-entity inventory profits in the subsidiary's beginning inventory (downstream sale) when the parent uses the equity method (***G**) is as follows:

Equity in Subsidiary Earnings	7,500	
Cost of Goods Sold		7,500.

In this case, Consolidation Entry I removes the *remaining* amount of the Equity in Subsidiary Earnings against the Investment in Subsidiary account. In either alternative adjustment for recognizing intra-entity inventory gross profits in beginning inventory, the final consolidated balances are exactly the same: Equity in Subsidiary Earnings = 0, Investment in Subsidiary = 0, and Cost of Goods Sold is reduced by $7,500.

The last sentence indicates that alternative approaches are available in computing the noncontrolling interest's share of a subsidiary's net income. According to this pronouncement, gross profits in inventory resulting from intra-entity transfers *may or may not* affect recognition of outside ownership. Because the amount attributed to a noncontrolling interest reduces consolidated net income, the handling of this issue can affect the reported profitability of a business combination.

To illustrate, assume that Large Company owns 70 percent of the voting stock of Small Company. To avoid extraneous complications, assume that no amortization expense resulted from this acquisition. Assume further that Large reports current net income (from its separate operations) of $500,000 while Small reports net income of $100,000. During the current period, intra-entity transfers of $200,000 occur with a total markup of $90,000. At the end of the year, a $40,000 intra-entity gross profit remains within the inventory accounts.

The consolidated net income prior to the reduction for the 30 percent noncontrolling interest is $560,000 computed as follows:

Net income reported by Large	$500,000
Net income reported by Small	100,000
Intra-entity ending inventory gross profit deferral	(40,000)
Consolidated net income	$560,000

The problem facing the accountant is the computation of the noncontrolling interest's share of Small's net income. Because of the flexibility allowed by the FASB ASC, this figure may be reported as either

- $30,000 (30 percent of Small's $100,000 net income), or
- $18,000 (30 percent of Small's $100,000 net income less $40,000 intra-entity gross profit in ending inventory).

To appropriately measure the noncontrolling interest income allocation, the direction of the intra-entity transfer must be considered. If a transfer is downstream (the parent sells inventory to the subsidiary), a logical view would seem to be that the intra-entity ending inventory gross profit deferral is attributable to the parent company. The parent made the original sale; therefore, the gross profit is included in its financial records. Because the subsidiary's net income is unaffected, little justification exists for adjusting the noncontrolling interest to reflect the deferral of the intra-entity gross profit. Consequently, in the example of Large and Small, if the transfers were downstream, the 30 percent noncontrolling interest would be $30,000 based on Small's reported net income of $100,000.

In contrast, when the subsidiary sells inventory to the parent (an upstream transfer), the subsidiary recognizes the entire gross profit in its financial records even though part of the gross profit is deferred from a consolidation perspective. A reasonable conclusion is that because the subsidiary created the gross profit, a portion of that profit is attributable to the noncontrolling interest.

In this textbook, the noncontrolling interest's share of consolidated net income is based on the reported net income of the subsidiary after adjusting for intra-entity gross profit in inventories from *upstream* sales. Returning to Large Company and Small Company, if the $40,000 intra-entity gross profit results from an upstream sale from subsidiary to parent, only $60,000 of Small's $100,000 net income should be recognized currently for consolidation purposes. The allocation to the noncontrolling interest is, therefore, reported as $18,000, or 30 percent of the $60,000 subsidiary net income after adjusting for the intra-entity profit remaining in ending inventory.

Although the noncontrolling interest figure is based here on the subsidiary's reported net income adjusted for the effects of upstream intra-entity transfers, GAAP, as quoted earlier, does not require this treatment. Giving effect to upstream transfers in this calculation but not to downstream transfers is simply an attempt to select the most logical approach among acceptable alternatives.[6]

[6] The 100 percent allocation of downstream profits to the parent affects its application of the equity method. As seen later in this chapter, in applying the equity method, the parent removes 100 percent of intra-entity profits resulting from downstream sales from its investment and equity earnings accounts rather than its percentage ownership in the subsidiary.

Intra-Entity Inventory Transfers Summarized

To assist in overcoming the complications created by intra-entity transfers, we demonstrate the consolidation process in three different ways:

1. Before proceeding to a numerical example, we review the impact of intra-entity transfers on consolidated figures. Ultimately, the accountant must understand how the balances reported by a business combination are derived when intra-entity gross profit in inventory result from either upstream or downstream sales.
2. Next, two alternative consolidation worksheets are produced: one for downstream transfers and the other for upstream. The various consolidation procedures used in these worksheets are explained and analyzed.
3. Finally, several of the consolidation worksheet entries are shown side by side to illustrate the differences created by the direction of the transfers.

The Development of Consolidated Totals

A summary of the effects of intra-entity inventory transfers on consolidated totals follows:

- *Revenues.* Parent and subsidiary balances are combined, but all intra-entity transfers are then removed.
- *Cost of Goods Sold.* Parent and subsidiary balances are combined, but all intra-entity transfers are removed. The resulting total is decreased by any intra-entity gross profit in beginning inventory (thus raising net income) and increased by any intra-entity gross profit in ending inventory (reducing net income).
- *Net Income Attributable to the Noncontrolling Interest.* The subsidiary's reported net income is adjusted for any excess acquisition-date fair-value amortizations and the effects of intra-entity gross profits in inventory from upstream transfers (but not downstream transfers) and then multiplied by the percentage of outside ownership.
- *Retained Earnings at the Beginning of the Year.* As discussed in previous chapters, if the equity method is applied, the parent's balance mirrors the consolidated total. When any other method is used, the parent's beginning Retained Earnings must be converted to the equity method by Entry ***C.** Accruals for this purpose must recognize (1) the effects on reported subsidiary net income of intra-entity gross profits in beginning inventory that arose from upstream sales in the prior year, and (2) prior years' excess acquisition-date fair-value amortizations.
- *Inventory.* Parent and subsidiary balances are combined. Any intra-entity gross profit remaining at the end of the current year is removed to adjust the reported balance to historical cost.
- *Noncontrolling Interest in Subsidiary at End of Year.* The final total begins with the noncontrolling interest at the beginning of the year. This figure is based on the subsidiary's book value on that date plus its share of any unamortized acquisition-date excess fair value less its share of gross profits in beginning inventory arising from prior year upstream sales. The beginning balance is updated by adding the portion of the subsidiary's net income assigned to these outside owners (as previously described) and subtracting the noncontrolling interest's share of subsidiary dividends.

Intra-Entity Inventory Transfers Illustrated: Parent Uses Equity Method

To examine the various consolidation procedures required by intra-entity inventory transfers, assume that Top Company acquires 80 percent of the voting stock of Bottom Company on January 1, 2020. The parent pays $400,000, and the acquisition-date fair value of the noncontrolling interest is $100,000. Top allocates the entire $50,000 excess fair value over book value to adjust a database owned by Bottom to fair value. The database has an estimated remaining life of 20 years. Top Company applies the equity method to its investment in Bottom.[7]

[7] Later in this chapter, we extend the example to when the parent applies the initial value method.

EXHIBIT 5.2
Intra-Entity Transfers

	2020	2021
Transfer prices	$80,000	$100,000
Historical cost	60,000	70,000
Gross profit	$20,000	$ 30,000
Inventory remaining at year-end (at transfer price)	$16,000	$ 20,000
Gross profit percentage	25%	30%
Gross profit remaining in year-end inventory	$ 4,000	$ 6,000

The subsidiary reports net income of $30,000 in 2020 and $70,000 in 2021, the current year. The subsidiary declares dividends of $20,000 in the first year and $50,000 in the second. After the takeover, intra-entity inventory transfers between the two companies occurred as shown in Exhibit 5.2. A $10,000 intra-entity receivable and payable also exists as of December 31, 2021.

The 2021 consolidation of Top and Bottom is presented twice. First, we assume the intra-entity transfers are downstream from parent to subsidiary. Second, consolidated figures are recomputed with the transfers being viewed as upstream. This distinction between upstream and downstream transfer becomes significant when the parent uses the equity method and in the presence of a noncontrolling interest.

Downstream Inventory Transfers: Parent Uses the Equity Method

To understand the consolidation procedures for intra-entity inventory transfers, it's useful first to analyze the parent's internal accounting for the investment. Under the equity method, the parent's investment-related accounts are subjected to (1) income accrual, (2) excess fair over book value amortization, (3) adjustments required by intra-entity gross profit in inventory, and (4) dividends. Exhibit 5.3 shows the changes to the Investment in Bottom Company from the acquisition date until the end of the current year (2021).

Note in particular the computations of Top's equity in earnings of Bottom Company in Exhibit 5.3. First, the calculations for equity method income are identical to those presented in Chapter 4, with the addition of an adjustment for intra-entity profits. Also observe that

EXHIBIT 5.3
Investment Balances—Equity Method—Downstream Sales

Investment in Bottom Company Analysis 1/1/20 to 12/31/21		
Consideration paid (fair value) 1/1/20		$400,000
Bottom Company reported net income for 2020	$30,000	
Database amortization	(2,500)	
Bottom Company adjusted 2020 net income	$27,500	
Top's ownership percentage	80%	
Top's share of Bottom Company's net income	$22,000	
Deferred profit from Top's 2020 downstream sales	(4,000)	
Equity in earnings of Bottom Company, 2020		$ 18,000
Top's share of Bottom Company dividends, 2020 (80%)		(16,000)
Balance 12/31/20		$402,000
Bottom Company reported net income for 2021	$70,000	
Database amortization	(2,500)	
Bottom Company adjusted 2021 net income	$67,500	
Top's ownership percentage	80%	
Top's share of Bottom Company's net income	$54,000	
Recognized profit from Top's 2020 downstream sales	4,000	
Deferred profit from Top's 2021 downstream sales	(6,000)	
Equity in earnings of Bottom Company, 2021		$ 52,000
Top's share of Bottom Company dividends, 2021 (80%)		(40,000)
Balance 12/31/21		$414,000

the $4,000 intra-entity profit deferred in 2020 is subsequently recognized in 2021. Thus, the $4,000 intra-entity profit is not eliminated but simply reallocated across time to the period when it is recognized by the consolidated entity. Next observe that, because the inventory transfers are downstream from parent to subsidiary, 100 percent of the profit deferral and subsequent recognition is allocated to the parent's equity earnings and investment account. As a result, the intra-entity profit reallocation across time affects neither Bottom's net income nor the noncontrolling interest.

Exhibit 5.4 presents the worksheet to consolidate these two companies for the year ending December 31, 2021. Most of the worksheet entries found in Exhibit 5.4 are described and analyzed in previous chapters of this textbook. Thus, we examine only three of these entries in detail along with the computation of the net income attributable to the noncontrolling interest.

First, Consolidation Entry ***G** adjusts for the intra-entity gross profit carried over in the beginning inventory from the 2020 intra-entity downstream transfers.

Consolidation Entry *G		
Investment in Bottom	4,000	
Cost of Goods Sold		4,000
To remove 2020 intra-entity gross profit in inventory from seller's beginning balance and recognize the gross profit in 2021 following sales to outsiders. Top uses the equity method, and intra-entity sales were downstream.		

The gross profit rate (Exhibit 5.2) on these items was 25 percent ($20,000 gross profit/$80,000 transfer price), indicating an intra-entity profit of $4,000 (25 percent of the remaining $16,000 in inventory). To recognize this gross profit in 2021, Entry ***G** reduces Cost of Goods Sold (or the beginning inventory component of that expense) by that amount. The reduction in Cost of Goods Sold creates an increase in current-year net income. From a consolidation perspective, the gross profit is correctly recognized in 2021 when the inventory is sold to an outside party. The debit to the Investment in Bottom account becomes part of the sequence of adjustments to bring that account to a zero balance in consolidation.

Consolidation Entry TI		
Sales	100,000	
Cost of Goods Sold		100,000
To eliminate current-year intra-entity sales/purchases.		

Entry **TI** eliminates the intra-entity sales/purchases for 2021. The entire $100,000 transfer recorded by the two parties during the current period is removed to arrive at consolidated figures for the business combination.

Consolidation Entry G		
Cost of Goods Sold	6,000	
Inventory		6,000
To defer intra-entity gross profit in ending inventory.		

Entry **G** defers the intra-entity gross profit remaining in ending inventory at the end of 2021. The $20,000 in transferred merchandise (Exhibit 5.2) that Bottom has not yet sold has a gross profit rate of 30 percent ($30,000 gross profit/$100,000 transfer price); thus, the intra-entity gross profit amounts to $6,000. On the worksheet, Entry **G** eliminates this overstatement in the Inventory asset balance as well as the ending inventory (credit) component of Cost of Goods Sold. Because the gross profit must be deferred, the increase in this expense appropriately decreases consolidated net income.

EXHIBIT 5.4 Downstream Inventory Transfers

TOP COMPANY AND BOTTOM COMPANY
Consolidation Worksheet
For Year Ending December 31, 2021

Investment: Equity Method — *Ownership: 80%*

Accounts	Top Company	Bottom Company	Consolidation Entries Debit	Consolidation Entries Credit	Noncontrolling Interest	Consolidated Totals
Income Statement						
Sales	(600,000)	(300,000)	(TI) 100,000			(800,000)
Cost of goods sold	320,000	180,000	(G) 6,000	(*G) 4,000 (TI) 100,000		402,000
Operating expenses	170,000	50,000	(E) 2,500			222,500
Equity in earnings of Bottom Company	(52,000)		(I) 52,000[‡]			–0–
Separate company net income	(162,000)	(70,000)				
Consolidated net income						(175,500)
Net income attributable to noncontrolling interest					(13,500)[†]	13,500
Net income to Top Company						(162,000)
Statement of Retained Earnings						
Retained earnings, 1/1/21						
Top Company	(652,000)					(652,000)
Bottom Company		(310,000)	(S) 310,000			
Net income (above)	(162,000)	(70,000)				(162,000)
Dividends declared	70,000	50,000		(D) 40,000	10,000	70,000
Retained earnings, 12/31/21	(744,000)	(330,000)				(744,000)
Balance Sheet						
Cash and receivables	280,000	120,000		(P) 10,000		390,000
Inventory	220,000	160,000		(G) 6,000		374,000
Investment in Bottom	414,000		(D) 40,000 (*G) 4,000	(I) 52,000 (S) 368,000 (A) 38,000		–0–
Land	410,000	200,000				610,000
Plant assets (net)	190,000	170,000				360,000
Database			(A) 47,500	(E) 2,500		45,000
Total assets	1,514,000	650,000				1,779,000
Liabilities	(340,000)	(170,000)	(P) 10,000			(500,000)
Noncontrolling interest in Bottom Company, 1/1/21				(S) 92,000 (A) 9,500	(101,500)	
Noncontrolling interest in Bottom Company, 12/31/21					(105,000)	(105,000)
Common stock	(430,000)	(150,000)	(S) 150,000			(430,000)
Retained earnings, 12/31/21 (above)	(744,000)	(330,000)				(744,000)
Total liabilities and equities	(1,514,000)	(650,000)	722,000	722,000		(1,779,000)

Note: Parentheses indicate a credit balance.

[†]Because intra-entity sales are made downstream (by the parent), the subsidiary's adjusted net income is the $70,000 reported less $2,500 excess amortization figure with a 20% allocation to the noncontrolling interest ($13,500).

[‡]Boxed items highlight differences with upstream transfers examined in Exhibit 5.6.

Consolidation entries:

(*G) Recognition of intra-entity beginning inventory gross profit in current-period consolidated net income. Downstream sales are attributed to parent.
(S) Elimination of subsidiary's stockholders' equity accounts along with recognition of the noncontrolling interest as of January 1.
(A) Allocation of excess fair value over subsidiary's book value, unamortized balance as of January 1.
(I) Elimination of intra-entity income remaining after *G elimination.
(D) Elimination of intra-entity dividend.
(E) Recognition of amortization expense for current year on excess fair value allocated to database.
(P) Elimination of intra-entity receivable/payable balances.
(TI) Elimination of intra-entity sales/purchases balances.
(G) Deferral of intra-entity ending inventory gross profit from current-period consolidated net income and removal of intra-entity gross profit from ending inventory.

Net Income Attributable to the Noncontrolling Interest

In this first illustration, the intra-entity transfers are downstream. Thus, the deferred intra-entity gross profits are considered to relate solely to the parent company, creating no effect on the subsidiary or the outside ownership. For this reason, the noncontrolling interest's share of consolidated net income is unaffected by the downstream intra-entity profit deferral and subsequent recognition. Therefore, Top allocates $13,500 of Bottom's net income to the noncontrolling interest computed as 20 percent of $67,500 ($70,000 reported net income less $2,500 current-year database excess fair-value amortization).

By including these entries along with the other routine worksheet eliminations and adjustments, the accounting information generated by Top and Bottom is brought together into a single set of consolidated financial statements. However, the effect of this process extends beyond the worksheet entries; it also affects reported net income. A $4,000 gross profit is removed on the worksheet from 2020 figures and subsequently recognized in 2021 (Entry ***G**). A $6,000 gross profit is deferred in a similar fashion from 2021 (Entry **G**) and subsequently recognized in 2022. However, these changes do not affect the noncontrolling interest because the transfers were downstream.

Special Equity Method Procedures for Deferred Intra-Entity Profits from Downstream Transfers

Exhibit 5.3 presents the parent's equity method investment accounting procedures in the presence of deferred intra-entity gross profits resulting from downstream inventory transfers. This application of the equity method differs from that presented in Chapter 1 for a significant influence (typically 20 to 50 percent ownership) investment. For significant influence investments, an investor company defers intra-entity gross profits in inventory only to the extent of its percentage ownership, regardless of whether the profits resulted from upstream or downstream transfers. In contrast, Exhibit 5.3 shows a 100 percent deferral in 2020, with a subsequent 100 percent recognition in 2021, for intra-entity gross profits resulting from Top's inventory transfers to Bottom, its 80 percent–owned subsidiary.

Why the distinction? When control (rather than just significant influence) exists, 100 percent of all intra-entity gross profits are removed from consolidated net income regardless of the direction of the underlying sale.[8] The 100 percent intra-entity profit deferral on Top's books for downstream sales ensures that none of the deferral will be allocated to the noncontrolling interest. As discussed previously, when the parent is the seller in an intra-entity transfer, little justification exists to allocate a portion of the gross profit deferral to the noncontrolling interest. In contrast, for an upstream sale, the subsidiary recognizes the gross profit on its books. Because the noncontrolling interest owns a portion of the subsidiary (but not of the parent), partial allocation of intra-entity gross profit deferrals and subsequent recognition to the noncontrolling interest is appropriate when resulting from upstream sales.

Upstream Inventory Transfers: Parent Uses the Equity Method

A different set of consolidation procedures is necessary if the intra-entity transfers are upstream from Bottom to Top. As previously discussed, upstream gross profits are attributed to the subsidiary rather than to the parent company. Therefore, had these transfers been upstream, both the $4,000 beginning inventory gross profit recognition (Entry ***G**) and the $6,000 intra-entity gross profit deferral (Entry **G**) would be considered adjustments to Bottom's reported totals.

In contrast to the downstream example in Exhibit 5.3, Exhibit 5.5 includes the intra-entity profit deferral and subsequent recognition in the adjustments to Bottom's net income. Because the inventory transfers are upstream from subsidiary to parent, only 80 percent of the profit deferral and subsequent recognition is allocated to the parent's equity earnings and

[8] When only significant influence is present, purchasing-related decisions are typically made in conjunction with the interests of other outside owners of the investee. Profits are partially deferred because sales are considered to be partially made to the other outside owners. When control is present, decision making usually rests exclusively with the majority owner, providing little basis for objective profit measurement in the presence of intra-entity sales.

EXHIBIT 5.5
Investment Balances—Equity Method—Upstream Sales

Investment in Bottom Company Analysis 1/1/20 to 12/31/21		
Consideration paid (fair value) 1/1/20		$400,000
Bottom Company reported net income for 2020	$30,000	
Database amortization	(2,500)	
Deferred profit from Bottom's 2020 upstream sales	(4,000)	
Bottom Company adjusted 2020 net income	$23,500	
Top's ownership percentage	80%	
Equity in earnings of Bottom Company, 2020		$ 18,800
Top's share of Bottom Company dividends, 2020 (80%)		(16,000)
Balance 12/31/20		$402,800
Bottom Company reported net income for 2021	$70,000	
Database amortization	(2,500)	
Recognized profit from Bottom's 2020 upstream sales	4,000	
Deferred profit from Bottom's 2021 upstream sales	(6,000)	
Bottom Company's adjusted 2021 net income	$65,500	
Top's ownership percentage	80%	
Equity in earnings of Bottom Company, 2021		$ 52,400
Top's share of Bottom Company dividends, 2021 (80%)		(40,000)
Balance 12/31/21		$415,200

investment account. As a result, the intra-entity profit reallocation across time affects both the subsidiary's reported net income and the noncontrolling interest. Similar to the previous example, the $4,000 intra-entity profit is not eliminated, but simply reallocated across time to the period when it is recognized by the consolidated entity.

To illustrate the effects of upstream inventory transfers, in Exhibit 5.6, we consolidate the financial statements of Top and Bottom again. *The individual records of the two companies are changed from Exhibit 5.4 to reflect the parent's application of the equity method for upstream sales.* This change creates several important differences between Exhibits 5.4 and 5.6.

Because the intra-entity sales are upstream, the $4,000 beginning intra-entity gross profit (Entry ***G**) deferral no longer involves a debit to the parent's Investment in Bottom account. Recall that Top and Bottom, as separate legal entities, maintain independent accounting information systems. Thus, when it transferred inventory to Top in 2020, Bottom recorded the transfer as a regular sale even though the counterparty (Top) is a member of the consolidated group. Because $16,000 of these transfers remain in Top's inventory, $4,000 of gross profit (25 percent) is deferred from a consolidated perspective as of January 1, 2021. Also from a consolidated standpoint, Bottom's January 1, 2021, Retained Earnings are overstated by the $4,000 gross profit from the 2020 intra-entity transfers. Thus, Exhibit 5.6 shows a worksheet adjustment that reduces Bottom's January 1, 2021, Retained Earnings balance. Similar to Exhibit 5.4, the credit to Cost of Goods Sold increases consolidated net income to recognize the profit in 2021 from sales to outsiders as follows:

Consolidation Entry *G		
Retained earnings—Bottom	4,000	
Cost of Goods Sold		4,000
To remove 2020 intra-entity gross profit in inventory from seller's beginning balance and recognize the gross profit in 2021 following sales to outsiders. Top uses the equity method, and intra-entity sales were upstream.		

Following this adjustment, Bottom's beginning Retained Earnings on the worksheet becomes $306,000. Reassigning the $4,000 gross profit from 2020 into 2021 dictates the adjustment of the subsidiary's beginning Retained Earnings balance (as the seller of the goods) to $306,000 from the $310,000 found in the company's separate records on the worksheet.

EXHIBIT 5.6 Upstream Inventory Transfers

TOP COMPANY AND BOTTOM COMPANY
Consolidation Worksheet
For Year Ending December 31, 2021

Investment: Equity Method | ***Ownership: 80%***

Accounts	Top Company	Bottom Company	Consolidation Entries Debit	Consolidation Entries Credit	Noncontrolling Interest	Consolidated Totals
Income Statement						
Sales	(600,000)	(300,000)	(TI) 100,000			(800,000)
Cost of goods sold	320,000	180,000	(G) 6,000	(*G) 4,000 (TI) 100,000		402,000
Operating expenses	170,000	50,000	(E) 2,500			222,500
Equity in earnings of Bottom	(52,400)		(I) 52,400‡			
Separate company net income	(162,400)	(70,000)				
Consolidated net income						(175,500)
Net income attributable to noncontrolling interest					(13,100)†	13,100
Net income to Top Company						(162,400)
Statement of Retained Earnings						
Retained earnings, 1/1/21						
Top Company	(652,800)					(652,800)
Bottom Company		(310,000)	(*G) 4,000 (S) 306,000			
Net income (above)	(162,400)	(70,000)				(162,400)
Dividends declared	70,000	50,000		(D) 40,000	10,000	70,000
Retained earnings, 12/31/21	(745,200)	(330,000)				(745,200)
Balance Sheet						
Cash and receivables	280,000	120,000		(P) 10,000		390,000
Inventory	220,000	160,000		(G) 6,000		374,000
Investment in Bottom	415,200		(D) 40,000	(I) 52,400 (S) 364,800 (A) 38,000		–0–
Land	410,000	200,000				610,000
Plant assets (net)	190,000	170,000				360,000
Database			(A) 47,500	(E) 2,500		45,000
Total assets	1,515,200	650,000				1,779,000
Liabilities	(340,000)	(170,000)	(P) 10,000			(500,000)
Noncontrolling interest in Bottom Company, 1/1/21				(S) 91,200 (A) 9,500	(100,700)	
Noncontrolling interest in Bottom Company, 12/31/21					(103,800)	(103,800)
Common stock	(430,000)	(150,000)	(S) 150,000			(430,000)
Retained earnings, 12/31/21 (above)	(745,200)	(330,000)				(745,200)
Total liabilities and equities	(1,515,200)	(650,000)	718,400	718,400		(1,779,000)

Note: Parentheses indicate a credit balance.

†Because intra-entity sales were upstream, the subsidiary's $70,000 net income is decreased for the $6,000 gross profit deferred into next year and increased for $4,000 gross profit deferred from the previous year. After further reduction for $2,500 excess amortization, the resulting $65,500 provides the noncontrolling interest with a $13,100 allocation (20%).

‡Boxed items highlight differences with downstream transfers examined in Exhibit 5.4.

Consolidation entries:

(*G) Recognition of intra-entity beginning inventory gross profit in current-period consolidated net income. Upstream sales are attributed to the subsidiary.
(S) Elimination of adjusted stockholders' equity accounts along with recognition of the noncontrolling interest as of January 1.
(A) Allocation of excess fair value over subsidiary's book value, unamortized balance as of January 1.
(I) Elimination of intra-entity income.
(D) Elimination of intra-entity dividends.
(E) Recognition of amortization expense for current year on database.
(P) Elimination of intra-entity receivable/payable balances.
(TI) Elimination of intra-entity sales/purchases balances.
(G) Deferral of intra-entity ending inventory gross profit from current-period consolidated net income and removal of intra-entity gross profit from ending inventory.

Consolidation Entry **S** eliminates a portion of the parent's investment account and provides the initial noncontrolling interest balance. This worksheet entry also removes the stockholders' equity accounts of the subsidiary as of the beginning of the current year. Thus, the above $4,000 reduction in Bottom's January 1, 2021, Retained Earnings to defer the intra-entity gross profit affects Entry **S.** After posting Entry ***G,** only $306,000 remains as the subsidiary's January 1, 2021, Retained Earnings, which along with Bottom's common stock is eliminated as follows:

Consolidation Entry S		
Common Stock—Bottom	150,000	
Retained earnings—Bottom	306,000	
Investment in Bottom		364,800
Noncontrolling Interest		91,200

This combined equity elimination figure ($456,000) above forms the basis for the 20 percent noncontrolling interest ($91,200) and the elimination of the 80 percent parent company investment ($364,800).

In comparing the consolidated totals across Exhibits 5.4 and 5.6, note that consolidated net income, inventory, total assets, and total liabilities and equities are all identical. The sole effect of the direction of the intra-entity inventory transfers (upstream or downstream) resides in the allocation of the temporary income effects of profit deferral and subsequent recognition to the controlling and noncontrolling interests.

Finally, to complete the consolidation, the noncontrolling interest's share of consolidated net income entered on the worksheet is $13,100, computed as follows:

Bottom reported net income, 2021	$70,000
Excess fair-value database amortization ($50,000/20 years)	(2,500)
2020 intra-entity gross profit recognized	4,000
2021 intra-entity gross profit deferred	(6,000)
Bottom 2021 net income adjusted	$65,500
Noncontrolling interest percentage	20%
Net income attributable to the noncontrolling interest, 2021	$13,100

Upstream transfers affect this computation although the downstream sales in the previous example did not. Thus, the noncontrolling interest balance reported previously in the income statement in Exhibit 5.4 differs from the allocation in Exhibit 5.6.

Consolidations—Downstream versus Upstream Transfers

To help clarify the effect of downstream and upstream transfers when the parent uses the equity method, we compare two of the worksheet entries in more detail:

Downstream Transfers			**Upstream Transfers**		
(Exhibit 5.4)			(Exhibit 5.6)		
Entry *G			**Entry *G**		
Investment in Bottom	4,000		Retained Earnings, 1/1/21—Bottom	4,000	
Cost of Goods Sold		4,000	Cost of Goods Sold		4,000
To remove 2020 intra-entity gross profit effect from seller's beginning balance and recognize the gross profit in 2021.			To remove 2020 intra-entity gross profit effect from seller's beginning balance and recognize the gross profit in 2021.		

(continued)

(continued)

Downstream Transfers			**Upstream Transfers**		
Entry S			**Entry S**		
Common stock—Bottom	150,000		Common stock—Bottom	150,000	
Retained Earnings, 1/1/21—Bottom	310,000		Retaining Earnings, 1/1/21—Bottom (as adjusted)	306,000	
Investment in Bottom (80%)		368,000	Investment in Bottom (80%)		364,800
Noncontrolling interest—1/1/21 (20%)		92,000	Noncontrolling interest—1/1/21 (20%)		91,200
To remove subsidiary's stockholders' equity accounts and portion of investment balance. Book value at beginning of year is appropriate.			To remove subsidiary's stockholders' equity accounts (as adjusted in Entry ***G**) and portion of investment balance. Adjusted book value at beginning of year is appropriate.		
Net Income Attributable to the Noncontrolling Interest = $13,500. 20% of Bottom's reported net income less excess database amortization.			**Net Income Attributable to the Noncontrolling Interest** = $13,100. 20% of Bottom's net income (after adjustment for intra-entity gross profit in inventory and excess database amortization).		

Effects of Alternative Investment Methods on Consolidation

In Exhibits 5.3 through 5.6, the parent company utilized the equity method. When the parent uses either the initial value or the partial equity method, consolidation procedures normally continue to follow the same patterns analyzed in the previous chapters of this textbook. However, these alternative methods lack the full accrual properties of the equity method. Therefore, an additional worksheet adjustment (***C**) is needed to ensure the consolidated financial statements reflect a full accrual GAAP basis. As was the case previously, the worksheet adjustments depend on whether the intra-entity inventories result from downstream or upstream sales.

Using the same example, we now assume the parent applies the **initial value method.** Given that the subsidiary declares and pays dividends of $20,000 in 2020 and $50,000 in 2021, Top records dividend income of $16,000 ($20,000 × 80%) and $40,000 ($50,000 × 80%) during these two years.

Exhibits 5.7 and 5.8 present the worksheets to consolidate these two companies for the year ending December 31, 2021. As in the previous examples, most of the worksheet entries found in Exhibits 5.7 and 5.8 are described and analyzed in previous chapters of this textbook. Additionally, many of the worksheet entries required by intra-entity sales are identical to those used when the parent applies the equity method. Thus, only Consolidation Entries ***C** and ***G** are examined in detail separately for downstream intra-entity sales (Exhibit 5.7) and upstream intra-entity sales (Exhibit 5.8).

*Downstream Transfers—Consolidation Entries *C and *G: Parent Uses Initial Value Method*

Consolidation Entry ***C** is required in periods subsequent to acquisition whenever the parent does not apply the equity method. This adjustment converts the parent's beginning Retained Earnings to a full-accrual consolidated total. In the current illustration, Top did not accrue its portion of the 2020 increase in Bottom's book value [($30,000 net income less $20,000 in dividends) × 80%, or $8,000] or record the $2,000 amortization expense for this same period.

EXHIBIT 5.7 Downstream Inventory Transfers

TOP COMPANY AND BOTTOM COMPANY
Consolidation Worksheet
For Year Ending December 31, 2021

Investment: Initial Value Method | ***Ownership: 80%***

Accounts	Top Company	Bottom Company	Consolidation Entries Debit	Consolidation Entries Credit	Noncontrolling Interest	Consolidated Totals
Income Statement						
Sales	(600,000)	(300,000)	(TI)100,000			(800,000)
Cost of goods sold	320,000	180,000	(G) 6,000	(*G) 4,000		402,000
				(TI)100,000		
Operating expenses	170,000	50,000	(E) 2,500			222,500
Dividend income	(40,000)		(I) 40,000			
Separate company net income	(150,000)	(70,000)				
Consolidated net income						(175,500)
Net income attributable to noncontrolling interest					(13,500)†	13,500
Net income to Top Company						(162,000)
Statement of Retained Earnings						
Retained Earnings, 1/1/21						
Top Company	(650,000)		(*G) 4,000	(*C) 6,000		(652,000)
Bottom Company		(310,000)	(S) 310,000‡			
Net income (above)	(150,000)	(70,000)				(162,000)
Dividends declared	70,000	50,000		(I) 40,000	10,000	70,000
Retained earnings, 12/31/21	(730,000)	(330,000)				(744,000)
Balance Sheet						
Cash and receivables	280,000	120,000		(P) 10,000		390,000
Inventory	220,000	160,000		(G) 6,000		374,000
Investment in Bottom	400,000		(*C) 6,000	(S) 368,000		–0–
				(A) 38,000		
Land	410,000	200,000				610,000
Plant assets (net)	190,000	170,000				360,000
Database	–0–	–0–	(A) 47,500	(E) 2,500		45,000
Total assets	1,500,000	650,000				1,779,000
Liabilities	(340,000)	(170,000)	(P) 10,000			(500,000)
Noncontrolling interest in Bottom Company, 1/1/21				(S) 92,000		
				(A) 9,500	(101,500)	
Noncontrolling interest in Bottom Company, 12/31/21					105,000	(105,000)
Common stock	(430,000)	(150,000)	(S) 150,000			(430,000)
Retained earnings, 12/31/21 (above)	(730,000)	(330,000)				(744,000)
Total liabilities and equities	(1,500,000)	(650,000)	676,000	676,000		(1,779,000)

Note: Parentheses indicate a credit balance.
†Because intra-entity sales are made downstream (by the parent), the subsidiary's adjusted net income is the $70,000 reported figure less $2,500 excess amortization with a 20% allocation to the noncontrolling interest ($13,500).
‡Boxed items highlight differences with upstream transfers examined in Exhibit 5.8.
Consolidation entries:
(*G) Recognition of intra-entity beginning inventory gross profit in current-period consolidated net income. Downstream sales are attributed to the parent.
(*C) Recognition of increase in book value and amortization relating to ownership of subsidiary for year prior to the current year.
(S) Elimination of subsidiary's stockholders' equity accounts along with recognition of the noncontrolling interest as of January 1.
(A) Allocation of subsidiary's fair value in excess of book value, unamortized balance as of January 1.
(I) Elimination of intra-entity dividends recorded by parent as dividend income.
(E) Recognition of amortization expense for current year on database.
(P) Elimination of intra-entity receivable/payable balances.
(TI) Elimination of intra-entity sales/purchases balances.
(G) Deferral of intra-entity ending inventory gross profit from current-period consolidated net income and removal of intra-entity gross profit from ending inventory.

EXHIBIT 5.8 Upstream Inventory Transfers

TOP COMPANY AND BOTTOM COMPANY
Consolidation Worksheet
For Year Ending December 31, 2021

Investment: Initial Value Method | *Ownership: 80%*

Accounts	Top Company	Bottom Company	Consolidation Entries Debit	Consolidation Entries Credit	Noncontrolling Interest	Consolidated Totals
Income Statement						
Sales	(600,000)	(300,000)	(TI) 100,000			(800,000)
Cost of goods sold	320,000	180,000	(G) 6,000	(*G) 4,000 (TI) 100,000		402,000
Operating expenses	170,000	50,000	(E) 2,500			222,500
Dividend income	(40,000)		(I) 40,000			
Separate company net income	(150,000)	(70,000)				
Consolidated net income						(175,500)
Net income attributable to noncontrolling interest					(13,100)†	13,100
Net income to Top Company						(162,400)
Statement of Retained Earnings						
Retained earnings, 1/1/21						
Top Company	(650,000)			(*C) 2,800		(652,800)
Bottom Company		(310,000)	(*G) 4,000 (S) 306,000‡			
Net income (above)	(150,000)	(70,000)				(162,400)
Dividends declared	70,000	50,000		(I) 40,000	10,000	70,000
Retained earnings, 12/31/21	(730,000)	(330,000)				(745,200)
Balance Sheet						
Cash and receivables	280,000	120,000		(P) 10,000		390,000
Inventory	220,000	160,000		(G) 6,000		374,000
Investment in Bottom	400,000		(*C) 2,800	(S) 364,800 (A) 38,000		–0–
Land	410,000	200,000				610,000
Plant assets (net)	190,000	170,000				360,000
Database	–0–	–0–	(A) 47,500	(E) 2,500		45,000
Total assets	1,500,000	650,000				1,779,000
Liabilities	(340,000)	(170,000)	(P) 10,000			(500,000)
Noncontrolling interest in Bottom Company, 1/1/21				(S) 91,200 (A) 9,500	(100,700)	
Noncontrolling interest in Bottom Company, 12/31/21					(103,800)	(103,800)
Common stock	(430,000)	(150,000)	(S) 150,000			(430,000)
Retained earnings, 12/31/21 (above)	(730,000)	(330,000)				(745,200)
Total liabilities and equities	(1,500,000)	(650,000)	668,800	668,800		(1,779,000)

Note: Parentheses indicate a credit balance.

†Because intra-entity sales were upstream, the subsidiary's $70,000 net income is decreased for the $6,000 gross profit deferred into next year and increased for $4,000 gross profit deferred from the previous year. After further reduction for $2,500 excess amortization, the resulting $65,500 provides the noncontrolling interest with a $13,100 allocation (20%).

‡Boxed items highlight differences with downstream transfers examined in Exhibit 5.7.

Consolidation entries:

(*G) Recognition of intra-entity beginning inventory gross profit in current-period consolidated net income. Upstream sales are attributed to the subsidiary.
(*C) Recognition of increase in book value and amortization relating to ownership of subsidiary for year prior to the current year.
(S) Elimination of adjusted stockholders' equity accounts along with recognition of the noncontrolling interest as of January 1.
(A) Allocation of subsidiary's fair value in excess of book value, unamortized balance as of January 1.
(I) Elimination of intra-entity dividends recorded by parent as dividend income.
(E) Recognition of amortization expense for current year on fair value allocated to value of database.
(P) Elimination of intra-entity receivable/payable balances.
(TI) Elimination of intra-entity sales/purchases balances.
(G) Deferral of intra-entity ending inventory gross profit from current-period consolidated net income and removal of intra-entity gross profit from ending inventory.

Discussion Question

WHAT PRICE SHOULD WE CHARGE OURSELVES?

Slagle Corporation is a large manufacturing organization. Over the past several years, it has obtained an important component used in its production process exclusively from Harrison, Inc., a relatively small company in Topeka, Kansas. Harrison charges $90 per unit for this part:

Variable cost per unit	$40
Fixed cost assigned per unit	30
Markup	20
Total price	$90

In hope of reducing manufacturing costs, Slagle purchases all of Harrison's outstanding common stock. This new subsidiary continues to sell merchandise to a number of outside customers as well as to Slagle. Thus, for internal reporting purposes, Slagle views Harrison as a separate profit center.

A controversy has now arisen among company officials about the amount that Harrison should charge Slagle for each component. The administrator in charge of the subsidiary wants to continue the $90 price. He believes this figure best reflects the division's profitability: "If we are to be judged by our profits, why should we be punished for selling to our own parent company? If that occurs, my figures will look better if I forget Slagle as a customer and try to market my goods solely to outsiders."

In contrast, the vice president in charge of Slagle's production wants the price set at variable cost, total cost, or some derivative of these numbers. "We bought Harrison to bring our costs down. It only makes sense to reduce the transfer price; otherwise the benefits of acquiring this subsidiary are not apparent. I pushed the company to buy Harrison; if our operating results are not improved, I will get the blame."

Will the decision about the transfer price affect consolidated net income? Which method would be easiest for the company's accountant to administer? As the company's accountant, what advice would you give to these officials?

Because the parent recognized neither number in its financial records, the worksheet process adjusts the parent's beginning retained earnings by $6,000 as follows:

Consolidation Entry *C		
Investment in Bottom	6,000	
Retained Earnings—Top		6,000
To convert Top's retained earnings to the accrual basis. Intra-entity sales were downstream and therefore do not affect the adjustment.		

The intra-entity inventory transfers do not affect this entry because they were downstream; the gross profits had no impact on the net income recognized by the subsidiary.

Under the initial value method, the parent makes no entries in its internal financial records to adjust for the intra-entity sales. Because in this case the sales are downstream, the parent's January 1, 2021, Retained Earnings will be overstated from a consolidated view by the intra-entity $4,000 gross profit in beginning inventory recognized from its 2020 intra-entity sales.

Consolidation Entry ***G** corrects this overstatement and appropriately recognizes (through the credit to Cost of Goods Sold) the profit in the current year as follows:

Consolidation Entry *G		
Retained Earnings—Top	4,000	
Cost of Goods Sold		4,000
To remove 2020 intra-entity gross profit in inventory from seller's beginning balance and recognize the gross profit in 2021 following sales to outsiders. Top uses the initial value method and intra-entity sales were downstream.		

Note that the preceding Entry ***G** simply reassigns the intra-entity beginning inventory gross profit from downstream transfers to 2021 from 2020.

*Upstream Transfers—Consolidation Entries *C and *G: Parent Uses Initial Value Method*

We now change the example by assuming the intra-entity transfers are upstream from Bottom to Top. In this case, the $4,000 intra-entity gross profit remaining in Top's 2020 ending inventory has been recorded by Bottom as part of its 2020 net income and retained earnings. Because $4,000 of Bottom's 2020 net income is deferred until 2021, the increase in the subsidiary's book value in the previous year is only $6,000 rather than $10,000 ($30,000 net income less $20,000 in dividends) as reported. Consequently, conversion to the equity method (Entry ***C**) requires an increase of just $2,800:

$6,000 net increase (after intra-entity profit deferral) in subsidiary's book value during 2020 × 80%	$ 4,800
2020 amortization expense (80% × $2,500)	(2,000)
Increase in parent's beginning retained earnings (Entry *C)	$ 2,800

In applying the initial value method in its financial records, the parent did not recognize the increase in subsidiary book value, excess fair-value amortization, or any effects from intra-entity transfers remaining in inventory. The worksheet process thus adjusts the parent's beginning retained earnings by $2,800 as shown here.

Consolidation Entry *C		
Investment in Bottom	2,800	
Retained Earnings—Top		2,800
To convert Top's retained earnings to the accrual basis. Intra-entity sales were upstream.		

In this case, the intra-entity inventory transfers affect Consolidation Entry ***C** because they were downstream; the gross profits directly affected the net income recognized by the subsidiary.

Using the initial value method, the parent makes no entries in its internal financial records to adjust for the intra-entity sales. Because in this case the sales are upstream, the subsidiary's January 1, 2021, Retained Earnings will be overstated from a consolidated view by the intra-entity gross profit in beginning inventory. Consolidation Entry ***G** corrects this overstatement and appropriately recognizes the profit in the current year as follows:

Consolidation Entry *G		
Retained Earnings—Bottom	4,000	
Cost of Goods Sold		4,000
To remove 2020 intra-entity gross profit in inventory from seller's beginning balance and recognize the gross profit in 2021 following sales to outsiders. Top uses the initial value method and intra-entity sales were upstream.		

Note again how the preceding Entry ***G** simply reassigns the intra-entity beginning inventory gross profit to 2021 from 2020.

Finally, if the parent had applied the **partial equity method** in its internal records, little would change in the consolidation processes previously described for the equity method. The primary change would involve inclusion of a Consolidation Entry ***C.** Because the parent would have recorded changes in reported subsidiary book value, the ***C** adjustment would be computed only for (1) previous years' excess fair over book value amortizations and (2) the immediate past year's intra-entity profit deferral.

LO 5-6

Prepare the consolidation entry to defer any gain created by an intra-entity transfer of land from the accounting records of the year of transfer and subsequent years.

Intra-Entity Land Transfers

Although not as prevalent as inventory transactions, intra-entity sales of other assets occur occasionally. The final two sections of this chapter examine the worksheet procedures that noninventory transfers necessitate. We first analyze land transactions and then discuss the effects created by the intra-entity sale of depreciable assets such as buildings and equipment.

Accounting for Land Transactions

The consolidation procedures necessitated by intra-entity land transfers partially parallel those for intra-entity inventory. As with inventory, the sale of land creates a series of effects on the individual records of the two companies. The worksheet process must then adjust the account balances to reflect the perspective of a single economic entity.

By reviewing the sequence of events occurring in an intra-entity land sale, the similarities to inventory transfers can be ascertained as well as the unique features of this transaction.

1. The original seller of the land reports a gain (losses are rare in intra-entity asset transfers), even though the transaction occurred between related parties. At the same time, the acquiring company capitalizes the inflated transfer price rather than the land's historical cost to the business combination.
2. The gain the seller recorded is closed into Retained Earnings at the end of the year. From a consolidated perspective, this account has been artificially increased by a related party. Thus, both the buyer's Land account and the seller's Retained Earnings account continue to contain the intra-entity gain.
3. The gain on the original transfer is recognized in consolidated net income only when the land is subsequently disposed of to an outside party. Therefore, appropriate consolidation techniques must be designed to eliminate the intra-entity gain each period until the time of resale.

Clearly, two characteristics encountered in inventory transfers also exist in intra-entity land transactions: inflated book values and intra-entity gains subsequently culminated through sales to outside parties. Despite these similarities, significant differences exist. Because of the nature of the transaction, the individual companies do not use sales/purchases accounts when land is transferred. Instead, the seller establishes a separate gain account when it removes the land from its books. And because it's an intra-entity gain, the balance must be eliminated when preparing consolidated statements.

In addition, the subsequent resale of land to an outside party does not always occur in the year immediately following the transfer. Although inventory is normally disposed of within a relatively short time, the buyer often holds land for years, if not permanently. Thus, the overvalued Land account can remain on the acquiring company's books indefinitely. As long as the land is retained, the effects of the intra-entity gain (the equivalent of Entry ***G** in inventory transfers) must be eliminated for each subsequent consolidation. By repeating this worksheet entry every year, the consolidated financial statements properly state both the Land and the Retained Earnings accounts.

Eliminating Intra-Entity Gains—Land Transfers

To illustrate these worksheet procedures, assume that Hastings Company and Patrick Company are related parties. On July 1, 2021, Hastings sold land that originally cost $60,000 to Patrick at a $100,000 transfer price. The seller reports a $40,000 gain; the buyer records the land at the $100,000 acquisition price. At the end of this fiscal period, the intra-entity effect of this transaction must be eliminated for consolidation purposes:

Consolidation Entry TL (year of transfer)		
Gain on Sale of Land	40,000	
Land		40,000
To eliminate effects of intra-entity transfer of land. (Labeled ***TL*** in reference to the transferred land.)		

This worksheet entry eliminates the intra-entity gain from the 2021 consolidated statements and returns the land to its recorded value at date of transfer, for consolidated purposes. However, as with the transfer of inventory, the effects created by the original transaction remain in the financial records of the individual companies for as long as the property is held. The gain recorded by Hastings carries through to Retained Earnings while Patrick's Land account retains the inflated transfer price. *Therefore, for every subsequent consolidation until the land is eventually sold, the elimination process must be repeated.* Including the following entry on each subsequent worksheet removes the intra-entity gain from the asset and from the earnings reported by the combination:

Consolidation Entry *GL (every year following transfer)		
Retained Earnings (beginning balance of seller)	40,000	
Land		40,000
To eliminate effects of intra-entity transfer of land made in a previous year. (Labeled ****GL*** in reference to the gain on a land transfer occurring in a prior year.)		

Note that the reduction in Retained Earnings is changed to an increase in the Investment in Subsidiary account when the original sale is downstream and the parent has applied the equity method. In that specific situation, equity method adjustments have already corrected the timing of the parent's intra-entity gain. Removing the gain has created a reduction in the Investment account that is appropriately allocated to the subsidiary's Land account on the worksheet. Conversely, if sales were upstream, the Retained Earnings of the seller (the subsidiary) continue to be overstated even if the parent applies the equity method.

One final consolidation concern exists in accounting for intra-entity transfers of land. If the property is ever sold to an outside party, the company making the sale records a gain or loss based on its recorded book value. However, this cost figure is actually the internal transfer price. The gain or loss being recognized is incorrect for consolidation purposes; it has not been computed by comparison to the land's historical cost. Again, the separate financial records fail to reflect the transaction from the perspective of the single economic entity.

Therefore, if the company eventually sells the land, it must recognize the gain deferred at the time of the original transfer. Gain recognition is appropriate once the property is sold to outsiders. On the worksheet, the gain is removed one last time from beginning Retained Earnings (or the investment account, if applicable). In this instance, though, the worksheet entry reclassifies the amount as a recognized gain. Thus, the gain recognition is reallocated from the year of transfer into the fiscal period in which the land is sold to the unrelated party.

Returning to the previous illustration, Hastings acquired land for $60,000 and sold it to Patrick, a related party, for $100,000. Consequently, the $40,000 intra-entity gain was eliminated on the consolidation worksheet in the year of transfer as well as in each succeeding period. However, if this land is subsequently sold to an outside party for $115,000, Patrick recognizes only a $15,000 gain. From the viewpoint of the business combination, the land (having been bought for $60,000) was actually sold at a $55,000 gain. To correct the reporting, the following consolidation entry must be made in the year that the property is sold to the unrelated party. This adjustment increases the $15,000 gain recorded by Patrick to the consolidated balance of $55,000:

Consolidation Entry *GL (year of sale to outside party)		
Retained Earnings (Hastings)	40,000	
Gain on Sale of Land		40,000
To remove intra-entity gain from year of transfer so that total profit can be recognized in the current period when land is sold to an outside party.		

As in the accounting for inventory transfers, the entire consolidation process demonstrated here accomplishes two major objectives:

1. It reports historical cost for the transferred land for as long as it remains within the business combination.
2. It defers income recognition until the land is sold to outside parties.

Recognizing the Effect on Noncontrolling Interest—Land Transfers

The preceding discussion of intra-entity land transfers ignores the possible presence of a noncontrolling interest. In constructing financial statements for an economic entity that includes outside ownership, the guidelines already established for inventory transfers remain applicable.

If the original sale was a *downstream* transaction, neither the annual deferral nor the eventual recognition of the intra-entity gain has any effect on the noncontrolling interest. The rationale for this treatment, as previously indicated, is that profits from downstream transfers relate solely to the parent company.

Conversely, if the transfer is made *upstream,* deferral and recognition of gains are attributed to the subsidiary and, hence, to the noncontrolling interest. As with inventory, all noncontrolling interest balances are computed on the reported earnings of the subsidiary after adjustment for any upstream transfers.

To reiterate, the accounting consequences stemming from land transfers are these:

1. In the year of transfer, any intra-entity gain is deferred, and the Land account is reduced to historical cost. When an upstream sale creates the gain, the amount also is excluded in calculating the noncontrolling interest's share of the subsidiary's net income for that year.
2. Each year thereafter, the intra-entity gain will be removed from the seller's beginning Retained Earnings. If the transfer was upstream, eliminating this earlier gain directly affects the balances recorded within both Entry ***C** (if conversion to the equity method is required) and Entry **S.** The additional equity accrual (Entry ***C,** if needed) as well as the elimination of beginning Stockholders' Equity (Entry **S**) must be based on the newly adjusted balance in the subsidiary's Retained Earnings. This deferral process also has an impact on the noncontrolling interest's share of the subsidiary's net income, but only in the year of transfer and the eventual year of sale.
3. If the land is ever sold to an outside party, the original gain is recognized and reported in consolidated net income.

Intra-Entity Transfer of Depreciable Assets

LO 5-7

Prepare the consolidation entries to remove the effects of upstream and downstream intra-entity fixed asset transfers across affiliated entities.

Just as related parties can transfer inventory and land, the intra-entity sale of a host of other assets is possible. Equipment, patents, franchises, buildings, and other long-lived assets can be involved. Accounting for such intra-entity transactions resembles that demonstrated for land sales. However, the subsequent calculation of depreciation or amortization provides an added challenge in the development of consolidated financial statements.[9]

[9] To avoid redundancy within this analysis, all further references are made to depreciation expense alone, although this discussion is equally applicable to the amortization of intangible assets and the depletion of wasting assets.

Deferral and Subsequent Recognition of Intra-Entity Gains

When faced with intra-entity sales of depreciable assets, financial reporting objectives remain unchanged: *defer intra-entity gains, reestablish historical cost balances, and recognize appropriate income within the consolidated financial statements.* More specifically, we defer gains created by intra-entity transfers until such time as the subsequent use or resale of the asset consummates the original transaction. For inventory sales, the culminating disposal normally occurs currently or in the year following the transfer. In contrast, transferred land may be kept indefinitely, thus deferring the recognition of the intra-entity profit indefinitely.

When depreciable asset sales occur across firms within a consolidated entity, the accounting effects for both the seller and buyer of the depreciable asset must be analyzed in preparing consolidated financial statements. For example, assume a parent company sells a delivery truck to its subsidiary at a transfer price in excess of the parent's carrying amount for the asset. In recording the sale, the parent recognizes a gain on its books. Clearly, this is an intra-entity gain that must be removed in consolidation.

In the subsidiary's financial records, the purchased truck is recorded at the transfer price and subsequently depreciated. However, because of the parent–subsidiary control relationship, no sale of the truck occurred with an outside entity. Consequently, from a consolidated reporting perspective, the carrying amount of the truck account becomes overstated and further results in overstated depreciation expense and accumulated depreciation. The resulting overstatements of the truck, depreciation expense, and accumulated depreciation must also be removed in consolidation.

However, as the subsidiary uses the truck to generate revenues over time, the decline in the truck's future economic benefit can be viewed as an indirect, gradual sale to outsiders. From a consolidated perspective, as the truck is consumed in producing revenues from outsiders, it becomes gradually "sold," and the intra-entity gain can be gradually recognized. Thus, for depreciable asset transfers, the ultimate recognition of any gain on sale typically occurs over a period of several years.

Because of the long-term nature of depreciable assets, so long as the entity owns the asset, the effects of an intra-entity transfer must be accounted for in preparing the consolidated entity's financial statements. In the year of the intra-entity fixed asset transfer, consolidation procedures to remove the intra-entity gain and its effects on the asset, depreciation expense, and accumulated depreciation are relatively straightforward. First, a worksheet entry eliminates the gain and returns the asset and accumulated depreciation accounts to their pre-transfer amounts. Then, a second worksheet entry accordingly reduces the overstated current year depreciation expense and related accumulated depreciation.

In years subsequent to the intra-entity asset transfer, we observe that the gain on sale recognized by the seller has now been closed to Retained Earnings. The overstated depreciation expense also has been closed to the Retained Earnings of the buyer. Consolidation worksheet entries thus reflect the net effect of the gain on sale and the overstated depreciation on the affiliate's separate accounting records. Next we provide an illustration of the consolidated worksheet entries in the year of the intra-entity transfer followed by the year subsequent to the intra-entity transfer.

Depreciable Asset Intra-Entity Transfers Illustrated

To examine the consolidation procedures required by the intra-entity transfer of a depreciable asset, assume that Able Company sells equipment to Baker Company at the current market value of $90,000. Able originally acquired the equipment for $100,000 several years ago; since that time, it has recorded $40,000 in accumulated depreciation. The transfer is made on January 1, 2020, when the equipment has a 10-year remaining life.[10]

[10] Although this example assumes an intra-entity gain on sale, intra-entity losses may occur as well. If the loss cannot be attributed to an asset impairment, then parallel consolidation procedures to those provided in the example, reflecting a loss, would be appropriate.

Year of Intra-Entity Transfer

The 2020 effects on the separate financial accounts of the two companies can be quickly enumerated:

1. Baker, as the buyer, enters the equipment into its records at the $90,000 transfer price. However, from a consolidated view, the asset has not been sold, and, therefore, the $60,000 book value ($100,000 cost less $40,000 accumulated depreciation) remains appropriate.
2. Able, as the seller, reports a $30,000 gain, although the consolidated entity has not yet sold the asset to outsiders. After preparation of the December 31, 2020, consolidated financial statements, Able then closes this gain to its Retained Earnings account.
3. Assuming application of the straight-line depreciation method with no salvage value, Baker records expense of $9,000 at the end of 2020 ($90,000 transfer price/10 years). The proper depreciation expense for consolidation, however, is based on the asset's carrying amount to the consolidated entity at the date of the intra-entity transfer. Consolidated depreciation expense for this asset would thus be $6,000 ($60,000 carrying amount/10 remaining years). This requires a $3,000 consolidated worksheet adjustment to depreciation expense.

To report these events as seen by the consolidated entity, we first acknowledge that an asset write-up cannot be recognized based on an intra-entity transfer. A consolidated worksheet entry must therefore return the asset to its pre-transfer carrying amount based on historical cost. Moreover, both the $30,000 intra-entity gain and the $3,000 overstatement in depreciation expense must be eliminated on the worksheet. The two consolidation entries for 2020 are shown:

Consolidation Entry TA (year of transfer)[11]		
Gain on Sale of Equipment	30,000	
Equipment	10,000	
Accumulated Depreciation		40,000
To remove intra-entity gain and return equipment accounts to balances based on original historical cost. (Labeled ***TA*** in reference to transferred asset.)		

Consolidation Entry ED (year of transfer)		
Accumulated Depreciation	3,000	
Depreciation Expense		3,000
To eliminate overstatement of depreciation expense caused by inflated transfer price. (Labeled **ED** in reference to excess depreciation.) *Entry must be repeated for all 10 years of the equipment's remaining life.*		

From the viewpoint of a single consolidated entity, these entries accomplish several objectives:

- Reinstate the asset's historical cost of $100,000.
- Return the January 1, 2020, book value to the appropriate $60,000 figure by recognizing accumulated depreciation of $40,000.
- Eliminate the $30,000 intra-entity gain recorded by Able so the amount does not appear in the consolidated income statement.

[11] If the worksheet uses only one account for a net depreciated asset, this entry would have been

Gain on sale	30,000	
Equipment (net)		30,000
To reduce the $90,000 to original $60,000 book value at date of transfer rather than reinstating original balances.		

- Reduce depreciation for the year from $9,000 to $6,000, the appropriate expense based on pre-transfer carrying amount of the asset.
- Although the gain is eliminated, the credit to depreciation expense increases consolidated net income serving as a partial recognition of the gain for 2020.

Over the remaining life of the asset, consolidation entries serve to reallocate the gain from the year of transfer to each of the 10 years following the transfer as the asset is consumed in the production process. Recall that for intra-entity gross profit in ending inventory, the ultimate recognition of the profit deferral was achieved on the consolidated worksheet through a credit to *cost of goods sold.* In a parallel fashion, deferred intra-entity profits on depreciable asset transfers are achieved on the consolidated worksheet through a credit to *depreciation expense.*

In the year of the intra-entity depreciable asset transfer, the preceding consolidation entries **TA** and **ED** are applicable regardless of whether the transfer was upstream or downstream. They are likewise applicable regardless of whether the parent applies the equity method, initial value method, or partial equity method of accounting for its investment. As discussed subsequently, however, in the years following the intra-entity transfer, we make a slight modification to consolidation entry ***TA** for downstream transfers when the equity method is applied.

Years Following the Intra-Entity Transfer

Again, the preceding worksheet entries do not actually remove the effects of the intra-entity transfer from the individual records of these two organizations. Both the intra-entity gain and the excess depreciation expense remain on the separate books and are closed into Retained Earnings of the respective companies at year-end. Similarly, the Equipment account with the related Accumulated Depreciation continues to hold balances based on the transfer price, not historical cost. *Thus, for every subsequent period, the separately reported figures must be adjusted on the worksheet to present the consolidated totals from a single entity's perspective.*

To derive worksheet entries at any future point, the balances in the accounts of the individual companies must be ascertained and compared to the figures appropriate for the consolidated entity. As an illustration, the separate records of Able and Baker two years after the transfer (December 31, 2021) follow. Consolidated totals are calculated based on the original historical cost of $100,000 and accumulated depreciation of $40,000.

Account	Individual Records	Consolidated Perspective	Worksheet Adjustments
Equipment 12/31/21	$ 90,000	$ 100,000	$ 10,000
Accumulated Depreciation 12/31/21	(18,000)	(52,000)*	(34,000)
Depreciation Expense for 2021	9,000	6,000	(3,000)
1/1/21 Retained Earnings effect	(21,000)†	6,000	27,000

Note: Parentheses indicate a credit balance.
*Accumulated depreciation before transfer $(40,000) plus 2 years × $(6,000).
†Intra-entity transfer gain ($30,000) less one year's depreciation of $9,000.

Because the intra-entity transfer's effects remain in the separate financial records, the various accounts must be adjusted in each subsequent consolidation. Moreover, the amounts involved must be updated every period because of the continual impact of depreciation recorded by the buyer. Continuing our example, to adjust the individual figures to the consolidated totals derived previously, the 2021 worksheet includes the following entries:

Consolidation Entry *TA (year following transfer)		
Equipment	10,000	
Retained Earnings, 1/1/21 (Able)	27,000	
Accumulated Depreciation		37,000
To return the Equipment account to original historical cost and adjust the 1/1/21 balances of Retained Earnings and Accumulated Depreciation.		

Consolidation Entry ED (year following transfer)		
Accumulated Depreciation	3,000	
Depreciation Expense		3,000
To remove excess depreciation expense on the intra-entity transfer price and adjust Accumulated Depreciation to its 12/31/21 consolidated balance.		
Note that the $34,000 increase in 12/31/21 consolidated Accumulated Depreciation results from a $37,000 credit in Entry ***TA** and a $3,000 debit in Entry **ED.**		

We observe that in consolidation entry ***TA,** $27,000 of the original intra-entity gain on sale is removed from Retained Earnings. Then, in consolidation entry **ED,** the $3,000 credit to Depreciation Expense serves to increase consolidated net income by $3,000. Essentially, the remaining intra-entity gain as of the beginning of the year is removed from Retained Earnings and partially recognized as a current-year increase in consolidated net income (via the decrease in depreciation expense).[12]

The ***TA** adjustment to the Equipment account remains constant over the life of the asset. However, the ***TA** adjustments to beginning Retained Earnings and Accumulated Depreciation vary with each succeeding consolidation. At December 31, 2020, the individual companies closed out both the intra-entity gain of $30,000 and $9,000 depreciation expense on their books. *Importantly, the $9,000 depreciation expense was overstated by $3,000 from a consolidated perspective.* Therefore, as reflected in Entry ***TA,** the beginning Retained Earnings account for the 2021 consolidation is overstated by a net amount of only $27,000 rather than $30,000. *Over the life of the asset, the intra-entity gain in consolidated retained earnings will be systematically reduced to zero as excess depreciation expense ($3,000) is closed out each year on the books of the company that possesses the asset.* Hence, on subsequent consolidation worksheets, the beginning Retained Earnings account decreases by this amount: $27,000 in 2021, $24,000 in 2022, $21,000 in the following period, and so on. This reduction continues until, at the end of 10 years, the intra-entity gain has been completely recognized in the consolidation process.

Similarly, the change in beginning Accumulated Depreciation varies with each succeeding consolidation. At December 31, 2020, the buyer recorded a $3,000 overstatement of depreciation expense and Accumulated Depreciation. Therefore, as reflected in Entry ***TA,** the Accumulated Depreciation account at the beginning of 2021 is undervalued by a net amount of only $37,000 rather than $40,000.

If this equipment is ever resold to an outside party, the remaining portion of the gain is immediately recognized by the consolidated entity. As in the previous discussion of land, the remaining intra-entity profit existing at the date of resale must be recognized on the consolidated income statement to arrive at the appropriate amount of gain or loss on the sale.

Years Following Downstream Intra-Entity Depreciable Asset Transfers—Parent Uses Equity Method

Consolidation entry ***TA** requires a slight modification when the intra-entity depreciable asset transfer is downstream and the parent uses the equity method. In applying the equity method, the parent adjusts its book income for both the original transfer gain and periodic depreciation expense adjustments. Thus, in downstream intra-entity transfers when the equity method is used, from a consolidated view, the parent's Retained Earnings balance has been already reduced for the gain. Therefore, continuing with the previous example, the following worksheet consolidation entries would be made for a downstream sale assuming that (1) Able is the parent and (2) Able has applied the equity method to account for its investment in Baker.

[12] Alternatively, because the straight-line method is used, the depreciation expense adjustment can also be computed as the original gain on sale divided by the remaining life of the transferred asset ($30,000/10 years).

Consolidation Entry *TA (year following transfer)

Equipment	10,000	
Investment in Baker	27,000	
Accumulated Depreciation		37,000

Consolidation Entry ED (year following transfer)

Accumulated Depreciation	3,000	
Depreciation Expense		3,000

In Entry ***TA,** note that the Investment in Baker account replaces the parent's Retained Earnings. This temporary increase to the Investment account then effectively allocates the adjustments necessitated by the intra-entity transfer to the appropriate subsidiary Equipment and Accumulated Depreciation accounts.

Effect on Noncontrolling Interest—Depreciable Asset Transfers

Because of the lack of official guidance, no easy answer exists as to the assignment of any income effects created within the consolidation process. Consistent with the previous sections of this chapter, all income is assigned here to the original seller. In Entry ***TA,** for example, the beginning Retained Earnings account of Able (the seller) is reduced. Both the intra-entity gain on the transfer and the excess depreciation expense subsequently recognized are assigned to that party.

Thus, again, downstream sales are assumed to have no effect on any noncontrolling interest values. The parent rather than the subsidiary made the sale. Conversely, the impact on net income created by upstream sales must be considered in computing the balances attributed to these outside owners. Currently, this approach is one of many acceptable alternatives. However, in its future deliberations on consolidation policies and procedures, the FASB could mandate a specific allocation pattern.

Summary

1. The transfer of assets, especially inventory, between the members of a consolidated entity is a common practice. In producing consolidated financial statements, any effects on the separate accounting records created by such transfers must be removed because the transactions did not occur with an outside unrelated party.
2. Inventory transfers are the most prevalent form of intra-entity asset transaction. Despite being only a transfer, one company records a sale while the other reports a purchase. These balances are reciprocals that must be offset on the worksheet in the process of producing consolidated figures.
3. Additional accounting problems result if inventory is transferred at a markup. Any portion of the merchandise still held at year-end is valued at more than historical cost because of the inflation in price. Furthermore, the gross profit that the seller reports on these goods must be deferred from a consolidation perspective. Thus, this gross profit must be removed from the ending Inventory account, a figure that appears as an asset on the balance sheet and as a negative component within cost of goods sold.
4. Intra-entity inventory gross profits in ending inventory also create a consolidation problem in the year following the transfer. Within the separate accounting systems, the seller closes the gross profit to Retained Earnings. The buyer's ending Inventory balance becomes the next period's beginning balance (within Cost of Goods Sold). Therefore, the inflation must be removed again but this time in the subsequent year. The seller's beginning Retained Earnings is decreased to eliminate the intra-entity gross profit while Cost of Goods Sold is reduced to remove the overstatement from the beginning inventory component. However, when the parent applies the equity method and sales are downstream, the parent's Retained Earnings are correctly stated from a consolidated view. Therefore, in this case, the Investment in Subsidiary account is used in the beginning intra-entity inventory profit adjustment, instead of the parent's Retained Earnings. Through this process, the intra-entity profit is deferred from the year of transfer so that recognition can be made at the point of disposal or consumption.

5. The deferral and subsequent recognition of intra-entity gross profits raise a question concerning the measurement of noncontrolling interest balances: Does the change in the period of recognition alter these calculations? Although the issue is currently under debate, no formal answer to this question is yet found in official accounting pronouncements. In this textbook, the deferral of profits from upstream transfers (from subsidiary to parent) is assumed to affect the noncontrolling interest, whereas downstream transactions (from parent to subsidiary) do not. When upstream transfers are involved, noncontrolling interest values are based on the gross profit recognized after adjustment for any intra-entity gross profit remaining in inventory.
6. Inventory is not the only asset that can be transferred between the members of a consolidated entity. For example, transfers of land sometimes occur. Again, if the transfer price exceeds original cost, the buyer's records state the asset at an inflated value while the seller recognizes an intra-entity gain. As with inventory, the consolidation process must return the asset's recorded balance to cost while deferring the gain. Repetition of this procedure is necessary in every consolidation for as long as the land remains within the consolidated entity.
7. The consolidation process required by the intra-entity transfer of depreciable assets differs somewhat from that demonstrated for inventory and land. The intra-entity gain created by the transaction must still be deferred along with an adjustment for the asset's overstatement. However, because of subsequent depreciation, these adjustments systematically change from period to period. Additionally, because the excess depreciation is closed annually to Retained Earnings, the overstatement of the equity account resulting from the intra-entity gain is constantly reduced. To produce consolidated figures at any point in time, the remaining overstatement in these figures (as well as in the current depreciation expense) must be determined and removed. Overall, the intra-entity gain is removed from the year of the depreciable asset transfer and subsequently recognized over the remaining life of the asset. Consolidation worksheet entries that serve to reduce depreciation expense become the vehicle for recognizing the annual portion of the intra-entity gain.

Comprehensive Illustration

Problem

(*Estimated Time: 45 to 65 Minutes*) On January 1, 2019, Daisy Company acquired 80 percent of Rose Company for $594,000 in cash. Rose's total book value on that date was $610,000, and the fair value of the noncontrolling interest was $148,500. The newly acquired subsidiary possessed a trademark (10-year remaining life) that, although unrecorded on Rose's accounting records, had a fair value of $75,000. Any remaining excess acquisition-date fair value was attributed to goodwill.

Daisy decided to acquire Rose so that the subsidiary could furnish component parts for the parent's production process. During the ensuing years, Rose sold inventory to Daisy as follows:

Year	Cost to Rose Company	Transfer Price	Gross Profit Rate	Transferred Inventory Still Held at End of Year (at transfer price)
2019	$100,000	$140,000	28.6%	$20,000
2020	100,000	150,000	33.3	30,000
2021	120,000	160,000	25.0	68,000

Any transferred merchandise that Daisy retained at year-end was always put into production during the following period.

On January 1, 2020, Daisy sold Rose several pieces of equipment that had a 10-year remaining life and were being depreciated on the straight-line method with no salvage value. This equipment was transferred at an $80,000 price, although it had an original $100,000 cost to Daisy and a $44,000 book value at the date of exchange.

On January 1, 2021, Daisy sold land to Rose for $50,000, its fair value at that date. The original cost had been only $22,000. By the end of 2021, Rose had made no payment for the land.

The following separate financial statements are for Daisy and Rose as of December 31, 2021. Daisy has applied the equity method to account for this investment.

	Daisy Company	Rose Company
Sales	$ (900,000)	$ (500,000)
Cost of goods sold	598,000	300,000
Operating expenses	210,000	80,000
Gain on sale of land	(28,000)	–0–
Equity in earnings of Rose Company	(60,000)	–0–
Net income	$ (180,000)	$ (120,000)
Retained earnings, 1/1/21	$ (620,000)	$ (430,000)
Net income	(180,000)	(120,000)
Dividends declared	55,000	50,000
Retained earnings, 12/31/21	$ (745,000)	$ (500,000)
Cash and accounts receivable	$ 348,000	$ 410,000
Inventory	430,400	190,000
Investment in Rose Company	737,600	–0–
Land	454,000	280,000
Equipment	270,000	190,000
Accumulated depreciation	(180,000)	(50,000)
Total assets	$ 2,060,000	$ 1,020,000
Liabilities	(715,000)	(120,000)
Common stock	(600,000)	(400,000)
Retained earnings, 12/31/21	(745,000)	(500,000)
Total liabilities and equities	$(2,060,000)	$(1,020,000)

Required

Answer the following questions:

a. By how much did Rose's book value increase during the period from January 1, 2019, through December 31, 2020?

b. During the initial years after the takeover, what annual amortization expense was recognized in connection with the acquisition-date excess of fair value over book value?

c. What amount of intra-entity gross profit exists within the parent's inventory figures at the beginning and at the end of 2021?

d. Equipment has been transferred between the companies. What amount of additional depreciation is recognized in 2021 because of this transfer?

e. The parent reports Income of Rose Company of $60,000 for 2021. How was this figure calculated?

f. Without using a worksheet, determine consolidated totals.

g. Prepare the December 31, 2021, worksheet entries required by the transfers of inventory, land, and equipment.

Solution

a. The subsidiary's acquisition-date book value is given as $610,000. At the beginning of 2021, the company's common stock and retained earnings total is $830,000 ($400,000 and $430,000, respectively). In the previous years, Rose's book value has apparently increased by $220,000 ($830,000 – $610,000).

b. To determine amortization, an allocation of Daisy's acquisition-date fair value must first be made. The $75,000 allocation needed to show Daisy's equipment at fair value leads to an additional annual expense of $7,500 for the initial years of the combination. The $57,500 assigned to goodwill is not subject to amortization.

Acquisition-Date Fair-Value Allocation and Excess Amortization Schedule

Consideration paid by Daisy for 80% of Rose	$594,000
Noncontrolling interest (20%) fair value	148,500
Rose's fair value at acquisition date	$742,500
Book value of Rose Company	(610,000)
Excess fair value over book value	$132,500

		Remaining Life (Years)	Annual Excess Amortizations	Excess Amortizations 2019–2021	Unamortized Balance, 12/31/21
Trademark	$ 75,000	10	$7,500	$22,500	$52,500
Goodwill	57,500	indefinite	–0–	–0–	57,500
Totals	$132,500		$7,500	$22,500	

c. Of the inventory transferred to Daisy during 2020, $30,000 is still held at the beginning of 2021. This merchandise contains an intra-entity gross profit of $10,000 ($30,000 × 33.3% gross profit rate for that year). At year-end, $17,000 ($68,000 remaining inventory × 25% gross profit rate) remains as intra-entity gross profit in the ending inventory.

d. Additional depreciation for the net addition of 2021 is $3,600. Equipment with a book value of $44,000 was transferred at a price of $80,000. The net of $36,000 to this asset's account balances would be written off over 10 years for an extra $3,600 per year during the consolidation process.

e. According to the separate statements given, the subsidiary reports net income of $120,000. However, in determining the net income allocation between the parent and the noncontrolling interest, this reported figure must be adjusted for the effects of *any upstream transfers.* Because Rose sold the inventory upstream to Daisy, the $10,000 gross profit deferred in requirement (*c*) from 2020 into the current period is attributed to the subsidiary (as the seller). Likewise, the $17,000 intra-entity gross profit at year-end is viewed as a reduction in Rose's net income.

All other transfers are downstream and not considered to have an effect on the subsidiary. Therefore, the Equity in earnings of Rose Company balance can be verified as follows:

Company's reported net income—2021	$120,000
Recognition of 2020 intra-entity gross profit	10,000
Deferral of 2021 intra-entity gross profit	(17,000)
Excess amortization expense—2021 (see requirement [*b*])	(7,500)
Recognized subsidiary net income from consolidated perspective	105,500
Parent's ownership percentage	80%
Equity income before downstream transfer effects	$ 84,400
Adjustments attributed to parent's ownership	
Deferral of intra-entity gain—land	(28,000)
Removal of excess depreciation (see requirement [*d*])	3,600
Equity in earnings of Rose Company—2021	$ 60,000

f. Each of the 2021 consolidated totals for this business combination can be determined as follows:

Sales = $1,240,000. The parent's balance is added to the subsidiary's balance less the $160,000 in intra-entity transfers for the period.

Cost of Goods Sold = $745,000. The computation begins by adding the parent's balance to the subsidiary's balance less the $160,000 in intra-entity transfers for the period. The $10,000 intra-entity gross profit in inventory from the previous year is deducted to recognize this income currently. Next, the $17,000 ending intra-entity gross profit is added to cost of goods sold to defer the income until a later year when the goods are sold to an outside party.

Operating Expenses = $293,900. The parent's balance is added to the subsidiary's balance. Annual excess fair-value amortization of $7,500 (see requirement [*b*]) is also included. Excess depreciation of $3,600 resulting from the transfer of equipment (see requirement [*e*]) is removed.

Gain on Sale of Land = 0. This amount is eliminated for consolidation purposes because the transaction was intra-entity.

Equity in Earnings of Rose Company = 0. The equity earnings figure is removed and replaced with the subsidiary's actual revenues and expenses in the consolidated financial statements.

Net Income Attributable to Noncontrolling Interest = $21,100. Requirement (*e*) shows the subsidiary's net income from a consolidated perspective as $105,500 after adjustments for intra-entity upstream gains and excess fair-value amortization. Because outsiders hold 20 percent of the subsidiary, a $21,100 allocation ($105,500 × 20%) is made.

Consolidated Net Income = $201,100 computed as Sales less Cost of Goods Sold and Operating Expenses. The consolidated net income is then distributed: $21,100 to the noncontrolling interest and $180,000 to the parent company owners.

Retained Earnings, 1/1/21 = $620,000. The equity method has been applied; therefore, the parent's balance equals the consolidated total.

Dividends Declared = $55,000. Only the parent's dividends are shown in the consolidated statements. Distributions from the subsidiary to the parent are eliminated as intra-entity transfers. Any dividends distributable to the noncontrolling interest reduce the ending balance attributed to these outside owners.

Cash and Accounts Receivable = $708,000. The two balances are added after removal of the $50,000 intra-entity receivable created by the transfer of land.

Inventory = $603,400. The two balances are added after removal of the $17,000 ending intra-entity gross profit (see requirement [*c*]).

Investment in Rose Company = 0. The investment balance is eliminated and replaced with actual assets and liabilities of the subsidiary.

Land = $706,000. The two balances are added. The $28,000 intra-entity gain created by the transfer is removed.

Equipment = $480,000. The two balances are added. Because of the intra-entity transfer, $20,000 must also be included to adjust the $80,000 transfer price to the original $100,000 cost of the asset.

Accumulated Depreciation = $278,800. The balances are combined and adjusted for $52,400 to reinstate the historical balance for the equipment transferred across affiliates ($56,000 written off at date of transfer less $3,600 for the previous year's depreciation on the intra-entity gain). Then, an additional $3,600 is removed for the current year's depreciation on the intra-entity gain.

Trademark = $52,500. The amount is from the original $75,000 acquisition-date excess fair-value allocation less three years' amortization at $7,500 per year.

Goodwill = $57,500. The amount is from the original allocation of Rose's acquisition-date fair value.

Total Assets = $2,328,600. This figure is a summation of the preceding consolidated assets.

Liabilities = $785,000. The two balances are added after removal of the $50,000 intra-entity payable created by the transfer of land.

Noncontrolling Interest in Subsidiary, 12/31/21 = $198,600. This figure is composed of several different balances:

Rose 20% book value (adjusted for upstream intra-entity profits) at 1/1/21	$164,000
20% of 1/1/21 unamortized excess fair-value allocation for Rose's net identifiable assets and goodwill ($117,500 × 20%)	23,500
Noncontrolling interest at 1/1/21	$187,500
2021 Rose net income allocation	21,100
Noncontrolling interest share of Rose dividends	(10,000)
December 31, 2021, balance	$198,600

Common Stock = $600,000. Only the parent company balance is reported within the consolidated statements.

Retained Earnings, 12/31/21 = $745,000. The retained earnings amount is found by adding the parent's (Daisy) share of consolidated net income to the beginning Retained Earnings balance and then subtracting the parent's dividends. All of these figures have been computed previously.

Total Liabilities and Equities = $2,328,600. This figure is the summation of all consolidated liabilities and equities.

g.

Consolidation Worksheet Entries to Adjust for Intra-Entity Transfers December 31, 2021

Inventory

Entry *G

Retained Earnings, 1/1/21—Subsidiary	10,000	
Cost of Goods Sold		10,000
To remove 2020 intra-entity gross profit from beginning balances of the current year. Because transfers were upstream, retained earnings of the subsidiary (as the original seller) are reduced. Balance is computed in requirement (c).		

(continued)

(continued)

Consolidation Worksheet Entries to Adjust for Intra-Entity Transfers December 31, 2021

Entry TI

Sales	160,000	
Cost of Goods Sold		160,000
To eliminate current-year intra-entity transfer of inventory.		

Entry G

Cost of Goods Sold	17,000	
Inventory		17,000
To remove 2021 intra-entity gross profit from ending accounts of the current year. Balance is computed in requirement (c).		

Land

Entry TL

Gain on Sale of Land	28,000	
Land		28,000
To eliminate gross profit created on first day of current year by an intra-entity transfer of land.		

Equipment

Entry *TA

Equipment	20,000	
Investment in Rose Company	32,400	
Accumulated Depreciation		52,400
To remove remaining gain (as of January 1, 2021) created by intra-entity transfer of equipment and to adjust equipment and accumulated depreciation to historical cost figures.		

Equipment is increased from the $80,000 transfer price to $100,000 cost.

Accumulated depreciation of $56,000 was eliminated at time of transfer. Excess depreciation of $3,600 per year has been recorded for the prior year ($3,600); thus, the accumulated depreciation is now only $52,400 less than the cost-based figure.

The intra-entity gain on the transfer was $36,000 ($80,000 less $44,000). That figure has now been reduced by one year of excess depreciation ($3,600). Because the parent used the equity method and this transfer was downstream, the adjustment here is to the investment account rather than the parent's beginning Retained Earnings.

Entry ED

Accumulated Depreciation	3,600	
Operating Expenses (depreciation)		3,600
To eliminate the current-year overstatement of depreciation created by inflated transfer price.		

Questions

1. Intra-entity transfers between the component companies of a business combination are quite common. Why do these intra-entity transactions occur so frequently?
2. Barker Company owns 80 percent of the outstanding voting stock of Walden Company. During the current year, intra-entity sales amount to $100,000. These transactions were made with a gross profit rate of 40 percent of the transfer price. In consolidating the two companies, what amount of these sales would be eliminated?
3. Padlock Corp. owns 90 percent of Safeco, Inc. During the year, Padlock sold 3,000 locking mechanisms to Safeco for $900,000. By the end of the year, Safeco had sold all but 500 of the locking mechanisms to outside parties. Padlock marks up the cost of its locking mechanisms by 60 percent in computing its sales price to affiliated and nonaffiliated customers. How much intra-entity profit remains in Safeco's inventory at year-end?
4. How are intra-entity inventory gross profits created, and what consolidation entries does the presence of these gross profits necessitate?

5. James, Inc., sells inventory to Matthews Company, a related party, at James's standard gross profit rate. At the current fiscal year-end, Matthews still holds some portion of this inventory. If consolidated financial statements are prepared, why are worksheet entries required in two different fiscal periods?
6. How do intra-entity profits present in any year affect the noncontrolling interest calculations?
7. A worksheet is being developed to consolidate Allegan, Incorporated, and Stark Company. These two organizations have made considerable intra-entity transactions. How would the consolidation process be affected if these transfers were downstream? How would consolidated financial statements be affected if these transfers were upstream?
8. King Company owns a 90 percent interest in the outstanding voting shares of Pawn Company. No excess fair-value amortization resulted from the acquisition. Pawn reports a net income of $110,000 for the current year. Intra-entity sales occur at regular intervals between the two companies. Intra-entity gross profits of $30,000 were present in the beginning inventory balances, whereas $60,000 in similar gross profits were recorded at year-end. What is the noncontrolling interest's share of consolidated net income?
9. When a subsidiary sells inventory to a parent, the intra-entity profit is removed from the subsidiary's net income for consolidation and reduces the income allocation to the noncontrolling interest. Is the profit permanently eliminated from the noncontrolling interest, or is it merely shifted from one period to the next? Explain.
10. The consolidation process applicable when intra-entity land transfers have occurred differs somewhat from that used for intra-entity inventory sales. What differences should be noted?
11. A subsidiary sells land to the parent company at a significant gain. The parent holds the land for two years and then sells it to an outside party, also for a gain. How does the business combination account for these events?
12. Why does an intra-entity sale of a depreciable asset (such as equipment or a building) require subsequent adjustments to depreciation expense within the consolidation process?
13. If a seller makes an intra-entity sale of a depreciable asset at a price above book value, the seller's beginning Retained Earnings is reduced when preparing each subsequent consolidation. Why does the amount of the adjustment change from year to year?

Problems

1. What is the primary reason we defer financial statement recognition of gross profits on intra-entity sales for goods that remain within the consolidated entity at year-end?

LO 5-1

   a. Revenues and COGS must be recognized for all intra-entity sales regardless of whether the sales are upstream or downstream.
   b. Intra-entity sales result in gross profit overstatements regardless of amounts remaining in ending inventory.
   c. Gross profits must be deferred indefinitely because sales among affiliates always remain in the consolidated group.
   d. When intra-entity sales remain in ending inventory, control of the goods has not changed.

LO 5-3

2. James Corporation owns 80 percent of Carl Corporation's common stock. During October, Carl sold merchandise to James for $250,000. At December 31, 40 percent of this merchandise remains in James's inventory. Gross profit percentages were 20 percent for James and 30 percent for Carl. The amount of intra-entity gross profit in inventory at December 31 that should be eliminated in the consolidation process is
   a. $24,000.
   b. $30,000.
   c. $20,000.
   d. $75,000.

LO 5-5

3. In computing the noncontrolling interest's share of consolidated net income, how should the subsidiary's net income be adjusted for intra-entity transfers?
   a. The subsidiary's reported net income is adjusted for the impact of upstream transfers prior to computing the noncontrolling interest's allocation.
   b. The subsidiary's reported net income is adjusted for the impact of all transfers prior to computing the noncontrolling interest's allocation.
   c. The subsidiary's reported net income is not adjusted for the impact of transfers prior to computing the noncontrolling interest's allocation.
   d. The subsidiary's reported net income is adjusted for the impact of downstream transfers prior to computing the noncontrolling interest's allocation.

Use the following information for Problems 4-6:

LO 5-2, 5-3

Alpha Company owns 80 percent of the voting stock of Beta Company. Alpha and Beta reported the following account information from their year-end separate financial records:

	Alpha	Beta
Inventory	$ 95,000	$ 88,000
Sales Revenue	800,000	300,000
Cost of Goods Sold	600,000	180,000

During the current year, Alpha sold inventory to Beta for $100,000. As of year end, Beta had resold only 60 percent of these intra-entity purchases. Alpha sells inventory to Beta at the same markup it uses for all of its customers.

4. What is the total for consolidated sales revenue?
   a. $800,000
   b. $970,000
   c. $1,000,000
   d. $1,100,000
5. What is the total for consolidated inventory?
   a. $143,000
   b. $173,000
   c. $175,000
   d. $183,000
6. What is the total for consolidated cost of goods sold?
   a. $670,000
   b. $690,000
   c. $788,000
   d. $790,000

LO 5-2, 5-3

7. Parkette, Inc., acquired a 60 percent interest in Skybox Company several years ago. During 2020, Skybox sold inventory costing $160,000 to Parkette for $200,000. A total of 18 percent of this inventory was not sold to outsiders until 2021. During 2021, Skybox sold inventory costing $297,500 to Parkette for $350,000. A total of 30 percent of this inventory was not sold to outsiders until 2022. In 2021, Parkette reported cost of goods sold of $607,500 while Skybox reported $450,000. What is the consolidated cost of goods sold in 2021?
   a. $698,950
   b. $720,000
   c. $1,066,050
   d. $716,050

LO 5-3, 5-4, 5-5

8. Angela, Inc., holds a 90 percent interest in Corby Company. During 2020, Corby sold inventory costing $77,000 to Angela for $110,000. Of this inventory, $40,000 worth was not sold to outsiders until 2021. During 2021, Corby sold inventory costing $72,000 to Angela for $120,000. A total of $50,000 of this inventory was not sold to outsiders until 2022. In 2021, Angela reported separate net income of $150,000 while Corby's net income was $90,000 after excess amortizations. What is the noncontrolling interest in the 2021 income of the subsidiary?
   a. $8,000
   b. $8,200
   c. $9,000
   d. $9,800

LO 5-7

9. Dunn Corporation owns 100 percent of Grey Corporation's common stock. On January 2, 2020, Dunn sold to Grey $40,000 of machinery with a carrying amount of $30,000. Grey is depreciating the acquired machinery over a five-year remaining life by the straight-line method. The net adjustments to compute 2020 and 2021 consolidated net income would be an increase (decrease) of

	2020	2021
a.	$(8,000)	$2,000
b.	$(8,000)	–0–
c.	$(10,000)	$2,000
d.	$(10,000)	–0–

(AICPA adapted)

LO 5-7

10. Thomson Corporation owns 70 percent of the outstanding stock of Stayer, Incorporated. On January 1, 2019, Thomson acquired a building with a 10-year life for $460,000. Thomson depreciated the building on the straight-line basis assuming no salvage value. On January 1, 2021, Thomson sold this building to Stayer for $430,400. At that time, the building had a remaining life of eight years but still no expected salvage value. In preparing financial statements for 2021, how does this transfer affect the computation of consolidated net income?
    a. Net income is reduced by $62,400.
    b. Net income is reduced by $59,440.
    c. Net income is reduced by $70,200.
    d. Net income is reduced by $54,600.

Use the following data for Problems 11–16:

On January 1, Jarel acquired 80 percent of the outstanding voting stock of Suarez for $260,000 cash consideration. The remaining 20 percent of Suarez had an acquisition-date fair value of $65,000. On January 1, Suarez possessed equipment (five-year remaining life) that was undervalued on its books by $25,000. Suarez also had developed several secret formulas that Jarel assessed at $50,000. These formulas, although not recorded on Suarez's financial records, were estimated to have a 20-year future life.

As of December 31, the financial statements appeared as follows:

	Jarel	Suarez
Revenues	$ (300,000)	$(200,000)
Cost of goods sold	140,000	80,000
Expenses	20,000	10,000
Net income	$ (140,000)	$(110,000)
Retained earnings, 1/1	$ (300,000)	$(150,000)
Net income	(140,000)	(110,000)
Dividends declared	–0–	–0–
Retained earnings, 12/31	$ (440,000)	$(260,000)
Cash and receivables	$ 210,000	$ 90,000
Inventory	150,000	110,000
Investment in Suarez	260,000	–0–
Equipment (net)	440,000	300,000
Total assets	$ 1,060,000	$ 500,000
Liabilities	$ (420,000)	$(140,000)
Common stock	(200,000)	(100,000)
Retained earnings, 12/31	(440,000)	(260,000)
Total liabilities and equities	$(1,060,000)	$(500,000)

Included in the preceding statements, Jarel sold inventory costing $80,000 to Suarez for $100,000. Of these goods, Suarez still owns 60 percent on December 31.

LO 5-2

11. What is the total of consolidated revenues?
    a. $500,000
    b. $460,000
    c. $420,000
    d. $400,000

LO 5-2, 5-3

12. What is the total of consolidated cost of goods sold?
    a. $140,000
    b. $152,000
    c. $132,000
    d. $145,000

LO 3-1
(Chapter 3)

13. What is the total of consolidated expenses?
    a. $30,000
    b. $36,000
    c. $37,500
    d. $39,000

LO 5-5

14. What is the consolidated total of noncontrolling interest appearing on the balance sheet?
    a. $85,500
    b. $83,100
    c. $87,000
    d. $70,500

LO 5-7

15. What is the consolidated total for equipment (net) at December 31?
    a. $735,000
    b. $740,000
    c. $760,000
    d. $765,000

LO 5-3

16. What is the consolidated total for inventory at December 31?
    a. $240,000
    b. $248,000
    c. $250,000
    d. $260,000

LO 5-2, 5-3, 5-5

17. The following are several figures reported for Allister and Barone as of December 31, 2021:

	Allister	Barone
Inventory	$ 500,000	$300,000
Sales	1,000,000	800,000
Investment income	not given	
Cost of goods sold	500,000	400,000
Operating expenses	230,000	300,000

Allister acquired 90 percent of Barone in January 2020. In allocating the newly acquired subsidiary's fair value at the acquisition date, Allister noted that Barone had developed a customer list worth $78,000 that was unrecorded on its accounting records and had a four-year remaining life. Any remaining excess fair value over Barone's book value was attributed to goodwill. During 2021, Barone sells inventory costing $130,000 to Allister for $180,000. Of this amount, 10 percent remains unsold in Allister's warehouse at year-end.

Determine balances for the following items that would appear on Allister's consolidated financial statements for 2021:

Inventory
Sales
Cost of Goods Sold
Operating Expenses
Net Income Attributable to Noncontrolling Interest

LO 5-3, 5-4, 5-5

18. On January 1, 2020, Corgan Company acquired 80 percent of the outstanding voting stock of Smashing, Inc., for a total of $980,000 in cash and other consideration. At the acquisition date, Smashing had common stock of $700,000, retained earnings of $250,000, and a noncontrolling interest fair value of $245,000. Corgan attributed the excess of fair value over Smashing's book value to various covenants with a 20-year remaining life. Corgan uses the equity method to account for its investment in Smashing.

During the next two years, Smashing reported the following:

	Net Income	Dividends Declared	Inventory Purchases from Corgan
2020	$150,000	$ 35,000	$100,000
2021	130,000	45,000	120,000

Corgan sells inventory to Smashing using a 60 percent markup on cost. At the end of 2020 and 2021, 40 percent of the current year purchases remain in Smashing's inventory.

a. Compute the equity method balance in Corgan's Investment in Smashing, Inc., account as of December 31, 2021.

b. Prepare the worksheet adjustments for the December 31, 2021, consolidation of Corgan and Smashing.

LO 5-1, 5-3, 5-4, 5-5, 5-6, 5-7

19. Placid Lake Corporation acquired 80 percent of the outstanding voting stock of Scenic, Inc., on January 1, 2020, when Scenic had a net book value of $400,000. Any excess fair value was assigned to intangible assets and amortized at a rate of $5,000 per year.

Placid Lake's 2021 net income before consideration of its relationship with Scenic (and before adjustments for intra-entity sales) was $300,000. Scenic reported net income of $110,000. Placid Lake declared $100,000 in dividends during this period; Scenic paid $40,000. At the end of 2021, selected figures from the two companies' balance sheets were as follows:

	Placid Lake	Scenic
Inventory	$140,000	$ 90,000
Land	600,000	200,000
Equipment (net)	400,000	300,000

During 2020, intra-entity sales of $90,000 (original cost of $54,000) were made. Only 20 percent of this inventory was still held within the consolidated entity at the end of 2020. In 2021, $120,000 in intra-entity sales were made with an original cost of $66,000. Of this merchandise, 30 percent had not been resold to outside parties by the end of the year.

Each of the following questions should be considered as an independent situation for the year 2021.

a. What is consolidated net income for Placid Lake and its subsidiary?

b. If the intra-entity sales were upstream, how would consolidated net income be allocated to the controlling and noncontrolling interest?

c. If the intra-entity sales were downstream, how would consolidated net income be allocated to the controlling and noncontrolling interest?

d. What is the consolidated balance in the ending Inventory account?

e. Assume that no intra-entity inventory sales occurred between Placid Lake and Scenic. Instead, in 2020, Scenic sold land costing $30,000 to Placid Lake for $50,000. On the 2021 consolidated balance sheet, what value should be reported for land?

f. Assume that no intra-entity inventory or land sales occurred between Placid Lake and Scenic. Instead, on January 1, 2020, Scenic sold equipment (that originally cost $100,000 but had a $60,000 book value on that date) to Placid Lake for $80,000. At the time of sale, the equipment had a remaining useful life of five years. What worksheet entries are made for a December 31, 2021, consolidation of these two companies to eliminate the impact of the intra-entity transfer? For 2021, what is the noncontrolling interest's share of Scenic's net income?

LO 5-2, 5-3, 5-4, 5-5

20. On January 1, 2020, Doone Corporation acquired 60 percent of the outstanding voting stock of Rockne Company for $300,000 consideration. At the acquisition date, the fair value of the 40 percent noncontrolling interest was $200,000, and Rockne's assets and liabilities had a collective net fair value of $500,000. Doone uses the equity method in its internal records to account for its investment in Rockne. Rockne reports net income of $160,000 in 2021. Since being acquired, Rockne has regularly supplied inventory to Doone at 25 percent more than cost. Sales to Doone amounted to $250,000 in 2020 and $300,000 in 2021. Approximately 30 percent of the inventory purchased during any one year is not used until the following year.

a. What is the noncontrolling interest's share of Rockne's 2021 income?

b. Prepare Doone's 2021 consolidation entries required by the intra-entity inventory transfers.

LO 5-3, 5-4, 5-5, 5-7

21. Protrade Corporation acquired 80 percent of the outstanding voting stock of Seacraft Company on January 1, 2020, for $612,000 in cash and other consideration. At the acquisition date, Protrade assessed Seacraft's identifiable assets and liabilities at a collective net fair value of $765,000, and the fair value of the 20 percent noncontrolling interest was $153,000. No excess fair value over book value amortization accompanied the acquisition.

The following selected account balances are from the individual financial records of these two companies as of December 31, 2021:

	Protrade	Seacraft
Sales	$880,000	$600,000
Cost of goods sold	410,000	317,000
Operating expenses	174,000	129,000
Retained earnings, 1/1/21	980,000	420,000
Inventory	370,000	144,000
Buildings (net)	382,000	181,000
Investment income	Not given	–0–

Each of the following problems is an independent situation:

a. Assume that Protrade sells Seacraft inventory at a markup equal to 60 percent of cost. Intra-entity transfers were $114,000 in 2020 and $134,000 in 2021. Of this inventory, Seacraft retained and then sold $52,000 of the 2020 transfers in 2021 and held $66,000 of the 2021 transfers until 2022.

Determine balances for the following items that would appear on consolidated financial statements for 2021:

Cost of Goods Sold
Inventory
Net Income Attributable to Noncontrolling Interest

b. Assume that Seacraft sells inventory to Protrade at a markup equal to 60 percent of cost. Intra-entity transfers were $74,000 in 2020 and $104,000 in 2021. Of this inventory, $45,000 of the 2020 transfers were retained and then sold by Protrade in 2021, whereas $59,000 of the 2021 transfers were held until 2022.

Determine balances for the following items that would appear on consolidated financial statements for 2021:

Cost of Goods Sold
Inventory
Net Income Attributable to Noncontrolling Interest

c. Protrade sells Seacraft a building on January 1, 2020, for $128,000, although its book value was only $74,000 on this date. The building had a five-year remaining life and was to be depreciated using the straight-line method with no salvage value.

Determine balances for the following items that would appear on consolidated financial statements for 2021:

Buildings (net)
Operating Expenses
Net Income Attributable to Noncontrolling Interest

LO 5-3, 5-4, 5-5

22. Akron, Inc., owns all outstanding stock of Toledo Corporation. Amortization expense of $15,000 per year for patented technology resulted from the original acquisition. For 2021, the companies had the following account balances:

	Akron	Toledo
Sales	$1,100,000	$600,000
Cost of goods sold	500,000	400,000
Operating expenses	400,000	220,000
Investment income	Not given	–0–
Dividends declared	80,000	30,000

Intra-entity sales of $320,000 occurred during 2020 and again in 2021. This merchandise cost $240,000 each year. Of the total transfers, $70,000 was still held on December 31, 2020, with $50,000 unsold on December 31, 2021.

a. For consolidation purposes, does the direction of the transfers (upstream or downstream) affect the balances to be reported here?

b. Prepare a consolidated income statement for the year ending December 31, 2021.

LO 5-7

23. On January 1, 2020, QuickPort Company acquired 90 percent of the outstanding voting stock of NetSpeed, Inc., for $810,000 in cash and stock options. At the acquisition date, NetSpeed had common stock of $800,000 and Retained Earnings of $40,000. The acquisition-date fair value of the 10 percent noncontrolling interest was $90,000. QuickPort attributed the $60,000 excess of NetSpeed's fair value over book value to a database with a five-year remaining life.

During the next two years, NetSpeed reported the following:

	Net Income	Dividends Declared
2020	$ 80,000	$8,000
2021	115,000	8,000

On July 1, 2020, QuickPort sold communication equipment to NetSpeed for $42,000. The equipment originally cost $48,000 and had accumulated depreciation of $9,000 and an estimated remaining life of three years at the date of the intra-entity transfer.

a. Compute the equity method balance in QuickPort's Investment in NetSpeed, Inc., account as of December 31, 2021.

b. Prepare the worksheet adjustments for the December 31, 2021, consolidation of QuickPort and NetSpeed.

LO 5-7

24. Padre holds 100 percent of the outstanding shares of Sonora. On January 1, 2019, Padre transferred equipment to Sonora for $95,000. The equipment had cost $130,000 originally but had a $50,000 book value and five-year remaining life at the date of transfer. Depreciation expense is computed according to the straight-line method with no salvage value.

Consolidated financial statements for 2021 currently are being prepared. What worksheet entries are needed in connection with the consolidation of this asset? Assume that the parent applies the partial equity method.

LO 5-7

25. On January 1, 2021, Ackerman sold equipment to Brannigan (a wholly owned subsidiary) for $200,000 in cash. The equipment had originally cost $180,000 but had a book value of only $110,000 when transferred. On that date, the equipment had a five-year remaining life. Depreciation expense is computed using the straight-line method.

Ackerman reported $300,000 in net income in 2021 (not including any investment income) while Brannigan reported $98,000. Ackerman attributed any excess acquisition-date fair value to Brannigan's unpatented technology, which was amortized at a rate of $4,000 per year.

a. What is consolidated net income for 2021?

b. What is the parent's share of consolidated net income for 2021 if Ackerman owns only 90 percent of Brannigan?

c. What is the parent's share of consolidated net income for 2021 if Ackerman owns only 90 percent of Brannigan and the equipment transfer was upstream?

d. What is the consolidated net income for 2022 if Ackerman reports $320,000 (does not include investment income) and Brannigan $108,000 in income? Assume that Brannigan is a wholly owned subsidiary and the equipment transfer was downstream.

LO 5-2, 5-3, 5-4, 5-7

26. Allison Corporation acquired 90 percent of Bretton on January 1, 2019. Of Bretton's total acquisition-date fair value, $60,000 was allocated to undervalued equipment (with a 10-year remaining life) and $80,000 was attributed to franchises (to be written off over a 20-year period).

Since the takeover, Bretton has transferred inventory to its parent as follows:

Year	Cost	Transfer Price	Remaining at Year-End
2019	$45,000	$90,000	$30,000 (at transfer price)
2020	48,000	80,000	35,000 (at transfer price)
2021	69,000	92,000	50,000 (at transfer price)

On January 1, 2020, Allison sold Bretton a building for $50,000 that had originally cost $70,000 but had only a $30,000 book value at the date of transfer. The building is estimated to have a five-year remaining life (straight-line depreciation is used with no salvage value).

Selected figures from the December 31, 2021, trial balances of these two companies are as follows:

	Allison	Bretton
Sales	$700,000	$400,000
Cost of goods sold	440,000	220,000
Operating expenses	120,000	80,000
Investment income	Not given	–0–
Inventory	210,000	90,000
Equipment (net)	140,000	110,000
Buildings (net)	350,000	190,000

Determine consolidated totals for each of these account balances.

LO 5-3, 5-4, 5-5, 5-7

27. On January 1, 2021, Sledge had common stock of $120,000 and retained earnings of $260,000. During that year, Sledge reported sales of $130,000, cost of goods sold of $70,000, and operating expenses of $40,000.

On January 1, 2019, Percy, Inc., acquired 80 percent of Sledge's outstanding voting stock. At that date, $60,000 of the acquisition-date fair value was assigned to unrecorded contracts (with a 20-year life) and $20,000 to an undervalued building (with a 10-year remaining life).

In 2020, Sledge sold inventory costing $9,000 to Percy for $15,000. Of this merchandise, Percy continued to hold $5,000 at year-end. During 2021, Sledge transferred inventory costing $11,000 to Percy for $20,000. Percy still held half of these items at year-end.

On January 1, 2020, Percy sold equipment to Sledge for $12,000. This asset originally cost $16,000 but had a January 1, 2020, book value of $9,000. At the time of transfer, the equipment's remaining life was estimated to be five years.

Percy has properly applied the equity method to the investment in Sledge.

a. Prepare worksheet entries to consolidate these two companies as of December 31, 2021.

b. Compute the net income attributable to the noncontrolling interest for 2021.

LO 5-1, 5-2, 5-3, 5-4, 5-5, 5-7

28. Pitino acquired 90 percent of Brey's outstanding shares on January 1, 2019, in exchange for $342,000 in cash. The subsidiary's stockholders' equity accounts totaled $326,000, and the noncontrolling interest had a fair value of $38,000 on that day. However, a building (with a nine-year remaining life) in Brey's accounting records was undervalued by $18,000. Pitino assigned the rest of the excess fair value over book value to Brey's patented technology (six-year remaining life).

Brey reported net income from its own operations of $64,000 in 2019 and $80,000 in 2020. Brey declared dividends of $19,000 in 2019 and $23,000 in 2020.

Brey sells inventory to Pitino as follows:

Year	Cost to Brey	Transfer Price to Pitino	Inventory Remaining at Year-End (at transfer price)
2019	$69,000	$115,000	$25,000
2020	81,000	135,000	37,500
2021	92,800	160,000	50,000

At December 31, 2021, Pitino owes Brey $16,000 for inventory acquired during the period.

The following separate account balances are for these two companies for December 31, 2021, and the year then ended. Credits are indicated by parentheses.

	Pitino	Brey
Sales revenues	$ (862,000)	$(366,000)
Cost of goods sold	515,000	209,000
Expenses	185,400	67,000
Equity in earnings of Brey	(68,400)	–0–
Net income	$ (230,000)	$ (90,000)
Retained earnings, 1/1/21	$ (488,000)	$(278,000)
Net income (above)	(230,000)	(90,000)
Dividends declared	136,000	27,000
Retained earnings, 12/31/21	$ (582,000)	$(341,000)

(continued)

(continued)

	Pitino	Brey
Cash and receivables	$ 146,000	$ 98,000
Inventory	255,000	136,000
Investment in Brey	450,000	–0–
Land, buildings, and equipment (net)	964,000	328,000
Total assets	$ 1,815,000	$ 562,000
Liabilities	$ (718,000)	$ (71,000)
Common stock	(515,000)	(150,000)
Retained earnings, 12/31/21	(582,000)	(341,000)
Total liabilities and equities	$(1,815,000)	$(562,000)

Answer each of the following questions:

a. What was the annual amortization resulting from the acquisition-date fair-value allocations?

b. Were the intra-entity transfers upstream or downstream?

c. What intra-entity gross profit in inventory existed as of January 1, 2021?

d. What intra-entity gross profit in inventory existed as of December 31, 2021?

e. What amounts make up the $68,400 Equity Earnings of Brey account balance for 2021?

f. What is the net income attributable to the noncontrolling interest for 2021?

g. What amounts make up the $450,000 Investment in Brey account balance as of December 31, 2021?

h. Prepare the 2021 worksheet entry to eliminate the subsidiary's beginning owners' equity balances.

i. Without preparing a worksheet or consolidation entries, determine the consolidation balances for these two companies.

LO 5-2, 5-3, 5-4

29. ProForm acquired 70 percent of ClipRite on June 30, 2020, for $910,000 in cash. Based on ClipRite's acquisition-date fair value, an unrecorded intangible of $400,000 was recognized and is being amortized at the rate of $10,000 per year. No goodwill was recognized in the acquisition. The noncontrolling interest fair value was assessed at $390,000 at the acquisition date. The 2021 financial statements are as follows:

	ProForm	ClipRite
Sales	$ (800,000)	$ (600,000)
Cost of goods sold	535,000	400,000
Operating expenses	100,000	100,000
Dividend income	(35,000)	–0–
Net income	$ (200,000)	$ (100,000)
Retained earnings, 1/1/21	$(1,300,000)	$ (850,000)
Net income	(200,000)	(100,000)
Dividends declared	100,000	50,000
Retained earnings, 12/31/21	$(1,400,000)	$ (900,000)
Cash and receivables	$ 400,000	$ 300,000
Inventory	290,000	700,000
Investment in ClipRite	910,000	–0–
Fixed assets	1,000,000	600,000
Accumulated depreciation	(300,000)	(200,000)
Totals	$ 2,300,000	$ 1,400,000
Liabilities	$ (600,000)	$ (400,000)
Common stock	(300,000)	(100,000)
Retained earnings, 12/31/21	(1,400,000)	(900,000)
Totals	$(2,300,000)	$(1,400,000)

ProForm sold ClipRite inventory costing $72,000 during the last six months of 2020 for $120,000. At year-end, 30 percent remained. ProForm sold ClipRite inventory costing $200,000 during 2021 for $250,000. At year-end, 10 percent is left. With these facts, determine the consolidated balances for the following:

Sales
Cost of Goods Sold
Operating Expenses
Dividend Income
Net Income Attributable to Noncontrolling Interest
Inventory
Noncontrolling Interest in Subsidiary, 12/31/21

LO 5-2, 5-3, 5-4, 5-5

30. Compute the balances in Problem 29 again, assuming that all intra-entity transfers were made from ClipRite to ProForm.

LO 5-1, 5-2, 5-3, 5-4, 5-5, 5-6, 5,7

31. Following are financial statements for Moore Company and Kirby Company for 2021:

	Moore	Kirby
Sales	$ (800,000)	$ (600,000)
Cost of goods sold	500,000	400,000
Operating and interest expenses	100,000	160,000
Net income	$ (200,000)	$ (40,000)
Retained earnings, 1/1/21	$ (990,000)	$ (550,000)
Net income	(200,000)	(40,000)
Dividends declared	130,000	–0–
Retained earnings, 12/31/21	$(1,060,000)	$ (590,000)
Cash and receivables	$ 217,000	$ 180,000
Inventory	224,000	160,000
Investment in Kirby	657,000	–0–
Equipment (net)	600,000	420,000
Buildings	1,000,000	650,000
Accumulated depreciation—buildings	(100,000)	(200,000)
Other assets	200,000	100,000
Total assets	$ 2,798,000	$ 1,310,000
Liabilities	$(1,138,000)	$ (570,000)
Common stock	(600,000)	(150,000)
Retained earnings, 12/31/21	(1,060,000)	(590,000)
Total liabilities and equity	$(2,798,000)	$(1,310,000)

- Moore purchased 90 percent of Kirby on January 1, 2020, for $657,000 in cash. On that date, the 10 percent noncontrolling interest was assessed to have a $73,000 fair value. Also at the acquisition date, Kirby held equipment (four-year remaining life) undervalued in its financial records by $20,000 and interest-bearing liabilities (five-year remaining life) overvalued by $40,000. The rest of the excess fair over book value was assigned to previously unrecognized brand names and amortized over a 10-year life.
- During 2020, Kirby reported a net income of $80,000 and declared no dividends.
- Each year, Kirby sells Moore inventory at a 20 percent gross profit rate. Intra-entity sales were $145,000 in 2020 and $160,000 in 2021. On January 1, 2021, 30 percent of the 2020 transfers were still on hand, and on December 31, 2021, 40 percent of the 2021 transfers remained.
- Moore sold Kirby a building on January 2, 2020. It had cost Moore $100,000 but had $90,000 in accumulated depreciation at the time of this transfer. The price was $25,000 in cash. At that time, the building had a five-year remaining life.

Determine all consolidated balances either computationally or by using a worksheet.

32. On January 1, 2020, McIlroy, Inc., acquired a 60 percent interest in the common stock of Stinson, Inc., for $372,000. Stinson's book value on that date consisted of common stock of $100,000 and retained earnings of $220,000. Also, the acquisition-date fair value of the 40 percent noncontrolling interest was $248,000. The subsidiary held patents (with a 10-year remaining life) that were undervalued within the company's accounting records by $70,000 and an unrecorded customer list (15-year remaining life) assessed at a $45,000 fair value. Any remaining excess acquisition-date fair value was assigned to goodwill. Since acquisition, McIlroy has applied the equity method to its Investment in Stinson account and no goodwill impairment has occurred. At year-end, there are no intra-entity payables or receivables.

Intra-entity inventory sales between the two companies have been made as follows:

Year	Cost to McIlroy	Transfer Price to Stinson	Ending Balance (at transfer price)
2020	$120,000	$150,000	$50,000
2021	112,000	160,000	40,000

The individual financial statements for these two companies as of December 31, 2021, and the year then ended follow:

	McIlroy, Inc.	Stinson, Inc.
Sales	$ (700,000)	$(335,000)
Cost of goods sold	460,000	205,000
Operating expenses	188,000	70,000
Equity in earnings in Stinson	(28,000)	–0–
Net income	$ (80,000)	$ (60,000)
Retained earnings, 1/1/21	$ (695,000)	$(280,000)
Net income	(80,000)	(60,000)
Dividends declared	45,000	15,000
Retained earnings, 12/31/21	$ (730,000)	$(325,000)
Cash and receivables	$ 248,000	$ 148,000
Inventory	233,000	129,000
Investment in Stinson	411,000	–0–
Buildings (net)	308,000	202,000
Equipment (net)	220,000	86,000
Patents (net)	–0–	20,000
Total assets	$ 1,420,000	$ 585,000
Liabilities	$ (390,000)	$(160,000)
Common stock	(300,000)	(100,000)
Retained earnings, 12/31/21	(730,000)	(325,000)
Total liabilities and equities	$(1,420,000)	$(585,000)

a. Show how McIlroy determined the $411,000 Investment in Stinson account balance. Assume that McIlroy defers 100 percent of downstream intra-entity profits against its share of Stinson's income.

b. Prepare a consolidated worksheet to determine appropriate balances for external financial reporting as of December 31, 2021.

LO 5-2, 5-3, 5-4, 5-5

33. On January 1, 2019, Plymouth Corporation acquired 80 percent of the outstanding voting stock of Sander Company in exchange for $1,200,000 cash. At that time, although Sander's book value was $925,000, Plymouth assessed Sander's total business fair value at $1,500,000. Since that time, Sander has neither issued nor reacquired any shares of its own stock.

The book values of Sander's individual assets and liabilities approximated their acquisition-date fair values except for the patent account, which was undervalued by $350,000. The undervalued patents had a five-year remaining life at the acquisition date. Any remaining excess fair value was attributed to goodwill. No goodwill impairments have occurred.

Sander regularly sells inventory to Plymouth. The following are details of the intra-entity inventory sales for the past three years:

Year	Intra-Entity Sales	Intra-Entity Ending Inventory at Transfer Price	Gross Profit Rate on Intra-Entity Inventory Transfers
2019	$125,000	$ 80,000	25%
2020	220,000	125,000	28
2021	300,000	160,000	25

Separate financial statements for these two companies as of December 31, 2021, follow:

	Plymouth	Sander
Revenues	$(1,740,000)	$ (950,000)
Cost of goods sold	820,000	500,000
Depreciation expense	104,000	85,000
Amortization expense	220,000	120,000
Interest expense	20,000	15,000
Equity in earnings of Sander	(124,000)	–0–
Net income	$ (700,000)	$ (230,000)
Retained earnings, 1/1/21	$(2,800,000)	$ (345,000)
Net income	(700,000)	(230,000)
Dividends declared	200,000	25,000
Retained earnings, 12/31/21	$(3,300,000)	$ (550,000)
Cash	$ 535,000	$ 115,000
Accounts receivable	575,000	215,000
Inventory	990,000	800,000
Investment in Sander	1,420,000	–0–
Buildings and equipment	1,025,000	863,000
Patents	950,000	107,000
Total assets	$ 5,495,000	$ 2,100,000
Accounts payable	$ (450,000)	$ (200,000)
Notes payable	(545,000)	(450,000)
Common stock	(900,000)	(800,000)
Additional paid-in capital	(300,000)	(100,000)
Retained earnings, 12/31/21	(3,300,000)	(550,000)
Total liabilities and stockholders' equity	$(5,495,000)	$(2,100,000)

a. Prepare a schedule that calculates the Equity in Earnings of Sander account balance.

b. Prepare a worksheet to arrive at consolidated figures for external reporting purposes. At year-end, there are no intra-entity payables or receivables.

LO 5-2, 5-3, 5-4, 5-5, 5-7

34. On January 1, 2019, Monica Company acquired 70 percent of Young Company's outstanding common stock for $665,000. The fair value of the noncontrolling interest at the acquisition date was $285,000. Young reported stockholders' equity accounts on that date as follows:

Common stock—$10 par value	$300,000
Additional paid-in capital	90,000
Retained earnings	410,000

In establishing the acquisition value, Monica appraised Young's assets and ascertained that the accounting records undervalued a building (with a five-year remaining life) by $50,000. Any remaining excess acquisition-date fair value was allocated to a franchise agreement to be amortized over 10 years.

During the subsequent years, Young sold Monica inventory at a 30 percent gross profit rate. Monica consistently resold this merchandise in the year of acquisition or in the period immediately following. Transfers for the three years after this business combination was created amounted to the following:

Year	Transfer Price	Inventory Remaining at Year-End (at transfer price)
2019	$60,000	$10,000
2020	80,000	12,000
2021	90,000	18,000

In addition, Monica sold Young several pieces of fully depreciated equipment on January 1, 2020, for $36,000. The equipment had originally cost Monica $50,000. Young plans to depreciate these assets over a six-year period.

In 2021, Young earns a net income of $160,000 and declares and pays $50,000 in cash dividends. These figures increase the subsidiary's Retained Earnings to a $740,000 balance at the end of 2021. During this same year, Monica reported dividend income of $35,000 and an investment account containing the initial value balance of $665,000. No changes in Young's common stock accounts have occurred since Monica's acquisition.

Prepare the 2021 consolidation worksheet entries for Monica and Young. In addition, compute the net income attributable to the noncontrolling interest for 2021.

LO 5-2, 5-3, 5-4, 5-5, 5-7

35. Assume the same basic information as presented in Problem 34 except that Monica employs the equity method of accounting. Hence, it reports $102,740 investment income for 2021 with an Investment account balance of $826,220. Under these circumstances, prepare the worksheet entries required for the consolidation of Monica Company and Young Company.

LO 5-1, 5-2, 5-3, 5-4, 5-5, 5-6, 5,7

excel

36. The individual financial statements for Gibson Company and Keller Company for the year ending December 31, 2021, follow. Gibson acquired a 60 percent interest in Keller on January 1, 2020, in exchange for various considerations totaling $570,000. At the acquisition date, the fair value of the noncontrolling interest was $380,000 and Keller's book value was $850,000. Keller had developed internally a customer list that was not recorded on its books but had an acquisition-date fair value of $100,000. This intangible asset is being amortized over 20 years. Gibson uses the partial equity method to account for its investment in Keller.

Gibson sold Keller land with a book value of $60,000 on January 2, 2020, for $100,000. Keller still holds this land at the end of the current year.

Keller regularly transfers inventory to Gibson. In 2020, it shipped inventory costing $100,000 to Gibson at a price of $150,000. During 2021, intra-entity shipments totaled $200,000, although the original cost to Keller was only $140,000. In each of these years, 20 percent of the merchandise was not resold to outside parties until the period following the transfer. Gibson owes Keller $40,000 at the end of 2021.

	Gibson Company	Keller Company
Sales	$ (800,000)	$ (500,000)
Cost of goods sold	500,000	300,000
Operating expenses	100,000	60,000
Equity in earnings of Keller	(84,000)	–0–
Net income	$ (284,000)	$ (140,000)
Retained earnings, 1/1/21	$(1,116,000)	$ (620,000)
Net income (above)	(284,000)	(140,000)
Dividends declared	115,000	60,000
Retained earnings, 12/31/21	$(1,285,000)	$ (700,000)
Cash	$ 177,000	$ 90,000
Accounts receivable	356,000	410,000
Inventory	440,000	320,000
Investment in Keller	726,000	–0–
Land	180,000	390,000
Buildings and equipment (net)	496,000	300,000
Total assets	$ 2,375,000	$ 1,510,000
Liabilities	$ (480,000)	$ (400,000)
Common stock	(610,000)	(320,000)
Additional paid-in capital	–0–	(90,000)
Retained earnings, 12/31/21	(1,285,000)	(700,000)
Total liabilities and equities	$(2,375,000)	$(1,510,000)

a. Prepare a worksheet to consolidate the separate 2021 financial statements for Gibson and Keller.

b. How would the consolidation entries in requirement (*a*) have differed if Gibson had sold a building on January 2, 2020, with a $60,000 book value (cost of $140,000) to Keller for $100,000 instead of land, as the problem reports? Assume that the building had a 10-year remaining life at the date of transfer.

LO 5-2, 5-3, 5-4, 5-6

37. On January 1, 2020, Panther, Inc., issued securities with a total fair value of $577,000 for 100 percent of Stark Corporation's outstanding ownership shares. Stark has long supplied inventory to Panther. The companies expect to achieve synergies with production scheduling and product development with this combination.

Although Stark's book value at the acquisition date was $300,000, the fair value of its trademarks was assessed to be $45,000 more than their carrying amounts. Additionally, Stark's patented technology was undervalued in its accounting records by $232,000. The trademarks were considered to have indefinite lives, and the estimated remaining life of the patented technology was eight years.

In 2020, Stark sold Panther inventory costing $75,000 for $125,000. As of December 31, 2020, Panther had resold 74 percent of this inventory. In 2021, Panther bought from Stark $140,000 of inventory that had an original cost of $70,000. At the end of 2021, Panther held $38,000 (transfer price) of inventory acquired from Stark, all from its 2021 purchases.

During 2021, Panther sold Stark a parcel of land for $88,000 and recorded a gain of $16,000 on the sale. Stark still owes Panther $62,000 (current liability) related to the land sale.

At the end of 2021, Panther and Stark prepared the following statements for consolidation.

	Panther, Inc.	Stark Corporation
Revenues	$ (710,000)	$(360,000)
Cost of goods sold	305,000	189,000
Other operating expenses	167,000	81,000
Gain on sale of land	(16,000)	–0–
Equity in Stark's earnings	(39,000)	–0–
Net income	$ (293,000)	$ (90,000)
Retained earnings, 1/1/21	$ (367,000)	$(292,000)
Net income	(293,000)	(90,000)
Dividends declared	80,000	25,000
Retained earnings, 12/31/21	$ (580,000)	$(357,000)
Cash and receivables	$ 102,000	$ 154,000
Inventory	311,000	110,000
Investment in Stark	691,000	–0–
Trademarks	–0–	58,000
Land, buildings, and equip. (net)	638,000	280,000
Patented technology	–0–	125,000
Total assets	$ 1,742,000	$ 727,000
Liabilities	$ (462,000)	$(220,000)
Common stock	(400,000)	(100,000)
Additional paid-in capital	(300,000)	(50,000)
Retained earnings, 12/31/21	(580,000)	(357,000)
Total liabilities and equity	$(1,742,000)	$(727,000)

a. Show how Panther computed its $39,000 equity in Stark's earnings balance.

b. Prepare a 2021 consolidated worksheet for Panther and Stark.

LO 5-2, 5-3, 5-4, 5-5

38. Kelly Company acquired 75 percent of Helton Company's outstanding voting shares on January 1, 2019, in exchange for $285,000 in cash. The subsidiary's stockholders' equity accounts totaled $326,000, and the noncontrolling interest had a fair value of $95,000 on that day. However, a building (with a 12-year remaining life) in Helton's accounting records was undervalued by $18,000. Kelly assigned the remaining excess fair over book value to Helton's patented technology (three-year remaining life).

Helton sold inventory to Kelly as follows:

Year	Cost to Helton	Transfer Price to Kelly	Inventory Held by Kelly at Year End (at transfer price)
2019	$69,000	$103,000	$18,000
2020	81,000	135,000	27,500
2021	40,000	100,000	50,000

Following are selected separate account balances for these two companies for the year ended December 31, 2021. Credit balances are indicated by parentheses.

	Kelly	Helton
Sales revenue	$ (962,000)	$ (466,000)
Cost of goods sold	515,000	210,000
Depreciation expense	81,100	32,500
Amortization expense	79,900	23,000
Other operating expenses	124,000	112,000
Equity in earnings of Helton	(42,000)	–0–
Net income	$ (204,000)	$ (88,500)

Prepare a consolidated income statement for Kelly Company and its subsidiary Helton for the year ended December 31, 2021. Include a proper title and line items allocating consolidated net income to the controlling and noncontrolling interests. Omit per share amounts.

Develop Your Skills

EXCEL CASE

CPA skills

On January 1, 2020, James Company purchased 100 percent of the outstanding voting stock of Nolan, Inc., for $1,000,000 in cash and other consideration. At the purchase date, Nolan had common stock of $500,000 and retained earnings of $185,000. James attributed the excess of acquisition-date fair value over Nolan's book value to a trade name with an estimated 25-year remaining useful life. James uses the equity method to account for its investment in Nolan.

During the next two years, Nolan reported the following:

	Income	Dividends Declared	Inventory Transfers to James at Transfer Price
2020	$78,000	$25,000	$190,000
2021	85,000	27,000	210,000

Nolan sells inventory to James after a markup based on a gross profit rate. At the end of 2020 and 2021, 30 percent of the current year purchases remain in James's inventory.

Required

Create an Excel spreadsheet that computes the following:

1. Equity method balance in James's Investment in Nolan, Inc., account as of December 31, 2021.
2. Worksheet adjustments for the December 31, 2021, consolidation of James and Nolan.

Formulate your solution so that Nolan's gross profit rate on sales to James is treated as a variable.

ANALYSIS AND RESEARCH CASE: ACCOUNTING INFORMATION AND SALARY NEGOTIATIONS

CPA *skills*

The Edison Eagles Players' Association and Mr. Sideline, the CEO and majority owner of Edison Eagles Soccer, Inc., ask your help in resolving a salary dispute. Mr. Sideline presents the following income statement to the players' representatives.

EDISON EAGLES SOCCER, INC.
Income Statement

Ticket revenues		$3,500,000
Stadium rent expense	$2,500,000	
Ticket expense	30,000	
Promotion expense	80,000	
Player salaries	700,000	
Staff salaries and miscellaneous	265,000	3,575,000
Net income (loss)		$ (75,000)

The players contend that their salaries are below market and a raise is warranted. Mr. Sideline argues that the Edison Eagles really lose money and, until ticket revenues increase, a salary hike is out of the question.

As a result of your inquiry, you discover that Edison Eagles Soccer owns 85 percent of the voting stock in Eagles Stadium, Inc. This venue is specifically designed for soccer and is where the Eagles play their entire home game schedule. However, Mr. Sideline does not wish to consider the profits of Eagles Stadium in the negotiations with the players. He claims that "the stadium is really a separate business entity that was purchased separately from the team and therefore does not concern the players. On top of that, we allocate all the ticket revenues to the team's income statement."

The Eagles Stadium income statement appears as follows:

EAGLES STADIUM, INC.
Income Statement

Stadium rent revenue	$2,500,000	
Concession revenue	875,000	
Parking revenue	95,000	$3,470,000
Cost of goods sold	270,000	
Depreciation expense	190,000	
Grounds maintenance expense	410,000	
Staff salaries and miscellaneous	200,000	1,070,000
Net income (loss)		$2,400,000

Required

1. What advice would you provide the negotiating parties regarding the issue of considering the Eagles Stadium income statement in their discussions? What authoritative literature could you cite in supporting your advice?
2. What other pertinent information would you need to provide a specific recommendation regarding players' salaries?

chapter

6

Variable Interest Entities, Intra-Entity Debt, Consolidated Cash Flows, and Other Issues

Learning Objectives

After studying this chapter, you should be able to:

LO 6-1 Describe a variable interest entity, a primary beneficiary, and the factors used to decide when a variable interest entity is subject to consolidation.

LO 6-2 Demonstrate the process to consolidate a primary beneficiary with a variable interest entity.

LO 6-3 Demonstrate the consolidation procedures to eliminate all intra-entity debt accounts and recognize any associated gain or loss created whenever one company acquires an affiliate's debt instrument from an outside party.

LO 6-4 Understand that subsidiary preferred stock not owned by the parent is a component of the noncontrolling interest and is initially measured at acquisition-date fair value.

LO 6-5 Prepare a consolidated statement of cash flows.

LO 6-6 Compute basic and diluted earnings per share for a business combination.

LO 6-7 Demonstrate the accounting effects of subsidiary stock transactions on the parent's financial records and consolidated financial statements.

The consolidation of financial information can be a highly complex process often encompassing a number of practical challenges. This chapter examines the procedures required by several additional issues:

- Variable interest entities.
- Intra-entity debt.
- Subsidiary preferred stock.
- The consolidated statement of cash flows.
- Computation of consolidated earnings per share.
- Subsidiary stock transactions.

Variable interest entities emerged over recent decades as a new type of business structure that provided effective control of one firm by another without overt ownership. In response to the evolving nature of control relationships among firms, the FASB expanded its definition of control beyond the long-standing criterion of a majority voting interest to include control exercised through variable interests. This topic and some of the more traditional advanced business combination subjects listed earlier provide for further exploration of the complexities faced by the financial reporting community in providing decision-useful information to users of consolidated financial reports.

Consolidation of Variable Interest Entities

Several decades ago, many firms began establishing separate business structures to help finance their operations at favorable rates. These structures became commonly known as *special-purpose entities* (SPEs), *special-purpose vehicles,* or *off-balance-sheet structures.* In this text, we refer to all such entities collectively as *variable interest entities,* or VIEs. Many firms routinely included their VIEs in their consolidated financial reports. However, others sought to avoid consolidation.

VIEs can help accomplish legitimate business purposes. Nonetheless, their use was widely criticized in the aftermath of Enron Corporation's 2001 collapse. Because many firms avoided consolidation and used VIEs

LO 6-1

Describe a variable interest entity, a primary beneficiary, and the factors used to decide when a variable interest entity is subject to consolidation.

for off-balance-sheet financing, such entities were often characterized as vehicles to hide debt and mislead investors. Other critics observed that firms with variable interests recorded questionable profits on sales to their VIEs that were not arm's-length transactions.[1] The FASB ASC "Variable Interest Entities" sections within the "Consolidations" topic were issued in response to such financial reporting abuses.

What Is a VIE?

A VIE can take the form of a trust, partnership, joint venture, or corporation, although sometimes it has neither independent management nor employees. Most are established for valid business purposes, and transactions involving VIEs have become widespread. Common examples of VIE activities include transfers of financial assets, leasing, hedging financial instruments, research and development, and other arrangements. An enterprise often creates a VIE to accomplish a well-defined and limited business activity and to provide low-cost financing.

Low-cost financing of asset purchases is frequently a benefit available through VIEs. Rather than engaging in the transaction directly, a business enterprise may establish a VIE to purchase and finance an asset acquisition. The VIE then leases the asset back to the business enterprise that established the VIE. This strategy saves the business enterprise money because the VIE is often eligible for a lower interest rate. This advantage is achieved for several reasons. First, the VIE typically operates with a very limited set of assets—in many cases, just one asset. By isolating an asset in a VIE, the asset's risk is isolated from the business enterprise's overall risk. Thus, the VIE creditors remain protected by the specific collateral in the asset. Second, the governing documents can strictly limit the actions of a VIE. These limits further protect lenders by preventing the VIE from engaging in any activities not specified in its agreements. As a major public accounting firm noted,

> The borrower/transferor gains access to a source of funds less expensive than would otherwise be available. This advantage derives from isolating the assets in an entity prohibited from undertaking any other business activity or taking on any additional debt, thereby creating a better security interest in the assets for the lender/investor.[2]

Because governing agreements limit activities and decision making in most VIEs, ownership of a VIE's common stock typically does not provide control of the VIE. In fact, the enterprise that created the VIE may own very little, if any, of the VIE's voting stock. Prior to current consolidation requirements for VIEs, many enterprises left such entities unconsolidated in their financial reports because technically they did not own a majority of the entity's voting stock. In utilizing the VIE as a conduit to provide financing, the related assets and debt were effectively removed from the enterprise's balance sheet.

In general, the party that primarily benefits (or risks losses) from the economic activities of the VIE and has the power to direct the VIE's activities is deemed to have a controlling financial interest in the VIE. We use the term **primary beneficiary** to designate the party with such financial control. The primary beneficiary (most often a business) typically exercises its financial control through governance documents or other contractual agreements that provide it with decision-making authority over the VIE. Once identified, the primary beneficiary must consolidate in its financial statements the VIE's assets, liabilities, revenues, expenses, and noncontrolling interest.

Characteristics of Variable Interest Entities

Similar to most business entities, VIEs generally have assets, liabilities, and investors with equity interests. Unlike most businesses, because a VIE's activities and decision making can be strictly limited, the role of the equity investors can be fairly minor. The VIE may have

[1] In its 2001 fourth-quarter 10-Q, Enron recorded earnings restatements of more than $400 million related to its failure to properly consolidate several of its SPEs (e.g., Chewco and LJM2). Enron also admitted an improper omission of $700 million of its SPE's debt. Within a month of the restatements, Enron filed for bankruptcy.

[2] KPMG, "Defining Issues: New Accounting for SPEs," March 1, 2002.

been created specifically by the primary beneficiary to provide it with low-cost financing. Thus, the equity investors may serve simply as a technical requirement to allow the VIE to function as a legal entity. Because they bear relatively low economic risk, equity investors may be provided only a small rate of return.

The small equity investments in a VIE normally are insufficient to induce lenders to provide financing for the VIE. As a result, another party (e.g., the primary beneficiary) must contribute substantial resources—often loans and/or guarantees—to enable the VIE to secure additional financing needed to accomplish its purpose. For example, the primary beneficiary may guarantee the VIE's debt, thus assuming the risk of default. Other contractual arrangements may limit returns to equity holders while participation rights or management fees provide increased profit potential and risks to the primary beneficiary. Risks and rewards such as these cause the primary beneficiary's economic interest to vary depending on the created entity's success—hence the term **variable interest entity**. In contrast to a traditional entity, a VIE's risks and rewards frequently are distributed not according to stock ownership but according to other variable interests. Exhibit 6.1 describes variable interests further and provides several examples.

Variable interests increase a firm's risk as the resources it provides (or guarantees) to the VIE increase. With increased risks come incentives to restrict the VIE's decision making. In fact, a firm with variable interests will regularly limit the equity investors' power through the VIE's governance documents. As noted by FASB ASC (810-10-05-13),

> If the total equity investment at risk is not sufficient to permit the legal entity to finance its activities, the parties providing the necessary additional subordinated financial support most likely will not permit an equity investor to make decisions that may be counter to their interests.

Although the equity investors are technically the owners of the VIE, in reality they may retain little of the traditional responsibilities, risks, and benefits of ownership. In fact, the equity investors sometimes cede financial control of the VIE to those with variable interests in exchange for a guaranteed rate of return. Alternatively, equity ownership is also a variable interest, and a minority equity holder may be the primary beneficiary and end up consolidating the VIE.

Consolidation of Variable Interest Entities

Prior to current financial reporting standards, assets, liabilities, and results of operations for VIEs and other entities frequently were not consolidated with those of the firm that controlled the entity. These firms invoked a reliance on voting interests, as opposed to variable

EXHIBIT 6.1
Examples of Variable Interests

Variable interests in a variable interest entity are contractual, ownership, or other pecuniary interests in an entity that change with changes in the entity's net asset value. Variable interests absorb portions of a variable interest entity's expected losses if they occur or receive portions of the entity's expected residual returns if they occur.

The following are some examples of variable interests and the related potential losses or returns:

Variable interests	Potential losses or returns
• Participation rights.	• Entitles holder to portions of profits.
• Asset purchase options.	• Entitles holder to benefit from increases in asset fair values.
• Debt or guarantee of debt.	• If a VIE cannot repay liabilities, non-repayment of a loan or honoring a debt guarantee will produce a loss.
• Subordinated debt instruments.	• If a VIE's cash flow is insufficient to repay all senior debt, subordinated debt may be required to absorb the loss.
• Lease residual value guarantees.	• If leased asset declines below the residual value, honoring the guarantee will produce a loss.
• Common stock.	• Entitles holder to residual profits, losses, and dividends.
• Management fee contracts.	• Entitles primary beneficiary to receive payment (often variable) from providing management services.

interests, to indicate a lack of a controlling financial interest. As legacy FASB standard *FIN 46R* observed,

> An enterprise's consolidated financial statements include subsidiaries in which the enterprise has a controlling financial interest. That requirement usually has been applied to subsidiaries in which an enterprise has a majority voting interest, but in many circumstances, the enterprise's consolidated financial statements do not include variable interest entities with which it has similar relationships. The voting interest approach is not effective in identifying controlling financial interests in entities that are not controllable through voting interests or in which the equity investors do not bear residual economic risk.[3]

Thus, a business enterprise is required to consolidate the assets and liabilities of a variable interest entity if it can exercise financial control through its role as a primary beneficiary. Variable interests often serve as the vehicle for a controlling financial interest, even in the absence of any equity investment whatsoever.

Business enterprises must first determine if they have a controlling financial interest in any affiliated entity by applying the variable interest model. Each enterprise involved with a VIE must evaluate whether it possesses a controlling financial interest and thus qualifies as the primary beneficiary of the VIE's activities. The VIE's primary beneficiary is then required to include the assets, liabilities, and results of the activities of the VIE in its consolidated financial statements. If the affiliated entity is not a VIE, then a voting interest model is utilized to assess whether financial control exists.

As noted by General Electric Company in a recent annual report:

> Our financial statements consolidate all of our affiliates—entities in which we have a controlling financial interest, most often because we hold a majority voting interest. To determine if we hold a controlling financial interest in an entity, we first evaluate if we are required to apply the variable interest entity (VIE) model to the entity, otherwise, the entity is evaluated under the voting interest model.
>
> Where we hold current or potential rights that give us the power to direct the activities of a VIE that most significantly impact the VIE's economic performance, combined with a variable interest that gives us the right to receive potentially significant benefits or the obligation to absorb potentially significant losses, we have a controlling financial interest in that VIE.

Identification of a Variable Interest Entity

An entity qualifies as a VIE if *either* of the following conditions exists:

- The total equity at risk is not sufficient to permit the entity to finance its activities without additional subordinated financial support provided by any parties, including equity holders. In most cases, if equity at risk is less than 10 percent of total assets, the risk is deemed insufficient.[4]
- The equity investors in the VIE, as a group, lack any one of the following three characteristics of a controlling financial interest:
  1. The power, through voting rights or similar rights, to direct the activities of an entity that most significantly impact the entity's economic performance.
  2. The obligation to absorb the expected losses of the entity (e.g., the primary beneficiary may guarantee a return to the equity investors).
  3. The right to receive the expected residual returns of the entity (e.g., the investors' return may be capped by the entity's governing documents or other arrangements with variable interest holders).

[3] (Summary, page 2) FASB *Interpretation No. 46R (FIN 46R),* "Consolidation of Variable Interest Entities," December 2003.

[4] Alternatively, a 10 percent or higher equity interest may also be insufficient. According to GAAP, "Some entities may require an equity investment greater than 10 percent of their assets to finance their activities, especially if they engage in high-risk activities, hold high-risk assets, or have exposure to risks that are not reflected in the reported amounts of the entities' assets or liabilities" (FASB ASC [para. 810-10-25-46]).

Identification of the Primary Beneficiary of the VIE

Once it is established that a firm has a relationship with a VIE, the firm must determine whether it qualifies as the VIE's primary beneficiary. According to FASB ASC (810-10-05-8A), an enterprise with a variable interest that provides it with a controlling financial interest in a variable interest entity is the primary beneficiary and will have both of the following characteristics:

- The power to direct the activities that most significantly impact the VIE's economic performance.
- The obligation to absorb losses of the VIE that could potentially be significant to the VIE or the right to receive benefits from the VIE that could potentially be significant to the VIE.

Note that these characteristics mirror those that the equity investors often lack in a VIE. Instead, the primary beneficiary will absorb a significant share of the VIE's losses or receive a significant share of the VIE's residual returns or both. The fact that the primary beneficiary may own no voting shares whatsoever becomes inconsequential because such shares do not effectively give the equity investors power to exercise control. Thus, a careful examination of the VIE's governing documents, contractual arrangements among parties involved, and who bears the risk is necessary to determine whether a reporting entity possesses control over a VIE.

The magnitude of the effect of consolidating an enterprise's VIEs can be large. For example, Walt Disney Company consolidates its Asian Theme Parks as variable interest entities. In its 2018 annual report, Disney states the following:

> The Company enters into relationships or investments with other entities that may be variable interest entities (VIE). A VIE is consolidated in the financial statements if the Company has the power to direct activities that most significantly impact the economic performance of the VIE and has the obligation to absorb losses or the right to receive benefits from the VIE that could potentially be significant (as defined by ASC 810-10-25-38) to the VIE. Hong Kong Disneyland Resort and Shanghai Disney Resort (collectively the Asia Theme Parks) are VIEs.

Because Disney has the ability to direct the day-to-day operations and to develop business strategies, and because it receives management fees, Disney consolidates the Asia Theme Parks in its financial statements. As a result of the 2018 consolidation of these VIEs, Disney's total assets increased by $10.31 billion while its total debt increased by $2.4 billion.

Example of a Primary Beneficiary and Consolidated Variable Interest Entity

Assume that Twin Peaks Electric Company seeks to acquire a generating plant for a negotiated price of $400 million from Ace Electric Company. Twin Peaks wishes to expand its market share and expects to be able to sell the electricity generated by the plant acquisition at a profit to its owners.

In reviewing financing alternatives, Twin Peaks observed that its general credit rating allowed for a 4 percent annual interest rate on a debt issue. Twin Peaks also explored the establishment of a separate legal entity whose sole purpose would be to own the electric generating plant and lease it back to Twin Peaks. Because the separate entity would isolate the electric generating plant from Twin Peaks's other risky assets and liabilities and provide specific collateral, an interest rate of 3 percent on the debt is available, producing before-tax savings of $4 million per year. To obtain the lower interest rate, however, Twin Peaks must guarantee the separate entity's debt. Twin Peaks must also maintain certain of its own predefined financial ratios and restrict the amount of additional debt it can assume.

To take advantage of the lower interest rate, on January 1, 2020, Twin Peaks establishes Power Finance Co., an entity designed solely to own, finance, and lease the electric generating plant to Twin Peaks. The documents governing the new entity specify the following:

- The sole purpose of Power Finance is to purchase the Ace electric generating plant, provide equity and debt financing, and lease the plant to Twin Peaks.
- An outside investor will provide $16 million in exchange for a 100 percent nonvoting equity interest in Power Finance.

- Power Finance will issue debt in exchange for $384 million. Because the $16 million equity investment by itself is insufficient to attract low-interest debt financing, Twin Peaks will guarantee the debt.
- Twin Peaks will lease the electric generating plant from Power Finance in exchange for payments of $12 million per year based on a 3 percent fixed interest rate for both the debt and equity investors for an initial lease term of five years.
- At the end of the five-year lease term (or any extension), Twin Peaks must do one of the following:
  - Renew the lease for five years, subject to the approval of the equity investor.
  - Purchase the electric generating plant for $400 million.
  - Sell the electric generating plant to an independent third party. If the proceeds of the sale are insufficient to repay the equity investor, Twin Peaks must make a payment of $16 million to the equity investor.

Once the purchase of the electric generating plant is complete and the equity and debt are issued, Power Finance Company reports the following balance sheet:

POWER FINANCE COMPANY
Balance Sheet
January 1, 2020

Electric Generating Plant	$400 million	Long-Term Debt	$384 million
		Owners' Equity	16 million
Total Assets	$400 million	Total Liabilities and OE	$400 million

Exhibit 6.2 shows the relationships between Twin Peaks, Power Finance, the electric generating plant, and the parties financing the asset purchase.

In evaluating whether Twin Peaks Electric Company must consolidate Power Finance Company, two conditions must be met. First, Power Finance must qualify as a VIE by either (1) an inability to secure financing without additional subordinated support or (2) a lack of either the risk of losses or entitlement to residual returns (or both). Second, Twin Peaks must qualify as the primary beneficiary of Power Finance.

EXHIBIT 6.2
Variable Interest Entity to Facilitate Financing

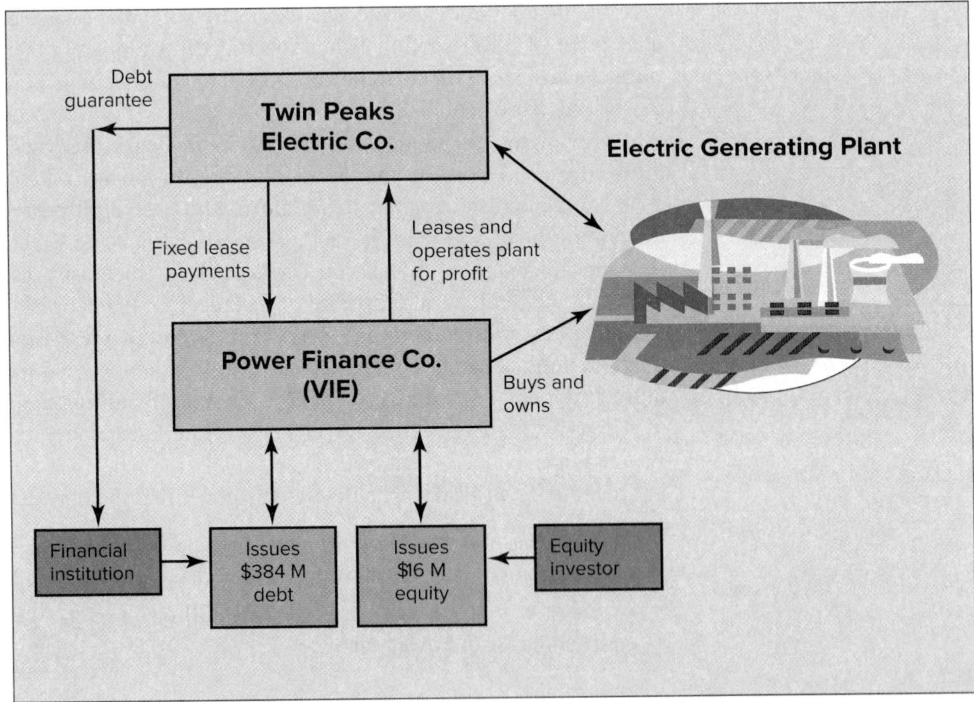

In assessing the first condition, several factors point to VIE status for Power Finance. Its owners' equity comprises only 4 percent of total assets, far short of the 10 percent benchmark. Moreover, Twin Peaks guarantees Power Finance's debt, suggesting insufficient equity to finance its operations without additional support. Finally, the equity investor appears to bear almost no risk with respect to the operations of the Ace electric plant. These characteristics indicate that Power Finance qualifies as a VIE.

In evaluating the second condition for consolidation, an assessment is made to determine whether Twin Peaks qualifies as Power Finance's primary beneficiary. Clearly, Twin Peaks has the power to direct Power Finance's activities. But to qualify for consolidation, Twin Peaks must also have the obligation to absorb losses or the right to receive returns from Power Finance—either of which could potentially be significant to Power Finance. But what possible losses or returns would accrue to Twin Peaks? What are Twin Peaks's variable interests that rise and fall with the fortunes of Power Finance?

As stated in the VIE agreement, Twin Peaks will pay a fixed fee to lease the electric generating plant. It will then operate the plant and sell the electric power in its markets. If the business plan is successful, Twin Peaks will enjoy residual profits from operating while Power Finance's equity investors receive the fixed fee. On the other hand, if prices for electricity fall, Twin Peaks may generate revenues insufficient to cover its lease payments while Power Finance's equity investors are protected from this risk. Moreover, if the plant's fair value increases significantly, Twin Peaks can exercise its option to purchase the plant at a fixed price and either resell it or keep it for its own future use. Alternatively, if Twin Peaks were to sell the plant at a loss, it must pay the equity investors all of their initial investment, furthering the loss to Twin Peaks. Each of these elements points to Twin Peaks as the primary beneficiary of its VIE through variable interests. As the primary beneficiary, Twin Peaks must consolidate the assets, liabilities, and results of operations of Power Finance with its own.

Procedures to Consolidate Variable Interest Entities

As Power Finance's balance sheet exemplifies, VIEs typically possess only a few assets and liabilities. Also, their business activities usually are strictly limited. Thus, the actual procedures to consolidate VIEs are relatively uncomplicated. Nonetheless, ASC (810-10-35-3) provides the following overall guidance:

> The principles of consolidated financial statements in this Topic apply to primary beneficiaries' accounting for consolidated variable interest entities (VIEs). After the initial measurement, the assets, liabilities, and noncontrolling interests of a consolidated VIE shall be accounted for in consolidated financial statements as if the VIE were consolidated based on voting interests . . . The consolidated entity shall follow the requirements for elimination of intra-entity balances and transactions and other matters . . . and existing practices for consolidated subsidiaries.

Initial Measurement Issues

As the ASC states, the financial reporting principles for consolidating variable interest entities require asset, liability, and noncontrolling interest valuations. These valuations initially, and with few exceptions, are based on fair values.

Recall that the acquisition method requires an allocation of the acquired business fair value based on the underlying fair values of its assets and liabilities. The fair-value principle applies to consolidating VIEs in the same manner as business combinations accomplished through voting interests. If the total business fair value of the VIE exceeds the collective fair values of its net assets, goodwill is recognized.[5] Conversely, if the collective fair values of the net assets exceed the total business fair value, then the primary beneficiary recognizes a gain on bargain purchase.

[5] The FASB in ASU 2017-01, *Business Combinations (Topic 805): Clarifying the Definition of a Business,* describes the requirement that a business include, at a minimum, an input and a substantive process that together significantly contribute to the ability to create outputs. If the activities of the VIE are so restricted that it does not qualify as a business, the excess fair value is recognized as an acquisition loss, as opposed to goodwill.

In the previous example, assuming that the debt and noncontrolling interests are stated at fair values, Twin Peaks simply includes in its consolidated balance sheet the Electric Generating Plant at $400 million, the Long-Term Debt at $384 million, and a noncontrolling interest of $16 million.

Consolidation of VIEs Subsequent to Initial Measurement

After the initial measurement, consolidations of VIEs with their primary beneficiaries should follow the same process as if the entity were consolidated based on voting interests. Importantly, all intra-entity transactions between the primary beneficiary and the VIE (including management fees, expenses, other sources of income or loss, and intra-entity inventory transfers, etc.) must be eliminated in consolidation. Finally, the VIE's income must be allocated among the parties involved (e.g., equity holders and the primary beneficiary). For a VIE, contractual arrangements, as opposed to ownership percentages, typically specify the distribution of its income. Therefore, a close examination of these contractual arrangements is needed to determine the appropriate allocation of VIE income to its equity owners and those holding variable interests.

LO 6-2

Demonstrate the process to consolidate a primary beneficiary with a variable interest entity.

Consolidation of a Primary Beneficiary and VIE Illustrated

The next example considers (1) the issues that arise when a primary beneficiary obtains control through variable interests of an existing business, and (2) financial reporting for a VIE in periods subsequent to obtaining control.

Assume that on January 1, 2018, Payton Corporation provides a $2,200,000 loan to Vicente, Inc., a business entity. The loan is due on January 1, 2023. Until receiving the loan from Payton, Vicente had been unable to secure the financing needed to continue its operations.

As part of the loan contract, Vicente agrees to provide the following to Payton during the next five years:

- 5 percent annual interest (market rate) on the $2,200,000 loan.
- Decision-making power over Vicente's operating and financing activities.
- An annual management fee equal to 10 percent of Vicente's sales.

At the end of the five-year agreement Payton has the option of either acquiring ownership of Vicente, Inc., for $500,000 or extending the original contract for an additional five years.

As a result of the agreement, Vicente is a variable interest entity, and Payton is its primary beneficiary. Upon consummation of the variable interest agreement, the companies' balance sheets appears as follows:

January 1, 2021	Payton	Vicente
Cash	$ 35,000	$ 2,308,000
Accounts receivable	33,000	145,000
Loan receivable from Vicente	2,200,000	–0–
Patented technology	–0–	9,000
Equipment (net)	2,245,000	400,000
Total assets	$ 4,513,000	$ 2,862,000
Accounts payable	$ (44,000)	$ (644,000)
Long-term debt	(955,000)	(2,200,000)
Common stock	(2,500,000)	(10,000)
Retained earnings, 1/1/21	(1,014,000)	(8,000)
Total liabilities and equity	$(4,513,000)	$(2,862,000)

At January 1, 2021, Payton estimated the fair value of Vicente's common stock at $143,000. The $125,000 difference between the fair value of the common stock and Vicente's book value ($143,000 – $18,000) was attributed entirely to the patented technology with a 10-year estimated remaining life.

Exhibit 6.3 shows the consolidation worksheet for Payton (the primary beneficiary) and Vicente (the variable interest entity) at January 1, 2021, the date Payton obtained financial control over Vicente.

EXHIBIT 6.3 Acquisition-Date Consolidation Worksheet—Primary Beneficiary and VIE

PAYTON AND VICENTE COMPANIES
Consolidation Worksheet
At January 1, 2021

Balance Sheet	Payton	Vicente	Consolidation Entries		Noncontrolling Interest	Consolidated Balance Sheet
Cash	35,000	2,308,000				2,343,000
Accounts receivable	33,000	145,000				178,000
Loan receivable from Vicente	2,200,000			(P)2,200,000		–0–
Patented technology		9,000	(A) 125,000			134,000
Equipment (net)	2,245,000	400,000				2,645,000
Total assets	4,513,000	2,862,000				5,300,000
Accounts payable	(44,000)	(644,000)				(688,000)
Long-term debt	(955,000)	(2,200,000)	(P)2,200,000			(955,000)
Common stock—Payton	(2,500,000)					(2,500,000)
Common stock—Vicente		(10,000)	(S) 10,000			
Retained earnings—Payton	(1,014,000)					(1,014,000)
Retained earning—Vicente		(8,000)	(S) 8,000			
Noncontrolling interest				(S) 18,000		
				(A) 125,000	(143,000)	(143,000)
Total liabilities and equity	(4,513,000)	(2,862,000)	2,343,000	2,343,000		(5,300,000)

Observe that in Exhibit 6.3,

- Consolidation Entry **S** eliminates the VIE's owners' equity account balances and recognizes the 100 percent equity ownership as a noncontrolling interest.
- Consolidation Entry **P** eliminates the intra-entity Long-Term Debt and Loan Receivable from Vicente.
- Consolidation Entry **A** allocates the excess fair over book value to Patented Technology with a corresponding increase in the noncontrolling interest.
- The noncontrolling interest appears in the consolidated balance sheet at its acquisition-date fair value of $143,000.

Consolidation of VIEs Subsequent to Initial Measurement

Following the first year of operations, Exhibit 6.4 shows the consolidation worksheet for December 31, 2021, at the end of the first year in which Payton obtained control of the variable interest entity. At the end of the year, Vicente paid

- A $5,000 dividend to its equity holders.
- The $40,000 management fee (10 percent of Vicente's sales) to Payton. The fee was recorded by Vicente as an other operating expense.
- The $110,000 interest due on the loan to Payton.

The following worksheet entries, as seen in Exhibit 6.4, are used to consolidate the financial statements of Payton Corporation and its VIE, Vicente, as of December 31, 2021:

Consolidation Entry S

Retained earnings—Vicente 1/1/21	8,000	
Common stock—Valente	10,000	
Noncontrolling interest		18,000

To eliminate the beginning stockholders' equity of the VIE and recognize the 100 percent equity ownership of the noncontrolling interest.

EXHIBIT 6.4 Consolidation Worksheet for Primary Beneficiary and VIE (Post-Control)

PAYTON AND VICENTE COMPANIES
Consolidation Worksheet
For the year ended, December 31, 2021

Income Statement	**Payton**	**Vicente**	**Consolidation Entries**		**Noncontrolling Interest**	**Consolidated**
Sales	(932,000)	(400,000)				(1,332,000)
Management fee	(40,000)	–0–	(F) 40,000			
Cost of goods sold	530,000	175,000				705,000
Other operating expenses	122,000	95,000	(E) 12,500	(F) 40,000		189,500
Interest income	(110,000)	–0–	(IE) 110,000			–0–
Interest expense	33,000	110,000		(IE) 110,000		33,000
Net income	(397,000)	(20,000)				
Consolidated net income						(404,500)
to noncontrolling interest					(7,500)	7,500
to controlling interest						(397,000)
Statement of Retained Earnings						
Retained earnings, 1/1	(1,014,000)	(8,000)	(S) 8,000			(1,014,000)
Net income	(397,000)	(20,000)				(397,000)
Dividends declared	36,000	5,000			5,000	36,000
Retained earnings, 12/31	(1,375,000)	(23,000)				(1,375,000)
Balance Sheet						
Cash	214,000	8,800				222,800
Accounts receivable	258,000	71,500				329,500
Loan receivable from Vicente	2,200,000	–0–		(P) 2,200,000		–0–
Patented technology		7,200	(A) 125,000	(E) 12,500		119,700
Equipment (net)	2,528,000	2,250,000				4,778,000
Total assets	5,200,000	2,337,500				5,450,000
Accounts payable	(425,000)	(104,500)				(529,500)
Long-term debt	(900,000)	(2,200,000)	(P) 2,200,000			(900,000)
Common stock	(2,500,000)	(10,000)	(S) 10,000			(2,500,000)
Retained earnings, 12/31	(1,375,000)	(23,000)				(1,375,000)
				(A) 125,000		
				(S) 18,000	(143,000)	
Noncontrolling interest					(145,500)	(145,500)
Total liabilities and equities	(5,200,000)	(2,337,500)	2,505,500	2,505,500		(5,450,000)

Consolidation Entry A

Patented technology	125,000	
Noncontrolling interest		125,000

To allocate the excess fair value to patented technology and credit the noncontrolling interest as part of their fair valuation as of the date Payton obtained control.

Consolidation Entry P

Long-term debt	2,200,000	
Loan receivable from Vicente		2,200,000

To eliminate the long-term receivable and debt representing Payton's initial investment in Vicente.

Consolidation Entry E		
Other operating expenses	12,500	
Patented technology		12,500
To amortize the excess fair value allocation to unpatented technology over its five-year remaining life.		

Consolidation Entry IE		
Interest income	110,000	
Interest expense		110,000
To eliminate the intra-entity interest related to the loan from Payton to Vicente.		

Consolidation Entry F		
Management fee	40,000	
Other operating expenses		40,000
To eliminate the intra-entity management fee.		

Consolidation Entry F is a new worksheet entry introduced to eliminate the management fee. Such management fees are a common arrangement between variable interest entities and their primary beneficiaries and are routinely eliminated in consolidation. As ASC (810-10-35-3) observes

> Fees or other sources of income or expense between a primary beneficiary and a consolidated VIE shall be eliminated against the related expense or income of the VIE. The resulting effect of that elimination on the net income or expense of the VIE shall be attributed to the primary beneficiary (and not to noncontrolling interests) in the consolidated financial statements.

Both the $40,000 management fee and the $110,000 intra-entity loan interest, although eliminated in consolidation, continue to be allocated to the primary beneficiary because of the contractual arrangement with the VIE. Although the effect of Consolidation Entry F and Consolidation Entry IE eliminations is to increase the VIE's net income by $150,000, none of this increase is attributed to the noncontrolling interest.

In Exhibit 6.4, the $7,500 income allocation to the NCI is computed as all of Vicente's $20,000 net income less the $12,500 control-date excess fair value amortization attributed to Vicente's patented technology. The entire $7,500 is allocated to the noncontrolling interest because Payton, the primary beneficiary, holds no equity interest in Vicente, the VIE. Overall, as shown by Exhibit 6.4, consolidation of a VIE with its primary beneficiary follows a similar process as if the entity were consolidated based on voting interests.

Variable Interest Entity Disclosure Requirements

VIE disclosure requirements are designed to provide users of financial statements with more transparent information about an enterprise's involvement in a VIE. The enhanced disclosures are required for any enterprise that holds a variable interest in a VIE.

Included among the enhanced disclosures are requirements to show:

- The VIE's nature, purpose, size, and activities.
- The significant judgments and assumptions made by an enterprise in determining whether it must consolidate a VIE and/or disclose information about its involvement in a VIE.
- The nature of restrictions on a consolidated VIE's assets and on the settlement of its liabilities reported by an enterprise in its statement of financial position, including the carrying amounts of such assets and liabilities.
- The nature of, and changes in, the risks associated with an enterprise's involvement with the VIE.
- How an enterprise's involvement with the VIE affects the enterprise's financial position, financial performance, and cash flows.

Comparisons with International Accounting Standards

Under both U.S. GAAP and IFRS, a controlling financial interest is the critical concept in assessing whether an entity should be consolidated by a reporting enterprise. Nonetheless, the FASB and IASB so far have employed different criteria to determine the existence of control. IFRS employs a single consolidation model for all entities regardless of whether control is evidenced by voting interests or variable interests. In contrast, U.S. GAAP employs separate models for assessing control for variable interest entities and voting interest entities. As a result, current reporting standards differ across jurisdictions for enterprises seeking to determine whether to consolidate another entity.

The International Accounting Standards Board *IFRS 10,* "Consolidated Financial Statements" and *IFRS 12,* "Disclosure of Interests in Other Entities" cover situations where financial control exists either through a majority voting share or through other means. These standards define control to encompass all possible ways (voting power, contractual power, decision-making rights, etc.) in which one entity can exercise power over another. In particular, the criteria for assessing control are

- Power over an investee—does the reporting entity have the current ability to direct activities that significantly affect another entity's returns?
- Exposure to, or rights to, variable returns from involvement with another entity
- Linkage between power and returns—does the investor have the ability to affect its returns through its power?

These criteria recognize one entity can control another through its power to direct its operating and financing activities. For example, even with less than majority ownership, voting interests can provide an enterprise control if the nonowned shares are diffusely held and lack arrangements to act in a coordinated manner. Control can also be achieved through obtaining decision-making rights that relate to the relevant activities of an investee. Importantly, such decision-making rights can extend beyond merely voting rights. By establishing a broad concept of control as opposed to a bright-line rule (e.g., consolidate if an entity has majority voting rights or the majority of risks and rewards), the IASB seeks to avoid standards that create structuring opportunities to achieve a particular accounting outcome.[6]

IFRS 12 provides for enhanced disclosures about the relationship between a parent and the entities it controls. These disclosures focus on helping investors understand first why a parent controls (or does not control) another entity and the claims of the noncontrolling interest. Second, the disclosures are designed to help investors evaluate the risks assumed by the parent.[7]

LO 6-3

Demonstrate the consolidation procedures to eliminate all intra-entity debt accounts and recognize any associated gain or loss created whenever one company acquires an affiliate's debt instrument from an outside party.

Intra-Entity Debt Transactions

The previous chapter explored the consolidation procedures required by the intra-entity transfer of inventory, land, and depreciable assets. In preparing consolidated financial statements, all resulting gains were deferred until either the asset was sold to an outside party or consumed through use. Deferral was necessary because these gains, although legitimately recognized by the individual companies, were based on activities of the consolidated entity with itself. The separate financial information of each company was adjusted on the worksheet to be consistent with treating the related companies as a single economic concern.

This same objective applies in consolidating all other intra-entity activities: The financial statements must represent the business combination as one enterprise rather than as a group of independent organizations. Consequently, in designing consolidation procedures for

[6] Patrick Finnegan, Board Member of the IASB. "At Long-Last—A Single Model for Consolidation," IFRS Foundation, May 2011 perspectives.

[7] Ibid.

intra-entity transactions, we first isolate the effects recorded by the individual companies. After analyzing the impact of each action, worksheet entries recast these events from the vantage point of the business combination. Although this process involves a number of nuances and complexities, the desire for reporting financial information solely from the perspective of the consolidated entity remains constant.

We introduced the intra-entity sales of inventory, land, and depreciable assets together (in Chapter 5) because these transfers result in similar consolidation procedures. In each case, one of the affiliated companies recognizes a gain prior to the time the consolidated entity is entitled to recognize it. The worksheet entries required by these transactions simply realign the separate financial information to agree with the viewpoint of the business combination. The gain is removed, and the inflated asset value is reduced to historical cost.

The next section of this chapter examines the intra-entity acquisition of bonds and notes. Although accounting for the related companies as a single economic entity continues to be the central goal, the consolidation procedures applied to intra-entity debt transactions stand in marked contrast to the process utilized in Chapter 5 for asset transfers.

Before delving into this topic, note that *direct* loans used to transfer funds between affiliated companies create no unique consolidation problems. Regardless of whether bonds or notes generate such amounts, the resulting receivable/payable balances are necessarily identical. Because no money is owed to or from an outside party, these reciprocal accounts must be eliminated in each subsequent consolidation. A worksheet entry simply offsets the two corresponding balances. Furthermore, the interest revenue/expense accounts associated with direct loans also agree and are removed in the same fashion.

Acquisition of Affiliate's Debt from an Outside Party

The difficulties encountered in consolidating intra-entity liabilities relate to a specific type of transaction: the purchase of an affiliate's debt instrument from an outside third party. For example, a subsidiary may have issued bonds in the past that continue to be traded in the open market. If the parent then purchases all or a portion of these outstanding subsidiary bonds in the open market, from a consolidated view, the combined entity (parent and subsidiary) has reacquired its own bonds. Nonetheless, because the companies maintain independent accounting systems, the parent records an Investment in Bonds account as well as periodic interest income. The subsidiary shows the bonds as still outstanding and records periodic interest expense.

Although the individual companies continue to carry both the debt and the investment on their individual financial records, *from a consolidation viewpoint, this liability is effectively retired as of the debt reacquisition date.* From that date forward, the debt is no longer owed to a party outside the business combination. Subsequent interest payments are simply intra-entity cash transfers. To create consolidated statements, worksheet entries must be developed to adjust the various balances to report the debt's effective retirement.

Acquiring an affiliate's bond or note from an unrelated party poses no significant consolidation problems if the purchase price equals the corresponding carrying amount of the liability. Reciprocal balances within the individual records would always be identical in value and easily offset in each subsequent consolidation.

Realistically, though, such reciprocity rarely occurs when a debt instrument is purchased from a third party. A variety of economic factors typically produce a difference between the price paid for the investment and the carrying amount of the obligation. The debt is originally sold under market conditions at a particular time. Any premium or discount associated with this issuance is then amortized over the life of the bond, creating a continuous adjustment to its carrying amount. The acquisition of this instrument at a later date is made at a price influenced by current economic conditions, prevailing interest rates, and myriad other financial and market factors.

Therefore, the cost paid to purchase the debt could be either more or less than the carrying amount of the liability currently found within the issuing company's financial records. *To the business combination, this difference is a gain or loss because the acquisition effectively retires the bond; the debt is no longer owed to an outside party.* For external reporting purposes, this gain or loss must be recognized immediately by the consolidated entity.

Accounting for Intra-Entity Debt Transactions—Individual Financial Records

The following accounting problems emerge in consolidating intra-entity debt transactions:

1. Intra-entity investments in debt securities and related debt accounts must be eliminated in consolidation despite their differing balances.
2. Intra-entity interest revenue/expense (as well as any interest receivable/payable accounts) must be removed although these balances also fail to agree in amount.
3. The amortization process for discounts and premiums causes continual changes in each of the preceding accounts.
4. The business combination must recognize the gain or loss on the effective retirement of the debt, even though it is not recognized within the financial records of either company.

To illustrate, assume that Alpha Company possesses an 80 percent interest in the outstanding voting stock of Omega Company. On January 1, 2018, Omega issued $1 million in 10-year bonds paying cash interest of 9 percent annually. Because of market conditions prevailing on that date, Omega sold the debt for $938,555 to yield an effective interest rate of 10 percent per year. Shortly thereafter, the interest rate began to fall, and by January 1, 2020, Omega made the decision to retire this debt prematurely and refinance it at a currently lower rate. To carry out this plan, Alpha purchased all of these bonds in the open market on January 1, 2020, for $1,057,466. This price was based on an effective yield of 8 percent, which is assumed to be in line with the interest rates at the time.

Many reasons could exist for having Alpha, rather than Omega, reacquire this debt. For example, company cash levels at that date could necessitate Alpha's role as the purchasing agent. Also, contractual limitations could prohibit Omega from repurchasing its own bonds.

In accounting for this business combination, Omega Company's bonds have been effectively retired. Thus, the difference between the $1,057,466 payment and the January 1, 2020, carrying amount of the liability must be recognized in the consolidated statements as a gain or loss. The carrying amount for the debt on that date depends on the amortization process. Exhibit 6.5 shows the bond amortization schedule for January 1, 2018, through December 31, 2021.[8]

As seen in Exhibit 6.5, the carrying amount of Omega Company's bonds has increased to $946,651 as of December 31, 2019, the date immediately before the day that Alpha Company acquired the bonds.

Because Alpha paid $110,815 in excess of the recorded liability ($1,057,466 – $946,651), the consolidated entity must recognize a loss of this amount. After the loss has been acknowledged, the bond is considered to be retired, and no further reporting is necessary by the *business combination* after January 1, 2020.

Despite the simplicity of this approach for consolidation, neither company separately accounts for the event in this manner. Omega retains the $1 million debt balance within its separate financial records and amortizes the remaining discount each year. Annual cash interest payments of $90,000 (9 percent) continue to be made. At the same time, Alpha records the investment at the historical cost of $1,057,466, an amount that also requires periodic

EXHIBIT 6.5
Omega Company Bond Issue Amortization Schedule

Date	Face Value	Unamortized Discount	Carrying Amount	Effective Interest	Cash Interest	Discount Amortized
01/01/18	$1,000,000	$61,445	$938,555			
12/31/18	1,000,000	57,590	942,410	$93,855	$90,000	$3,855
12/31/19	1,000,000	53,349	946,651	94,241	90,000	4,241
12/31/20	1,000,000	48,684	951,316	94,665	90,000	4,665
12/31/21	1,000,000	43,552	956,448	95,132	90,000	5,132

[8] The effective rate method of amortization is demonstrated here because this approach is theoretically preferable. However, the straight-line method can be applied if the resulting balances are not materially different from the figures computed using the effective rate method.

amortization. Furthermore, as the owner of these bonds, Alpha receives the $90,000 interest payments made by Omega.

To organize the accountant's approach to this consolidation, we analyze the subsequent financial records for each company. Omega records only two journal entries during 2020, assuming that interest is paid each December 31:

	Omega Company's Financial Records		
12/31/20	Interest Expense	90,000	
	Cash		90,000
	To record payment of annual cash interest on $1 million, 9 percent bonds payable.		
12/31/20	Interest Expense	4,665	
	Discount on Bonds Payable		4,665
	To adjust interest expense to effective rate based on original yield rate of 10 percent ($946,651 carrying amount for 2017 × 10% = $94,665). Carrying amount increases to $951,316.		

Concurrently, Alpha journalizes entries to record its ownership of this investment:

	Alpha Company's Financial Records		
1/1/20	Investment in Omega Company Bonds	1,057,466	
	Cash		1,057,466
	To record acquisition of $1,000,000 in Omega Company bonds paying 9 percent cash interest, acquired to yield an effective rate of 8 percent.		
12/31/20	Cash	90,000	
	Interest Income		90,000
	To record receipt of cash interest from Omega Company bonds ($1,000,000 × 9%).		
12/31/20	Interest Income	5,403	
	Investment in Omega Company Bonds		5,403
	To reduce $90,000 interest income to effective rate based on original yield rate of 8 percent ($1,057,466 carrying amount for 2017 × 8% = $84,597). Carrying amount decreases to $1,052,063.		

Even a brief review of these entries indicates that the reciprocal accounts to be eliminated within the consolidation process do not agree in amount. You can see the dollar amounts appearing in each set of financial records in Exhibit 6.6. Despite the presence of these recorded balances, none of the four intra-entity accounts (the bond liability, investment,

EXHIBIT 6.6

ALPHA COMPANY AND OMEGA COMPANY
Effects of Intra-Entity Debt Transaction 2020

	Omega Company Reported Debt	Alpha Company Investment
2020 interest expense*	$ 94,665	$ –0–
2020 interest income†	–0–	(84,597)
Bonds payable	(1,000,000)	–0–
Discount on bonds payable*	48,684	–0–
Investment in bonds, 12/31/20†	–0–	1,052,063
Loss on retirement	–0–	–0–

Note: Parentheses indicate a credit balance.
*Company total is adjusted for 2020 amortization of $4,665 (see journal entry).
†Adjusted for 2020 amortization of $5,403 (see journal entry).

interest expense, and interest revenue) appear in the consolidated financial statements. *The only figure that the business combination reports is the $110,815 loss created by the effective extinguishment of this debt.*

Effects on Consolidation Process

As previous discussions indicated, consolidation procedures convert information generated by the individual accounting systems to the perspective of a single economic entity. A worksheet entry is therefore required on December 31, 2020, to eliminate the intra-entity balances shown in Exhibit 6.6 and to recognize the loss resulting from the effective retirement. Mechanically, the differences in the liability and investment balances as well as the interest expense and interest income accounts stem from the $110,815 difference between the purchase price of the investment and the carrying amount of the liability. Recognition of this loss, in effect, bridges the gap between the divergent figures.

Consolidation Entry B (December 31, 2020)		
Bonds Payable	1,000,000	
Interest Income	84,597	
Loss on Retirement of Bonds	110,815	
Discount on Bond Payable		48,684
Investment in Omega Company Bonds		1,052,063
Interest Expense		94,665
To eliminate intra-entity bonds and related interest accounts and to recognize loss on effective retirement. (Labeled **B** in reference to bonds.)		

The preceding entry successfully transforms the separate financial reporting of Alpha and Omega to that appropriate for the business combination. The objective of the consolidation process has been met: The statements present the bonds as having been retired on January 1, 2020. The debt and the corresponding investment are eliminated along with both interest accounts. Only the loss now appears on the worksheet to be reported within the consolidated financial statements.

Assignment of Retirement Gain or Loss

An issue in accounting for intra-entity debt repurchases concerns the assignment of any retirement gains or losses. Should the $110,815 loss just reported be attributed to Alpha or to Omega? From a practical perspective, this assignment affects only the consolidated net income allocation to the controlling and noncontrolling interests. In the absence of FASB guidance on the assignment of retirement gain or loss, all income effects in this textbook relating to intra-entity debt transactions are assigned solely to the parent company. Such treatment is consistent with the perspective that the parent company ultimately controls the repurchase decision.

Intra-Entity Debt Transactions—Years Subsequent to Effective Retirement

Even though the preceding Entry **B** correctly eliminates Omega's bonds in the year of retirement for consolidation purposes, the debt remains within the financial accounts of both companies until maturity. Therefore, in each succeeding time period, all balances must again be consolidated so that the liability is always reported as having been extinguished on January 1, 2020. Unfortunately, a simple repetition of Entry **B** is not possible. Developing the appropriate worksheet entry is complicated by the amortization process that produces continual change in the various account balances. Thus, as a preliminary step in each subsequent consolidation, current carrying amounts, as reported by the two parties, must be identified.

Discussion Question

WHO LOST THIS $300,000?

Several years ago, Penston Company purchased 90 percent of the outstanding shares of Swansan Corporation. Penston made the acquisition because Swansan produced a vital component used in Penston's manufacturing process. Penston wanted to ensure an adequate supply of this item at a reasonable price. The former owner, James Swansan, retained the remaining 10 percent of Swansan's stock and agreed to continue managing this organization. He was given responsibility for the subsidiary's daily manufacturing operations but not for any financial decisions.

Swansan's takeover has proven to be a successful undertaking for Penston. The subsidiary has managed to supply all of the parent's inventory needs and distribute a variety of items to outside customers.

At a recent meeting, Penston's president and the company's chief financial officer began discussing Swansan's debt position. The subsidiary had a debt-to-equity ratio that seemed unreasonably high considering the significant amount of cash flows being generated by both companies. Payment of the interest expense, especially on the subsidiary's outstanding bonds, was a major cost, one that the corporate officials hoped to reduce. However, the bond indenture specified that Swansan could retire this debt prior to maturity only by paying 107 percent of face value.

This premium was considered prohibitive. Thus, to avoid contractual problems, Penston acquired a large portion of Swansan's liability in the open market for 101 percent of face value. Penston's purchase created an effective loss of $300,000 on the debt, the excess of the price over the carrying amount of the debt, as reported on Swansan's books.

Company accountants currently are computing the noncontrolling interest's share of consolidated net income to be reported for the current year. They are unsure about the impact of this $300,000 loss. The subsidiary's debt was retired, but officials of the parent company made the decision. Who lost this $300,000?

To illustrate, the 2021 journal entries for Alpha and Omega follow. Exhibit 6.7 shows the resulting account balances as of the end of that year.

EXHIBIT 6.7

ALPHA COMPANY AND OMEGA COMPANY
Effects of Intra-Entity Debt Transactions 2021

	Omega Company Reported Debt	Alpha Company Investment
2021 interest expense*	$ 95,132	$ –0–
2021 interest income†	–0–	(84,165)
Bonds payable	(1,000,000)	–0–
Discount on bonds payable*	43,552	–0–
Investment in bonds, 12/31/21†	–0–	1,046,228
Income effect within retained earnings, 1/1/21‡	94,665	(84,597)

Note: Parentheses indicate a credit balance.
*Company total is adjusted for 2021 amortization of $5,132 (see journal entry).
† Adjusted for 2021 amortization of $5,835 (see journal entry).
‡ The balance shown for the Retained Earnings account of each company represents the 2020 reported interest figures.

Omega Company's Financial Records—December 31, 2021		
Interest Expense	90,000	
Cash		90,000
To record payment of annual cash interest on $1 million, 9 percent bonds payable.		
Interest Expense	5,132	
Discount on Bonds Payable		5,132
To adjust interest expense to effective rate based on an original yield rate of 10 percent ($951,316 carrying amount for 2021 × 10% = $95,132). Carrying amount increases to $956,448.		

Alpha Company's Financial Records—December 31, 2021		
Cash	90,000	
Interest Income		90,000
To record receipt of cash interest from Omega Company bonds.		
Interest Income	5,835	
Investment in Omega Company Bonds		5,835
To reduce $90,000 interest income to effective rate based on an original yield rate of 8 percent ($1,052,063 carrying amount for 2021 × 8% = $84,165). Carrying amount decreases to $1,046,228.		

After assembling the information in Exhibit 6.7, the necessary December 31, 2021, consolidation entry is prepared. We first assume that the parent applies either the initial value or the partial equity method to its Investment in Omega account. We then show this final consolidation entry assuming the parent applies the equity method.

Parent Applies the Initial Value or Partial Equity Method

To recognize the January 1, 2020, effective retirement on the December 31, 2021, consolidated financial statements, the individual affiliate's balances for the intra-entity bonds and interest income and expense must be removed. Because neither the initial value nor the partial equity method recognizes the retirement loss, the parent's retained earnings will fail to reflect the prior year effective retirement loss. However, retained earnings will reflect past interest income and expense to the extent of any discount or premium amortization.[9] A worksheet adjustment therefore reduces Alpha's January 1, 2021, retained earnings by $110,815 to reflect the original loss net of the prior year's discount and premium amortizations.

Consolidation Entry *B, When Parent Uses the Initial Value or Partial Equity Method (December 31, 2021)		
Bonds Payable	1,000,000	
Interest Income	84,165	
Retained Earnings—Alpha	100,747	
Discount on Bond Payable		43,552
Investment in Omega Company Bonds		1,046,228
Interest Expense		95,132
To eliminate intra-entity bond and related interest accounts and to adjust Alpha's Retained Earnings from $10,068 (currently recorded net debit balance) to $110,815. (Labeled ***B** in reference to prior year bond transaction.)		

Analysis of this latest consolidation entry should emphasize several important factors:

1. The individual account balances change during the present fiscal period so that the current consolidation entry differs from Entry **B.** These alterations are a result of the amortization

[9] If there is no discount or premium amortization, interest revenue will simply offset interest expense, leaving no net effect on retained earnings.

process. To ensure the accuracy of the worksheet entry, the adjusted balances are isolated in Exhibit 6.7.

2. As indicated previously, all income effects arising from intra-entity debt transactions are assigned to the parent company. For this reason, the adjustment to beginning Retained Earnings in Entry ***B** is attributed to Alpha, as is the $10,967 increase in current income ($95,132 interest expense elimination less the $84,165 interest revenue elimination).[10] Consequently, the noncontrolling interest balances are not altered by Entry ***B.**
3. The 2021 reduction to beginning Retained Earnings in Entry ***B** ($100,747) does not agree with the original $110,815 retirement loss. The individual companies have recorded a net deficit balance of $10,068 (the amount by which previous interest expense exceeds interest revenue) at the start of 2021. To achieve the proper consolidated total, an adjustment of only $100,747 is required ($110,815 − $10,068).

Retained earnings balance—consolidation perspective (loss on retirement of debt)		$110,815
Individual retained earnings balances, 1/1/21:		
Omega Company (interest expense—2020)	$ 94,665	
Alpha Company (interest income—2020)	(84,597)	10,068
Adjustment to consolidated retained earnings, 1/1/21		$100,747

Note: Parentheses indicate a credit balance

The periodic amortization of both the bond payable discount and the premium on the investment impacts the interest expense and revenue recorded by the two companies. As this schedule shows, these two interest accounts do not offset exactly; a $10,068 net residual amount remains in Retained Earnings after the first year. Because this balance continues to increase each year, the subsequent consolidation adjustments to record the loss decrease to $100,747 in 2021 and constantly lesser thereafter. *Over the life of the bond, the amortization process gradually brings the totals in the individual Retained Earnings accounts into agreement with the consolidated balance.*

Parent Applies the Equity Method

Entry ***B** as shown is appropriate for consolidations in which the parent has applied either the initial value or the partial equity method. However, a deviation is required if the parent uses the equity method for internal reporting purposes. Properly applying the equity method ensures that the parent's income and, hence, its retained earnings are correctly stated prior to consolidation. Alpha would have already recognized the loss in accounting for this investment. Consequently, when the parent applies the equity method, no adjustment to Retained Earnings is needed. In this one case, the $100,747 debit in Entry ***B** is made to the Investment in Omega Company (instead of Retained Earnings) because the loss has become a component of that account.

Consolidation Entry *B, When Parent Uses the Equity Method (December 31, 2021)

Bonds Payable	1,000,000	
Interest Income	84,165	
Investment in Omega	100,747	
Discount on Bond Payable		43,552
Investment in Omega Company Bonds		1,046,228
Interest Expense		95,132
To eliminate intra-entity bond and related interest accounts and to adjust the Investment in Omega from $10,068 (currently recorded net debit balance) to $110,815. (Labeled "***B**" in reference to prior year bond transaction.)		

[10] Had the effects of the retirement been attributed solely to the original issuer of the bonds, the $10,967 addition to current income would have been assigned to Omega (the subsidiary), thus creating a change in the noncontrolling interest computations.

The Entry *B debit to the Investment in Omega account then serves as part of the investment account elimination sequence.

LO 6-4

Understand that subsidiary preferred stock not owned by the parent is a component of the noncontrolling interest and is initially measured at acquisition-date fair value.

Subsidiary Preferred Stock

Although both small and large corporations routinely issue preferred shares, their presence within a subsidiary's equity structure adds a new dimension to the consolidation process. What accounting should be made of a subsidiary's preferred stock and the parent's payments that are made to acquire these shares?

Recall that preferred shares, although typically nonvoting, possess other "preferences" over common shares such as a cumulative dividend preference or participation rights. Some preferred shares even offer limited voting rights. Regardless, preferred shares are part of the subsidiary's stockholders' equity and are treated as such in consolidated financial reports.

The existence of subsidiary preferred shares does little to complicate the consolidation process. The acquisition method measures all business acquisitions (whether 100 percent or less than 100 percent acquired) at their full fair values. In accounting for the acquisition of a subsidiary with preferred stock, the essential process of determining the acquisition-date business fair value of the subsidiary remains intact. Any preferred shares not owned by the parent simply become a component of the noncontrolling interest and are included in the subsidiary business fair-value calculation. The acquisition-date fair value for any subsidiary common and/or preferred shares owned by outsiders becomes the basis for the noncontrolling interest valuation in the parent's consolidated financial reports.

To illustrate, assume that on January 1, 2020, High Company acquires control over Low Company by purchasing 80 percent of its outstanding common stock and 60 percent of its nonvoting, cumulative, preferred stock. Low owns land undervalued in its records by \$100,000, but all other assets and liabilities have fair values equal to their book values. High paid \$1 million for the common shares and \$62,400 for the preferred shares. On the acquisition date, the 20 percent noncontrolling interest in the common shares had a fair value of \$250,000, and the 40 percent preferred stock noncontrolling interest had a fair value of \$41,600.

Low's capital structure immediately prior to the acquisition is as follows:

Common stock, \$20 par value (20,000 shares outstanding)	\$ 400,000
Preferred stock, 6% cumulative with a par value of \$100 (1,000 shares outstanding)	100,000
Additional paid-in capital	200,000
Retained earnings	516,000
Total stockholders' equity (book value)	\$1,216,000

Exhibit 6.8 shows High's calculation of the acquisition-date fair value of Low and the allocation of the difference between the fair and book values to land and goodwill.

As seen in Exhibit 6.8, the subsidiary's ownership structure (i.e., comprising both preferred and common shares) does not affect the fair-value principle for determining the basis for consolidating the subsidiary. Moreover, the acquisition method follows the same procedure for calculating business fair value regardless of the various preferences the preferred shares may possess. Any cumulative or participating preferences (or other rights) attributed to the preferred shares are assumed to be captured by the acquisition-date fair value of the shares and thus automatically incorporated into the subsidiary's valuation basis for consolidation.

By utilizing the preceding information, we next construct a basic worksheet entry as of January 1, 2020 (the acquisition date). In the presence of both common and preferred subsidiary shares, combining the customary consolidation entries S and A avoids an unnecessary allocation of the subsidiary's retained earnings across these equity shares. The combined

EXHIBIT 6.8

LOW COMPANY
Acquisition-Date Fair Value
January 1, 2020

Consideration transferred for 80% interest in Low's common stock	$1,000,000
Consideration transferred for 60% interest in Low's preferred stock	62,400
Noncontrolling interest in Low's common stock (20%)	250,000
Noncontrolling interest in Low's preferred stock (40%)	41,600
Total fair value of Low on 1/1/20	$1,354,000

HIGH'S ACQUISITION OF LOW
Excess Fair Value Over Book Value Allocation
January 1, 2020

Low Company business fair value		$1,354,000
Low Company book value		1,216,000
Excess acquisition-date fair value over book value		$ 138,000
Assigned to land	$100,000	
Assigned to goodwill	38,000	138,000
		$ -0-

consolidation entry also recognizes the allocations made to the undervalued land and goodwill. No other consolidation entries are needed because no time has passed since the acquisition took place.

Consolidation Entries S and A (combined)		
Common Stock (Low)	400,000	
Preferred Stock (Low)	100,000	
Additional Paid-In Capital (Low)	200,000	
Retained Earnings (Low)	516,000	
Land	100,000	
Goodwill	38,000	
Investment in Low's Common Stock		1,000,000
Investment in Low's Preferred Stock		62,400
Noncontrolling Interest		291,600
To eliminate the subsidiary's common and preferred shares, recognize the fair values of the subsidiary's assets, and recognize the outside ownership.		

The preceding combined consolidation entry recognizes the noncontrolling interest as the total of acquisition-date fair values of $250,000 for the common stock and $41,600 for the preferred shares. Consistent with previous consolidation illustrations throughout the text, the entire subsidiary's stockholders' equity section is eliminated along with the parent's investment accounts—in this case, for both the common and preferred shares.

Allocation of Subsidiary Income

The final factor influencing a consolidation that includes subsidiary preferred shares is the allocation of the company's income between the two types of stock. A division must be made for every period subsequent to the takeover (1) to compute the noncontrolling interest's share and (2) for the parent's own recognition purposes. For a cumulative nonparticipating preferred stock such as the one presently being examined, only the specified annual dividend is attributed to the preferred stock with all remaining income assigned to common stock. Consequently, if we assume that Low reports earnings of $100,000 in 2020 while declaring and paying the annual $6,000 dividend on its preferred stock, we allocate income for consolidation purposes as follows:

	Income
Subsidiary total	$100,000
Preferred stock (6% dividend × $100,000 par value of the stock)	$ 6,000
Common stock (residual amount).	94,000

During 2020, High Company, as the parent, is entitled to $3,600 in dividends ($6,000 × 60%) from Low's preferred stock because of its 60 percent ownership. In addition, High holds 80 percent of Low's common stock so that another $75,200 of the income ($94,000 × 80%) is attributed to the parent. The noncontrolling interest in consolidated net income can be calculated in a similar fashion:

		Percentage Outside Ownership	Noncontrolling Interest
Preferred stock dividend.	$ 6,000	40%	$ 2,400
Income attributed to common stock	94,000	20	18,800
Noncontrolling interest in consolidated net income			$21,200

LO 6-5

Prepare a consolidated statement of cash flows.

Consolidated Statement of Cash Flows

Current accounting standards require that companies include a statement of cash flows among their consolidated financial reports. The main purpose of the statement of cash flows is to provide information about the entity's cash receipts and cash payments during a period. The statement is also designed to show why an entity's net income is different from its operating cash flows. For a consolidated entity, the cash flows relate to the entire business combination, including the parent and all of its subsidiaries.

The statement of cash flows allocates the consolidated entity's overall change in cash during a period to three separate categories:

1. Cash flows from operating activities.
2. Cash flows from investing activities.
3. Cash flows from financing activities.

The cash flows from operating activities can be shown using either the indirect method or the direct method. The indirect method begins with consolidated net income and then adds and subtracts various items to adjust the accrual number to a cash flow amount. The direct method examines cash flows directly from distinct sources that typically include revenues, purchases of inventory, and cash payments of other expenses. However, firms using the direct method must also supplement the statement with the calculation of cash flows from operating activities using the indirect method.

The consolidated statement of cash flows is not prepared from the individual cash flow statements of the separate companies. Instead, the consolidated income statements and balance sheets are first brought together on the worksheet. The cash flows statement is then based on the resulting consolidated figures. Thus, this statement is not actually produced by a consolidation worksheet but is created from numbers generated by the process. Because special accounting procedures are needed in the period when the parent acquires a subsidiary, we first discuss preparation of the consolidated statement of cash flows for periods in which an acquisition takes place, followed by statement preparation in periods subsequent to acquisition.

Acquisition Period Statement of Cash Flows

If a business combination occurs during a particular reporting period, the consolidated cash flow statement must properly reflect several considerations. For many business combinations, the following issues frequently are present.

Business Acquisitions in Exchange for Cash

Cash purchases of businesses are an investing activity. The *net cash outflow* (cash paid less subsidiary cash acquired) is reported as the amount paid in a business acquisition.[11]

Operating Cash Flow Adjustments

Keeping in mind that the focus is on the consolidated entity's cash flows (not just the parent's), consolidated net income is the starting point for the indirect calculation of consolidated operating cash flows. Recall that consolidated net income includes only postacquisition subsidiary revenues and expenses. Therefore, the adjustment to the accrual-based income number must also reflect only postacquisition amounts for the subsidiary. One important category of adjustments to consolidated net income to arrive at cash flows from operations involves changes in current operating accounts (e.g., accounts receivable, accounts payable, etc.).

For example, an increase in an accounts receivable balance typically indicates that a firm's accrual-based sales exceed the actual cash collections for sales during a period. Therefore, in computing operating cash flows, the increase in accounts receivable are deducted from the sales amount (direct method) or the net income (indirect method). However, when an acquisition takes place, the change in accounts receivable will often include amounts from the newly acquired subsidiary. Because the consolidated entity recognizes only postacquisition subsidiary revenues, such acquired receivables do not reflect sales that have been made by the consolidated entity. Therefore, any subsidiary acquisition-date current operating account balances must be removed before calculating the change in accounts receivable.

In fact, any changes in operating balance sheet accounts (accounts receivable, inventory, accounts payable, etc.) must be computed net of the amounts acquired in the combination. Use of the direct method of presenting operating cash flows also reports the separate computations of cash collected from customers and cash paid for inventory net of acquisition-date balances of newly acquired businesses.

Excess Fair-Value Amortizations

Any adjustments arising from the subsidiary's revenues or expenses (e.g., depreciation, amortization) must reflect only postacquisition amounts. Closing the subsidiary's books at the date of acquisition facilitates the determination of the appropriate current year postacquisition subsidiary effects on the consolidated entity's cash flows.

Subsidiary Dividends Paid

The cash outflow from subsidiary dividends only leaves the consolidated entity when paid to the noncontrolling interest. Thus, dividends paid by a subsidiary to its parent do not appear as financing outflows. However, subsidiary dividends paid to the noncontrolling interest are a component of cash outflows from financing activities.

Intra-Entity Transfers

A significant volume of transfers between affiliated companies comprising a business combination often occurs. The resulting effects of intra-entity activities are eliminated in the preparation of consolidated statements. Likewise, the consolidated statement of cash flows does not include the impact of these transfers. Intra-entity sales and purchases do not change the amount of cash held by the business combination when viewed as a whole. Because the statement of cash flows is derived from the consolidated balance sheet and income statement, the impact of all transfers is already removed. Therefore, the proper presentation of cash flows

[11] For acquisitions that do not involve cash, or only partially involve cash, the details of the acquisitions should be provided in a supplemental disclosure to the statement of cash flows for "significant noncash investing and financing activities."

requires no special adjustments for intra-entity transfers. The worksheet entries produce correct balances for the consolidated statement of cash flows.

Consolidated Statement of Cash Flows Illustration

Assume that on July 1, 2020, Pinto Company acquires 90 percent of Salida Company's outstanding stock for $774,000 in cash. At the acquisition date, the 10 percent noncontrolling interest has a fair value of $86,000. Exhibit 6.9 shows book and fair values of Salida's assets and liabilities and Pinto's acquisition-date fair-value allocation schedule.

At the end of 2020, the following comparative balance sheets and consolidated income statement are available:

PINTO COMPANY AND SUBSIDIARY SALIDA COMPANY
Comparative Balance Sheets

	Pinto Co. January 1, 2020	Consolidated December 31, 2020
Cash	$ 170,000	$ 431,000
Accounts receivable (net)	118,000	319,000
Inventory	310,000	395,000
Land	250,000	370,000
Buildings (net)	350,000	426,000
Equipment (net)	1,145,000	1,380,000
Database	–0–	49,000
Total assets	$2,343,000	$3,370,000
Accounts payable	$ 50,000	$ 45,000
Long-term liabilities	18,000	522,000
Common stock	1,500,000	1,500,000
Noncontrolling interest	–0–	98,250
Retained earnings	775,000	1,204,750
Total liabilities and equities	$2,343,000	$3,370,000

PINTO COMPANY AND SUBSIDIARY SALIDA COMPANY
Consolidated Income Statement (partial presentation)
For the Year Ended December 31, 2020

Revenues		$1,255,000
Cost of goods sold	$600,000	
Depreciation	124,000	
Database amortization	1,000	
Interest and other expenses	35,500	760,500
Consolidated net income		$ 494,500

Additional Information for 2020

- The consolidated income statement totals include Salida's postacquisition revenues and expenses.
- During the year, Pinto paid $50,000 in dividends. On August 1, Salida paid a $25,000 dividend.
- During the year, Pinto issued $504,000 in long-term debt at par value.
- No asset purchases or dispositions occurred during the year other than Pinto's acquisition of Salida.

In preparing the consolidated statement of cash flows, note that each adjustment derives from the consolidated income statement or changes from Pinto's January 1, 2020, balance sheet to the consolidated balance sheet at December 31, 2020.

EXHIBIT 6.9

SALIDA COMPANY
Book and Fair Values
July 1, 2020

Account	Book Value	Fair Value
Cash	$ 35,000	$ 35,000
Accounts receivable	145,000	145,000
Inventory	90,000	90,000
Land	100,000	120,000
Buildings	136,000	136,000
Equipment	259,000	299,000
Database	–0–	50,000
Accounts payable	(15,000)	(15,000)
Net book value	$750,000	$860,000

PINTO'S ACQUISITION OF SALIDA
Excess Fair Value over Book Value Allocation
July 1, 2020

Consideration transferred by Pinto		$774,000
Noncontrolling interest fair value		86,000
Salida's total fair value		$860,000
Salida's book value		750,000
Excess fair over book value		$110,000
To land	$ 20,000	
To equipment (5-year remaining life)	40,000	
To database (25-year remaining life)	50,000	110,000
		$ –0–

Depreciation and Amortization

These expenses do not represent current operating cash outflows and thus are added back to convert accrual basis income to cash provided by operating activities.

Increases in Accounts Receivable, Inventory, and Accounts Payable (net of acquisition)

Changes in balance sheet accounts affecting operating cash flows must take into account amounts acquired in business acquisitions. In this case, note that the changes in Accounts Receivable, Inventory, and Accounts Payable are computed as follows:

	Accounts Receivable	Inventory	Accounts Payable
Pinto's balance, 1/1/20	$118,000	$310,000	$50,000
Increase from Salida acquisition	145,000	90,000	15,000
Adjusted beginning balance	263,000	400,000	65,000
Consolidated balance, 12/31/20	319,000	395,000	45,000
Operating cash flow adjustment	$ 56,000	$ 5,000	$20,000

Acquisition of Salida Company

The Investing Activities section of the cash flow statement shows increases and decreases in assets purchased or sold involving cash. The cash outflow from the acquisition of Salida Company is determined as follows:

Cash paid for 90% interest in Salida	$774,000
Cash acquired	(35,000)
Net cash paid for Salida investment	$739,000

Note here that although Pinto acquires only 90 percent of Salida, 100 percent of Salida's cash is offset against the cash consideration paid in the acquisition in determining the investing cash outflow. Ownership divisions between the noncontrolling and controlling interests do not affect reporting for the entity's investing cash flows.

Issue of Long-Term Debt

Pinto Company's issuance of long-term debt represents a cash inflow from financing activities.

Dividends

The dividends paid to Pinto Company owners ($50,000) combined with the dividends paid to the noncontrolling interest ($2,500) represent cash outflows from financing activities.

Based on the consolidated totals from the comparative balance sheets and the consolidated income statement, the following consolidated statement of cash flows is then prepared. Pinto chooses to use the indirect method of reporting cash flows from operating activities.

PINTO COMPANY AND SUBSIDIARY SALIDA COMPANY
Consolidated Statement of Cash Flows (partial presentation)
For the Year Ended December 31, 2020

Consolidated net income		$ 494,500
Depreciation expense	$ 124,000	
Amortization expense	1,000	
Increase in accounts receivable (net of acquisition effects)	(56,000)	
Decrease in inventory (net of acquisition effects)	5,000	
Decrease in accounts payable (net of acquisition effects)	(20,000)	54,000
Net cash provided by operating activities		$ 548,500
Purchase of Salida Company (net of cash acquired)		
Net cash used in investing activities	$(739,000)	(739,000)
Issue long-term debt	$ 504,000	
Dividends	(52,500)	
Net cash provided by financing activities		451,500
Increase in Cash, 1/1/20 to 12/31/20		**$261,000**

Statement of Cash Flows in Periods Subsequent to Acquisition

Preparing a consolidated statement of cash flows during periods of no acquisition is relatively uncomplicated. As before, consolidated net income is the starting point for the indirect calculation of consolidated operating cash flows. If the operating accounts (e.g., accounts receivable, accounts payable, etc.) do not include amounts acquired in a business combination, then no further special adjustments are required. Because the consolidation process eliminates intra-entity balances, preparation of the operating activity section of the statement of cash flows typically proceeds in a straightforward manner using the already available consolidated income statement and balance sheet amounts. Finally, subsidiary dividends paid to the noncontrolling interest are shown as a component of cash outflows from financing activities.

LO 6-6

Compute basic and diluted earnings per share for a business combination.

Consolidated Earnings per Share

The consolidation process affects one other intermediate accounting topic, the computation of earnings per share (EPS). Publicly held companies must disclose EPS each period.

The following steps calculate such figures:

- Determine basic EPS by dividing the parent's share of consolidated net income (after reduction for preferred stock dividends) by the weighted-average number of common stock shares outstanding for the period. If the reporting entity has no dilutive options, warrants, or other convertible items, only basic EPS is presented on the face of the income statement. However, diluted EPS also must be presented if any dilutive convertibles are present.

- Compute diluted EPS by combining the effects of *any dilutive securities* with basic earnings per share. Stock options, stock warrants, convertible debt, and convertible preferred stock often qualify as dilutive securities.[12]

In most instances, the computation of EPS for a business combination follows the same general pattern. Consolidated net income attributable to the parent company owners, along with the number of outstanding parent shares, provides the basis for calculating basic EPS. Any convertibles, warrants, or options for the parent's stock that can possibly dilute the reported figure must be included as described earlier in determining diluted EPS.

However, a problem arises if warrants, options, or convertibles that can dilute the subsidiary's earnings are outstanding. Although the parent company is not directly affected, the potential impact of these items on its share of consolidated net income must be given weight in computing diluted EPS for the consolidated income statement. Because of possible conversion, the subsidiary earnings figure included in consolidated net income is not necessarily applicable to the diluted EPS computation. *Thus, the accountant must separately determine the parent's share of subsidiary income that should be used in deriving diluted EPS.*

Finally, the focus is on earnings per share for the parent company stockholders, even in the presence of a noncontrolling interest. As stated in FASB ASC (para. 260-10-45-11A):

> For purposes of computing EPS in consolidated financial statements (both basic and diluted), if one or more less-than-wholly-owned subsidiaries are included in the consolidated group, income from continuing operations and net income shall exclude the income attributable to the noncontrolling interest in subsidiaries.

Thus, consolidated income attributable to the parent's interest forms the basis for the numerator in all EPS calculations for consolidated financial reporting.

Earnings per Share Illustration

Assume Big Corporation has 100,000 shares of its common stock outstanding during the current year. The company also has issued 20,000 shares of nonvoting preferred stock, paying an annual cumulative preferred dividend of $5 per share ($100,000 total). Each of these preferred shares is convertible into two shares of Big's common stock.

Assume also that Big owns 90 percent of Little's common stock and 60 percent of its preferred stock (which pays $12,000 in preferred dividends per year). Annual amortization is $26,000, attributable to various intangibles. Big is preparing its EPS computations for 2020. During the year, Big reported separate income of $600,000, and Little earned $100,000. A simplified consolidation of the figures for the year indicates consolidated net income attributable to Big of $663,000:

Big's separate income for 2020		$600,000
Little's separate income for 2020	$100,000	
Amortization expense resulting from original fair-value allocation	(26,000)	
Little's income after excess fair-value amortization		74,000
Consolidated net income		$674,000
Noncontrolling interest in Little—common stock (10% × $62,000 [$74,000 income less $12,000 preferred stock dividends])	$ (6,200)	
Noncontrolling interest in Little—preferred stock (40% of dividends)	(4,800)	
Net income attributable to the noncontrolling interest		(11,000)
Net income attributable to Big (parent)		$663,000

[12] Complete coverage of the EPS computation can be found in virtually any intermediate accounting textbook. To adequately understand this process, a number of complex procedures must be mastered, including calculating the weighted-average number of common shares outstanding and understanding the method of including stock rights, convertible debt, and convertible preferred stock within the computation of diluted EPS.

Little has 20,000 shares of common stock and 4,000 shares of preferred stock outstanding. The preferred shares pay a $3 per year dividend, and each can be converted into two shares of common stock (or 8,000 shares in total). Because Big owns only 60 percent of Little's preferred stock, a $4,800 dividend is distributed each year to the outside owners (40 percent of the $12,000 total payment).

Assume finally that the subsidiary also has $200,000 in convertible bonds outstanding that were originally issued at face value. This debt has both a cash and an effective interest rate of 10 percent ($20,000 per year) and can be converted by the owners into 9,000 shares of Little's common stock. Big owns none of these bonds. Little's tax rate is 21 percent.

To better visualize these factors, the convertible items are scheduled as follows:

Company	Item	Interest or Dividend	Conversion	Big Owns
Big	Preferred stock	$100,000/year	40,000 shares	Not applicable
Little	Preferred stock	12,000/year	8,000 shares	60%
Little	Bonds	15,800/year*	9,000 shares	–0–

*Interest on the bonds is shown net of the 21 percent tax effect ($20,000 interest less $4,200 tax savings). No tax is computed for the preferred shares because distributed dividends do not create a tax impact.

Because the subsidiary has convertible items that can affect the company's outstanding shares and net income, Little's diluted earnings per share must be derived *before* Big's diluted EPS can be determined. As shown in Exhibit 6.10, Little's diluted EPS are $2.43. Two aspects of this schedule should be noted:

- The individual impact of the convertibles ($1.50 for the preferred stock and $1.76 for the bonds) did not raise the EPS figures above the $3.10 basic EPS. Thus, neither the preferred stock nor the bonds are antidilutive, and both are properly included in these computations.
- Absent the presence of the subsidiary's convertible bonds and preferred stock, the parent's share of consolidated net income would form the basis for computing EPS.

As shown in Exhibit 6.10, Little's income is $89,800 for diluted EPS. The issue then becomes how much of this amount should be included in computing the parent's diluted EPS. This allocation is based on the percentage of shares controlled by the parent. Note that if the subsidiary's preferred stock and bonds are converted into common shares, Big's ownership falls from 90 to 62 percent. For diluted EPS, 37,000 shares are appropriate. Big's 62 percent ownership (22,800/37,000) is the basis for allocating the subsidiary's $89,800 income to the parent.

EXHIBIT 6.10
Subsidiary's Diluted Earnings per Share

LITTLE COMPANY
Basic and Diluted Earnings per Common Share
For Year Ending December 31, 2020

	Earnings		Shares	
Little's income after amortization . . .	$74,000		20,000	
Preferred stock dividends	(12,000)			
Basic EPS	$62,000		20,000	$3.10 ($62,000/20,000)
Effect of possible preferred stock conversion:				
Dividends saved	$12,000	New shares	8,000	$1.50 impact ($12,000/8,000)
Effect of possible bond conversion:				
Interest saved (net of taxes)	$15,800		9,000	$1.76 impact ($15,800/9,000)
Diluted EPS	$89,800		37,000	$ 2.43 (rounded)

EXHIBIT 6.11

BIG COMPANY AND CONSOLIDATED SUBSIDIARY
Basic Earnings per Common Share
For Year Ending December 31, 2020

	Earnings		Shares	
Consolidated net income (to Big). . .	$663,000			
Big's shares outstanding			100,000	
Preferred stock dividends (Big) . . .	(100,000)			
Basic EPS	$563,000		100,000	$5.63

Diluted Earnings per Common Share
For Year Ending December 31, 2020

	Earnings		Shares	
Computed below	$655,676*			
Big's shares outstanding			100,000	
Preferred stock dividends (Big) . . .	(100,000)			
Effect of possible preferred stock (Big) conversion:				
Dividends saved	100,000	New shares	40,000	$2.50 impact (100,000/40,000)
Diluted EPS.	$655,676		140,000	$4.68 (rounded)

*Net income computation:

Big's separate income	$600,000	
Portion of Little's income assigned to diluted earnings per share calculation	55,676	(computed in supporting calculations)
Earnings of the business combination applicable to diluted earnings per share	$655,676	

Supporting Calculations for Diluted Earnings per Share

	Little Company Shares	Big's Percentage	Big's Ownership
Common stock	20,000	90%	18,000
Possible new shares—preferred stock	8,000	60	4,800
Possible new shares—bonds	9,000	–0–	–0–
Total	37,000		22,800

Big's ownership (diluted): 22,800/37,000 = 62% (rounded)
Income assigned to Big (diluted earnings per share computation): $89,800 × 62% = $55,676

We can now determine Big Company's EPS. Only $55,676 of subsidiary income is appropriate for computing diluted EPS. Because separate income figures are utilized, Exhibit 6.11 above shows separate basic and diluted EPS calculations. Consequently, Big Company reports basic EPS of $5.63 and diluted earnings per share of $4.68.

LO 6-7

Demonstrate the accounting effects of subsidiary stock transactions on the parent's financial records and consolidated financial statements.

Subsidiary Stock Transactions

A note to the financial statements of Gerber Products Company disclosed a transaction carried out by one of the organization's subsidiaries: "The Company's wholly owned Mexican subsidiary sold previously unissued shares of common stock to Grupo Coral, S.A., a Mexican food company, at a price in excess of the shares' net book value." The note added that Gerber had increased consolidated Additional Paid-In Capital by $432,000 as a result of this stock sale.

As this illustration shows, subsidiary stock transactions can alter the level of parent ownership. A subsidiary, for example, can decide to sell previously unissued stock to raise needed capital. Although the parent company can acquire a portion or even all of these new shares, such issues frequently are marketed entirely to outsiders. A subsidiary could also be legally forced to sell additional shares of its stock. As an example, companies holding control over foreign subsidiaries occasionally encounter this problem because of laws in the individual localities. Regulations requiring a certain percentage of local ownership as a prerequisite for operating within a country can mandate issuance of new shares. Of course, changes in the level of parent ownership do not result solely from stock sales: A subsidiary also can repurchase its own stock. The acquisition, as well as the possible retirement, of such treasury shares serves as a means of reducing the percentage of outside ownership.

Changes in Subsidiary Value—Stock Transactions

When a subsidiary subsequently buys or sells its own stock, a nonoperational increase or decrease occurs in the company's fair and book value. Because the transaction need not involve the parent, the parent's investment account does not automatically reflect the effect of this change. However, the parent's percentage ownership of the subsidiary may change. *Thus, a separate adjustment must be recorded to maintain reciprocity between the subsidiary's stockholders' equity accounts and the parent's investment balance.* The accountant measures the impact the stock transaction has on the parent to ensure that this effect is appropriately recorded in the parent's investment account and then reflected in the consolidation process.

An overall perspective of accounting for subsidiary stock transactions follows from the fundamental notion that the parent establishes the subsidiary's valuation basis at fair value as of the acquisition date. Over time, the parent adjusts this initial fair value for subsidiary income less excess amortization and subsidiary dividends. If the subsidiary issues (or buys) any of its own stock subsequent to acquisition, the effect on the parent will depend on whether the price received (or paid) is greater or less than the per-share subsidiary adjusted fair value at that point in time.

An example demonstrates the mechanics of this issue. Assume that on January 1, 2020, Giant Company acquires in the open market 60,000 of Small Company's outstanding 80,000 shares and prepares the following fair-value allocation schedule:

Consideration transferred by Giant	$480,000	
Noncontrolling interest fair value	160,000	
Small Company acquisition-date fair value		$640,000
Small Company acquisition-date book value		
Common stock (80,000 shares outstanding)	$ 80,000	
Additional paid-in capital	200,000	
Retained earnings, 1/1/20	260,000	540,000
Excess fair value assigned to trademark (10-year remaining life)		$100,000

Assuming Small reports earnings of $50,000 in 2020 and pays no dividends, Giant prepares the following routine consolidation entries for the December 31, 2020, worksheet. Giant uses the equity method to account for its 75 percent interest in Small.

December 31, 2020, Consolidation Worksheet Entries

Consolidation Entry S		
Common Stock (Small Company)	80,000	
Additional Paid-In Capital (Small Company)	200,000	
Retained Earnings, 1/1/20 (Small Company)	260,000	
Investment in Small Company (75%)		405,000
Noncontrolling Interest in Small Company (25%)		135,000
To eliminate subsidiary's stockholders' equity accounts and recognize noncontrolling interest beginning balance in Small's book value.		

Consolidation Entry A		
Trademark	100,000	
Investment in Small Company (75%)		75,000
Noncontrolling Interest in Small Company (25%)		25,000
To recognize the excess acquisition-date fair value assigned to Small's trademark with allocations to the controlling and noncontrolling interest.		

Consolidation Entry I		
Equity in Small's Earnings	30,000	
Investment in Small Company		30,000
To eliminate Giant's equity in Small's earnings [75% × ($50,000 less $10,000 trademark excess amortization)].		

Consolidation Entry E		
Amortization Expense	10,000	
Trademark		10,000
To recognize the excess trademark amortization ($100,000 ÷ 10 years).		

We now introduce a subsidiary stock transaction to demonstrate the effect created on the consolidation process. Assume that on January 1, 2021, Giant announces plans for expansion of Small's operations. To help finance the expansion, Small sells 20,000 previously unissued shares of its common stock to outside parties for $10 per share. After the stock issue, Small's book value is as follows:

Common stock ($1.00 par value with 100,000 shares issued and outstanding)	$100,000
Additional paid-in capital	380,000
Retained earnings, 1/1/21	310,000
Total stockholders' equity, 1/1/21	$790,000

Note that the common stock and additional paid-in capital balances reflect increases from the new stock issue. Retained earnings have also increased from Small's $50,000 income in 2020 (no dividends). Although Small's book value is now $790,000, its valuation for the consolidated entity is derived from its acquisition-date fair value as adjusted through time as follows:

Consideration transferred	$480,000
Noncontrolling interest acquisition-date fair value	160,000
2017 Small income less excess amortization	40,000
Adjusted subsidiary value, 1/1/21	$680,000
Stock issue proceeds ($10 × 20,000 shares)	200,000
Subsidiary valuation basis, 1/1/21	$880,000

Because of Small's stock issue, Giant no longer possesses a 75 percent interest. Instead, the parent now holds 60 percent (60,000 shares of a total of 100,000 shares) of Small Company. The effect on the parent's ownership can be computed as follows:

Small's valuation basis, 1/1/21 (above)	$880,000
Giant's post-issue ownership (60,000 shares ÷ 100,000 shares)	60%
Giant's post, stock issue ownership balance	$528,000
Giant's equity-adjusted investment account [$480,000 + (75% × $40,000)]	510,000
Required adjustment—increase in Giant's additional paid-in capital	$ 18,000

Independent of any action by the parent company, the assigned fair-value equivalency of this investment has risen from $510,000 to $528,000. Small's ability to sell shares of stock at more than the per-share consolidated subsidiary value ($680,000 ÷ 80,000 shares = $8.50 per share) created an increased value for the parent. Therefore, Giant records the $18,000 increment as an adjustment to both its investment account (because the underlying value of the subsidiary has increased) and additional paid-in capital:

Giant Company's Financial Records—January 1, 2021		
Investment in Small Company	18,000	
Additional Paid-In Capital (Giant Company)		18,000
To recognize change in equity of business combination created by Small Company issuing 20,000 additional shares of common stock at above the previously assigned fair value.		

Note that the parent reports a change in stockholders' equity (i.e., Additional Paid-In Capital) for effects from subsidiary stock transactions. GAAP literature states that

> [c]hanges in a parent's ownership interest while the parent retains its controlling financial interest in its subsidiary shall be accounted for as equity transactions (investments by owners and distributions to owners acting in their capacity as owners). Therefore, no gain or loss shall be recognized in consolidated net income or comprehensive income. The carrying amount of the noncontrolling interest shall be adjusted to reflect the change in its ownership interest in the subsidiary. Any difference between the fair value of the consideration received or paid and the amount by which the noncontrolling interest is adjusted shall be recognized in equity attributable to the parent. (FASB ASC [para. 810-10-45-23])

Consistent with this view, this textbook treats the effects from subsidiary stock transactions on the consolidated entity as adjustments to Additional Paid-In Capital.

After the change in the parent's records has been made, the consolidation process can proceed in a normal fashion. Assuming Small reports earnings of $85,000 in 2021 and pays no dividends, Giant prepares the following routine consolidation entries for the December 31, 2021, worksheet. *Although the investment and subsidiary equity accounts are removed here, the change recorded earlier in Giant's Additional Paid-In Capital remains within the consolidated figures.*

December 31, 2021, Consolidation Worksheet Entries

Consolidation Entry S		
Common Stock (Small Company)	100,000	
Additional Paid-In Capital (Small Company)	380,000	
Retained Earnings (Small Company)	310,000	
Investment in Small Company (60%)		474,000
Noncontrolling Interest in Small Company (40%)		316,000
To eliminate subsidiary's stockholders' equity accounts and recognize noncontrolling interest book value beginning balance. Small's capital accounts have been updated to reflect the issuance of 20,000 shares of $1 par value common stock at $10 per share.		

Consolidation Entry A		
Trademark	90,000	
Investment in Small Company (60%)		54,000
Noncontrolling Interest in Small Company (40%)		36,000
To recognize the unamortized excess acquisition-date fair value assigned to Small's trademark as of the beginning of the period with allocations to the controlling and noncontrolling interests' adjusted ownership percentages.		

Consolidation Entry I		
Equity in Small's Earnings	45,000	
Investment in Small Company		45,000
To eliminate Giant's equity in Small's earnings [60% × ($85,000 – $10,000 trademark excess amortization)].		

Consolidation Entry E		
Amortization Expense	10,000	
Trademark		10,000
To recognize the excess trademark amortization ($100,000 ÷ 10 years).		

The noncontrolling interest now stands at 40 percent ownership. Because these 40 percent owners will share in the profits generated by the subsidiary's trademark, they are allocated a 40 percent share to their overall equity balance in the consolidated financial statements. The noncontrolling interest is also assigned 40 percent of the excess fair-value trademark amortization.

Subsidiary Stock Transactions—Illustrated

No single example can demonstrate the many possible variations that different types of subsidiary stock transactions could create. To provide a working knowledge of this process, we analyze four additional cases briefly, each based on the following scenario.

Assume that Antioch Company acquires 90 percent of the common stock of Westminster Company on January 1, 2020, in exchange for $1,350,000 cash. The acquisition-date fair value of the 10 percent noncontrolling interest is $150,000. At that date, Westminster has the following stockholders' equity accounts:

Common stock—100,000 shares outstanding	$ 200,000
Additional paid-in capital	450,000
Retained earnings, 1/1/20	750,000
Total stockholders' equity	$1,400,000

The $100,000 excess acquisition-date fair over book value was allocated to a customer list with a five-year remaining life. In 2020, Westminster reports $190,000 in earnings and declares a $30,000 dividend. Antioch accrues its share of Westminster's income (less excess fair-value amortization related to the customer list) through application of the equity method. Antioch's equity method balance for its investment in Westminster is computed as follows:

Consideration transferred for 90% of Westminster	$1,350,000
Equity earnings of Westminster [90% × ($190,000 – $20,000 excess amortization)]	153,000
Dividends from Westminster (90% × $30,000)	(27,000)
Equity method balance, 12/31/20	$1,476,000

View each of the following cases as an independent situation.

Case 1

Assume that on January 1, 2021, Westminster Company sells 25,000 shares of previously unissued common stock to outside parties for $14.40 per share. This stock issue changes both the parent's percentage interest in the subsidiary and the subsidiary's consolidated valuation basis. The parent's percentage ownership declines to 72 percent (90,000 shares ÷ 125,000 total shares). The subsidiary's valuation basis for consolidation becomes the following:

Consideration transferred	$1,350,000
Noncontrolling interest acquisition-date fair value	150,000
2020 Westminster income less excess amortization	170,000
Westminster dividends	(30,000)
Stock issue proceeds ($14.40 × 25,000 shares)	360,000
Subsidiary valuation basis, 1/1/21	$2,000,000

Next, the effect on the parent's ownership can be computed as follows:

Westminster's valuation basis, 1/1/21 (above)	$2,000,000
Antioch's post, stock issue ownership (90,000 shares ÷ 125,000 shares)	72%
Antioch's post, stock issue ownership balance	$1,440,000
Antioch's pre, stock issue equity-adjusted investment account (above)	1,476,000
Required adjustment—decrease in Antioch's additional paid-in capital	$ 36,000

To reflect this effect of the stock issue change on its valuation of the subsidiary, the parent makes the following journal entry on its financial records.

Antioch Company's Financial Records		
Additional Paid-In Capital (Antioch Company)	36,000	
Investment in Westminster Company		36,000
To recognize change in equity of business combination created by issuance of 25,000 additional shares of Westminster's common stock.		

Case 2

Assume that on January 1, 2021, Westminster issues 20,000 new shares of common stock for $16 per share. Of this total, Antioch acquires 18,000 shares to maintain its 90 percent level of ownership. Antioch pays a total of $288,000 (18,000 shares × $16) for this additional stock. Outside parties buy the remaining shares.

Under these circumstances, the stock transaction alters the consolidated valuation basis of the subsidiary but not the percentage owned by the parent. Thus, only the subsidiary value must be updated prior to determining the necessity of an equity revaluation:

Consideration transferred	$1,350,000
Noncontrolling interest acquisition-date fair value	150,000
2020 Westminster income less excess amortization	170,000
Westminster dividends	(30,000)
Stock issue proceeds ($16 × 20,000 shares)	320,000
Subsidiary valuation basis 1/1/21	$1,960,000

The effect on the parent's ownership is computed as follows:

Westminster's valuation basis 1/1/21 (above)		$1,960,000
Antioch's post, stock issue ownership (108,000 shares ÷ 120,000 shares)		90%
Antioch's post, stock issue ownership balance		$1,764,000
Antioch's equity-adjusted investment account before stock purchase	$1,476,000	
Additional payment for 18,000 shares of Westminster	288,000	1,764,000
Required adjustment		$ –0–

This case requires no adjustment because Antioch's underlying interest remains aligned with the subsidiary's consolidated valuation basis. Any purchase of new stock by the parent in the same ratio as previous ownership does not affect consolidated Additional Paid-In Capital. The transaction creates no proportionate increase or decrease.

Case 3

Assume that instead of issuing new stock, on January 1, 2021, Westminster reacquires all 10,000 shares owned by the noncontrolling interest. It pays $16 per share for this treasury stock.

This illustration presents another type of subsidiary stock transaction: the acquisition of treasury stock. In this case, the effect on the parent can be computed by reference to the amount of noncontrolling interest that must be reduced to zero in the consolidated financial statements.

Noncontrolling interest (NCI) acquisition-date fair value	$ 150,000
NCI share of 2020 Westminster income less excess amortization ($170,000 × 10%)	17,000
NCI share of Westminster dividends ($30,000 × 10%)	(3,000)
Noncontrolling interest valuation basis at 1/1/21	$ 164,000
Treasury stock purchase ($16 × 10,000 shares)	(160,000)
Required adjustment—increase in Antioch's additional paid-in capital	$ 4,000

The consolidated entity paid $160,000 to reduce a $164,000 owners' equity interest (the noncontrolling interest) to zero, thus increasing its own equity by $4,000. As usual, the increase in equity is attributed to additional paid-in capital and is recorded on the parent's records.

Antioch Company's Financial Records		
Investment in Westminster Company	4,000	
Additional Paid-In Capital (Antioch Company)		4,000
To recognize change in equity of business combination created by acquisition of 10,000 treasury shares by Westminster.		

This third illustration represents a newly introduced subsidiary stock transaction, the purchase of treasury stock. Therefore, display of consolidation Entries **S** and **A** are also presented. These entries demonstrate the worksheet eliminations required when the subsidiary holds treasury shares:

Consolidation Entry S		
Common Stock (Westminster Company)	200,000	
Additional Paid-In Capital (Westminster Company)	450,000	
Retained Earnings, 1/1/21 (Westminster Company)	910,000	
Treasury Stock		160,000
Investment in Westminster Company		1,400,000
To eliminate equity accounts of Westminster Company.		

Consolidation Entry A		
Customer List	80,000	
Investment in Westminster Company		80,000
To recognize the beginning-of-year unamortized excess acquisition-date fair value allocated to the customer list.		

Note first the absence of a noncontrolling interest entry. Also note that the sum of the credits to the Investment in Westminster account is $1,480,000, which is the pretreasury stock purchase equity method balance of $1,476,000 plus the $4,000 addition from the acquisition of the noncontrolling interest.

Case 4

Assume that on January 1, 2021, Westminster issues a 10 percent stock dividend (10,000 new shares) to its owners when the stock's fair value is $15 per share.

This final case illustrates another example of a subsidiary stock transaction producing no effect on the parent's records. Stock dividends, whether large or small, capitalize a portion of the issuing company's retained earnings without altering total book value. Shareholders recognize the receipt of a stock dividend as a change in the per share value rather than as an adjustment to the investment balance. Because neither party perceives a net effect, the consolidation process proceeds in a routine fashion. Therefore, a subsidiary stock dividend requires no special treatment prior to development of a worksheet.

Consideration transferred	$1,350,000
Noncontrolling interest acquisition-date fair value	150,000
2020 Westminster income less excess amortization	170,000
Westminster dividends	(30,000)
Subsidiary valuation basis, 1/1/21	$1,640,000
Antioch's ownership (adjusted for 10% stock dividend 99,000 ÷ 110,000 shares)	90%
Antioch's post, stock dividend ownership interest	$1,476,000
Antioch's equity-adjusted investment account	1,476,000
Adjustment required by stock dividend	$ –0–

The consolidation Entries **S** and **A** made just after the stock dividend follow. The $1,404,000 component of the investment account is offset against the stockholders' equity of the subsidiary. Although the stock dividend did not affect the parent's investment, the equity accounts of the subsidiary have been realigned in recognition of the $150,000 stock dividend (10,000 shares of $2 par value stock valued at $15 per share):

Consolidation Entry S		
Common Stock (Westminster Company)	220,000	
Additional Paid-In Capital (Westminster Company)	580,000	
Retained Earnings, 1/1/21 (Westminster Company)	760,000	
Investment in Westminster Company (90%)		1,404,000
Noncontrolling Interest (10%)		156,000

Consolidation Entry A		
Customer List	80,000	
Investment in Westminster Company		72,000
Noncontrolling Interest		8,000
To recognize the beginning-of-year unamortized excess fair value attributable to the customer list.		

Note here that the sum of the credits to the Investment in Westminster account is $1,476,000, which equals the pre–stock dividend equity method balance.

Summary

1. Variable interest entities (VIEs) typically take the form of a trust, partnership, joint venture, or corporation. In most cases, a sponsoring firm creates these entities to engage in a limited and well-defined set of business activities. Control of VIEs, by design, often does not rest with their equity holders. Instead, control is exercised through contractual arrangements with the sponsoring firm that becomes the entity's "primary beneficiary." These contracts can take the form of leases, participation rights, guarantees, or other residual interests. Through contracting, the primary beneficiary bears a significant portion of the risks and receives a significant portion of the rewards of the entity, often without owning any voting shares. Current accounting standards require a business that has a controlling financial interest in a VIE to consolidate the financial statements of the VIE with its own.
2. In periods after the primary beneficiary gains control over a VIE, consolidation procedures follow a similar process as if the entity were controlled by voting interests. All intra-entity transactions between the primary beneficiary and the VIE must be eliminated in consolidation. The consolidated net income distribution to the noncontrolling interest, however, must be based on the contractual agreement with the primary beneficiary, rather than voting interests.
3. If one member of a business combination acquires an affiliate's debt instrument (e.g., a bond or note) from an outside party, the purchase price usually differs from the carrying amount of the liability. Thus, a gain or loss has been incurred from the perspective of the business combination. However, both the debt and investment remain in the individual financial accounts of the two companies, but the gain or loss goes unrecorded. The consolidation process must adjust all balances to reflect the effective retirement of the debt.
4. Following a related party's acquisition of a company's debt, Interest Income and Expense are recognized. Because these accounts result from intra-entity transactions, they also must be removed in every subsequent consolidation along with the debt and investment figures. Retained Earnings also requires adjustment in each year after the purchase to record the impact of the gain or loss.
5. Amortization of intra-entity debt/investment balances often is necessary because of discounts and/or premiums. Consequently, the Interest Income and Interest Expense figures reported by the two parties will not agree. The closing of these two accounts into Retained Earnings each year gradually reduces the consolidation adjustment that must be made to this equity account.
6. When acquired, many subsidiaries have preferred stock outstanding as well as common stock. The existence of subsidiary preferred shares does little to complicate the consolidation process. The acquisition method values all business acquisitions at their full fair values. If a subsidiary has preferred stock, the essential process of determining its acquisition-date business fair value remains intact. Any preferred shares not owned by the parent simply become a component of the noncontrolling interest and are included in the acquisition-date measure of subsidiary fair value.
7. Every business combination must prepare a statement of cash flows. This statement is not created by consolidating the individual cash flows of the separate companies. Instead, both a consolidated income statement and balance sheet are produced, and the cash flows statement is developed from these figures. Dividends paid to the noncontrolling interest are listed as a financing activity.
8. For most business combinations, the determination of earnings per share (EPS) follows the normal pattern presented in intermediate accounting textbooks. However, if the subsidiary has potentially dilutive items outstanding (stock warrants, convertible preferred stock, convertible bonds, etc.), a different process must be followed. The subsidiary's own diluted EPS is computed as a preliminary procedure. The parent and the outside owners then allocate the earnings used in each of these calculations based on the ownership levels of the subsidiary's shares and the dilutive items. The determination of the EPS figures to be reported for the business combination is based on the portion of consolidated net income assigned to the parent.
9. After the combination is created, a subsidiary may enter into stock transactions such as issuing additional shares or acquiring treasury stock. Such actions normally create a proportional increase or decrease in the subsidiary's equity when compared with the parent's investment. The change is measured and then reflected in the consolidated statements through the Additional Paid-In Capital account. To achieve the appropriate accounting, the parent adjusts the Investment in Subsidiary account as well as its own Additional Paid-In Capital. Because the worksheet does not eliminate this equity balance, the required increase or decrease carries over to the consolidated figures.

Comprehensive Illustration

(*Estimated Time: 35 to 45 Minutes*) Pop, Inc., acquires 90 percent of the 20,000 shares of Son Company's outstanding common stock on December 31, 2019. Of the acquisition-date fair value, it allocates $80,000 to trademarks, a figure amortized at the rate of $2,000 per year. Comparative consolidated balance sheets for 2021 and 2020 are as follows:

Problem: Consolidated Statement of Cash Flows and Earnings per Share

	2021	2020
Cash	$ 210,000	$ 130,000
Accounts receivable	350,000	220,000
Inventory	320,000	278,000
Land, buildings, and equipment (net)	1,090,000	1,120,000
Trademarks	78,000	80,000
Total assets	$2,048,000	$1,828,000
Accounts payable	$ 290,000	$ 296,000
Long-term liabilities	650,000	550,000
Noncontrolling interest	37,800	34,000
Preferred stock (10% cumulative)	100,000	100,000
Common stock (26,000 shares outstanding)	520,000	520,000
Retained earnings, 12/31	450,200	328,000
Total liabilities and stockholders' equity	$2,048,000	$1,828,000

Additional Information for 2021

- Consolidated net income (after adjustments for all intra-entity items) was $178,000.
- Consolidated depreciation and amortization equaled $52,000.
- On April 10, Son sold a building with a $40,000 book value, receiving cash of $50,000. Later that month, Pop borrowed $100,000 from a local bank and purchased equipment for $60,000. These transactions were all with outside parties.
- During the year, Pop declared and paid $40,000 dividends on its common stock and $10,000 on its preferred stock, and Son declared and paid a $20,000 dividend on its common stock.
- Son has long-term convertible debt of $180,000 outstanding included in consolidated liabilities. It recognized interest expense of $16,000 (net of taxes) on this debt during the year. This debt can be exchanged for 10,000 shares of the subsidiary's common stock. Pop owns none of this debt.
- Son recorded $60,000 net income from its own operations. Noncontrolling interest in consolidated net income was $5,800.
- Pop recorded $4,000 in profits on sales of goods to Son. These goods remain in Son's warehouse at December 31.
- Pop applies the equity method to account for its investment in Son. On its own books, Pop recognized $48,200 equity in earnings from Son [90% × ($60,000 less $2,000 amortization) and $4,000 intra-entity gross profit in inventory from its sales to Son].

Required

a. Prepare a consolidated statement of cash flows for Pop, Inc., and Son Company for the year ending December 31, 2018. Use the indirect method for determining the amount of cash provided from operations.[13]

b. Compute basic earnings per share and diluted earnings per share for Pop, Inc.

[13] Prior to attempting this problem, a review of an intermediate accounting textbook might be useful to obtain a complete overview of the production of a statement of cash flows.

Solution

a. *Consolidated Statement of Cash Flows*

The problem specifies that the indirect method should be used in preparing the consolidated statement of cash flows. Therefore, all items that do not represent cash flows from operations must be removed from the $178,000 consolidated net income. For example, both the depreciation and amortization are eliminated (noncash items) as well as the gain on the sale of the building (a nonoperational item). In addition, each of the changes in consolidated Accounts Receivable, Inventory, and Accounts Payable produces a noncash impact on net income. The increase in Accounts Receivable, for example, indicates that the sales figure for the period was larger than the amount of cash collected so that adjustment is required in producing this statement.

From the information given, several nonoperational changes in cash can be determined: the bank loan, the acquisition of equipment, the sale of a building, the dividend paid by Son to the noncontrolling interest, and the dividend paid by the parent. Each of these transactions is included in the consolidated statement of cash flows shown in Exhibit 6.12, which explains the $80,000 increase in cash experienced by the entity during 2021.

b. *Earnings per Share*

The subsidiary's convertible debt has a potentially dilutive effect on earnings per share. Therefore, diluted EPS cannot be determined for the business combination directly from consolidated net income. First, the diluted EPS figure must be calculated for the subsidiary. This information is then used in the computations made by the consolidated entity.

Diluted EPS of $2.47 for the subsidiary is determined as follows:

Son Company—Diluted Earnings per Share

	Earnings		Shares	
As reported less excess amortization	$58,000		20,000	$2.90
Effect of possible debt conversion:				
Interest saved (net of taxes)	16,000	New shares	10,000	$1.60 impact (16,000/10,000)
Diluted EPS.	$74,000		30,000	$2.47 (rounded)

EXHIBIT 6.12

POP, INC., AND SON COMPANY
Consolidated Statement of Cash Flows
Year Ending December 31, 2021

Cash flows from operating activities		
Consolidated net income		$ 178,000
Adjustments to reconcile consolidated net income to net cash provided by operating activities:		
Depreciation and amortization.	$ 52,000	
Gain on sale of building.	(10,000)	
Increase in accounts receivable	(130,000)	
Increase in inventory	(42,000)	
Decrease in accounts payable.	(6,000)	(136,000)
Net cash provided from operations.		$ 42,000
Cash flows from investing activities		
Purchase of equipment	$ (60,000)	
Sale of building	50,000	
Net cash used in investing activities		(10,000)
Cash flows from financing activities		
Payment of cash dividends—Pop	$ (50,000)	
Payment of cash dividend to noncontrolling owners of Son . . .	(2,000)	
Borrowed from bank	100,000	
Net cash provided by financing activities.		48,000
Net increase in cash.		$ 80,000
Cash, January 1, 2021.		130,000
Cash, December 31, 2021		$ 210,000

EXHIBIT 6.13

POP, INC., AND SON COMPANY
Earnings per Share Year Ending
December 31, 2021

	Earnings	Shares	
	Basic Earnings per Share		
Pop's share of consolidated net income	$172,200		
Preferred dividend declared by Pop	(10,000)		
Basic EPS	162,200	26,000	$6.24 (rounded)
	Diluted Earnings per Share		
Pop's share of consolidated net income	$172,200		
Remove equity income	(48,200)		
Remove intra-entity gross profit	(4,000)		
Preferred stock dividend	(10,000)		
Common shares outstanding (Pop, Inc.)		26,000	
Common stock income—Pop (for EPS computations)	$110,000		
Income of Son (for diluted EPS)	44,400		
Diluted EPS	$154,400	26,000	$5.94 (rounded)

The parent owns none of the convertible debt included in computing diluted EPS. Pop holds only 18,000 (90 percent of the outstanding common stock) of the 30,000 shares used in this EPS calculation. Consequently, in determining diluted EPS for the parent company, only $44,400 of the subsidiary's income is applicable:

$$\$74{,}000 \times 18{,}000/30{,}000 = \$44{,}400$$

Exhibit 6.13 reveals basic EPS of $6.24 and diluted EPS of $5.94. Because the subsidiary's earnings figure is included separately in the computation of diluted EPS, the parent's individual income must be identified in the same manner. Thus, the effect of the equity income and intra-entity (downstream) transactions are taken into account in arriving at the parent's separate earnings.

Questions

1. What is a variable interest entity (VIE)?
2. What are variable interests in an entity, and how might they provide financial control over an entity?
3. When is a firm required to consolidate the financial statements of a VIE with its own financial statements?
4. A parent company acquires from a third party bonds that had been issued originally by one of its subsidiaries. What accounting problems are created by this purchase?
5. In Question 4, why is the consolidation process simpler if the bonds had been acquired directly from the subsidiary than from a third party?
6. When a company acquires an affiliated company's debt instruments from a third party, how is the gain or loss on extinguishment of the debt calculated? When should this balance be recognized?
7. Several years ago, Bennett, Inc., bought a portion of the outstanding bonds of Smith Corporation, a subsidiary organization. The acquisition was made from an outside party. In the current year, how should these intra-entity bonds be accounted for within the consolidation process?
8. One company purchases the outstanding debt instruments of an affiliated company on the open market. This transaction creates a gain that is appropriately recognized in the consolidated financial statements of that year. Thereafter, a worksheet adjustment is required to correct the beginning balance of consolidated Retained Earnings (or the parent's Investment in Subsidiary account when the equity method is employed). Why is the amount of this adjustment reduced from year to year?
9. A parent acquires the outstanding bonds of a subsidiary company directly from an outside third party. For consolidation purposes, this transaction creates a gain of $45,000. Should this gain be allocated to the parent or the subsidiary? Why?
10. Perkins Company acquires 90 percent of the outstanding common stock of the Butterfly Corporation as well as 55 percent of its preferred stock. How should these preferred shares be accounted for within the consolidation process?

11. The income statement and the balance sheet are produced using a worksheet, but a consolidated statement of cash flows is not. What process is followed in preparing a consolidated statement of cash flows?
12. How do noncontrolling interest balances affect the consolidated statement of cash flows?
13. In many cases, EPS is computed based on the parent's portion of consolidated net income and parent company shares and convertibles. However, a different process must be used for some business combinations. When is this alternative approach required?
14. A subsidiary has (1) a convertible preferred stock and (2) a convertible bond. How are these items factored into the computation of earnings per share for the parent company?
15. Why might a subsidiary decide to issue new shares of common stock to parties outside the business combination?
16. Washburn Company owns 75 percent of Metcalf Company's outstanding common stock. During the current year, Metcalf issues additional shares to outside parties at a price more than its per share consolidated value. How does this transaction affect the business combination? How is this impact recorded within the consolidated statements?
17. Assume the same information as in Question 16 except that Metcalf issues a 10 percent stock dividend instead of selling new shares of stock. How does this transaction affect the business combination?

Problems

LO 6-1

1. An enterprise that holds a variable interest in a variable interest entity (VIE) is required to consolidate the assets, liabilities, revenues, expenses, and noncontrolling interest of that entity if
   a. The VIE has issued no voting stock.
   b. The variable interest held by the enterprise involves a lease.
   c. The enterprise has a controlling financial interest in the VIE.
   d. Other equity interests in the VIE have the obligation to absorb the expected losses of the VIE.

LO 6-2

2. Prairie Corporation is a primary beneficiary for Vintage Company, a variable interest entity. When Prairie obtained financial control over Vintage, any excess fair value over Prairie's book value was attributed solely to goodwill. Prairie owns 15 percent of Vintage Company's common stock and participation rights that entitle it to an additional 40 percent of Vintage's net income. In the current year, Prairie reports $400,000 of net income before consideration of its investment in Vintage. Vintage Company reports net income of $100,000. What amount of consolidated net income is attributable to the noncontrolling interest?
   a. $15,000
   b. $45,000
   c. $60,000
   d. $85,000

LO 6-3

3. A parent company buys bonds on the open market that had been previously issued by its subsidiary. The price paid by the parent is less than the carrying amount of the bonds on the subsidiary's records. How should the parent report the difference between the price paid and the carrying amount of the bonds on its consolidated financial statements?
   a. As a loss on retirement of the bonds.
   b. As a gain on retirement of the bonds.
   c. As an increase to interest expense over the remaining life of the bonds.
   d. Because the bonds now represent intra-entity debt, the difference is not reported.

LO 6-3

4. A subsidiary has a debt outstanding that was originally issued at a discount. At the beginning of the current year, the parent company acquired the debt at a slight premium from outside parties. Which of the following statements is true?
   a. Whether the balances agree or not, both the subsequent interest income and interest expense should be reported in a consolidated income statement.
   b. The interest income and interest expense will agree in amount and should be offset for consolidation purposes.
   c. In computing any noncontrolling interest allocation, the interest income should be included but not the interest expense.
   d. Although subsequent interest income and interest expense will not agree in amount, both balances should be eliminated for consolidation purposes.

LO 6-4

5. The parent company acquires all of a subsidiary's common stock but only 70 percent of its preferred shares. This preferred stock pays a 7 percent annual cumulative dividend. No dividends are in arrears at the current time. How is the noncontrolling interest's share of the subsidiary's income computed?
   a. As 30 percent of the subsidiary's preferred dividend.
   b. No allocation is made because the dividends have been paid.
   c. As 30 percent of the subsidiary's income after all dividends have been subtracted.
   d. Income is assigned to the preferred stock based on total par value, and 30 percent of that amount is allocated to the noncontrolling interest.

LO 6-5

6. Aceton Corporation owns 80 percent of the outstanding stock of Voctax, Inc. During the current year, Voctax made $140,000 in sales to Aceton. How does this transfer affect the consolidated statement of cash flows?
   a. The transaction should be included if payment has been made.
   b. Only 80 percent of the transfers should be included because the subsidiary made the sales.
   c. Because the transfers were from a subsidiary organization, the cash flows are reported as investing activities.
   d. Because of the intra-entity nature of the transfers, the amount is not reported in the consolidated cash flow statement.

Problems 7 and 8 are based on the following information.

Comparative consolidated balance sheet data for Iverson, Inc., and its 80 percent–owned subsidiary Oakley Co. follow:

	2021	2020
Cash	$ 7,000	$ 20,000
Accounts receivable (net)	55,000	38,000
Merchandise inventory	85,000	45,000
Buildings and equipment (net)	95,000	105,000
Trademark	85,000	100,000
Totals	$327,000	$308,000
Accounts payable	$ 75,000	$ 63,000
Notes payable, long-term	–0–	25,000
Noncontrolling interest	39,000	35,000
Common stock, $10 par	200,000	200,000
Retained earnings (deficit)	13,000	(15,000)
Totals	$327,000	$308,000

Additional Information for Fiscal Year 2021

- Iverson and Oakley's consolidated net income was $45,000.
- Oakley paid $5,000 in dividends during the year. Iverson paid $12,000 in dividends.
- Oakley sold $11,000 worth of merchandise to Iverson during the year.
- There were no purchases or sales of long-term assets during the year.

In the 2021 consolidated statement of cash flows for Iverson Company:

LO 6-5

7. Net cash flows from operating activities were
   a. $12,000.
   b. $20,000.
   c. $24,000.
   d. $25,000.

LO 6-5

8. Net cash flows from financing activities were
   a. $(25,000).
   b. $(37,000).
   c. $(38,000).
   d. $(42,000).

LO 6-6

9. Bensman Corporation is computing EPS. One of its subsidiaries has stock warrants outstanding. How do these convertible items affect Bensman's EPS computation?
   a. No effect is created because the stock warrants were for the subsidiary company's shares.
   b. The stock warrants are not included in the computation unless they are antidilutive.
   c. The effect of the stock warrants must be computed in deriving the amount of subsidiary income to be included in making the diluted EPS calculation.
   d. The stock warrants are included only in basic EPS but never in diluted EPS.

LO 6-7

10. Arcola, Inc., acquires all 40,000 shares of Tuscola Company for $725,000. A year later, when Arcola's equity-adjusted balance in its investment in Tuscola equals $800,000, Tuscola issues an additional 10,000 shares to outside investors for $25 per share. Which of the following best describes the effect of Tuscola's stock issue on Arcola's investment account?
    a. There is no effect because the shares were all sold to outside parties.
    b. The investment account is reduced because Arcola now owns a smaller percentage of Tuscola.
    c. The investment account is increased because Arcola's share of Tuscola's value has increased.
    d. There is no effect because Arcola maintains control over Tuscola despite the new stock issue.

LO 6-3

11. Dane, Inc., owns Carlton Corporation. For the current year, Dane reports net income (without consideration of its investment in Carlton) of $185,000, and the subsidiary reports $105,000. The parent had a bond payable outstanding on January 1, with a carrying amount of $209,000. The subsidiary acquired the bond on that date for $196,000. During the current year, Dane reported interest expense of $18,000 while Carlton reported interest income of $19,000, both related to the intra-entity bond payable. What is consolidated net income?
    a. $289,000
    b. $291,000
    c. $302,000
    d. $304,000

LO 6-6

12. Mattoon, Inc., owns 80 percent of Effingham Company. For the current year, this combined entity reported consolidated net income of $500,000. Of this amount, $465,000 was attributable to Mattoon's controlling interest while the remaining $35,000 was attributable to the noncontrolling interest. Mattoon has 100,000 shares of common stock outstanding, and Effingham has 25,000 shares outstanding. Neither company has issued preferred shares or has any convertible securities outstanding. On the face of the consolidated income statement, how much should be reported as Mattoon's earnings per share?
    a. $5.00
    b. $4.65
    c. $4.00
    d. $3.88

LO 6-3

13. Aaron Company's books show current earnings of $430,000 and $46,000 in cash dividends. Zeese Company earns $164,000 in net income and declares $11,500 in dividends. Aaron has held a 70 percent interest in Zeese for several years, an investment with an acquisition-date excess fair over book value attributable solely to goodwill. Aaron uses the initial value method to account for these shares and includes dividend income in its internal earnings reports.

    On January 1 of the current year, Zeese acquired in the open market $64,400 of Aaron's 8 percent bonds. The bonds had originally been issued several years ago at 92, reflecting a 10 percent effective interest rate. On the date of purchase, the carrying amount of the bonds payable was $60,200. Zeese paid $56,000 based on a 12 percent effective interest rate over the remaining life of the bonds.

    What is consolidated net income for this year?
    a. $598,900
    b. $589,450
    c. $438,050
    d. $590,850

LO 6-3

14. Redfield Company reports current earnings of $420,000 while declaring $52,000 in cash dividends. Snedeker Company earns $147,000 in net income and declares $13,000 in dividends. Redfield has held a 70 percent interest in Snedeker for several years, an investment with an acquisition-date excess fair over book value attributable solely to goodwill. Redfield uses the initial value method to account for these shares.

On January 1 of the current year, Snedeker acquired in the open market $51,600 of Redfield's 8 percent bonds. The bonds had originally been issued several years ago at 92, reflecting a 10 percent effective interest rate. On the date of purchase, the carrying amount of the bonds payable was $50,400. Snedeker paid $49,200 based on a 12 percent effective interest rate over the remaining life of the bonds.

What is the noncontrolling interest's share of consolidated net income?

a. $40,200
b. $44,100
c. $40,560
d. $44,460

LO 6-3

15. Pesto Company possesses 80 percent of Salerno Company's outstanding voting stock. Pesto uses the initial value method to account for this investment. On January 1, 2017, Pesto sold 9 percent bonds payable with a $10 million face value (maturing in 20 years) on the open market at a premium of $600,000. On January 1, 2020, Salerno acquired 40 percent of these same bonds from an outside party at 96.6 percent of face value. Both companies use the straight-line method of amortization. For a 2021 consolidation, what adjustment should be made to Pesto's beginning Retained Earnings as a result of this bond acquisition?
    a. $320,000 increase
    b. $326,000 increase
    c. $331,000 increase
    d. $340,000 increase

LO 6-4

16. On January 1, Tesco Company spent a total of $4,384,000 to acquire control over Blondel Company. This price was based on paying $424,000 for 20 percent of Blondel's preferred stock and $3,960,000 for 90 percent of its outstanding common stock. At the acquisition date, the fair value of the 10 percent noncontrolling interest in Blondel's common stock was $440,000. The fair value of the 80 percent of Blondel's preferred shares not owned by Tesco was $1,696,000. Blondel's stockholders' equity accounts at January 1 were as follows:

Preferred stock—9%, $100 par value, cumulative and participating; 10,000 shares outstanding	$1,000,000
Common stock—$50 par value; 40,000 shares outstanding	2,000,000
Retained earnings	3,000,000
Total stockholders' equity	$6,000,000

Tesco believes that all of Blondel's accounts approximate their fair values within the company's financial statements. What amount of consolidated goodwill should be recognized?

a. $ 300,000
b. $ 316,000
c. $ 364,000
d. $ 520,000

LO 6-4

17. On January 1, Coldwater Company has a net book value of $2,174,000 as follows:

2,000 shares of preferred stock; par value $100 per share; cumulative, nonparticipating, nonvoting; call value $108 per share	$ 200,000
34,500 shares of common stock; par value $40 per share	1,380,000
Retained earnings	594,000
Total	$2,174,000

Westmont Company acquires all outstanding preferred shares for $214,000 and 60 percent of the common stock for $1,253,280. The acquisition-date fair value of the noncontrolling interest in Coldwater's common stock was $835,520. Westmont believed that one of Coldwater's buildings, with a 12-year remaining life, was undervalued by $63,600 on the company's financial records.

What amount of consolidated goodwill would be recognized from this acquisition?

a. $61,600
b. $65,200
c. $60,400
d. $59,200

LO 6-5

18. Premier Company owns 90 percent of the voting shares of Stanton, Inc. Premier reports sales of $480,000 during the current year, and Stanton reports $264,000. Stanton sold inventory costing $28,800 to Premier (upstream) during the year for $57,600. Of this amount, 25 percent is still in ending inventory at year-end. Total receivables on the consolidated balance sheet were $81,800 at the first of the year and $119,100 at year-end. No intra-entity debt existed at the beginning or end of the year. Using the direct method, what is the consolidated amount of cash collected by the business combination from its customers?
    a. $706,700
    b. $649,100
    c. $686,400
    d. $744,000

LO 6-7

19. Aaron owns 100 percent of the 12,000 shares of Veritable, Inc. The Investment in Veritable account has a balance of $588,000, corresponding to the subsidiary's unamortized acquisition-date fair value of $49 per share. Veritable issues 3,000 new shares to the public for $50 per share. How does this transaction affect the Investment in Veritable account?
    a. It is not affected because the shares were sold to outside parties.
    b. It should be increased by $2,400.
    c. It should be increased by $3,000.
    d. It should be decreased by $117,600.

Problems 20 through 22 are based on the following information.

Neill Company purchases 80 percent of the common stock of Stamford Company on January 1, 2020, when Stamford has the following stockholders' equity accounts:

Common stock—40,000 shares outstanding	$100,000
Additional paid-in capital	75,000
Retained earnings, 1/1/20	540,000
Total stockholders' equity	$715,000

To acquire this interest in Stamford, Neill pays a total of $592,000. The acquisition-date fair value of the 20 percent noncontrolling interest was $148,000. Any excess fair value was allocated to goodwill, which has not experienced any impairment.

On January 1, 2021, Stamford reports retained earnings of $620,000. Neill has accrued the increase in Stamford's retained earnings through application of the equity method.

View the following problems as independent situations:

LO 6-7

20. On January 1, 2021, Stamford issues 10,000 additional shares of common stock for $25 per share. Neill acquires 8,000 of these shares. How will this transaction affect the parent company's Additional Paid-In Capital account?
    a. Has no effect on it
    b. Increases it by $20,500
    c. Increases it by $36,400
    d. Increases it by $82,300

LO 6-7

21. On January 1, 2021, Stamford issues 10,000 additional shares of common stock for $15 per share. Neill does not acquire any of this newly issued stock. How does this transaction affect the parent company's Additional Paid-In Capital account?
    a. Has no effect on it
    b. Increases it by $44,000
    c. Decreases it by $35,200
    d. Decreases it by $55,000

LO 6-7

22. On January 1, 2021, Stamford reacquires 8,000 of the outstanding shares of its own common stock for $24 per share. None of these shares belonged to Neill. How does this transaction affect the parent company's Additional Paid-In Capital account?
    a. Has no effect on it
    b. Decreases it by $55,000
    c. Decreases it by $35,000
    d. Decreases it by $28,000

LO 6-2

23. Paige Clothing Company (Paige) helped form Apparel Media LLC, a company that will conduct e-commerce sales for Paige through a dedicated internet site. Two outside investors contributed $50,000 in start-up capital to Apparel Media as the sole owners of the company. Apparel Media's governing contract stipulates the following:
    - Paige is to be Apparel Media's sole client, and Paige must approve any expenditures by Apparel Media.
    - Apparel Media will receive a fee of 5 percent of all sales revenue generated through its e-commerce internet site up to a maximum fee of $30,000 per year. The maximum fee will increase by 4 percent per year.
    - Paige and Apparel Media will pay 50 percent of the costs to maintain the internet site. However, if Apparel Media's fees are insufficient to cover its 50 percent share of the costs, Paige will reimburse Apparel Media for the loss.

    Explain whether Apparel Media qualifies as a variable interest entity. Explain whether Paige should consolidate Apparel Media.

LO 6-2

24. The following describes a set of arrangements between TecPC Company and a variable interest entity (VIE) as of December 31, 2020. TecPC agrees to design and construct a new research and development (R&D) facility. The VIE's sole purpose is to finance and own the R&D facility and lease it to TecPC Company after construction is completed. Payments under the operating lease are expected to begin in the first quarter of 2022.

    The VIE has financing commitments sufficient for the construction project from equity and debt participants (investors) of $4 million and $42 million, respectively. TecPC, in its role as the VIE's construction agent, is responsible for completing construction by December 31, 2020. TecPC has guaranteed a portion of the VIE's obligations during the construction and post-construction periods.

    TecPC agrees to lease the R&D facility for five years with multiple extension options. The lease is a variable rate obligation indexed to a three-month market rate. As market interest rates increase or decrease, the payments under this operating lease also increase or decrease, sufficient to provide a return to the investors. If all extension options are exercised, the total lease term is 35 years.

    At the end of the first five-year lease term or any extension, TecPC may choose one of the following:
    - Renew the lease at fair value subject to investor approval.
    - Purchase the facility at its original construction cost.
    - Sell the facility on the VIE's behalf to an independent third party. If TecPC sells the project and the proceeds from the sale are insufficient to repay the investors their original cost, TecPC may be required to pay the VIE up to 85 percent of the project's cost.

    a. What is the purpose of reporting consolidated statements for a company and the entities that it controls?

    b. When should a VIE's financial statements be consolidated with those of another company?

    c. Identify the risks of ownership of the R&D facility that (1) TecPC has effectively shifted to the VIE's owners and (2) remain with TecPC.

    d. What characteristics of a primary beneficiary does TecPC possess?

LO 6-2

25. On December 31, 2020, Petra Company invests $20,000 in Valery, a variable interest entity. In contractual agreements completed on that date, Petra established itself as the primary beneficiary of Valery. Previously, Petra had no equity interest in Valery. Immediately after Petra's investment, Valery presents the following balance sheet:

Cash	$ 20,000	Long-term debt	$120,000
Marketing software	140,000	Noncontrolling interest	60,000
Computer equipment	40,000	Petra equity interest	20,000
Total assets	$200,000	Total liabilities and equity	$200,000

    Each of the amounts represents an assessed fair value at December 31, 2020, except for the marketing software. The December 31 business fair value of Valery is assessed at $80,000.

    a. If the carrying amount of the marketing software was undervalued by $25,000, what amounts for Valery would appear in Petra's December 31, 2020, consolidated financial statements?

    b. If the carrying amount of the marketing software was overvalued by $25,000, what amounts for Valery would appear in Petra's December 31, 2020, consolidated financial statements?

LO 6-2

26. On January 1, 2021, Access IT Company exchanged $1,000,000 for 40 percent of the outstanding voting stock of Net Connect. Especially attractive to Access IT was a research project underway at Net Connect that would enhance both the speed and quantity of client-accessible data. Although not recorded in Net Connect's financial records, the fair value of the research project was considered to be $1,960,000.

In contractual agreements with the sole owner of the remaining 60 percent of Net Connect, Access IT was granted (1) various decision-making rights over Net Connect's operating decisions and (2) special service purchase provisions at below-market rates. As a result of these contractual agreements, Access IT established itself as the primary beneficiary of Net Connect. Immediately after the purchase, Access IT and Net Connect presented the following balance sheets:

	Access IT	Net Connect
Cash	$ 61,000	$ 41,000
Investment in Net Connect	1,000,000	
Capitalized software	981,000	156,000
Computer equipment	1,066,000	56,000
Communications equipment	916,000	336,000
Patent		191,000
Total assets	$ 4,024,000	$ 780,000
Long-term debt	(941,000)	(616,000)
Common stock—Access IT	(2,660,000)	
Common stock—Net Connect		(41,000)
Retained earnings	(423,000)	(123,000)
Total liabilities and equity	$(4,024,000)	$(780,000)

Each of the above amounts represents a fair value at January 1, 2021. The fair value of the 60 percent of Net Connect shares not owned by Access IT was estimated at $1,500,000.

Prepare an acquisition-date consolidation worksheet for Access IT and its variable interest entity.

LO 6-2

27. On January 1, 2021, Pikes Corporation loaned Venti Company $300,000 and agreed to guarantee all of Venti's long-term debt in exchange for (1) decision-making authority over all of Venti's activities and (2) an annual management fee of 25 percent of Venti's annual revenues. As a result of the agreement, Pikes becomes the primary beneficiary of Venti (now a variable interest entity). Pikes' loan to Venti stipulated a 7 percent (market) rate of interest to be paid annually with principal due in 10 years.

On January 1, 2021, Pikes estimated that the fair value of Venti's equity shares equaled $75,000 while Venti's book value was $55,000. Any excess fair over book value at that date was attributed to Venti's trademark with an indefinite life. Because Pikes owns no equity in Venti, all of the acquisition-date excess fair over book value is allocated to the noncontrolling interest.

Venti paid Pikes 25 percent of its 2021 revenues at the end of the year and recorded the payment in other operating expenses. Venti also paid the interest to Pikes for the loan. On December 31, 2021, Pikes and Venti submitted the following statements for consolidation. (Parentheses indicate credit balances.)

	Pikes	Venti
Revenues	(792,000)	(216,000)
Management fee	(54,000)	–0–
Cost of good sold	621,000	89,000
Other operating expenses	76,000	64,000
Interest income	(21,000)	–0–
Interest expense	–0–	39,000
Net income	(170,000)	(24,000)
Retained earnings, 1/1	(1,380,000)	(40,000)
Net income	(170,000)	(24,000)
Dividends declared	75,000	–0–
Retained earnings, 12/31	(1,475,000)	(64,000)

(continued)

(continued)

	Pikes	Venti
Current assets	360,000	73,000
Loan receivable from Venti	300,000	–0–
Equipment (net)	895,000	527,000
Trademark	–0–	125,000
Total assets	1,555,000	725,000
Current liabilities	(30,000)	(92,000)
Loan payable to Pikes	–0–	(300,000)
Other long-term debt	–0–	(254,000)
Common stock	(50,000)	(15,000)
Retained earnings, 12/31	(1,475,000)	(64,000)
Total liabilities and equity	(1,555,000)	(725,000)

Prepare the December 31, 2021, consolidation worksheet for Pikes and its variable interest entity Venti.

LO 6-3

28. Cairns owns 75 percent of the voting stock of Hamilton, Inc. The parent's interest was acquired several years ago on the date that the subsidiary was formed. Consequently, no goodwill or other allocation was recorded in connection with the acquisition. Cairns uses the equity method in its internal records to account for its investment in Hamilton.

    On January 1, 2017, Hamilton sold $1,000,000 in 10-year bonds to the public at 105. The bonds had a cash interest rate of 9 percent payable every December 31. Cairns acquired 40 percent of these bonds at 96 percent of face value on January 1, 2019. Both companies utilize the straight-line method of amortization. Prepare the consolidation worksheet entries to recognize the effects of the intra-entity bonds at each of the following dates.

    a. December 31, 2019
    b. December 31, 2020
    c. December 31, 2021

LO 6-3

29. Highlight, Inc., owns all outstanding stock of Kiort Corporation. The two companies report the following balances for the year ending December 31, 2020:

	Highlight	Kiort
Revenues and interest income	$(670,000)	$(390,000)
Operating and interest expense	540,000	221,000
Other gains and losses	(120,000)	(32,000)
Net income	$(250,000)	$(201,000)

On January 1, 2020, Highlight acquired on the open market bonds for $108,000 originally issued by Kiort. This investment had an effective rate of 8 percent. The bonds had a face value of $100,000 and a cash interest rate of 9 percent. At the date of acquisition, these bonds were shown as liabilities by Kiort with a carrying amount of $84,000 (based on an effective rate of 11 percent). Determine the balances that should appear on a consolidated income statement for 2020.

LO 6-3

30. Several years ago, Brant, Inc., sold $900,000 in bonds to the public. Annual cash interest of 9 percent ($81,000) was to be paid on this debt. The bonds were issued at a discount to yield 12 percent. At the beginning of 2019, Zack Corporation (a wholly owned subsidiary of Brant) purchased $180,000 of these bonds on the open market for $201,000, a price based on an effective interest rate of 7 percent. The bond liability had a carrying amount on that date of $760,000. Assume Brant uses the equity method to account internally for its investment in Zack.

    a. What consolidation entry would be required for these bonds on December 31, 2019?
    b. What consolidation entry would be required for these bonds on December 31, 2021?

LO 6-3

31. Paulina, Incorporated, owns 90 percent of Southport Company. On January 1, 2021, Paulina acquires half of Southport's $500,000 outstanding 13-year bonds. These bonds had been sold on the

open market on January 1, 2018, at a 12 percent effective rate. The bonds pay a cash interest rate of 10 percent every December 31 and are scheduled to come due on December 31, 2030. Southport issued this debt originally for $435,765. Paulina paid $283,550 for this investment, indicating an 8 percent effective yield.

a. Assuming that both parties use the effective rate method, what gain or loss from the retirement of this debt should be reported on the consolidated income statement for 2020?

b. Assuming that both parties use the effective rate method, what balances should appear in the Investment in Southport Bonds account on Paulina's records and the Bonds Payable account of Southport as of December 31, 2021?

c. Assuming that both parties use the straight-line method, what consolidation entry would be required on December 31, 2021, because of these bonds? Assume that the parent is not applying the equity method.

LO 6-4

32. Hepner Corporation has the following stockholders' equity accounts:

Preferred stock (6% cumulative dividend)	$500,000
Common stock	750,000
Additional paid-in capital	300,000
Retained earnings	950,000

The preferred stock is participating. Wasatch Corporation buys 80 percent of this common stock for $1,600,000 and 70 percent of the preferred stock for $630,000. The acquisition-date fair value of the noncontrolling interest in the common shares was $400,000 and was $270,000 for the preferred shares. All of the subsidiary's assets and liabilities are viewed as having fair values equal to their book values. What amount is attributed to goodwill on the date of acquisition?

LO 6-4

33. Smith, Inc., has the following stockholders' equity accounts as of January 1, 2021:

Preferred stock—$100 par, nonvoting and nonparticipating, 8% cumulative dividend	$2,000,000
Common stock—$20 par value	4,000,000
Retained earnings	10,000,000

Haried Company purchases all of Smith's common stock on January 1, 2021, for $14,040,000. The preferred stock remains in the hands of outside parties. Any excess acquisition-date fair value will be assigned to franchise contracts with a 40-year remaining life.

During 2021, Smith reports earning $450,000 in net income and declares $360,000 in cash dividends. Haried applies the equity method to this investment.

a. What is the noncontrolling interest's share of consolidated net income for this period?

b. What is the balance in the Investment in Smith account as of December 31, 2021?

c. What consolidation entries are needed for 2021?

LO 6-4

34. Through the payment of $10,468,000 in cash, Drexel Company acquires voting control over Young Company. This price is paid for 60 percent of the subsidiary's 100,000 outstanding common shares ($40 par value) as well as all 10,000 shares of 8 percent, cumulative, $100 par value preferred stock. Of the total payment, $3.1 million is attributed to the fully participating preferred stock with the remainder paid for the common. This acquisition is carried out on January 1, 2021, when Young reports retained earnings of $10 million and a total book value of $15 million. The acquisition-date fair value of the noncontrolling interest in Young's common stock was $4,912,000. On this same date, a building owned by Young (with a five-year remaining life) is undervalued in the financial records by $200,000, while equipment with a 10-year remaining life is overvalued by $100,000. Any further excess acquisition-date fair value is assigned to a brand name with a 20-year remaining life.

During 2021, Young reports net income of $900,000 while declaring $400,000 in cash dividends. Drexel uses the initial value method to account for both of these investments.

Prepare appropriate consolidation entries for 2021.

LO 6-5

35. The following information has been taken from the consolidation worksheet of Peak and its 90 percent–owned subsidiary, Valley:

- Peak reports a $12,000 gain on the sale of a building. The building had a book value of $32,000 but was sold for $44,000 cash.
- Intra-entity inventory transfers of $129,000 occurred during the current period.

- Valley declared and paid a $30,000 dividend during the year, with $27,000 of this amount going to Peak.
- Amortization of an intangible asset recognized by Peak's worksheet was $16,000 for the current period.
- Consolidated accounts payable decreased by $11,000 during the year.

Indicate how to reflect each of these events on a consolidated statement of cash flows.

LO 6-5

36. Alford Company and its 80 percent–owned subsidiary, Knight, have the following income statements for 2021:

	Alford	Knight
Revenues	$(500,000)	$(230,000)
Cost of goods sold	300,000	140,000
Depreciation and amortization	40,000	10,000
Other expenses	20,000	20,000
Gain on sale of equipment	(30,000)	–0–
Equity in earnings of Knight	(36,200)	–0–
Net income	$(206,200)	$ (60,000)

Additional Information for 2021

- Intra-entity inventory transfers during the year amounted to $90,000. All intra-entity transfers were downstream from Alford to Knight.
- Intra-entity gross profits in inventory at January 1 were $6,000, but at December 31 they are $9,000.
- Annual excess amortization expense resulting from the acquisition is $11,000.
- Knight paid dividends totaling $20,000.
- The noncontrolling interest's share of the subsidiary's income is $9,800.
- During the year, consolidated inventory rose by $11,000 while accounts receivable and accounts payable declined by $8,000 and $6,000, respectively.

Using either the direct or indirect method, compute net cash flows from operating activities during the period for the business combination.

LO 6-6

37. Porter Corporation owns all 30,000 shares of the common stock of Street, Inc. Porter has 60,000 shares of its own common stock outstanding. During the current year, Porter earns net income (without any consideration of its investment in Street) of $150,000 while Street reports $130,000. Annual amortization of $10,000 is recognized each year on the consolidation worksheet based on acquisition-date fair-value allocations. Both companies have convertible bonds outstanding. During the current year, bond-related interest expense (net of taxes) is $32,000 for Porter and $24,000 for Street. Porter's bonds can be converted into 8,000 shares of common stock; Street's bonds can be converted into 10,000 shares. Porter owns none of these bonds. What are the earnings per share amounts that Porter should report in its current year consolidated income statement?

LO 6-6

38. Primus, Inc., owns all outstanding stock of Sonston, Inc. For the current year, Primus reports net income (exclusive of any investment income) of $600,000. Primus has 100,000 shares of common stock outstanding. Sonston reports net income of $200,000 for the period, with 40,000 shares of common stock outstanding. Sonston also has 10,000 stock warrants outstanding that allow the holder to acquire shares at $10 per share. The value of this stock was $20 per share throughout the year. Primus owns 2,000 of these warrants. What amount should Primus report for diluted earnings per share?

LO 6-6

39. Bravo, Inc., owns all of the stock of Echo, Inc. For 2021, Bravo reports income (exclusive of any investment income) of $480,000. Bravo has 80,000 shares of common stock outstanding. It also has 5,000 shares of preferred stock outstanding that pay a dividend of $15,000 per year. Echo reports net income of $290,000 for the period with 80,000 shares of common stock outstanding. Echo also has a liability from its 10,000, $100 bonds that pay annual interest of $8 per bond. Each of these bonds can be converted into two shares of common stock. Bravo owns none of these bonds. Assume a tax rate of 21 percent. What amount should Bravo report as diluted earnings per share?

LO 6-6

40. The following separate income statements are for Burks Company and its 80 percent–owned subsidiary, Foreman Company:

	Burks	Foreman
Revenues	$(430,000)	$(330,000)
Expenses	280,000	240,000
Gain on sale of equipment	–0–	(30,000)
Equity earnings of subsidiary	(64,000)	–0–
Net income	$(214,000)	$(120,000)
Outstanding common shares	65,000	40,000

Additional Information

- Amortization expense resulting from Foreman's excess acquisition-date fair value is $40,000 per year.
- Burks has convertible preferred stock outstanding. Each of these 8,000 shares is paid a dividend of $4 per year. Each share can be converted into four shares of common stock.
- Stock warrants to buy 20,000 shares of Foreman are also outstanding. For $15, each warrant can be converted into a share of Foreman's common stock. The fair value of this stock is $20 throughout the year. Burks owns none of these warrants.
- Foreman has convertible bonds payable that paid interest of $45,000 (after taxes) during the year. These bonds can be exchanged for 10,000 shares of common stock. Burks holds 10 percent of these bonds, which it bought at book value directly from Foreman.

Compute basic and diluted EPS for Burks Company.

LO 6-7

41. DeMilo, Inc., owns 100 percent of the 40,000 outstanding shares of Ricardo, Inc. DeMilo currently carries the Investment in Ricardo account at $490,000 using the equity method.

Ricardo issues 10,000 new shares to the public for $15.75 per share. How does this transaction affect the Investment in Ricardo account that appears on DeMilo's financial records?

LO 6-7

42. Albuquerque, Inc., acquired 16,000 shares of Marmon Company several years ago for $600,000. At the acquisition date, Marmon reported a book value of $710,000, and Albuquerque assessed the fair value of the noncontrolling interest at $150,000. Any excess of acquisition-date fair value over book value was assigned to broadcast licenses with indefinite lives. Since the acquisition date and until this point, Marmon has issued no additional shares. No impairment has been recognized for the broadcast licenses.

At the present time, Marmon reports $800,000 as total stockholders' equity, which is broken down as follows:

Common stock ($10 par value)	$200,000
Additional paid-in capital	230,000
Retained earnings	370,000
Total	$800,000

View the following as independent situations:

a. Marmon sells 5,000 shares of previously unissued common stock to the public for $47 per share. Albuquerque purchased none of this stock. What journal entry should Albuquerque make to recognize the impact of this stock transaction?

b. Marmon sells 4,000 shares of previously unissued common stock to the public for $33 per share. Albuquerque purchased none of this stock. What journal entry should Albuquerque make to recognize the impact of this stock transaction?

LO 6-7

43. On January 1, 2019, Aronsen Company acquired 90 percent of Siedel Company's outstanding shares. Siedel had a net book value on that date of $480,000: common stock ($10 par value) of $200,000 and retained earnings of $280,000.

Aronsen paid $584,100 for this investment. The acquisition-date fair value of the 10 percent noncontrolling interest was $64,900. The excess fair value over book value associated with the acquisition was used to increase land by $89,000 and to recognize copyrights (16-year remaining life) at $80,000. Subsequent to the acquisition, Aronsen applied the initial value method to its investment account.

In the 2019–2020 period, the subsidiary's retained earnings increased by $100,000. During 2021, Siedel earned income of $80,000 while declaring $20,000 in dividends. Also, at the beginning of 2021, Siedel issued 4,000 new shares of common stock for $38 per share to finance the expansion of its corporate facilities. Aronsen purchased none of these additional shares and therefore recorded no entry. Prepare the appropriate 2021 consolidation entries for these two companies.

LO 6-3

44. Pavin acquires all of Stabler's outstanding shares on January 1, 2018, for $460,000 in cash. Of this amount, $30,000 was attributed to equipment with a 10-year remaining life and $40,000 was assigned to trademarks expensed over a 20-year period. Pavin applies the partial equity method so that income is accrued each period based solely on the earnings reported by the subsidiary.

On January 1, 2021, Pavin reports $300,000 in bonds outstanding with a carrying amount of $282,000. Stabler purchases half of these bonds on the open market for $145,500.

During 2021, Pavin begins to sell merchandise to Stabler. During that year, inventory costing $80,000 was transferred at a price of $100,000. All but $10,000 (at sales price) of these goods were resold to outside parties by year-end. Stabler still owes $33,000 for inventory shipped from Pavin during December.

The following financial figures are for the two companies for the year ending December 31, 2021. Dividends were both declared and paid during the current year. Prepare a worksheet to produce consolidated balances. (Credits are indicated by parentheses.)

	Pavin	Stabler
Revenues	$ (740,000)	$(505,000)
Cost of goods sold	455,000	240,000
Expenses	125,000	158,500
Interest expense—bonds	36,000	–0–
Interest income—bond investment	–0–	(16,500)
Loss on extinguishment of bonds	–0–	–0–
Equity in Stabler's income	(123,000)	–0–
Net income	$ (247,000)	$(123,000)
Retained earnings, 1/1/21	$ (345,000)	$(361,000)
Net income (above)	(247,000)	(123,000)
Dividends declared	155,000	61,000
Retained earnings, 12/31/21	$ (437,000)	$(423,000)
Cash and receivables	$ 217,000	$ 35,000
Inventory	175,000	87,000
Investment in Stabler	613,000	–0–
Investment in Pavin bonds	–0–	147,000
Land, buildings, and equipment (net)	245,000	541,000
Trademarks	–0–	–0–
Total assets	$ 1,250,000	$ 810,000
Accounts payable	$ (225,000)	$(167,000)
Bonds payable	(300,000)	(100,000)
Discount on bonds	12,000	–0–
Common stock	(300,000)	(120,000)
Retained earnings (above)	(437,000)	(423,000)
Total liabilities and stockholders' equity	$(1,250,000)	$(810,000)

LO 6-3

45. Fred, Inc., and Herman Corporation formed a business combination on January 1, 2019, when Fred acquired a 60 percent interest in Herman's common stock for $312,000 in cash. The book value of Herman's assets and liabilities on that day totaled $300,000, and the fair value of the noncontrolling interest was $208,000. Patents being held by Herman (with a 12-year remaining life) were undervalued by $90,000 within the company's financial records, and a customer list (10-year life) worth $130,000 was also recognized as part of the acquisition-date fair value.

Intra-entity inventory transfers occur regularly between the two companies. Merchandise carried over from one year to the next is always sold in the subsequent period.

Year	Original Cost to Herman	Transfer Price to Fred	Ending Balance at Transfer Price
2019	$ 80,000	$100,000	$20,000
2020	100,000	125,000	40,000
2021	90,000	120,000	30,000

Fred had not paid for half of the 2021 inventory transfers by year-end.

On January 1, 2020, Fred sold $15,000 in land to Herman for $22,000. Herman is still holding this land.

On January 1, 2021, Herman acquired $20,000 (face value) of Fred's bonds in the open market. These bonds had an 8 percent cash interest rate. On the date of repurchase, the liability was shown within Fred's records at $21,386, indicating an effective yield of 6 percent. Herman's acquisition price was $18,732 based on an effective interest rate of 10 percent.

Herman indicated earning a net income of $25,000 within its 2021 financial statements. The subsidiary also reported a beginning Retained Earnings balance of $300,000, dividends of $4,000, and common stock of $100,000. Herman has not issued any additional common stock since its takeover. The parent company has applied the equity method to record its investment in Herman.

a. Prepare consolidation worksheet adjustments for 2021.

b. Calculate the amount of consolidated net income attributable to the noncontrolling interest for 2021. In addition, determine the ending 2021 balance for noncontrolling interest in the consolidated balance sheet.

c. Determine the consolidation worksheet adjustments needed in 2022 in connection with the intra-entity bonds.

LO 6-3, 6-4

46. On January 1, 2020, Mona, Inc., acquired 80 percent of Lisa Company's common stock as well as 60 percent of its preferred shares. Mona paid $65,000 in cash for the preferred stock, with a call value of 110 percent of the $50 per share par value. The remaining 40 percent of the preferred shares traded at a $34,000 fair value. Mona paid $552,800 for the common stock. At the acquisition date, the noncontrolling interest in the common stock had a fair value of $138,200. The excess fair value over Lisa's book value was attributed to franchise contracts of $40,000. This intangible asset is being amortized over a 40-year period. Lisa pays all preferred stock dividends (a total of $8,000 per year) on an annual basis. During 2020, Lisa's book value increased by $50,000.

On January 2, 2020, Mona acquired one-half of Lisa's outstanding bonds payable to reduce the business combination's debt position. Lisa's bonds had a face value of $100,000 and paid cash interest of 10 percent per year. These bonds had been issued to the public to yield 14 percent. Interest is paid each December 31. On January 2, 2020, these bonds had a total $88,350 carrying amount. Mona paid $53,310, indicating an effective interest rate of 8 percent.

On January 3, 2020, Mona sold Lisa fixed assets that had originally cost $100,000 but had accumulated depreciation of $60,000 when transferred. The transfer was made at a price of $120,000. These assets were estimated to have a remaining useful life of 10 years.

The individual financial statements for these two companies for the year ending December 31, 2021, are as follows:

	Mona, Inc.	Lisa Company
Sales and other revenues	$ (500,000)	$ (200,000)
Expenses	220,000	120,000
Dividend income—Lisa common stock	(8,000)	–0–
Dividend income—Lisa preferred stock	(4,800)	–0–
Net income	$ (292,800)	$ (80,000)
Retained earnings, 1/1/21	$ (700,000)	$ (500,000)
Net income (above)	(292,800)	(80,000)
Dividends declared—common stock	92,800	10,000
Dividends declared—preferred stock	–0–	8,000
Retained earnings, 12/31/21	$ (900,000)	$ (562,000)

(continued)

(continued)

	Mona, Inc.	Lisa Company
Current assets	$ 130,419	$ 500,000
Investment in Lisa—common stock	552,800	–0–
Investment in Lisa—preferred stock	65,000	–0–
Investment in Lisa—bonds	51,781	–0–
Fixed assets	1,100,000	800,000
Accumulated depreciation	(300,000)	(200,000)
Total assets	$ 1,600,000	$ 1,100,000
Accounts payable	$ (400,000)	$ (144,580)
Bonds payable	–0–	(100,000)
Discount on bonds payable	–0–	6,580
Common stock	(300,000)	(200,000)
Preferred stock	–0–	(100,000)
Retained earnings, 12/31/21	(900,000)	(562,000)
Total liabilities and equities	$(1,600,000)	$(1,100,000)

a. What consolidation worksheet adjustments would have been required as of January 1, 2020, to eliminate the subsidiary's common and preferred stocks?

b. What consolidation worksheet adjustments would have been required as of December 31, 2020, to account for Mona's purchase of Lisa's bonds?

c. What consolidation worksheet adjustments would have been required as of December 31, 2020, to account for the intra-entity sale of fixed assets?

d. Assume that consolidated financial statements are being prepared for the year ending December 31, 2021. Calculate the consolidated balance for each of the following accounts:

Franchises
Fixed Assets
Accumulated Depreciation
Expenses

LO 6-5

47. Bolero Company holds 80 percent of the common stock of Rivera, Inc., and 40 percent of this subsidiary's convertible bonds. The following consolidated financial statements are for 2020 and 2021 (credit balances indicated by parentheses):

Bolero Company and Consolidated Subsidiary Rivera

	2020	2021
Revenues	$ (900,000)	$(1,030,000)
Cost of goods sold	610,000	650,000
Depreciation and amortization	100,000	120,000
Gain on sale of building	–0–	(30,000)
Interest expense	40,000	40,000
Consolidated net income	(150,000)	(250,000)
to noncontrolling interest	19,000	21,000
to parent company	$ (131,000)	$ (229,000)
Retained earnings, 1/1	$ (310,000)	$ (381,000)
Net income	(131,000)	(229,000)
Dividends declared	60,000	110,000
Retained earnings, 12/31	$ (381,000)	$ (500,000)
Cash	$ 90,000	$ 180,000
Accounts receivable	170,000	150,000
Inventory	210,000	360,000
Buildings and equipment (net)	650,000	710,000
Databases	170,000	155,000
Total assets	$1,290,000	$ 1,555,000

(continued)

(continued)

Bolero Company and Consolidated Subsidiary Rivera		
	2020	2021
Accounts payable	$ (160,000)	$ (110,000)
Bonds payable	(410,000)	(520,000)
Noncontrolling interest in Rivera	(42,000)	(61,000)
Common stock	(110,000)	(140,000)
Additional paid-in capital	(187,000)	(224,000)
Retained earnings	(381,000)	(500,000)
Total liabilities and equities	$(1,290,000)	$(1,555,000)

Additional Information for 2021

- The parent issued bonds during the year for cash.
- Amortization of databases amounts to $15,000 per year.
- The parent sold a building with a cost of $80,000 but a $40,000 book value for cash on May 11.
- The subsidiary purchased equipment on July 23 for $205,000 in cash.
- Late in November, the parent issued stock for cash.
- During the year, the subsidiary paid dividends of $10,000. Both parent and subsidiary pay dividends in the same year as declared.

Prepare a consolidated statement of cash flows for this business combination for the year ending December 31, 2021. Use the indirect method to compute cash flow from operating activities.

LO 6-6

48. Following are separate income statements for Austin, Inc., and its 80 percent–owned subsidiary, Rio Grande Corporation as well as a consolidated statement for the business combination as a whole (credit balances indicated by parentheses).

	Austin	Rio Grande	Consolidated
Revenues	$(700,000)	$(500,000)	$(1,200,000)
Cost of goods sold	400,000	300,000	700,000
Operating expenses	100,000	70,000	195,000
Equity in earnings of Rio Grande	(84,000)		
Individual company net income	$(284,000)	$(130,000)	
Consolidated net income			$ (305,000)
Noncontrolling interest in consolidated net income			(21,000)
Consolidated net income attributable to Austin			$ (284,000)

Additional Information

- Annual excess fair over book value amortization of $25,000 resulted from the acquisition.
- The parent applies the equity method to this investment.
- Austin has 50,000 shares of common stock and 10,000 shares of preferred stock outstanding. Owners of the preferred stock are paid an annual dividend of $40,000, and each share can be exchanged for two shares of common stock.
- Rio Grande has 30,000 shares of common stock outstanding. The company also has 5,000 stock warrants outstanding. For $10, each warrant can be converted into a share of Rio Grande's common stock. Austin holds half of these warrants. The price of Rio Grande's common stock was $20 per share throughout the year.
- Rio Grande also has convertible bonds, none of which Austin owned. During the current year, total interest expense (net of taxes) was $22,000. These bonds can be exchanged for 10,000 shares of the subsidiary's common stock.

Determine Austin's basic and diluted EPS.

LO 6-4

49. On January 1, Paisley, Inc., paid $560,000 for all of Skyler Corporation's outstanding stock. This cash payment was based on a price of $180 per share for Skyler's $100 par value preferred stock and $38 per share for its $20 par value common stock. The preferred shares are voting, cumulative, and fully participating. At the acquisition date, the book values of Skyler's accounts equaled their fair values. Any excess fair value is assigned to an intangible asset and will be amortized over a 10-year period.

During the year, Skyler sold inventory costing $60,000 to Paisley for $90,000. All but $18,000 (measured at transfer price) of this merchandise has been resold to outsiders by the end of the year. At the end of the year, Paisley continues to owe Skyler for the last shipment of inventory priced at $28,000.

Also, on January 2, Paisley sold Skyler equipment for $20,000 although it had a carrying amount of only $12,000 (original cost of $30,000). Both companies depreciate such property according to the straight-line method with no salvage value. The remaining life at this date was four years.

The following financial statements are for each company for the year ending December 31 (credit balances indicated by parentheses). Determine consolidated financial totals for this business combination.

	Paisley, Inc.	Skyler Corporation
Sales	$ (800,000)	$(400,000)
Cost of goods sold	528,000	260,000
Expenses	180,000	130,000
Gain on sale of equipment	(8,000)	–0–
Net income	$ (100,000)	$ (10,000)
Retained earnings, 1/1	$ (400,000)	$(150,000)
Net income	(100,000)	(10,000)
Dividends declared	60,000	–0–
Retained earnings, 12/31	$ (440,000)	$(160,000)
Cash	$ 30,000	$ 40,000
Accounts receivable	300,000	100,000
Inventory	260,000	180,000
Investment in Skyler Corporation	560,000	–0–
Land, buildings, and equipment	680,000	500,000
Accumulated depreciation	(180,000)	(90,000)
Total assets	$ 1,650,000	$ 730,000
Accounts payable	$ (140,000)	$ (90,000)
Long-term liabilities	(240,000)	(180,000)
Preferred stock	–0–	(100,000)
Common stock	(620,000)	(200,000)
Additional paid-in capital	(210,000)	–0–
Retained earnings, 12/31	(440,000)	(160,000)
Total liabilities and equity	$(1,650,000)	$(730,000)

LO 6-5

50. On June 30, 2021, Plaster, Inc., paid $916,000 for 80 percent of Stucco Company's outstanding stock. Plaster assessed the acquisition-date fair value of the 20 percent noncontrolling interest at $229,000. At acquisition date, Stucco reported the following book values for its assets and liabilities:

Cash	$ 60,000
Accounts receivable	127,000
Inventory	203,000
Land	65,000
Buildings	175,000
Equipment	300,000
Accounts payable	(35,000)

On June 30, Plaster allocated the excess acquisition-date fair value over book value to Stucco's assets as follows:

Equipment (3-year remaining life)	$ 75,000
Database (10-year remaining life)	175,000

At the end of 2021, the following comparative (2020 and 2021) balance sheets and consolidated income statement were available:

	Plaster, Inc. December 31, 2020	Consolidated December 31, 2021
Cash	$ 43,000	$ 242,850
Accounts receivable (net)	362,000	485,400
Inventory	415,000	720,000
Land	300,000	365,000
Buildings (net)	245,000	370,000
Equipment (net)	1,800,000	2,037,500
Database	–0–	166,250
Total assets	$3,165,000	$4,387,000
Accounts payable	$ 80,000	$ 107,000
Long-term liabilities	400,000	1,200,000
Common stock	1,800,000	1,800,000
Noncontrolling interest	–0–	255,500
Retained earnings	885,000	1,024,500
Total liabilities and equities	$3,165,000	$4,387,000

PLASTER, INC., AND SUBSIDIARY STUCCO COMPANY
Consolidated Income Statement
For the Year Ended December 31, 2021

Revenues		$1,217,500
Cost of goods sold	$737,500	
Depreciation	187,500	
Database amortization	8,750	
Interest and other expenses	9,750	943,500
Consolidated net income		$ 274,000

Additional Information for 2021

- On December 1, Stucco paid a $40,000 dividend. During the year, Plaster paid $100,000 in dividends.
- During the year, Plaster issued $800,000 in long-term debt at par.
- Plaster reported no asset purchases or dispositions other than the acquisition of Stucco.

Prepare a 2021 consolidated statement of cash flows for Plaster and Stucco. Use the indirect method of reporting cash flows from operating activities.

Develop Your Skills

EXCEL CASE: INTRA-ENTITY BONDS

CPA *skills*

Place Company owns a majority voting interest in Sassano, Inc. On January 1, 2019, Place issued $1,000,000 of 11 percent 10-year bonds at $943,497.77 to yield 12 percent. On January 1, 2021, Sassano purchased all of these bonds in the open market at a price of $904,024.59 with an effective yield of 13 percent.

Required

Using an Excel spreadsheet, do the following:

1. Prepare amortization schedules for the Place Company bonds payable and the Investment in Place Bonds for Sassano, Inc.

2. Using the values from the amortization schedules, compute the worksheet adjustment for a December 31, 2021, consolidation of Place and Sassano to reflect the effective retirement of the Place bonds. Formulate your solution to be able to accommodate various yield rates (and therefore prices) on the repurchase of the bonds.

Hints

Present value of 1 = $1/(1 + r)n$
Present value of an annuity of 1 = $[1 - 1/(1 + r)n]/r$
Where r = effective yield and n = years remaining to maturity

RESEARCH CASE: STATEMENT OF CASH FLOWS

CPA skills

Download a recent copy of Pfizer's annual report (search Pfizer Investor Relations). Locate the firm's consolidated statement of cash flows and answer the following:

- Does the firm employ the direct or indirect method of accounting for operating cash flows?
- Why does the firm account for the changes in balances in operating accounts (e.g., accounts receivable, inventory, accounts payable) in determining operating cash flows as net of acquisitions and divestitures?
- Describe the accounting for cash paid for business acquisitions in the statement of cash flows.
- Describe the accounting for any noncontrolling subsidiary interest and any other business combination–related items in the consolidated statement of cash flows.

FINANCIAL REPORTING RESEARCH AND ANALYSIS CASE

CPA skills

The FASB ASC Subtopic "Variable Interest Entities" affects thousands of business enterprises that now, as primary beneficiaries, consolidate entities that qualify as controlled VIEs. Retrieve a recent annual report of one or more of the following companies (or any others you may find) that consolidate VIEs:

- The Walt Disney Company.
- General Electric.
- Harley-Davidson.

Required

Write a brief report that describes

1. The reasons for consolidation of the company's VIE(s).
2. The effect of the consolidation of the VIE(s) on the company's financial statements.

chapter

7

Consolidated Financial Statements—Ownership Patterns and Income Taxes

Learning Objectives

After studying this chapter, you should be able to:

LO 7-1 Demonstrate the consolidation process when indirect control is present in a father-son-grandson ownership configuration.

LO 7-2 Demonstrate the consolidation process when a corporate ownership structure is characterized by a connecting affiliation.

LO 7-3 Demonstrate the consolidation process when a corporate ownership structure is characterized by mutual ownership.

LO 7-4 List the criteria for membership in an affiliated group for income tax filing purposes.

LO 7-5 Compute taxable income and deferred tax amounts for an affiliated group based on information presented in a consolidated set of financial statements.

LO 7-6 Compute taxable income and deferred tax amounts to be recognized when separate tax returns are filed by any of the affiliates of a business combination.

LO 7-7 Determine the deferred tax consequences for temporary differences generated when a business combination is created.

LO 7-8 Explain the impact that a net operating loss of an acquired affiliate has on consolidated figures.

Chapter 7 concludes coverage of the accounting for business combinations by analyzing two additional aspects of consolidated financial statements. First, we present the various ownership patterns that can exist within a combination. We examine indirect control of a subsidiary, connecting affiliations, and mutual ownership as well as the consolidation procedures applicable to each organizational structure. The chapter then provides an overview of the income tax considerations relevant to the members of a business combination. We discuss income tax accounting for both consolidated and separate corporate returns in light of current laws.

Indirect Subsidiary Control

Chapters 2 through 5 focus primarily on one particular type of financial control structure for a consolidated entity. Specifically, a parent holds a direct majority voting interest in a single subsidiary. This ownership pattern expedites the explanation of consolidation theories and techniques. In practice, though, more elaborate corporate ownership structures commonly exist. Alphabet, Inc., for example, controls several subsidiaries. However, Alphabet does not directly own voting stock in many of these companies. It maintains control through indirect ownership because Alphabet's subsidiaries are majority stockholders of many of the companies within the consolidated entity. For example, Alphabet, the parent company, owns Google, which in turn has controlling financial interests in other companies such as Android and YouTube. This type of corporate configuration is referred to as a *father-son-grandson relationship* because of the pattern the descending tiers create. Other examples of such ownership structures can be found at Ford, Berkshire Hathaway, General Electric, and many more corporations.

The formation of a business combination (the acquisition of a controlling financial interest) through indirect ownership is not an unusual practice. Many businesses organize their operations in this manner to group individual companies along product lines, geographic districts, or other logical criteria. The philosophy behind this structuring is that placing direct control in proximity to each subsidiary can develop clearer lines of communication and responsibility reporting. However, other indirect ownership patterns are simply the result of years of acquisition and growth. As an example, when

Procter & Gamble acquired the Gillette Company, it gained control over Gillette's subsidiaries including Oral-B Laboratories, Braun AG, and others. Procter & Gamble did not achieve this control directly, but indirectly through the acquisition of the parent company.

LO 7-1

Demonstrate the consolidation process when indirect control is present in a father-son-grandson ownership configuration.

The Consolidation Process When Indirect Control Is Present

Regardless of a company's reason for establishing indirect control over a subsidiary, a new accounting challenge emerges: The parent must consolidate financial information from each of the connecting corporations into a single set of financial statements. Fortunately, indirect ownership does not introduce any new conceptual issues but affects only the mechanical elements of this process. For example, in preparing consolidated statements, the parent company must allocate acquisition-date fair values and recognize any related excess amortizations for each affiliate, regardless of whether control is direct or indirect. In addition, all worksheet entries previously demonstrated continue to apply. For consolidated entities involving indirect control, the entire consolidation process is basically repeated for each separate affiliate.

Calculation of Subsidiary Income

Although the presence of an indirect ownership does not change most consolidation procedures, a calculation of each subsidiary's accrual-based income does pose some difficulty. Appropriate income determination is essential for calculating (1) equity income accruals and (2) the net income attributable to the noncontrolling interest.

In consolidated entities with indirect control, at least one company (and possibly many) holds both a parent and a subsidiary position. A company in that position must first recognize the equity income accruing from its subsidiaries before computing its own net income total. The process begins with the grandson, then moves to the son, and finishes with the father. Only by following this systematic approach is the correct amount of accrual-based net income determined for each individual company.

In computing consolidated net income, we adjust the subsidiary's reported earnings for excess fair-value amortizations and any upstream intra-entity transfers. In consolidated entities with indirect control, these same adjustments are made for each company's separate income, beginning at the lowest level. The respective accrual-based income figures for each affiliate in the consolidated entity therefore must take into account

- Excess acquisition-date fair over book value amortizations.
- Deferrals and subsequent income recognition from intra-entity transfers. The income effects can include gains from long-term asset transfers or gross profits from inventory transfers. In subsequent illustrations, we refer to both types as "gains."

Income Computation Illustrated

For example, assume that three companies form a business combination: Top Company owns 70 percent of Midway Company—which, in turn, possesses 60 percent of Bottom Company. As the following display indicates, Top controls both subsidiaries, although the parent's relationship with Bottom is only of an indirect nature.

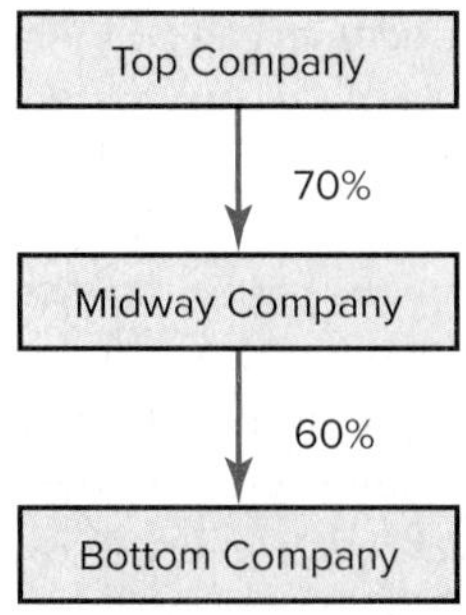

Assume next that the following information comes from the 2021 individual financial records of the three companies making up this combination:

	Top Company	Midway Company	Bottom Company
Separate company net income (before investment income)	$600,000	$300,000	$100,000
Dividend income from investment in subsidiary (based on initial value method)	80,000	50,000	
Internally calculated net income	$680,000	$350,000	$100,000
Additional information:			
Amortization expense from acquisition-date excess fair over book value		$ 30,000	$ 25,000
Net deferred intra-entity gains within current year income	$110,000	80,000	20,000

As specified, we begin with the grandson of the organization and calculate each company's 2021 accrual-based income. From the perspective of the consolidated entity, Bottom's income for the period is only $55,000 after deferring the $20,000 in net intra-entity gains and recognizing the $25,000 excess amortization associated with the acquisition by Midway. Thus, $55,000 is the basis for the equity accrual by its parent and noncontrolling interest recognition. Once the grandson's income has been derived, this figure then is used to compute the accrual-based earnings of the son, Midway:

Separate company net income—Midway Company		$300,000
Equity income accruing from Bottom Company—		
Bottom's income from internal records	$100,000	
Excess amortization related to Midway acquisition	(25,000)	
Net intra-entity gain deferral	(20,000)	
Bottom's accrual-based net income	$ 55,000	
Midway's percentage ownership	60%	
Midway's share of Bottom's net income		33,000
Excess amortization from Top's acquisition of Midway		(30,000)
Deferral of Midway's intra-entity gain (above)		(80,000)
Accrual-based net income of Midway Company		$223,000

Midway's $223,000 accrual-based income differs from its separate internally calculated profit of $350,000. The difference reflects a consolidated perspective for the entire ownership structure including excess amortization and intra-entity transfers. Continuing with the successive derivation of each company's net income, we now can determine Top Company's net income. After computing the son's net income, the father's net income is derived as follows:

Separate company income—Top Company	$600,000
Equity income accruing from Midway Company—70% of $223,000 (above)	156,100
Deferral of Top's net intra-entity gain (above)	(110,000)
Accrual-based net income of Top Company	$646,100

We should note several aspects of the accrual-based income data:

1. The 2021 income statement for Top Company and its consolidated subsidiaries discloses an $88,900 balance as the "net income attributable to the noncontrolling interest."

The total accrual-based income figures of the two subsidiaries provide the basis for the calculation as follows:

	Accrual-Based Income	Outside Ownership	Noncontrolling Interest in Net Income
Bottom Company	$ 55,000	40%	$22,000
Midway Company	223,000	30	66,900
Total			$88,900

2. Although this illustration applies the initial value method to both investments, the parent's individual accounting does not affect accrual-based income totals. The initial value figures are simply replaced with equity accruals in preparation for consolidation. The selection of a particular method is relevant only for internal reporting purposes; earnings, as shown here, are based entirely on the equity income accruing from each subsidiary.
3. As demonstrated previously, if appropriate equity accruals are recognized, the sum of the parent's accrual-based net income and the noncontrolling interest net income share serves as a "proof figure" for the consolidated total. Thus, if the consolidation process is performed correctly, the earnings this entire organization reports should equal $735,000 ($646,100 + $88,900). Observe that consolidated net income can also be computed as follows:

Sum of Top, Midway, and Bottom separate company incomes	$1,000,000
Less: Combined excess fair-value amortizations	(55,000)
Less: Combined net intra-entity gain deferrals	(210,000)
Consolidated net income	$ 735,000

4. Although Midway possesses 60 percent of Bottom's voting stock, only 42 percent of Bottom's income is attributed to Top's controlling interest (70% direct ownership of Midway × 60% indirect ownership of Bottom). The subsidiary's remaining income is assigned to the noncontrolling interest.

   To demonstrate the accuracy of this percentage, we construct a brief example. Assume that neither Top nor Midway reports any earnings during the year but that Bottom has $100 in accrual-based income. If Bottom declares a $100 cash dividend, $60 goes to Midway, and the remaining $40 goes to Bottom's noncontrolling interest. Assuming then that Midway uses this $60 to pay its own dividend, $42 (70 percent) is transferred to Top, and $18 goes to Midway's outside owners.

   Thus, 58 percent of Bottom's income is attributed to parties outside the consolidated entity. An initial 40 percent belongs to Bottom's own noncontrolling interest, and an additional 18 percent accrues to Midway's other shareholders. Only 42 percent of Bottom's original income is considered attributable to the consolidated entity. Consolidated financial statements reflect this allocation by including 100 percent of the subsidiary's revenues and expenses and allocating 58 percent of the subsidiary's net income to the noncontrolling interest.

Consolidation Process—Indirect Control

After analyzing the income calculations within a father-son-grandson configuration, a full-scale consolidation can be produced. As demonstrated, this type of ownership pattern does not significantly alter the worksheet process. Most worksheet entries are simply made twice: first for the son's investment in the grandson and then for the father's ownership of the son.

Although this sudden doubling of entries may seem overwhelming, close examination reveals that the individual procedures remain unaffected.

To illustrate, assume that on January 1, 2019, Big acquires 80 percent of Middle's outstanding common stock for $640,000. On that date, Middle has a book value (total stockholders' equity) of $700,000, and the 20 percent noncontrolling interest has a fair value of $160,000. The resulting excess of subsidiary fair value over book value is assigned to franchises and amortized at the rate of $10,000 per year.

Following the acquisition, Middle's book value rises to $1,080,000 by the end of 2021, denoting a $380,000 increment during this three-year period ($1,080,000 – $700,000). Big applies the partial equity method; therefore, the parent accrues a $304,000 ($380,000 × 80%) increase in the investment account (to $944,000) over this same time span.

On January 1, 2020, Middle acquires 70 percent of Little for $462,000. Little's stockholders' equity accounts total $630,000, and the fair value of the 30 percent noncontrolling interest is $198,000. Middle allocates this entire $30,000 excess fair value to franchises so that, over a six-year assumed remaining life, the consolidated entity recognizes amortization expense of $5,000 each year. During 2020–2021, Little's book value increases by $150,000, to a $780,000 total. Because Middle also applies the partial equity method, it adds $105,000 ($150,000 × 70%) to the investment account to arrive at a $567,000 balance ($462,000 + $105,000).

To complete the introductory information for this illustration, assume that a number of intra-entity upstream transfers occurred over the past two years. The following table shows the dollar volume of these transactions and the intra-entity gross profit in each year's ending inventory:

	Little Company Transfers to Middle Company		Middle Company Transfers to Big Company	
Year	Transfer Price	Year-End Deferred Gross Profit	Transfer Price	Year-End Deferred Gross Profit
2020	$ 75,000	$17,500	$200,000	$30,000
2021	120,000	25,000	250,000	40,000

Exhibit 7.1 presents the worksheet to consolidate these three companies for the year ending December 31, 2021. The first three columns represent the individual statements for each entity. The entries required to consolidate the various balances follow this information. To identify the separate procedures, entries concerning the relationship between Big (father) and Middle (son) are marked with a "B," whereas an "L" denotes Middle's ownership of Little (grandson). Duplicate entries in this exhibit are designed to facilitate a clearer understanding of this consolidation. A number of these dual entries can be combined later.

To arrive at consolidated figures, Exhibit 7.1 incorporates the worksheet entries described next. Analyzing each of these adjustments and eliminations can identify the consolidation procedures necessitated by a father-son-grandson ownership pattern. Despite the presence of indirect control over Little, financial statements are created for the consolidated entity as a whole utilizing the process described in previous chapters.

*Consolidation Entry *G*

Entry ***G** defers the intra-entity gross profits contained in the beginning financial figures. Within their separate accounting systems, two of the companies prematurely recorded income ($17,500 by Little and $30,000 by Middle) in 2020 at the transfer. For consolidation purposes, a 2020 worksheet entry eliminates these gross profits from both beginning Retained Earnings as well as Cost of Goods Sold (the present location of the beginning inventory). Consequently, the consolidated income statement recognizes the appropriate gross profit for the current period.

EXHIBIT 7.1

Indirect Control: Father-Son-Grandson
Investment: Partial Equity Method

BIG COMPANY AND CONSOLIDATED SUBSIDIARIES
Consolidation Worksheet
For Year Ending December 31, 2021

Accounts	Big Company	Middle Company	Little Company	Consolidation Entries Debit	Consolidation Entries Credit	Noncontrolling Interest	Consolidated Totals
Income Statement							
Sales	(800,000)	(500,000)	(300,000)	(LTI) 120,000 (BTI) 250,000			(1,230,000)
Cost of goods sold	300,000	220,000	140,000	(LG) 25,000 (BG) 40,000	(L*L) 17,500 (LTI) 120,000 (B*G) 30,000 (BTI) 250,000		307,500
Expenses	200,000	80,000	60,000	(LE) 5,000 (BE) 10,000			355,000
Income of Little Company	–0–	(70,000)	–0–	(LI) 70,000			–0–
Income of Middle Company	(216,000)	–0–	–0–	(BI) 216,000			–0–
Separate company net income	(516,000)	(270,000)	100,000				
Consolidated net income							(567,500)
Net income attributable to noncontrolling interest (Little)						(26,250)	26,250
Net income attributable to noncontrolling interest (Middle)						(48,250)	48,250
Net income attributable to Big Company							(493,000)
Statement of Retained Earnings							
Retained earnings, 1/1/21:							
Big Company	(900,000)	–0–	–0–	(B * C) 52,600			(847,400)
Middle Company	–0–	(800,000)	–0–	(B * G) 30,000 (L * C) 15,750 (BS) 754,250			–0–
Little Company	–0–	–0–	(600,000)	(L * L) 17,500 (LS) 582,500		–0–	
Net income (from above)	(516,000)	(270,000)	(100,000)				(493,000)
Dividends declared:							
Big Company	120,000	–0–	–0–				120,000
Middle Company	–0–	90,000	–0–		(BD) 72,000	18,000	–0–
Little Company	–0–	–0–	50,000		(LD) 35,000	15,000	–0–
Retained earnings, 12/31/21	(1,296,000)	(980,000)	(650,000)				(1,220,400)

(continued)

EXHIBIT 7.1 (Continued)

Accounts	Big Company	Middle Company	Little Company	Consolidation Entries Debit	Consolidation Entries Credit	Noncontrolling Interest	Consolidated Totals
BalanceSheet							
Cash and receivables	600,000	300,000	280,000				1,180,000
Inventory	300,000	260,000	290,000		(LG) 25,000 (BG) 40,000		785,000
Investment in Middle Company	944,000	–0–	–0–	(BD) 72,000	(B * C) 52,600 (BS) 683,400 (BI) 216,000 (BA) 64,000		–0–
Investmentin Little Company	–0–	567,000	–0–	(LD) 35,000	(L * C) 15,750 (LS) 498,750 (LI) 70,000 (LA) 17,500		–0–
Land, buildings, equipment	192,000	153,000	510,000				855,000
Franchises	–0–	–0–	–0–	(LA) 25,000 (BA) 80,000	(LE) 5,000 (BE) 10,000		90,000
Totalassets	2,036,000	1,280,000	1,080,000				2,910,000
Liabilities	(340,000)	(200,000)	(300,000)				(840,000)
Noncontrolling interest in Little Company, 1/1/21	–0–	–0–	–0–		(LS) 213,750 (LA) 7,500	(221,250)	
Noncontrolling interest in Middle Company, 1/1/21	–0–	–0–	–0–		(BS) 170,850 (BA) 16,000	(186,850)	
Total noncontrolling interest, 12/31/21	–0–	–0–	–0–			(449,600)	(449,600)
Common stock:							
Big Company	(400,000)	–0–	–0–				(400,000)
Middle Company	–0–	(100,000)	–0–	(BS) 100,000			–0–
Litte Company	–0–	–0–	(130,000)	(LS) 130,000			–0–
Retained earnings (above)	(1,296,000)	(980,000)	(650,000)				(1,220,400)
Total liabilities and equities	(2,036,000)	(1,280,000)	(1,080,000)	2,630,600	2,630,600		(2,910,000)

Note: Parentheses indicate a credit balance.

Consolidation entries: Entries labeled with a "B" refer to the investment relationship between Big and Middle. Entries with an "L" refer to Middle's ownership of Little.

(*G) Removal of intra-entity gross profit from beginning inventory figures so that it can be recognized in current period.
(*C) Conversion of partial equity method to equity method. Amortization for prior years is recognized along with effects of beginning intra-entity upstream gross profits.
(S) Elimination of subsidiaries' stockholders' equity accounts along with recognition of January 1 noncontrolling interests.
(A) Allocation to franchises, unamortized balance being recognized as of January 1.
(I) Elimination of intra-entity income accrued during the period.
(D) Elimination of intra-entity dividends.
(E) Recognition of amortization expense for the current period.
(TI) Elimination of intra-entity sales/purchases balances created by the transfer of inventory.
(G) Deferral of intra-entity inventory gross profit from ending figures to be recognized in subsequent periods.

*Consolidation Entry *C*

Neither Big nor Middle applies the full equity method to its investments; therefore, the figures recognized during the years prior to the current period (2021) must now be updated on the worksheet. This process begins with the son's ownership of the grandson. Hence, Middle must reduce its 2020 income (now closed into Retained Earnings) by $3,500 to reflect the amortization applicable to that year. Middle did not record this expense in applying the partial equity method.

In addition, because $17,500 of Little's previously reported earnings have just been deferred (in preceding Entry ***G**), the effect of this reduction on Middle's ownership must also be recognized. The parent's original equity accrual for 2020 is based on reported rather than accrual-based profit, thus recording too much income. Little's deferral necessitates Middle's parallel $12,250 decrease ($17,500 × 70%). Consequently, the worksheet reduces Middle's Retained Earnings balance as of January 1, 2021, and the Investment in Little account by a total of $15,750:

Reduction in Middle's Beginning Retained Earnings

2020 amortization expense ($5,000 × 70%).	$ 3,500
Income effect created by Little's deferral of 2020 intra-entity gross profit (reduction of previous accrual) ($17,500 × 70%).	12,250
Required reduction to Middle's beginning retained earnings (Entry **L*C**)	$15,750

A similar equity adjustment is required in connection with Big's ownership of Middle. The calculation of the specific amount to be recorded follows the same procedure identified earlier for Middle's investment in Little. Again, amortization expense for all prior years (2019 and 2020, in this case) is brought into the consolidation as well as the income reduction created by the deferral of Middle's $30,000 intra-entity gross profit (Entry ***G**). *However, recognition also must be given to the effects associated with the $15,750 decrease in Middle's pre-2021 earnings described in the previous paragraph.* Although entered only on the worksheet, this adjustment is a change in Middle's originally reported income. To reflect Big's ownership of Middle, the effect of this reduction must be included in determining the income balances actually accruing to the parent company. Thus, a $52,600 decrease is needed in Big's beginning Retained Earnings to establish the proper accounting for its subsidiaries:

Reduction in Big's Beginning Retained Earnings

Amortization expense relating to Middle Company acquisition—2019–2020 ($10,000 per year × 80%).	$16,000
Income effect created by Middle Company's deferral of intra-entity gross profit ($30,000 × 80%)	24,000
Income effect created by Middle Company's adjustment to its prior year's investment income ($15,750 × 80%) (above)	12,600
Required reduction to Big's beginning retained earnings (Entry **B*C**)	$52,600

Consolidation Entry S

The beginning stockholders' equity accounts of each subsidiary are eliminated here, and noncontrolling interest balances as of the beginning of the year are recognized. As in previous chapters, the preliminary adjustments described earlier directly affect the amounts involved in this entry. Because Entry ***G** removed a $17,500 beginning inventory profit, Little's January 1, 2021, book value on the worksheet is $712,500, not $730,000. This total is the basis for the $213,750 beginning noncontrolling interest (30 percent) and the $498,750 elimination (70 percent) from the parent's investment account.

Similarly, Entries ***G** ($30,000) and ***C** ($15,750) have already decreased Middle's book value by $45,750. Thus, this company's beginning stockholders' equity accounts are now adjusted to a total of $854,250 ($900,000 – $45,750). This balance leads to a $170,850 initial noncontrolling interest valuation (20 percent) and a $683,400 (80 percent) offset against Big's Investment in Middle account.

Consolidation Entry A

The unamortized franchise balances remaining as of January 1, 2021, are removed from the two investment accounts so that this intangible asset can be identified separately on the consolidated balance sheet. Because Entry *C already recognizes amortization expense for the previous periods, only beginning totals for the year of $25,000 ($30,000 – $5,000) and $80,000 ($100,000 – $20,000) still remain from the original amounts paid. These totals are allocated across the controlling and noncontrolling interests.

Consolidation Entry I

This entry eliminates the current intra-entity income figures accrued by each parent through its application of the partial equity method.

Consolidation Entry D

Intra-entity dividends declared are removed here from the consolidated financial totals.

Consolidation Entry E

The annual amortization expense relating to each of the franchise balances is recognized.

Consolidation Entry TI

The intra-entity sales/purchases figures created by the transfer of inventory during 2021 are eliminated on the worksheet.

Consolidation Entry G

This final consolidation entry defers the intra-entity gross profits that remain in inventory as of December 31, 2021. The profit on these transfers is removed until the merchandise is subsequently sold to unrelated parties or consumed by the affiliate receiving the transfer.

Noncontrolling Interests' Share of Consolidated Net Income

To complete the steps that constitute this consolidation worksheet, the 2021 income accruing to owners outside the consolidated entity must be recognized. This allocation is based on the accrual-based earnings of the two subsidiaries, which, as previously discussed, are calculated beginning with the grandson (Little) followed by the son (Middle):

Little Company's Accrual-Based Income and Noncontrolling Interest

Little Company separate income (from Exhibit 7.1)	$100,000
Excess fair-value franchise amortization from acquisition by Middle	(5,000)
Recognition of previously deferred gross profits from 2020 (Entry **L*G**)	17,500
Deferral of intra-entity gross profits as of 12/31/21 (Entry **LG**)	(25,000)
Little Company's accrual-based net income, 2021	$ 87,500
Outside ownership	30%
Net income attributable to the noncontrolling interest (Little Company)	$ 26,250

Middle Company's Accrual-Based Income and Noncontrolling Interest

Middle Company separate income (from Exhibit 7.1 after removing income of Little Company)	$200,000
Excess fair-value franchise amortization from acquisition by Big	(10,000)
Recognition of gross profits previously deferred from 2020 (Entry **B*G**)	30,000
Deferral of intra-entity gross profits as of 12/31/21 (Entry **BG**)	(40,000)
Equity income accruing from Little Company (70% of $87,500 accrual-based net income [above])	61,250
Middle Company's accrual-based net income, 2021	$241,250
Outside ownership	20%
Net income attributable to the noncontrolling interest (Middle Company)	$ 48,250

Although computation of Big's earnings is not required here, this figure, along with the consolidated net income allocations to the noncontrolling interests, verifies the accuracy of the worksheet process:

Big Company's Accrual-Based Income

Big Company separate income (from Exhibit 7.1, not including income of Middle Company)	$300,000
Equity income accruing from Middle Company (80% of $241,250 accrual-based net income [prior schedule])	193,000
Big Company's accrual-based net income, 2021	$493,000

This $493,000 figure represents the income derived by the parent from its own operations plus the earnings accrued from the company's two subsidiaries (one directly owned and the other indirectly controlled). This balance equals Big Company's share of the consolidated net income of the consolidated entity. As Exhibit 7.1 shows, the income reported by Big Company does, indeed, net to this same total: $493,000.

LO 7-2

Demonstrate the consolidation process when a corporate ownership structure is characterized by a connecting affiliation.

Indirect Subsidiary Control—Connecting Affiliation

The father-son-grandson organization is only one of many corporate ownership patterns. The number of possible configurations found in today's business world is almost limitless. To illustrate the consolidation procedures that accompany these alternative patterns, we briefly discuss a second basic ownership structure referred to as a *connecting affiliation.*

A connecting affiliation exists when two or more companies within a consolidated entity own an interest in another member of that organization. The simplest form of this configuration is frequently drawn as a triangle:

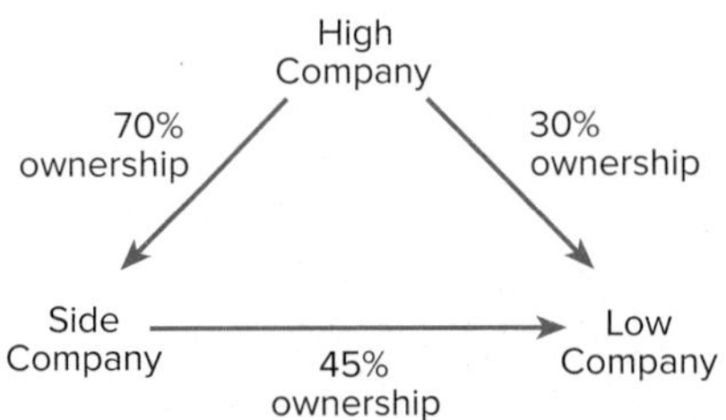

In this example, both High Company and Side Company maintain an ownership interest in Low Company, thus creating a connecting affiliation. Although neither of these individual companies possesses enough voting stock to establish direct control over Low's operations, the consolidated entity's members hold a total of 75 percent of the outstanding shares. Consequently, control lies within the single economic entity's boundaries and requires inclusion of Low's financial information as a part of consolidated statements.

On the date the parent obtains control, the valuation basis for the subsidiary in the parent's consolidated statements is established. For Low, we assume that Side Company's ownership preceded that of High's. Subsequently, High obtained control upon acquiring its 30 percent interest in Low, and the valuation basis for inclusion of Low's assets and liabilities (and related excess fair value over book value amortization) was established at that date.

The process for consolidating a connecting affiliation is essentially the same as for a father-son-grandson organization. Perhaps the most noticeable difference is that more than two investments are always present. In this triangular consolidated entity, High owns an interest in both Side and Low while Side also maintains an investment in Low. Thus, unless combined in some manner, three separate sets of consolidation entries appear on the worksheet. Although the added number of entries certainly provides a degree of mechanical complication, the basic concepts involved in the consolidation process remain the same regardless of the number of investments.

As with the father-son-grandson structure, one key aspect of the consolidation process warrants additional illustration: the determination of accrual-based income figures for each individual company. Therefore, assume that High, Side, and Low have separate incomes (without inclusion of any earnings from their subsidiaries) of $300,000, $200,000, and $100,000, respectively. Each company also retains a $30,000 net intra-entity gain in its current-year income figures. Assume that annual amortization expense of $10,000 has been identified within the acquisition-date excess fair value over book value for each of the two subsidiaries.

In the same manner as a father-son-grandson organization, determining accrual-based earnings begins with any companies solely in a subsidiary position (Low in this case). Next, companies that are both parents and subsidiaries (Side) compute their accrual-based income. Finally, this same calculation is made for the one company (High) that has ultimate control over the entire consolidated entity. Accrual-based income figures for the three companies in this consolidated entity are derived as follows.

Low Company's Accrual-Based Income and Noncontrolling Interest

Low Company separate income	$100,000
Amortization expense from High and Side Companies' acquisition	(10,000)
Deferral of Low Company's net intra-entity gain	(30,000)
Low Company's accrual-based net income	$ 60,000
Outside ownership	25%
Net income attributable to the noncontrolling interest (Low Company)	$ 15,000

Side Company's Accrual-Based Income and Noncontrolling Interest

Side Company separate income	$200,000
Amortization expense relating to High Company's acquisition	(10,000)
Deferral of Side Company's net intra-entity gain	(30,000)
Equity income accruing from Low Company (45% × $60,000) (above)	27,000
Side Company's accrual-based net income	$187,000
Outside ownership	30%
Net income attributable to the noncontrolling interest (Side Company)	$ 56,100

High Company's Accrual-Based Income

High Company separate income	$300,000
Deferral of High Company's net intra-entity gain	(30,000)
Equity income accruing from Side Company (70% × $187,000) (above)	130,900
Equity income accruing from Low Company—direct ownership (30% × $60,000) (above)	18,000
High Company's net income	$418,900

Although in this illustration a connecting affiliation exists, the basic tenets of the consolidation process remain the same:

- Remove all effects from intra-entity transfers.
- Adjust the parents' beginning retained earnings to recognize the equity income resulting from ownership of the subsidiaries in prior years. Determining accrual-based earnings for this period properly aligns the balances with the perspective of a single economic entity.
- Eliminate the beginning stockholders' equity accounts of each subsidiary and recognize the noncontrolling interests' figures as of the first day of the year.
- Enter all unamortized balances created by the original acquisition-date excess of fair value over book value onto the worksheet and allocated to controlling and noncontrolling interests.

- Recognize amortization expense for the current year.
- Remove intra-entity income and dividends.
- Compute the net income attributable to the noncontrolling interest (as just shown), and include it in the consolidated entity's financial statements.

LO 7-3

Demonstrate the consolidation process when a corporate ownership structure is characterized by mutual ownership.

Mutual Ownership

One specific corporate structure that requires further analysis is a mutual ownership. This type of configuration exists when two companies within a business combination hold an equity interest in each other. This ownership pattern is sometimes created as a result of financial battles that occur during takeover attempts. A defensive strategy (often called the *Pac-Man Defense*) is occasionally adopted whereby the target company attempts to avoid takeover by reversing roles and acquiring shares of its investor. Consequently, the two parties hold shares of each other, and one usually gains control.

Two typical mutual ownership patterns follow. In situation A, the parent and the subsidiary possess a percentage of each other's voting shares; in situation B, the mutual ownership exists between two subsidiary companies:

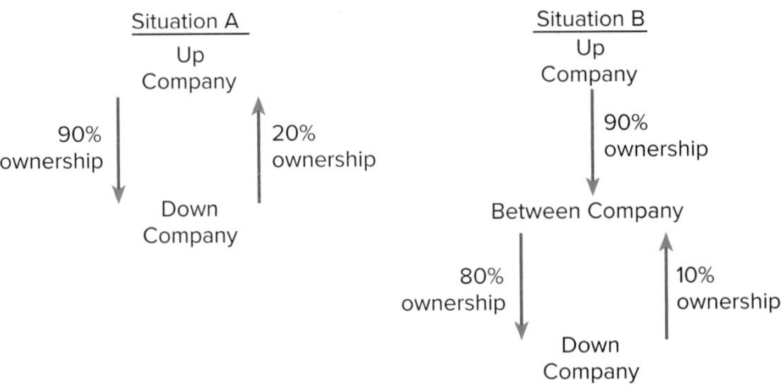

Accounting for mutual ownership raises unique conceptual issues. These concerns center on handling any parent company stock owned by a subsidiary. According to FASB ASC 810-10-45-5,

> shares of the parent held by a subsidiary shall not be treated as outstanding shares in the consolidated statement of financial position and, therefore, shall be eliminated in the consolidated financial statements and reflected as treasury shares.

This approach has theoretical merit because ownership of parent shares by its subsidiary does not involve parties outside of the affiliated group. For consolidation purposes, no accounting distinction is drawn between the parent reacquiring its own shares and the same transaction made by its subsidiary. The acquisition of treasury shares by either a parent or its controlled subsidiary represents an identical economic event that should have identical financial reporting implications.

Treasury Stock Approach

The treasury stock approach to mutual ownership focuses on the parent's control over the subsidiary. Although the affiliated companies maintain separate legal incorporation, only a single economic entity exists, and the parent dominates it. Hence, either company can purchase stock or other items, but all reporting for the business combination must be from the parent's perspective. The focus on the parent's perspective is underscored by the fundamental purpose of consolidated financial statements, as observed in FASB ASC 810-10-10-1:

> The purpose of consolidated financial statements is to present, primarily for the benefit of the owners and creditors of the parent, the results of operations and the financial position of a parent and all its subsidiaries as if the consolidated group were a single economic entity.

Therefore, as a single economic entity, the purchase of the parent's shares by any of the affiliated members is reported as treasury stock in the consolidated financial statements.

The treasury stock approach has always been common in practice, although its popularity was undoubtedly based as much on the ease of application as on theoretical merit. *The cost of parent shares held by the subsidiary is simply reclassified on the worksheet into a treasury stock account.* Any dividend declarations on this stock are considered intra-entity transfers that must be eliminated. This reporting technique is straightforward, and the shares are indeed no longer accounted for as if they were outstanding.

Mutual Ownership Illustrated

To illustrate the treasury stock approach, assume that on January 1, 2019, Sun Company purchased 10 percent of Pop Company. Sun paid $120,000 for these shares, an amount that exactly equaled Pop's proportionate book value. Many possible reasons exist for this transaction. The acquisition could be simply an investment or an attempt to forestall a takeover move by Pop. To simplify the illustration, it is assumed that Pop's shares are not traded actively, and, therefore, continuous market values are unavailable. Under these circumstances, Sun's books appropriately carry the investment in Pop at the $120,000 initial value.

On January 1, 2020, Pop manages to gain control over Sun by acquiring a 70 percent ownership interest, an acquisition that requires consolidation. Details of the acquisition are as follows:

Consideration transferred for 70% interest	$504,000
30% noncontrolling interest acquisition-date fair value	216,000
Sun Company total fair value	$720,000
Sun Company's reported book value	600,000
Excess fair value over book value—assigned to franchise contracts (40-year remaining life)	$120,000
Annual additional amortization ($120,000 over 40 years)	$ 3,000
Investment is accounted for internally by the initial value method.	

During the ensuing years, the two companies report these balances and transactions:

	Sun Company			Pop Company		
Year	Reported Separate Income	Dividend Income (10% ownership)	Dividends Declared	Reported Separate Income	Dividend Income (70% ownership)	Dividends Declared
2019	$20,000	$3,000	$ 8,000	$ 90,000	$ –0–	$30,000
2020	30,000	5,000	10,000	130,000	7,000	50,000
2021	40,000	8,000	15,000	160,500	10,500	80,000

Treasury Stock Approach Illustrated

Exhibit 7.2 presents the consolidation of Pop and Sun for 2021. This worksheet has been developed under the treasury stock approach to mutual ownership so that Pop's investment in Sun is consolidated along routine lines.

Following the calculation of the franchise value and amortization, regular worksheet entries are developed for Pop's investment. Because the initial value method is applied, the $7,000 dividend income recognized in the prior years of ownership (only 2020, in this case) is converted to an equity accrual in Entry ***C.** The parent should recognize 70 percent of the subsidiary's $35,000 income for 2020, or $24,500.[1] However, inclusion of the $2,100

[1] Although an intra-entity transfer, the $5,000 dividend from Pop is included here in measuring the subsidiary's previous income. This dividend increased Sun's book value; thus, some accounting must be made within the consolidation process. In addition, at the time of declaration, the parent reduced its Retained Earnings. Hence, the intra-entity portion of this dividend must be reinstated or consolidated Retained Earnings will be too low.

EXHIBIT 7.2

Investment: Initial Value Method
Mutual Ownership: Treasury Stock Approach

POP AND CONSOLIDATED SUBSIDIARY
Consolidation Worksheet
For Year Ending December 31, 2021

Accounts	Pop Company	Sun Company	Consolidation Entries: Debit	Consolidation Entries: Credit	Noncontrolling Interest	Consolidated Totals
Income Statement						
Revenues	(900,000)	(400,000)				(1,300,000)
Expenses	739,500	360,000	(E) 3,000			1,102,500
Dividend income	(10,500)	(8,000)	(I) 18,500			–0–
Separate company net income	(171,000)	(48,000)				
Consolidated net income						(197,500)
Net income attributable to the noncontrolling interest [($48,000 – 3,000) × 30%]					(13,500)	13,500
Net income attributable to Pop Company						(184,000)
Statement of Retained Earnings						
Retained earnings, 1/1/21:						
Pop Company	(747,000)	–0–		(*C) 15,400		(762,400)
Sun Company	–0–	(425,000)	(S) 425,000			–0–
Net income (above)	(171,000)	(48,000)				(184,000)
Dividends declared:						
Pop Company	80,000	–0–		(I) 8,000		72,000
Sun Company	–0–	15,000		(I) 10,500	4,500	–0–
Retained earnings, 12/31/21	(838,000)	(458,000)				(874,400)
Balance Sheet						
Current assets	842,000	332,000				1,174,000
Investment in Sun Company	504,000	–0–	(*C) 15,400	(S) 437,500 (A) 81,900		–0–
Investment in Pop Company	–0–	120,000		(TS) 120,000		–0–
Land, buildings, equipment (net)	642,000	516,000				1,158,000
Franchises	–0–	–0–	(A) 117,000	(E) 3,000		114,000
Total assets	1,988,000	968,000				2,446,000
Liabilities	(550,000)	(310,000)				(860,000)
Noncontrolling interest in Sun Company, 1/1/21	–0–	–0–		(S) 187,500 (A) 35,100	(222,600)	
Noncontrolling interest in Sun Company, 12/31/21	–0–	–0–			(231,600)	(231,600)
Common stock	(600,000)	(200,000)	(S) 200,000			(600,000)
Retained earnings, 12/31/21 (above)	(838,000)	(458,000)				(874,400)
Treasury stock	–0–	–0–	(TS) 120,000			120,000
Total liabilities and equities	(1,988,000)	(968,000)	898,900	898,900		(2,446,000)

Note: Parentheses indicate a credit balance.
Consolidation entries:
(*C) Conversion of initial value method to equity method. This entry recognizes 70 percent of the increase in Sun Company's book value less amortization expense applicable to the previous year [70% ($25,000 – $3,000)].
(S) Elimination of subsidiary's stockholders' equity accounts along with recognition of January 1, noncontrolling interest.
(TS) Reclassification of Sun Company's ownership in Pop Company into a treasury stock account.
(A) Allocation to franchises, unamortized balance recognized as of January 1.
(I) Elimination of intra-entity dividend income for the period.
(E) Recognition of amortization expense for the current year.

amortization expense (the parent's 70 percent share) dictates that $22,400 is the appropriate equity accrual. Because the parent has already recognized $7,000 in dividend income, Entry *C records the necessary increase as $15,400 ($22,400 – $7,000).[2]

The remaining entries relating to Pop's investment are standard: The subsidiary's stockholders' equity accounts are eliminated (Entry **S**), the franchises' allocation is recognized (Entry **A**), and so on. The existence of the mutual ownership actually affects only two facets of Exhibit 7.2. First, Sun's $120,000 payment made for the parent's shares is reclassified into a treasury stock account (through Entry **TS**). Second, the $8,000 intra-entity dividend flowing from Pop to Sun during the current year of 2021 is eliminated within Entry **I** (used because the collection was recorded as income). The simplicity of applying the treasury stock approach should be apparent from this one example.

Before leaving the treasury stock approach, a final comment is needed regarding the computation of the noncontrolling interest's share of consolidated net income. In Exhibit 7.2, this balance is recorded as $13,500, or 30 percent of the subsidiary's $45,000 adjusted net income ($48,000 reported net income less $3,000 excess fair-value amortization). A question can be raised as to the validity of including the $8,000 dividend within this income total because that amount is eliminated within the consolidation.

These dividends, although intra-entity in nature, increase the subsidiary company's book value (see footnote 1). Therefore, the increment must be reflected in some manner to indicate the change in the amount attributed to the outside owners. For example, the increase could be recognized as a direct adjustment of $2,400 (30 percent of $8,000) in the noncontrolling interest balance. More often, as shown here, such cash transfers are considered to be income *when viewed from the perspective of these other unrelated parties.*

Income Tax Accounting for a Consolidated Entity

To this point, this textbook has refrained from analyzing the income tax consequences of corporate mergers and acquisitions. Only a comprehensive tax course can cover the tax law complexities inherent in this area. Furthermore, essential accounting issues can be overshadowed by intermingling an explanation of the financial reporting process with an in-depth study of related tax consequences.

Despite the attention focused on basic accounting issues associated with consolidated entities, income tax effects cannot be ignored. Certain tax considerations have a direct impact on the financial reporting of any consolidated entity. At a minimum, a fair presentation of the consolidated entity's financial statements requires recognition of income tax expense figures and deferred income taxes. Therefore, a fundamental knowledge of the income tax effects of a consolidated entity is necessary to understand the consolidated financial reporting process.

As discussed in Chapter 2, U.S. GAAP requires all entities under common control to report their financial statements on a consolidated basis. GAAP consolidated financial statements must report the income taxes payable by the affiliated firms both currently and in the future. However, to properly understand the tax implications of a consolidated entity requires that we first focus on the differences across the consolidation rules for GAAP and federal tax purposes.

[2] The necessary adjustment to beginning retained earnings also can be computed as follows:

Income of subsidiary—2020	$ 35,000
Dividends declared	(10,000)
Increase in book value	$ 25,000
Ownership percentage	70%
Income accrual	$ 17,500
Amortization—2020 (70% × $3,000)	(2,100)
Increase in 2021 beginning retained earnings	$ 15,400

LO 7-4

List the criteria for membership in an affiliated group for income tax filing purposes.

Affiliated Groups

A central issue in accounting for the income taxes of an affiliated group involves the entity filing its tax returns. Many consolidated entities require only a single consolidated return; in other cases, some, or even all, of the component corporations prepare separate returns. According to current tax laws, a consolidated entity may elect to file a consolidated return encompassing all companies that compose an *affiliated group* as defined by the Internal Revenue Code. The Code automatically requires all other corporations to submit separate income tax returns. Consequently, a first step in the taxation process is to delineate the boundaries of an affiliated group. Because of specific requirements outlined in the tax laws, this designation does not necessarily cover the same constituents as a consolidated entity.

According to the Internal Revenue Code, the essential criterion for including a subsidiary within an affiliated group is the parent's ownership of at least 80 percent of the voting stock and at least 80 percent of each class of nonvoting stock. This ownership may be direct or indirect, although the parent must meet these requirements in connection with at least one directly owned subsidiary. As another condition, each company in the affiliated group must be a domestic (rather than a foreign) corporation. A company's options can be described as follows:

- *Domestic subsidiary, 80 percent to 100 percent owned:* May file as part of consolidated return or may file separately.
- *Domestic subsidiary, less than 80 percent owned:* Must file separately.
- *Foreign subsidiary:* Must file separately.

Clearly, a distinction exists between consolidated entities (identified for financial reporting) and affiliated groups as defined for tax purposes. Chapter 2 described a consolidated entity as comprising all subsidiaries controlled by a parent company unless control is only temporary. The possession (either directly or indirectly) of a mere majority of voting stock normally supports control. Conversely, the Internal Revenue Code's 80 percent rule creates a smaller circle of companies qualifying for inclusion in an affiliated group.

As noted earlier, a parent company is not required to file a consolidated tax return. However, for the companies of an affiliated group, the following represent distinct benefits associated with a consolidated tax return:

- Intra-entity profits are not taxed until the asset leaves the consolidated entity; similarly, intra-entity losses (which are rare) are not deducted until the asset leaves the consolidated entity.
- Losses incurred by one affiliated company can be used to reduce taxable income recognized by other group members.

LO 7-5

Compute taxable income and deferred tax amounts for an affiliated group based on information presented in a consolidated set of financial statements.

Deferred Income Taxes

Some deviations between generally accepted accounting principles and income tax laws create *temporary differences* whereby (1) a variation between an asset or liability's recorded book value and its tax basis exists, and (2) this difference results in taxable or deductible amounts in future years. When a temporary difference is present, financial reporting principles require recognizing a deferred tax asset or liability. The specific amount of this income tax deferral depends somewhat on whether the consolidated reporting entity files consolidated or separate returns. Thus, we analyze here the tax consequences of several common transactions to demonstrate a consolidated entity's income tax expense reporting.

Intra-Entity Dividends

For financial reporting, dividends between the members of a consolidated entity always are eliminated; they represent intra-entity cash transfers. For tax accounting, dividends also are removed from income but only if at least 80 percent of the subsidiary's stock is held. Consequently, at this ownership level, no difference between financial and tax reporting exists; both eliminate all intra-entity dividends. Income tax expense is not recorded on the intra-entity dividends. Deferred tax recognition is also ignored because no temporary difference has been created.

However, if less than 80 percent of a subsidiary's stock is held, tax recognition becomes necessary. Intra-entity dividends are taxed partially because, at that ownership level, 35 percent is taxable. The dividends-received deduction on the tax return (the nontaxable portion) is only 65 percent.[3] Thus, an income tax liability is immediately created for the recipient. *In addition, deferred income taxes are required for any of the subsidiary's income not paid currently as a dividend.* A temporary difference is created because tax payments will occur in future years when the subsidiary's earnings eventually are distributed to the parent. Hence, a tax liability is recorded based on the dividends collected, and a deferred tax liability is recorded for the taxable portion of any income not paid to the parent during the year.

The Impact of Goodwill

Current law allows, in some cases, the amortization of goodwill and other purchased intangibles (referred to as *Section 197 property*) over a 15-year period. For financial reporting, goodwill is written off if it is impaired or if the related business is disposed of in some manner. Because of the difference in the periods in which taxable income and financial income are reduced, the presence of tax-deductible goodwill creates a temporary difference that necessitates recognizing deferred income taxes. A temporary difference will also exist for other purchased intangibles that qualify as *Section 197* property.

Intra-Entity Profits

Taxes on intra-entity profits that result from transfers between related companies within a consolidated entity create a special accounting situation. As discussed next, the accounting for the tax consequences of intra-entity transfers depend on the nature of the transferred items. Differential accounting standards apply to taxes on intra-entity inventory transfers vs. other type of assets such as fixed assets, intellectual property, licenses, and financial assets.

Intra-Entity Inventory Profits On consolidated financial statements, recall that we defer recognition of any gross profit on intra-entity transferred inventory until the inventory leaves the group (either through sale or use). The same is true for a consolidated tax return; intra-entity gross profits in inventory are removed until the transferred asset leaves the group. No temporary difference is created.

If separate tax returns are filed, though, tax laws require the inclusion of intra-entity inventory profits in taxable income in the period of inventory transfer even though not yet recognized by the consolidated entity. Thus, the income is taxed immediately, although no sale is recognized from a financial reporting perspective. As observed by FASB ASC (810-10-45-8):

> If income taxes have been paid on intra-entity profits on inventory remaining within the consolidated group, those taxes shall be deferred.[4]

Thus, a "prepayment" of the tax on intra-entity inventory profits creates a deferred income tax asset based on the amount of taxes paid on the deferred profits by the selling affiliate.

Other than Inventory Intra-Entity Profits For intra-entity transfers of assets other than inventory (e.g., equipment, intellectual property, etc.), the ASC requires companies to recognize the related income tax effects in the period in which the transfer occurs. Thus, tax expense on an intra-entity transfer of equipment, for example, is recognized in the period of the transfer and is not deferred. However, following the intra-entity transfer, the buyer recognizes a temporary difference based on the difference between the tax basis of the asset in the buyer's jurisdiction and its financial reporting carrying value in the consolidated financial statements.[5]

[3] If less than 20 percent of a company's stock is owned, the dividends-received deduction is only 50 percent. However, this level of ownership is not applicable to a subsidiary within a business combination.

[4] The ASC also allows for the direct reduction of intra-entity inventory profits eliminated in consolidation as an alternative to tax deferral.

[5] FASB Accounting Standards Update *2016-16 Income Taxes (Topic 740): Intra-Entity Transfers of Assets Other than Inventory.*

Consolidated Tax Returns—Illustration

To illustrate accounting effects created by filing a consolidated tax return, assume that Allan Company possesses 90 percent of Brady Company's voting and nonvoting stocks. Subsequent to the acquisition, the two companies continue normal operations, which includes significant intra-entity transactions. Each company's separate operating and dividend incomes for the current time period are presented as follows, along with the effects of intra-entity inventory profits. No income tax accruals have been recognized within these totals:

	Allan Company (Parent)	**Brady Company (90% owned subsidiary)**
Separate operating income (excludes equity or dividend income from subsidiary)	$160,000	$40,000
Net intra-entity gross profits on inventory remaining in the consolidated entity (included in separate operating income above)	30,000	8,000
Dividends received (from Brady)	9,000	–0–
Dividends paid.	20,000	10,000

From the perspective of the single economic entity, consolidated pretax income is computed as follows:

Separate operating income—Allan	$160,000	
Net intra-entity inventory profit—Allan.	(30,000)	$130,000
Separate operating income—Brady	40,000	
Net intra-entity inventory profits—Brady.	(8,000)	$ 32,000
Pretax consolidated net income.		$162,000

Thus, the pretax income to report in consolidated financial statements before the reduction for the noncontrolling interest is $162,000. For financial reporting, both intra-entity dividends and the effects of intra-entity inventory profits are excluded from this total. Pretax income prior to the noncontrolling interest is computed here because any allocation to these other owners is not deductible for tax purposes.

Because the parent owns more than 80 percent of Brady's stock, dividends from the subsidiary are tax-free. Likewise, intra-entity inventory profits are not taxable presently because a consolidated return is filed. Consequently, *financial and tax accounting are the same for both items;* neither of these items produces a temporary difference, and deferred income taxes are not needed.

The affiliated group pays taxes on $162,000 and, assuming a statutory tax rate of 21 percent, must convey $34,020 ($162,000 × 21%) to the federal government this year. Because no temporary differences exist, deferred income tax recognition is not applicable. Consequently, $34,020 is the reported GAAP tax expense. The consolidated entity recognizes this tax expense by means of a worksheet entry or through individual accruals by each company.

Income Tax Expense Assignment

After computing its income taxes for financial reporting purposes, a parent company includes a single total income tax expense figure on its consolidated income statement. This total income tax expense is then allocated across the members of the affiliated group. This figure is especially important to the subsidiary if it must produce separate financial statements for a loan or a future issuance of equity. The subsidiary's expense also serves as a basis for calculating the net income attributable to the noncontrolling interest.

Several techniques are available to accomplish the tax expense allocation across affiliated companies. For example, the expense charged to a subsidiary often is based on the percentage of the total taxable income from each affiliated company (the percentage allocation method) or on the appropriate taxable income figures if separate returns were filed (the separate return method).

To illustrate, we again use the figures from Allan and Brady in the previous example. Allan owns 90 percent of Brady's outstanding stock. Based on filing a consolidated return, total GAAP income tax expense of $34,020 was recognized. How should these two companies allocate this figure?

Percentage Allocation Method

The percentage allocation method attributes the GAAP tax expense based on the relative contribution of each affiliate to taxable income. Total taxable income on this consolidated return was $162,000. Of this amount, $130,000 was applied to the parent (separate operating income after deferral of intra-entity inventory profits), and $32,000 came from the subsidiary (computed in the same manner). Thus, 19.753 percent ($32,000 ÷ $162,000) of total expense should be assigned to the subsidiary, an amount that equals $6,720 (19.753 percent of $34,020).

Separate Return Method

An alternative allocation technique uses the taxable income that results from filing separate tax returns. On separate returns, intra-entity profits are taxable. Therefore, the separate returns of these two companies appear as follows:

	Allan	Brady	Total
Taxable income (separate operating income)	$160,000	$40,000	
Tax rate	21%	21%	
Income tax expense—separate returns	$ 33,600	$ 8,400	$42,000

By filing a consolidated return, an expense of only $34,020 is recorded for the consolidated entity. Because 20 percent of income tax expense on the separate returns ($8,400 ÷ $42,000) came from the subsidiary, $6,804 of the expense ($34,020 × 20%) is assigned to Brady.

Under this second approach, the noncontrolling interest's share of consolidated net income is computed as follows:

Brady Company—reported operating income	$40,000
Less: Intra-entity profits on inventory remaining in the consolidated entity	(8,000)
Less: Assigned income tax expense	(6,804)
Brady Company—adjusted income	$25,196
Outside ownership	10%
Net income attributable to the noncontrolling interest (rounded)	$ 2,520

LO 7-6

Compute taxable income and deferred tax amounts to be recognized when separate tax returns are filed by any of the affiliates of a consolidated entity.

Filing of Separate Tax Returns

Despite the advantages of filing as an affiliated group, a single consolidated return cannot always encompass every member of a consolidated entity. Separate returns are mandatory for foreign subsidiaries and for domestic corporations not meeting the 80 percent ownership rule.[6] Also, a company may still elect to file separately even if it meets the conditions for inclusion within an affiliated group. If all companies in an affiliated group are profitable and few intra-entity transactions occur, they may prefer separate returns. Filing in this manner gives the various companies more flexibility in their choice of accounting methods and fiscal tax years. Tax laws, though, do not allow a company to switch back and forth between consolidated and separate returns. Once a company elects to file a consolidated tax return as part of an affiliated group, obtaining Internal Revenue Service permission to file separately can be difficult.

When members of a consolidated entity do file separate tax returns, temporary differences often emerge across income recognized for consolidated financial reporting and for income tax reporting. The sources of such differences include (1) the immediate taxation of intra-entity profits (and losses) and (2) possible future tax effects of subsidiary income in excess

[6] Canadian and Mexican subsidiaries can qualify for treatment as domestic companies for purposes of filing a consolidated return.

of dividend payments. Differences in the timing of income recognition across consolidated reporting and income tax purposes create deferred tax assets and/or liabilities. For example, intra-entity profits and losses must be included on a separate tax return at the time of transfer rather than when the goods are sold to outside customers or consumed within the consolidated entity. Because the tax is paid in the current year, but the profit is not recognized until a subsequent year, a deferred tax asset is created—similar to a prepaid item. On the other hand when a parent recognizes subsidiary profits for financial reporting purposes, both current net income and net assets increase. But if the parent delays paying tax on the profits until the subsidiary pays a dividend, the parent also needs to account for the delayed tax effect. Accordingly the parent recognizes and reports a deferred tax liability.

However, not all subsidiary dividend distributions result in deferred taxes. For dividend payments, deferred taxes are not required when ownership equals or exceeds 80 percent. Because the tax law provides a 100 percent dividends-received deduction, the transfer is nontaxable even on a separate return; no expense recognition is required.

If the amount distributed by a less than 80 percent–owned subsidiary equals current earnings, 35 percent of the dividend is taxed immediately to the recipient, but no temporary difference is created because no future tax effect is produced. Hence, again, deferred income tax recognition is not appropriate.

Conceptually, questions about the recognition of deferred taxes arise when a less than 80 percent–owned subsidiary pays less in dividends than its current net income. If a subsidiary earns $100,000, for example, but pays dividends of only $60,000, will the parent's share of the $40,000 remainder ever become taxable income? Do these undistributed earnings represent temporary differences? If so, immediate recognition of the associated tax effect is required even though payment of this $40,000 is not anticipated for the foreseeable future.

FASB ASC 740-30-25-4 addresses this issue as follows: "A deferred tax liability shall be recognized for . . . an excess of the amount for financial reporting over the tax basis of an investment in a domestic subsidiary." Therefore, other than one exception noted later in this chapter, any portion of the subsidiary's income not distributed in the form of dividends creates a temporary difference but is not taxed until a later date; thus, a deferred tax liability is created. Because many companies retain a substantial portion of their income to finance growth, an expense recognized here may not be paid for many years.

Deferred Tax on Undistributed Earnings—Illustrated

Assume that Perry Company owns 70 percent of Simon Company, a domestic entity. Because ownership is less than 80 percent, the two companies must file separate tax returns. In the current year, Perry's separate operating earnings (excluding taxes and any income from this investment) amount to $200,000, and Simon reports a pretax net income of $100,000. During the period, the subsidiary paid a total of $20,000 in cash dividends, $14,000 (70 percent) to Perry, and the remainder to the other owners. To avoid complications in this initial example, we assume that no intra-entity profits and losses are present.

The reporting of Simon's income taxes does not provide a significant difficulty because it involves no temporary differences. Using a statutory tax rate of 21 percent, the subsidiary accrues income tax expense of $21,000 ($100,000 × 21%), leaving an after-tax profit of $79,000. *Because it paid only $20,000 in dividends, undistributed earnings for the period amount to $59,000.*

For Perry, Simon's undistributed earnings represent a temporary tax difference. The following schedules have been developed to calculate Perry's current tax liability and deferred tax liability.

Income Tax Currently Payable—Parent Company

Reported separate operating income—Perry Company		$200,000
Dividends received	$14,000	
Less: Dividends-received deduction (65%)	(9,100)	4,900
Taxable income—current year		$204,900
Tax rate		21%
Income tax payable (Perry)		$ 43,029

Deferred Income Tax Payable—Parent Company

Undistributed earnings of subsidiary Simon Company	$59,000
Perry Company's ownership	70%
Undistributed earnings accruing to Perry	$41,300
Dividends-received deduction upon eventual distribution (65%)	(26,845)
Income to be taxed—subsequent dividend payments	$14,455
Tax rate	21%
Deferred income tax payable	$ 3,036

The preceding computations show a total income tax expense of $46,065: a current tax liability of $43,029 and a deferred tax liability of $3,036. The deferred tax balance results entirely from Simon's undistributed earnings. Although the subsidiary has a $79,000 after-tax income, it distributes only $20,000 in the form of dividends. The $59,000 that Simon retains represents a temporary difference to the stockholders. Thus, Simon recognizes the deferred income tax associated with these undistributed earnings. The income is recognized now; therefore, the liability is recorded in the current period.

Separate Tax Returns Illustrated

A separate complete example best demonstrates the full accounting impact when affiliated firms file separate tax returns. As a basis for this illustration, assume that Parco Corporation reported the following data with its 60 percent–owned domestic subsidiary, Subco Company, for the current year:

	Parco Corporation (Parent)	Subco Company (60% owned by Parco)
Separate company operating income	$500,000	$200,000
Intra-entity gross profits in ending inventory (included in separate operating income)	45,000	30,000
Dividend income from Subco Company	24,000	Not applicable
Dividends paid	Not applicable	40,000
Applicable tax rate	21%	21%

Subsidiary's Income Tax Expense

Because the companies must file separate tax returns, they do not defer the intra-entity gross profits in ending inventory but instead leave them in both companies' separate operating incomes. Thus, Subco's taxable income is $200,000, an amount that creates a current payable of $42,000 ($200,000 × 21%). The intra-entity inventory gross profit is a temporary difference for financial reporting purposes, creating a deferred income tax asset (payment of the tax comes before the income actually is recognized) of $6,300 ($30,000 × 21%). Therefore, the subsidiary recognizes only $35,700 of tax expense.

Income Tax Expense—Subco

Income currently taxable	$200,000	
Tax rate	21%	$42,000
Temporary difference (intra-entity gross profit is taxed before the asset leaves the consolidated group—either through sale or use)	$ (30,000)	
Tax rate	21%	(6,300)
Income tax expense—Subco		$35,700

Consequently, Subco reports after-tax income of $134,300 ($200,000 separate operating income less $30,000 intra-entity gross profit less $35,700 in income tax expense). This profit figure is the basis for recognizing $53,720 ($134,300 × 40% outside ownership) as the noncontrolling interest's share of consolidated income.

Parent's Income Tax Expense

On Parco's separate return, its own intra-entity gross profits remain within income. The taxable portion of the dividends received from Subco also must be included. Hence, the parent's taxable earnings total $508,400, a balance that creates a $106,764 current tax liability for the company.

Income Tax Currently Payable—Parco

Separate operating income—Parco Corporation (includes $45,000 intra-entity inventory gross profit)		$500,000
Dividends received from Subco Company (60%)	$24,000	
Less: 65% dividends-received deduction	(15,600)	8,400
Taxable income		$508,400
Tax rate		21%
Income tax payable (Parco)		$106,764

Although we present Parco's tax return information here, Parco determines its total tax expense for the period only by accounting for the impact of the two temporary differences: the parent's $45,000 in intra-entity gross profits in ending inventory and the undistributed earnings of the subsidiary. Parco's share of undistributed earnings amount to $56,580, computed as follows:

After-tax income of Subco (above)	$134,300
Dividends paid	(40,000)
Undistributed earnings	$ 94,300
Parco's ownership	60%
Parco's portion of undistributed earnings	$ 56,580

Now the parent can derive its deferred income tax effects for financial reporting.

Deferred Income Taxes—Parco Company

Intra-Entity Gross Profits in Ending Inventory	
Amount taxable now prior to financial statement recognition	$45,000
Tax rate	21%
Deferred income tax asset	$ 9,450

Undistributed Earnings of Subsidiary	
Undistributed earnings of Subco—to be taxed later (computed above)	$56,580
Dividends-received deduction upon eventual distribution (65%)	(36,777)
Income eventually taxable	$19,803
Tax rate	21%
Deferred income tax liability	$ 4,159

The two temporary differences exert opposite effects on Parco's reported income taxes. Because the firms file separate returns, the intra-entity gross profits in ending inventory are taxable in the current period despite not actually having been sold to an outside customer or consumed internally within the consolidated entity. From an accounting perspective, paying the tax on these gross profits now creates a deferred income tax asset of $9,450 ($45,000 × 21%). In contrast, the parent currently recognizes the undistributed earnings (through consolidation of the investment). However, this portion of the subsidiary's income is not yet taxable to the parent. Because the tax payment is not due until the parent receives the dividends, a $4,159 (rounded) deferred income tax liability ($19,803 × 21%) occurs.

The parent reports the deferred tax asset relating to inventory, whereas the deferred tax liability relates to the eventual tax to be paid upon distribution of Subco's income. Parco's reported income tax expense results from the creation of these three accounts:

Parco's Financial Records		
Deferred Income Tax Asset	9,450	
Income Tax Expense	101,473	
Deferred Income Tax Liability		4,159
Income Tax Payable		106,764
To record tax payable and deferred taxes of parent company.		

LO 7-7

Determine the deferred tax consequences for temporary differences generated when a business combination is created.

Temporary Differences Generated by Business Combinations

Based on the transaction's nature, the tax laws deem some acquisitions to be tax-free (to the seller) but others to be taxable. In most tax-free acquisitions and in a few taxable acquisitions, the resulting book values of the acquired company's assets and liabilities differ from their tax bases. Such differences result because the subsidiary's cost is retained for tax purposes (in tax-free exchanges) or because the allocations for tax purposes vary from those used for financial reporting (a situation found in some taxable transactions).

Thus, formation of a business combination can create temporary differences. Any deferred income tax assets and liabilities the subsidiary previously recorded are not at issue; the parent consolidates these accounts in the same manner as other subsidiary assets and liabilities. The question here concerns differences in book value and tax basis that stem from the takeover.

As an illustration, assume that Saul Company owns a single asset, a building that has a $150,000 tax basis (cost less accumulated depreciation) but presently has a $250,000 fair value. Pierce Corporation conveys a total value of $300,000 to acquire Saul Company and assigns any excess fair value to nondeductible goodwill. The exchange is structured to be tax-free. After this transaction, the building continues to have a tax basis of only $150,000. However, its consolidated book value is $250,000, an amount $100,000 more than the figure applicable for tax purposes. How does this $100,000 difference affect the consolidated statements?

GAAP provides extensive guidance on reporting deferred tax assets and deferred tax liabilities created in a business combination. According to FASB ASC 805-740-25-2,

> an acquirer shall recognize a deferred tax asset or deferred tax liability arising from the assets acquired and liabilities assumed in a business combination and shall account for the potential tax effects of temporary differences, carryforwards, and any income tax uncertainties of an acquiree that exist at the acquisition date.

Thus, any temporary difference that is found in Pierce's acquisition of Saul creates a deferred tax asset or liability. Because the asset's tax basis is $150,000 but its recorded value within consolidated statements is $250,000, a temporary difference of $100,000 exists. Assuming a 21 percent applicable tax rate, the newly formed consolidated entity must recognize a deferred income tax liability of $21,000 ($100,000 × 21%).

Consequently, in a consolidated balance sheet prepared immediately after Pierce obtains control over Saul, the building is recorded at $250,000 fair value. In addition, Pierce reports the new deferred tax liability of $21,000. Because the net value of these two accounts is $229,000, goodwill of $71,000 emerges as the figure remaining from the $300,000 acquisition value as shown here:

Consideration transferred (cash)		$300,000
to building at fair value	$250,000	
to deferred tax liability on building [($250,000 – $150,000) × 21%]	(21,000)	229,000
Goodwill		$ 71,000

This $21,000 deferred tax liability systematically declines to zero over the building's life. The consolidated entity must compute depreciation for tax purposes based on the $150,000 basis and is, therefore, less each year than the expense shown for financial reporting purposes (based on $250,000). With less tax basis depreciation, taxable income is more than book income for the remaining years of the asset's life. However, the extra tax payment that results is not charged to expense but instead reduces the deferred tax liability initially established at the acquisition date. To illustrate, assume that this building generates revenues of $40,000 per year. Assume also that it has a 10-year life and that the company uses the straight-line method of depreciation.

	Financial Reporting	Income Tax Reporting	Temporary Difference
Revenues	$40,000	$40,000	$ –0–
Depreciation expense:			
10% of $250,000	25,000		
10% of $150,000		15,000	10,000
Income	$15,000	$25,000	$10,000
Tax rate	21%	21%	21%
Tax effect	$ 3,150	$ 5,250	$ 2,100

Although the consolidated entity must pay $5,250 to the government, the financial reporting tax expense is only $3,150. The other $2,100 ($10,000 reversal of temporary difference × 21%) resulted because of the use of the previous basis for tax purposes. Therefore, the following entry is made:

Income Tax Expense	3,150	
Deferred Income Tax Liability (to remove part of balance created at acquisition date)	2,100	
Income Tax Payable		5,250
To accrue income tax expense as well as impact of temporary difference in the subsidiary's assets.		

LO 7-8

Explain the impact that a net operating loss of an acquired affiliate has on consolidated figures.

Consolidated Entities and Operating Loss Carryforwards

Tax laws in the United States provide a measure of relief for companies incurring net operating losses (NOLs) when they file current tax returns. Companies may carry forward (in time) such losses for an indefinite period and apply them as a reduction to future taxable income figures. This procedure generates a cash refund of income taxes the company paid during these earlier periods.[7]

Carrying the loss forward reduces subsequent taxable income levels until the NOL is entirely eliminated or the time period expires. *Thus, NOL carryforwards can benefit the company only if it has future positive taxable income.* The recognition of future tax savings associated with NOL carryforwards has always been controversial because it requires the company to anticipate positive taxable income.

In the past, some companies created business combinations, at least in part, to take advantage of tax carryforwards. If an acquired company had an unused NOL while the parent projected significant profitability, the consolidated entity could use the acquired company's NOL to offset the parent's taxable income after the acquisition. U.S. laws were changed so that only the company that reported the loss can use virtually all of an NOL carryforward. Hence, acquiring companies with an NOL carryforward has ceased to be a popular business strategy. However, because the practice has not disappeared, reporting rules for a subsidiary's NOL carryforward are still needed.

[7] For tax years beginning after December 31, 2017, the federal *Tax Cuts and Jobs Act* (TCJA) limits the NOL deduction in any particular year to 80 percent of that year's taxable income. Also, the TCJA eliminated the previous two-year carry-back provision but allows for an indefinite carry-forward.

FASB ASC *Topic 740: Income Taxes* requires an acquiring firm to recognize a deferred income tax asset for any NOL carryforward. However, a valuation allowance also must be recognized

> if, based on the weight of available evidence, it is *more likely than not* (a likelihood of more than 50 percent) that some portion or all of the deferred tax assets will not be realized. The valuation allowance should be sufficient to reduce the deferred tax asset to the amount that is more likely than not to be realized. (FASB ASC 740-10-30-5)

As an example, assume that a company has one asset (a building) worth $500,000, which is also its tax basis. Because of recent losses, this company has a $200,000 NOL carryforward. The assumed tax rate is 21 percent so that the company will derive $42,000 in future tax savings ($200,000 × 21%) if it earns sufficient future taxable income.

Assume that the parent acquired this company for $640,000. In accounting for the acquisition, the parent must anticipate the likelihood that the new subsidiary will utilize some or all of the NOL carryforward. If it is more likely than not that the benefit will be realized, goodwill of $98,000 results:

Consideration transferred		$640,000
Subsidiary assets:		
Building	$500,000	
Deferred income tax asset (NOL carryforward)	42,000	542,000
Goodwill		$ 98,000

Conversely, if the chances that this subsidiary will use the NOL carryforward are 50 percent or less, the parent must record a valuation allowance against the NOL carryforward deferred tax asset. This will cause the recognition of $140,000 of consolidated goodwill.

Consideration transferred			$640,000
Subsidiary assets:			
Building		$500,000	
Deferred income tax asset	$42,000		
Valuation allowance	(42,000)	–0–	500,000
Goodwill			$140,000

In this second case, a question arises if this carryforward successfully reduces future taxes: How should the company remove the valuation allowance? Any changes in a valuation allowance for an acquired entity's deferred tax asset must be reported as a reduction or increase to income tax expense.[8] However, changes within the measurement period that result from new information about facts and circumstances that existed at the acquisition date are recognized through a corresponding adjustment to goodwill.[9]

Income Taxes and Consolidated Entities—Comparisons with International Accounting Standards

U.S. GAAP on accounting for income taxes and *International Accounting Standard (IAS) 12* each require consolidated entities to recognize both current tax effects and anticipated future tax consequences using deferred tax assets and liabilities. For many financial reporting tax issues that arise with consolidated entities, the standards are the same.

[8] Alternatively, a postacquisition change in the valuation allowance may result in a direct adjustment to contributed capital if the original transaction was accounted for directly through other comprehensive income or other elements of stockholders' equity.

[9] However, once goodwill is reduced to zero, an acquirer recognizes any additional decrease in the valuation allowance as a bargain purchase.

Intra-Entity Inventory Tax Effects

One area, however, where a difference remains concerns taxes on intra-entity asset transfers that remain within the consolidated group. The difference relates to intra-entity profits on inventory. U.S. GAAP requires the deferral of intra-entity profits on inventory that have been transferred across affiliates until the inventory is sold to a third party or consumed within the consolidated group. Moreover, the selling firm defers any related current tax payments on the transfer until the inventory leaves the consolidated group, In contrast, IFRS requires the taxes paid by the selling firm on intra-entity profits to be recognized as a current expense. Further, although prohibited by U.S. GAAP, IFRS requires tax deferral on temporary differences between the tax bases of assets transferred across entities (and tax jurisdictions) that remain within the consolidated group.[10]

Intra-Entity Tax Effects Other than Inventory

In 2016, the FASB issued Accounting Standards Update (ASU) *2016-16 Income Taxes (Topic 740): Intra-Entity Transfers of Assets Other than Inventory.* Thus, U.S accounting standards now differ across the intra-entity tax effects for inventory vs. asset transfers (e.g., fixed assets) across affiliated entities. The Accounting Standard Codification now requires the current and deferred tax consequences of intra-entity fixed asset transfers to be recognized currently.

The update has converged the IFRS and U.S. GAAP treatment for the tax effect of asset intra-entity transfers other than inventory. First, the selling affiliate in an intra-entity fixed asset transfer would recognize an expense for current income taxes incurred in its jurisdiction resulting from the transfer. Then, the buying affiliate would recognize tax deferrals on intra-entity transfers that remain within its possession. Further, the update now requires that the income tax rate in the buyer's tax jurisdiction (as opposed to the seller's) be used to calculate the deferred taxes reported in the consolidated financial statements. The ASU particularly affects cross-border intra-entity transfers where income tax rates differ across jurisdictions.

The convergence in the treatment of intra-entity profits, however, does not extend to inventory. According to the FASB,

> The Board decided to require that an entity recognize the income tax consequences of an intra-entity asset transfer, other than an intra-entity asset transfer of inventory, when the transfer occurs. For intra-entity asset transfers of inventory, the Board decided to retain current GAAP, which requires an entity to recognize the income tax consequences when the inventory has been sold to an outside party.[11]

Thus, the FASB excludes the recognition of the income tax consequences of intra-entity transfers of inventory when the transfer occurs. As a result, the convergence between U.S. GAAP and IFRS from the 2016 update is applicable to the tax treatment of intra-entity transfers of long-term assets, but not inventories.

Summary

1. For consolidation purposes, a parent need not possess majority ownership of each of the component companies constituting a business combination. Often control is indirect: One subsidiary owns a majority of an affiliated subsidiary's shares. Although the parent might own stock in only one of these companies, control has been established over both. Such an arrangement often is referred to as a *father-son-grandson configuration.*
2. The consolidation of financial information for a father-son-grandson business combination does not differ conceptually from a consolidation involving only direct ownership. All intra-entity, reciprocal balances are eliminated. Goodwill, other allocations, and amortization usually must be recognized if an acquisition has taken place. Because more than one investment is involved, the number of worksheet entries increases, but that is more of a mechanical inconvenience than a conceptual concern.
3. One aspect of a father-son-grandson consolidation that warrants attention is determining accrual-based income figures for each subsidiary. Any company within a business combination that holds both a parent and subsidiary position must determine the income accruing from ownership of its subsidiary before computing its own earnings. This procedure is important because net income is the basis for each parent's equity accruals and noncontrolling interest allocations.

[10] Ernst & Young LLP, *US GAAP vs. IFRS: The Basics,* January 2019.

[11] FASB Action Alert, Tentative Board Decisions, June 15, 2016 FASB Board Meeting.

4. If a subsidiary possesses shares of its parent, a mutual affiliation exists. This investment is intra-entity in nature and must be eliminated for consolidation purposes. The treasury stock approach reclassifies the cost of these shares as treasury stock with no equity accrual recorded.
5. Under present tax laws, an affiliated group of only domestic corporations can file a single consolidated income tax return. The parent must control 80 percent of the voting stock as well as 80 percent of the nonvoting stock (either directly or indirectly). A consolidated return allows the companies to defer recognition of intra-entity gains and gross profits until sold to an outside customer or consumed internally within the consolidated group. Furthermore, losses incurred by one member of the group reduce taxable income recognized by the others. Intra-entity dividends are also nontaxable on a consolidated return, although such distributions are never taxable when paid between companies within an affiliated group.
6. Separate tax returns apply to some members of a business combination. Foreign corporations and any company not meeting the 80 percent ownership rule, as examples, must report in this manner. In addition, a company might simply elect to file in this manner if a consolidated return provides no advantages. For financial reporting purposes, a separate return often necessitates recognition of deferred income taxes because temporary differences can result from intra-entity transfer gains as well as intra-entity dividends (if 80 percent ownership is not held).
7. When a business combination is created, the subsidiary's assets and liabilities sometimes have a tax basis that differs from their assigned values. In such cases, the company must recognize a deferred tax asset or liability at the time of acquisition to reflect the tax impact of these differences.

Comprehensive Illustration

Problem

(*Estimated Time: 60 to 75 Minutes*) On January 1, 2019, Gold Company acquired 90 percent of Silver Company. Details of the acquisition are as follows:

Consideration transferred by Gold	$576,000
Noncontrolling interest acquisition-date fair value	64,000
Silver total fair value	$640,000
Silver book value	600,000
Excess fair value over book value assigned to brand name (20-year life)	$ 40,000

Subsequently, on January 1, 2020, Silver purchased 10 percent of Gold for $150,000. This price equaled the book value of Gold's underlying net assets and no allocation was made to either goodwill or any specific accounts.

On January 1, 2021, Gold and Silver each acquired 30 percent of the outstanding shares of Bronze for $105,000 apiece, which resulted in Gold obtaining control over Bronze. Details of this acquisition are as follows:

Consideration transferred by Gold and Silver ($105,000 each)	$210,000
Noncontrolling interest acquisition-date fair value	140,000
Bronze total fair value	$350,000
Bronze book value	300,000
Excess fair value over book value assigned to copyright (10-year life)	$ 50,000

After the formation of this business combination, Silver made significant intra-entity inventory sales to Gold. The volume of these transfers follows:

Year	Transfer Price to Gold Company	Markup on Transfer Price	Inventory Retained at Year-End (at transfer price)
2019	$100,000	30%	$ 60,000
2020	160,000	25	90,000
2021	200,000	28	120,000

In addition, on July 1, 2021, Gold sold Bronze a tract of land for $25,000. This property cost $12,000 when the parent acquired it several years ago.

The initial value method is used to account for all investments. The individual firms recognize income from the investments when dividends are declared. Because consolidated statements are prepared for the business combination, accounting for the investments affects internal reporting only. During 2019 and 2020, Gold and Silver individually reported the following information:

	Gold Company	Silver Company
2019:		
Separate company income	$180,000	$120,000
Dividend income—Silver Company (90%)	36,000	–0–
Dividends declared	80,000	40,000
2020:		
Separate company income	240,000	150,000
Dividend income—Gold Company (10%)	–0–	9,000
Dividend income—Silver Company (90%)	27,000	–0–
Dividends declared	90,000	30,000

The 2021 financial statements for each of the three companies comprising this business combination are presented in Exhibit 7.3. These figures ignore income tax effects.

Required

a. Prepare worksheet entries to consolidate the 2021 financial statements for this combination. Assume that the mutual ownership between Gold and Silver is accounted for by means of the treasury stock approach. Compute the noncontrolling interests in consolidated net income from Bronze's income and in Silver's income.

b. Assume the effective tax rate is 21 percent and that Gold and Silver file a consolidated tax return but Bronze files separately. Calculate the income tax expense recognized within the consolidated income statement for 2021.

EXHIBIT 7.3
Individual Financial Statements—2021

	Gold Company	Silver Company	Bronze Company
Sales	$ (800,000)	$ (600,000)	$ (300,000)
Cost of goods sold	380,000	300,000	120,000
Operating expenses	193,000	100,000	90,000
Gain on sale of land	(13,000)	–0–	–0–
Dividend income from Gold Company	–0–	(10,000)	–0–
Dividend income from Silver Company	(36,000)	–0–	–0–
Dividend income from Bronze Company	(6,000)	(6,000)	–0–
Net income	$ (282,000)	$ (216,000)	$ (90,000)
Retained earnings, 1/1/21	$ (923,200)	$ (609,000)	$ (200,000)
Net income (above)	(282,000)	(216,000)	(90,000)
Dividends declared	100,000	40,000	20,000
Retained earnings, 12/31/21	$ (1,105,200)	$ (785,000)	$ (270,000)
Cash and receivables	$ 289,000	$ 190,000	$ 130,000
Inventory	459,000	410,000	110,000
Investment in Silver Company	576,000	–0–	–0–
Investment in Gold Company	–0–	150,000	–0–
Investment in Bronze Company	105,000	105,000	–0–
Land, buildings, and equipment (net)	980,000	670,000	380,000
Total assets	$ 2,409,000	$ 1,525,000	$ 620,000
Liabilities	$ (603,800)	$ (540,000)	$ (250,000)
Common stock	(700,000)	(200,000)	(100,000)
Retained earnings, 12/31/21	(1,105,200)	(785,000)	(270,000)
Total liabilities and equities	$ (2,409,000)	$ (1,525,000)	$ (620,000)

Note: Parentheses indicate a credit balance.

Solution

a. The 2021 consolidation entries for Gold, Silver, and Bronze follow.

Entry *G

The consolidation process begins with Entry ***G,** which recognizes the intra-entity gross profit (on transfers from Silver to Gold) created in the previous period. The intra-entity gross profit within ending inventory is deferred from the previous period into the current period.

Consolidation Entry *G

Retained earnings, 1/1/21 (Silver Company)	22,500	
Cost of goods sold		22,500
To recognize gross profits on intra-entity sales made from Silver to Gold during the preceding year (25% markup × $90,000).		

Consolidation Entry *C (Gold)

Investment in Silver Company	164,250	
Retained earnings, 1/1/21 (Gold Company)		164,250
To convert Gold's investment income figures for the two preceding years to equity income accruals computed as follows:		
Increase in Silver's book value from 1/1/19 to 1/1/21 ($809,000 – 600,000)	$209,000	
Excess fair-value amortization ($2,000 × 2 years)	(4,000)	
Deferral of 12/31/20 intra-entity inventory profit (25% × $90,000)	(22,500)	
Silver's increase in book value adjusted for accruals recognized in combination	$182,500	
Gold's ownership percentage	90%	
Conversion from initial value method to equity method	$164,250	

Consolidation Entry S1

Common stock (Silver Company)	200,000	
Retained earnings, 1/1/21 (Silver Company)	586,500	
Investment in Silver Company (90%)		707,850
Noncontrolling interest in Silver Company, 1/1/21 (10%)		78,650
To eliminate the beginning stockholders' equity accounts of Silver and to recognize a 10 percent noncontrolling interest in the subsidiary. Retained earnings has been adjusted for Entry ***G.**		

Consolidation Entry S2

Common stock (Bronze Company)	100,000	
Retained earnings, 1/1/21 (Bronze Company)	200,000	
Investment in Bronze Company (60%)		180,000
Noncontrolling interest in Bronze Company, 1/1/21 (40%)		120,000
To eliminate Bronze's beginning stockholders' equity accounts and to recognize outside ownership of the company's remaining shares. The investments of both Gold and Silver are accounted for concurrently through this one entry.		

Consolidation Entry TS

Treasury stock	150,000	
Investment in Gold		150,000
To reclassify Silver's investment in Gold as treasury stock.		

Consolidation Entry A

Brand name	36,000	
Copyright	50,000	
Investment in Silver		32,400
Noncontrolling interest in Silver		3,600
Investment in Bronze		30,000
Noncontrolling interest in Bronze		20,000
To recognize unamortized beginning-of-the-year balances from the excess fair value over book value acquisition-date allocations.		

Consolidation Entry I

Dividend income from Gold Company	10,000	
Dividend income from Silver Company	36,000	
Dividend income from Bronze Company	12,000	
Dividends declared (Gold Company)		10,000
Dividends declared (Silver Company)		36,000
Dividends declared (Bronze Company)		12,000

To eliminate intra-entity dividend transfers recorded as income based on application of the initial value method.

Consolidation Entry E

Amortization expense	7,000	
Brand name		2,000
Copyright		5,000

To recognize current year amortizations of the acquisition-date excess fair-value allocations.

Consolidation Entry TI

Sales	200,000	
Cost of goods sold		200,000

To eliminate the intra-entity transfer of inventory made in the current year by Silver.

Consolidation Entry G

Cost of goods sold	33,600	
Inventory		33,600

To defer intra-entity gross profits remaining in Gold's December 31 current-year inventory (28% gross profit rate × the parent's $120,000 ending inventory balance).

Consolidation Entry GL

Gain on sale of land	13,000	
Land		13,000

To defer gross profit on intra-entity transfer of land from Gold to Bronze during the year.

Net Income Attributable to the Noncontrolling Interest (Bronze Company)

As in all previous examples, the noncontrolling interest calculates its claim to a portion of consolidated income based on the subsidiary's income after amortizations and intra-entity profit deferrals and recognitions. Because this subsidiary has no intra-entity profits, the $90,000 income figure reported in Exhibit 7.3 is applicable and is adjusted only for the $5,000 excess fair-value amortization. Thus, Bronze's noncontrolling interest in consolidated net income is $34,000 [40% × ($90,000 – $5,000)].

Net Income Attributable to the Noncontrolling Interest (Silver Company)

Again, the noncontrolling interest calculates its claim to a portion of consolidated income based on the subsidiary's income after amortizations and intra-entity profit deferrals and recognitions. For Silver Company the adjustments are as follows:

Silver's separate company net income	$210,000
Excess fair-value amortization	(2,000)
Equity in earnings of Bronze (30%)	27,000
Beginning inventory intra-entity profit recognized	22,500
Ending inventory intra-entity profit deferral	(33,600)
Silver's income adjusted for combination accruals	$223,900
Noncontrolling interest percentage	10%
Net income attributable to the noncontrolling interest (Silver Company)	$ 22,390

b. No differences exist between Bronze's book values and tax basis. No computation of deferred income taxes is required; thus, this company's separate tax return is relatively straightforward. The $90,000 income figure creates a current tax liability of $18,900 (using the 21 percent tax rate).

In contrast, the consolidated tax return filed for Gold and Silver must include the following financial information. When applicable, figures reported in Exhibit 7.3 have been combined for the two companies.

Tax Return Information—Consolidated Return

Sales	$1,400,000	
Less: Intra-entity sales (2021)	(200,000)	$1,200,000
Cost of goods sold	$ 680,000	
Less: 2021 intra-entity purchases	(200,000)	
Less: 2020 intra-entity inventory gross profits recognized in 2021 ($90,000 × 25%)	(22,500)	
Add: 2021 intra-entity inventory gross profits ($120,000 × 28%)	33,600	491,100
Gross profit		$ 708,900
Operating expenses (including amortization)		300,000
Operating income		$ 408,900
Other income (since Bronze is not part of affiliated group):		
Gain on sale of land		13,000
Dividend income—Bronze Company	$ 12,000	
Less: 65% dividends-received deduction	(7,800)	4,200
Taxable income		$ 426,100
Tax rate		21%
Income tax payable by Gold Company and Silver Company for 2021		$ 89,481

Members of this business combination must pay a total of $108,381 to the government in 2021 ($18,900 for Bronze and $89,481 in connection with the consolidated return of Gold and Silver). Any temporary differences that originate or reverse during the year necessitate accounting for deferred income tax assets and/or liabilities. *In this illustration, only the dividend payments from Bronze and the intra-entity gain on the sale of land to Bronze actually create such differences.* For example, amortization of the intangible assets is the same for book and tax purposes. Other items encountered do not lead to deferred income taxes:

- Because Gold and Silver file a consolidated return, they defer the intra-entity inventory gross profits for both tax purposes and financial reporting so that no difference is created.
- The dividends that Silver pays to Gold are not subject to taxation because these distributions were made between members of an affiliated group.

However, recognition of a deferred tax liability is required because Bronze's $71,100 adjusted income ($90,000 after income tax expense of $18,900) is higher than its $20,000 dividend distribution. Gold and Silver's 60% share thus includes $42,660 ($71,100 × 60%) of Bronze's adjusted income. Because this figure is $30,660 more than the amount of dividends it paid Gold and Silver ($12,000, or 60 percent of $20,000), a deferred tax liability is required. The temporary difference is actually $10,731 (35 percent of $30,660) because of the 65 percent dividends-received deduction. The future tax effect on this difference is $2,254 based on the 21 percent tax rate applied.

A deferred tax asset also is needed in connection with Gold's intra-entity sale of land to Bronze. These companies file separate returns. Thus, the gain is taxed immediately, although this $13,000 is not recognized for reporting purposes until a future resale occurs. From an accounting perspective, the tax of $2,730 ($13,000 × 21%) is prepaid in 2021.

Recognition of the current payable as well as the two deferrals leads to an income tax expense of $107,905:

Income Tax Expense	107,905	
Deferred Income Tax—Asset	2,730	
Income Taxes Payable—Current		108,381
Deferred Income Tax—Liability		2,254

Questions

1. What is a *father-son-grandson relationship?*
2. When an indirect ownership is present, why is a specific ordering necessary for determining the incomes of the component corporations?
3. Able Company owns 70 percent of the outstanding voting stock of Baker Company, which, in turn, holds 80 percent of Carter Company. Carter possesses 60 percent of Dexter Company's capital stock. How much income actually accrues to the consolidated entity from each of these companies after considering the various noncontrolling interests?
4. How does the presence of an indirect ownership (such as a father-son-grandson relationship) affect the mechanical aspects of the consolidation process?
5. What is the difference between a connecting affiliation and a mutual ownership?
6. In accounting for mutual ownerships, what is the treasury stock approach?
7. For income tax purposes, how is *affiliated group* defined?
8. What are the advantages to a business combination filing a consolidated tax return? Considering these advantages, why do some members of a business combination file separate tax returns?
9. Why is the allocation of the income tax expense figure between the members of a business combination important? By what methods can this allocation be made?
10. If a parent and its subsidiary file separate income tax returns, why will the parent frequently have to recognize deferred income taxes? Why might the subsidiary have to recognize deferred income taxes?
11. In a recent acquisition, the consolidated value of a subsidiary's assets exceeded the basis appropriate for tax purposes. How does this difference affect the consolidated balance sheet?
12. Jones acquires Wilson, in part because the new subsidiary has an unused net operating loss carry-forward for tax purposes. How does this carry-forward affect the consolidated figures at the acquisition date?
13. A subsidiary that has a net operating loss carry-forward is acquired. The related deferred income tax asset is $230,000. Because the parent believes that a portion of this carry-forward likely will never be used, it also recognizes a valuation allowance of $150,000. At the end of the first year of ownership, the parent reassesses the situation and determines that the valuation allowance should be reduced to $110,000. What effect does this change have on the business combination's reporting?

Problems

LO 7-1

1. In a father-son-grandson business combination, which of the following is true?
   a. The father company always must have its total accrual-based income computed first.
   b. The computation of a company's accrual-based net income has no effect on the accrual-based net income of other companies within a business combination.
   c. A father-son-grandson configuration does not require consolidation unless one company owns shares in all of the other companies.
   d. All companies solely in subsidiary positions must have their accrual-based net income computed first within the consolidation process.

LO 7-3

2. A subsidiary owns shares of its parent company. Which of the following is true concerning the treasury stock approach?
   a. It is one of several options to account for mutual holdings available under current accounting standards.
   b. The original cost of the subsidiary's investment is a reduction in consolidated stockholders' equity.
   c. The subsidiary accrues income on its investment by using the equity method.
   d. The treasury stock approach eliminates these shares entirely within the consolidation process.

LO 7-3

3. On January 1, Balanger Company buys 10 percent of the outstanding shares of its parent, Altgeld, Inc. Although the total book and fair values of Altgeld's net assets equaled $3.2 million, the price paid for these shares was $340,000. During the year, Altgeld reported $415,000 of separate operating income (no subsidiary income was included) and declared dividends of $35,000. How are the shares of the parent owned by the subsidiary reported at December 31?
   a. Consolidated stockholders' equity is reduced by $340,000.
   b. An investment balance of $378,000 is eliminated for consolidation purposes.
   c. Consolidated stockholders' equity is reduced by $378,000.
   d. An investment balance of $358,000 is eliminated for consolidation purposes.

LO 7-4

4. Which of the following is correct for two companies that want to file a consolidated tax return as an affiliated group?
   a. One company must hold at least 51 percent of the other company's voting stock.
   b. One company must hold at least 65 percent of the other company's voting stock.
   c. One company must hold at least 80 percent of the other company's voting stock.
   d. They cannot file one unless one company owns 100 percent of the other's voting stock.

LO 7-5

5. How does the amortization of tax-deductible goodwill affect the computation of a parent company's income taxes?
   a. It is a deductible expense only if the parent owns at least 80 percent of the subsidiary's voting stock.
   b. It is deductible only as impairments are recognized.
   c. It is a deductible item over a 15-year period.
   d. It is deductible only if a consolidated tax return is filed.

LO 7-4

6. Which of the following is *not* a reason for two companies to file separate tax returns?
   a. The parent owns 68 percent of the subsidiary.
   b. They have no intra-entity transactions.
   c. Intra-entity dividends are tax-free only on separate returns.
   d. Neither company historically has had an operating tax loss.

LO 7-1

7. Diamond Company owns 80 percent of Emerald, and Emerald owns 90 percent of Sapphire, Inc. Separate operating income totals for the current year follow; they contain no investment income. None of these acquisitions required amortization expense. Included in Sapphire's income is a $50,000 intra-entity gain on transfers to Emerald still in Emerald's possession.

	Diamond	Emerald	Sapphire
Separate operating income	$348,000	$228,000	$210,000

   What is Diamond's accrual-based net income for the year?
   a. $658,400
   b. $674,400
   c. $666,800
   d. $645,600

LO 7-1

8. Arnold Corporation holds 70 percent of Belvista, which, in turn, owns 70 percent of Stang. Separate operating income figures (excluding investment income) and intra-entity upstream gains (on assets remaining within the consolidated group) included in the income for the current year follow:

	Arnold	Belvista	Stang
Separate operating income	$625,000	$305,000	$240,000
Intra-entity gains	–0–	18,000	50,000

   What is the amount of consolidated net income attributable to the noncontrolling interests?
   a. $143,100
   b. $163,500
   c. $183,000
   d. $213,900

LO 7-3

9. Arryn, Inc., owns 95 percent of Stark Corporation's voting stock. The acquisition price exceeded book and fair value by $85,500, which was appropriately attributed to goodwill. Stark holds 15 percent of Arryn's voting stock. The price paid for the shares by Stark equaled 15 percent of the parent's book value and the net fair values of its assets and liabilities.

   During the current year, Arryn reported separate operating income of $228,000 and dividend income from Stark of $52,500. At the same time, Stark reported separate operating income of $78,000 and dividend income from Arryn of $18,000.

   What is the net income attributable to the noncontrolling interest under the treasury stock approach?
   a. $4,800
   b. $2,700
   c. $24,600
   d. $26,700

LO 7-7

10. Kyle, Inc., owns 75 percent of CRT Company. During the current year, CRT reported net income of $425,000 but paid a total cash dividend of only $105,000. What deferred income tax liability must be recognized in the consolidated balance sheet? Assume the tax rate is 21 percent.
    a. $23,520
    b. $17,640
    c. $34,440
    d. $50,400

LO 7-7

11. Paloma, Inc., owns 85 percent of Blanca Corporation. Both companies have been profitable for many years. During the current year, the parent sold merchandise to the subsidiary at a transfer price of $175,000. In recording the transfer, the parent recognized cost of goods sold of $125,000. At the end of the year, the subsidiary still held 20 percent of this merchandise in its inventory. Assume that the tax rate is 21 percent and that separate tax returns are filed. What deferred income tax asset amount is created?
    a. –0–
    b. $1,785
    c. $2,100
    d. $8,925

LO 7-5

12. What would be the answer to Problem 11 if a consolidated tax return were filed?
    a. –0–
    b. $1,785
    c. $2,100
    d. $8,925

LO 7-7

13. Lanister Company purchases all of Mountain Company for $401,600 in cash. On that date, the subsidiary has net assets with a $355,000 fair value but a $315,000 book value and tax basis. The tax rate is 21 percent. Neither company has reported any deferred income tax assets or liabilities. What amount of goodwill should be recognized on the date of the acquisition?
    a. –0–
    b. $55,000
    c. $74,550
    d. $121,550

LO 7-1

14. On January 1, 2019, Aspen Company acquired 80 percent of Birch Company's voting stock for $288,000. Birch reported a $300,000 book value, and the fair value of the noncontrolling interest was $72,000 on that date. Then, on January 1, 2020, Birch acquired 80 percent of Cedar Company for $104,000 when Cedar had a $100,000 book value and the 20 percent noncontrolling interest was valued at $26,000. In each acquisition, the subsidiary's excess acquisition-date fair over book value was assigned to a trade name with a 30-year remaining life.

    These companies report the following financial information. Investment income figures are not included.

	2019	2020	2021
Sales:			
Aspen Company	$ 415,000	$545,000	$688,000
Birch Company	200,000	280,000	400,000
Cedar Company	Not available	160,000	210,000
Expenses:			
Aspen Company	$ 310,000	$420,000	$510,000
Birch Company	160,000	220,000	335,000
Cedar Company	Not available	150,000	180,000
Dividends declared:			
Aspen Company	$ 20,000	$ 40,000	$ 50,000
Birch Company	10,000	20,000	20,000
Cedar Company	Not available	2,000	10,000

Assume that each of the following questions is independent:

a. If all companies use the equity method for internal reporting purposes, what is the December 31, 2020, balance in Aspen's Investment in Birch Company account?

b. What is the consolidated net income for this business combination for 2021?

c. What is the net income attributable to the noncontrolling interest in 2021?

d. Assume that Birch made intra-entity inventory transfers to Aspen that have resulted in the following intra-entity gross profits in inventory at the end of each year:

Date	Amount
12/31/19	$10,000
12/31/20	16,000
12/31/21	25,000

What is the accrual-based net income of Birch in 2020 and 2021, respectively?

LO 7-3

15. On January 1, 2019, Uncle Company purchased 80 percent of Nephew Company's capital stock for $500,000 in cash and other assets. Nephew had a book value of $600,000, and the 20 percent noncontrolling interest fair value was $125,000 on that date. On January 1, 2021, Nephew had acquired 30 percent of Uncle for $280,000. Uncle's appropriately adjusted book value as of that date was $900,000.

Separate operating income figures (not including investment income) for these two companies follow. In addition, Uncle declares and pays $20,000 in dividends to shareholders each year and Nephew distributes $5,000 annually. Any excess fair-value allocations are amortized over a 10-year period.

Year	Uncle Company	Nephew Company
2019	$ 90,000	$30,000
2020	120,000	40,000
2021	140,000	50,000

a. Assume that Uncle applies the equity method to account for this investment in Nephew. What is the subsidiary's income recognized by Uncle in 2021?

b. What is the net income attributable to the noncontrolling interest for 2021?

LO 7-1

16. Boulder, Inc., obtained 90 percent of Rock Corporation on January 1, 2019. Annual amortization of $22,000 is applicable on the allocations of Rock's acquisition-date business fair value. On January 1, 2020, Rock acquired 75 percent of Stone Company's voting stock. Excess business fair-value amortization on this second acquisition amounted to $8,000 per year. For 2021, each of the three companies reported the following information accumulated by its separate accounting system. Separate operating income figures do not include any investment or dividend income.

	Separate Operating Income	Dividends Declared
Boulder	$245,000	$120,000
Rock	85,000	28,000
Stone	150,000	42,000

a. What is consolidated net income for 2021?

b. How is consolidated net income distributed to the controlling and noncontrolling interests?

LO 7-2

17. Baxter, Inc., owns 90 percent of Wisconsin, Inc., and 20 percent of Cleveland Company. Wisconsin, in turn, holds 60 percent of Cleveland's outstanding stock. No excess amortization resulted from these acquisitions. During the current year, Cleveland sold a variety of inventory items to Wisconsin for $40,000, although the original cost was $30,000. Of this total, Wisconsin still held $12,000 in inventory (at transfer price) at year-end.

During this same period, Wisconsin sold merchandise to Baxter for $100,000, although the original cost was only $70,000. At year-end, $40,000 of these goods (at the transfer price) was still on hand.

The initial value method was used to record each of these investments. None of the companies holds any other investments.

Using the following separate income statements, determine the figures that would appear on a consolidated income statement (credit balances indicated by parentheses):

	Baxter	Wisconsin	Cleveland
Sales	$(1,000,000)	$(450,000)	$(280,000)
Cost of goods sold	670,000	280,000	190,000
Expenses	110,000	60,000	30,000
Dividend income:			
Wisconsin	(36,000)	–0–	–0–
Cleveland	(4,000)	(12,000)	–0–
Net income	$ (260,000)	$(122,000)	$ (60,000)

LO 7-8

18. Sienna Company developed a specialized banking application software program that it licenses to various financial institutions through multiple-year agreements. On January 1, 2021, these licensing agreements have a fair value of $900,000 and represent Sienna's sole asset. Although Sienna currently has no liabilities, the company has a $155,000 net operating loss (NOL) carry-forward because of recent operating losses.

    On January 1, 2021, Paoli, Inc., acquired all of Sienna's voting stock for $1,120,000. Paoli expects to extract operating synergies by integrating Sienna's software into its own products. Paoli also hopes that Sienna will be able to receive a future tax reduction from its NOL. Assume an applicable federal income tax rate of 21 percent.

    a. If there is a greater than 50 percent chance that the subsidiary will be able to utilize the NOL carry-forward, how much goodwill should Paoli recognize from the acquisition?

    b. If there is a less than 50 percent chance that the subsidiary will be able to utilize the NOL carry-forward, how much goodwill should Paoli recognize from the acquisition?

LO 7-6

19. Arriba and its 80 percent–owned subsidiary (Abajo) reported the following figures for the year ending December 31, 2021 (credit balances indicated by parentheses). Abajo paid dividends of $30,000 during this period.

	Arriba	Abajo
Sales	$ (600,000)	$ (300,000)
Cost of goods sold	300,000	140,000
Operating expenses	174,000	60,000
Dividend income	(24,000)	–0–
Net income	$ (150,000)	$ (100,000)

    In 2020, intra-entity gross profits of $30,000 on upstream transfers of $90,000 were deferred into 2021. In 2021 intra-entity gross profits of $40,000 on upstream transfers of $110,000 were deferred into 2022.

    a. What amounts appear for each line in a consolidated income statement? Explain your computations.

    b. What income tax expense should appear on the consolidated income statement if each company files a separate return? Assume that the tax rate is 21 percent.

LO 7-5, 7-6

20. Martin has a controlling interest in Rowen's outstanding stock. At the current year-end, the following information has been accumulated for these two companies:

	Separate Operating Income	Dividends Paid
Martin	$500,000 (includes a $90,000 net gross profit in intra-entity ending inventory)	$90,000
Rowen	240,000	80,000

Martin uses the initial value method to account for the investment in Rowen. The separate operating income figures just presented include neither dividend nor other investment income. The effective tax rate for both companies is 21 percent.

a. Assume that Martin owns 100 percent of Rowen's voting stock and is filing a consolidated tax return. What income tax amount does this affiliated group pay for the current period?

b. Assume that Martin owns 92 percent of Rowen's voting stock and is filing a consolidated tax return. What amount of income taxes does this affiliated group pay for the current period?

c. Assume that Martin owns 80 percent of Rowen's voting stock, but the companies elect to file separate tax returns. What is the total amount of income taxes that these two companies pay for the current period?

d. Assume that Martin owns 70 percent of Rowen's voting stock, requiring separate tax returns. What is the total amount of income tax expense to be recognized in the consolidated income statement for the current period?

e. Assume that Martin owns 70 percent of Rowen's voting stock so that separate tax returns are required. What amount of income taxes does Martin have to pay for the current year?

LO 7-5, 7-6

21. On January 1, 2020, Abbey acquires 90 percent of Benjamin's outstanding shares. Financial information for these two companies for the years 2020 and 2021 follows (credit balances indicated by parentheses):

	2020	2021
Abbey Company:		
Sales	$ (500,000)	$ (700,000)
Operating expenses	300,000	400,000
Intra-entity gross profits in ending inventory (included in above figures)	(120,000)	(150,000)
Dividend income—Benjamin Company	(18,000)	(36,000)
Benjamin Company:		
Sales	(210,000)	(270,000)
Operating expenses	130,000	170,000
Dividends paid	(20,000)	(40,000)

Assume that a tax rate of 21 percent is applicable to both companies.

a. On consolidated financial statements for 2021, what are the income tax expense and the income tax currently payable if Abbey and Benjamin file a consolidated tax return as an affiliated group?

b. On consolidated financial statements for 2021, what are the income tax expense and income tax currently payable if they choose to file separate returns?

LO 7-6

22. Lake acquired a controlling interest in Boxwood several years ago. During the current fiscal period, the two companies individually reported the following income (exclusive of any investment income):

Lake	$300,000
Boxwood	100,000

Lake paid a $90,000 cash dividend during the current year, and Boxwood distributed $10,000.

Boxwood sells inventory to Lake each period. Intra-entity gross profits of $18,000 were present in Lake's beginning inventory for the current year, and its ending inventory carried $32,000 in intra-entity gross profits.

View each of the following questions as an independent situation. The effective tax rate for both companies is 21 percent.

a. If Lake owns a 60 percent interest in Boxwood, what total income tax expense must be reported on a consolidated income statement for this period?

b. If Lake owns a 60 percent interest in Boxwood, what total amount of income taxes must be paid by these two companies for the current year?

c. If Lake owns a 90 percent interest in Boxwood and a consolidated tax return is filed, what amount of income tax expense would be reported on a consolidated income statement for the year?

LO 7-5, 7-6

23. Garrison holds a controlling interest in Robertson's outstanding stock. For the current year, the following information has been gathered about these two companies:

	Garrison	Robertson
Separate operating income (includes $50,000 intra-entity gross profit in ending inventory)	$300,000	$200,000
Dividends paid	32,000	50,000
Tax rate	21%	21%

Garrison uses the initial value method to account for the investment in Robertson. Garrison's separate operating income figure does not include dividend income for the current year.

a. Assume that Garrison owns 80 percent of Robertson's voting stock. On a consolidated tax return, what amount of income tax is paid?

b. Assume that Garrison owns 80 percent of Robertson's voting stock. On separate tax returns, what total amount of income tax is paid?

c. Assume that Garrison owns 70 percent of Robertson's voting stock. What total amount of income tax expense does a consolidated income statement recognize?

d. Assume that Garrison holds 60 percent of Robertson's voting stock. On a separate income tax return, what amount of income tax does Garrison have to pay?

LO 7-6

24. King's Road recently acquired all of Oxford Corporation's stock and is now consolidating the financial data of this new subsidiary. King's Road paid a total of $850,000 for Oxford, which has the following accounts:

	Fair Value	Tax Basis
Accounts receivable	$ 153,000	$153,000
Inventory	141,000	141,000
Land	136,000	136,000
Buildings	276,000	221,000
Equipment	233,000	160,000
Liabilities	(281,000)	(281,000)

a. What amount of deferred tax liability arises in the acquisition?

b. What amounts will be used to consolidate Oxford with King's Road at the date of acquisition?

c. On a consolidated balance sheet prepared immediately after this takeover, how much goodwill should King's Road recognize? Assume a 21 percent effective tax rate.

LO 7-2

25. House Corporation has been operating profitably since its creation in 1960. At the beginning of 2019, House acquired a 70 percent ownership in Wilson Company. At the acquisition date, House prepared the following fair-value allocation schedule:

Consideration transferred for 70% interest in Wilson		$ 707,000
Fair value of the 30% noncontrolling interest		303,000
Wilson business fair value		$1,010,000
Wilson book value		790,000
Excess fair value over book value		$ 220,000
Assignments to adjust Wilson's assets to fair value:		
To buildings (20-year remaining life)	$60,000	
To equipment (4-year remaining life)	(20,000)	
To franchises (10-year remaining life)	40,000	80,000
To goodwill (indefinite life)		$ 140,000

House regularly buys inventory from Wilson at a markup of 25 percent more than cost. House's purchases during 2019 and 2020 and related ending inventory balances follow:

Year	Intra-Entity Purchases	Remaining Intra-Entity Inventory—End of Year (at transfer price)
2019	$120,000	$40,000
2020	150,000	60,000

On January 1, 2021, House and Wilson acted together as co-acquirers of 80 percent of Cuddy Company's outstanding common stock. The total price of these shares was $240,000, indicating neither goodwill nor other specific fair-value allocations. Each company put up one-half of the consideration transferred. During 2021, House acquired additional inventory from Wilson at a price of $200,000. Of this merchandise, 45 percent is still held at year-end.

Using the three companies' following financial records for 2021, prepare a consolidation worksheet. The partial equity method based on *separate company incomes* has been applied to each investment.

	House Corporation	Wilson Company	Cuddy Company
Sales and other revenues	$ (900,000)	$ (700,000)	$ (300,000)
Cost of goods sold	551,000	300,000	140,000
Operating expenses	219,000	270,000	90,000
Income of Wilson Company	(91,000)	–0–	–0–
Income of Cuddy Company	(28,000)	(28,000)	–0–
Net income	$ (249,000)	$ (158,000)	$ (70,000)
Retained earnings, 1/1/21	$ (820,000)	$ (590,000)	$ (150,000)
Net income (above)	(249,000)	(158,000)	(70,000)
Dividends declared	100,000	96,000	50,000
Retained earnings, 12/31/21	$ (969,000)	$ (652,000)	$ (170,000)
Cash and receivables	$ 220,000	$ 334,000	$ 67,000
Inventory	390,200	320,000	103,000
Investment in Wilson Company	807,800	–0–	–0–
Investment in Cuddy Company	128,000	128,000	–0–
Buildings	385,000	320,000	144,000
Equipment	310,000	130,000	88,000
Land	180,000	300,000	16,000
Total assets	$ 2,421,000	$ 1,532,000	$ 418,000
Liabilities	$ (632,000)	$ (570,000)	$ (98,000)
Common stock	(820,000)	(310,000)	(150,000)
Retained earnings, 12/31/21	(969,000)	(652,000)	(170,000)
Total liabilities and equities	$ (2,421,000)	$ (1,532,000)	$ (418,000)

Credit balances are indicated by parentheses.

LO 7-3

26. Mighty Company purchased a 60 percent interest in Lowly Company on January 1, 2020, for $420,000 in cash. Lowly's book value at that date was reported as $600,000, and the fair value of the noncontrolling interest was assessed at $280,000. Any excess acquisition-date fair value over Lowly's book value is assigned to trademarks to be amortized over 20 years. Subsequently, on January 1, 2021, Lowly acquired a 20 percent interest in Mighty. The price of $240,000 was equivalent to 20 percent of Mighty's book and fair value.

Neither company has paid dividends since these acquisitions occurred. On January 1, 2021, Lowly's book value was $800,000, a figure that rises to $840,000 (common stock of $300,000 and retained earnings of $540,000) by year-end. Mighty's book value was $1.7 million at the beginning of 2021 and $1.8 million (common stock of $1 million and retained earnings of $800,000) at December 31, 2021. No intra-entity transactions have occurred, and no additional stock has been sold. Each company applies the initial value method in accounting for the individual investments. What worksheet entries are required to consolidate these two companies for 2021? What is the net income attributable to the noncontrolling interest for this year?

LO 7-1, 7-5, 7-6

27. On January 1, 2020, Travers Company acquired 90 percent of Yarrow Company's outstanding stock for $720,000. The 10 percent noncontrolling interest had an assessed fair value of $80,000 on that date. Any acquisition-date excess fair value over book value was attributed to an unrecorded customer list developed by Yarrow with a remaining life of 15 years.

On the same date, Yarrow acquired an 80 percent interest in Stookey Company for $344,000. At the acquisition date, the 20 percent noncontrolling interest fair value was $86,000. Any excess fair value was attributed to a fully amortized copyright that had a remaining life of 10 years. Although both investments are accounted for using the initial value method, neither Yarrow nor Stookey has distributed dividends since the acquisition date. Travers has a policy to declare and pay cash dividends each year equal to 40 percent of its separate company operating earnings. Reported income totals for 2020 follow:

Travers Company	$300,000
Yarrow Company	160,000
Stookey Company	120,000

The following are the 2021 financial statements for these three companies (credit balances indicated by parentheses). Stookey has transferred numerous amounts of inventory to Yarrow since the takeover amounting to $80,000 (2020) and $100,000 (2021). These transactions include the same markup applicable to Stookey's outside sales. In each year, Yarrow carried 20 percent of this inventory into the succeeding year before disposing of it. An effective tax rate of 21 percent is applicable to all companies. All dividend declarations are paid in the same period.

	Travers Company	Yarrow Company	Stookey Company
Sales	$ (900,000)	$ (600,000)	$ (500,000)
Cost of goods sold	480,000	320,000	260,000
Operating expenses	100,000	80,000	140,000
Net income	$ (320,000)	$ (200,000)	$ (100,000)
Retained earnings, 1/1/21	$ (700,000)	$ (600,000)	$ (300,000)
Net income (above)	(320,000)	(200,000)	(100,000)
Dividends declared	128,000	–0–	–0–
Retained earnings, 12/31/21	$ (892,000)	$ (800,000)	$ (400,000)
Current assets	$ 444,000	$ 380,000	$ 280,000
Investment in Yarrow Company	720,000	–0–	–0–
Investment in Stookey Company	–0–	344,000	–0–
Land, buildings, and equipment (net)	949,000	836,000	520,000
Total assets	$ 2,113,000	$ 1,560,000	$ 800,000
Liabilities	$ (721,000)	$ (460,000)	$ (200,000)
Common stock	(500,000)	(300,000)	(200,000)
Retained earnings, 12/31/21	(892,000)	(800,000)	(400,000)
Total liabilities and equities	$ (2,113,000)	$ (1,560,000)	$ (800,000)

a. Prepare the business combination's 2021 consolidation worksheet; ignore income tax effects.

b. Determine the amount of income tax for Travers and Yarrow on a consolidated tax return for 2021.

c. Determine the amount of Stookey's income tax on a separate tax return for 2021.

d. Based on the answers to requirements (*b*) and (*c*), what journal entry does this combination make to record 2021 income tax?

LO 7-5, 7-6

28. Parson Company acquired an 80 percent interest in Syber Company on January 1, 2020. Any portion of Syber's business fair value in excess of its corresponding book value was assigned to trademarks. This intangible asset has subsequently undergone annual amortization based on a 15-year life. Over the past two years, regular intra-entity inventory sales transpired between the two companies. No payment has yet been made on the latest transfer. All dividends are paid in the same period as declared.

The individual financial statements for the two companies as well as consolidated totals for 2021 follow (credit balances indicated by parentheses):

	Parson Company	Syber Company	Consolidated Totals
Sales	$ (800,000)	$ (600,000)	$(1,280,000)
Cost of goods sold	500,000	400,000	784,000
Operating expenses	100,000	100,000	202,500
Income of Syber	(74,800)	–0–	–0–
Separate company net income	$ (274,800)	$ (100,000)	
Consolidated net income			$ (293,500)
Net income attributable to noncontrolling interest			18,700
Net income attributable to Parson Company			$ (274,800)
Retained earnings, 1/1/21	$ (611,600)	$ (290,000)	$ (611,600)
Net income (above)	(274,800)	(100,000)	(274,800)
Dividends declared	70,000	30,000	70,000
Retained earnings, 12/31/21	$ (816,400)	$ (360,000)	$ (816,400)
Cash and receivables	$ 298,000	$ 80,000	$ 358,000
Inventory	190,000	160,000	338,000
Investment in Syber Company	368,400	–0–	–0–
Land, buildings, and equipment	380,000	260,000	640,000
Trademarks	–0–	–0–	32,500
Total assets	$ 1,236,400	$ 500,000	$ 1,368,500
Liabilities	$ (270,000)	$ (60,000)	$ (310,000)
Common stock	(120,000)	(80,000)	(120,000)
Additional paid-in capital	(30,000)	–0–	(30,000)
Noncontrolling interest in Syber	–0–	–0–	(92,100)
Retained earnings (above)	(816,400)	(360,000)	(816,400)
Total liabilities and equities	$(1,236,400)	$ (500,000)	$(1,368,500)

a. What method does Parson use to account for its investment in Syber?

b. What is the balance of the intra-entity inventory gross profit deferred at the end of the current period?

c. What amount was originally allocated to the trademarks?

d. What is the amount of the current-year intra-entity inventory sales?

e. Were the intra-entity inventory sales made upstream or downstream?

f. What is the balance of the intra-entity liability at the end of the current year?

g. What amount of intra-entity gross profit was deferred from the preceding period and recognized in the current period?

h. How was the ending Noncontrolling Interest in Syber Company computed?

i. With a tax rate of 21 percent, what income tax journal entry is recorded if the companies prepare a consolidated tax return?

j. With a tax rate of 21 percent, what income tax journal entry is recorded if these two companies prepare separate tax returns?

LO 7-1

29. On January 1, 2019, Alpha acquired 80 percent of Delta. Of Delta's total business fair value, $125,000 was allocated to copyrights with a 20-year remaining life. Subsequently, on January 1, 2020, Delta obtained 70 percent of Omega's outstanding voting shares. In this second acquisition, $120,000 of Omega's total business fair value was assigned to copyrights that had a remaining life of 12 years. Delta's book value was $490,000 on January 1, 2019, and Omega reported a book value of $140,000 on January 1, 2020.

Delta has made numerous inventory transfers to Alpha since the business combination was formed. Intra-entity gross profits of $15,000 were present in Alpha's inventory as of January 1, 2021. During the year, $200,000 in additional intra-entity sales were made with $22,000 in intra-entity gross profits in inventory remaining at the end of the period.

Both Alpha and Delta utilized the partial equity method to account for their investment balances.

Following are the individual financial statements for the companies for 2021 with consolidated totals (credit balances indicated by parentheses). Develop the worksheet entries necessary to derive these reported balances:

	Alpha Company	Delta Company	Omega Company	Consolidated Totals
Sales	$ (900,000)	$ (500,000)	$ (200,000)	$(1,400,000)
Cost of goods sold	500,000	240,000	80,000	627,000
Operating expenses	294,000	129,000	50,000	489,250
Income of subsidiary	(144,000)	(49,000)	–0–	–0–
Separate company net income	$ (250,000)	$ (180,000)	$ (70,000)	
Consolidated net income				$ (283,750)
Net income attributable to noncontrolling interest (Delta Company)				31,950
Net income attributable to noncontrolling interest (Omega Company)				18,000
Net income attributable to Alpha Company				$ (233,800)
Retained earnings, 1/1/21	$ (600,000)	$ (400,000)	$ (100,000)	$ (572,400)
Net income (above)	(250,000)	(180,000)	(70,000)	(233,800)
Dividends declared	50,000	40,000	50,000	50,000
Retained earnings, 12/31/21	$ (800,000)	$ (540,000)	$ (120,000)	$ (756,200)
Cash and receivables	$ 262,000	$ 206,000	$ 70,000	$ 538,000
Inventory	290,000	310,000	160,000	738,000
Investment in Delta Company	628,000	–0–	–0–	–0–
Investment in Omega Company	–0–	238,000	–0–	–0–
Property, plant, and equipment	420,000	316,000	270,000	1,006,000
Copyrights	–0–	–0–	–0–	206,250
Total assets	$ 1,600,000	$ 1,070,000	$ 500,000	$ 2,488,250
Liabilities	$ (600,000)	$ (410,000)	$ (280,000)	$(1,290,000)
Common stock	(200,000)	(120,000)	(100,000)	(200,000)
Retained earnings, 12/31/21	(800,000)	(540,000)	(120,000)	(756,200)
Noncontrolling interest in Delta Company, 12/31/21	–0–	–0–	–0–	(146,050)
Noncontrolling interest in Omega Company, 12/31/21	–0–	–0–	–0–	(96,000)
Total liabilities and equities	$ (1,600,000)	$ (1,070,000)	$ (500,000)	$(2,488,250)

Develop Your Skills

EXCEL CASE: INDIRECT SUBSIDIARY CONTROL

CPA skills

Highpoint owns a 95 percent majority voting interest in Middlebury. In turn, Middlebury owns an 80 percent majority voting interest in Lowton. In the current year, each firm reports the following income and dividends. Separate Company income figures do not include any investment or dividend income.

	Separate Company Income	Dividends Declared
Highpoint	$425,000	$200,000
Middlebury	340,000	150,000
Lowton	250,000	75,000

In addition, in computing its income on a full accrual basis, Middlebury's acquisition of Lowton necessitates excess acquisition-date fair value over book value amortizations of $25,000 per year. Similarly, Highpoint's acquisition of Middlebury requires $20,000 of excess fair-value amortizations.

Required

Prepare an Excel spreadsheet that computes the following:

1. Middlebury's net income including its equity in Lowton earnings.
2. Highpoint's net income including its equity in Middlebury's total earnings.
3. Total entity net income for the three companies.
4. Net income attributable to the noncontrolling interests.
5. Difference between these elements:
   - Highpoint's net income.
   - Total entity net income for the three companies less net income attributable to the noncontrolling interests of the total entity.

   (*Hint:* The difference between these two amounts should be zero.)

RESEARCH CASE: CONSOLIDATED TAX EXPENSE

Access a recent copy of The Coca-Cola Company's financial statements (www.coca-colacompany.com). Identify and discuss the following aspects of consolidated tax expense disclosed in the financial statements:

1. Loss carry-forwards.
2. Components of deferred tax assets and liabilities.
3. Deferred tax impacts of stock sales by equity investees.
4. Deferred tax impacts of sales of interests in investees.
5. Valuation allowances on deferred taxes.

Segment and Interim Reporting

chapter 8

As one of the largest companies in the United States, The Walt Disney Company reported consolidated revenues of $55.1 billion in 2017. The Walt Disney Company is well known as a filmmaker and operator of theme parks, but it is perhaps less well known as the owner of the ESPN and ABC television networks. How much of the company's consolidated revenues did these different lines of business generate? Knowing this could be very useful to potential investors because opportunities for future growth and profitability in these different industries could differ significantly.

To comply with U.S. GAAP, Disney disaggregated its 2017 consolidated operating revenues and reported that the company's revenues were generated from four different operating segments. Approximately $23.5 billion in operating revenue came from Media Networks, $18.4 billion from Parks and Resorts, $8.4 billion from Studio Entertainment, and $4.8 billion from Consumer Products and Interactive Media. Additional information disclosed by Disney indicated that $41.9 billion of consolidated revenues were generated in the United States and Canada, $6.5 billion in Europe, $5.1 billion in Asia Pacific, and $1.6 billion in Latin America and other parts of the world. Such information, describing the various components of Disney's operations (both by operating segment and by geographic area), can be more useful to an analyst than the single revenue figure reported in the consolidated income statement.

In its 2017 Annual Report, the Boeing Company reported net earnings of $10,278 million for the year ended December 31, 2017. This information was not made available to the public until early in 2018 after the company had closed the books and prepared audited financial statements for the prior year. To provide more timely information on which investors could base their decisions about the company throughout the year, Boeing published separate interim reports for each of the first three quarters of 2017. Earnings from operations increased steadily from $2,024 million in the first quarter, to $2,535 million in the second quarter, to $2,689 million in the third quarter, and then peaked at $3,030 million in the fourth quarter. Information about the results of operations for time intervals of less than one year can be very useful to an analyst.

The first part of this chapter examines the specific requirements for disaggregating financial statement information as required by authoritative accounting literature. Companies must disclose specific items of information for each reportable operating segment and provide additional enterprisewide disclosures. The second part of the chapter concentrates on the special rules required to be applied in preparing interim reports. All publicly traded companies in the United States are required to prepare interim reports on a quarterly basis.

Learning Objectives

After studying this chapter, you should be able to:

LO 8-1 Understand how an enterprise determines its operating segments.

LO 8-2 Apply the three tests that are used to determine which operating segments are of significant size to warrant separate disclosure.

LO 8-3 List the basic disclosure requirements for operating segments.

LO 8-4 Determine when and what types of information must be disclosed for geographic areas.

LO 8-5 Apply the criterion for determining when disclosure of a major customer is required.

LO 8-6 Understand and apply procedures used in interim financial reports to treat an interim period as an integral part of the annual period.

LO 8-7 List the minimum disclosure requirements for interim financial reports.

LO 8-1

Understand how an enterprise determines its operating segments.

Segment Reporting

According to FASB *Accounting Standards Codification*® (ASC) Topic 280, "Segment Reporting," the objective of segment reporting is to provide information about the different business activities in which an enterprise engages and the different economic environments in which it operates to help users of financial statements

- Better understand the enterprise's performance.
- Better assess its prospects for future net cash flows.
- Make more informed judgments about the enterprise as a whole.

The Management Approach

To achieve this objective, U.S. GAAP follows a management approach for determining segments. The management approach is based on the way that management disaggregates the enterprise for making operating decisions. These disaggregated components are *operating segments,* which will be evident from the enterprise's organization structure. More specifically, an operating segment is a component of an enterprise if

- It engages in business activities from which it recognizes revenues and incurs expenses.
- The chief operating decision maker regularly reviews its operating results to assess performance and make resource allocation decisions.
- Its discrete financial information is available.

An organizational unit can be an operating segment even if all of its revenues or expenses result from transactions with other segments as might be the case in a vertically integrated company. However, not all parts of a company are necessarily included in an operating segment. For example, a research and development unit that incurs expenses but does not recognize revenues would not be an operating segment. Similarly, corporate headquarters might not recognize revenues or might recognize revenues that are only incidental to the enterprise's activities and therefore would not be considered an operating segment.

For many companies, only one set of organizational units qualifies as operating segments. In some companies, however, business activities are disaggregated in more than one way, and the chief operating decision maker uses multiple sets of reports. For example, a company might generate reports by geographic region *and* by product line. In those cases, two additional criteria must be considered to identify operating segments:

1. An operating segment has a segment manager who is directly accountable to the chief operating decision maker for its financial performance. If more than one set of organizational units exist but segment managers are held responsible for only one set, that set constitutes the operating segments.
2. If segment managers exist for two or more overlapping sets of organizational units (as in a matrix form of organization), the nature of the business activities must be considered, and the organizational units based on products and services constitute the operating segments. For example, if certain managers are responsible for different product lines and other managers are responsible for different geographic areas, the enterprise components based on products would constitute the operating segments.

LO 8-2

Apply the three tests that are used to determine which operating segments are of significant size to warrant separate disclosure.

Determination of Reportable Operating Segments

After a company has identified its operating segments based on its internal reporting system, management must decide which segments to report separately. Generally, information must be reported separately for each operating segment that meets one or more quantitative thresholds. *However, if two or more operating segments have essentially the same business activities in essentially the same economic environments, information for those individual segments may be combined.* For example, a retail chain may have five stores, each of which meets the definition of an operating segment, but each store is essentially the same as the others. In that case, the benefit to be derived from separately reporting each operating segment would not justify the cost of disclosure. In determining whether business activities and environments are similar, management must consider these aggregation criteria:

1. The nature of the products and services provided by each operating segment.
2. The nature of the production process.
3. The type or class of customer.
4. The distribution methods.
5. If applicable, the nature of the regulatory environment.

Segments must be similar in each and every one of these areas to be combined. However, aggregation of similar segments is not required.

Quantitative Thresholds

After determining whether any segments are to be combined, management next must decide which of its operating segments are significant enough to justify separate disclosure. The FASB established three tests for identifying operating segments for which separate disclosure is required:

1. A revenue test.
2. A profit or loss test.
3. An asset test.

An operating segment needs to satisfy only one of these tests to be considered of significant size to necessitate separate disclosure.

To apply these three tests, a segment's revenues, profit or loss, and assets (before any intra-entity eliminations) must be determined. Additionally, general corporate (nontraceable) revenues and expenses are not considered in conducting these tests because corporate headquarters is not a separate unit for segment reporting. Authoritative literature does not stipulate a specific measure of profit or loss, such as operating profit or income before taxes, to be used in applying these tests. Instead, the profit measure used by the chief operating decision maker in evaluating operating segments is to be used. An operating segment is considered to be significant if it meets any one of the following tests:

1. *Revenue test.* Segment revenues, both external and intersegment, are 10 percent or more of the combined revenue, internal and external, of all reported operating segments.
2. *Profit or loss test.* Segment profit or loss is 10 percent or more of the larger (in absolute terms) of the combined reported profit of all profitable segments or the combined reported loss of all segments incurring a loss.
3. *Asset test.* Segment assets are 10 percent or more of the combined assets of all operating segments.

Application of the revenue and asset tests appears to pose few challenges. In contrast, the profit or loss test is more complicated and warrants illustration. For this purpose, assume that Durham Company has five separate operating segments with the following profits or losses:

Durham Company Segments—Profits and Losses

Soft drinks	$1,700,000
Wine	(600,000)
Food products	240,000
Paper packaging	880,000
Recreation parks	(130,000)
Net operating profit	$2,090,000

Three of these industry segments (soft drinks, food products, and paper packaging) report profits that total $2,820,000. The two remaining segments have losses of $730,000 for the year.

Profits		Losses	
Soft drinks	$1,700,000	Wine	$600,000
Food products	240,000	Recreation parks	130,000
Paper packaging	880,000		
Total	$2,820,000	Total	$730,000

Consequently, $2,820,000 serves as the basis for the profit or loss test because that amount is larger in absolute terms than $730,000. Based on the 10 percent threshold, any operating segment with either a profit *or loss* of more than $282,000 (10% × $2,820,000) is considered material and, thus, must be disclosed separately. According to this one test, the soft drinks and paper packaging segments (with operating profits of $1.7 million and $880,000, respectively) are both judged to be reportable, as is the wine segment, despite having a loss of $600,000.

Operating segments that do not meet any of the quantitative thresholds may be combined to produce a reportable segment if they share *a majority* of the aggregation criteria listed earlier. Durham Company's food products and recreation parks operating segments do not meet any of the aggregation criteria. Operating segments that are not individually significant and that cannot be aggregated with other segments are combined and disclosed in an *All Other* category. The sources of the revenues included in the All Other category must be disclosed.

Testing Procedures—Complete Illustration

To provide a comprehensive example of all three of these testing procedures, assume that Atkinson Company is a large business combination comprising six operating segments: automotive, furniture, textbook, motion picture, appliance, and finance. Complete information about each of these segments, as reported internally to the chief operating decision maker, appears in Exhibit 8.1.

The Revenue Test

In applying the revenue test to Atkinson Company's operating segments, the combined revenue of all segments must be determined:

Operating Segment	Total Revenues
Automotive	$41.6*
Furniture	9.0
Textbook	6.8
Motion picture	22.8
Appliance	5.3
Finance	12.3
Combined total	$97.8

*All figures are in millions.

Because these six segments have total revenues of $97.8 million, that amount is used in applying the revenue test. Based on the 10 percent significance level, any segment with revenues of more than $9.78 million qualifies for required disclosure. Accordingly, the automotive, motion picture, and finance segments have satisfied this particular criterion. Atkinson must present appropriate disaggregated information for each of these three operating segments within its financial statements.

The Profit or Loss Test

Subtracting segment expenses from total segment revenues determines the profit or loss of each operating segment. Common costs are not required to be allocated to individual segments to determine segment profit or loss if this is not normally done for internal purposes.

EXHIBIT 8.1 Reportable Segment Testing

ATKINSON COMPANY

	Automotive	Furniture	Textbook	Motion Picture	Appliance	Finance
Revenues:						
Sales to outsiders	$32.6*	$6.9	$ 6.6	$22.2	$3.1	$ -0-
Intersegment transfers	6.6	1.2	-0-	-0-	1.9	-0-
Interest revenue—outsiders	2.4	0.9	0.2	0.6	0.3	8.7
Interest revenue—intersegment loans	-0-	-0-	-0-	-0-	-0-	3.6
Total revenues	$41.6	$9.0	$ 6.8	$22.8	$5.3	$12.3
Expenses:						
Operating expenses—outsiders	$14.7	$3.3	$ 7.2	$21.0	$3.4	$ 1.8
Operating expenses—intersegment transfers	4.8	1.0	-0-	-0-	0.8	0.8
Depreciation and amortization	2.4	0.3	0.1	3.0	0.2	0.5
Interest expense	2.1	1.0	2.2	4.6	-0-	6.1
Income taxes	6.6	1.4	(1.5)	(3.1)	0.4	0.1
Total expenses	$30.6	$7.0	$ 8.0	$25.5	$4.8	$ 9.3
Profit (loss)	$11.0	$2.0	$(1.2)	$ (2.7)	$0.5	$ 3.0
Assets:						
Tangible	$ 9.6	$1.1	$ 0.8	$10.9	$0.9	$ 9.2
Intangible	1.8	0.2	0.7	3.6	0.1	-0-
Intersegment loans	-0-	-0-	-0-	-0-	-0-	5.4
Total assets	$11.4	$1.3	$ 1.5	$14.5	$1.0	$14.6

*All figures are in millions.

For example, an enterprise that accounts for pension expense only on a consolidated basis is not required to allocate pension expense to each operating segment. Any allocations of common costs that are made must be done on a reasonable basis. Moreover, segment profit or loss does not have to be calculated in accordance with generally accepted accounting principles if the measure reported internally is calculated on another basis. To assist the readers of financial statements in understanding segment disclosures, any differences in the basis of measurement between segment and consolidated amounts must be disclosed.

Each operating segment's profit or loss is calculated as follows:

Operating Segment	Total Revenues	Total Expenses	Profit	Loss
Automotive	$41.6*	$30.6	$11.0	$-0-
Furniture	9.0	7.0	2.0	-0-
Textbook	6.8	8.0	-0-	1.2
Motion picture	22.8	25.5	-0-	2.7
Appliance	5.3	4.8	0.5	-0-
Finance	12.3	9.3	3.0	-0-
Totals	$97.8	$85.2	$16.5	$ 3.9

*All figures are in millions.

The $16.5 million in total profit is larger in an absolute sense than the $3.9 million in losses. Therefore, this larger balance is the basis for the second quantitative test. As a result of the 10 percent criterion, either a profit or loss of $1.65 million or more qualifies a segment for disaggregation. According to the profit or loss totals just calculated, Atkinson Company's automotive, furniture, motion picture, and finance segments are large enough to warrant separate disclosure.

The Asset Test

The final test is based on the operating segments' combined total assets:

Operating Segment	Assets
Automotive	$11.4*
Furniture	1.3
Textbook	1.5
Motion picture	14.5
Appliance	1.0
Finance	14.6
Combined total	$44.3

*All figures are in millions.

Because 10 percent of the combined total equals $4.43 million, any segment holding at least that amount of assets is viewed as a reportable segment. Consequently, according to this final significance test, the automotive, motion picture, and finance segments are all considered of sufficient size to require disaggregation. The three remaining segments do not have sufficient assets to pass this particular test.

Summary of Test Results

A summary of all three significance tests as applied to Atkinson Company follows:

Operating Segments	Revenue Test	Profit or Loss Test	Asset Test
Automotive	✓	✓	✓
Furniture		✓	
Textbook			
Motion picture	✓	✓	✓
Appliance			
Finance	✓	✓	✓

Four of this company's operating segments meet at least one of the quantitative thresholds (automotive, furniture, motion picture, and finance) and therefore are separately reportable. Because neither the textbook nor the appliance segment has met any of these three tests, disaggregated information describing their *individual* operations is not required. However, the financial data accumulated from these two nonsignificant segments still have to be presented. The amounts for these two segments can be combined and disclosed as aggregate amounts in an All Other category with appropriate disclosure of the source of revenues.

In fact, this is the approach taken by Ford Motor Company in its 2017 annual report, as stated in the following disclosure (which also reflects Ford's application of the management approach in determining reportable segments):

> Reflecting the manner in which our Chief Operating Decision Maker manages our businesses, including resource allocation and performance assessment, we have four operating segments that represent the primary businesses reported in our consolidated financial statements. These operating segments are: Automotive, Financial Services, Ford Smart Mobility LLC, and Central Treasury Operations.
>
> Automotive and Financial Services comprise separate reportable segments. Ford Smart Mobility LLC and Central Treasury Operations did not meet the quantitative thresholds in this reporting period to qualify as reportable segments; therefore, these operating segments are combined and disclosed below as All Other.[1]

[1] Ford Motor Company, 2017 Annual Report, page FS-61.

Other Guidelines

Additional guidelines apply to the disclosure of operating segment information. These rules are designed to ensure that the disaggregated data are consistent from year to year and relevant to the needs of financial statement users. For example, any operating segment that has been reportable in the past and is judged by management to be of continuing significance should be disclosed separately in the current financial statements regardless of the outcome of the testing process. This ensures the ongoing usefulness of segment information, especially for comparison purposes.

In a similar manner, if an operating segment newly qualifies for disclosure in the current year, prior period segment data presented for comparative purposes must be restated to reflect the newly reportable segment as a separate segment. Again, the comparability of information has high priority in setting the standards for disclosure.

Another issue concerns the number of operating segments that should be disclosed. To enhance the value of the disaggregated information, a substantial portion of a company's operations should be presented individually. A sufficient number of segments is presumed to be included only if the combined segment sales to unaffiliated customers are at least 75 percent of total company consolidated sales made to outsiders. If this lower limit is not achieved, additional segments must be disclosed separately despite their failure to satisfy even one of the three quantitative thresholds.

As an illustration, assume that Brendan Corporation identified seven operating segments that generated revenues as follows (in millions):

Operating Segments	Sales to Unaffiliated Customers	Intersegment Transfers	Segment Revenues (and percentage of total)	
Housewares	$ 5.5	$ 1.6	$ 7.1	9.3%
Toys	6.2	–0–	6.2	8.1
Pottery	3.4	7.9	11.3	14.8 ✓
Lumber	6.6	10.4	17.0	22.3 ✓
Lawn mowers	7.2	–0–	7.2	9.4
Appliances	2.1	6.2	8.3	10.9 ✓
Construction	19.2	–0–	19.2	25.2 ✓
Totals	$50.2	$26.1	$76.3	100

Based on the 10 percent revenue test, four of these segments are reportable (because each has total revenues of more than $7.63 million): pottery, lumber, appliances, and construction. Assuming that none of the other segments qualify as significant in either of the two remaining tests, disclosure of disaggregated data is required for only these four segments. However, the 75 percent rule has not been met; the reportable segments generate just 62.4 percent of the company's total sales to unrelated parties (in millions):

Reportable Segments	Sales to Unaffiliated Customers
Pottery	$ 3.4
Lumber	6.6
Appliances	2.1
Construction	19.2
Total	$31.3

Information being disaggregated: $31.3 million/$50.2 million = 62.4%

To satisfy the 75 percent requirement, Brendan Corporation must also include the lawn mowers segment within the disaggregated data. With the addition of this nonsignificant segment, sales of $38.5 million ($31.3 + $7.2) to outside parties now are disclosed. This amounts to 76.7 percent of the company total ($38.5 million/$50.2 million). The two remaining segments—housewares and toys—could still be included separately within the disaggregated data; disclosure is not prohibited. However, information for these two segments probably would be combined and reported as aggregate amounts in an All Other category.

One final aspect of these reporting requirements should be mentioned. Some companies might be organized in such a fashion that a relatively large number of operating segments exist. The authoritative guidance suggests that there could be a practical limit to the number of operating segments that should be reported separately. Beyond that limit, the information becomes too detailed to be useful. Although a maximum number is not prescribed, FASB ASC 280-10-50-18 suggests that 10 separately reported segments might be the practical limit. Exhibit 8.2 provides a flowchart summarizing the procedures for determining separately reportable operating segments.

EXHIBIT 8.2 Flowchart for Determining Reportable Operating Segments

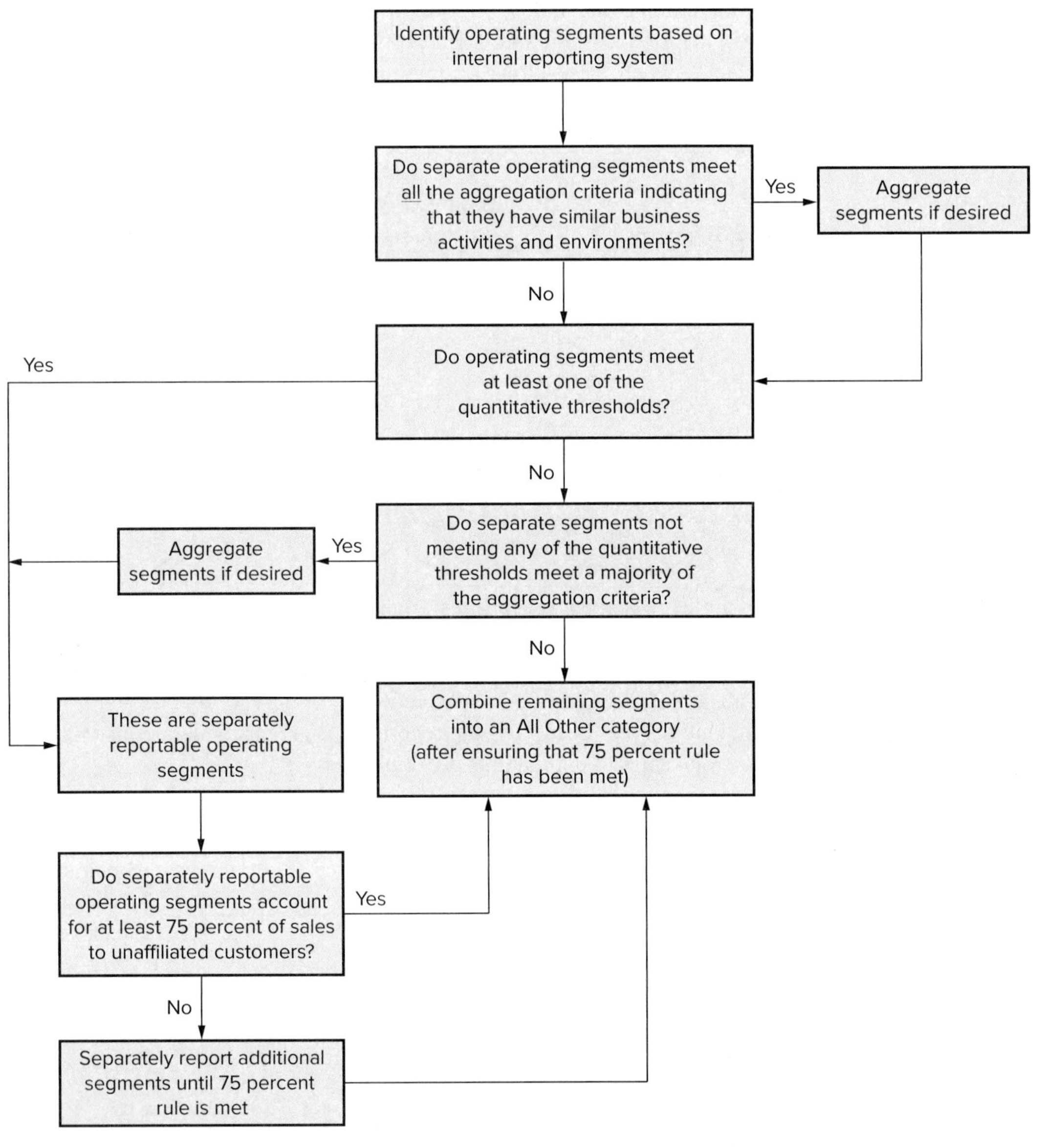

LO 8-3

List the basic disclosure requirements for operating segments.

Information to Be Disclosed by Reportable Operating Segments

A significant amount of information is required to be disclosed for each operating segment:

1. *General information* about the operating segment:
   - Factors used to identify reportable operating segments.
   - Types of products and services from which each operating segment reported derives its revenues.
2. *Segment profit or loss* and each of the following if it is regularly provided to or included in the measure of segment profit or loss reviewed by the chief operating decision maker:
   - Revenues from external customers.
   - Revenues from transactions with other operating segments.
   - Interest revenue and interest expense (reported separately); net interest revenue may be reported for finance segments if this measure is used internally for evaluation.
   - Depreciation, depletion, and amortization expenses.
   - Unusual items.
   - Equity in the net income of investees accounted for by the equity method.
   - Income tax expense or benefit.
   - Other significant noncash items included in segment profit or loss.
3. *Total segment assets* and the following related items:
   - Investment in equity method affiliates.
   - Expenditures for additions to long-lived assets.

The measure of segment profit or loss and segment assets disclosed must be the same as the measure reported to the chief operating decision maker for the purpose of assessing performance and allocating resources to segments. If, for example, the chief operating decision maker evaluates segment performance on the basis of earnings before interest, taxes, depreciation, and amortization (EBITDA), then EBITDA must be disclosed for each reportable segment. In that case, interest revenue and interest expense; income tax expense or benefit; and depreciation, depletion, and amortization need not be disclosed by segment, unless these amounts are reported to the chief operating decision maker in addition to EBITDA.

Authoritative guidance does not specifically require cash flow information to be reported for each operating segment because this information often is not generated by segment for internal reporting purposes. The requirement to disclose significant noncash items other than depreciation is an attempt to provide information that might enhance users' ability to estimate cash flow from operations.

Immaterial items need not be disclosed. For example, some segments do not have material amounts of interest revenue and expense, and therefore disclosure of these items of information is not necessary. In addition, if the internal financial reporting system does not generate information for an item on a segment basis, that item need not be disclosed. This is consistent with the rationale that segment reporting should create as little additional cost to an enterprise as possible.

To demonstrate how the operating segment information might be disclosed, we return to the Atkinson Company example introduced earlier in this chapter. Application of the quantitative threshold tests resulted in four separately reportable segments (automotive, furniture, motion picture, and finance). The nonsignificant operating segments (textbook and appliance) are combined in an All Other category. Exhibit 8.3 shows the operating segment disclosures included in Atkinson's financial statements. Depreciation and amortization, interest, and income taxes are disclosed for each segment because these expenses are included in the measure of segment profit or loss reported to the chief operating decision maker.

In addition to the information in Exhibit 8.1, data on other significant noncash items, and expenditures for long-lived segment assets were gathered for each operating segment to comply with the disclosure requirements. Only the automotive segment has other significant noncash items, and none of the segments have equity method investments. Atkinson had no unusual items during the year.

EXHIBIT 8.3 Operating Segment Disclosures

ATKINSON COMPANY					
	Operating Segment				
	Automotive	Furniture	Motion Picture	Finance	All Other
Segment profit (loss)	**$11.0***	**$2.0**	**$(2.7)**	**$3.0**	**$(0.7)**
Revenues from external customers.	32.6*	6.9	22.2	—	9.7
Intersegment revenues	6.6	1.2	–0–	—	1.9
Interest revenue	2.4	0.9	0.6	—	0.5
Interest expense	2.1	1.0	4.6	—	2.2
Net interest revenue.	—	—	—	6.2	—
Depreciation and amortization	2.4	0.3	3.0	0.5	0.3
Other significant noncash items:					
Cost in excess of billings on long-term contracts.	0.8	–0–	–0–	–0–	–0–
Income tax expense (benefit)	6.6	1.4	(3.1)	0.1	(1.1)
Segment assets	**11.4**	**1.3**	**14.5**	**14.6**	**2.5**
Expenditures for long-lived segment assets. . .	3.5	0.4	3.7	1.7	1.3

*All figures are in millions.

To determine whether a sufficient number of segments is reported separately, the ratio of combined sales to unaffiliated customers for the separately reported operating segments must be compared with total company sales made to outsiders. The combined amount of revenues from external customers disclosed for the automotive, furniture, motion picture, and finance segments is $61.7 million. Total revenues from external customers are $71.4 million:

$$\$61.7 \text{ million}/\$71.4 \text{ million} = 86.4\%$$

Because 86.4 percent exceeds the lower limit of 75 percent, Atkinson's level of disaggregation is adequate.

Reconciliations to Consolidated Totals

As noted earlier, segment information is to be provided as the company's internal reporting system prepares it, even if not based on GAAP. Preparing segment information in accordance with authoritative accounting literature used at the consolidated level is difficult in some cases because some GAAP is not intended to apply at the segment level. Examples are accounting for (1) inventory on a LIFO basis when inventory pools include items in more than one segment, (2) companywide pension plans, and (3) litigation obligations. Accordingly, allocation of these items to individual operating segments is not required.

However, the total of the reportable segments' revenues must be reconciled to consolidated revenues, the total of the reportable segments' profit or loss must be reconciled to consolidated income before tax, and the total of the reportable segments' assets must be reconciled to consolidated total assets. To carry out this reconciliation, adjustments and eliminations that have been made to prepare consolidated financial statements in compliance with GAAP must be identified. Examples are the elimination of intersegment revenues and an adjustment for companywide pension expense.

In addition, in reconciling the total of segments' revenues, profit or loss, and assets to the consolidated totals, the aggregate amount of revenues, profit or loss, and assets from immaterial operating segments must be disclosed. The company also must disclose assets, revenues, expenses, gains, losses, interest expense, and depreciation, depletion, and amortization expense for components of the enterprise that are not operating segments. This includes, for example, assets and expenses associated with corporate headquarters. See Exhibit 8.4 for an example of how Atkinson might present these reconciliations.

Atkinson Company must make four types of adjustments in reconciling segment results with consolidated totals. The first type of adjustment is to eliminate intra-entity revenues, profit or loss, and assets that are not included in consolidated totals. The elimination of intersegment

EXHIBIT 8.4
Reconciliation of Segment Results to Consolidated Totals

ATKINSON COMPANY	
Revenues:	
Total segment revenues	$97.8*
Elimination of intersegment revenues	(13.3)
Total consolidated revenues	$84.5
Profit or loss:	
Total segment profit or loss	$12.6
Total segment income taxes	3.9
Total segment profit before income taxes	$16.5
Elimination of intersegment profits	(5.9)
Unallocated amounts:	
Litigation settlement received	3.6
Other corporate expenses	(2.7)
Adjustment to pension expense in consolidation	(0.8)
Consolidated income before income taxes	$10.7
Assets:	
Total for reported segments	$44.3
Elimination of intersegment loans	(5.4)
Other corporate assets	5.8
Total consolidated assets	$44.7

*All figures are in millions.

revenues includes intersegment transfers amounting to $9.7 million plus $3.6 million of intersegment interest revenue generated by the finance segment (total $13.3 million). Likewise, intersegment loans made by the finance segment must be eliminated to reconcile to total consolidated assets. The second adjustment adds total segment income taxes back to total segment profit to be able to reconcile to income before tax for the company as a whole. The third type of adjustment relates to corporate items that have not been allocated to the operating segments, including a litigation settlement received by the company, and corporate headquarters expenses and assets. The fourth adjustment reconciles differences in segment accounting practices from accounting practices used in the consolidated financial statements. The only adjustment of this nature that Atkinson made relates to the accounting for pension expense. Individual operating segments measure pension expense based on cash payments made to the pension plan. Because GAAP requires measuring pension expense on an accrual basis, an adjustment for the amount of pension expense to be recognized in the consolidated statements is necessary.

Explanation of Measurement

In addition to the operating segment disclosures and reconciliation of segment results to consolidated totals, companies also must explain the measurement of segment profit or loss and segment assets, including a description of any differences in measuring (1) segment profit or loss and consolidated income before tax, (2) segment assets and consolidated assets, and (3) segment profit or loss and segment assets. An example of this last item would be the allocation of depreciation expense to segments in determining segment profit or loss even though the related depreciable assets are not included in segment assets. The basis of accounting for intersegment transactions also must be described.

Examples of Operating Segment Disclosures

A majority of companies are organized along product and/or service lines. Exhibit 8.5 shows selected operating segment disclosures for Fluor Corporation. Fluor provides a reconciliation of total segment profit to consolidated earnings from continuing operations before taxes in its segment disclosures. Because Fluor measures segment profit on a before-tax basis, it does not

EXHIBIT 8.5 **Fluor Corporation's Operating Segment Disclosures**

15. Operations by Business Segment and Geographical Area

The company provides professional services in the fields of engineering, procurement, construction, fabrication and modularization, commissioning and maintenance, as well as project management, on a global basis and serves a diverse set of industries worldwide.

Operating Information by Segment

	Year Ended December 31,		
(in millions)	**2017**	**2016**	**2015**
External revenue			
Energy, Chemicals & Mining	**$ 9,376.7**	$ 9,754.2	$11,865.4
Industrial, Infrastructure & Power	**4,367.5**	4,094.5	2,264.0
Government	**3,232.7**	2,720.0	2,557.4
Diversified Services	**2,544.1**	2,467.8	1,427.2
Total external revenue	**$19,521.0**	$19,036.5	$18,114.0
Segment profit (loss)			
Energy, Chemicals & Mining	**$ 454.7**	$ 401.5	$ 866.6
Industrial, Infrastructure & Power	**(170.8)**	135.8	(44.9)
Government	**127.9**	85.1	83.1
Diversified Services	**133.6**	121.9	127.4
Total segment profit	**$ 545.4**	$ 744.3	$ 1,032.2
Depreciation and amortization of fixed assets			
Energy, Chemicals & Mining	**$ —**	$ —	$ —
Industrial, Infrastructure & Power	**4.7**	3.9	4.0
Government	**2.8**	2.3	3.2
Diversified Services	**137.6**	139.5	113.4
Corporate and other	**61.0**	65.4	68.1
Total depreciation and amortization of fixed assets	**$ 206.1**	$ 211.1	$ 188.7
Capital expenditures			
Energy, Chemicals & Mining	**$ —**	$ —	$ —
Industrial, Infrastructure & Power	**27.7**	2.2	6.1
Government	**4.2**	2.1	3.9
Diversified Services	**187.1**	153.1	158.9
Corporate and other	**64.1**	78.5	71.3
Total capital expenditures	**$ 283.1**	$ 235.9	$ 240.2
Total assets			
Energy, Chemicals & Mining	**$ 1,815.2**	$ 2,348.0	
Industrial, Infrastructure & Power	**926.3**	750.1	
Government	**732.0**	493.7	
Diversified Services	**2,120.4**	1,952.7	
Corporate and other	**3,733.8**	3,671.9	
Total assets	**$ 9,327.7**	$ 9,216.4	

The reportable segments follow the same accounting policies as those described in Major Accounting Policies. Management evaluates a segment's performance based upon segment profit. The company incurs cost and expenses and holds certain assets at the corporate level that relate to its business as a whole. Certain of these amounts have been charged to the company's business segments by various methods, largely on the basis of usage. Total assets not allocated to segments and held in "Corporate and other" primarily include cash, marketable securities, income-tax related assets, pension assets, deferred compensation trust assets and corporate property, plant, and equipment.

(continued)

EXHIBIT 8.5 **(Continued)**

Reconciliation of Segment Information to Consolidated Amounts

	Year Ended December 31,		
(in millions)	**2017**	**2016**	**2015**
Total segment profit	**$545.4**	$744.3	$1,032.2
Gain related to a partial sale of a subsidiary	—	—	68.2
Pension settlement charge	—	—	(239.9)
Corporate general and administrative expense	**(192.2)**	(191.1)	(168.3)
Interest income (expense), net	**(39.9)**	(52.6)	(28.1)
Earnings attributable to noncontrolling interests	**73.1**	46.0	62.5
Earnings from continuing operations before taxes	**$386.4**	$546.6	$ 726.6

Source: Fluor Corporation, 2017 Annual Report, pages F-46 and F-47.

report income tax expense or benefit by operating segment. A significant amount of corporate general and administrative expense is not allocated to individual operating segments. Likewise, net interest expense and noncontrolling interests are treated as corporate level items, and the company thus does not disclose these amounts by operating segment.

Some companies, such as Apple, Coca-Cola, McDonald's, and Nike, are organized geographically and define operating segments as regions of the world. Apple has identified five operating segments: Americas, Europe, Greater China, Japan, and Rest of Asia Pacific. Some companies report a combination of products or services and international segments. Walmart has three operating segments: Walmart U.S., Walmart International, and Sam's Club. PepsiCo has six reportable segments: Frito-Lay North America (FLNA); Quaker Foods North America (QFNA); North America Beverages (NAB); Latin America; Europe Sub-Saharan Africa (ESSA); and Asia, Middle East, and North Africa (AMENA). The nature of these companies' segmentation provides considerable insight into the way upper management views and evaluates the various parts of the consolidated enterprise.

Entitywide Information

Information about Products and Services

The authoritative literature recognizes that some enterprises are not organized along product or service lines. For example, some enterprises are organized geographically. Moreover, some enterprises may have only one operating segment yet provide a range of different products and services. To provide some comparability between enterprises, FASB ASC 280-10-50-40 requires *disclosure of revenues derived from transactions with external customers from each product or service* if operating segments have not been determined based on differences in products or services. An enterprise with only one operating segment also must disclose revenues from external customers on the basis of product or service. However, providing this information is not required if impracticable; that is, the information is not available and the cost to develop it would be excessive.

Lowe's Companies, Inc., operates in only one segment; nevertheless, it reported "sales by product category," as required in its 2017 annual report. See Exhibit 8.6 for that information.

LO 8-4

Determine when and what types of information must be disclosed for geographic areas.

Information about Geographic Areas

For those companies with international activities, two items of information—revenues from external customers and long-lived assets—must be reported (1) for the *domestic country* and (2) for *all foreign countries in total* in which the enterprise derives revenues or holds assets. In addition, if revenues from external customers attributed to an *individual foreign country* are material, the specific country and amount of revenues must be disclosed separately as

EXHIBIT 8.6 Lowe's Companies' Sales by Product Category

	Sales by Product Category					
	2017		2016		2015	
(Dollars in millions)	Total Sales	%	Total Sales	%	Total Sales	%
Lumber & Building Materials	$ 9,508	14%	$ 8,505	13%	$ 7,007	12%
Appliances	7,696	11	7,037	11	6,477	11
Seasonal & Outdoor Living	7,165	10	6,996	11	6,623	11
Tools & Hardware	6,713	10	6,359	10	5,686	10
Fashion Fixtures	6,429	9	6,303	10	5,806	10
Rough Plumbing & Electrical	6,149	9	5,741	9	5,203	9
Paint	5,321	8	5,183	8	4,742	8
Millwork	5,308	8	5,236	8	4,957	8
Lawn & Garden	5,251	8	5,109	8	4,732	8
Flooring	4,363	6	4,227	6	3,887	7
Kitchens	3,644	5	3,532	5	3,276	5
Other	1,072	2	789	1	678	1
Totals	**$68,619**	**100%**	**$65,017**	**100%**	**$59,074**	**100%**

must a material amount of long-lived assets located in an individual foreign country. Even if the company has only one operating segment and therefore does not otherwise provide segment information, it must report geographic area information.

Thus, U.S.-based companies are required to disclose the amount of revenues generated and long-lived assets held in (1) the United States, (2) all other countries in total, and (3) each material foreign country. Requiring disclosure at the individual country level is a significant change from previous accounting standards, which required disclosures according to groups of countries in the same region of the world (such as Asia-Pacific). Current U.S. GAAP does not preclude companies from continuing to provide information by region, and for consistency purposes many companies continue to do so even if they determine no single foreign country to be material. The reporting requirement was changed from geographic regions to individual countries because reporting information about individual countries has two benefits. First, it reduces the burden on financial statement preparers because most companies likely have material operations in only a few countries, perhaps only their country of domicile. Second, and more important, country-specific information is easier to interpret and therefore more useful. Individual countries within a region of the world often experience very different rates of economic growth and economic conditions. Disclosures by individual country rather than groups of countries provide investors and other financial statement readers better information for assessing the risk level associated with a company's foreign operations.

Although a 10 percent threshold was considered for determining when a country is material, ultimately the FASB decided to leave this to management's judgment. In determining materiality, management should apply the concept that an item is material if its omission could change a user's decision about the enterprise as a whole. U.S. GAAP does not provide more specific guidance on this issue.

Considerable variation exists with respect to how companies apply the materiality rule for determining separately reportable countries. For example, International Business Machines Corporation (IBM) provides disclosures only for those countries with 10 percent or more of revenues or net plant, property, and equipment. Exhibit 8.7 contains the geographic area information included in IBM's 2017 Annual Report. With respect to revenue, only the United States and Japan meet the company's materiality threshold of 10 percent. As a result, the location of more than 50 percent of IBM's revenues is not disclosed. Only the United States meets the 10 percent threshold for net plant, property, and equipment.

Also using a 10 percent materiality threshold, Hewlett Packard Enterprises (HPE) stated in Note 3 of its 2017 Form 10-K: "For each of the fiscal years of 2017, 2016 and 2015, other than the U.S., no country represented more than 10% of Hewlett Packard Enterprise's net

Discussion Question

HOW DOES A COMPANY DETERMINE WHETHER A FOREIGN COUNTRY IS MATERIAL?

Segment reporting can provide useful information for investors and competitors. Segment disclosures could result in competitive harm for the company making the disclosures. By analyzing segment information, potential competitors can identify and concentrate on the more successful areas of a disclosing company's business. Indeed, the FASB recognized competitive harm as an issue of concern for companies disclosing segment information. In developing the current segment reporting guidelines, the FASB considered but ultimately decided not to provide companies an exemption from providing segment information if they believed that doing so would result in competitive harm. The FASB believed that such an exemption would be inappropriate because it would provide a means for broad noncompliance with the standard.

The previous segment reporting standard required geographic segments with 10 percent or more of total firm revenues, operating profit, or identifiable assets to be reported separately. In contrast, the current guidelines require disclosures to be provided by country when revenues or long-lived assets in an individual country are material. However, U.S. GAAP does not specify what is material for this purpose but leaves this to management judgment. Some commentators have expressed a concern that firms might use high materiality thresholds to avoid making individual country disclosures, perhaps to avoid potential competitive harm. Anecdotally, the very different levels of disclosure provided in 2017 by IBM and Abbott shown in Exhibits 8.7 and 8.8, respectively, show that companies define materiality differently.

What factors might a company consider in determining whether an individual foreign country is material to its operations? Should U.S. GAAP require a percentage test to determine when an individual country is material?

EXHIBIT 8.7
IBM Corporation's Geographic Area Disclosures

INTERNATIONAL BUSINESS MACHINES CORPORATION
GEOGRAPHIC INFORMATION

The following provides information for those countries that are 10 percent or more of the specific category.

Revenue* ($ in millions) **For the year ended December 31:**	**2017**	**2016**	**2015**
United States	**$29,759**	$30,194	$30,514
Japan	**8,239**	8,339	7,544
Other countries	**41,141**	41,386	43,683
Total IBM consolidated revenue	**$79,139**	$79,919	$81,741

Plant and Other Property—Net ($ in millions) **At December 31:**	**2017**	**2016**	**2015**
United States	**$ 4,670**	$ 4,701	$ 4,644
Other countries	**5,985**	5,607	5,532
Total	**$10,655**	$10,308	$10,176

*Revenues are attributed to countries based on the location of the client.

revenue." As a result, for 2017, HPE reported $9,913 million in net revenue in the United States and $18,958 million in net revenue from Other Countries, with no disclosure of net revenue in any individual foreign country.

In contrast, Exhibit 8.8 provides the net sales by geographic area disclosures made by Abbott Laboratories in its 2017 Annual Report. In providing this information, Abbott appears to define materiality at about 1.5 percent. Abbott provided disclosures for 15 individual countries (including the United States) that comprised 79 percent of the company's total net sales in 2017.

For export sales, companies must choose whether to attribute the sales revenue to the country in which the selling entity is located or to the country in which the customer is located, and the basis for identifying the location of sales must be disclosed. IBM provides a footnote to its geographic information that indicates revenue is attributed to the country in which the customer (client) is located. In contrast, Abbott indicates that sales are attributed to the country that sold the product.

LO 8-5

Apply the criterion for determining when disclosure of a major customer is required.

Information about Major Customers

FASB ASC 280-10-50-42 requires one final but important disclosure. A reporting entity must indicate its reliance on any major external customer. *Presentation of this information is required whenever 10 percent or more of a company's consolidated revenues is derived from a single external customer.* The existence of all major customers must be disclosed along with the related amount of revenues and the identity of the operating segment generating the revenues. Interestingly enough, the company need not reveal the customer's identity.

The 2017 Annual Report of toy manufacturer Hasbro, Inc., provides an example of how this information is disclosed. Although not required to do so, Hasbro has elected to disclose the names of its major customers. In Note 20, "Segment Reporting," Hasbro discloses:

> Sales to the Company's three largest customers, Wal-Mart Stores, Inc., Toys 'R' Us, Inc. and Target Corporation, amounted to 19%, 9% and 9%, respectively, of consolidated net revenues during 2017, 18%, 9% and 9%, respectively, of consolidated net revenues during 2016, and 16%, 9% and 9%, respectively, of consolidated net revenues during 2015. These sales were primarily within the U.S. and Canada segment.

EXHIBIT 8.8 Abbott Laboratories' Geographic Area Information

ABBOTT LABORATORIES AND COMPANY

	Geographic Area Information		
	Net Sales to External Customers*		
(in millions)	**2017**	**2016**	**2015**
United States	**$ 9,673**	$ 6,486	$ 6,270
China	**2,146**	1,728	1,796
Germany	**1,366**	1,044	1,004
Japan	**1,255**	924	895
India	**1,237**	1,114	1,053
The Netherlands	**929**	830	855
Switzerland	**841**	766	784
Russia	**664**	554	483
France	**628**	352	375
Brazil	**541**	410	381
Italy	**507**	365	383
United Kingdom	**498**	377	430
Colombia	**494**	424	388
Canada	**443**	408	428
Vietnam	**427**	434	331
All Other Countries	**5,741**	4,637	4,549
Consolidated	**$27,390**	$20,853	$20,405

*Sales by country are based on the country that sold the product.

The authoritative literature requires major customer disclosures even if a company operates in only one segment and therefore does not provide segment information. Also, to avoid any confusion, a group of entities under common control is considered to be a single customer, and federal, state, local, and foreign governments are each considered to be a single customer.

International Financial Reporting Standard 8—Operating Segments

IFRS 8, "Operating Segments," went into effect in 2009 and substantially converged IFRS with U.S. GAAP. *IFRS 8* requires disclosures to be provided for separately reportable operating segments as well as certain enterprisewide disclosures. Paragraph 1 establishes the "core principle" of *IFRS 8* to be the following:

> An entity shall disclose information to enable users of its financial statements to evaluate the nature and financial effects of the business activities in which it engages and the economic environments in which it operates.

The major differences between *IFRS 8* and U.S. GAAP are the following:

1. *IFRS 8* requires disclosure of total assets and total liabilities by operating segment, but only if such information is provided to the chief operating decision maker. U.S. GAAP requires disclosure of segment assets in general and is silent with respect to the disclosure of liabilities, even if this information is provided to the chief operating decision maker.
2. *IFRS 8* indicates that intangible assets are to be included in providing disclosure of long-lived assets attributable to geographic segments. In contrast, U.S. GAAP does not define what is intended to be included in long-lived assets. However, FASB ASC 280-10-55-23 indicates long-lived assets "implies hard assets that cannot be readily removed, which would exclude intangibles." Many U.S. companies define long-lived assets as property, plant, and equipment only, which is inconsistent with *IFRS 8.*
3. When a company has a matrix form of organization, *IFRS 8* indicates operating segments are to be determined based on the core principle of the standard. As a result, operating segments can be based on either products and services or geographic areas. U.S. GAAP stipulates that in a matrix form of organization, segments must be based on products and services, not geographic areas.

Interim Reporting

LO 8-6

Understand and apply procedures used in interim financial reports to treat an interim period as an integral part of the annual period.

To give investors and creditors more timely information than an annual report provides, companies publish financial information for periods of less than one year. The SEC requires publicly traded companies in the United States to provide financial statements on a quarterly basis. Unlike annual financial statements, financial statements included in quarterly reports filed with the SEC need not be audited. This allows companies to disseminate the information to investors and creditors as quickly as possible. FASB ASC Topic 270, "Interim Reporting," provides guidance to companies as to how to prepare interim statements, and also stipulates minimum disclosures to be provided in interim statements.

Some inherent problems are associated with determining the results of operations for time periods of less than one year, especially with regard to expenses that do not occur evenly throughout the year. Two approaches can be followed in preparing interim reports: (1) Treat the interim period as a **discrete** accounting period, standing on its own, or (2) treat it as an **integral** portion of a longer period. Considering the annual bonus a company pays to key employees in December of each year illustrates the distinction between these two approaches. Under the *discrete* period approach, the company reports the entire bonus as an expense in December, reducing fourth-quarter income only. Under the *integral* part of an annual period approach, a company accrues a portion of the bonus to be paid in December as an expense in each of the first three quarters of the year. Application of the integral approach requires estimating the annual bonus early in the year and developing a method for allocating the bonus to the four quarters of the year. The advantage of this approach is that there is less volatility in quarterly earnings as irregularly occurring costs are spread over the entire year.

FASB ASC 270 requires companies to treat interim periods as integral parts of an annual period rather than as discrete accounting periods in their own right. Generally speaking, companies should prepare interim financial statements following the same accounting principles and practices they use in preparing annual statements. However, deviation from this general rule is necessary for several items so that the interim statements better reflect the expected annual amounts. Special rules related to revenues, inventory and cost of goods sold, other costs and expenses, income taxes, accounting changes, and seasonal items are discussed in turn in the following sections.

Revenues

Companies should recognize revenues in interim periods the same way they recognize revenues on an annual basis. For example, revenues from a long-term construction contract that includes performance obligations that are satisfied by a company over time should be recognized in interim periods on the same basis as such revenues are recognized for the full year. Moreover, a company should recognize projected losses on long-term construction contracts to their full extent in the interim period in which it becomes apparent that a loss will arise.

Inventory and Cost of Goods Sold

Interim period accounting for inventory and cost of goods sold requires several modifications to procedures used on an annual basis. The modifications relate to (1) a LIFO liquidation, (2) application of the lower-of-cost-or-net realizable value rule, and (3) standard costing.

1. *LIFO liquidation:* Companies using the last-in, first-out (LIFO) cost-flow assumption to value inventory experience a LIFO liquidation at the end of an interim period when the number of units of inventory sold exceeds the number of units added to inventory during the period. When prices are rising, matching beginning inventory cost (carried at low LIFO amounts) against the current period sales revenue results in an unusually high amount of gross profit. If the company expects to replace by year-end the units of beginning inventory sold, there is no LIFO liquidation on an annual basis. In that case, gross profit for the interim period should not reflect the temporary LIFO liquidation, and inventory reported on the interim balance sheet should include the expected cost to replace the beginning inventory sold.

To illustrate, assume that Liquid Products Company began the first quarter with 100 units of inventory that cost $10 per unit. During the first quarter, it purchased 200 units at a cost of $15 per unit and sold 240 units at $20 per unit. During the first quarter, the company experienced a liquidation of 40 units of beginning inventory. It calculates gross profit as follows:

Sales (240 units @ $20).		$4,800
Cost of goods sold:		
200 units @ $15	$ 3,000	
40 units @ $10 (LIFO historical cost).	400	3,400
Gross profit.		$1,400

However, during the second quarter, the company expects to replace the units of beginning inventory sold at a cost of $17 per unit and that inventory at year-end will be at least 100 units. Therefore, it calculates gross profit for the first quarter as follows:

Sales (240 units @ $20).		$4,800
Cost of goods sold:		
200 units @ $15	$ 3,000	
40 units @ $17 (replacement cost)	680	3,680
Gross profit.		$1,120

The journal entry to record cost of goods sold in the first quarter is as follows:

Cost of Goods Sold	3,680	
Inventory		3,400
Excess of Replacement Cost over Historical Cost of LIFO Liquidation		280
To record cost of goods sold with a historical cost of $3,400 and an excess of replacement cost over historical cost for beginning inventory liquidated of $280 [($17 – $10) × 40 units].		

Thus, ending inventory is still reported at the original LIFO cost. The LIFO liquidation account will be removed in the second quarter when new goods are purchased.

2. *Lower-of-cost-or-net realizable value:* If at the end of an interim period, the net realizable value of inventory is less than its cost, the company normally should write down inventory and recognize a loss. However, if the company expects the net realizable value to recover above the inventory's original cost by year-end, it should not write down inventory and recognize a loss at the interim balance sheet date. Instead, it should continue to carry inventory at cost.

3. *Standard costing:* A company should not reflect in interim financial statements planned price, volume, or capacity variances arising from the use of a standard cost system that are expected to be absorbed by the end of the annual period. However, it should report unplanned variances at the end of the interim period in the same fashion as it would in the annual financial statements.

Other Costs and Expenses

A company should charge costs and expenses not directly matched with revenues to income in the interim period in which they occur unless they can be identified with activities or benefits of other interim periods. In that case, the cost should be allocated among interim periods on a reasonable basis through the use of accruals and deferrals. For example, assume that a company required to prepare quarterly financial statements pays annual property taxes of $100,000 on April 10. One-fourth of the estimated property tax should be accrued as expense in the first quarter of the year. When it makes the payment, it should apply one-fourth against the accrued property tax payable from the previous quarter and charge one-fourth to second-quarter income. The company should defer one-half of the payment as a prepaid expense to be allocated to the third and fourth quarters of the year. The following journal entries demonstrate the procedures for ensuring that the company recognizes one-fourth of the annual payment as expense in each quarter of the year.

March 31

Property Tax Expense	25,000	
Accrued Property Tax Payable		25,000
To accrue one-fourth of the estimated annual property tax as expense for the quarter ended March 31.		

April 10

Accrued Property Tax Payable	25,000	
Property Tax Expense	25,000	
Prepaid Property Tax (Current Asset)	50,000	
Cash		100,000
To record the payment of the annual property tax, recognize one-fourth as property tax expense for the quarter ending June 30, and defer one-half as a prepaid expense.		

September 30

Property Tax Expense	25,000	
Prepaid Property Tax.		25,000
To record property tax expense for the quarter ended September 30.		

December 31

Property Tax Expense	25,000	
Prepaid Property Tax.		25,000
To record property tax expense for the quarter ended December 31.		

Other items requiring similar treatment include annual major repairs and advertising. In addition, a number of adjustments such as bad debt expense, executive bonuses, and quantity discounts based on annual sales volume that are normally made at year-end actually relate to the entire year. To the extent that the company can estimate annual amounts, it should make adjustments at the end of each interim period so that the interim periods bear a reasonable portion of the expected annual amount.

Income Taxes

Companies should compute income tax related to ordinary income at an estimated *annual* effective tax rate. At the end of each interim period, a company makes its best estimate of the effective tax rate for the entire year. The effective tax rate reflects anticipated tax credits, foreign tax rates, and tax planning activities for the year. It then applies this rate to the pretax ordinary income earned to date during the year, resulting in the cumulative income tax expense to recognize to date. The difference between the cumulative income tax recognized to date and income tax recognized in earlier interim periods is the amount of income tax expense recognized in the current interim period.

Assume that Viertel Company estimated its effective annual tax rate at 25 percent in the first quarter of 2020. Pretax income for the first quarter was $500,000. At the end of the second quarter of 2020, the company expects its effective annual tax rate will be only 22 percent because of the planned usage of foreign tax credits. Pretax income in the second quarter of 2020 is also $500,000. No items require net-of-tax presentation in either quarter. The income tax expense recognized in each of the first two quarters of 2020 is determined as follows:

First Quarter	
Pretax income for first quarter of 2020.	$500,000
Estimated annual income tax rate	25%
Income tax expense.	$125,000

Second Quarter		
Pretax income for first quarter of 2020.	$500,000	
Pretax income for second quarter of 2020	500,000	
Year-to-date pretax income		$1,000,000
Estimated annual income tax rate		22%
Year-to-date income tax expense		$ 220,000
Income tax expense recognized in first quarter		125,000
Income tax expense recognized in second quarter.		$ 95,000

The same process is followed for the third and fourth quarters of the year.

Discontinued operations should be reported in net income on a *net of tax* basis in the interim period in which a business component is discontinued or classified as held-for-sale.

The income tax on an interim period discontinued operation is calculated at the margin as the difference between income tax on income including discontinued operations and income tax on income excluding discontinued operations.

Change in Accounting Principle

Current accounting guidelines require retrospective application of a new accounting principle to prior periods' financial statements. *Retrospective application* means that comparative financial statements will be restated as if the new accounting principle had always been used. Whether an accounting change occurs in the first or in a subsequent interim period has no bearing on the manner in which the change is reflected in the interim financial statements. Changes in accounting principle, regardless of when the accounting change is made, are handled as follows (according to FASB ASC 250-10-45-5):

a. The cumulative effect of the change to the new accounting principle on periods prior to those presented is reflected in the carrying amounts of assets and liabilities as of the beginning of the first period presented.
b. An offsetting adjustment, if any, is made to the opening balance of retained earnings (or other appropriate components of equity or net assets in the statement of financial position) for that period.
c. Financial statements for each individual prior period are adjusted to reflect the period-specific effects of applying the new accounting principle.

When the accounting change takes place in other than the first interim period, current guidelines require information for the interim periods prior to the change to be reported by retrospectively applying the new accounting principle to those prechange interim periods. If retrospective application is impracticable, the accounting change is not allowed to be made in an interim period but may be made at the beginning of the next fiscal year. Situations in which the retrospective application of a new accounting principle to prechange interim periods is not feasible should be rare.

Illustration of Accounting Change Made in Other Than First Interim Period

Modal Company began operations on January 1, 2019. The company's interim income statements as originally reported under the LIFO inventory valuation method follow:

	2019				2020
	1stQ	**2ndQ**	**3rdQ**	**4thQ**	**1stQ**
Sales	$2,000	$2,000	$2,000	$2,000	$2,200
Cost of goods sold (LIFO)	900	950	1,000	1,000	1,050
Operating expenses	500	500	500	500	600
Income before income taxes	$ 600	$ 550	$ 500	$ 500	$ 550
Income taxes (40%)	240	220	200	200	220
Net income	$ 360	$ 330	$ 300	$ 300	$ 330

Modal has 500 shares of common stock outstanding. The company's interim report for the first quarter of 2020 included the following information:

	Three Months Ended March 31	
	2019	**2020**
Net income	$ 360	$ 330
Net income per common share	$0.72	$0.66

In June 2020, Modal adopts the FIFO method of inventory valuation for both financial reporting and tax purposes. Retrospective application of the FIFO method to previous quarters results in the following amounts of cost of goods sold:

	2019				2020
	1stQ	2ndQ	3rdQ	4thQ	1stQ
Cost of goods sold (FIFO)	$800	$850	$1,000	$900	$950

Retrospective application of the FIFO method results in the following restatements of income:

	2019				2020
	1stQ	2ndQ	3rdQ	4thQ	1stQ
Sales	$2,000	$2,000	$2,000	$2,000	$2,200
Cost of goods sold (FIFO)	800	850	1,000	900	950
Operating expenses.	500	500	500	500	600
Income before income taxes	$ 700	$ 650	$ 500	$ 600	$ 650
Income taxes (40%).	280	260	200	240	260
Net income.	$ 420	$ 390	$ 300	$ 360	$ 390

Sales for the second quarter of 2020 are $2,400, cost of goods sold under the FIFO method is $1,000, and operating expenses are $600. Income before income taxes in the second quarter of 2020 is $800, income taxes are $320, and net income is $480.

To prepare interim statements for the second quarter of 2020 in accordance with U.S. GAAP, net income as originally reported in the first and second quarters of 2019, as well as in the first quarter of 2020, is restated to reflect the change to FIFO. The manner in which the accounting change is reflected in the second quarter of 2020, with year-to-date information, and comparative information for similar periods in 2019 follow:

	Three Months Ended June 30		Six Months Ended June 30	
	2019	2020	2019	2020
Net income.	$390	$480	$810	$870
Net income per common share	0.78	0.96	1.62	1.74

Seasonal Items

The sales volume of some companies experiences significant seasonal variation. Summer sports equipment manufacturers, for example, are likely to have a significant upward spike in sales during the second quarter of the year. To avoid the risk that investors and creditors will be misled into believing that second-quarter earnings indicate earnings for the entire year, FASB ASC 270-10-45 requires companies to disclose the seasonal nature of their business operations. In addition, such companies should consider supplementing their interim reports with reports on the 12-month period ended at the interim date for both the current and preceding years. An excerpt from the seasonality disclosure provided by Callaway Golf Company in its Form 10-Q for the quarter ended June 30, 2018 (page 33), is shown here:

> **Seasonality.**
> ***Golf Clubs and Golf Balls***
> In most of the regions where the Company conducts business, the game of golf is played primarily on a seasonal basis. Weather conditions generally restrict golf from being played year-round, except in a few markets, with many of the Company's on-course customers closing for the cold weather months. The Company's golf clubs and golf ball businesses are therefore subject to

seasonal fluctuations . . . The Company's fourth-quarter sales are generally less than the other quarters due to the end of the golf season in many of the Company's key regions . . .

Gear, Accessories and Other

Sales of the Company's lifestyle and golf-related apparel, gear and accessories, historically followed the golf clubs and golf balls seasonality, where most of the sales and profitability occurred during the first half of the year.

LO 8-7

List the minimum disclosure requirements for interim financial reports.

Minimum Disclosures in Interim Reports

Many companies provide summary financial statements and notes in their interim reports that contain less information than is included in the annual financial statements. FASB ASC 270-10-50 requires companies to provide the following minimum information in their interim reports:

- Sales or gross revenues, provision for income taxes, net income, and comprehensive income.
- Basic and diluted earnings per share.
- Seasonal revenues and expenses.
- Significant changes in estimates or provisions for income taxes.
- Disposal of a component of the business and unusual or infrequently occurring items.
- Contingent items.
- Changes in accounting principles or estimates.
- Significant changes in financial position.

Other FASB ASC topics require certain disclosures related to postretirement benefit plans, fair-value measurements, derivative and other financial instruments, financing receivables, and impairments. FASB guidelines also encourage, but do not require, companies to publish balance sheet and cash flow information in interim reports. If they do not include this information, companies must disclose significant changes since the last period in cash and cash equivalents, net working capital, and long-term liabilities.

The SEC also requires interim reports to include a reconciliation of changes in stockholders' equity. For each line item in equity, a company must reconcile the beginning balance to the ending balance for the current quarter as well as for the year-to-date. In a third-quarter report, for example, companies must explain the change in each equity item from the beginning of the third quarter (July 1) to the end of the third quarter (September 30) as well as the change from the beginning of the year (January 1) to the end of the third quarter (September 30). The reconciliations may be presented in two separate statements (for the period July 1 to September 30 and for the period January 1 to September 30), or in a single statement that shows the changes in stockholders' equity from January 1 to September 30 that also includes separate subtotals for each of the first two quarters of the year.

Companies that provide interim reports on a quarterly basis are not required to publish a fourth-quarter report because this coincides with the end of the annual period. When a company does not provide a separate fourth-quarter report, it should disclose special accounting items occurring in the fourth quarter in the notes to financial statements in the annual report. These items include unusual and infrequently occurring items, disposals of a component of the business, and the aggregate effect of year-end adjustments that are material to the results of the fourth quarter.

The SEC requires companies to include selected quarterly financial data in their annual report to shareholders. Southwest Airlines Co. provided quarterly data in its 2017 Annual Report as shown in Exhibit 8.9.

Segment Information in Interim Reports

The management approach to determining operating segments results in readily available information for disclosure because, by definition, management already collects this data. Because the information is available on a timely basis, segment disclosures also must be

EXHIBIT 8.9
Southwest Airlines Co.'s Quarterly Financial Data

QUARTERLY FINANCIAL DATA (unaudited)

	Three Months Ended			
(in millions, except per share amounts)	**March 31**	**June 30**	**Sept. 30**	**Dec. 31**
2017				
Operating revenues	$4,883	$5,744	$5,271	$5,274
Operating income.	658	1,250	834	773
Income before income taxes	553	1.170	791	737
Net income.	351	746	503	1,888(a)
Net income per share, basic.	0.57	1.24	0.84	3.19(a)
Net income per share, diluted	0.57	1.23	0.84	3.18(a)

(a)Includes a $1.4 billion reduction in Provision for income taxes related to the Tax Cuts and Jobs Act legislation enacted in December 2017, which resulted in a remeasurement of the Company's deferred tax assets and liabilities at the new federal corporate tax rate of 21 percent.

included in interim reports. U.S. GAAP requires that the following information be included in interim reports for each operating segment:

- Revenues from external customers.
- Intersegment revenues.
- Segment profit or loss.
- Total assets, if there has been a material change from the last annual report.

In addition, an enterprise must reconcile total segments' profit or loss to the company's total income before taxes and disclose any change from the last annual report in the basis for measuring segment profit or loss. Requiring only a few items of information in interim reports is a compromise between users' desire to have the same information as is provided in annual financial statements and preparers' cost in reporting the information. There is no requirement to provide information about geographic areas or major customers in interim reports.

International Accounting Standard 34—Interim Financial Reporting

In contrast to U.S. GAAP, which does not require the presentation of financial statements *per se* in an interim report, *IAS 34,* "Interim Financial Reporting," provides guidance with respect to the form and content of interim financial statements, and the recognition and measurement principles to be followed in preparing them.[2] *IAS 34* requires the following minimum components in an interim report:

- A condensed statement of financial position (balance sheet).
- A condensed statement of comprehensive income, presented as:
  a. A condensed single statement of net income and comprehensive income, or
  b. Separate condensed statements of net income and comprehensive income.
- A condensed statement of changes in equity.
- A condensed statement of cash flows.
- Selected explanatory notes.

Unlike U.S. GAAP, *IAS 34* requires each interim period to be treated as a discrete period in determining the amounts to be recognized. Thus, expenses that are incurred in one quarter are recognized in full in that quarter, even though the expenditure benefits the entire year. In addition, there is no accrual in earlier quarters for expenses expected to be incurred in a later quarter of the year. The only exception to this rule is the accrual of income tax expense at the end of each interim period.

[2] Note that the IASB has no jurisdictional authority to require the preparation of interim reports; it simply provides requirements (through *IAS 34*) for how those reports should be prepared. *IAS 34* must be followed in those jurisdictions that require the use of IFRS and require the preparation of interim reports.

Summary

1. The consolidation of information from varied operations into a set of consolidated financial statements tends to camouflage the characteristics of the individual components. FASB ASC 280, "Segment Reporting," requires enterprises to follow a management approach in providing disaggregated information by operating segment.
2. The management approach to disaggregating information bases operating segments on a company's organization structure and internal reporting system. The management approach should enhance the usefulness of segment information because it highlights the risks and opportunities that management believes are important and allows the analyst to see the company through management's eyes. This approach also has the advantage of reducing the cost of providing segment information because that information already is being produced for internal use.
3. Once operating segments have been identified, a company must determine which segments are of significant magnitude to warrant separate disclosure. Three quantitative threshold tests (revenue, profit or loss, and asset) are used to identify reportable segments. A segment need satisfy only one of these tests to be considered of sufficient size to necessitate disclosure. Each test is based on identifying segments that meet a 10 percent minimum of the related combined total. The profit and loss test has a 10 percent criterion based on the higher (in an absolute sense) of the total profit from all segments with profits or the total loss from all segments with losses.
4. Companies must report several information types for each reportable operating segment—including selected revenues, profit or loss, selected expenses, assets, capital expenditures, and equity method investment and income. Companies must report revenues from external customers separately from intersegment revenues. In addition, the types of products and services from which each segment derives its revenues must be disclosed.
5. A set of parameters determines the number of segments an enterprise reports. As a minimum, the separately disclosed units must generate at least 75 percent of the total sales made to unaffiliated parties. For an upper limit, authoritative literature suggests that the disclosure of more than 10 operating segments reduces the usefulness of the information.
6. Companies must reconcile the total of all segments' revenues, profit or loss, and assets to the consolidated totals. The major reconciliation adjustments relate to intra-entity revenues, profit or loss, and assets eliminated in consolidation; revenues, profit or loss, and assets that have not been allocated to individual operating segments; and differences in accounting methods used by segments and in preparing consolidated financial statements.
7. U.S. GAAP requires several entitywide disclosures. If an enterprise does not define operating segments internally on a product-line basis or has only one operating segment, disclosure of revenues derived from each product or service is required.
8. In addition, companies must report revenues from external customers and long-lived assets for the domestic country, for each foreign country that generates a material amount of revenues or holds assets, and for all foreign countries in total. Current guidelines do not provide any threshold tests for determining when operations in a foreign country are material. Instead, determining materiality is left to management's judgment.
9. The reporting entity also must indicate the existence of major customers when 10 percent or more of consolidated revenues are derived from a single unaffiliated party. However, the identity of the major customer need not be disclosed.
10. To converge with U.S. GAAP, the IASB issued *IFRS 8,* "Operating Segments." The major differences between IFRS and U.S. GAAP are that *IFRS 8* (a) requires the disclosure of liabilities by operating segment if this information is reported to the chief operating decision maker, (b) requires the inclusion of intangible assets in the disclosure of long-lived assets by geographic area, and (c) allows companies with matrix organizations to define operating segments on the basis of either products and services or geographic areas.
11. For interim reporting purposes, U.S. GAAP requires time intervals of less than one year to be treated as an integral part of the annual period.
12. Costs and expenses not directly matched with revenues should be charged to income in the interim period in which they occur unless they can be identified with activities or benefits of other interim periods. In that case, the cost should be allocated among interim periods on a reasonable basis by using accruals and deferrals. Items related to the whole year but recorded as an adjustment only at year-end should be estimated and accrued in each interim period of the year.
13. Companies determine interim period income tax expense by applying the estimated annual effective income tax rate to year-to-date pretax ordinary income, resulting in the cumulative income tax expense to be recognized to date. The cumulative income tax to be recognized to date less income tax recognized in earlier interim periods is the amount of income tax expense recognized in the current interim period.

14. When an accounting change is made in other than the first interim period, information for the prechange interim periods should be reported based on retrospective application of the new accounting principle to those periods. An accounting change may be made only at the beginning of a fiscal year if retrospective application of the new accounting principle to prechange interim periods is not practicable.
15. The minimum information to disclose in interim reports includes sales, income taxes, net income, earnings per share, seasonal revenues and expenses, and significant changes in financial position. Publication of balance sheet and cash flow information in interim reports is not required. However, if this information is not included, any significant changes since the last period in cash and cash equivalents, net working capital, long-term liabilities, and stockholders' equity must be disclosed.
16. Certain segment information items need to be disclosed in interim reports. Specifically, companies must disclose revenues from outside customers, intersegment revenues, and segment profit or loss in interim reports for each operating segment. In addition, companies must report total assets by segment if a material change occurred since the last annual report.
17. Unlike U.S. GAAP, the IASB's *IAS 34,* "Interim Financial Reporting," requires the presentation of condensed financial statements in an interim report. Also, each interim period should be treated as a discrete period rather than as an integral part of an annual period in determining amounts to be recognized. The exception to this rule is the accrual of income tax expense to determine net income for each interim period.

Comprehensive Illustration

Problem

(*Estimated Time: 25 to 40 Minutes*) Battey Corporation manufactures several products: natural fibers, synthetic fibers, leather, plastics, and wood. It is organized into five operating divisions based on these different products. The company has a number of subsidiaries that perform operations throughout the world. At the end of 2020, as part of the internal reporting process, Battey reported the revenues, profits, and assets (in millions) to the chief operating decision maker:

Revenues by Operating Segment	United States	Canada	Mexico	France	Italy	Brazil
Natural fibers:						
Sales to external customers	$1,739	$–0–	$342	$606	$–0–	$1,171
Intersegment sales	–0–	–0–	–0–	–0–	–0–	146
Synthetic fibers:						
Sales to external customers	290	116	–0–	–0–	–0–	37
Intersegment sales	12	5	–0–	–0–	–0–	–0–
Leather:						
Sales to external customers	230	–0–	57	–0–	278	55
Intersegment sales	22	–0–	9	–0–	34	9
Plastics:						
Sales to external customers	748	286	–0–	83	92	528
Intersegment sales	21	12	–0–	–0–	–0–	72
Wood:						
Sales to external customers	116	22	–0–	–0–	–0–	149
Intersegment sales	17	3	–0–	–0–	–0–	28

Operating Profit or Loss by Operating Segment	United States	Canada	Mexico	France	Italy	Brazil
Natural fibers	$ 526	$–0–	$ 92	$146	$–0–	$ 404
Synthetic fibers	21	8	–0–	–0–	–0–	10
Leather	70	–0–	27	–0–	94	24
Plastics	182	74	–0–	18	24	68
Wood	18	5	–0–	–0–	–0–	37

Assets by Operating Segment	United States	Canada	Mexico	France	Italy	Brazil
Natural fibers	$1,005	$–0–	$223	$296	$–0–	$ 817
Synthetic fibers	163	50	–0–	–0–	–0–	74
Leather	146	–0–	41	–0–	150	38
Plastics	425	173	–0–	54	58	327
Wood	66	19	–0–	–0–	–0–	143

Required

a. Determine the operating segments that should be reported separately in Battey's 2020 financial statements.

b. Determine the countries for which Battey should report revenues separately in its 2020 financial statements. Assume that Battey has elected to define a material country as one in which sales to external customers are 10 percent or more of consolidated sales.

c. Determine the volume of revenues that a single customer must generate to necessitate disclosure of a major customer.

Solution

a. Battey Corporation determines its reportable operating segments by following a three-step process. First, it identifies operating segments. Second, it examines aggregation criteria to determine whether any operating segments may be combined. Third, it determines reportable operating segments by applying the three quantitative threshold tests.

Identification of Operating Segments Battey's internal reporting system provides information to the chief operating decision maker by operating division and by country. Either of these components conceivably could be identified as operating segments for segment reporting purposes. However, U.S. GAAP stipulates that, in this situation, the components based on products and services constitute the operating segments. Thus, the five operating divisions are identified as Battey's operating segments.

Aggregation Criteria Aggregation criteria are examined next to determine whether any operating segments can be combined. Management determines that the economic characteristics of the natural fibers and synthetic fibers operating divisions are very similar. In addition, they are considerably similar with regard to the nature of the product, production process, customers, and distribution methods. Because each aggregation criterion is met, Battey elects to combine these two segments into a single fibers category.

Quantitative Threshold Tests Determining Battey's reportable operating segments depends on the three materiality tests described in this chapter. The revenue test can be performed directly from the information provided. Any operating segment with total revenues (including intersegment sales) equal to 10 percent or more of combined revenue (internal and external) must be reported separately:

Revenue Test (in millions)

Operating Segments	Total Revenues (including intersegment)	
Fibers	$4,464	60.8%
Leather	694	9.5
Plastics	1,842	25.1
Wood	335	4.6
Total combined revenues	$7,335	100.0%

Reportable segments are fibers and plastics.

The profit or loss test is performed next. Battey must separately report any operating segment with profit or loss equal to 10 percent or more of the larger, in absolute amount, of combined segment profit (for those segments with a profit) or combined segment loss (for those segments with a loss). Because each of Battey's operating segments generated a profit in 2020, this test can be applied by determining the total combined profit:

Profit or Loss Test (in millions)

Operating Segments	Total Profit or Loss	
Fibers	$1,207	65.3%
Leather	215	11.6
Plastics	366	19.8
Wood	60	3.3
Total combined segment profit	$1,848	100.0%

Reportable segments are fibers, leather, and plastics.

Finally, Battey performs the asset test:

Asset Test (in millions)

Operating Segments	Total Assets	
Fibers	$2,628	61.6%
Leather	375	8.8
Plastics	1,037	24.3
Wood	228	5.3
Total combined segment assets	$4,268	100.0%

Reportable segments are fibers and plastics.

Based on these three tests, data about the fibers, leather, and plastics operating segments must be reported separately. Information on the immaterial wood segment need not be reported. However, the revenues, profit, and assets of this segment are included in reconciliations to consolidated totals.

b. Battey must report sales to external customers for the United States, for each individual foreign country in which the company generates a material amount of revenues, and for all foreign countries in total. Authoritative accounting literature does not provide quantitative tests for determining when a foreign country is material but leaves this to management's judgment. Battey has decided to define *materiality* as sales to external customers equal to 10 percent or more of consolidated revenues.

Revenue Test (in millions)

Country	Sales to External Customers	
United States	$3,123	45.0%
Canada	424	6.1
Mexico	399	5.8
France	689	9.9
Italy	370	5.3
Brazil	1,940	27.9
Total consolidated revenues	$6,945	100.0%

Using this criterion, Battey reports results for the United States and Brazil separately and combines the remaining countries into an All Other category. Alternatively, if Battey had established a materiality threshold of 5 percent, it would report separately each of the foreign countries in which it generates revenues. Again, determination of materiality is left to management's judgment.

c. The significance test for disclosure of a major customer is 10 percent of consolidated revenues. Battey must report the existence of any major customer from which it generated $694.5 million or more in revenues during 2020.

Questions

1. How does the consolidation process tend to disguise information needed to analyze the financial operations of a diversified organization?
2. What is disaggregated financial information?
3. According to the FASB, what is the major objective of segment reporting?
4. The management approach requires a firm to define segments on the basis of its internal organizational structure. What are the advantages in defining segments on this basis?
5. What is an operating segment?
6. How should a company determine operating segments when it organizes business activities in more than one way and the chief operating decision maker uses multiple sets of reports?
7. Describe the three tests to identify reportable operating segments.

8. What information must an enterprise provide for each of its separately reportable operating segments?
9. Under what conditions must an enterprise provide information about products and services?
10. Under what conditions must an enterprise provide information about geographic areas?
11. What information must an enterprise report by geographic area?
12. To satisfy geographic area disclosure requirements, what are the minimum and maximum numbers of countries for which information should be reported separately?
13. Under what conditions should a company disclose the amount of sales from a major customer?
14. What are the major differences between U.S. GAAP and *IFRS 8* with respect to the disclosures that are required to be provided for each separately reportable operating segment?
15. Why are publicly traded companies in the United States required to prepare interim reports on a quarterly basis?
16. What approach are companies required to follow in preparing interim financial statements?
17. How should a company handle a LIFO liquidation in an interim period when the liquidated inventory is expected to be replaced by year-end?
18. How does a company determine the amount of income tax expense to report in an interim period?
19. What procedures must companies follow to account for a change in accounting principle made in other than the first interim period of the year?
20. What minimum information must an enterprise provide in an interim report?
21. What type of segment information must companies provide in interim financial statements?
22. How would an annual bonus paid at year-end be treated under *IAS 34,* and how does this treatment differ from what is required under U.S. GAAP?

Problems

LO 8-1

1. Which of the following does U.S. GAAP *not* consider to be an objective of segment reporting?
   a. It helps users better understand the enterprise's performance.
   b. It helps users better assess the enterprise's prospects for future cash flows.
   c. It helps users make more informed judgments about the enterprise as a whole.
   d. It helps users make comparisons between a segment of one enterprise and a similar segment of another enterprise.

LO 8-3

2. Under current U.S. accounting guidelines, which of the following items of information is a company *not* required to disclose, even if it were material in amount?
   a. Revenues generated from sales of its consumer products line of goods
   b. Revenues generated by its Japanese subsidiary
   c. Revenues generated from export sales
   d. Revenues generated from sales to Walmart

LO 8-3

3. Which of the following operating segment disclosures is *not* required under current U.S. accounting guidelines?
   a. Liabilities
   b. Interest expense
   c. Intersegment sales
   d. Unusual items

LO 8-2

4. In determining whether a particular operating segment is of significant size to warrant disclosure, which of the following is true?
   a. Three tests are applied, and all three must be met.
   b. Four tests are applied, and only one must be met.
   c. Three tests are applied, and only one must be met.
   d. Four tests are applied, and all four must be met.

LO 8-1, 8-3, 8-4

5. Which of the following statements is *not* true under U.S. GAAP?
   a. Operating segments can be determined by looking at a company's organization chart.
   b. Companies must combine individual foreign countries into geographic areas to comply with the geographic area disclosure requirements.

c. Companies that define their operating segments by product lines must provide revenue and asset information for the domestic country, for all foreign countries in total, and for each material foreign country.

d. Companies must disclose total assets, investment in equity method affiliates, and total expenditures for long-lived assets by operating segment.

LO 8-1

6. Which of the following is *not* necessarily true for an operating segment?
   a. An operating segment earns revenues and incurs expenses.
   b. The chief operating decision maker regularly reviews an operating segment to assess performance and make resource-allocation decisions.
   c. Discrete financial information generated by the internal accounting system is available for an operating segment.
   d. An operating segment regularly generates a profit from its normal ongoing operations.

LO 8-2

7. Which of the following is a criterion for determining whether an operating segment is separately reportable?
   a. Segment liabilities are 10 percent or more of consolidated liabilities.
   b. Segment profit or loss is 10 percent or more of consolidated net income.
   c. Segment assets are 10 percent or more of combined segment assets.
   d. Segment revenues from external sales are 5 percent or more of combined segment revenues from external sales.

LO 8-1, 8-3, 8-4, 8-5

8. Which of the following statements concerning FASB ASC 280 is true?
   a. Does not require segment information to be reported in accordance with generally accepted accounting principles
   b. Does not require a reconciliation of segment assets to consolidated assets
   c. Requires geographic area information to be disclosed in interim financial statements
   d. Requires disclosure of a major customer's identity

LO 8-3

9. Plume Company has a paper products operating segment. Which of the following items does it *not* have to report for this segment?
   a. Interest expense
   b. Research and development expense
   c. Depreciation and amortization expense
   d. Interest income

LO 8-4

10. Which of the following items is required to be disclosed by geographic area?
    a. Total assets
    b. Revenues from external customers
    c. Profit or loss
    d. Capital expenditures

LO 8-4

11. For a U.S.-based company, which of the following would be an acceptable presentation of countries for providing information by geographic area?
    a. United States, Mexico, Japan, Spain, All Other Countries
    b. United States, Canada and Mexico, Germany, Italy
    c. Europe, Asia, Africa
    d. Canada, Germany, France, All Other Countries

LO 8-4

12. What information about revenues by geographic area should a company present?
    a. Disclose separately the amount of sales to unaffiliated customers and the amount of intra-entity sales between geographic areas.
    b. Disclose as a combined amount sales to unaffiliated customers and intra-entity sales between geographic areas.
    c. Disclose separately the amount of sales to unaffiliated customers but not the amount of intra-entity sales between geographic areas.
    d. No disclosure of revenues from foreign operations need be reported.

LO 8-5

13. Which of the following information items with regard to a major customer must be disclosed?
    a. The identity of the major customer
    b. The percentage of total sales derived from the major customer

c. The operating segment making sales to the major customer

d. The geographic area in which sales to the major customer are made

LO 8-1

14. Which of the following statements is true for a company that has managers responsible for product and service lines of business and managers responsible for geographic areas (matrix form of organization)?

a. Under U.S. GAAP, the company must base operating segments on geographic areas.

b. Under IFRS, the company must base operating segments on product and service lines of business.

c. Under U.S. GAAP, the company may choose to define operating segments on the basis of either products and services or geographic areas.

d. Under IFRS, the company must refer to the core principle of *IFRS 8* to determine operating segments.

LO 8-6

15. In considering interim financial reporting, how does current U.S. GAAP require that such reporting be viewed?

a. As a special type of reporting that need not follow generally accepted accounting principles

b. As useful only if activity is evenly spread throughout the year, making estimates unnecessary

c. As reporting for a basic accounting period

d. As reporting for an integral part of an annual period

LO 8-6

16. How should material seasonal variations in revenue be reflected in interim financial statements?

a. The seasonal nature should be disclosed, and the interim report should be supplemented with a report on the 12-month period ended at the interim date for both the current and preceding years.

b. The seasonal nature should be disclosed, but no attempt should be made to reflect the effect of past seasonality on financial statements.

c. The seasonal nature should be reflected by providing pro forma financial statements for the current interim period.

d. No attempt should be made to reflect seasonality in interim financial statements.

LO 8-6

17. For interim financial reporting, a gain from the sale of land occurring in the second quarter should be

a. Recognized ratably over the last three quarters.

b. Recognized ratably over all four quarters, with the first quarter being restated.

c. Recognized in the second quarter.

d. Disclosed by footnote only in the second quarter.

LO 8-7

18. Which of the following items must be disclosed in interim reports?

a. Total assets

b. Total liabilities

c. Cash flow from operating activities

d. Gross revenues

LO 8-7

19. Which of the following items is *not* required to be reported in interim financial statements for each material operating segment?

a. Revenues from external customers

b. Intersegment revenues

c. Segment assets

d. Segment profit or loss

LO 8-6

20. Niceville Company pays property taxes of $100,000 in the second quarter of the year. Which of the following statements is true with respect to the recognition of property tax expense in interim financial statements?

a. Under U.S. GAAP, the company would report property tax expense of $100,000 in the second quarter of the year.

b. Under IFRS, the company would report property tax expense of $100,000 in the second quarter of the year.

c. Under U.S. GAAP, the company would report property tax expense of $33,333 in each of the second, third, and fourth quarters of the year.

d. Under IFRS, the company would report property tax expense of $25,000 in the first quarter of the year.

LO 8-2

21. Livro Company has three operating segments with the following information:

	Books	Calendars	Bags
Sales to outsiders	$12,000	$9,000	$8,000
Intersegment transfers	1,000	500	1,500

In addition, corporate headquarters generates revenues of $2,000.

What is the minimum amount of revenue that each of these segments must generate to be considered separately reportable?

a. $2,900
b. $3,200
c. $3,300
d. $3,400

LO 8-5

22. Nottage Company has four separate operating segments:

	East	West	North	South
Sales to outsiders	$188,000	$126,000	$65,000	$43,000
Intersegment transfers	16,000	6,000	13,000	8,000

What revenue amount must one customer generate before it must be identified as a major customer?

a. $39,600
b. $42,200
c. $46,500
d. $49,200

LO 8-2

23. Howard Corporation has six different operating segments reporting the following operating profit and loss figures:

A	$ 80,000 profit	D	$440,000 loss
B	140,000 loss	E	50,000 profit
C	100,000 profit	F	170,000 profit

With respect to the profit or loss test, which of the following statements is *not* true?

a. A is a reportable segment based on this one test.
b. C is not a reportable segment based on this one test.
c. E is not a reportable segment based on this one test.
d. F is a reportable segment based on this one test.

LO 8-2

24. Hyams Corp. engages solely in manufacturing operations. The following data pertain to the operating segments for the current year:

Operating Segment	Total Revenues	Profit (Loss)	Assets at 12/31
U	$13,000,000	$2,000,000	$15,000,000
V	9,500,000	1,200,000	11,000,000
W	5,500,000	(1,000,000)	3,000,000
X	3,000,000	600,000	7,500,000
Y	2,000,000	400,000	4,500,000
Z	2,000,000	300,000	2,000,000
Total	$35,000,000	$3,500,000	$43,000,000

In its segment information for the current year, how many reportable segments does Hyams have?

a. Three
b. Four
c. Five
d. Six

LO 8-2

25. What is the minimum number of operating segments that must be separately reported?
    a. Ten.
    b. Segments with at least 75 percent of revenues as measured by the revenue test.
    c. At least 75 percent of the segments must be separately reported.
    d. Segments with at least 75 percent of the revenues generated from outside parties.

LO 8-2

26. Chambers Company has seven operating segments but only four (One, Two, Three, and Four) are of significant size to warrant separate disclosure. As a whole, the segments generated revenues of $1,010,000 ($780,000 + $230,000) from sales to outside customers. In addition, the segments had $300,000 in intersegment sales ($250,000 + $50,000).

	Outside Sales	Intersegment Sales
One	$270,000	$110,000
Two	200,000	70,000
Three	160,000	40,000
Four	150,000	30,000
Totals	$780,000	$250,000
Five	$100,000	$ 20,000
Six	80,000	10,000
Seven	50,000	20,000
Totals	$230,000	$ 50,000

    Which of the following statements is true?
    a. A sufficient number of segments is being reported because those segments have $1,030,000 in total sales of a total of $1,310,000 for the company as a whole.
    b. Not enough segments are being reported because those segments have $780,000 in outside sales of a total of $1,010,000 for the company as a whole.
    c. Not enough segments are being reported because those segments have $1,030,000 in total revenues of a total of $1,310,000 for the company as a whole.
    d. A sufficient number of segments is being reported because those segments have $780,000 in outside sales of a total of $1,010,000 for the company as a whole.

LO 8-6

27. Baton Company estimates that the amounts for total depreciation expense for the year ending December 31 will be $120,000 and for year-end bonuses to employees will be $200,000. What total amount of expense relating to these two items should Baton report in its quarterly income statement for the three months ended March 31?
    a. $0
    b. $30,000
    c. $50,000
    d. $80,000

LO 8-6

28. Rouge Company's $250,000 net income for the quarter ended September 30 included the following after-tax items:
    - A $20,000 cumulative effect loss resulting from a change in inventory valuation method made on September 1.
    - $0 of the $60,000 annual property taxes paid on February 1.

    For the quarter ended September 30, the amount of net income that Rouge should report is
    a. $235,000.
    b. $250,000.
    c. $255,000.
    d. $270,000.

LO 8-6

29. In March of the current year, Mooney Company estimated its year-end executive bonuses to be $800,000. The executive bonus paid in the previous year was $950,000. What amount of bonus expense, if any, should Mooney recognize in determining net income for the first quarter of the current calendar year?
    a. -0-
    b. $200,000
    c. $237,500
    d. $800,000

Use the following information for Problems 30 and 31.

On March 15, Calloway, Inc., paid property taxes of $480,000 for the calendar year.

LO 8-6

30. How much of this expense should Calloway's income statement reflect for the quarter ending March 31?
    a. –0–
    b. $40,000
    c. $120,000
    d. $480,000

LO 8-6

31. The journal entry at March 15 to record the payment of property taxes would include which of the following?
    a. A debit to Property Tax Expense of $480,000
    b. A credit to Cash of $120,000
    c. A debit to Prepaid Property Taxes of $360,000
    d. A credit to Prepaid Property Taxes of $40,000

Use the following information for Problems 32 and 33.

Tristan, Inc., uses the LIFO cost-flow assumption to value inventory. It began the current year with 2,000 units of inventory carried at LIFO cost of $20 per unit. During the first quarter, it purchased 8,000 units at an average cost of $40 per unit and sold 9,500 units at $60 per unit.

LO 8-6

32. Assume the company does not expect to replace the units of beginning inventory sold; it plans to reduce inventory by year-end to 500 units. What amount of cost of goods sold should be recorded for the quarter ended March 31?
    a. $335,000
    b. $350,000
    c. $380,000
    d. $387,500

LO 8-6

33. Assume the company expects to replace the units of beginning inventory sold in April at a cost of $45 per unit and expects inventory at year-end to be between 2,100 and 2,500 units. What amount of cost of goods sold should be recorded for the quarter ended March 31?
    a. $335,000
    b. $350,000
    c. $380,000
    d. $387,500

LO 8-2

34. Vehicle Corporation is organized into four operating segments. The internal reporting system generated the following segment information:

	Revenues from Outsiders	Intersegment Transfers	Operating Expenses
Autos	$4,000,000	$100,000	$3,600,000
Trucks	3,500,000	200,000	4,000,000
SUVs	2,600,000	–0–	2,000,000
Motorcycles	900,000	50,000	1,020,000

The company incurred additional operating expenses (of a general nature) of $1,200,000.

Perform the profit or loss test to determine which of these segments is separately reportable.

LO 8-2

35. Ecru Company has identified five industry segments: plastics, metals, lumber, paper, and finance. It appropriately consolidated each of these segments in producing its annual financial statements. Information describing each segment (in thousands) follows:

	Plastics	Metals	Lumber	Paper	Finance
Sales to outside parties	$6,694	$2,354	$711	$422	$–0–
Intersegment transfers	148	173	138	150	–0–
Interest income from outside parties	–0–	34	21	–0–	42

(continued)

(continued)

	Plastics	Metals	Lumber	Paper	Finance
Interest income from intersegment loans.	–0–	–0–	–0–	–0–	201
Operating expenses.	4,214	1,762	1,066	654	31
Interest expense	76	31	66	28	102
Tangible assets	1,501	3,196	524	771	179
Intangible assets	87	403	–0–	63	–0–
Intersegment loans (debt) . .	–0–	–0–	–0–	–0–	706

Ecru does not allocate its $1,460,000 in common expenses to the various segments.

Perform testing procedures to determine Ecru's reportable operating segments.

LO 8-2, 8-5

36. The following is financial information describing the six operating segments that make up Fairfield, Inc. (in thousands):

	Segments					
	Red	Blue	Green	Pink	Black	White
Sales to outside parties . . .	$1,811	$812	$514	$309	$121	$ 99
Intersegment revenues . . .	16	91	109	–0–	16	302
Salary expense	614	379	402	312	317	62
Rent expense.	139	166	81	92	42	31
Interest expense	65	59	82	49	14	5
Income tax expense (savings)	141	87	61	(86)	(64)	–0–

Consider the following questions independently. None of the six segments have a primarily financial nature.

a. What minimum revenue amount must any one segment generate to be of significant size to require disaggregated disclosure?

b. If only Red, Blue, and Green necessitate separate disclosure, is Fairfield disclosing disaggregated data for enough segments?

c. What volume of revenues must a single customer generate to necessitate disclosing the existence of a major customer?

d. Now assume each of these six segments has a profit or loss (in thousands) as follows, which warrants separate disclosure?

Segment	Profit (Loss)	Segment	Profit (Loss)	Segment	Profit (Loss)
Red	$1,074	Green	$140	Black	$(222)
Blue	449	Pink	(94)	White	308

LO 8-2

37. Mason Company has prepared consolidated financial statements for the current year and is now gathering information in connection with the following five operating segments it has identified.

Determine the reportable segments by performing each applicable test. Also, describe the procedure utilized to ensure that a sufficient number of segments are being separately disclosed. (Figures are in thousands.)

	Company Total	Books	Computers	Maps	Travel	Finance
Sales to outside parties	$1,547	$121	$ 696	$416	$314	$ –0–
Intersegment sales	421	24	240	39	118	–0–
Interest income—external	97	60	–0–	–0–	–0–	37
Interest income—intersegment loans.	147	–0–	–0–	–0–	–0–	147
Assets	3,398	206	1,378	248	326	1,240
Operating expenses.	1,460	115	818	304	190	33

(continued)

(continued)

	Company Total	Books	Computers	Maps	Travel	Finance
Expenses—intersegment sales	198	70	51	31	46	–0–
Interest expense—external	107	–0–	–0–	–0–	–0–	107
Interest expense—intersegment loans	147	21	71	38	17	–0–
Income tax expense (savings)	21	12	(41)	27	31	(8)
General corporate expenses	55					
Unallocated operating costs	80					

LO 8-4

38. Taft Corporation operates primarily in the United States. However, a few years ago it opened a plant in Spain to produce merchandise to sell there. This foreign operation has been so successful that during the past 24 months the company started a manufacturing plant in Italy and another in Greece. Financial information for each of these facilities follows:

	Spain	Italy	Greece
Sales	$175,000	$600,000	$450,000
Intersegment transfers	–0–	100,000	60,000
Operating expenses	172,000	206,000	190,000
Interest expense	16,000	29,000	19,000
Income taxes	67,000	19,000	34,000
Long-lived assets	91,000	150,000	100,000

The company's domestic (U.S.) operations reported the following information for the current year:

Sales to unaffiliated customers	$4,500,000
Intersegment transfers	427,000
Operating expenses	2,410,000
Interest expense	136,000
Income taxes	819,000
Long-lived assets	2,200,000

Taft has adopted the following criteria for determining the materiality of an individual foreign country: (1) Sales to unaffiliated customers within a country are 10 percent or more of consolidated sales, or (2) long-lived assets within a country are 10 percent or more of consolidated long-lived assets.

Apply Taft's materiality tests to identify the countries to report separately with respect to (a) revenues and (b) long-lived assets.

LO 8-6

39. Solaris Corporation prepared the following estimates for the four quarters of the current year:

	First Quarter	Second Quarter	Third Quarter	Fourth Quarter
Sales	$1,300,000	$1,560,000	$1,820,000	$2,080,000
Cost of goods sold	430,000	510,000	580,000	630,000
Administrative costs	310,000	185,000	190,000	200,000
Advertising costs	–0–	100,000	–0–	–0–
Executive bonuses	–0–	–0–	–0–	76,000
Provision for bad debts	–0–	–0–	–0–	64,000
Annual maintenance costs	72,000	–0–	–0–	–0–

Additional Information

- First-quarter administrative costs include the $160,000 annual insurance premium.
- Advertising costs paid in the second quarter relate to television advertisements that will be broadcast throughout the entire year.

- No special items affect income during the year.
- The company estimates an effective income tax rate for the year of 25 percent.

a. Assuming that actual results do *not* vary from the estimates provided, determine the amount of net income to be reported each quarter of the current year.

b. Assume that actual results do *not* vary from the estimates provided except for that in the third quarter, the estimated annual effective income tax rate is revised downward to 22 percent. Determine the amount of net income to be reported each quarter of the current year.

LO 8-6

40. Volata Company began operations on January 1, 2019. In the second quarter of 2020, it adopted the FIFO method of inventory valuation. In the past, it used the LIFO method. The company's interim income statements as originally reported under the LIFO method follow:

	2019				2020
	1stQ	**2ndQ**	**3rdQ**	**4thQ**	**1stQ**
Sales	$10,000	$12,000	$14,000	$16,000	$18,000
Cost of goods sold (LIFO).	4,000	5,000	5,800	7,000	8,500
Operating expenses. . . .	2,000	2,200	2,600	3,000	3,200
Income before income taxes	$ 4,000	$ 4,800	$ 5,600	$ 6,000	$ 6,300
Income taxes (25%).	1,000	1,200	1,400	1,500	1,575
Net income.	$ 3,000	$ 3,600	$ 4,200	$ 4,500	$ 4,725

If the FIFO method had been used since the company began operations, cost of goods sold in each of the previous quarters would have been as follows:

	2019				2020
	1stQ	**2ndQ**	**3rdQ**	**4thQ**	**1stQ**
Cost of goods sold (FIFO) . .	$3,800	$4,600	$5,200	$6,000	$7,400

Sales for the second quarter of 2020 are $20,000, cost of goods sold under the FIFO method is $9,000, and operating expenses are $3,400. The effective tax rate remains 25 percent. Volata Company has 1,000 shares of common stock outstanding.

Prepare a schedule showing the calculation of net income and earnings per share that Volata reports for the three-month period and the six-month period ended June 30, 2020.

LO 8-6

41. The following information for Dorado Corporation relates to the three-month period ending September 30.

	Units	**Price per Unit**
Sales	425,000	$36
Beginning inventory	35,000	18
Purchases.	400,000	24
Ending inventory	10,000	?

Dorado expects to purchase 150,000 units of inventory in the fourth quarter of the current calendar year at a cost of $25 per unit, and to have on hand 40,000 units of inventory at year-end. Dorado uses the last-in, first-out (LIFO) method to account for inventory costs.

Determine the cost of goods sold and gross profit amounts Dorado should record for the three months ending September 30. Prepare journal entries to reflect these amounts.

Develop Your Skills

RESEARCH CASE 1—SEGMENT REPORTING

CPA skills

Many companies make annual reports available on their corporate website. Annual reports also can be accessed through the SEC's EDGAR system at www.sec.gov (under Filing Type, search for 10-K).

Access the most recent annual report for a company with which you are familiar to complete the following requirements.

Required

Prepare a short report describing your findings for the following:

1. The company's reported operating segments and whether they are based on product lines, geographic areas, or some other basis.
2. The importance of each operating segment for the company as a whole in terms of revenues, income, and assets.
3. Whether the company provides any enterprisewide disclosures in addition to disclosures related to its operating segments, and which ones.
4. Whether the company provides disclosures about major customers.

RESEARCH CASE 2—INTERIM REPORTING

CPA skills

Many companies make quarterly reports available on their corporate website. Quarterly reports also can be accessed through the SEC's EDGAR system at www.sec.gov (under Filing Type, search for 10-Q).

Access the most recent quarterly report for a company with which you are familiar to complete the following requirements.

Required

Prepare a short report describing your findings for the following:

1. Whether the company provides the minimum disclosures required for interim reports.
2. Any disclosures the company provides that exceed the minimum disclosures required.
3. The various year-to-year comparisons that can be made using the disclosures provided in the quarterly report.

RESEARCH CASE 3—OPERATING SEGMENTS

Many companies make annual reports available on their corporate website. Annual reports also can be accessed through the SEC's EDGAR system at www.sec.gov (under Filing Type, search for 10-K). Access the most recent annual report for each of the following companies to complete the requirements:

Eaton
United Technologies

Required

Prepare a short report summarizing your findings for the most recent year for the following:

1. The two largest operating segments in terms of percentage of total net sales.
2. The two operating segments with the largest year-to-year change in net sales.
3. The two most profitable operating segments in terms of profit margin (operating profit/net sales).

RESEARCH CASE 4—COMPARABILITY OF GEOGRAPHIC AREA INFORMATION

Many companies make annual reports available on their corporate website. Annual reports also can be accessed through the SEC's EDGAR system at www.sec.gov (under Filing Type, search for 10-K). Access the most recent annual report for each of the following companies:

Eli Lilly
Merck
Pfizer

Required

Prepare a short report describing the extent to which direct comparisons can be made of the geographic area information provided by these companies.

EVALUATION CASE—OPERATING SEGMENT DISCLOSURES

Corcoran Heavy Industries Company (CHIC) is organized into four divisions, each of which operates in a different industry. The types of customer served and the method used to distribute products differ across all four of these industries. In addition, each division must comply with its own unique set of industry regulations related to issues such as safety and recyclability of materials.

Operating profit before depreciation and amortization is the measure of profit regularly used by the chief operating decision maker for evaluating the performance of each of these divisions. In addition, information for each division on capital expenditures and depreciation and amortization is routinely provided by corporate headquarters to the chief operating decision maker. A summary of the information provided to the chief operating decision maker at the end of the current year is as follows:

	Division				
($ in thousands)	Automobiles	Trucks	Helicopters	Ships	Total
Sales to outside parties	**$4,007,304**	**$3,796,432**	**$1,411,235**	**$1,003,809**	**$10,218,780**
Intersegment sales	644,243	307,982	—	—	952,225
Total sales	$ 4,651,547	$ 4,104,414	$ 1,411,235	$ 1,003,809	$ 11,171,005
Operating expenses—external	3,480,666	3,147,086	1,004,464	958,743	8,590,959
Operating expense—internal	289,589	500,798	57,893	103,945	952,225
Operating profit before depreciation and amortization	$ 881,292	$ 456,530	$ 348,878	$ (58,879)	$ 1,627,821
Depreciation and amortization	180,345	170,976	97,638	58,617	507,576
Interest expense					130,655
Income before tax					$ 989,590
Income taxes					376,044
Profit (loss)					$ 613,546
Segment assets	**$3,987,776**	**$3,209,078**	**$1,587,006**	**$1,209,970**	**$ 9,993,830**
Corporate headquarters assets					1,008,988
Total assets					$ 11,002,818
Capital expenditures	$ 349,776	$ 365,543	$ 276,655	$ 23,695	$ 1,015,669

In compiling notes to the financial statements, CHIC's accountants prepared the following Note to comply with the operating segment disclosure requirements of ASC Topic 280, "Segment Reporting."

Note X. Operating Segments

($ in thousands)	Automobiles	Trucks	Other
Revenues	$4,651,547	$4,104,414	$2,415,044
Segment Profit (Loss)	$ 881,292	$ 456,530	$ 289,999
Assets	$3,987,776	$3,209,078	$2,796,976

Required

1. Prepare a report for CHIC's management evaluating whether the operating segments disclosures prepared by CHIC's accountants comply with ASC 280.
2. Prepare a revised operating segments note to comply with ASC 280. CHIC does not have any unusual or extraordinary items, significant noncash items other than depreciation and amortization, or equity method affiliates.

ACCOUNTING STANDARDS CASE 1—SEGMENT REPORTING

CPA *skills*

Nuland International Corporation recently acquired 40 percent of Scott Trading Company and appropriately accounts for this investment under the equity method. Nuland's corporate controller is in the process of determining the company's operating segments for purposes of preparing financial statements for the current year. He has determined that the investment in Scott meets the definition of an operating segment (i.e., Scott earns revenues and incurs expenses, Nuland's chief operating officer regularly reviews Scott's operating results, and Scott provides Nuland with a complete set of financial statements). However, because Nuland does not control Scott, the controller is not sure whether the investment in Scott can be considered a separate operating segment.

Required

Search current U.S. authoritative accounting literature to determine whether an equity method investment can be treated as an operating segment for financial reporting purposes. If so, explain the conditions under which this would be possible. Identify the source of guidance for answering this question.

ACCOUNTING STANDARDS CASE 2—INTERIM REPORTING

CPA *skills*

Caplan Pharma, Inc., recently was sued by a competitor for possible infringement of the competitor's patent on a top-selling flu vaccine. The plaintiff is suing for damages of $15 million. Caplan's CFO has discussed the case with legal counsel, who believes it is possible that Caplan will not be able to successfully defend the lawsuit. The CFO knows that current U.S. accounting guidelines require that contingencies (such as lawsuits) must be disclosed in the annual report when a loss is possible. However, she is unsure whether this rule must be applied in the preparation of interim financial statements. She also knows that disclosure is necessary only if the amount is material, but she is unsure whether materiality should be assessed in relation to results for the interim period or for the entire year.

Required

Search current U.S. accounting standards to determine whether contingencies are required to be disclosed in interim reports and, if so, how materiality is to be determined. Identify the source of guidance for answering these questions.

ANALYSIS CASE 1—WALMART INTERIM AND SEGMENT REPORTING

The following information was extracted from quarterly reports for Walmart Inc. (amounts in millions):

	Three Months Ended April 30, 2017		Three Months Ended July 31, 2017		Three Months Ended October 31, 2017	
	Net Sales	Operating Income	Net Sales	Operating Income	Net Sales	Operating Income
Walmart U.S..	$75,436	$4,269	$78,738	$4,618	$77,724	$4,030
Walmart International	27,097	1,163	28,331	1,592	29,548	1,249
Sam's Club	13,993	414	14,880	404	14,864	447

The following information was extracted from the notes to the financial statements in the Walmart Inc., Annual Report (for the fiscal year ended January 31, 2018, amounts in millions):

Note 15. Segments Fiscal Year Ended January 31, 2018

	Walmart U.S.	Walmart International	Sam's Club	Corporate and Support	Consolidated
Net sales.	$318,477	$118,068	$59,216	—	$495,761
Operating income (loss)	17,869	5,352	982	(3,766)	20,437
Total assets.	104,347	81,549	13,418	5,208	204,522

Note 17. Quarterly Financial Data (unaudited)

	Fiscal Year Ended January 31, 2018			
	Q1	**Q2**	**Q3**	**Q4**
Net sales.	$116,526	$121,949	$122,136	$135,150
Cost of sales	87,688	91,521	91,547	102,640
Consolidated net income	3,152	3,104	1,904	2,363

Required

1. Assess the seasonal nature of Walmart's sales and income for the company as a whole and by operating segment.
2. Assess Walmart's profitability by quarter and by operating segment.

ANALYSIS CASE 2—COCA-COLA OPERATING SEGMENT INFORMATION

CPA *skills*

The Coca-Cola Company is organized geographically and defines reportable operating segments as regions of the world. The following information was extracted from Note 19 Operating Segments in the Coca-Cola Company 2017 Annual Report:

Information about our Company's continuing operations by operating segment as of and for the years ended December 31, 2017, 2016, and 2015, is as follows (in millions):

	Europe, Middle East & Africa	Latin America	North America	Asia Pacific	Bottling Investments	Corporate	Eliminations	Consolidated
2017								
Net operating revenues:								
Third party	$7,332	$3,956	$8,651	$4,767	$10,524	$ 138	$ —	$35,368
Intersegment	42	73	1,986	409	81	—	(2,549)	42
Total net operating revenues	7,374	4,029	10,637	5,176	10,605	138	(2,549)	35,410
Operating income (loss)	3,646	2,214	2,578	2,163	(1,117)	(1,983)	—	7,501
Interest income	—	—	44	—	—	633	—	677
Interest expense	—	—	—	—	—	841	—	841
Depreciation and amortization	91	37	411	65	454	202	—	1,260
Equity income (loss)—net	48	(3)	(3)	11	878	140	—	1,071
Income (loss) from continuing operations before income taxes	3,706	2,211	2,307	2,179	(2,345)	(1,316)	—	6,742
Identifiable operating assets	5,475	1,896	17,619	2,072	4,493	27,060	—	58,615
Investments	1,238	891	112	177	15,998	3,536	—	21,952
Capital expenditures	81	55	541	50	662	286	—	1,675
2016								
Net operating revenues:								
Third party	$7,014	$3,746	$6,437	$4,788	$19,751	$ 127	$ —	$41,863
Intersegment	264	73	3,773	506	134	5	(4,755)	—
Total net operating revenues	7,278	3,819	10,210	5,294	19,885	132	(4,755)	41,863
Operating income (loss)	3,676	1,951	2,582	2,224	(137)	(1,670)	—	8,626
Interest income	—	—	27	—	—	615	—	642
Interest expense	—	—	—	—	—	733	—	733
Depreciation and amortization	93	35	426	80	1,013	140	—	1,787
Equity income (loss)—net	62	18	(17)	9	648	115	—	835
Income (loss) from continuing operations before income taxes	3,749	1,966	2,560	2,338	(1,923)	(454)	—	8,136
Identifiable operating assets	4,067	1,785	16,566	2,024	15,973	29,606	—	70,021
Investments	1,302	804	109	164	11,456	3,414	—	17,249
Capital expenditures	62	45	438	107	1,329	281	—	2,262
2015								
Net operating revenues:								
Third party	$6,966	$3,999	$5,581	$4,707	$22,885	$ 156	$ —	$44,294
Intersegment	621	75	4,259	545	178	10	(5,688)	—
Total net operating revenues	7,587	4,074	9,840	5,252	23,063	166	(5,688)	44,294
Operating income (loss)	3,875	2,169	2,366	2,189	124	(1,995)	—	8,728
Interest income	—	—	9	—	—	604	—	613
Interest expense	—	—	—	—	—	856	—	856
Depreciation and amortization	103	41	373	85	1,211	157	—	1,970
Equity income (loss)—net	39	(7)	(18)	9	426	40	—	489
Income (loss) from continuing operations before income taxes	3,923	2,164	2,356	2,207	(427)	(618)	—	9,605
Identifiable operating assets	4,156	1,627	16,396	1,639	22,688	27,702	—	74,208
Investm[illegible]	1,138	657	[illegible]07	158	8,084	5,644	—	15,[illegible]
Capital [illegible]nditures	54	70	[illegible]77	81	1,699	272	—	2[illegible]

Required

1. Calculate the following measures for each of Coca-Cola's operating segments (excluding Bottling Investments and Corporate):
   - Percentage of total net operating revenues, 2016 and 2017.
   - Percentage change in total net operating revenues, 2015 to 2016 and 2016 to 2017.
   - Operating income as a percentage of total net operating revenues (profit margin), 2013 and 2014.
2. Determine whether you believe Coca-Cola should attempt to expand its operations in a particular region of the world to increase net operating revenues and operating income.
3. List any additional information you would like to have to conduct your analysis.

chapter

9

Foreign Currency Transactions and Hedging Foreign Exchange Risk

Today, international business transactions such as export sales and import purchases are a regular occurrence. In its 2017 annual report, Lockheed Martin Corporation reported export sales of $15 billion, representing 29 percent of total sales. Some businesses are very significantly involved in transactions occurring throughout the world as evidenced by this excerpt from the fiscal year 2018 annual report of Cirrus Logic, Inc.: "Sales to non-U.S. customers, principally located in Asia . . . were approximately $1.5 billion in fiscal years 2018 and 2017 and $1.1 billion in fiscal year 2016, representing 98 percent of net sales in each of fiscal years 2018 and 2017, and 94 percent of net sales in fiscal year 2016."

Collections from export sales or payments for imported items might not be made in U.S. dollars but in pesos, pounds, yen, and the like, depending on the negotiated terms of the transaction. As foreign currency exchange rates fluctuate, so does the U.S. dollar value of these export sales and import purchases. Companies often find it necessary to engage in some form of hedging activity to reduce losses arising from fluctuating exchange rates. At the end of fiscal year 2017, in conjunction with foreign currency hedging activities, Lockheed Martin reported having outstanding foreign currency hedges with a notional value of $4.1 billion, while Apple, Inc., had outstanding foreign exchange contracts with a notional value of $56.2 billion.

This chapter covers accounting issues related to foreign currency transactions and foreign currency hedging activities. To provide background for subsequent discussions of the accounting issues, the chapter begins by describing foreign exchange markets. The chapter then discusses accounting for foreign currency–denominated import and export transactions, followed by coverage of various hedging techniques. Because they are most popular, the discussion concentrates on foreign currency forward contracts and foreign currency options. Understanding how to account for these items is important for any company engaged in international transactions.

Learning Objectives

After studying this chapter, you should be able to:

LO 9-1 Understand concepts related to foreign currency, exchange rates, and foreign exchange risk.

LO 9-2 Account for foreign currency transactions using the two-transaction perspective, accrual approach.

LO 9-3 Account for foreign currency borrowings.

LO 9-4 Understand the different types of foreign exchange risk that can be hedged and how foreign currency forward contracts and foreign currency options can be used to hedge those risks.

LO 9-5 Understand the accounting guidelines for derivative financial instruments.

LO 9-6 Understand the basic concepts of hedge accounting.

LO 9-7 Account for forward contracts and options used as hedges of foreign currency–denominated assets and liabilities.

LO 9-8 Account for forward contracts and options used as hedges of foreign currency firm commitments.

LO 9-9 Account for forward contracts and options used as hedges of forecasted foreign currency transactions.

LO 9-1

Understand concepts related to foreign currency, exchange rates, and foreign exchange risk.

Foreign Exchange Markets

Each country (or group of countries) uses its own currency as the unit of value for the purchase and sale of goods and services. The currency used in the United States is the U.S. dollar, the currency used in Mexico is the Mexican peso, the currency used by a subset of European Union countries is the euro, and so on. If a U.S. citizen travels to Mexico and wishes to purchase local goods, Mexican merchants require payment to be made in Mexican pesos. To make a purchase in Mexico, a U.S. citizen would need to acquire pesos using U.S. dollars. The foreign currency *exchange rate* is the price at which the foreign currency can be acquired (or sold). A variety of factors determine the exchange rate between two currencies; unfortunately for those engaged in international business, the exchange rate can fluctuate over time.[1]

Exchange Rate Mechanisms

Exchange rates have not always fluctuated. During the period 1945–1973, countries fixed the value of their currency in terms of the U.S. dollar, and the value of the U.S. dollar was fixed in terms of gold. In March 1973, most countries allowed their currencies to float in value. Today, several different currency arrangements exist. Some of the more important ones and the countries affected follow:

1. *Independent float:* The value of the currency is allowed to fluctuate freely according to market forces with little or no intervention from the central bank (example countries include Australia, Brazil, Canada, Japan, Sweden, Switzerland, the United Kingdom, and the United States).
2. *Pegged to another currency:* The value of the currency is fixed (pegged) in terms of a particular foreign currency, and the central bank intervenes as necessary to maintain the fixed value. For example, Bahrain, Hong Kong, Panama, and Saudi Arabia peg their currency to the U.S. dollar.
3. *European Monetary System (euro):* In 1998, those European Union countries comprising the European Monetary System adopted a common currency called the *euro* and established a European Central Bank.[2] On January 1, 2002, local currencies (such as the French franc, German mark, and Spanish peseta) disappeared, and the euro became the currency in 12 European Union countries. Today, 19 countries are part of the euro zone. The value of the euro floats freely against other currencies such as the Swiss franc, British pound, Japanese yen, and U.S. dollar.

Foreign Exchange Rates

Exchange rates between the U.S. dollar and many foreign currencies are readily available online at websites such as www.oanda.com and www.x-rates.com. To illustrate exchange rates and the foreign currency market, next we take a look at exchange rates for selected currencies reported for September 13 and 14, 2018, as shown in Exhibit 9.1.

The exchange rates shown in Exhibit 9.1 are for trades between banks; that is, these are *interbank* or wholesale prices. Prices charged by banks to retail customers, such as companies engaged in international business, are higher. Exhibit 9.1 shows *ask* rates at which banks will *sell* currency to one another. The prices at which banks are willing to buy foreign currency (bid rates) are somewhat less than the selling rates. The difference between the buying and selling rates is the spread through which banks earn a profit on foreign exchange trades. For example, the September 13, 2018, U.S. dollar selling (ask) rate for the euro was $1.1656,

[1] Several theories attempt to explain exchange rate fluctuations but with little success, at least in the short term. An understanding of the causes of exchange rate changes is not necessary to comprehend the concepts underlying the accounting for changes in exchange rates.

[2] Most longtime members of the European Union (EU) are "euro zone" countries. The major exception is the United Kingdom (U.K.), which elected not to participate. (The U.K. subsequently exited the EU in 2019). Switzerland is another important European country not part of the euro zone because it is not a member of the EU.

EXHIBIT 9.1
Exchange Rates for Selected Currencies (September 13–14, 2018)

	September 13, 2018		September 14, 2018	
Currency	Direct*	Indirect†	Direct*	Indirect†
Euro	1.1656	0.8579	1.1671	0.8568
British pound	1.3073	0.7649	1.3099	0.7634
Canadian dollar	0.7691	1.3002	0.7684	1.3014
Brazilian real	0.2398	4.1700	0.2387	4.1894
Hong Kong dollar	0.1274	7.8493	0.1274	7.8493

Source: www.oanda.com/currency/historical-rates.
*www.oanda.com/currency/historical-rates.
†Indirect quotes have been calculated by the author and rounded to four digits behind the decimal point.

while the the buying (bid) rate was $1.1654. On that date, banks were willing to buy euros for $1.1656 and sell them for $1.1654, earning a profit of $0.0002 per euro.

Two columns of information are shown for each day's exchange rates. The first column reports *direct quotes,* which indicate the number of U.S. dollars needed to purchase one unit of foreign currency. The direct quote for the Brazilian real (BRL) on September 13 was $0.2398; in other words, 1.0 Brazilian real could be purchased for $0.2398. The second column reports *indirect quotes,* which indicate the number of foreign currency units that could be purchased with one U.S. dollar. These rates are simply the inverse of direct quotes (indirect quote = 1 ÷ direct quote). If one BRL can be purchased with $0.2398, then 4.17 BRL can be purchased with $1.00. To avoid confusion, *direct quotes are used exclusively in this chapter.*

The third and fourth columns in Exhibit 9.1 show exchange rates for September 14, 2018. Two of the currencies shown increased in U.S. dollar price (appreciated) from September 13 to September 14, namely the euro and British pound. For example, the euro increased in price by $0.0013 from one day to the next. As a result, the purchase of 100,000 euros on September 14, 2018, would have cost $130 more than on the previous day. In contrast, the U.S. dollar price for two currencies decreased (depreciated) from one day to the next, namely the Canadian dollar and Brazilian real. The Hong Kong dollar did not change in U.S. dollar value from one day to the next because this currency was effectively pegged to the U.S. dollar.

Foreign Currency Forward Contracts

Foreign currency trades can be executed on a spot or forward basis. The *spot rate* is the price at which a foreign currency can be purchased or sold today. In contrast, the *forward rate* is the price available today at which foreign currency can be purchased or sold sometime in the future. Because many international business transactions take some time to be completed, the ability to lock in a price today at which foreign currency can be purchased or sold at some future date has definite advantages.

A *foreign currency forward contract* can be negotiated by a firm with its bank to exchange foreign currency for U.S. dollars, or vice versa, on a specified future date at a predetermined exchange rate. A forward contract can be written for whatever currency and for whatever future date is required. Entering into a forward contract has no up-front cost; the firm and its bank simply agree today to exchange foreign currency for U.S. dollars at the forward rate on a future date. Similar to how banks make a profit in the spot market, there is a spread between the buying and selling rates in the forward market. For example, on February 1, a bank might agree to buy 500,000 British pounds in three months from one customer at a forward rate of $1.30 per British pound and simultaneously agree to sell 500,000 British pounds in three months to another customer at a rate of $1.31 per British pound. In this way, the bank generates a profit of $5,000 ($0.01 × 500,000 British pounds) from entering into these two forward contracts.

The difference between the forward rate and the spot rate for a currency on a given date is referred to as *forward points,* which can be either positive or negative. When the forward rate exceeds the spot rate on a given date, positive forward points exist and the foreign currency is said to be selling at a *premium* in the forward market. When the forward rate is less than the spot rate, negative forward points exist and the currency is selling at a *discount.* Currencies sell at a premium or a discount in the forward market because of differences in interest rates between two countries. When the interest rate in the foreign country exceeds the domestic interest rate, the foreign currency sells at a discount in the forward market. Conversely, if the foreign interest rate is less than the domestic rate, the foreign currency sells at a premium.[3]

The forward exchange rate for a specific future settlement date will change over time due to changes in the spot exchange rate and/or changes in the differential interest rates between two countries. For example, assume on April 15 the U.S. dollar (USD) per Mexican peso (MXN) spot rate is $0.11 and the forward rate for a forward contract to be settled on June 15 is $0.105. The peso is selling at a discount of $0.005 in the two-month forward market due to a higher interest rate in Mexico than in the United States. If the USD/MXN spot rate decreases to $0.08 on May 15, the forward rate for a June 15 settlement-date forward contract also will decrease, to an amount less than $0.08. The peso will continue to sell at a discount in the one-month forward market because of the higher interest rate in Mexico.

Foreign Currency Options

To provide companies more flexibility than exists with a forward contract, a market for *foreign currency options* was created. A foreign currency option gives the holder of the option *the right but not the obligation* to trade foreign currency in the future. A *put* option is for the sale of foreign currency by the holder of the option; a *call* option is for the purchase of foreign currency by the holder of the option. The *strike price* is the exchange rate at which the option will be executed if the option holder decides to exercise the option. The strike price is similar to a forward rate. There are generally several strike prices to choose from on a particular date. Foreign currency options can be purchased on the Philadelphia Stock Exchange or the Chicago Mercantile Exchange, but most foreign currency options are purchased directly from a bank in the so-called over-the-counter (OTC) market. Options purchased in the OTC market usually have a strike price that is equal to the spot rate on that date. These options are said to be "at the money."

Unlike a forward contract, for which banks earn their profit through the spread between buying and selling rates, options are purchased by paying an *option premium,* which is a function of two components: intrinsic value and time value. An option's *intrinsic value* is equal to the gain that could be realized by exercising the option immediately. For example, if the spot rate for the euro is $1.15, a *call* option (to purchase euros) with a strike price of $1.12 has an intrinsic value of $0.03 per euro. Euros can be purchased for $1.12 and sold for $1.15, generating a gain of $0.03 per euro. On the other hand, when the spot rate for the euro is $1.15, a *put* option (to sell euros) with a strike price of $1.12 has an intrinsic value of zero. An option with a positive intrinsic value is said to be "in-the-money." The *time value* of an option relates to the fact that the spot rate can change over time and cause the option's intrinsic value to increase. Even though a call option (to purchase euros) with a strike price of $1.12 has zero intrinsic value when the spot rate is $1.12, it has a positive time value because there is a chance that the spot rate could increase over the next 90 days and bring the option into the money. As time passes, the time value of an option decreases because there is less time remaining for the option to increase in intrinsic value. On the option's expiration date, the time value is zero because there is no time remaining for the option to become more valuable. It is important to remember that the *fair value of a foreign currency option on a specific date is the sum of its intrinsic and time values on that date, and the time value of the option decreases to zero over the life of the option.*

The fair value of a foreign currency option can be determined by applying an adaptation of the Black-Scholes option pricing formula. This formula is discussed in detail in international finance books. In very general terms, the value of an option is a function of several factors: the difference between the current spot rate and strike price, the difference between domestic and foreign interest rates, the length of time to expiration, and the potential volatility of changes in the spot rate. For purposes of this book, the premium originally paid for a foreign currency option and its subsequent fair value up to the date of expiration derived from applying the option pricing formula will be given.

[3] This relationship is based on the theory of interest rate parity that indicates the difference in national interest rates should be equal to, but opposite in sign to, the forward rate discount or premium. This topic is covered in detail in international finance textbooks.

LO 9-2

Account for foreign currency transactions using the two-transaction perspective, accrual approach.

Foreign Currency Transactions

Export sales and import purchases are international transactions; they are components of what is called *international trade*. When two parties from different countries enter into a transaction, they must decide which of the two countries' currencies to use to settle the transaction. For example, if a U.S. computer manufacturer sells to a customer in Japan, the parties must decide whether the transaction will be denominated (payment will be made) in U.S. dollars or in Japanese yen.

Assume that a U.S.-based trading company (Eximco) sells goods to a British customer that will pay in British pounds (£). In this situation, Eximco has entered into a foreign currency transaction. It must restate the British pound amount that it actually will receive into U.S. dollars to account for this transaction. This is necessary because Eximco keeps its books and prepares financial statements in U.S. dollars. Although the British customer has entered into an international transaction, it does not have a foreign currency transaction (payment will be made in its currency), and no restatement is necessary.

Assume that, as is customary in its industry, Eximco does not require immediate payment and allows its British customer 30 days to pay for its purchases. By doing this, Eximco runs the risk that the British pound might depreciate (decrease in value) against the U.S. dollar between the sale date and the date of payment. If so, the sale would generate fewer U.S. dollars than it would have had the British pound not decreased in value, and the sale is less profitable because it was made on a credit basis. In this situation, Eximco is said to have an *exposure to foreign exchange risk*. Specifically, Eximco has a foreign currency *transaction exposure* that can be summarized as follows:

- *Export sale:* A foreign currency transaction exposure exists when the exporter *allows the buyer to pay in a foreign currency* and *allows the buyer to pay sometime after the sale has been made*. The exporter is exposed to the risk that the foreign currency might depreciate (decrease in value) between the date of sale and the date payment is received, thereby decreasing the U.S. dollars ultimately collected.
    - Note that there is no exposure to foreign exchange risk if the exporter requires the foreign customer to make payment on the date of sale. In that case, the exporter would receive foreign currency and immediately convert it into U.S. dollars at the spot rate on the date of sale.
- *Import purchase:* A foreign currency transaction exposure exists when the importer *is required to pay in foreign currency* and *is allowed to pay sometime after the purchase has been made*. The importer is exposed to the risk that the foreign currency might appreciate (increase in price) between the date of purchase and the date of payment, thereby increasing the U.S. dollars that have to be paid for the imported goods.
    - Note that there is no exposure to foreign exchange risk if the importer makes payment in foreign currency on the date of purchase. In that case, the importer converts U.S. dollars into foreign currency at the spot rate on the date of purchase and immediately makes payment.

Accounting Issue

The major issue in accounting for foreign currency transactions is how to deal with the change in U.S. dollar value of the sales revenue and account receivable resulting from the export sale when the foreign currency changes in value. (The corollary issue is how to deal with the change in the U.S. dollar value of the account payable and goods acquired in an import purchase.) For example, assume that Eximco, a U.S. company, sells goods to a British customer at a price of 1 million British pounds when the spot exchange rate is $1.300 per pound. If payment were received at the sale date, Eximco could have converted 1 million British pounds into $1,300,000; this amount clearly would be the amount at which the sales revenue would be recognized. Instead, Eximco allows the British customer 30 days to pay for its purchase. At the end of 30 days, the British pound has depreciated to $1.285, and Eximco is able to convert the 1 million pounds received on that date into only $1,285,000. How should Eximco account for this $15,000 decrease in value?

FASB ASC 830-20 Foreign Currency Matters–Foreign Currency Transactions requires companies to use what can be referred to as a *two-transaction perspective* in accounting for foreign currency transactions. This perspective treats the export sale and the subsequent collection of cash as two separate transactions. Because management has made two decisions—(1) to make the export sale and (2) to extend credit in foreign currency to the customer—the company should report the income effect from each of these decisions separately. The U.S. dollar value of the sale is recorded at the date the sale occurs. At that point, the sale has been completed; there are no subsequent adjustments to the Sales account. Any difference between the number of U.S. dollars that could have been received at the date of sale and the number of U.S. dollars actually received at the date of collection due to fluctuations in the exchange rate is a result of the decision to extend foreign currency credit to the customer. This difference is recognized in a Foreign Exchange Gain or Loss account that is reported separately from Sales in the income statement.

Similarly, an import purchase denominated in a foreign currency and the subsequent payment of cash must be accounted for separately. The U.S. dollar value of the goods purchased is recorded at the date of purchase, with no subsequent adjustments to the Cost of Goods Sold account. Any difference between the number of U.S. dollars that could have been paid on the date of purchase and the actual number of U.S. dollars that is paid on the payment date due to a change in the exchange rate is recognized in a separate Foreign Exchange Gain or Loss account.

Using the two-transaction perspective to account for its export sale to the British customer, Eximco would make the following journal entries:

Date of Sale:	Accounts Receivable (£)........................	1,300,000	
	Sales		1,300,000
	To record the sale and euro receivable at the spot rate of $1.300.		
Date of Collection:	Foreign Exchange Gain or Loss..................	15,000	
	Accounts Receivable (£)		15,000
	To adjust the value of the £ receivable to the new spot rate of $1.285 and recognize a foreign exchange loss resulting from the depreciation in the £.		
	Cash	1,285,000	
	Accounts Receivable (£)		1,285,000
	To record the receipt of 1 million British pounds and conversion into U.S. dollars at the spot rate of $1.285.		

Sales are reported in net income at the amount that would have been received if the customer had not been given 30 days to pay the 1 million pounds—that is, $1,300,000. A separate foreign exchange loss of $15,000 is reported in net income to indicate that because of the decision to extend foreign currency credit to the British customer and because the pound decreased in value, Eximco actually received fewer U.S. dollars.[4]

Note that Eximco creates an "Account" account, which is separate from its U.S. dollar receivables. Companies engaged in international trade need to keep separate receivable and payable accounts in each of the currencies in which they have transactions. Each foreign currency receivable and payable should have a separate account number in the company's chart of accounts.

The loss on the account receivable is recorded in a Foreign Exchange Gain or Loss account, which will have either a debit (net loss) or credit (net gain) balance at the end of each accounting period. If the British pound had appreciated against the U.S. dollar from the date of sale to the date of collection, Eximco would have made a credit to the Foreign Exchange Gain or Loss account to recognize the gain.

[4] Note that the foreign exchange loss results because the customer is allowed to pay in foreign currency and is given 30 days to pay. If the transaction were denominated in U.S. dollars, no loss would result, nor would there be a loss if the foreign currency had been received at the date the sale was made.

We can summarize the relationship between fluctuations in exchange rates and foreign exchange gains and losses as follows:

		Foreign Currency (FC)	
Transaction	**Type of Exposure**	**Appreciates**	**Depreciates**
Export sale	Asset (receivable)	Gain	Loss
Import purchase	Liability (payable)	Loss	Gain

A foreign currency receivable arising from an export sale creates an *asset exposure* to foreign exchange risk. If the foreign currency appreciates, the foreign currency asset increases in U.S. dollar value and a foreign exchange gain arises; depreciation of the foreign currency causes a foreign exchange loss. A foreign currency payable arising from an import purchase creates a *liability exposure* to foreign exchange risk. If the foreign currency appreciates, the foreign currency liability increases in U.S. dollar value and a foreign exchange loss results; depreciation of the currency results in a foreign exchange gain.

Balance Sheet Date before Date of Payment

The question arises as to what adjustments should be made if a balance sheet date falls between the date of sale (or purchase) and the date of collection (or payment). For example, assume that Eximco shipped goods to its British customer on December 1, 2020, with payment to be received on March 1, 2021. Assume that at December 1, the spot rate for the British pound was $1.300, but by December 31, the pound has depreciated to $1.285. Is any adjustment needed at December 31, 2020, when the books are closed, to account for the fact that the foreign currency receivable has changed in U.S. dollar value since December 1?

Authoritative accounting literature requires foreign currency balances such as a foreign currency receivable or a foreign currency payable to be revalued at the balance sheet date to account for the change in exchange rates. Under the two-transaction perspective, this means that a foreign exchange gain or loss arises at the balance sheet date. The next question then is what should be done with these foreign exchange gains and losses that have not yet been realized in cash. Should they be included in net income?

U.S. GAAP requires unrealized foreign exchange gains and losses to be reported in net income in the period in which the exchange rate changes. This is consistent with accrual accounting as it results in reporting the effect of a rate change that will have an impact on cash flow in the period when the event causing the impact takes place. Thus, any change in the exchange rate from the date of sale to the balance sheet date results in a foreign exchange gain or loss to be reported in net income in that period. Any change in the exchange rate from the balance sheet date to the date of collection results in a second foreign exchange gain or loss that is reported in net income in the second accounting period. Eximco makes the following journal entries under this approach:

12/1/20	Accounts Receivable (£).	1,300,000	
	Sales		1,300,000
	To record the sale and euro receivable at the spot rate of $1.300.		
12/31/20	Foreign Exchange Gain or Loss	15,000	
	Accounts Receivable (£)		15,000
	To adjust the value of the £ receivable to the new spot rate of $1.285 and record a foreign exchange loss in 2020 net income resulting from the depreciation in the £ since December 1.		
3/1/21	Foreign Exchange Gain or Loss	13,000	
	Accounts Receivable (£)		13,000
	To adjust the value of the £ receivable to the new spot rate of $1.272 and record a foreign exchange loss in 2021 net income resulting from the depreciation in the £ since December 31.		

(continued)

(continued)

Cash	1,272,000	
Accounts Receivable (£)		1,272,000
To record the receipt of £1 million and conversion at the spot rate of $1.272.		

The net impact on income in 2020 is a sale of $1,300,000 and a foreign exchange loss of $15,000; in 2021, Eximco records a foreign exchange loss of $13,000. This results in a net increase of $1,272,000 in Retained Earnings that is balanced by an equal increase in Cash over the two-year period. Over the two-year period, Eximco recognizes a net foreign exchange loss of $28,000.

Restatement at the balance sheet date is required for all foreign currency assets and liabilities carried on a company's books. In addition to foreign currency payables and receivables arising from import and export transactions, companies might have dividends receivable from foreign subsidiaries, loans payable to foreign lenders, or lease payments receivable from foreign customers that are denominated in a foreign currency and therefore must be restated at the balance sheet date. Each of these foreign currency–denominated assets and liabilities is exposed to foreign exchange risk; therefore, fluctuation in exchange rates result in foreign exchange gains and losses on all foreign currency–denominated assets and liabilities.

Many U.S. companies report foreign exchange gains and losses on the income statement in a line item often titled "Other income (expense)." Companies include other incidental gains and losses such as gains and losses on sales of assets in this line item as well. Companies are required to disclose the magnitude of foreign exchange gains and losses if material. For example, in the Notes to Financial Statements in its 2017 annual report, Merck & Co., Inc., indicated that the income statement item "Other (Income) Expense, Net," included a net exchange gain of $11 million in 2017, and net exchange losses of $174 million in 2016 and $1,277 million in 2015.

International Accounting Standard 21—The Effects of Changes in Foreign Exchange Rates

Similar to U.S. GAAP, *IAS 21,* "The Effects of Changes in Foreign Exchange Rates," also requires the use of a two-transaction perspective in accounting for foreign currency transactions with unrealized foreign exchange gains and losses accrued in net income in the period of exchange rate change. There are no substantive differences between IFRS and U.S. GAAP in the accounting for foreign currency transactions.

LO 9-3

Account for foreign currency borrowings.

Foreign Currency Borrowing

In addition to the receivables and payables that arise from import and export activities, companies often must account for foreign currency borrowings, another type of foreign currency transaction. Companies borrow foreign currency from foreign lenders either to finance foreign operations or perhaps to take advantage of more favorable interest rates. The facts that both the principal and interest are denominated in foreign currency and both create an exposure to foreign exchange risk complicate accounting for a foreign currency borrowing.

To demonstrate the accounting for foreign currency debt, assume that on July 1, 2020, Multicorp International borrowed 1 billion Japanese yen (¥) on a one-year note at an interest rate of 5 percent per annum. Interest is payable and the note comes due on July 1, 2021. The following exchange rates apply:

Date	U.S. Dollars per Japanese Yen Spot Rate
July 1, 2020	$0.00921
December 31, 2020	0.00932
July 1, 2021	0.00937

On July 1, 2020, Multicorp borrows ¥1 billion and converts it into $9,210,000 in the spot market. On December 31, 2020, Multicorp must revalue the Japanese yen note payable with an offsetting foreign exchange gain or loss reported in income and must accrue interest expense and interest payable. Interest is calculated by multiplying the loan principal in yen by the relevant interest rate. The amount of interest payable in yen is then translated to U.S. dollars at the spot rate to record the accrual journal entry. On July 1, 2021, any difference between the amount of interest accrued at year-end and the actual U.S. dollar amount that must be spent to pay the accrued interest is recognized as a foreign exchange gain or loss. These journal entries account for this foreign currency borrowing:

Date	Account	Debit	Credit
7/1/20	Cash	9,210,000	
	Note Payable (¥)		9,210,000
	To record the ¥ note payable at the spot rate of $0.00921 and the conversion of ¥1 billion into U.S. dollars.		
12/31/20	Interest Expense	233,000	
	Accrued Interest Payable (¥)		233,000
	To accrue interest for the period July 1–December 31, 2020: ¥1 billion × 5% × ½ year = ¥25 million × $0.00932 = $233,000.		
	Foreign Exchange Gain or Loss	110,000	
	Note Payable (¥)		110,000
	To revalue the ¥ note payable at the spot rate of $0.00932 and record a foreign exchange loss of $110,000 [¥1 billion × ($0.00932 – $0.00921)].		
7/1/21	Interest Expense	234,250	
	Accrued Interest Payable (¥)		234,250
	To accrue interest for the period January 1–July 1, 2021: ¥1 billion × 5% × ½ year = ¥25 million × $0.00937 = $234,250.		
	Foreign Exchange Gain or Loss	1,250	
	Accrued Interest Payable (¥)		1,250
	To revalue the ¥ interest payable that was accrued on December 31, 2020, at the spot rate of $0.00937 and record a foreign exchange loss of $1,250 [¥25 million × ($0.00937 – $0.00932)].		
	Accrued Interest Payable (¥)	468,500	
	Cash		468,500
	To record the cash interest payment of $468,500 [¥50 million × the spot rate of $0.00937] and remove the ¥ accrued interest payable from the books.		
	Foreign Exchange Gain or Loss	50,000	
	Note Payable (¥)		50,000
	To revalue the ¥ note payable at the spot rate of $0.00937 and record a foreign exchange loss of $50,000 [¥1 billion × ($0.00937 – $0.00932)].		
	Note Payable (¥)	9,370,000	
	Cash		9,370,000
	To record repayment of the ¥1 billion note through purchase of ¥1 billion at the spot rate of $0.00937 and remove the ¥ note payable from the books.		

The total U.S. dollar borrowing cost on the 1 billion Japanese yen note payable is equal to the difference between the U.S. dollar cash outflows and cash inflow: $9,370,000 + $468,500 – $9,210,000 = $628,500. This borrowing cost is reflected in Multicorp's financial statements as a combination of interest expense ($467,250) and foreign exchange loss ($161,250). Taking the exchange rate effect on the cost of borrowing into consideration results in an "effective" interest rate of 6.8 percent ($628,500/$9,210,000), even though the stated interest rate is only 5 percent.

Foreign Currency Loan

At times, companies lend foreign currency to related parties, creating the opposite situation from a foreign currency borrowing. The accounting involves keeping track of a note receivable and related interest receivable, both of which are denominated in foreign currency. Fluctuations in the U.S. dollar value of the principal and interest generally give rise to foreign exchange gains and losses that would be included in net income. An exception arises when the foreign currency loan is made on a long-term basis to a foreign branch, subsidiary, or equity method affiliate. Foreign exchange gains and losses on "intra-entity foreign currency transactions that are of a long-term investment nature (that is, settlement is not planned or anticipated in the foreseeable future)" are deferred in accumulated other comprehensive income until the loan is repaid.[5] Only the foreign exchange gains and losses related to the interest receivable are recorded currently in net income.

LO 9-4

Understand the different types of foreign exchange risk that can be hedged and how foreign currency forward contracts and foreign currency options can be used to hedge those risks.

Hedges of Foreign Exchange Risk

In the example provided in the earlier section on foreign currency transactions, Eximco has an asset exposure in British pounds when it sells goods to the U.K. customer and allows the customer three months to pay for its purchase. If the British pound depreciates over the next three months, Eximco will incur a net foreign exchange loss. For many companies, the uncertainty of not knowing exactly how many U.S. dollars an export sale will generate is of great concern. (Similarly, not knowing exactly how many U.S. dollars a foreign currency–denominated import purchase will cost is also of concern.) To avoid this uncertainty, companies often use derivative financial instruments to hedge against the effect of unfavorable changes in the value of foreign currencies. A derivative financial instrument, or simply derivative, derives its value from some "underlying." In the case of foreign currency derivatives, the underlying is the currency exchange rate. The two most common derivatives used to hedge foreign exchange risk are *foreign currency forward contracts* and *foreign currency options.*

In our example, Eximco will receive British pounds in three months when it collects the receivable, and it will need to sell those pounds at that time. Through a forward contract, Eximco can lock in the price at which it will sell the pounds it receives in three months. Alternatively, an option establishes a price at which Eximco will be able, but is not required, to sell the pounds it receives in three months. If Eximco enters into a forward contract or purchases a put option on the date the sale is made, the derivative is being used as a *hedge of a recognized foreign currency–denominated asset* (the British pound account receivable).

Companies engaged in foreign currency activities often enter into hedging arrangements as soon as they receive a noncancelable sales order or place a noncancelable purchase order. A noncancelable order that specifies the foreign currency price and date of delivery is known as a *foreign currency firm commitment.* Assume that on June 1, Eximco accepts an order to sell parts to a customer in South Korea at a price of 5 million Korean won. The parts will be delivered and payment will be received on August 15. On June 1, when the order is accepted but before the sale has been made, Eximco enters into a forward contract to sell 5 million Korean won on August 15. In this case, Eximco is using a foreign currency derivative as a *hedge of an unrecognized foreign currency firm commitment.*

Some companies have foreign currency transactions that occur on a regular basis and can be reliably forecasted. For example, Eximco regularly purchases materials from a supplier in Hong Kong for which it pays in Hong Kong dollars. Even if Eximco has no contract to make future purchases, it has an exposure to foreign currency risk if it plans to continue making purchases from the Hong Kong supplier. Assume that on October 1, Eximco forecasts that it will make a purchase from the Hong Kong supplier in three months. To hedge against a possible increase in the price of the Hong Kong dollar, Eximco acquires a call option on October 1

[5] FASB ASC (para. 830-20-35-3b).

to purchase Hong Kong dollars in three months. The foreign currency option represents a *hedge of a forecasted foreign currency–denominated transaction.*

To summarize, there are three points in time at which a company might choose to initiate a hedge of the foreign exchange risk associated with a foreign currency transaction, resulting in these three types of hedges:

1. Hedge of a recognized foreign currency–denominated asset or liability.
2. Hedge of an unrecognized foreign currency firm commitment.
3. Hedge of a forecasted foreign currency transaction.

The following timeline illustrates how these hedges differ in terms of timing.

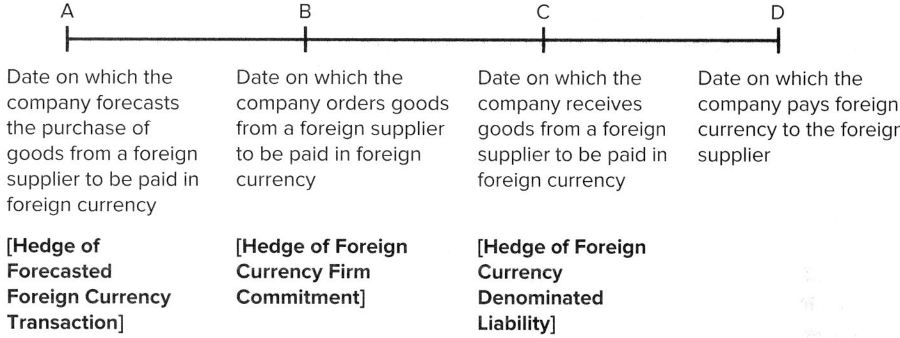

The company can enter into a hedge at any of the dates A, B, or C.

LO 9-5

Understand the accounting guidelines for derivative financial instruments.

Derivatives Accounting

FASB ASC Topic 815, "Derivatives and Hedging," governs the accounting for derivatives, including those used to hedge foreign exchange risk. This authoritative literature provides guidance for hedges of the following sources of foreign exchange risk:

1. Recognized foreign currency–denominated assets and liabilities.
2. Unrecognized foreign currency–denominated firm commitments.
3. Foreign currency–denominated forecasted transactions.
4. Net investments in foreign operations.

Different accounting applies to each type of foreign currency hedge. This chapter demonstrates the accounting for the first three types of hedges. The next chapter covers hedges of net investments in foreign operations.

Fundamental Requirement of Derivatives Accounting

The fundamental requirement of FASB ASC 815 is that companies carry all derivatives on the balance sheet at their fair value. Derivatives are reported on the balance sheet as assets when they have a positive fair value and as liabilities when they have a negative fair value. The first issue in accounting for derivatives is the determination of fair value.

The fair value of derivatives can change over time, causing adjustments to be made to the carrying values of the assets and liabilities. The second issue in accounting for derivatives is the treatment of the gains and losses that arise from these fair value changes.

Determination of Fair Value of Derivatives

Foreign Currency Forward Contract

The *fair value of a foreign currency forward contract* is determined by reference to changes in the forward rate over the life of the contract (discounted to present value). Three pieces of information are needed to determine the fair value of a forward contract at any point in time:

1. The forward rate when the forward contract was entered into.
2. The current forward rate for a contract that matures on the same date as the forward contract entered into.
3. A discount rate—typically, the company's incremental borrowing rate.

Assume that International Company enters into a forward contract with its bank on December 1 to sell 1 million Mexican pesos (MXN) on March 1 at a forward rate of $0.085 per peso, or a total of $85,000. International Company incurs no cost to enter into the forward contract, and the forward contract has no value on December 1.

U.S. dollar (USD) per MXN exchange rates over the life of the forward contract are as follows:

Date	Spot Rate	Forward Rate to March 1
December 1	$0.086	$0.085
December 31	$0.0835	$0.082
March 1	$0.0818	n/a

The USD per MXN spot rate on December 1 is $0.086, so the peso sold at a forward discount. The forward points component of the forward contract is negative $1,000 [MXN 1,000,000 × ($0.086 – $0.085)]. In other words, this forward contract includes a discount of $1,000.

On December 31, when International Company closes its books to prepare financial statements, the forward rate to sell Mexican pesos on March 1 has changed to $0.082. On that date, a forward contract for the delivery of MXN 1 million could be signed, resulting in a cash inflow of only $82,000 on March 1. This represents a favorable change in the value of International Company's forward contract of $3,000 ($85,000 – $82,000), because International Company has contracted to sell pesos for $85,000.

The undiscounted fair value of the forward contract on December 31 is $3,000. Assuming that the company's incremental borrowing rate is 4 percent per annum, the undiscounted fair value of the forward contract should be discounted at 0.3333 percent per month for two months (from the current date of December 31 to the settlement date of March 1). The fair value of the forward contract at December 31 is $2,980.10 ($3,000 × 0.993367).[6] Thus, the change in fair value since December 1 also is $2,980.10, because the fair value on December 1 was $0.

Authoritative literature indicates that the fair value of a derivative should be measured on a discounted (present value) basis. However, in a low interest rate environment, the difference between measuring a derivative on a discounted or undiscounted basis can be immaterial. For simplicity, examples presented later in this chapter recognize the fair value of derivatives at undiscounted amounts. Discounting to present value is ignored.

Foreign Currency Option

As noted earlier in this chapter, the fair value of a foreign currency option is composed of two components: intrinsic value and time value. The manner in which the *fair value of a foreign currency option* is determined depends on whether the option is traded on an exchange or has been acquired in the over-the-counter market. The fair value of an exchange-traded foreign currency option is its current market price quoted on the exchange. For over-the-counter options, fair value usually can be determined by obtaining a price quote from the option dealer. If dealer price quotes are unavailable, the company can estimate the value of an option using the modified Black-Scholes option pricing model (briefly mentioned earlier). Regardless of who does the calculation, principles similar to those of the Black-Scholes pricing model can be used to determine the fair value of the option.

[6] The present value factor for two months at 0.3333 percent per month is calculated as $1/1.003333^2$, or 0.993367.

Accounting for Changes in the Fair Value of Derivatives

Changes in the fair value of derivatives must be included in *comprehensive income,* which consists of two components: *Net Income* and *Other Comprehensive Income.* Other Comprehensive Income (OCI) consists of income items that authoritative accounting literature requires to be deferred in stockholders' equity such as unrealized gains and losses on available-for-sale debt securities. OCI is accumulated and closed to a separate line in the stockholders' equity section of the balance sheet titled *Accumulated Other Comprehensive Income* (AOCI).

In accordance with U.S. GAAP, gains and losses arising from changes in the fair value of derivatives are recognized initially either (1) in Net Income (closed to Retained Earnings on the balance sheet) or (2) in Other Comprehensive Income (reflected on the balance sheet in Accumulated Other Comprehensive Income). Recognition treatment depends partly on whether a derivative is used for hedging or for speculation.

Using derivatives for speculation is not commonly done by companies other than financial institutions. Financial institutions might acquire derivative financial instruments as investments for speculative purposes. For example, assume that the three-month U.S. dollar–euro forward exchange rate is $1.12, and a speculator believes the U.S. dollar–euro spot rate in three months will be $1.10. In that case, the speculator would enter into a three-month forward contract to sell euros. At the future date, the speculator purchases euros at the spot rate of $1.10 and sells them at the contracted forward rate of $1.12, realizing a gain of $0.02 per euro. Of course, such an investment might just as easily generate a loss if the spot rate does not move in the expected direction. For speculative derivatives, the change in the fair value of the derivative must be recognized immediately as a foreign exchange gain or loss in net income.[7]

The accounting for changes in the fair value of derivatives used for hedging depends on a variety of factors, including whether the derivative qualifies for *hedge accounting.*

LO 9-6

Understand the basic concepts of hedge accounting.

Hedge Accounting

Companies enter into hedging relationships to minimize the adverse effect that changes in exchange rates have on cash flows and net income. As such, companies would like to account for hedges in a way that recognizes the gain or loss from the hedging instrument in net income in the same period as the loss or gain on the risk being hedged. This approach is known as *hedge accounting.* U.S. GAAP allows hedge accounting for foreign currency derivatives only if three conditions are satisfied:

1. The derivative is used to hedge either a cash flow exposure or a fair value exposure to foreign exchange risk.
2. The derivative is highly effective in offsetting changes in the cash flows or fair value related to the hedged item.
3. The derivative is properly documented as a hedge.

Each of these conditions is discussed in turn.[8]

Nature of the Hedged Risk

Derivatives for which companies wish to use hedge accounting must be designated as either a *cash flow hedge* or a *fair value hedge.* For hedges of recognized foreign currency–denominated assets and liabilities and hedges of foreign currency–denominated firm commitments, companies may choose between the two types of designation. Hedges of forecasted foreign currency–denominated transactions can qualify only as cash flow hedges. Accounting procedures differ for the two types of hedges. In general, gains and losses on cash flow

[7] In the next section, we will see that the change in fair value of a derivative designated as the fair value hedge of a foreign currency–denominated asset or liability also is recognized immediately in net income.

[8] The requirements to qualify for hedge accounting are rigorous, and companies must expend resources to meet them. Not all hedges that are effective in minimizing risk will qualify for hedge accounting, and in some cases, companies might decide not to pursue hedge accounting because the cost to do so exceeds the benefit.

hedges are included in other comprehensive income (and deferred on the balance sheet in Accumulated Other Comprehensive Income), and gains and losses on fair value hedges are recognized immediately in net income (and closed to Retained Earnings).

A *fair value exposure* exists if changes in exchange rates can affect the fair value of an asset or liability reported on the balance sheet. To qualify for hedge accounting, the fair value risk must have the potential to affect net income if it is not hedged. For example, a fair value risk is associated with a recognized foreign currency account receivable. If the foreign currency depreciates, the receivable must be written down with an offsetting loss recognized in net income. Authoritative literature has determined that a fair value exposure also exists for unrecognized foreign currency firm commitments.

A *cash flow exposure* exists if changes in exchange rates can affect the amount of cash flow to be realized from a foreign currency transaction with changes in cash flow reflected in net income. A foreign currency account receivable, for example, has both a fair value exposure and a cash flow exposure. A cash flow exposure exists for (1) recognized foreign currency assets and liabilities, (2) unrecognized foreign currency firm commitments, and (3) forecasted foreign currency transactions.

Hedge Effectiveness

For hedge accounting to be used initially, the derivative hedging instrument must be expected to be *highly effective* in mitigating foreign exchange risk related to the fair value or cash flow of the item being hedged. To continue to apply hedge accounting over the life of the derivative, the derivative instrument's effectiveness must be evaluated at each subsequent balance sheet date (including when interim financial statements are prepared). If a derivative instrument is deemed no longer to be highly effective at a subsequent balance sheet date, hedge accounting must be discontinued and the instrument's change in fair value is recognized immediately in net income.

At inception, a foreign currency derivative can be considered to be highly effective as a hedge if the *critical terms* of the hedging instrument match those of the hedged item. Critical terms include the currency type, currency amount, and settlement date. For example, a forward contract to purchase 100,000 Canadian dollars in one year would be a highly effective hedge of a 100,000 Canadian dollar liability that is payable in one year.

In practice, assessing hedge effectiveness for many derivative hedging instruments can be rather complicated, and could include the use of regression analysis or other quantitative methods. The FASB allows firms to avoid quantitative analysis of effectiveness when a derivative is perfectly effective—that is, the critical terms of the hedging instrument are exactly the same as the hedged item.

Exclusion of Components from Hedge Effectiveness Assessment

In general terms, the assessment of hedge effectiveness involves comparing the change in fair value of the hedging instrument with the change in fair value of the item being hedged. Accounting guidelines allow a reporting entity to exclude these components of the hedging instrument from the assessment of hedge effectiveness:

- Forward points (discount or premium)—when a forward contract is the hedging instrument.
- Time value—when an option is the hedging instrument.

In other words, an entity may choose to designate only the spot component of a forward contract as the hedging instrument, and may choose to designate only the intrinsic value of an option as the hedging instrument. When this choice is made, the excluded components (forward points, time value) must be recognized in net income using one of two approaches:

- The initial value of the excluded component is amortized to net income using a systematic and rationale method (such as straight-line) over the life of the hedging instrument.
- The change in fair value of the excluded component is recognized currently in net income.

Under either approach, the total amount of the excluded component will be recognized in net income over the life of the hedging instrument; only the pattern of income recognition will differ between the two approaches.

Conceptually, excluding forward points and time value from the hedging instrument and then allocating the excluded element to net income over its life is analogous to treating the hedging instrument as an insurance contract.

When a foreign currency option is purchased "at the money" (strike price equals spot rate), the option's purchase price is solely attributable to time value (intrinsic value is zero). Thus, the original time value of the option is the amount paid for "insurance." The cost of normal insurance, such as fire insurance, is recognized as insurance expense over the life of the insurance contract. Allocating the cost of a foreign currency option over its life is analogous to treating the option as insurance. A similar conceptual argument can be made for allocating the forward points on a forward contract to net income over the life of the forward contract.

The only difference between the accounting for normal insurance and allocating the excluded component to net income is that the FASB requires the amortization of the derivative instrument's excluded component to be recognized in the same line item in the income statement as the item that is being hedged. For example, if a forecasted foreign currency export sale is being hedged, the amortization of the derivative instrument's excluded component must be reported in Sales. Similarly, if a forecasted foreign currency import purchase of inventory is being hedged, the amortization of the derivative instrument's excluded component must be reported in Cost of Goods Sold. Conversely, when a recognized foreign currency–denominated asset or liability is being hedged, the excluded component is allocated to the Foreign Exchange Gain or Loss line item in net income.

Hedge Documentation

For hedge accounting to be applied, U.S. GAAP requires formal documentation of the hedging relationship at the inception of the hedge (i.e., on the date a foreign currency forward contract is entered into or a foreign currency option is acquired). The hedging company must prepare a document that identifies the hedged item (for example, a 100,000 Canadian dollar liability), the hedging instrument (a forward contract to purchase 100,000 Canadian dollars), the nature of the risk being hedged (a cash flow exposure), how the hedging instrument's effectiveness will be assessed (through comparison of critical terms), and the risk management objective and strategy for undertaking the hedge (to minimize risk associated with a possible Canadian dollar appreciation).

Hedging Combinations

The specific accounting procedures followed and journal entries needed to account for a foreign currency hedging relationship are determined by a combination of the following factors:

1. The type of foreign currency item being hedged:
   a. Foreign currency–denominated asset or liability.
   b. Foreign currency–denominated firm commitment.
   c. Forecasted foreign currency–denominated transaction.
2. The nature of the risk exposure being hedged:
   a. Fair value exposure.
   b. Cash flow exposure.
3. The nature of the foreign currency item being hedged:
   a. Asset (or future sale).
   b. Liability (or future purchase).
4. The type of derivative hedging instrument used:
   a. Forward contract.
   b. Option.
5. The component(s) of the derivative identified as the hedging instrument:
   a. Forward contract—spot component only or spot and forward components.
   b. Option—intrinsic value component only or intrinsic and time value components.

In the next several sections in this chapter, we discuss the accounting for hedges of (1) recognized foreign currency assets and liabilities, (2) unrecognized foreign currency firm commitments, and (3) forecasted foreign currency transactions. We demonstrate through examples the use of both forward contracts and options to hedge these items, and we selectively demonstrate the accounting for both cash flow and fair value hedges. For simplicity, we focus on examples in which only the spot component (forward contract) or intrinsic value component (option) has been identified as the hedging instrument. Also, for simplicity, we ignore discounting to present value in determining the fair value of forward contracts and firm commitments.

We focus on hedges entered into by an exporter that has a current or future foreign currency asset (receivable) that is exposed to foreign exchange risk. The comprehensive illustration at the end of this chapter demonstrates the accounting for hedges entered into by an importer that has an existing or future foreign currency liability (payable).

Exhibit 9.2 provides an overall summary of the procedures followed in accounting for hedges of foreign exchange risk for those combinations presented in this chapter. By examining this exhibit, the similarities and differences in the procedures followed and accounting entries prepared to account for each hedge combination can be discerned.

LO 9-7

Account for forward contracts and options used as hedges of foreign currency–denominated assets and liabilities.

Hedges of Foreign Currency–Denominated Assets and Liabilities

Hedges of foreign currency–denominated assets and liabilities, such as accounts receivable and accounts payable, can qualify as either *cash flow hedges* or *fair value hedges.* To qualify as a cash flow hedge, the hedging instrument must completely offset the variability in the cash flows associated with the foreign currency receivable or payable. If the hedging instrument does not qualify as a cash flow hedge or if the company elects not to designate the hedging instrument as a cash flow hedge, the hedge is designated as a fair value hedge. The following summarizes the basic accounting for the two types of hedges of foreign currency–denominated assets and liabilities, assuming that forward points (forward contract) and time value (option) are excluded in assessing hedge effectiveness.

Cash Flow Hedge

At each balance sheet date, the following procedures are required:

1. The hedged asset (foreign currency account receivable) or liability (foreign currency account payable) is adjusted to fair value based on changes in the spot exchange rate, and a foreign exchange gain or loss is recognized in net income (Cash Flow Hedge Step B.1 in Exhibit 9.2).
2. To comply with the fundamental requirement of derivatives accounting, the derivative hedging instrument (forward contract or option) is adjusted to fair value (resulting in an asset or liability reported on the balance sheet) with the counterpart recognized as a change in other comprehensive income (OCI) (Cash Flow Hedge Step B.2 in Exhibit 9.2).
3. To achieve hedge accounting, a foreign exchange gain or loss related to the hedging instrument is recognized to offset the foreign exchange loss or gain on the hedged asset or liability, with the counterpart recorded in OCI (Cash Flow Hedge Step B.3 in Exhibit 9.2).
4. An additional foreign exchange loss is recognized in net income (with the counterpart in OCI) to reflect (a) the current period's amortization of the original discount or premium on the forward contract (if a forward contract is the hedging instrument) or (b) the change in the *time value* of the option (if an option is the hedging instrument) (Cash Flow Hedge Step B.4 in Exhibit 9.2).

Fair Value Hedge

At each balance sheet date, the following procedures are required:

1. Adjust the hedged asset or liability to fair value based on changes in the spot exchange rate and recognize a foreign exchange gain or loss in net income (Fair Value Hedge Step B.1 in Exhibit 9.2).

EXHIBIT 9.2 Summary of Accounting for Hedges of Foreign Exchange Risk

Date	Hedge of a Foreign Currency–Denominated Asset or Liability				Hedge of a Foreign Currency Firm Commitment		Hedge of a Forecasted Foreign Currency Transaction	
	Cash Flow Hedge		Fair Value Hedge		Fair Value Hedge		Cash Flow Hedge	
	Forward Contract	Option	Forward Contract	Option	Forward Contract	Option	Forward Contract	Option
A. Initiation Date	1. Recognize the transaction (sale or purchase) and foreign currency–denominated asset or liability	1. Recognize the transaction (sale or purchase) and foreign currency–denominated asset or liability	1. Recognize the transaction (sale or purchase) and foreign currency–denominated asset or liability	1. Recognize the transaction (sale or purchase) and foreign currency–denominated asset or liability	1. No entry related to the firm commitment (zero value)	1. No entry related to the firm commitment	1. No entry related to the forecasted transaction	1. No entry related to the forecasted transaction
	2. No entry related to forward contract (zero fair value)	2. Recognize option as an asset (purchase price is fair value)	2. No entry related to forward contract (zero fair value)	2. Recognize option as an asset (purchase price is fair value)	2. No entry related to forward contract (zero fair value)	2. Recognize option as an asset (purchase price is fair value)	2. No entry related to forward contract (zero fair value)	2. Recognize option as an asset (purchase price is fair value)
B. Balance Sheet Date	1. Adjust hedged asset or liability to fair value, with counterpart (change in fair value) reported as foreign exchange gain or loss in net income	1. Adjust hedged asset or liability to fair value, with counterpart (change in fair value) reported as foreign exchange gain or loss in net income	1. Adjust hedged asset or liability to fair value, with counterpart (change in fair value) reported as foreign exchange gain or loss in net income	1. Adjust hedged asset or liability to fair value, with counterpart (change in fair value) reported as foreign exchange gain or loss in net income	1. Adjust forward contract to fair value (either an asset or a liability), with counterpart (change in fair value) reported as foreign exchange gain or loss in net income	1. Adjust option to fair value (either an asset or zero value), with counterpart (change in fair value) reported as foreign exchange gain or loss in net income	1. N/A	1. N/A
	2. Adjust forward contract to fair value (either an asset or a liability), with counterpart (change in fair value) reported in OCI	2. Adjust option to fair value (either an asset or zero value), with counterpart (change in fair value) reported in OCI	2. Adjust forward contract to fair value (either an asset or a liability), with counterpart (change in fair value) reported as foreign exchange gain or loss in net income	2. Adjust option to fair value (either an asset or zero value), with counterpart (change in fair value) reported as foreign exchange gain or loss in net income	2. Adjust firm commitment to fair value (based on change in forward rate), with counterpart (change in fair value) reported as foreign exchange gain or loss in net income	2. Adjust firm commitment to fair value (based on change in spot rate), with counterpart (change in fair value) reported as foreign exchange gain or loss in net income	2. Adjust forward contract to fair value (either an asset or a liability), with counterpart (change in fair value) reported in OCI	2. Adjust option to fair value (either an asset or zero value), with counterpart (change in fair value) reported in OCI

(continued)

EXHIBIT 9.2 (Continued)

	Hedge of a Foreign Currency–Denominated Asset or Liability				Hedge of a Foreign Currency Firm Commitment		Hedge of a Forecasted Foreign Currency Transaction	
	Cash Flow Hedge		Fair Value Hedge		Fair Value Hedge		Cash Flow Hedge	
Date	Forward Contract	Option	Forward Contract	Option	Forward Contract	Option	Forward Contract	Option
	3. Recognize a loss or gain related to the hedging instrument (with counterpart reported in OCI) to offset the foreign exchange gain or loss on the hedged item recognized in B.1	3. Recognize a loss or gain related to the hedging instrument (with counterpart reported in OCI) to offset the foreign exchange gain or loss on the hedged item recognized in B.1	3. N/A	3. N/A	3. N/A	3. N/A	3. N/A	3. N/A
	4. Recognize a portion of the forward points (discount or premium) in net income with the counterpart reported in OCI	4. Recognize a portion of the time value of the option in net income with the counterpart reported in OCI	4. Adjust the already recognized net foreign exchange gain or loss to reflect the current period's allocation of forward points in net income, with the counterpart reported in OCI	4. Adjust the already recognized net foreign exchange gain or loss to reflect the current period's allocation of option time value in net income, with the counterpart reported in OCI (this step is needed only when the option has no intrinsic value)	4. N/A	4. N/A	4. Recognize a portion of the forward points (discount or premium) in net income with counterpart reported in OCI	4. Recognize a portion of the time value of the option in net income with counterpart reported in OCI

(continued)

EXHIBIT 9.2 (Continued)

Date	Hedge of a Foreign Currency–Denominated Asset or Liability				Hedge of a Foreign Currency Firm Commitment		Hedge of a Forecasted Foreign Currency Transaction	
	Cash Flow Hedge		Fair Value Hedge		Fair Value Hedge		Cash Flow Hedge	
	Forward Contract	Option	Forward Contract	Option	Forward Contract	Option	Forward Contract	Option
C. Settlement Date	1–4. Repeat steps B.1–B.4	1–4. Repeat steps B.1–B.4	1–2. Repeat steps B.1 and B.2	1–2. Repeat steps B.1 and B.2	1–2. Repeat steps B.1 and B.2	1–2. Repeat steps B.1 and B.2	1–2. Repeat steps B.2 and B.4	1–2. Repeat steps B.2 and B.4
	5. Recognize settlement of the foreign currency–denominated asset or liability	5. Recognize settlement of the foreign currency	3. Transfer the amount in AOCI (as a result of step B.4) to net income to reflect the current period's allocation of forward points	3. Transfer the amount in AOCI (as a result of step B.4) to net income to reflect the current period's allocation of option time value	3. Recognize the transaction (sale or purchase)	3. Recognize the transaction (sale or purchase)	3. Recognize the transaction (sale or purchase)	3. Recognize the transaction (sale or purchase)
	6. Recognize settlement of the forward contract*	6. Recognize exercise (or expiration) of the option*	4. Recognize settlement of the foreign currency–denominated asset or liability	4. Recognize settlement of the foreign currency–denominated asset or liability	4. Recognize settlement of the forward contract#	4. Recognize exercise (or expiration) of the option#	4. Recognize settlement of the forward contract#	4. Recognize exercise (or expiration) of the option#
			5. Recognize settlement of the forward contract†	5. Recognize exercise (or expiration) of the option†	5. Close the balance in the firm commitment account as an adjustment to net income	5. Close the balance in the firm commitment account as an adjustment to net income	5. Close the balance in AOCI related to the forward contract as an adjustment to net income	5. Close the balance in AOCI related to the option as an adjustment to net income

*Step 6 precedes step 5 in the case of a foreign currency–denominated liability.
†Step 4 precedes step 3 in the case of a foreign currency–denominated liability.
#Step 4 precedes step 3 in the case of a foreign currency purchase transaction.

2. Adjust the derivative hedging instrument to fair value (resulting in an asset or liability reported on the balance sheet) and recognize the counterpart as a foreign exchange gain or loss in net income (Fair Value Hedge Step B.2 in Exhibit 9.2).
3. Adjust the net foreign exchange gain or loss thus far recognized to properly reflect (a) the current period's amortization of the original discount or premium on the forward contract (if a forward contract is the hedging instrument) or (b) the change in the *time value* of the option (if an option is the hedging instrument) (Fair Value Hedge Step B.4 in Exhibit 9.2).

Forward Contract Hedge of a Foreign Currency–Denominated Asset

We now return to the Eximco example in which the company has a foreign currency account receivable to demonstrate the accounting for a hedge of a recognized foreign currency–denominated asset.[9] In the preceding example, Eximco has an asset exposure in British pounds when it sells goods to the U.K. customer and allows the customer three months to pay for its purchase. To hedge its exposure to a possible decline in the U.S. dollar value of the British pound, Eximco enters into a forward contract.

Assume that on December 1, 2020, the three-month forward rate for British pounds is $1.288 and Eximco signs a contract with New World Bank to deliver 1 million British pounds in three months in exchange for $1,288,000. No cash changes hands on December 1, 2020. Because the spot rate on December 1 is $1.300, the British pound (£) is selling at a discount in the three-month forward market (the forward rate is less than the spot rate). Because the British pound is selling at a discount of $0.012 ($1.300 – $1.288) per pound, Eximco receives $12,000 less than it would have if payment had been received at the date the goods are delivered ($1,288,000 versus $1,300,000). This $12,000 can be viewed as the "insurance" that Eximco pays to avoid the risk that the British pound could depreciate over the next three months. The $12,000 reduction in cash flow also is the cost of extending foreign currency credit to the foreign customer.[10] Conceptually, this cost is similar to the transaction loss that arises on the export sale. It exists only because the transaction is denominated in a foreign currency. The major difference is that Eximco knows the exact amount of the loss at the date of sale, whereas when it is left unhedged, the company does not know the size of the transaction loss until three months pass. (In fact, it is possible that the unhedged receivable could result in a transaction gain rather than a transaction loss.)

Because the future spot rate turns out to be only $1.272, selling British pounds at a forward rate of $1.288 is better than leaving the British pound receivable unhedged: Eximco will receive $16,000 more as a result of the hedge. This can be viewed as an economic gain resulting from the use of the forward contract. Unlike the discount loss, however, the exact size of this gain is not known until three months pass. (In fact, it is possible that use of the forward contract could result in an additional loss. This would occur if the spot rate on March 1, 2021, is higher than the forward rate of $1.288.)

Eximco must account for its foreign currency transaction and the related forward contract simultaneously but separately. The process can be better understood by referring to the steps involving the three parties—Eximco, the British customer, and New World Bank—shown in Exhibit 9.3.

Because the critical terms (currency type, currency amount, and settlement date) of the forward contract match the corresponding terms of the account receivable, the hedge is assessed as being highly effective. If Eximco properly designates the forward contract as a hedge of its British pound account receivable position, it may apply hedge accounting. Because it completely offsets the variability in the cash flows related to the account receivable, Eximco may

[9] The comprehensive illustration at the end of this chapter demonstrates the accounting for the hedge of a foreign currency–denominated liability.

[10] This should not be confused with the cost associated with normal credit risk—that is, the risk that the customer will not pay for its purchase. That is a separate issue unrelated to the currency in which the transaction is denominated.

EXHIBIT 9.3
Hedge of a Foreign Currency Account Receivable with a Forward Contract

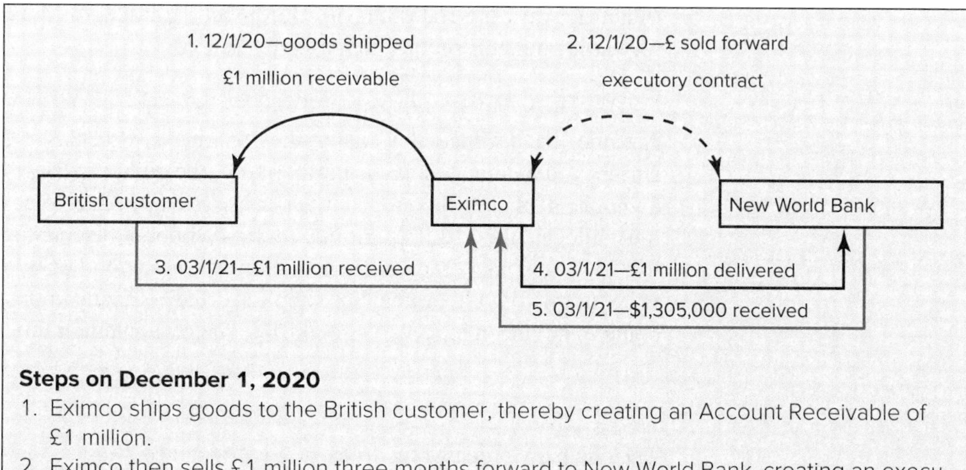

Steps on December 1, 2020

1. Eximco ships goods to the British customer, thereby creating an Account Receivable of £1 million.
2. Eximco then sells £1 million three months forward to New World Bank, creating an executory contract to pay £1 million and receive $1,288,000.

Steps on March 1, 2021

3. The British customer remits £1 million to Eximco—the £ Account Receivable has been received and Eximco has £1 million reflected in an account titled Foreign Currency (£).
4. Eximco delivers £1 million to New World Bank.
5. New World Bank pays Eximco $1,288,000.

designate the forward contract as a cash flow hedge. Alternatively, because changes in the spot rate affect not only the cash flows but also the fair value of the foreign currency receivable, Eximco may elect to account for this forward contract as a fair value hedge.

In either case, Eximco determines the fair value of the forward contract by referring to the change in the forward rate for a contract maturing on March 1, 2021. The relevant exchange rates, U.S. dollar value of the British pound receivable, and fair value of the forward contract are determined as follows:

		Account Receivable (£)		Forward	Forward Contract	
Date	Spot Rate	U.S. Dollar Value	Change in U.S. Dollar Value	Rate to 3/1/21	Fair Value	Change in Fair Value
12/1/20	$1.300	$1,300,000	—	$1.288	$ –0–	—
12/31/20	1.285	1,285,000	–$15,000	1.278	10,000*	+$10,000
3/1/21	1.272	1,272,000	– 13,000	1.272 (spot)	16,000†	+ 6,000

*$1,288,000 – $1,278,000 = $10,000. For simplicity, discounting to present value is ignored.
†$1,288,000 – $1,272,000 = $16,000.

Eximco pays nothing to enter into the forward contract at December 1, 2020, and the forward contract has a fair value of zero on that date. The original discount on the forward contract is $12,000, determined by the difference in the British pound spot rate and three-month forward rate on December 1, 2020 [($1.300 – $1.288) × £1 million]. At December 31, 2020, the forward rate for a contract to deliver British pounds on March 1, 2021, is $1.278. Eximco could enter into a forward contract on December 31, 2020, to sell 1 million British pounds for $1,278,000 on March 1, 2021. Because Eximco has contracted to sell 1 million British pounds for $1,288,000, the value of the forward contract is $10,000.[11] Because the fair value is positive, the forward contract is recognized as an asset on December 31, 2020. On March 1, 2021, the forward rate to sell British pounds on that date is, by definition, the spot rate of $1.272. At that rate, Eximco could sell 1 million British pounds for $1,272,000. Because Eximco has a contract to sell British pounds for $1,288,000, the fair value of the forward contract on

[11] Conceptually, the undiscounted value of the forward contract should be discounted to its present value. However, in the current low-interest environment, the difference between the discounted and undiscounted values is immaterial. For simplicity, we ignore discounting in determining the fair value of a forward contract.

March 1, 2021, is $16,000. From December 31, 2020, to March 1, 2021, the fair value of the forward contract asset has increased by $6,000.

Forward Contract Designated as Cash Flow Hedge

Assume that Eximco designates the forward contract as a *cash flow hedge* of a foreign currency–denominated asset. Furthermore, the company elects to exclude the forward points component of the forward contract in assessing hedge effectiveness. In this case, Eximco must allocate the $12,000 original forward contract discount as a loss to net income over the life of the contract using either an amortization method or by referring to changes in the fair value of the forward points. For simplicity, the company chooses to amortize the forward discount to net income using a straight-line method on a monthly basis, as follows:

2020: $12,000 × ⅓ = $4,000 (one month of amortization)

2021: $12,000 × ⅔ = $8,000 (two months of amortization)

The company prepares the following journal entries to account for the foreign currency transaction and the related forward contract:

2020 Journal Entries—Forward Contract Designated as a Cash Flow Hedge

Date	Account	Debit	Credit
12/1/20	Accounts Receivable (£)...............................	1,300,000	
	Sales..		1,300,000
	To record the sale and £1 million account receivable at the spot rate of $1.300 (Cash Flow Hedge Step A.1 in Exhibit 9.2).		
	The company makes no formal entry for the forward contract because it is an executory contract (no cash changes hands) and has a fair value of zero (Cash Flow Hedge Step A.2 in Exhibit 9.2).		

Eximco prepares a memorandum designating the forward contract as a hedge of the risk of changes in the cash flow to be received on the foreign currency account receivable resulting from changes in the U.S. dollar–British pound exchange rate. Following steps B.1–B.4 in accounting for a cash flow hedge presented in Exhibit 9.2, the company prepares the following journal entries on December 31:

Date	Account	Debit	Credit
12/31/20	Foreign Exchange Gain or Loss.......................	15,000	
	Accounts Receivable (£)		15,000
	To adjust the value of the £ receivable to the new spot rate of $1.285 and recognize a foreign exchange loss resulting from the depreciation of the £ since December 1 (Cash Flow Hedge Step B.1 in Exhibit 9.2).		
	Forward Contract	10,000	
	Other Comprehensive Income (OCI)...............		10,000
	To record the forward contract as an asset at its fair value of $10,000 with a corresponding credit to OCI (Cash Flow Hedge Step B.2 in Exhibit 9.2).		
	Other Comprehensive Income (OCI)...................	15,000	
	Foreign Exchange Gain or Loss..................		15,000
	To record a foreign exchange gain related to the forward contract to offset the foreign exchange loss on the account receivable with a corresponding debit to OCI (Cash Flow Hedge Step B.3 in Exhibit 9.2).		
	Foreign Exchange Gain or Loss.......................	4,000	
	Other Comprehensive Income (OCI)...............		4,000
	To amortize the forward contract discount to net income over the life of the contract using the straight-line method with a corresponding credit to OCI (Cash Flow Hedge Step B.4 in Exhibit 9.2).		

The first entry at December 31, 2020, serves to revalue the foreign currency account receivable and recognize a foreign exchange loss of $15,000 in net income. Because the forward contract has a positive fair value of $10,000, it must be recognized on the balance sheet as an asset. Thus, the second entry makes a debit of $10,000 to Forward Contract (an asset account). Under cash flow hedge accounting, the change in the fair value of the forward contract, which has gone from $0 to $10,000, is not recognized immediately in net income, but instead is recognized in Other Comprehensive Income (OCI), which is subsequently closed to Accumulated Other Comprehensive Income (AOCI) in stockholders' equity.

The third entry achieves the objective of hedge accounting by recognizing a $15,000 foreign exchange gain on the forward contract with the counterpart reported in OCI. As a result of this entry, the foreign exchange gain on forward contract of $15,000 and the foreign exchange loss on the account receivable of $15,000 exactly offset one another, and the impact on net income is zero. The gain on forward contract and loss on account receivable are both recorded in the Foreign Exchange Gain or Loss account, which will have either a debit (net loss), credit (net gain), or zero balance at the end of the period.

The last entry uses the straight-line method to amortize a portion of the $12,000 forward contract discount to net income (Foreign Exchange Gain or Loss). By making the credit in this entry to OCI, the correct amounts are reported in net income and on the balance sheet, and the balance sheet remains in balance.

The impact on net income for the year 2020 follows:

Sales	$1,300,000
Net foreign exchange gain (loss)	(4,000)
Impact on net income	$1,296,000

Assets		Liabilities and Stockholders' Equity	
Accounts receivable (£)	$1,285,000	Retained earnings	$1,296,000
Forward contract	10,000	AOCI	(1,000)
	$1,295,000		$1,295,000

The impact on net income is closed to Retained Earnings and the debit balance of $1,000 in OCI is closed to AOCI. The overall impact on the December 31, 2020, balance sheet is as follows:

2021 Journal Entries—Forward Contract Designated as Cash Flow Hedge

From December 31, 2020, to March 1, 2021, the British pound account receivable decreases in value by $13,000 and the forward contract increases in value by $6,000. In addition, on March 1, 2021, the remaining discount on forward contract must be amortized to net income. The company prepares the following journal entries on March 1, 2021, to reflect these changes:

Date	Account	Debit	Credit
3/1/21	Foreign Exchange Gain or Loss	13,000	
	Accounts Receivable (£)		13,000
	To adjust the value of the £ receivable to the new spot rate of $1.272 and recognize a foreign exchange loss resulting from the depreciation of the £ since December 31 (Cash Flow Hedge Step C.1 in Exhibit 9.2).		
	Forward Contract	6,000	
	Other Comprehensive Income (OCI)		6,000
	To adjust the carrying value of the forward contract to its current fair value of $16,000 with a corresponding credit to OCI (Cash Flow Hedge Step C.2 in Exhibit 9.2).		

(continued)

(continued)

		Debit	Credit
	Other Comprehensive Income (OCI)	13,000	
	Foreign Exchange Gain or Loss		13,000
	To record a foreign exchange gain on forward contract to offset the foreign exchange loss on account receivable with a corresponding debit to OCI (Cash Flow Hedge Step C.3 in Exhibit 9.2).		
	Foreign Exchange Gain or Loss	8,000	
	Other Comprehensive Income (OCI)		8,000
	To amortize the remaining forward contract discount to net income with a corresponding credit to OCI (Cash Flow Hedge Step C.4 in Exhibit 9.2).		

This series of journal entries results in a net credit to OCI of $1,000 in 2021. Once this net credit to OCI is closed to AOCI, the balance in AOCI is reduced to zero.

The next two journal entries record the receipt of British pounds from the customer, close out the British pound account receivable, and record the settlement of the forward contract.

		Debit	Credit
3/1/21	Foreign Currency (£)	1,272,000	
	Accounts Receivable (£)		1,272,000
	To record receipt of £1 million from the British customer as an asset (Foreign Currency) at the spot rate of $1.272 (Cash Flow Hedge Step C.5 in Exhibit 9.2).		
	Cash	1,288,000	
	Foreign Currency (£)		1,272,000
	Forward Contract		16,000
	To record settlement of the forward contract (i.e., record receipt of $1,282,000 in exchange for delivery of £1 million) and remove the forward contract from the accounts (Cash Flow Hedge Step C.6 in Exhibit 9.2).		

The impact on net income for the year 2021 follows:

Net foreign exchange gain (loss)	$(8,000)
Impact on net income	$(8,000)

The net foreign exchange loss of $8,000 in 2021 is solely attributable to the current period's amortization of the forward contract discount.

Over the two accounting periods, Eximco reports sales of $1,300,000 and a cumulative net foreign exchange loss of $12,000. The net foreign exchange loss is equal to the original forward contract discount and reflects the cost of extending credit to the British customer. It also reflects the amount of cost the company incurred as "insurance" to hedge the foreign exchange risk associated with a foreign currency receivable. The net effect on the balance sheet over the two years is an increase in Cash of $1,288,000 with a corresponding increase in Retained Earnings of $1,288,000 ($1,296,000 – $8,000).

The net benefit from entering into the forward contract is $16,000. This "gain" is not directly reflected in net income. However, it can be calculated as the fair value of the forward contract immediately prior to its settlement.

Forward Contract Premium

What if the forward rate on December 1, 2020, had been $1.306 rather than $1.288 (i.e., the British pound was selling at a premium in the forward market)? In that case, Eximco would receive $6,000 more through the forward sale of British pounds ($1,306,000) than if it had received the British pounds at the date of sale ($1,300,000). Eximco would allocate the forward contract premium as an increase in net income at the rate of $2,000 per month: $2,000 at December 31, 2020, and $4,000 at March 1, 2021.

Forward Contract Designated as Fair Value Hedge

Now assume that Eximco designates the forward contract as a fair value hedge rather than as a cash flow hedge. In that case, the company recognizes the change in fair value of the forward contract as a foreign exchange gain or loss directly in net income. Eximco chooses to exclude the forward component in assessing hedge effectiveness and to recognize the forward discount in net income on a straight-line basis. However, the company does not need to make a separate entry to amortize the original discount on the forward contract. Instead, the company will make an adjustment to the net foreign exchange gain or loss otherwise recognized to properly recognize a discount loss.

2020 Journal Entries—Forward Contract Designated as a Fair Value Hedge

12/1/20	Accounts Receivable (£)............................	1,300,000	
	Sales..		1,300,000
	To record the sale and £1 million account receivable at the spot rate of $1.30 (Fair Value Hedge Step A.1 in Exhibit 9.2).		

The forward contract requires no formal entry (Fair Value Hedge Step A.2 in Exhibit 9.2). A memorandum designates the forward contract as a hedge of the risk of changes in the fair value of the foreign currency account receivable resulting from changes in the U.S. dollar–British pound exchange rate.

Following the two steps in accounting for a fair value hedge presented in Exhibit 9.2, the company prepares the following entries on December 31:

12/31/20	Foreign Exchange Gain or Loss........................	15,000	
	Accounts Receivable (£)...........................		15,000
	To adjust the value of the £ receivable to the new spot rate of $1.285 and record a foreign exchange loss resulting from the depreciation of the £ since December 1 (Fair Value Hedge Step B.1 in Exhibit 9.2).		
	Forward Contract....................................	10,000	
	Foreign Exchange Gain or Loss....................		10,000
	To record the forward contract as an asset at its fair value of $10,000 and recognize a forward contract gain for the change in the fair value of the forward contract since December 1 (Fair Value Hedge Step B.2 in Exhibit 9.2).		

The first entry at December 31, 2020, serves to revalue the foreign currency account receivable and recognize a foreign exchange loss of $15,000. The second entry recognizes the forward contract as an asset of $10,000 on the balance sheet. At this point, the company has recognized a net foreign exchange loss of $5,000. The current period's amortization of forward contract discount is only $4,000 ($12,000 × ⅓), so the following adjustment must be made:

12/31/20	Other Comprehensive Income (OCI)....................	1,000	
	Foreign Exchange Gain or Loss....................		1,000
	To adjust the amount recognized as foreign exchange loss to reflect the current period's amortization of the forward contract discount in net income with a corresponding debit to OCI (Fair Value Hedge Step B.4 in Exhibit 9.2).		

As a result of this entry, a net foreign exchange loss of $4,000 ($5,000 – $1,000), equal to the current period's amortization of forward contract discount, is reported in net income.

The impact on net income for the year 2020 is as follows:

Sales	$1,300,000
Net foreign exchange gain (loss)	(4,000)
Impact on net income	$1,296,000

Once net income and OCI are closed to Retained Earnings and AOCI, respectively, the effect on the December 31, 2020, balance sheet is as follows:

Assets		Liabilities and Stockholders' Equity	
Accounts receivable (£)	$1,285,000	Retained earnings	$1,296,000
Forward contract	10,000	AOCI	(1,000)
	$1,295,000		$1,295,000

2021 Journal Entries—Forward Contract Designated as a Fair Value Hedge

The company prepares the following entries on March 1:

3/1/21	Foreign Exchange Gain or Loss	13,000	
	Accounts Receivable (£)		13,000
	To adjust the value of the £ receivable to the new spot rate of $1.272 and record a foreign exchange loss resulting from the depreciation of the £ since December 31 (Fair Value Hedge Step C.1 in Exhibit 9.2).		
	Forward Contract	6,000	
	Foreign Exchange Gain or Loss		6,000
	To adjust the carrying value of the forward contract to its current fair value of $16,000 and record a forward contract gain for the change in the fair value since December 31 (Fair Value Hedge Step C.2 in Exhibit 9.2).		
	Foreign Exchange Gain or Loss	1,000	
	Accumulated Other Comprehensive Income (AOCI)		1,000
	To transfer the amount deferred in AOCI to net income to accurately reflect the current period's amortization of forward contract discount (Fair Value Hedge Step C.3. in Exhibit 9.2).		
	Foreign Currency (£)	1,272,000	
	Accounts Receivable (£)		1,272,000
	To record receipt of £1 million from the German customer as an asset at the spot rate of $1.272 (Fair Value Hedge Step C.4. in Exhibit 9.2).		
	Cash	1,288,000	
	Foreign Currency (£)		1,272,000
	Forward Contract		16,000
	To record settlement of the forward contract (i.e., record receipt of $1,288,000 in exchange for delivery of £1 million) and remove the forward contract from the accounts (Fair Value Hedge Step C.5. in Exhibit 9.2).		

The first three entries result in the recognition of a net foreign exchange loss of $8,000 ($13,000 – $6,000 +$1,000), which is equal to the current period's amortization of forward contract discount.

The impact on net income for the year 2021 follows:

Net foreign exchange gain (loss)	$(8,000)
Impact on net income	$(8,000)

Discussion Question

DO WE HAVE A GAIN OR WHAT?

Ahnuld Corporation, a health juice producer, recently expanded its sales through exports to foreign markets. Earlier this year, the company negotiated the sale of several thousand cases of turnip juice to a retailer in the country of Tcheckia. The customer is unwilling to assume the risk of having to pay in U.S. dollars. Desperate to enter the Tcheckian market, the vice president for international sales agrees to denominate the sale in tchecks, the national currency of Tcheckia. The current exchange rate for 1 tcheck is $2.00. In addition, the customer indicates that it cannot pay until it sells all of the juice. Payment of 100,000 tchecks is scheduled for six months from the date of sale.

Fearful that the tcheck might depreciate in value over the next six months, the head of the risk management department at Ahnuld Corporation enters into a forward contract to sell tchecks in six months at a forward rate of $1.80. The forward contract is designated as a fair value hedge of the tcheck receivable. Six months later, when Ahnuld receives payment from the Tcheckian customer, the exchange rate for the tcheck is $1.70. The corporate treasurer calls the head of the risk management department into her office.

Treasurer: I see that your decision to hedge our foreign currency position on that sale to Tcheckia was a bad one.

Department head: What do you mean? We have a gain on that forward contract. We're $10,000 better off from having entered into that hedge.

Treasurer: That's not what the books say. The accountants have recorded a net loss of $20,000 on that particular deal. I'm afraid I'm not going to be able to pay you a bonus this year. Another bad deal like this one and I'm going to have to demote you back to the interest rate swap department.

Department head: Those bean counters have messed up again. I told those guys in international sales that selling to customers in Tcheckia was risky, but at least by hedging our exposure, we managed to receive a reasonable amount of cash on that deal. In fact, we ended up with a gain of $10,000 on the hedge. Tell the accountants to check their debits and credits again. I'm sure they just put a debit in the wrong place or some accounting thing like that.

Have the accountants made a mistake? Does the company have a loss, a gain, or both from this forward contract?

Over the two periods, Eximco has recognized a total net foreign exchange loss of $12,000, which is equal to the original discount on forward contract, and accurately reflects the cost of extending credit to the British customer. (The company receives only $1,288,000 in cash rather than $1,300,000 if it had received payment on the date of sale.)

The net effect on the balance sheet for the two periods is an increase in Cash of $1,288,000 with a corresponding increase in Retained Earnings of $1,288,000 ($1,296,000 in 2020 less $8,000 in 2021). The fair value of the forward contract of $16,000 reflects the net benefit (increase in cash inflow) from Eximco's decision to hedge the British pound receivable. (The company receives $1,288,000 from entering into a forward contract rather than $1,272,000 if it had not hedged the British pound account receivable.)

Companies often cannot (or do not bother to) designate as hedges the forward contracts they use to hedge foreign currency–denominated assets and liabilities. In those cases, the company accounts for the forward contract as if it were a speculative investment. The company reports an undesignated forward contract on the balance sheet at fair value as an asset or liability and immediately recognizes changes in the fair value of the forward contract in net income. This accounting treatment is the same as if the forward contract had been designated as a fair value hedge. However, there would be no adjustment to Foreign Exchange Gain or Loss to reflect the current period's amortization of forward contract discount. Therefore, the only difference between a forward contract designated as a fair value hedge of a foreign currency–denominated asset or liability and an undesignated (speculative) forward contract is the pattern in which the company recognizes the original forward discount in net income.

Option Hedge of a Foreign Currency–Denominated Asset

As an alternative to a forward contract, Eximco could hedge its exposure to foreign exchange risk arising from the British pound account receivable by purchasing a foreign currency put option. A put option would give Eximco the right but not the obligation to sell 1 million British pounds on March 1, 2021, at a predetermined strike price. Assume that on December 1, 2020, Eximco purchases an over-the-counter option from its bank with a strike price of \$1.300 when the spot rate is \$1.300 and pays a premium of \$0.020 per British pound.[12] Thus, the purchase price for the option is \$20,000 (\$0.020 × £1 million).

Because the strike price and spot rate are the same, no intrinsic value is associated with this option. The premium is based solely on time value; that is, it is possible that the British pound will depreciate and the spot rate on March 1, 2021, will be less than \$1.300, in which case the option will be "in the money." If the spot rate for British pounds on March 1, 2021, is less than the strike price of \$1.300, Eximco will exercise its option and sell its 1 million British pounds at the strike price of \$1.300. Conversely, if the spot rate for British pounds in three months is more than the strike price of \$1.300, Eximco will not exercise its option but will sell the British pounds it receives at the higher spot rate. By purchasing this option, Eximco is guaranteed a minimum cash flow from the export sale of \$1,280,000 (\$1,300,000 from exercising the option less the \$20,000 cost of the option). There is no limit to the maximum number of U.S. dollars that Eximco could receive.

As is true for other derivative financial instruments, authoritative accounting literature requires foreign currency options to be reported on the balance sheet at fair value. The fair value of a foreign currency option at the balance sheet date is determined by reference to the premium quoted by banks on that date for an option with a similar expiration date. Banks (and other sellers of options) determine the current premium by incorporating relevant variables at the balance sheet date into the modified Black-Scholes option pricing model. Changes in value for the British pound account receivable and the foreign currency option are summarized as follows:

		Account Receivable (£)		Option	Foreign Currency Option	
Date	Spot Rate	U.S. Dollar Value	Change in U.S. Dollar Value	Premium for 3/1/21	Fair Value	Change in Fair Value
12/1/20	\$1.300	\$1,300,000	\$ –0–	\$0.0200	\$20,000	\$ –0–
12/31/20	1.285	1,285,000	−15,000	0.0245	24,500	+4,500
3/1/21	1.272	1,272,000	−13,000	N/A	28,000	+3,500

The fair value of the foreign currency put option at December 1 is its cost of \$20,000. The spot rate for the British pound decreases during December, which causes an increase in the fair value of the put option; the right to sell British pounds at \$1.300 is of more value when the spot rate is \$1.285 (on December 31) than when the spot rate was \$1.300 (on December 1). The bank determines the fair value of the option at December 31 to be \$24,500. By March 1, the British pound spot rate has decreased to \$1.272. By exercising its option on March 1 at the

[12] The seller of the option determined the price of the option (the premium) by using a variation of the Black-Scholes option pricing formula.

strike price of $1.300, Eximco will receive $1,300,000 from its export sale, rather than only $1,272,000 if it were required to sell British pounds in the spot market on March 1. Thus, the option has a fair value of $28,000 on March 1.

We can decompose the fair value of the foreign currency option into its intrinsic value and time value components as follows:

Date	Fair Value	Intrinsic Value	Time Value	Change in Time Value
12/1/20	$20,000	$ –0–	$20,000	$ –0–
12/31/20	24,500	15,000	9,500	–10,500
3/1/21	28,000	28,000	–0–	–9,500

Because the option strike price of $1.300 is higher than the spot rate of $1.285 on December 31, the option has an intrinsic value of $15,000 on that date. The time value of the option decreases from $20,000 on December 1 to $9,500 on December 31. On March 1, the date of expiration, no time value remains, and the entire amount of fair value for the option is attributable to intrinsic value.

Option Designated as Cash Flow Hedge

Assume that Eximco designates the foreign currency option as a *cash flow hedge* of a foreign currency–denominated asset. Eximco has elected to exclude the time value of the option from the assessment of hedge effectiveness. Furthermore, the company has chosen to recognize the change in the option's time value in net income (rather than apply straight-line amortization). The company prepares the following journal entries to account for the foreign currency transaction and the related foreign currency option:

2020 Journal Entries—Option Designated as a Cash Flow Hedge

Date	Account	Debit	Credit
12/1/20	Accounts Receivable (£)	1,300,000	
	Sales		1,300,000
	To record the sale and £1 million account receivable at the spot rate of $1.300 (Cash Flow Hedge Step A.1 in Exhibit 9.2).		
	Foreign Currency Option	20,000	
	Cash		20,000
	To record the purchase of the foreign currency option as an asset at its fair value of $20,000 (Cash Flow Hedge Step A.2 in Exhibit 9.2).		

From December 1 to December 31, the British pound account receivable decreases in value by $15,000, and the option increases in value by $4,500. The company prepares the following journal entries on December 31 to reflect these changes:

Date	Account	Debit	Credit
12/31/20	Foreign Exchange Gain or Loss	15,000	
	Accounts Receivable (£)		15,000
	To adjust the value of the £ receivable to the new spot rate of $1.285 and recognize a foreign exchange loss resulting from the depreciation of the £ since December 1 (Cash Flow Hedge Step B.1 in Exhibit 9.2).		
	Foreign Currency Option	4,500	
	Other Comprehensive Income (OCI)		4,500
	To adjust the fair value of the option from $20,000 to $24,500 and recognize the change in fair value in OCI (Cash Flow Hedge Step B.2 in Exhibit 9.2).		

(continued)

(continued)

	Other Comprehensive Income (OCI)	15,000	
	Foreign Exchange Gain or Loss		15,000
	To record a foreign exchange gain on the foreign currency option (to offset the foreign exchange loss on the account receivable) with a corresponding debit to OCI (Cash Flow Hedge Step B.3 in Exhibit 9.2).		
	Foreign Exchange Gain or Loss	10,500	
	Other Comprehensive Income (OCI)		10,500
	To recognize the change in the time value of the option as a decrease in net income with a corresponding credit to OCI (Cash Flow Hedge Step B.4 in Exhibit 9.2).		

The first three journal entries prepared on December 31 result in the British pound account receivable and the foreign currency option being reported on the balance sheet at fair value with a net foreign exchange gain (loss) of zero reflected in net income, which is consistent with the concept of hedge accounting. The final entry serves to recognize a portion of the option cost in net income, in the same line item in which changes in the $ value of the account receivable are recognized.

The impact on net income for the year 2020 follows:

Sales	$1,300,000
Net foreign exchange gain (loss)	(10,500)
Impact on net income	$1,289,500

The effect on the December 31, 2020, balance sheet is as follows:

Assets		**Liabilities and Stockholders' Equity**	
Cash	$ (20,000)	Retained earnings	$1,289,500
Accounts receivable (£)	1,285,000		
Foreign currency option	24,500		
	$1,289,500		

At March 1, 2021, the option has increased in fair value by $3,500—intrinsic value increases by $13,000 and time value decreases by $9,500. The accounting entries made in 2021 are presented next.

2021 Journal Entries—Option Designated as a Cash Flow Hedge

3/1/21	Foreign Exchange Gain or Loss	13,000	
	Accounts Receivable (£)		13,000
	To adjust the value of the £ receivable to the spot rate of $1.272 and recognize a foreign exchange loss resulting from the depreciation of the £ since December 31 (Cash Flow Hedge Step C.1 in Exhibit 9.2).		
	Foreign Currency Option	3,500	
	Other Comprehensive Income (OCI)		3,500
	To adjust the fair value of the option from $24,500 to $28,000 and recognize the change in fair value in OCI (Cash Flow Hedge Step C.2 in Exhibit 9.2).		
	Other Comprehensive Income (OCI)	13,000	
	Foreign Exchange Gain or Loss		13,000
	To record a foreign exchange gain on the foreign currency option (to offset the foreign exchange loss on the account receivable) with a corresponding debit to OCI (Cash Flow Hedge Step C.3 in Exhibit 9.2).		

(continued)

(*continued*)

	Foreign Exchange Gain or Loss	9,500	
	Other Comprehensive Income (OCI).		9,500
	To recognize the change in the time value of the option as a decrease in net income with a corresponding credit to OCI (Cash Flow Hedge Step C.4 in Exhibit 9.2).		

The first three entries on March 1 result in the British pound account receivable and the foreign currency option being reported at their fair values, with a net gain (loss) of zero. The fourth entry serves to recognize the remaining cost of the option in net income.

The next two journal entries recognize the receipt of British pounds from the customer, close out the British pound account receivable, and record the exercise of the foreign currency option.

3/1/21	Foreign Currency (£).	1,272,000	
	Accounts Receivable (£)		1,272,000
	To record receipt of £1 million as an asset at the spot rate of $1.300 (Cash Flow Hedge Step C.5 in Exhibit 9.2).		
	Cash	1,300,000	
	Foreign Currency (£).		1,272,000
	Foreign Currency Option.		28,000
	To record exercise of the option (i.e., record receipt of $1,300,000 in exchange for delivery of £1 million) and remove the foreign currency option from the accounts (Cash Flow Hedge Step C.6 in Exhibit 9.2).		

The impact on net income for the year 2021 is

Net foreign exchange gain (loss).	$(9,500)
Impact on net income	$(9,500)

Over the two accounting periods, Eximco reports sales of $1,300,000 and a cumulative net foreign exchange loss of $20,000. The net foreign exchange loss is equal to the original cost of the foreign currency option. The net effect on the balance sheet is an increase in Cash of $1,280,000 ($1,300,000 – $20,000) with a corresponding increase in Retained Earnings.

The net benefit from having acquired the option is $8,000. This is the difference between the net amount Eximco received from executing the option ($1,280,000) and the amount Eximco would have received if it had not acquired the option ($1,272,000). This "gain" is equal to the increase in fair value of the option over its life, and is not directly reflected in net income.

Option Designated as Fair Value Hedge

Assume that Eximco decides not to designate the foreign currency option as a cash flow hedge but to treat it as a fair value hedge. In that case, the company recognizes the change in fair value of the option directly to net income. Furthermore, the company excludes the time value of the option in assessing hedge effectiveness and recognizes each period's change in time value in net income. The journal entries for 2020 are shown next.

2020 Journal Entries—Option Designated as a Fair Value Hedge

12/1/20	Accounts Receivable (£).	1,300,000	
	Sales		1,300,000
	To record the sale and £1 million account receivable at the spot rate of $1.300 (Fair Value Hedge Step A.1 in Exhibit 9.2).		

(*continued*)

(continued)

Date	Account	Debit	Credit
	Foreign Currency Option.	20,000	
	Cash		20,000
	To record the purchase of the foreign currency option as an asset at its fair value of $20,000 (Fair Value Hedge Step A.2 in Exhibit 9.2).		
12/31/20	Foreign Exchange Gain or Loss.	15,000	
	Accounts Receivable (£)		15,000
	To adjust the value of the £ receivable to the new spot rate of $1.285 and recognize a foreign exchange loss resulting from the depreciation of the £ since December 1 (Fair Value Hedge Step B.1 in Exhibit 9.2).		
	Foreign Currency Option.	4,500	
	Foreign Exchange Gain or Loss.		4,500
	To adjust the fair value of the option from $20,000 to $24,500 and recognize the change in fair value of the option since December 1 as a gain (Fair Value Hedge Step B.2 in Exhibit 9.2).		

The two journal entries on December 31, 2020 serve to (a) measure the foreign currency account receivable and foreign currency option at their fair values, and (b) simultaneously recognize the change in the time value of the option in net income. The net foreign exchange loss recognized in 2020 is $10,500 ($15,000 – $4,500), which equals the change in the time value of the option for that year. There is no need to record any additional journal entries.

The impact on net income for the year 2020 follows:

Sales	$1,300,000
Net foreign exchange gain (loss).	(10,500)
Impact on net income	$1,289,500

2021 Journal Entries—Option Designated as a Fair Value Hedge

Date	Account	Debit	Credit
3/1/21	Foreign Exchange Gain or Loss.	13,000	
	Accounts Receivable (£)		13,000
	To adjust the value of the £ receivable to the new spot rate of $1.272 and recognize a foreign exchange loss resulting from the depreciation of the £ since December 31 (Fair Value Hedge Step C.1 in Exhibit 9.2).		
	Foreign Currency Option.	3,500	
	Foreign Exchange Gain or Loss.		3,500
	To adjust the fair value of the option from $24,500 to $28,000 and recognize the change in fair value of the option since December 31 as a gain (Fair Value Hedge Step C.2 in Exhibit 9.2).		
	Foreign Currency (£).	1,272,000	
	Accounts Receivable (£)		1,272,000
	To record receipt of £1 million as an asset at the spot rate of $1.272 (Fair Value Hedge Step C.3 in Exhibit 9.2).		
	Cash	1,300,000	
	Foreign Currency (£).		1,272,000
	Foreign Currency Option.		28,000
	To record exercise of the option (i.e., record receipt of $1,300,000 in exchange for delivery of £1 million) and remove the foreign currency option from the accounts (Fair Value Hedge Step C.4 in Exhibit 9.2).		

The impact on net income for the year 2021 is	
Net foreign exchange gain (loss)	$(9,500)
Impact on net income	$(9,500)

Over the two accounting periods, Eximco reports sales of $1,300,000 and a cumulative net foreign exchange loss of $20,000 ($10,500 in 2020 and $9,500 in 2021). The net effect on the balance sheet is an increase in Cash of $1,280,000 ($1,300,000 – $20,000) with a corresponding increase in Retained Earnings.

The accounting for an option used as a fair value hedge of a foreign currency–denominated asset or liability is the same as if the option had been considered a speculative derivative. The only possible advantage to designating the option as a fair value hedge would relate to the disclosures made in the notes to the financial statements explaining the hedging relationship.

Spot Rate Exceeds Strike Price

If the spot rate on March 1, 2021, had turned out to be $1.302 (i.e., higher than the strike price of $1.300), Eximco would allow its option to expire unexercised. Instead it would sell the foreign currency (£) it receives on March 1, 2021, at the spot rate on that date. In this case, the company will realize a net cash inflow of $1,282,000 ($1,302,000 less $20,000 for the option). The fair value of the foreign currency option on March 1, 2021, would be zero. The journal entries for 2020 to reflect this scenario would be the same as the preceding ones. The option would be reported as an asset on the December 31, 2020, balance sheet at $24,500, and the £ receivable would have a carrying value of $1,285,000. The entries on March 1, 2021, assuming a spot rate on that date of $1.302 (rather than $1.272), would be as follows:

3/1/21	Accounts Receivable (£)	17,000	
	Foreign Exchange Gain or Loss		17,000
	To adjust the value of the £ receivable to the new spot rate of $1.302 and record a foreign exchange gain resulting from the appreciation of the £ since December 31 (Fair Value Hedge Step C.1. in Exhibit 9.2).		
	Foreign Exchange Gain or Loss	24,500	
	Foreign Currency Option		24,500
	To adjust the fair value of the option from $24,500 to $0 and recognize a loss for the change in fair value since December 31 (Fair Value Hedge Step C.2. in Exhibit 9.2).		

The above two entries result in a net foreign exchange loss of $7,500 recognized in 2021, which results in a cumulative net loss of $18,000 since December 1, 2020. This accurately measures the net cost of extending credit to the British customer ($1,282,000 in net cash inflow versus $1,300,000). There is no need to adjust the net foreign exchange loss to reflect the current period's change in the time value of the option.

The next two journal entries recognize the receipt of British pounds from the customer, close out the British pound account receivable, and record the sale of British pounds at the current spot rate.

	Foreign Currency (£)	1,302,000	
	Accounts Receivable (£)		1,302,000
	To record receipt of £1 million as an asset at the spot rate of $1.302 (Fair Value Hedge Step C.3 in Exhibit 9.2).		
	Cash	1,302,000	
	Foreign Currency (£)		1,302,000
	To record the sale of £1 million at the spot rate of $1.302 (Fair Value Hedge Step C.4 in Exhibit 9.2).		

The overall impact on net income for the year 2021 is:	
Net foreign exchange gain (loss)	$(7,500)
Impact on net income	$(7,500)

In this situation, over the two accounting periods, Eximco reports Sales of $1,300,000 and a cumulative net foreign exchange loss of $18,000 ($10,500 in 2020 and $7,500 in 2021). The net effect on the balance sheet is an increase in Cash of $1,282,000 ($1,302,000 – $20,000) with a corresponding increase in Retained Earnings.

LO 9-8

Account for forward contracts and options used as hedges of foreign currency firm commitments.

Hedge of Unrecognized Foreign Currency Firm Commitment

In the examples thus far, Eximco does not enter into a hedge of its export sale until it actually makes the sale. Assume now that on December 1, 2020, Eximco receives and accepts an order from a British customer to deliver goods on March 1, 2021, at a price of 1 million British pounds. Assume further that under the terms of the sale agreement, Eximco will ship the goods to the British customer on March 1, 2021, and will receive immediate payment on delivery. Although Eximco will not make the sale until March 1, 2021, it has a firm commitment to make the sale and receive 1 million British pounds in three months. This creates a British pound asset exposure to foreign exchange risk as of December 1, 2020. On that date, Eximco wants to hedge against an adverse change in the value of the British pound over the next three months. This is known as a *hedge of a foreign currency–denominated firm commitment*. U.S. GAAP allows hedges of firm commitments to be designated either as cash flow or fair value hedges. However, because the results of fair value hedge accounting are intuitively more appealing, we do not cover cash flow hedge accounting for firm commitments.

A firm commitment is an executory contract; the company has not delivered goods nor has the customer paid for them. Normally, executory contracts are not recognized in financial statements. However, when a firm commitment is hedged using a derivative financial instrument, hedge accounting requires explicit recognition on the balance sheet at fair value of both the derivative financial instrument (forward contract or option) and the firm commitment. The change in fair value of the firm commitment results in a gain or loss that offsets the loss or gain on the hedging instrument (forward contract or option), thus achieving the goal of hedge accounting. This raises the conceptual question of how to measure the fair value of the firm commitment. When a forward contract is used as the hedging instrument, the fair value of the firm commitment is determined through reference to changes in the forward exchange rate. Changes in the spot exchange rate are used to determine the fair value of the firm commitment when a foreign currency option is the hedging instrument.

Forward Contract Fair Value Hedge of a Firm Commitment

To hedge its firm commitment exposure to a decline in the U.S. dollar value of the British pound, Eximco decides to enter into a forward contract on December 1, 2020. As in previous examples, assume that on that date, the spot rate for British pounds is $1.300 and the three-month forward rate is $1.288. Eximco signs a contract with New World Bank to deliver 1 million British pounds in three months in exchange for $1,288,000. No cash changes hands on December 1, 2020. Eximco measures the fair value of the firm commitment through changes in the forward exchange rate. Because the fair value of the forward contract also is measured using changes in the forward rate, the gains and losses on the firm commitment and forward contract exactly offset. The fair value of the forward contract and firm commitment are determined as follows:

		Forward Contract		Firm Commitment	
Date	Forward Rate to 3/1/21	Fair Value	Change in Fair Value	Fair Value	Change in Fair Value
12/1/20	$1.277	$ –0–	$ –0–	$ –0–	$ –0–
12/31/20	1.278	10,000*	+10,000	(10,000)*	–10,000
3/1/21	1.272 (spot)	16,000†	+ 6,000	(16,000)†	– 6,000

*$1,288,000 – $1,278,000 = $10,000. Discounting to present value is ignored for simplicity.
†$1,288,000 – $1,272,000 = $16,000.

Eximco pays nothing to enter into the forward contract at December 1, 2020. Both the forward contract and the firm commitment have a fair value of zero on that date. As a result, there are no journal entries needed on December 1, 2020. At December 31, 2020, the forward rate for a contract to deliver British pounds on March 1, 2021, is $1.278. A forward contract could be entered into on December 31, 2020, to sell 1 million British pounds for $1,278,000 on March 1, 2021. Because Eximco is committed to sell 1 million British pounds for $1,288,000, the value of the forward contract is $10,000. The fair value of the firm commitment is also measured through reference to changes in the forward rate. At December 31, 2020, the firm commitment is a liability of $(10,000). To apply the steps in accounting for a fair value hedge of a firm commitment at the balance sheet date, on December 31, 2020, Eximco will

1. Adjust the forward contract to fair value, which results in the recognition of an asset of $10,000, and recognize the counterpart as a foreign exchange loss in net income (Fair Value Hedge Step B.1 in Exhibit 9.2).
2. Adjust the firm commitment to fair value, which results in the recognition of a liability of $10,000, and recognize the counterpart as a foreign exchange gain in net income (Fair Value Hedge Step B.2 in Exhibit 9.2).

Because changes in the fair value of the firm commitment are measured using changes in the forward exchange rate, the original forward points may not be excluded from the assessment of hedge effectiveness. Thus, the *forward contract discount is not separately amortized to net income.*

The journal entries in 2020 to account for the forward contract fair value hedge of a foreign currency firm commitment are as follows.

2020 Journal Entries—Forward Contract Fair Value Hedge of Firm Commitment

Date	Account / Explanation	Debit	Credit
12/1/20	There is no entry to record either the sales agreement or the forward contract because both are executory contracts.		
	A memorandum designates the forward contract as a hedge of the risk of changes in the fair value of the firm commitment resulting from changes in the U.S. dollar–British pound forward exchange rate (Fair Value Hedge Steps A.1 and A.2 in Exhibit 9.2).		
12/31/20	Forward Contract	10,000	
	Foreign Exchange Gain or Loss		10,000
	To record the forward contract as an asset at its fair value of $10,000 and recognize the change in fair value since December 1 as a gain (Fair Value Hedge Step B.1 in Exhibit 9.2).		
	Foreign Exchange Gain or Loss	10,000	
	Firm Commitment		10,000
	To record the firm commitment as a liability at fair value of $10,000 and recognize the change in fair value since December 1 as a loss (Fair Value Hedge Step B.2 in Exhibit 9.2).		

Eximco reports the forward contract as an asset and reports the firm commitment as a liability on the December 31, 2020, balance sheet. Consistent with the objective of hedge accounting, the loss on the firm commitment offsets the gain on the forward contract such that the impact on net income is zero.

On March 1, 2021, the forward rate to sell British pounds on that date, by definition, is the spot rate, $1.272. At that rate, Eximco could sell 1 million British pounds for $1,272,000. Because Eximco has a contract to sell British pounds for $1,282,000, the fair value of the forward contract on March 1, 2021, is $16,000. The firm commitment has a value of $(16,000).

On March 1, 2021, Eximco recognizes changes in the fair value of the forward contract and firm commitment since December 31. The company then records the sale and the settlement of the forward contract. Finally, the balance in the firm commitment account is closed to net income (as an adjustment to Sales). The required journal entries are as follows.

2021 Journal Entries—Forward Contract Fair Value Hedge of Firm Commitment

Date	Account	Debit	Credit
3/1/21	Forward Contract	6,000	
	Foreign Exchange Gain or Loss		6,000
	To adjust the fair value of the forward contract asset from $10,000 to $16,000 and recognize the change in fair value since December 31 as a gain (Fair Value Hedge Step C.1 in Exhibit 9.2).		
	Foreign Exchange Gain or Loss	6,000	
	Firm Commitment		6,000
	To adjust the fair value of the firm commitment liability from $10,000 to $16,000 and recognize the change in fair value since December 31 as a loss (Fair Value Hedge Step C.2 in Exhibit 9.2).		
	Foreign Currency (£)	1,272,000	
	Sales		1,272,000
	To record the sale and the receipt of €1 million as an asset at the spot rate of $1.30 (Fair Value Hedge Step C.3 in Exhibit 9.2).		
	Cash	1,288,000	
	Foreign Currency (£)		1,272,000
	Forward Contract		16,000
	To record settlement of the forward contract (receipt of $1,305,000 in exchange for delivery of £1 million) and remove the forward contract asset from the accounts (Fair Value Hedge Step C.4 in Exhibit 9.2).		
	Firm Commitment	16,000	
	Sales		16,000
	To transfer the balance in the firm commitment account to net income (as an adjustment to Sales) (Fair Value Hedge Step C.5 in Exhibit 9.2).		

As a result of these entries, Sales are effectively recognized at the forward exchange rate ($1.288 forward rate × £1 million = $1,288,000), which is exactly equal to the increase in Cash resulting from the export sale. Once again, the gain on forward contract and the loss on firm commitment offset. The original forward contract discount has not been separately recognized in net income.

Option Fair Value Hedge of Firm Commitment

Now assume that to hedge its firm commitment exposure to a decline in the U.S. dollar value of the British pound, Eximco purchases a put option to sell 1 million British pounds on March 1, 2021, at a strike price of $1.300. The premium for such an option on December 1, 2020, is $0.020 per British pound. With this option, Eximco is guaranteed a minimum cash flow from the export sale of $1,280,000 ($1,300,000 from option exercise less $20,000 cost of the option).

In this case, Eximco measures the fair value of the firm commitment by referring to changes in the U.S. dollar–British pound spot rate. The fair value and changes in fair value for the foreign currency option and firm commitment are summarized here:

		Foreign Currency Option			Firm Commitment	
Date	Option Premium for 3/1/21	Fair Value	Change in Fair Value	Spot Rate	Fair Value	Change in Fair Value
12/1/20	$0.0200	$20,000	$ –0–	$1.300	$ –0–	$ –0–
12/31/20	0.0245	24,500	+4,500	1.285	(15,000)*	–15,000
3/1/21	0.0280	28,000	+3,500	1.272	(28,000)†	–13,000

*$1,300,000 – $1,285,000 = $15,000. Discounting to present value is ignored for simplicity.
†$1,300,000 – $1,272,000 = $28,000.

At December 1, 2020, given the spot rate of $1.300, the firm commitment to receive 1 million British pounds in three months would generate a cash flow of $1,300,000. At December 31, 2020, the cash flow that the firm commitment could generate decreases by $15,000 to $1,285,000. Therefore, the fair value of the firm commitment at December 31, 2020, is $15,000. On March 1, 2021, when the spot rate is $1.272, the fair value of the firm commitment is $1,272,000 $(20,000) on March 1, 2021.

Because changes in the fair value of the firm commitment are measured using changes in the spot exchange rate, the time value of the option may be excluded from the assessment of hedge effectiveness. Through the process of revaluing the option and firm commitment over time, and as long as the option has a positive intrinsic value, the company will automatically recognize the change in the option's time value in net income. There is no need to record an additional entry related to the excluded component. However, an additional entry to adjust the net amount recognized as foreign exchange loss is necessary when the intrinsic value of the option is zero.

The journal entries to account for the foreign currency option and related foreign currency firm commitment are discussed next.

2020 Journal Entries—Option Fair Value Hedge of Firm Commitment

12/1/20	Foreign Currency Option.	20,000	
	Cash		20,000
	To record the purchase of the foreign currency option as an asset (Fair Value Hedge Step A.2 in Exhibit 9.2).		
	There is no entry to record the sales agreement because it is an executory contract (Fair Value Hedge Step A.1 in Exhibit 9.2). Eximco prepares a memorandum to designate the option as a hedge of the risk of changes in the fair value of the firm commitment resulting from changes in the spot exchange rate.		

12/31/20	Foreign Currency Option.	4,500	
	Foreign Exchange Gain or Loss.		4,500
	To adjust the fair value of the option from $20,000 to $24,500 and record the change in the value of the option since December 1 as a foreign exchange gain (Fair Value Hedge Step B.1 in Exhibit 9.2).		
	Foreign Exchange Gain or Loss.	15,000	
	Firm Commitment.		15,000
	To record the firm commitment as a liability at its fair value of $15,000 and record the change in fair value of the firm commitment since December 1 as a foreign exchange loss (Fair Value Hedge Step B.2 in Exhibit 9.2).		

Because the fair value of the firm commitment is based on changes in the spot rate whereas the fair value of the option is based on a variety of factors, the loss on the firm commitment and gain on the option do not exactly offset. The difference between the gain and the loss is

$10,500, which effectively recognizes the current period's change in time value of the option in net income. No additional entry is needed.

The impact on net income for the year 2020 is as follows:

Net foreign exchange gain (loss)	$(10,500)
Impact on net income	$(10,500)

The effect on the December 31, 2020, balance sheet follows:

Assets		Liabilities and Stockholders' Equity	
Cash	$(20,000)	Firm commitment	$ 15,000
Foreign currency option	24,500	Retained earnings	(10,500)
	$ 4,500		$ 4,500

On March 1, 2021, following fair value hedge accounting procedures, Eximco first recognizes changes in the fair value of the option and the fair value of the firm commitment since December 31. The company then records the sale and the exercise of the option. Finally, the $28,000 balance in the firm commitment account is closed to net income (as an adjustment to Sales). The required journal entries are as follows.

2021 Journal Entries—Option Fair Value Hedge of Firm Commitment

3/1/21	Foreign Currency Option	3,500	
	Foreign Exchange Gain or Loss		3,500
	To adjust the fair value of the foreign currency option from $24,500 to $28,000 and recognize the change in fair value since December 31 as a foreign exchange gain (Fair Value Hedge Step C.1 in Exhibit 9.2)		
	Foreign Exchange Gain or Loss	13,000	
	Firm Commitment		13,000
	To adjust the fair value of the firm commitment from $(15,000) to $(28,000) and recognize the change in fair value since December 31 as a foreign exchange loss (Fair Value Hedge Step C.2 in Exhibit 9.2)		
	Foreign Currency (£)	1,272,000	
	Sales		1,272,000
	To record the sale and the receipt of £1 million as an asset at the spot rate of $1.272 (Fair Value Hedge Step C.3 in Exhibit 9.2).		
	Cash	1,300,000	
	Foreign Currency (£)		1,272,000
	Foreign Currency Option		28,000
	To record exercise of the foreign currency option (receipt of $1,300,000 in exchange for delivery of £1 million) and remove the foreign currency option from the accounts (Fair Value Hedge Step C.4 in Exhibit 9.2).		
	Firm Commitment	28,000	
	Sales		28,000
	To close the firm commitment to net income (as an adjustment to Sales) (Fair Value Hedge Step C.5 in Exhibit 9.2).		

As a result of these entries, Sales are effectively recognized at the strike price on the option ($1.30 strike price × £1 million = $1,300,000). The difference ($9,500) between the gain on the option and the loss on the firm commitment serves to recognize the current period's change in time value of the option in net income. The following is the impact on net income for the year 2021:

Sales	$1,300,000
Net foreign exchange gain (loss)	(9,500)
Impact on net income	$1,290,500

The net increase in net income over the two accounting periods is $1,280,000 ($1,290,500 increase in 2021 less $10,500 decrease in 2020), which exactly equals the net cash flow realized on the export sale ($1,300,000 from exercising the option less $20,000 to purchase the option).

LO 9-9

Account for forward contracts and options used as hedges of forecasted foreign currency transactions.

Hedge of Forecasted Foreign Currency Transaction

Cash flow hedge accounting also is used for foreign currency derivatives used to hedge the cash flow risk associated with a forecasted foreign currency transaction. For hedge accounting to apply, the forecasted transaction must be probable (likely to occur), the hedge must be highly effective in offsetting fluctuations in the cash flow associated with the foreign currency risk, and the hedging relationship must be properly documented.

Accounting for a hedge of a forecasted transaction differs from accounting for a hedge of a foreign currency firm commitment in two ways:

1. Unlike the accounting for a firm commitment, there is no recognition of the forecasted transaction or gains and losses on the forecasted transaction. (Because there is no recognition of an asset or liability, there is no fair value exposure to foreign exchange risk. Thus, fair value hedge accounting is not appropriate for hedges of forecasted transactions.)
2. The company reports the hedging instrument (forward contract or option) at fair value and recognizes changes in the fair value of the hedging instrument in other comprehensive income. On the projected date of the forecasted transaction, the company transfers the cumulative change in the fair value of the hedging instrument from accumulated other comprehensive income (balance sheet) to net income (income statement). The impact on net income is reported in the same line item in which the income effect of the forecasted transaction is reflected.

Forward Contract Cash Flow Hedge of a Forecasted Transaction

To demonstrate the accounting for a hedge of a forecasted foreign currency transaction, assume that Eximco has a long-term relationship with its British customer and can reliably forecast that the customer will require delivery of goods costing 1 million British pounds in March 2021. Confident that it will receive 1 million British pounds on March 1, 2021, Eximco enters into a forward contract on December 1, 2020, to sell 1 million British pounds on March 1, 2021, at a forward rate of $1.288. The facts are essentially the same as those for the hedge of a firm commitment except that Eximco does not receive a sales order from the British customer until late February 2021. Relevant exchange rates and the fair value of the forward contract are as follows:

		Forward Contract	
Date	Forward Rate to 3/1/21	Fair Value	Change in Fair Value
12/1/20	$1.288	$ -0-	$ -0-
12/31/20	1.278	10,000*	+10,000
3/1/21	1.272 (spot)	16,000†	+ 6,000

*$1,288,000 – $1,278,000 = $10,000. Discounting to present value is ignored for simplicity.
†$1,288,000 – $1,272,000 = $16,000.

The company elects to exclude the forward points from assessment of hedge effectiveness, and chooses to amortize the forward contract discount using the straight-line method on a monthly basis. The original discount on the forward contract is determined by the difference in the £ spot rate and the three-month forward rate on December 1, 2020: ($1.300 – $1.288) × £1 million = $12,000. The discount will be amortized at the rate of $4,000 per month.

2020 Journal Entries—Forward Contract Hedge of a Forecasted Transaction

12/1/20	There is no entry to record either the forecasted sale or the forward contract. A memorandum designates the spot component of the forward contract as a hedge of the risk of changes in the cash flows related to the forecasted sale, and indicates that the forward component of the forward contract will be systematically amortized to net income (Cash Flow Hedge Steps A.1 and A.2 in Exhibit 9.2).		

On December 31, the forward contract is recognized as an asset at its fair value, with the counterpart reflected in other comprehensive income (OCI). The forward contract discount is amortized to net income (as an adjustment to Sales), with the counterpart also reflected in OCI. The necessary journal entries are as follows:

12/31/20	Forward Contract	10,000	
	Other Comprehensive Income (OCI).		10,000
	To record the forward contract as an asset at its fair value of $10,000 with a corresponding credit to OCI (Cash Flow Hedge Step B.2 in Exhibit 9.2).		
	Sales	4,000	
	Other Comprehensive Income (OCI).		4,000
	To record straight-line amortization of the forward contract discount: $12,000 × ⅓ = $4,000 (Cash Flow Hedge Step B.4 in Exhibit 9.2).		

The debit to Sales reduces 2020 net income by $4,000. After net income is closed to Retained Earnings and OCI is closed to Accumulated Other Comprehensive Income (AOCI), the impact on the December 31, 2020, balance sheet is as follows:

Assets		**Liabilities and Stockholders' Equity**	
Forward contract.	$10,000	Retained earnings.	$(4,000)
	$10,000	AOCI	14,000
			$10,000

On March 1, 2021, the carrying value of the forward contract asset is adjusted to fair value, and the forward contract discount is amortized to net income (as an adjustment to Sales). Then the sale and the settlement of the forward contract are recorded. Finally, the balance in AOCI related to the hedge of the forecasted transaction is closed as an adjustment to net income (Sales). The following entries are required:

2021 Journal Entries—Forward Contract Hedge of a Forecasted Transaction

3/1/21	Forward Contract	6,000	
	Other Comprehensive Income (OCI).		6,000
	To adjust the carrying value of the forward contract to its current fair value of $16,000 with a corresponding credit to OCI (Cash Flow Hedge Step C.1 in Exhibit 9.2).		
3/1/21	Sales	8,000	
	Other Comprehensive Income (OCI).		8,000
	To record straight-line amortization of the forward contract discount: $12,000 × ⅔ = $8,000 (Cash Flow Hedge Step C.2 in Exhibit 9.2).		

(continued)

(continued)

		Debit	Credit
	Foreign Currency (£)	1,272,000	
	Sales		1,272,000
	To record the sale and the receipt of £1 million as an asset at the spot rate of $1.272 (Cash Flow Hedge Step C.3 in Exhibit 9.2).		
	Cash	1,288,000	
	Foreign Currency (£)		1,272,000
	Forward Contract		16,000
	To record settlement of the forward contract (receipt of $1,288,000 in exchange for delivery of £1 million) and remove the forward contract from the accounts (Cash Flow Hedge Step C.4 in Exhibit 9.2).		
	Accumulated Other Comprehensive Income (AOCI)	28,000	
	Sales		28,000
	To close AOCI as an adjustment to net income (Cash Flow Hedge Step C.5 in Exhibit 9.2).		

Note that prior to the final entry on March 1, 2021, OCI was closed to AOCI, which then had a credit balance of $28,000 ($14,000 in 2020 plus $14,000 in 2021).

As a result of these entries, the forward contract asset has been reduced to zero, as has been the balance in AOCI related to this forward contract.

The impact on net income for the year 2021 follows:

Sales	$1,292,000
Impact on net income	$1,292,000

Over the two accounting periods, $1,288,000 has been recognized in Sales, which equals the amount of net cash inflow realized from the sale.

Option Cash Flow Hedge of a Forecasted Transaction

Now assume that Eximco hedges its forecasted foreign currency transaction by purchasing a 1 million British pound put option on December 1, 2020. The option, which expires on March 1, 2021, has a strike price of $1.30 and a premium of $0.020 per British pound. The fair value of the option at relevant dates is as follows (same as in previous examples):

		Foreign Currency Option				
Date	Option Premium for 3/1/21	Fair Value	Change in Fair Value	Intrinsic Value	Time Value	Change in Time Value
12/1/20	$0.0200	$20,000	$ –0–	$ –0–	$20,000	$ –0–
12/31/20	0.0245	24,500	+ 4,500	15,000	9,500	–10,500
3/1/21	0.0280	28,000	+ 3,500	28,000	–0–	– 9,500

2020 Journal Entries—Option Hedge of a Forecasted Transaction

		Debit	Credit
12/1/20	Foreign Currency Option	20,000	
	Cash		20,000
	To record the purchase of the foreign currency option as an asset (Cash Flow Hedge Step A.2 in Exhibit 9.2).		
	There is no entry to record the forecasted sale. A memorandum designates the foreign currency option as a hedge of the risk of changes in the cash flows related to the forecasted sale and indicates that changes in the option's time value will be recognized in net income (Cash Flow Hedge Step A.1 in Exhibit 9.2).		

At December 31, the carrying value of the option is increased for the change in fair value since December 1, and the change in the time value of the option since December 1 is recognized in net income (as an adjustment to Sales). The required journal entries are as follows:

12/31/20	Foreign Currency Option.	4,500	
	Other Comprehensive Income (OCI).		4,500
	To adjust the carrying value of the option to its fair value with a corresponding credit to OCI (Cash Flow Hedge Step B.2. in Exhibit 9.2).		
	Sales	10,500	
	Other Comprehensive Income (OCI).		10,500
	To recognize the change in the time value of the option as a decrease in net income with a corresponding credit to OCI (Cash Flow Hedge Step B.4 in Exhibit 9.2).		

The impact on net income for the year 2020 follows:

Sales	$(10,500)
Impact on net income	$(10,500)

On the December 31, 2020, balance sheet, Cash is decreased by $20,000 and Foreign Currency Option is reported as $24,500, for a net increase in assets of $4,500. Retained Earnings is decreased by $10,500, while AOCI is increased by $15,000, for a net increase in stockholders' equity of $4,500.

On March 1, 2021, first, the carrying value of the option is adjusted to fair value, and the change in the time value of the option is recognized in net income (as an adjustment to Sales). Then the sale and the exercise of the foreign currency option are recorded. Finally, the balance in AOCI related to the hedge of the forecasted transaction is closed to net income (as an adjustment to Sales). The following entries are required:

2021 Journal Entries—Option Hedge of a Forecasted Transaction

3/1/21	Foreign Currency Option.	3,500	
	Other Comprehensive Income (OCI).		3,500
	To adjust the carrying value of the option to its fair value with a corresponding credit to OCI (Cash Flow Hedge Step C.1 in Exhibit 9.2).		
	Sales	9,500	
	Other Comprehensive Income (OCI).		9,500
	To recognize the change in the time value of the option as a decrease in net income with a corresponding credit to AOCI (Cash Flow Hedge Step C.2 in Exhibit 9.2).		
	Foreign Currency (£).	1,272,000	
	Sales		1,272,000
	To record the sale and the receipt of £1 million as an asset at the spot rate of $1.272 (Cash Flow Hedge Step C.3 in Exhibit 9.2).		
	Cash	1,300,000	
	Foreign Currency (£).		1,272,000
	Foreign Currency Option.		28,000
	To record the exercise of the foreign currency option (receipt of $1,300,000 in exchange for delivery of £1 million) and remove the foreign currency option from the accounts (Cash Flow Hedge Step C.4 in Exhibit 9.2).		
	Accumulated Other Comprehensive Income (AOCI)	28,000	
	Sales		28,000
	To close AOCI as an adjustment to net income (Cash Flow Hedge Step C.5 in Exhibit 9.2).		

Note that prior to the final entry on March 1, 2021, AOCI had a credit balance of $28,000 ($15,000 beginning credit balance from 2020 plus $13,000 from closing OCI in 2021).

As a result of these entries, the net amount recognized as Sales over the two periods is $1,280,000 ($1,290,500 net credit in 2021 less $10,500 debit in 2020), which is equal to the net increase in Cash realized from the export sale ($1,300,000 from exercising the option less $20,000 for the cost of the option).

Use of Hedging Instruments

There are probably as many different corporate strategies regarding hedging foreign exchange risk as there are companies exposed to that risk. Some companies require hedges of all foreign currency transactions. Others require the use of a forward contract hedge when the forward rate results in a larger cash inflow or smaller cash outflow than with the spot rate. Still other companies have proportional hedging policies that require hedging on some predetermined percentage (e.g., 50 percent, 60 percent, or 70 percent) of transaction exposure. For example, on page 56 of its 2017 annual report, Johnson Controls, Inc., discloses: "The Company hedges 70% to 90% of the nominal amount of each of its known foreign exchange transactional exposures."

Companies are required to provide information on the use of derivative financial instruments to hedge foreign exchange risk in the notes to financial statements. Exhibit 9.4 presents disclosures made by Abbott Laboratories in its 2017 annual report. Abbott uses forward contracts to hedge foreign exchange risk associated with anticipated foreign currency transactions, foreign currency–denominated payables and receivables, and foreign currency borrowings. Much of its hedging activity relates to intra-entity transactions involving foreign subsidiaries. The table in Exhibit 9.4 discloses that (1) Abbott's forward contracts primarily are to sell foreign currencies to receive U.S. dollars, (2) 72 percent of Abbott's

EXHIBIT 9.4 Disclosures Related to Hedging Foreign Exchange Risk in Abbott Laboratories' 2017 Annual Report

Foreign Currency Sensitive Financial Instruments

Certain Abbott foreign subsidiaries enter into foreign currency forward exchange contracts to manage exposures to changes in foreign exchange rates for anticipated intercompany purchases by those subsidiaries whose functional currencies are not the U.S. dollar. These contracts are designated as cash flow hedges of the variability of the cash flows due to changes in foreign exchange rates and are marked-to-market with the resulting gains or losses reflected in Accumulated other comprehensive income (loss). Gains or losses will be included in Cost of products sold at the time the products are sold, generally within the next 12 to 18 months. At December 31, 2017 and 2016, Abbott held $3.3 billion and $2.6 billion, respectively, of such contracts. Contracts held at December 31, 2017, will mature in 2018 or 2019 depending on the contract. Contacts held at December 31, 2016, matured in 2017 or will mature in 2018, depending upon the contract.

Abbott enters into foreign currency forward exchange contracts to manage its exposure to foreign currency–denominated intercompany loans and trade payables and third-party trade payables and receivables. The contracts are marked-to-market, and resulting gains or losses are reflected in income and are generally offset by losses or gains on the foreign currency exposure being managed. At December 31, 2017 and 2016, Abbott held $20.1 billion and $14.9 billion, respectively, of such contracts, which generally mature in the next 12 months.

The following table reflects the total foreign currency forward contracts outstanding at December 31, 2017.

(dollars in millions)	Contract Amount	Weighted Average Exchange Rate	Fair and Carrying Value Receivable/ (Payable)
Receive primarily U.S. Dollars in exchange for the following currencies:			
Euro	$16,877	1.1861	$(24)
British pound	609	1.3300	(5)
Japanese yen	1,109	110.5370	15
Canadian dollar	597	1.2799	(4)
All other currencies	4,245	N/A	(49)
Total	$23,437		$(67)

Source: Abbott Laboratories, 2017 Annual Report, page 60.

Part B

The facts are the same as in Part A with the exception that Felix designates the forward contract as a *fair value hedge* of the Chinese yuan liability exposure.

Part C

On August 1, Felix imports inventory from its Chinese supplier at a price of 1 million Chinese yuan. It receives the inventory on August 1 but does not pay for it until October 31. On August 1, Felix purchases a three-month call option on 1 million Chinese yuan with a strike price of $0.143. The option is appropriately designated as a *cash flow hedge* of the Chinese yuan liability exposure. Because the critical terms of the hedging instrument match those of the hedged item, the option is a highly effective hedge. Felix excludes the time value of the option from the assessment of hedge effectiveness and recognizes the change in option time value in net income. The inventory is sold in November.

Part D

On August 1, Felix orders inventory from its Chinese supplier at a price of 1 million Chinese yuan. On that date, Felix enters into a forward contract to purchase 1 million yuan on October 31. The company designates the forward contract as a *fair value hedge* of the Chinese yuan firm commitment exposure. Because the critical terms of the hedging instrument match those of the hedged item, the forward contract is a highly effective hedge. Felix measures the fair value of the foreign currency firm commitment using forward exchange rates. As a result, the forward points may not be excluded from the assessment of hedge effectiveness, and therefore are not amortized to net income. Felix receives the inventory and pays for it on October 31. The inventory is sold in November.

Part E

On August 1, Felix orders inventory from its Chinese supplier at a price of 1 million Chinese yuan. On that date, Felix purchases a three-month call option on 1 million Chinese yuan with a strike price of $0.143. The company designates the option as a *fair value hedge* of the Chinese yuan firm commitment exposure. Because the critical terms of the hedging instrument match those of the hedged item, the option is a highly effective hedge. Felix excludes the time value of the option from the assessment of hedge effectiveness and recognizes the change in option time value in net income. Felix measures the fair value of the firm commitment using spot exchange rates. The company receives the inventory and pays for it on October 31. The inventory is sold in November.

Part F

Felix anticipates that it will import inventory from its Chinese supplier in the near future. On August 1, Felix purchases a three-month call option on 1 million Chinese yuan with a strike price of $0.143. The company appropriately designates the option as a *cash flow hedge* of a forecasted Chinese yuan transaction. Because the critical terms of the hedging instrument match those of the hedged item, the option is a highly effective hedge. Felix excludes the time value of the option from the assessment of hedge effectiveness and recognizes the change in option time value in net income. Felix receives the inventory and pays for it on October 31. The inventory is sold in November.

Required

Prepare journal entries for each of these independent situations in accordance with U.S. GAAP, and determine the impact each situation has on the third-quarter (September 30) and year-end (December 31) trial balances. Ignore any discounting to present values.

Solution

Part A. Forward Contract Cash Flow Hedge of a Recognized Foreign Currency Liability

8/1	Inventory	143,000	
	Accounts Payable (CNY)		143,000
	To record the purchase of inventory and a CNY account payable at the spot rate of $0.143.		

The forward contract requires no formal entry. Felix prepares a memorandum to designate the forward contract as a hedge of the risk of changes in the cash flow to be paid on the foreign currency payable resulting from changes in the U.S. dollar–Chinese yuan exchange rate, indicating that the forward points are excluded from hedge effectiveness, and will be amortized to net income on a straight-line basis.

9/30	Foreign Exchange Gain or Loss	6,000	
	Accounts Payable (CNY)		6,000
	To adjust the value of the CNY account payable to the new spot rate of $0.149 and record a foreign exchange loss resulting from the appreciation of the yuan since August 1.		
	Forward Contract	3,000	
	Other Comprehensive Income (OCI).		3,000
	To record the forward contract as an asset at its fair value of $3,000 with a corresponding credit to OCI.		

Felix determines the fair value of the forward contract by referring to the change in the forward rate for a contract that settles on October 31: ($0.151 – $0.148) × CNY 1 million = $3,000. The difference in the undiscounted and discounted fair value is immaterial; therefore, for simplicity, discounting to present value is ignored.

9/30	Other Comprehensive Income (OCI).	6,000	
	Foreign Exchange Gain or Loss.		6,000
	To record a gain on forward contract to offset the foreign exchange loss on account payable with a corresponding debit to OCI.		
	Foreign Exchange Gain or Loss	3,333	
	Other Comprehensive Income (OCI).		3,333
	To allocate the forward contract premium to net income over the life of the contract using a straight-line method on a monthly basis ($5,000 × ⅔ = $3,333).		

The original premium on the forward contract is determined by the difference in the U.S. dollar–Chinese yuan three-month forward rate and the spot rate on August 1: ($0.148 – $0.143) × CNY 1 million = $5,000.

Trial Balance—September 30	**Debit**	**Credit**
Inventory.	$143,000	$ –0–
Forward Contract (asset)	3,000	–0–
Accounts Payable (CNY)	–0–	149,000
AOCI		333
Foreign exchange gain (loss)	3,333	–0–
Total	$149,333	$149,333

10/31	Foreign Exchange Gain or Loss	5,000	
	Accounts Payable (CNY)		5,000
	To adjust the value of the CNY account payable to the new spot rate of $0.154 and record a foreign exchange loss resulting from the appreciation of the CNY since September 30.		
	Forward Contract	3,000	
	Other Comprehensive Income (OCI).		3,000
	To adjust the carrying value of the forward contract to its current fair value of $6,000 with a corresponding credit to OCI.		

The current fair value of the forward contract is determined by referring to the difference in the spot rate on October 31 and the original forward rate: ($0.154 – $0.148) × CNY 1 million = $6,000. The forward contract adjustment on October 31 is calculated as the difference in the current fair value and the carrying value at September 30: $6,000 – $3,000 = $3,000.

10/31	Other Comprehensive Income (OCI).	5,000	
	Foreign Exchange Gain or Loss.		5,000
	To record a foreign exchange gain on forward contract to offset the foreign exchange loss on account payable with a corresponding debit to OCI.		

(continued)

(continued)

Date	Account	Debit	Credit
	Foreign Exchange Gain or Loss	1,667	
	Other Comprehensive Income (OCI)		1,667
	To allocate the forward contract premium to income over the life of the contract using a straight-line method on a monthly basis ($5,000 × ⅓ = $1,667).		
	Foreign Currency (CNY)	154,000	
	Cash		148,000
	Forward Contract		6,000
	To record settlement of the forward contract: Record payment of $148,000 in exchange for CNY 1 million, record the receipt of CNY 1 million as an asset at the spot rate of $0.154, and remove the forward contract from the accounts.		
	Accounts Payable (CNY)	154,000	
	Foreign Currency (CNY)		154,000
	To record remittance of CNY 1 million to the Chinese supplier.		
11/30	Cost of Goods Sold	143,000	
	Inventory		143,000
	To transfer the carrying value of inventory to cost of goods sold (at the time inventory is sold).		

Trial Balance—December 31	Debit	Credit
Cash	$ –0–	$148,000
Retained earnings, 9/30	3,333	–0–
Cost of goods sold	143,000	–0–
Foreign exchange gain (loss)	1,667	–0–
Total	$148,000	$148,000

Part B. Forward Contract Fair Value Hedge of a Recognized Foreign Currency Liability

Date	Account	Debit	Credit
8/1	Inventory	143,000	
	Accounts Payable (CNY)		143,000
	To record the purchase of inventory and a CNY account payable at the spot rate of $0.143.		

The forward contract requires no formal entry. Felix prepares a memorandum to designate the forward contract as a hedge of the risk of changes in the cash flow to be paid on the foreign currency payable resulting from changes in the U.S. dollar–Chinese yuan exchange rate, indicating that the forward points are excluded from hedge effectiveness and will be amortized to net income on a straight-line basis.

Date	Account	Debit	Credit
9/30	Foreign Exchange Gain or Loss	6,000	
	Accounts Payable (CNY)		6,000
	To adjust the value of the CNY payable to the new spot rate of $0.149 and record a foreign exchange loss resulting from the appreciation of the CNY since August 1.		
	Forward Contract	3,000	
	Foreign Exchange Gain or Loss		3,000
	To record the forward contract as an asset at its fair value of $3,000 and record a forward contract gain for the change in the fair value of the forward contract since August 1.		
	Foreign Exchange Gain or Loss	333	
	Other Comprehensive Income (OCI)		333
	To adjust the amount recognized as the current period's amortization of the forward contract discount in net income with a corresponding debit to OCI (which is subsequently closed to AOCI).		

As a result of the third entry, a net foreign exchange loss of $3,333 is reported in third-quarter net income, which equals the current period's amortization of forward contract premium ($5,000 × ⅔ = $3,333).

Trial Balance—September 30	**Debit**	**Credit**
Inventory	$143,000	$ –0–
Forward contract (asset)	3,000	–0–
Accounts payable (CNY)		149,000
Accumulated other comprehensive income (AOCI)	–0–	333
Foreign exchange gain (loss)	3,333	–0–
Total	$149,333	$149,333

10/31	Foreign Exchange Gain or Loss	5,000	
	Accounts Payable (CNY)		5,000
	To adjust the value of the CNY account payable to the new spot rate of $0.154 and record a foreign exchange loss resulting from the appreciation of the CNY since September 30.		
	Forward Contract	3,000	
	Foreign Exchange Gain or Loss		3,000
	To adjust the carrying value of the forward contract to its current fair value of $6,000 and record a foreign exchange gain for the change in fair value since September 30.		
	Accumulated Other Comprehensive Income (AOCI)	333	
	Foreign Exchange Gain or Loss		333
	To adjust the amount recognized as the current period's amortization of the forward contract discount by transferring the credit balance in AOCI to net income.		
	Foreign Currency (CNY)	154,000	
	Cash		148,000
	Forward Contract		6,000
	To record settlement of the forward contract: Record payment of $154,000 in exchange for CNY 1 million, record the receipt of CNY 1 million as an asset at the spot rate of $0.154, and remove the forward contract from the accounts.		
	Accounts Payable (CNY)	154,000	
	Foreign Currency (CNY)		154,000
	To record remittance of CNY 1 million to the Chinese supplier.		
11/30	Cost of Goods Sold	143,000	
	Inventory		143,000
	To transfer the carrying value of inventory to cost of goods sold (at the time inventory is sold).		

Trial Balance—December 31	**Debit**	**Credit**
Cash	$ –0–	$148,000
Retained earnings, 9/30	3,333	–0–
Cost of goods sold	143,000	–0–
Foreign exchange gain (loss)	1,667	–0–
Total	$148,000	$148,000

Part C. Option Cash Flow Hedge of a Recognized Foreign Currency Liability

The following schedule summarizes the changes in the components of the fair value of the Chinese yuan call option with a strike price of $0.143:

Date	Spot Rate	Option Premium	Fair Value	Change in Fair Value	Intrinsic Value	Time Value	Change in Time Value
8/1	$0.143	$0.0081	$ 8,100	$ –0–	$ –0–	$8,100*	$ –0–
9/30	0.149	0.0123	12,300	+4,200	6,000†	6,300†	–1,800
10/31	0.154	n/a	11,000	–1,300	11,000	–0–‡	–6,300

*Because the strike price and spot rate are the same, the option has no intrinsic value. Fair value is attributable solely to the time value of the option.

†With a spot rate of $0.149 and a strike price of $0.143, the option has an intrinsic value of $6,000. The remaining $6,300 of fair value is attributable to time value.

‡The time value of the option at maturity is zero.

Date	Account	Debit	Credit
8/1	Inventory	143,000	
	Accounts Payable (CNY)		143,000
	To record the purchase of inventory and a CNY account payable at the spot rate of $0.143.		
	Foreign Currency Option	8,100	
	Cash		8,100
	To record the purchase of a foreign currency option as an asset.		
9/30	Foreign Exchange Gain or Loss	6,000	
	Accounts Payable (CNY)		6,000
	To adjust the value of the CNY account payable to the new spot rate of $0.149 and record a foreign exchange loss resulting from the appreciation of the CNY since August 1.		
	Foreign Currency Option	4,200	
	Other Comprehensive Income (OCI)		4,200
	To adjust the fair value of the option from $8,100 to $12,300 with a corresponding credit to OCI.		
	Other Comprehensive Income (OCI)	6,000	
	Foreign Exchange Gain or Loss		6,000
	To record a foreign exchange gain on foreign currency option to offset the foreign exchange loss on account payable with a corresponding debit to OCI.		
	Foreign Exchange Gain or Loss	1,800	
	Other Comprehensive Income (OCI)		1,800
	To recognize the change in the time value of the foreign currency option since August 1 as an adjustment to net income with a corresponding credit to OCI.		

Trial Balance—September 30	Debit	Credit
Cash	$ –0–	$ 8,100
Inventory	143,000	–0–
Foreign currency option (asset)	12,300	–0–
Accounts payable (CNY)	–0–	149,000
Foreign exchange gain (loss)	1,800	–0–
Total	$157,100	$157,100

Date	Account	Debit	Credit
10/31	Foreign Exchange Gain or Loss	5,000	
	Accounts Payable (CNY)		5,000
	To adjust the value of the CNY account payable to the new spot rate of $0.154 and record a foreign exchange loss resulting from the appreciation of the CNY since September 30.		

(continued)

(continued)

Date	Account	Debit	Credit
	Foreign Currency Option	1,300	
	Other Comprehensive Income (OCI)		1,300
	To adjust the carrying value of the foreign currency option to its current fair value of $11,000 with a corresponding credit to OCI.		
	Other Comprehensive Income (OCI)	5,000	
	Foreign Exchange Gain or Loss		5,000
	To record a foreign exchange gain on foreign currency option to offset the foreign exchange loss on account payable with a corresponding debit to OCI.		
	Foreign Exchange Gain or Loss	6,300	
	Other Comprehensive Income (OCI)		6,300
	To recognize the change in the time value of the foreign currency option since September 30 in net income with a corresponding credit to OCI.		
	Foreign Currency (CNY)	154,000	
	Cash		143,000
	Foreign Currency Option		11,000
	To record exercise of the foreign currency option: Record payment of $154,000 in exchange for CNY 1 million, record the receipt of CNY 1 million as an asset at the spot rate of $0.154, and remove the option from the accounts.		
	Accounts Payable (CNY)	91,000	
	Foreign Currency (CNY)		91,000
	To record remittance of CNY 1 million to the Chinese supplier.		
11/30	Cost of Goods Sold	143,000	
	Inventory		143,000
	To transfer the carrying value of inventory to cost of goods sold (at the time inventory is sold).		

Trial Balance—December 31	**Debit**	**Credit**
Cash ($5,200 credit balance + $143,000 credit)	$ –0–	$151,100
Retained earnings, 9/30	1,800	–0–
Cost of goods sold	143,000	–0–
Foreign exchange gain (loss)	6,300	–0–
Total	$151,100	$151,100

Part D. Forward Contract Fair Value Hedge of a Foreign Currency Firm Commitment

Date	Account	Debit	Credit
8/1	There is no entry to record either the purchase order or the forward contract because both are executory contracts. A memorandum designates the forward contract as a fair value hedge of the risk of changes in the fair value of the firm commitment resulting from changes in the U.S. dollar–Chinese yuan forward exchange rate, and indicates that the firm commitment will be measured using forward exchange rates.		
9/30	Forward Contract	3,000	
	Foreign Exchange Gain or Loss		3,000
	To record the forward contract as an asset at its fair value of $3,000 and record a forward exchange gain for the change in the fair value of the forward contract since August 1.		
	Foreign Exchange Gain or Loss	3,000	
	Firm Commitment		3,000
	To record the firm commitment as a liability at its fair value of $3,000 based on changes in the forward rate and record a foreign exchange loss on firm commitment for the change in fair value since August 1.		

Trial Balance—September 30	Debit	Credit
Forward contract (asset)	$3,000	$ –0–
Firm commitment (liability)	–0–	3,000
Total	$3,000	$3,000

Date	Account	Debit	Credit
10/31	Forward Contract	3,000	
	Foreign Exchange Gain or Loss		3,000
	To adjust the carrying value of the forward contract to its current fair value of $6,000 and record a foreign exchange gain for the change in fair value since September 30.		
	Foreign Exchange Gain or Loss	3,000	
	Firm Commitment		3,000
	To adjust the carrying value of the firm commitment to $6,000 based on changes in the forward rate and record a foreign exchange loss for the change in fair value since September 30.		
	Foreign Currency (CNY)	154,000	
	Cash		148,000
	Forward Contract		6,000
	To record settlement of the forward contract: Record payment of $148,000 in exchange for CNY 1 million, record the receipt of CNY 1 million as an asset at the spot rate of $0.154, and remove the forward contract from the accounts.		
	Inventory	154,000	
	Foreign Currency (CNY)		154,000
	To record the purchase of inventory through the payment of CNY 1 million to the Chinese supplier.		
11/30	Cost of Goods Sold	154,000	
	Inventory		154,000
	To transfer the carrying value of inventory to cost of goods sold (at the time inventory is sold).		
	Firm Commitment	6,000	
	Cost of Goods Sold		6,000
	To close the firm commitment account to net income (as an adjustment to cost of goods sold).		

(*Note:* The final entry to close the Firm Commitment account to Cost of Goods sold is made *only* in the period in which Inventory affects net income through Cost of Goods Sold. The Firm Commitment account remains on the books as a liability until that point in time.)

Trial Balance—December 31	Debit	Credit
Cash	$ –0–	$148,000
Cost of goods sold	148,000	–0–
Total	$148,000	$148,000

Part E. Option Fair Value Hedge of a Foreign Currency Firm Commitment

Date	Account	Debit	Credit
8/1	Foreign Currency Option	8,100	
	Cash		8,100
	To record the purchase of a foreign currency option as an asset.		
9/30	Foreign Currency Option	4,200	
	Foreign Exchange Gain or Loss		4,200
	To adjust the fair value of the option from $8,100 to $12,300 and record a foreign exchange gain on option for the change in fair value since August 1.		

(continued)

(continued)

		Debit	Credit
	Foreign Exchange Gain or Loss	6,000	
	Firm Commitment		6,000
	To record the firm commitment as a liability at its fair value of $6,000 based on changes in the spot rate and record a foreign exchange loss on firm commitment for the change in fair value since August 1.		

The fair value of the firm commitment on September 30 is determined by referring to changes in the spot rate from August 1 to September 30: ($0.143 – $0.149) × CNY 1 million = $(6,000).

Trial Balance—September 30	Debit	Credit
Cash	$ –0–	$ 8,100
Foreign currency option (asset)	12,300	–0–
Firm commitment (liability)	–0–	6,000
Foreign exchange gain (loss)	1,800	–0–
Total	$14,100	$14,100

		Debit	Credit
10/31	Foreign Exchange Gain or Loss	1,300	
	Foreign Currency Option		1,300
	To adjust fair value of the foreign currency option from $12,300 to $11,000 and record a foreign exchange loss for the change in fair value since September 30.		
	Foreign Exchange Gain or Loss	5,000	
	Firm Commitment		5,000
	To adjust the fair value of the firm commitment liability from $6,000 to $11,000 and record a foreign exchange loss for the change in fair value since September 30.		

The fair value of the firm commitment is determined by referring to changes in the spot rate from August 1 to October 31: ($0.143 – $0.154) × CNY 1 million = $(11,000).

		Debit	Credit
10/31	Foreign Currency (CNY)	154,000	
	Cash		143,000
	Foreign Currency Option		11,000
	To record exercise of the foreign currency option: Record payment of $143,000 in exchange for CNY 1 million, record the receipt of CNY 1 million as an asset at the spot rate of $0.154, and remove the option from the accounts.		
	Inventory	154,000	
	Foreign Currency (CNY)		154,000
	To record the purchase of inventory through the payment of CNY 1 million to the Chinese supplier.		
11/30	Cost of Goods Sold	154,000	
	Inventory		154,000
	To transfer the carrying value of inventory to cost of goods sold (at the time inventory is sold).		
	Firm Commitment	11,000	
	Cost of Goods Sold		11,000
	To close the firm commitment account to net income (as an adjustment to cost of goods sold).		

(*Note:* The final entry to close the Firm Commitment to Cost of Goods Sold is made *only* in the period in which Inventory affects net income through Cost of Goods Sold. The Firm Commitment account remains on the books as a liability until that point in time.)

Trial Balance—December 31	Debit	Credit
Cash ($8,100 credit balance + $143,000 credit)	$ –0–	$151,100
Retained earnings, 9/30	1,800	–0–
Cost of goods sold	143,000	–0–
Foreign exchange gain (loss)	6,300	–0–
Total	$151,100	$151,100

Part F. Option Cash Flow Hedge of a Forecasted Foreign Currency Transaction

Date	Account	Debit	Credit
8/1	Foreign Currency Option	8,300	
	Cash		8,300
	To record the purchase of a foreign currency option as an asset.		
9/30	Foreign Currency Option	4,200	
	Other Comprehensive Income (OCI)		4,200
	To adjust the fair value of the option from $5,200 to $9,500 with a corresponding adjustment to OCI.		
	Cost of Goods Sold	1,800	
	Other Comprehensive Income (OCI)		1,800
	To recognize the change in the time value of the foreign currency option in net income (in the same line item that will be affected by the import purchase—i.e., cost of goods sold) with a corresponding credit to OCI.		

Trial Balance—September 30	Debit	Credit
Cash	$ –0–	$ 8,100
Foreign currency option (asset)	12,300	–0–
Accumulated other comprehensive income (AOCI)	–0–	6,000
Cost of goods sold	1,800	–0–
Total	$14,100	$14,100

Date	Account	Debit	Credit
10/31	Other Comprehensive Income (OCI)	1,300	
	Foreign Currency Option		1,300
	To adjust the fair value of the foreign currency option asset from $12,300 to $11,000 with a corresponding adjustment to OCI.		
	Cost of Goods Sold	6,300	
	Other Comprehensive Income (OCI)		6,300
	To recognize the change in the time value of the foreign currency option in net income with a corresponding credit to OCI.		
	Foreign Currency (CNY)	154,000	
	Cash		143,000
	Foreign Currency Option		11,000
	To record exercise of the foreign currency option: Record payment of $143,000 in exchange for CNY 1 million, record the receipt of CNY 1 million as an asset at the spot rate of $0.154, and remove the option from the accounts.		
	Inventory	154,000	
	Foreign Currency (CNY)		154,000
	To record the purchase of inventory through the payment of CNY 1 million to the Chinese supplier.		

(continued)

(continued)

		Debit	Credit
	Accumulated Other Comprehensive Income (AOCI)	11,000	
	Cost of Goods Sold		11,000
	To close the balance in AOCI (after closing the current period's OCI) to net income (as an adjustment to cost of goods sold).		
11/30	Cost of Goods Sold	154,000	
	Inventory.		154,000
	To transfer the carrying value of inventory to cost of goods sold (at the time inventory is sold).		

(*Note:* The entry to close AOCI to Cost of Goods Sold is made at the date that the forecasted transaction was expected to occur, regardless of when the inventory affects net income.)

Trial Balance—December 31	Debit	Credit
Cash ($8,100 credit balance + $143,000 credit)...............	$ –0–	$151,100
Retained earnings, 9/30	1,800	–0–
Cost of goods sold	149,300	–0–
Total	$151,100	$151,100

Questions

1. What concept underlies the two-transaction perspective in accounting for foreign currency transactions?
2. A company makes an export sale denominated in a foreign currency and allows the customer one month to pay. Under the two-transaction perspective, accrual approach, how does the company account for fluctuations in the exchange rate for the foreign currency?
3. What factors create a foreign exchange gain on a foreign currency transaction? What factors create a foreign exchange loss?
4. In what way is the accounting for a foreign currency borrowing more complicated than the accounting for a foreign currency account payable?
5. What does the term *hedging* mean? Why do companies elect to follow this strategy?
6. How does a foreign currency option differ from a foreign currency forward contract?
7. How does the timing of hedges of (*a*) foreign currency–denominated assets and liabilities, (*b*) foreign currency firm commitments, and (*c*) forecasted foreign currency transactions differ?
8. Why would a company prefer a foreign currency option over a forward contract in hedging a foreign currency firm commitment? Why would a company prefer a forward contract over an option in hedging a foreign currency asset or liability?
9. How do companies report foreign currency derivatives, such as forward contracts and options, on the balance sheet?
10. How does a company determine the fair value of a foreign currency forward contract? How does it determine the fair value of an option?
11. What is hedge accounting?
12. Under what conditions can companies use hedge accounting to account for a foreign currency option used to hedge a forecasted foreign currency transaction?
13. Under what conditions can a foreign currency derivative be considered "highly effective" as a hedge without conducting a quantitative assessment?
14. What are the differences in accounting for a forward contract used as (*a*) a cash flow hedge and (*b*) a fair value hedge of a foreign currency–denominated asset or liability?
15. How does the accounting for a hedge of a foreign currency firm commitment affect assets and liabilities reported on the balance sheet differently from the accounting for a hedge of a forecasted foreign currency transaction?
16. How are changes in the fair value of an option accounted for in a cash flow hedge? In a fair value hedge?

Problems

LO 9-1

1. Which of the following combinations correctly describes the relationship between foreign currency transactions, exchange rate changes, and foreign exchange gains and losses?

Type of Transaction	Foreign Currency	Foreign Exchange Gain or Loss
a. Export sale	Appreciates	Loss
b. Import purchase	Appreciates	Gain
c. Import purchase	Depreciates	Gain
d. Export sale	Depreciates	Gain

LO 9-2

2. In accounting for foreign currency transactions, which of the following approaches is used in the United States?

   a. One-transaction perspective; accrue foreign exchange gains and losses

   b. One-transaction perspective; defer foreign exchange gains and losses

   c. Two-transaction perspective; defer foreign exchange gains and losses

   d. Two-transaction perspective; accrue foreign exchange gains and losses

LO 9-2

3. On October 1, Tile Co., a U.S. company, purchased products from Azulejo, a Portuguese company, with payment due on December 1. If Tile's operating income included no foreign exchange gain or loss, the transaction could have

   a. Been denominated in U.S. dollars.

   b. Resulted in an unusual gain.

   c. Generated a foreign exchange gain to be reported in accumulated other comprehensive income on the balance sheet.

   d. Generated a foreign exchange loss to be reported as a separate component of stockholders' equity.

LO 9-2

4. Brief, Inc., had a receivable from a foreign customer that is payable in the customer's local currency. On December 31, 2020, Brief correctly included this receivable for 200,000 local currency units (LCU) in its balance sheet at $110,000. When Brief collected the receivable on February 15, 2021, the U.S. dollar equivalent was $120,000. In Brief's 2021 consolidated income statement, how much should it report as a foreign exchange gain?

   a. $–0–

   b. $10,000

   c. $15,000

   d. $25,000

LO 9-2, 9-3

5. On July 1, 2020, Mifflin Company borrowed 200,000 euros from a foreign lender evidenced by an interest-bearing note due on July 1, 2021. The note is denominated in euros. The U.S. dollar equivalent of the note principal is as follows:

Date	Amount
July 1, 2020 (date borrowed)	$225,000
December 31, 2020 (Mifflin's year-end)	220,000
July 1, 2021 (date repaid)	210,000

In its 2021 income statement, what amount should Mifflin include as a foreign exchange gain or loss on the note?

   a. $15,000 gain

   b. $15,000 loss

   c. $10,000 gain

   d. $10,000 loss

LO 9-1, 9-2

6. Grace Co. had a Chinese yuan payable resulting from imports from China and a Mexican peso receivable resulting from exports to Mexico. Grace recorded foreign exchange losses related to both

its yuan payable and peso receivable. Did the foreign currencies increase or decrease in dollar value from the date of the transaction to the settlement date?

Yuan	Peso
a. Increase	Increase
b. Increase	Decrease
c. Decrease	Increase
d. Decrease	Decrease

LO 9-2, 9-3

7. Matthias Corp. had the following foreign currency transactions during 2020:
   - Purchased merchandise from a foreign supplier on January 20 for the U.S. dollar equivalent of $60,000 and paid the invoice on April 20 at the U.S. dollar equivalent of $50,000.
   - On September 1, borrowed the U.S. dollar equivalent of $300,000 evidenced by a note that is payable in the lender's local currency in one year. On December 31, the U.S. dollar equivalent of the principal amount was $320,000.

   In Matthias's 2020 income statement, what amount should be included as a net foreign exchange gain or loss?
   a. $10,000 gain
   b. $10,000 loss
   c. $20,000 gain
   d. $30,000 loss

LO 9-7

8. A U.S. exporter has a Thai baht account receivable resulting from an export sale on June 1 to a customer in Thailand. The exporter signed a forward contract on June 1 to sell Thai baht and designated it as a cash flow hedge of a recognized Thai baht receivable. The spot rate was $0.022 on that date, and the forward rate was $0.021. Forward points are excluded from the assessment of hedge effectiveness. Which of the following is true with respect to the forward points on this contract? The forward points are a
   a. Forward contract discount that is recognized in net income as a foreign exchange loss.
   b. Forward contract discount that is recognized in net income as a foreign exchange gain.
   c. Forward contract premium that is recognized in net income as a foreign exchange loss.
   d. Forward contract premium that is recognized in net income as a foreign exchange gain.

LO 9-8

9. Monument Company (a U.S.-based company) ordered a machine costing €100,000 from a foreign supplier on January 15, when the spot rate was $1.20 per €. A one-month forward contract was signed on that date to purchase €100,000 at a forward rate of $1.23. The forward contract is properly designated as a fair value hedge of the €100,000 firm commitment. On February 15, when the company receives the machine, the spot rate is $1.22. At what amount should Monument Company capitalize the machine on its books?
   a. $120,000
   b. $121,000
   c. $122,000
   d. $123,000

LO 9-5

10. On December 1, 2020, Venice Company (a U.S.-based company) entered into a three-month forward contract to purchase 1,000,000 pesos on March 1, 2021. The following U.S. dollar per peso exchange rates apply:

Date	Spot Rate	Forward Rate (to March 1, 2021)
December 1, 2020	$0.088	$0.094
December 31, 2020	0.095	0.098
March 1, 2021	0.105	N/A

Ignoring present values, which of the following correctly describes the manner in which Venice Company will report the forward contract on its December 31, 2020, balance sheet?
   a. As an asset in the amount of $1,000
   b. As an asset in the amount of $4,000
   c. As a liability in the amount of $1,000
   d. As a liability in the amount of $4,000

Use the following information for Problems 11 and 12.

Brandt Corp. (a U.S.-based company) sold parts to a South Korean customer on December 1, 2020, with payment of 10 million South Korean won to be received on March 31, 2021. The following exchange rates apply:

Date	Spot Rate	Forward Rate (to March 31, 2021)
December 1, 2020	$0.0035	$0.0034
December 31, 2020	0.0033	0.0032
March 31, 2021	0.0038	N/A

LO 9-2

11. Assuming that Brandt did not hedge its foreign exchange risk, how much foreign exchange gain or loss should it report on its 2020 income statement with regard to this transaction?
    a. $5,000 gain
    b. $3,000 gain
    c. $2,000 loss
    d. $1,000 loss

LO 9-7

12. Assuming that Brandt entered into a forward contract to sell 10 million South Korean won on December 1, 2020, as a fair value hedge of a foreign currency receivable, what is the net impact on its net income in 2020 resulting from a fluctuation in the value of the won? Brandt amortizes forward points on a monthly basis using a straight-line method. Ignore present values.
    a. No impact on net income
    b. $100 decrease in net income
    c. $250 decrease in net income
    d. $2,000 increase in net income

LO 9-9

13. On March 1, Derby Corporation (a U.S.-based company) expects to order merchandise from a supplier in Norway in three months. On March 1, when the spot rate is $0.10 per Norwegian krone, Derby enters into a forward contract to purchase 500,000 Norwegian kroner at a three-month forward rate of $0.12. Forward points are excluded in assessing the forward contract's effectiveness as a hedge, and are amortized to net income on a straight-line basis. At the end of three months, when the spot rate is $0.115 per Norwegian krone, Derby orders and receives the merchandise, paying 500,000 kroner. The merchandise is sold within 30 days. What amount(s) does Derby report in net income as a result of this cash flow hedge of a forecasted transaction and the related purchase and sale of merchandise?
    a. Cost of goods sold of $60,000
    b. Cost of goods sold of $57,500 plus foreign exchange loss of $2,500
    c. Cost of goods sold of $50,000 plus foreign exchange loss of $10,000
    d. Cost of goods sold of $60,000 less foreign exchange gain of $10,000

LO 9-9

14. Shandra Corporation (a U.S.-based company) expects to order goods from a foreign supplier at a price of 100,000 pounds, with delivery and payment to be made on April 20. On February 20, when the spot rate is $1.00 per pound, Shandra purchases a two-month call option on 100,000 pounds and designates this option as a cash flow hedge of a forecasted foreign currency transaction. The time value of the option is excluded in assessing hedge effectiveness; the change in time value is recognized in net income over the life of the option. The option has a strike price of $1.00 per pound and costs $1,000. The goods are received and paid for on April 20. Shandra sells the imported goods in the local market by May 31. The spot rate for pounds is $1.02 on April 20. What amount will Shandra Corporation report as foreign exchange gain or loss in net income for the quarter ended June 30?
    a. $0
    b. $500
    c. $1,000
    d. $2,000

Use the following information for Problems 15 through 17.

On September 1, 2020, Stone Company received an order to sell a machine to a customer in Australia at a price of 100,000 Australian dollars. Stone shipped the machine and received payment on March 1, 2021. On September 1, 2020, Stone purchased a put option giving it the right to sell 100,000 Australian dollars on March 1, 2021, at a price of $80,000. Stone properly designated the option as a fair value hedge of the Australian dollar firm commitment. The option's time value is excluded in assessing hedge effectiveness, and the change in time value is recognized in net income over the life of the option. The option cost $2,000 and had a fair value of $2,300 on December 31, 2020. The fair value of the firm commitment was measured by referring to changes in the spot rate (discounting to present value is ignored). The following spot exchange rates apply:

Date	U.S. Dollar per Australian Dollar (AUD)
September 1, 2020	$0.80
December 31, 2020	0.79
March 1, 2021	0.77

LO 9-8

15. What was the net impact on Stone Company's 2020 income as a result of this fair value hedge of a firm commitment?
   a. $–0–
   b. $700 decrease in income
   c. $300 increase in income
   d. $700 increase in income

LO 9-8

16. What was the net impact on Stone Company's 2021 income as a result of this fair value hedge of a firm commitment and export sale?
   a. $–0–.
   b. $1,300 decrease in income
   c. $78,000 increase in income
   d. $78,700 increase in income

LO 9-8

17. What was the net increase or decrease in cash flow from having purchased the foreign currency option to hedge this exposure to foreign exchange risk?
   a. $–0–
   b. $1,000 increase in cash flow
   c. $1,500 decrease in cash flow
   d. $3,000 increase in cash flow

Use the following information for Problems 18 through 20.

On June 1, 2020, Munchkin Corp. received an order for finished goods from a Turkish customer at a price of 500,000 Turkish lira with a delivery date of July 31, 2020. On June 1, when the U.S. dollar–Turkish lira spot rate is $0.230, Munchkin Corp. entered into a two-month forward contract to sell 500,000 lira at a forward rate of $0.240 per lira. Munchkin designates the forward contract as a fair value hedge of the firm commitment to receive lira. The fair value of the firm commitment is measured by referring to changes in the lira forward rate, so forward points must be included in assessing hedge effectiveness of the forward contract. Munchkin delivers the goods and receives payment on July 31, 2020, when the U.S. dollar–Turkish lira spot rate is $0.236. On June 30, 2020, the Turkish lira spot rate is $0.246, and the forward contract has a fair value of $2,400.

LO 9-8

18. What is the net impact on Munchkin's net income for the quarter ended June 30, 2020, as a result of this forward contract hedge of a firm commitment?
   a. $–0–
   b. $2,400 increase in net income
   c. $4,000 decrease in net income
   d. $8,000 increase in net income

LO 9-8

19. What is the net impact on Munchkin's net income for the quarter ended September 30, 2020, as a result of this forward contract hedge of a firm commitment and export sale?
   a. $–0–
   b. $115,000 increase in net income
   c. $118,000 increase in net income
   d. $120,000 increase in net income

LO 9-8

20. What is Munchkin's net increase or decrease in cash flow from having entered into this forward contract hedge?
    a. $–0–
    b. $1,000 increase in cash flow
    c. $1,500 decrease in cash flow
    d. $2,000 increase in cash flow

Use the following information for Problems 21 and 22.

On November 1, 2020, Good Life Company forecasts the purchase of raw materials from a Chilean supplier on February 1, 2021, at a price of 20,000,000 Chilean pesos. On November 1, 2020, Good Life pays $1,500 for a three-month call option on 20,000,000 pesos with a strike price of $0.0015 per peso. On December 31, 2020, the option has a fair value of $1,100. The following spot exchange rates apply:

Date	U.S. Dollar per Chilean Peso (CLP)
November 1, 2020	$0.0015
December 31, 2020	0.0013
February 1, 2021	0.0016

Good Life properly designates the option as a cash flow hedge of a forecasted foreign currency transaction. The time value of the option is excluded from the assessment of hedge effectiveness, and the change in time value is recognized in net income over the life of the option. Raw materials are received and paid for on February 1, 2021, and the finished goods into which the materials are incorporated are sold by March 30, 2021.

LO 9-9

21. What is the net impact on Good Life Company's 2020 net income as a result of this hedge of a forecasted foreign currency transaction?
    a. $–0–
    b. $400 decrease in net income
    c. $1,000 decrease in net income
    d. $1,400 decrease in net income

LO 9-9

22. What is the net impact on Good Life Company's 2021 net income as a result of this hedge of a forecasted foreign currency transaction and import purchase? Assume that the raw materials are consumed and become a part of the cost of goods sold in 2021.
    a. $30,000 decrease in net income
    b. $30,600 decrease in net income
    c. $31,100 decrease in net income
    d. $33,100 decrease in net income

LO 9-2

23. Bento Corporation (a U.S.-based company) acquired merchandise on account from a foreign supplier on November 1, 2020, for 100,000 crowns. It paid the foreign currency account payable on January 15, 2021. The following exchange rates are relevant:

Date	U.S. Dollar per Crown
November 1, 2020	$0.754
December 31, 2020	0.742
January 15, 2021	0.747

a. How does the fluctuation in the U.S. dollar per crown exchange rate affect Bento's 2020 income statement?

b. How does the fluctuation in the U.S. dollar per crown exchange rate affect Bento's 2021 income statement?

LO 9-2

24. On December 20, 2020, Momeier Company (a U.S.-based company) sold parts to a foreign customer at a price of 50,000 rials. Payment is received on January 10, 2021. Currency exchange rates are as follows:

Date	U.S. Dollar per Rial
December 20, 2020	$1.05
December 31, 2020	1.02
January 10, 2021	0.98

a. How does the fluctuation in the U.S. dollar per rial exchange rate affect Momeier's 2020 income statement?

b. How does the fluctuation in the U.S. dollar per rial exchange rate affect Momeier's 2021 income statement?

LO 9-2

25. Peerless Corporation (a U.S.-based company) made a sale to a foreign customer on September 15, for 100,000 crowns. It received payment on October 15. The following exchange rates for 1 crown apply:

Date	U.S. Dollar per Crown
September 15	$0.60
September 30	0.66
October 15	0.62

Prepare all journal entries for Peerless Corporation in connection with this export sale, assuming that the company closes its books on September 30 to prepare interim financial statements.

LO 9-2

26. On December 15, 2020, Lisbeth Inc. (a U.S.-based company) purchases merchandise inventory from a foreign supplier for 50,000 schillings. Lisbeth agrees to pay in 45 days, after it sells the merchandise. Lisbeth makes sales rather quickly and pays the entire obligation on January 25, 2021. Currency exchange rates for 1 schilling are as follows:

Date	U.S. Dollar per Schilling
December 15, 2020	$0.28
December 31, 2020	0.30
January 25, 2021	0.33
January 31, 2021	0.34

Prepare all journal entries for Lisbeth Company in connection with this purchase and payment.

LO 9-2

27. Voltac Corporation (a U.S.-based company) has the following import/export transactions denominated in Mexican pesos in 2020:

March 1	Bought inventory costing 100,000 pesos on credit.
May 1	Sold 60 percent of the inventory for 80,000 pesos on credit.
August 1	Collected 70,000 pesos from customers.
September 1	Paid 60,000 pesos to suppliers.

Currency exchange rates for 1 peso for 2020 are as follows:

Date	U.S. Dollar per Peso
March 1	$0.10
May 1	0.12
August 1	0.13
September 1	0.14
December 31	0.15

For each of the following accounts, what amount will Voltac report on its 2020 financial statements?

a. Inventory.

b. Cost of Goods Sold.

c. Sales.

d. Accounts Receivable.

e. Accounts Payable.

f. Cash.

LO 9-3

28. On April 1, 2020, Mendoza Company (a U.S.-based company) borrowed 500,000 euros for one year at an interest rate of 5 percent per annum. Mendoza must make its first interest payment on the loan on October 1, 2020, and will make a second interest payment on March 31, 2021, when the loan is repaid. Mendoza prepares U.S. dollar financial statements and has a December 31 year-end. Prepare all journal entries related to this foreign currency borrowing assuming the following exchange rates for 1 euro:

Date	U.S. Dollar per Euro
April 1, 2020	$1.10
October 1, 2020	1.20
December 31, 2020	1.24
March 31, 2021	1.28

LO 9-2

29. Spindler, Inc. (a U.S.-based company), imports surfboards from a supplier in Brazil and sells them in the United States. Purchases are denominated in terms of the Brazilian real (BRL). During 2020, Spindler acquires 200 surfboards at a price of BRL 1,600 per surfboard, for a total of BRL 320,000. Spindler will pay for the surfboards when it sells them. Relevant exchange rates are as follows:

Date	U.S. Dollar per Brazilian Real (BRL)
September 1, 2020	$0.230
December 1, 2020	0.220
December 31, 2020	0.240
March 1, 2021	0.225

a. Assume that Spindler acquired the surfboards on September 1, 2020, and made payment on December 1, 2020. What is the effect of the exchange rate fluctuations on reported income in 2020?

b. Assume that Spindler acquired the surfboards on December 1, 2020, and made payment on March 1, 2021. What is the effect of the exchange rate fluctuations on reported income in 2020 and 2021?

c. Assume that Spindler acquired the surfboards on September 1, 2020, and made payment on March 1, 2021. What is the effect of the exchange rate fluctuations on reported income in 2020 and in 2021?

LO 9-3

30. On September 30, 2020, Peace Frog International (PFI) (a U.S.-based company) negotiated a two-year, 1,000,000 Chinese yuan loan from a Chinese bank at an interest rate of 2 percent per year. The company makes interest payments annually on September 30 and will repay the principal on September 30, 2022. PFI prepares U.S. dollar financial statements and has a December 31 year-end. Relevant exchange rates are as follows:

Date	U.S. Dollar per Chinese Yuan (CNY)
September 30, 2020	$0.100
December 31, 2020	0.105
September 30, 2021	0.120
December 31, 2021	0.125
September 30, 2022	0.150

a. Prepare all journal entries related to this foreign currency borrowing.

b. Taking the exchange rate effect on the cost of borrowing into consideration, determine the effective interest rate in U.S. dollars on the loan in each of the three years 2020, 2021, and 2022.

LO 9-7

31. Icebreaker Company (a U.S.-based company) sells parts to a foreign customer on December 1, 2020, with payment of 16,000 dinars to be received on March 1, 2021. Icebreaker enters into a forward contract on December 1, 2020, to sell 16,000 dinars on March 1, 2021. The forward points on the forward contract are excluded in assessing hedge effectiveness and are amortized to net income using a straight-line method on a monthly basis. Relevant exchange rates for the dinar on various dates are as follows:

Date	Spot Rate	Forward Rate (to March 1, 2021)
December 1, 2020	$2.70	$2.775
December 31, 2020	2.80	2.900
March 1, 2021	2.95	N/A

Icebreaker must close its books and prepare financial statements at December 31.

a. Assuming that Icebreaker designates the forward contract as a cash flow hedge of a foreign currency receivable, prepare journal entries for the sale and foreign currency forward contract in U.S. dollars. What is the impact on 2020 net income? What is the impact on 2021 net income? What is the impact on net income over the two accounting periods?

b. Assuming that Icebreaker designates the forward contract as a fair value hedge of a foreign currency receivable, prepare journal entries for the sale and foreign currency forward contract in U.S. dollars. What is the impact on 2020 net income? What is the impact on 2021 net income? What is the impact on net income over the two accounting periods?

LO 9-7

32. Use the same facts as in Problem 31 except that Icebreaker Company purchases materials from a foreign supplier on December 1, 2020, with payment of 16,000 dinars to be made on March 1, 2021. The materials are consumed immediately and recognized as cost of goods sold at the date of purchase. On December 1, 2020, Brandlin enters into a forward contract to purchase 16,000 dinars on March 1, 2021.

a. Assuming that Icebreaker designates the forward contract as a cash flow hedge of a foreign currency payable, prepare journal entries for the import purchase and foreign currency forward contract in U.S. dollars. What is the impact on 2020 net income? What is the impact on 2021 net income? What is the impact on net income over the two accounting periods?

b. Assuming that Icebreaker designates the forward contract as a fair value hedge of a foreign currency payable, prepare journal entries for the import purchase and foreign currency forward contract in U.S. dollars. What is the impact on net income in 2020 and in 2021? What is the impact on net income over the two accounting periods?

LO 9-7

33. On June 1, Maxwell Corporation (a U.S.-based company) sold goods to a foreign customer at a price of 1,000,000 pesos and will receive payment in three months on September 1. On June 1, Maxwell acquired an option to sell 1,000,000 pesos in three months at a strike price of $0.062. The time value of the option is excluded from the assessment of hedge effectiveness, and the change in time value is recognized in net income over the life of the option. Relevant exchange rates and option premia for the peso are as follows:

Date	Spot Rate	Put Option Premium for September 1 (strike price $0.062)
June 1	$0.062	$0.0025
June 30	0.061	0.0022
September 1	0.060	N/A

Maxwell must close its books and prepare its second-quarter financial statements on June 30.

a. Assuming that Maxwell designates the foreign currency option as a cash flow hedge of a foreign currency receivable, prepare journal entries for the export sale and related hedge in U.S. dollars. What is the impact on net income over the two accounting periods?

b. Assuming that Maxwell designates the foreign currency option as a fair value hedge of a foreign currency receivable, prepare journal entries for the export sale and related hedge in U.S. dollars. What is the impact on net income over the two accounting periods?

LO 9-7

34. On September 1, Westbrook Corporation purchased goods from a foreign supplier at a price of 1,000,000 francs and will make payment in three months on December 1. On September 1, Westbrook acquired an option to purchase 1,000,000 francs in three months at a strike price of $0.852. The time value of the option is excluded from the assessment of hedge effectiveness, and the change in time value is recognized in net income over the life of the option. Relevant exchange rates and option premia for the franc are as follows:

Date	Spot Rate	Call Option Premium for December 1 (strike price $0.852)
September 1	$0.852	$0.0020
September 30	0.858	0.0075
December 1	0.870	N/A

Westbrook must close its books and prepare its third-quarter financial statements on September 30. The goods purchased on September 1 are sold in December.

a. Assuming that Westbrook designates the foreign currency option as a cash flow hedge of a foreign currency payable, prepare journal entries for the import purchase and related hedge in U.S. dollars. What is the impact on net income over the two accounting periods?

b. Assuming that Westbrook designates the foreign currency option as a fair value hedge of a foreign currency payable, prepare journal entries for the import purchase and related hedge in U.S. dollars. What is the impact on net income over the two accounting periods?

LO 9-7

35. On November 1, 2020, Cheng Company (a U.S.-based company) forecasts the purchase of goods from a foreign supplier for 100,000 yuan. Cheng expects to receive the goods on April 30, 2021, and make immediate payment. On November 1, 2020, Cheng enters into a six-month forward contract to buy 100,000 yuan. The company properly designates the forward contract as a cash flow hedge of a forecasted foreign currency transaction. Forward points are excluded in assessing hedge effectiveness and are amortized to net income using a straight-line method on a monthly basis over the life of the contract. The following U.S. dollar–Yuan exchange rates apply:

Date	Spot Rate	Forward Rate (to April 30, 2021)
November 1, 2020	$0.21	$0.195
December 31, 2020	0.19	0.170
April 30, 2021	0.18	N/A

As expected, Cheng receives goods from the foreign supplier on April 30, 2021, and pays 100,000 yuan immediately. Cheng sells the imported goods in the local market in May 2021.

a. Prepare all journal entries, including December 31 adjusting entries, to record the foreign currency forward contract and import purchase.

b. What is the impact on net income in 2020?

c. What is the impact on net income in 2021?

LO 9-7

36. On November 30, 2020, Walter Corporation (a U.S.-based company) forecasts the sale of equipment to a foreign customer at a price of 500,000 crowns. The equipment is expected to be delivered on January 31, 2021, with payment received upon delivery. Also on November 30, 2020, Walter pays $3,000 for an option to sell 500,000 crowns on January 31, 2021, at a strike price of $0.52. Walter properly designates its foreign currency option as a cash flow hedge of a forecasted foreign currency transaction. The time value of the option is excluded in assessing hedge effectiveness, and the change in time value is recognized in net income over the life of the option. The following U.S. dollar–crown exchange rates apply:

Date	Spot Rate	Put Option Premium for January 31, 2021 (strike price $0.52)
November 30, 2020	$0.53	$0.006
December 31, 2020	0.50	0.024
January 31, 2021	0.49	N/A

Walter delivers the equipment to the foreign customer on January 31, 2021, and immediately receives 500,000 crowns.

a. Prepare all journal entries, including December 31 adjusting entries, to record the foreign currency option and export sale.

b. What is the impact on net income in 2020?

c. What is the impact on net income in 2021?

LO 9-7, 9-8

37. On October 1, 2020, Mertag Company (a U.S.-based company) receives an order from a customer in Poland to deliver goods on January 31, 2021, for a price of 1,000,000 Polish zlotys (PLN). Mertag enters into a forward contract on October 1, 2020, to sell PLN 1,000,000 in four months (on January 31, 2021). U.S. dollar–Polish zloty exchange rates are as follows:

Date	Spot Rate	Forward Rate (to January 31, 2021)
October 1, 2020	$0.25	$0.29
December 31, 2020	0.28	0.31
January 31, 2021	0.30	N/A

Mertag designates the forward contract as a fair value hedge of a foreign currency firm commitment. The fair value of the firm commitment is measured by referring to changes in the forward rate, and, therefore, forward points are included in assessing hedge effectiveness. Mertag must close its books and prepare financial statements on December 31. Discounting to present value can be ignored.

a. Prepare journal entries for the foreign currency forward contract, foreign currency firm commitment, and export sale.

b. Determine the net benefit, if any, realized by Mertag from entering into the forward contract.

LO 9-8

38. On August 1, Pure Joy Corporation (a U.S.-based importer) placed an order to purchase merchandise from a foreign supplier at a price of 400,000 pounds. Pure Joy will receive and make payment for the merchandise in three months on October 31. On August 1, Pure Joy entered into a forward contract to purchase 400,000 pounds in three months at a forward rate of $0.60 per pound. The company properly designates the forward contract as a fair value hedge of a foreign currency firm commitment. The fair value of the firm commitment is measured by referring to changes in the forward rate, and, therefore, forward points are included in assessing hedge effectiveness. Relevant U.S. dollar exchange rates for the pound are as follows:

Date	Spot Rate	Forward Rate (to October 31)
August 1	$0.60	$0.60
September 30	0.63	0.66
October 31	0.68	N/A

Pure Joy must close its books and prepare its third-quarter financial statements on September 30. The merchandise is received and paid for on October 31 and sold to local customers in November. Discounting to present value can be ignored.

a. Prepare journal entries for the foreign currency forward contract, foreign currency firm commitment, and import purchase.

b. What is the impact on net income over the two accounting periods?

c. What is the amount of net cash outflow resulting from the purchase of merchandise from the foreign supplier?

LO 9-8

39. On June 1, Parker-Mae Corporation (a U.S.-based company) received an order to sell goods to a foreign customer at a price of 100,000 francs. Parker-Mae will ship the goods and receive payment in three months, on September 1. On June 1, Parker-Mae purchased an option to sell 100,000 francs in three months at a strike price of $1.00. The company designated the option as a fair value hedge of a foreign currency firm commitment. The option's time value is excluded in assessing hedge effectiveness, and the change in time value is recognized in net income. The fair value of the

firm commitment is measured by referring to changes in the spot rate (discounting to present value is ignored). Relevant exchange rates and option premiums for the franc are as follows:

Date	Spot Rate	Put Option Premium for September 1 (strike price $1.00)
June 1	$1.00	$0.020
June 30	0.94	0.072
September 1	0.90	N/A

Parker-Mae Corporation must close its books and prepare its second-quarter financial statements on June 30.

a. Prepare journal entries for the foreign currency option, foreign currency firm commitment, and export sale.

b. What is the impact on net income in each of the two accounting periods?

c. What is the amount of net cash inflow resulting from the sale of goods to the foreign customer?

LO 9-8

40. Amaretta Company (a U.S.-based company) ordered merchandise from a foreign supplier on November 20 at a price of 1,000,000 rupees when the spot rate was $0.050 per rupee. Delivery and payment were scheduled for December 20. On November 20, Amaretta acquired a call option on 1,000,000 rupees at a strike price of $0.050, paying a premium of $0.001 per rupee. The company designates the option as a fair value hedge of a foreign currency firm commitment. The fair value of the firm commitment is measured by referring to changes in the spot rate. The option's time value is excluded from the assessment of hedge effectiveness, and the change in time value is recognized in net income. The merchandise arrives, and Amaretta makes payment according to schedule. Amaretta sells the merchandise by December 31, when it closes its books.

a. Assuming a spot rate of $0.053 per rupee on December 20, prepare all journal entries to account for the foreign currency option, foreign currency firm commitment, and purchase of inventory.

b. Assuming a spot rate of $0.048 per rupee on December 20, prepare all journal entries to account for the foreign currency option, foreign currency firm commitment, and purchase of inventory.

LO 9-9

41. Based on past experience, Maas Corp. (a U.S.-based company) expects to purchase raw materials from a foreign supplier at a cost of 1,000,000 francs on March 15, 2021. To hedge this forecasted transaction, on December 15, 2020, the company acquires a call option to purchase 1,000,000 francs in three months. Maas selects a strike price of $0.58 per franc when the spot rate is $0.58 and pays a premium of $0.005 per franc. The spot rate increases to $0.584 at December 31, 2020, causing the fair value of the option to increase to $7,500. By March 15, 2021, when the raw materials are purchased, the spot rate has climbed to $0.59, resulting in a fair value for the option of $10,000. The raw materials are used in assembling finished products, which are sold by December 31, 2021, when Maas prepares its annual financial statements.

a. Prepare all journal entries for the option hedge of a forecasted transaction and for the purchase of raw materials.

b. What is the overall impact on net income over the two accounting periods?

c. What is the net cash outflow to acquire the raw materials?

LO 9-2, 9-7, 9-8

42. Pacifico Company, a U.S.-based importer of beer and wine, purchased 1,000 cases of Oktoberfest-style beer from a German supplier for 50,000 euros. Relevant U.S. dollar exchange rates for the euro are as follows:

Date	Spot Rate	Forward Rate to October 15	Call Option Premium for October 15 (strike price $1.10)
August 15	$1.10	$1.16	$0.05
September 30	1.15	1.19	0.06
October 15	1.18	1.18 (spot)	N/A

The company closes its books and prepares third-quarter financial statements on September 30.

a. Assume that the beer arrived on August 15, and the company made payment on October 15. There was no attempt to hedge the exposure to foreign exchange risk. Prepare journal entries to account for this import purchase.

b. Assume that the beer arrived on August 15, and the company made payment on October 15. On August 15, the company entered into a two-month forward contract to purchase 50,000 euros. The company designated the forward contract as a cash flow hedge of a foreign currency payable. Forward points are excluded in assessing hedge effectiveness and amortized to net income using a straight-line method on a monthly basis. Prepare journal entries to account for the import purchase and foreign currency forward contract.

c. Assume that the company ordered the beer on August 15. The beer arrived and the company paid for it on October 15. On August 15, the company entered into a two-month forward contract to purchase 50,000 euros. The company designated the forward contract as a fair value hedge of a foreign currency firm commitment. The fair value of the firm commitment is measured by referring to changes in the forward rate. Forward points are not excluded in assessing hedge effectiveness. Prepare journal entries to account for the foreign currency forward contract, foreign currency firm commitment, and import purchase.

d. Assume that the company ordered the beer on August 15. The beer arrived and the company paid for it on October 15. On August 15, the company purchased a two-month call option on 50,000 euros. The company designated the option as a fair value hedge of a foreign currency firm commitment. The fair value of the firm commitment is measured by referring to changes in the spot rate. The time value of the option is excluded from the assessment of hedge effectiveness, and the change in time value is recognized in net income over the life of the option. Prepare journal entries to account for the foreign currency option, foreign currency firm commitment, and import purchase.

e. Assume that, on August 15, the company forecasted the purchase of beer on October 15. On August 15, the company acquired a two-month call option on 50,000 euros. The company designated the option as a cash value hedge of a forecasted foreign currency transaction. The time value of the option is excluded from the assessment of hedge effectiveness, and the change in time value is recognized in net income over the life of the option. Prepare journal entries to account for the foreign currency option and import purchase.

Develop Your Skills

RESEARCH CASE—INTERNATIONAL FLAVORS AND FRAGRANCES

CPA skills

Many companies make annual reports available on their corporate website. Annual reports also can be accessed through the SEC's EDGAR system at www.sec.gov (under Filing Type, search for 10-K).

Access the most recent annual report for International Flavors and Fragrances Inc. (IFF) to complete the following requirements.

Required

1. Identify the location(s) in the annual report where IFF provides disclosures related to its management of foreign exchange risk.
2. Determine the types of hedging instruments the company uses and the types of hedges in which it engages.
3. Determine the manner in which the company discloses the fact that its foreign exchange hedges are effective in offsetting gains and losses on the underlying items being hedged.

ACCOUNTING STANDARDS CASE—FORECASTED TRANSACTIONS

CPA skills

Fergusson Corporation, a U.S. company, manufactures components for the automobile industry. In the past, Fergusson purchased actuators used in its products from a supplier in the United States. The company plans to shift its purchases to a supplier in Portugal. Fergusson's CFO expects to place an order with the Portuguese supplier in the amount of 200,000 euros in three months. In contemplation of this future import, the CFO purchased a euro call option to hedge the cash flow risk that the euro might appreciate against the U.S. dollar over the next three months. The CFO is aware that a foreign currency option used to hedge the cash flow risk associated with a forecasted foreign currency transaction may be designated as a hedge for accounting purposes only if the forecasted transaction is probable. However, he is unsure how he should demonstrate that the anticipated import purchase from Portugal is likely to occur. He wonders whether management's intention to make the purchase is sufficient.

Required

Search current U.S. authoritative accounting literature to determine whether management's intent is sufficient to assess that a forecasted foreign currency transaction is likely to occur. If not, what additional evidence must be considered? Identify the FASB ASC guidance for answering these questions.

ANALYSIS CASE—CASH FLOW HEDGE

CPA skills

On February 1, 2020, when the spot rate was $1.00 per Swiss franc, Blue Bogey Company (BBC) forecasted the purchase of component parts on May 1, 2020, at a price of 100,000 Swiss francs. On that date, BBC entered into a forward contract to purchase 100,000 Swiss francs on May 1, 2020, and designated the forward contract as a cash flow hedge of the forecasted transaction. The forward points are excluded from the assessment of hedge effectiveness and are straight-line amortized on a monthly basis. On May 1, 2020, the forward contract was settled, and the component parts were received and paid for. The parts were used in the assembly of finished goods that were sold by June 30, 2020.

BBC's trial balance at March 31 (end of the first quarter) reported the following amounts related to this cash flow hedge (credit balance in parentheses):

Trial Balance	March 31, 2020
Forward contract (asset)	$ 2,000
Cost of goods sold	6,000
Other comprehensive income (OCI)	(8,000)
Total	$ –0–

Required

Answer the following questions:

1. On February 1, 2020, was the Swiss franc selling at a discount or at a premium in the three-month forward market?
2. On February 1, 2020, what was the U.S. dollar per Swiss franc forward rate to May 1, 2020?
3. On March 31, 2020, what was the U.S. dollar per Swiss franc forward rate to May 1, 2020?
4. What amount did BBC recognize as Cost of Goods Sold in the second quarter of 2020?

INTERNET CASE—HISTORICAL EXCHANGE RATES

The Cinco Centavo Company (CCC), a U.S. company, made credit sales to four customers in Asia on September 15, 2018, and received payment on October 15, 2018. Information related to these sales is as follows:

Customer	Location	Invoice Price
Surat Ltd.	Mumbai, India	7,195,000 Indian rupees (INR)
Cebu Group	Cebu City, Philippines	5,417,000 Philippine pesos (PHP)
Hayagawa Company	Osaka, Japan	11,210,000 Japanese yen (JPY)
Senai Berhad	Johor Bahru, Malaysia	414,000 Malaysian ringgits (MYR)

CCC's fiscal year ends September 30.

Required

1. Use historical exchange rate information available on the Internet at www.x-rates.com, Historical Lookup, to find exchange rates between the U.S. dollar and each foreign currency for September 15, September 30, and October 15, 2018.

2. Determine the foreign exchange gains and losses that CCC would have recognized in net income in the fiscal years ended September 30, 2018, and September 30, 2019, and the overall foreign exchange gain or loss for each transaction. Determine for which transaction, if any, it would have been important for CCC to hedge its foreign exchange risk.
3. CCC could have acquired a one-month put option on September 15, 2018, to hedge the foreign exchange risk associated with each of the four export sales. In each case, the put option would have cost $100 with the strike price equal to the September 15, 2018, spot rate. Determine for which hedges, if any, CCC would have realized a net cash flow benefit from the foreign currency option.

COMMUNICATION CASE—FORWARD CONTRACTS AND OPTIONS

CPA skills

Palmetto Bug Extermination Corporation (PBEC), a U.S. company, regularly purchases chemicals from a supplier in Switzerland with the invoice price denominated in Swiss francs. PBEC has experienced several foreign exchange losses in the past year due to increases in the U.S. dollar price of the Swiss currency. As a result, Dewey Nukem, PBEC's CEO, has asked you to investigate the possibility of using derivative financial instruments, specifically foreign currency forward contracts and foreign currency options, to hedge the company's exposure to foreign exchange risk.

Required

Draft a memo to CEO Nukem comparing the advantages and disadvantages of using forward contracts and options to hedge foreign exchange risk. Recommend the type of hedging instrument you believe the company should employ, and justify your recommendation.

chapter 10

Translation of Foreign Currency Financial Statements

- Germany's Bayer will wrap up the $62.5 billion takeover of Monsanto on Thursday this week and also retire the name of the U.S. seeds maker, it said on Monday.[1]
- Walmart Inc. and Flipkart Group this weekend announced the closing of the $16 billion deal that makes Walmart the largest shareholder in Flipkart, with 77% of shares in the India-based e-commerce company.[2]
- Coca-Cola Co. is making an audacious move into coffee and retail outlets with the 3.9 billion-pound ($5.1 billion) purchase of U.K. chain Costa, its biggest acquisition in eight years and a push into the fiercely competitive java market.[3]

Learning Objectives

After studying this chapter, you should be able to:

LO 10-1 Explain the theoretical underpinnings and the limitations of the current rate and temporal methods.

LO 10-2 Describe guidelines for determining when foreign currency financial statements are to be translated using the current rate method and when they are to be remeasured using the temporal method.

LO 10-3 Translate a foreign subsidiary's financial statements into its parent's reporting currency using the current rate method and calculate the related translation adjustment.

LO 10-4 Remeasure a foreign subsidiary's financial statements using the temporal method and calculate the associated remeasurement gain or loss.

LO 10-5 Understand the rationale for hedging balance sheet exposure to foreign exchange risk and describe the treatment of gains and losses on hedges used for this purpose.

LO 10-6 Prepare a consolidation worksheet for a parent and its foreign subsidiary.

Recent announcements such as these are common in today's global economy. Companies establish operations in foreign countries for a variety of reasons including to develop new markets for their products, take advantage of lower production costs, or gain access to raw materials. Some multinational companies have reached a stage in their development in which domestic operations are no longer considered to be of higher priority than international operations. For example, in 2017, New York–headquartered International Flavors and Fragrances, Inc., had operations in 39 countries and generated 74 percent of its net sales outside North America; Merck & Co., Inc., generated 57 percent of its sales and had 35 percent of its property, plant, and equipment outside of the United States.

Foreign operations create numerous managerial problems for the parent company that do not exist for domestic operations. Some of these problems arise from cultural differences between the home and foreign countries. Other problems exist because foreign operations generally are required to comply with the laws and regulations of the foreign country. For example, most countries require companies to prepare financial statements in the local currency using local accounting rules.

[1] Reuters U.S. Edition Online, "Bayer to close Monsanto takeover, to retire target's name," June 4, 2018, www.reuters.com.

[2] Supermarket News, "Walmart completes acquisition of India's Flipkart," August 20, 2018, www.supermarketnews.com.

[3] Bloomberg, "Coke makes $5.1 billion bet on coffee market with Costa deal," August 31, 2018, www.bloomberg.com.

To prepare worldwide consolidated financial statements, a U.S. parent company must (1) convert the foreign GAAP financial statements of its foreign operations into U.S. GAAP and (2) translate the financial statements from the foreign currency into U.S. dollars. This conversion and translation process must be carried out regardless of whether the foreign operation is a branch, joint venture, majority-owned subsidiary, or affiliate accounted for under the equity method. This chapter deals with the issue of translating foreign currency financial statements into the parent's reporting currency.

Two major theoretical issues are related to the translation process: (1) which *translation method* should be used (the current rate method or the temporal method) and (2) where the resulting *translation adjustment* should be reported in the consolidated financial statements (as a translation gain/loss in net income or as a component of accumulated other comprehensive income in equity). In this chapter, these two issues are examined first from a conceptual perspective and second by the manner in which the FASB in the United States has resolved these issues. The chapter also discusses IFRS on this topic.

Exchange Rates Used in Translation

Two methods currently are used in the United States and most other countries to translate foreign currency financial statements into the parent company's reporting currency, and *two types of exchange rates* are used in applying these methods:

1. *Historical exchange rate:* the exchange rate that existed when a transaction occurred.
2. *Current exchange rate:* the exchange rate that exists at the balance sheet date.

Translation methods differ as to which balance sheet and income statement accounts are translated at historical exchange rates and which are translated at current exchange rates. Before continuing on to the next paragraph, please read the Discussion Question: How Do We Report This?

Assume that the company described in the Discussion Question began operations in Gualos on December 31, 2019, when the exchange rate was $0.20 per vilsek. When Southwestern Corporation prepared its consolidated balance sheet at December 31, 2019, it had no choice about the exchange rate used to translate the Land account into U.S. dollars. It translated the Land account carried on the foreign subsidiary's books at 150,000 vilseks at an exchange rate of $0.20; $0.20 was both the *historical* and *current* exchange rate for the Land account at December 31, 2019.

Consolidated Balance Sheet: 12/31/19	
Land (150,000 vilseks × $0.20)	$30,000

During the first quarter of 2020, the vilsek appreciates relative to the U.S. dollar by 15 percent; the exchange rate at March 31, 2020, is $0.23 per vilsek. In preparing its balance sheet at the end of the first quarter of 2020, Southwestern must decide whether the Land account carried on the subsidiary's balance sheet at 150,000 vilseks should be translated into dollars using the *historical exchange rate* of $0.20 or the *current exchange rate* of $0.23.

If the historical exchange rate is used at March 31, 2020, Land continues to be carried on the consolidated balance sheet at $30,000 with no change from December 31, 2019.

Historical Rate—Consolidated Balance Sheet: 3/31/20	
Land (150,000 vilseks × $0.20)	$30,000

Discussion Question

HOW DO WE REPORT THIS?

Southwestern Corporation operates throughout Texas, buying and selling widgets. To expand into more profitable markets, the company recently decided to open a small subsidiary in the nearby country of Gualos. The currency in Gualos is the vilsek. For some time, the government of that country held the exchange rate constant: 1 vilsek equaled $0.20 (or 5 vilseks equaled $1.00). Initially, Southwestern invested cash in this new operation; its $90,000 was converted into 450,000 vilseks ($90,000 × 5). Southwestern used one-third of this money (150,000 vilseks, or $30,000) to purchase land to hold for the possible construction of a plant, invested one-third in short-term marketable securities, and spent one-third in acquiring inventory for future resale.

Shortly thereafter, the Gualos government officially revalued the currency so that 1 vilsek was worth $0.23. Because of the strength of the local economy, the vilsek gained buying power in relation to the U.S. dollar. The vilsek then was considered more valuable than in the past. Southwestern's accountants realized that a change had occurred; each of the assets (land, inventory, and marketable securities) was now worth more in U.S. dollars than the original $30,000 investment: 150,000 vilseks × $0.23 = $34,500. Two of the company's top officers met to determine the appropriate method for reporting this change in currency values.

Controller: Nothing has changed. Our cost is still $30,000 for each item. That's what we spent. Accounting uses historical cost wherever possible. Thus, we should do nothing.

Finance director: Yes, but the old rates are meaningless now. We would be foolish to report figures based on a rate that no longer exists. The cost is still 150,000 vilseks for each item. You are right, the cost has not changed. However, the vilsek is now worth $0.23, so our reported value must change.

Controller: The new rate affects us only if we take money out of the country. We don't plan to do that for many years. The rate will probably change 20 more times before we remove money from Gualos. We've got to stick to our $30,000 historical cost. That's our cost, and that's good, basic accounting.

Finance director: You mean that for the next 20 years we will be translating balances for external reporting purposes using an exchange rate that has not existed for years? That doesn't make sense. I have a real problem using an antiquated rate for the inventory and marketable securities. They will be sold for cash when the new rate is in effect. These balances have no remaining relation to the original exchange rate.

Controller: You misunderstand the impact of an exchange rate fluctuation. Within Gualos, no impact occurs. One vilsek is still one vilsek. The effect is realized only when an actual conversion takes place into U.S. dollars at a new rate. At that point, we will properly measure and report the gain or loss. That is when realization takes place. Until then, our cost has not changed.

Finance director: I simply see no value at all in producing financial information based entirely on an exchange rate that does not exist. I don't care when realization takes place.

Controller: You've got to stick with historical cost; believe me. The exchange rate today isn't important unless we actually convert vilseks to dollars.

How should Southwestern report each of these three assets on its current balance sheet? Does the company have a gain because the value of the vilsek has increased relative to the U.S. dollar?

If the current exchange rate is used, Land is carried on the consolidated balance sheet at $34,500, an increase of $4,500 from December 31, 2019.

Current Rate—Consolidated Balance Sheet: 3/31/20	
Land (150,000 vilseks × $0.23)	$34,500

Translation Adjustments

To keep the accounting equation (A = L + SE) in balance, the increase of $4,500 in the Land account on the asset (A) side of the consolidated balance sheet when the current exchange rate is used must be offset by an equal $4,500 *increase* in stockholders' equity (SE) on the other side of the balance sheet. The increase in stockholders' equity is called a *positive translation adjustment.* It has a *credit* balance.

The increase in dollar value of the Land due to the vilsek's appreciation creates a positive translation adjustment. This is true for any asset on the Gualos subsidiary's balance sheet that is translated at the *current* exchange rate. *Assets translated at the current exchange rate when the foreign currency has appreciated generate a positive (credit) translation adjustment.*

Liabilities on the Gualos subsidiary's balance sheet that are translated at the current exchange rate also increase in dollar value when the vilsek appreciates. For example, Southwestern would report Notes Payable of 10,000 vilseks at $2,000 on the December 31, 2019, balance sheet and at $2,300 on the March 31, 2020, balance sheet. To keep the accounting equation in balance, the increase in liabilities (L) must be offset by a *decrease* in owners' equity (OE), giving rise to a *negative translation adjustment.* This has a *debit* balance. *Liabilities translated at the current exchange rate when the foreign currency has appreciated generate a negative (debit) translation adjustment.*

Balance Sheet Exposure

Balance sheet items (assets and liabilities) translated at the *current* exchange rate change in dollar value from balance sheet to balance sheet as a result of the change in exchange rate. These items are *exposed* to translation adjustment. Balance sheet items translated at *historical* exchange rates do not change in dollar value from one balance sheet to the next. These items are *not* exposed to translation adjustment. Exposure to translation adjustment is referred to as *balance sheet, translation,* or *accounting exposure. Transaction exposure,* discussed in the previous chapter, arises when a company has foreign currency receivables and payables and can be contrasted with *balance sheet exposure* in the following way: *Transaction exposure gives rise to foreign exchange gains and losses that are ultimately realized in cash; translation adjustments arising from balance sheet exposure do not directly result in cash inflows or outflows.*

Each item translated at the current exchange rate is exposed to translation adjustment. In effect, a separate translation adjustment exists for each of these exposed items. However, negative translation adjustments on liabilities offset positive translation adjustments on assets when the foreign currency appreciates. If total exposed assets equal total exposed liabilities throughout the year, the translation adjustments (although perhaps significant on an individual basis) net to a zero balance. The *net* translation adjustment needed to keep the consolidated balance sheet in balance is based solely on the *net asset* or *net liability* exposure.

A foreign operation has a *net asset balance sheet exposure* when assets translated at the current exchange rate are higher in amount than liabilities translated at the current exchange rate. A *net liability balance sheet exposure* exists when liabilities translated at the current exchange rate are higher than assets translated at the current exchange rate. The following summarizes the relationship between exchange rate fluctuations, balance sheet exposure, and translation adjustments:

Balance Sheet Exposure	**Foreign Currency (FC)**	
	Appreciates	**Depreciates**
Net asset	Positive translation adjustment	Negative translation adjustment
Net liability	Negative translation adjustment	Positive translation adjustment

Exactly how to handle the translation adjustment in the consolidated financial statements is a matter of some debate. The major issue is whether the translation adjustment should be treated as a *translation gain or loss reported in net income* (and then closed to retained earnings) or whether the translation adjustment should be treated as a *direct adjustment to owners' equity* (in accumulated other comprehensive income) *without affecting net income.* We consider this issue in more detail later, after examining methods of translation.

LO 10-1

Explain the theoretical underpinnings and the limitations of the current rate and temporal methods.

Translation Methods

Two major translation methods are currently used: (1) the current rate method and (2) the temporal method. (Although standard setters do not specifically use these names in their authoritative guidance, *current rate method* and *temporal method* provide a useful shorthand for describing the procedures required.) In this section, we discuss the concepts and basic procedures of each method from the perspective of a U.S.-based multinational company translating foreign currency financial statements into U.S. dollars.

Current Rate Method

The basic assumption underlying the *current rate method* is that a company's *net investment* in a foreign operation is *exposed* to foreign exchange risk. In other words, a foreign operation represents a foreign currency net asset, and if the foreign currency *decreases* in value against the U.S. dollar, a *decrease in the U.S. dollar value of the foreign currency net asset* occurs. This decrease in U.S. dollar value of the net investment will be reflected by reporting a *negative* (debit balance) translation adjustment in the consolidated financial statements. If the foreign currency *increases* in value, an *increase in the U.S. dollar value of the net asset* occurs and will be reflected through a *positive* (credit balance) translation adjustment.

To measure the net investment's exposure to foreign exchange risk, *all assets and all liabilities* of the foreign operation are translated at the *current* exchange rate. Stockholders' equity items are translated at historical rates. *The balance sheet exposure under the current rate method is equal to the foreign operation's net asset (total assets minus total liabilities) position.*[4]

Total assets > Total liabilities → Net asset exposure

A positive translation adjustment arises when the foreign currency appreciates, and a negative translation adjustment arises when the foreign currency depreciates.

To reiterate, assets and liabilities are translated at the current rate and stockholders' equity is translated at historical rates to reflect the fact that the current rate method assumes that the company's net investment in a foreign operation is exposed to foreign exchange risk; net investment is equal to stockholders' equity.

Another reason to translate equity accounts at historical rates is so that the translated amount for the subsidiary's equity accounts will be equal to the original amount of the investment in subsidiary on the parent's balance sheet. Otherwise, the parent will not be able to exactly eliminate the investment in subsidiary account against the subsidiary's stockholders' equity accounts on the consolidation worksheet.

As mentioned, the major difference between the translation adjustment and a foreign exchange gain or loss is that the translation adjustment is not necessarily realized through inflows and outflows of cash. The translation adjustment that arises when using the current rate method is unrealized. It can become a realized gain or loss only if the foreign operation is sold (for its book value) and the foreign currency proceeds from the sale are converted into U.S. dollars.

The current rate method requires translation of all income statement items at the exchange rate in effect at the date of accounting recognition. For example, January 1 sales revenue should be translated at the January 1 exchange rate, January 2 sales at the January 2 exchange rate, and so on. With so many transactions, this would be overly burdensome. Thus, in many cases, an assumption can be made that the revenue or expense is incurred evenly throughout

[4] In rare cases, a foreign subsidiary could have liabilities higher than assets (negative stockholders' equity). In those cases, a net liability exposure exists under the current rate method.

the accounting period and a weighted average-for-the-period exchange rate can be used for translation. However, when an income account, such as a gain or loss, occurs at a specific point in time, the exchange rate at that date should be used for translation.

Temporal Method

The basic objective underlying the *temporal method* of translation is to produce a set of U.S. dollar–translated financial statements as if the foreign subsidiary had actually used U.S. dollars in conducting its operations. Continuing with the Gualos subsidiary example, Southwestern, the U.S. parent, should report the Land account on the consolidated balance sheet at the amount of U.S. dollars that it would have spent if it had sent dollars to the subsidiary to purchase land. Because the land cost 150,000 vilseks at a time when one vilsek could be acquired with $0.20, the parent would have sent $30,000 to the subsidiary to acquire the land; this is the land's historical cost *in U.S. dollar terms.* The following rule is consistent with the temporal method's underlying objective:

1. Assets and liabilities carried on the foreign operation's balance sheet at *historical cost* are translated at *historical* exchange rates to yield an equivalent historical cost in U.S. dollars.
2. Conversely, assets and liabilities carried at a *current or future value* are translated at the *current* exchange rate to yield an equivalent current value in U.S. dollars.

Application of this rule maintains the underlying valuation method (current value or historical cost) that the foreign subsidiary uses in accounting for its assets and liabilities. In addition, stockholders' equity accounts are translated at historical exchange rates. Similar to the current rate method, this ensures that the translated amount of subsidiary's stockholders' equity is equal to the original amount of the investment in subsidiary on the parent's balance sheet.

Cash, marketable securities, receivables, and most liabilities are carried at current or future value and translated at the *current* exchange rate under the temporal method.[5] The temporal method generates either a net asset or a net liability balance sheet exposure, depending on whether cash plus marketable securities plus receivables are more than or less than liabilities.

Cash + Marketable securities + Receivables > Liabilities → Net asset exposure
Cash + Marketable securities + Receivables < Liabilities → Net liability exposure

Because the amount of liabilities (current plus long term) translated at the current exchange rate usually exceeds the amount of assets translated at the current exchange rate, *a net liability exposure generally exists when the temporal method is used.*

One way to understand the concept of exposure underlying the temporal method is to suppose that the parent actually carries on its balance sheet the foreign operation's cash, marketable securities, receivables, and payables. For example, consider the Japanese subsidiary of a U.S. parent company. The Japanese subsidiary's yen receivables that result from sales in Japan may be thought of as Japanese yen receivables of the U.S. parent that result from export sales to Japan. If the U.S. parent had yen receivables on its balance sheet, a decrease in the yen's value would result in a *foreign exchange loss.* A foreign exchange loss also occurs on the Japanese yen held in cash by the U.S. parent and on the Japanese yen–denominated marketable securities. A foreign exchange gain on the parent's Japanese yen payables resulting from foreign purchases would offset these foreign exchange losses. Whether a net gain or a net loss exists depends on the relative amount of yen cash, marketable securities, and receivables versus yen payables. Under the temporal method, the translation adjustment measures the "net foreign exchange gain or loss" on the

[5] Under current authoritative literature, all marketable equity securities and marketable debt securities that are classified as "trading" or "available for sale" are carried at fair value. Marketable debt securities classified as "held to maturity" are carried at amortized cost. Throughout the remainder of this chapter, we will assume that all marketable securities are reported at fair value.

foreign operation's cash, marketable securities, receivables, and payables, *as if those items were actually carried on the parent's books.*

Again, the major difference between the translation adjustment resulting from the use of the temporal method and a foreign exchange gain or loss is that the translation adjustment is not necessarily realized through inflows or outflows of cash. The U.S. dollar translation adjustment in this case *is realized* only if (1) the parent sends U.S. dollars to the Japanese subsidiary to pay all of its yen liabilities, and (2) the subsidiary converts its yen receivables and marketable securities into yen cash and then sends this amount plus the amount in its yen cash account to the U.S. parent, which converts it into U.S. dollars.

The temporal method translates income statement items at exchange rates that exist when the revenue is generated or the expense is incurred. For most items, an assumption can be made that the revenue or expense is incurred evenly throughout the accounting period and an average-for-the-period exchange rate can be used for translation. However, some expenses are related to assets carried at historical cost—for example, cost of goods sold, depreciation of property, plant, and equipment, and amortization of intangibles. Because the related assets are translated at historical exchange rates, these expenses must be translated at historical rates as well.

The current rate method and temporal method are the two methods currently used in the United States and in all countries that have adopted International Financial Reporting Standards as their local GAAP. A summary of the appropriate exchange rates for selected financial statement items under these two methods is presented in Exhibit 10.1.

Translation of Retained Earnings

Stockholders' equity items are translated at historical exchange rates under both the current rate and temporal methods. This creates somewhat of a problem in translating retained earnings.

EXHIBIT 10.1
Exchange Rates for Selected Financial Statement Items

	Temporal Method Exchange Rate	**Current Rate Method Exchange Rate**
	Balance Sheet	**Balance Sheet**
Assets		
Cash and receivables	Current	Current
Marketable securities	Current*	Current
Inventory at net realizable value	Current	Current
Inventory at cost	Historical	Current
Prepaid expenses	Historical	Current
Property, plant, and equipment	Historical	Current
Intangible assets	Historical	Current
Liabilities		
Current liabilities	Current	Current
Deferred income	Historical	Current
Long-term debt	Current	Current
Stockholders' equity		
Capital stock	Historical	Historical
Additional paid-in capital	Historical	Historical
Retained earnings	Composite	Composite
Dividends	Historical	Historical
	Income Statement	**Income Statement**
Revenues	Average	Average
Most expenses	Average	Average
Cost of goods sold	Historical	Average
Depreciation of property, plant, and equipment	Historical	Average
Amortization of intangibles	Historical	Average

*Marketable debt securities classified as held to maturity are carried at amortized cost and translated at the historical exchange rate under the temporal method.

Retained earnings is an accumulation of all of the net income less dividends declared by a company since its inception. At the end of the first year of a company's operations, foreign currency (FC) retained earnings (R/E) is translated as follows:

Net income in FC	[translated per method used to translate income statement items]	= Net income in $
– Dividends in FC	× historical exchange rate when declared	= –Dividends in $
Ending R/E in FC		Ending R/E in $

The ending dollar amount of retained earnings in Year 1 becomes the beginning dollar retained earnings for Year 2, and the translated retained earnings in Year 2 (and subsequent years) are then determined as follows:

Beginning R/E in FC	(carried forward from last year's translation)	= Beginning R/E in $
+ Net income in FC	[translated per method used to translate income statement items]	= + Net income in $
– Dividends in FC	× historical exchange rate when declared	= – Dividends in $
Ending R/E in FC		Ending R/E in $

The same approach translates retained earnings under both the current rate and the temporal methods. The only difference is that translation of the current period net income is calculated differently under the two methods.

Complicating Aspects of the Temporal Method

Under the temporal method, keeping a record of the acquisition date exchange rates is necessary when translating inventory, prepaid expenses, property, plant, and equipment, and intangible assets because these assets, carried at historical cost, are translated at historical exchange rates. Keeping track of the historical rates for these assets is not necessary under the current rate method. Translating these assets at historical rates makes the application of the temporal method more complicated than the current rate method.

Calculation of Cost of Goods Sold

Under the *current rate method,* the account Cost of Goods Sold (COGS) in foreign currency (FC) is simply translated using the average-for-the-period exchange rate (ER):

COGS in FC × Average ER = COGS in $

Under the *temporal method,* no single exchange rate can be used to directly translate COGS in FC into COGS in dollars. Instead, COGS must be decomposed into beginning inventory, purchases, and ending inventory, and each component of COGS must then be translated at its appropriate historical rate. For example, if a company acquires beginning inventory (FIFO basis) in the year 2020 evenly throughout the fourth quarter of 2019, then it uses the average exchange rate in the fourth quarter of 2019 to translate beginning inventory. Likewise, it uses the fourth-quarter (4thQ) 2020 exchange rate to translate ending inventory. When purchases can be assumed to have been made evenly throughout 2020, the average 2020 exchange rate is used to translate purchases:

Beginning inventory in FC	×	Historical ER (4thQ 2019)	=	Beginning inventory in $
+ Purchases in FC	×	Average ER (2017)	=	+ Purchases in $
– Ending inventory in FC	×	Historical ER (4thQ 2020)	=	– Ending inventory in $
COGS in FC				COGS in $

Application of the Lower-of-Cost-or-Net-Realizable-Value Rule

Under the *current rate method,* the ending inventory reported on the foreign currency balance sheet is translated at the current exchange rate regardless of whether it is carried at cost or a lower net realizable value. Application of the *temporal method* requires the inventory's foreign currency cost to be translated into U.S. dollars at the historical exchange rate and foreign currency net realizable value to be translated into U.S. dollars at the current exchange rate. The *lower of the dollar cost and dollar net realizable value* is reported on the consolidated balance sheet. As a result, inventory can be carried at foreign currency cost on the foreign currency balance sheet and at U.S. dollar–translated net realizable value on the U.S. dollar consolidated balance sheet, and vice versa.

Property, Plant, and Equipment, Depreciation, and Accumulated Depreciation

The *temporal method* requires translating property, plant, and equipment acquired at different times at different (historical) exchange rates. The same is true for depreciation of property, plant, and equipment and accumulated depreciation related to property, plant, and equipment.

For example, assume that a company purchases a piece of equipment on January 1, 2018, for FC 1,000 when the exchange rate is \$1.00 per FC. It purchases another item of equipment one year later on January 1, 2019, for FC 5,000 when the exchange rate is \$1.20 per FC. Both pieces of equipment have a five-year useful life. The temporal method reports the amount of the equipment on the consolidated balance sheet on December 31, 2020, when the exchange rate is \$1.50 per FC, as follows:

FC 1,000	× \$1.00	=	\$1,000
5,000	× 1.20	=	6,000
FC 6,000			\$7,000

Depreciation expense for 2020 under the temporal method is calculated as shown here:

FC 200	× \$1.00	=	\$ 200
1,000	× 1.20	=	1,200
FC 1,200			\$1,400

Accumulated depreciation under the temporal method is calculated as shown:

FC 600	× \$1.00	=	\$ 600
2,000	× 1.20	=	2,400
FC 2,600			\$3,000

Similar procedures apply for intangible assets as well.

The *current rate method* reports equipment on the December 31, 2020, balance sheet at \$9,000 (FC 6,000 × \$1.50). Depreciation expense is translated at the average exchange rate of \$1.40 to be \$1,680 (FC 1,200 × \$1.40), and accumulated depreciation is \$3,900 (FC 2,600 × \$1.50 = \$3,900).

In this example, the foreign subsidiary has only two pieces of equipment requiring translation. In comparison with the current rate method, the temporal method can require substantial additional work for subsidiaries that own hundreds and thousands of items of property, plant, and equipment.

Gain or Loss on the Sale of an Asset

Assume that a foreign subsidiary sells land that cost FC 1,000 at a selling price of FC 1,200. The subsidiary reports an FC 200 gain on the sale of land on its income statement. It acquired the land when the exchange rate was \$1.00 per FC; it made the sale when the exchange rate was \$1.20 per FC; and the exchange rate at the balance sheet date is \$1.50 per FC. How should the gain on the sale of an asset be translated into U.S. dollars?

The *current rate method* translates the gain on sale of land at the exchange rate in effect at the date of sale:

$$FC\ 200 \times \$1.20 = \$240$$

The *temporal method* cannot translate the gain on the sale of land directly. Instead, it requires translating the cash received and the cost of the land sold into U.S. dollars separately, with the difference being the U.S. dollar value of the gain. In accordance with the rules of the temporal method, the Cash account is translated at the exchange rate on the date of sale, and the Land account is translated at the historical rate:

Cash	FC1,200 ×	$1.20 =	$1,440
Land	1,000 ×	1.00 =	1,000
Gain	FC 200		$ 440

Treatment of Translation Adjustment

The *first issue* related to the translation of foreign currency financial statements is selecting the appropriate method. The *second issue* in financial statement translation relates to deciding *where to report the resulting translation adjustment in the consolidated financial statements.* There are two prevailing schools of thought with regard to this second issue:

1. *Translation gain or loss:* This treatment considers the translation adjustment to be a gain or loss analogous to the gains and losses arising from foreign currency transactions and reports it in net income in the period in which the fluctuation in the exchange rate occurs.

The first of two conceptual problems with treating translation adjustments as gains or losses in income is that the gain or loss is unrealized; that is, no cash inflow or outflow accompanies it. The second problem is that the gain or loss could be inconsistent with economic reality. For example, the depreciation of a foreign currency can have a *positive* impact on the foreign operation's export sales and income, but the particular translation method used gives rise to a translation *loss.*

2. *Cumulative translation adjustment in other comprehensive income:* The alternative to reporting the translation adjustment as a gain or loss in net income is to include it in other comprehensive income. In effect, this treatment defers the gain or loss in stockholders' equity (Accumulated Other Comprehensive Income, or AOCI) until it is realized in some way. As a balance sheet account, the cumulative translation adjustment (CTA) is not closed at the end of an accounting period and fluctuates in amount over time.

The two major translation methods and the two possible treatments for the translation adjustment give rise to these four possible combinations:

Combination	Translation Method	Treatment of Translation Adjustment
A	Temporal	Gain or loss in Net Income
B	Temporal	CTA in Other Comprehensive Income
C	Current rate	Gain or loss in Net Income
D	Current rate	CTA in Other Comprehensive Income

Authoritative Guidance

Prior to 1975, the United States had no authoritative guidance on which translation method to use or where to report the translation adjustment in the consolidated financial statements. Different companies used different combinations. As an indication of the importance of this particular accounting issue, the first official pronouncement issued by the newly created FASB in 1974 was *SFAS 1,* "Disclosure of Foreign Currency Translation Information." It did not express a preference for any particular combination but simply required disclosure of the method used and the treatment of the translation adjustment.

The use of different combinations by different companies created a lack of comparability across companies. To eliminate this noncomparability, in 1975 the FASB issued *SFAS 8,* "Accounting for the Translation of Foreign Currency Transactions and Foreign Currency Financial Statements." It mandated use of the *temporal method* with all companies reporting *translation gains or losses* in net income for all foreign operations.

U.S. multinational companies (MNCs) strongly opposed *SFAS 8.* Specifically, they considered reporting translation gains and losses in income to be inappropriate because they are unrealized. Moreover, because currency fluctuations often reversed themselves in subsequent quarters, artificial volatility in quarterly earnings resulted.

After releasing two exposure drafts proposing new translation rules, the FASB finally issued *SFAS 52,* "Foreign Currency Translation," in 1981. This resulted in a complete overhaul of U.S. GAAP with regard to foreign currency translation. A narrow four-to-three vote of the board approving *SFAS 52* indicates how contentious the issue of foreign currency translation has been. Despite the narrow vote, *SFAS 52* has stood the test of time and was incorporated into the FASB *Accounting Standards Codification®* (ASC) in 2009 as part of Topic 830, "Foreign Currency Matters."

LO 10-2

Describe guidelines for determining when foreign currency financial statements are to be translated using the current rate method and when they are to be remeasured using the temporal method.

Determining the Appropriate Translation Method

Implicit in the *temporal method* is the assumption that foreign subsidiaries of U.S. MNCs have very close ties to their parent companies and that they would actually carry out their day-to-day operations and keep their books in the U.S. dollar if they could. To reflect the integrated nature of the foreign subsidiary with its U.S. parent, the translation process should create a set of U.S. dollar–translated financial statements as if the foreign subsidiary had actually used the dollar in carrying out its activities. This is the *U.S. dollar perspective* to translation.

In developing the current authoritative guidance, the FASB recognized two types of foreign entities. First, some foreign entities are so closely integrated with their parents that they conduct much of their business in U.S. dollars. *Second, other foreign entities are relatively self-contained and integrated with the local economy; primarily, they use a foreign currency in their daily operations.* For the first type of entity, the FASB determined that the U.S. dollar perspective still applies, and, therefore, use of the *temporal method* with translation gains and losses reported in *net income* (and closed to retained earnings) is still relevant.

For the second relatively independent type of entity, a *local currency perspective* to translation is applicable. For this type of entity, the FASB determined that a different translation methodology, namely the *current rate method,* should be used for translation. Furthermore, translation adjustments should be reported in *other comprehensive income* and then closed out to a *separate component of stockholders' equity (accumulated other comprehensive income)* on the balance sheet.

Functional Currency

To determine whether a specific foreign operation is integrated with its parent or self-contained and integrated with the local economy, the FASB created the concept of the *functional currency.* The functional currency is defined as the currency of the foreign entity's primary economic operating environment. It can be either the parent's currency (U.S. dollar for a U.S.-based company) or a foreign currency (generally the local currency). The functional currency orientation results in the following rule:

Functional Currency	Translation Method	Translation Adjustment
U.S. dollar	Temporal method	Gain (loss) in Net Income (closed to Retained Earnings)
Foreign currency	Current rate method	Separate component of Other Comprehensive Income (closed to Accumulated Other Comprehensive Income)

In addition to introducing the concept of the *functional currency,* the FASB introduced some new terminology. The *reporting currency* is the currency in which the entity prepares its financial statements. For U.S.-based corporations, this is the U.S. dollar. If a foreign operation's functional currency is the U.S. dollar, foreign currency balances must be *remeasured* into U.S. dollars using the temporal method with translation adjustments reported as *remeasurement gains and losses* in net income (and closed to retained earnings). When a foreign currency is the functional currency, foreign currency balances are *translated* using the current rate method, and a *translation adjustment* is reported in other comprehensive income (and closed to accumulated other comprehensive income (AOCI)).

The functional currency is essentially a matter of fact. However, in some cases, the facts will not clearly indicate a single functional currency. Management's judgment is essential in assessing the facts to determine a foreign entity's functional currency. Indicators provided by the FASB to guide parent company management in its determination of a foreign entity's functional currency are presented in Exhibit 10.2. ASC 830-10-55-5 states that these indicators, "and possibly others, should be considered individually and collectively when determining the functional currency." However, the FASB provides no guidance as to how to weight these indicators in determining the functional currency. Leaving the decision about identifying the functional currency up to management allows some flexibility in this process.

Highly Inflationary Economies

Multinationals do not need to determine the functional currency of those foreign entities located in a *highly inflationary economy.* In those cases, entities must use the *temporal method with remeasurement gains or losses reported in net income.*

A country is defined as having a *highly inflationary economy* when its cumulative three-year inflation exceeds 100 percent. With compounding, this equates to an average of approximately 26 percent per year for three years in a row. Countries that have met this definition at some time include Argentina, Brazil, Israel, Mexico, and Turkey. In any given year, a country may or may not be classified as highly inflationary, depending on its most recent three-year experience with inflation.

One reason for this rule is to avoid a "disappearing plant problem" caused by using the current rate method in a country with high inflation. Remember that under the current rate method, all assets (including fixed assets) are translated at the current exchange rate. To see the problem this creates in a highly inflationary economy, consider the following hypothetical example.

The Brazilian subsidiary of a U.S. parent purchased land at the end of 1984 for 10,000,000 cruzeiros (Cr$) when the exchange rate was $0.001 per Cr$. Under the *current rate method,* Land is reported in the parent's consolidated balance sheet (B.S.) at $10,000:

	Historical Cost		Current ER		Consolidated B.S.
1984	Cr$ 10,000,000	×	$0.001	=	$10,000

In 1985, Brazil experienced roughly 200 percent inflation. Accordingly, with the forces of purchasing power parity at work, the cruzeiro plummeted against the U.S. dollar to a value of

EXHIBIT 10.2
Indicators for Determining the Functional Currency

	Indication That Functional Currency Is the:	
Indicator	**Foreign Currency**	**Parent's Currency**
Cash flow	Primarily in FC and does not affect parent's cash flows	Directly impacts parent's cash flows on a current basis
Sales price	Not affected on short-term basis by changes in exchange rate	Affected on short-term basis by changes in exchange rate
Sales market	Active local sales market	Sales market mostly in parent's country or sales denominated in parent's currency
Expenses	Primarily local costs	Primarily costs for components obtained from parent's country
Financing	Primarily denominated in foreign currency and FC cash flows adequate to service obligations	Primarily from parent or denominated in parent currency or FC cash flows not adequate to service obligations
Intra-entity transactions	Low volume of intra-entity transactions, not extensive interrelationship with parent's operations	High volume of intra-entity transactions and extensive interrelationship with parent's operations

$0.00025 at the end of 1985. Under the current rate method, the parent's consolidated balance sheet reports Land at $2,500, and a negative translation adjustment of $7,500 results:

	Historical Cost		Current ER		Consolidated B.S.
1985	Cr$ 10,000,000	×	$0.00025	=	$2,500

Using the current rate method, 75 percent of the Land's U.S. dollar value "disappeared" in one year—and land is not even a depreciable asset!

In the exposure draft that led to the current authoritative guidance on translation, the FASB proposed requiring companies with operations in highly inflationary countries to first *restate* the foreign financial statements for inflation and then *translate* all financial statement accounts using the current exchange rate. For example, with 200 percent inflation in 1985, the Land account would have been written up to Cr$ 40,000,000 and then translated at the current exchange rate of $0.00025, producing a U.S. dollar–translated amount of $10,000, the same as in 1984.

Companies objected to making inflation adjustments, however, because of a lack of reliable inflation indices in many countries. The FASB backed off from requiring the *restate/translate* approach; instead it requires using the temporal method in highly inflationary countries. In the previous example, under the *temporal method,* a firm uses the historical rate of $0.001 to translate the land value year after year. The firm carries land on the consolidated balance sheet at $10,000 each year, thereby avoiding the disappearing plant problem.

Once a country is classified as highly inflationary, a decrease in the cumulative three-year inflation rate below 100 percent is not necessarily sufficient to remove it from this classification. FASB ASC 830-10-55-25 and the SEC staff suggest that if there is no evidence to suggest that the drop below 100 percent is "other than temporary," the country should continue to be viewed as highly inflationary. The magnitude of the decrease below 100 percent, the length of time the rate is less than 100 percent, and the country's current economic conditions should be taken into account in the "other than temporary" analysis.

In recent years, few countries have met the FASB's definition of highly inflationary. One of the most significant countries regularly exceeding this threshold is Venezuela, which has been identified as highly inflationary since January 2010.[6] Many U.S. companies, especially those in the energy industry, have subsidiaries in Venezuela. In 2010, those U.S. parent companies that previously designated their Venezuelan operation as having the local currency as functional currency, and therefore used the current rate method for translation, were compelled to change their translation method to the temporal method and begin reporting remeasurement gains and losses in net income.

More recently, in June 2018, each of the major public accounting firms concluded that Argentina had reached the threshold of having a cumulative three-year inflation exceeding 100 percent. "Therefore, we would expect a company that reports on a calendar year-end basis to conclude that Argentina is highly inflationary no later than the quarter ended June 30, 2018. This would require that it applies the accounting guidance for highly inflationary economies during its fiscal quarter beginning July 1, 2018."[7]

Appropriate Exchange Rate

In some countries, such as Venezuela, there is more than one rate at which the local currency can be converted into foreign currency. Often there is an "official rate" that is available from the Central Bank, and a "parallel rate" that is available in the open (sometimes illegal) market. Or in some countries there is one rate for certain types of transactions and another rate for

[6] The International Practices Task Force (IPTF) of the Center for Audit Quality (CAQ) SEC Regulations Committee monitors the inflationary status of certain countries and identifies those that meet the FASB's definition of highly inflationary. In May 2018, Angola, South Sudan, Suriname, and Venezuela were the only countries identified by the IPTF with three-year cumulative inflation rates exceeding 100 percent. Source: Center for Audit Quality, "Monitoring Inflation in Certain Countries," May 16, 2018, available at www.thecaq.org/our-committees/international-practices-task-force.

[7] KPMG, "Defining Issues: Financial reporting considerations for companies with operations in Argentina," July 5, 2018, available at https://frv.kpmg.us/reference-library/2018/defining-issues-18-11-argentina-inflation.html.

other transactions. For example, in January 2010, in conjunction with an official devaluation of the local currency, the Venezuelan government established an exchange rate of 2.6 bolivar fuertes (BsF) per one U.S. dollar for *essential* imports (such as food and medicine), and an exchange rate of BsF 4.3 per U.S. dollar for the import of *nonessential* goods. The existence of multiple exchange rates raises the question of which exchange rate to use in the financial statement translation process.

When the temporal method is used, ASC 830-20-30-3 indicates that the appropriate rate to use is the applicable rate at which a transaction could be settled, which is a matter for management judgment. In the case of Venezuela, for example, the Center for Audit Quality's International Practices Task Force (IPTF) determined that while Venezuelan law generally requires foreign currency transactions to be settled at the official exchange rate, because some transactions denominated in U.S. dollars may be settled using the parallel rate of exchange, either exchange rate might be appropriate for the translation of U.S. dollar–denominated assets and liabilities.

In contrast, when the current rate method is used, ASC 830-30-45-6 states that the exchange rate applicable for converting dividend remittances into U.S. dollars should be used to translate financial statements. Generally, this will be the official exchange rate established by the Central Bank or other governmental authority.

International Accounting Standard 21—The Effects of Changes in Foreign Exchange Rates

IAS 21, "The Effects of Changes in Foreign Exchange Rates," provides guidance in IFRS with respect to the translation of foreign currency financial statements. *IAS 21* generally follows the functional currency approach introduced by the FASB. Under *IAS 21,* as is true under U.S. GAAP, a foreign subsidiary's financial statements are translated using the current rate method when a foreign currency is the functional currency and are remeasured using the temporal method when the parent company's currency is the functional currency. Significant differences between IFRS and U.S. GAAP relate to (1) the hierarchy of factors used to determine the functional currency and (2) the method used to translate the foreign currency statements of a subsidiary located in a hyperinflationary country.

Although stated differently, the factors to be considered in determining the functional currency of a foreign subsidiary in *IAS 21* generally are consistent with U.S. GAAP functional currency indicators. Specifically, *IAS 21* indicates that the *primary* factors to be considered are the following:

1. The currency that mainly influences sales price.
2. The currency of the country whose competitive forces and regulations mainly determine sales price.
3. The currency that mainly influences labor, material, and other costs of providing goods and services.

Other factors to be considered are the following:

1. The currency in which funds from financing activities are generated.
2. The currency in which receipts from operating activities are retained.
3. Whether the foreign operation carries out its activities as an extension of the parent or with a significant degree of autonomy.
4. The volume of transactions with the parent.
5. Whether cash flows generated by the foreign operation directly affect the cash flows of the parent.
6. Whether cash flows generated by the foreign operation are sufficient to service its debt.

IAS 21 states that when the preceding indicators are mixed and the functional currency is not obvious, the parent must give priority to the primary indicators in determining the foreign entity's functional currency.

As noted earlier, U.S. GAAP is silent with respect to weights to be assigned to various indicators to determine the functional currency, and there is no hierarchy provided. Because of this difference in the functional currency determination process, it is possible that a foreign subsidiary could be determined to have a functional currency under IFRS that would be different from the functional currency determined under U.S. GAAP.

Under *IAS 21,* the financial statements of a foreign subsidiary located in a hyperinflationary economy are translated into the parent's currency using a two-step process. First, the financial statements are restated for local inflation in accordance with *IAS 29,* "Financial Reporting in Hyperinflationary Economies." Second, each financial statement line item, which has now been restated for local inflation, is translated using the current exchange rate. In effect, neither the temporal method nor the current rate method is used when the subsidiary is located in a country experiencing hyperinflation. Because all balance sheet accounts, including stockholders' equity, are translated at the current exchange rate, a translation adjustment does not exist. Unlike U.S. GAAP, IFRS does not provide a bright-line threshold to identify a hyperinflationary economy. Instead, *IAS 29* provides a list of characteristics that indicate hyperinflation, including (1) the general population prefers to keep its wealth in a relatively stable foreign currency; (2) interest rates, wages, and other prices are linked to a price index; and (3) the cumulative rate of inflation over three years is approaching, or exceeds, 100 percent. As noted earlier in this chapter, under current U.S. GAAP, the financial statements of a foreign subsidiary located in a highly inflationary economy must be translated using the temporal method, and high inflation is defined as a cumulative three-year inflation of 100 percent or more.

The Translation Process Illustrated

To provide a basis for demonstrating the translation and remeasurement procedures prescribed by current authoritative literature, assume that USCO (a U.S.-based company) forms a wholly owned subsidiary in Switzerland (SWISSCO) on December 31, 2019. On that date, USCO invested $300,000 in exchange for all of the subsidiary's common stock. Given the exchange rate of $0.60 per Swiss franc (CHF), the initial capital investment was CHF 500,000, of which CHF 150,000 was immediately invested in inventory and the remainder held in cash. Thus, SWISSCO began operations on January 1, 2020, with stockholders' equity (net assets) of CHF 500,000 and net monetary assets of CHF 350,000. (Recall that monetary assets consist primarily of cash, receivables, and marketable securities.)

SWISSCO
Opening Balance Sheet
January 1, 2020

Assets	CHF	Liabilities and Equity	CHF
Cash	CHF 350,000	Common stock	CHF 100,000
Inventory	150,000	Additional paid-in capital	400,000
	CHF 500,000		CHF 500,000

During 2020, SWISSCO purchased property, plant, and equipment, acquired a patent, and purchased additional inventory, primarily on account. It negotiated a five-year loan to help finance the purchase of equipment. It sold goods, primarily on account, and incurred expenses. It generated income after taxes of CHF 470,000 and declared dividends of CHF 150,000 on October 1, 2020.

As a company incorporated in Switzerland, SWISSCO accounts for its activities using IFRS, which differs from U.S. GAAP in many respects. As noted in the introduction to this chapter, to prepare consolidated financial statements, USCO must first convert SWISSCO's financial statements to a U.S. GAAP basis.[8] SWISSCO's U.S. GAAP financial statements for the year 2020 in Swiss francs appear in Exhibit 10.3.

[8] Differences in accounting rules across countries are discussed in more detail in Chapter 11.

EXHIBIT 10.3
Foreign Currency Financial Statements

SWISSCO
Income Statement
For Year Ending December 31, 2020

	CHF
Sales	4,000,000
Cost of goods sold	(3,000,000)
Gross profit	1,000,000
Depreciation expense	(100,000)
Amortization expense	(10,000)
Other expenses	(220,000)
Income before income taxes	670,000
Income taxes	(200,000)
Net income	470,000

Statement of Retained Earnings
For Year Ending December 31, 2020

	CHF
Retained earnings, 1/1/20	–0–
Net income, 2020	470,000
Less: Dividends, 10/1/20	(150,000)
Retained earnings, 12/31/20	320,000

Balance Sheet December 31, 2020

Assets	CHF	Liabilities and Equity	CHF
Cash	130,000	Accounts payable	600,000
Accounts receivable	200,000	Total current liabilities	600,000
Inventory*	400,000	Long-term debt	250,000
Total current assets	730,000	Total liabilities	850,000
Property, plant and equipment	1,000,000	Common stock	100,000
Accumulated depreciation	(100,000)	Additional paid-in capital	400,000
Patents, net	40,000	Retained earnings	320,000
Total assets	1,670,000	Total equity	820,000
		Total liabilities and equity	1,670,000

Statement of Cash Flows
For Year Ending December 31, 2020

	CHF
Operating activities:	
Net income	470,000
Add: Depreciation expense	100,000
Amortization expense	10,000
Increase in accounts receivable	(200,000)
Increase in inventory	(250,000)
Increase in accounts payable	600,000
Net cash from operations	730,000
Investing activities:	
Purchase of property, plant and equipment	(1,000,000)
Acquisition of patent	(50,000)
Net cash from investing activities	(1,050,000)

*Inventory is valued at FIFO cost under the lower-of-cost-or-market-value rule; ending inventory was acquired evenly throughout the fourth quarter.

(continued)

(*continued*)

Statement of Cash Flows For Year Ending December 31, 2020	
Financing activities:	
Proceeds from long-term debt	250,000
Payment of dividends	(150,000)
Net cash from financing activities	100,000
Decrease in cash	(220,000)
Cash at 12/31/19	350,000
Cash at 12/31/20	130,000

To properly translate the Swiss franc financial statements into U.S. dollars, USCO must gather exchange rates between the Swiss franc and U.S. dollar at various points in time. Relevant exchange rates (in U.S. dollars) are as follows:

January 1, 2020	$1.00
Rate when property, plant and equipment was acquired and long-term debt was incurred, March 15, 2020	1.01
Rate when patent was acquired, April 10, 2020	1.02
Average 2020	1.05
Rate when dividends were declared, October 1, 2020	1.07
Average fourth quarter 2020	1.08
December 31, 2020	1.10

The Swiss franc steadily appreciated against the dollar during the year, from a value of $1.00 on January 1 to $1.10 on December 31.

LO 10-3

Translate a foreign subsidiary's financial statements into its parent's reporting currency using the current rate method and calculate the related translation adjustment.

Translation of Financial Statements—Current Rate Method

The first step in translating foreign currency financial statements is to determine the functional currency. Assuming that the Swiss franc is the functional currency, the current rate method must be used with the cumulative translation adjustment reported in a separate component of stockholders' equity on the balance sheet. The amount of the cumulative translation adjustment can be determined indirectly as the amount that is needed to keep the translated balance sheet in balance. Translating the income statement first, followed by the statement of retained earnings, and then the balance sheet, facilitates the translation adjustment being reported in the balance sheet. (Conversely, the balance sheet is remeasured first when the temporal method is used.) Translation of the income statement and statement of retained earnings into U.S. dollars using the current rate method is shown in Exhibit 10.4.

All revenues and expenses are translated at the exchange rate in effect at the date of accounting recognition. We utilize the weighted average exchange rate for 2020 here because each revenue and expense in this illustration would have been recognized evenly throughout the year. However, when an income account, such as a gain or loss, occurs at a specific point in time, the exchange rate as of that date is applied. Depreciation and amortization expenses also are translated at the average rate for the year. These expenses accrue evenly throughout the year even though the journal entry to recognize them might not have been made until year-end for convenience.

The translated amount of net income for 2020 is brought down from the income statement into the statement of retained earnings. Dividends are translated at the exchange rate on the date of declaration.

EXHIBIT 10.4
Translation of Income Statement and Statement of Retained Earnings—Current Rate Method

SWISSCO
Income Statement
For Year Ending December 31, 2020

	CHF	Translation Rate*	U.S.$
Sales	CHF 4,000,000	1.05 A	$4,200,000
Cost of goods sold	(3,000,000)	1.05 A	(3,150,000)
Gross profit	1,000,000		1,050,000
Depreciation expense	(100,000)	1.05 A	(105,000)
Amortization expense	(10,000)	1.05 A	(10,500)
Other expenses	(220,000)	1.05 A	(231,000)
Income before income taxes	670,000		703,500
Income taxes	(200,000)	1.05 A	(210,000)
Net income	CHF 470,000		$ 493,500

Statement of Retained Earnings
For Year Ending December 31, 2020

	CHF	Translation Rate*	U.S.$
Retained earnings, 1/1/20	CHF –0–		$ –0–
Net income, 2020	470,000	From income statement	493,500
Dividends, 10/1/20	(150,000)	1.07 H	(160,500)
Retained earnings, 12/31/20	CHF 320,000		$ 333,000

*Indicates the exchange rate used and whether the rate is the current (C), average (A), or historical (H) rate.

Translation of the Balance Sheet

Looking at SWISSCO's translated balance sheet in Exhibit 10.5, note that all assets and liabilities are translated at the current exchange rate. Common stock and additional paid-in capital are translated at the exchange rate on the day the common stock was originally acquired by the parent company. Retained earnings at December 31, 2020, is brought down from the statement of retained earnings. Application of these procedures results in total assets of $1,837,000 and total liabilities and equities of $1,768,000. The balance sheet is brought into balance by creating a positive translation adjustment of $69,000 that is treated as an increase in stockholders' equity.

Note that the translation adjustment for 2020 is a *positive* $69,000 (credit balance). The sign of the translation adjustment (positive or negative) is a function of two factors: (1) the nature of the balance sheet exposure (asset or liability) and (2) the change in the exchange rate (appreciation or depreciation). In this illustration, SWISSCO has a *net asset exposure* (total assets translated at the current exchange rate are more than total liabilities translated at the current exchange rate), and the Swiss franc has *appreciated,* creating a *positive translation adjustment.*

The translation adjustment can be derived as the amount needed to bring the balance sheet back into balance. The translation adjustment also can be calculated by considering the impact of exchange rate changes on the beginning balance and subsequent changes in the net asset position, summarized as follows:

1. Translate the net asset balance of the subsidiary at the beginning of the year at the exchange rate in effect on that date (*a*).
2. Translate individual increases and decreases in the net asset balance during the year at the rates in effect when those increases and decreases occurred (*b*). Only a few events, such as net income, dividends, stock issuance, and the acquisition of treasury stock, actually change net assets. Transactions such as the acquisition of equipment or the payment of a liability have no effect on total net assets.

EXHIBIT 10.5
Translation of Balance Sheet—Current Rate Method

SWISSCO
Balance Sheet
December 31, 2020

	CHF	Translation Rate	U.S.$
Assets			
Cash	CHF 130,000	1.10 C	$ 143,000
Accounts receivable	200,000	1.10 C	220,000
Inventory	400,000	1.10 C	440,000
Total current assets	730,000		803,000
Property, plant, and equipment	1,000,000	1.10 C	1,100,000
Less: Accumulated depreciation	(100,000)	1.10 C	(110,000)
Patents, net	40,000	1.10 C	44,000
Total assets	CHF 1,670,000		$1,837,000
Liabilities and Equities			
Accounts payable	CHF 600,000	1.10 C	$ 660,000
Total current liabilities	600,000		660,000
Long-term debt	250,000	1.10 C	275,000
Total liabilities	850,000		935,000
Common stock	100,000	1.00 H	100,000
Additional paid-in capital	400,000	1.00 H	400,000
Retained earnings	320,000	From statement of R/E	333,000
Cumulative translation adjustment		To balance	69,000
Total equity	820,000		902,000
Total liabilities and equity	CHF 1,670,000		$1,837,000

3. Combine the translated beginning net asset balance (*a*) and the translated value of the individual changes (*b*) to arrive at the relative value of the net assets being held prior to the impact of any exchange rate fluctuations during the year (*c*).
4. Translate the ending net asset balance at the current exchange rate to determine the reported value after all exchange rate changes have occurred (*d*).
5. Compare the translated value of the net assets prior to any rate changes (*c*) with the ending translated value (*d*). The difference is the result of exchange rate changes during the period. If (*c*) is higher than (*d*), a negative (debit) translation adjustment arises. If (*d*) is higher than (*c*), a positive (credit) translation adjustment results.

Computation of Translation Adjustment

Based on the process just described, the translation adjustment for SWISSCO in this example is calculated as follows:

Net asset balance, 1/1/20	CHF 500,000	× 1.00	=	$500,000	(*a*)
Change in net assets:					
Net income, 2020	470,000	× 1.05	=	493,500	(*b*)
Dividends declared, 10/1/20	(150,000)	× 1.07	=	(160,500)	(*b*)
Net asset balance, 12/31/20	CHF 820,000			$833,000	(*c*)
Net asset balance, 12/31/20 at current exchange rate	CHF 820,000	× 1.10	=	902,000	(*d*)
Translation adjustment, 2020 (positive)				$ (69,000)	

The process just described and demonstrated is used to calculate the current period's translation adjustment. Because SWISSCO began operations at the beginning of the current year, the $69,000 translation adjustment is the only amount that will be needed to keep the U.S. dollar consolidated balance sheet in balance. In subsequent years, a cumulative translation adjustment comprising the current year's translation adjustment plus translation adjustments from prior years will be included in stockholders' equity on the U.S. dollar consolidated balance sheet. Companies report the cumulative translation adjustment in Accumulated Other Comprehensive Income (AOCI), along with unrealized foreign exchange gains and losses, gains and losses on cash flow hedges, unrealized gains and losses on available-for-sale marketable securities, and adjustments for pension accounting.

The cumulative translation adjustment remains within AOCI only until the foreign operation is sold or liquidated. In the period in which sale or liquidation occurs, the cumulative translation adjustment related to the particular foreign entity is removed from AOCI and included as part of the gain or loss on the sale of the investment. In effect, the accumulated unrealized foreign exchange gain or loss that has been deferred in AOCI becomes realized when the entity is disposed of.

Translation of the Statement of Cash Flows

The current rate method requires translating all operating items in the statement of cash flows at the average-for-the-period exchange rate (see Exhibit 10.6). This is the same rate used for translating income statement items. Although the ending balances in Accounts Receivable, Inventory, and Accounts Payable on the balance sheet are translated at the current exchange rate, the average rate is used for the *changes* in these accounts because those changes are caused by operating activities (such as sales and purchases) that are translated at the average rate.

Investing and financing activities are translated at the exchange rate on the day the activity took place. Although long-term debt is translated in the balance sheet at the current rate, in the statement of cash flows, it is translated at the historical rate when the debt was incurred.

EXHIBIT 10.6
Translated Statement of Cash Flows—Current Rate Method

SWISSCO
Statement of Cash Flows
For Year Ending December 31, 2020

	CHF	Translation Rate	U.S.$
Operating activities:			
Net income	CHF 470,000	1.05 A	$ 493,500
Add: Depreciation	100,000	1.05 A	105,000
Amortization	10,000	1.05 A	10,500
Increase in accounts receivable	(200,000)	1.05 A	(210,000)
Increase in inventory	(250,000)	1.05 A	(262,500)
Increase in accounts payable	600,000	1.05 A	630,000
Net cash from operations	730,000		766,500
Investing activities:			
Purchase of property, plant, and equipment	(1,000,000)	1.01 H	(1,010,000)
Acquisition of patent	(50,000)	1.02 H	(51,000)
Net cash from investing activities	(1,050,000)		(1,061,000)
Financing activities:			
Proceeds from long-term debt	250,000	1.01 H	252,500
Payment of dividends	(150,000)	1.07 H	(160,500)
Net cash from financing activities	100,000		92,000
Decrease in cash	(220,000)		(202,500)
Effect of exchange rate change on cash		To balance	(4,500)
Cash at December 31, 2019	CHF 350,000	1.00 H	350,000
Cash at December 31, 2020	CHF 130,000	1.10 C	$ 143,000

The $(4,500) "effect of exchange rate change on cash" is a part of the overall translation adjustment of $69,000. It represents that part of the translation adjustment attributable to a decrease in Cash and is derived as a balancing amount.

LO 10-4

Remeasure a foreign subsidiary's financial statements using the temporal method and calculate the associated remeasurement gain or loss.

Remeasurement of Financial Statements—Temporal Method

Now assume that a careful examination of the functional currency indicators in Exhibit 10.2 leads USCO's management to conclude that SWISSCO's functional currency is the U.S. dollar. In that case, the Swiss franc financial statements must be remeasured into U.S. dollars using the temporal method, and the remeasurement gain or loss must be reported in income. To ensure that the remeasurement gain or loss is reported in income, it is easiest to remeasure the balance sheet first (as shown in Exhibit 10.7).

According to the procedures outlined in Exhibit 10.1, the temporal method remeasures cash, receivables, and liabilities into U.S. dollars using the current exchange rate of $1.10. Inventory (carried at FIFO cost); property, plant, and equipment; patents; and contributed capital (common stock and additional paid-in capital) are remeasured at historical rates. These procedures result in total assets of $1,744,800, total liabilities of $935,000, and contributed capital of $500,000. To balance the balance sheet, retained earnings must total $309,800. We verify the accuracy of this amount later.

Remeasurement of the Income Statement

Exhibit 10.8 shows the remeasurement of SWISSCO's income statement and statement of retained earnings. Revenues and expenses incurred evenly throughout the year (sales, other expenses, and income taxes) are remeasured at the average exchange rate of $0.65. Expenses related to assets remeasured at historical exchange rates (depreciation expense and amortization expense) are remeasured at relevant historical rates.

EXHIBIT 10.7
Remeasurement of Balance Sheet—Temporal Method

SWISSCO
Balance Sheet
December 31, 2020

	CHF	Remeasurement Rate	U.S.$
Assets			
Cash	CHF 130,000	1.10 C	$ 143,000
Accounts receivable	200,000	1.10 C	220,000
Inventory	400,000	1.08 H	432,000
Total current assets	730,000		795,000
Property, plant, and equipment	1,000,000	1.01 H	1,010,000
Less: Accumulated depreciation	(100,000)	1.01 H	(101,000)
Patents, net	40,000	1.02 H	40,800
Total assets	CHF 1,670,000		$1,744,800
Liabilities and Equities			
Accounts payable	CHF 600,000	1.10 C	$ 660,000
Total current liabilities	600,000		660,000
Long-term debt	250,000	1.10 C	275,000
Total liabilities	850,000		935,000
Common stock	100,000	1.00 H	100,000
Additional paid-in capital	400,000	1.00 H	400,000
Retained earnings	320,000	To balance	309,800
Total equity	820,000		809,800
Total liabilities and equity	CHF 1,670,000		$1,744,800

EXHIBIT 10.8
Remeasurement of Income Statement and Statement of Retained Earnings—Temporal Method

SWISSCO
Income Statement
For Year Ending December 31, 2020

	CHF	Remeasurement Rate	U.S.$
Sales	CHF 4,000,000	1.05 A	$4,200,000
Cost of goods sold	(3,000,000)	Calculation	(3,130,500)
Gross profit	1,000,000		1,069,500
Depreciation expense	(100,000)	1.01 H	(101,000)
Amortization expense	(10,000)	1.02 H	(10,200)
Other expenses	(220,000)	1.05 A	(231,000)
Income before income taxes	670,000		727,300
Income taxes	(200,000)	1.05 A	(210,000)
Income before remeasurement loss	470,000		517,300
Remeasurement Loss		To balance	(47,000)
Net income	CHF 470,000	Below	$ 470,300

Statement of Retained Earnings
For Year Ending December 31, 2020

	CHF	Remeasurement Rate	U.S.$
Retained earnings, 1/1/20	CHF –0–		$ –0–
Net income, 2020	470,000	To balance	470,300
Dividends	(150,000)	1.07 H	(160,500)
Retained earnings, 12/31/20	CHF 320,000	Above	$ 309,800

The following procedure remeasures cost of goods sold at historical exchange rates. Beginning inventory acquired on January 1 is remeasured at the exchange rate on that date ($1.00). Purchases made evenly throughout the year are remeasured at the average rate for the year ($1.05). Ending inventory (at FIFO cost) is purchased evenly throughout the fourth quarter of 2020, and the average exchange rate for the quarter ($1.08) is used to remeasure that component of cost of goods sold. These procedures result in cost of goods sold of $3,130,500, calculated as follows:

Beginning inventory, 1/1/20	CHF 150,000	× 1.00 =	$ 150,000
Plus: Purchases, 2020	3,250,000	× 1.05 =	3,412,500
Less: Ending inventory, 12/31/20	(400,000)	× 1.08 =	(432,000)
Cost of goods sold, 2020	CHF 3,000,000		$3,130,500

The ending balances in retained earnings on the balance sheet and on the statement of retained earnings must reconcile with one another. Because dividends are remeasured into a U.S. dollar equivalent of $160,500 and the ending balance in retained earnings on the balance sheet is $309,800, net income must be $470,300.

Reconciling the amount of income reported in the statement of retained earnings and in the income statement requires a remeasurement loss of $47,000 in calculating net income. Without this remeasurement loss, the income statement, statement of retained earnings, and balance sheet are not consistent with one another.

The remeasurement loss can be calculated by considering the impact of exchange rate changes on the subsidiary's balance sheet exposure. Under the temporal method, SWISSCO's balance sheet exposure is defined by its net monetary asset or net monetary liability position. SWISSCO began 2020 with net monetary assets (cash) of CHF 350,000. During the year, however, expenditures of cash and the incurrence of liabilities caused monetary liabilities (accounts payable + long-term debt = CHF 850,000) to exceed monetary assets (cash + accounts receivable = CHF 330,000). A net monetary liability position of CHF 520,000 exists at December 31, 2020. The remeasurement loss is computed by translating the beginning net monetary asset position and subsequent changes in monetary items at appropriate exchange rates and then comparing this with the dollar value of net monetary liabilities at year-end based on the current exchange rate:

Computation of Remeasurement Loss

Net monetary assets, 1/1/20	CHF 350,000 × 1.00 =	$ 350,000
Increase in monetary assets:		
Sales, 2020	4,000,000 × 1.05 =	4,200,000
Decreases in monetary assets and increases in monetary liabilities:		
Purchases, 2020	(3,250,000) × 1.05 =	(3,412,500)
Other expenses, 2020	(220,000) × 1.05 =	(231,000)
Income taxes, 2020	(200,000) × 1.05 =	(210,000)
Purchase of property, plant, and equipment, 3/15/20	(1,000,000) × 1.01 =	(1,010,000)
Acquisition of patent, 4/10/20	(50,000) × 1.02 =	(51,000)
Dividends, 10/1/20	(150,000) × 1.07 =	(160,500)
Net monetary liabilities, 12/31/20	CHF (520,000)	$(525,000)
Net monetary liabilities, 12/31/20 at the current exchange rate	CHF (520,000) × 1.10 =	(572,000)
Remeasurement loss		$ 47,000

Had SWISSCO maintained its net monetary asset position of CHF 350,000 for the entire year, a $35,000 remeasurement gain would have resulted. The CHF held in cash was worth $350,000 (CHF 350,000 × $1.00) at the beginning of the year and $385,000 (CHF 350,000 × $1.10) at year-end. However, the net monetary asset position is not maintained because of changes during the year in monetary items other than the original cash balance. Indeed, a net monetary liability position arises over the course of the year. The foreign currency *appreciation* coupled with an increase in *net monetary liabilities* generates a *remeasurement loss* for the year.

Remeasurement of the Statement of Cash Flows

In remeasuring the statement of cash flows (shown in Exhibit 10.9), the U.S. dollar value for net income comes directly from the remeasured income statement. Depreciation and amortization are remeasured at the rates used in the income statement, and the remeasurement loss is added back to net income because it is a noncash item. The increases in accounts receivable and accounts payable relate to sales and purchases and therefore are remeasured at the average rate. The U.S. dollar value for the increase in inventory is determined by referring to the remeasurement of the cost of goods sold.

The resulting U.S. dollar amount of "net cash from operations" ($766,500) is exactly the same as when the current rate method was used in translation. In addition, the investing and financing activities are translated in the same manner under both methods. This makes sense; the amount of cash inflows and outflows is a matter of fact and is not affected by the particular translation methodology employed.

Nonlocal Currency Balances

One additional issue related to the translation of foreign currency financial statements needs to be considered. How should a company deal with nonlocal currency balances in the foreign currency financial statements of their foreign operations? For example, if any of the accounts of the Swiss subsidiary are denominated in a currency other than the Swiss franc, those balances would first have to be restated into francs in accordance with the rules discussed in the previous chapter. Both the foreign currency balance and any related foreign exchange gain or loss would then be translated (or remeasured) into U.S. dollars.

EXHIBIT 10.9
Remeasurement of Statement of Cash Flows—Temporal Method

SWISSCO
Statement of Cash Flows
For Year Ending December 31, 2020

	CHF	Remeasurement Rate	U.S.$
Operating activities:			
Net income	CHF 470,000	From I/S	$ 470,300
Add: Depreciation expense	100,000	1.01 H	101,000
Amortization expense	10,000	1.02 H	10,200
Remeasurement loss		From I/S	47,000
Increase in accounts receivable	(200,000)	1.05 A	(210,000)
Increase in inventory	(250,000)	*	(282,000)
Increase in accounts payable	600,000	1.05 A	630,000
Net cash from operations	730,000		766,500
Investing activities:			
Purchase of property and equipment	(1,000,000)	1.01 H	(1,010,000)
Acquisition of patent	(50,000)	1.02 H	(51,000)
Net cash from investing activities	(1,050,000)		(1,061,000)
Financing activities:			
Proceeds from long-term debt	250,000	1.01 H	252,500
Payment of dividends	(150,000)	1.07 H	(160,500)
Net cash from financing activities	100,000		92,000
Decrease in cash	(220,000)		(202,500)
Effect of exchange rate changes on cash		To balance	(4,500)
Cash at December 31, 2019	CHF 350,000	1.00 H	$ 350,000
Cash at December 31, 2020	CHF 130,000	1.10 C	$ 143,000

*In remeasuring cost of goods sold earlier, beginning inventory was remeasured as $150,000, and ending inventory was remeasured as $432,000: an increase of $282,000.

For example, assume that SWISSCO borrows 100,000 euros on January 1, 2020. Exchange rates in 2020 between the Swiss franc (CHF) and euro (€) and between the CHF and U.S. dollar ($) are as follows:

	CHF per €	$ per CHF
January 1, 2020	CHF 1.15	$1.00
Average, 2020	CHF 1.18	$1.05
December 31, 2020	CHF 1.20	$1.10

On December 31, 2020, SWISSCO remeasures the €100,000 note payable into CHF using the current rate as follows: €100,000 × CHF 1.20 = CHF 120,000. SWISSCO also recognizes a CHF 5,000 [€100,000 × (CHF 1.20 – CHF 1.15)] foreign exchange loss. To consolidate Swissco's CHF financial statements with those of its parent, the note payable remeasured in CHF is then translated into U.S. dollars using the current exchange rate, and the related foreign exchange loss in CHF is translated into U.S. dollars using the average exchange rate, as follows:

Note payable	CHF 120,000 × $1.10 C = $132,000
Foreign exchange loss	CHF 5,000 × $1.05 A = $5,250

A note payable of $132,000 will be reported on the consolidated balance sheet, and a loss of $5,250 will be reflected in the measurement of consolidated net income.

The comprehensive illustration at the end of this chapter further demonstrates how nonlocal currency balances of a foreign entity are treated in the preparation of consolidated financial statements.

Comparison of the Results from Applying the Two Different Methods

The determination of the foreign subsidiary's functional currency (and the use of different translation methods) can have a significant impact on consolidated financial statements. The following chart shows differences for SWISSCO in several key items under the two different translation methods:

	Translation Method		
Item	**Current Rate**	**Temporal**	**Difference**
Net income (NI)	$ 493,500	$ 470,300	+ 4.7%
Total assets (TA)	1,837,000	1,744,800	+ 5.0%
Total equity (TE)	902,000	809,800	+ 10.2%
Return on equity (NI/TE)	54.7%	58.1%	− 6.1%

In this illustration, if the Swiss franc is determined to be SWISSCO's functional currency (and the current rate method is applied), net income reported in the consolidated income statement would be 4.7 percent more than if the U.S. dollar is the functional currency (and the temporal method is applied). In addition, total assets would be 5.0 percent more and total equity would be 10.2 percent more using the current rate method. Because of the larger amount of equity, return on equity (net income/total equity) using the current rate method is 6.1 percent less.

Note that the current rate method does not always result in higher net income and a higher amount of equity than the temporal method. For example, had SWISSCO maintained its net monetary asset position, it would have computed a remeasurement gain under the temporal method leading to higher income than under the current rate method. Moreover, if the Swiss franc had depreciated during 2020, the temporal method would have resulted in higher net income.

The important point is that determining the functional currency and resulting translation method can have a significant impact on the amounts a parent company reports in its consolidated financial statements. The appropriate determination of the functional currency is an important issue.

> "Within rather broad parameters," says Peat, Marwick, Mitchell partner James Weir, "choosing the functional currency is basically a management call. So much so, in fact, that Texaco, Occidental, and Unocal settled on the dollar as the functional currency for most of their foreign operations, whereas competitors Exxon, Mobil, and Amoco chose primarily the local currencies as the functional currencies for their foreign businesses."[9]

Different functional currencies selected by different companies in the same industry could have a significant impact on the comparability of financial statements within that industry. Indeed, one concern that those FASB members dissenting on the current standard raised was that the functional currency rules might not result in similar accounting for similar situations.

In addition to differences in amounts reported in the consolidated financial statements, the results of the SWISSCO illustration demonstrate several conceptual differences between the two translation methods.

Underlying Valuation Method

Using the temporal method, SWISSCO remeasured its property, plant, and equipment as follows:

Property, plant, and equipment CHF 1,000,000 × $1.01 H = $1,010,000

[9] John Heins, "Plenty of Opportunity to Fool Around," *Forbes*, June 2, 1986, p. 139.

By multiplying the historical cost in Swiss francs by the historical exchange rate, $1,010,000 represents the U.S. dollar–equivalent historical cost of this asset. It is the amount of U.S. dollars that the parent company would have had to pay to acquire assets having a cost of CHF 1,000,000 when the exchange rate was $1.01 per Swiss franc.

Property, plant, and equipment was translated under the current rate method as follows:

Property, plant, and equipment CHF 1,000,000 × $1.10 C = $1,100,000

The $1,100,000 amount is not readily interpretable. It does not represent the U.S. dollar–equivalent historical cost of the asset; that amount is $1,010,000. Nor does it represent the U.S. dollar–equivalent fair value of the asset because CHF 1,000,000 is not the fair value of the asset in Switzerland. The $1,100,000 amount is simply the product of multiplying two numbers together!

Underlying Relationships

The following table reports the values for selected financial ratios calculated from the original foreign currency financial statements and from the U.S. dollar–translated statements using the two different translation methods:

Ratio	CHF	U.S.$ Current Rate	U.S.$ Temporal
Current ratio (current assets/current liabilities)	1.22	1.22	1.20
Debt/equity ratio (total liabilities/total equities)	1.04	1.04	1.15
Gross profit ratio (gross profit/sales)	25.0%	25.0%	25.5%
Return on equity (net income/total equity)	57.3%	54.7%	58.1%

The temporal method distorts all of the ratios measured in the foreign currency. The subsidiary appears to be less liquid, more highly leveraged, and more profitable than it does in Swiss franc terms.

The current rate method maintains the first three ratios but distorts return on equity. The distortion occurs because income was translated at the average-for-the-period exchange rate whereas total equity was translated at the current exchange rate. In fact, the use of the average rate for income and the current rate for assets and liabilities distorts any ratio combining balance sheet and income statement figures, such as turnover ratios.

LO 10-5

Understand the rationale for hedging balance sheet exposure to foreign exchange risk and describe the treatment of gains and losses on hedges used for this purpose.

Hedging Balance Sheet Exposure

When the U.S. dollar is the functional currency (or when a foreign operation is located in a highly inflationary economy), remeasurement gains and losses are reported in net income. Management of U.S. multinational companies could wish to avoid reporting remeasurement losses in net income because of the perceived negative impact this has on the company's stock price. Likewise, when the foreign currency is the functional currency, management could wish to avoid negative translation adjustments because of the adverse impact these have on the debt-to-equity ratio.

Translation adjustments and remeasurement gains or losses are functions of two factors: (1) changes in the exchange rate and (2) balance sheet exposure. Although a company can do little if anything to influence exchange rates, parent companies can use several techniques to hedge the balance sheet exposures of their foreign operations.

Parent companies can hedge balance sheet exposure by using a derivative financial instrument, such as a forward contract or a foreign currency option, or a nonderivative hedging instrument, such as a foreign currency borrowing. To illustrate the latter, assume that SWISSCO's functional currency is the Swiss franc, which means that the current rate method will be used to translate the Swiss franc financial statements; this creates a net asset balance sheet exposure. USCO believes that the Swiss franc will depreciate against the U.S. dollar over the course of the coming year, thereby generating a negative translation adjustment that will reduce USCO's consolidated stockholders' equity. USCO could hedge this Swiss franc net asset balance sheet exposure by borrowing Swiss francs for a period of time, thus creating an offsetting Swiss franc liability exposure. As the Swiss franc depreciates, the U.S. dollar value of the Swiss franc borrowing decreases, and USCO will be able to repay the Swiss franc borrowing using fewer U.S. dollars. This generates a foreign exchange gain, which offsets the negative translation adjustment arising from the translation of SWISSCO's financial statements.

As an alternative to the Swiss franc borrowing, USCO might have acquired a Swiss franc put option to hedge its Swiss franc net asset balance sheet exposure. A put option gives the company the right to sell Swiss francs at a predetermined strike price, creating a potential Swiss franc liability. As the Swiss franc depreciates, the fair value of the put option increases, resulting in a gain, which offsets the negative translation adjustment.

The paradox of hedging a balance sheet exposure is that in the process of avoiding an unrealized negative translation adjustment (or unrealized remeasurement loss), realized foreign exchange gains and losses can result. Consider USCO's foreign currency borrowing to hedge a Swiss franc net asset balance sheet exposure. At the initiation of the loan, USCO converts the borrowed Swiss francs into U.S. dollars at the spot exchange rate. When the liability matures, USCO purchases Swiss francs at the spot rate prevailing at that date to repay the loan. The change in the U.S. dollar/Swiss franc exchange rate over the life of the loan generates a *realized* gain or loss. If the Swiss franc depreciates as expected, a realized foreign exchange gain that offsets the negative translation adjustment reported in AOCI results. Although the net effect on AOCI is zero, a net increase in cash occurs as a result of the hedge. If the Swiss franc unexpectedly appreciates, a realized foreign exchange loss occurs. This is offset by a positive translation adjustment in AOCI, but a net decrease in cash exists. While a hedge of a balance sheet exposure eliminates the possibility of reporting a negative translation adjustment in AOCI, gains and losses realized in cash can result.

Accounting for Hedges of Remeasurement-Related Balance Sheet Exposure

When a foreign entity's financial statements are remeasured using the temporal method, a net liability balance sheet exposure normally exists. A foreign currency borrowing, which creates an additional foreign currency liability, would not be effective in hedging this type of balance sheet exposure. However, either a forward contract or an option to *purchase* foreign currency in the future creates a foreign currency asset exposure and would act as a hedge against the remeasurement-based net liability balance sheet exposure.

Following the proper accounting for derivative financial instruments, the gain/loss on a foreign currency option or forward contract is reported in net income and offsets the remeasurement loss/gain that also is reported in net income. Thus, there is no need for the FASB to allow hedge accounting to be applied in accounting for hedges of remeasurement-related balance sheet exposure.

Accounting for Hedges of Translation-Related Balance Sheet Exposure

When a foreign entity's financial statements are translated using the current rate method, the resulting translation adjustment is reported in AOCI. Normally, the gain or loss on a financial instrument is reflected in net income. However, when such a financial instrument is effective and properly designated as a hedge of translation-related balance sheet exposure, ASC 815-35-35 indicates that hedge accounting applies. In this case, the gain or loss on the hedging instrument should be reported in the same manner as the translation adjustment being hedged—that is, in AOCI. The FASB describes this type of hedge as a *hedge of the net investment in a foreign operation.*

Thus, returning to the hedge of SWISSCO's translation-related balance sheet exposure described earlier, the foreign exchange gain on the Swiss franc borrowing (or the gain on the foreign currency option) would be included in AOCI along with the negative translation adjustment arising from the translation of SWISSCO's financial statements.

To demonstrate the accounting for a hedge of a net investment, assume that SWISSCO has net assets of CHF 820,000 on January 1, 2021, when the exchange rate is $1.10 per CHF. USCO is concerned that the Swiss franc will depreciate against the U.S. dollar and wishes to hedge against reporting a negative translation adjustment in the quarter ending March 31, 2021. On January 1, 2021, USCO negotiates a 5 percent, 90-day note payable for CHF 820,000 with its bank and properly designates this borrowing as a hedge of a net investment. The journal entry to record this foreign currency borrowing is as follows:

1/1/21	Cash	902,000	
	Note Payable (CHF)		902,000
	To record the Swiss franc note payable at the spot rate of $1.10 and the conversion of CHF 820,000 into U.S. dollars.		

Assuming that SWISSCO maintains net assets of CHF 820,000 during the first quarter of 2021, the negative translation adjustment for that time period resulting from the decrease in value of the Swiss franc is calculated as follows:

Net assets × Exchange rate at 3/31/21	CHF 820,000 × $1.04 = $852,800
Less: Net assets × Exchange rate at 1/1/21	CHF 820,000 × $1.10 = 902,000
Translation adjustment (negative – debit)	$ (49,200)

The summary entry to recognize the first quarter 2021 translation adjustment on USCO's books is as follows:

3/31/21	Translation Adjustment (AOCI)	49,200	
	Net Investment in SWISSCO		49,200
	To record the negative translation adjustment resulting from a decrease in U.S. dollar value of the Swiss franc.		

On March 31, 2021, USCO purchases CHF 820,000 at the spot of $1.04 for $852,800 and delivers them to the bank to extinguish the note payable. On that date, USCO acquires an additional CHF 10,250 for $10,660 to cover the accrued interest on the loan. The entries related to the foreign currency borrowing used as a net investment hedge are the following:

3/31/21	Foreign currency (CHF)	863,460	
	Cash		863,460
	To record the purchase of CHF 830,250 at the spot rate of $1.04.		
	Note payable (CHF)	902,000	
	Foreign currency (CHF)		852,800
	Translation adjustment (AOCI)		49,200
	To record payment of CHF 820,000 to extinguish the CHF note payable, and recognize the resulting transaction gain as an adjustment to the translation adjustment component of AOCI.		
	Interest expense	10,660	
	Foreign currency (CHF)		10,660
	To record the cash interest payment of CHF 10,250 and recognize interest expense.		

As a result of the net investment hedge, the net translation adjustment reflected in AOCI is zero ($49,200 – $49,200). However, avoiding the recognition of a negative translation adjustment in the first quarter of 2021 cost USCO a total of $10,660 in cash interest paid.

Many U.S. companies regularly hedge their net investments in foreign operations. For example, in its 2017 annual report, McDonald's Corporation disclosed: "The Company primarily uses foreign currency denominated debt (third party and intercompany) to hedge its investments in certain foreign subsidiaries and affiliates." In its 2017 annual report, Hewlett Packard Enterprises Company stated: "The Company uses forward contracts designated as net investment hedges to hedge net investments in certain foreign subsidiaries whose functional currency is the local currency."

International Financial Reporting Standard 9–Financial Instruments

As noted in the previous chapter, there is considerable similarity between IFRS and U.S. GAAP with respect to the accounting for derivative financial instruments used to hedge foreign exchange risk. Similar to U.S. GAAP, *IFRS 9* also allows hedge accounting for hedges of net investments in a foreign operation. The gain or loss on the hedging instrument is recognized in Accumulated Other Comprehensive Income (AOCI) along with the translation adjustment that is being hedged. Under both IFRS and U.S. GAAP, the cumulative translation adjustment and cumulative net gain or loss on the net investment hedge are transferred from AOCI to net income when the foreign subsidiary is sold or otherwise disposed of.

Disclosures Related to Translation

Current standards require firms to present an analysis of the change in the cumulative translation adjustment account in the financial statements or notes thereto. Many companies comply with this requirement directly in their statement of comprehensive income. Other companies provide separate disclosure in the notes. Exhibit 10.10 provides an example of note disclosure for Mondelēz International, Inc.

That exhibit shows that the company's cumulative translation adjustment account had a negative (debit) balance of $(5,042) on January 1, 2015, which increased to $(8,006) on December 31, 2015. The negative balance in this account further increased to $(8,914) by the end of 2016, and then decreased to $(7,741) on December 31, 2017. An analysis of the *Currency translation adjustments* row in Exhibit 10.10 indicates negative translation adjustments of $2,905 million and $847 million in 2015 and 2016, respectively, and a positive translation adjustment of $987 million in 2017. From the signs of these translation adjustments, one can infer that, in aggregate, the foreign currencies in which Mondelēz has operations decreased in value against the U.S. dollar in both 2015 and 2016, with a much larger decrease in value in 2015, and then appreciated in value against the U.S. dollar in 2017. The negative translation adjustment of $2,905 million in 2015 in particular is quite large, being equal to 10.4 percent of total equity at January 1, 2015.

In 2015, Mondelēz's Venezuelan subsidiaries were deconsolidated because of a loss of control and an other-than-temporary lack of currency exchangeability. This deconsolidation resulted in the cumulative translation adjustment of $99 million related to Venezuelan operations being

EXHIBIT 10.10
Mondelēz International, Inc., Analysis of Change in Cumulative Translation Adjustment

Excerpt from Note 13. Reclassifications from Accumulated Other Comprehensive Income
The following table summarizes the changes in the accumulated balances of each component of accumulated other comprehensive earnings / (losses) attributable to Mondelēz International.

	For the Years Ended December 31,		
	2017	**2016**	**2015**
Currency Translation Adjustments:		**(in millions)**	
Balance at beginning of period	$(8,914)	$(8,006)	$(5,042)
Currency translation adjustments	987	(847)	(2,905)
Reclassification to earnings related to:			
Venezuela deconsolidation			99
Equity method investment transactions		57	
Tax (expense) / benefit	214	(135)	(184)
Other comprehensive earnings / (losses)	1,201	(925)	(2,990)
Less: (earnings) / loss attributable to noncontrolling interests	(28)	17	26
Balance at end of period	$(7,741)	$(8,914)	$(8,006)

Source: Mondelēz International, Inc., 2017 Form 10-K, page 108.

reclassified from AOCI to net income. In 2016, transactions involving equity method investees located in foreign countries resulted in the transfer of $57 million from AOCI to net income.

Although not specifically required to do so, many companies describe their translation procedures in their "summary of significant accounting policies" in the notes to the financial statements. The following excerpt from International Business Machines (IBM) Corporation's 2017 annual report illustrates this type of disclosure. Note that IBM uses the terms *translated* and *translation gains and losses* (rather than remeasured and remeasurment gains and losses) in describing its accounting policy with regard to foreign entities that operate in U.S. dollars:

> **Translation of Non-U.S. Currency Amounts**—Assets and liabilities of non-U.S. subsidiaries that have a local functional currency are translated to United States (U.S.) dollars at year-end exchange rates. Translation adjustments are recorded in OCI. Income and expense items are translated at weighted-average rates of exchange prevailing during the year.
>
> Inventories, property, plant and equipment—net, and other non-monetary assets and liabilities of non-U.S. subsidiaries and branches that operate in U.S. dollars are translated at the approximate exchange rates prevailing when the company acquired the assets or liabilities. All other assets and liabilities denominated in a currency other than U.S. dollars are translated at year-end exchange rates with the transaction gain or loss recognized in other (income) and expense. Income and expense items are translated at the weighted-average rates of exchange prevailing during the year. These translation gains and losses are included in net income for the period in which exchange rates change.

LO 10-6

Prepare a consolidation worksheet for a parent and its foreign subsidiary.

Consolidation of a Foreign Subsidiary

This section of the chapter demonstrates the procedures used to consolidate a foreign subsidiary's financial statements with those of its parent. The treatment of the excess of fair value over book value requires special attention. As an item denominated in foreign currency, translation of the excess gives rise to a translation adjustment recorded on the consolidation worksheet.

On January 1, 2020, Altman, Inc., a U.S.-based manufacturing firm, acquired 100 percent of Bradford Ltd. in Great Britain. Altman paid 25 million British pounds (£25,000,000), which was equal to Bradford's fair value. Bradford's balance sheet on January 1, 2020, which reflects a book value of £22,700,000, showed the following totals:

Cash	£ 925,000	Accounts payable	£ 675,000
Accounts receivable	1,400,000	Long-term debt	4,000,000
Inventory	6,050,000	Common stock	20,000,000
Property, plant and equipment (net)	19,000,000	Retained earnings	2,700,000
Total	£27,375,000	Total	£27,375,000

The £2,300,000 excess of fair value over book value resulted from undervalued land (part of Property, plant and equipment) and therefore is not subject to amortization. Altman uses the equity method to account for its investment in Bradford.

On December 31, 2021, two years after the acquisition date, Bradford submitted the following trial balance for consolidation (credit balances are in parentheses):

Cash	£ 600,000
Accounts receivable	2,700,000
Inventory	9,000,000
Property, plant and equipment (net)	17,200,000
Accounts payable	(500,000)
Long-term debt	(2,000,000)
Common stock	(20,000,000)
Retained earnings, 1/1/21	(3,800,000)
Sales	(13,900,000)
Cost of goods sold	8,100,000
Depreciation expense	900,000
Other expenses	950,000
Dividends declared, 6/30/21	750,000
	£ –0–

Although Bradford generated net income of £1,100,000 in 2020, it neither declared nor paid dividends that year. Other than the payment of dividends in 2021, no intra-entity transactions occurred between the two affiliates. Altman has determined the British pound to be Bradford's functional currency.

Relevant exchange rates for the British pound were as follows:

	January 1	June 30	December 31	Average
2020	$1.51	N/A	$1.56	$1.54
2021	1.56	$1.58	1.53	1.55

Translation of Foreign Subsidiary Trial Balance

The initial step in consolidating the foreign subsidiary is to translate its trial balance from British pounds into U.S. dollars. Because the British pound has been determined to be the functional currency, this translation uses the current rate method. The historical exchange rate for translating Bradford's common stock and January 1, 2020, retained earnings is the exchange rate that existed at the acquisition date—$1.51.

	British Pounds	Rate	U.S. Dollars
Cash	£ 600,000	1.53 C	$ 918,000
Accounts receivable	2,700,000	1.53 C	4,131,000
Inventory	9,000,000	1.53 C	13,770,000
Property, plant and equipment (net)	17,200,000	1.53 C	26,316,000
Accounts payable	(500,000)	1.53 C	(765,000)
Long-term debt	(2,000,000)	1.53 C	(3,060,000)
Common stock	(20,000,000)	1.51 H	(30,200,000)
Retained earnings, 1/1/21	(3,800,000)	*	(5,771,000)
Sales	(13,900,000)	1.55 A	(21,545,000)
Cost of goods sold	8,100,000	1.55 A	12,555,000
Depreciation expense	900,000	1.55 A	1,395,000
Other expenses	950,000	1.55 A	1,472,500
Dividends declared, 6/30/21	750,000	1.58 H	1,185,000
Cumulative translation adjustment			(401,500)
	£ –0–		$ –0–
*Retained Earnings, 1/1/20	£2,700,000	1.51 H	$4,077,000
Net Income, 2020	1,100,000	1.54 A	1,694,000
Retained Earnings, 12/31/20	£3,800,000		$5,771,000

A positive (credit balance) cumulative translation adjustment of $401,500 is required to make the trial balance actually balance. The cumulative translation adjustment is calculated as follows:

Net assets, 1/1/20	£22,700,000	1.51 H	$34,277,000	
Change in net assets, 2020				
Net income, 2020	1,100,000	1.54 A	1,694,000	
Net assets, 12/31/20	£23,800,000		$35,971,000	
Net assets, 12/31/20, at current exchange rate	£23,800,000	1.56 C	37,128,000	
Translation adjustment, 2020 (positive)				$(1,157,000)
Net assets, 1/1/21	£23,800,000	1.56 H	$37,128,000	
Change in net assets, 2021				
Net income, 2021	3,950,000	1.55 A	6,122,500	
Dividends, 6/30/21	(750,000)	1.58 H	(1,185,000)	
Net assets, 12/31/21	£27,000,000		$42,065,500	
Net assets, 12/31/21, at current exchange rate	£27,000,000	1.53 C	$41,310,000	
Translation adjustment, 2021 (negative)				755,500
Cumulative translation adjustment, 12/31/21 (positive)				$ (401,500)

The translation adjustment in 2020 is positive because the British pound appreciated against the U.S. dollar that year; the translation adjustment in 2021 is negative because the British pound depreciated against the U.S. dollar that year.

Determination of Balance in Investment Account—Equity Method

The original value of the investment in Bradford, the net income earned by Bradford, and the dividends paid by Bradford are all denominated in British pounds. Relevant amounts must be translated from pounds into U.S. dollars so Altman can account for its investment in Bradford under the equity method. In addition, the translation adjustment calculated each year is included in the Investment in Bradford account to update the foreign currency investment to its U.S. dollar equivalent. The counterpart is recorded as a translation adjustment on Altman's books:

12/31/20	Investment in Bradford	$1,157,000	
	Cumulative Translation Adjustment		$1,157,000
	To record the positive translation adjustment related to the investment in a British subsidiary when the British pound appreciated.		
12/31/21	Cumulative Translation Adjustment	$755,500	
	Investment in Bradford		$755,500
	To record the negative translation adjustment related to the investment in a British subsidiary when the British pound depreciated.		

As a result of these two journal entries, Altman has a cumulative translation adjustment of $401,500 on its separate balance sheet.

The carrying value of the investment account in U.S. dollar terms at December 31, 2021, is determined as follows:

Investment in Bradford	British Pounds	Exchange Rate	U.S. Dollars
Original value	£25,000,000	1.51 H	$37,750,000
Bradford net income, 2020	1,100,000	1.54 A	1,694,000
Translation adjustment, 2020			1,157,000
Balance, 12/31/20	£26,100,000		$40,601,000
Bradford net income, 2021	3,950,000	1.55 A	6,122,500
Bradford dividends, 6/30/21	(750,000)	1.58 H	(1,185,000)
Translation adjustment, 2021			(755,500)
Balance, 12/31/21	£29,300,000		$44,783,000

In addition to Altman's $44,783,000 investment in Bradford, it has equity income on its December 31, 2021, trial balance in the amount of $6,122,500.

Consolidation Worksheet

Once the subsidiary's trial balance has been translated into dollars and the carrying value of the investment is known, the consolidation worksheet at December 31, 2021, can be prepared. As is true in the consolidation of domestic subsidiaries, the investment account, the subsidiary's equity accounts, and the effects of intra-entity transactions must be eliminated. The excess of fair value over book value at the date of acquisition also must be allocated to the appropriate accounts (in this example, Property, plant and equipment).

Unique to the consolidation of foreign subsidiaries is the fact that the excess of fair value over book value, denominated in foreign currency, also must be translated into the parent's reporting currency. When the foreign currency is the functional currency, the excess is translated at the current exchange rate with a resulting translation adjustment. The excess is not carried on either the parent's or the subsidiary's books but is recognized only in the consolidation worksheet. *Neither the parent nor the subsidiary has recorded the translation adjustment related to the excess, and it also must be entered in the consolidation worksheet.* Exhibit 10.11 presents the consolidation worksheet of Altman and Bradford at December 31, 2021.

EXHIBIT 10.11 Consolidation Worksheet—Parent and Foreign Subsidiary

ALTMAN, INC., AND BRADFORD LTD.
Consolidation Worksheet
For Year Ending December 31, 2021

Accounts	Altman	Bradford	Consolidation Entries: Debits	Consolidation Entries: Credits	Consolidated Totals
Income Statement					
Sales	$ (32,489,000)	$ (21,545,000)			$ (54,034,000)
Cost of goods sold	16,000,000	12,555,000			28,555,000
Depreciation expense	9,700,000	1,395,000			11,095,000
Other expenses	2,900,000	1,472,500			4,372,500
Equity income	(6,122,500)		(I) 6,122,500		–0–
Net income	$ (10,011,500)	$ (6,122,500)			$ (10,011,500)
Statement of Retained Earnings					
Retained earnings, 1/1/21	$ (25,194,000)	$ (5,771,000)	(S) 5,771,000		$ (25,194,000)
Net income (above)	(10,011,500)	(6,122,500)			(10,011,500)
Dividends	1,500,000	1,185,000		(D) 1,185,000	1,500,000
Retained earnings, 12/31/21	$ (33,705,500)	$ (10,708,500)			$ (33,705,500)
Balance Sheet					
Cash	$ 3,649,800	$ 918,000			$ 4,567,800
Accounts receivable	3,100,000	4,131,000			7,231,000
Inventory	11,410,000	13,770,000			25,180,000
Investment in Bradford	44,783,000			(S) 35,971,000	–0–
				(A) 3,473,000	
			(D) 1,185,000	(I) 6,122,500	
				(T) 401,500	
Property, plant and equipment (net)	39,500,000	26,316,000	(A) 3,473,000		
			(E) 46,000		69,335,000
Total assets	$ 102,442,800	$ 45,135,000			$ 106,313,800
Accounts payable	$ (2,500,000)	$ (765,000)			$ (3,265,000)
Long-term debt	(22,728,800)	(3,060,000)			(25,788,800)
Common stock	(43,107,000)	(30,200,000)	(S) 30,200,000		(43,107,000)
Retained earnings, 12/31/21 (above)	(33,705,500)	(10,708,500)			(33,705,500)
Cumulative translation adjustment	(401,500)	(401,500)	(T) 401,500	(E) 46,000	(447,500)
Total liabilities and equities	$ (102,422,800)	$ (45,135,000)	$47,199,000	$47,199,000	$ (106,313,800)

Explanation of Consolidation Entries

S—Eliminates the subsidiary's stockholders' equity accounts as of the beginning of the current year along with the equivalent book value component within the original value of the Investment in Bradford account.

A—Allocates the excess of fair value over book value at the date of acquisition to land (Property, plant and equipment) and eliminates that amount within the original value of the Investment in Bradford account.

I—Eliminates the amount of equity income recognized by the parent in the current year and included in the Investment in Bradford account under the equity method.

D—Eliminates the subsidiary's dividend payment that was a reduction in the Investment in Bradford account under the equity method.

T—Eliminates the cumulative translation adjustment included in the Investment in Bradford account under the equity method and the cumulative translation adjustment on the subsidiary's translated books.

E—Revalues the excess of fair value over book value for the change in exchange rate since the date of acquisition with the counterpart recognized as an increase in the consolidated cumulative translation adjustment. The revaluation is calculated as follows:

Excess of Fair Value over Book Value			
U.S. dollar equivalent at 12/3121	£2,300,000 × $1.53	=	$3,519,000
U.S. dollar equivalent at 1/1/20	2,300,000 × $1.51	=	3,473,000
Cumulative translation adjustment related to excess, 12/31/21			$ 46,000

Summary

1. Because many companies have significant financial involvement in foreign countries, the process by which foreign currency financial statements are translated into U.S. dollars has special accounting importance. The two major issues related to the translation process are (a) which method to use and (b) where to report the resulting translation adjustment in the consolidated financial statements.
2. Translation methods differ on the basis of which accounts are translated at the current exchange rate and which are translated at historical rates. Accounts translated at the current exchange rate are exposed to translation adjustment. Different translation methods give rise to different concepts of balance sheet exposure and translation adjustments of differing signs and magnitude.
3. The temporal method translates assets carried at current value (cash, marketable securities, receivables) and liabilities at the current exchange rate. This method translates assets carried at historical cost and stockholders' equity at historical exchange rates. When liabilities are more than the sum of cash, marketable securities, and receivables, a net liability balance sheet exposure exists. Foreign currency appreciation results in a negative translation adjustment (remeasurement loss). Foreign currency depreciation results in a positive translation adjustment (remeasurement gain). By translating assets carried at historical cost at historical exchange rates, the temporal method maintains the underlying valuation method used by the foreign operation but distorts relationships in the foreign currency financial statements.
4. The current rate method translates all assets and liabilities at the current exchange rate, giving rise to a net asset balance sheet exposure. Foreign currency appreciation results in a positive translation adjustment. Foreign currency depreciation results in a negative translation adjustment. By translating assets carried at historical cost at the current exchange rate, the current rate method maintains relationships in the foreign currency financial statements but distorts the underlying valuation method used by the foreign operation.
5. Current U.S. accounting procedures require two separate procedures for translating foreign currency financial statements into the parent's reporting currency. *Translation* through use of the current rate method is appropriate when the foreign operation's functional currency is a foreign currency. In this case, the translation adjustment is reported in the Accumulated Other Comprehensive Income (AOCI) account and reflected on the balance sheet as a separate component of stockholders' equity. *Remeasurement* by using the temporal method is appropriate when the operation's functional currency is the U.S. dollar. Remeasurement also is applied when the operation is in a country with a highly inflationary economy. In these situations, the translation adjustment is treated as a remeasurement gain or loss in net income.
6. IFRS and U.S. GAAP have broadly similar rules with regard to the translation of foreign currency financial statements. Differences exist with respect to the determination of functional currency, with *IAS 21* establishing a hierarchy of functional currency indicators, and in translating financial statements of foreign entities located in high-inflation countries. For these entities, *IAS 21* requires financial statements to first be restated for local inflation and then be translated into the parent's currency using the current exchange rate for all financial statement items.
7. Some companies hedge their balance sheet exposures to avoid reporting remeasurement losses in net income and/or negative translation adjustments in stockholders' equity. When a remeasurement-related balance sheet exposure is hedged, both the gain/loss on the hedging instrument and the remeasurement gain/loss are reported in net income. When a translation-related balance sheet exposure is hedged (referred to by the FASB as a *hedge of a net investment in a foreign operation*), hedge accounting is appropriate and the gain/loss on the hedging instrument is reported in AOCI along with the translation adjustment being hedged.

Comprehensive Illustration

(*Estimated Time: 55 to 65 Minutes*) Arlington Company is a U.S.-based organization with numerous foreign subsidiaries. As a preliminary step in preparing consolidated financial statements for 2020, it must translate the financial information from each foreign operation into its reporting currency, the U.S. dollar.

Arlington owns a Swedish subsidiary that has been in business for several years. On December 31, 2019, this entity's balance sheet was translated from Swedish kroner (SEK), its functional currency, into U.S. dollars as prescribed by U.S. GAAP. Equity accounts at that date follow (all credit balances):

Common stock	SEK 110,000 =	$21,000
Retained earnings	194,800 =	36,100
Cumulative translation adjustment		3,860

At the end of 2020, the Swedish subsidiary produced the following trial balance. These figures include all of the entity's transactions for the year except for the results of several transactions related to sales made to a Chinese customer. A separate ledger has been maintained for these transactions denominated in Chinese renminbi (RMB). This ledger follows the company's trial balance.

Trial Balance—Swedish Subsidiary
December 31, 2020

	Debit	Credit
Cash	SEK 41,000	
Accounts receivable	126,000	
Inventory	128,000	
Property, plant, and equipment	388,000	
Accumulated depreciation		SEK 98,100
Accounts payable		39,000
Notes payable		56,000
Bonds payable		125,000
Common stock		110,000
Retained earnings, 1/1/20		194,800
Sales		350,000
Cost of goods sold	165,000	
Depreciation expense	10,900	
Salary expense	36,000	
Rent expense	12,000	
Interest expense	10,000	
Other expenses	31,000	
Dividends, 7/1/20	25,000	
Totals	SEK 972,900	SEK 972,900

Ledger—Transactions in Chinese Renminbi
December 31, 2020

	Debit	Credit
Cash	RMB 10,000	
Accounts receivable	28,000	
Property, plant, and equipment	20,000	
Accumulated depreciation		RMB 4,000
Notes payable		15,000
Sales		44,000
Depreciation expense	4,000	
Interest expense	1,000	
Totals	RMB 63,000	RMB 63,000

Additional Information

- The Swedish subsidiary began selling to the Chinese customer at the beginning of the current year. At that time, it borrowed 20,000 RMB to acquire a truck for delivery purposes. It paid one-fourth of that debt before the end of the year. The subsidiary made sales to China evenly during the period.

- The U.S. dollar exchange rates for 1 SEK are as follows:

January 1, 2020	$0.200 = 1.00 SEK
Weighted average rate for 2020	0.192 = 1.00
July 1, 2020	0.190 = 1.00
December 31, 2020	0.182 = 1.00

- The exchange rates applicable for the remeasurement of 1 RMB into Swedish kroner are as follows:

January 1, 2020	1.25 SEK	= 1.00 RMB
Weighted average rate for 2020	1.16	= 1.00
December 1, 2020	1.101	= 1.00
December 31, 2020	1.04	= 1.00

- The Swedish subsidiary expended SEK 10,000 during the year on development activities. In accordance with IFRS, this cost has been capitalized within the Property, plant, and equipment account. This expenditure had no effect on the depreciation recognized for the year.

Required

a. Prepare the Swedish kroner trial balance for the Swedish subsidiary for the year ending December 31, 2020. Verify, through separate calculation, the amount of remeasurement gain/loss derived as a plug figure in the trial balance.

b. Translate the Swedish kroner trial balance into U.S. dollars to facilitate Arlington Company's preparation of consolidated financial statements. Verify, through separate calculation, the amount of cumulative translation adjustment derived as a plug figure in the trial balance.

Solution

Part A

Remeasurement of Foreign Currency Balances

A portion of the Swedish subsidiary's operating results is presently stated in Chinese renminbi. These balances must be remeasured into the functional currency, the Swedish krona, before the translation process can begin. In remeasuring these accounts using the temporal method, the krona value of the monetary assets and liabilities is determined by using the current (C) exchange rate (1.04 SEK per RMB) whereas all other accounts are remeasured at historical (H) or average (A) rates.

Remeasurement of Foreign Currency Balances

	Renminbi			Kroner	
	Debit	Credit	Rate	Debit	Credit
Cash	10,000		× 1.04 C =	10,400	
Accounts receivable	28,000		× 1.04 C =	29,120	
Property, plant, and equipment	20,000		× 1.25 H =	25,000	
Accumulated depreciation		4,000	× 1.25 H =		5,000
Notes payable		15,000	× 1.04 C =		15,600
Sales		44,000	× 1.16 A =		51,040
Depreciation expense	4,000		× 1.25 H =	5,000	
Interest expense	1,000		× 1.16 A =	1,160	
	63,000	63,000		70,680	71,640
Remeasurement loss				960	
Total				71,640	71,640

Remeasurement Loss for 2020

Net monetary asset balance, 1/1/20	–0–		–0–
Increases in net monetary items:			
Operations (sales less interest expense)	RMB 43,000	× 1.16 A =	SEK 49,880
Decreases in net monetary items:			
Purchased truck, 1/1/20	(20,000)	× 1.25 H =	(25,000)
Net monetary assets, 12/31/20	RMB 23,000		SEK 24,880
Net monetary assets, 12/31/20, at current exchange rate	RMB 23,000	× 1.04 C =	SEK 23,920
Remeasurement loss (gain)			SEK 960

The net monetary asset exposure (cash and accounts receivable > notes payable) and depreciation of the Chinese renminbi create a remeasurement loss of SEK 960.

The remeasured figures from the Chinese operation must be combined in some manner with the subsidiary's trial balance denominated in Swedish kroner. For example, a year-end adjustment can be recorded in the Swedish subsidiary's accounting system to add the remeasured balances for financial reporting purposes, as follows:

	Kroner	
12/31/20 Adjustment	**Debit**	**Credit**
Cash	10,400	
Accounts receivable	29,120	
Property, plant, and equipment	25,000	
Depreciation expense	5,000	
Interest expense	1,160	
Remeasurement loss	960	
Accumulated depreciation		5,000
Notes payable		15,600
Sales		51,040
To record in Swedish kroner the foreign currency transactions originally denominated in renminbi.		

One more adjustment is necessary before translating the subsidiary's Swedish krona financial statements into the parent's reporting currency. The development costs incurred by the Swedish entity should be reclassified as an expense as required by U.S. authoritative literature. After this adjustment, the Swedish subsidiary's statements conform with U.S. GAAP.

	Kroner	
12/31/20 Adjustment	**Debit**	**Credit**
Other expenses	10,000	
Property, plant, and equipment		10,000
To adjust property, plant, and equipment and expenses in Swedish kroner to be in compliance with U.S. GAAP.		

Alternatively, the results from remeasuring the Chinese renminbi balances into Swedish kroner and reclassification of development costs can be added to the Swedish subsidiary's unadjusted trial balance as follows:

Preparation of Adjusted Trial Balance in Swedish Kroner

	Unadjusted		Adjustments		Adjusted	
	Debit	**Credit**	**Debit**	**Credit**	**Debit**	**Credit**
Cash	41,000		10,400		51,400	
Accounts receivable	126,000		29,120		155,120	
Inventory	128,000				128,000	
Property, plant, and equipment	388,000		25,000	10,000	403,000	
Accumulated depreciation		98,100		5,000		103,100
Accounts payable		39,000				39,000
Notes payable		56,000		15,600		71,600
Bonds payable		125,000				125,000
Common stock		110,000				110,000
Retained earnings, 1/1/20		194,800				194,800
Sales		350,000		51,040		401,040
Cost of goods sold	165,000				165,000	
Depreciation expense	10,900		5,000		15,900	
Salary expense	36,000				36,000	
Rent expense	12,000				12,000	
Interest expense	10,000		1,160		11,160	

(continued)

(continued)

	Unadjusted		Adjustments		Adjusted	
	Debit	Credit	Debit	Credit	Debit	Credit
Other expenses	31,000		10,000		41,000	
Remeasurement loss			960		960	
Dividends, 7/1/20	25,000				25,000	
Total	972,900	972,900	81,640	81,640	1,044,540	1,044,540

Having established all account balances in the functional currency (Swedish kroner), the subsidiary's trial balance now can be translated into U.S. dollars. Under the current rate method, the dollar values to be reported for income statement items are based on the average exchange rate for the current year. All assets and liabilities are translated at the current exchange rate at the balance sheet date, and equity accounts are translated at historical rates in effect at the date of accounting recognition.

Part B

Translation of Swedish Kroner Trial Balance into U.S. Dollars

	Swedish Kroner					U.S. Dollars	
	Debit	Credit	Rate			Debit	Credit
Cash	51,400		× 0.182	C	=	9,354.80	
Accounts receivable	155,120		× 0.182	C	=	28,231.84	
Inventory	128,000		× 0.182	C	=	23,296.00	
Property, plant, and equipment	403,000		× 0.182	C	=	73,346.00	
Accumulated depreciation		103,100	× 0.182	C	=		18,764.20
Accounts payable		39,000	× 0.182	C	=		7,098.00
Notes payable		71,600	× 0.182	C	=		13,031.20
Bonds payable		125,000	× 0.182	C	=		22,750.00
Common stock		110,000	**Given**				21,000.00
Retained earnings, 1/1/20		194,800	**Given**				36,100.00
Sales		401,040	× 0.192	A	=		76,999.68
Cost of goods sold	165,000		× 0.192	A	=	31,680.00	
Depreciation expense	15,900		× 0.192	A	=	3,052.80	
Salary expense	36,000		× 0.192	A	=	6,912.00	
Rent expense	12,000		× 0.192	A	=	2,304.00	
Interest expense	11,160		× 0.192	A	=	2,142.72	
Other expenses	41,000		× 0.192	A	=	7,872.00	
Remeasurement loss	960		× 0.192	A	=	184.32	
Dividends, 7/1/20	25,000		× 0.190	H	=	4,750.00	
Total	1,044,540	1,044,540				193,126.48	195,743.08
Cumulative translation adjustment						2,616.60	
Total						195,743.08	195,743.08

The cumulative translation adjustment at 12/31/20 comprises the beginning balance (given) plus the translation adjustment for the current year:

Cumulative Translation Adjustment	
Balance, 1/1/20	$3,860.00
Translation adjustment for 2020	(6,476.60)
Balance, 12/31/20	$(2,616.60)

The negative translation adjustment for 2020 of $6,476.60 is calculated by considering the effect of exchange rate changes on net assets:

Translation Adjustment for 2020

Net assets, 1/1/20	SEK 304,800*	×	0.200 C	=	$60,960.00
Increase in net assets:					
Net income, 2020.	119,020	×	0.192 A	=	22,851.84
Decrease in net assets:					
Dividends, 7/1/20.	(25,000)	×	0.190 H	=	(4,750.00)
Net assets, 12/31/20	SEK 398,820†				$79,061.84
Net assets, 12/31/20, at current exchange rate	SEK 398,820	×	0.182 C	=	72,585.24
Translation adjustment, 2020—negative					$ 6,476.60

*Indicated by January 1, 2020, stockholders' equity balances—Common Stock, SEK 110,000; Retained Earnings, SEK 194,800.

† Indicated by December 31, 2020, stockholders' equity balances—Common Stock, SEK 110,000; Retained Earnings, SEK 288,820.

Questions

1. What are the two major issues related to the translation of foreign currency financial statements?
2. What causes balance sheet exposure to foreign exchange risk? How does balance sheet exposure compare with transaction exposure?
3. What concept underlies the current rate method of translation? What concept underlies the temporal method of translation? How does balance sheet exposure differ under these two methods?
4. What are the major procedural differences in applying the current rate and temporal methods of translation?
5. In translating the financial statements of a foreign subsidiary, why is the value assigned to retained earnings especially difficult to determine? How is this problem normally resolved?
6. Clarke Company has a subsidiary operating in a foreign country. In relation to this subsidiary, what does the term *functional currency* mean? How is the functional currency determined?
7. When is remeasurement rather than translation appropriate? How does remeasurement differ from translation?
8. A translation adjustment must be calculated and disclosed when financial statements of a foreign subsidiary are translated into the parent's reporting currency. How is this translation adjustment computed, and where is the amount reported in the financial statements?
9. Which translation method does U.S. GAAP require for operations in highly inflationary countries? What is the rationale for mandating use of this method?
10. In what ways does IFRS differ from U.S. GAAP with respect to the translation of foreign currency financial statements?
11. Why might a company want to hedge its balance sheet exposure? What is the paradox associated with hedging balance sheet exposure?
12. How are gains and losses on financial instruments used to hedge the balance sheet exposure of a foreign operation reported in the consolidated financial statements?
13. In preparing the consolidation worksheet for a parent company and its foreign subsidiary, what consolidation entries are made related to the cumulative translation adjustment?

Problems

LO 10-2

1. What is a subsidiary's functional currency?
   a. The parent's reporting currency
   b. The currency used by the parent to acquire the subsidiary
   c. The currency in which the entity primarily generates and expends cash
   d. Always the currency of the country in which the company has its headquarters

LO 10-3, 10-4

2. In comparing the current rate and temporal methods of translation, which of the following is true?
   a. The reported balance of accounts receivable is normally the same under both methods.
   b. The reported balance of inventory is normally the same under both methods.

c. The reported balance of equipment is normally the same under both methods.

d. The reported balance of depreciation expense is normally the same under both methods.

LO 10-3

3. Which of the following statements is true for the translation process using the current rate method?

   a. A translation adjustment can affect consolidated net income.

   b. Equipment is translated at the historical exchange rate in effect at the date of its purchase.

   c. A translation adjustment is created by the change in the relative value of a subsidiary's monetary assets and monetary liabilities caused by exchange rate fluctuations.

   d. A translation adjustment is created by the change in the relative value of a subsidiary's net assets caused by exchange rate fluctuations.

LO 10-2, 10-3

4. A foreign subsidiary of Thun Corporation has one asset (inventory) and no liabilities. The functional currency for this subsidiary is the yuan. The inventory was acquired for 100,000 yuan when the exchange rate was $0.16 = 1 yuan. Consolidated statements are to be produced, and the current exchange rate is $0.12 = 1 yuan. Which of the following statements is true for the consolidated financial statements?

   a. A remeasurement gain must be reported.

   b. A positive translation adjustment must be reported.

   c. A negative translation adjustment must be reported.

   d. A remeasurement loss must be reported.

LO 10-3

5. At what rates should the following balance sheet accounts in foreign statements be translated (using the current rate method) into U.S. dollars?

	Equipment	Accumulated Depreciation—Equipment
a.	Current	Current
b.	Current	Average for year
c.	Historical	Current
d.	Historical	Historical

Problems 6 and 7 are based on the following information.

Certain balance sheet accounts of a foreign subsidiary of Orchid Company have been stated in U.S. dollars as follows:

	Stated at	
	Current Rates	Historical Rates
Accounts receivable, current	$200,000	$220,000
Accounts receivable, long term	100,000	110,000
Land	50,000	55,000
Patents	80,000	85,000
	$430,000	$470,000

LO 10-2, 10-3

6. This subsidiary's functional currency is a foreign currency. What total should Orchid's balance sheet include for the preceding items?

   a. $430,000

   b. $435,000

   c. $440,000

   d. $450,000

LO 10-2, 10-4

7. This subsidiary's functional currency is the U.S. dollar. What total should Orchid's balance sheet include for the preceding items?

   a. $430,000

   b. $435,000

   c. $440,000

   d. $450,000

Problems 8 and 9 are based on the following information.

Newberry, Inc., whose reporting currency is the U.S. dollar, has a subsidiary in Argentina, whose functional currency also is the U.S. dollar. The subsidiary acquires inventory on credit on November 1, 2020, for 100,000 pesos that is sold on January 17, 2021, for 130,000 pesos. The subsidiary pays for the inventory on January 31, 2021. Currency exchange rates are as follows:

November 1, 2020	\$0.16 = 1 peso
December 31, 2020	0.17 = 1
January 17, 2021	0.18 = 1
January 31, 2021	0.19 = 1

LO 10-2, 10-4

8. What amount does Newberry's consolidated balance sheet report for this inventory at December 31, 2020?
   a. \$16,000
   b. \$17,000
   c. \$18,000
   d. \$19,000

LO 10-2, 10-4

9. What amount does Newberry's consolidated income statement report for cost of goods sold for the year ending December 31, 2021?
   a. \$16,000
   b. \$17,000
   c. \$18,000
   d. \$19,000

Problems 10 and 11 are based on the following information.

A Clarke Corporation subsidiary buys marketable equity securities and inventory on April 1, 2020, for 100,000 won each. It pays for both items on June 1, 2020, and they are still on hand at year-end. Inventory is carried at cost under the lower-of-cost-or-net realizable rule. Currency exchange rates in 2020 follow:

January 1	\$0.15 = 1 won
April 1	0.16 = 1
June 1	0.17 = 1
December 31	0.19 = 1

LO 10-2, 10-3

10. Assume that the won is the subsidiary's functional currency. What balances does a consolidated balance sheet report as of December 31, 2020?
    a. Marketable equity securities = \$16,000 and Inventory = \$16,000.
    b. Marketable equity securities = \$17,000 and Inventory = \$17,000.
    c. Marketable equity securities = \$19,000 and Inventory = \$16,000.
    d. Marketable equity securities = \$19,000 and Inventory = \$19,000.

LO 10-2, 10-4

11. Assume that the U.S. dollar is the subsidiary's functional currency. What balances does a consolidated balance sheet report as of December 31, 2020?
    a. Marketable equity securities = \$16,000 and Inventory = \$16,000
    b. Marketable equity securities = \$17,000 and Inventory = \$17,000
    c. Marketable equity securities = \$19,000 and Inventory = \$16,000
    d. Marketable equity securities = \$19,000 and Inventory = \$19,000

LO 10-2, 10-4

12. A U.S. company's foreign subsidiary had these amounts in local currency units (LCU) in 2020:

Cost of goods sold	LCU 5,000,000
Beginning inventory	500,000
Ending inventory	600,000

The average exchange rate during 2020 was \$1.00 = LCU 1. The beginning inventory was acquired when the exchange rate was \$0.80 = LCU 1. Ending inventory was acquired when the exchange rate was \$1.10 = LCU 1. The exchange rate at December 31, 2020, was \$1.15 = LCU 1. Assuming that the foreign country is highly inflationary, at what amount should the foreign subsidiary's cost of goods sold be reflected in the U.S. dollar income statement?

a. $4,440,000

b. $4,840,000

c. $5,000,000

d. $5,750,000

LO 10-3

13. Yang Corporation starts a foreign subsidiary on January 1 by investing 20,000 rand. Yang owns all of the shares of the subsidiary's common stock. The foreign subsidiary generates 40,000 rand of net income throughout the year and pays no dividends. The rand is the foreign subsidiary's functional currency. Currency exchange rates for 1 rand are as follows:

January 1	$0.25 = 1 rand
Average for the year	0.28 = 1
December 31	0.31 = 1

In preparing consolidated financial statements, what translation adjustment will Yang report at the end of the current year?

a. $400 positive (credit)

b. $1,000 positive (credit)

c. $1,400 positive (credit)

d. $2,400 positive (credit)

LO 10-1

14. In the translated financial statements, which method of translation maintains the underlying valuation methods used in preparing the foreign currency financial statements?

a. Current rate method; income statement translated at average exchange rate for the year

b. Current rate method; income statement translated at exchange rate at the balance sheet date

c. Temporal method

d. Monetary/nonmonetary method

LO 10-4

15. Charleston Corporation operates a branch operation in a foreign country. Although this branch operates in euros, the U.S. dollar is its functional currency. Thus, a remeasurement is necessary to produce financial information for external reporting purposes. The branch began the year with 500,000 euros in cash and no other assets or liabilities. However, the branch immediately used 300,000 euros to acquire a warehouse. On May 1, it purchased inventory costing 100,000 euros for cash that it sold on July 1 for 160,000 euros cash. The branch transferred 10,000 euros to the parent on October 1 and recorded depreciation on the warehouse of 10,000 euros for the year. U.S dollar exchange rates for 1 euro follow:

January 1	$1.14 = 1 euro
May 1	1.18 = 1
July 1	1.20 = 1
October 1	1.18 = 1
December 31	1.16 = 1
Average for the year	1.19 = 1

What is the remeasurement gain or loss to be recognized in the consolidated income statement?

a. $100 gain

b. $200 gain

c. $100 loss

d. $200 loss

LO 10-4

16. Which of the following items is remeasured using the current exchange rate under the temporal method?

a. Bonds payable

b. Dividends declared

c. Additional paid-in capital

d. Amortization of intangibles

LO 10-2

17. In accordance with U.S. generally accepted accounting principles, which translation combination is appropriate for a foreign operation whose functional currency is the U.S. dollar?

	Method	Treatment of Translation Adjustment
a.	Current rate	Other comprehensive income
b.	Current rate	Gain or loss in net income
c.	Temporal	Other comprehensive income
d.	Temporal	Gain or loss in net income

LO 10-3

18. A foreign subsidiary's functional currency is its local currency, which has not experienced significant inflation. The current exchange rate at the balance sheet date is the appropriate exchange rate for translating which of the following:

	Insurance Expense	Prepaid Insurance
a.	Yes	Yes
b.	Yes	No
c.	No	Yes
d.	No	No

LO 10-5

19. The functional currency of Bertrand, Inc.'s Irish subsidiary is the euro. Bertrand borrowed euros as a partial hedge of its investment in the subsidiary. Since then, the euro has decreased in value. Bertrand's negative translation adjustment on its investment in the subsidiary exceeded its foreign exchange gain on its euro borrowing. How should Bertrand report the effects of the negative translation adjustment and foreign exchange gain in its consolidated financial statements?
   a. Report the translation adjustment in accumulated other comprehensive income on the balance sheet and the foreign exchange gain as a gain on the income statement.
   b. Report the translation adjustment in the income statement and defer the foreign exchange gain in accumulated other comprehensive income on the balance sheet.
   c. Report the translation adjustment less the foreign exchange gain in accumulated other comprehensive income on the balance sheet.
   d. Report the translation adjustment less the foreign exchange gain in the income statement.

Problems 20 and 21 are based on the following information.

McCarthy, Inc.'s Brazilian subsidiary borrowed 100,000 euros on January 1, 2020. Exchange rates between the Brazilian real (BRL) and euro (€) and between the U.S. dollar ($) and BRL are as follows:

	BRL per €	US$ per BRL
January 1, 2020	BRL 4.2	$ 0.28
Average, 2020	BRL 4.3	$ 0.25
December 31, 2020	BRL 4.6	$ 0.20

LO 10-4

20. At what amount should the Brazilian subsidiary's euro note payable be reported on McCarthy's December 31, 2020, consolidated balance sheet?
   a. $84,000.
   b. $86,000.
   c. $92,000.
   d. $128,800.

LO 10-4

21. What amount of foreign exchange gain or loss should be reflected in McCarthy's 2020 consolidated net income?
   a. $8,000 loss.
   b. $10,000 loss.
   c. $2,000 gain.
   d. $5,000 gain.

LO 10-3

22. On January 1, Narnevik Corporation formed a subsidiary in a foreign country. On April 1, the subsidiary purchased inventory on account at a cost of 250,000 local currency units (LCU). One-fifth of this inventory remained unsold on December 31, while 30 percent of the account payable had not yet been paid. The U.S.dollar–per-LCU exchange rates were as follows:

January 1	$0.60
April 1	0.58
Average for the current year	0.56
December 31	0.54

At what amounts should the December 31 balances in inventory and accounts payable be translated into U.S. dollars using the current rate method?

LO 10-3, 10-4

23. The following accounts are denominated in rubles as of December 31, 2020. For reporting purposes, these accounts need to be stated in U.S. dollars. For each account, indicate the exchange rate that would be used to translate the ruble balance into U.S. dollars under the current rate method. Then, again for each account, indicate the exchange rate that would be used to remeasure the ruble balance to U.S. dollars using the temporal method. The company was started in 2015. The buildings were acquired in 2016 and the patents in 2018.

	Translation	Remeasurement
Accounts payable		
Accounts receivable		
Accumulated depreciation—buildings		
Advertising expense		
Amortization expense (patents)		
Buildings		
Cash		
Common stock		
Depreciation expense		
Dividends (10/1/20)		
Notes payable—due in 2023		
Patents (net)		
Salary expense		
Sales		

Exchange rates for 1 ruble are as follows:

2015	1 ruble = $0.28
2016	1 = 0.26
2018	1 = 0.25
January 1, 2020	1 = 0.24
April 1, 2020	1 = 0.23
July 1, 2020	1 = 0.22
October 1, 2020	1 = 0.20
December 31, 2020	1 = 0.16
Average for 2020	1 = 0.19

LO 10-1, 10-3, 10-4

24. On December 18, 2020, Stephanie Corporation acquired 100 percent of a Swiss company for 4.0 million Swiss francs (CHF), which is indicative of book and fair value. At the acquisition date, the exchange rate was $1.00 = CHF 1. On December 18, 2020, the book and fair values of the subsidiary's assets and liabilities were as follows:

Cash	CHF 800,000
Inventory	1,300,000
Property, plant, and equipment	4,000,000
Notes payable	(2,100,000)

Stephanie prepares consolidated financial statements on December 31, 2020. By that date, the Swiss franc has appreciated to $1.10 = CHF 1. Because of the year-end holidays, no transactions took place prior to consolidation.

a. Determine the translation adjustment to be reported on Stephanie's December 31, 2020, consolidated balance sheet, assuming that the Swiss franc is the Swiss subsidiary's functional currency. What is the economic relevance of this translation adjustment?

b. Determine the remeasurement gain or loss to be reported in Stephanie's 2020 consolidated net income, assuming that the U.S. dollar is the functional currency. What is the economic relevance of this remeasurement gain or loss?

LO 10-3, 10-4

25. The Isle of Palms Company (IOP), a U.S.-based entity, has a wholly owned subsidiary in Israel that has been determined as having the Israeli shekel (ILS) as its functional currency. On October 1, 2019, the Israeli subsidiary borrowed 500,000 Swiss francs (CHF) from a bank in Geneva for two years at an interest rate of 5 percent per year. The note payable and accrued interest are payable at the date of maturity. On December 31, 2020, the Israeli subsidiary has the following foreign currency balances on its books:

Interest expense	CHF 25,000
Interest payable	CHF 31,250
Note payable	CHF 500,000

Relevant exchange rates between the Israeli shekel (ILS) and Swiss franc (CHF), and between the U.S. dollar (USD) and Israeli shekel (ILS) follow:

	ILS per CHF	USD per ILS
October 1, 2019	3.86	0.30
January 1, 2020	3.91	0.29
Average for 2020	3.95	0.27
December 31, 2020	4.02	0.25

a. Determine the Israeli shekel amounts at which the Swiss franc balances should be reported on the Israel subsidiary's December 31, 2020, trial balance.

b. Determine the U.S. dollar amounts at which the Swiss franc balances should be included in IOP's 2020 consolidated financial statements.

LO 10-3

26. Sullivan's Island Company began operating a subsidiary in a foreign country on January 1, 2020, by investing capital in the amount of 60,000 pounds. The subsidiary immediately borrowed 140,000 pounds on a five-year note with 10 percent interest payable annually beginning on January 1, 2021. The subsidiary then purchased for 200,000 pounds a building that had a 10-year expected life and no salvage value and is to be depreciated using the straight-line method. Also on January 1, 2020, the subsidiary rented the building for three years to a group of local attorneys for 8,000 pounds per month. By year-end, rent payments totaling 80,000 pounds had been received, and 16,000 pounds was in accounts receivable. On October 1, 2020, 4,000 pounds was paid for a repair made to the building. The subsidiary transferred a cash dividend of 12,000 pounds back to Sullivan's Island Company on December 31, 2020. The functional currency for the subsidiary is the pound. Currency exchange rates for 1 pound follow:

January 1, 2020	$2.00 = 1 pound
October 1, 2020	2.05 = 1
December 31, 2020	2.08 = 1
Average for 2020	2.04 = 1

Prepare an income statement, statement of retained earnings, and balance sheet for this subsidiary in pounds, and then translate these amounts into U.S. dollars.

LO 10-3

27. Refer to the information in problem 26. Prepare a statement of cash flows in pounds for Sullivan's Island Company's foreign subsidiary, and then translate this statement into U.S. dollars.

LO 10-3, 10-4

28. Rolfe Company (a U.S.-based company) has a subsidiary in Nigeria, where the local currency unit is the naira (NGN). On December 31, 2019, the subsidiary had the following balance sheet (amounts are in thousands [000s]):

Cash	NGN 16,000	Note payable	NGN 20,000
Inventory	10,000	Common stock	20,000
Land	4,000	Retained earnings	10,000
Building	40,000		
Accumulated depreciation	(20,000)		
	NGN 50,000		NGN 50,000

The subsidiary acquired the inventory on August 1, 2019, and the land and building in 2013. It issued the common stock in 2011. During 2020, the following transactions took place:

2020	
Feb. 1	Paid 8,000,000 NGN on the note payable.
May 1	Sold entire inventory for 16,000,000 NGN on account.
June 1	Sold land for 6,000,000 NGN cash.
Aug. 1	Collected all accounts receivable.
Sept. 1	Signed long-term note to receive 8,000,000 NGN cash.
Oct. 1	Bought inventory for 20,000,000 NGN cash.
Nov. 1	Bought land for 3,000,000 NGN on account.
Dec. 1	Declared and paid 3,000,000 NGN cash dividend to parent.
Dec. 31	Recorded depreciation for the entire year of 2,000,000 NGN.

The U.S dollar ($) exchange rates for 1 NGN are as follows:

2011	NGN 1 = $0.0048
2013	1 = 0.0042
August 1, 2019	1 = 0.0062
December 31, 2019	1 = 0.0064
February 1, 2020	1 = 0.0066
May 1, 2020	1 = 0.0068
June 1, 2020	1 = 0.0070
August 1, 2020	1 = 0.0074
September 1, 2020	1 = 0.0076
October 1, 2020	1 = 0.0078
November 1, 2020	1 = 0.0080
December 1, 2020	1 = 0.0082
December 31, 2020	1 = 0.0084
Average for 2020	1 = 0.0074

a. Assuming the NGN is the subsidiary's functional currency, what is the translation adjustment determined solely for 2020?

b. Assuming the U.S.$ is the subsidiary's functional currency, what is the remeasurement gain or loss determined solely for 2020?

LO 10-3, 10-4

29. Zugar Company is domiciled in a country whose currency is the dinar. Zugar begins 2020 with three assets: Cash of 20,000 dinars, Accounts receivable of 80,000 dinars, and Land that cost 200,000 dinars when acquired on April 1, 2019. On January 1, 2020, Zugar has a 150,000 dinar Note payable, and no other liabilities. On May 1, 2020, Zugar renders services to a customer for 120,000 dinars, which was immediately paid in cash. On June 1, 2020, Zugar incurred a 100,000 dinar operating expense, which was immediately paid in cash. No other transactions occurred during the year. Currency exchange rates for 1 dinar follow:

April 1, 2019	$0.33 = 1 dinar
January 1, 2020	0.36 = 1
May 1, 2020	0.37 = 1
June 1, 2020	0.39 = 1
December 31, 2020	0.41 = 1

a. Assume that Zugar is a foreign subsidiary of a U.S. multinational company that uses the U.S. dollar as its reporting currency. Assume also that the dinar is the subsidiary's functional currency. What is the translation adjustment for this subsidiary for the year 2020?

b. Assume that Zugar is a foreign subsidiary of a U.S. multinational company that uses the U.S. dollar as its reporting currency. Assume also that the U.S. dollar is the subsidiary's functional currency. What is the remeasurement gain or loss for 2020?

c. Assume that Zugar is a foreign subsidiary of a U.S. multinational company. On the December 31, 2020, balance sheet, what is the *translated* value of the Land account? On the December 31, 2020, balance sheet, what is the *remeasured* value of the Land account?

LO 10-3, 10-4

30. Lancer, Inc. (a U.S.-based company), establishes a subsidiary in Croatia on January 1, 2019. The following account balances for the year ending December 31, 2020, are stated in kuna (K), the local currency:

Sales	K 200,000
Inventory (bought on 3/1/20)	100,000
Equipment (bought on 1/1/19)	80,000
Rent expense	10,000
Dividends (declared on 10/1/20)	20,000
Notes receivable (to be collected in 2023)	30,000
Accumulated depreciation—equipment	24,000
Salary payable	5,000
Depreciation expense	8,000

The following U.S.$ per kuna exchange rates are applicable:

January 1, 2019	$0.13
Average for 2019	0.14
January 1, 2020	0.18
March 1, 2020	0.19
October 1, 2020	0.21
December 31, 2020	0.22
Average for 2020	0.20

Lancer is preparing account balances to produce consolidated financial statements.

a. Assuming that the kuna is the functional currency, what exchange rate would be used to report each of these accounts in U.S. dollar consolidated financial statements?

b. Assuming that the U.S. dollar is the functional currency, what exchange rate would be used to report each of these accounts in U.S. dollar consolidated financial statements?

LO 10-3, 10-5

31. Christina Company (a U.S.-based company) has a subsidiary in Canada that began operations at the start of 2020 with assets of 132,000 Canadian dollars (CAD) and liabilities of CAD 54,000. During this initial year of operation, the subsidiary reported a profit of CAD 26,000. It distributed two dividends, each for CAD 5,000 with one dividend declared on March 1 and the other on October 1. Applicable U.S. dollar ($) exchange rates for 1 Canadian dollar follow:

January 1, 2020 (start of business)	$0.80
March 1, 2020	0.78
Weighted average rate for 2020	0.77
October 1, 2020	0.76
December 31, 2020	0.75

a. Assume that the Canadian dollar is this subsidiary's functional currency. What translation adjustment would the company report for the year 2020?

b. Assume that on October 1, 2020, Christina entered into a forward exchange contract to hedge the net investment in this subsidiary. On that date, the company agreed to sell CAD 400,000 in three months at a forward exchange rate of $0.76/CAD 1. Prepare the journal entries required by this forward contract.

c. Compute the net translation adjustment the company will report in accumulated other comprehensive income for the year 2020 under this second set of circumstances.

LO 10-3, 10-4

32. Kingsfield establishes a subsidiary operation in a foreign country on January 1, 2020. The country's currency is the rial (R). To start this business, Kingsfield invests 10,000 rials. Of this amount, it spends 3,000 rials immediately to acquire equipment. Later, on April 1, 2020, it also purchases land. All subsidiary operational activities occur at an even rate throughout the year. Kingsfield uses the U.S. dollar as its reporting currency. The U.S. dollar ($) exchange rates for the rial for 2020 follow:

January 1	$1.71
April 1	1.59
June 1	1.66
Weighted average	1.64
December 31	1.62

As of December 31, 2020, the subsidiary reports the following trial balance:

	Debits	Credits
Cash	R 8,000	
Accounts receivable	9,000	
Equipment	3,000	
Accumulated depreciation		R 600
Land	5,000	
Accounts payable		3,000
Notes payable (due 2028)		5,000
Common stock		10,000
Dividends declared (6/1/20)	4,000	
Sales		25,000
Salary expense	5,000	
Depreciation expense	600	
Miscellaneous expenses	9,000	
Totals	R 43,600	R 43,600

a. Assume that the subsidiary's functional currency is the rial (R). Prepare a trial balance for it in U.S. dollars so that 2020 consolidated financial statements can be prepared.

b. Assume that the subsidiary's functional currency is the U.S. dollar. Prepare a trial balance for it in U.S. dollars so that 2020 consolidated financial statements can be prepared.

LO 10-3

33. Livingston Company is a wholly owned subsidiary of Rose Corporation. Livingston operates in a foreign country with financial statements recorded in pounds (P), the company's functional currency. Financial statements for the year 2020 are as follows:

Income Statement
For Year Ending December 31, 2020

Sales	P 270,000
Cost of goods sold	(155,000)
Gross profit	115,000
Less: Operating expenses	(54,000)
Gain on sale of equipment	10,000
Net income	P 71,000

Statement of Retained Earnings
For Year Ending December 31, 2020

Retained earnings, 1/1/20	P 216,000
Net income	71,000
Less: Dividends	(26,000)
Retained earnings, 12/31/20	P 261,000

Balance Sheet
December 31, 2020

Assets	
Cash	P 44,000
Receivables	116,000
Inventory	58,000
Property, plant, and equipment (net)	339,000
Total assets	P 557,000
Liabilities and Equities	
Liabilities	P 176,000
Common stock	120,000
Retained earnings, 12/31/20	261,000
Total liabilities and equities	P 557,000

Additional Information

- The common stock was issued in 2013 when the exchange rate was $2.08 per pound; property, plant, and equipment was acquired in 2014 when the rate was $2.00 per pound.
- As of January 1, 2020, the retained earnings balance was translated as $396,520.
- The U.S. dollar–per-pound exchange rates for 2020 follow:

January 1	$1.67
April 1	1.61
September 1	1.72
December 31	1.54
Weighted average	1.59

- Inventory was acquired evenly throughout the year.
- The December 31, 2019, balance sheet reported a translation adjustment with a debit balance of $85,000.
- Dividends were declared on April 1, 2020, and a piece of equipment was sold on September 1, 2020.

Assume that the pound is Livingston Company's functional currency. Translate the 2020 foreign currency financial statements into the parent's reporting currency, the U.S. dollar.

LO 10-3, 10-4

34. The following account balances are for the Agee Company as of January 1, 2020, and December 31, 2020. All amounts are denominated in kroner (Kr).

	January 1, 2020	December 31, 2020
Accounts payable	(15,000)	(25,000)
Accounts receivable	54,000	104,000
Accumulated depreciation—buildings	(45,000)	(50,000)
Accumulated depreciation—equipment	–0–	(7,500)
Bonds payable—due 2023	(64,000)	(64,000)
Buildings	134,000	105,000
Cash	60,000	10,500
Common stock	(69,000)	(82,000)
Depreciation expense	–0–	40,000
Dividends (10/1/20)	–0–	57,000
Equipment	–0–	64,000
Gain on sale of building	–0–	(8,500)
Rent expense	–0–	21,500
Retained earnings	(55,000)	(55,000)
Salary expense	–0–	45,000
Sales	–0–	(162,000)
Utilities expense	–0–	7,000

Additional Information

- Agee issued additional shares of common stock during the year on April 1, 2020. Common stock at January 1, 2020, was sold at the start of operations in 2013.
- Agee purchased buildings in 2014 and sold one building with a book value of Kr 1,500 on July 1 of the current year.
- Equipment was acquired on April 1, 2020.

Relevant exchange rates for 1 Kr were as follows:

2013	$2.90
2014	2.70
January 1, 2020	3.00
April 1, 2020	3.10
July 1, 2020	3.30
October 1, 2020	3.40
December 31, 2020	3.50
Average for 2020	3.20

a. Assuming the U.S. dollar is the functional currency, what is the remeasurement gain or loss for 2020? The December 31, 2019, U.S. dollar–translated balance sheet reported retained earnings of $145,200, which included a remeasurement loss of $28,300.

b. Assuming the foreign currency is the functional currency, what is the translation adjustment for 2020? The December 31, 2019, U.S. dollar–translated balance sheet reported retained earnings of $162,250 and a cumulative translation adjustment of $9,650 (credit balance).

LO 10-3, 10-4

35. Sendelbach Corporation is a U.S.-based organization with operations throughout the world. One of its subsidiaries is headquartered in Toronto. Although this wholly owned company operates primarily in Canada, it engages in some transactions through a branch in Mexico. Therefore, the subsidiary maintains a ledger denominated in Mexican pesos (Ps) and a general ledger in Canadian dollars (C$). As of December 31, 2020, the subsidiary is preparing financial statements in anticipation of consolidation with the U.S. parent corporation. Both ledgers for the subsidiary are as follows:

Main Operation—Canada

	Debit	Credit
Accounts payable		C$ 35,000
Accumulated depreciation		27,000
Buildings and equipment	C$167,000	
Cash	26,000	
Common stock		50,000
Cost of goods sold	203,000	
Depreciation expense	8,000	
Dividends, 4/1/20	28,000	
Gain on sale of equipment, 6/1/20		5,000
Inventory	98,000	
Notes payable—due in 2023		76,000
Receivables	68,000	
Retained earnings, 1/1/20		135,530
Salary expense	26,000	
Sales		312,000
Utility expense	9,000	
Branch operation	7,530	
Totals	C$640,530	C$640,530

Branch Operation—Mexico

	Debit	Credit
Accounts payable		Ps 49,000
Accumulated depreciation		19,000
Building and equipment	Ps 40,000	
Cash	59,000	
Depreciation expense	2,000	
Inventory (beginning—income statement)	23,000	
Inventory (ending—income statement)		28,000
Inventory (ending—balance sheet)	28,000	
Purchases	68,000	
Receivables	21,000	
Salary expense	9,000	
Sales		124,000
Main office		30,000
Totals	Ps 250,000	Ps 250,000

Additional Information

- The Canadian subsidiary's functional currency is the Canadian dollar, and Sendelbach's reporting currency is the U.S. dollar. The Canadian and Mexican operations are not viewed as separate accounting entities.
- The building and equipment used in the Mexican operation were acquired in 2010 when the currency exchange rate was C$0.25 = Ps 1.
- Purchases of inventory were made evenly throughout the fiscal year.
- Beginning inventory was acquired evenly throughout 2019; ending inventory was acquired evenly throughout 2020.
- The Main Office account on the Mexican records should be considered an equity account. This balance was remeasured into C$7,530 on December 31, 2020.
- Currency exchange rates for 1 Ps applicable to the Mexican operation follow:

Weighted average rate for 2019	C$0.30
January 1, 2020	0.32
Weighted average rate for 2020	0.34
December 31, 2020	0.35

- The December 31, 2019, consolidated balance sheet reported a cumulative translation adjustment with a $36,950 credit (positive) balance.
- The subsidiary's common stock was issued in 2007 when the exchange rate was $0.45 = C$1.
- The subsidiary's December 31, 2019, retained earnings balance was C$135,530, an amount that has been translated into U.S. $70,421.
- The applicable currency exchange rates for 1 C$ for translation purposes are as follows:

January 1, 2020	US$0.70
April 1, 2020	0.69
June 1, 2020	0.68
Weighted average rate for 2020	0.67
December 31, 2020	0.65

a. Remeasure the Mexican operation's account balances into Canadian dollars. (Note: Back into the beginning net monetary asset or liability position.)

b. Prepare financial statements (income statement, statement of retained earnings, and balance sheet) for the Canadian subsidiary in its functional currency, Canadian dollars.

c. Translate the Canadian dollar functional currency financial statements into U.S. dollars so that Sendelbach can prepare consolidated financial statements.

LO 10-3, 10-6

36. On January 1, 2019, Cayce Corporation acquired 100 percent of Simbel Company for consideration transferred with a fair value of $126,000. Cayce is a U.S.-based company headquartered in Buffalo, New York, and Simbel is in Cairo, Egypt. Cayce accounts for its investment in Simbel under the initial value method. Any excess of fair value of consideration transferred over book value is attributable to undervalued land on Simbel's books. Simbel had no retained earnings at the date of acquisition. The following are the 2020 financial statements for the two operations. Information for Cayce and for Simbel is in U.S. dollars ($) and Egyptian pounds (£E), respectively.

	Cayce Corporation	Simbel Company
Sales	$ 200,000	£E 800,000
Cost of goods sold	(93,800)	(420,000)
Salary expense	(19,000)	(74,000)
Rent expense	(7,000)	(46,000)
Other expenses	(21,000)	(59,000)
Dividend income—from Simbel	13,750	–0–
Gain on sale of building, 10/1/20	–0–	30,000
Net income	$ 72,950	£E 231,000
Retained earnings, 1/1/20	$ 318,000	£E 133,000
Net income	72,950	231,000
Dividends	(24,000)	(50,000)
Retained earnings, 12/31/20	$ 366,950	£E 314,000
Cash and receivables	$ 110,750	£E 146,000
Inventory	98,000	297,000
Prepaid expenses	30,000	–0–
Investment in Simbel (initial value)	126,000	–0–
Property, plant, and equipment (net)	398,000	455,000
Total assets	$ 762,750	£E 898,000
Accounts payable	$ 60,800	£E 54,000
Notes payable—due in 2023	132,000	140,000
Common stock	120,000	240,000
Additional paid-in capital	83,000	150,000
Retained earnings, 12/31/20	366,950	314,000
Total liabilities and equities	$ 762,750	£E 898,000

Additional Information

- During 2019, the first year of joint operation, Simbel reported income of £E 163,000 earned evenly throughout the year. Simbel declared a dividend of £E 30,000 to Cayce on June 1 of that year. Simbel also declared the 2020 dividend on June 1.
- On December 9, 2020, Simbel classified a £E 10,000 expenditure as a rent expense, although this payment related to prepayment of rent for the first few months of 2021.
- The exchange rates for 1 £E are as follows:

January 1, 2019	$0.300
June 1, 2019	0.290
Weighted average rate for 2019	0.288
December 31, 2019	0.280
June 1, 2020	0.275
October 1, 2020	0.273
Weighted average rate for 2020	0.274
December 31, 2020	0.270

Translate Simbel's 2020 financial statements into U.S. dollars and prepare a consolidation worksheet for Cayce and its Egyptian subsidiary. Assume that the Egyptian pound is the subsidiary's functional currency.

LO 10-1, 10-3, 10-4

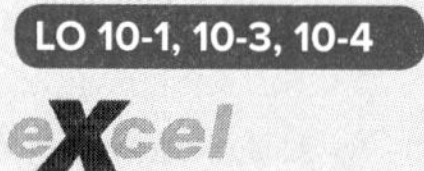

37. Diekmann Company, a U.S.-based company, acquired a 100 percent interest in Rakona A.S. in the Czech Republic on January 1, 2019, when the exchange rate for the Czech koruna (Kčs) was $0.05. Rakona's financial statements as of December 31, 2020, two years later, follow:

Balance Sheet
December 31, 2020

Assets	
Cash	Kčs 2,000,000
Accounts receivable (net)	3,300,000
Inventory	8,500,000
Equipment	25,000,000
Less: Accumulated depreciation	(8,500,000)
Buildings	72,000,000
Less: Accumulated depreciation	(30,300,000)
Land	6,000,000
Total assets	Kčs 78,000,000
Liabilities and Stockholders' Equity	
Accounts payable	Kčs 2,500,000
Long-term debt	50,000,000
Common stock	5,000,000
Additional paid-in capital	15,000,000
Retained earnings	5,500,000
Total liabilities and stockholders' equity	Kčs 78,000,000

Income Statement
For Year Ending December 31, 2020

Sales	Kčs 25,000,000
Cost of goods sold	(12,000,000)
Depreciation expense—equipment	(2,500,000)
Depreciation expense—buildings	(1,800,000)
Research and development expense	(1,200,000)
Other expenses (including taxes)	(1,000,000)
Net income	Kčs 6,500,000
Plus: Retained earnings, 1/1/20	500,000
Less: Dividends, 2020	(1,500,000)
Retained earnings, 12/31/20	Kčs 5,500,000

Additional Information

- The January 1, 2020, beginning inventory of Kčs 6,000,000 was acquired on December 18, 2019, when the exchange rate was $0.043. Purchases of inventory were acquired uniformly during 2020. The December 31, 2020, ending inventory of Kčs 8,500,000 was acquired in the latter part of 2020 when the exchange rate was $0.032. All depreciable assets (equipment and buildings) were on the books when the subsidiary was acquired—except for Kčs 5,000,000 of equipment acquired on January 3, 2020, when the exchange rate was $0.036, and Kčs 12,000,000 in buildings acquired on March 5, 2020, when the exchange rate was $0.034. Straight-line depreciation is 10 years for equipment and 40 years for buildings. A full year's depreciation is taken in the year of acquisition.
- Dividends were declared and paid on December 15, 2020, when the exchange rate was $0.031.
- Other exchange rates for 1 Kčs follow:

January 1, 2020	$0.040
Average 2020	0.035
December 31, 2020	0.030

Part I. Translate the Czech koruna financial statements at December 31, 2020, in the following three situations:

a. The Czech koruna is the functional currency. The December 31, 2019, U.S. dollar–translated balance sheet reported retained earnings of $22,500. The December 31, 2019, cumulative translation adjustment was negative $202,500 (debit balance).

b. The U.S. dollar is the functional currency. The December 31, 2019, U.S. dollar–remeasured balance sheet reported retained earnings (including a 2019 remeasurement gain) of $353,000.

c. The U.S. dollar is the functional currency. Rakona has no long-term debt. Instead, it has common stock of Kčs 20,000,000 and additional paid-in capital of Kčs 50,000,000. The December 31, 2019, U.S. dollar–remeasured balance sheet reported a negative balance in retained earnings of $147,000 (including a 2019 remeasurement loss).

Part II. Explain the positive or negative sign of the translation adjustment in Part I(*a*), and explain why a remeasurement gain or loss exists in Parts I(*b*) and I(*c*).

LO 10-3, 10-4

38. Millager Company is a U.S.-based multinational corporation with the U.S. dollar (USD) as its reporting currency. To prepare consolidated financial statements for 2020, the company must translate the accounts of its subsidiary in Mexico, Cadengo S.A. On December 31, 2019, Cadengo's balance sheet was translated from Mexican pesos (MXN) (its functional currency) into U.S. dollars as prescribed by U.S. GAAP. Equity accounts at that date follow:

December 31, 2019	MXN	USD
Common stock	12,000,000	1,000,000
Retained earnings	2,500,000	200,000
Cumulative translation adjustment (debit balance)		(40,000)

Early in 2020, Cadengo negotiated a 5,000 Brazilian real (BRL) loan from a bank in Rio de Janeiro and established a sales office in Brazil.

At the end of 2020, Cadengo provided Millager a trial balance that includes all of Cadengo's Mexican peso–denominated transactions for the year. A separate ledger has been maintained for transactions carried out by the Brazilian sales office that are denominated in BRL. A trial balance for the Brazilian real-denominated transactions follows Cadengo's MXN trial balance.

CADENGO S.A.
Trial Balance
December 31, 2020

	Debit	Credit
Cash	MXN 1,000,000	
Accounts receivable	3,000,000	
Inventory	5,000,000	
Land	2,000,000	
Machinery and equipment	15,000,000	
Accumulated depreciation		MXN 6,000,000
Accounts payable		1,500,000
Notes payable		4,000,000
Common stock		12,000,000
Retained earnings, 1/1/20		2,500,000
Sales		34,000,000
Cost of goods sold	28,000,000	
Depreciation expense	600,000	
Rent expense	3,000,000	
Interest expense	400,000	
Dividends, 7/1/20	2,000,000	
Total	MXN 60,000,000	MXN 60,000,000

BRAZILIAN SALES OFFICE
Trial Balance
December 31, 2020

	Debit	Credit
Cash	BRL 5,500	
Accounts receivable	28,000	
Notes payable		BRL 5,000
Sales		35,000
Rent expense	6,000	
Interest expense	500	
Total	BRL 40,000	BRL 40,000

Additional Information

The Mexican peso exchange rate for 1 Brazilian real (MXN/BRL) and the U.S. dollar exchange rate for 1 Mexican peso (USD/MXN) during 2020 follow:

Date	MXN/BRL	USD/MXN
January 1, 2020	6.00	0.080
Average 2020	6.20	0.075
July 1, 2020	6.28	0.073
December 31, 2020	6.30	0.072

a. Using an electronic spreadsheet, prepare the Mexican peso trial balance for Cadengo S.A. for the year ending December 31, 2020. Verify the amount of remeasurement gain/loss derived as a plug figure in the spreadsheet through separate calculation.

b. Using a second electronic worksheet, translate Cadengo S.A.'s Mexican peso trial balance into U.S. dollars to facilitate Millager Company's preparation of consolidated financial statements. Verify the amount of cumulative translation adjustment derived as a plug figure in the spreadsheet through separate calculation. Note: An additional row must be inserted in the trial balance for the remeasurement gain/loss calculated in part *a.*

Develop Your Skills

RESEARCH CASE 1—FOREIGN CURRENCY TRANSLATION AND HEDGING DISCLOSURES

CPA skills

Many companies make annual reports available on their corporate website. Annual reports on Form 10-K also can be accessed through the SEC's EDGAR system at www.sec.gov (under Filing Type, search for 10-K).

Access the most recent annual report for a U.S.-based multinational company with which you are familiar to complete the following requirements.

Required

a. Identify the location(s) in the annual report that provides disclosures related to the translation of foreign currency financial statements and foreign currency hedging.

b. Determine whether the company's foreign operations have a predominant functional currency.

c. List the amount of translation adjustment, if any, reported in other comprehensive income in each of the three most recent years. Explain the sign (positive or negative) of the translation adjustment in each of the three most recent years.

d. Determine whether the company hedges net investments in foreign operations. If so, determine the type(s) of hedging instrument used.

RESEARCH CASE 2—FOREIGN CURRENCY TRANSLATION AND HEDGING DISCLOSURES

CPA skills

Many companies make annual reports (sometimes on Form 10-K) available on their corporate website. Access the annual report indicated for each of the following U.S.-based multinational corporations to complete the requirements:

International Business Machines Corporation, 2017 Annual Report.

Oracle Corporation, Form 10-K for the Fiscal Year Ended May 31, 2018.

Required

a. Identify the location(s) in the annual report that provides disclosures related to foreign currency translation and foreign currency hedging.

b. Determine whether the company's foreign operations have a predominant functional currency.

c. List the amount of translation adjustment, if any, reported in other comprehensive income in each of the three most recent years. Explain the sign (positive or negative) of the translation adjustment in each of the three most recent years.

d. Determine whether each company hedges net investments in foreign operations. If so, determine the type(s) of hedging instrument used.

ACCOUNTING STANDARDS CASE 1—MORE THAN ONE FUNCTIONAL CURRENCY

CPA skills

Lynch Corporation has a wholly owned subsidiary in Mexico (Lynmex) with two distinct and unrelated lines of business. Lynmex's Small Appliance Division manufactures small household appliances such as toasters and coffeemakers at a factory in Monterrey, Nuevo Leon, and sells them directly to retailers such as Gigantes throughout Mexico. Lynmex's Electronics Division imports finished products produced by Lynch Corporation in the United States and sells them to a network of distributors operating throughout Mexico.

Lynch's CFO believes that the two divisions have different functional currencies. The functional currency of the Small Appliance Division is the Mexican peso, whereas the functional currency of the Electronics Division is the U.S. dollar. The CFO is unsure whether to designate the Mexican peso or the U.S. dollar as Lynmex's functional currency, or whether the subsidiary can be treated as two separate foreign operations with different functional currencies.

Required

Search current U.S. authoritative accounting literature to determine how the functional currency should be determined for a foreign entity that has more than one distinct and separable operation. Identify the source of guidance for answering this question.

ACCOUNTING STANDARDS CASE 2—CHANGE IN FUNCTIONAL CURRENCY

CPA skills

Hughes Inc. has a wholly owned subsidiary in Canada that previously had been determined as having the Canadian dollar as its functional currency. Due to a recent restructuring, Hughes Inc.'s CFO believes that the functional currency of the Canadian company has changed to the U.S. dollar. A large cumulative translation adjustment related to the Canadian subsidiary is included in accumulated other comprehensive income on Hughes Inc.'s balance sheet. The CFO is unsure whether the cumulative translation adjustment should be removed from equity, and if so, to what other account it should be transferred. He also questions whether the change in functional currency qualifies as a change in accounting principle, which would require retrospective application of the temporal method in translating the Canadian subsidiary's financial statements. He wonders, for example, whether the

Canadian subsidiary's nonmonetary assets need to be restated as if the temporal method had been applied in previous years.

Required

Search current U.S. authoritative accounting literature for guidance on how to handle a change in functional currency from a foreign currency to the U.S. dollar. Summarize that guidance to answer the CFO's questions. Identify the source of guidance for answering these questions.

EXCEL CASE—TRANSLATING FOREIGN CURRENCY FINANCIAL STATEMENTS

Charles Edward Company established a subsidiary in a foreign country on January 1, 2020, by investing FC 3,200,000 when the exchange rate was \$0.50/FC. Charles Edward negotiated a bank loan of FC 3,000,000 on January 5, 2020, and purchased plant and equipment in the amount of FC 6,000,000 on January 8, 2020. It depreciated plant and equipment on a straight-line basis over a 10-year useful life. It purchased its beginning inventory of FC 1,000,000 on January 10, 2020, and acquired additional inventory of FC 4,000,000 at three points in time during the year at an average exchange rate of \$0.43/FC. It uses the first-in, first-out (FIFO) method to determine cost of goods sold. Additional exchange rates per FC 1 during the year 2020 follow:

January 1–31, 2020	\$0.50
Average 2020	0.45
December 31, 2020	0.38

The foreign subsidiary's income statement for 2020 and balance sheet at December 31, 2020, follow:

INCOME STATEMENT
For the Year Ended December 31, 2020
FC (in thousands)

Sales	FC 5,000
Cost of goods sold	3,000
Gross profit	2,000
Selling expense	400
Depreciation expense	600
Income before tax	1,000
Income taxes	300
Net income	700
Retained earnings, 1/1/20	–0–
Retained earnings, 12/31/20	FC 700

BALANCE SHEET
At December 31, 2020
FC (in thousands)

Cash	FC 1,000
Inventory	2,000
Property, plant & equipment	6,000
Less: Accumulated depreciation	(600)
Total assets	FC 8,400
Current liabilities	FC 1,500
Long-term debt	3,000
Contributed capital	3,200
Retained earnings	700
Total liabilities and stockholders' equity	FC 8,400

As the controller for Charles Edward Company, you have evaluated the characteristics of the foreign subsidiary to determine that the FC is the subsidiary's functional currency.

Required

a. Use Excel to translate the foreign subsidiary's FC financial statements into U.S. dollars at December 31, 2020, in accordance with U.S. GAAP. Insert a row in the spreadsheet after retained earnings and before total liabilities and stockholders' equity for the cumulative translation adjustment. Calculate the translation adjustment separately to verify the amount obtained as a balancing figure in the translation worksheet.

b. Use Excel to remeasure the foreign subsidiary's FC financial statements in U.S. dollars at December 31, 2020, assuming that the U.S. dollar is the subsidiary's functional currency. Insert a row in the spreadsheet after depreciation expense and before income before taxes for the remeasurement gain (loss).

c. Prepare a report for James Benjamin, CEO of Charles Edward, summarizing the differences that will be reported in the company's 2020 consolidated financial statements because the FC, rather than the U.S. dollar, is the foreign subsidiary's functional currency. In your report, discuss the relationship between the current ratio, the debt-to-equity ratio, and profit margin calculated from the FC financial statements and from the translated U.S. dollar financial statements. Also discuss the meaning of the translated U.S. dollar amounts for inventory and for fixed assets.

COMMUNICATION CASE—FUNCTIONAL CURRENCY OF A FOREIGN SUBSIDIARY

Earlier this year, Alltime Company (headquartered in Kansas City, Missouri) acquired a small watch manufacturer in Berlin, Germany, that keeps its books in euros. (This is the first foreign direct investment made by Alltime.) The end of the fiscal year is approaching, and the company's CFO is beginning to plan for the financial statement consolidation of the Germany subsidiary. The CFO has heard that she must determine the "functional currency" of the foreign subsidiary to be able to comply with U.S. GAAP, and she has asked you to provide her with answers to the following questions.

1. What is the functional currency of a foreign subsidiary?
2. Why must the functional currency of a foreign subsidiary be determined?
3. How is the functional currency of a foreign subsidiary determined?

Required

Draft a memorandum to the company's CFO answering the preceding questions.

EXCEL AND ANALYSIS CASE—PARKER, INC., AND SUFFOLK PLC

On January 1, 2019, Parker, Inc., a U.S.-based firm, acquired 100 percent of Suffolk PLC located in Great Britain for consideration paid of 52,000,000 British pounds (£), which was equal to fair value. The excess of fair value over book value is attributable to land (part of property, plant, and equipment) and is not subject to depreciation. Parker accounts for its investment in Suffolk at cost. On January 1, 2019, Suffolk reported the following balance sheet:

Cash	$ 2,000,000	Accounts payable	$ 1,000,000
Accounts receivable	3,000,000	Long-term debt	8,000,000
Inventory	14,000,000	Common stock	44,000,000
Property, plant, and equipment (net)	40,000,000	Retained earnings	6,000,000
	$59,000,000		$59,000,000

Suffolk's 2019 income was recorded at £2,000,000. It declared and paid no dividends in 2019.

On December 31, 2020, two years after the date of acquisition, Suffolk submitted the following trial balance to Parker for consolidation:

Cash	$ 1,500,000
Accounts Receivable	5,200,000
Inventory	18,000,000
Property, Plant, and Equipment (net)	36,000,000
Accounts Payable	(1,450,000)
Long-Term Debt	(5,000,000)
Common Stock	(44,000,000)
Retained Earnings, 1/1/20	(8,000,000)
Sales	(28,000,000)
Cost of Goods Sold	16,000,000
Depreciation	2,000,000
Other Expenses	6,000,000
Dividends, 1/30/20	1,750,000
	–0–

Other than paying dividends, no intra-entity transactions occurred between the two companies. Relevant U.S. dollar exchange rates for the British pound follow:

	January 1	January 30	Average	December 31
2019	$1.60	$1.61	$1.62	$1.64
2020	1.64	1.65	1.66	1.68

The December 31, 2020, financial statements (before consolidation with Suffolk) follow. Dividend income is the U.S. dollar amount of dividends received from Suffolk translated at the $1.65/£ exchange rate at January 30, 2020. The amounts listed for dividend income and all affected accounts (i.e., net income, December 31 retained earnings, and cash) reflect the $1.65/£ exchange rate at January 30, 2020. Credit balances are in parentheses.

	Parker
Sales	$ (70,000,000)
Cost of goods sold	34,000,000
Depreciation	20,000,000
Other expenses	6,000,000
Dividend income	(2,887,500)
Net income	$ (12,887,500)
Retained earnings, 1/1/20	$ (48,000,000)
Net income, 2020	(12,887,500)
Dividends, 1/30/20	4,500,000
Retained earnings, 12/31/20	$ (56,387,500)
Cash	$ 3,687,500
Accounts receivable	10,000,000
Inventory	30,000,000
Investment in Suffolk	83,200,000
Plant and equipment (net)	105,000,000
Accounts payable	(25,500,000)
Long-term debt	(50,000,000)
Common stock	(100,000,000)
Retained earnings, 12/31/20	(56,387,500)
	–0–

Parker's chief financial officer (CFO) wishes to determine the effect that a change in the value of the British pound would have on consolidated net income and consolidated stockholders' equity. To help assess the foreign currency exposure associated with the investment in Suffolk, the CFO requests assistance in comparing consolidated results under actual exchange rate fluctuations with results that would have occurred had the dollar value of the pound remained constant or declined during the first two years of Parker's ownership.

Required

Use Excel to complete the following four parts:

Part I. Given the relevant exchange rates presented,

a. Translate Suffolk's December 31, 2020, trial balance from British pounds to U.S. dollars. The British pound is Suffolk's functional currency.

b. Prepare a schedule that details the change in Suffolk's cumulative translation adjustment (beginning net assets, income, dividends, etc.) for 2019 and 2020.

c. Prepare the December 31, 2020, consolidation worksheet for Parker and Suffolk.

d. Prepare the 2020 consolidated income statement and the December 31, 2020, consolidated balance sheet.

Note: Worksheets should possess the following qualities:

- Each spreadsheet should be programmed so that all relevant amounts adjust appropriately when different values of exchange rates (subsequent to January 1, 2019) are entered into it.
- Be sure to program Parker's dividend income, cash, and retained earnings to reflect the dollar value of alternative January 30, 2020, exchange rates.

Part II. Repeat tasks (*a*), (*b*), (*c*), and (*d*) from Part I to determine consolidated net income and consolidated stockholders' equity if the exchange rate had remained at $1.60/£ over the period 2019 to 2020.

Part III. Repeat tasks (*a*), (*b*), (*c*), and (*d*) from Part I to determine consolidated net income and consolidated stockholders' equity if the following exchange rates had existed:

	January 1	January 30	Average	December 31
2019	$1.60	$1.59	$1.58	$1.56
2020	1.56	1.55	1.54	1.52

Part IV. Prepare a report that provides Parker's CFO the risk assessments requested. Focus on profitability, cash flow, and the debt-to-equity ratio.

chapter 11

Worldwide Accounting Diversity and International Standards

Learning Objectives

After studying this chapter, you should be able to:

LO 11-1 Explain the major factors influencing the international development of accounting systems.

LO 11-2 Understand the problems created by differences in accounting across countries and the reasons to develop a set of internationally accepted accounting standards.

LO 11-3 List the types of authoritative pronouncements that constitute International Financial Reporting Standards (IFRS).

LO 11-4 Describe the ways and the extent to which IFRS Standards are used around the world.

LO 11-5 Explain the purpose of IFRS for SMEs and how it differs from full IFRS.

LO 11-6 Understand the steps to be taken in preparing IFRS financial statements for the first time.

LO 11-7 Describe the FASB–IASB convergence process and SEC recognition of IFRS.

LO 11-8 Recognize acceptable accounting treatments under IFRS and identify key differences between IFRS and U.S. GAAP.

LO 11-9 Determine the impact that specific differences between IFRS and U.S. GAAP have on financial statements and prepare adjustments to convert IFRS balances to U.S. GAAP.

Historically, considerable differences have existed across countries with respect to how financial reports are prepared and presented. For example, many European companies present intangible assets first and cash last in the balance sheet, and some include a line item in the income statement labeled "own work performed and capitalized." A significant number of U.S. companies use LIFO in measuring inventory, whereas this method is not acceptable in most other countries in the world. The first part of this chapter presents additional evidence of accounting diversity, explores the reasons for that diversity, and describes problems historically caused by accounting diversity.

Efforts have been underway for over four decades to reduce the differences that exist in financial reporting across countries and converge on a single set of global accounting standards. The most important of these efforts has been the work that was begun by the International Accounting Standards Committee (IASC) and continues with the International Accounting Standards Board (IASB) to develop International Financial Reporting Standards (IFRS). Today, publicly traded companies in more than 100 countries around the world are using IFRS to prepare consolidated financial statements. The second part of this chapter describes the process of international convergence of financial reporting, focusing on the work of the IASB and recent efforts to converge U.S. GAAP with IFRS.

IFRS and U.S. GAAP are not fully converged, and many differences exist between these two sets of standards. Many accountants involved in the preparation of consolidated financial statements find it necessary to understand these differences to be able to convert IFRS balances to a U.S. GAAP basis, or vice versa. The latter part of this chapter focuses on differences between IFRS and U.S. GAAP and illustrates the process of converting from one set of standards to the other. The comprehensive illustration at the end of the chapter provides additional examples of this conversion process.

Evidence of Accounting Diversity

Exhibit 11.1 presents the 2017 consolidated balance sheet for Jardine Matheson Holdings Limited, a diversified company incorporated in Bermuda with significant investments in Asia. Jardine Matheson is one of the thousands of companies around the world that prepares its consolidated

EXHIBIT 11.1
Jardine Matheson Holdings Limited Balance Sheet

Consolidated Balance Sheet at 31st December 2017

	Note	2017 US$m	2016 US$m
Assets			
Intangible assets	12	**3,009**	2,825
Tangible assets	13	**7,008**	6,239
Investment properties	14	**33,538**	28,609
Bearer plants	15	**498**	497
Associates and joint ventures	16	**13,088**	10,595
Other investments	17	**2,673**	1,369
Non-current debtors	18	**3,042**	2,936
Deferred tax assets	19	**404**	375
Pension assets	20	**14**	5
Non-current assets		**63,274**	53,450
Properties for sale	21	**2,947**	2,315
Stocks and work in progress	22	**3,470**	3,281
Current debtors	18	**6,921**	6,697
Current investments	17	**22**	65
Current tax assets		**164**	169
Bank balances and other liquid funds	23		
– nonfinancial services companies		**5,764**	5,314
– financial services companies		**241**	229
		6,005	5,543
		19,529	18,070
Assets classified as held for sale		**11**	3
Current assets		**19,540**	18,073
Total assets		**82,814**	71,523
Equity			
Share capital	24	**181**	178
Share premium and capital reserves	26	**188**	175
Revenue and other reserves		**30,015**	25,547
Own shares held	28	**(4,715)**	(4,100)
Shareholders' funds		**25,669**	21,800
Noncontrolling interests	29	**32,101**	27,937
Total equity		**57,770**	49,737
Liabilities			
Long-term borrowings	30		
– nonfinancial services companies		**5,975**	5,343
– financial services companies		**1,487**	1,518
		7,462	6,861
Deferred tax liabilities	19	**544**	500
Pension liabilities	20	**385**	419
Non-current creditors	31	**255**	440
Non-current provisions	32	**175**	151
Non-current liabilities		**8,821**	8,371
Current creditors	31	**10,352**	8,714
Current borrowings	30		
– nonfinancial services companies		**3,195**	2,058
– financial services companies		**2,154**	2,265
		5,349	4,323
Current tax liabilities		**362**	266
Current provisions	32	**154**	112
		16,217	13,415

(continued)

(continued)

Consolidated Balance Sheet at 31st December 2017	Note	2017 US$m	2016 US$m
Liabilities classified as held for sale		**6**	-
Current liabilities		**16,223**	13,415
Total liabilities		**25,044**	21,786
Total equity and liabilities		**82,814**	71,523

Source: *Jardine Matheson Holdings Limited, Annual Report 2017, pages 30–31.*

financial statements in accordance with IFRS. A quick examination of this financial statement reveals several format and terminology differences compared with what is usually found in the balance sheets of U.S.-based companies. The company classifies assets as current and noncurrent but lists them in reverse order of liquidity starting with intangibles. Likewise, it lists long-term liabilities before current liabilities, both of which are reported below stockholders' equity.

Property, plant, and equipment is referred to as *tangible assets,* receivables are called *debtors,* and inventories are reported as *stocks and work in progress.* Cash and cash equivalents are called *bank balances and other liquid funds.* Accounts payable are referred to as *creditors. Provisions,* found in both noncurrent and current liabilities, are estimated obligations related to things such as warranties and restructuring plans. *Share capital* reflects the par value of common stock, and *share premium* shows the paid-in capital in excess of par value. Retained earnings are not reported separately but are included in *revenue and other reserves.* One of the *other reserves* is related to the revaluation of assets, which is an unacceptable practice in the United States. Treasury stock is aptly called *own shares held.*

Exhibit 11.2 presents the 2017 consolidated income statement for the Dutch company Heineken N.V., the producer of one of the most popular brands of beer in the world. Heineken also uses IFRS in preparing its consolidated financial statements. Inspection of this statement

EXHIBIT 11.2
Heineken N.V. Income Statement

Consolidated Income Statement			
In Millions of Euros	**Note**	**2017**	**2016**
Revenue	5	**21,888**	**20,792**
Other income	8	**141**	**46**
Raw materials, consumables, and services	9	(13,540)	(13,003)
Personnel expenses	10	(3,550)	(3,263)
Amortisation, depreciation and impairments	11	(1,587)	(1,817)
Total expenses		**(18,677)**	**(18,083)**
Operating profit		**3,352**	**2,755**
Interest income	12	72	60
Interest expenses	12	(468)	(419)
Other net finance income/(expenses)	12	(123)	(134)
Net finance expenses		**(519)**	**(493)**
Share of profit of associates and joint ventures and impairments thereof (net of income tax)	16	75	150
Profit before income tax		**2,908**	**2,412**
Income tax expense	13	(755)	(673)
Profit		**2,153**	**1,739**
Attributable to:			
Equity holders of the company (net profit)		1,935	1,540
Noncontrolling interests		218	199
Profit		**2,153**	**1,739**

Source: *Heineken N.V., Annual Report 2017, page 57.*

reveals a significant difference in format compared with the format normally found in the United States. U.S. companies typically report operating expenses on the income statement according to their function, as follows:

Sales
Less: Cost of goods sold
Gross profit
Less: General, selling, and administrative expenses
Operating profit

This typical U.S. format combines manufacturing costs (materials and supplies, labor costs, and overhead) and reports them as cost of goods sold. Selling costs and administrative costs (which also consist of supplies, labor costs, and overhead) are reported separately from cost of goods sold. Gross profit is reported as the difference between sales and cost of goods sold.

Heineken does not report operating expenses on the basis of their function but on the basis of their nature. Materials costs are reported as *raw material, consumables and service;* labor costs are reported as *personnel expenses;* and overhead is reported in these line items as well as in *amortisation, depreciation, and impairments.* Each of these line items includes amounts that cut across functional areas. *Personnel expenses,* for example, includes the wages, salaries, and benefits paid to employees involved in manufacturing, selling, and administration. As a result, cost of goods sold is not reported as a separate amount, and, therefore, gross profit cannot be calculated. The nature of expenses format used by Heineken in preparing its income statement is the format traditionally used in continental European countries. Today, however, it is common to find companies in the Netherlands, France, Germany, and other European countries using the function of expenses (or cost of goods sold) format familiar in the United States. Both formats for presenting expenses are acceptable under both IFRS and U.S. GAAP.

The examples of accounting diversity demonstrated thus far relate to differences in terminology and presentation in the financial statements. However, as already alluded to, differences also exist across countries with regard to the recognition and measurement principles followed in determining the amounts reported in financial statements.

Foreign companies whose stock is listed on a U.S. stock exchange are required to be registered and file financial statements with the U.S. Securities and Exchange Commission (SEC). Foreign registrants must file their annual report with the SEC on Form 20-F. The financial statements included in Form 20-F may be prepared in accordance with U.S. GAAP, IFRS, or some other foreign GAAP. The SEC requires companies using some other foreign GAAP to reconcile income and stockholders' equity to U.S. GAAP. Companies using IFRS are not subject to this requirement. Examination of these U.S. GAAP reconciliations provides considerable insight into the significant differences that exist in recognition and measurement principles between U.S. GAAP and accounting principles in other countries.

As an example, Exhibit 11.3 presents the reconciliation of net income provided by Ecopetrol S.A., the largest petroleum company in Colombia, in its 2014 Form 20-F. Adjustments are made for 28 differences between Colombian Government Entity GAAP and U.S. GAAP.)[1] Some of the accounting differences requiring the largest adjustments relate to deferred charges; deferred income taxes; revenue recognition; and depreciation, depletion, and amortization. Note that net income under U.S. GAAP is less than net income under Colombian GAAP in 2014, but the opposite is true in 2013 and 2012.

In addition to providing the reconciliation schedule as shown in Exhibit 11.3, Ecopetrol also provides notes that explain the accounting differences that underlie each adjustment. For example, the company provided the following disclosure related to a portion of the adjustment for depreciation, depletion, and amortization (item xv.):

> Under Colombian Government Entity GAAP, all tangible equipment, including those used in crude oil and natural gas, exploration and development, are depreciated on a straight-line basis over the related estimated useful lives . . . Under U.S. GAAP, all assets, including tangible

[1] In 2015, Ecopetrol switched to using IFRS and therefore no longer provides a reconciliation to U.S. GAAP.

EXHIBIT 11.3 Ecopetrol S.A., 2014 Reconciliation of Net Income to U.S. GAAP

	2014	2013	2012
Consolidated net income under Colombian Government Entity GAAP	$ 7,510,270	$ 13,106,503	$ 14,778,947
i. Investment securities:			
a. Unrealized gain (loss)	(1,608)	75,458	(45,199)
b. Impairment	(3,197)	65,921	(34,657)
ii. Investments in nonmarketable securities:			
a. Equity method	240,419	66,558	(109,749)
b. Variable interest entity (VIE)	–	13	–
c. Impairment	(294,931)	(51,664)	9
iii. Derivatives	3,160	(3)	(4,709)
v. Deferred charges	521,356	476,091	493,159
vi. Employee benefit plans	(105,137)	(40,439)	(157,893)
vii. Provisions and contingencies	273,446	802,341	141,755
viii. Assets and liabilities present value	(1,157)	(39,029)	(99,188)
ix. Deferred income taxes	1,076,387	(685,981)	(392,593)
x. Revenue recognition:			
a. Cost of sales—over and under deliveries	(29,522)	296,317	208,644
b. Other income	(28,096)	28,242	6,100
xi. Inflation adjustment	37,282	46,283	165,867
xii. Inventories	(9,124)	30,289	(16,699)
xiii. Lease accounting	(45,470)	(50,101)	(75,203)
xiv. Property, plant, and equipment:			
a. Interest	(272,907)	(480,513)	(607,200)
b. Impairment	(159,300)	(188,615)	(43,609)
d. Capitalized expenses	(39,104)	(53,987)	17,685
e. Exchange difference	(2,366,138)	(17,953)	28,793
xv. Depreciation, depletion, and amortization	82,035	(33,177)	239,571
xvi. Asset retirement obligations	(46,104)	(41,964)	(117,988)
xvii. Equity contributions:			
a. Incorporated institutional equity	11,100	9,113	14,195
b. Reversal of concession rights contributed as capital	1,780	2,280	2,725
xviii. Indebtedness cost	5,131	1,385	(36)
xix. Business combinations:			
a. Goodwill	221,771	403,460	275,271
xx. Noncontrolling interest	91,868	147,177	227,514
xxi. Cumulative translation adjustment	145,340	72,850	(199,863)
Consolidated net income under U.S. GAAP attributable to Ecopetrol	**$6,819,550**	**$13,946,855**	**$14,695,649**

Source. *Ecopetrol S.A., 2014 Form 20-F, page F-49*

equipment, used in crude oil and natural gas producing activities are required to be depreciated or depleted using a units-of-production method, using proved reserves calculated in accordance with SEC requirements. Therefore, an adjustment to net income per U.S. GAAP has been recorded to account for the difference in depreciation, depletion and amortization expense based on the above-described differences in the methods used.[2]

LO 11-1

Explain the major factors influencing the international development of accounting systems.

Reasons for Accounting Diversity

As will be discussed later in this chapter, many countries now require publicly traded (that is, stock exchange–listed) companies to use IFRS in preparing their consolidated financial statements. However, this is a fairly recent phenomenon, which has accelerated in the 21st

[2] Ecopetrol S.A., 2014 Form 20-F, p. F-77.

century. Historically, each country had its own national GAAP that was required to be used by both public and private companies and that differed from the accounting standards followed in other countries. Brazilian GAAP, Canadian GAAP, French GAAP, German GAAP, Turkish GAAP, and so on were different from one another. Indeed, many countries continue to have a national GAAP that must be used by private companies as well as by public companies in preparing separate parent company financial statements.[3]

What are the historical reasons for different financial reporting practices across countries? Accounting scholars have hypothesized numerous influences on the national development of accounting systems including factors as varied as the nature of the country's political system, the stage of economic development, and the state of accounting education and research. A survey of the relevant literature identified the following five items as major factors influencing the development of a country's financial reporting practices: (1) legal system, (2) taxation, (3) financing system, (4) inflation, and (5) political and economic ties.[4]

Legal System

The two major types of legal systems used around the world are common law and codified Roman law. Common law began in England and is found primarily in the English-speaking countries of the world. Common law countries rely on a limited amount of statute law interpreted by the courts. A system of code law, followed in most non-English-speaking countries, originated in the Roman *jus civile.* Code law countries tend to have relatively more statute or codified law governing a wider range of human activity.

What does a country's legal system have to do with accounting? Code law countries generally have a corporation law (sometimes called a *commercial code* or *companies act*) that establishes the basic legal parameters governing business enterprises. Corporation law often stipulates which financial statements must be published in accordance with a prescribed format. Additional accounting measurement and disclosure rules are included in an accounting law that has been debated and passed by the national legislature. The accounting profession tends to have little influence on the development of accounting standards. In countries with a tradition of common law, although a corporation law laying the basic framework for accounting might exist (such as in the United Kingdom), the profession or an independent, nongovernmental body representing a variety of constituencies establishes specific accounting rules. Thus, the type of legal system in a country historically determined whether the primary source of accounting rules was the government or the accounting profession or other nongovernmental body.

In code law countries, the accounting law tends to be rather general and does not provide much guidance regarding specific accounting practices. Germany is a good example of a code law country. Its accounting law (*Bilanzrichtliniengesetz*), passed in 1985; was only 47 pages long; and was silent with regard to issues such as leases, foreign currency translation, and a cash flows statement.[5] In those situations for which the law provided no guidance, German companies found it necessary to refer to other sources, including tax law and opinions of the German auditing profession, to decide how to do their accounting. Although publicly traded companies in Germany now must use IFRS in preparing consolidated financial statements, these same companies must comply with German accounting law in their parent company statements, as must private companies in Germany. Historically, common law countries, where a nongovernment organization developed accounting standards, have had much more detailed rules. The extreme case might be the FASB in the United States. The FASB *Accounting Standards Codification*® provides much more guidance than the German accounting law, and the FASB has been described as producing overly rules-based standards.

[3] Some countries require publicly traded companies to prepare two sets of financial statements. In one set, investments in subsidiaries are not consolidated but are reflected in a single line item in the balance sheet and income statement—often these are referred to as parent company financial statements. A second set of financial statements is prepared on a consolidated basis.

[4] Gary K. Meek and Sharokh M. Saudagearan, "A Survey of Research on Financial Reporting in a Transnational Context," *Journal of Accounting Literature,* 1990, pp. 145–82.

[5] Jermyn Paul Brooks and Dietz Mertin, *Neues Deutsches Bilanzrecht* (Düsseldorf: IDW-Verlag GmbH, 1986).

Taxation

In some countries, parent company financial statements are the basis for taxation, whereas in other countries, financial statements are adjusted for tax purposes and submitted to the government separately from the reports sent to stockholders. Continuing to focus on Germany, prior to 2009, the reverse conformity principle (*umgekehrte Massgeblichkeitsprinzip*) required that, in most cases, an expense had to be recognized in accounting income to be deductible for tax purposes. Well-managed German companies attempted to minimize income for tax purposes, for example, by using accelerated depreciation to reduce their tax liability. As a result of the reverse conformity principle, accelerated depreciation also had to be recognized in calculating accounting income. As part of the accounting modernization law (*Bilanzrechtsmodernisierungsgesetz*), passed in 2009, the reverse conformity requirement was removed, thereby reducing the influence that taxation has on financial reporting in Germany.

In the United States, on the other hand, conformity between the tax statement and financial statements is required only for the use of the LIFO inventory cost-flow assumption. U.S. companies are allowed, for example, to use accelerated depreciation for tax purposes and straight-line depreciation in the financial statements. All else being equal, prior to 2009, the reverse conformity principle in Germany was likely to result in a U.S. company reporting a larger net income than its German counterpart.

Financing System

It has been argued that differences in the purpose for financial reporting across countries is the major reason for international differences in financial reporting, and that the most relevant factor in determining the purpose of financial reporting is the nature of a country's financing system.[6] Specifically, whether or not a country has a strong equity financing system with large numbers of outside shareholders determines the type of financial reporting system a country uses. Countries with a strong equity-outsider financing system tend to have an accounting system that is less conservative, provides more disclosure, and does not follow tax rules. Australia, the United States, and the United Kingdom are examples of countries with strong equity-outsider financing systems. Countries with a weak equity-outsider financing system have an accounting system that is more conservative; disclosure is not as extensive and financial reporting more closely follows tax rules. France, Germany, and Italy are examples of countries with weak equity-outsider financing systems.

Inflation

Historically, countries with chronically high rates of inflation were compelled to develop accounting rules that required the inflation adjustment of historical cost amounts. This was especially true in Latin America, which as a region has had more inflation than any other part of the world. For example, prior to economic reform in the mid-1990s, Brazil regularly experienced annual inflation rates exceeding 100 percent. Double- and triple-digit inflation rates render historical costs meaningless. Historically, this factor primarily distinguished accounting in Latin America from the rest of the world. However, inflation has been brought under control in most countries. and inflation accounting has been abandoned throughout Latin America.

Political and Economic Ties

Accounting is a technology that can be borrowed relatively easily from or imposed on another country. Through political and economic linkages, accounting rules historically have been conveyed from one country to another. For example, through previous colonialism, both England and France transferred their accounting frameworks to a variety of countries around the world. British-style accounting systems can be found in countries as far-flung as Australia and Zimbabwe. French accounting is prevalent in the former French colonies of western Africa. More recently, the member nations of the European Union (which is a political and economic union) have adopted a common set of accounting standards—that is, IFRS—for publicly traded companies.

[6] Christopher W. Nobes, "Towards a General Model of the Reasons for International Differences in Financial Reporting," *Abacus,* September 1998, pp. 162–87.

LO 11-2

Understand the problems created by differences in accounting across countries and the reasons to develop a set of internationally accepted accounting standards.

Problems Caused by Diverse Accounting Practices

Diversity in accounting across countries causes problems for both preparers and users of financial statements. One problem relates to the preparation of consolidated financial statements by companies with foreign operations. Consider The Coca-Cola Company, which has subsidiaries in more than 40 countries around the world. Each subsidiary incorporated in the country in which it is located is required to prepare financial statements in accordance with local regulations. These regulations often require companies to keep books in the local currency and follow local accounting principles. Thus, Coca-Cola Italia S.r.L. prepares financial statements in euros using Italian accounting rules, and Coca-Cola India Private Limited prepares financial statements in Indian rupees using Indian accounting standards. To prepare consolidated financial statements in the United States, in addition to translating the foreign currency balances into U.S. dollars, the parent company also must convert the financial statements of its foreign subsidiaries into U.S. GAAP. Each foreign subsidiary must either maintain two sets of books prepared in accordance with both local and U.S. GAAP or, as is more common, convert local GAAP financial statements to U.S. GAAP at the balance sheet date. In either case, considerable effort and cost are involved; company personnel must develop an expertise in more than one set of accounting standards.

A second problem relates to companies gaining access to foreign capital markets. If a company desires to obtain capital by selling stock or borrowing money in a foreign country, it might be required to present a set of financial statements prepared in accordance with the accounting standards in the country in which the capital is being obtained. For example, to have stock listed on a U.S. stock exchange, prior to 2008, foreign companies were required to reconcile their local-GAAP financial statements to U.S. accounting standards. Preparation of a U.S. GAAP reconciliation can be quite costly. For example, to prepare for a New York Stock Exchange (NYSE) listing in 1993, the German automaker Daimler-Benz estimated it spent $60 million to prepare U.S. GAAP financial statements.[7] Since 2008, foreign companies listed on a U.S. stock exchange that use IFRS to prepare financial statements are no longer required to provide a reconciliation to U.S. GAAP. However, foreign companies using a local GAAP other than IFRS continue to be required to provide a U.S. GAAP reconciliation. As an example, in conjunction with the Colombian energy company Ecopetrol S.A.'s listing on the New York Stock Exchange in 2014, the company provided a note in the financial statements it filed with the U.S. Securities and Exchange Commission (SEC) that was 50 pages in length. A portion of this note was shown earlier in this chapter in Exhibit 11.3.

A third problem arising from accounting diversity relates to the lack of comparability of financial statements between companies using different accounting standards. This complicates international investors' job of deciding which foreign companies to invest in. It is very difficult, if not impossible, for a potential investor to directly compare the financial position and performance of, for example, automobile manufacturers in Germany (BMW), Japan (Toyota), and the United States (Ford) because these three countries have different financial accounting and reporting standards.

Because of the problems associated with worldwide accounting diversity, work to reduce accounting differences across countries and establish a single set of global accounting standards has been ongoing for more than four decades. The ultimate goal is to have all companies in the world following one set of accounting standards. While numerous organizations have been involved in the international convergence of financial reporting over the years, the most important players in this effort have been the International Accounting Standards Board and its predecessor, the International Accounting Standards Committee.

[7] Allan B. Afterman, *International Accounting, Financial Reporting, and Analysis* (New York: Warren, Gorham & Lamont, 1995), pp. C1–17 and C1–22.

International Accounting Standards Committee

In hopes of eliminating the diversity of principles used throughout the world, the International Accounting Standards Committee (IASC) was formed in June 1973 by accountancy bodies in Australia, Canada, France, Germany, Japan, Mexico, the Netherlands, the United Kingdom and Ireland, and the United States. The IASC operated until April 1, 2001, when it was succeeded by the International Accounting Standards Board (IASB).

Based in London, the IASC's primary objective was to develop international accounting standards (IASs). The IASC had no power to require the use of its standards, but member accountancy bodies pledged to work toward adoption of IASs in their countries. IASs were approved by a board consisting of representatives from 14 countries. The part-time board members normally met only three times a year for three or four days. The publication of a final IAS required approval of at least 11 of the 14 board members.

Early IASs tended to follow a lowest-common-denominator approach and often allowed at least two methods for dealing with a particular accounting issue. For example, *IAS 2,* originally issued in 1975, allowed the use of specific identification, FIFO, LIFO, average cost, and the base stock method for valuing inventories, effectively sanctioning most of the alternative methods in worldwide use. For the same reason, the IASC initially allowed both the traditional U.S. treatment of expensing goodwill over a period of up to 40 years and the U.K. approach of writing off goodwill directly to stockholders' equity. Although perhaps necessary from a political perspective, such compromise brought the IASC under heavy criticism.

The IOSCO Agreement

The International Organization of Securities Commissions (IOSCO) is composed of the stock exchange regulators in more than 100 countries, including the U.S. SEC. As one of its objectives, IOSCO works to facilitate cross-border securities offerings and listings by multinational issuers. To this end, IOSCO supported the IASC's efforts at developing IASs that foreign issuers could use in lieu of local accounting standards when entering capital markets outside of their home country. "This could mean, for example, that if a French company had a simultaneous stock offering in the United States, Canada, and Japan, financial statements prepared in accordance with international standards could be used in all three nations."[8]

IOSCO supported the IASC's Comparability Project (begun in 1987) "to eliminate most of the choices of accounting treatment currently permitted under International Accounting Standards."[9] As a result of the Comparability Project, 10 revised IASs were approved in 1993 to become effective in 1995. In 1993, IOSCO and the IASC agreed upon a list of "core" standards to use in financial statements of companies involved in cross-border securities offerings and listings. Upon their completion, IOSCO agreed to evaluate the core standards for possible endorsement for cross-border listing purposes.

The IASC accelerated its pace of standards development, issuing or revising 16 standards in the period 1997–1998. With the publication of *IAS 39* in December 1998, the IASC completed its work program to develop the core set of standards. In 2000, IOSCO's Technical Committee recommended that securities regulators permit foreign issuers to use IASC standards to gain access to a country's capital market as an alternative to using local standards, and many stock exchanges around the world implemented this recommendation.

International Accounting Standards Board and IFRS

On completion of its core set of standards, the IASC proposed a new structure that would allow it and national standard setters to better work together toward global harmonization. The restructuring created the International Accounting Standards Board (IASB), which is

[8] Stephen H. Collins, "The SEC on Full and Fair Disclosure," *Journal of Accountancy,* January 1989, p. 84.

[9] International Accounting Standards Committee, *International Accounting Standards 1990* (London: IASC, 1990), p. 13.

governed by the IFRS Foundation. In April 2001, the IASB assumed accounting standard-setting responsibilities from its predecessor body, the IASC.

The IFRS Foundation's Constitution indicates that the IASB shall be comprised of 16 members, up to three of whom may be part-time. To ensure the IASB's independence, all full-time members are required to sever their employment relationships with former employers and are not allowed to hold any position giving rise to perceived economic incentives that might call their independence into question. The primary qualifications for IASB membership are professional competence and practical experience. To ensure a broad international representation, normally there should be four IASB members from Europe, four from North America, four from the Asia/Oceania region, one from Africa, one from South America, and two from any area to achieve geographic balance. Passage of a new standard requires affirmation of at least 10 IASB members. However, the Constitution notes that at any point in time the IASB might have fewer than 16 members, in which case nine yes votes are required to approve a standard.

LO 11-3

List the types of authoritative pronouncements that constitute International Financial Reporting Standards (IFRS).

International Financial Reporting Standards (IFRS)

In April 2001, the IASB adopted all international accounting standards (IASs) issued by the IASC and announced that its accounting standards would be called *international financial reporting standards* (IFRS). *IAS 1,* "Presentation of Financial Statements," was amended in 2003 and defines IFRS as standards and interpretations adopted by the IASB. The authoritative pronouncements that make up IFRS consist of the following:

- International Financial Reporting Standards (IFRSs) issued by the IASB.
- International Accounting Standards (IASs) issued by the IASC (and adopted by the IASB).
- Interpretations issued by the International Financial Reporting Interpretations Committee (IFRICs).
- Interpretations issued by the Standing Interpretations Committee (SICs) (and adopted by the IASB).

The IASC issued 41 IASs from 1975 to 2001, and the IASB had issued 17 IFRSs by the end of 2018. Several IASs have been withdrawn or superseded by subsequent standards. For example, later standards dealing with property, plant, and equipment and intangible assets have superseded *IAS 4,* "Depreciation Accounting," originally issued in 1976. Other IASs have been revised one or more times since their original issuance. For example, *IAS 2,* "Inventories," was originally issued in 1975 but was revised in 1993 and updated in 2003. Of the 41 IASs issued by the IASC, only 25 were still in force as of January 2019. The IASB issued the first IFRS in 2003; it deals with the important question of how a company should restate its financial statements when it adopts IFRS for the first time.

Exhibit 11.4 provides a complete list of the IASs still in effect and the IFRSs issued (and in effect) as of January 2019. In addition, 20 Interpretations (15 IFRICs and 5 SICs) were in effect on that date. Together, the two sets of standards and two sets of interpretations comprise what the IASB refers to as "IFRS Standards." IFRS Standards constitute a comprehensive set of financial reporting standards that covers most major accounting issues. In addition, the IASB's *Conceptual Framework for Financial Reporting,* which is very similar in scope to the FASB's conceptual framework, provides a basis for determining the appropriate accounting treatment for items not covered by a specific standard or interpretation. As was true for its predecessor, the IASB does not have the ability to enforce its standards. It develops IFRS Standards for the public good and makes them available to any organization or nation that wishes to use them.

The IASB *Conceptual Framework for Financial Reporting* states that "the objective of general purpose financial reporting is to provide financial information about the reporting entity that is useful to existing and potential investors, lenders and other creditors in making decisions relating to providing resources to the entity."[10] The framework further states that "other parties, such as regulators and members of the public other than investors, lenders and other creditors, may also find general purpose financial reports useful. However, those reports are not primarily directed to these other groups."[11]

[10] IASB, *Conceptual Framework for Financial Reporting,* Chapter 1, para. 1.2, March 2018.

[11] Ibid., para. 1.10.

EXHIBIT 11.4
IFRS Standards as of January 2019

	Title	Originally Issued
IAS 1	Presentation of Financial Statements	1975
IAS 2	Inventories	1975
IAS 7	Statement of Cash Flows	1977
IAS 8	Accounting Policies, Changes in Accounting Estimates and Errors	1978
IAS 10	Events after the Reporting Period	1978
IAS 12	Income Taxes	1979
IAS 16	Property, Plant, and Equipment	1982
IAS 19	Employee Benefits	1983
IAS 20	Accounting for Government Grants and Disclosure of Government Assistance	1983
IAS 21	The Effects of Changes in Foreign Exchange Rates	1983
IAS 23	Borrowing Costs	1984
IAS 24	Related Party Disclosures	1984
IAS 26	Accounting and Reporting by Retirement Benefit Plans	1987
IAS 27	Separate Financial Statements	1989
IAS 28	Investments in Associates and Joint Ventures	1989
IAS 29	Financial Reporting in Hyperinflationary Economies	1989
IAS 32	Financial Instruments: Presentation	1995
IAS 33	Earnings per Share	1997
IAS 34	Interim Financial Reporting	1998
IAS 36	Impairment of Assets	1998
IAS 37	Provisions, Contingent Liabilities and Contingent Assets	1998
IAS 38	Intangible Assets	1998
IAS 39	Financial Instruments: Recognition and Measurement	1998
IAS 40	Investment Property	2000
IAS 41	Agriculture	2001
IFRS 1	First-Time Adoption of IFRS	2003
IFRS 2	Share-Based Payment	2004
IFRS 3	Business Combinations	2004
IFRS 5	Noncurrent Assets Held for Sale and Discontinued Operations	2004
IFRS 6	Exploration for and Evaluation of Mineral Resources	2004
IFRS 7	Financial Instruments: Disclosures	2005
IFRS 8	Operating Segments	2006
IFRS 9	Financial Instruments	2009
IFRS 10	Consolidated Financial Statements	2011
IFRS 11	Joint Arrangements	2011
IFRS 12	Disclosure of Interests in Other Entities	2011
IFRS 13	Fair Value Measurement	2011
IFRS 14	Regulatory Deferral Accounts	2014
IFRS 15	Revenue from Contracts with Customers	2014
IFRS 16	Leases	2016
IFRS 17	Insurance Contracts	2017

LO 11-4

Describe the ways and the extent to which IFRS Standards are used around the world.

Use of IFRS Standards

A country can use IFRS Standards (or simply, IFRS) in a number of different ways. For example, a country could (1) adopt IFRS as its national GAAP, (2) *require* domestic listed companies to use IFRS in preparing their *consolidated* financial statements, (3) *permit* domestic listed companies to use IFRS, and/or (4) require or allow *foreign* companies listed on a domestic stock exchange to use IFRS. See Exhibit 11.5 for a summary of the extent to which IFRS are required or permitted to be used by domestic listed companies in preparing consolidated financial statements in countries around the world.

As of the beginning of 2019, of the 149 countries included in Exhibit 11.5, 105 required all or most domestic listed companies to use IFRS. Most significant among this group of

EXHIBIT 11.5
Use of IFRS Standards in Preparing Consolidated Financial Statements

IFRS Required for All or Most Domestic Listed Companies			
Anguilla	Dominican Republic	Kuwait	Philippines
Antigua & Barbuda	Ecuador	Kyrgzstan	Poland*
Argentina	Estonia*	Latvia*	Portugal*
Armenia	Fiji	Lebanon	Qatar
Australia	Finland*	Libya	Romania*
Austria*	France*	Liechtenstein	Russia
Azerbaijan	Georgia	Lithuania*	Saudi Arabia
Bahamas	Germany*	Luxembourg*	Serbia
Bahrain	Ghana	Macedonia	Sierra Leone
Bangladesh	Greece*	Malaysia	Singapore
Barbados	Grenada	Malawi	Slovakia*
Belarus	Guatemala	Malta*	Slovenia*
Belgium*	Guyana	Mauritius	South Africa
Bosnia & Herzegovina	Honduras	Mexico	Spain*
Botswana	Hong Kong	Moldova	Sri Lanka
Brazil	Hungary*	Mongolia	St. Kitts and Nevis
Bulgaria*	Iceland	Montenegro	Sweden*
Cambodia	Iraq	Namibia	Taiwan
Canada	Ireland*	Netherlands*	Tajikistan
Chile	Israel	New Zealand	Tanzania
Colombia	Italy*	Nigeria	Trinidad & Tobago
Costa Rica	Jamaica	Norway	United Arab Emirates
Croatia*	Jordan	Oman	United Kingdom*
Cyprus*	Kazakhstan	Panama	Venezuela
Czech Republic*	Kenya	Papua New Guinea	West Bank/Gaza
Denmark*	Korea (South)	Peru	Zambia
Dominica			
IFRS Required for Some Domestic Companies Only			
Angola	Morocco	Pakistan	Ukraine
IFRS Permitted for Domestic Listed Companies			
Bermuda	Japan[§]	Netherlands Antilles	Turkey
Bolivia	Lesotho	Nicaragua	Uganda
Cayman Islands	Maldives	Paraguay	Zimbabwe
El Salvador	Mozambique	Suriname	
Haiti	Myanmar	Swaziland	
India	Nepal	Switzerland[§]	
IFRS Not Permitted for Domestic Listed Companies			
Bhutan	Egypt	Senegal	United States
Burkina Faso	Indonesia	Thailand	Uruguay
Cote D'Ivoire	Iran	Togo	Uzbekistan
China[‡]	Mali	Tunisia	Vietnam
Cuba	Niger	Turkmenistan	

*Denotes EU membership. The EU has not adopted portions of *IAS 39*.
[§] Japan and Switzerland allow the use of IFRS, U.S. GAAP, or local (Japanese or Swiss, respectively) GAAP.
[‡] While China has not adopted IFRS *per se*, its standards are substantially converged with IFRS.
Sources: IFRS Foundation, *Use of IFRS Standards by Jurisdiction*, www.ifrs.org, and Deloitte, *Use of IFRS by Jurisdiction*, www.iasplus.com, accessed October 2, 2018.

IFRS users are the 28 countries of the European Union (EU). All publicly traded companies in the EU have been required to use IFRS to prepare their consolidated financial statements since January 1, 2005. In some EU countries, such as France and Germany, publicly traded companies continue to use domestic GAAP to prepare separate parent-company financial statements, which often serve as the basis for taxation. With the EU's adoption of IFRS, the IASB gained a substantial amount of legitimacy as the global accounting standard setter.

By 2019, most countries of economic importance required or permitted domestic listed companies to use IFRS in preparing consolidated financial statements (or were in the process of doing so). The most important exceptions were China and the United States, the two largest economies in the world. In recent years, China developed a completely new set of Accounting Standards for Business Enterprises (ASBE), which, while not IFRS, is substantially converged with IFRS. In addition, Chinese companies listed on the Hong Kong stock exchange are permitted to use either Hong Kong GAAP or IFRS. More than 250 Chinese companies listed in Hong Kong prepare IFRS financial statements in addition to financial reports prepared in accordance with ASBE for their listing in China. (The process of IFRS convergence in the United States is described in the next section of this chapter.)

There are two primary methods used by countries to incorporate IFRS into their financial reporting requirements for listed companies: (1) full adoption of IFRS as issued by the IASB, without any intervening review or approval by a local body, and (2) adoption of IFRS after some form of jurisdictional review and approval process. As an example, Mexico has followed the first method by requiring companies listed on the Mexican stock exchange (*Bolsa Mexicana de Valores*) to apply the official English version of IFRS as issued by the IASB. In contrast, the EU follows the second method with individual IFRSs going through a multistep process of review and formal endorsement by the European Commission (EC). The EC has adopted all IFRSs as issued by the IASB without modification, with one exception. Certain provisions on hedge accounting in *IAS 39,* "Financial Instruments: Recognition and Measurement," have been carved out from the standard endorsed by the EC. Typically, auditor reports of EU-based companies are careful to state that the company's consolidated financial statements comply with IFRS *as adopted by the European Union.*

LO 11-5

Explain the purpose of *IFRS for SMEs* and how it differs from full IFRS.

IFRS for SMEs

The vast majority of companies in the world are *not* publicly traded. The 52 largest stock exchanges globally are estimated to have about 45,000 listed companies. In contrast, there are approximately 28 million private (non–publicly traded) companies in Europe and another 25 million in the United States, not to mention other parts of the world.[12] Nonpublic companies often are referred to as small and medium-sized entities (SMEs). Full IFRS are primarily designed to meet the needs of large public companies. To meet the needs of smaller, nonpublic companies, the IASB created a less complex set of standards in 2009 (which was revised in 2015). *IFRS for SMEs* is a self-contained book of standards less than 250 pages in length that differs from full IFRS in the following ways:

- Topics in full IFRS not deemed to be relevant for private companies are omitted. Examples include earnings per share, interim reporting, and segment reporting.
- Significantly fewer disclosures are required. There are approximately 300 disclosures in *IFRS for SMEs* compared to around 3,000 in full IFRS.
- Some principles for recognizing and measuring assets, liabilities, income, and expenses in full IFRS are simplified. Examples include the following:
    - Borrowing costs: all borrowing costs are expensed as incurred (full IFRS requires some borrowing costs to be capitalized).
    - Development costs: all development costs are expensed as incurred (full IFRS requires some development costs to be capitalized).
    - Goodwill: amortized over useful life (full IFRS requires testing goodwill for impairment without amortization).
    - Property, plant, and equipment: cost model must be used (full IFRS allows choice between cost and revaluation models).
    - Defined benefit plans: actuarial gains and losses are recognized immediately (full IFRS allows choice between immediate recognition or deferral and amortization).

IFRS for SMEs is available for any country to adopt, regardless of whether it has adopted full IFRS. To date, a smaller number of countries has opted to require private companies to use *IFRS for SMEs* than the number of countries that requires public companies to use full IFRS.

[12] IFRS Foundation, *The IFRS for SMEs: A Resource for Accounting Educators,* presented by Paul Pacter in Santiago, Chile, December 5, 2011.

An IFRS Foundation study conducted in 2015 identified 73 jurisdictions out of 139 surveyed that require or permit the use of IFRS for SMEs by private companies. Of these jurisdictions:

- Five require *IFRS for SMEs* for all private companies that are not required to use full IFRS;
- 50 allow a choice between full IFRS or *IFRS for SMEs;*
- 17 allow a choice to use either full IFRS or local GAAP instead of *IFRS for SMEs;* and
- One requires an SME to use local GAAP if it does not choose *IFRS for SMEs.*[13]

First-Time Adoption of IFRS

LO 11-6

Understand the steps to be taken in preparing IFRS financial statements for the first time.

Publicly traded companies in more than 100 countries around the world have been required to discontinue using their old accounting standards and adopt IFRS in preparing their consolidated financial statements. The process of converting from one set of accounting standards to another is quite complex, and there are many questions to be answered. To provide guidance on this issue, the first standard developed by the IASB was *IFRS 1,* "First-Time Adoption of IFRS." *IFRS 1* establishes the procedures to be followed in converting from previously used accounting standards to IFRS for the first time and introduces the concept of the "opening balance sheet."

IFRS 1 requires companies transitioning to IFRS to prepare an *opening balance sheet* at the "date of transition." The transition date is the beginning of the earliest period for which an entity presents full comparative information under IFRS. The following timeline shows how the transition date is determined:

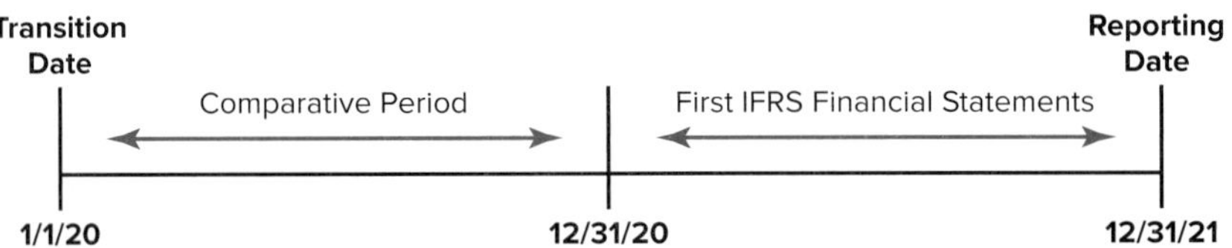

If a company is preparing financial statements using IFRS for the first time for the year ended December 31, 2021 (the reporting date), under *IFRS 1,* it also must provide comparative financial statements for the year ended December 31, 2020. January 1, 2020, is the beginning of the earliest period for which comparative information must be provided and, therefore, is the transition date. This means that a company must begin using IFRS prior to January 1, 2020, to be able to prepare IFRS financial statements for 2021.

An entity must complete the following steps to prepare the opening IFRS balance sheet:

Step 1—Determine Applicable IFRS Accounting Policies Based on Standards in Force on the Reporting Date.

This requirement implies that companies must know on the transition date what the applicable standards will be on the reporting date. For example, in preparing the opening balance sheet at January 1, 2020, a company would need to determine what IFRS policies will be in effect on December 31, 2021. As a result, companies adopting IFRS must keep track of the date on which new standards go into effect.

Step 2—Recognize Assets and Liabilities Required to Be Recognized under IFRS That Were Not Recognized under Previous GAAP and Derecognize Assets and Liabilities Previously Recognized That Are Not Allowed to Be Recognized under IFRS.

Let's assume that a company previously using U.S. GAAP is adopting IFRS. *Deferred development costs* is an example of an intangible asset recognized under IFRS that is not recognized as an asset under U.S. GAAP. A U.S.-GAAP company transitioning to IFRS on January 1, 2020, would be required to assess whether development costs incurred in prior years met the criteria for capitalization in *IAS 38,* "Intangible Assets." If so, then the costs previously expensed would be reversed and recognized on the opening balance sheet as an asset. The counterpart

[13] IFRS Foundation, *Financial Reporting Standards for the World Economy,* June 2015, p. 17.

would be an adjustment to stockholders' equity. Restructuring of operations is an area in which a U.S. company might need to derecognize a liability because a restructuring charge and related liability can be recognized at an earlier date under U.S. GAAP than under IFRS. Going forward, new IFRS adopters need to amend their asset and liability recognition policies to make sure that they are in compliance with IFRS. For example, development costs incurred after the transition date of January 1, 2020, would have to be evaluated for possible capitalization.

Step 3—Measure Assets and Liabilities Recognized on the Opening Balance Sheet in Accordance with IFRS.

An entity must retrospectively apply applicable IASB standards to each asset and liability reported on the opening balance sheet. As an example, a U.S.-GAAP company previously using LIFO to measure inventory would have to select a method acceptable under IFRS (FIFO or weighted average cost) and retroactively apply that method to the inventory carried on the opening balance sheet. This represents a change in accounting principle. *IFRS 1* indicates that the effect of the change should be recognized in stockholders' equity on the opening balance sheet, and not in net income.

In preparing the opening balance sheet, *IFRS 1* provides several optional exemptions from complying with IFRS where retrospective application would be extremely difficult and the informational benefit to users is unlikely to exceed the cost. First-time adopters of IFRS have an option *not* to (1) adjust the carrying amount of goodwill recognized under previous GAAP, (2) restate a business combination originally accounted for under the pooling method, (3) retrospectively apply *IFRS 2* to stock options, or (4) recognize any cumulative translation adjustment for foreign subsidiaries.

Step 4—Reclassify Items Previously Classified in a Different Manner from What Is Acceptable under IFRS.

There are several situations in which accounting elements are classified differently under IFRS and U.S. GAAP. For example, U.S.-GAAP companies classify bank overdrafts as a current liability. *IAS 7,* "Statement of Cash Flows" stipulates that bank overdrafts that form an integral part of an entity's cash management should be classified as a reduction in cash and cash equivalents. In this case, to comply with IFRS, bank overdrafts classified as a current liability under U.S. GAAP would have to be reclassified as a reduction in cash and cash equivalents on the IFRS opening balance sheet. As another example, in some cases, a portion of the fair value of convertible debt that is classified as a liability under U.S. GAAP would have to be reclassified as equity under IFRS.

Step 5—Comply with All Presentation and Disclosure Requirements.

First-time adopters of IFRS must be careful to comply with all presentation and disclosure requirements, especially those contained in *IAS 1,* "Presentation of Financial Statements." As an example, *IAS 1,* para. 113, requires companies to cross-reference each item in each of the financial statements to any related information in the notes. A similar presentation requirement does not exist in U.S. GAAP. Several public accounting firms provide IFRS disclosure checklists that can be used by IFRS adopters for the purpose of determining whether applicable presentation and disclosure requirements have been met.[14]

Once the opening IFRS balance sheet has been prepared (for example, on January 1, 2020), the company continues to use IFRS for the next two years so that comparative information can be included in the first set of annual financial statements prepared under IFRS (for example, for the year ended December 31, 2021). *IFRS 1* also requires a company to provide the following reconciliations in its first set of IFRS financial statements:

1. Reconciliation of total equity measured under previous GAAP to total equity measured under IFRS at
   (a) the date of transition (e.g., January 1, 2020), and
   (b) the end of the comparative period (e.g., December 31, 2020).

[14] For example, KPMG's International Standards Group prepared a "Guide to Annual Financial Statements—Disclosure Checklist" dated September 2018, which is available for download at www.kpmg.com.

2. Reconciliation of net income measured under previous GAAP to net income measured under IFRS for the comparative period (e.g., for the year ended December 31, 2020).

IFRS 1 also requires disclosures explaining the company's adoption of IFRS, including notes to accompany the IFRS reconciliations.

Exhibit 11.6 presents Note 4 from the 2005 Annual Report of the Spanish airline company Iberia, Líneas Aéreas de España, S.A. In accordance with European Union

EXHIBIT 11.6
Iberia Group 2005 Annual Report

4. Reconciliation of the Beginning and Ending Balances for 2004 per Spanish GAAP and IFRSs

Reconciliation of equity at 1 January 2004 and at 31 December 2004

	Thousands of Euros	
Concept	**Equity at 1 January 2004**	**Equity at 31 December 2004**
Balance per Spanish GAAP in force at that date[(a)]	1,432,760	1,645,765
Impacts due to transition to IFRSs[(b)]		
Derecognition of amortisation of goodwill	(98,098)	(91,485)
Reversal of provisions and other contingent liabilities	116,682	124,507
Derecognition of deferred income	19,090	1,981
Reversal of provision for major repairs	5,114	—
Conversion to IFRSs of financial statements of companies accounted for using the equity method	4,618	2,262
Derecognition of negative consolidation differences	1,494	998
Derecognition of deferred charges and start-up expenses	(1,905)	(5,189)
Other	—	6
Total impact on equity	46,995	33,080
Minority interests	9,204	5,324
Balance per IFRSs	1,488,959	1,684,169

[(a)] Obtained from the consolidated financial statements at the date shown, as approved by the shareholders at the related Annual General Meetings.
[(b)] Taking into consideration tax effects.

Reconciliation of profit for 2004

	Thousands of Euros
Concept	**Increase/ (Reduction) 2004 Profit**
Balance per Spanish GAAP in force at that date[(*)]	218,402
Impacts due to transition to IFRSs:	
Amortisation of goodwill	6,613
Provisions and other contingent liabilities	7,825
Derecognition of deferred income	(17,109)
Reversal of provision for major repairs	(3,521)
Conversion to IFRSs of financial statements of companies accounted for using the equity method	(2,356)
Share options	(4,969)
Derecognition of negative consolidation differences	(496)
Derecognition of deferred charges and start-up expenses	(3,284)
Other	6
Total impact on equity/profit	(17,291)
Balance per IFRSs	201,111

[(*)] Obtained from the consolidated financial statements at the date shown, as approved by the shareholders at the related Annual General Meeting.

(continued)

EXHIBIT 11.6
(Continued)

The main changes arose in the following items:

Goodwill

Goodwill was calculated as the positive difference between the amount paid by Iberia, Líneas Aéreas de España, S.A. for the acquisition of 67% of Aviación y Comercio, S.A. and the related underlying carrying amount at 31 December 1997. This goodwill was attributed basically to the value of the market presence, size and image of Aviación y Comercio, S.A. at that date. Since it was not possible to reasonably allocate these items to a single cash-generating unit on the basis of which to evaluate possible changes in value in the future, the Company opted to write this goodwill off against the reserves for first-time application of IFRSs. Also, the Group reversed EUR 6,613 thousand relating to the amortisation recognised in 2004 in accordance with Spanish GAAP.

Provisions and Other Contingent Liabilities

The Group reversed, with a credit to reserves, certain provisions recorded to cover potential contingencies which do not meet all the requirements under *IAS 37* to be recognised in the financial statements.

Deferred Income

In accordance with *IAS 17*, the gains recognised as a result of a sale and operating leaseback transaction, which until 2004 were recognised over the subsequent lease term, must be recognised in the income statement at the moment when the transaction is arranged. The Group therefore eliminated the deferred gains with a charge to reserves on first-time application of IFRSs. Also, the deferred income credited to the income statement in this connection in 2004 was reversed.

Source: *Iberia Group, 2005 Annual Report, p. 105*

regulations, Iberia adopted IFRS for the year ended December 31, 2005, with January 1, 2004, as the transition date. Note 4 provides the reconciliation of equity and net income from Spanish GAAP to IFRS for the comparative period 2004 and explains the major adjustments made. The notes indicate that Iberia opted not to restate goodwill and instead wrote existing goodwill off against equity on the opening balance sheet. In addition, the notes explain that the company retroactively applied IFRS to remeasure the amounts reported on the opening balance sheet for provisions and other contingent liabilities, and deferred income.

IFRS Accounting Policy Hierarchy

With respect to the issue of determining appropriate accounting policies to use in preparing IFRS financial statements, *IAS 8*, "Accounting Policies, Changes in Accounting Estimates and Errors," establishes the following hierarchy that firms must follow:

1. Apply *specifically relevant* IFRS standards (IASs, IFRSs, SICs, or IFRICs) dealing with an accounting issue.
2. Refer to *other* IFRS standards dealing with similar or related issues.
3. Refer to the definitions, recognition criteria, and measurement concepts in the IASB *Conceptual Framework for Financial Reporting.*
4. Consider the most recent pronouncements of other standard-setting bodies that use a similar conceptual framework, other accounting literature, and accepted industry practice to the extent that these do not conflict with sources in items 2 and 3 above.

Two aspects of this hierarchy are noteworthy. First, the Conceptual Framework is specifically listed as part of the hierarchy and must be consulted before considering sources of guidance listed in item 4. In contrast, the FASB's concepts statements are not a part of U.S. GAAP. Second, because the FASB and IASB conceptual frameworks are similar, step 4 provides an opportunity for entities using IFRS to adopt FASB standards in dealing with accounting issues where steps 1 through 3 are not helpful.

In establishing accounting policies to be followed in adopting IFRS for the first time, the two extreme approaches that companies can follow are

1. *Minimize change.* Under this approach, a company would adopt accounting policies consistent with IFRS that are most consistent with the company's current accounting policies.
2. *Fresh start.* Under this approach, a company would ignore its current accounting policies and adopt accounting policies consistent with IFRS that best reflect economic reality.

The first approach is likely to be less costly than the second approach. However, many commentators encourage companies to take advantage of the opportunity to start from a clean slate and adopt a fresh-start approach.

LO 11-7

Describe the FASB–IASB convergence process and SEC recognition of IFRS.

FASB–IASB Convergence

At a joint meeting in Norwalk, Connecticut, in September 2002, the FASB and IASB agreed to "use their best efforts to (a) make their existing financial reporting standards fully compatible as soon as is practicable and (b) to coordinate their work program to ensure that once achieved, compatibility is maintained."[15] This so-called "Norwalk Agreement" set the FASB and IASB along the path of *convergence* of accounting standards. Convergence can occur by the FASB adopting an existing IASB standard, the IASB adopting an existing FASB standard, or the two Boards working together to develop a new standard. The idea behind convergence is to have similar, but not necessarily identical, standards. Indeed, the Boards acknowledge that the issuance of identical standards, even if jointly developed, is not realistic.

The FASB–IASB convergence process resulted in changes made to U.S. GAAP, IFRS, or both in a number of important areas. Exhibit 11.7 summarizes some of the key accomplishments from this process. As shown in this exhibit, in many cases, convergence did not result in complete elimination of differences between the applicable IFRS and U.S. GAAP. For example, although both standard setters adopted the acquisition method for business combinations and require noncontrolling interest to be classified as equity, *IFRS 3* allows companies to choose from two different methods to measure noncontrolling interest, whereas FASB *ASC Topic 805* only allows one method. As a result, both noncontrolling interest and goodwill can be measured two different ways under IFRS but only one way under U.S. GAAP.

Another example of the difficulty the Boards have had in developing a common standard relates to leases. In 2006, the FASB and IASB added a joint project on leases to their agendas. This project was intended to develop a principle-based model to replace the rule-based lease classification model used in both IFRS and U.S. GAAP at the time. After years of joint work, the Boards issued an exposure draft in 2010 proposing a new standard that would require lessees to capitalize all leases. Based on comments received, the Boards made changes to their proposal and issued a revised exposure draft in 2013. Subsequently, the FASB decided to retain a version of the existing model in which lessees capitalize some leases but treat others as operating leases. The IASB, on the other hand, continued to support a model in which lessees would capitalize all leases. This joint project was concluded with the IASB issuing *IFRS 16,* "Leases," and the FASB issuing *Accounting Standards Update 2016-02,* "Leases," in 2016. While the new standards are substantially similar with respect to lessor accounting, essentially retaining the existing accounting requirements, lessee accounting now differs between IFRS and U.S. GAAP. Under IFRS, lessees treat all leases as finance leases both on the balance sheet and in the measurement of net income. Under U.S. GAAP, lessees continue to classify leases as either finance or operating. The major difference from prior lease accounting requirements in U.S. GAAP is that operating leases are reflected on the balance sheet as both an asset and a liability, similar to a finance lease, but continue to be treated as a traditional operating lease in the measurement of net income.

Perhaps the most significant successful FASB–IASB joint project was the development of a new revenue recognition model embodied in "Revenue from Contracts with Customers" issued

[15] FASB–IASB, *Memorandum of Understanding,* "The Norwalk Agreement," available at www.fasb.org/resources/ccurl/443/883/memorandum.pdf.

EXHIBIT 11.7 Successful FASB–IASB Convergence Projects

Issue	Year—New Standard(s)	Remaining Differences
Share-based payment	2004—IASB issued *IFRS 2* "Share-based Payment" and FASB revised *SFAS 123* "Share-Based Payment"	Some differences in the measurement of share-based payment expense
Discontinued operations	2004—IASB issued *IFRS 5* "Noncurrent Assets Held for Sale and Discontinued Operations" to converge with *SFAS 144* (issued in 2001)	Some differences in the definition of a discontinued operation and its presentation on the income statement
Segment reporting	2006—IASB issued *IFRS 8* "Operating Segments" to converge with *SFAS 133* (issued in 1997)	Minor differences in identification of operating segments and required disclosures
Business combinations	2007—IASB revised *IFRS 3* "Business Combinations" and FASB revised *SFAS 141* "Business Combinations" to converge on a common method of accounting for business combinations	Differences in the measurement of noncontrolling interest and goodwill with IFRS allowing choices; difference in the level at which goodwill impairment testing is conducted
Fair value option	2007—FASB issued *SFAS 159* "The Fair Value Option for Financial Assets and Financial Liabilities" to converge with *IAS 39* (revised in 2003)	Some differences in the financial instruments eligible for the fair value option
Borrowing costs	2009—IASB amended *IAS 23* "Borrowing Costs" to require capitalization of borrowing costs and converge with *SFAS 34* (issued in 1979)	Some differences in the definition of borrowing costs that are eligible for capitalization
Comprehensive income	2011—IASB revised *IAS 1* "Presentation of Financial Statements" and FASB issued *ASU 2011-05* to amend Comprehensive Income (ASC Topic 220) to reduce options for presentation of comprehensive income	Some differences in the requirements for reclassifying other comprehensive income items into net income
Joint ventures	2011—IASB issued *IFRS 11* "Joint Arrangements," which eliminates the option of proportionate consolidation for joint ventures	Complete convergence on use of the equity method for joint ventures
Fair value measurement	2011—IASB issued *IFRS 13* "Fair Value Measurement" and FASB issued *ASU 2011-04* to amend Fair Value Measurement (ASC Topic 820)	Essentially word-for-word convergence
Revenue recognition	2014—IASB issued *IFRS 15* "Revenue from Contracts with Customers" and FASB issued *ASU 2014-09* (same title) creating ASC Topic 606	Essentially word-for-word convergence
Leases	2016—IASB issued *IFRS 16* "Leases" and FASB issued *ASU 2016-02* "Leases"	Convergence on lessees bringing all leases onto the balance sheet but IASB adopted a single model for income recognition whereas FASB adopted a dual model

simultaneously by the two Boards in 2014. The new revenue recognition standard was issued by the IASB as *IFRS 15* and by the FASB as *ASC Topic 606.* Other successful convergence projects of particular importance include business combinations and fair value measurement.

Areas in which the Boards tried but were unable to agree on a common approach include impairment, derecognition, income taxes, research and development, post-employment benefits, and insurance contracts. By 2016, the FASB and IASB had completed work on their joint projects and had no plans to add future projects to their work agendas.

Although the formal FASB–IASB convergence project has come to an end, each Board could continue to refer to the other's standards when making improvements, and convergence is likely to continue on a less formal basis. Evidence of this can be found in several Accounting Standards Updates (ASU) issued by the FASB outside the scope of the convergence project, including

- *ASU 2015-01* "Income Statement—Extraordinary and Unusual Items (Subtopic 225-20)—Simplifying Income Statement Presentation by Eliminating the Concept of Extraordinary Items," eliminates the classification of income statement items as extraordinary, consistent with IFRS.
- *ASU 2015-11* "Inventory (Topic 330)—Simplifying the Measurement of Inventory," requires inventory to be measured at the lower of cost or net realizable value (rather than at the lower of cost or market), consistent with IFRS.

Both of these changes stemmed from the FASB's Simplification Initiative, the objective of which is to identify areas in U.S. GAAP where cost and complexity can be reduced while maintaining or improving the usefulness of information provided to financial statement users. In each case, however, the ASU not only simplifies U.S. GAAP, but also converges U.S. GAAP with IFRS. The FASB acknowledges this in each of these updates. For example, in partial answer to the question posed in the Summary in *ASU 2015-01,* "Why is the FASB issuing this Accounting Standards Update?" the FASB responded:

> This Update will align more closely GAAP income statement presentation guidance with IAS 1, Presentation of Financial Statements, which prohibits the presentation and disclosure of extraordinary items.[16]

SEC Recognition of IFRS

As a result of the IOSCO agreement discussed earlier, the SEC's early focus on international accounting standards related to whether it should allow *foreign* companies to use IFRS without reconciliation to U.S. GAAP. The SEC began formal consideration of this question in 2000 and finally issued a rule in 2007 aptly titled "Acceptance from Foreign Private Issuers of Financial Statements Prepared in Accordance with International Financial Reporting Standards without Reconciliation to U.S. GAAP." Beginning with financial statements filed for fiscal years ending after November 15, 2007, foreign companies using IFRS no longer provide U.S. GAAP information in their annual reports filed with the SEC. However, foreign companies using *foreign GAAP other than IFRS* must continue to provide a U.S. GAAP reconciliation in their Form 20-F.

Elimination of the U.S. GAAP reconciliation requirement for foreign filers using IFRS resulted in an asymmetric situation for U.S. domestic companies that are required to use U.S. GAAP. To level the playing field, the SEC issued a Concept Release in July 2007 to solicit public comment on the idea of allowing U.S. companies to choose between U.S. GAAP and IFRS. A majority of comment letters were not in favor of allowing a *choice* between IFRS or U.S. GAAP, but instead recommended that the SEC *require* the use of IFRS by U.S. companies. Even the chairmen of the FASB and the Financial Accounting Foundation (FAF), which

[16] FASB Accounting Standards Update No. 2015-01, ""Income Statement—Extraordinary and Unusual Items (Subtopic 225-20)—Simplifying Income Statement Presentation by Eliminating the Concept of Extraordinary Items," January 2015, p. 2.

oversees the FASB, expressed approval for a move toward the use of IFRS in the United States. They concluded that "Investors would be better served if all U.S. public companies used accounting standards promulgated by a single global standard setter as the basis for preparing their financial reports. This would be best accomplished by *moving U.S. public companies to an improved version of International Financial Reporting Standards (IFRS)*" (emphasis added).[17] However, they also noted that the switch to IFRS would be a complex, multiyear process that would involve significant changes to the U.S. financial reporting system, including changes in auditing standards, licensing requirements, and how accountants are educated.

IFRS Roadmap

In reaction to the support expressed for IFRS, the SEC issued a proposed rule for the potential use of IFRS by U.S. public companies in November 2008.[18] This so-called IFRS Roadmap sets forth several milestones that, if achieved, could lead to the *required* use of IFRS by U.S. issuers. The SEC indicated that it would monitor these milestones until 2011, and if significant progress had been made at that time, the SEC would then require the mandatory adoption of IFRS by U.S. public companies over a three-year phase-in period. The roadmap indicated 2014 as the first year of IFRS adoption, but a subsequent SEC Release in February 2010 pushed that date back to "approximately 2015 or 2016."[19]

A Possible Framework for Incorporating IFRS into U.S. Financial Reporting

As the self-imposed deadline for monitoring roadmap milestones approached, the SEC staff published a discussion paper in May 2011 that suggested a possible alternative framework for incorporating IFRS into the U.S. financial reporting system.[20] This framework combined the existing FASB–IASB convergence project with the endorsement process followed in many countries and the EU. Some refer to this method as "condorsement." The framework would retain both U.S. GAAP and the FASB as the U.S. accounting standard setter. At the end of a transition period, a U.S. company following U.S. GAAP also would be able to represent that its financial statements are in compliance with IFRS.

The proposed condorsement framework was not adopted. The 2011 deadline established by the SEC in its IFRS Roadmap came and went without the Commission making a decision whether to require the use of IFRS in the United States. In July 2012, the SEC staff issued a Final Staff Report[21] that identified several unresolved issues related to the possible use of IFRS by U.S. companies including the following:

1. The diversity in how IFRS are interpreted, applied, and enforced in various jurisdictions.
2. The potential cost to U.S issuers of adopting or incorporating IFRS.
3. Investor education.

The Final Staff Report did not include conclusions or recommendation for action by the Commission with regard to adoption of IFRS and did not provide insight into the nature or timetable for next steps.

[17] Letter to Ms. Nancy M. Morris, Securities and Exchange Commission, signed by Robert E. Denham, Chairman, Financial Accounting Foundation, and Robert H. Herz, Chairman, Financial Accounting Standards Board, dated November 7, 2007 (accessed December 6, 2007, at www.fasb.org/FASB_FAF_Response_SEC_Release_msw.pdf).

[18] The SEC's "Roadmap for the Potential Use of Financial Statements Prepared in Accordance with International Financial Reporting Standards by U.S. Issuers" is available at www.sec.gov/rules/proposed/2008/33-8982.pdf.

[19] *SEC Release Nos. 33-9109; 34-61578* , "Commission Statement in Support of Convergence and Global Accounting Standards," February 2010, p. 15, available at www.sec.gov.

[20] SEC, "Work Plan for the Consideration of Incorporating International Financial Reporting Standards into the Financial Reporting System for U.S. Issuers: Exploring a Possible Method of Incorporation," SEC Staff Paper, May 26, 2011, available at http://www.sec.gov/spotlight/globalaccountingstandards/ifrs-work-plan-paper-052611.pdf.

[21] SEC, "Work Plan for Consideration of Incorporating International Financial Reporting Standards into the Financial Reporting System for U.S. Issuers" Final Staff Report," July 13, 2012, available at www.sec.gov/spotlight/globalaccountingstandards/ifrs-work-plan-final-report.pdf.

Several public statements made by SEC Chief Accountants suggest that the SEC is unlikely to require U.S. public companies to adopt IFRS anytime soon. In May 2015, SEC Chief Accountant James Schnurr said that he probably would not recommend that U.S. companies be required or allowed to use IFRS in preparing financial statements. In a speech given in December 2016, SEC Chief Accountant Wesley Bricker said: "I believe that for at least the foreseeable future, the FASB's independent standard setting process and U.S. GAAP will continue to best serve the needs of investors and other users who rely on financial reporting by U.S. issuers."[22] However, in December 2017, Bricker indicated that "we will continue to encourage the FASB and the IASB to work together to keep converged standards converged, to reduce differences in standards where they continue to exist, and to continually look for opportunities to improve standards in producing decision-useful information for investors."[23]

Relevance of IFRS for U.S. Accountants

Notwithstanding the fact that it appears unlikely that the SEC will require or even allow U.S. public companies to use IFRS in preparing financial statements, a working knowledge of IFRS is still important for many U.S. accountants. In response to the question "Where do entry-level CPAs currently work with IFRS?" the American Institute of Certified Public Accountants (AICPA) responded as follows:

> In many settings. For example, in US companies that are owned by international entities, entry-level CPAs use IFRS in preparing reporting packages; in US companies that own international entities, entry-level CPAs work on converting IFRS financials to US GAAP. In addition, entry-level CPA auditors use IFRS when auditing companies or subsidiaries that report in IFRS.[24]

Because of the relevance of IFRS for many entry-level accountants, the AICPA began testing IFRS on the Uniform CPA Examination in 2011. More specifically, the AICPA indicates that CPA exam candidates will be expected to be able to:

- Identify accounting and reporting differences between IFRS and U.S. GAAP, and
- Determine the impact of the differences between IFRS and U.S. GAAP on the financial statements.[25]

LO 11-8

Recognize acceptable accounting treatments under IFRS and identify key differences between IFRS and U.S. GAAP.

Differences between IFRS and U.S. GAAP

IFRS and U.S. GAAP share a similar conceptual framework and are designed to provide useful information to providers of financing. Moreover, the IASB and FASB worked for over a decade to converge IFRS and U.S. GAAP. As a result, there are more similarities than differences between the two sets of standards. However, as the adage goes, "the devil is in the details," and numerous differences between the two sets of standards continue to exist. Exhibit 11.8 summarizes some of the key differences between IFRS and U.S. GAAP. These are only a few of the differences that remain between the two sets of standards.

The types of differences that exist between IFRS and U.S. GAAP generally can be classified as follows:

1. Recognition differences.
2. Measurement differences.
3. Classification, presentation, and disclosure differences.

Examples of each type of difference are described next.

[22] Wesley Bricker, "Working Together to Advance High Quality Information in the Capital Markets," December 5, 2016, available at www.sec.gov, accessed October 2, 2018.

[23] Wesley Bricker, "Statement in Connection with the 2017 AICPA Conference on Current SEC and PCAOB Developments," December 4, 2017, accessed October 2, 2018 at www.sec.gov.

[24] American Institute of Certified Public Accountants, "Uniform CPA Examination FAQs—International Financial Reporting Standards (IFRS)," undated, accessed January 22, 2016 at www.aicpa.org.

[25] American Institute of Certified Public Accountants, "Uniform CPA Examination Blueprints," approved May 31, 2018, p. 70, accessed October 2, 2018 at www.aicpa.org.

EXHIBIT 11.8 Some Key Differences between IFRS and U.S. GAAP

Accounting Item	IFRS	U.S. GAAP
Cash and cash equivalents		
Bank overdrafts that are an integral part of cash management	Report as a reduction in cash and cash equivalents	Report as a current liability
Inventory		
Subsequent measurement	LIFO not allowed	LIFO allowed
Reversal of inventory write-down	Required if certain criteria are met	Not allowed
Property, plant, and equipment		
Subsequent measurement	Based on historical cost or a revalued amount	Based on historical cost
Component depreciation	Required when an asset comprises components	Permitted, but not commonly used
Major inspection or overhaul costs	Generally capitalized	Either capitalized or expensed
Impairment		
Indication of impairment	Asset's carrying value exceeds the higher of its (1) value in use (discounted expected future cash flows) or (2) fair value less costs to sell	Asset's carrying value exceeds the undiscounted expected future cash flows from the asset
Subsequent reversal of an impairment loss	Required if certain criteria are met	Not allowed
Research and development costs		
Development costs	Capitalized if certain criteria are met	Expensed immediately (except computer software development)
Defined benefit plans		
Recognition of past (prior) service cost*	Recognized immediately in net income	Amortized to net income over the remaining service period or life expectancy of affected employees
Measurement of net defined benefit asset	Lesser of (a) FVPA less PVDBO or (b) "asset ceiling"†	Fair value of plan assets (FVPA) less present value of defined benefit obligation (PVDBO)
Income taxes		
Recognition of deferred tax assets	Recognized only if realization of tax benefit is probable	Always recognized but a valuation allowance is provided
Tax laws and rates used to measure current and deferred taxes	Enacted or substantively enacted tax laws and rates	Enacted tax laws and rates only
Leases		
Lessee accounting	All leases treated as finance (capital) leases on both balance sheet and income statement	Leases classified as finance or operating. Operating leases treated as such in the income statement but capitalized on the balance sheet
Compound financial instruments		
Convertible debt	Split into debt and equity components	Treated as debt only
Preferred shares		
Redeemable at the option of the shareholder	Classified as a liability	Classified as equity
Loss Contingencies		
Criterion for financial statement recognition of a contingent liability and loss	An outflow of resources is probable, which is defined as "more likely than not"	An outflow of resources is "probable," which is undefined
Measurement of recognized contingent liability and loss when range of outcomes is possible	Midpoint of range	Minimum amount in range

(continued)

EXHIBIT 11.8 Continued

Accounting Item	IFRS	U.S. GAAP
Consolidated financial statements		
Model for determining whether an entity must be consolidated	Single model for determining control for all entities	Separate models for determining control of (a) voting interest entity or (b) variable interest entity
Different accounting policies of parent and subsidiaries	Must conform policies	No requirement to conform policies
Foreign currency translation		
Financial statements of foreign operations in highly inflationary environment	Remeasured for local inflation and then translated into the parent's reporting currency using an all current rate approach	Translated into the parent's reporting currency using the temporal method
Definition of a discontinued operation	A reportable business or geographic segment	A reportable segment, operating segment, reporting unit, subsidiary, or asset group
Interim reporting	Interim period treated as discrete accounting period	Interim period treated as integral part of full year
Statement of cash flows		
Classification of:		
• Interest paid	Operating or financing	Operating
• Interest received	Operating or investing	Operating

*IFRS uses the term *past* service cost, whereas U.S. GAAP calls this *prior* service cost.

†The "asset ceiling" is the present value of any economic benefits available in the form of refunds from the defined benefit plan or reduction in future contributions to the plan.

Recognition Differences

Several differences between IFRS and U.S. GAAP relate to (1) whether an item is recognized or not, (2) how it is recognized, or (3) when it is recognized. A prime example of this type of difference relates to the accounting for research and development (R&D) costs. Under U.S. GAAP, R&D costs must be expensed immediately. The only exception relates to costs incurred in developing computer software, which must be capitalized as an intangible asset when several restrictive criteria are met. *IAS 38,* "Intangible Assets," also requires immediate expensing of all research costs. Development costs, on the other hand, must be recognized as an internally generated intangible asset when certain criteria are met. Deferred development cost (an intangible asset) is amortized over its useful life but not to exceed 20 years. Development costs include all costs directly attributable to or that can be reasonably allocated to development activities including personnel costs, materials and services costs, depreciation on fixed assets, amortization of patents and licenses, and overhead costs other than general administration. The types of development costs that might qualify as an internally generated intangible asset under *IAS 38* include computer software costs, patents and copyrights, customer or supplier relationships, market share, fishing licenses, and franchises. Brands, advertising costs, training costs, and customer lists that are internally generated are specifically excluded from recognition as an intangible asset.

Other recognition differences relate to (1) past service costs related to defined benefit plans, (2) deferred tax assets, and (3) loss contingencies (refer to Exhibit 11.8).

Measurement Differences

Measurement differences result in the recognition of different amounts in the financial statements under IFRS and U.S. GAAP. In some cases, these differences result from different measurement methods required under the two sets of standards. For example, when a contingent liability meets the criteria to be recognized as a liability on the balance sheet and a range of possible cash outflows exists, IFRS requires the liability to be measured at the midpoint of the range of cash outflows when all points in the range are equally likely. In contrast, U.S. GAAP requires use of the low end of the range rather than the midpoint to measure the liability.

Discussion Question

WHICH ACCOUNTING METHOD REALLY IS APPROPRIATE?

In this era of rapidly changing technology, research and development (R&D) expenditures represent one of the most important factors in the future success of many companies. Organizations that spend too little on R&D risk being left behind by the competition. Conversely, companies that spend too much may waste money or not be able to make efficient use of the results.

In the United States, except for costs related to computer software development, all R&D expenditures are expensed as incurred. However, expensing all R&D costs is not an approach used in much of the world. Firms using IFRS must capitalize development costs as an intangible asset when they can demonstrate (1) the technical feasibility of completing the project, (2) the intention to complete the project, (3) the ability to use or sell the intangible asset, (4) how the intangible asset will generate future benefits, (5) the availability of adequate resources to complete the asset, and (6) the ability to measure development costs associated with the intangible asset.

Should any portion of R&D costs be capitalized as an asset? Is expensing all R&D expenditures the best method of reporting these costs? Is the U.S. approach better than the international standard? Which approach provides the best representation of a company's activities?

In other cases, measurement differences can exist because of alternatives allowed by one set of standards but not the other. Permitting the use of LIFO under U.S. GAAP but not allowing its use under IFRS is an example of this type of difference.

One of the greatest potential differences between the application of IFRS and U.S. GAAP is found in *IAS 16,* "Property, Plant, and Equipment." In measuring fixed assets subsequent to acquisition, *IAS 16* allows companies to choose between two approaches: (1) the cost model and (2) the revaluation model. Under the cost model, property, plant, and equipment is measured and carried on the balance sheet at cost less accumulated depreciation and any impairment losses. This is consistent with U.S. GAAP. Under the revaluation model, property, plant, and equipment is carried on the balance sheet subsequent to acquisition at a revalued amount, which is measured as fair value at the date of revaluation less any subsequent accumulated depreciation and impairment losses. If a company adopts the revaluation model, it must make revaluations regularly enough that the carrying value reported on the balance sheet does not differ materially from fair value. Companies following the revaluation model need not adopt this treatment for all classes of property, plant, and equipment. However, they must apply it to all items within a class of assets. A company could choose to revalue land but not buildings, for example, but it would need to revalue each and every parcel of land it owns at the same time.

Classification, Presentation, and Disclosure Differences

Classification, presentation, and disclosure relate to the manner in which items are classified or presented on the financial statements or disclosed in the notes to the financial statements. As one might expect, numerous specific disclosure differences exist between IFRS and U.S. GAAP. Classification and presentation differences also exist between the two sets of standards.

Splitting convertible debt into separate liability and equity components under IFRS but classifying this item as a liability only under U.S. GAAP is one example of a classification difference. Another example is the classification of bank overdrafts as a liability under U.S. GAAP; bank overdrafts that are part of an entity's cash management are classified as a reduction in cash and cash equivalents under IFRS. A third difference relates to what is considered a discontinued operation and therefore presented separately on the income statement. The U.S. GAAP definition of a discontinued operation is less restrictive than the definition in IFRS.

Perhaps the greatest difference between IFRS and U.S. GAAP with respect to presentation is the fact that IFRS contain a single standard—*IAS 1,* "Presentation of Financial Statements"—that governs the presentation of financial statements. U.S. GAAP has no equivalent to *IAS 1*.

IAS 1, "Presentation of Financial Statements"

IAS 1, "Presentation of Financial Statements," provides guidance with respect to the following issues:

1. *Purpose of financial statements:* Financial statements provide information about the financial position, financial performance, and cash flows useful to a wide range of users in making economic decisions.
2. *Overriding principle of fair presentation:* Financial statements should present fairly an entity's financial position, financial performance, and cash flows. Compliance with IFRS generally ensures fair presentation. In extremely rare circumstances, an entity might need to depart from IFRS to ensure fair presentation.
3. *Basic principles and assumptions: IAS 1* emphasizes the going concern assumption, the accrual basis of accounting, the consistency principle, the principle of comparative information, and the separate presentation of material items. The standard also precludes the offsetting of assets and liabilities and of revenues and expenses unless specifically permitted by another standard.
4. *Components of financial statements: IAS 1* requires a complete set of financial statements to include
   a. A statement of financial position (balance sheet).
   b. A statement of comprehensive income (or a separate income statement and statement of comprehensive income).
   c. A statement of changes in equity.
   d. A statement of cash flows.
   e. Accompanying notes, including a summary of significant accounting policies.
5. *Structure and content of financial statements: IAS 1* also provides guidance with respect to the structure of each financial statement and prescribes items that must be presented (*a*) on the face of financial statements and (*b*) either on the face of financial statements or disclosed in the notes.

IAS 1 requires an entity to classify assets and liabilities as current and noncurrent unless presentation according to liquidity provides more reliable information. The income statement can be presented using either a *function of expenses* (cost of sales) format or a *nature of expenses* format. See Exhibit 11.9 for illustrations of the alternative formats for classifying expenses on the income statement. Note that the amount reported as *operating income (loss)* and all line items below operating income (loss) are the same under both formats. Additional required disclosures must be made either on the face of the income statement or in the notes. For example, a company using the function of expenses format must disclose additional information on the nature of expenses, including depreciation and amortization expense and employee benefits expense. For both formats, the total amount distributed as dividends as well as dividends per share must be disclosed. In addition, *IAS 33,* "Earnings per Share," requires basic and diluted earnings per share to be reported on the face of the income statement.

Conversion of IFRS Financial Statements to U.S. GAAP

LO 11-9

Determine the impact that specific differences between IFRS and U.S. GAAP have on financial statements, and prepare adjustments to convert IFRS balances to U.S. GAAP.

Several thousand U.S.-based companies have subsidiaries overseas that must be included in consolidated financial statements. Many of these foreign subsidiaries use IFRS in preparing their financial statements. For U.S. public companies, the IFRS financial statements of foreign subsidiaries must be converted to a U.S. GAAP basis before they can be consolidated. As a result, many U.S. accountants involved in the preparation of consolidated financial statements

EXHIBIT 11.9
Illustrative IFRS Income Statements

IFRS COMPANY
Income Statement for the Year Ended
December 31, Year 1 (in thousands of currency units)

Nature of Expenses Format	*Function of Expenses Format*
Revenue	**Revenue**
Other income	Cost of sales
Changes in inventories of finished goods and work in progress	**Gross profit**
Raw materials and consumables used	Other income
Employee benefits expense	Distribution costs
Depreciation and amortization expense	Administrative expenses
Other expenses	Other expenses
Operating income (loss)	**Operating income (loss)**
Finance costs	Finance costs
Equity method income (loss)	Equity method income (loss)
Profit (or loss) before tax	**Profit (or loss) before tax**
Income tax expense	Income tax expense
Profit (loss) for the period	**Profit (loss) for the period**
Attributable to:	Attributable to:
Parent company shareholders	Parent company shareholders
Noncontrolling interest	Noncontrolling interest

Source: *IAS 1*, "Presentation of Financial Statements," paras. 102, 103.

need to be "bilingual" in both U.S. GAAP and IFRS. Accountants and other finance professionals involved in cross-border merger and acquisition decisions also find it important to be able to convert IFRS balances to U.S. GAAP as part of the due diligence process. Using IFRS-based financial statement amounts as inputs into valuation models that have been developed for U.S. GAAP can result in suboptimal investment decisions.[26]

Unfortunately, converting IFRS-based amounts to U.S. GAAP is not as easy as, say, converting kilometers to miles. It is not possible to employ a simple decision rule such as "take IFRS net income and add 10 percent" to approximate U.S. GAAP net income. Converting financial statements from IFRS to U.S. GAAP requires not only an expertise in both sets of accounting standards, but also the analytical ability to determine how to get from point A (IFRS) to point B (U.S. GAAP). This section demonstrates the process for determining the adjustments needed to convert IFRS amounts to U.S. GAAP focusing on differences that exist between the two sets of standards with regard to the recognition and measurement of loss contingencies. The comprehensive illustration at the end of this chapter provides additional examples of this process.

Illustrative Example—Loss Contingency (First Year)

Amarcord Corporation (a U.S.-based company) owns 100 percent of Moravia SE, which is located in a foreign country that uses IFRS. At the beginning of 2020, Moravia had assets of 1,000,000, liabilities of 400,000, capital stock of 100,000, and retained earnings of 500,000. (All amounts in this illustrative example are in euros, Moravia's reporting currency.)

Early in 2020, Moravia acquired a piece of land in a neighboring country that was the site of a former manufacturing facility. In October 2020, Moravia was informed by the Ministry for Environment in the neighboring country that the land Moravia now owns is contaminated and that Moravia is legally obligated to remediate the environmental contamination. Moravia hired a team of environmental engineers to assess the extent of contamination and estimate the cost to remediate the situation. The engineers estimate that the cost could be as low as 50,000 and as high as 150,000, with all amounts in that range being equally likely. Moravia

[26] For a discussion of this issue, see PricewaterhouseCoopers, "The Importance of Being Financially Bilingual: How Financial Reporting Differences Can Affect Cross-Border Deal Value," May 2017, available online at www.pwc.com/us/en/cfodirect/issues/ifrs-adoption-convergence/ifrs-financially-bilingual.html.

plans to appeal the Ministry for Environment's ruling and has engaged a law firm in the neighboring country to provide an opinion on the likelihood that Moravia will be successful in this matter. In late December 2020, the law firm provides its opinion that it is more likely than not (about 60 percent probable) that Moravia will lose the appeal and that the company will be required to clean up the environmental contamination.

IFRS Treatment

In preparing financial statements for the year ended December 31, 2020, Moravia's accountants applied relevant IFRS guidance to determine the appropriate financial reporting treatment for this environmental remediation loss contingency. In loss contingency situations, *IAS 37,* "Provisions, Contingent Liabilities and Contingent Assets," requires recognition of a provision (liability) and a loss when it is *probable* that an outflow of resources will be required to settle the obligation. To implement this principle, *IAS 37,* para. 23 defines probable as "more likely than not," which is interpreted as a probability of more than 50 percent. A loss and provision must be recognized at the best estimate of the expenditure that will be required to settle the obligation. *IAS 37,* para. 39 indicates: "Where there is a continuous range of possible outcomes, and each point in that range is as likely as any other, the mid-point of the range is used." Applying this guidance, Moravia's accountants recognized a provision and a loss on December 31, 2020, in the amount of 100,000, which is the midpoint in the 50,000 to 150,000 range of cost estimated by the environmental engineers. The journal entry was as follows:

Environmental Remediation Loss.	100,000	
Provision for Environmental Remediation (liability).		100,000

The environmental remediation loss reduced Moravia's 2020 pretax income, which resulted in a reduction in income tax expense of 25,000 (the corporate income tax rate in Moravia's home country is 25 percent). Because the loss contingency was not deductible for tax purposes, a temporary tax difference exists and a deferred tax asset of 25,000 was recognized. The journal entry to reflect this was the following:

Deferred Tax Asset.	25,000	
Income Tax Expense		25,000

For consolidation purposes, Moravia's accountants have provided Amarcord, its parent company, with IFRS financial statements for the year ended December 31, 2020. Exhibit 11.10 presents the worksheet used by Amarcord's accountants to convert Moravia's IFRS financial statements to U.S. GAAP. The IFRS column in Exhibit 11.10 shows the balances provided by Moravia's accountants. Amounts in parentheses have credit balances; amounts without parentheses have debit balances. The accounts affected by the preceding journal entries are highlighted in **bold.**

U.S. GAAP Treatment

FASB *ASC 450,* "Contingencies," requires the accrual of a contingent loss when it is *probable* that an outflow of resources will occur (*ASC* 450-20-25-2). However, probable is not specifically defined, and it is common for companies to use a threshold of 70 percent or more in determining whether a contingency should be recognized. Accordingly, Amarcord Corporation has adopted a corporate policy of recognizing loss contingencies when the probability of a negative outcome exceeds 70 percent. Consistent with this policy, Amarcord's accountants have determined that Moravia's environmental remediation contingency would not have been recognized in 2020 under U.S. GAAP.

Conversion from IFRS to U.S. GAAP

From a U.S. GAAP perspective, Moravia's December 31, 2020, financial statements

a. Overstate environmental remediation loss by 100,000,

b. Overstate provision for environmental remediation by 100,000,

EXHIBIT 11.10
Moravia SE's IFRS to U.S. GAAP Conversion Worksheet for the Year Ending December 31, 2020

MORAVIA SE
IFRS to U.S. GAAP Conversion Worksheet
For the Year Ending December 31, 2020

(amounts in euros)		**Conversion Entries**		
Accounts	**IFRS**	**Debit**	**Credit**	**U.S. GAAP**
Income Statement				
Revenues	(3,000,000)			(3,000,000)
Expenses	2,000,000			2,000,000
Environmental remediation loss	**100,000**		(1) 100,000	**–0–**
Income before tax	(900,000)			(1,000,000)
Income tax expense	**225,000**	(2) 25,000		**250,000**
Net income	(675,000)			(750,000)
Statement of Retained Earnings				
Retained earnings, 1/1	(500,000)			(500,000)
Net income (from above)	(675,000)			(750,000)
Retained earnings, 12/31	(1,175,000)			(1,250,000)
Balance Sheet				
Assets	1,750,000			1,750,000
Deferred tax asset	**25,000**		(2) 25,000	**–0–**
Total assets	1,775,000			1,750,000
Liabilities	(400,000)			(400,000)
Provision for environmental remediation	**(100,000)**	(1) 100,000		**–0–**
Total liabilities	(500,000)			(400,000)
Capital stock	(100,000)			(100,000)
Retained earnings, 12/31 (from above)	(1,175,000)			(1,250,000)
Total liabilities and equity	(1,775,000)			(1,750,000)
		125,000	125,000	

c. Overstate deferred tax asset by 25,000, and
d. Understate income tax expense by 25,000.

The net effect of (a) and (d) is that Net Income is understated by 75,000 (100,000 – 25,000), and therefore Retained Earnings at December 31, 2020, is understated by 75,000. The U.S. GAAP column in Exhibit 11.10 shows the balances that would be reported by Moravia under U.S. GAAP.

To restate from IFRS to U.S. GAAP, Amarcord's accountants would simply reverse the loss contingency recognition entries made by Moravia's accountants as follows:

Conversion Entry (1)		
Provision for Environmental Remediation (liability)	100,000	
Environmental Remediation Loss		100,000

Conversion Entry (2)		
Income Tax Expense	25,000	
Deferred Tax Asset		25,000

Exhibit 11.10 shows that these conversion entries eliminate the Loss on Environmental Remediation from the Income Statement, and the Provision for Environmental Remediation and Deferred Tax Asset from the balance sheet. There is a net increase of 75,000 in 2020 Net Income and in the December 31, 2020, balance in Retained Earnings.

Illustrative Example—Loss Contingency (Second Year)

In January 2021, Moravia appealed the Department for Environment's ruling to the regional judicial body in the neighboring country. On March 15, 2021, the regional judicial body informed Moravia that its appeal had been denied and that the company must remediate the environmental contamination by June 15, 2021. Moravia's environmental engineers conduct a more extensive study of the situation and now estimate that the cost of remediation will be somewhere between 90,000 and 190,000, with all amounts in that range being equally likely.

IFRS Treatment

In preparing the company's interim financial statements for the quarter ending March 31, 2021, Moravia's accountants applied relevant guidance in IFRS to determine the appropriate financial reporting treatment for its Provision for Environmental Remediation. *IAS 37*, para. 59 states: "Provisions shall be reviewed at the end of each reporting period and adjusted to reflect the current best estimate." Consistent with this guidance, Moravia's accountants increased the Provision for Environmental Remediation to 140,000, which is the new midpoint [(90,000 + 190,000) / 2] in the estimated range of cleanup cost. An additional Environmental Remediation Loss of 40,000 also was recognized. The journal entry to achieve this was:

Environmental Remediation Loss.	40,000	
Provision for Environmental Remediation		40,000

The additional environmental remediation loss reduces first quarter 2021 pre-tax income by 40,000 and income tax expense by 10,000 [40,000 × 25% tax rate]. Because the remediation loss is not tax deductible, a temporary tax difference arises and an additional deferred tax asset is recognized. The tax effect of the loss is reflected in the following entry:

Deferred Tax Asset.	10,000	
Income Tax Expense		10,000

Moravia's accountants have provided Amarcord with IFRS financial statements for consolidation purposes for the quarter ending March 31, 2021. The IFRS column in Exhibit 11.11 shows these financial statements.

U.S. GAAP Treatment

At March 31, 2021, given the negative ruling by the regional judicial body, Amarcord's accountants now believe it is probable (more than 70 percent likely) that Moravia will incur costs to remediate the environmental damage and a loss contingency should be recognized. FASB *ASC* 450-20-30-1 states: "If some amount within a range of loss appears at the time to be a better estimate than any other amount within the range, that amount shall be accrued. When no amount within the range is a better estimate than any other amount, however, the minimum amount in the range shall be accrued." Following this guidance, Amarcord's accountants determine that Moravia should report a loss and a liability in the amount of 90,000, which is the minimum amount in the range of the cleanup cost estimate. The loss would reduce income tax expense by 22,500 (90,000 × 25%), and a deferred tax asset of 22,500 must be recognized. The journal entries to recognize the loss contingency on March 31, 2021, under U.S. GAAP are as follows:

Environmental Remediation Loss.	90,000	
Environmental Remediation Liability		90,000

Deferred Tax Asset.	22,500	
Income Tax Expense		22,500

EXHIBIT 11.11
Moravia SE's IFRS to U.S. GAAP Conversion Worksheet for the Quarter Ending March 31, 2021

MORAVIA SE
IFRS to U.S. GAAP Conversion Worksheet
For the Quarter Ending March 31, 2021

(amounts in euros)		Restatement Entries		
Accounts	**IFRS**	**Debit**	**Credit**	**U.S. GAAP**
Income Statement				
Revenues	(1,000,000)			(1,000,000)
Expenses	600,000			600,000
Environmental remediation loss	**40,000**	(1) 50,000		**90,000**
Income before tax	(360,000)			(310,000)
Income tax expense	**90,000**		(1) 12,500	**77,500**
Net income	(270,000)			(232,500)
Statement of Retained Earnings				
Retained earnings, 1/1	(1,175,000)		(1) 75,000	(1,250,000)
Net income	(270,000)			(232,500)
Retained earnings, 12/31	(1,445,000)			(1,482,500)
Balance Sheet				
Assets	2,050,000			2,050,000
Deferred tax asset	**35,000**		(1) 12,500	**22,500**
Total assets	2,085,000			2,072,500
Liabilities	(400,000)			(400,000)
Provision for environmental remediation	**(140,000)**	(1) 50,000		**(90,000)**
Total liabilities	(540,000)			(490,000)
Capital stock	(100,000)			(100,000)
Retained earnings, 12/31	(1,445,000)			(1,482,500)
Total liabilities and equity	(2,085,000)			(2,072,500)
		100,000	100,000	

Conversion from IFRS to U.S. GAAP

From a U.S. GAAP perspective, Moravia's March 31, 2021, IFRS financial statements:

a. Understate Environmental Remediation Loss by 50,000 (90,000 – 40,000),
b. Overstate Provision for Environmental Remediation by 50,000 (90,000 – 140,000),
c. Overstate Deferred Tax Asset by 12,500 (22,500 – 35,000),
d. Overstate Income Tax Expense by 12,500, and
e. Understate the January 1, 2021, balance in Retained Earnings by 75,000.

The net effect of (a) and (d) is that Net Income in the first quarter 2021 is overstated by 37,500. The balance in Retained Earnings at March 31, 2021, is understated by 37,500.

To convert from IFRS to U.S. GAAP, Amarcord's accountants made the following entry in the March 31, 2021, conversion worksheet (see Exhibit 11.11):

Conversion Entry (1)		
Environmental Remediation Loss	50,000	
Provision for Environmental Remediation	50,000	
Retained Earnings, 1/1/21		75,000
Deferred Tax Asset		12,500
Income Tax Expense		12,500

The U.S. GAAP column in Exhibit 11.11 shows that this entry results in the correct amounts being reported in Moravia's first quarter 2021 financial statements in accordance with U.S. GAAP. Environmental Remediation Loss and Provision for Environmental Remediation are reported at 90,000. Deferred Tax Asset is reported at 22,500, and net income is 37,500 smaller than under IFRS.

Obstacles to Worldwide Comparability of Financial Statements

Comparability of financial statements across countries is one of the goals of a common set of global accounting standards. IFRS is the dominant set of accounting standards used in the world. Does that mean that the goal of comparability across companies using IFRS has been achieved? The use of a common set of accounting standards is a necessary but perhaps not a sufficient condition for ensuring worldwide comparability. Several obstacles stand in the way of a common set of standards being interpreted and applied in a consistent manner across all countries.[27]

Translation of IFRS into Other Languages

IFRS are written in English and therefore must be translated into other languages for use by non-English-speaking accountants. The IASB created an official translation process in 1997, and by 2016, IFRS had been translated into more than 40 other languages. Most translations are into European languages because of the European Union's required usage of IFRS. However, IFRS also have been translated into Chinese, Japanese, and Arabic, among other languages. Despite the care the IASB took in the translation process, several research studies suggest that certain English-language expressions used in IFRS are difficult to translate without some distortion of meaning. In one study, Canadian researchers examined English-speaking and French-speaking students' interpretations of probability expressions such as *probable, not likely,* and *reasonable assurance* used to establish recognition and disclosure thresholds in IASs.[28] English-speaking students' interpretations of these expressions differed significantly from the interpretations made by French-speaking students of the French-language translation. In another study, German accountants fluent in English assigned values to both the English original and the German translation of probability expressions used in IFRS.[29] For several expressions, the original and translation were interpreted differently, suggesting that the German translation distorted the original meaning.

The SEC implicitly acknowledged the potential problem in translating IFRS to other languages in its rule eliminating the U.S. GAAP reconciliation requirement for foreign registrants. That rule applies only to those foreign companies that prepare financial statements in accordance with the *English language version* of IFRS.

The Impact of Culture on Financial Reporting

Even if translating IFRS into languages other than English was not difficult, differences in national culture values could lead to differences in the interpretation and application of IFRS. In 1988, Gray proposed a model that hypothesizes a relationship between cultural values, accounting values, and the financial reporting rules developed in a country.[30] More recently, Gray's model was extended to hypothesize that accounting values affect not only a country's

[27] The following discussion is based on George T. Tsakumis, David R. Campbell Sr., and Timothy S. Doupnik, "IFRS: Beyond the Standards," *Journal of Accountancy,* February 2009, pp. 34–39.

[28] Ronald A. Davidson and Heidi Hadlich Chrisman, "Interlinguistic Comparison of International Accounting Standards: The Case of Uncertainty Expressions," *The International Journal of Accounting* 28 (1993), pp. 1–16.

[29] Timothy S. Doupnik and Martin Richter, "Interpretation of Uncertainty Expressions: A Cross-National Study," *Accounting, Organizations and Society* 28 (2003), pp. 15–35.

[30] Sidney J. Gray, "Towards a Theory of Cultural Influence on the Development of Accounting Systems Internationally," *Abacus,* March 1988, pp. 1–15.

accounting rules but also the manner in which those rules are applied.[31] This hypothesis has important implications for a world in which countries with different national cultures use the same accounting standards. It implies that for accounting issues in which accountants must use their judgment in applying an accounting principle, culturally based biases could cause accountants in one country to apply the standard differently from accountants in another country.

Several research studies support this hypothesis.[32] For example, one study found that, given the same set of facts, accountants in France and Germany estimated higher amounts of warranty expense than did accountants in the United Kingdom.[33] This result was consistent with differences in the level of the accounting value of conservatism across these countries resulting from differences in their cultural values.

Auditors, both internal and external, who are auditing financial statements prepared in different countries under IFRS should be aware of the inherent biases that national culture might introduce into application of the standards. Financial statement users need to be aware that the use of a common set of accounting standards (that is, IFRS) might not necessarily result in complete financial statement comparability across countries. However, a greater degree of comparability exists than if each country were to continue to use a different set of standards.

Summary

1. Historically, considerable diversity existed with respect to financial reporting across countries. Differences include the format and presentation of financial statements, the measurement and recognition rules followed in preparing financial statements, disclosures provided in the notes to financial statements, and even the terminology used to describe items reported on financial statements.
2. Accounting systems differ across countries partially because of differences in environmental factors such as the type of legal system followed in the country, the importance of equity as a source of financing, and the extent to which accounting statements serve as the basis for taxation.
3. The worldwide diversity in accounting practices causes problems that can be quite serious for some parties. Parent companies with foreign subsidiaries must convert from foreign GAAP to parent company GAAP to prepare worldwide consolidated financial statements. To gain access to a foreign capital market, companies often find it necessary to prepare information based on foreign GAAP. Accounting diversity makes it difficult for potential investors to compare financial statements between companies from different countries in making international investment decisions.
4. The International Accounting Standards Committee (IASC) was formed in 1973 to develop international accounting standards (IASs) universally acceptable in all countries. The so-called IOSCO agreement significantly enhanced the IASC's legitimacy as the international accounting standard setter.
5. In 2001, the International Accounting Standards Board (IASB) replaced the IASC and adopted the IASs developed by its predecessor. The IASB creates its own international financial reporting standards (IFRSs). Together, IASs, IFRSs, and Interpretations make up IFRS Standards, which are referred to collectively as IFRS.
6. The IASB does not have the ability to require the use of its standards. However, more than 100 countries either require or allow publicly traded domestic companies to use IFRS. Since 2005, all publicly traded companies in the European Union have been required to use IFRS in preparing their consolidated financial statements.
7. The IASB has a simplified version of full IFRS for use by small and medium-sized entities called *IFRS for SMEs*.
8. *IFRS 1* establishes procedures to be followed in the first-time adoption of IFRS. *IFRS 1* requires the preparation of an opening IFRS balance sheet two years prior to when a company publishes

[31] Timothy S. Doupnik and George T. Tsakumis, "A Critical Review of Tests of Gray's Theory," *Journal of Accounting Literature,* 2001.

[32] See Joseph J. Schultz and Thomas J. Lopez, "The Impact of National Influence on Accounting Estimates: Implications for International Accounting Standard-Setters," *The International Journal of Accounting* 36 (2001), pp. 271–90; Timothy S. Doupnik and Martin Richter, "The Impact of Culture on the Interpretation of "In Context" Verbal Probability Expressions," *Journal of International Accounting Research* 3, no. 1 (2004), pp. 1–20; and George T. Tsakumis, "The Influence of Culture on Accountants' Application of Financial Reporting Rules," *Abacus,* March 2007, pp. 27–48.

[33] Schultz and Lopez, "The Impact of National Influence on Accounting Estimates."

its first set of IFRS financial statements. In preparing the opening IFRS balance sheet, a company would need to (a) recognize assets and liabilities required by IFRS but not by previous GAAP and derecognize items previously recognized that are not allowed under IFRS, (b) measure assets and liabilities in accordance with IFRS, (c) reclassify items previously classified in a different manner from what it required by IFRS, and (d) comply with all presentation and disclosure requirements.

9. In 2002, the FASB and the IASB announced the Norwalk Agreement to converge their financial reporting standards as soon as is practicable. Convergence involves the IASB adopting an FASB standard, the FASB adopting an IASB standard, or the two boards jointly developing a new standard. Several joint projects have resulted in new standards being issued simultaneously by the IASB and FASB. Formal FASB–IASB convergence concluded in 2016.
10. In 2007, the U.S. SEC eliminated the U.S. GAAP reconciliation requirement for foreign companies that use IFRS, and in 2008 it issued an IFRS Roadmap that proposed the use of IFRS by U.S. companies. In 2011, the SEC staff suggested a "condorsement" approach to incorporating IFRS into U.S. financial reporting. More recently, however, the SEC's chief accountants have indicated that the SEC is not likely to require or allow the use of IFRS by U.S. publicly traded companies.
11. Although IFRS and U.S. GAAP are similar in many ways, numerous differences continue to exist between the two sets of standards. These differences can be categorized as relating to (a) recognition, (b) measurement, and (c) classification, presentation, or disclosure. Recognizing development costs as an asset when certain criteria are met under IFRS while requiring they be expensed under U.S. GAAP is an example of a recognition difference. Carrying property, plant, and equipment on the balance sheet at revalued amounts under IFRS versus depreciated historical cost under U.S. GAAP is a measurement difference. Classifying convertible bonds as both debt and equity under IFRS but only as equity under U.S. GAAP is a classification difference.
12. Many foreign subsidiaries of U.S. parent companies use IFRS. To prepare consolidated financial statements, a foreign subsidiary's IFRS financial statements must be restated to U.S. GAAP. As a result, many U.S. accountants involved in the preparation of consolidated financial statements must have an expertise in both U.S. GAAP and IFRS.
13. The use of the same set of accounting standards by all companies is a necessary but possibly insufficient condition for achieving the goal of worldwide comparability of financial statements. Translation and culture are two obstacles in achieving this goal. It might not be possible to translate IFRS into non-English languages without some distortion of meaning. Differences in societal values across countries might lead to culturally determined biases in interpreting and applying a common set of standards. However, although these obstacles exist, worldwide adoption of a single set of standards results in a greater degree of comparability than existed when a different set of standards was used by each country.

Comprehensive Illustration

Problem

(*Estimated Time: 120 to 180 minutes*) Jameson Company is a U.S.-based company that prepares consolidated financial statements in accordance with U.S. GAAP. At the beginning of 2020, Jameson paid cash for all of the outstanding common stock of Ammer Limited. In accordance with the financial reporting requirements of its home country, Ammer uses IFRS to prepare its financial statements. Jameson's CFO has given you the task of converting Ammer's financial statements from IFRS to U.S. GAAP to be able to consolidate the two companies. Based on information provided by Ammer's accountants, you have identified the following areas in which Ammer's accounting principles based on IFRS differ from U.S. GAAP.

- **Cash and cash equivalents**—classification of bank overdraft
- **Property, plant, and equipment**—component depreciation, revaluation
- **Intangible assets**—impairment, research and development expenditures
- **Compound financial instruments**—convertible bonds
- **Defined benefit pension plan**—past service cost
- **Business combination**—noncontrolling interest and goodwill

Required

Based upon information provided, use your knowledge of IFRS and U.S. GAAP to determine the adjustments needed to convert Ammer's financial statements to a U.S. GAAP basis on December 31, 2020, and December 31, 2021. For each item, determine (a) the appropriate accounting treatment under IFRS, (b) the appropriate accounting treatment under U.S. GAAP, (c) the debit/credit entry needed to convert

Ammer's financial statement balances from IFRS to U.S. GAAP, and (d) prepare a partial conversion worksheet summarizing the impact each adjustment has on Ammer's financial statements.

Additional information:

- Because there is no corporate income tax in Ammer's home country, there are no tax implications associated with the adjustments made to convert the financial statements from IFRS to U.S. GAAP.
- Ammer's financial statement balances are reported in dollars ($).

Solution

Cash and Cash Equivalents—Bank Overdraft

On December 31, 2020, Ammer had an overdraft of $8,000 on one of its bank accounts. Bank overdrafts are an integral part of the company's cash management, with the bank account fluctuating from having a positive balance to being overdrawn over time. On December 31, 2021, the company had a positive balance in its bank account.

IFRS Treatment

IAS 7, "Statement of Cash Flows," states that bank overdrafts that are an integral part of an entity's cash management should be included as a component of cash and cash equivalents, rather than being treated as a borrowing. Therefore, Ammer has deducted the $8,000 bank overdraft from the balance in Cash and Cash Equivalents on its December 31, 2020, balance sheet.

U.S. GAAP Treatment

Under U.S. GAAP, bank overdrafts are treated as a short-term borrowing (current liability).

Conversion from IFRS to U.S. GAAP—2020

To reclassify the bank overdraft as a short-term borrowing, the following entry must be made in an IFRS-to-U.S.-GAAP conversion worksheet on December 31, 2020:

Cash and Cash Equivalents.	8,000	
Short-term Borrowings.		8,000

This adjustment has no impact on net income or retained earnings. Total assets and total liabilities both increase by $8,000.

Conversion from IFRS to U.S. GAAP—2021

Because Ammer's bank account has a positive balance on December 31, 2021, no overdraft exists and there is no classification difference between IFRS and U.S. GAAP on that date. Therefore, no adjustment is needed to convert from IFRS to U.S. GAAP on December 31, 2021.

Property, Plant, and Equipment—Component Depreciation

Ammer acquired a major piece of manufacturing machinery on January 1, 2020, at an original cost of $1,000,000. The machinery has an overall estimated useful life of 20 years and no salvage value. However, individual components in the machinery will need to be replaced periodically for the machinery to achieve its estimated useful life. The company has determined that the machinery comprises three significant components with the following original costs and estimated useful lives (each component has zero salvage value):

Component	Cost	Useful Life
Housing	$ 200,000	20 years
Control unit	300,000	5 years
Motor	500,000	10 years
Total	$1,000,000	

IFRS Treatment

IAS 16, "Property, Plant and Equipment," indicates that when an item of property, plant, and equipment is made up of individual components for which different depreciation methods or useful lives are appropriate, each component must be depreciated separately. This is commonly referred to as *component depreciation.* Because the machinery acquired on January 1, 2020, comprises three separate components with significantly different useful lives, Ammer appropriately calculates depreciation expense for 2020 as $120,000, as shown here:

Component	Cost	Useful Life	Depreciation
Housing	$ 200,000	20 years	$ 10,000
Control unit	300,000	5 years	60,000
Motor	500,000	10 years	50,000
Total	$1,000,000		$120,000

The journal entries Ammer prepared in 2020 related to the machinery are the following:

January 1, 2020

Machinery	1,000,000	
Cash		1,000,000
To recognize the cash purchase of machinery.		

December 31, 2020

Depreciation Expense	120,000	
Accumulated Depreciation—Machinery		120,000
To recognize depreciation expense on machinery using the component method.		

These entries result in a decrease in net income and retained earnings of $120,000, as well as a decrease in total assets of the same amount (+$1,000,000 – $1,000,000 – $120,000).

U.S. GAAP Treatment

U.S. GAAP allows but does not require component depreciation. Jameson has a corporate policy of using straight-line depreciation for machinery and equipment and plans to extend this policy to Ammer Limited. On a straight-line basis, the depreciation recognized in 2020 related to the manufacturing machinery would be $50,000 ($1,000,000 original cost/20-year estimated useful life). The appropriate journal entries under U.S. GAAP would be the following:

January 1, 2020

Machinery	1,000,000	
Cash		1,000,000

December 31, 2020

Depreciation Expense	50,000	
Accumulated Depreciation—Machinery		50,000

These entries result in a decrease in net income and retained earnings of $50,000, as well as a $50,000 decrease in total assets.

Conversion from IFRS to U.S. GAAP—2020

Depreciation expense and accumulated depreciation must be reduced by $70,000 to convert Ammer's financial statements from IFRS to U.S. GAAP. The conversion entry is as follows:

Accumulated Depreciation—Machinery	70,000	
Depreciation Expense		70,000

The December 31, 2020, partial conversion worksheet (focusing on component depreciation) shown next isolates the effect machinery depreciation has on Ammer's financial statements. (Note that worksheet amounts in parentheses indicate credit balances; amounts without parentheses are debits. Accounts affected by the conversion entry are highlighted in **bold.**)

Partial Conversion Worksheet, 12/31/20 (Component Depreciation)

Account	IFRS	Conversion Entry Debit	Conversion Entry Credit	U.S. GAAP
Depreciation expense	**120,000**		70,000	**50,000**
Net income (negative)	120,000			50,000
Retained earnings, 1/1	–0–			–0–
Retained earnings, 12/31 (negative)	120,000			50,000
Cash	(1,000,000)			(1,000,000)
Machinery	1,000,000			1,000,000
Accumulated Depreciation—Machinery	**(120,000)**	70,000		(50,000)
Total assets	(120,000)			(50,000)
Total liabilities	–0–			–0–
Retained earnings, 12/31 (above)	120,000			50,000
Total liabilities and equity	120,000			50,000
		70,000	70,000	

The IFRS column in the December 31, 2020, partial conversion worksheet (component depreciation) shows that component depreciation expense of $120,000 has a negative effect on net income (debit balance), which in turn has a negative impact on ending retained earnings (debit balance). The payment of $1,000,000 cash for machinery has a zero net effect on total assets. However, accumulated depreciation on the machinery results in a negative impact (credit) on total assets of $120,000.

The U.S. GAAP column in the preceding worksheet shows that straight-line depreciation has a negative impact on net income of $50,000. Ending retained earnings and total assets also are negatively affected by $50,000. The worksheet clearly demonstrates that adjusting the balances in the IFRS column by the debit/credit conversion entry results in the appropriate amounts being reported in the U.S. GAAP column.

Conversion from IFRS to U.S. GAAP—2021

In 2021, depreciation expense of $120,000 is recognized under IFRS ,but only $50,000 of depreciation would be recognized under U.S. GAAP. Therefore, the IFRS-to-U.S.-GAAP conversion entry at December 31, 2021, should once again credit depreciation expense by $70,000. Accumulated depreciation at December 31, 2021, is now $140,000 ($70,000 × 2 years) higher under IFRS than it would be under U.S. GAAP. A debit of $140,000 to accumulated depreciation is required to convert to U.S. GAAP. Because IFRS net income in 2021 was understated from a U.S. GAAP perspective by $70,000, the January 1, 2021, IFRS balance in retained earnings also is understated by the same amount. A credit of $70,000 to January 1 retained earnings is needed to increase the balance in this account from negative $120,000 to negative $70,000 on that date. The conversion entry at December 31, 2021 is as follows:

	Debit	Credit
Accumulated Depreciation—Machinery	140,000	
Depreciation Expense		70,000
Retained Earnings, 1/1/21		70,000

The December 31, 2021, partial conversion worksheet (component depreciation) next shows that this entry results in the correct amounts being reported under U.S. GAAP.

Partial Conversion Worksheet, 12/31/21 (Component Depreciation)

Account	IFRS	Conversion Entry Debit	Conversion Entry Credit	U.S. GAAP
Depreciation expense	**120,000**		70,000	**50,000**
Net income (negative)	120,000			50,000
Retained earnings, 1/1 (negative)	**120,000**		70,000	**50,000**
Retained earnings, 12/31 (negative)	240,000			100,000
Cash	(1,000,000)			(1,000,000)
Machinery	1,000,000			1,000,000
Accumulated Depreciation—Machinery	**(240,000)**	140,000		**(100,000)**
Total assets	(240,000)			(100,000)
Total liabilities	–0–			–0–
Retained earnings, 12/31 (above)	240,000			100,000
Total liabilities and equity	240,000			100,000
		140,000	140,000	

Property, Plant, and Equipment—Revaluation

Ammer acquired a building at the beginning of 2019 at a cost of $500,000. The building has an estimated useful life of 25 years and an estimated residual value of $100,000 and is depreciated on a straight-line basis. The company recorded $16,000 [($500,000 – $100,000)/25 years] of depreciation on the building in 2019, and the building had a carrying amount of $484,000 ($500,000 cost less $16,000 of accumulated depreciation) on December 31, 2019. At the beginning of 2020, the building was appraised and determined to have a fair value of $700,000, an estimated residual value of $100,000, and a remaining useful life of 24 years.

IFRS Treatment

IAS 16, "Property, Plant and Equipment," requires entities to choose between (a) the *cost model* or (b) the *revaluation model* to determine the carrying amount of property, plant, and equipment (PPE) subsequent to acquisition. The cost model carries an item of PPE at its cost less accumulated depreciation and any accumulated impairment losses. The revaluation model carries an item of PPE at a revalued amount, which is its fair value at the date of the revaluation, less any subsequent accumulated depreciation and subsequent accumulated impairment losses. Revaluations must be made with sufficient regularity to ensure that the *carrying amount* is not materially different from *fair value.* If an item of PPE is revalued, the entire class of assets to which that asset belongs must be revalued. The amount by which assets are revalued is recorded as a *revaluation surplus,* which is a component of accumulated other comprehensive income (AOCI).

Ammer has elected to use the revaluation model in measuring the carrying amount of its building, but uses the cost model for machinery and equipment. Therefore, Ammer revalued the building at the beginning of 2020. The company made the following journal entries related to revaluation of buildings in 2020:

January 1, 2020

	Debit	Credit
Accumulated Depreciation—Buildings	16,000	
Buildings		16,000
To eliminate accumulated depreciation on the building to be revalued, reducing the balance in Buildings to $484,000 ($500,000 – $16,000).		

	Debit	Credit
Buildings	216,000	
Revaluation Surplus (AOCI)		216,000
To revalue buildings to fair value on the revaluation date ($700,000 – $484,000 = $216,000) and recognize an increase in AOCI.		

December 31, 2020

Depreciation Expense	25,000	
Accumulated Depreciation—Buildings		25,000
To recognize annual depreciation based on the revalued amount of buildings [($700,000 – $100,000 salvage value)/24-year remaining life].		

As a result of applying the revaluation model, Ammer includes depreciation expense of $25,000 in 2020 net income, a revaluation surplus of $216,000 in AOCI, and carries the building on its December 31, 2020, balance sheet at $675,000 ($700,000 – $25,000).

U.S. GAAP Treatment

The revaluation of property, plant, and equipment is not allowed under U.S. GAAP. In 2020, the original cost of the building would continue to be depreciated at the rate of $16,000 per year, and the carrying amount of the building at December 31, 2020, would be $468,000 ($500,000 cost – $32,000 accumulated depreciation).

Conversion from IFRS to U.S. GAAP—2020

From a U.S. GAAP perspective, the revaluation model overstates 2020 depreciation expense by $9,000 ($25,000 – $16,000), overstates AOCI by $216,000, and overstates the carrying amount of buildings by $207,000 ($675,000 – $468,000). The following adjustment is needed to convert from IFRS to U.S. GAAP:

Revaluation Surplus (AOCI)	216,000	
Buildings		200,000
Accumulated Depreciation—Buildings		7,000
Depreciation Expense		9,000

As shown in the December 31, 2020, partial conversion worksheet (revaluation of buildings), this conversion entry increases net income and retained earnings by $9,000 (from negative $25,000 to negative $16,000) and decreases AOCI by $216,000. This results in a net decrease in equity of $207,000 (from positive $175,000 to negative $32,000). The net decrease in equity is offset on the other side of the balance sheet by an equal decrease in total assets of $207,000.

Partial Conversion Worksheet, 12/31/20 (Revaluation of Buildings)

		Conversion Entry		
Account	**IFRS**	**Debit**	**Credit**	**U.S. GAAP**
Depreciation expense	**25,000**		9,000	**16,000**
Net income, 2020 (negative)	25,000			16,000
Retained earnings, 1/1/20* (negative)	16,000			16,000
Retained earnings, 12/31/20 (negative)	41,000			32,000
Revaluation surplus	**(216,000)**	216,000		**–0–**
AOCI, 1/1/20	–0–			–0–
AOCI, 12/31/20	(216,000)			–0–
Cash	(500,000)			(500,000)
Buildings	**700,000**		200,000	**500,000**
Accumulated depreciation-buildings	**(25,000)**		7,000	**(32,000)**
Total assets	175,000			(32,000)
Total liabilities	–0–			–0–
Retained earnings, 12/31/20 (above)	41,000			–0–
AOCI, 12/31/20 (above)	(216,000)			–0–
Total liabilities and equity	(175,000)			32,000
		216,000	216,000	

*This reflects depreciation expense of $16,000 recognized in 2019.

Conversion from IFRS to U.S. GAAP—2021

In 2021, Ammer recognizes an additional $25,000 in depreciation expense on the revalued building. As a result, the building's carrying amount under IFRS on December 31, 2021, is $650,000 [$700,000 – $50,000 (= $25,000 × 2 years)]. Under U.S. GAAP, depreciation expense on the building would be $16,000, resulting in a carrying amount for the building on December 31, 2021, of $452,000 [($500,000 – $48,000 (= $16,000 × 3 years)]. The difference in carrying amount for the building is $198,000, composed of a $200,000 difference between cost and the revaluation amount, and a $2,000 difference in accumulated depreciation.

From a U.S. GAAP perspective, Ammer's beginning retained earnings in 2021 under IFRS is understated by $9,000, which is the difference in net income reported under the two sets of standards in 2020. In addition, the beginning balance in AOCI is overstated by $216,000 from a U.S. GAAP perspective. To convert from IFRS to U.S. GAAP, the worksheet entry at December 31, 2021 is as follows:

	Debit	Credit
AOCI, 1/1/21	216,000	
Accumulated Depreciation	2,000	
Equipment		200,000
Depreciation Expense		9,000
Retained Earnings, 1/1/21		9,000

The following December 31, 2021, partial conversion worksheet (revaluation of buildings) shows the amounts reported by Ammer under IFRS and the amounts that would be reported under U.S. GAAP. Posting the conversion entry to this worksheet results in the correct U.S. GAAP balances being reported.

Partial Conversion Worksheet, 12/31/21 (Revaluation of Buildings)

		Conversion Entry		
Account	**IFRS**	**Debit**	**Credit**	**U.S. GAAP**
Depreciation expense	**25,000**		9,000	**16,000**
Net income, 2021 (negative)	25,000			16,000
Retained earnings, 1/1/21 (negative)	**41,000**		9,000	**32,000**
Retained earnings, 12/31/21 (negative)	66,000			48,000
AOCI, 1/1/21	**(216,000)**	216,000		**–0–**
AOCI, 12/31/21	(216,000)			–0–
Cash	(500,000)			(500,000)
Buildings	**700,000**		200,000	**500,000**
Accumulated depreciation-equipment	**(50,000)**	2,000		**(48,000)**
Total assets	150,000			(48,000)
Total liabilities	–0–			–0–
AOCI, 12/31/21 (above)	(216,000)			–0–
Retained earnings, 12/31/21 (above)	66,000			48,000
Total liabilities and equity	(150,000)			48,000
		218,000	218,000	

Intangible Assets—Impairment

Ammer owns a brand (an indefinite-lived intangible asset) that it acquired for $440,000. On December 31, 2020, the brand is expected to generate future cash flows of $450,000, and it is estimated to have a fair value, after deducting costs to sell, of $360,000. The present value of expected future cash flows is $375,000.

IFRS Treatment

Under *IAS 36,* "Impairment of Assets," an asset is impaired when its carrying amount exceeds its recoverable amount. The *recoverable amount* of an asset is the *higher* of (a) its fair value less costs of disposal and (b) its value in use. *Value in use* is defined as the present value of the future cash flows expected to be derived from an asset.

The brand has a value in use of $375,000, and its fair value less costs of disposal is $360,000, so the recoverable amount is $375,000. Ammer recognized an impairment loss of $65,000 ($440,000 – $375,000) in determining 2020 net income, with a corresponding reduction in the carrying amount for the brand. The journal entry to record this is as follows:

Impairment Loss	65,000	
Brand		65,000
To recognize the impairment of a brand.		

U.S. GAAP Treatment

An asset is impaired under U.S. GAAP when its carrying amount exceeds its expected future cash flows, undiscounted to present value. Because the future cash flows expected to be generated by the brand of $450,000 exceed the carrying amount of $440,000, the brand is not impaired under U.S. GAAP, and no journal entry would be recorded.

Conversion from IFRS to U.S. GAAP—2020

To convert from IFRS to U.S. GAAP, the impairment loss recognized by Ammer must be reversed, and the carrying amount of the brand increased by $65,000. The conversion entry at December 31, 2020, is as follows:

Brand	65,000	
Impairment Loss		65,000

This entry increases assets, net income, and retained earnings by $65,000.

Conversion from IFRS to U.S. GAAP—2021

The impairment loss recognized by Ammer in 2020 was closed to retained earnings. From a U.S. GAAP perspective, Ammer's January 1, 2021, balance in retained earnings is understated, as is the carrying amount for the brand. The conversion entry needed at December 31, 2021, to convert from IFRS to U.S. GAAP is as follows:

Brand	65,000	
Retained Earnings, 1/1/21		65,000

Intangible Assets—Research and Development Expenditures

Ammer incurred the following costs in 2020 related to the research and development of a new product.

• Research expenditures, January–April	$8,000
• Development expenditures, May–June	8,000
• Development expenditures, July	4,000
• Development expenditures, August–October	5,000
• Construction of prototype, November	3,000
• Testing of prototype, December	2,000

The technical feasibility of the product was demonstrated on July 1, and a business plan detailing the feasibility of producing, financing, and selling the new product was written by August 1. The new product was brought to market at the beginning of 2021 and is expected to generate sales for five years.

IFRS Treatment

IAS 38, "Intangible Assets," requires *research expenditures* to be expensed as incurred. *Development expenditures,* on the other hand, are recognized as an intangible asset when an entity can demonstrate all of the following:

a. The technical feasibility of completing the intangible asset so that it will be available for use or sale.

b. Its intention to complete the intangible asset and use or sell it.

c. Its ability to use or sell the intangible asset.

d. How the intangible asset will generate probable future economic benefits. Among other things, the enterprise should demonstrate the existence of a market for the output of the intangible asset or the existence of the intangible asset itself or, if it is to be used internally, the usefulness of the intangible asset.

e. The availability of adequate technical, financial, and other resources to complete the development and to use or sell the intangible asset.

f. Its ability to measure the expenditure attributable to the intangible asset during its development reliably.

Ammer determined that all of the criteria for recognition of development expenditures as an intangible asset were met once the company finished its business plan related to the new product. Therefore, the company expensed the research and development costs incurred January–July ($20,000), and recognized an intangible asset for the development expenditures and prototype construction and testing costs incurred August–December ($10,000). Because Ammer had not yet begun sale of the new product, no amortization of the intangible asset was necessary in 2020. The company prepared the following journal entry in 2020:

Research and Development Expense	20,000	
Deferred Development Costs (intangible assets)	10,000	
Cash		30,000
To recognize a portion of research and development expenditures as expense and capitalize a portion as an intangible asset.		

U.S. GAAP Treatment

Other than computer software development costs, all research and development costs must be expensed immediately under U.S. GAAP. Thus, the entire $30,000 of research and development costs would be recognized as expense in 2020.

Conversion from IFRS to U.S. GAAP—2020

The following conversion worksheet entry is needed to derecognize the development costs deferred as an intangible asset under IFRS and recognize additional research and development expense under U.S. GAAP:

Research and Development Expense	10,000	
Deferred Development Costs (intangible assets)		10,000

This adjustment results in a decrease in net income and retained earnings of $10,000, offset by an equal decrease in assets.

Conversion from IFRS to U.S. GAAP—2021

Under IFRS, the deferred development cost intangible asset must be amortized over its useful life of five years (the number of years it is expected to generate sales). In 2021, Ammer recognizes amortization expense of $2,000, and the intangible asset has a carrying amount of $8,000 on December 31, 2021. From a U.S. GAAP perspective, neither the intangible asset nor its amortization should be recognized. In addition, Ammer's January 1, 2021, retained earnings balance is overstated by $10,000, the difference in 2020 net income under IFRS and U.S. GAAP. The December 31, 2021, entry necessary to convert IFRS balances to U.S. GAAP is as follows:

Retained earnings, 1/1/21	10,000	
Intangible Assets (deferred development costs)		8,000
Amortization Expense		2,000

Compound Financial Instruments—Convertible Bonds

Ammer issued $200,000 of convertible bonds at face value at the end of 2020. The bonds have a 10-year life with interest payable annually at an interest rate of 5 percent. Each bond has a face value of $1,000 and can be converted into 200 shares of common stock at any time up to maturity. At the date of issue, the prevailing rate for similar debt without a conversion feature is 6 percent, and the fair value of Ammer's common stock is $20 per share.

IFRS Treatment

Convertible bonds are a compound financial instrument, which *IAS 32*, "Financial Instruments: Presentation," requires to be split into a liability component and an equity component. The liability component is measured as the fair value of similar bonds that do not have an equity component. The equity component is the residual amount after subtracting the liability component from the fair value of the compound financial instrument as a whole. Applying this methodology, Ammer splits the $200,000 fair value of the convertible bonds into liability and equity components as follows:

Fair value of convertible bonds (original selling price)	$ 200,000
Liability component*	(185,280)
Equity component	$ 14,720

* Present value of $200,000 face value bonds with 10-year life paying 5 percent annual interest ($10,000), discounted at 6 percent: [$200,000 × (1/1.06)^{10})] + {[$10,000 × (1 – (1/1.06)^{10}] /0.06}

Ammer prepared the following journal entry to record the issuance of convertible bonds:

	Debit	Credit
Cash	200,000	
Bonds Payable		185,280
Additional Paid-in Capital—Convertible Bonds		14,720
To recognize the issuance of convertible bonds as separate liability and equity components.		

U.S. GAAP Treatment

Split accounting for convertible debt is not allowed under U.S. GAAP. The entire face value of the bonds ($200,000) must be recognized as a noncurrent liability, as follows:

	Debit	Credit
Cash	200,000	
Bonds Payable		200,000

Conversion from IFRS to U.S. GAAP—2020 and 2021

The following conversion worksheet entry must be made on December 31, 2020, to reclassify the equity component of the convertible bonds recognized under IFRS as a liability under U.S. GAAP:

	Debit	Credit
Additional Paid-in Capital—Convertible Bonds	14,720	
Bonds Payable		14,720

This adjustment has no effect on net income or retained earnings; noncurrent liabilities increase by $14,720 and stockholders' equity decreases by the same amount. The same conversion entry would be made at December 31, 2021.

Defined Benefit Pension Plan—Past Service Cost

At the beginning of 2020, Ammer amended its defined benefit pension plan creating a past service cost of $120,000. The average remaining number of years to be worked by the employees affected by the plan amendment is 15 years. The company has no retired employees.

IFRS Treatment

IAS 19, "Employee Benefits," requires past service cost to be recognized as expense when the plan amendment occurs. Therefore, in 2020, Ammer increased its defined benefit pension obligation and recognized past service cost expense in the amount of $120,000, as follows:

	Debit	Credit
Past Service Cost Expense	120,000	
Defined Benefit Obligation		120,000
To recognize past service cost expense and an increase in defined benefit obligation resulting from a defined benefit plan amendment.		

U.S. GAAP Treatment

Under U.S. GAAP, past service cost (referred to as prior service cost by the FASB) must be amortized to expense over the remaining service life of those employees affected by the plan amendment. As a result, only $8,000 [$120,000/15 years] of past service cost expense would be recognized in net income in 2020. The remaining $112,000 of past service cost to be recognized in net income over the next 14 years is treated as a component of accumulated other comprehensive income (AOCI) in 2020. The defined benefit pension obligation is increased by $120,000. The following journal entries would be made under U.S. GAAP:

January 1, 2020		
Deferred Past Service Costs (AOCI)	120,000	
Defined Benefit Obligation		120,000

December 31, 2020		
Past Service Cost Expense	8,000	
Deferred Past Service Costs (AOCI)		8,000

Conversion from IFRS to U.S. GAAP—2020

To convert to U.S. GAAP, $112,000 of past service cost expense recognized under IFRS must be deferred in AOCI. The following entry makes this conversion:

Deferred Past Service Costs (AOCI)	112,000	
Past Service Cost Expense		112,000

The December 31, 2020, partial conversion worksheet (past service cost) is shown next. The entry to convert from IFRS to U.S. GAAP increases net income and ending retained earnings by $112,000 (from negative $120,000 to negative $8,000). The conversion entry also decreases AOCI by the same amount (from $0 to negative $112,000). The increase in retained earnings and decrease in AOCI offset such that total equity is unaffected by this adjustment. Total assets and total liabilities also are unaffected.

Partial Conversion Worksheet, 12/31/20 (Past Service Cost)

		Conversion Entries		
Account	**IFRS**	**Debit**	**Credit**	**U.S. GAAP**
Past service cost expense	**120,000**		112,000	**8,000**
Net income, 2020 (negative)	120,000			8,000
Retained earnings, 1/1/20	–0–			–0–
Retained earnings, 12/31/20 (negative)	120,000			8,000
Deferred past service cost (AOCI)	**–0–**	112,000		**112,000**
AOCI, 1/1/20	–0–			–0–
AOCI, 12/31/20	–0–			112,000
Total assets	–0–			–0–
Defined benefit obligation	(120,000)			(120,000)
Total liabilities	(120,000)			(120,000)
AOCI, 12/31/20 (above)	–0–			112,000
Retained earnings, 12/31/20 (above)	120,000			8,000
Total liabilities and equity	–0–			–0–
		112,000	112,000	

Conversion from IFRS to U.S. GAAP—2021

Because the entire amount of past service cost was expensed in 2020, no further entries are needed in 2021 under IFRS. Under U.S. GAAP, an additional $8,000 of past service cost expense must be recognized in 2021 with an offsetting reduction in the deferred past service cost (AOCI). The following entry would be made under U.S. GAAP at December 31, 2021:

Past Service Cost Expense	8,000	
Deferred Past Service Cost (AOCI)		8,000

This entry reduces the carrying amount of deferred past service cost (a debit balance in AOCI) to $104,000 [$120,000 – $16,000 (= $8,000 × 2 years)].

From a U.S. GAAP perspective, the IFRS balances understate 2021 past service cost expense by $8,000 and beginning retained earnings by $112,000 (the difference in 2020 net income between IFRS and U.S. GAAP). In addition, AOCI is overstated by $104,000 (AOCI has a zero balance under IFRS but has a debit balance of $104,000 under U.S GAAP). The conversion entries needed at December 31, 2021, to convert from IFRS to U.S. GAAP are the following:

AOCI, 1/1/21	112,000	
Retained Earnings, 1/1/21		112,000

Past Service Cost Expense	8,000	
Deferred Past Service Cost (AOCI)		8,000

The December 31, 2021, partial conversion worksheet (past service cost) presented below reflects Ammer's account balances under IFRS and shows that the above conversion entries result in the correct balances being reported under U.S. GAAP.

Partial Conversion Worksheet, 12/31/21 (Past Service Cost)

		Conversion Entries		
Account	**IFRS**	**Debit**	**Credit**	**U.S. GAAP**
Past service cost expense	**–0–**	8,000		**8,000**
Net income, 2021 (negative)	–0–			8,000
Retained earnings, 1/1/21 (negative)	**120,000**		112,000	**8,000**
Retained earnings, 12/31/21 (negative)	120,000			16,000
Deferred past service cost (AOCI)	**–0–**		8,000	**(8,000)**
AOCI, 1/1/21	**–0–**	112,000		**112,000**
AOCI, 12/31/21	–0–			104,000
Total assets	–0–			–0–
Defined benefit obligation	(120,000)			(120,000)
Total liabilities	(120,000)			(120,000)
AOCI, 12/31/21 (above)	–0–			104,000
Retained earnings, 12/31/21 (above)	120,000			16,000
Total liabilities and equity	–0–			–0–
		120,000	120,000	

Business Combination—Noncontrolling Interest and Goodwill

Ammer acquired 90 percent of the outstanding shares of Ober AG at the end of 2020 by paying $360,000 in cash. At the date of acquisition, the book value of Ober's assets was $320,000, which was equal to fair value. The book value of Ober's liabilities was $40,000, which also was equal to fair value. Ammer must measure noncontrolling interest and goodwill at the date of acquisition.

IFRS Treatment

IFRS 3, "Business Combinations," allows noncontrolling interest to be measured either at (a) fair value (including goodwill) or (b) the proportionate interest in the values assigned to the assets acquired (excluding goodwill) and liabilities assumed. The acquirer can choose which of these treatments to follow. The amount recognized as goodwill depends upon the method selected to determine noncontrolling interest.

Ammer elected to measure noncontrolling interest in Ober using the "proportionate interest" approach. The acquisition-date amount of noncontrolling interest and goodwill were calculated as follows:

Fair value of net assets (excluding any goodwill) [$320,000 – $40,000]	$280,000
Noncontrolling interest %.	×10%
Fair value of noncontrolling interest	$ 28,000

Fair value of consideration transferred by Ammer (cash paid).	360,000
Plus: Fair value of noncontrolling interest.	28,000
Subtotal.	388,000
Less: Fair value of Ober's net assets (excluding goodwill)	280,000
Goodwill	$108,000

Under this approach, Ammer recognized noncontrolling interest in Ober of $28,000. Goodwill is measured as $108,000, which is the amount of goodwill deemed to have been acquired by Ammer in the business combination.

U.S. GAAP Treatment

Under U.S. GAAP, noncontrolling interest must be measured at fair value. Jameson's accountants have determined that this can best be measured based on the fair value of consideration transferred by Ammer to acquire a 90 percent interest in Ober. Because Ammer paid $360,000 for 90 percent of Ober, 100 percent of Ober has a fair value of $400,000 ($360,000/90%). Therefore, 10 percent of Ober has a fair value of $40,000 ($400,000 × 10%). This is the amount at which noncontrolling interest is measured. Accordingly, goodwill is determined as follows:

Fair value of controlling interest (cash paid by Ammer).	$360,000
Plus: Fair value of noncontrolling interest.	40,000
Total fair value of Ober AG	400,000
Less: Fair value of Ober's net assets (excluding goodwill)	280,000
Goodwill	$120,000

Under this approach, goodwill of $120,000 comprises $108,000 (90 percent) paid for by Ammer plus $12,000 (10 percent) attributed to the noncontrolling interest.

Conversion from IFRS to U.S. GAAP—2020 and 2021

To convert from IFRS to U.S. GAAP, both goodwill and noncontrolling interest must be increased on Ammer's consolidated balance sheet. This is accomplished with the following entry made on the December 31, 2020, conversion worksheet:

Goodwill	12,000	
Noncontrolling Interest		12,000

This adjustment has no effect on net income or retained earnings; total assets and total equity both increase by $12,000. A similar entry would be made on the December 31, 2021, conversion worksheet.

Questions

1. Historically, what factors contributed to the diversity of accounting systems worldwide?
2. Nestlé S.A. is a very large company headquartered in a very small country (Switzerland). It has operations in more than 50 different countries around the world. Much of the company's international expansion has been through the acquisition of local (i.e., foreign) companies. What problems does worldwide accounting diversity cause for a company like Nestlé?
3. Why were several original standards issued by the IASC revised in 1993?
4. In what ways does the IASB differ from the IASC?
5. What authoritative pronouncements make up International Financial Reporting Standards (IFRS)?
6. What are the different ways a country might use IFRS?
7. In general terms, how does *IFRS for SMEs* differ from full IFRS?
8. Some say that IFRS are now GAAP in the European Union. How is this statement true, and how is it false?
9. What are two countries that do not allow domestic publicly traded companies to use IFRS to prepare consolidated financial statements?
10. What are the steps that a company must follow in preparing its initial set of IFRS financial statements upon the company's first-time adoption of IFRS?
11. Under what circumstances might it be acceptable for a company preparing IFRS financial statements to follow an accounting treatment developed by the FASB?
12. When should a company begin gathering information about differences between IFRS and its existing GAAP to assist in its first-time adoption of IFRS?
13. What are the two extreme approaches that a company might follow in determining appropriate accounting policies for preparing its initial set of IFRS financial statements?
14. What did the FASB and IASB agree to do in the Norwalk Agreement?
15. Was the IASB–FASB convergence process successful?
16. How are IFRS currently used in the United States?
17. Why is it important for U.S. accountants to be familiar with IFRS?
18. What are two differences between IFRS and U.S. GAAP with respect to the recognition of financial statement items?
19. What are two differences between IFRS and U.S. GAAP with respect to the measurement of financial statement items?
20. What are two differences between IFRS and U.S. GAAP with respect to the classification of financial statement items?
21. Even if all companies in the world were to use IFRS, what are two obstacles to the worldwide comparability of financial statements?

Problems

LO 11-1

1. Which of the following historical reasons for accounting diversity could explain why accounting standards would be more detailed in some countries than in others?
   a. Different rates of inflation across countries
   b. Different legal systems across countries
   c. Differences across countries in the extent to which financial statements are the basis for taxation
   d. Political and economic ties between countries

LO 11-2

2. Which of the following is *not* a potential problem caused by differences in financial reporting practices across countries?
   a. Consolidation of financial statements by firms with foreign operations is more difficult.
   b. Firms incur additional costs when attempting to obtain financing in foreign countries.
   c. Firms face double taxation on income earned by foreign operations.
   d. Comparisons of financial ratios across firms in different countries may not be meaningful.

LO 11-2

3. Which of the following is *not* a reason for establishing international accounting standards?
   a. Some countries do not have the resources to develop accounting standards on their own.
   b. Comparability of financial reporting is needed between companies operating in different areas of the world.
   c. It would simplify the preparation of consolidated financial statements by multinational corporations.
   d. Demand in the United States is heavy for an alternative to U.S. generally accepted accounting principles.

LO 11-3

4. According to the IASB, IFRS comprise interpretations issued by the SIC and IFRIC, and
   a. International financial reporting standards issued by the IASB only.
   b. International accounting standards issued by the IASC only.
   c. International financial reporting standards issued by the IASB and international accounting standards issued by the IASC.
   d. International financial reporting standards issued by the IASB and statements of financial accounting standards issued by the FASB.

LO 11-4

5. Which of the following countries uses IFRS?
   a. Canada.
   b. Mexico.
   c. Brazil.
   d. All of these answer choices are correct.

LO 11-4

6. According to the IFRS Foundation, approximately how many countries either require or permit the use of IFRS by publicly traded companies?
   a. 40 countries
   b. 80 countries
   c. 130 countries
   d. 195 countries

LO 11-5

7. For which of the following types of companies is *IFRS for SMEs* intended?
   a. Private companies
   b. Publicly traded companies
   c. Multinational corporations
   d. Foreign companies

LO 11-5

8. For which of the following does *IFRS for SMEs* not provide a simplification of full IFRS?
   a. Goodwill
   b. Borrowing costs
   c. Development costs
   d. Inventory

LO 11-6

9. A company must prepare IFRS financial statements for the first time on December 31, 2022. According to *IFRS 1,* what is the date of transition to IFRS for this company?
   a. January 1, 2020
   b. January 1, 2021
   c. December 31, 2021
   d. December 31, 2022

LO 11-6

10. Which of the following does *not* accurately describe a requirement that a company must fulfill when adopting IFRS for the first time?
    a. The company must prepare an opening IFRS balance sheet at the beginning of the year for which the company is preparing its first set of IFRS financial statements.
    b. At the IFRS transition date, the company must select IFRS accounting policies based on those that will be in effect for the accounting period that will be covered by the first set of IFRS financial statements.
    c. At the IFRS transition date, the company must derecognize assets and liabilities that were recognized under previous GAAP that are not allowed to be recognized under IFRS.
    d. The company must provide a reconciliation of net income and stockholders' equity under previous GAAP to net income and stockholders' equity under IFRS in its first set of IFRS financial statements.

LO 11-6

11. Which of the following statements is correct with respect to the IFRS accounting policy hierarchy in situations where a specifically relevant IASB standard dealing with an accounting issue does not exist?
    a. The IASB *Conceptual Framework for Financial Reporting* takes precedence over other IASB standards that deal with related issues.
    b. The IASB *Conceptual Framework for Financial Reporting* takes precedence over standards developed by standard-setting bodies in other countries that deal with the specific accounting issue.

c. The most recent specifically relevant pronouncement of any other standard-setting body may be used when neither IASB standards nor the IASB *Conceptual Framework for Financial Reporting* provide helpful guidance.

d. IFRSs take precedence over IASs and Interpretations in identifying appropriate guidance.

LO 11-7

12. What was the so-called Norwalk Agreement?
    a. An agreement between the FASB and SEC to allow foreign companies to use IFRS in their filing of financial statements with the SEC
    b. An agreement between the U.S. FASB and the U.K. Accounting Standards Board to converge their respective accounting standards as soon as practicable
    c. An agreement between the SEC chairman and the EU Internal Market commissioner to allow EU companies to list securities in the United States without providing a U.S. GAAP reconciliation
    d. An agreement between the FASB and the IASB to make their existing standards compatible as soon as practicable and to work together to ensure compatibility in the future.

LO 11-7

13. Which of the following statements is true for a foreign company registered with the U.S. SEC to list its stock on the New York Stock Exchange?
    a. The company must file an annual report with the SEC that is prepared in accordance with U.S. GAAP.
    b. The company may file an annual report with the SEC that is prepared in accordance with IFRS but must also provide a reconciliation of IFRS to U.S. GAAP.
    c. The company must file an annual report with the SEC that is prepared in accordance with IFRS but must also provide a reconciliation of IFRS to U.S. GAAP.
    d. The company may file an annual report with the SEC that is prepared in accordance with IFRS but need not also provide a reconciliation of IFRS to U.S. GAAP.

LO 11-7

14. Which of the following best describes the extent to which the SEC requires or permits the use of IFRS by U.S. public companies?
    a. U.S. public companies are required to use IFRS.
    b. U.S. public companies may choose between IFRS and U.S. GAAP.
    c. U.S. public companies may use IFRS, but must also provide a reconciliation to U.S. GAAP.
    d. U.S. public companies are neither required nor allowed to use IFRS.

LO 11-7

15. Which companies are required to provide a U.S. GAAP reconciliation in their annual report filed with the SEC?
    a. All foreign companies listed on a U.S. securities exchange
    b. Foreign companies listed on a U.S. securities exchange that use IFRS in preparing financial statements
    c. Domestic U.S. companies listed on a U.S. securities exchange that use IFRS in preparing financial statements
    d. Foreign companies listed on a U.S. securities exchange that use financial reporting standards other than U.S. GAAP or IFRS in preparing financial statements

LO 11-8

16. Under IFRS, when an entity chooses the revaluation model as its accounting policy for measuring property, plant, and equipment, which of the following statements is correct?
    a. When an asset is revalued, the entire class of property, plant, and equipment (such as Land) to which that asset belongs must be revalued.
    b. When an asset is revalued, it is reported on the balance sheet at its current replacement cost.
    c. Revaluations of property, plant, and equipment must be made at least every three years.
    d. The revalued assets must be reported in a special section of the balance sheet separate from those assets measured using the cost model.

LO 11-8

17. In which of the following areas does the IASB *not* allow firms to choose between two acceptable treatments?
    a. Measuring property, plant, and equipment subsequent to acquisition.
    b. Measuring noncontrolling interest in a business combination.
    c. Recognizing development costs that meet criteria for capitalization as an asset.
    d. Classifying interest paid in the statement of cash flows.

Problems 18–24 assume that a foreign company using IFRS is owned by a company using U.S. GAAP. Thus, IFRS balances must be converted to U.S. GAAP to prepare consolidated financial statements. Ignore income taxes for each problem.

LO 11-9

18. Izmir A.S. issued convertible bonds at their face value of 100,000 lira on December 31, 2020. The bonds have a 10-year life with interest of 10 percent payable annually. At the date of issue, the prevailing interest rate for similar debt without a conversion option was 12 percent.
    a. Determine the appropriate accounting for this compound financial instrument for the year ending December 31, 2020, under (1) IFRS and (2) U.S. GAAP.
    b. Prepare the entry(ies) that the U.S. parent would make on the December 31, 2020, conversion worksheet to convert IFRS balances to U.S. GAAP.

LO 11-9

19. Surat Limited paid cash to acquire an aircraft on January 1, 2020, at a cost of 30,000,000 rupees. The aircraft has an estimated useful life of 40 years and no salvage value. The company has determined that the aircraft is composed of three significant components with the following original costs (in rupees) and estimated useful lives:

Component	Cost	Useful Life
Fuselage	10,000,000	40 years
Engines	15,000,000	30 years
Interior	5,000,000	20 years
	30,000,000	

The U.S. parent of Surat does not depreciate assets on a component basis, but instead depreciates assets over their estimated useful life as a whole.
    a. Determine the appropriate accounting for this aircraft for the years ending December 31, 2020, and December 31, 2021, under (1) IFRS and (2) U.S. GAAP.
    b. Prepare the entry(ies) that the U.S. parent would make on the December 31, 2020, and December 31, 2021, conversion worksheets to convert IFRS balances to U.S. GAAP.

LO 11-9

20. On January 1, 2020, Xiamen Company made amendments to its defined benefit pension plan that resulted in 60,000 yuan of past service cost. The plan has 5,000 active employees with an average expected remaining working life of 15 years. There currently are no retirees under the plan.
    a. Determine the appropriate accounting for the past service cost for the years ending December 31, 2020, and December 31, 2021, under (1) IFRS and (2) U.S. GAAP.
    b. Prepare the entry(ies) that the U.S. parent would make on the December 31, 2020, and December 31, 2021, conversion worksheets to convert IFRS balances to U.S. GAAP.

LO 11-9

21. Mikkeli OY acquired a brand name with an indefinite life in 2021 for 40,000 markkas. At December 31, 2020, the brand name could be sold for 35,000 markkas, with zero costs to sell. Expected cash flows from the continued use of the brand are 42,000 markkas, and the present value of this amount is 34,000 markkas.
    a. Determine the appropriate accounting for this brand name for the year ending December 31, 2020, under (1) IFRS and (2) U.S. GAAP.
    b. Prepare the entry(ies) that the U.S. parent would make on the December 31, 2020, conversion worksheet to convert IFRS balances to U.S. GAAP.

LO 11-9

22. Llungby AB spent 1,000,000 krone in 2020 on the development of a new product. The company determined that 25 percent of this amount was incurred after the criteria in *IAS 36* for capitalization as an intangible asset had been met. The newly developed product is brought to market in January 2021 and is expected to generate sales revenue for five years.
    a. Determine the appropriate accounting for development costs for the years ending December 31, 2020, and December 31, 2021, under (1) IFRS and (2) U.S. GAAP.
    b. Prepare the entry(ies) that the U.S. parent would make on the December 31, 2020, and December 31, 2021, conversion worksheets to convert IFRS balances to U.S. GAAP.

LO 11-9

23. Sapporo K.K. was sued by a competitor in late 2020, and company management concluded that there was a 55 percent probability that the company would lose the lawsuit. The best estimate of the loss on December 31, 2020, was 4,000,000 yen. In 2021, the lawsuit is concluded with Sapporo paying its competitor 5,000,000 yen on May 15, 2021.

a. Determine the appropriate accounting for this lawsuit for the years ending December 31, 2020, and December 31, 2021, under (1) IFRS and (2) U.S. GAAP.

b. Prepare the entry(ies) that the U.S. parent would make on the December 31, 2020, and December 31, 2021, conversion worksheets to convert IFRS balances to U.S. GAAP.

LO 11-9

24. Tapatio S.A. de C.V. acquired a new piece of manufacturing equipment on January 1, 2019, for a cash price of 500,000 pesos. The equipment was expected to have a useful life of 10 years and no residual value, and is being depreciated on a straight-line basis. On January 1, 2020, the equipment was appraised and determined to have a fair value of 540,000 pesos, zero salvage value, and a remaining useful life of 9 years. Tapatio uses the revaluation model in *IAS 16* to measure equipment subsequent to acquisition. Any revaluation surplus will be recycled to retained earnings when the equipment is disposed of.

    a. Determine the appropriate accounting for this equipment for the years ending December 31, 2020, and December 31, 2021, under (1) IFRS and (2) U.S. GAAP.

    b. Prepare the entry(ies) that the U.S. parent would make on the December 31, 2020, and December 31, 2021, conversion worksheets to convert IFRS balances to U.S. GAAP.

Problems 25–28 assume that a U.S.-based company is issuing securities to foreign investors who require financial statements prepared in accordance with IFRS. Thus, adjustments to convert from U.S. GAAP to IFRS must be made. Ignore income taxes for each problem.

LO 11-9

25. Harrington Company was sued by an employee in late 2020. General counsel concluded that there was an 80 percent probability that the company would lose the lawsuit. The range of possible loss is estimated to be $20,000 to $70,000, with no amount in the range more likely than any other. The lawsuit was settled in 2021, with Harrington making a payment of $60,000.

    a. Determine the appropriate accounting for this lawsuit for the years ending December 31, 2020, and December 31, 2021, under (1) U.S. GAAP and (2) IFRS.

    b. Prepare the entry(ies) that Harrington would make on the December 31, 2020, and December 31, 2021, conversion worksheets to convert U.S. GAAP balances to IFRS.

LO 11-9

26. Parnell Company acquired construction equipment on January 1, 2020, at a cost of $78,400. The equipment was expected to have a useful life of six years and a residual value of $10,000 and is being depreciated on a straight-line basis. On January 1, 2021, the equipment was appraised and determined to have a fair value of $74,500, a salvage value of $10,000, and a remaining useful life of five years. In measuring property, plant, and equipment subsequent to acquisition under IFRS, Parnell would opt to use the revaluation model in *IAS 16*.

    a. Determine the appropriate accounting for this equipment for the years ending December 31, 2020, and December 31, 2021, under (1) U.S. GAAP and (2) IFRS.

    b. Prepare the entry(ies) that Parnell would make on the December 31, 2021, conversion worksheet to convert U.S. GAAP balances to IFRS.

LO 11-9

27. Trecek Corporation incurs research and development costs of $650,000 in 2020, 30 percent of which relate to development activities subsequent to *IAS 36* criteria having been met that indicate an intangible asset has been created. The newly developed product is brought to market in January 2021 and is expected to generate sales revenue for 10 years.

    a. Determine the appropriate accounting for research and development costs for the years ending December 31, 2020, and December 31, 2021, under (1) U.S. GAAP and (2) IFRS.

    b. Prepare the entry(ies) that Trecek would make on the December 31, 2020, and December 31, 2021, conversion worksheets to convert U.S. GAAP balances to IFRS.

LO 11-9

28. Hirsch Company acquired equipment at the beginning of 2020 at a cost of $135,000. The equipment has a five-year life with no expected salvage value and is depreciated on a straight-line basis. At December 31, 2020, Hirsch compiled the following information related to this equipment:

Expected future cash flows from use of the equipment	$116,000
Present value of expected future cash flows from use of the equipment	100,000
Fair value (selling price less costs to dispose)	96,600

    a. Determine the appropriate accounting for this equipment for the years ending December 31, 2020, and December 31, 2021, under (1) U.S. GAAP and (2) IFRS.

    b. Prepare the entry(ies) that Hirsch would make on the December 31, 2020, and December 31, 2021, conversion worksheets to convert U.S. GAAP balances to IFRS. Ignore the possibility of any additional impairment at the end of 2021.

Develop Your Skills

ANALYSIS CASE 1—APPLICATION OF *IAS 16*

CPA skills

Abacab Company's shares are listed on the New Market Stock Exchange, which allows the use of either IFRS or U.S. GAAP. On January 1, Year 1, Abacab Company acquired a building at a cost of $10 million. The building has a 20-year useful life and no residual value and is depreciated on a straight-line basis. On January 1, Year 3, the company hired an appraiser who determines the fair value of the building (net of any accumulated depreciation) to be $12 million.

IAS 16, "Property, Plant, and Equipment," requires assets to be initially measured at cost. Subsequent to initial recognition, assets may be carried either at cost less accumulated depreciation and any impairment losses (the cost model) or at a revalued amount equal to fair value at the date of the revaluation less any subsequent accumulated depreciation and impairment losses (the revaluation model). If a firm chooses to use the revaluation model, the counterpart to the revaluation of the asset is recorded as an increase in stockholders' equity (as a component of Accumulated Other Comprehensive Income). Subsequent depreciation is based on the revalued amount less any residual value.

U.S. GAAP requires items of property, plant, and equipment to be initially measured at cost. U.S. GAAP does not allow property, plant, and equipment to be revalued above original cost at subsequent balance sheet dates. The cost of property, plant, and equipment must be depreciated on a systematic basis over its useful life. Subsequent to initial recognition, assets must be carried at cost less accumulated depreciation and any impairment losses.

Required

a. Determine the amount of depreciation expense recognized in Year 2, Year 3, and Year 4 under (1) the revaluation model in *IAS 16* and (2) U.S. GAAP.

b. Determine the book value of the building under the two different sets of accounting rules at January 2, Year 3; December 31, Year 3; and December 31, Year 4.

c. Summarize the difference in net income and in stockholders' equity over the 20-year life of the building using the two different sets of accounting rules.

ANALYSIS CASE 2—RECONCILIATION OF IFRS TO U.S. GAAP

CPA skills

Vitous Ltd. began operations on January 1, 2018, and uses IFRS to prepare its consolidated financial statements. Although not required to do so, to facilitate comparisons with companies in the United States, Vitous keeps its books in U.S. dollars ($), and reconciles its net income and stockholders' equity to U.S. GAAP. Information relevant for preparing this reconciliation is as follows:

1. Vitous carries fixed assets at revalued amounts. Fixed assets were revalued upward on January 1, 2020, by $35,000. At that time, fixed assets had a remaining useful life of 10 years.
2. On January 1, 2019, Vitous issued $50,000 of convertible bonds. The company measured the liability component of the bonds to be $45,000, and the equity component of the bonds as $5,000.
3. Vitous capitalized development costs related to a new pharmaceutical product in 2019 in the amount of $80,000. Vitous began selling the new product on January 1, 2020, and expects the product to be marketable for a total of five years.

Net income under IFRS in 2020 is $100,000, and stockholders' equity under IFRS at December 31, 2020, is $1,000,000. Ignore income taxes.

Required

a. Prepare a schedule to reconcile Vitous's 2020 net income and December 31, 2020, stockholders' equity under IFRS to U.S. GAAP.

b. Provide a brief title/description for each reconciling adjustment made, indicate the U.S. dollar amount of the adjustment, and calculate total amounts for net income and stockholders' equity under U.S. GAAP.

RESEARCH CASE—DIFFERENCES BETWEEN IFRS AND U.S. GAAP

CPA skills

A company located in a foreign country is preparing for a listing of its common shares on the New York Stock Exchange in the United States. The company must decide whether to use U.S. GAAP or IFRS in preparing the financial statements that will accompany its registration with the U.S. Securities and Exchange Commission and has hired you to research several accounting issues related to making this decision. The accounting issues and specific questions the company would like you to research are the following:

1. The equity method of accounting is used to account for investments in investee companies over which the investor has significant influence. Should "potential voting rights" be considered in determining whether the investor has significant influence?
2. Contingent liabilities (provisions) must be recognized on the balance sheet when certain conditions are met. Should contingent liabilities (provisions) be measured at a discounted amount (that is, at present value)?
3. Some gains and losses are included in other comprehensive income (rather than net income). Should these items be accumulated and reported separately on the statement of financial position (balance sheet)?
4. An event that occurs after the balance sheet date that provides additional evidence about conditions existing at the balance sheet date usually requires an adjustment to the financial statements. What is the post-balance-sheet cutoff date for determining events that require an adjustment?

Comparisons of U.S. GAAP and IFRS prepared by international public accounting firms are readily available on the internet. An example is the "US GAAP/IFRS Accounting Differences Identifier Tool: January 2019" prepared by Ernst & Young LLP (EY), available at www.ey.com.

Required

Prepare a brief report answering the questions in items 1–4 for both IFRS and U.S. GAAP. Summarize the implications any differences between the two sets of standards with regard to these questions would have for financial reporting.

INTERNET CASE 1—FOREIGN COMPANY ANNUAL REPORT

CPA skills

Many non-U.S. companies make annual reports available on their corporate website. Access the financial statements from the most recent annual report for a non-U.S. company with which you are familiar to complete this assignment.

Required

a. Determine the set of accounting rules (GAAP) the company uses to prepare its financial statements.

b. Determine whether the company provides a set of financial statements comparable to the set of financial statements provided by U.S. companies.

c. List differences between the company's income statement and the income statement of a typical U.S. corporation.

d. List differences between the company's balance sheet and the balance sheet of a typical U.S. corporation.

e. Determine whether the scope and content of the information provided in the notes to the financial statements are comparable to the information provided in the notes to the financial statements by a typical U.S. corporation.

f. Evaluate the overall presentation of financial statements and notes to financial statements by the company in comparison with a typical U.S. corporation.

INTERNET CASE 2—IFRS WEBSITE

The IFRS Foundation and IASB maintain a website at www.ifrs.org. Go to this website and access "Use of IFRS Standards by jurisdiction" (click on the "Around the World" tab). Select a country of interest, and access its "Jurisdictional Profile" (available as PDF file) to complete this assignment.

Required

Prepare a short report summarizing the extent to which full IFRS and *IFRS for SMEs* are used in your country of interest.

chapter

12

Financial Reporting and the Securities and Exchange Commission

The Securities and Exchange Commission was born on June 6, 1934—a time of despair in the markets. Americans were still suffering from the 1929 market crash after a roaring 1920s when they bought about $50 billion in new securities—half of which turned out to be worthless. Their confidence also was eroded by the 1932 indictment (later acquittal) of Samuel Insull for alleged wrongs in the collapse of his utility "empire" and by the 1933–34 Senate hearings on improper market activity.

The financing of U.S. industry depends on raising vast amounts of capital. During every business day in the United States, many billions of dollars of stocks, bonds, and other securities are sold to thousands of individuals, corporations, trust funds, pension plans, mutual funds, and other investors. Such investors cannot be expected to venture their money without forethought. They have to be able to assess the risks involved: the possibility of either a profit or loss being returned to them as well as the expected amount.

Consequently, disclosure of sufficient, accurate information is needed to stimulate the inflow of large quantities of capital. Enough data must be available to encourage investors to consider buying and selling securities in hopes of generating profits. With inadequate or unreliable information on which to base these decisions, investing becomes little more than gambling.

Learning Objectives

After studying this chapter, you should be able to:

- **LO 12-1** Understand the origin and expansive role of the Securities and Exchange Commission.
- **LO 12-2** Describe the purpose(s) of various federal securities laws.
- **LO 12-3** Understand the Congressional rationale for enacting the Sarbanes–Oxley Act and the responsibilities of the Public Company Accounting Oversight Board.
- **LO 12-4** Describe the SEC's role in establishing generally accepted accounting principles (GAAP).
- **LO 12-5** Define and describe an issuer's filings with the Securities and Exchange Commission.
- **LO 12-6** Describe an issuer's registration process, various forms used by the issuers, and the exemption(s) from registration.

The Work of the Securities and Exchange Commission

In the United States, the responsibility for ensuring that complete and reliable information is available to investors lies with the Securities and Exchange Commission (SEC), an independent agency of the federal government created by the Securities Exchange Act of 1934. Although the SEC's authority applies mainly to publicly held companies, the commission's guidelines and requirements have had a major influence in the United States on the development of all generally accepted accounting principles (GAAP).

As described on the SEC's website:

> The mission of the U.S. Securities and Exchange Commission is to protect investors, maintain fair, orderly, and efficient markets, and facilitate capital formation.
>
> As more and more first-time investors turn to the markets to help secure their futures, pay for homes, and send children to college, our investor protection mission is more compelling than ever.

LO 12-1

Understand the origin and expansive role of the Securities and Exchange Commission.

> As our nation's securities exchanges mature into global for-profit competitors, there is even greater need for sound market regulation.
>
> And the common interest of all Americans in a growing economy that produces jobs, improves our standard of living, and protects the value of our savings means that all of the SEC's actions must be taken with an eye toward promoting the capital formation that is necessary to sustain economic growth.
>
> The world of investing is fascinating and complex, and it can be very fruitful. But unlike the banking world, where deposits are guaranteed by the federal government, stocks, bonds and other securities can lose value. There are no guarantees. That's why investing is not a spectator sport. By far the best way for investors to protect the money they put into the securities markets is to do research and ask questions.
>
> The laws and rules that govern the securities industry in the United States derive from a simple and straightforward concept: all investors, whether large institutions or private individuals, should have access to certain basic facts about an investment prior to buying it, and so long as they hold it. To achieve this, the SEC requires public companies to disclose meaningful financial and other information to the public. This provides a common pool of knowledge for all investors to use to judge for themselves whether to buy, sell, or hold a particular security. Only through the steady flow of timely, comprehensive, and accurate information can people make sound investment decisions.[1]

The SEC is headed by five commissioners appointed by the president of the United States (with the consent of the Senate) to serve five-year staggered terms. To ensure the bipartisan nature of this group, no more than three of these individuals can belong to the same political party. The chairman is from the same political party as the president. The commissioners provide leadership for an agency that has grown over the years into an organization with approximately 4,600 employees in 11 regional locations. Despite its importance, the SEC is a relatively small component of the federal government. However, the SEC generates significant fees primarily from issuers, relative to 8-K, 10-K, 10-Q, and registration statement fees. This results in a fully self-funded SEC.

The SEC is composed of five divisions and 23 offices including the following:

- The *Division of Corporation Finance* has responsibility to ensure that publicly held companies meet disclosure requirements. This division reviews registration statements, annual and quarterly filings, proxy materials, annual reports, and tender offers.
- The *Division of Trading and Markets* oversees the securities markets in this country and is responsible for registering and regulating brokerage firms. This division also oversees the Securities Investor Protection Corporation (SIPC), a nonprofit corporation that provides insurance for cash and securities held by customers in member brokerage firms. This insurance protects ("insures") against the failure of the member brokerage firms.
- The *Division of Enforcement* helps to ensure compliance with federal securities laws. This division investigates possible violations of securities laws and recommends appropriate remedies. The most common issues facing this division are insider trading, misrepresentation or omission of important information about securities, manipulation of the market price of a security, and issuance of securities without proper registration. According to the SEC Division of Enforcement's 2018 annual report, 821 investigations of possible violations were initiated in 2018.
- The *Division of Investment Management* oversees the $66.8 trillion[2] investment management industry and administers the securities laws affecting investment companies including mutual funds and investment advisers. This division also interprets laws and regulations for the public and the SEC staff.
- The *Division of Economic and Risk Analysis* assists the SEC in efforts to protect investors, maintain efficient markets, and facilitate capital creation. This Division interacts with every SEC Division and office and provides access to sophisticated economic and risk analysis to help advise and inform policymakers and rule makers.

[1] The U.S. Securities and Exchange Commission, SEC website, March 2019. Available at www.sec.gov/Article/whatwedo.html.

[2] Ibid.

- The *Office of Information Technology* supports the SEC and its staff in all aspects of information technology. This office operates the Electronic Data Gathering Analysis and Retrieval (EDGAR) system, which electronically receives, processes, and disseminates more than half a million financial statements every year. This office also maintains a very active website that contains a tremendous amount of data about the SEC and the securities industry and free access to EDGAR.[3]
- The *Office of Compliance Inspections and Examinations* determines whether brokers, dealers, and investment companies and advisers comply with federal securities laws. One of the most important goals of this office is the quick and often informal correction of compliance problems.
- The *Office of the Chief Accountant* is the principal adviser to the commission on accounting and auditing matters that arise in connection with the securities laws. The office also works closely with private sector bodies such as the FASB and the AICPA that set various accounting and auditing standards.

This chapter provides an overview of the workings of the Securities and Exchange Commission as well as the agency's relationship to the accounting profession. Because complete examination of the organization is beyond the scope of this textbook, we discuss only a portion of the SEC's extensive functions here. This coverage introduces the role the agency currently plays in the world of U.S. business.

LO 12-2

Describe the purpose(s) of various federal securities laws.

Purpose of the Federal Securities Laws

Before examining the SEC and its various functions in more detail, a historical perspective should be established. The development of laws regulating companies involved in interstate commerce was discussed as early as 1885. In fact, the Industrial Commission created by Congress suggested in 1902 that all publicly held companies should be required to disclose material information including annual financial reports. However, the crisis following the stock market crash of 1929 and the widespread fraud that was subsequently discovered were necessary to prompt Congress to act in hope of reestablishing the trust and stability needed for the capital markets.

> Before the Great Crash of 1929, there was little support for federal regulation of the securities markets. This was particularly true during the post–World War I surge of securities activity. Proposals that the federal government require financial disclosure and prevent the fraudulent sale of stock were never seriously pursued.
>
> Tempted by promises of "rags to riches" transformations and easy credit, most investors gave little thought to the systemic risk that arose from widespread abuse of margin financing and unreliable information about the securities in which they were investing. During the 1920s, approximately 20 million large and small shareholders took advantage of post-war prosperity and set out to make their fortunes in the stock market. It is estimated that of the $50 billion in new securities offered during this period, half became worthless.
>
> When the stock market crashed in October 1929, public confidence in the markets plummeted . . . There was a consensus that for the economy to recover, the public's faith in the capital markets needed to be restored.[4]

As a result, Congress enacted two primary pieces of securities legislation designed to restore investor trust in the capital markets by providing more structure and government oversight:

- The Securities Act of 1933, often referred to as the *truth in securities law,* regulates the initial offering of securities by a company or underwriter.
- The Securities Exchange Act of 1934, which actually created the SEC, regulates the subsequent trading of securities through brokers and exchanges.

These laws criminalized many abuses that had been common practices such as the manipulation of stock market prices and the misuse of corporate information by officials and directors

[3] For EDGAR Search Tools, see www.sec.gov/edgar/searchedgar/webusers.htm.

[4] U.S. Securities and Exchange Commission, SEC website, March 2016. Available at www.sec.gov/Article/whatwedo.html#create.

(often referred to as *inside parties*)[5] for their own personal gain. Just as important, these two legislative actions were designed to help rebuild public confidence in the capital market system. Because of the large losses suffered during the 1929 market crash and the subsequent depression, fewer investors bought stocks, bonds, or other securities.

This reduction in the pool of available capital dramatically compounded the economic problems of the day.

The creation of federal securities laws did not end with the 1933 Act and the 1934 Act. During the decades since the first commissioners were appointed, the SEC has administered rules and regulations created by a number of different congressional actions. Despite the passage of subsequent legislation, this organization's major objectives have remained relatively constant. Over the years, the SEC has attempted to achieve several interconnected goals, including

- Ensuring that full and fair information is disclosed to all investors before the securities of a company are allowed to be bought and sold.
- Prohibiting the dissemination of materially misstated information.
- Preventing the misuse of information, especially by inside parties.
- Regulating the operation of securities markets such as the New York Stock Exchange and the various over-the-counter exchanges.

In many regards, the SEC's work has been a success. However, a cloud has rested over the entire U.S. capital market system. In the early 2000s, a number of highly publicized corporate scandals shook public confidence in the financial information available for decision-making purposes. Where once most investors appeared to believe in the overall integrity of the stock markets, that faith clearly diminished, although the problem did not reach the magnitude seen in the 1930s. This lack of confidence was a drag on the general willingness to invest and, thus, on the economy as a whole.

A number of reasons can be put forth for these scandals. Some of them are

- Greed by corporate executives.
- Failure in the corporate governance process as practiced by many boards of directors.
- Failure of public accounting firms to apply appropriate quality control measures to ensure independent judgments.
- Shortcomings in promulgated standards used to self-regulate the accounting profession.
- Unreasonable market expectations brought on by years of skyrocketing stock values fueled in part by technology stocks.
- A workload that overburdened the Securities and Exchange Commission, which the relatively small agency could not handle in an adequate fashion.

As a result, on July 30, 2002, President George W. Bush signed the Sarbanes–Oxley Act of 2002. This wide-ranging legislation was designed to end many of the problems that had plagued corporate reporting and the securities markets in the early 2000's in the hope of restoring public confidence. This law has had an enormous impact on public accounting as well as the reporting required in connection with the issuance of securities.

Full and Fair Disclosure

No responsibility of the SEC is more vital than that of ensuring that a company has disclosed sufficient, reliable information before its stocks, bonds, or other securities are publicly traded. Reporting problems that became the scandals at companies such as Enron, WorldCom, Adelphia, and Tyco still draw increased attention to this role.

[5] *Inside parties* usually are identified as the officers of a company as well as its directors and any owners of more than 10 percent of any class of equity security. An individual's level of ownership is measured by a person's own holdings of equity securities as well as ownership by related parties such as a spouse, minor children, relatives living in the same house as the person in question, or a trust in which the person is the beneficiary.

Unless specifically exempted, all publicly held companies (frequently referred to as *issuers* or *registrants*) must periodically file detailed reports with the SEC. The SEC requires these filings as a result of laws passed by Congress in the 1930s and the following decades.

1. *Securities Act of 1933*: Requires the registration of new securities offered for public sale so that potential investors can have adequate information. The act is also intended to prevent deceit and misrepresentation in connection with the sale of securities.[6]
2. *Securities Exchange Act of 1934*: Created the SEC and empowered it to require reporting by publicly owned companies and registration of securities, security exchanges, and certain brokers and dealers. This act prohibits fraudulent and unfair behavior such as sales practice abuses and insider trading.
3. *Public Utility Holding Company Act of 1935*: Requires registration of interstate holding companies of public utilities covered by this law. This act was passed because of abuses in the 1920s in which huge, complex utility empires were created to minimize the need for equity financing.
4. *Trust Indenture Act of 1939*: Requires registration of trust indenture documents and supporting data in connection with the public sale of bonds, debentures, notes, and other debt securities.
5. *Investment Company Act of 1940*: Requires registration of investment companies, including mutual funds, that engage in investing and trading in securities. This act is designed in part to minimize conflicts of interest that arise with fund management.
6. *Investment Advisers Act of 1940* and *Securities Investor Protection Act of 1970*: Require investment advisers to register and to follow certain standards created to protect investors.
7. *Foreign Corrupt Practices Act of 1977*: Affects registration indirectly through amendment to the Securities Exchange Act of 1934. This act requires the maintenance of accounting records and adequate internal accounting controls.
8. *Insider Trading Sanctions Act of 1984* and *Insider Trading and Securities Fraud Enforcement Act of 1988*: Also affect registration indirectly. Increase the penalties against persons who profit from illegal use of inside information and who are associated with market manipulation and securities fraud.
9. *Sarbanes–Oxley Act of 2002*: Designed as an answer to the numerous corporate accounting scandals that came to light in 2001 and 2002. As discussed in a later section of this chapter, this act mandated a number of reforms to bolster corporate responsibility, strengthen disclosure, and combat fraud. It also created the Public Company Accounting Oversight Board (PCAOB) to oversee the accounting profession.
10. *Dodd–Frank Act*: In light of additional financial market scandals, Congress passed and President Obama signed the Wall Street Reform and Consumer Protection Act of 2010.[7] This new legislation marked a significant expansion of the federal government's role in regulating corporate governance, required both stress tests and so-called living wills as safety valves designed to plan for financial disaster for banks that are deemed too important to the financial system to fail, established the Consumer Financial Protection Bureau (CFPB), and provided expanded authority to the SEC to require extensive disclosures concerning corporate compensation. However, in May 2018, both chambers of Congress passed, with bipartisan support, and President Trump signed into law, a partial rollback of Dodd–Frank, largely based on concerns that it placed unnecessary burdens on small and medium-sized lenders, such as community banks, which had forced consolidation of the banking system. The CFPB and the additional disclosure requirements were left largely intact, however.

[6] Interestingly, one of the provisions originally suggested for this act would have created a federal corps of auditors. The defeat of this proposal (after some debate) has allowed for the rise of the independent auditing profession as it is currently structured in the United States. For more information, see Mark Moran and Gary John Previts, "The SEC and the Profession, 1934–1984: The Realities of Self-Regulation," *Journal of Accountancy*, July 1984.

[7] Public Law No. 111–203, 124 stat. 1376 (2010). This statute is commonly referred to as the "Dodd–Frank Act."

SEC Requirements

Based on the previous list of statutes, and corresponding agency regulations, the SEC administers extensive filing requirements. Accountants who specialize in working with the federal securities laws must develop a broad knowledge of a great many reporting rules and regulations. The SEC specifies most of these disclosure requirements in two basic documents, *Regulation S-K* and *Regulation S-X,* which are supplemented by periodic releases and staff bulletins.

Regulation S-K established requirements for all nonfinancial information contained in filings with the SEC. Descriptions of the registrant's business and its securities are just two items covered by these regulations. A partial list of other nonfinancial data to be disclosed includes specified data about the company's directors, officers, and other management; management's discussion and analysis of the current financial condition and the results of operations; and descriptions of both legal proceedings and the company's properties.

Regulation S-X prescribed the form and content of the financial statements (and the accompanying notes and related schedules) included in the various reports filed with the SEC. Thus, before being accepted, all financial information must meet a number of clearly specified requirements established by Regulation S-X.

The SEC's Impact on Financial Reporting to Stockholders

The SEC's disclosure and accounting requirements are not limited to the filings made directly with that body. *Rule 14c-3* of the 1934 Act states that the annual reports of publicly held companies should include financial statements that have been audited. This information (referred to as *proxy information* because it accompanies the management's request to cast votes for absentee stockholders at the annual shareholders meeting) must present balance sheets as of the end of the two most recent fiscal years along with income statements and cash flow statements for the three most recent fiscal years. *Rule 14c-3* also states that additional information, as specified in *Regulation S-K,* should be included in this annual report. The result has been a significant demand for CPAs to provide services as independent auditors.

Over the years, the SEC has moved toward an *integrated disclosure system.* Under this approach, much of the same reported information that the SEC requires must also go to the shareholders. Thus, the overall reporting process is simplified because only a single set of information must be generated in most cases. The integrated disclosure system is also intended as a way to improve the quality of the disclosures received directly by the shareholders.

Information required in proxy statements, which the shareholders receive directly, includes the following:

1. Five-year summary of operations including sales, total assets, income from continuing operations, and cash dividends per share.
2. Description of the business activities, including principal products and sources and availability of raw materials.
3. Three-year summary of industry segments, export sales, and foreign and domestic operations.
4. List of company directors and executive officers.
5. Market price of the company's common stock for each quarterly period within the two most recent fiscal years.
6. Any restrictions on the company's ability to continue paying dividends.
7. Management's discussion and analysis of financial condition, changes in financial condition, and results of operations. This discussion should include liquidity, trends and significant events, and causes of material changes in the financial statements.

In addition, even prior to passage of the Sarbanes–Oxley Act, the SEC required certain disclosures in proxy statements describing the services provided by the registrant's independent external auditor. This information helped to ensure that true independence was not endangered.

Such disclosure must include the following:

1. All nonaudit services provided by the independent audit firm.
2. A statement as to whether the board of directors (or its audit committee) approved all non-audit services after considering the possibility that such services might impair the external auditor's independence.
3. The percentage of nonaudit fees to the total annual audit fee. This disclosure helps indicate the importance of the audit work to the firm versus the reward from any other services provided to the registrant.
4. Individual nonaudit fees that are more than 3 percent of the annual audit fee.

LO 12-3

Understand the Congressional rationale for enacting the Sarbanes–Oxley Act and the responsibilities of the Public Company Accounting Oversight Board.

Corporate Accounting Scandals and the Sarbanes–Oxley Act

When William H. Donaldson entered his cavernous corner office on the sixth floor of the Securities and Exchange Commission in 2003, he headed an agency at one of its lowest points since its creation 80 years ago.[8]

Enron's former chairman and chief executive, Kenneth Lay, received $152.7 million in payments and stock in the year leading up to the company's collapse amid revelations that it hid debt and inflated profit for years. Lay's take in 2001 was more than 11,000 times the maximum amount of severance paid to laid-off workers.

Former WorldCom CEO Bernard Ebbers borrowed $408 million from the telecommunications company that had improperly accounted for $9 billion and was forced into bankruptcy. Ebbers had pledged company shares as collateral, but with those shares, once valued at $286 million, worthless, he was said to be considering forgoing his $1.5 million annual pension to help settle the debt.

Adelphia Communications's founder and former CEO, John J. Rigas, allegedly conspired with four other executives to loot the company, leading prosecutors to seek the forfeiture of more than $2.5 billion.[9]

Hardly a day passed during 2002 without a new revelation of corporate wrongdoing. The list of companies whose executives virtually robbed the corporate treasury or whose accounting practices ranged from dubious to outrageous is unfortunately long. Throughout this excruciating disclosure process, many in the investing public began to raise two related questions:

Why didn't independent auditors stop these practices?

How can the SEC allow such activities to occur?

As indicated previously, a number of reasons were suggested for the cause of the ethical meltdown during this period, ranging from human greed to inappropriate auditing practices. In truth, as the history of this time continues to unfold, a variety of culprits share the blame for such reprehensible behavior at both the corporate and the individual levels.

Regardless of the reasons, drastic actions had to be taken to reduce or eliminate future abuses (actual and perceived) to begin restoring public confidence in publicly traded entities and their disclosed accounting information. A capitalistic economy functions well only if investors believe they can make wise decisions to buy and sell securities based on the information available. Thus, Congress passed the Sarbanes–Oxley Act in July 2002[10] by a virtually unanimous vote. The scope and potential consequences of this legislation are extremely broad. "The Sarbanes–Oxley Act of 2002 is a major reform package mandating the most far-reaching changes Congress has imposed on the business world since FDR's New Deal."[11]

[8] Stephen Labaton, "Can a Bloodied S.E.C. Dust Itself Off and Get Moving?" *The New York Times,* December 16, 2002, p. C-2.

[9] Brad Foss, "Unearthing of Corporate Scandals Exposed Market's Vulnerabilities," Associated Press Newswires, December 12, 2002.

[10] Public Law 107–204; 107th Congress, July 30, 2002.

[11] Richard I. Miller and Paul H. Pashkoff, "Regulations under the Sarbanes–Oxley Act," *Journal of Accountancy,* October 2002, p. 33.

The act is so wide-ranging that this text describes only a general overview of some of the more frequently discussed statutory provisions here.

Creation of the Public Company Accounting Oversight Board

The public accounting profession had long taken pride in its own self-regulation. Through its major professional body, the American Institute of Certified Public Accountants (AICPA), the profession has established and enforced its own code of conduct and, through its Auditing Standards Board (ASB), created its own auditing standards for decades. The maintenance of public trust was often heard as a litany for the creation of such professional guidelines. Unfortunately, self-regulation was not always successful in the public auditing arena. One of the inherent flaws in the system was that the professional body, the AICPA, was less powerful than many of the international audit firms that it sought to control. Discipline and conformity are difficult to maintain when the entities being regulated are bigger, richer, and more powerful than the regulator.

The Sarbanes–Oxley Act created the Public Company Accounting Oversight Board (PCAOB) to oversee auditors of public companies. The creation of the Oversight Board—a governmental board under the control of the SEC—effectively minimizes self-regulation in the accounting profession. The board

- Has five members appointed by the SEC to staggered five-year terms.[12]
- Allows only two members to be accountants, past or present.[13]
- Enforces auditing, quality control, and independence standards and rules.
- Is under the oversight and enforcement authority of the SEC.
- Is funded from fees levied on all publicly traded companies.

These few provisions show that this Oversight Board, rather than the accounting profession, is now ultimately in charge of regulating public accounting firms whose clients are publicly traded companies. Although the board itself is not a government agency, the SEC exercises power over it. For example, the SEC selects the five members of the board (after consultation with the chair of the Board of Governors of the Federal Reserve System and the secretary of the U.S. Department of the Treasury). The act requires the board members to be prominent individuals of integrity and good reputation who must cease all other professional and business activities to help ensure independence and adequate time commitment.

One of the most interesting issues is how the Oversight Board interacts with the Auditing Standards Board to promulgate audit and attestation standards. While the AICPA authorizes the ASB to issue such pronouncements, the mandate of the Sarbanes–Oxley Act requires the Oversight Board to play a significant role in this process. Although directed to cooperate with the accounting profession, the PCAOB has the authority to amend, modify, repeal, or reject any auditing standard.[14] ASB standards, unless later modified or superseded by the PCAOB, are adopted for audits of securities issuers. The Oversight Board has since taken an active role in developing its own pronouncements, and many new ASB pronouncements apply only to nonissuers.

Registration of Public Accounting Firms

Registration of public accounting firms is required only of firms that prepare, issue, or participate in preparing an audit report for issuers—entities which trade on publicly traded exchanges. Virtually all public accounting firms of significant size must register; but most small firms do not need to register. Even foreign firms that play a substantial role in the audit of an organization that has securities registered in the United States must register with the PCAOB and follow the rules of the Sarbanes–Oxley Act. This act has a significant impact on the activities of foreign companies that sell their securities on U.S. markets, an impact not necessarily appreciated outside the United States. "Under the law, CEOs are required to

[12] Sarbanes–Oxley Act of 2002, Sec. 101(e)(1).

[13] Ibid., Sec. 101(e)(2).

[14] Ibid., Sec. 103(a)(1).

vouch for financial statements, boards must have audit committees drawn from independent directors, and companies can no longer make loans to corporate directors. All of that conflicts with some other countries' rules and customs."[15]

The application process for PCAOB registration provides the Oversight Board a significant amount of information about the audit firms. The firms must identify each of their audit clients that qualifies as an issuer and the Oversight Board then assesses an annual fee on the issuer based on the size of its market capitalization. These fees serve, in part, as the financial support for the work of the Oversight Board.[16]

Other information required of the accounting firms in this application process includes the following:

- A list of all accountants participating in the audit report of any client qualifying as an issuer.
- Annual fees received from each issuer with the amounts separated as to audit and nonaudit services.
- Information about any criminal, civil, or administrative actions pending against the firm or any person associated with the firm.
- Information regarding disagreements between issuers and the auditing firm during the previous year.

Inspections of Registered Firms

After registration, each audit firm is subject to periodic inspections by the PCAOB. Any firm that audits more than 100 issuers per year is inspected annually. All other registered firms are inspected every three years. The Oversight Board has the power to take disciplinary action as a result of the findings of these inspections. In addition, deficiencies can be made public if the firm does not address them in an appropriate fashion within 12 months.

The PCAOB's power is not limited just to reacting to the findings of annual inspections.

> The new board has a full range of sanctions at its disposal, including suspension or revocation of registration, censure, and significant fines. It has authority to investigate any act or practice that may violate the act, the new board's rules, the provisions of the federal securities laws relating to audit reports, or applicable professional standards.[17]

Clearly, Congress provided the new Oversight Board extensive powers to enable it to clean up any problems it discovers in public accounting.

Auditor Independence

One of the most discussed issues surrounding accounting scandals was the failure of audit firms to act independently in dealing with audit clients. Not surprisingly, a significant portion of the Sarbanes–Oxley Act ensures that public accounting firms are, indeed, independent. Certain services that could previously have been provided to an audit client are now forbidden.[18] These include financial information system design and implementation as well as internal audit outsourcing. The client's audit committee must preapprove any allowed services and disclose them in reports to the SEC.

Audit committees long were considered an important element in maintaining an appropriate distance between the external auditors and the management of the client. Audit committees were generally composed of members of the company's board of directors and served as a liaison with the auditors. However, the work and the composition of the audit committees tended to vary greatly from company to company until the Sarbanes–Oxley Act formalized the liaison role by making the audit committee responsible for the appointment and compensation of the external auditor. To help ensure impartiality, the committee now must be made up of individuals who are independent from management. The act now directs the auditor to

[15] Louis Lavelle and Mike McNamee, "Will Overseas Boards Play by American Rules?" *BusinessWeek*, December 16, 2002, p. 36.

[16] Sarbanes–Oxley Act of 2002, Sec. 102(b)(2).

[17] Miller and Pashkoff, "Regulations under the Sarbanes–Oxley Act," pp. 35 and 36.

[18] Sarbanes–Oxley Act of 2002, Sec. 201.

report to the audit committee, rather than to company management. To further ensure independence from management, the lead partner of the audit engagement must rotate off the audit engagement after five years.[19]

These provisions, as well as the many other elements of the Sarbanes–Oxley Act, have changed public accounting from how it was in the past. Drastic action was needed and was taken.[20] This Act strengthened independent audits and helped eliminate some dubious practices that haunted public accounting. Some of these steps may not have been necessary; but the need to reestablish public confidence in the capital market system forced the legislators to avoid any "quick-fix" solutions.

LO 12-4

Describe the SEC's role in establishing generally accepted accounting principles (GAAP).

The SEC's Authority and SEC Filings

The SEC's Authority over Generally Accepted Accounting Principles

The primary focus of the Sarbanes–Oxley Act was on the regulation of independent auditors and auditing standards. Therefore, it had little impact on accounting standards and on the regulations for the registration of securities. Those regulations continue to evolve over time. Because financial reporting standards can be changed merely by amending *Regulation S-X,* the SEC holds the ultimate legal authority for establishing accounting principles for most publicly held companies in this country. In the past, the SEC has usually restricted the application of this power to disclosure issues while looking to the private sector (with the SEC's oversight) to formulate accounting principles. For this reason, the FASB rather than the SEC is generally viewed as the main standards-setting body for financial accounting in the United States. "Under federal law, the SEC has the mandate to determine accounting principles for publicly traded companies. But it has generally ceded that authority to private-sector accounting bodies such as the Financial Accounting Standards Board."[21]

On the accounting side of self-regulation, from its inception, the FASB has been a freestanding organization entirely separate from the AICPA. As we discuss later, the SEC has always had the ability to significantly impact accounting standards. Furthermore, the problems that led to the largest corporate scandals were more about audit failures than about accounting rules. Some observers, however, believe that U.S. generally accepted accounting principles encourage income manipulation, which also could lead to more investigative activity by the SEC in this area.

However, the SEC does retain the ability to exercise its power with regard to the continuing evolution of accounting principles. The chief accountant of the SEC (described earlier in this chapter) is responsible for providing the commissioners and the commission staff with advice on all current accounting and auditing matters and helps to draft rules for the form and content of financial statement disclosure and other reporting requirements. Because he or she is the principal adviser to the SEC on all accounting and auditing matters,[22] the most powerful accounting position in the United States is that of chief accountant of the SEC. The work of the chief accountant can lead the SEC to pass amendments as needed to alter various aspects of *Regulation S-X.*

The SEC has issued *Financial Reporting Releases (FRRs)* to supplement *Regulation S-X* and *Regulation S-K.*[23] In addition, the staff of the SEC publishes a series of *Staff Accounting Bulletins (SABs)* as a means of informing the financial community of its positions.

[19] Ibid., Sec. 203.

[20] The Sarbanes–Oxley Act, especially the Section 404 requirements, added significant costs to reporting operations for public companies. However, the SEC attempted to provide "Section 404 relief" from the "multi-million-dollar expenses," while still ensuring proper disclosure. See "Getting It Right," *Journal of Accountancy,* March 2007, p. 29.

[21] Kevin G. Salwen and Robin Goldwyn Blumenthal, "Tackling Accounting, SEC Pushes Changes with Broad Impact," *The Wall Street Journal,* September 27, 1990, p. A1.

[22] www.sec.gov/about/whatwedo.shtml, March 2016.

[23] From 1937 until 1982, the SEC issued more than 300 *Accounting Series Releases* (ASRs) to (1) amend *Regulation S-X,* (2) express interpretations regarding accounting and auditing issues, and (3) report disciplinary actions against public accountants. The SEC codified the ASRs that dealt with financial reporting matters of continuing interest and issued it as *Financial Reporting Release No. 1.*

> Staff Accounting Bulletins reflect the SEC staff's views regarding accounting-related disclosure practices. They represent interpretations and policies followed by the Division of Corporation Finance and the Office of the Chief Accountant in administering the disclosure requirements of the federal securities laws.[24]
>
> In addition, the SEC's Office of the Chief Accountant (OCA), the Chief Accountant, and OCA staff regularly communicate about accounting and auditing issues. These can and do take the form of Staff Accounting Bulletins; but also may be disseminated in the form of speeches or staff letters to industry, among others.[25]

SEC Content in the FASB's Accounting Standards Codification® (ASC)

In addition to authoritative financial accounting and reporting guidance that has been issued by the FASB ("FASB guidance"), the FASB's Accounting Standards Codification® (ASC) includes relevant portions of financial accounting and reporting guidance that has been issued by the SEC and its staff ("SEC guidance").

In the Codification, SEC guidance is organized in the same manner as—but separate from—FASB guidance. The distinction between FASB and SEC guidance is made at the Section level of the Codification content's hierarchy (Topic–Subtopic–Section–Paragraph). SEC Sections are identified with the same standardized two-digit Section numbers and titles as FASB Sections, except that the Section number is preceded by the letter "S." Additionally, Section S99, SEC Materials, is also an SEC Section; there is no FASB Section that corresponds to it.

According to the FASB:

> All authoritative guidance issued by the FASB is included in the Codification. The SEC and its staff issue many kinds of guidance that apply to its registrants; the Codification includes relevant portions of authoritative content issued by the SEC and selected SEC staff interpretations and administrative guidance that pertain to financial accounting and reporting, but it does not include other kinds of SEC guidance.
>
> Examples of included SEC content are:
>
> 1. Regulation S-X (SX)
> 2. Financial Reporting Releases (FRR)/Accounting Series Releases (ASR)
> 3. Interpretive Releases (IR)
> 4. SEC Staff guidance in:
>   a. Staff Accounting Bulletins (SAB)
>   b. EITF Topic D and SEC Staff Observer comments.
>
> The SEC guidance that is included in the Codification does not originate with the FASB—it is provided on a "pass through" basis merely as a convenience to Codification users. The SEC Sections do not contain the entire population of SEC rules, regulations, interpretive releases, and staff guidance. For example, the Codification does not include all content related to matters outside the basic financial statements, such as Management's Discussion and Analysis (MD&A), or to auditing or independence matters.[26]

Additional Disclosure Requirements

Historically, the SEC has restricted the use of its authority to the gray areas of accounting for which official guidance is not available. New reporting problems arise each year while no authoritative body has ever completely addressed many other accounting issues, even after years of discussion. As another response to such problems, the SEC often requires the disclosure of additional data if current rules are viewed as insufficient.

As an example pertaining to disclosures contained in financial statement notes, in the early part of 1997, while the FASB worked on a project concerning the accounting for derivatives, the SEC approved rules so that more information would be available immediately. Note disclosure in financial statements had to include more information about accounting policies used. In addition, information about the risk of loss from market rate or price changes inherent in derivatives and other financial instruments was required.

[24] https://www.sec.gov/interps/account.shtml

[25] https://www.sec.gov/page/staff-communications-and-guidance

[26] https://asc.fasb.org/help&cid=1175804733747#.

Moratorium on Specific Accounting Practices

The commission also can exert its power by declaring a moratorium on the use of specified accounting practices. When authoritative guidance is not present, the SEC can simply prohibit a particular method from being applied. As an example, in the 1980s, companies utilized a variety of procedures to account for internal computer software costs because no official pronouncement had yet been issued. Consequently, the SEC

> imposed a moratorium that will prohibit companies that plan to go public from capitalizing the internal costs of developing computer software for sale or lease or marketed to customers in other ways. . . .The decision doesn't prevent companies currently capitalizing internal software expenses from continuing, but the companies must disclose the effect of not expensing such costs as incurred. The moratorium continues until the Financial Accounting Standards Board issues a standard on the issue.[27]

Two years later, when the FASB eventually arrived at a resolution of this question and issued *SFAS 86,* "Accounting for the Costs of Computer Software to Be Sold, Leased, or Otherwise Marketed," the SEC dropped the moratorium. Hence, the FASB set the accounting rule, but the SEC moratorium probably hastened resolution of this issue by the FASB and ensured appropriate reporting until that time.

Challenging Individual Statements

As described, officially requiring additional disclosure and prohibiting the application of certain accounting practices are two methods the SEC uses to control the financial reporting process. Forcing a specific registrant to change its filed statements is another, less formal approach that can create the same control. For example,

> Advanced Micro Devices, Inc., agreed to settle an investigation by the Securities and Exchange Commission of the semiconductor company's public disclosures. The SEC found AMD "made inaccurate and misleading statements" concerning development of its 486 microprocessor. In 1992 and 1993, AMD "led the public to believe that it was independently designing the microcode for its 486 microprocessor without access" to the code of its rival chipmaker, Intel Corp., the SEC said, "when, in fact, AMD had provided its engineers . . . with Intel's copyrighted 386 microcode to accelerate the company's development efforts." Without admitting or denying the commission's findings, AMD, based in Sunnyvale, California, consented to an order barring it from committing future violations of SEC rules. No fines were imposed.[28]

Following the SEC's action, any company involved in a similar event would certainly be well advised to provide the suggested disclosure. Failing to do so could result in the SEC's refusal to approve an issuer's future registrations.

The Dodd–Frank Act strengthened the SEC's role in challenging, or at least questioning, financial statements. Dodd–Frank added a new provision to the Securities Exchange Act, pursuant to which the SEC may require listed companies to adopt and publish policies by which they will disgorge or "claw back" executive compensation when restated financial statements are necessitated by executive misconduct. Failure to adopt such policies results in mandatory delisting.[29]

Overruling the FASB

The SEC's actions are not necessarily limited, however, to the gray areas of accounting. Although the commission generally has allowed the FASB (and previous authoritative groups) to establish accounting principles, the SEC retains the authority to override or negate any pronouncements produced in the private sector. This power was dramatically demonstrated in 1977 when the FASB issued *SFAS 19,* "Financial Accounting and Reporting by Oil and Gas Producing Companies." After an extended debate over the merits of alternative methods, the FASB issued this statement requiring oil- and gas-producing companies to apply the successful-efforts method preferred by large, integrated oil companies in the

[27] "SEC Imposes 'Software Costs' Moratorium," *Journal of Accountancy,* September 1983, p. 3.

[28] "SEC Inquiry on Disclosure to Public Is Being Settled," *The Wall Street Journal,* October 1, 1996, p. B4.

[29] Dodd–Frank §954.

United States when accounting for unsuccessful exploration and drilling costs, rather than the full cost method preferred by smaller U.S. oil companies.

In response, the SEC almost immediately invoked a moratorium on the use of this practice until an alternative approach could be evaluated. Thus, companies filing with the SEC were not allowed to follow the method established by the FASB (after years of formal study and deliberation by that body). Although the commission's reaction toward the accounting profession was a unique instance, the handling of this one issue clearly demonstrates the veto power that the SEC maintains over the work of the FASB.[30]

SEC and PCAOB Fees and Budgets

The SEC charges a registration fee based on the value of the securities offered.[31] This fee is a very small fraction of the value of the securities being issued. In 2013, it was $136.40 for each $1 million of security offering; for 2019 (2018), this fee was set at $121.20 ($124.20) per million dollars, which was expected to raise $660 million for the U.S. Treasury in fiscal 2018.

Before the Sarbanes–Oxley Act, the SEC collected fees vastly in excess of its operating costs and, in fact, has a net position at the end of most fiscal years. For years, the existence of this surplus caused debate. Some viewed it as a source of general revenue for the federal government, while others argued that it indicated that corporations were overcharged for the registration and periodic filing processes. However, another possibility emerged following the corporate accounting scandals in 2001 and 2002. Such a surplus may have indicated that inadequate resources were invested in the SEC's work and that the agency could not meet its responsibilities with the money allotted. Not surprisingly, the Sarbanes–Oxley Act authorized a 77 percent increase in the agency's budget as well as a substantial increase in the size of its staff. However, this authorization did not necessarily mean that the SEC would actually receive more money in the Congressional budgeting process.

> Instead of supporting the 77 percent budget hike promised by Congress, the White House wants the SEC to make do with a more modest $568 million next year. The Commission's 2002 budget was $438 million. While this might seem like a lot, Harvey Goldschmid [SEC Commissioner] said that it is not enough to pay for the effective policing of 17,000 companies, 34,000 investment portfolios, and 7,500 financial advisers, especially in a climate where so much emphasis is placed on the quality of oversight.[32]

More recently, the U.S. Congress has increased appropriations for the SEC. For fiscal 2018, the SEC expended over $1.8 billion on its total program costs.[33] In addition, the PCAOB's 2019 budget, approved by the SEC, includes accounting support fees that are assessed annually on issuers and registered broker-dealers. For 2019, these SEC-approved accounting support fees were $262.9 million, approximately 12 percent higher than the 2018 accounting support fee of $235.3 million.[34] In contrast, the 2018 budgeted Accounting Support Fees that make up most of the budget of the Financial Accounting Standards Board (FASB) were $29 million (and 2018 budgeted Accounting Support Fees for the Governmental Accounting Standards Board [GASB] were $8 million).[35] Of course, the FASB and GASB only set accounting standards—they do not review company filings, do inspections of accounting firms, or conduct enforcement activities like the SEC and the PCAOB do.

[30] For a detailed account of the activities surrounding the SEC's rejection of *SFAS 19,* see Donald Gorton, "The SEC Decision Not to Support SFAS 19: A Case Study of the Effect of Lobbying on Standard Setting," *Accounting Horizons,* March 1991.

[31] Self-Regulatory Organizations also impose similar fees. For instance, the National Association of Security Dealers imposes a 0.01 percent initial filing fee (with a $75,000.00 cap) based on the proposed maximum aggregate offering price. This permits the NASD to fulfill its functions in regard to its role with the SEC. (SEC Release No. 34-50984, File No. SR-NASD-2004-177.)

[32] Howard Stock, "Don't Short-Change SEC, Goldschmid Tells Bush," Investors Relations Business, December 16, 2002.

[33] SEC Agency Financial Report for Fiscal Year 2018 (Year Ended September 30, 2018), p. 59.

[34] Press Release, "SEC Approves 2019 PCAOB Budget and Accounting Support Fee," SEC.gov, March 24, 2019, www.sec.gov/news/press-release/2018-292.

[35] Financial Accounting Foundation, Summarized Budget Information for the year ending December 31, 2018, p. 4.

LO 12-5

Define and describe an issuer's filings with the Securities and Exchange Commission.

Filings with the SEC

Because of legislation and regulations, registrants may be required to make numerous different filings with the SEC. The SEC actually receives hundreds of thousands of filings per year. However, for the overview presented here, the reporting process is divided into two very broad categories:

1. Registration statements.
2. Periodic filings.

Registration statements ensure the disclosure of sufficient, relevant financial data before either a company or its underwriters can *initially offer* a security to the public. The Securities Act of 1933 mandates dissemination of such information. Registration is necessary except in certain situations described at a later point in this chapter.

After initial registration, a number of federal laws, the most important of which is the Securities Exchange Act of 1934, require registrants to provide periodic filings. This legislation has resulted in the *continual reporting of specific data* by all companies that have securities publicly traded on either a national securities exchange or an over-the-counter market.

For registration statements as well as periodic filings, the SEC has established forms that give the format and content to be followed in providing required information. "These forms contain no blanks to be filled in as do tax forms. Instead, they are narrative in character, giving general instructions about the items of information to be furnished. Detailed information must be assembled by the companies using the form for the type of security being offered as well as the type of company making the offer."[36]

Registration Statements (1933 Act)

As indicated, a registration statement must be filed with and made effective by the Securities and Exchange Commission before a company can offer a security publicly. A security is very broadly defined to include items such as a note, stock, treasury stock, bond, debenture, investment contract, evidence of indebtedness, or transferable share.

The SEC's role is not to evaluate the quality of the investment. Rather, the SEC seeks to ensure that the content and disclosure of the filing comply with all applicable regulations. The responsibility for the information always rests with corporate officials. The SEC is charged with ensuring full and fair disclosure of relevant financial information. The registrant has the responsibility to provide such data, but the decision to invest must remain with the public.

- S-1 Used when no other form is prescribed. Usually used by new registrants or by companies that have been filing reports with the SEC for less than 36 months.
- S-3 Used by companies that are large and already have a significant following in the stock market (at least $75 million of the voting stock is held by nonaffiliates). Disclosure is reduced for these organizations because the public is assumed to already have access to a considerable amount of information. Form F-3 is used if registration is by a foreign issuer.
- S-4 Used for securities issued in connection with business combination transactions.
- S-8 Used as a registration statement for employee stock plans.
- S-11 Used for the registration of securities by certain real estate companies.

The use of several of these forms, especially Form S-3, offers a distinct advantage to established companies that are issuing securities. Rather than duplicate voluminous information already disclosed in other filings with the SEC—frequently the annual report to shareholders—the registrant can simply indicate the location of the data in these other documents, a process referred to as *incorporation by reference*.

LO 12-6

Describe an issuer's registration process, various forms used by the issuers, and the exemption(s) from registration.

Registration Procedures

The actual registration process is composed of a series of events leading up to the SEC's permission to "go effective." Because the registrant is seeking to obtain significant financial

[36] K. Fred Skousen, *An Introduction to the SEC* (Cincinnati: South-Western Publishing, 1991), p. 47.

resources through the issuance of new securities in public markets, each of these procedures is vitally important.

After selecting the appropriate form, the company accumulates information according to the requirements of *Regulation S-K* and *Regulation S-X.* If it anticipates problems or questions, the company may request a prefiling conference with the SEC staff to seek guidance prior to beginning the registration. For example, if uncertainty concerning the handling or disclosure of an unusual transaction exists, a prefiling conference can save all parties considerable time and effort.

> The Commission has a long-established policy of holding its staff available for conferences with prospective registrants or their representatives in advance of filing a registration statement. These conferences may be held for the purpose of discussing generally the problems confronting a registrant in effecting registration or to resolve specific problems of an unusual nature which are sometimes presented by involved or complicated financial transactions.[37]

When the SEC receives it, the Division of Corporation Finance reviews the registration statement.[38] An analyst determines whether all nonfinancial information complies with the SEC's disclosure requirements in *Regulation S-K.* At the same time, an accountant verifies that the financial statements included in the filing meet the standards of *Regulation S-X* and were prepared according to generally accepted accounting principles. *Because the SEC does not conduct a formal audit, the report of the company's independent CPA is essential to this particular evaluation.* In addition, an SEC lawyer reviews the registration statement to verify its legal aspects.

The Division of Corporation Finance regularly requests clarifications, changes, or additional information, especially for those filings involving an initial registration. A *letter of comments* (also known as a *deficiency letter*) is issued to the company to communicate these findings. In most cases, the registrant attempts to provide the necessary data or changes to expedite the process. However, in controversial areas, the issuer may begin discussions directly with the SEC staff in hope of resolving the problem without making the requested adjustments or disclosure or, at least, with limited inconvenience.

When the Division of Corporation Finance is eventually satisfied that the company has fulfilled all SEC regulations, the registration statement is made effective and the securities can be sold. *Effectiveness does not, however, indicate an endorsement of the securities by the SEC.* With most offerings, the company actually sells the stock using one or more underwriters (stock brokerage firms) that market the shares to their clients to earn commissions.

For convenience, and to save time and money, large companies are allowed to use a process known as *shelf registration.* They file once with the SEC and are then allowed to offer those securities at any time over the subsequent two years without having to go back to the SEC. For example, "Enterprise Products Partners L. P. announced today that it has filed an $800 million universal shelf registration statement with the Securities and Exchange Commission for the proposed sale of debt and equity securities over the next two years."[39]

The registration statement is physically composed of two parts. Part I, referred to as a *prospectus,* contains extensive information that includes these items:

1. Financial statements for the issuing company audited by an independent CPA along with appropriate supplementary data.
2. An explanation of the intended use of the proceeds to be generated by the sale of the new securities.
3. A description of the risks associated with the securities.
4. A description of the business and the properties owned by the issuer.

The registrant must furnish every potential buyer of the securities with a copy of this prospectus, thus ensuring the adequate availability of information for its investment analysis.

[37] Stanley Weinstein, Daniel Schechtman, and Michael A. Walker, *SEC Compliance,* vol. 4 (Englewood Cliffs, NJ: Prentice Hall, 1999), para. 30, 641.

[38] All registration statements filed by issuers offering securities to the public for the first time are reviewed. Subsequent registration statements and periodic filings are reviewed only on a selective basis.

[39] "Enterprise Files $800 Million Universal Shelf Registration with SEC," *Business Wire,* December 27, 1999.

Part II of the registration statement is primarily for the informational needs of the SEC staff. Additional data should be disclosed about the company and the securities being issued, such as marketing arrangements, expenses of issuance, sales to special parties, and the like. The registrant is not required to provide this information to prospective buyers, although the entire registration statement is available to the public through the SEC.

Securities Exempt from Registration According to the 1933 Act, not all securities issued by companies and their underwriters require registration prior to their sale. For example, securities sold to the residents of the state in which the issuing company is chartered and principally doing business are exempted. However, these offerings may still be regulated by the securities laws of the individual states (commonly known as *blue sky laws*), which vary significantly.[40]

Other exempt offerings include but are not limited to the following:

- Securities issued by governments, banks, and savings and loan associations. (However, offerings of bank holding companies are not exempt.)
- Securities issued that are restricted to a company's own existing stockholders for which no commission is paid to solicit the exchange.
- Securities, such as bonds, issued by nonprofit organizations such as religious, educational, or charitable groups.
- Revised Regulation A: Regulation A is an exemption from the requirement to register public offerings. In March 2015, the SEC implemented Section 401 of the Jumpstart Our Business Startups (JOBS) Act by amending Regulation A to create two offering tiers. Tier 1 provides exemption for up to $20 million of securities in a 12-month period. Tier 2 provides exemption for up to $50 million of securities in a 12-month period. Both Tier 1 and Tier 2 securities may be offered publicly utilizing general solicitation and advertising and offered to non-accredited investors.
- Regulation D—Rule 504: Offerings of no more than $1 million made to any number of investors within a 12-month period. No specific disclosure of information is required. General solicitations are allowed. The issuer must give notice of the offering to the SEC within 15 days of the first sale.
- Regulation D—Rule 505: Offerings of no more than $5 million made to 35 or fewer non-accredited and an unlimited number of accredited purchasers in a 12-month period. No general solicitation is allowed for securities issued in this manner. Non-accredited investors must still be furnished an audited balance sheet and other specified information. Parties making purchases have to hold the securities for at least two years or the issuing firm will lose the filing exemption.
- Regulation D—Rule 506: The private placement of any dollar amount of issuance to unlimited non-accredited investors and no more than 35 sophisticated investors (having knowledge and experience in financial matters) who already have sufficient information available to them about the issuing company. General solicitation is not permitted, although solicitation is permitted if the entire issuance is to accredited investors. These private placement rules have become quite important in recent years.

Periodic Filings with the SEC

Once a company has issued securities that are publicly traded on a securities exchange or an over-the-counter market, it must continually file information with the SEC so that adequate disclosure is available. As with registration statements, several different forms are utilized for this purpose. However, for most companies with actively traded securities, three of these are common: Form 10-K (an annual report), Form 10-Q (a quarterly report), and Form 8-K (disclosure of significant events). Smaller businesses use Form 10-KSB for annual reports and Form 10-QSB for quarterly reports.

[40] "These early laws became known as 'blue sky' laws after a judicial decision characterized some transactions as 'speculative schemes which have no more basis than so many feet of blue sky.'" (Skousen, *An Introduction to the SEC,* p. 3.)

In addition, as mentioned previously, proxy statements must be filed with the SEC. Management or another interested party issues these statements to a company's owners in hope of securing voting rights to be used at stockholders' meetings.

Form 10-K A 10-K form is an annual report filed with the SEC to provide information and disclosures required by *Regulation S-K* and *Regulation S-X.* Fortunately, because of the integrated disclosure system, the annual report distributed by companies to their stockholders now includes most of the basic financial disclosures required by the SEC in Form 10-K. Thus, many companies simply attach the stockholders' annual report to the Form 10-K each year and use the incorporation by reference procedure to meet most of the SEC's filing requirements. This process is sometimes known as a *wraparound filing.*

Form 10–K, as with the various other SEC filings, is constantly undergoing assessment to determine whether it is meeting investor needs.[41]

The SEC is especially interested in the quality of the information provided by the MD&A section of a registrant's filings. Basically, management should describe the company's past, present, and future. This information can furnish investors with a feel for the prospects of the company; it is a candid narrative to provide statement readers with a sense of management's priorities, accomplishments, and concerns. The SEC staff carefully reviews the MD&A feature.

Form 10-Q A 10-Q form contains condensed interim financial statements for the registrant and must be filed with the SEC shortly after the end of each quarter. However, no Form 10-Q is required following the fourth quarter of the year since a Form 10-K is forthcoming shortly thereafter. A Form 10-Q does not have to be audited by an independent CPA.

Information to be contained in each Form 10-Q includes the following:

- Income statements must be included for the most recent quarter and for the year to date as well as for the comparative periods in the previous year.
- A statement of cash flows is also necessary, but only for the year to date as well as for the corresponding period in the preceding year.
- Two balance sheets are reported: one as of the end of the most recent quarter and the second showing the company's financial position at the end of the previous fiscal year.
- Each Form 10-Q should also include any needed disclosures pertaining to the current period including the MD&A of the financial condition of the company and results of operations.

Form 8-K An 8-K form is used to disclose a unique or significant happening.[42] Consequently, the 8-K is not filed at regular time intervals but within 15 calendar days of the event (or within five business days in certain specified instances). The SEC receives thousands of 8-K reports each year. According to the SEC's guidelines, Form 8-K may be filed to report any action that company officials believe is important to security holders. However, the following events are designated for required disclosure in this manner:

- Resignation of a director.
- Changes in control of the registrant.
- Acquisition or disposition of assets.
- Changes in the registrant's certified public accountants (independent auditors).
- Bankruptcy or receivership.

In the last two decades, the disclosures made on Form 8-K have expanded through regulation. First, in August 2000, the SEC promulgated Regulation FD (Fair Disclosure), ordinarily referred to as Regulation FD or Reg FD.[43] Regulation FD prohibits public companies from disclosing material information that was previously nonpublic to certain parties, unless the public first receives the information first or receives it simultaneously. The intent of Regulation FD

[41] The current Form 10-K instructions can be viewed at www.sec.gov/about/forms/form10-K.pdf. This version of the Form 10-K has been approved for use through October 31, 2021.

[42] The current Form 8–K instructions can be viewed at www.sec.gov/about/forms/form8-K.pdf.

[43] Regulation FD is codified as 17 C.F.R.243.

was to eliminate selective disclosure, where some investors (often large institutional investors) received information before others (often small individual investors). Under Regulation FD, selective disclosure is still acceptable if the company obtains a confidentiality agreement from the other party (or the other party is already subject to a duty of trust and confidence). While the agreement need not include an undertaking not to trade on the information, Regulation FD makes it easier to prosecute recipients of selective information for insider trading, because in many instances, only persons who owe a duty of confidentiality are subject to such prosecution. The General Instructions to Form 8-K state that "Form 8-K shall be used for current reports under Section 13 or 15(d) of the Securities Exchange Act of 1934 . . . and for reports of nonpublic information required to be disclosed by Regulation FD."

Second, as part of the Sarbanes-Oxley Act, Congress enacted new rules for publicly traded firms requiring greater use of real-time disclosures for material changes in their financial condition or operations between periodic 10-K and 10-Q filings. The Securities and Exchange Commission (SEC) implemented these rules by increasing the reporting requirements for Form 8-K filings effective August 23, 2004. These requirements increased both the scope of economic events subject to mandatory 8-K filing requirements, as well as the timeliness of these disclosures, by mandating the prompt filing of additional information that firms previously had reserved for their 10-Ks and 10-Qs. These rules required timelier disclosures of performance information, as well as disclosures of a broad range of economic events useful in forecasting firms' future performance. For example, the rules required real-time disclosures of terminated material definitive agreements (for example, licensing contracts).

Proxy Statements As previously mentioned, most of the significant actions undertaken by a company first must be approved at stockholders' meetings. For example, the members of the board of directors are elected in this meeting to oversee the company's operations. Although such votes are essential to the operations of a business, few major companies could possibly assemble enough shareholders at any one time and place for a voting quorum. The geographic distances are often too great. Hence, before each of the periodic meetings, the management (or any other interested party) usually requests signed proxies from shareholders granting the legal authority to cast votes for the owners in connection with the various actions to be taken at such stockholders' meetings.[44]

Because of the power conveyed by a proxy, any such solicitation sent to shareholders (by any party) must include specific information as the SEC required in its *Regulation 14A*. This proxy statement has to be filed with the SEC at least 10 days before being distributed. In addition to the disclosed items previously described, other data must be reported to the owners:

- The proxy statement needs to indicate on whose behalf the solicitation is being made.
- The proxy statement must disclose fully all matters that are to be voted on at the meeting.
- In most cases, the proxy statement has to be accompanied (or preceded) by an annual report to the shareholders.

As with all areas of disclosure, the SEC's regulation of proxy statements has greatly enhanced the information available to investors. Historically, shareholders have not always been able to get adequate information.

> Thus was the president of one company able to respond cavalierly to a shareholder's request for information, "I can assure you that the company is in a good financial position. I trust that you will sign and mail your proxy at an early date." Quaint. But that was nothing. One unlisted company printed its proxy on the back of the dividend check—so when you endorsed the check you voted for management.[45]
>
> From a 1902 annual report to shareholders: "The settled plan has been to withhold all information from stockholders and others that is not called for by the stockholders in a body. So far no request for information has been made in the manner prescribed by the directors."[46]

[44] Any person who owns at least 5 percent of the company's stock or has been an owner for six months or longer has the right to look at a list of shareholders to make a proxy solicitation.

[45] Laura Jereski, "You've Come a Long Way, Shareholder," *Forbes,* July 13, 1987, p. 282.

[46] Skousen, *An Introduction to the SEC,* p. 75.

Discussion Question

IS THE DISCLOSURE WORTH THE COST?

Filing with the SEC requires a very significant amount of time and effort on the registrant's part. Companies frequently resist attempts by the SEC to increase the levels of disclosure. Usually, they argue that additional information will not necessarily be useful to a great majority of investors. Regardless of the issue being debated, critics claim that the cost of the extra data far outweighs any benefits that might be derived from this disclosure.

Such contentions are not necessarily made just to avoid disclosing information. This cost analysis has continued for most of the past four decades. One survey from the late 1970s estimated the cost of SEC disclosures to be more than $400 million in 1975 alone.

> The table reports an estimated $213,500,000 for the fully variable costs of 10-K, 10-Q, and 8-K disclosures in 1975. To this should be added the separate estimate (not shown) of $191,900,000 for disclosure related to new issues in 1975, for a total estimate of about $400,000,000 for SEC disclosure costs in 1975. These estimates are biased downward because they do not include various fixed costs.*

Such costs are either passed along to the consumer in the form of higher prices or serve to retard the growth of the reporting company.

Additional SEC requirements continue to concern issuers, many of which conclude that "the costs of mandatory SEC disclosures outweigh the benefits" and accept delisting from the various exchanges rather than incurring the costs of such disclosure.† SEC revenues, which constitute real out-of-pocket costs to issuers, exceeded $3 billion in 2012. This represents a 15-fold increase in the past 40 years.

The author of one survey (that has been widely discussed and debated over the years) held that federal securities laws are not actually helpful to investors.

> I found that there was little evidence of fraud related to financial statements in the period prior to the enactment of the Securities Acts. Nor was there a widespread lack of disclosure. . . . Hence, I conclude that there was little justification for the accounting disclosure required by the Acts. . . . These findings indicate that the data required by the SEC do not seem to be useful to investors.‡

The SEC was created, in part, to ensure that the public has fair and full disclosure about companies whose securities are publicly traded. However, the commission must be mindful of the cost of such disclosures.

How can the SEC determine whether the cost of a proposed disclosure is more or less than the benefits to be derived by the public? After all, despite SEC investigations, Bernard Madoff avoided detection for decades.

*J. Richard Zecher, "An Economic Perspective of SEC Corporate Disclosure," *The SEC and Accounting: The First 50 Years,* ed. Robert H. Mundheim and Noyes E. Leech (Amsterdam: North-Holland, 1985), pp. 75–76.
†Brian J. Bushee and Christian Leuz, "Economic Consequences of SEC Disclosure Regulation," The Wharton School, University of Pennsylvania, February 2004, p. 3.
‡George J. Benston, "The Value of the SEC's Accounting Disclosure Requirements," *The Accounting Review,* July 1969, p. 351.

Electronic Data Gathering, Analysis, and Retrieval System (EDGAR)

During recent years, the SEC has been almost overwhelmed by the sheer mountains of documents that it receives, reviews, and makes available to the public. Filings with the SEC contain millions of pieces of paper each year. Not surprisingly, some problems in the capital markets in the past may have been blamed, in part, on this overload. "[The SEC's] corporation finance division cannot keep up with the deluge of company filings."[47]

In 1984, the SEC began to develop an electronic data gathering, analysis, and retrieval system nicknamed EDGAR. As originally envisioned, all filings would arrive at the SEC on disks or through some other electronic transmission. Each filing could be reviewed, analyzed, and stored by SEC personnel on a computer so they would no longer constantly have to sift through stacks of paper. Perhaps more important, investors would have the ability to access these data through the Internet. Thus, investors throughout the world could have information available for their decisions literally minutes after the documents are made effective by the SEC.

Because of the ambitious nature of the EDGAR project, approximately a decade was required to get the system effectively operational. For years, EDGAR was the object of much scorn; "one member of the House Energy and Commerce Committee suggested renaming the project Mr. Ed, 'since the SEC has a much better chance of finding a talking horse than it does of achieving an efficient computer filing system.'"[48] However, the beginning of the explosive use of the Internet in the mid-1990s corresponded with the widespread availability of information on EDGAR. Not surprisingly, EDGAR's popularity has expanded.

> If you're suspicious about a certain stock, then go to the Securities and Exchange Commission's EDGAR database—chockablock with annual reports, prospectuses and all the other paperwork demanded of public companies.[49]
>
> Since Congress went to all the trouble in the 1930s of creating the SEC and requiring these corporate disclosures, it seems like somebody should give them an occasional good read.

> The EDGAR database at the SEC's Web site gives any individual free access to the filings of thousands of public companies. . . . It's sometimes amazing what kind of information typing someone's name, address or phone number into an EDGAR search engine can generate.[50]

Today virtually all publicly held companies are required to file their SEC reports electronically. Paper filings, when permitted, are also converted to electronic files and available to the general public.[51] The resultant EDGAR filings are typically available via the SEC's website within 24 hours of filing. These public filings, combined with the ease of access via the Internet, have resulted in the virtually immediate dissemination of vital investment-related data to accounting professionals, financial advisers, government regulators, and the investing public. EDGAR users can locate filings based on entity names, standard industrial classification (SIC) codes, central index keys (CIK), addresses, date–time frames, and a variety of other variables. This extensive database has helped move financial reporting to a significantly higher level of transparency.

Summary

1. In the United States, the Securities and Exchange Commission (SEC) has been entrusted with the responsibility for ensuring that complete and reliable information is available to investors who buy and sell securities in public capital markets. Since being created in 1934, this agency has administered numerous reporting rules and regulations created by congressional actions starting with the Securities Act of 1933 and the Securities Exchange Act of 1934.
2. The corporate accounting scandals that rocked the U.S. financial community during 2001 and 2002 led Congress to pass the Sarbanes–Oxley Act. This legislation addressed a number of problems. One main provision was the creation of the Public Company Accounting Oversight Board to monitor and regulate the auditors of public companies. Audit firms of public companies must register with this board and are subject to periodic inspections as well as various types of possible disciplinary actions. This act also contains rules to help ensure the independence of the external auditor.

[47] Stephen Labaton, "Can a Bloodied S.E.C. Dust Itself Off and Get Moving?" *The New York Times,* December 16, 2002.

[48] Sandra Block, "SEC Gets Closer to Electronic Filing," *The Wall Street Journal,* August 30, 1991, p. C1.

[49] Joseph R. Garber, "Click Before You Leap," *Forbes,* February 24, 1997, p. 162.

[50] John Emshwiller, "Financial Filings Hold Key to Investigative Pieces, Big and Small," *The Wall Street Journal,* May 31, 2005.

[51] www.sec.gov/edgar/quickedgar.htm.

3. Before a company's securities (either equity or debt) can be publicly traded, appropriate filings must be made with the SEC to ensure that sufficient data are made available to potential investors. Disclosure requirements for this process are outlined in two documents: *Regulation S-K* (for nonfinancial information) and *Regulation S-X* (describing the form and content of all included financial statements).
4. The ability to require the reporting of special information gives the SEC enormous legal power over accounting standards in the United States. Traditionally, this authority has been wielded only on rare occasions and only to increase disclosure requirements and to provide guidance where none was otherwise available. However, in a significant demonstration of its authority, the SEC overruled the FASB's decision in 1977 as to the appropriate method to account for unsuccessful exploration and drilling costs incurred by oil- and gas-producing companies.
5. Filings with the SEC are divided generally into two broad categories: registration statements and periodic filings. Registration statements are designed to provide information about a company prior to its issuance of a security to the public. Depending on the circumstances, several different registration forms are available for this purpose. After the registrant produces the statement and the SEC initially reviews it, a letter of comments describing desired explanations or changes is furnished. These concerns must be resolved before the security can be sold.
6. Not all securities issued in the United States require registration with the SEC. As an example, formal registration is not necessary for securities sold by either government units or banks. Certain issues for relatively small amounts are also exempt although some amount of disclosure is normally required. Securities sold solely within the state in which the business operates are not subject to federal securities laws but must comply with state laws frequently referred to as *blue sky laws.*
7. Companies whose stocks or bonds are publicly traded on a securities exchange must also submit periodic filings to the SEC to ensure that adequate disclosure is constantly maintained. Among the most common of these filings are Form 10-K (an annual report) and Form 10-Q (condensed interim financial information). Form 8-K also is required to report any significant events that occur. In addition, proxy statements (documents that are used to solicit votes at stockholders' meetings) also come under the filing requirements monitored by the SEC.
8. The SEC created the EDGAR database to allow companies to make electronic filings with the commission. More importantly, EDGAR allows any person with access to the Internet to review these documents in a timely fashion. Thus, access to financial and other information about filing entities has become much more widely available.

Questions

(Students should visit the SEC website, www.sec.gov, for supplemental resources.)

1. Why were federal securities laws originally enacted by Congress?
2. What are some of the possible reasons for the numerous corporate accounting scandals discovered during 2001 and 2002?
3. List several provisions of the Sarbanes–Oxley Act that are designed to restore public confidence in the U.S. capital market system.
4. What is the SEC's relationship to the Public Company Accounting Oversight Board?
5. Who must register with the Public Company Accounting Oversight Board?
6. What is the impact of being registered with the PCAOB?
7. How has the Sarbanes–Oxley Act attempted to ensure that external auditors will be completely independent in the future?
8. What is the purpose of the inspection process created by the Sarbanes–Oxley Act?
9. What is covered by *Regulation S-K?*
10. What is covered by *Regulation S-X?*
11. What are some of the major divisions and offices within the SEC?
12. What does the Securities Act of 1933 cover?
13. What does the Securities Exchange Act of 1934 cover?
14. What are the goals of the SEC?
15. What information is required in a proxy statement?
16. Why is the content of a proxy statement considered to be so important?
17. How does the SEC affect the development of generally accepted accounting principles in the United States?

18. What is the purpose of *Financial Reporting Releases* and *Staff Accounting Bulletins?*
19. What was the SEC's response to the FASB's handling of accounting for oil- and gas-producing companies, and why was this action considered so significant?
20. What is the purpose of a registration statement?
21. Under what law is a registration statement filed?
22. What are the two parts of a registration statement? What does each part contain?
23. How does the SEC generate revenues?
24. Two forms commonly used in the registration process are Form S-1 and Form S-3. Which registrants should use each form?
25. What is incorporation by reference?
26. What is a prefiling conference, and why might it be helpful to a registrant?
27. What is a letter of comments? By what other name is it often called?
28. What is a prospectus? What does a prospectus contain?
29. Under what circumstances is a company exempt from filing a registration statement with the SEC prior to the issuance of securities?
30. What is a private placement of securities?
31. What are blue sky laws?
32. What is a wraparound filing?
33. When is a Form 8-K issued by a company? What specific information does a Form 8-K convey?
34. What is the purpose of the Management's Discussion and Analysis?
35. What is the difference between a Form 10-K and a Form 10-Q?
36. What was the purpose of creating the EDGAR system?

Problems

LO 12-1

1. Which of the following statements is true?
   a. The Securities Exchange Act of 1934 regulates intrastate stock offerings made by a company.
   b. The Securities Act of 1933 regulates the subsequent public trading of securities through brokers and markets.
   c. The Securities Exchange Act of 1934 is commonly referred to as blue sky legislation.
   d. The Securities Act of 1933 regulates the initial offering of securities by a company.

LO 12-2

2. What is the purpose of *Regulation S-K?*
   a. Defines generally accepted accounting principles in the United States
   b. Establishes required disclosure of nonfinancial information with the SEC
   c. Establishes required financial disclosures with the SEC
   d. Indicates which companies must file with the SEC on an annual basis

LO 12-2

3. What is the difference between *Regulation S-K* and *Regulation S-X?*
   a. *Regulation S-K* establishes reporting requirements for companies in their initial issuance of securities, whereas *Regulation S-X* is directed toward the subsequent issuance of securities.
   b. *Regulation S-K* establishes reporting requirements for companies smaller than a certain size, whereas *Regulation S-X* is directed toward companies larger than that size.
   c. *Regulation S-K* establishes regulations for nonfinancial information filed with the SEC, whereas *Regulation S-X* prescribes the form and content of financial statements included in SEC filings.
   d. *Regulation S-K* establishes reporting requirements for publicly held companies, whereas *Regulation S-X* is directed toward private companies.

LO 12-2

4. The Securities Exchange Act of 1934
   a. Regulates the public trading of previously issued securities through brokers and exchanges.
   b. Prohibits blue sky laws.
   c. Regulates the initial offering of securities by a company.
   d. Requires the registration of investment advisers.

LO 12-3

5. Which of the following is a requirement of the Sarbanes–Oxley Act of 2002?
   a. Registration of all auditing firms with the Public Company Accounting Oversight Board
   b. Annual inspection of all auditing firms registered with the Public Company Accounting Oversight Board

c. A monetary fee assessed on organizations issuing securities

d. Overall assessment of the work of the SEC each year

LO 12-3

6. Which of the following is *not* correct with regard to the Public Company Accounting Oversight Board?

a. The board can expel a registered auditing firm without SEC approval.

b. All registered auditing firms must be inspected at least every three years.

c. The board members must be appointed by Congress.

d. The board has the authority to set auditing standards rather than utilize the work of the Auditing Standards Board.

LO 12-3

7. Which of the following is *not* a way by which the Sarbanes–Oxley Act attempts to ensure auditor independence from an audit client?

a. The auditing firm must be appointed by the client's audit committee.

b. Audit fees must be approved by the Public Company Accounting Oversight Board.

c. The audit committee must be composed of members of the client's board of directors who are independent of the management.

d. The external auditor cannot also perform financial information system design and implementation work.

LO 12-5

8. What is a registration statement?

a. A statement that must be filed with the SEC before a company can begin an initial offering of securities to the public

b. A required filing with the SEC before a large amount of stock can be obtained by an inside party

c. An annual filing made with the SEC

d. A filing made by a company with the SEC to indicate that a significant change has occurred

LO 12-5

9. Which of the following is a registration statement used by large companies that already have a significant following in the stock market?

a. Form 8-K

b. Form 10-K

c. Form S-1

d. Form S-3

LO 12-4

10. What was the significance of the controversy in 1977 over the appropriate accounting principles to be used by oil- and gas-producing companies?

a. Several major lawsuits resulted.

b. Companies refused to follow the SEC's dictates.

c. Partners of a major accounting firm were indicted on criminal charges.

d. The SEC overruled the FASB on its handling of this matter.

LO 12-6

11. Which of the following must be provided to every potential buyer of a new security?

a. A letter of comments

b. A deficiency letter

c. A prospectus

d. A Form S-16

LO 12-5

12. What does the term *incorporation by reference* mean?

a. The legal incorporation of a company in more than one state

b. Filing information with the SEC by indicating that the information is already available in another document

c. A reference guide indicating informational requirements specified in *Regulation S-X*

d. Incorporating a company in a state outside of its base of operations

LO 12-6

13. What is a letter of comments?

a. A letter the SEC sends to a company indicating needed changes or clarifications in a registration statement

b. A questionnaire supplied to the SEC by a company suggesting changes in *Regulation S-X*

c. A letter included in a Form 10-K to indicate the management's assessment of the company's financial position

d. A letter composed by a company asking for information or clarification prior to the filing of a registration statement

LO 12-6

14. What is a prospectus?
    a. A document attached to a Form 8-K
    b. A potential stockholder, as defined by *Regulation S-K*
    c. A document a company files with the SEC prior to filing a registration statement
    d. The first part of a registration statement that a company must furnish to all potential buyers of a new security

LO 12-6

15. Which of the following is *not* exempt from registration with the SEC under the Securities Act of 1933?
    a. Securities issued by a nonprofit religious organization
    b. Securities issued by a government unit
    c. A public offering of $40 million to unaccredited investors under Regulation A
    d. An offering to 40 sophisticated investors

LO 12-6

16. Which of the following is usually *not* filed with the SEC on a regular periodic basis?
    a. A Form 10-Q
    b. A prospectus
    c. A proxy statement
    d. A Form 10-K

LO 12-6

17. What is a shelf registration?
    a. A registration statement that the SEC formally rejects
    b. A registration statement that the SEC rejects due to the lapse of a specified period of time
    c. A registration process for large companies that allows them to offer securities over a period of time without seeking additional approval by the SEC
    d. A registration form that is withdrawn by the registrant without any action having been taken

LO 12-6

18. What is EDGAR?
    a. A system the SEC uses to reject registration statements that do not contain adequate information
    b. The enforcement arm of the SEC
    c. A system designed by the SEC to allow electronic filings
    d. A branch of the government that oversees the work of the SEC

LO 12-1, 12-3, 12-5, 12-6

19. Identify each of the following as they pertain to the SEC.
    a. Blue sky laws
    b. S-8 Statement
    c. Letter of comments
    d. Public Company Accounting Oversight Board
    e. Prospectus

LO 12-2

20. Discuss the objectives of the Securities Act of 1933 and the Securities Exchange Act of 1934. How are these objectives accomplished?

LO 12-6

21. What are the general steps involved in filing a registration statement with the SEC?

LO 12-4

22. Discuss the methods by which the SEC can influence the development of generally accepted accounting principles in the United States.

LO 12-6

23. Which forms do most companies file with the SEC on a periodic basis? Explain the purpose of each form and its primary contents.

LO 12-5

24. Which forms do most companies file with the SEC in connection with the offering of securities to the public?

LO 12-6

25. What is the importance of a Form 8-K? What is the importance of a proxy statement?

LO 12-3

26. Describe the provisions of the Sarbanes–Oxley Act as they relate to the creation and responsibilities of the Public Company Accounting Oversight Board.

LO 12-1, 12-2, 12-4, 12-5, 12-6

27. Explain each of the following items:
    a. Staff Accounting Bulletins
    b. Wraparound filing
    c. Incorporation by reference
    d. Division of Corporation Finance
    e. Integrated disclosure system
    f. Management's discussion and analysis
    g. Chief accountant of the SEC

LO 12-6

28. Which organizations are normally exempted from the SEC's registration requirements?

Develop Your Skills

RESEARCH CASE 1

Domer Corporation is preparing to issue a relatively small amount of securities and does not want to go to the trouble and expense of filing a registration statement with the SEC. Company officials hope to be exempt under provisions of Regulation A. These officials want to be certain that they meet these provisions precisely so that no later legal problems arise.

Required

Go to the website www.sec.gov and select "Corporate Finance under Divisions." Then select the link for "Statutes, Rules, and Forms," followed by the "Rules, Regulations, and Schedules" link. Based on the information provided for Regulation A (click on "General Rules and Regulations, Securities Act of 1933"), prepare a report for Domer Corporation officials as to the requirements for exemption and advise as to the maximum amount of capital that may be raised through such issuance. Assuming that Domer Corporation is a development-stage company, revise the report. Note specifically Regulation §230.251.

RESEARCH CASE 2

Tasch Corporation, a multilevel marketing and sales organization, plans to sell approximately $10,000,000 worth of "service agreements" to many of its customers. These service agreements guarantee a set return to the customer in exchange for an up-front purchase price, with Tasch Corporation managing the various business interests of its customers. Jerry Tasch, the corporation's president, needs advice concerning the necessity of SEC filings prior to the sale of these service agreements.

Required

Assume that the only (initial) question to be addressed is whether the service agreements constitute securities under the Securities Act of 1933. Perform research utilizing an Internet search engine to determine whether the service agreements are in fact securities. Note that courts interpret statutes and regulations, so it is often useful to look at judicial determinations to reach a conclusion. To that end, consider locating and reviewing the following case: *SEC v. Calvo,* 378 F.3d 1211 (11th Cir. 2004). Students can locate this case using many web links including FINDLAW and LexisNexis. This web link will direct the student directly to the specific opinion (https://law.resource.org/pub/us/case/reporter/F3/378/378.F3d.1211.02-13445.html).

ANALYSIS CASE 1

Go to the website www.sec.gov and, under the Filings heading, click on "Filings" and then click on "Company Filing Search." Enter the name of a well-known company such as Facebook. A list of available documents should be shown for that company.

Required

Using these available documents, answer the following questions:

1. Has the company filed an 8-K during the most recent time period? If so, open that document and determine the reason that the form was filed with the SEC.
2. Has the company filed a 10-K during the recent time period? If so, open that document and determine the total reported net income for the latest period of time.
3. Has the company filed a 10-Q during the most recent time period? If so, open that document and determine what issues were addressed and disclosed.

COMMUNICATION CASE 1

The senior partner of Wojtysiak & Co., CPAs, has been approached by a small, publicly traded corporation wishing to change auditors. The Wojtysiak firm does not audit any other public companies. Because of the Sarbanes–Oxley Act of 2002, Mike Wojtysiak, the senior partner, needs to know the regulatory issues facing his firm if it accepts the new engagement.

Required

Draft a report that outlines the Sarbanes–Oxley considerations for a firm such as the Wojtysiak firm. Locate the actual act (Public Law 107-204), or perform a thorough summary and review it prior to preparing the report. The full act may be found at www.gpo.gov/fdsys/pkg/PLAW-107publ204/pdf/PLAW-107publ204.pdf.

chapter 13

Accounting for Legal Reorganizations and Liquidations

Learning Objectives

After studying this chapter, you should be able to:

- **LO 13-1** Describe both the history and current status of bankruptcy and bankruptcy laws.
- **LO 13-2** Describe the reporting actions that accountants should consider before a troubled company declares bankruptcy.
- **LO 13-3** Explain the difference between a voluntary bankruptcy and an involuntary bankruptcy.
- **LO 13-4** Identify the various types of creditors based on their status during a bankruptcy.
- **LO 13-5** Describe the difference between a Chapter 7 bankruptcy and a Chapter 11 bankruptcy.
- **LO 13-6** Account for a company as it enters bankruptcy.
- **LO 13-7** Account for the liquidation of a company in bankruptcy especially when using the liquidation basis of accounting.
- **LO 13-8** Discuss the provisions often found in a bankruptcy reorganization plan.
- **LO 13-9** Account for a company as it moves through reorganization.
- **LO 13-10** Describe the financial reporting for a company that successfully exits bankruptcy as a reorganized entity.

One common thread running through a significant portion of this textbook is the financial reporting of an organization when viewed as a whole.[1] Several chapters examine the consolidation of financial information generated by two or more companies united in a business combination. Although that coverage includes the reporting of many specific accounts, the primary emphasis is on producing financial statements for multiple organizations that form a single economic entity.

Likewise, coverage of foreign currency translation describes the procedures used in consolidating the assets, liabilities, and operating results of a subsidiary conducting business in a different functional currency than that of its parent.

The textbook also includes explanations of various reporting requirements for disaggregated information to show the many distinct ways a single organization can be presented. Again, the accounting goal is to convey data that enables decision makers to evaluate the entire operation.

Continuing with this theme, subsequent chapters present the specialized accounting used by partnerships, state and local government units, not-for-profit organizations, estates, and trusts. Clearly, the presentation of financial data to describe a particular type of organization does not rely on a rigid structure. Accounting is adaptable.

Numerous factors influence specific reporting requirements: the purpose of the information, the nature and environment of the organization, and so on. In reporting the operations, cash flows, and financial position of a business combination, a foreign subsidiary, an operating segment, a partnership, a state or local government unit, an estate, or a not-for-profit organization, accountants must develop unique techniques to address particular reporting needs and problems.

The current chapter extends this coverage of organizations as a whole by examining the accounting procedures required for financially troubled companies. In such circumstances, both owners and creditors face the prospect of incurring significant losses. Once again, the accountant must adapt financial reporting to meet varied informational needs. The failure of a significant number of prominent companies during the past decade has made this accounting process especially relevant.

[1] Intermediate accounting textbooks, in contrast, tend to examine the reporting of specific assets and liabilities such as leases, pensions, deferred income taxes, bonds, and the like.

LO 13-1

Describe both the history and current status of bankruptcy and bankruptcy laws.

Overview of Bankruptcy in the United States

The most widely-accepted theory on the origin of the word "bankruptcy" comes from a mixing of the ancient Latin words *bancus* (bench or table) and *ruptus* (broken). When a banker, who originally conducted his public marketplace transactions on a bench, was unable to continue lending and meet obligations, his bench was broken in a symbolic show of failure and inability to negotiate. As a result of the frequency of this practice in Medieval Italy, the current term bankrupt is commonly believed to spring specifically from the translation of *banco rotto,* Italian for broken bank.[2]

A basic assumption of accounting is that a business is a *going concern* unless evidence to the contrary is discovered. As a result, assets such as inventory, land, buildings, and equipment are traditionally reported based on historical cost rather than the net realizable value they could command at the current time. Unfortunately, not all organizations prove to be going concerns.[3] The number of companies experiencing financial difficulties varies from year to year as the economy and other conditions change. During the 12 months ending September 30, 2018, 13,682 U.S. businesses filed for Chapter 7 bankruptcy, and another 5,962 filed for Chapter 11 bankruptcy.[4]

The sheer size of the more renowned bankruptcies is often astronomical. Many of the 10 largest U.S. bankruptcies occurred in the last 15 years, but none since 2014.

- Lehman Brothers Holdings Inc., September 15, 2008, $691 billion in assets.
- Washington Mutual Inc., September 26, 2008, $328 billion.
- WorldCom Inc., July 21, 2002, $104 billion.
- General Motors Corp., June 1, 2009, $82 billion.
- CIT Group, Inc., November 1, 2009, $71 billion.
- Enron Corp., December 2, 2001, $66 billion.
- Conseco Inc., December 17, 2002, $61 billion.
- Energy Future Holdings Corp., April 29, 2014, $41 billion.
- MF Global Holdings, LTD, October 31, 2011, $41 billion.
- Chrysler LLC, April 30, 2009, $39 billion.[5]

Although not of the size of the previous companies, several prominent businesses filed for bankruptcy during 2018 including Sears Holdings, Nine West, Claire's, Bon-Ton, Brookstone, and Rockport. Some of these failures likely reflect the changing face of retail sales.

What happens to these businesses after they fail? Is bankruptcy the equivalent of a death sentence? Who gets any assets that remain? Are creditors protected? During this period, how does the accountant reflect the economic plight of the company?

Virtually all businesses undergo occasional financial difficulties. Economic downturns, poor product performance, intense competition, rapid technological changes, unwise acquisitions, and litigation losses can create cash flow difficulties for even the best-managed organizations. Management teams will attempt remedial actions in hopes of returning operations to normal profitability. Unfortunately, not every company is able to solve its difficulties. If problems persist, a company can eventually become *insolvent,* unable to pay debts as the obligations come due. When creditors are not paid, they take whatever actions they can to protect their financial interests in hopes of reducing possible losses. They might seek recovery from

[2] BankruptcyData a division of New Generation Research, Inc. www.bankruptcydata.com/Ch11History.htm.

[3] A short history of bankruptcies and bankruptcy law over the past 2,000 years can be found at http://www.bankruptcydata.com/Ch11History.htm.

[4] United States Courts "Caseload Statistics Data Tables," http://www.uscourts.gov/sites/default/files/data_tables/bf_f5a_0930.2018.pdf.

[5] Amanda Harding, "The Biggest Bankruptcies in America's History Prove No One is 'Too Big to Fail'" *The Cheat Sheet,* September 13, 2018. https://www.cheatsheet.com/money-career/the-biggest-bankruptcies-in-americas-history-prove-no-one-is-too-big-to-fail.html/.

the distressed company in several ways including repossessing assets, filing lawsuits, foreclosing on loans, and so on. An insolvent company can quickly become besieged by its creditors.

If left unchecked, pandemonium is likely be the outcome of a company's insolvency. As a result, some creditors, stockholders, and the company itself could be treated unfairly. One party might collect debts in full while another is left with a total loss. Not surprisingly, bankruptcy laws have been established in the United States to structure this process, provide protection for all parties, and ensure fair and equitable treatment.

Although a complete coverage of bankruptcy statutes is more appropriate for a business law textbook, significant aspects of this process directly involve accountants.

> In many small business situations, the company accountant is the sole outside financial adviser and the first to recognize that the deteriorating financial picture mandates consideration of bankruptcy in one form or another. In many such situations, the accountant's role in convincing management that a timely reorganization under the bankruptcy law is the sole means of salvaging any part of the business may be critical.[6]

Describe the reporting actions that accountants should consider before a troubled company declares bankruptcy.

Preliminary Reporting Considerations for a Troubled Company

Companies rarely fall into bankruptcy because of a single, sudden action. Typically, management will struggle for months if not years to keep operations viable. During that time, a number of reporting actions can become necessary. For example, the possible demise of the company might force an accounting reassessment of several assets.

Goodwill is one obvious asset that accountants must monitor. As discussed in an earlier chapter, entities are required to test goodwill annually for impairment. More frequent testing is necessary if circumstances or events indicate that the fair value of an individual reporting unit is more likely than not to have fallen below its carrying amount. If possible bankruptcy looms, accountants should not wait to begin testing for goodwill impairment. "It is common for goodwill to be impaired prior to the bankruptcy filing."[7]

Another asset balance that requires reporting attention in troubled times is a deferred income tax asset. As covered in intermediate accounting textbooks, a valuation allowance must be recognized to offset the impact of this future tax benefit but only if it is more likely than not that the asset will not be realized. The possibility that an entity will not be able to make use of a temporary tax difference (a warranty expense, for example) to reduce future amounts of taxable income increases as the financial outlook becomes more uncertain. Accountants weigh all available factors to assess the need for creating a valuation allowance to offset the financial effect of tax assets. If the possibility of bankruptcy looms, the likelihood of that recognition increases.

FASB also provides additional structure for the reporting of troubled companies. A formal warning is necessary when bankruptcy becomes a possibility so that outside decision makers are not caught unaware. Accounting Standards Update 2014-15 ("Disclosure of Uncertainties about an Entity's Ability to Continue as a Going Concern") describes situations of uncertainty that warrant investigation and the related disclosures needed to inform financial statement readers of going-concern issues.

According to this update to U.S. GAAP, conditions or events can arise that, in the aggregate, cast substantial doubt on an entity's ability to continue as a going concern for a reasonable period of time. Substantial doubt is said to exist when evidence shows that an entity will probably be unable to meet its financial obligations as they come due during a period that extends one year from the date of the financial statements.

Several of the conditions or events that could signal an entity's inability to meet debts as they come due include the following. They are obviously signs of possible future trouble.

- Recurring operating losses.
- Working capital deficiencies.

[6] John K. Pearson, "The Role of the Accountant in Business Bankruptcies," *The National Public Accountant,* November 1982, p. 22.

[7] PWC, "Bankruptcies and Liquidations," *Accounting Guide,* October 2018. pp. 2–3, https://www.pwc.com/us/en/cfodirect/assets/pdf/accounting-guides/pwc-guide-bankruptcies-and-liquidations.pdf.

- Negative cash flows from operating activities.
- Loan default.
- Work stoppages or other labor difficulties.
- Legal proceedings.
- Loss of a key asset such as a patent or franchise.[8]

If substantial doubt exists about the ability of a reporting entity to continue as a going concern, management must evaluate any plans that are in place to avoid the possibility of failing to meet obligations as they come due. For financial reporting purposes, two questions must be addressed:

1. First, is it probable that the entity can effectively implement these plans within the one-year period? Plans provide no benefit if described actions cannot or will not be taken.
2. Second, is it probable that the plans will mitigate the conditions or events that have raised substantial doubts? The plans must provide a genuine likelihood of success.

What are possible plans that a management team might create to address the substantial doubt that the entity will be able to make its debt payments within one year from the issuance of current financial statements? Many possibilities exist. Management could develop plans to dispose of assets to raise needed cash and reduce costs. Management might also plan to borrow money, seek a restructuring of debt agreements, reduce expenditures, or increase outside ownership. All of these possibilities could raise the funds necessary to reduce the level of uncertainty.

However, plans alone are not sufficient. Management must also present evidence to show that it can probably implement the plans, and if so, that they will probably mitigate the conditions or events that have created the high level of doubt.

Interestingly, the reporting entity must disclose the going-concern problem even if implementation of the plans is probable and mitigation of the potential crisis is probable. Once substantial doubt has been raised, certain information must be included in the financial reporting to make outside decision makers aware of the situation.

- If substantial doubt is raised but alleviated by management's plans, the reporting entity discloses the conditions that caused the concern along with management's evaluation of their significance and the plans that are expected to address the problems.
- If substantial doubt is raised that is not alleviated by management's plans, the entity provides the same information as noted earlier. In addition, management must include a clear statement in the footnotes to disclose that substantial doubt exists about the entity's ability to continue as a going concern for one year from the issuance date of the financial statements. The statements provide readers with an adequate warning.

In both cases, outside decision makers are made aware of the concern. Furthermore, if that concern has not been mitigated, a warning of the current substantial doubt is included in financial statement note disclosures.

U.S. Bankruptcy Laws

> Over the ages debtors who found themselves unable to meet obligations were dealt with harshly. Not only were all their assets taken from them, but they were given little or no relief through legal forgiveness of debts. Many of them ended up in debtors' prisons with all means of rehabilitation removed. A large number of the early settlers in this country left their homelands to escape such a fate.[9]

Based on an original provision in the U.S. Constitution, Congress (rather than the individual state governments) is responsible for creating bankruptcy laws. Nevertheless, virtually no federal bankruptcy laws were passed until the Bankruptcy Act of 1898 (revised in 1938 by the

[8] FASB, *ASC* 205-40-55-2, "Disclosure of Uncertainties about an Entity's Ability to Continue as a Going Concern."

[9] Homer A. Bonhiver, *The Expanded Role of the Accountant under the 1978 Bankruptcy Code* (New York: Deloitte Haskins & Sells, 1980), p. 7.

Chandler Act). Later, following a decade of study and debate, the Bankruptcy Reform Act of 1978 replaced these laws. Congress has amended this act several times since 1978.[10]

Consequently, the Bankruptcy Reform Act of 1978 as amended continues to provide legal structure for most bankruptcy proceedings in the United States. *The laws strive to achieve two goals in connection with insolvency cases: (1) the fair distribution of assets to creditors and (2) the discharge of an honest debtor from debt.*

LO 13-3

Explain the difference between a voluntary bankruptcy and an involuntary bankruptcy.

Voluntary and Involuntary Petitions

When insolvency occurs, every interested party has the right to seek protection under the Bankruptcy Reform Act.[11] The company itself can file a petition with the court to begin bankruptcy proceedings. If the company is the initiator, the process is referred to as a *voluntary bankruptcy*. In such cases, the petition must be accompanied by exhibits listing all assets and debts.[12] Company officials also must respond to questions concerning various aspects of the business's affairs. Such questions include

- When did the business commence?
- In whose possession are the books of account and records?
- When was the last inventory of property taken?

Creditors also can seek to force a debtor into bankruptcy (known as an *involuntary bankruptcy*) in hopes of reducing their potential losses. To avoid nuisance actions, bankruptcy laws regulate the filing of involuntary petitions. If a company has 12 or more unsecured creditors, at least 3 must sign the petition. The creditors that sign must have unsecured debts of at least $16,750.[13] If fewer than 12 unsecured creditors exist, only a single signer is required, but the $16,750 minimum debt limit remains.

Neither a voluntary nor an involuntary petition automatically creates a bankruptcy case. Bankruptcy courts can reject voluntary petitions if the action is considered detrimental to the creditors. Involuntary petitions also can be rejected unless evidence exists to indicate that the debtor is not actually able to meet obligations as they come due. Merely being slow to make payments is not sufficient. Debtors may well fight an involuntary petition fearing that their reputation will be tainted.

If the court accepts the petition, an *order for relief* is granted which creates an automatic stay that halts all actions against the debtor. This stay provides time for the various parties to consider what steps should be taken to limit losses. The company comes under the authority of the bankruptcy court so that any asset distributions must be made in a fair manner.

> To prevent creditors from seizing whatever is handy once the bankruptcy is filed, the Bankruptcy Code provides for an automatic stay or injunction that prohibits actions by creditors to collect debts from the debtor or the debtor's property without the court's permission. The automatic stay bars any creditor (including governmental creditors such as the Internal Revenue Service) from taking any action against the debtor or the debtor's property.[14]

[10] An excellent overview of the bankruptcy process from a legal perspective, "Bankruptcy Basics" by the Administrative Office of the U.S. Courts can be found at http://www.uscourts.gov/FederalCourts/Bankruptcy/BankruptcyBasics.aspx. Bankruptcy can be viewed in an entirely different light in the book *Comic Wars* by Dan Raviv ©2002 Broadway Books. *Comic Wars* follows the battle between several financial icons as they seek to gain control over Marvel Entertainment as the company struggles to avoid liquidation.

[11] Insolvency (not being able to pay debts as they come due) is not necessary for filing a bankruptcy petition. During the 1980s, such companies as Manville Corporation, Texaco, and A. H. Robins filed for protection under the Bankruptcy Reform Act in hopes of settling massive litigation claims.

[12] The bankruptcy petition filed by Circuit City on November 10, 2008, can be found at http://www.creditslips.org/creditslips/CircuitCity.pdf. This document shows that the company held total assets of $3.4 billion and total debt of $2.3 billion. The document indicates that off-balance-sheet debts (such as operating leases) have not been included in this total. On that day, the company owed Hewlett-Packard, its biggest unsecured creditor, $118,797,964. The petition originally sought a reorganization, but that quickly became a liquidation in January 2009, after an unsuccessful attempt to generate a significant amount of cash from Christmas sales.

[13] Throughout the bankruptcy laws, a number of monetary thresholds exist. These dollar amounts are adjusted for inflation every three years based on the Consumer Price Index for All Urban Consumers. The $16,750 figure was established on April 1, 2019.

[14] Pearson, "The Role of the Accountant," p. 24.

LO 13-4

Identify the various types of creditors based on their status during a bankruptcy.

Classification of Creditors

Following the issuance of an order for relief, the possibility of loss influences each party's view of a bankruptcy case. However, some creditors might have already obtained a measure of security for themselves. When parties create a debt, they can agree to attach a mortgage lien or security interest to specified assets (known as *collateral*) owned by the debtor. This action is most likely to occur when the amounts involved are great or the debtor is experiencing financial difficulty. Subsequently, if the liability is not paid when due, the creditor can force the sale (or, in some cases, the return) of the pledged property with the proceeds used to satisfy all or part of the obligation. In bankruptcy proceedings, a secured creditor holds a much less vulnerable position than an unsecured creditor.

Because of the possible presence of liens, all loans and other liabilities are reported to the bankruptcy court according to their degree of protection against loss. Some are identified as *fully secured* to indicate that the net realizable value of the collateral exceeds the amount of the obligation. Despite the debtor's insolvency, these creditors will suffer no loss. They are protected by the pledged property. Any money received from the collateral in excess of the debt balance is used to pay unsecured creditors.

A liability is viewed as *partially secured* if the value of the collateral covers only a portion of the obligation. The remainder is considered *unsecured.* The creditor risks losing some or all of the additional amount. For example, assume a bank holds a $90,000 loan due from an insolvent party. The creditor is protected by a lien attached to land valued at $64,000. The debt is only partially secured. Proceeds from the sale of the land will not satisfy the other $26,000 of the balance. This residual portion is reported to the court as unsecured.

All other liabilities are unsecured. These creditors have no legal right to any of the debtor's specific assets. They are only entitled to share in any funds that might remain after all secured claims have been settled. Unsecured creditors are in a precarious position. Unless a debtor's assets greatly exceed secured liabilities (which is unlikely in most insolvency cases), unsecured creditors can expect significant losses if liquidation becomes necessary. For example, the liquidation plan approved for Circuit City asserted, "unsecured creditors, such as suppliers, should get between 10 percent and 32 percent of the amount they are owed."[15]

Hence, an important aspect of the bankruptcy laws is the ranking of unsecured claims. The Bankruptcy Reform Act identifies several types of unsecured liabilities that have priority and must be paid before other unsecured debts are settled. *These obligations are ranked with each level to be satisfied in full before any payment is made to the next.* Only in this manner is a systematic distribution of any remaining assets possible.

Unsecured Liabilities Having Priority

The following liabilities have priority in a bankruptcy:[16]

1. Claims for administrative expenses such as the costs of preserving and liquidating available property. It also includes amounts owed to vendors for inventory delivered to the debtor within 20 days of the filing. All trustee expenses and the costs of outside attorneys, accountants, or other consultants logically fall within this category. Without this high-priority ranking, insolvent companies would have difficulty convincing qualified individuals to serve in these essential positions.

   > Ms. Goldstein's firm received $389 million in fees and expenses in its 3 ½ years as lead counsel in the Lehman Brothers bankruptcy, just a piece of the more than $1.4 billion in total fees paid out to all of the professional firms on Lehman's tab.[17]

2. Obligations arising between the date a petition is filed with the bankruptcy court and the appointment of a trustee or the issuance of an order for relief. In voluntary cases, such

[15] Louis Llovio, "Circuit City Liquidation Plan Approved in Bankruptcy Court," *Richmond Times-Dispatch* (online), September 9, 2010.

[16] Only the most significant unsecured liabilities given legal priority are included here. For a complete list, review a current business law textbook.

[17] Jacqueline Palank, "$1,000/Hour Bankruptcies: Attorneys Justify Their Fees," *Wall Street Journal,* June 4, 2012, p. B-6.

claims are rare because an order for relief is usually entered when the petition is filed. This provision is important in helping the debtor continue operations if an involuntary petition is presented but legal action is not immediately taken (often because the debtor resists possible court action). With this high ranking, the debtor can hope to continue to buy goods on credit in order to stay in business while resisting the involuntary petition.

3. Employee claims for wages earned during the 180 days preceding the filing of a petition. The amount of this priority is limited, though, to $13,650 per individual. (The limit was $12,475 until raised in 2016 to $12,850. That limit remained until set at $13,650 in 2019.) This priority ranking does not include officers' salaries. Employees are not company creditors in the traditional sense of that term. They did not enter employment to serve as lenders to the business. This designation prevents employees from being penalized too heavily because of the company's problems. It also encourages them to continue working until the bankruptcy issue is settled.
4. Employee claims for contributions to benefit plans earned during the 180 days preceding the filing of a petition. Again, a $13,650 limit per individual (reduced by certain specified payments) is enforced.
5. Claims for the return of deposits made by customers to acquire property or services that the debtor never delivered or provided. The priority figure here is limited to $3,025. These claimants did not intend to be creditors. They were merely trying to make a purchase.
6. Government claims for unpaid taxes.

All of the remaining obligations of an insolvent company are classified as general unsecured claims that will be repaid only after all creditors with priority have been satisfied. *If the funds that remain are not sufficient to settle all of these general unsecured claims, the available money must be divided proportionally.*

In practice, bankruptcies can be quite complicated. As an example, officials took almost eight months to sort out the affairs of RadioShack's bankruptcy. Many of the chain's 4,000 stores were saved but only under new ownership. Some creditors were paid in full. Unfortunately, the results were not as good for the unsecured creditors of the 95-year-old retailer. Not surprisingly, the company did not have sufficient assets at the end to pay the $1 billion in debt that it carried. The bankruptcy was only finalized when unsecured creditors agreed to drop lawsuits against secured creditors. In exchange, approximately $9 million was set aside for the unsecured creditors to limit their losses somewhat.

LO 13-5

Describe the difference between a Chapter 7 bankruptcy and a Chapter 11 bankruptcy.

An essential decision in any bankruptcy filing (either voluntary or involuntary) is the method by which the debtor will be discharged from its obligations. One obvious option is to liquidate the company's assets with the proceeds distributed to creditors based on their secured positions and the priority ranking system just outlined. However, an important alternative to liquidation does exist. A debtor organization might be able to survive insolvency and continue operating if the parties involved will accept a proposal for *reorganization.*

Legal guidelines for the liquidation of a debtor are contained in Chapter 7 of Title I of the Bankruptcy Reform Act. Chapter 11 describes the reorganization process. Consequently, the proceedings have come to be referred to as a Chapter 7 bankruptcy (liquidation) or as a Chapter 11 bankruptcy (reorganization).

Not everyone agrees with the wisdom of allowing troubled businesses to reorganize and continue operating. This argument holds that keeping inefficient organizations alive and competing does not serve the industry or the economy well.

> There are many reasons why a business gets sick, but they don't necessarily mean it should be destroyed. Hundreds of thousands of businesses that at one time or another had financial difficulties survive today as the result of Chapter 11 proceedings. They continue to contribute to employment, to tax revenues, to overall growth. It's counterproductive to destroy the business value of an asset by liquidating it and paying it out in a Chapter 7 if that company shows signs of being able to recover in a reorganization.[18]

[18] James A. Goodman as interviewed by Robert A. Mamis, "Why Bankruptcy Works," *Inc.*, October 1996, p. 39.

Discussion Question

WHAT DO WE DO NOW?

The Toledo Shirt Company manufactures men's shirts sold to department stores and other outlets throughout Ohio, Illinois, and Indiana. For the past 14 years, one of Toledo's major customers has been Abraham and Sons, a chain of nine stores selling men's clothing. Mr. Abraham retired 18 months ago, and his two sons took complete control of the organization. Since that time, they have invested significant sums of money in an attempt to expand each store by also selling women's clothing. Success in this new market has proven difficult. Abraham and Sons is not known for selling women's clothing, and no one in the company has much expertise in the area.

Approximately seven months ago, James Thurber, Toledo's chief financial officer, began to notice that Abraham and Sons was taking longer than usual to make payments. Instead of the normal 30 days, the retailer was taking 45 days—and frequently longer—to pay each invoice. Because of the amount of money involved, Thurber began to monitor the balance daily. When the age of the receivable ($467,000) hit 60 days, he called Abraham and Sons. The treasurer assured him that the company was merely having seasonal cash flow issues but that payments would soon be back on a normal schedule.

Thurber was still concerned and shortly thereafter placed Abraham and Sons on a "cash and carry" basis. No new sales were to be made unless cash was collected in advance. The company's treasurer immediately called Thurber to complain bitterly. "We have been one of your best customers for well over a decade, but now that we have gotten into a bit of trouble you stab us in the back. When we finish straightening things out here, we will remember this. We can get our shirts from someone else. Our expansions are now complete. We have hired an expert to help us better market women's clothing. We can see the light at the end of the tunnel. Abraham and Sons will soon be more profitable than ever." In hopes of appeasing the customer while still protecting his own financial position, Thurber agreed to sell merchandise to Abraham and Sons on a very limited credit basis.

A few days later, Thurber received a disturbing phone call from the vice president of another clothing manufacturer. "We've got to force Abraham and Sons into involuntary bankruptcy immediately to protect ourselves. Those guys are running their father's company into the ground. They owe me $270,000, and I can only hope to collect a small portion of the money now. I need two other creditors to sign the petition, and I want Toledo Shirt to be one of them. Abraham and Sons has already mortgaged all of its buildings and equipment so we cannot get anything from those assets. Their inventory stocks are dwindling, and sales have disappeared since they've tried to change the image of their stores. We can still get some of our money, but if we wait much longer, nothing will be left but the bones."

Should Toledo Shirt Company be loyal to a customer that has been excellent in the past or start the bankruptcy process to protect itself? What actions should Thurber take?

Contrast that statement with the following:

> The efficiency of Chapter 11 is undergoing scrutiny. A particular concern, in industries such as telecoms and now airlines, is that bankrupt firms will return with manageable debts and thus be better able to compete, with the result that they force hitherto healthier rivals into bankruptcy in their turn. Does Chapter 11 create zombie companies that live on, only to drag other firms into their graves?[19]

[19] "The Night of the Killer Zombies," *The Economist*, December 14, 2002.

Discussion Question

HOW MUCH IS THAT BUILDING REALLY WORTH?

Viron, Inc., was created in 2011 to recycle plastic products and manufacture a variety of new items. The actual production process was quite complex because old plastic had to be divided into categories and then reclaimed based on the composition. Viron made new products based on the type of plastic available and the market demand.

In December 2015, the company spent $10.5 million to construct a building for manufacturing purposes. It was designed specifically to meet Viron's needs. The building was constructed near Gaffney, South Carolina, to take advantage of a large labor force available because of unemployment in the area.

Unfortunately, Viron was unable to generate sufficient revenues quickly enough to reach the break-even point and was forced to file for bankruptcy. An accountant was hired to aid the parties in deciding whether to liquidate or attempt a reorganization.

In producing an initial report for the court and the parties involved, the accountant needed to establish a liquidation value for the building in Gaffney, the company's largest asset. A real estate appraiser was brought in, and she made the following comments about the structure:

> The building is well constructed and practically new. It is clearly worth in excess of $10 million. However, I doubt that anyone is going to pay that much for it. We don't get a lot of new industry in this area. Not many companies need to buy large buildings. Even if a buyer is found, a significant amount of money will be required to convert the property into a different usage. Unless a company wants to recycle plastics, the building will have to be completely adapted to any other purpose. To be honest, I am not sure it can be sold at any price. There are a lot of abandoned buildings in this area of South Carolina. Of course, if someone wants to recycle plastics, it just might bring in $10 million.

In producing financial information for this company, how should the accountant report this building?

Under most reorganization plans, creditors agree to absorb a partial loss rather than force the insolvent company to liquidate. Before accepting such an arrangement, creditors (as well as the bankruptcy court) must be convinced that helping to rehabilitate the debtor will lead to a higher return (or a smaller loss). One potential benefit associated with reorganizations is that the creditor might be able to retain the insolvent company as a customer. In many cases, continuation of the relationship is an important concern if the debtor has been a good client in the past. Furthermore, the priority ranking system for debts often leaves general unsecured creditors with little to gain by trying to force a liquidation.

Accountants face two entirely different reporting situations depending on whether a Chapter 7 or a Chapter 11 bankruptcy is encountered. However, in both cases, accountants must keep all parties informed about relevant events as they occur.

LO 13-6

Account for a company as it enters bankruptcy.

Statement of Financial Affairs

> A federal bankruptcy judge on Friday granted a 30-day extension, to February 27, for AMR Corp.'s filing of schedules of assets and liabilities and a statement of financial affairs in its Chapter 11 bankruptcy restructuring.[20]

[20] D. R. Stewart, "AMR Gets Extension for Filing Key Papers," *McClatchy-Tribune Regional News,* January 28, 2012.

At the start of bankruptcy proceedings, the debtor normally prepares a statement of financial affairs. This schedule provides vital information about the company's financial position and helps guide all parties as they consider what actions to take. This statement is especially important in assisting unsecured creditors as they decide whether to push for reorganization or liquidation. To assist in these assessments, the debtor's assets and liabilities are reported according to the classifications that are relevant to a liquidation.

Consequently, on a statement of financial affairs, assets are labeled as follows:

1. Pledged with fully secured creditors.
2. Pledged with partially secured creditors.
3. Free assets available to pay priority liabilities with any remaining amount then used to pay some or all of the other unsecured creditors. This category consists of both assets that have not been pledged on debts and the excess value of any pledged assets. Excess value exists when an asset can be liquidated for more money than the debt it secures.

The company's debts are listed in a similar fashion:

1. Liabilities with priority.
2. Fully secured creditors.
3. Partially secured creditors.
4. Unsecured creditors. For convenience, stockholders are included in this final group.

The statement of financial affairs is produced under the assumption that liquidation will occur. Historical cost figures are not relevant. The parties to the bankruptcy desire information that reflects (1) the net realizable value of the debtor's assets and (2) the potential application of these proceeds to the various liabilities. With this knowledge, creditors and stockholders can estimate the monetary resources that will be available after all secured claims and priority liabilities have been settled. By comparing this total with the amount of unsecured liabilities, interested parties can approximate the eventual loss they face.

The information found in a statement of financial affairs can affect the outcome of a bankruptcy. If, for example, the statement indicates that unsecured creditors are destined to suffer a substantial loss from a liquidation, this group might well favor reorganizing the company in hopes of averting that consequence. Conversely, if the statement shows that all creditors will be paid in full and that a distribution to the stockholders is also possible, liquidation becomes a much more viable option. Thus, all parties involved with an insolvent company should study the statement of financial affairs before deciding the fate of the operation.

Statement of Financial Affairs Illustrated

For illustration purposes, assume that Chaplin Company recently experienced severe financial difficulties and is currently insolvent. It will soon file a voluntary bankruptcy petition. Company officials are trying to decide whether to seek liquidation or reorganization. They have asked their accounting firm to produce a statement of financial affairs to assist them in formulating an appropriate strategy. A current balance sheet for Chaplin, prepared as if the company were a going concern, is presented in Exhibit 13.1.

Assume that the following information about Chaplin Company has been accumulated as a preliminary step in creating the statement of financial affairs:

- The equity method investment reported on the balance sheet has appreciated in value since being acquired and is now worth $20,000. Dividends of $500 are currently due from this investment, although Chaplin has not yet recognized the revenue.
- Officials estimate that $12,000 of the company's accounts receivable can still be collected despite the bankruptcy proceedings.
- By spending $5,000 for repairs and marketing, Chaplin can sell its inventory for $50,000.
- The company will receive a $2,000 refund from the various prepaid expenses, but its intangible assets have no resale or other monetary value.
- The land and building are in an excellent location and can be sold for 10 percent more than net book value. However, the equipment was specially designed for Chaplin. The

EXHIBIT 13.1
Financial Position Prior to Bankruptcy Petition

CHAPLIN COMPANY
Balance Sheet
June 30, 2020

Assets		
Current assets:		
Cash	$ 2,000	
Investment (equity method)	15,000	
Accounts receivable (net)	23,000	
Inventory	41,000	
Prepaid expenses	5,000	$ 86,000
Land, building, equipment, and other assets:		
Land	100,000	
Building (net)	110,000	
Equipment (net)	80,000	
Intangible assets	15,000	305,000
Total assets		$391,000
Liabilities and Stockholders' Equity		
Current liabilities:		
Notes payable (secured by inventory)	$ 75,000	
Accounts payable	59,000	
Accrued expenses	21,000	$155,000
Long-term liabilities:		
Notes payable (secured by lien on land and buildings)		200,000
Stockholders' equity:		
Common stock	100,000	
Retained earnings (deficit)	(64,000)	36,000
Total liabilities and stockholders' equity		$391,000

company's management anticipates having trouble finding a buyer for this equipment unless the price is reduced considerably. Only 40 percent of the current net book value is expected from these assets.

- Administrative costs of $20,500 are projected if the company is liquidated.
- Accrued expenses are listed on the balance sheet as $21,000. That amount includes employee salaries of $16,000. This figure includes one person who is owed $14,650 but is the only employee due an amount more than $13,650. Other accrued expenses total $5,000. In addition, payroll taxes of $2,000 have been withheld from these wages but not yet paid to the government or recorded as a liability.
- Interest of $5,000 on the company's long-term liabilities has not yet been accrued for the first six months of 2020.

Using this information, the statement of financial affairs presented in Exhibit 13.2 can be prepared for the Chaplin Company. Several aspects of this statement should be specifically noted:

1. The current and noncurrent distinctions usually applied to reported assets and liabilities are omitted from this statement. Because the company is on the verge of going out of business, such classifications are meaningless. Instead, the statement is designed to separate secured from unsecured balances.
2. Book values are included on the side of the schedule but only for informational purposes. These figures are not relevant in a bankruptcy. *Assets are reported at estimated net realizable value. Liabilities are shown at the amount required for settlement.*
3. Both the dividend receivable and the interest payable are included in Exhibit 13.2, although neither was recorded by the company on its balance sheet. The payroll tax liability is reported at the amount the company presently owes. The statement of financial affairs is designed to disclose currently updated figures.

EXHIBIT 13.2

CHAPLIN COMPANY
Statement of Financial Affairs
June 30, 2020

Book Values			Available for Unsecured Creditors	
	Assets			
	Pledged with fully secured creditors:			
$210,000	Land and building	$ 231,000		
	Less: Notes payable (long term)	(200,000)		
	Interest payable	(5,000)	$ 26,000	
	Pledged with partially secured creditors:			
41,000	Inventory	$ 45,000		
	Less: Notes payable (current)	(75,000)	–0–	
	Free assets:			
2,000	Cash		2,000	
15,000	Investment in marketable securities		20,000	
-0-	Dividends receivable		500	
23,000	Accounts receivable		12,000	
5,000	Prepaid expenses		2,000	
80,000	Equipment		32,000	
15,000	Intangible assets		-0-	
	Total available to pay liabilities with priority and unsecured creditors		94,500	
	Less: Liabilities with priority (see Ⓐ below in Liabilities)		(37,500)	Ⓑ
	Available for unsecured creditors		57,000	Ⓓ
	Estimated deficiency		38,000	Ⓔ
$391,000			$ 95,000	

Book Values			Unsecured—Nonpriority Liabilities	
	Liabilities and Stockholders' Equity			
	Liabilities with priority:			
$ -0-	Administrative expenses (estimated)	$ 20,500		
16,000	Salaries payable (accrued expenses)	15,000	$ 1,000	©
-0-	Payroll taxes payable (accrued expenses)	2,000		
	Total	$ 37,500 Ⓐ		
	Fully secured creditors:			
200,000	Notes payable	$ 200,000		
-0-	Interest payable	5,000		
	Less: Land and building	(231,000)	-0-	
	Partially secured creditors:			
75,000	Notes payable	$ 75,000		
	Less: Inventory	(45,000)	30,000	
	Unsecured creditors:			
59,000	Accounts payable		59,000	
5,000	Accrued expenses (other than salaries and payroll taxes)		5,000	
36,000	Stockholders' equity		-0-	
$391,000			$ 95,000	

4. Liabilities having priority are individually identified within the liability section (Point A). Because these claims will be paid before other unsecured creditors, the $37,500 total is subtracted directly from the free assets (Point B). Although not yet incurred, estimated administrative costs are included in this category because such expenses will be necessary for liquidation. Salaries are appropriately considered as priority liabilities. However, the $1,000 owed to one employee in excess of the individual $13,650 limit is separated and shown as an unsecured claim (Point C).
5. According to this statement, if the liquidation process occurs as expected, Chaplin will have $57,000 in free assets remaining after settling all liabilities with priority (Point D). Because the liability section shows unsecured claims of $95,000, these creditors face a $38,000 loss ($95,000 – $57,000) if the company is liquidated (Point E). This final distribution is often stated as a percentage:

$$\frac{\text{Free assets}}{\text{Unsecured claims}} = \frac{\$57{,}000}{\$95{,}000} = 60\%$$

   Unsecured creditors can anticipate receiving 60 percent of their claims. A creditor, for example, to whom this company owes an unsecured balance of $400 should anticipate collecting $240 ($400 × 60%) following liquidation. However, this figure is merely an estimate.
6. If the statement of financial affairs had shown the company with more free assets (after subtracting liabilities with priority) than the total amount of unsecured claims, all of the creditors could expect to be paid in full with any excess money going to Chaplin's stockholders.

LO 13-7

Account for the liquidation of a company in bankruptcy especially when using the liquidation basis of accounting.

Liquidation—Chapter 7 Bankruptcy

When an insolvent company is to be liquidated, the provisions established by Chapter 7 of the Bankruptcy Reform Act regulate the process. These laws were created to provide an orderly and equitable structure for selling assets and settling debts. To achieve this end, several events occur after the court enters an order for relief in either a voluntary or involuntary liquidation.

To begin, the court appoints an interim trustee to oversee the company and its liquidation. This individual is charged with preserving the assets and preventing loss of the estate. Creditors are protected from detrimental actions that management, the ownership, or any of the other creditors might undertake. The interim trustee (as well as the permanent trustee, if the creditors subsequently select one) normally performs a number of tasks, including changing locks, securing all assets, and gaining possession of the financial records and other official documents.[21]

The court then calls for a meeting of all creditors who have appropriately filed a proof of claim against the debtor. To ensure fairness during the liquidation process, a committee of unsecured creditors is selected to help protect the financial interests of all unsecured creditors. The committee consults with the trustee and makes recommendations about the administration of the estate.[22]

Role of the Trustee

In a liquidation, the trustee is a central figure. This individual must recover all property belonging to the insolvent company, preserve the estate from any deterioration, liquidate noncash assets, and make proper distributions to the various claimants. The trustee might need to continue operating the company to complete business activities that were in progress when the order for relief was entered. To accomplish such a multitude of objectives, this individual holds wide-ranging authority.

[21] Bonhiver, *The Expanded Role of the Accountant*, pp. 50–51.

[22] Ibid., p. 26.

The trustee can also void any transfer of property (known as a *preference*) made by the debtor within 90 days *prior* to the filing of the bankruptcy petition if the company was already insolvent at the time. The recipient must return these transfers so that the money or other property can be returned to the debtor's estate.[23]

> The preference avoidance statute is designed to ensure that any distributions from a bankruptcy estate are made in accordance with the scheme established by Congress. The preference avoidance statute looks back for a period of 90 days to a full year before the bankruptcy filing to examine whether any creditors received more than their proportionate share of the debtor's assets during that time. If a creditor did receive more than its fair share of the debtor's assets, the bankruptcy trustee is empowered to void such transactions and to recover the value of the transfers from the recipient for the benefit of the debtor's bankruptcy estate as a whole.[24]

Return of the asset is not necessary if the transfer was for no more than would have been paid to this party in an organized liquidation.

Not surprisingly, the trustee must record all activities and report them periodically to the court and other interested parties. Historically, a wide variety of statements has been utilized to report ongoing liquidations. Trustees often prepare *a statement of realization and liquidation* as a quick method to report the impact of events as they occur during the liquidation process. This statement is used mostly to report smaller concerns that are not required to follow U.S. GAAP. Many bankruptcy cases involve small concerns where a simple statement of realization and liquidation is appropriate.

The statement of realization and liquidation is designed to convey significant information such as

- Account balances reported by the company at the date on which the order for relief was filed.
- Cash receipts generated by the sale of the debtor's property.
- Cash disbursements made to wind up the affairs of the business and pay secured creditors.
- Any other transactions such as the write-off of assets and the recognition of unrecorded liabilities.

Any cash that remains following this series of events is distributed to the unsecured creditors after all priority claims have been settled.

As will be discussed later, to be in conformity with U.S. GAAP, a statement of net assets in liquidation and a statement of changes in net assets in liquidation must, at a minimum, be presented based on application of the liquidation basis of accounting. However, many small operations do not need that degree of financial reporting as they go through the process of ending their business. They can opt to report only a statement of realization and liquidation.

Statement of Realization and Liquidation Illustrated

To demonstrate the production of a statement of realization and liquidation, the information previously presented for Chaplin Company will be extended into a liquidation.

The dollar amounts resulting from this liquidation will not necessarily agree with the balances used in creating the statement of financial affairs in Exhibit 13.2. The previous statement was based on projected sales and other estimations. A statement of realization and liquidation reports the actual transactions and other events as they occur. Differences between actual figures and the expected amounts are normal. Assume the following transactions occur in liquidating this company:

[23] The 90-day limit is extended to one year if the transfer is made to an inside party such as an officer or a director or an affiliated company. The one-year limit also applies to any transfer made by the debtor with the intent to defraud another party. Transfers of less than $5,000 cannot be challenged as preferences.

[24] Bradley S. Schmarak and Tracy L. Treger, "Avoiding the Preference Pitfall in Workouts," *Commercial Lending Review,* October 11, 1997, p. 37.

Liquidation Transactions of Chaplin Company—2020

July 1	The accounting records in Exhibit 13.1 are adjusted to the appropriate balances as of June 30, 2020, the date on which the order for relief was entered. Hence, the previously unrecorded dividends receivable, interest payable, and additional payroll tax liability are now recognized.
July 23	The trustee expends $7,000 to dispose of the company's inventory at a negotiated price of $51,000. The net cash is applied to the notes payable for which the inventory served as partial security.
July 29	A cash dividend of $500, accrued as of June 30, is collected. The related investments (reported at $15,000) are then sold for $19,600.
Aug. 17	Accounts receivable of $16,000 are collected. The remaining balances are written off as uncollectible.
Aug. 30	The trustee determines that no refund is available from any of the company's prepaid expenses. The intangible assets are removed from the financial records because they have no cash value. The land and building are sold for $208,000. The trustee uses $205,000 of this money to pay off the secured creditors.
Oct. 9	After an extended search for a buyer, the equipment is sold for $42,000 in cash.
Nov. 1	A $24,900 invoice is received for various administrative expenses incurred in liquidating the company. The trustee also reclassifies the remaining portion of the partially secured liabilities as unsecured.
Nov. 9	Noncash assets have now been converted into cash and all secured claims settled, so the trustee begins to distribute any remaining funds. The liabilities with priority are paid first. The excess is then applied to the claims of unsecured nonpriority creditors.

Because the process is not structured according to U.S. GAAP, the physical layout used to prepare a statement of realization and liquidation can vary significantly. For example, the various account groups can be presented on a horizontal plane with the liquidating transactions shown vertically. The accountants can then record events as they occur to show their effects on each account classification. Exhibit 13.3 displays the liquidation of the Chaplin Company.

Probably the most significant information presented in this statement is the measurement and classification of the company's liabilities. Once again, fully and partially secured claims are reported separately from liabilities with priority and unsecured nonpriority claims.

For Chaplin Company, Exhibit 13.3 discloses $137,900 in debts as of November 9 ($41,900 in priority claims and $96,000 in unsecured nonpriority liabilities). After satisfying all secured liabilities, the company holds only $83,100 in cash. The trustee must first use this remaining money to pay the three liabilities with priority according to the following ranking:

Administrative expenses (adjusted from original estimation)	$24,900
Salaries payable (within the $13,650 per person limitation)	15,000
Payroll taxes payable	2,000
Total	$41,900

These disbursements leave the company with $41,200 in cash ($83,100 – $41,900) but $96,000 in unsecured liabilities. Consequently, the unsecured creditors will receive only 42.9 percent of their claims against Chaplin Company:

$$\frac{\$41,200}{\$96,000} = 42.9\% \text{ (rounded)}$$

EXHIBIT 13.3 Final Statement of Realization and Liquidation

CHAPLIN COMPANY
Statement of Realization and Liquidation
June 30, 2020, to November 9, 2020

Date		Cash	Noncash Assets	Liabilities with Priority	Fully Secured Creditors	Partially Secured Creditors	Unsecured—Nonpriority Liabilities	Stockholders' Equity (Deficit)
6/30/20	Book balances	$ 2,000	$ 389,000	$ 15,000*	$ 200,000	$ 75,000	$65,000†	$ 36,000
7/1/20	Adjustments for unrecorded dividends, interest, and payroll taxes		500	2,000	5,000			(6,500)
7/1/20	Adjusted book balances	2,000	389,500	17,000	205,000	75,000	65,000	29,500
7/23/20	Inventory sold—recorded net of disposal costs	44,000	(41,000)					3,000
7/23/20	Proceeds from inventory paid to secured creditors	(44,000)				(44,000)		
7/29/20	Investments sold and dividends received	20,100	(15,500)					4,600
8/17/20	Receivables collected with remainder written off	16,000	(23,000)					(7,000)
8/30/20	Intangible assets and prepaid expenses written off		(20,000)					(20,000)
	Land and building sold	208,000	(210,000)					(2,000)
	Proceeds from land and building paid to secured creditors	(205,000)			(205,000)			
10/9/20	Equipment sold	42,000	(80,000)					(38,000)
11/1/20	Administrative expenses accrued			24,900				(24,900)
11/1/20	Excess of partially secured liabilities reclassified as an unsecured claim					(31,000)	31,000	
11/9/20	Final balances remaining for unsecured creditors	$ 83,100	$ –0–	$ 41,900	$ –0–	$ –0–	$96,000	$(54,800)

*Includes salaries payable of $15,000 (amount due employees but limited to $13,650 per individual). In addition, payroll taxes have not yet been recorded.
†Accounts payable of $60,000 plus accrued expenses other than salaries payable (within $13,650 per person limitation) of $1,000 and other accrued expenses of $4,000.

Because all liabilities are not paid in full, stockholders receive nothing, a common outcome for a bankruptcy liquidation.

At a 42.9 percent collection rate, the unsecured nonpriority creditors receive a smaller percentage of their claims than the 60 percent figure projected in the statement of financial affairs (Exhibit 13.2). Although this earlier statement plays an important role in bankruptcy planning and proceedings, the ability to anticipate future events limits the statement's accuracy.

The Liquidation Basis of Accounting

In 2013, FASB issued *Accounting Standards Update No. 2013-07,* "Liquidation Basis of Accounting." Official reporting standards prior to this pronouncement had been virtually nonexistent for companies in the process of being liquidated. A number of high-profile liquidations at the time (such as Circuit City and Hostess Brands) pointed to a need for authoritative guidance to help the parties involved. In this Update, FASB addresses four essential questions about the reporting of a company being liquidated:

1. When does a company qualify as being in liquidation so that the liquidation basis of accounting is necessary?
2. At a minimum, what statements should a company report during liquidation to be in conformity with U.S. GAAP?
3. How should a company report its assets during liquidation?
4. How should a company report its liabilities during this liquidation?

According to *ASU* No. 2013-07, the liquidation basis is not applied until liquidation becomes imminent. This condition is said to exist when a plan of liquidation is approved by the court or by the people who have such authority, and there is only a remote chance that (1) the plan will be blocked or (2) the entity will return from liquidation. Thus, the proper approval of a liquidation plan is usually the point at which the liquidation basis of reporting becomes required by U.S. GAAP. Until that point, traditional accounting rules for a going concern continue to be applied.

Once the liquidation basis is appropriate, the company's financial reporting must include (1) a statement of changes in net assets in liquidation and (2) a statement of net assets in liquidation.

- The first statement reports all changes during the period in the net assets available for distribution to investors and other claimants. It shows the expected amount of net assets and the changes that occur in anticipated balances. Because the company is going out of business, neither an income statement nor a statement of cash flows is relevant to the interested parties.
- The second statement provides information about the net assets held by the company that are available for distribution.

The statement of net assets in liquidation reports assets at the estimated amount of cash (or other consideration) that the company expects to receive as a result of the liquidation process. That is the information that interested parties want to know. This figure is not necessarily the same as fair value. Liquidations often take place quickly so that the amount obtained might be far less than an asset's fair value. The statement reports only the assets expected to generate cash during the liquidation process.

In reporting liabilities, no attempt is made to anticipate the legal release that might result from the bankruptcy process. Liabilities continue to be reported in a normal fashion unless actual changes in debt balances take place. To help decision makers understand the impact of actions that will occur during liquidation, the company accrues all estimated costs to dispose of its assets and any other costs that are expected.

Exhibits 13.4 and 13.5 present these statements using the liquidation basis so that they are in conformity with U.S. GAAP. The assumption here is that liquidation has become imminent for the Winslow Corporation.

EXHIBIT 13.4
Statement of Changes in Net Assets in Liquidation

WINSLOW CORPORATION Statement of Changes in Net Assets in Liquidation for the Three Months Ending December 31, 2020	
Net assets in liquidation as of October 1, 2020	$3,422,960
Adjustment for additional accrued liquidation costs	(211,000)
Adjustment in expected net realizable value of assets	35,000
Adjustment in amount of valid liability claims	(20,000)
Net assets in liquidation as of December 31, 2020	$3,226,960

EXHIBIT 13.5
Statement of Net Assets in Liquidation

WINSLOW CORPORATION December 31, 2020	
Cash	$ 74,000
Accounts receivable	218,000
Inventory	610,540
Land, buildings, and equipment	2,873,220
Intangible assets	120,000
Accounts payable	(148,390)
Taxes payable	(124,130)
Accrued liquidation costs	(396,280)
Net assets in liquidation as of December 31, 2020	$3,226,960

In examining these two financial statements, several distinct characteristics should be noted:

1. Even though liquidation is termed as *imminent,* the actual time for the process to be completed may take well over 12 months. New statements will need to be created periodically during that period of time.
2. Any financial statements prepared before the liquidation basis became necessary are not retroactively adjusted. They are still viewed as being presented fairly based on the facts known at that time.
3. The net assets in liquidation figure ($3,226,960) represents the amount that the company expects to remain after the liquidation of all assets and the settlement of all liabilities.
4. Reported assets often include items not reported as assets in earlier statements. Internally developed intangibles, for example, can have a significant cash value even though previously reported as expenses based on U.S. GAAP for a going concern.
5. All of the asset figures reflect the amounts the company expects to collect. Therefore, the recording of depreciation or impairment is no longer relevant. Because these accounts are equal to the expected liquidation value, no further gains and losses are expected. Adjustments of these balances because of new information will impact the amount reported for net assets in liquidation.
6. Liabilities continue to be shown at the amounts due until they are settled. However, estimated amounts (such as warranties) may require adjustment because of changes occurring during the remaining time of the company's existence.
7. All disposal costs should be anticipated in advance and recognized as a liability so that the amount of cash expected to remain after liquidation can be determined. The same reporting is true for operating costs. For example, if employees will remain at work during this period and be paid $10,000, that obligation is recognized as soon as it is estimated rather than when earned.
8. Equity accounts are usually not reported because that information is not relevant to the parties involved in a liquidation.

LO 13-8

Discuss the provisions that are often found in a bankruptcy reorganization plan.

Reorganization—Chapter 11 Bankruptcy

> Reorganization under the federal Bankruptcy Code is a way to salvage a company rather than liquidate it. Although the original owners of a company rescued in this way are often left without anything, others whose livelihoods depend on the company's fortunes may come out with their interests intact. The company's creditors, for example, may take over as the new owners. Its suppliers might be able to maintain the company as a customer. Its customers still may count on the company as a supplier. And perhaps most important, many of its employees may be able to keep the jobs that otherwise would have been sacrificed in a liquidation.[25]

As indicated at the beginning of this chapter, for the 12 months ended September 30, 2018, 5,962 Chapter 11 business reorganizations were begun in the United States.[26] Reorganizations allow the parties a chance to salvage the business so that operations can continue. Although this legal procedure offers the hope of survival, reorganization is no guarantee of future prosperity. Companies that attempt to reorganize are often eventually liquidated. A timeline for the demise of Toys R Us shows the speed at which a company can fail.

- September 5, 2017—Reports break that Toys R Us is considering filing for bankruptcy.
- September 18, 2017—Company files for Chapter 11 protection.
- December 2017—Holiday sales fail to produce adequate cash inflows.
- January 24, 2018—Company announces plans to close 180 stores.
- March 15, 2018—Toys R Us moves to liquidate U.S. business.[27]

Obviously, the activities and events surrounding a reorganization differ significantly from a liquidation. One important distinction is that control over the company normally stays with the ownership (referred to as a *debtor in possession*). However, if fraud or gross mismanagement is proven, the court has the authority to appoint an independent trustee to assume control.

Unless replaced, the debtor in possession continues to operate the company and has the primary responsibility for developing an acceptable plan of reorganization. Not everyone, though, agrees with the wisdom of leaving operational control in the hands of management: "One philosophical objection raised increasingly often is the rule that puts the debtor in control of the bankruptcy process, an idea that often leaves foreigners 'stunned,' says one bankruptcy lawyer. This typically means that the managers who bankrupt a firm can have a go at restructuring it to keep it alive."[28]

While a reorganization is in process, owners and managers are legally required to preserve the company's estate as of the date that the order for relief is entered by the court. Liabilities must be separated into those occurring before the bankruptcy filing (often called "prepetition liabilities") and after the filing ("postpetition liabilities"). In this way, bankruptcy laws seek to reduce the losses that creditors and stockholders will have to absorb when either reorganization or liquidation eventually occurs.

The Plan for Reorganization

> The plan is the heart of every Chapter 11 reorganization. The provisions of the plan specify the treatment of all creditors and equity holders upon its approval by the Bankruptcy Court. Moreover, the plan shapes the financial structure of the entity that emerges.[29]

The most intriguing aspect of a Chapter 11 bankruptcy is the plan developed to rescue the company from insolvency. Initially, only the debtor in possession can file proposals with the

[25] John Robbins, Al Goll, and Paul Rosenfield, "Accounting for Companies in Chapter 11 Reorganization," *Journal of Accountancy,* January 1991, p. 75.

[26] United States Courts "Caseload Statistics Data Tables," http://www.uscourts.gov/sites/default/files/data_tables/bf_f5a_0930.2018.pdf.

[27] Ben Unglesbee "One Year Later: Toys R Us' Fatal Journey Through Chapter 11," *Retail Dive,* September 18, 2018.

[28] "The Night of the Killer Zombies," *The Economist* , December 14, 2002.

[29] FASB ASC (para. 852-10-05-4).

court. If a plan for reorganization is not put forth within 120 days of the order for relief or accepted within 180 days (unless the court grants an extension, although the debtor's exclusivity to propose a plan cannot be extended beyond 18 months), any interested party has the right to prepare and file a proposal.

A recent trend has been to push for quicker reorganization by threatening to move the process to a liquidation. "Most companies that file for bankruptcy these days have debts that far exceed their assets. That means they probably won't be able to pay off their lenders in full, let alone more-junior creditors like suppliers, no matter how long they stay in bankruptcy proceedings. As a result, banks and other lenders, who often are owed millions of dollars and get first dibs on any sale proceeds, are using their clout for a speedy sale."[30]

A reorganization plan can contain an unlimited number of provisions: proposed changes in the company, additional financing arrangements, alterations in the debt structure, and the like. Regardless of the specific details, the intent of all such plans is to provide a feasible long-term solution to the company's monetary difficulties. To gain acceptance by the parties involved, a plan must present convincing evidence that the business will emerge from bankruptcy as a viable going concern.

Although no definitive list of inclusions in a reorganization proposal is possible, the following are some of the most common:

1. *Plans proposing changes in the company's operations.* In hopes of improving liquidity, officials often decide to introduce new product lines or sell off unprofitable assets or even entire businesses. Selling or closing failing operations is common because that reduces costs and might generate needed cash. A debtor in possession bears the burden of proving that the problems that led to insolvency can be eliminated by the proposed actions.

> Kodak has agreed to sell some of its document imaging assets to Brother Industries Ltd. for about $210 million, its latest deal as it seeks to exit bankruptcy protection. Japan-based Brother also would assume the business's deferred service revenue liability, which totaled about $67 million as of Dec. 31, the companies said Monday. Kodak's document imaging business provides scanners, capture software and related services. Brother makes laser, label and multi-function printers, along with fax machines and sewing machines. Eastman Kodak Co. filed for Chapter 11 bankruptcy protection in January 2012.[31]

2. *Plans for generating additional monetary resources.* Companies facing insolvency must develop new sources of cash, often in a short period of time. Loans and the sale of both common and preferred stocks are frequently negotiated during reorganization to provide funding to continue the business. "The U.S. government will take about a 61 percent stake in the new GM after lending the automaker more than $50 billion."[32]

3. *Plans for changes in company management.* In many cases, a financial crisis is blamed on poor leadership. For that reason, proposing to reorganize a company with the management team intact is probably not a practical suggestion. Many plans include hiring new individuals to implement the reorganization and run important aspects of the company. These changes may also affect the board of directors as shown in this remark about the Tribune Co. as it goes through reorganization:

> The publisher of the *Chicago Tribune* and *Los Angeles Times* will soon turn to naming a new board and possibly a new chief executive as it wrestles with the fate of a sprawling empire of newspapers and television stations across the U.S.[33]

4. *Plans to settle debts that existed when the order for relief was entered.* No element of a reorganization plan is more important than the proposal for satisfying the claims of the

[30] Jacqueline Palank, "Companies in Chapter 11 Face Express Trip to Auction Block," *Wall Street Journal,* January 14, 2013, p. B1.

[31] Associated Press, "Kodak Selling Document Imaging Assets for $210M," April 15, 2013.

[32] Mike Spector, "GM Asset Sale Gets Judge's Nod," *Wall Street Journal,* July 6, 2009, p. B-1.

[33] Keith Hagey and Mike Spector, "Tribune Nears Chapter 11 Exit," *Wall Street Journal,* July 16, 2012, p. B5.

company's creditors. Their agreement is usually necessary before the court will confirm any plan of reorganization.

- Assets can be transferred to creditors who accept this payment in exchange for extinguishing a specified amount of debt. The liability being canceled is typically higher (often substantially higher) than the fair value of the assets surrendered. Most parties to a bankruptcy expect to incur significant losses.
- An equity interest (such as common stock, preferred stock, or stock rights) can be conveyed to creditors to settle outstanding debt.

> Remington Outdoor, one of the country's oldest and largest gun makers, said this week that a bankruptcy judge had approved its reorganization plan, which will transfer ownership of the company to creditors including JPMorgan. After a court hearing in Delaware on Wednesday, Remington said it expected to emerge from Chapter 11 bankruptcy proceedings by the end of the month with more than $775 million in debt wiped from its balance sheet. Remington, which sought bankruptcy protection in March after sales fell and its debt piled up, will no longer be owned by the private equity firm Cerberus Capital Management. Instead, some of its creditors, including JPMorgan's asset management arm, will take control.[34]

- The terms of outstanding liabilities can be modified: maturity dates extended, interest rates lowered, face values reduced, accrued interest forgiven, and so on.

One interesting development over the last few years is the use of prepackaged or prearranged bankruptcies where the company and creditors agree on the terms of a reorganization plan before the bankruptcy petition is signed. The parties enter bankruptcy with an agreement to present to the court. Using this strategy, extensive legal fees can be avoided. An increasing number of these bankruptcy reorganizations take only two to three months instead of years. Furthermore, the parties have more protection because the Bankruptcy Court is likely to accept the plan without requiring extensive changes or revisions.

> Prearranged bankruptcies are on the rise and for good reason. A well-executed prearranged bankruptcy—where most of the biggest creditors agree to a reorganization plan before going to court—allows a company to secure attractive financing, maintain the trust of employees, customers and suppliers, and move through the bankruptcy process much more quickly and inexpensively than a standard filing.[35]

Acceptance and Confirmation of Reorganization Plan

The creation of a plan for reorganization does not guarantee acceptance. A plan must be voted on by both the company's creditors and stockholders before possible confirmation by the court. *To be accepted, each class of creditors must vote for the plan.* Acceptance requires the approval of two-thirds in dollar amount and more than one-half in the number of claims that cast votes. A separate vote is also required of each class of shareholders. For approval, at least two-thirds (measured by the number of shares held) of the owners who vote must agree to the proposed reorganization. Convincing parties to support a specific plan is normally not an easy task. Agreement often means accepting a significant loss. Eventually, though, acceptance of some plan is necessary if progress is to be made and liquidation avoided.

Although a specific plan may gain creditor and stockholder approval, court confirmation is still required. The court reviews the proposal and can reject a reorganization plan if a claimant (who did not vote for acceptance) would receive more through liquidation.

[34] Tiffany Hsu, "After Emerging from Bankruptcy, Remington, One of the Country's Oldest Gun Manufacturers, Will be Owned by Creditors Including JPMorgan," *New York Times* May 3, 2018, http://www.nytimes.com/2018/05/03/business/remington-bankruptcy-chapter-11.html.

[35] Jim Hogan, "Keys to a Prearranged Bankruptcy: A Powerful Tool to Move a Company through Chapter 11 Proceedings Quickly, Inexpensively and with Minimal Disruption to the Business," *Investment Dealers Digest,* March 25, 2011.

The court also has the authority to confirm a reorganization plan that was not accepted by a particular class of creditors or stockholders. This provision is referred to as a *cram down* and occurs when the court determines that a rejected plan is fair and equitable. The court may also convert a Chapter 11 reorganization into a Chapter 7 liquidation at any time if the development of an acceptable plan does not appear possible. That threat should encourage the parties to join together to achieve a workable resolution.

LO 13-9

Account for a company as it moves through reorganization.

Financial Reporting during Reorganization

Developing and then gaining approval for a reorganization plan can take years. During that time, operations continue under the assumption that a reorganized company will eventually emerge from the bankruptcy proceedings. For that reason, most account balances are reported in the same manner as with any ongoing operation. Nevertheless, during this period, companies do face several significant accounting questions:

- Should the income resulting from continuing operating activities be differentiated from transactions connected solely with the reorganization process? If so, how are those reorganization items identified?
- How should liabilities be reported? Some debts might not be paid for years and then require payment of an amount considerably less than face value. How is this information presented?
- Does reorganization necessitate a change in the reporting basis of the company's assets? Is the previous carrying value still relevant?

Answers to such questions can be found in FASB's *Accounting Standards Codification®*, Topic 852, "Reorganizations," which provides official guidance for the preparation of financial statements at two times:

1. During the period when an entity is going through reorganization.
2. At the point that the entity emerges from reorganization.

Income Statement Reporting during Reorganization

According to U.S. GAAP, any gains, losses, revenues, and expenses resulting from the reorganization are known as *reorganization items,* and the company should report them separately from normal operating activities (although they still appear on the income statement before any income tax expense or benefits).[36]

Reorganization items include gains and losses on the sale of assets but only if the sale is a direct result of the bankruptcy proceedings as approved by the bankruptcy court. In addition, as mentioned previously, professional fees can be incurred that are often of significant size. Such costs are not capitalized regardless of the monetary amount but, rather, included within the reorganization items. "Judgment is required in determining which statement of operations items should be reported as reorganization items. As a general rule, only incremental costs directly related to the reporting entity's bankruptcy filings, such as professional fees for bankruptcy services, should be presented as a reorganization item. Recurring internal costs of normal operations should not be presented as reorganization items."[37]

U.S. GAAP also establishes approved reporting for both interest expense and interest revenue. During reorganization, interest expense usually does not accrue on debts owed at the date on which the automatic stay is granted. The amount of these liabilities is frozen until reorganization or liquidation occurs. Recognition of interest expense is necessary only if payment will be made (for example, on debts incurred after the order for relief is granted). That expense is shown on the income statement but is not included within the reorganization items. Therefore, the interest expense reported on the income statement is often quite small.

[36] In a similar manner, the statement of cash flows is constructed so that reorganization items are shown separately within the operating, investing, and financing categories.

[37] PWC ,"Bankruptcies and liquidations, " 2018, pp. 3–16, https://www.pwc.com/us/en/cfodirect/assets/pdf/accounting-guides/pwc-guide-bankruptcies-and-liquidations.pdf.

For informational purposes, the contractual interest that would have accrued except for the bankruptcy must be disclosed.

In contrast, interest revenue can grow to a substantial amount during reorganization. Because the company is not forced to pay debts incurred prior to the date of the automatic stay, cash reserves accumulate so that the resulting interest revenue can become significant. For this reason, any interest revenue that would not have been earned except for the bankruptcy is reported as a reorganization item.

To illustrate the reporting of an income statement during reorganization, assume that Crawford Corporation files a voluntary petition of bankruptcy and is granted an order for relief on January 1, 2020. Thereafter, ownership and management begin to work on a reorganization plan to rehabilitate the company. Accountants, lawyers, and other professionals are hired to assist in the reorganization. At the end of 2020, the bankruptcy is still in progress. The company prepares an income statement that is structured so that the reader can distinguish the results of operating activities as separate from reorganization items (see Exhibit 13.6).

Balance Sheet Reporting during Reorganization

A new entity is not created when a company moves *into* reorganization. Therefore, most traditional generally accepted accounting principles continue to apply. Assets, for example, are still reported at their net book values.

However, a successful reorganization plan will likely reduce the payments to be made on many of the company's debts. According to U.S. GAAP, liabilities that are subject to compromise must be shown separately and at the expected amount of allowable claims rather than estimated settlement figures. Thus, the company does not anticipate the payments required by a final plan but simply discloses the amount of the claims. As of April 30, 2018, iHeartMedia, Inc., (in monthly filings with the SEC) reported liabilities subject to compromise of $17.4 billion. Unsecured and partially secured obligations existing as of the granting of the order for relief fall into this category. Fully secured liabilities and all debts incurred subsequent to that date are not subject to compromise and should be reported in a normal manner as either current ($332 million) or noncurrent ($603 million).

EXHIBIT 13.6
Income Statement during Reorganization

CRAWFORD CORPORATION
(Debtor in Possession)
Income Statement
for Year Ended December 31, 2020
(In thousands except for the loss per common share)

Revenues:		
Sales		$ 650,000
Cost and expenses:		
Cost of goods sold	$346,000	
General and administrative expenses	165,000	
Selling expenses	86,000	
Interest expense ($15,000 contractual amount)	4,000	601,000
Earnings before reorganization items and tax effects		49,000
Reorganization items:		
Attorney and other legal fees	(81,000)	
Accounting and other professional fees	(70,000)	
Interest revenue	16,000	(135,000)
Loss before income tax benefit		(86,000)
Income tax benefit		18,800
Net loss		$ (67,200)
Loss per common share		$ (0.56)

On August 31, 2013, when Eastman Kodak was ready to emerge from reorganization, its liabilities were reported on its balance sheet as follows:

(in millions)	
Current liabilities	$ 317
Short-term borrowings and current portion of long-term debt	681
Other current liabilities	600
Liabilities held for sale	45
Total current liabilities	$1,643
Long-term debt, net of current portion	370
Pension and other postretirement liabilities	411
Other long-term liabilities	318
Liabilities subject to compromise	2,475
Total liabilities	$5,217

LO 13-10

Describe the financial reporting for a company that successfully exits bankruptcy as a reorganized entity.

Financial Reporting for Companies Emerging from Reorganization

Is a company that successfully exits Chapter 11 status a new entity so that fair values should be assigned to its asset and liability accounts (referred to as *fresh start reporting*)? Or is the company simply a continuation of the organization that entered bankruptcy so that historical figures remain appropriate.

According to U.S. GAAP, the assets and liabilities of a reorganized company should be adjusted to fair value if two criteria are met:

1. The total reorganization (or fair) value of the assets of the emerging company is less than the total of the allowed claims as of the date of the order for relief plus liabilities incurred subsequently.
2. The previous owners of all voting stock are left with less than 50 percent of the voting stock of the company when it emerges from bankruptcy.

Meeting the first criterion shows that the predecessor company could not have continued in business as a going concern because it would have had a negative net worth. The second criterion indicates that control of the successor company has changed.

Many, if not most, Chapter 11 bankruptcies meet these two criteria. Consequently, the emerging entity reports as if it were a brand new business. For example, Ayana Holdings Corp. exited bankruptcy reorganization on November 28, 2017. Afterwards, a note to the company's financial statements explains, "Upon the Emergence Date, the Company applied fresh start accounting, which resulted in a new basis of accounting and the Company becoming a new entity for financial reporting purposes. As a result of the application of fresh start accounting . . ., the Consolidated Financial Statements after the Emergence Date, are not comparable with the Consolidated Financial Statements on or before that date."

In applying fresh start accounting, the reorganization value of the entity that emerges from bankruptcy must first be determined. This reorganization value is an estimate of the amount a willing buyer would pay for the company's assets after restructuring. This total value is then assigned to the specific tangible and intangible assets of the company in the same way as in a business combination as described in earlier chapters of this book.

Unfortunately, determining the reorganization value for a large and complex business can be a difficult assignment. The 2010 financial statements for General Motors describe its approach to this computation:

Our reorganization value was determined using the sum of:

- Our discounted forecast of expected future cash flows from our business subsequent to the 363 Sale,[38] discounted at rates reflecting perceived business and financial risks;

[38] A 363 Sale refers to the section of the bankruptcy code that allows the old company to sell its assets to the new company as a means of going forward with the business.

- The fair value of operating liabilities;
- The fair value of our non-operating assets, primarily our investments in nonconsolidated affiliates and cost method investments; and
- The amount of cash we maintained at July 10, 2009, that we determined to be in excess of the amount necessary to conduct our normal business activities.

During this process, the reorganization value is usually reported to the court as a range of possibilities. When the company emerges from bankruptcy, a best figure within that range is selected. This single number is often based on the determination of the emerging company's enterprise value. A company's enterprise value represents the fair value of its interest-bearing debt plus its shareholders' equity. In most bankruptcy proceedings, a valuation specialist will determine the emerging entity's enterprise value. The reorganization value can then be derived from the enterprise value by including liabilities other than interest-bearing debt.

In applying fresh start accounting, the assets held by a company on the day it exits from reorganization should be reported based on individual current values, not historical book values. *The entity is viewed as a newly created organization.* For that reason, Kmart Holdings indicated when it emerged from reorganization that the "fair value adjustments included the recognition of approximately $2.2 billion of intangible assets that were previously not recorded in the Predecessor Company's financial statements, such as favorable leasehold interests, Kmart brand rights, pharmacy customer relationships and other lease and license agreements." As with a consolidation, any unallocated portion of the reorganization value is reported as goodwill. General Motors reported goodwill of $30.5 billion upon application of fresh start accounting whereas Eastman Kodak recognized only $88 million.

At the same time, all liabilities (except for deferred income taxes) are reported at the present value of the future cash payments.

Because the company is viewed as a new entity, it leaves reorganization with a zero balance reported for retained earnings. Changes in asset balances made as a result of fresh start accounting are normally shown as changes in additional paid-in capital.

Fresh Start Accounting Illustrated

Assume that the Hayes Company has the following trial balance just prior to emerging from bankruptcy:

	Debit	Credit
Current assets	$ 50,000	
Land	100,000	
Buildings	400,000	
Equipment	250,000	
Accounts payable (incurred since the order for relief was granted)		$ 100,000
Liabilities when the order for relief was granted:		
Accounts payable		60,000
Accrued expenses		50,000
Notes payable (due in 3 years)		300,000
Bonds payable (due in 5 years)		600,000
Common stock (50,000 shares with a $1 par value)		50,000
Additional paid-in capital		40,000
Retained earnings (deficit)	400,000	
Totals	$1,200,000	$1,200,000

Other Information

- *Assets.* The company's land has a fair value of $120,000, whereas the building has a value of $500,000. Other listed assets are worth the same as their book values. In addition, a trademark is worth $10,000 although not previously recorded by the company. A bankruptcy expert has calculated the reorganization value of the company's assets to be between $900,000 and $1.3 million. A $1 million figure is selected when the company exits bankruptcy by determining the enterprise value on that day and also by the use of discounted cash flows.

- *Liabilities.* The $100,000 in accounts payable incurred after the order for relief was granted must be paid in full as the individual balances come due. Liabilities existing when the order for relief was granted total $1,010,000 ($60,000 + $50,000 + $300,000 + $600,000). The accounts payable and accrued expenses owed at that time will be converted into one-year notes with a face value of $70,000 and an annual interest rate of 10 percent. The company will convert the $300,000 in notes payable listed on the trial balance into a 10-year $100,000 note paying annual interest of 8 percent. These note holders also get 20,000 shares of stock that the common stockholders return in to the company. Finally, the $600,000 of bonds payable will be converted into eight-year, 9 percent notes with a face value of $430,000. The bondholders also get 15,000 shares of common stock turned in by the current owners. All of these interest rates are assumed to be reasonable so that no present value calculation is needed.
- *Stockholders' equity:* The owners of common stock will return 70 percent of their shares (35,000) to the company to be reissued as specified above. As mentioned, the reorganization value of the assets is set at $1,000,000. The remaining debts of the company after these events total $700,000 ($100,000 + $70,000 + $100,000 + $430,000). Stockholders' equity must be the $300,000 difference in the assets and liabilities. Because all of the shares (with a $50,000 par value) will still be outstanding, Additional Paid-In Capital (APIC) is adjusted to $250,000 ($300,000 for the total stockholders' equity less the $50,000 par value of the common stock). Retained earnings is zero to show that the company coming out of bankruptcy is a new entity. If present, accumulated other comprehensive income is also zero.

In reporting this reorganized company, the initial question to be resolved is always whether fresh start accounting is appropriate.

- The first criterion is met because the reorganization value of the assets ($1,000,000) is less than the sum of all postpetition liabilities ($100,000 in Accounts Payable) plus allowed claims (the $1,010,000 total of liabilities remaining from the date of the order for relief before any write-downs).
- The second criterion is also met because the previous stockholders retain less than 50 percent of the shares after the plan takes effect. At that point, they hold only 15,000 of the 50,000 outstanding shares.

To implement fresh start accounting, the company adjusts each asset account to fair value rather than retain the historical book value. Although the reorganization value is $1 million, the individual assets' fair value totals only $930,000 (current assets $50,000, trademark $10,000, land $120,000 [adjusted], buildings $500,000 [adjusted], and equipment $250,000). Goodwill is recognized for the $70,000 portion of the company's reorganization value in excess of the value assigned to specific assets.

Adjustment is necessary only when fair value differs from book value. Because the retained earnings balance will be placed at zero, asset changes affect additional paid-in capital.

Trademark	10,000	
Land	20,000	
Buildings	100,000	
Goodwill	70,000	
Additional Paid-In Capital		200,000
To adjust asset accounts from book value to fair value based on fresh start accounting and to recognize excess value as goodwill.		

Next, the 35,000 shares of common stock (with a $1 per share par value) returned to the company by the previous owners are eliminated from the financial records as follows:

Common Stock	35,000	
Additional Paid-In Capital		35,000
To remove shares of common stock returned to the company by owners as part of the reorganization agreement.		

Liability accounts must now be adjusted to reflect the provisions of the reorganization plan. Because the new debts in this illustration bear a reasonable interest rate, present value computations are not necessary. The first entry is a straight conversion of the accounts payable and accrued expenses with a gain recorded for the difference between the old debt and the new. Any write-down of a liability is this process is a recognized gain.

Accounts Payable	60,000	
Accrued Expenses	50,000	
Notes Payable (1 year)		70,000
Gain on Debt Discharge		40,000
To convert liabilities to a 1-year note as per reorganization plan.		

According to the information provided, the two remaining debts (the note payable and the bond payable) are exchanged, at least in part, for a total of 35,000 shares of common stock held previously by the owners at the time of the bankruptcy. Each of these stock entries requires a computation of the amount to be assigned to additional paid-in capital (APIC). The reported total of APIC for the company was calculated previously as $250,000 (reported assets less reported liabilities and less par value of outstanding shares of common stock).

Because the holders of the notes are to receive 20,000 shares of stock (or 40 percent of the company's 50,000 share total), this stock is assigned APIC of $100,000 (40 percent of the determined total). The holders of the bonds receive 15,000 shares (30 percent of the total). APIC of $75,000 (30 percent of the company total) is recorded. Gains are recognized for the differences.

Notes Payable (3 years)	300,000	
Notes Payable (10 years)		100,000
Common Stock (par value of 20,000 shares)		20,000
Additional Paid-In Capital (40% of company total)		100,000
Gain on Debt Discharge		80,000
To record exchange with gain recorded for difference between book value of old note payable and the amount recorded for new note and shares of stock.		
Bonds Payable	600,000	
Notes Payable (8 years)		430,000
Common Stock (par value of 15,000 shares)		15,000
Additional Paid-In Capital (30% of company total)		75,000
Gain on Debt Discharge		80,000
To record exchange with gain recorded for difference between book value of old bonds and the amount recorded for new notes and shares of stock.		

At this point in this illustration, all asset, liability, and common stock amounts are reported appropriately for the company as it leaves reorganization. Only additional paid-in capital and retained earnings remain to be finalized. Additional Paid-In Capital now has a balance of $450,000 ($40,000 beginning balance plus $200,000 for adjusting assets to fair value plus $35,000 for shares returned by owners plus $100,000 because of common stock shares issued

6. Liquidation is not the only outcome available to an insolvent business. The company may seek to survive by developing a reorganization plan (a Chapter 11 bankruptcy). Reorganization is possible only if creditors, shareholders, and the court accept the plan. While a reorganization is in process, the owners and management must preserve the company's estate as of the date on which the order of relief was entered. Although ownership has the initial opportunity to create a proposal for action, any interested party has the right to file a reorganization plan after a specified period of time.
7. Reorganization plans usually contain a number of provisions for modifying operations, disposing of unsuccessful properties, generating new financing by equity or debt, and settling the liabilities existing when the order for relief was entered. To be accepted, each class of creditors and shareholders must support the agreement. Thereafter, the court must confirm the reorganization plan.
8. During reorganization, a company reports its liabilities as either those subject to compromise or not subject to compromise. The first category includes all unsecured and partially secured debts that existed on the day the order for relief was granted. The balance to be reported is the total of allowed claims rather than the estimated amount of settlement. Liabilities not subject to compromise are those debts fully secured or incurred following the granting of the order for relief.
9. An income statement prepared during reorganization should report operating activities separately from reorganization items. Professional fees associated with the reorganization such as lawyers' fees are classified as reorganization items and recorded as expenses as incurred. Interest revenue earned during this period because of an increase in the company's cash reserves is another reorganization item.
10. Many companies that emerge from reorganization proceedings must apply fresh start accounting as a new entity. Such companies report all assets at fair value. Goodwill is recognized if the reorganization value is greater than the fair value of the identified assets. Liabilities (except for deferred income taxes) are reported at the present value of required cash flows. Any retained earnings balance (or a deficit) is eliminated. Additional paid-in capital is adjusted to keep the balance sheet in equilibrium.

Comprehensive Illustration

Problem

(*Estimated Time: 50 to 65 Minutes*) Roth Company is insolvent and in the process of filing for relief under the provisions of the Bankruptcy Reform Act. Roth has no cash, and the company's balance sheet shows accounts payable of $48,000. Roth owes an additional $8,000 in connection with various expenses but has not yet recorded these debts. The book value and anticipated net realizable value of the company's assets are as follows:

	Book Value	Expected Net Realizable Value
Accounts receivable	$ 31,000	$ 9,000
Inventory	48,000	36,000
Investments	10,000	18,000
Land	80,000	75,000
Buildings	190,000	160,000
Accumulated depreciation	(38,000)	
Equipment	110,000	20,000
Accumulated depreciation	(61,000)	
Other assets	5,000	–0–
Totals	$375,000	$318,000

Roth has three notes payable, each with a different maturity date:

- Note 1 due in 5 years—$220,000, secured by a mortgage lien on Roth's land and buildings.
- Note 2 due in 8 years—$30,000, secured by Roth's investments.
- Note 3 due in 10 years—$35,000, unsecured.

Of the accounts payable that Roth owes, $10,000 represents salaries to employees. However, no individual is entitled to receive more than $4,100. Another $3,000 due to the U.S. government in connection with taxes is included in this liability amount.

The company is reporting a total for stockholders' equity of $42,000 at the current date: common stock of $140,000 and a deficit of $98,000. Officials believe that liquidating the company will lead to administrative expenses of approximately $20,000.

Required

a. Prepare a statement of financial affairs for Roth to indicate the expected availability of funds if the company is liquidated.

b. Assume that Roth owes Philip, Inc., $2,000. This liability is unsecured. If Roth is liquidated, what amount can Philip expect to receive?

c. What amount will be paid on note 2 if Roth is liquidated?

d. Assume that Roth is immediately reorganized. Assume that the company has a reorganization value of $330,000, based on discounted cash flows, and each asset is to be recorded at its estimated net realizable value. By agreement of the parties, the accounts payable and accrued expenses are reduced to a total of $20,000. Note 1 is decreased to a $130,000 note due in four years with a 7 percent annual interest rate. This creditor also receives half of the company's outstanding stock from the owners. Note 2 is reduced to a $12,000 note due in five years with an 8 percent annual interest rate. This creditor also receives 10 percent of the outstanding stock of the company from the owners. Note 3 is decreased to $5,000 due in three years with a 9 percent annual interest rate. All interest rates are considered reasonable.

Prepare a trial balance for this company after it emerges from bankruptcy.

Solution

a. To develop a statement of financial affairs for the Roth Company, the following preliminary actions must be taken:

- The $8,000 total for the unrecorded accounts payable is entered into the company's accounting records. Because these debts were incurred in connection with expenses, the deficit is increased by a corresponding amount.
- Unsecured liabilities that have priority are identified:

Administrative costs (estimated)	$ 20,000
Salaries payable	10,000
Amount due to government for taxes	3,000
Total liabilities with priority	$ 33,000

- Secured claims should be classified as follows. With this information, the statement of financial affairs in Exhibit 13.7 can be produced.

  Note 1 is fully secured. Roth's land and buildings can be sold for an amount in excess of the $220,000 balance.

  Note 2 is only partially secured. Roth's investments are worth less than the $30,000 debt balance.

b. Based on the information provided by the statement of financial affairs, Roth anticipates having $47,000 (Point A) in free assets remaining at the end of the liquidation. This amount must be distributed to unsecured creditors with total claims of $90,000 (Point B). Therefore, only 52.2 percent of each obligation can be paid based on these projections:

$$\frac{\$47,000}{\$90,000} = 52.2\% \text{ (rounded)}$$

Philip, Inc., should receive 52.2 percent of its $2,000 unsecured claim, or $1,044.

EXHIBIT 13.7

ROTH COMPANY
Statement of Financial Affairs

Book Values	Assets		Available for Unsecured Creditors
	Pledged with fully secured creditors:		
$232,000	Land and buildings	$235,000	
	Less: Note payable 1	(220,000)	$ 15,000
	Pledged with partially secured creditors:		
10,000	Investments	18,000	
	Less: Note payable 2	(30,000)	–0–
	Free assets:		
31,000	Accounts receivable		9,000
48,000	Inventory		36,000
49,000	Equipment		20,000
5,000	Other assets		–0–
	Total available for liabilities with priority and unsecured creditors		80,000
	Less: Liabilities with priority (listed below)		(33,000)
	Available for unsecured creditors		47,000 (A)
	Estimated deficiency		43,000
$375,000			$ 90,000

Book Values	Liabilities and Stockholders' Equity		Available for Nonpriority Liabilities
	Liabilities with priority:		
$ –0–	Administrative expenses (estimated)	$ 20,000	
	Liabilities with priority currently owed:		
10,000	Salaries payable	10,000	
3,000	Taxes payable	3,000	
	Total	$ 33,000	
	Fully secured creditors:		
220,000	Note payable 1	220,000	
	Less: Land and buildings	(235,000)	$ –0–
	Partially secured creditors:		
30,000	Note payable 2	30,000	
	Less: Investments	(18,000)	12,000
	Unsecured creditors:		
35,000	Note payable 3		35,000
43,000	Accounts payable (other than salaries and taxes plus $8,000 in previously unrecorded liabilities)		43,000
34,000	Stockholders' equity (adjusted for unrecorded liabilities)		–0–
$375,000			$ 90,000 (B)

c. The $30,000 note payable is partially secured by Roth's investments, an asset having an estimated net realizable value of only $18,000. The remaining $12,000 is an unsecured claim, which (as computed in the previous requirement) will be paid 52.2 percent of face value. The holder of this note can expect to receive $24,264:

Net realizable value of investments	$18,000
Payment on $12,000 unsecured claim (52.2%)	6,264
Amount to be received	$24,264

d. Fresh start accounting is appropriate. The reorganization value of $330,000 is less than the $341,000 total amount of claims (no liabilities after the issuance of the order for relief are indicated).

Accounts payable	$ 48,000
Accrued expenses	8,000
Note 1	220,000
Note 2	30,000
Note 3	35,000
Total claims	$341,000

In addition, the original owners retain only 40 percent of the stock after the company exits from bankruptcy. For fresh start reporting, the following information is necessary.

The company's assets are assigned values equal to their net realizable value based on the information provided. Because the reorganization value of $330,000 is $12,000 in excess of the $318,000 total net realizable value of company assets, goodwill is recognized for that amount.

Each liability is adjusted to the newly agreed-on amounts. Present value computations are not required because a reasonable interest rate is included in each case. These debts now total $167,000 ($20,000 + $130,000 + $12,000 + $5,000).

The reorganization value is $330,000 and the liabilities are $167,000 so that stockholders' equity must be $163,000 ($330,000 – $167,000). The number of outstanding shares of common stock has not changed and retains its balance of $140,000. The other $23,000 of stockholders' equity is recorded as additional paid-in capital leaving the proper zero balance for retained earnings. (If appropriate, any accumulated other comprehensive income total is now also adjusted to a zero balance.)

	Debit	Credit
Accounts receivable	$ 9,000	
Inventory	36,000	
Investments	18,000	
Land	75,000	
Buildings	160,000	
Equipment	20,000	
Goodwill	12,000	
Accounts payable and accrued expenses		$ 20,000
Note payable 1		130,000
Note payable 2		12,000
Note payable 3		5,000
Common stock		140,000
Additional paid-in capital		23,000
Totals	$330,000	$330,000

Questions

1. What does the term *insolvent* mean?
2. Why should a company monitor the reporting of goodwill prior to the filing of a bankruptcy petition?
3. What situations might raise substantial doubt that a company can meet its financial obligations as they come due for one year from the issuance of the financial statements?
4. A company believes that there might be substantial doubt that it can meet its financial obligations as they come due for one year from the issuance of its financial statements. What plans might mitigate this concern?

5. A company's management believes that substantial doubt exists that the company can meet its financial obligations as they come due for a one-year period from the issuance of its financial statements. Management is studying the plans that have been developed to avoid this problem. What two decisions must management make?
6. A company's management believes that substantial doubt exists that the company can meet its financial obligations as they come due for a one-year period from the issuance of its financial statements. What possible disclosures are required?
7. What federal legislation governs most bankruptcy proceedings?
8. What are the primary objectives of a bankruptcy proceeding?
9. A bankruptcy case can begin with either a voluntary or an involuntary petition. What is the difference? What are the requirements for an involuntary petition?
10. A bankruptcy court enters an order for relief. How does this action affect an insolvent company and its creditors?
11. What is the difference between fully secured liabilities, partially secured liabilities, and unsecured liabilities?
12. In a bankruptcy proceeding, what is the significance of a liability with priority? What are the general categories of liabilities that have priority in a liquidation?
13. Why are administrative expenses incurred during a liquidation classified legally as liabilities having priority?
14. What is the difference between a Chapter 7 bankruptcy and a Chapter 11 bankruptcy?
15. What is the purpose of a statement of financial affairs? Why might this statement be prepared before a bankruptcy petition is filed?
16. In a bankruptcy liquidation, what actions does the trustee perform?
17. A trustee for a company that is being liquidated voids a preference transfer. What has happened? Why did the trustee take this action?
18. If a company is not required to follow U.S. GAAP, a statement of realization and liquidation can be prepared during liquidation. What information can interested parties gain from this statement?
19. When is a company required to use the liquidation basis of accounting to be in conformity with U.S. GAAP?
20. In determining whether a company needs to use the liquidation basis of accounting, how does an accountant determine that liquidation is imminent?
21. In following the liquidation basis of accounting, what financial statements must be presented?
22. How does a company report its assets when the liquidation basis of accounting is applied? How does a company report its liabilities when the liquidation basis of accounting is applied?
23. What does *debtor in possession* mean?
24. Who can develop a reorganization plan in a Chapter 11 bankruptcy?
25. What types of proposals might a reorganization plan include?
26. Under normal conditions, how does a reorganization plan become effective?
27. In a bankruptcy proceeding, what is a *cram down?*
28. While a company goes through a bankruptcy reorganization, how should its assets and liabilities be reported?
29. During reorganization, how should a company's income statement be structured?
30. What accounting is made of the professional fees incurred during a reorganization?
31. What is meant by *fresh start accounting*?
32. Under what conditions must a company emerging from a bankruptcy reorganization apply fresh start accounting?
33. When a company uses fresh start accounting, how does it report assets and liabilities?
34. How is goodwill computed if fresh start accounting is applied to a company emerging from bankruptcy reorganization?

Problems

LO 13-1

1. What are the objectives of the bankruptcy laws in the United States?
   a. Provide relief for the court system and ensure that all debtors are treated the same.
   b. Distribute assets fairly and discharge honest debtors from their obligations.
   c. Protect the economy and stimulate growth.
   d. Prevent insolvency and protect shareholders.

LO 13-2

2. A company's management has monitored recent events that indicate that substantial doubt exists that the company can pay its debts as they come due over the following year. What should management do next?
   a. Management should disclose that substantial doubt exists that the company can remain in existence.
   b. Management should examine the plans created to address the concern.
   c. Management should adjust all asset balances to fair value.
   d. Management should adjust all liabilities to expected settlement amounts.

LO 13-2

3. A company's management has uncovered events that indicate that substantial doubt exists that the company can pay its debts as they come due over the following year. Management studies the plans created internally to address this risk. How can the company avoid disclosing that this substantial doubt exists?
   a. The plans must be reviewed by the chief financial officer.
   b. It must be probable that the plans will be implemented, and it must be probable that the plans will mitigate the conditions that raised substantial doubt.
   c. Disclosure of the substantial doubt is required regardless of the availability of the plans.
   d. The plans must have been tested before the end of the financial year by a liquidity expert.

LO 13-1, 13-3, 13-4 13-5, 13-6

4. In a bankruptcy case, which of the following statements is true?
   a. An order for relief results only from a voluntary petition.
   b. Creditors entering an involuntary petition must have debts totaling at least $21,625.
   c. Secured notes payable are considered liabilities with priority on a statement of affairs.
   d. A liquidation is referred to as a *Chapter 7 bankruptcy,* and a reorganization is referred to as a *Chapter 11 bankruptcy.*

LO 13-7

5. The Jackston Company is to be liquidated as a result of bankruptcy. Until the liquidation occurs, on what basis are its assets reported?
   a. Present value calculated using an appropriate effective rate
   b. Net realizable value
   c. Historical cost
   d. Book value

LO 13-3

6. An involuntary bankruptcy petition must be filed by
   a. The insolvent company's attorney.
   b. The holders of the insolvent company's debenture bonds.
   c. Unsecured creditors with total debts of at least $16,750.
   d. The company's management.

LO 13-3

7. An order for relief creates an automatic stay. This automatic stay
   a. Prohibits creditors from taking action to collect from an insolvent company without court approval.
   b. Calls for the immediate distribution of free assets to unsecured creditors.
   c. Can be entered only in an involuntary bankruptcy proceeding.
   d. Provides an insolvent company with time to file a voluntary bankruptcy petition.

LO 13-4

8. Which of the following is *not* a liability that has priority in a liquidation?
   a. Administrative expenses incurred during the liquidation
   b. Salary payable of $1,250 per person owed to 26 employees
   c. Payroll taxes due to the federal government
   d. Advertising expense incurred before the company became insolvent but not recorded until after the order of relief

LO 13-3

9. Which of the following is the minimum limitation necessary for filing an involuntary bankruptcy petition in connection with a company that has 57 unsecured creditors?
   a. The signature of 12 creditors to whom the debtor owes at least $14,775 in unsecured debt
   b. The signature of six creditors to whom the debtor owes at least $18,250 in unsecured debt
   c. The signature of three creditors to whom the debtor owes at least $16,750 in unsecured debt
   d. The signature of nine creditors to whom the debtor owes at least $23,225 in unsecured debt

LO 13-6

10. On a statement of financial affairs, how are liabilities classified?
   a. Current and noncurrent
   b. Secured and unsecured
   c. Monetary and nonmonetary
   d. Historic and futuristic

LO 13-6

11. What is a *debtor in possession?*
   a. The holder of a note receivable issued by an insolvent company prior to the granting of an order for relief
   b. A fully secured creditor
   c. The ownership of an insolvent company that continues to control the organization during a bankruptcy reorganization
   d. The stockholders in a Chapter 7 bankruptcy

LO 13-6

12. How are anticipated administrative expenses reported on a statement of financial affairs?
   a. As a footnote until actually incurred
   b. As a liability with priority
   c. As a partially secured liability
   d. As an unsecured liability

LO 13-7

13. Prior to filing a voluntary Chapter 7 bankruptcy petition, Haynes Company pays a supplier $13,000 to satisfy an unsecured claim. Haynes was insolvent at the time. Subsequently, the trustee appointed to oversee this liquidation forces the return of the $13,000 by the supplier. Which of the following is true?
   a. A preference transfer has been voided.
   b. All transactions just prior to a voluntary bankruptcy proceeding must be nullified.
   c. The supplier should sue for the return of this money.
   d. The $13,000 claim becomes a liability with priority.

LO 13-7

14. Which of the following is *not* an expected function of a bankruptcy trustee?
   a. Filing a plan of reorganization
   b. Recovering all property belonging to a company
   c. Liquidating noncash assets
   d. Distributing assets to the proper claimants

LO 13-6

15. What is an inherent limitation of the statement of financial affairs?
   a. Many of the amounts reported are only estimates that might prove to be inaccurate.
   b. The statement is applicable only to a Chapter 11 bankruptcy.
   c. The statement covers only a short time, whereas a bankruptcy may last much longer.
   d. The figures on the statement vary depending on whether it is a voluntary or an involuntary bankruptcy.

LO 13-8

16. What is a *cram down?*
   a. An agreement about the total amount of money to be reserved to pay creditors who have priority
   b. The bankruptcy court's confirmation of a reorganization even though a class of creditors or stockholders did not accept it
   c. The filing of an involuntary bankruptcy petition, especially by the holders of partially secured debts
   d. The court's decision as to whether a particular creditor has priority

LO 13-9

17. On a balance sheet prepared for a company during reorganization, how are liabilities reported?
   a. As current and long term
   b. As monetary and nonmonetary
   c. As subject to compromise and not subject to compromise
   d. As equity related and debt related

LO 13-7

18. When does the liquidation basis of accounting first have to be applied to financial statements to be viewed as in conformity with U.S. GAAP?
    a. When an involuntary bankruptcy petition is approved by the court
    b. When liquidation is imminent
    c. When the first asset is sold
    d. At least 90 days before the final asset is sold

LO 13-7

19. What financial statements must a company report when applying the liquidation basis of accounting?
    a. Statement of activities and a statement of financial position
    b. Income statement and balance sheet
    c. Statement of liquidating cash flows and statement of current position during liquidation
    d. Statement of changes in net assets in liquidation and statement of net assets in liquidation

LO 13-7

20. When a company applies the liquidation basis of accounting, what reporting is appropriate for its assets?
    a. At cost less accumulated depreciation
    b. At the estimated amount of cash to be received
    c. At fair value
    d. At the lower of cost or market value

LO 13-7

21. The New England Company has a debt to a bank of $55,000. The company is being liquidated, and officials believe that between $12,000 and $20,000 will be paid on that debt. According to the liquidation basis of accounting, what amount is reported for this liability?
    a. $12,000
    b. $16,000
    c. $20,000
    d. $55,000

LO 13-9

22. On a balance sheet prepared for a company during reorganization, at what balance are liabilities reported?
    a. At the expected amount of the allowed claims
    b. At the present value of the expected future cash flows
    c. At the expected amount of the settlement
    d. At the amount of the anticipated final payment

LO 13-9

23. Which of the following is *not* a reorganization item for purposes of reporting a company's income statement during a Chapter 11 bankruptcy?
    a. Professional fees
    b. Interest revenue
    c. Interest expense
    d. Gains and losses on closing facilities

LO 13-9

24. What accounting is made for professional fees incurred during a bankruptcy reorganization?
    a. They must be expensed immediately.
    b. They must be capitalized and written off over 180 months or less.
    c. They must be capitalized until the company emerges from the reorganization.
    d. They are either expensed or capitalized, depending on the nature of the expenditure.

LO 13-10

25. Which of the following is necessary for a company to use fresh start accounting?
    a. The previous owners must hold at least 50 percent of the stock of the company when it emerges from bankruptcy.
    b. The reorganization value of the company must exceed the value of all assets.
    c. The reorganization value of the company must exceed the value of all liabilities.
    d. The original owners must hold less than 50 percent of the stock of the company when it emerges from bankruptcy.

LO 13-10

26. If the reorganization value of a company emerging from bankruptcy is larger than the fair values that can be assigned to specific assets, what accounting is made of the difference?
    a. Because of conservatism, the difference is simply ignored.
    b. The difference is recorded as an expense immediately.
    c. The difference is capitalized as goodwill.
    d. The difference is recorded as a professional fee.

LO 13-10

27. How should a company emerging from bankruptcy reorganization report its liabilities (other than deferred income taxes)?
    a. At their historical value
    b. At zero because of fresh start accounting
    c. At the present value of the future cash flows
    d. At the negotiated value less all professional fees incurred in the reorganization

LO 13-4, 13-6, 13-7

28. The Walston Company is to be liquidated. It has the following liabilities:

Income taxes	$ 8,000
Notes payable (secured by land)	120,000
Accounts payable	85,000
Salaries payable (evenly divided between two employees)	6,000
Bonds payable	70,000
Administrative expenses for liquidation	20,000

The company has the following assets:

	Book Value	Fair Value
Current assets	$ 80,000	$ 35,000
Land	100,000	90,000
Buildings and equipment	100,000	110,000

How much money will the holders of the notes payable collect following liquidation?

LO 13-4, 13-7

29. Shi Company is going through a Chapter 7 bankruptcy. All assets have been liquidated, and the company retains only $26,200 in free cash. The following debts, totaling $43,050, remain:

Government claims to unpaid taxes	$ 7,000
Salary during last month owed to Mr. Key (not an officer)	19,200
Administrative expenses	3,450
Salary during last month owed to Ms. Rankin (not an officer)	5,850
Unsecured accounts payable	7,550

Indicate how much money will be paid to the creditor associated with each debt.

LO 13-4, 13-6, 13-7

30. Ataway Company has suffered severe financial difficulties and is considering filing a bankruptcy petition. It has the following assets and liabilities. The assets are stated at net realizable value.

Assets (pledged against debts of $70,000)	$116,000
Assets (pledged against debts of $130,000)	50,000
Other assets	80,000
Liabilities with priority	42,000
Other unsecured creditors	200,000

In a liquidation, how much money would be paid on the partially secured debt?

LO 13-4, 13-6, 13-7

31. Chesterfield Company holds cash of $60,000, inventory worth $110,000, and a building worth $140,000. Unfortunately, the company also has accounts payable of $190,000, a note payable of $90,000 (secured by the inventory), liabilities with priority of $22,800, and a bond payable of $170,000 (secured by the building). In a Chapter 7 bankruptcy, how much money should the holder of the bond expect to receive?

LO 13-4, 13-7

32. Mondesto Company has the following debts:

Unsecured creditors	$230,000
Liabilities with priority	110,000
Secured liabilities:	
Debt 1, $210,000; value of pledged asset	180,000
Debt 2, $170,000; value of pledged asset	100,000
Debt 3, $120,000; value of pledged asset	140,000

The company also has a number of other assets that are not pledged in any way. The creditors holding Debt 2 want to receive at least $142,000. For how much do the free assets have to be sold so that the creditors associated with Debt 2 will receive exactly $142,000?

LO 13-4, 13-7

33. A statement of financial affairs created for an insolvent corporation that is beginning the process of liquidation discloses the following data. The assets are shown at net realizable values.

Assets pledged with fully secured creditors	$220,000
Fully secured liabilities	160,000
Assets pledged with partially secured creditors	390,000
Partially secured liabilities	510,000
Assets not pledged	310,000
Unsecured liabilities with priority	182,800
Accounts payable (unsecured)	400,000

a. The company owes $13,000 on an account payable to an unsecured creditor (without priority). How much money can this creditor expect to collect?

b. The company owes $120,000 to a bank on a note payable that is secured by a security interest attached to property with an estimated net realizable value of $90,000. How much money can the bank expect to collect?

LO 13-4, 13-7

34. A company preparing for a Chapter 7 liquidation has listed the following liabilities:

- Note payable A of $90,000 secured by land having a book value of $50,000 and a fair value of $70,000.
- Note payable B of $120,000 secured by a building having a $60,000 book value and a $40,000 fair value.
- Note payable C of $60,000, unsecured.
- Administrative expenses payable of $20,000.
- Accounts payable of $120,000.
- Income taxes payable of $30,000.

The company also has these other assets:

- Cash of $10,000.
- Inventory of $100,000 but with a net realizable value of $60,000.
- Equipment of $90,000 but with a net realizable value of $50,000.

Based on this information, how much will each of the company's liabilities be paid at liquidation?

LO 13-7

35. Olds Company declares Chapter 7 bankruptcy. The following are the book values of the asset and liability accounts at that time. A bankruptcy expert estimates that administrative expense will total $20,000.

Cash	$ 32,000	
Accounts receivable	68,000	(valued at $36,000)
Inventory	78,000	(valued at $64,000)
Land (secures note A)	208,000	(valued at $168,000)
Building (secures bonds)	408,000	(valued at $336,000)
Equipment	128,000	(value unknown)
Accounts payable	188,000	
Taxes payable to government	28,000	
Note payable A	186,000	
Note payable B	258,000	
Bonds payable	308,000	

The holders of note payable B want to collect at least $129,000. To achieve this goal, how much does the company have to receive in the liquidation of its equipment?

LO 13-4, 13-7

36. A company going through a Chapter 7 bankruptcy has the following account balances:

Cash	$ 30,000
Receivables (30% collectible)	50,000
Inventory (worth $39,000)	90,000
Land (worth $120,000) (secures note payable)	100,000
Buildings (worth $180,000) (secures bonds payable)	200,000
Salaries payable (Four workers owed equal amounts for last two weeks)	10,000

(Continued)

(*Continued*)

Accounts payable	90,000
Note payable (secured by land)	110,000
Bonds payable (secured by building)	300,000
Common stock	100,000
Retained earnings	(140,000)

How much will be paid to each of the following?

Salaries payable
Accounts payable
Note payable
Bonds payable

LO 13-9

37. Pumpkin Company is going through bankruptcy reorganization. It signed a $200,000 note payable prior to the order for relief. The company believes that this note will be settled for $60,000 in cash. It is also possible that the creditor will instead take a piece of land that cost the company $50,000 but is valued at $72,000. On a balance sheet prepared during the reorganization period, how will this debt be reported?

LO 13-10

38. The Larisa Company is exiting bankruptcy reorganization with the following accounts:

	Book Value	Fair Value
Receivables	$ 80,000	$ 90,000
Inventory	200,000	210,000
Buildings	300,000	400,000
Liabilities	300,000	300,000
Common stock	330,000	
Additional paid-in capital	20,000	
Retained earnings (deficit)	(70,000)	

The company's assets have a $760,000 reorganization value. As part of the reorganization, the company's owners transferred 80 percent of the outstanding stock to the creditors.

Prepare the journal entry (or entries) necessary to adjust the company's records to fresh start accounting.

LO 13-9

39. Addison Corporation is currently going through a Chapter 11 bankruptcy reorganization. The company has the following account balances for the current year. Prepare an income statement for this organization. The effective tax rate is 20 percent (realization of any tax benefits is anticipated).

	Debit	Credit
Advertising expense	$ 24,000	
Cost of goods sold	211,000	
Depreciation expense	22,000	
Interest expense	4,000	
Interest revenue		$ 32,000
Loss on closing of branch as part of reorganization	109,000	
Professional fees	71,000	
Rent expense	16,000	
Revenues		467,000
Salaries expense	70,000	

LO 13-10

40. Kansas City Corporation holds three assets when it emerges from Chapter 11 bankruptcy reorganization:

	Book Value	Fair Value
Inventory	$ 86,000	$ 50,000
Land and buildings	250,000	400,000
Equipment	123,000	110,000

The company has a reorganization value of $600,000.

a. Describe the rules to determine whether to apply fresh start accounting to Kansas City.

b. If fresh start accounting is appropriate, how will this company's assets be reported?

c. If a goodwill account is recognized in a reorganization, where should it be reported? What happens to this balance?

LO 13-9

41. Jaez Corporation is in the process of going through a reorganization. As of December 31, 2020, the company's accountant has determined the following information although the company is still several months away from emerging from the bankruptcy proceeding. Prepare a balance sheet in the appropriate form.

	Book Value	Fair Value
Assets		
Cash	$ 23,000	$ 23,000
Inventory	45,000	47,000
Land	140,000	210,000
Buildings	220,000	260,000
Equipment	154,000	157,000

	Allowed Claims	Expected Settlement
Liabilities as of the date of the order for relief		
Accounts payable	$ 123,000	$ 20,000
Accrued expenses	30,000	4,000
Income taxes payable	22,000	18,000
Note payable (due 2023, secured by land)	100,000	100,000
Note payable (due 2025)	170,000	80,000
Liabilities since the date of the order for relief		
Accounts payable	$ 60,000	
Note payable (due 2022)	110,000	
Stockholders' equity		
Common stock	$ 200,000	
Deficit	(233,000)	

LO 13-10

42. Ristoni Company is in the process of emerging from a Chapter 11 bankruptcy. It will apply fresh start accounting as of December 31, 2020. The company currently has 30,000 shares of common stock outstanding with a $240,000 par value. As part of the reorganization, the owners will contribute 18,000 shares of this stock back to the company. A retained earnings deficit balance of $330,000 exists at the time of this reorganization.

The company has the following asset accounts:

	Book Value	Fair Value
Accounts receivable	$ 100,000	$ 80,000
Inventory	112,000	90,000
Land and buildings	420,000	500,000
Equipment	78,000	65,000

The company's liabilities will be settled as follows. Assume that all notes will be issued at reasonable interest rates.

- Accounts payable of $80,000 will be settled with a note for $5,000. These creditors will also get 1,000 shares of the stock contributed by the owners.
- Accrued expenses of $35,000 will be settled with a note for $4,000.

- Note payable of $100,000 (due 2024) was fully secured and has not been renegotiated.
- Note payable of $200,000 (due 2023) will be settled with a note for $50,000 and 10,000 shares of the stock contributed by the owners.
- Note payable of $185,000 (due 2021) will be settled with a note for $71,000 and 7,000 shares of the stock contributed by the owners.
- Note payable of $200,000 (due 2022) will be settled with a note for $110,000.

The company has a reorganization value of $780,000.

Prepare all journal entries for Ristoni so that the company can emerge from the bankruptcy proceeding.

LO 13-10

43. Smith Corporation has gone through bankruptcy and is ready to emerge as a reorganized entity on December 31, 2020. On this date, the company has the following assets (fair value is based on discounting the anticipated future cash flows):

	Book Value	Fair Value
Accounts receivable.	$ 20,000	$ 18,000
Inventory.	143,000	111,000
Land and buildings	250,000	278,000
Machinery.	144,000	121,000
Patents	100,000	125,000

The company has a reorganization value of $800,000.

Smith has 50,000 shares of $10 par value common stock outstanding. A deficit retained earnings balance of $670,000 also is reported. The owners will distribute 30,000 shares of this stock as part of the reorganization plan.

The company's liabilities will be settled as follows:

- Accounts payable of $180,000 (existing at the date on which the order for relief was granted) will be settled with an 8 percent, two-year note for $35,000.
- Accounts payable of $97,000 (incurred since the date on which the order for relief was granted) will be paid in the regular course of business.
- Note payable—First Metropolitan Bank of $200,000 will be settled with an 8 percent, five-year note for $50,000 and 15,000 shares of the stock contributed by the owners.
- Note payable—Northwestern Bank of Tulsa of $350,000 will be settled with a 7 percent, eight-year note for $100,000 and 15,000 shares of the stock contributed by the owners.

a. How does Smith Corporation's accountant know that fresh start accounting must be utilized?

b. Prepare a balance sheet for Smith Corporation upon its emergence from reorganization.

LO 13-4, 13-7

44. Ambrose Corporation reports the following information:

	Book Value	Liquidation Value
Assets pledged with fully secured creditors	$220,000	$245,000
Assets pledged with partially secured creditors	111,000	103,000
Other assets.	140,000	81,000
Liabilities with priority.	36,000	
Fully secured liabilities.	200,000	
Partially secured liabilities	180,000	
Accounts payable (unsecured).	283,000	

In liquidation, what amount of cash should each class of liabilities expect to collect?

LO 13-4, 13-6

45. The following balance sheet has been prepared by the accountant for Limestone Company as of June 3, 2020, the date on which the company is to file a voluntary petition of bankruptcy:

LIMESTONE COMPANY Balance Sheet June 3, 2020	
Assets	
Cash	$ 3,000
Accounts receivable (net)	65,000
Inventory	88,000
Land	100,000
Buildings (net)	300,000
Equipment (net)	180,000
Total assets	$736,000
Liabilities and Equities	
Accounts payable	$ 98,000
Notes payable—current (secured by equipment)	250,000
Notes payable—long term (secured by land and buildings)	190,000
Common stock	120,000
Retained earnings	78,000
Total liabilities and equities	$736,000

Additional Information

- If the company is liquidated, administrative expenses are estimated at $18,000.
- The accounts payable figure includes $10,000 in wages earned by the company's 12 employees during May. No one earned more than $2,200.
- Liabilities do not include taxes of $14,000 owed to the U.S. government.
- Company officials estimate that 40 percent of the accounts receivable will be collected in a liquidation and that the inventory disposal will bring $80,000. The land and buildings will be sold together for approximately $310,000; the equipment should bring $130,000 at auction.

Prepare a statement of financial affairs for Limestone Company as of June 3, 2020.

LO 13-4, 13-6, 13-7

46. Creditors of Jones Corporation are considering petitioning the courts to force the company into Chapter 7 bankruptcy. The following information has been determined. Administrative expenses in connection with the liquidation are estimated to be $22,000. Indicate the amount of money that each class of creditors can anticipate receiving.

	Book Value	Net Realizable Value
Cash	$ 6,000	$ 6,000
Accounts receivable	32,000	18,000
Inventory	45,000	31,000
Supplies	3,000	–0–
Investments	2,000	8,000
Land	60,000	72,000
Buildings	90,000	68,000
Equipment	50,000	35,000
Notes payable (secured by land)	65,000	
Notes payable (secured by buildings)	78,000	
Bonds payable (secured by equipment)	115,000	
Accounts payable	70,000	
Salaries payable (two weeks' salary for three employees)	6,000	
Taxes payable	10,000	

LO 13-6, 13-7, 13-10

47. Anteium Company owes $80,000 on a note payable that is currently due. The note is held by a local bank and is secured by a mortgage lien attached to three acres of land worth $48,000. The land originally cost Anteium $31,000 when acquired several years ago. The only other account balances for this company are investments of $20,000 (but worth $25,000), accounts payable of $20,000, common stock of $40,000, and a deficit of $89,000. Anteium is insolvent and attempting to arrange a bankruptcy reorganization so the business can continue to operate and the employees can retain their jobs. The reorganization value of the company is $82,000.

View each of the following as an independent situation:

a. On a statement of financial affairs, how would this note be reported? How would the land be shown?

b. Assume that Anteium develops an acceptable reorganization plan. Sixty percent of the common stock is transferred to the bank to settle that particular obligation. A 7 percent, three-year note payable for $5,000 is used to settle the accounts payable. How would Anteium record the reorganization?

c. Assume that Anteium is liquidated. The land and investments are sold for $50,000 and $26,000, respectively. Administrative expenses amount to $11,000. How much will the various parties collect?

LO 13-4, 13-7

48. The following balance sheet has been produced for Litz Corporation as of August 8, 2020, the date on which the company is to begin selling assets as part of a corporate liquidation:

LITZ CORPORATION
Balance Sheet
August 8, 2020

Assets	
Cash	$ 16,000
Accounts receivable (net)	82,000
Investments	32,000
Inventory (net realizable value is expected to approximate cost)	69,000
Land	30,000
Buildings (net)	340,000
Equipment (net)	210,000
Total assets	$779,000
Liabilities and Equities	
Accounts payable	$150,000
Notes payable—current (secured by inventory)	132,000
Notes payable—long term [secured by land and buildings (valued at $300,000)]	259,000
Common stock	135,000
Retained earnings	103,000
Total liabilities and equities	$779,000

The following events occur during the liquidation process:

- The investments are sold for $39,000.
- The inventory is sold at auction for $48,000.
- The money derived from the inventory is applied against the current notes payable.
- Administrative expenses of $15,000 are incurred in connection with the liquidation.
- The land and buildings are sold for $315,000. The long-term notes payable are paid.
- The accountant determines that $34,000 of the accounts payable are liabilities with priority.
- The company's equipment is sold for $84,000.
- Accounts receivable of $34,000 are collected. The remainder of the receivables is considered uncollectible.
- The administrative expenses are paid.

a. Prepare a statement of realization and liquidation for the period just described.

b. What percentage of their claims should the unsecured creditors receive?

LO 13-8, 13-10

49. Becket Corporation's accountant has prepared the following balance sheet as of November 10, 2020, the date on which the company is to release a plan for reorganizing operations under Chapter 11 of the Bankruptcy Reform Act:

BECKET CORPORATION
Balance Sheet
November 10, 2020

Assets	
Cash	$ 12,000
Accounts receivable (net)	61,000
Investments	26,000
Inventory (net realizable value is expected to approximate 80% of cost)	80,000
Land	57,000
Buildings (net)	248,000
Equipment (net)	117,000
Total assets	$ 601,000
Liabilities and Equities	
Accounts payable	$ 129,000
Notes payable—current (secured by equipment)	220,000
Notes payable—(due in 2023) (secured by land and buildings)	325,000
Common stock ($10 par value)	60,000
Retained earnings (deficit)	(133,000)
Total liabilities and equities	$ 601,000

The company has presented the following proposal:

- The reorganization value of the company's assets prior to issuing additional shares mentioned later in the proposal, selling the company's investment, and conveying title to the land is set at $650,000 based on discounted future cash flows.
- Accounts receivable of $20,000 are written off as uncollectible. Investments are worth $40,000, land is worth $80,000, the buildings are worth $300,000, and the equipment is worth $86,000.
- An outside investor has been found to buy 7,000 shares of common stock at $11 per share.
- The company's investments are to be sold for $40,000 in cash with the proceeds going to the holders of the current note payable. The remainder of these short-term notes will be converted into $130,000 of notes due in 2024 that pay 10 percent annual cash interest.
- All accounts payable will be exchanged for $40,000 in notes payable due in 2021 that pay 8 percent annual cash interest.
- Title to land costing $20,000 but worth $50,000 will be transferred to the holders of the note payable due in 2023. In addition, these creditors will receive $180,000 in notes payable (paying 10 percent annual interest) coming due in 2027. These creditors also are issued 3,000 shares of previously unissued common stock. Becket retains the remainder of its land.

Prepare journal entries for Becket to record the transactions as put forth in this reorganization plan.

LO 13-4, 13-6

50. Oregon Corporation has filed a voluntary petition to reorganize under Chapter 11 of the Bankruptcy Reform Act. Its creditors are considering an attempt to force liquidation. The company currently holds cash of $6,000 and accounts receivable of $25,000. In addition, the company owns four plots of land. The first two (labeled A and B) cost $8,000 each. Plots C and D cost the company $20,000 and $25,000, respectively. A mortgage lien is attached to each parcel of land as security for four different notes payable of $15,000 each. Presently, the land can be sold for the following:

Plot A	$16,000
Plot B	$11,000
Plot C	$14,000
Plot D	$27,000

Another $25,000 note payable is unsecured. Accounts payable at this time total $32,000. Of this amount, $12,000 is salary owed to the company's workers. No employee is due more than $3,400.

The company expects to collect $12,000 from the accounts receivable if liquidation becomes necessary. Administrative expenses required for liquidation are anticipated to be $16,000.

a. Prepare a statement of financial affairs for Oregon Corporation.

b. If the company is liquidated, how much cash would be paid on the note payable secured by plot B?

c. If the company is liquidated, how much cash would be paid on the unsecured note payable?

d. If the company is liquidated and plot D is sold for $30,000, how much cash would be paid on the note payable secured by plot B?

LO 13-4, 13-6

51. Lynch, Inc., is a hardware store operating in Boulder, Colorado. Management recently made some poor inventory acquisitions that have loaded the store with unsalable merchandise. Because of the drop in revenues, the company is now insolvent. The entire inventory can be sold for only $33,000. The following is a trial balance as of March 14, 2020, the day the company files for a Chapter 7 liquidation:

	Debit	Credit
Accounts payable		$ 33,000
Accounts receivable	$ 25,000	
Accumulated depreciation, building		50,000
Accumulated depreciation, equipment		16,000
Additional paid-in capital		8,000
Advertising payable		4,000
Building	80,000	
Cash	1,000	
Common stock		50,000
Equipment	30,000	
Inventory	100,000	
Investments	15,000	
Land	10,000	
Note payable—Colorado Savings and Loan (secured by lien on land and building)		70,000
Note payable—First National Bank (secured by equipment)		150,000
Payroll taxes payable		1,000
Retained earnings (deficit)	126,000	
Salaries payable (owed equally to two employees)		5,000
Totals	$387,000	$387,000

Company officials believe that 60 percent of the accounts receivable can be collected if the company is liquidated. The building and land have a fair value of $75,000, and the equipment is worth $19,000. The investments represent shares of a nationally traded company that can be sold at the current time for $21,000. Administrative expenses necessary to carry out a liquidation would approximate $16,000.

Prepare a statement of financial affairs for Lynch, Inc., as of March 14, 2020.

LO 13-4, 13-7

52. Use the trial balance presented for Lynch, Inc., in problem (51). Assume that the company will be liquidated and the following transactions will occur:

- Accounts receivable of $18,000 are collected with remainder written off.
- All of the company's inventory is sold for $40,000.
- Additional accounts payable of $10,000 incurred for various expenses, such as utilities and maintenance, are discovered.
- The land and building are sold for $71,000.
- The note payable due to the Colorado Savings and Loan is paid.
- The equipment is sold at auction for only $11,000 with the proceeds applied to the note owed to the First National Bank.

- The investments are sold for $21,000.
- Administrative expenses total $20,000 as of July 23, 2020, but no payment has been made yet.

a. Prepare a statement of realization and liquidation for the period from March 14, 2020, through July 23, 2020.

b. How much cash would be paid to an unsecured, nonpriority creditor that Lynch, Inc., owes a total of $1,000?

LO 13-4, 13-8, 13-9, 13-10

53. Holmes Corporation files a voluntary petition with the bankruptcy court in hopes of reorganizing. Company officials prepare a statement of financial affairs showing these debts:

Liabilities with priority:	
Salaries payable	$ 18,000
Fully secured creditors:	
Notes payable (secured by land and buildings valued at $84,000)	70,000
Partially secured creditors:	
Notes payable (secured by inventory valued at $30,000)	140,000
Unsecured creditors:	
Notes payable	50,000
Accounts payable	10,000
Accrued expenses	4,000

Holmes has 10,000 shares of common stock outstanding with a par value of $5 per share. In addition, the company currently reports a deficit balance of $132,000.

In hopes of emerging from Chapter 11 bankruptcy, officials propose the following reorganization plan:

- The company's assets have a total book value of $210,000, an amount considered to be equal to fair value. The reorganization value of business assets as a whole is set at $225,000.
- Employees will receive a one-year note in lieu of all salaries owed. Interest will be paid at a 10 percent annual rate, a normal rate for this type of liability.
- Future interest on the fully secured note will drop from a 15 percent annual rate, which is now unrealistic, to a 10 percent rate.
- The company will issue a new six-year $30,000 note paying 10 percent annual interest to replace the partially secured note payable. In addition, this creditor will receive 5,000 new shares of Holmes's common stock.
- An outside investor will buy 6,000 new shares of common stock at $6 per share.
- The unsecured creditors will receive an offer of 20 cents on the dollar to settle the remaining liabilities.

Assume that all interested parties accept this plan of reorganization and it becomes effective. What journal entries will Holmes Corporation record?

Develop Your Skills

RESEARCH CASE 1

CPA skills

Aberdeen Corporation is considering the possibility of filing a voluntary petition of bankruptcy because of a particularly high level of debt. The company is publicly traded on a national stock exchange, and, therefore, company officials are concerned about the role of the U.S. Securities and Exchange Commission in this legal action.

Required

Go to the following website: www.sec.gov/investor/pubs/bankrupt.htm. List the information that the SEC provides in connection with the bankruptcy of a publicly held company.

RESEARCH CASE 2

An investment analyst has been studying the long-term prospects of Six Flags Entertainment Corporation and has asked for assistance. Go to www.sixflags.com and click on "Investors" at the top of the page. Then, click on "Financial Information" on the left side of the next page and then on "Annual Reports." Finally, scroll down to a list of annual reports and click on "2013 Annual Report." Scroll down and locate note 2 to the financial statements on page 48 of the annual report, "Chapter 11 Reorganization."

Required

Write a memo to summarize the information found in this note and the impact on the financial statements of applying fresh start accounting.

ANALYSIS CASE 1

Go to the following story about the bankruptcy filing of Sears Holdings Corp., https://www.cnbc.com/2018/10/15/sears-files-for-bankruptcy.html. Search for other stories about the bankruptcy of Sears Holdings.

Next, go to the Securities and Exchange Commission website (www.sec.gov) and click on "Search for Company Filings" under "Filings." Then click on "Company or Fund Name" and enter "Sears Holdings." Click on the most recent 10-K form. What information is available in this document about the company's bankruptcy reorganization plan?

Required

Assume a client of your firm holds an ownership stake in Sears Holdings. Based on these searches, write a memo to the client to describe the information available about the bankruptcy filing of Sears Holdings Corp.

ANALYSIS CASE 2

Go to www.epiqbankruptcysolutions.com or www.kccllc.net. Look through the list of active bankruptcy cases, and select one to research.

Required

Read through the information that is available for the case that selected. Assume your boss needs information about the current status of this particular bankruptcy. Compose a memo to present the information that can be uncovered about this company and its bankruptcy.

COMMUNICATION CASE 1

Go to www.epiqbankruptcysolutions.com or www.kccllc.net and select a current active bankruptcy case. If available, go to an online business publication database such as Factiva or ABI-Inform. Search for articles that discuss the issues and problems that led the selected company to file for bankruptcy and any progress that has been made since that time.

Required

Write a report on the selected company and the problems and mistakes that led to insolvency and the declaration of bankruptcy. If possible, indicate actions that the company might be required to take as a result of filing for bankruptcy.

COMMUNICATION CASE 2

Read several of the following articles as well as any other published pieces that describe the work of the accountant in bankruptcy cases:

Restructuring for a Positive Return," *CMA Management,* December 2005/January 2006.

"Alternatives to Bankruptcy Liquidation," *Agency Sales,* February 2005.

"The Use of Crystal Balls in Financial Reporting: The Case Against Three Recent FASB Developments," *Internal Auditing,* March/April 2015.

"Fresh-Start Reporting: An Opportunity for Debtor Companies Emerging from Bankruptcy," *American Bankruptcy Journal,* July/August 2009.

"Statements of Financial Affairs and Schedules as a Corporate X-Ray," *American Bankruptcy Institute Journal,* March 2010.

"Predicting the Financial Failure of Retail Companies in the United States," *Journal of Business & Economics Research,* August 2013.

"Fresh-Start Accounting Becomes Part of the Daily Financial Intake," *American Bankruptcy Institute Journal,* February 2010.

"Assisting Troubled Business Clients: A Midsize Dilemma for CPAs," *Journal of Accountancy,* March 2008.

"Stanford Business School Research: Financial Statements Are Still Valuable Tools for Predicting Bankruptcy," *Business Wire,* May 12, 2006.

Required

Write a report describing the services an accountant can perform before and during a corporate bankruptcy. Include activities to be carried out prior to filing a petition and thereafter.

chapter 14

Partnerships: Formation and Operation

A reader of college accounting textbooks might well conclude that business activity is carried out exclusively by corporations. Because most large companies are legally incorporated, a vast majority of textbook references and illustrations concern corporate organizations. Contrary to the perception being relayed, partnerships (as well as sole proprietorships) make up a vital element of the business community. The Internal Revenue Service projects that by 2025, more than 4.7 million partnership income tax returns will be filed (as compared to over 7.5 million projected corporation income tax returns).[1]

The partnership form serves a wide range of business activities, from small local operations to worldwide enterprises. The following examples exist in the U.S. economy:

- Individual proprietors often join together to form a partnership as a way to reduce expenses, expand services, and add increased expertise. As will be discussed, partnerships also provide important tax benefits.
- A partnership is a common means by which friends and relatives can easily create and organize a business endeavor.
- Historically, doctors, lawyers, and other professionals have formed partnerships because of legal prohibitions against the incorporation of their practices. Although most states now permit alternative forms for such organizations, operating as a partnership or sole proprietorship is still necessary in many areas.

Over the years, some partnerships have grown to enormous sizes. Buckeye Partners, for example, primarily operates pipeline systems in the United States; in 2018, Buckeye had revenues of more than $4 billion. The professional services firm of PricewaterhouseCoopers, a partnership, recently reported revenues of more than $41 billion.[2] In 2018, Deloitte indicated operations in more than 150 countries,[3] and Ernst & Young reported having more than 260,000 employees around the world.[4]

[1] Internal Revenue Service, Publication 6292 (Rev. 8-2018), *Fiscal Year Return Projections for the United States: 2018–2025,* Washington D.C. 20224

[2] "Global Annual Review 2018," pwc.com.

[3] "Deloitte 2018 Global Impact Report," deloitte.com.

[4] "EY at a Glance," ey.com.

Learning Objectives

After studying this chapter, you should be able to:

LO 14-1 Explain the advantages and disadvantages of the partnership versus the corporate form of business.

LO 14-2 Describe the purpose of the articles of partnership and list specific items that should be included in this agreement.

LO 14-3 Prepare the journal entry to record the initial capital investment made by a partner.

LO 14-4 Use both the bonus method and the goodwill method to record a partner's capital investment.

LO 14-5 Demonstrate the impact that the allocation of partnership income has on the partners' individual capital balances.

LO 14-6 Allocate income to partners when interest and/or salary factors are included.

LO 14-7 Explain the meaning of partnership dissolution and understand that a dissolution will often have little or no effect on the operations of the partnership business.

LO 14-8 Prepare journal entries to record the acquisition by a new partner of either all or a portion of a current partner's interest.

LO 14-9 Prepare journal entries to record a new partner's admission by a contribution made directly to the partnership.

LO 14-10 Prepare journal entries to record the withdrawal of a current partner.

LO 14-1

Explain the advantages and disadvantages of the partnership versus the corporate form of business.

Partnerships—Advantages and Disadvantages

The popularity of partnerships derives from several advantages inherent to this type of organization. An analysis of these attributes explains why millions of enterprises in the United States are partnerships rather than corporations.

One of the most common motives is the ease of formation. Only an oral agreement is necessary to create a legally binding partnership. In contrast, depending on specific state laws, incorporation requires filing a formal application and completing various other forms and documents. Operators of small businesses may find the convenience and reduced cost involved in creating a partnership to be an especially appealing characteristic. Tax advantages also can be found in the partnership form of business. As articulated by the American Bar Association:

> The principal advantage of partnerships is the ability to make virtually any arrangements defining their relationship to each other that the partners desire. There is no necessity, as there is in a corporation, to have the ownership interest in capital and profits proportionate to the investment made; and losses can be allocated on a different basis from profits. It is also generally much easier to achieve a desirable format for control of the business in a partnership than in a corporation, since the control of a corporation, which is based on ownership of voting stock, is much more difficult to alter.
>
> Partnerships are taxed on a conduit or flow-through basis under subchapter K of the Internal Revenue Code. This means that the partnership itself does not pay any taxes. Instead the net income and various deductions and tax credits from the partnership are passed through to the partners based on their respective percentage interest in the profits and losses of the partnership, and the partners include the income and deductions in their individual tax returns.[5]

Thus, partnership revenue and expense items (as defined by the tax laws) must be assigned directly each year to the individual partners who pay the income taxes. Passing income balances through to the partners in this manner avoids double taxation of the profits that are earned by a business and then distributed to its owners. A corporation's income is taxed twice: when earned and again when conveyed as a dividend. A partnership's income is taxed only at the time that the business initially earns it.

For example, assume that a business earns $100. After paying any income taxes, the remainder is immediately conveyed to its owners. An income tax rate of 25 percent (combined federal and state) is assumed for corporations and individuals. The tax rate on corporate dividends is assumed to be 15 percent.[6] As the following table shows, if this business is a partnership rather than a corporation, the owners have $11.25 more expendable income, which is 11.25 percent of the business income. Although potentially significant in amount, this difference narrows as tax rates are lowered.

	Partnership	Corporation
Income before income taxes	$100.00	$100.00
Income taxes paid by business (25%)	–0–	(25.00)
Income distributed to owners	$100.00	$ 75.00
Income taxes paid by owners*	(25.00)	(11.25)
Expendable income	$ 75.00	$ 63.75

*25 percent assumed rate on ordinary income. 15 percent assumed rate on dividend income.

Historically, another tax advantage has long been associated with partnerships. Because income is taxable to the partners as the business earns it, any operating losses can be used to reduce their personal taxable income directly. In contrast, a corporation is viewed as legally

[5] American Bar Association, *Family Legal Guide,* 3rd ed. (New York: Random House Reference, 2004).

[6] Corporate dividends paid to shareholders are taxed either 0 percent, 15 percent, or 20 percent depending on their overall earnings level.

separate from its owners, so losses cannot be passed through to them. A corporation has the ability to carry forward indefinitely operating losses to decrease future taxable income (up to a maximum of 80 percent in any particular year). However, if a corporation is newly formed or has not been profitable, operating losses provide no immediate benefit to a corporation or its owners as losses do for a partnership.

The tax advantage of deducting partnership losses is limited, however. For tax purposes, ownership of a partnership is labeled as a passive activity unless the partner materially participates in the actual business activities. Passive activity losses thus serve only to offset other passive activity profits. In most cases, these partnership losses cannot be used to reduce earned income such as salaries. Thus, unless a taxpayer has significant passive activity income (from rents, for example), losses reported by a partnership create little or no tax advantage unless the partner materially participates in the actual business activity.

A more recent partnership tax advantage was created by the 2017 Tax Cuts and Jobs Act.[7] Eligible taxpayers, including those with partnership income, may be entitled to a deduction of up to 20 percent of qualified income from domestic "pass-through" businesses. Partnerships (along with other tax entities) must be considered a qualified trade or business for their owners to benefit from the 20 percent deduction. Even though many partnerships will be unable to qualify (e.g., health, law, accounting, financial services, etc.), others may qualify and thus entitle their partners to the 20 percent deduction for pass-through businesses.

The partnership form of business also has certain significant disadvantages. Perhaps the most severe problem is the unlimited liability that each partner automatically incurs. Partnership law specifies that any partner can be held personally liable for *all* debts of the business. The potential risk is especially significant when coupled with the concept of *mutual agency*. This legal term refers to the right that each partner has to incur liabilities in the name of the partnership. Consequently, partners acting within the normal scope of the business have the power to obligate the company for any amount. If the partnership fails to pay these debts, creditors can seek satisfactory remuneration from any partner that they choose.

Such legal concepts as unlimited liability and mutual agency describe partnership characteristics that have been defined and interpreted over a number of years. To provide consistent application across state lines in regard to these terms as well as many other legal aspects of a partnership, the Uniform Partnership Act (UPA) was created. This act, which was first proposed in 1914 (and revised in 1997), now has been adopted by all states in some form. It establishes uniform standards in such areas as the nature of a partnership, the relationship of the partners to outside parties, and the dissolution of the partnership. For example, Section 6 of the act provides the most common legal definition of a partnership: "an association of two or more persons to carry on a business as co-owners for profit."

Alternative Legal Forms

Because of the possible owner liability, partnerships often experience difficulty in attracting large amounts of capital. Potential partners frequently prefer to avoid the risk that is a basic characteristic of a partnership. However, the tax benefits of avoiding double taxation still provide a strong pull toward the partnership form. Hence, in recent years, a number of alternative types of organizations have been developed. The availability of these legal forms depends on state laws as well as applicable tax laws. In each case, however, the purpose is to limit the owners' personal liability while providing the tax benefits of a partnership.[8]

[7] *Tax Cuts and Jobs Act, Provision 11011 Section 199A—Qualified Business Income Deduction FAQs*, www.irs.gov.

[8] Many factors should be considered in choosing a specific legal form for an organization. The information shown here is merely an overview. For more information, consult a tax guide or a business law textbook. Also see Hopson and Hopson, "Making the Right Choice of Business Entity," *CPA Journal*, October 2014, pp. 42–47.

Subchapter S Corporation

A Subchapter S corporation (often referred to as an *S corporation*) is created as a corporation and, therefore, has all of the legal characteristics of that form.[9] According to U.S. tax laws, if the corporation meets certain regulations, it will be taxed in virtually the same way as a partnership. Thus, the Subchapter S corporation pays no income taxes, although any income (and losses) pass directly through to the taxable income of the individual owners. This form avoids double taxation, and the owners do not face unlimited liability. To qualify, the business can have only one class of stock and is limited to 100 stockholders. All owners must be individuals, estates, certain tax-exempt entities, or certain types of trusts. The most significant problem associated with this business form is that its growth potential is limited because of the restriction on the number and type of owners.

Limited Partnerships (LPs)

A *limited partnership* is a type of investment designed primarily for individuals who want the tax benefits of a partnership but who do not wish to work in a partnership or have unlimited liability. In such organizations, a number of limited partners invest money as owners but are not allowed to participate in the company's management. These partners can still incur a loss on their investment, but the amount is restricted to what has been contributed. To protect the creditors of a limited partnership, one or more general partners must be designated to assume responsibility for all obligations created in the name of the business.

Buckeye Partners, L.P., is an example of a limited partnership that trades on the New York Stock Exchange. Buckeye's December 31, 2018, balance sheet reported capital of $4.16 billion for its limited partners.

Many limited partnerships were originally formed as tax shelters to create immediate losses (to reduce the taxable income of the partners) with profits spread out into the future. As mentioned earlier, tax laws limit the deduction of passive activity losses, and this significantly reduced the formation of limited partnerships.

Limited Liability Partnerships (LLPs)

The *limited liability partnership* has most of the characteristics of a general partnership except that it significantly reduces the partners' liability. Partners may lose their investment in the business and are responsible for the contractual debts of the business. The advantage here is created in connection with any liability resulting from damages. In such cases, the partners are responsible for only their own acts or omissions plus the acts and omissions of individuals under their supervision.

As Section 306(c) of the Uniform Partnership Act notes,

> An obligation of a partnership incurred while the partnership is a limited liability partnership, whether arising in contract, tort, or otherwise, is solely the obligation of the partnership. A partner is not personally liable, directly or indirectly, by way of contribution or otherwise, for such an obligation solely by reason of being or so acting as a partner.

Thus, a partner in the Houston office of a public accounting firm would probably not be held liable for a poor audit performed by that firm's San Francisco office. Not surprisingly, limited liability partnerships have become very popular with professional service organizations that have multiple offices. For example, all of the four largest accounting firms are LLPs.

Limited Liability Companies (LLCs)

The limited liability company was first seen in the United States in 1977. By 1996, all 50 states had LLC statutes approved. Currently, it is estimated that two-thirds of all new companies in the United States are LLCs.[10] An LLC is classified as a partnership for tax purposes and court purposes. However, depending on state laws, the owners risk only their own investments. Thus, similar to a Subchapter S entity, the LLC provides liability protection for its owners and managers. In contrast to a Subchapter S corporation, the number of owners is not usually restricted, so growth may be easier to accomplish.

[9] Unless a corporation qualifies as a Subchapter S corporation or some other legal variation, it is referred to as a *Subchapter C corporation.* Therefore, a vast majority of all businesses are C corporations.

[10] "The History of LLCS," *IncNow,* January 18, 2018.

Partnership Accounting—Capital Accounts

Despite legal distinctions, questions should be raised as to the need for an entirely separate study of partnership accounting:

- Does an association of two or more persons require accounting procedures significantly different from those of a corporation?
- Does proper accounting depend on the legal form of an organization?

The answers to these questions are both yes and no. Accounting procedures are normally standardized for assets, liabilities, revenues, and expenses, regardless of the legal form of a business. *Partnership accounting, though, does exhibit unique aspects that warrant study, but they lie primarily in the handling of the partners' capital accounts.*

The stockholders' equity accounts of a corporation do not correspond directly with the capital balances found in a partnership's financial records. The various equity accounts reported by an incorporated enterprise display a greater range of information. This characteristic reflects the wide variety of equity transactions that can occur in a corporation as well as the influence of state and federal laws. Government regulation has had an enormous effect on the accounting for corporate equity transactions in that extensive disclosure is required to protect stockholders and other outside parties such as potential investors.

To provide adequate information and to meet legal requirements, corporate accounting must provide details about a variety of equity transactions and account balances. For example, the amount of a corporation's paid-in capital is shown separately from earned capital (retained earnings) and accumulated other comprehensive income; the par value of each class of stock is disclosed; treasury stock, stock options, stock dividends, and other capital transactions are reported based on prescribed accounting principles.

In contrast, partnerships provide only a limited equity disclosures primarily in the form of individual capital accounts that are accumulated for every partner or every class of partners. These balances measure each partner's or group's interest in the book value of the net assets of the business. Thus, the equity section of a partnership balance sheet is composed solely of capital accounts that can be affected by many different events: contributions from partners as well as distributions to them, earnings, and any other equity transactions.

However, partnership accounting does not differentiate between the various sources of ownership capital. Disclosing the composition of the partners' capital balances has not been judged necessary because partnerships have historically tended to be small with equity transactions that were rarely complex. Additionally, absentee ownership is not common, a factor that minimizes both the need for government regulation and outside interest in detailed information about the capital balances.

Articles of Partnership

LO 14-2

Describe the purpose of the articles of partnership and list specific items that should be included in this agreement.

Because the demand for information about capital balances is limited, accounting principles specific to partnerships are based primarily on traditional approaches that have evolved over the years rather than on official pronouncements. These procedures attempt to mirror the relationship between the partners and their business, especially as defined by the partnership agreement. This legal covenant, which may be either oral or written, is often referred to as the *articles of partnership* and forms the central governance for a partnership's operation. The financial arrangements spelled out in this contract establish guidelines for the various capital transactions. Therefore, the articles of partnership, rather than either laws or official rules, provide much of the underlying basis for partnership accounting.

Because the articles of partnership are a negotiated agreement that the partners create, an unlimited number of variations can be encountered in practice. Partners' rights and responsibilities frequently differ from business to business. Consequently, firms often hire accountants in an advisory capacity to participate in creating this document to ensure the equitable treatment of all parties. Although the articles of partnership may contain a number of provisions, an explicit understanding should always be reached in regards to the following:

- Name and address of each partner.
- Business location.
- Description of the nature of the business.

Discussion Question

WHAT KIND OF BUSINESS IS THIS?

After graduating from college, Shelley Williams held several different jobs but found that she did not enjoy working for other people. Finally, she and Yvonne Hargrove, her college roommate, decided to start a business of their own. They rented a small building and opened a florist shop selling cut flowers such as roses and chrysanthemums that they bought from a local greenhouse.

Williams and Hargrove agreed orally to share profits and losses equally, although they also decided to take no money from the operation for at least four months. No other arrangements were made, but the business did reasonably well, and after the first four months had passed, each began to draw out $500 in cash every week.

At year-end, they took their financial records to a local accountant so that they could get their income tax returns completed. He informed them that they had been operating as a partnership and that they should draw up formal articles of partnership agreement or consider incorporation or some other legal form of organization. They confessed that they had never really considered the issue and asked for his advice on the matter.

What advice should the accountant give to these clients?

- Rights and responsibilities of each partner.
- Initial contribution to be made by each partner and the method to be used for valuation.
- Specific method by which profits and losses are to be allocated.
- Periodic withdrawal of assets by each partner.
- Procedure for admitting new partners.
- Method for arbitrating partnership disputes.
- Life insurance provisions enabling remaining partners to acquire the interest of any deceased partner.
- Method for settling a partner's share in the business upon withdrawal, retirement, or death.

Accounting for Capital Contributions

LO 14-3

Prepare the journal entry to record the initial capital investment made by a partner.

Several types of capital transactions occur in a partnership: allocation of profits and losses, retirement of a current partner, admission of a new partner, and so on. The initial transaction, however, is the contribution the original partners make to begin the business. In the simplest situation, the partners invest only cash amounts. For example, assume that Carter and Green form a business to be operated as a partnership. Carter contributes $50,000 in cash, and Green invests $20,000. The initial journal entry to record the creation of this partnership follows:

Cash	70,000	
Carter, Capital		50,000
Green, Capital		20,000
To record cash contributed to start new partnership.		

The assumption that the partners invested only cash avoids complications in this first illustration. Often, though, one or more of the partners transfers noncash assets such as inventory, land, equipment, or a building to the business. Although partnerships record asset contributions at fair value, a case could be developed for initially valuing any contributed asset at the partner's current book value. According to the concept of unlimited liability (as well as present tax laws), a partnership does not exist as an entity apart from its owners. A logical extension of the idea is that the investment of an asset is not a transaction occurring between two independent parties such as would warrant revaluation. This contention holds that the semblance of an arm's-length transaction is necessary to justify a change in the book value of any account.

Although retaining the recorded value for assets contributed to a partnership may seem reasonable, this method of valuation proves to be inequitable to any partner investing appreciated property. A $50,000 capital balance always results from a cash investment of that amount, but recording other assets depends entirely on the original book value.

For example, should a partner who contributes a building having a recorded value of $18,000 but a fair value of $50,000 be credited with only an $18,000 interest in the partnership? Because $50,000 in cash and $50,000 in appreciated property are equivalent contributions, a $32,000 difference in the partners' capital balances cannot be justified. To prevent such inequities, each item transferred to a partnership is initially recorded for external reporting purposes at current value.[11]

Requiring revaluation of contributed assets can, however, be advocated for reasons other than just the fair treatment of all partners. Despite some evidence to the contrary, a partnership can be viewed legitimately as an entity standing apart from its owners. As an example, a partnership maintains legal ownership of its assets and (depending on state law) can initiate lawsuits. For this reason, accounting practice traditionally has held that the contribution of assets (and liabilities) to a partnership is an exchange between two separately identifiable parties that should be recorded based on fair values.

Determining an appropriate valuation for each capital balance is more than just an accounting exercise. Over the life of a partnership, these figures serve in a number of important capacities:

1. The totals in the individual capital accounts often influence the assignment of profits and losses to the partners.
2. The capital account balance is usually one factor in determining the final distribution that will be received by a partner at the time of withdrawal or retirement.
3. Ending capital balances indicate the allocation to be made of any assets that remain following the liquidation of a partnership.

To demonstrate, assume that Carter invests $50,000 in cash to begin the previously discussed partnership and Green contributes the following assets:

	Book Value to Green	Fair Value
Inventory	$ 9,000	$10,000
Land	14,000	11,000
Building	32,000	46,000
Totals	$55,000	$67,000

As an added factor, Green's building is encumbered by a $23,600 mortgage that the partnership has agreed to assume.

Green's net investment is equal to $43,400 ($67,000 less $23,600). The following journal entry records the formation of the partnership created by these contributions:

	Debit	Credit
Cash	50,000	
Inventory	10,000	
Land	11,000	
Building	46,000	
Mortgage Payable		23,600
Carter, Capital		50,000
Green, Capital		43,400
To record properties contributed to start partnership. Assets and liabilities are recorded at fair value.		

[11] For federal income tax purposes, the $18,000 book value is retained as the basis for this building, even after transfer to the partnership. Within the tax laws, no difference is seen between partners and their partnership, so no adjustment to fair value is warranted.

We should make one additional point before leaving this illustration. Although having contributed inventory, land, and a building, Green holds no further right to these individual assets; they now belong to the partnership. The $43,400 capital balance represents an ownership interest in the business as a whole but does not constitute a specific claim to any asset. Having transferred title to the partnership, Green has no more right to these assets than does Carter.

LO 14-4

Use both the bonus method and the goodwill method to record a partner's capital investment.

Intangible Contributions

In forming a partnership, the contributions made by one or more of the partners may go beyond assets and liabilities. A doctor, for example, can bring a particular line of expertise to a partnership, and a practicing dentist might have already developed an established patient list. These attributes, as well as many others, are frequently as valuable to a partnership as cash and fixed assets. *Hence, formal accounting recognition of such special contributions may be appropriately included as a provision of any partnership agreement.*

To illustrate, assume that James and Joyce plan to open an advertising agency, and they decide to organize the endeavor as a partnership. James contributes cash of $70,000, and Joyce invests only $10,000. Joyce, however, is an accomplished graphic artist, a skill that is considered especially valuable to this business. Therefore, in producing the articles of partnership, the partners agree to start the business with equal capital balances. Often such decisions result only after long, and sometimes heated, negotiations. Because the value assigned to an intangible contribution such as artistic talent is arbitrary at best, proper reporting depends on the partners' ability to arrive at an equitable arrangement.

In recording this agreement, James and Joyce have two options: (1) the bonus method and (2) the goodwill method. Each of these approaches achieves the desired result of establishing equal capital account balances. Recorded figures can vary significantly, however, depending on the procedure selected. Thus, the partners should reach an understanding prior to beginning business operations as to the method to be used. The accountant can help avoid conflicts by assisting the partners in evaluating the impact created by each of these alternatives.

The Bonus Method The bonus method assumes that a specialization such as Joyce's artistic abilities does *not* constitute a recordable partnership asset with a measurable cost. Hence, this approach recognizes only the assets that are physically transferred to the business (such as cash, patents, and inventory). Although these contributions determine total partnership capital, the establishment of specific capital balances is viewed as an independent process based solely on the partners' agreement. Because the initial equity figures result from negotiation, they do not need to correspond directly with the individual investments.

James and Joyce have contributed a total of $80,000 in identifiable assets to their partnership and have decided on equal capital balances. According to the bonus method, this agreement is fulfilled simply by splitting the $80,000 capital evenly between the two partners. The following entry records the formation of this partnership under this assumption:

	Debit	Credit
Cash	80,000	
James, Capital		40,000
Joyce, Capital		40,000
To record cash contributions with bonus to Joyce because of artistic abilities.		

Joyce received a *capital bonus* here of $30,000 (the $40,000 recorded capital balance in excess of the $10,000 cash contribution) from James in recognition of the artistic abilities she brought into the business.

The Goodwill Method The goodwill method is based on the assumption that an implied value can be calculated mathematically and recorded for any intangible contribution made by a partner. In the present illustration, Joyce invested $60,000 less cash than James but receives an equal amount of capital according to the partnership agreement. Proponents of the goodwill method argue that Joyce's artistic talent has an apparent value of $60,000, a figure that should be included as part of this partner's capital investment. If not recorded, Joyce's primary contribution to the business is ignored completely within the accounting records.

Cash	80,000	
Goodwill	60,000	
James, Capital		70,000
Joyce, Capital		70,000
To record cash contributions with goodwill attributed to Joyce in recognition of artistic abilities.		

Comparison of Methods Both approaches achieve the intent of the partnership agreement: to record equal capital balances despite a difference in the partners' cash contributions. The bonus method allocates the $80,000 invested capital according to the percentages designated by the partners, whereas the goodwill method capitalizes the implied value of Joyce's intangible contribution.

Although nothing prohibits the use of either technique, the recognition of goodwill poses definite theoretical problems. In previous discussions of both the equity method (Chapter 1) and business combinations (Chapter 2), goodwill was recognized but only as a result of an acquisition made by the reporting entity. Consequently, this asset had a historical cost in the traditional accounting sense. Partnership goodwill has no such cost; the business recognizes an asset even though no funds have been spent.

The partnership of James and Joyce, for example, is able to record $60,000 in goodwill without any expenditure. Furthermore, the value attributed to this asset is based solely on a negotiated agreement between the partners; the $60,000 balance has no objectively verifiable basis. Thus, although partnership goodwill is sometimes encountered in actual practice, this "asset" should be viewed with a strong degree of professional skepticism.

Additional Capital Contributions and Withdrawals

Subsequent to forming a partnership, the owners may choose to contribute additional capital amounts during the life of the business. These investments can be made to stimulate expansion or to assist the business in overcoming working capital shortages or other problems. Regardless of the reason, the contribution is again recorded as an increment in the partner's capital account based on fair value. For example, in the previous illustration, assume that James decides to invest another $5,000 cash in the partnership to help finance the purchase of new office furnishings. The partner's capital account balance is immediately increased by this amount to reflect the transfer to the partnership.[12]

In many instances, the articles of partnership allow withdrawals on a regular periodic basis as a reward for ownership or as compensation for work performed for the business. Often such distributions are recorded initially in a separate drawing account that is closed into the individual partner's capital account at year-end. Assume for illustration purposes that James and Joyce take out $1,200 and $1,500, respectively, from their business. The journal entry to record these payments is as follows:

James, Drawing	1,200	
Joyce, Drawing	1,500	
Cash		2,700
To record withdrawal of cash by partners.		

Larger amounts might also be withdrawn from a partnership on occasion. A partner may have a special need for money or just desire to reduce the basic investment that has been made in the business. Such transactions are usually sporadic occurrences and entail amounts significantly higher than the partner's periodic drawing. The articles of partnership may require prior approval by the other partners.

[12] The partners also may reverse this process by withdrawing assets from the business for their own personal use. To protect the interests of the other partners, the articles of partnership should clearly specify the amount and timing of such withdrawals.

Discussion Question

HOW WILL THE PROFITS BE SPLIT?

James J. Dewars has been the sole owner of a small CPA firm for the past 20 years. Now 52 years old, Dewars is concerned about the continuation of his practice after he retires. He would like to begin taking more time off now although he wants to remain active in the firm for at least another 8 to 10 years. He has worked hard over the decades to build up the practice so that he presently makes a profit of $180,000 annually.

Lewis Huffman has been working for Dewars for the past four years. He now earns a salary of $68,000 per year. He is a very dedicated employee who generally works 44 to 60 hours per week. In the past, Dewars has been in charge of the larger, more profitable audit clients whereas Huffman, with less experience, worked with the smaller clients. Both Dewars and Huffman do some tax work although that segment of the business has never been emphasized.

Sally Scriba has been employed for the past seven years with another CPA firm as a tax specialist. She has no auditing experience but has a great reputation in tax planning and preparation. She currently earns an annual salary of $80,000.

Dewars, Huffman, and Scriba are negotiating the creation of a new CPA firm as a partnership. Dewars plans to reduce his time in this firm although he will continue to work with many of the clients that he has served for the past two decades. Huffman will begin to take over some of the major audit jobs. Scriba will start to develop an extensive tax practice for the firm.

Because of the changes in the firm, the three potential partners anticipate earning a total net income in the first year of operations of between $130,000 and $260,000. Thereafter, they hope that profits will increase at the rate of 10 to 20 percent annually for the next five years or so.

How should this new partnership allocate its future net income among these partners?

LO 14-5

Demonstrate the impact that the allocation of partnership income has on the partners' individual capital balances.

Allocation of Income

At the end of each fiscal period, partnership revenues and expenses are closed out, accompanied by an allocation of the resulting net income or loss to the partners' capital accounts. Because a separate capital balance is maintained for each partner, a method must be devised for this assignment of annual income. Because of the importance of the process, the articles of partnership should always stipulate the procedure the partners established. If no arrangement has been specified, state partnership law normally holds that all partners receive an equal allocation of any income or loss earned by the business. If the partnership agreement specifies only the division of profits, then losses must be divided in the same manner as directed for profit allocation.

The profit allocation pattern can be important to the success of any organization because it can help emphasize and reward outstanding performance. Therefore, many partner compensation plans recognize contributions to revenue, growth, time spent with the firm, management skill development, or any other attribute the partnership deems important. Profit allocations plans can thus become complex in attempting to recognize and reward the various elements of each partner's contributions to the firm's success. Alternatively, partnerships can avoid all complications by assigning net income on an equal basis among all partners.

As an initial illustration, assume that Tinker, Evers, and Chance form a partnership by investing cash of $120,000, $90,000, and $75,000, respectively. The articles of partnership agreement specifies that Evers will be allotted 40 percent of all profits and losses because of previous business experience. Tinker and Chance are to divide the remaining 60 percent equally. This agreement also stipulates that each partner is allowed to withdraw $10,000 in cash annually from the business. The amount of this withdrawal does not directly depend on the method utilized for income allocation. *From an accounting perspective, the assignment of income and the setting of withdrawal limits are two separate decisions.*

At the end of the first year of operations, the partnership reports net income of $60,000. To reflect the changes made in the partners' capital balances, the closing process consists of the following two journal entries. The assumption is made here that each partner has taken the allowed amount of drawing during the year. In addition, for convenience, all revenues and expenses already have been closed into the Income Summary account.

Tinker, Capital	10,000	
Evers, Capital	10,000	
Chance, Capital	10,000	
Tinker, Drawing		10,000
Evers, Drawing		10,000
Chance, Drawing		10,000
To close out drawing accounts recording payments made to the three partners.		

Income Summary	60,000	
Tinker, Capital (30%)		18,000
Evers, Capital (40%)		24,000
Chance, Capital (30%)		18,000
To allocate net income based on provisions of partnership agreement.		

Statement of Partners' Capital

Because a partnership does not separately disclose a retained earnings balance, the statement of retained earnings usually reported by a corporation is replaced by a statement of partners' capital. The following financial statement is based on the data presented for the partnership of Tinker, Evers, and Chance. The changes made during the year in the individual capital accounts are outlined along with totals representing the partnership as a whole:

TINKER, EVERS, AND CHANCE
Statement of Partners' Capital
For Year Ending December 31, Year 1

	Tinker, Capital	Evers, Capital	Chance, Capital	Totals
Capital balances beginning of year	$120,000	$ 90,000	$75,000	$285,000
Allocation of net income	18,000	24,000	18,000	60,000
Drawings	(10,000)	(10,000)	(10,000)	(30,000)
Capital balances end of year	$128,000	$104,000	$83,000	$315,000

LO 14-6

Allocate income to partners when interest and/or salary factors are included.

Alternative Allocation Techniques—Example 1

Assigning net income based on a ratio may be simple, but this approach is not necessarily equitable to all partners. For example, assume that Tinker does not participate in the partnership's operations but is the contributor of the highest amount of capital. Evers and Chance both work full-time in the business, but Evers has considerably more experience in this line of work.

Under these circumstances, no single ratio is likely to reflect properly the various contributions made by each partner. Indeed, an unlimited number of alternative allocation plans could be devised in hopes of achieving fair treatment for all parties. For example, because of the different levels of capital investments, consideration should be given to including interest within the allocation process to reward the contributions. A compensation allowance is also a possibility, usually in an amount corresponding to the number of hours worked or the level of a partner's business expertise.

To demonstrate one possible option, assume that Tinker, Evers, and Chance begin their partnership based on the original facts except that they arrive at a more detailed method of allocating profits and losses. After considerable negotiation, an articles of partnership agreement credits each partner annually for interest in an amount equal to 10 percent of that partner's beginning capital balance for the year. Evers and Chance also will be allotted $15,000 each as a compensation allowance in recognition of their participation in daily operations. Any remaining profit or loss will be split 3:4:3, with the largest share going to Evers because of the work experience that this partner brings to the business. As with any appropriate allocation, this pattern attempts to provide fair treatment for all three partners.

Under this arrangement, the $60,000 net income earned by the partnership in the first year of operation would be allocated as follows. The sequential alignment of the various provisions is irrelevant except that the ratio, which is used to assign the remaining profit or loss, must be calculated last.

Allocation of Partnership Net Income	**Tinker**	**Evers**	**Chance**	**Total**
Net Income				$ 60,000
Interest (10% of beginning capital)	$12,000	$9,000	$7,500	(28,500)
Net income remaining after interest				$ 31,500
Compensation allowance	–0–	15,000	15,000	(30,000)
Net income remaining after interest and compensation				$ 1,500
Remaining income distribution	450 (30%)	600 (40%)	450 (30%)	(1,500)
Net income allocation totals	$12,450	$24,600	$22,950	$ –0–

Importantly, the schedule computing the division of income must be completed prior to determining the final capital balances for the partners. For the Tinker, Evers, and Chance partnership, the allocations just calculated lead to the following year-end closing entry:

Income Summary	60,000	
Tinker, Capital		12,450
Evers, Capital		24,600
Chance, Capital		22,950
To allocate income for the year to the individual partners' capital accounts based on partnership agreement.		

Alternative Allocation Techniques—Example 2

As the preceding illustration indicates, the assignment process is no more than a series of mechanical steps reflecting the change in each partner's capital balance resulting from the provisions of the partnership agreement. The number of different allocation procedures that could be employed is limited solely by the partners' imagination. Although interest, compensation allowances, and various ratios are the predominant factors encountered in practice, other possibilities exist. Therefore, another approach to the allocation process is presented to further illustrate some of the variations that can be utilized. A two-person partnership is used here to simplify the computations.

Assume that Webber and Rice formed a partnership several years ago to operate a coffee shop. Webber contributed the initial capital, and Rice manages the business. With the assistance of their accountant, they wrote an articles of partnership agreement that contains the following provisions:

1. Each partner is allowed to draw $1,000 in cash from the business every month. Any withdrawal in excess of that figure will be accounted for as a direct reduction to the partner's capital balance.
2. Partnership profits and losses will be allocated each year according to the following plan:
   a. Each partner will earn 15 percent interest based on the monthly average capital balance for the year (calculated without regard for normal drawings or current income).

b. As a reward for operating the business, Rice is to receive credit for a bonus equal to 20 percent of the year's net income. However, no bonus is earned if the partnership reports a net loss.
c. The two partners will divide any remaining profit or loss equally.

Assume that Webber and Rice subsequently begin the current year with capital balances of $150,000 and $30,000, respectively. On April 1 of the current year, Webber invests an additional $8,000 cash in the business, and on July 1, Rice withdraws $6,000 in excess of the specified drawing allowance. Assume further that the partnership reports income of $30,000 for the current year.

Because the interest factor established in this allocation plan is based on a monthly average figure, the specific amount to be credited to each partner is determined by means of a preliminary calculation:

Webber—Interest Allocation

Beginning balance . . .	$150,000 × 3 months =	$ 450,000
Balance, April 1.	$158,000 × 9 months =	1,422,000
		1,872,000
		× 1/12
Monthly average capital balance		156,000
Interest rate.		× 15%
Interest credited to Webber		$ 23,400

Rice—Interest Allocation

Beginning balance . . .	$30,000 × 6 months =	$180,000
Balance, July 1	$24,000 × 6 months =	144,000
		324,000
		× 1/12
Monthly average capital balance		27,000
Interest rate.		× 15%
Interest credited to Rice		$ 4,050

Following this initial computation, the actual income assignment can proceed according to the provisions specified in the articles of partnership. The stipulations drawn by Webber and Rice must be followed exactly, even though the business's $30,000 profit for the current year is not sufficient to cover both the interest and the bonus. Income allocation is a mechanical process that should always be carried out as stated in the articles of partnership without regard to the specific level of income or loss.

Based on the plan that was created, Webber's capital increases by $21,675 during the current year, but Rice's account increases by only $8,325:

Allocation of Partnership Net Income	Weber	Rice	Total
Net Income			$ 30,000
Interest (above).	$23,400	$4,050	(27,450)
Net income remaining after interest.			$ 2,550
Bonus to Rice (20% × $30,000)	0	6,000	(6,000)
Net income (loss) remaining after interest and bonus.			(3,450)
Remaining income (loss) distribution	(1,725) (50%)	(1,725) (50%)	$ 3,450
Net income allocation totals	$21,675	$8,325	$ -0-

As discussed earlier, the interest and bonus allocations sum to $33,450 and thus exceed the available net income of $30,000. The remaining overallocation of $3,450 is then treated as a loss in allocating the partnership's income to the individual partners.

LO 14-7

Explain the meaning of partnership dissolution and understand that a dissolution will often have little or no effect on the operations of the partnership business.

Accounting for Partnership Dissolution

Many partnerships limit capital transactions almost exclusively to contributions, drawings, and profit and loss allocations. Normally, though, over any extended period, changes in the members who make up a partnership occur. Employees may be promoted into the partnership or new owners brought in from outside the organization to add capital or expertise to the business. Current partners eventually retire, die, or simply elect to leave the partnership. Large operations may even experience such changes on a routine basis.

Regardless of the nature or the frequency of the event, any alteration in the specific individuals composing a partnership automatically leads to legal dissolution. In many instances, the breakup is merely a prerequisite to the formation of a new partnership. For example, if Abernethy and Chapman decide to allow Miller to become a partner in their business, the legally recognized partnership of Abernethy and Chapman has to be dissolved first. The business property as well as the right to future profits can then be conveyed to the newly formed partnership of Abernethy, Chapman, and Miller. The change is a legal one. Actual operations of the business would probably continue unimpeded by this alteration in ownership.

Conversely, should the partners so choose, dissolution can be a preliminary step in the termination and liquidation of the business. The death of a partner, lack of sufficient profits, or internal management differences can lead the partners to break up the partnership business. Under this circumstance, the partnership sells properties, pays debts, and distributes any remaining assets to the individual partners. Thus, in liquidations (which are analyzed in detail in the next chapter), both the partnership and the business cease to exist.

Dissolution—Admission of a New Partner

One of the most prevalent changes in the makeup of a partnership is the addition of a new partner. An employee may have worked for years to gain this opportunity, or a prospective partner might offer the new investment capital or business experience necessary for future business success. An individual can gain admittance to a partnership in one of two ways: (1) by purchasing an ownership interest from a current partner or (2) by contributing assets directly to the business.

In recording either type of transaction, the accountant has the option, once again, to retain the book value of all partnership assets and liabilities (as exemplified by the bonus method) or revalue these accounts to their present fair values (the goodwill method). The decision as to a theoretical preference between the bonus and goodwill methods hinges on one single question: *Should the dissolved partnership and the newly formed partnership be viewed as two separate reporting entities?*

If the new partnership is merely an extension of the old, no basis exists for restatement. The transfer of ownership is a change only in a legal sense and has no direct impact on business assets and liabilities. However, if the continuation of the business represents a legitimate transfer of property from one partnership to another, revaluation of all accounts and recognition of goodwill can be justified.

Because both approaches are encountered in practice, this textbook presents each. However, the concerns previously discussed in connection with partnership goodwill still exist: Recognition is not based on historical cost, and no objective verification of the capitalized amount can be made. One alternative revaluation approach that attempts to circumvent the problems involved with partnership goodwill has been devised. This hybrid method revalues all partnership assets and liabilities to fair value without making any corresponding recognition of goodwill.

LO 14-8

Prepare journal entries to record the acquisition by a new partner of either all or a portion of a current partner's interest.

Admission through Purchase of a Current Interest

As mentioned, one method of gaining admittance to a partnership is by the purchase of a current interest. One or more partners can choose to sell their portion of the business to an outside party. This type of transaction is most common in operations that rely primarily on monetary capital rather than on the business expertise of the partners.

In making a transfer of ownership, a partner can actually convey only three rights:

1. *The right of co-ownership in the business property.* This right justifies the partner's periodic drawings from the business as well as the distribution settlement paid at liquidation or at the time of a partner's withdrawal.

2. *The right to share in profits and losses as specified in the articles of partnership.*
3. *The right to participate in the management of the business.*

Unless restricted by the articles of partnership, every partner has the power to sell or assign the first two of these rights at any time. Their transfer poses no threat of financial harm to the remaining partners. In contrast, partnership law states that the right to participate in the management of the business can be conveyed only with the consent of all partners. This particular right is considered essential to the future earning power of the enterprise as well as the maintenance of business assets. Therefore, current partners are protected from the intrusion of parties who might be considered detrimental to the management of the company.

As an illustration, assume that Scott, Thompson, and York formed a partnership several years ago. Subsequently, York decides to leave the partnership and offers to sell his interest to Morgan. Although York may transfer the right of property ownership as well as the specified share of future profits and losses, the partnership does not automatically admit Morgan. York legally remains a partner until such time as both Scott and Thompson agree to allow Morgan to participate in the management of the business.

To demonstrate the accounting procedures applicable to the transfer of a partnership interest, assume that the following information is available relating to the partnership of Scott, Thompson, and York:

Partner	Capital Balance	Profit and Loss Ratio
Scott	$ 50,000	20%
Thompson	30,000	50
York	20,000	30
Total capital	$100,000	

As often happens, the relationship of the capital accounts to one another does not correspond with the partners' profit and loss ratio. Capital balances are historical cost figures. They result from contributions and withdrawals made throughout the life of the business as well as from the allocation of partnership income. Therefore, any correlation between a partner's recorded capital at a particular point in time and the profit and loss percentage would probably be coincidental. Scott, for example, has 50 percent of the current partnership capital ($50,000/$100,000) but is entitled to only a 20 percent allocation of income.

Instead of York selling his interest to Morgan, assume that each of these three partners elects to transfer a 20 percent interest to Morgan for a total payment of $30,000. According to the sales contract, *the money is to be paid directly to the owners.*

One approach to recording this transaction is that, because Morgan's purchase is carried out between the individual parties, the acquisition has no impact on partnership assets and liabilities. Because the business is not involved directly, the transfer of ownership requires a simple capital reclassification without any accompanying revaluation. This approach is similar to the bonus method; only a legal change in ownership is occurring so that revaluation of neither assets or liabilities nor goodwill is appropriate.

Book Value Method

	Debit	Credit
Scott, Capital (20% of capital balance)	10,000	
Thompson, Capital (20%)	6,000	
York, Capital (20%)	4,000	
Morgan, Capital (20% of total)		20,000
To reclassify capital to reflect Morgan's acquisition. Money is paid directly to partners.		

An alternative for recording Morgan's acquisition relies on a different perspective of the new partner's admission. Legally, the partnership of Scott, Thompson, and York is transferring all assets and liabilities to the partnership of Scott, Thompson, York, and Morgan.

Therefore, according to the logic underlying the goodwill method, a transaction is occurring between two separate reporting entities, an event that necessitates the complete revaluation of all assets and liabilities.

Because Morgan is paying $30,000 for a 20 percent interest in the partnership, the implied value of the business as a whole is $150,000 ($30,000/20%). However, the book value is only $100,000; thus, a $50,000 upward revaluation is indicated. This adjustment is reflected by restating specific partnership asset and liability accounts to fair value with any remaining balance recorded as goodwill.

Goodwill (Revaluation) Method		
Goodwill (or specific accounts)	50,000	
Scott, Capital (20% of goodwill)		10,000
Thompson, Capital (50%)		25,000
York, Capital (30%)		15,000
To recognize goodwill and revaluation of assets and liabilities based on value of business implied by Morgan's purchase price.		

Note that this entry credits the $50,000 revaluation to the original partners based on the profit and loss ratio rather than on capital percentages. Recognition of goodwill (or an increase in the book value of specific accounts) indicates that unrecorded gains have accrued to the business during previous years of operation. Therefore, the equitable treatment is to allocate this increment among the partners according to their profit and loss percentages. After the implied value of the partnership is established, the reclassification of ownership can be recorded based on the new capital balances as follows:

Scott, Capital (20% × new $60,000 capital balance)	12,000	
Thompson, Capital (20% × $55,000)	11,000	
York, Capital (20% × $35,000)	7,000	
Morgan, Capital (20% × $150,000 new total)		30,000
To reclassify capital to reflect Morgan's acquisition. Money is paid directly to partners.		

LO 14-9

Prepare journal entries to record a new partner's admission by a contribution made directly to the partnership.

Admission by a Contribution Made to the Partnership

Entrance into a partnership is not limited solely to the purchase of a current partner's interest. An outsider may be admitted to the ownership by contributing cash or other assets directly to the business rather than to the partners. For example, assume that King and Wilson maintain a partnership and presently report capital balances of $80,000 and $20,000, respectively. According to the articles of partnership, King is entitled to 60 percent of all profits and losses with the remaining 40 percent credited each year to Wilson. By agreement of the partners, Goldman is allowed to enter the partnership for a payment of $20,000 *with this money going into the business.* Based on negotiations that preceded the acquisition, all parties have agreed that Goldman receives an initial 10 percent interest in the net assets of the partnership.

Bonus Credited to Original Partners The bonus (or no revaluation) method maintains the same recorded value for all partnership assets and liabilities despite Goldman's admittance. The capital balance for this new partner is simply set at the appropriate 10 percent level based on the total net assets of the partnership after the payment is recorded. Because $20,000 is invested, total reported capital increases to $120,000. Thus, Goldman's 10 percent interest is computed as $12,000. *The $8,000 difference between the amount contributed and this allotted capital balance is viewed as a bonus.* Because Goldman is willing to accept a capital balance that is less than his investment, this bonus is attributed to the original partners (again based on their profit and loss ratio). As a result of the nature of the transaction, no need exists to recognize goodwill or revalue any of the assets or liabilities.

Cash	20,000	
Goldman, Capital (10% of total capital)		12,000
King, Capital (60% of bonus)		4,800
Wilson, Capital (40% of bonus)		3,200
To record Goldman's entrance into partnership with $8,000 extra payment recorded as a bonus to the original partners.		

Goodwill Credited to Original Partners The goodwill method views Goldman's payment as evidence that the partnership as a whole possesses an actual value of $200,000 ($20,000/10%). Because—even with the new partner's investment—only $120,000 in net assets is reported, a valuation adjustment of $80,000 is implied.[13] Over the previous years, unrecorded gains have apparently accrued to the business. This $80,000 figure might reflect the need to revalue specific accounts such as inventory or equipment, although the entire amount, or some portion of it, may simply be recorded as goodwill.

Goodwill (or specific accounts)	80,000	
King, Capital (60% of goodwill)		48,000
Wilson, Capital (40%)		32,000
To recognize goodwill based on Goldman's purchase price.		
Cash	20,000	
Goldman, Capital		20,000
To record Goldman's admission into partnership.		

Comparison of Bonus Method and Goodwill Method Completely different capital balances as well as asset and liability figures result from these two approaches. In both cases, however, the new partner is credited with the appropriate 10 percent of total partnership capital.

	Bonus Method	Goodwill Method
Assets less liabilities (as reported)	$100,000	$100,000
Goldman's contribution	20,000	20,000
Goodwill	–0–	80,000
Total	$120,000	$200,000
Goldman's capital	$ 12,000	$ 20,000

Because Goldman contributed an amount more than 10 percent of the partnership's resulting book value, this business is perceived as being worth more than the recorded accounts indicate. Therefore, the bonus in the first instance and the goodwill in the second were both assumed as accruing to the two original partners. Such a presumption is not unusual in an established business, especially if profitable operations have developed over a number of years.

Hybrid Method of Recording Admission of New Partner One other approach to Goldman's admission can be devised. Assume that the assets and liabilities of the King and Wilson partnership have a book value of $100,000, as stated earlier. Also assume that a piece of land held by the business is actually worth $30,000 more than its currently recorded book value. Thus, the identifiable assets of the partnership are worth $130,000. Goldman pays $20,000 for a 10 percent interest.

[13] In this example, because $20,000 is invested in the business, total capital to be used in the goodwill computation has increased to $120,000. If, as in the previous illustration, payment had been made directly to the partners, the original capital of $100,000 is retained in determining goodwill.

In this approach, the identifiable assets (such as land) are revalued, but no goodwill is recognized.

	Debit	Credit
Land	30,000	
King, Capital (60% of revaluation)		18,000
Wilson, Capital (40%)		12,000
To record current fair value of land in preparation for admission of new partner.		

The admission of Goldman and the payment of $20,000 bring the total capital balance to $150,000. Because Goldman is acquiring a 10 percent interest, a capital balance of $15,000 is recorded. The extra $5,000 payment ($20,000 – $15,000) is attributed as a bonus to the original partners. In this way, asset revaluation and a capital bonus are both used to align the accounts.

	Debit	Credit
Cash	20,000	
Goldman, Capital (10% of total capital)		15,000
King, Capital (60% of bonus)		3,000
Wilson, Capital (40% of bonus)		2,000
To record entrance of Goldman into partnership and bonus assigned to original partners.		

Bonus or Goodwill Credited to New Partner As previously discussed, Goldman also may be contributing some attribute other than tangible assets to this partnership. Therefore, the articles of partnership may be written to credit the new partner, rather than the original partners, with either a bonus or goodwill. Because of an excellent professional reputation, valuable business contacts, or myriad other possible factors, Goldman might be able to negotiate a beginning capital balance in excess of the $20,000 cash contribution. This same circumstance may also result if the business is desperate for new capital and is willing to offer favorable terms as an enticement to the potential partner.

To illustrate, assume that Goldman receives a 20 percent interest in the partnership (rather than the originally stated 10 percent) in exchange for the $20,000 cash investment. The specific rationale for the higher ownership percentage need not be identified.

The bonus method sets Goldman's initial capital at $24,000 (20 percent of the $120,000 book value). To achieve this balance, a capital bonus of $4,000 must be credited to Goldman and taken from the present partners:

	Debit	Credit
Cash	20,000	
King, Capital (60% of bonus)	2,400	
Wilson, Capital (40% of bonus)	1,600	
Goldman, Capital		24,000
To record Goldman's entrance into partnership with reduced payment reported as a bonus from original partners.		

If goodwill rather than a bonus is attributed to the *entering partner,* a mathematical problem arises in determining the implicit value of the business as a whole. In the current illustration, Goldman paid $20,000 for a 20 percent interest. Therefore, the value of the company is calculated as only $100,000 ($20,000/20%), a figure that is less than the $120,000 in net assets reported after the new contribution. Negative goodwill appears to exist. One possibility is that individual partnership assets are overvalued and require reduction. As an alternative, the cash contribution might not be an accurate representation of the new partner's investment. Goldman could be bringing an intangible contribution (goodwill) to the business along with the $20,000. This additional amount must be determined algebraically:

$$\text{Goldman's capital} = 20\% \text{ of partnership capital}$$

Therefore:

$$\$20{,}000 + \text{Goodwill} = 0.20\ (\$100{,}000 + \$20{,}000 + \text{Goodwill})$$
$$\$20{,}000 + \text{Goodwill} = \$20{,}000 + \$4{,}000 + 0.20\ \text{Goodwill}$$
$$0.80\ \text{Goodwill} = \$4{,}000$$
$$\text{Goodwill} = \$5{,}000$$

If the partners determine that Goldman is, indeed, making an intangible contribution (a particular skill, for example, or a loyal clientele), Goldman should be credited with a $25,000 capital investment: $20,000 cash and $5,000 goodwill. When added to the original $100,000 in net assets reported by the partnership, this contribution raises the total capital for the business to $125,000. As the articles of partnership specified, Goldman's interest now represents a 20 percent share of the partnership ($25,000/$125,000).

Recognizing $5,000 in goodwill has established the proper relationship between the new partner and the partnership. Therefore, the following journal entry reflects this transaction:

Cash	20,000	
Goodwill	5,000	
Goldman, Capital		25,000
To record Goldman's entrance into partnership with goodwill attributed to this new partner.		

LO 14-10

Prepare journal entries to record the withdrawal of a current partner.

Dissolution—Withdrawal of a Partner

Admission of a new partner is not the only method by which a partnership can undergo a change in composition. Over the life of the business, partners might leave the organization. Death or retirement can occur, or a partner may simply elect to withdraw from the partnership. The articles of partnership also can allow for the expulsion of a partner under certain conditions. Again, any change in membership legally dissolves the partnership, although its operations usually continue uninterrupted under the remaining partners' ownership.

Regardless of the reason for dissolution, some method of establishing an equitable settlement of the withdrawing partner's interest in the business is necessary. Often, the partner (or the partner's estate) may simply sell the interest to an outside party, with approval, or to one or more of the remaining partners. As an alternative, the business can distribute cash or other assets as a means of settling a partner's right of co-ownership. Consequently, many partnerships hold life insurance policies solely to provide adequate cash to liquidate a partner's interest upon death.

Whether death or some other reason caused the withdrawal, a final distribution will not necessarily equal the book value of the partner's capital account. A capital balance is only a recording of historical transactions and rarely represents the true value inherent in a business. Instead, payment is frequently based on the value of the partner's interest as ascertained by either negotiation or appraisal. Because a settlement determination can be derived in many ways, the articles of partnership should contain exact provisions regulating this procedure.

The withdrawal of an individual partner and the resulting distribution of partnership property can, as before, be accounted for by either the bonus (no revaluation) method or the goodwill (revaluation) method. Again, a hybrid option is also available.

As in earlier illustrations, if a bonus is recorded, the amount can be attributed to either of the parties involved: the withdrawing partner or the remaining partners. Conversely, any revaluation of partnership property (as well as the establishment of a goodwill balance) is allocated among all partners to recognize possible unrecorded gains. The hybrid approach restates assets and liabilities to fair value but does not record goodwill. This last alternative reflects the legal change in ownership but avoids the theoretical problems associated with partnership goodwill.

Accounting for the Withdrawal of a Partner

To demonstrate the various approaches that can be taken to account for a partner's withdrawal, assume that the partnership of Duncan, Smith, and Windsor has existed for a number of years. At the present time, the partners have the following capital balances as well as the indicated profit and loss percentages:

Partner	Capital Balance	Profit and Loss Ratio
Duncan	$ 70,000	50%
Smith	20,000	30
Windsor	10,000	20
Total capital	$100,000	

Windsor decides to withdraw from the partnership, but Duncan and Smith plan to continue operating the business. As per the original partnership agreement, a final settlement distribution for any withdrawing partner is computed based on the following specified provisions:

- An independent expert will appraise the business to determine its estimated fair value.
- Any individual who leaves the partnership will receive cash or other assets equal to that partner's current capital balance after including an appropriate share of any adjustment indicated by the previous valuation. The allocation of unrecorded gains and losses is based on the normal profit and loss ratio.

Following Windsor's decision to withdraw from the partnership, its property is immediately appraised. Total fair value is estimated at $180,000, a figure $80,000 in excess of book value. According to this valuation, land held by the partnership is currently worth $50,000 more than its original cost. In addition, $30,000 in goodwill is attributed to the partnership based on its value as a going concern. *Therefore, Windsor receives $26,000 on leaving the partnership: the original $10,000 capital balance plus a 20 percent share of this $80,000 increment.* The amount of payment is not in dispute, but the method of recording the withdrawal is.

Bonus Method Applied If the partnership used the bonus method to record this transaction, the extra $16,000 paid to Windsor is simply assigned as a decrease in the remaining partners' capital accounts. Historically, Duncan and Smith have been credited with 50 percent and 30 percent of all profits and losses, respectively. This same relative ratio is used now to allocate the reduction between these two remaining partners on a ⅝ and ⅜ basis:

Bonus Method		
Windsor, Capital (to remove account balance)	10,000	
Duncan, Capital (⅝ of excess distribution)	10,000	
Smith, Capital (⅜ of excess distribution)	6,000	
Cash		26,000
To record Windsor's withdrawal with $16,000 excess distribution taken from remaining partners.		

Goodwill Method Applied This same transaction can also be accounted for by means of the goodwill (or revaluation) approach. The appraisal indicates that land is undervalued on the partnership's records by $50,000 and that goodwill of $30,000 has apparently accrued to the business over the years. The first two of the following entries recognize these valuations. The adjustments properly equate Windsor's capital balance with the $26,000 cash amount to be distributed. Windsor's equity balance is merely removed in the final entry at the time of payment.

Land Revaluation		
Land	50,000	
Duncan, Capital (50%)		25,000
Smith, Capital (30%)		15,000
Windsor, Capital (20%)		10,000
To recognize land value as a preliminary step to Windsor's withdrawal.		
Goodwill Recognition		
Goodwill	30,000	
Duncan, Capital (50%)		15,000
Smith, Capital (30%)		9,000
Windsor, Capital (20%)		6,000
To recognize goodwill at the time of ownership change.		
Windsor, Capital (to remove account balance)	26,000	
Cash		26,000
To distribute cash to Windsor in settlement of partnership interest.		

After the land revaluation, Windsor's recorded capital balance increases to $20,000. The remaining unrecorded increase in partnership value is then assigned to the intangible asset goodwill. Goodwill represents an asset that captures the intangible increase in partnership value attributable to the past efforts of the individual partners.[14] Upon withdrawal, a partner is entitled to share in any unrecorded increase in partnership value based on his or her profit and loss ratio. The extra $6,000 paid to Windsor (beyond the $20,000 adjusted capital balance) thus is consistent with the $30,000 overall recognition of partnership goodwill: ($6,000 ÷ 20%) = $30,000.

The implied value of a partnership as a whole, however, cannot be determined directly from the amount distributed to a withdrawing partner. For example, paying Windsor $26,000 did not indicate that total capital should be $130,000 ($26,000 ÷ 20%). This computation is appropriate only when (1) a new partner is admitted or (2) the percentage of capital is the same as the profit and loss ratio. Here, an outside valuation of the business indicated that it was worth $80,000 more than book value. As a 20 percent owner, Windsor was entitled to $16,000 of that amount, raising the partner's capital account from $10,000 to $26,000, the amount of the final payment.

Hybrid Method Applied As indicated previously, a hybrid approach also can be adopted to record a partner's withdrawal. It also recognizes asset and liability revaluations but ignores goodwill. A bonus must then be recorded to reconcile the partner's adjusted capital balance with the final distribution.

The following journal entry, for example, does not record goodwill. However, the book value of the land is increased by $50,000 in recognition of present worth. This adjustment increases Windsor's capital balance to $20,000, a figure that is still less than the $26,000 distribution. The $6,000 difference is recorded as a bonus taken from the remaining two partners according to their relative profit and loss ratio.

Hybrid Method		
Land	50,000	
Duncan, Capital (50%)		25,000
Smith, Capital (30%)		15,000
Windsor, Capital (20%)		10,000
To adjust Land account to fair value as a preliminary step in Windsor's withdrawal.		

(continued)

[14] The value of many partnerships derives overwhelmingly from intangibles such as professional reputation and expertise. Because increases in intangible partnership value are difficult to quantify on an ongoing basis, they typically go unrecorded until a change in partnership ownership forces a reckoning.

(continued)

Windsor, Capital (to remove account balance)	20,000	
Duncan, Capital (5/8 of bonus)	3,750	
Smith, Capital (3/8 of bonus)	2,250	
Cash		26,000
To record final distribution to Windsor with $6,000 bonus taken from remaining partners.		

Summary

1. A partnership is defined as "an association of two or more persons to carry on a business as co-owners for profit." This form of business organization exists throughout the U.S. economy ranging in size from small, part-time operations to international enterprises. The partnership format is popular for many reasons, including the ease of creation and the avoidance of the double taxation that is inherent in corporate ownership. However, the unlimited liability incurred by each general partner normally restricts the growth potential of most partnerships. Thus, although the number of partnerships in the United States is large, the size of each tends to be small.
2. Over the years, a number of different types of organizations have been developed to take advantage of both the single taxation of partnerships and the limited liability afforded to corporate stockholders. Such legal forms include S corporations, limited partnerships, limited liability partnerships, and limited liability companies.
3. The unique elements of partnership accounting are found primarily in the capital accounts accumulated for each partner. The basis for recording these balances is the articles of partnership, a document that should be established as a prerequisite to the formation of any partnership. One of the principal provisions of this agreement is each partner's initial investment. Noncash contributions such as inventory or land are entered into the partnership's accounting records at fair value.
4. In forming a partnership, the partners' contributions need not be limited to tangible assets. A particular line of expertise possessed by a partner and an established clientele are attributes that can have a significant value to a partnership. Two methods of recording this type of investment are found in practice. The bonus method recognizes only identifiable assets. The capital accounts are then aligned to indicate the balances negotiated by the partners. According to the goodwill approach, all contributions (even those of a nebulous nature such as expertise) are valued and recorded, often as goodwill.
5. Another accounting issue to be resolved in forming a partnership is the allocation of annual net income. In closing out the revenue and expense accounts at the end of each period, some assignment must be made to the individual capital balances. Although an equal division can be used to allocate any profit or loss, partners frequently devise unique plans in an attempt to be equitable. Such factors as time worked, expertise, and invested capital should be considered in creating an allocation procedure.
6. Over time, changes occur in the makeup of a partnership because of death or retirement or because of the admission of new partners. Such changes dissolve the existing partnership, although the business frequently continues uninterrupted through a newly formed partnership. If, for example, a new partner is admitted by the acquisition of a present interest, the capital balances can simply be reclassified to reflect the change in ownership. As an alternative, the purchase price may be viewed as evidence of the underlying value of the organization as a whole. Based on this calculation, asset and liability balances are adjusted to fair value, and any residual goodwill is recognized.
7. Admission into an existing partnership also can be achieved by a direct capital contribution from the new partner. Because of the parties' negotiations, the amount invested will not always agree with the beginning capital balance attributed to the new partner. The bonus method resolves this conflict by simply reclassifying the various capital accounts to align the balances with specified totals and percentages. No revaluation is carried out under this approach. Conversely, according to the goodwill method, all asset and liability accounts are adjusted first to fair value. The price the new partner paid is used to compute an implied value for the partnership, and any excess over fair value is recorded as goodwill.
8. The composition of a partnership also can undergo changes because of the death or retirement of a partner. Individuals may decide to withdraw. Such changes legally dissolve the partnership, although business operations frequently continue under the remaining partners' ownership. In compensating the departing partner, the final asset distribution may differ from the ending capital balance. This disparity can, again, be accounted for by means of the bonus method, which adjusts the remaining capital accounts to absorb the bonus. The goodwill approach by which all assets and liabilities are restated to fair value with any goodwill being recognized also can be applied. Finally, a hybrid method revalues the assets and liabilities but ignores goodwill. Under this last approach, any amount paid to the departing partner in excess of the newly adjusted capital balance is accounted for by means of the bonus method.

Comprehensive Illustration

Problem

(*Estimated Time: 30 to 55 Minutes*) Heyman and Mullins begin a partnership on January 1, 2020. Heyman invests $40,000 cash and inventory costing $15,000 but with a current appraised value of only $12,000. Mullins contributes a building with a $40,000 book value and a $48,000 fair value. The partnership also accepts responsibility for a $10,000 note payable owed in connection with this building.

The partners agree to begin operations with equal capital balances. The articles of partnership also provide that at each year-end, profits and losses are allocated as follows:

1. For managing the business, Heyman is credited with a bonus of 10 percent of partnership income after subtracting the bonus. No bonus is accrued if the partnership records a loss.
2. Both partners are entitled to interest equal to 10 percent of the average monthly capital balance for the year without regard for the income or drawings of that year.
3. Any remaining profit or loss is divided 60 percent to Heyman and 40 percent to Mullins.
4. Each partner is allowed to withdraw $800 per month in cash from the business.

On October 1, 2020, Heyman invested an additional $12,000 cash in the business. For 2020, the partnership reported income of $33,000.

Lewis, an employee, is allowed to join the partnership on January 1, 2021. The new partner invests $66,000 directly into the business for a one-third interest in the partnership property. The revised partnership agreement still allows for both the bonus to Heyman and the 10 percent interest, but all remaining profits and losses are now split 40 percent each to Heyman and Lewis with the remaining 20 percent to Mullins. Lewis is also entitled to $800 per month in drawings.

Mullins chooses to withdraw from the partnership a few years later. After negotiations, all parties agree that Mullins should be paid a $90,000 settlement. The capital balances on that date were as follows:

Heyman, Capital	$88,000
Mullins, Capital	78,000
Lewis, Capital	72,000

Required:

a. Assuming that this partnership uses the bonus method exclusively, make all necessary journal entries. Entries for the monthly drawings of the partners are not required.

b. Assuming that this partnership uses the goodwill method exclusively, make all necessary journal entries. Again, entries for the monthly drawings are not required.

Solution

a. **Bonus Method**
2020

Jan. 1 All contributed property is recorded at fair value. Under the bonus method, total capital is then divided as specified between the partners.

	Debit	Credit
Cash	40,000	
Inventory	12,000	
Building	48,000	
Note Payable		10,000
Heyman, Capital (50%)		45,000
Mullins, Capital (50%)		45,000
To record initial contributions to partnership along with equal capital balances.		

Oct. 1

	Debit	Credit
Cash	12,000	
Heyman, Capital		12,000
To record additional investment by partner.		

Dec. 31 Both the bonus assigned to Heyman and the interest accrual must be computed as preliminary steps in the income allocation process. Because the bonus is based on income after subtracting the bonus, the amount must be calculated algebraically:

$$\text{Bonus} = 0.10\ (\$33{,}000 - \text{Bonus})$$
$$\text{Bonus} = \$3{,}300 - 0.10\ \text{Bonus}$$
$$1.10\ \text{Bonus} = \$3{,}300$$
$$\text{Bonus} = \$3{,}000$$

According to the articles of partnership, the interest allocation is based on a monthly average figure. Mullins's capital balance of $45,000 did not change during the year; therefore, $4,500 (10 percent) is the appropriate interest accrual for that partner. However, because of the October 1, 2020, contribution, Heyman's interest must be determined as follows:

Beginning balance	$45,000 × 9 months =	$405,000
New balance	$57,000 × 3 months =	171,000
		576,000
		× 1/12
Monthly average—capital balance		48,000
Interest rate		× 10%
Interest credited to Heyman		$ 4,800

Following the bonus and interest computations, the $33,000 income earned by the business is allocated according to the previously specified arrangement:

	Heyman	Mullins	Totals
Net Income			$ 33,000
Bonus to Heyman	3,000		(3,000)
Income remaining after bonus			$ 30,000
Interest on monthly average capital balance	4,800	4,500	(9,300)
Income remaining after bonus and interest			$ 20,700
Remaining income allocation	12,420 (60%)	8,280 (40%)	(20,700)
Net income allocation total	$20,220	$12,780	$ 0

The partnership's closing entries for the year would be recorded as follows:

Heyman, Capital	9,600	
Mullins, Capital	9,600	
Heyman, Drawing		9,600
Mullins, Drawing		9,600
To close out $800 per month drawing accounts for the year.		
Income Summary	33,000	
Heyman, Capital		20,220
Mullins, Capital		12,780
To close out profit for year to capital accounts as computed above.		

At the end of this initial year of operation, the partners' capital accounts hold these balances:

	Heyman	Mullins	Totals
Beginning balance	$45,000	$45,000	$ 90,000
Additional investment	12,000	–0–	12,000
Drawing	(9,600)	(9,600)	(19,200)
Net income (above)	20,220	12,780	33,000
Total capital	$67,620	$48,180	$115,800

2021

Jan. 1 Lewis contributed $66,000 to the business for a one-third interest in the partnership property. Combined with the $115,800 balance previously computed, the partnership now has total capital of $181,800. Because no revaluation is recorded under the bonus approach, a one-third interest in the partnership equals $60,600 ($181,800 × ⅓). Lewis has invested $5,400 in excess of this amount, a balance viewed as a bonus accruing to the original partners:

Cash	66,000	
Lewis, Capital		60,600
Heyman, Capital (60% of bonus)		3,240
Mullins, Capital (40% of bonus)		2,160
To record Lewis's entrance into partnership with bonus to original partners.		

Several years later The final event in this illustration is Mullins's withdrawal from the partnership. Although this partner's capital balance reports only $78,000, the final distribution is set at $90,000. The extra $12,000 payment represents a bonus assigned to Mullins, an amount that decreases the capital of the remaining two partners. Because Heyman and Lewis have previously accrued equal 40 percent shares of all profits and losses, the reduction is split evenly between the two.

Mullins, Capital	78,000	
Heyman, Capital (½ of bonus payment)	6,000	
Lewis, Capital (½ of bonus payment)	6,000	
Cash		90,000
To record withdrawal of Mullins with a bonus from remaining partners.		

b. **Goodwill Method**

2020

Jan. 1 The fair value of Heyman's contribution is $52,000, whereas Mullins is investing only a net $38,000 (the value of the building less the accompanying debt). Because the capital accounts are initially to be equal, Mullins is presumed to be contributing goodwill of $14,000.

Cash	40,000	
Inventory	12,000	
Building	48,000	
Goodwill	14,000	
Note payable		10,000
Heyman, Capital		52,000
Mullins, Capital		52,000
Creation of partnership with goodwill attributed to Mullins.		

Oct. 1

Cash	12,000	
Heyman, Capital		12,000
To record additional contribution by partner.		

Dec. 31 Although Heyman's bonus is still $3,000 as derived in requirement (*a*), the interest accruals must be recalculated because the capital balances are different. Mullins's capital for the entire year was $52,000; thus, interest of $5,200 (10 percent) is appropriate. However, Heyman's balance changed during the year, so a monthly average must be determined as a basis for computing interest:

Beginning balance	$52,000 × 9 months =	$468,000
New balance	$64,000 × 3 months =	192,000
		660,000
		× 1⁄12
Monthly average—capital balance		55,000
Interest rate		× 10%
Interest credited to Heyman		$ 5,500

The $33,000 partnership income is allocated as follows:

	Heyman	Mullins	Totals
Net Income			$33,000
Bonus to Heyman	$ 3,000		(3,000)
Income remaining after bonus			$30,000
Interest on monthly average capital balance	5,500	5,200	(10,700)
Income remaining after bonus and interest			$19,300
Remaining income allocation	11,580 (60%)	7,720 (40%)	(19,300)
Net income allocation total	$20,080	$12,920	$ 0

The closing entries made under the goodwill approach would be as follows:

Heyman, Capital	9,600	
Mullins, Capital	9,600	
Heyman, Drawing		9,600
Mullins, Drawing		9,600
To close out drawing accounts for the year.		
Income Summary	33,000	
Heyman, Capital		20,080
Mullins, Capital		12,920
To assign profits per allocation schedule.		

After the closing process, the capital balances are composed of the following items:

	Heyman	Mullins	Totals
Beginning balance	$52,000	$52,000	$104,000
Additional investment	12,000	–0–	12,000
Drawing	(9,600)	(9,600)	(19,200)
Net income	20,080	12,920	33,000
Total capital	$74,480	$55,320	$129,800

2021

Jan. 1 Lewis's investment of $66,000 for a one-third interest in the partnership property implies that the business as a whole is worth $198,000 ($66,000 divided by ⅓). After adding Lewis's contribution to the present capital balance of $129,800, the business reports total net assets of only $195,800. Thus, a $2,200 increase in value ($198,000 – $195,800) is indicated and will be recognized at this time. Under the assumption that all partnership assets and liabilities are valued appropriately, this entire balance is attributed to goodwill.

Goodwill	2,200	
Heyman, Capital (60%)		1,320
Mullins, Capital (40%)		880
To recognize goodwill based on Lewis's acquisition price.		
Cash	66,000	
Lewis, Capital		66,000
To admit Lewis to the partnership.		

Several years later To conclude this illustration, Mullins's withdrawal must be recorded. This partner is to receive a distribution that is $12,000 more than the corresponding capital balance of $78,000. Because Mullins is entitled to a 20 percent share of profits and losses, the additional $12,000 payment indicates that the partnership as a whole is undervalued by $60,000 ($12,000/20%). Only in that circumstance would the extra payment to Mullins be justified. Therefore, once again, goodwill is recognized and is followed by the final distribution.

	Debit	Credit
Goodwill	60,000	
Heyman, Capital (40%)		24,000
Mullins, Capital (20%)		12,000
Lewis, Capital (40%)		24,000
Recognition of goodwill based on withdrawal amount paid to Mullins.		
Mullins, Capital	90,000	
Cash		90,000
To distribute money to partner.		

Questions

1. What are the advantages of operating a business as a partnership rather than as a corporation? What are the disadvantages?
2. How does partnership accounting differ from corporate accounting?
3. What information do the capital accounts found in partnership accounting convey?
4. Describe the differences between a Subchapter S corporation and a Subchapter C corporation.
5. A company is being created, and the owners are trying to decide whether to form a general partnership, a limited liability partnership, or a limited liability company. What are the advantages and disadvantages of each of these legal forms?
6. What is an articles of partnership agreement, and what information should this document contain?
7. What valuation should be recorded for noncash assets transferred to a partnership by one of the partners?
8. If a partner is contributing attributes to a partnership such as an established clientele or a particular expertise, what two methods can be used to record the contribution? Describe each method.
9. What is the purpose of a drawing account in a partnership's financial records?
10. At what point in the accounting process does the allocation of partnership income become significant?
11. What provisions in a partnership agreement can be used to establish an equitable allocation of income among all partners?
12. If no agreement exists in a partnership as to the allocation of income, what method is appropriate?
13. What is a partnership dissolution? Does dissolution automatically necessitate the cessation of business and the liquidation of partnership assets?
14. By what methods can a new partner gain admittance into a partnership?
15. When a partner sells an ownership interest in a partnership, what rights are conveyed to the new owner?
16. A new partner enters a partnership, and goodwill is calculated and credited to the original partners. How is the specific amount of goodwill assigned to these partners?
17. Under what circumstance might goodwill be allocated to a new partner entering a partnership?
18. When a partner withdraws from a partnership, why is the final distribution often based on the appraised value of the business rather than on the book value of the capital account balance?

Problems

LO 14-1

1. Which of the following is *not* a reason for the popularity of partnerships as a legal form for businesses?
   a. Partnerships may be formed merely by an oral agreement.
   b. Partnerships can more easily generate significant amounts of capital.
   c. Partnerships avoid the double taxation of income that is found in corporations.
   d. In some cases, losses may be used to offset gains for tax purposes.

LO 14-1

2. How does partnership accounting differ from corporate accounting?
   a. The matching principle is not considered appropriate for partnership accounting.
   b. Revenues are recognized at a different time by a partnership than is appropriate for a corporation.
   c. Individual capital accounts replace the contributed capital and retained earnings balances found in corporate accounting.
   d. Partnerships report all assets at fair value as of the latest balance sheet date.

LO 14-2

3. Which of the following best describes the articles of partnership agreement?
   a. The purpose of the partnership and partners' rights and responsibilities are required elements of the articles of partnership.
   b. The articles of partnership are a legal covenant and must be expressed in writing to be valid.
   c. The articles of partnership are an agreement that limits partners' liability to partnership assets.
   d. The articles of partnership are a legal covenant that may be expressed orally or in writing, and form the central governance for a partnership's operations.

LO 14-9

4. Pat, Jean Lou, and Diane are partners with capital balances of $50,000, $30,000, and $20,000, respectively. These three partners share profits and losses equally. For an investment of $50,000 cash (paid to the business), MaryAnn will be admitted as a partner with a one-fourth interest in capital and profits. Based on this information, which of the following best justifies the amount of MaryAnn's investment?
   a. MaryAnn will receive a bonus from the other partners upon her admission to the partnership.
   b. Assets of the partnership were overvalued immediately prior to MaryAnn's investment.
   c. The book value of the partnership's net assets was less than the fair value immediately prior to MaryAnn's investment.
   d. MaryAnn is apparently bringing goodwill into the partnership, and her capital account will be credited for the appropriate amount.

LO 14-10

5. A partnership has the following capital balances with partners' profit and loss percentages indicated parenthetically:

Henry (50%)	$135,000
Thomas (30%)	85,000
Catherine (20%)	80,000

   Anne is going to invest $125,000 into the business to acquire a 40 percent ownership interest. Goodwill is to be recorded. What will be Anne's beginning capital balance?
   a. $125,000
   b. $170,000
   c. $200,000
   d. $245,000

LO 14-8

6. A partnership has the following capital balances with partners' profit and loss percentages indicated parenthetically:

Burks (35%)	$280,000
Donovan (40%)	300,000
Watkins (25%)	170,000

   Ranzilla agrees to pay a total of $245,000 directly to these three partners to acquire a 25 percent ownership interest from each. The partnership will record goodwill based on the new partner's payment. What is Donovan's capital balance after the transaction?
   a. $225,000
   b. $294,000
   c. $392,000
   d. $398,000

LO 14-9

7. The capital balance for Maxwell is $110,000 and for Russell is $40,000. These two partners share profits and losses 70 percent (Maxwell) and 30 percent (Russell). Evan invests $50,000 in cash into the partnership for a 30 percent ownership. The bonus method will be used. What is Russell's capital balance after Evan's investment?
   a. $35,000
   b. $37,000
   c. $40,000
   d. $43,000

LO 14-9

8. Patrick has a capital balance of $120,000 in a local partnership, and Caitlin has a $90,000 balance. These two partners share profits and losses by a ratio of 60 percent to Patrick and 40 percent to Caitlin. Camille invests $60,000 in cash in the partnership for a 20 percent ownership. The goodwill method will be used. What is Caitlin's capital balance after this new investment?
   a. $99,600
   b. $102,000
   c. $112,000
   d. $126,000

LO 14-9

9. The capital balance for Messalina is $210,000 and for Romulus is $140,000. These two partners share profits and losses 60 percent (Messalina) and 40 percent (Romulus). Claudius invests $100,000 in cash in the partnership for a 20 percent ownership. The bonus method will be used. What are the capital balances for Messalina, Romulus, and Claudius after this investment is recorded?
   a. $216,000, $144,000, $90,000
   b. $218,000, $142,000, $88,000
   c. $222,000, $148,000, $80,000
   d. $240,000, $160,000, $100,000

LO 14-6

10. A partnership begins its first year with the following capital balances:

Alexander, Capital	$ 90,000
Bertrand, Capital	100,000
Coloma, Capital	160,000

The articles of partnership stipulate that profits and losses be assigned in the following manner:

- Each partner is allocated interest equal to 5 percent of the beginning capital balance.
- Bertrand is allocated compensation of $45,000 per year.
- Any remaining profits and losses are allocated on a 3:3:4 basis, respectively.
- Each partner is allowed to withdraw up to $25,000 cash per year.

Assuming that the net income is $115,000 and that each partner withdraws the maximum amount allowed, what is the balance in Coloma's capital account at the end of the year?
   a. $143,000
   b. $135,000
   c. $168,000
   d. $164,000

LO 14-4, 14-5, 14-6

11. A partnership begins its first year of operations with the following capital balances:

Winston, Capital	$110,000
Durham, Capital	80,000
Salem, Capital	110,000

According to the articles of partnership, all profits will be assigned as follows:

- Winston will be awarded an annual salary of $20,000 with $10,000 assigned to Salem.
- The partners will be attributed interest equal to 10 percent of the capital balance as of the first day of the year.
- The remainder will be assigned on a 5:2:3 basis, respectively.
- Each partner is allowed to withdraw up to $10,000 per year.

The net loss for the first year of operations is $20,000, and net income for the subsequent year is $40,000. Each partner withdraws the maximum amount from the business each period. What is the balance in Winston's capital account at the end of the second year?
   a. $102,600
   b. $104,400
   c. $108,600
   d. $109,200

LO 14-10

12. A partnership has the following capital balances:

Allen, Capital	$60,000
Burns, Capital	30,000
Costello, Capital	90,000

Profits and losses are split as follows: Allen (20 percent), Burns (30 percent), and Costello (50 percent). Costello wants to leave the partnership and is paid $100,000 from the business based on provisions in the articles of partnership. If the partnership uses the bonus method, what is the balance of Burns's capital account after Costello withdraws?
   a. $24,000
   b. $27,000
   c. $33,000
   d. $36,000

Problems 13 and 14 are *independent* problems based on the following scenario:

At year-end, the Circle City partnership has the following capital balances:

Manning, Capital	$130,000
Gonzalez, Capital	110,000
Clark, Capital	80,000
Freeney, Capital	70,000

Profits and losses are split on a 3:3:2:2 basis, respectively. Clark decides to leave the partnership and is paid $90,000 from the business based on the original contractual agreement.

LO 14-10

13. The payment made to Clark beyond his capital account was for Clark's share of previously unrecognized goodwill. After recognizing partnership goodwill, what is Manning's capital balance after Clark withdraws?
    a. $133,000
    b. $137,500
    c. $140,000
    d. $145,000

LO 14-10

14. If instead the partnership uses the bonus method, what is the balance of Manning's capital account after Clark withdraws?
    a. $100,000
    b. $126,250
    c. $130,000
    d. $133,750

Problems 15 and 16 are *independent* problems based on the following capital account balances and profit and loss percentages (indicated parenthetically):

William (40%)	$ 220,000
Jennings (40%)	160,000
Bryan (20%)	110,000

LO 14-8

15. Darrow invests $270,000 in cash for a 30 percent ownership interest. The money goes to the original partners. Goodwill is to be recorded. How much goodwill should be recognized, and what is Darrow's beginning capital balance?
    a. $410,000 and $270,000
    b. $140,000 and $270,000
    c. $140,000 and $189,000
    d. $410,000 and $189,000

LO 14-9

16. Darrow invests $250,000 in cash for a 30 percent ownership interest. The money goes to the business. No goodwill or other revaluation is to be recorded. After the transaction, what is Jennings's capital balance?
    a. $160,000
    b. $168,000
    c. $170,200
    d. $171,200

LO 14-9

17. Lear is to become a partner in the WS partnership by paying $80,000 in cash to the business. At present, the capital balance for Hamlet is $70,000 and for MacBeth is $40,000. Hamlet and MacBeth share profits on a 7:3 basis. Lear is acquiring 40 percent of the new partnership.
    a. If the goodwill method is applied, what will the three capital balances be following the payment by Lear?
    b. If the bonus method is applied, what will the three capital balances be following the payment by Lear?

LO 14-9

18. The Distance Plus partnership has the following capital balances at the beginning of the current year along with respective profit and loss percentages:

Tiger (50%)	$85,000
Phil (30%)	60,000
Ernie (20%)	55,000

Each of the following questions should be viewed independently.

a. If Sergio invests $100,000 in cash in the business for a 25 percent interest, what journal entry is recorded? Assume that the bonus method is used.

b. If Sergio invests $60,000 in cash in the business for a 25 percent interest, what journal entry is recorded? Assume that the bonus method is used.

c. If Sergio invests $72,000 in cash in the business for a 25 percent interest, what journal entry is recorded? Assume that the goodwill method is used.

LO 14-9

19. A partnership has the following account balances: Cash, $50,000; Other Assets, $600,000; Liabilities, $240,000; Nixon, Capital (50 percent of profits and losses), $200,000; Hoover, Capital (20 percent), $120,000; and Polk, Capital (30 percent), $90,000. Each of the following questions should be viewed as an independent situation:

a. Grant invests $80,000 in the partnership for an 18 percent capital interest. Goodwill is to be recognized. What are the capital accounts thereafter?

b. Grant invests $100,000 in the partnership to get a 20 percent capital balance. Goodwill is not to be recorded. What are the capital accounts thereafter?

LO 14-5, 14-6, 14-9

20. The Prince-Robbins partnership has the following capital account balances on January 1, 2021:

Prince, Capital	$70,000
Robbins, Capital	60,000

Prince is allocated 80 percent of all profits and losses with the remaining 20 percent assigned to Robbins after interest of 10 percent is given to each partner based on beginning capital balances.

On January 2, 2021, Jeffrey invests $37,000 cash for a 20 percent interest in the partnership. This transaction is recorded by the goodwill method. After this transaction, 10 percent interest is still to go to each partner. Profits and losses will then be split as follows: Prince (50 percent), Robbins (30 percent), and Jeffrey (20 percent). In 2021, the partnership reports a net income of $15,000.

a. Prepare the journal entry to record Jeffrey's entrance into the partnership on January 2, 2021.

b. Prepare a schedule showing how the 2021 net income allocation to the partners should be determined.

LO 14-6

21. The partnership agreement of Jones, King, and Lane provides for the annual allocation of the business's profit or loss in the following sequence:

- Jones, the managing partner, receives a bonus equal to 20 percent of the business's profit.
- Each partner receives 15 percent interest on average capital investment.
- Any residual profit or loss is divided equally.

The average capital investments for 2021 were as follows:

Jones	$100,000
King	200,000
Lane	300,000

The partnership earned $90,000 net income for 2021. Prepare a schedule showing how the 2021 net income should be allocated to the partners.

LO 14-4, 14-5, 14-6

22. Purkerson, Smith, and Traynor have operated a bookstore for a number of years as a partnership. At the beginning of 2021, capital balances were as follows:

Purkerson	$60,000
Smith	40,000
Traynor	20,000

Due to a cash shortage, Purkerson invests an additional $8,000 in the business on April 1, 2021.

Each partner is allowed to withdraw $1,000 cash each month.

The partners have used the same method of allocating profits and losses since the business's inception:

- Each partner is given the following compensation allowance for work done in the business: Purkerson, $18,000; Smith, $25,000; and Traynor, $8,000.
- Each partner is credited with interest equal to 10 percent of the average monthly capital balance for the year without regard for normal drawings.
- Any remaining profit or loss is allocated 4:2:4 to Purkerson, Smith, and Traynor, respectively. The net income for 2021 is $23,600. Each partner withdraws the allotted amount each month.

Prepare a schedule showing calculations for the partners' 2021 ending capital balances.

LO 14-4, 14-5, 14-6

23. On January 1, 2020, the dental partnership of Angela, Diaz, and Krause was formed when the partners contributed $30,000, $58,000, and $60,000, respectively. Over the next three years, the business reported net income and (loss) as follows:

2020	$70,000
2021	42,000
2022	(25,000)

During this period, each partner withdrew cash of $15,000 per year. Krause invested an additional $5,000 in cash on February 9, 2021.

At the time that the partnership was created, the three partners agreed to allocate all profits and losses according to a specified plan written as follows:

- Each partner is entitled to interest computed at the rate of 10 percent per year based on the individual capital balances at the beginning of that year.
- Because of prior work experience, Angela is entitled to an annual salary allowance of $12,000 per year, and Diaz is entitled to an annual salary allowance of $9,000 per year.
- Any remaining profit will be split as follows: Angela, 20 percent; Diaz, 40 percent; and Krause, 40 percent. If a net loss remains after the initial allocations to the partners, the balance will be allocated: Angela, 30 percent; Diaz, 50 percent; and Krause, 20 percent.

Prepare a schedule that determines the ending capital balance for each partner as of the end of each of these three years.

LO 14-10

24. The E.N.D. partnership has the following capital balances as of the end of the current year:

Pineda	$230,000
Adams	190,000
Fergie	160,000
Gomez	140,000
Total capital	$720,000

Answer each of the following *independent* questions:

a. Assume that the partners share profits and losses 3:3:2:2, respectively. Fergie retires and is paid $190,000 based on the terms of the original partnership agreement. If the goodwill method is used, what is the capital balance of the remaining three partners?

b. Assume that the partners share profits and losses 4:3:2:1, respectively. Pineda retires and is paid $280,000 based on the terms of the original partnership agreement. If the bonus method is used, what is the capital balance of the remaining three partners?

LO 14-10

25. The partnership of Matteson, Richton, and O'Toole has existed for a number of years. At the present time, the partners have the following capital balances and profit and loss sharing percentages:

Partner	Capital Balance	Profit and Loss Percentage
Matteson	$ 90,000	30%
Richton	150,000	50
O'Toole	100,000	20

O'Toole elects to withdraw from the partnership, leaving Matteson and Richton to operate the business. Following the original partnership agreement, when a partner withdraws, the partnership and all of its individual assets are to be reassessed to current fair values by an independent appraiser. The withdrawing partner will receive cash or other assets equal to that partner's current capital balance after including an appropriate share of any adjustment indicated by the appraisal. Gains and losses indicated by the appraisal are allocated using the regular profit and loss percentages.

An independent appraiser is hired and estimates that the partnership as a whole is worth $600,000. Regarding the individual assets, the appraiser finds that a building with a book value of $180,000 has a fair value of $220,000. The book values for all other identifiable assets and liabilities are the same as their appraised fair values.

Accordingly, the partnership agrees to pay O'Toole $120,000 upon withdrawal. Matteson and Richton, however, do not wish to record any goodwill in connection with the change in ownership.

Prepare the journal entry to record O'Toole's withdrawal from the partnership.

LO 14-2, 14-4, 14-6, 14-9

26. In the early part of 2021, the partners of Hugh, Jacobs, and Thomas sought assistance from a local accountant. They had begun a new business in 2020 but had never used an accountant's services.

Hugh and Jacobs began the partnership by contributing $150,000 and $100,000 in cash, respectively. Hugh was to work occasionally at the business, and Jacobs was to be employed full-time. They decided that year-end profits and losses should be assigned as follows:

- Each partner was to be allocated 10 percent interest computed on the beginning capital balances for the period.
- A compensation allowance of $5,000 was to go to Hugh with a $25,000 amount assigned to Jacobs.
- Any remaining income would be split on a 4:6 basis to Hugh and Jacobs, respectively.

In 2020, revenues totaled $175,000, and expenses were $146,000 (not including the partners' compensation allowance). Hugh withdrew cash of $9,000 during the year, and Jacobs took out $14,000. In addition, the business paid $7,500 for repairs made to Hugh's home and charged it to repair expense.

On January 1, 2021, the partnership sold a 15 percent interest to Thomas for $64,000 cash. This money was contributed to the business with the bonus method used for accounting purposes.

Answer the following questions:

a. Why was the original profit and loss allocation, as just outlined, designed by the partners?

b. Why did the drawings for 2020 not agree with the compensation allowances provided for in the partnership agreement?

c. What journal entries should the partnership have recorded on December 31, 2020?

d. What journal entry should the partnership have recorded on January 1, 2021?

LO 14-3, 14-9, 14-10

27. The following is the current balance sheet for a local partnership of doctors:

Cash and current assets	$ 30,000	Liabilities	$ 40,000
Land	180,000	A, Capital	20,000
Building and equipment (net)	100,000	B, Capital	40,000
		C, Capital	90,000
		D, Capital	120,000
Totals	$310,000	Totals	$310,000

The following questions represent *independent* situations:

a. E is going to invest enough money in this partnership to receive a 25 percent interest. No goodwill or bonus is to be recorded. How much should E invest?

b. E contributes $36,000 in cash to the business to receive a 10 percent interest in the partnership. Goodwill is to be recorded. Profits and losses have previously been split according to the following percentages: A, 30 percent; B, 10 percent; C, 40 percent; and D, 20 percent. After E makes this investment, what are the individual capital balances?

c. E contributes $42,000 in cash to the business to receive a 20 percent interest in the partnership. Goodwill is to be recorded. The four original partners share all profits and losses equally. After E makes this investment, what are the individual capital balances?

d. E contributes $55,000 in cash to the business to receive a 20 percent interest in the partnership. No goodwill or other asset revaluation is to be recorded. Profits and losses have previously been split according to the following percentages: A, 10 percent; B, 30 percent; C, 20 percent; and D, 40 percent. After E makes this investment, what are the individual capital balances?

e. C retires from the partnership and, as per the original partnership agreement, is to receive cash equal to 125 percent of her final capital balance. No goodwill or other asset revaluation is to be recognized. All partners share profits and losses equally. After the withdrawal, what are the individual capital balances of the remaining partners?

LO 14-5, 14-6, 14-9

28. Gorman and Morton form a partnership on May 1, 2019. Gorman contributes cash of $50,000; Morton conveys title to the following properties to the partnership:

	Book Value	Fair Value
Equipment	$15,000	$28,000
Licensing agreements	35,000	36,000

The partners agree to start their partnership with equal capital balances. No goodwill is to be recognized.

According to the articles of partnership written by the partners, profits and losses are allocated based on the following formula:

- Gorman receives a compensation allowance of $1,000 per month.
- All remaining profits and losses are split 40:60 between Gorman and Morton, respectively.
- Each partner can make annual cash drawings of $25,000 beginning in 2020.

Net income of $11,000 is earned by the business during 2019.

Steele is invited to join the partnership on January 1, 2020. Because of her business reputation and financial expertise, she is given a 40 percent interest for $54,000 cash. The bonus approach is used to record this investment, made directly to the business. The articles of partnership are amended to give Steele a $2,000 compensation allowance per month and an annual cash drawing of $20,000. Remaining profits are now allocated:

Gorman	12%
Morton	48
Steele	40

All drawings are taken by the partners during 2020. At year-end, the partnership reports net income of $86,000.

On January 1, 2021, Frank (previously a partnership employee) is admitted into the partnership. Each partner transfers 10 percent to Frank, who makes the following payments directly to the partners:

Gorman	$5,216
Morton	4,724
Steele	9,560

Once again, the articles of partnership must be amended to allow for the entrance of the new partner. This change entitles Frank to a compensation allowance of $800 per month and an annual drawing of $14,000. Profits and losses are now assigned as follows:

Gorman	13.5%
Morton	40.5
Steele	36.0
Frank	10.0

For the year of 2021, the partnership earned a profit of $40,000, and each partner withdrew the allowed amount of cash.

Prepare schedules that determine the capital balances for the individual partners as of the end of each year 2019 through 2021.

LO 14-4, 14-5, 14-6, 14-9

29. Kimble, Sykes, and Gerard open an accounting practice on January 1, 2019, in Chicago, Illinois, to be operated as a partnership. Kimble and Sykes will serve as the senior partners because of their years of experience. To establish the business, Kimble, Sykes, and Gerard contribute cash and other properties valued at $208,000, $180,000, and $92,000, respectively. An articles of partnership agreement is drawn up stipulating the following:

- Personal drawings are allowed annually up to an amount equal to 10 percent of the partner's beginning capital balance for the year.
- Profits and losses are allocated according to the following plan:
  1. Each partner receives an annual salary allowance of $55 per billable hours worked.
  2. Interest is credited to the partners' capital accounts at the rate of 12 percent of the beginning capital balance for the year.
  3. Kimble and Sykes are eligible for an annual bonus of 10 percent of net income after subtracting the bonus, salary allowance, and interest. The agreement also states that there will be no bonus if there is a net loss or if salary and interest result in a negative remainder of net income to be distributed.
  4. Any remaining partnership profit or loss is to be divided evenly among all partners.

On January 1, 2020, the partners admit Nichols to the partnership. Nichols contributes cash directly to the business in an amount equal to a 25 percent interest in the book value of the partnership property subsequent to this contribution. The partnership profit and loss sharing agreement is not altered upon Nichols' entrance into the firm; the general provisions continue to be applicable.

The billable hours for the partners during the first three years of operation follow:

	2019	2020	2021
Kimble	1,700	1,800	1,880
Sykes	1,440	1,500	1,620
Gerard	1,300	1,380	1,310
Nichols	–0–	1,560	1,550

The partnership reports net income (loss) for 2019 through 2021 as follows:

2019	$282,000
2020	(12,400)
2021	477,000

Each partner withdraws the maximum allowable amount each year.

a. Prepare schedules that allocate each year's net income to the partners (to the nearest dollar).

b. Prepare in appropriate form a statement of partners' capital for the year ending December 31, 2021.

LO 14-8, 14-9, 14-10

30. A partnership of attorneys in the St. Louis, Missouri, area has the following balance sheet accounts as of January 1, 2021:

Assets	$320,000	Liabilities	$120,000
		Athos, capital	80,000
		Porthos, capital	70,000
		Aramis, capital	50,000

According to the articles of partnership, Athos is to receive an allocation of 50 percent of all partnership profits and losses, while Porthos receives 30 percent, and Aramis, 20 percent. The book value of each asset and liability should be considered an accurate representation of fair value.

For each of the following *independent* situations, prepare the journal entry or entries to be recorded by the partnership. (Round to nearest dollar.)

a. Porthos, with permission of the other partners, decides to sell half of his partnership interest to D'Artagnan for $50,000 in cash. No asset revaluation or goodwill is to be recorded by the partnership.

b. All three of the present partners agree to sell 10 percent of each partnership interest to D'Artagnan for a total cash payment of $25,000. Each partner receives a negotiated portion of this amount. Goodwill is recorded as a result of the transaction.

c. D'Artagnan is allowed to become a partner with a 10 percent ownership interest by contributing $30,000 in cash directly into the business. The bonus method is used to record this admission.

d. Use the same facts as in requirement (*c*) except that the entrance into the partnership is recorded by the goodwill method.

e. D'Artagnan is allowed to become a partner with a 10 percent ownership interest by contributing $12,222 in cash directly to the business. The goodwill method is used to record this transaction.

f. Aramis decides to retire and leave the partnership. An independent appraisal of the business and its assets indicates a current fair value of $280,000. Goodwill is to be recorded. Aramis will then be given the exact amount of cash that will close out his capital account.

LO 14-2, 14-3, 14-5, 14-6, 14-8, 14-10

31. Steve Reese is a well-known interior designer in Fort Worth, Texas. He wants to start his own business and convinces Rob O'Donnell, a local merchant, to contribute the capital to form a partnership. On January 1, 2019, O'Donnell invests a building worth $52,000 and equipment valued at $16,000 as well as $12,000 in cash. Although Reese makes no tangible contribution to the partnership, he will operate the business and be an equal partner in the beginning capital balances.

To entice O'Donnell to join this partnership, Reese draws up the following profit and loss agreement:

- O'Donnell will be credited annually with interest equal to 20 percent of the beginning capital balance for the year.
- O'Donnell will also have added to his capital account 15 percent of partnership income each year (without regard for the preceding interest figure) or $4,000, whichever is larger. All remaining income is credited to Reese.
- Neither partner is allowed to withdraw funds from the partnership during 2019. Thereafter, each can draw $5,000 annually or 20 percent of the beginning capital balance for the year, whichever is larger.

The partnership reported a net loss of $10,000 during the first year of its operation. On January 1, 2020, Terri Dunn becomes a third partner in this business by contributing $15,000 cash to the partnership. Dunn receives a 20 percent share of the business's capital. The profit and loss agreement is altered as follows:

- O'Donnell is still entitled to (1) interest on his beginning capital balance as well as (2) the share of partnership income just specified.
- Any remaining profit or loss will be split on a 6:4 basis between Reese and Dunn, respectively.

Partnership income for 2020 is reported as $44,000. Each partner withdraws the full amount that is allowed.

On January 1, 2021, Dunn becomes ill and sells her interest in the partnership (with the consent of the other two partners) to Judy Postner. Postner pays $46,000 directly to Dunn. Net income for 2021 is $61,000 with the partners again taking their full drawing allowance.

On January 1, 2022, Postner withdraws from the business for personal reasons. The articles of partnership state that any partner may leave the partnership at any time and is entitled to receive cash in an amount equal to the recorded capital balance at that time plus 10 percent.

a. Prepare journal entries to record the preceding transactions on the assumption that the bonus (or no revaluation) method is used. Drawings need not be recorded, although the balances should be included in the closing entries.

b. Prepare journal entries to record the previous transactions on the assumption that the goodwill (or revaluation) method is used. Drawings need not be recorded, although the balances should be included in the closing entries.

(Round all amounts to the nearest dollar.)

Develop Your Skills

RESEARCH CASE

Go to the Buckeye Partners, L.P., website where forms filed with the SEC are available through the Investor Center. Find Buckeye's recent annual financial statements in their 10–K report for the partnership.

Required

Review Buckeye's financial statements as well as the accompanying notes. List and briefly discuss information included for this partnership that would typically not appear in financial statements produced for a corporation.

ANALYSIS CASE

Erin Carson, Megyn Delaney, and Caitlin Erikson form a partnership as a first step in creating a business. Carson invests most of the capital but does not plan to be actively involved in the day-to-day operations. Delaney has had some experience and is expected to do a majority of the daily work. Erikson has been in this line of business for some time and has many connections. Therefore, she will devote a majority of her time to getting new clients.

Required

Write a memo to these three partners suggesting at least two different ways in which the profits of the partnership can be allocated each year in order to be fair to all parties.

COMMUNICATION CASE 1

Kelly Fernandez and Michael Webster have decided to create a business. They have financing available and have a well-developed business plan. However, they have not yet decided which type of legal business structure would be best for them.

Required

Write a report for these two individuals outlining the types of situations in which the corporate form of legal structure would be the best choice.

COMMUNICATION CASE 2

Use the information in Communication Case 1.

Required

Write a report for these two individuals outlining the types of situations in which the partnership form of legal structure would be the best choice.

EXCEL CASE

The Ace and Deuce partnership has been created to operate a law firm. The partners are attempting to devise a fair system to allocate profits and losses. Ace plans to work more billable hours each year than Deuce. However, Deuce has more experience and can charge a higher hourly rate. Ace expects to invest more money in the business than Deuce.

Required

Build a spreadsheet that can be used to allocate profits and losses to these two partners each year. The spreadsheet should be constructed so that the following variables can be entered:

Net income for the year.
Number of billable hours for each partner.
Hourly rate for each partner.
Capital investment by each partner.
Interest rate on capital investment.
Profit and loss ratio.

Use this spreadsheet to determine the allocation if partnership net income for the current year is $200,000, the number of billable hours is 2,000 for Ace and 1,500 for Deuce, the hourly rate for Ace is $20 and for Deuce is $30, and investment by Ace is $80,000 and by Deuce is $50,000. Interest on capital will be accrued each year at 10 percent of the beginning balance. Any remaining income amount will be split 50–50.

Use the spreadsheet a second time but make these changes: Deuce reports 1,700 billable hours, Ace invests $100,000, and interest will be recognized at a 12 percent annual rate. How do these three changes impact the allocation of the $200,000?

chapter 15

Partnerships: Termination and Liquidation

Partnerships can be rather frail organizations. Termination of business activities followed by the liquidation of partnership property can take place for a variety of reasons, both legal and personal. Although a business organized as a partnership can exist indefinitely through periodic changes within the ownership, the actual cessation of operations is not an uncommon occurrence. "Sooner or later, all partnerships end, whether a partner dies, moves to Hawaii, or gets into a different line of business."[1] The partners simply might become incompatible and choose to cease operations. The same decision could be made if profits fail to reach projected levels.

The termination of a partnership occurs when business operations are discontinued. The subsequent liquidation of a partnership generally involves three important steps:

1. Noncash partnership assets are sold for cash. Gains and losses on the asset sales are allocated to the capital accounts of individual partners on the basis of their profit and loss ratios.
2. Partnership liabilities and expenses incurred during the liquidation are paid from the partnership's available cash. Liquidation expenses are allocated to partners' capital accounts on the basis of profit and loss ratios.
3. Any partnership cash remaining after paying liabilities and liquidation expenses is distributed to the individual partners on the basis of their respective capital balances.

The accountant can summarize and keep track of these steps in a *statement of partnership liquidation.*

The liquidation of a partnership becomes more complicated when

- One or more partners has a negative (deficit) capital balance. A deficit (debit) capital balance can exist either at the beginning of the liquidation process or can arise during the liquidation as partners' capital balances absorb losses from noncash asset sales and liquidation expenses. In some cases, a partner with a deficit capital balance will have sufficient personal assets to be able to make a contribution to the partnership to offset the deficit. In other cases, a partner will be personally insolvent, and the other partners will have to absorb the deficit through reductions in their capital accounts.

Learning Objectives

After studying this chapter, you should be able to:

- **LO 15-1** Determine amounts to be paid to partners in a liquidation.
- **LO 15-2** Prepare journal entries to record the transactions incurred in the liquidation of a partnership.
- **LO 15-3** Prepare a statement of partnership liquidation that summarizes transactions occurring during the liquidation of a partnership.
- **LO 15-4** Determine the distribution of available cash when one or more partners have a deficit capital balance.
- **LO 15-5** Calculate the safe payments that can be made to individual partners from cash that becomes available prior to final liquidation.
- **LO 15-6** Prepare a proposed schedule of liquidation to determine an equitable preliminary distribution of available partnership assets.
- **LO 15-7** Develop a predistribution plan to guide the distribution of cash in a partnership liquidation.

[1] Camilla Cornell, "Breaking Up (with a Business Partner) Is Hard to Do," *Profit,* November 2004, p. 69.

- The liquidation takes place over an extended period of time. In this case, the partners are likely to request that cash be distributed to them as it becomes available through the liquidation of partnership assets. The accountant can facilitate the distribution of cash in installments by calculating the *safe payments* that can be made without running the risk that an individual partner will incur a deficit capital balance, and then by preparing a series of *proposed statements of liquidation* based on those calculations. Or the accountant might choose to prepare a cash *predistribution plan* in advance of any sales of noncash assets to guide the distribution of installment payments during the course of the partnership liquidation.

Termination and Liquidation—Protecting the Interests of All Parties

As the chapter on bankruptcy discussed, accounting for the termination and liquidation of a business can prove to be a delicate task. Beyond the goal of merely reporting transactions, the accountant must work to ensure the equitable treatment of all parties involved in the liquidation. The accounting records are the basis for allocating available assets to creditors and to the individual partners. If assets are limited, the accountant also might have to make recommendations as to the appropriate method for distributing any remaining funds. Protecting the interests of partnership creditors is an especially significant duty because the Uniform Partnership Act specifies that they have first priority to the assets held by the business at dissolution.

Not only the creditors but also the partners themselves have a great interest in the financial data produced during the period of liquidation. They must be concerned with the possibility of incurring substantial monetary losses. The potential for loss is especially significant because of the unlimited liability to which the partners are exposed.

As long as a partnership can meet all of its obligations, the risk to partners is normally no more than that of corporate stockholders; the most they can lose is their capital investment. However, should the partnership become insolvent (that is, have insufficient cash to pay its obligations), *each* partner faces the possibility of having to satisfy *all* remaining partnership obligations personally. Although any partner suffering more than a proportionate share of these losses can seek legal remedy from the other partners, this process is not always effective. The other partners may themselves be personally insolvent, or anticipated legal costs might discourage the damaged partner from seeking recovery. Therefore, each partner usually has a keen interest in monitoring the progress of a liquidation as it transpires.

LO 15-1

Determine amounts to be paid to partners in a liquidation.

Partnership Liquidation Procedures

The procedures involved in terminating and liquidating a partnership are basically mechanical. Partnership assets are converted into cash that is then used to pay partnership liabilities as well as any liquidation expenses. *Any remaining cash is distributed to the individual partners based on their final capital balances.* Once all cash has been distributed, the partnership's books are permanently closed. If each partner has a capital balance large enough to absorb all liquidation losses and expenses, the accountant should experience little difficulty in recording this series of transactions.

To illustrate a simple liquidation process, assume that Morgan and Houseman have been operating an art gallery as a partnership for a number of years. Morgan and Houseman allocate all profits and losses on a 60%:40% basis, respectively. On May 1, 2020, the partners decide to terminate business activities, liquidate all noncash assets, and dissolve their partnership. Although they give no specific explanation for this action, any number of reasons could exist. The partners, for example, could have come to a disagreement so that they no longer believe they can work together. Another possibility is that business profits have become inadequate to warrant the continuing investment of their time and capital.

The following is a balance sheet for the partnership of Morgan and Houseman as of the termination date (that is, the date the partners close the art gallery). The partnership has $75,000 of noncash assets to be liquidated. The revenue, expense, and partner's drawing accounts have been closed as a preliminary step in terminating the business. A separate reporting of the gains and losses that occur during the liquidation process will subsequently be made.

MORGAN AND HOUSEMAN
Balance Sheet
May 1, 2020

Assets		Liabilities and Capital	
Cash	$ 45,000	Liabilities	$ 32,000
Accounts receivable	12,000	Morgan, capital	50,000
Inventory	22,000	Houseman, capital	38,000
Land, building, and equipment (net)	41,000		
Total assets	$120,000	Total liabilities and capital	$120,000

The liquidation of Morgan and Houseman proceeds in an orderly fashion through the following events:

June 1	The inventory is sold at auction for $15,000.
June 15	Of the total accounts receivable, the partnership collected $9,000 and wrote off the remainder as being uncollectible.
July 1	The land, building, and equipment are sold for a total of $29,000.
July 5	All partnership liabilities are paid.
July 10	A total of $3,000 in liquidation expenses is paid to cover accounting and legal fees as well as the sales commissions incurred in disposing of partnership property.
July 12	All remaining cash is distributed to the owners based on their final capital account balances.

The partnership of Morgan and Houseman incurred a number of losses in liquidating its assets. Losses often are expected because the need for immediate sale usually holds a high priority in a liquidation. Furthermore, a portion of the assets used by any business, such as its equipment and buildings, could have value that is strictly limited to a particular type of operation. If the assets are not easily adaptable for other uses, disposal at any reasonable price often proves to be difficult.

LO 15-2

Prepare journal entries to record the transactions incurred in the liquidation of a partnership.

To record the liquidation of Morgan and Houseman, the following journal entries would be made. Rather than report specific income and expense balances, gains and losses are recorded directly to the partners' capital accounts, allocated on the basis of the partners' profit and loss ratio. Because operations have ceased, determination of a separate net income figure for this period is unnecessary, as it would provide little informational value. *Instead, a primary concern of the parties involved in any liquidation is keeping track of the continuing changes in each partner's capital balance.*

6/1/20	Cash	15,000	
	Morgan, Capital (60% of loss)	4,200	
	Houseman, Capital (40% of loss)	2,800	
	Inventory		22,000
	To record sale of partnership inventory at a $7,000 loss.		

(continued)

(continued)

Date	Account	Debit	Credit
6/15/20	Cash	9,000	
	Morgan, Capital	1,800	
	Houseman, Capital	1,200	
	Accounts Receivable		12,000
	To record collection of accounts receivable with write-off of remaining $3,000 in accounts as being uncollectible.		
7/1/20	Cash	29,000	
	Morgan, Capital	7,200	
	Houseman, Capital	4,800	
	Land, Building, and Equipment (net)		41,000
	To record sale of land, building, and equipment and allocation of $12,000 loss.		
7/5/20	Liabilities	32,000	
	Cash		32,000
	To record payment made to settle the liabilities of the partnership.		

Date	Account	Debit	Credit
7/10/20	Morgan, Capital	1,800	
	Houseman, Capital	1,200	
	Cash		3,000
	To record payment of liquidation expenses with the amounts recorded as direct reductions to the partners' capital accounts.		

After liquidating the partnership assets and paying off all partnership liabilities, the $63,000 cash that remains can be distributed to Morgan and Houseman on the basis of their capital balances. The following schedule determines the partners' ending capital account balances and, thus, the appropriate distribution of the final cash balance.

Cash and Capital Account Balances

	Cash	Morgan, Capital	Houseman, Capital
Beginning balances*	$45,000	$50,000	$38,000
Sold inventory	15,000	(4,200)	(2,800)
Collected accounts receivable	9,000	(1,800)	(1,200)
Sold fixed assets	29,000	(7,200)	(4,800)
Paid liabilities	(32,000)	–0–	–0–
Paid liquidation expenses	(3,000)	(1,800)	(1,200)
Final balances	$63,000	$35,000	$28,000

*Because of the presence of other assets as well as liabilities, the beginning balances in Cash and in the capital accounts are not equal.

After the final capital balances have been calculated, the remaining cash can be distributed to the partners to close out the financial records of the partnership:

Date	Account	Debit	Credit
7/12/20	Morgan, Capital	35,000	
	Houseman, Capital	28,000	
	Cash		63,000
	To record distribution of cash to partners in accordance with final capital balances.		

LO 15-3

Prepare a statement of partnership liquidation that summarizes transactions occurring during the liquidation of a partnership.

Statement of Partnership Liquidation

Liquidation can take a considerable length of time to complete. Because the various parties involved seek continually updated financial information, the accountant should produce frequent reports summarizing transactions as they occur. Consequently, a statement (often referred to as a *statement of partnership liquidation*) can be prepared at periodic intervals to reflect:

- Transactions to date.
- Assets still held by the partnership.
- Liabilities remaining to be paid.
- Current cash and capital balances.

Although the preceding Morgan and Houseman example has been condensed into a few events occurring during a relatively brief period of time, partnership liquidations usually require numerous transactions that transpire over months and, perhaps, even years. By receiving frequent statements of partnership liquidation, both the creditors and the partners are able to stay apprised of the results of this lengthy process.

Exhibit 15.1 shows the final statement of partnership liquidation for the partnership of Morgan and Houseman. The accountant should have distributed previous statements at each important juncture of this liquidation to meet the informational needs of the parties involved. Exhibit 15.1 demonstrates the stair-step approach incorporated in preparing a statement of liquidation. The effects of each transaction (or group of transactions) are outlined in a horizontal fashion so that current account balances and all prior transactions are evident. This structuring also facilitates the preparation of future statements: A new layer summarizing recent events can simply be added at the bottom each time a new statement is to be produced.

LO 15-4

Determine the distribution of available cash when one or more partners have a deficit capital balance.

Deficit Capital Balances

During the liquidation process, one or more partners could have a negative (deficit) balance in their capital account. Such deficits are most likely to occur when the partnership has incurred significant operating losses that have negatively affected partners' capital balances or when the sale of noncash assets during the liquidation process results in material losses.

EXHIBIT 15.1

MORGAN AND HOUSEMAN
Statement of Partnership Liquidation

	Cash	Noncash Assets	Liabilities	Morgan, Capital (60%)	Houseman, Capital (40%)
Beginning balances, 5/1/20	$ 45,000	$ 75,000	$ 32,000	$ 50,000	$ 38,000
Sold inventory, 6/1/20	15,000	(22,000)	–0–	(4,200)	(2,800)
Updated balances	60,000	53,000	32,000	45,800	35,200
Collected receivables, 6/15/20	9,000	(12,000)	–0–	(1,800)	(1,200)
Updated balances	69,000	41,000	32,000	44,000	34,000
Sold land, building, and equipment, 7/1/20	29,000	(41,000)	–0–	(7,200)	(4,800)
Updated balances	98,000	–0–	32,000	36,800	29,200
Paid liabilities, 7/5/20	(32,000)		(32,000)	–0–	–0–
Updated balances	66,000	–0–	–0–	36,800	29,200
Paid liquidation expenses, 7/10/20	(3,000)			(1,800)	(1,200)
Updated balances	63,000	–0–	–0–	35,000	28,000
Distributed remaining cash, 7/12/20	(63,000)			(35,000)	(28,000)
Closing balances	$ –0–	$ –0–	$ –0–	$ –0–	$ –0–

Discussion Question

WHAT HAPPENS IF A PARTNER BECOMES INSOLVENT?

In 2010, three dentists—Ben Rogers, Judy Wilkinson, and Henry Walker—formed a partnership to open a practice in Toledo, Ohio. The partnership's primary purpose was to reduce expenses by sharing building and equipment costs, supplies, and the services of a clerical staff. Each contributed $70,000 in cash and, with the help of a bank loan, constructed a building and acquired furniture, fixtures, and equipment. Because the partners maintained their own separate clients, annual net income has been allocated as follows: Each partner receives the specific amount of revenues that he or she generated during the period less one-third of all expenses. From the beginning, the partners did not anticipate expansion of the practice; consequently, they could withdraw cash each year up to 90 percent of their share of income for the period.

The partnership had been profitable for a number of years. Over the years, Rogers has used much of his income to speculate in real estate in the Toledo area. By 2020 he was spending less time with the dental practice so that he could concentrate on his investments. Unfortunately, a number of these real estate deals proved to be bad decisions, and he incurred significant losses. On November 8, 2020, while Rogers was out of town, his personal creditors filed a $97,000 claim against the partnership's assets. Unbeknownst to Wilkinson and Walker, Rogers had become personally insolvent.

Wilkinson and Walker hurriedly met to discuss the problem because Rogers could not be located. Rogers's capital account was currently at $105,000, but the partnership had only $27,000 in cash and liquid assets. The partners knew that Rogers's dental equipment had been used for many years and could be sold for relatively little. In contrast, the building had appreciated in value, and Rogers's creditors' claims could be satisfied by selling the property. However, this action would have a tremendously adverse impact on the dental practice of the remaining two partners.

What alternatives are available to Wilkinson and Walker to deal with this situation, and what are the advantages and disadvantages of each?

In some cases, partners with deficit capital balances will make a cash contribution to the partnership to offset their deficit. When a deficit partner lacks sufficient cash (is insolvent) or is simply unwilling to make a contribution, remaining partners must absorb that partner's deficit as losses to their capital accounts. This section demonstrates the procedures for dealing with three different scenarios:

1. One partner has a deficit capital balance; that partner makes a contribution to the partnership to offset the deficit.
2. One partner has a deficit capital balance; other partners absorb that deficit as a loss.
3. Two partners have deficit capital balances; only one partner makes a contribution to offset the deficit.

Recognize that these are only three of an infinite number of possible situations involving deficit capital balances.

Partner with Deficit—Contribution to Partnership

To illustrate the situation in which a partner with a deficit capital balance makes a cash contribution to the partnership, assume that the partnership of Holland, Dozier, and Ross was terminated at the beginning of the current year. Business activities ceased and all noncash assets were subsequently converted into cash. During the liquidation process, the partnership incurred a number of large losses that have been allocated to the partners' capital accounts on a 4:4:2 basis, respectively. A portion of the resulting cash is then used to pay all partnership liabilities and liquidation expenses.

Following these transactions, only the following four account balances remain open within the partnership's records:

Cash	$20,000	Holland, capital	$ (6,000)
		Dozier, capital	15,000
		Ross, capital	11,000
		Total	$20,000

Holland has a negative capital balance of $6,000; the share of partnership losses allocated to Holland has exceeded this partner's capital balance at the date the partnership terminated. Holland is personally solvent and agrees to contribute $6,000 to the partnership to offset the negative capital balance. This contribution raises the cash balance to $26,000, which allows a complete distribution of cash to be made to Dozier ($15,000) and Ross ($11,000) based on their capital account balances. The journal entries for these final payments close out the partnership records:

Cash	6,000	
Holland, Capital		6,000
To record contribution made by Holland to extinguish negative capital balance.		
Dozier, Capital	15,000	
Ross, Capital	11,000	
Cash		26,000
To record distribution of remaining cash to partners in accordance with their ending capital balances.		

Partner with Deficit—Loss to Remaining Partners

An alternative scenario could easily arise for the previous partnership liquidation. Assume that although Holland's capital account shows a $6,000 deficit balance, this partner is personally insolvent and is unable to make a cash contribution.

In this case, Dozier and Ross must absorb a $6,000 loss on the basis of their relative profit and loss ratio (4:2, or ⅔:⅓). This is reflected in the following journal entry:

Dozier, Capital (⅔ of loss)	4,000	
Ross, Capital (⅓ of loss)	2,000	
Holland, Capital		6,000
To record allocation of deficit capital balance of insolvent partner.		

After posting this entry to the accounts, Dozier has a capital balance of $11,000 ($15,000 – $4,000) and Ross has a capital balance of $9,000 ($11,000 – $2,000). One final entry records the distribution of the $20,000 ending cash balance to the remaining partners and serves to close out the partnership books.

Dozier, Capital	11,000	
Ross, Capital	9,000	
Cash		20,000
To record distribution of remaining cash to partners in accordance with their ending capital balances.		

Two Partners with Deficit Capital Balances

Now we consider a different partnership in which two partners have negative ending capital balances. The following balance sheet is presented for the medical practice partnership of Morris, Newton, Olsen, and Prince and indicates the applicable profit and loss percentages.

Cash	$ 10,000	Liabilities	$ 70,000
Noncash assets	140,000	Morris, capital (40%)	15,000
		Newton, capital (20%)	10,000
		Olsen, capital (20%)	23,000
		Prince, capital (20%)	32,000
Total assets	$150,000	Total liabilities and capital	$150,000

Both Morris and Prince are personally insolvent. Morris's personal creditors have brought an $8,000 claim against the partnership's assets, and Prince's creditors are seeking $15,000. These claims have forced the partnership to terminate operations so that the business property can be liquidated and the insolvent partners can settle their personal obligations. The question arises as to how much cash each partner is entitled to as a result of the liquidation.

Assume that the partnership sells the noncash assets for a total of $80,000, creating a $60,000 loss, and pays all its liabilities. The partnership records these two events as follows:

Cash	80,000	
Morris, Capital (40% of loss)	24,000	
Newton, Capital (20% of loss)	12,000	
Olsen, Capital (20% of loss)	12,000	
Prince, Capital (20% of loss)	12,000	
Noncash Assets		140,000
To record sale of noncash assets and allocation of resulting $60,000 loss.		
Liabilities	70,000	
Cash		70,000
To record payment of partnership liabilities.		

As a result of these two transactions, the partnership's cash balance has increased from $10,000 to $20,000.

After allocation of the loss on the sale of the noncash assets, the capital accounts for Morris and Newton have deficit balances of $9,000 ($15,000 – $24,000) and $2,000 ($10,000 – $12,000), respectively. Although Newton is personally solvent and therefore will make a cash contribution to the partnership, Morris's personal financial condition does not allow for any further contribution. Therefore, Newton, Olsen, and Prince must absorb Morris's $9,000 deficit. Because each of these three partners has a 20 percent share of partnership profits and losses, they share this deficit equally:

Newton, Capital (⅓ of loss)	3,000	
Olsen, Capital (⅓ of loss)	3,000	
Prince, Capital (⅓ of loss)	3,000	
Morris, Capital		9,000
To record write-off of deficit capital balance of insolvent partner.		

This allocation increases Newton's deficit to a $5,000 balance ($2,000 + $3,000), an amount that this partner now contributes to the partnership.

Cash	5,000	
Newton, Capital		5,000
To record contribution from solvent partner necessitated by negative capital balance.		

EXHIBIT 15.2

ORRIS, NEWTON, OLSEN, AND PRINCE PARTNERSHIP
Statement of Partnership Liquidation

	Cash	Noncash Assets	Liabilities	Morris, Capital (40%)	Newton, Capital (20%)	Olsen, Capital (20%)	Prince, Capital (20%)
Beginning balances	$ 10,000	$ 140,000	$(70,000)	$ 15,000	$ 10,000	$ 23,000	$ 32,000
Sold noncash assets	80,000	(140,000)	–0–	(24,000)	(12,000)	(12,000)	(12,000)
Updated balances	90,000	–0–	(70,000)	(9,000)	(2,000)	11,000	20,000
Paid liabilities	(70,000)	–0–	70,000	–0–	–0–	–0–	–0–
Updated balances	20,000	–0–	–0–	(9,000)	(2,000)	11,000	20,000
Default by Morris	–0–	–0–	–0–	9,000	(3,000)	(3,000)	(3,000)
Updated balances	20,000	–0–	–0–	–0–	(5,000)	8,000	17,000
Contribution by Newton	5,000	–0–	–0–	–0–	5,000	–0–	–0–
Updated balances	25,000	–0–	–0–	–0–	–0–	8,000	17,000
Distribute remaining cash	(25,000)	–0–	–0–	–0–	–0–	(8,000)	(17,000)
Closing balances	$ –0–	$ –0–	$ –0–	$ –0–	$ –0–	$ –0–	$ –0–

Exhibit 15.2 presents the statement of partnership liquidation summarizing the series of transactions that takes place in the liquidation of this partnership.

The journal entry to close this partnership's books is as follows:

Olsen, Capital	8,000	
Prince, Capital	17,000	
Cash		25,000
To record distribution of remaining cash based upon final capital account balances.		

Although $8,000 of the partnership's remaining cash is paid directly to Olsen, the $17,000 attributed to Prince is first subjected to the claims of the partner's personal creditors. Because of their claims, $15,000 of this amount must be used to satisfy these obligations, with only the final $2,000 actually being paid directly to Prince. Because Morris receives no distribution of cash from the partnership, no assets become available to settle claims of this partner's personal creditors.

Safe Payments to Partners

LO 15-5

Calculate the safe payments that can be made to individual partners from cash that becomes available prior to final liquidation.

In the earlier scenarios in which one of the partners in the law firm of Holland, Dozier, and Ross had a deficit capital balance, no cash was distributed to any partner until the deficit capital balance had been resolved—either by Holland making a contribution to the partnership or by the other partners absorbing Holland's deficit. Recall that the partnership had the following balances after liquidation of noncash assets and payment of liabilities and expenses:

Cash	$20,000	Holland, capital	$ (6,000)
		Dozier, capital	15,000
		Ross, capital	11,000
		Total	$20,000

While awaiting the final resolution of Holland's capital deficit, no compelling reason exists for the partnership to continue holding $20,000 in cash. These funds eventually will be paid to Dozier and Ross regardless of whether Holland makes a contribution or not. An immediate transfer of cash should be made to these two partners to allow them the use of their money. However, because Dozier has a $15,000 capital account balance and Ross currently has $11,000, a complete distribution to close their capital accounts is not possible. A method must be devised, therefore, to allow for a fair allocation of the available $20,000.

To ensure the equitable treatment of all parties, this initial distribution is based on the assumption that the $6,000 deficit capital balance will prove to be a total loss to the partnership. By making this conservative presumption, the accountant is able to calculate the lowest possible amounts (or *safe capital balances*) that Dozier and Ross must retain in their capital accounts to be able to absorb all future losses. Based upon these safe capital balances, the accountant can determine the amount of *safe payments* that can be made to Dozier and Ross without running the risk that future losses will cause either of these partners to have a deficit capital balance.

Calculation of Safe Payments

Should Holland's $6,000 deficit (or any portion of it) prove uncollectible, the loss will be written off against the capital accounts of Dozier and Ross based on their relative profit and loss ratio. Dozier and Ross are credited with 40 percent and 20 percent of partnership income, respectively, which equates to ⅔:⅓ split between the two of them. Thus, if no part of the $6,000 deficit balance is ever recovered from Holland, $4,000 (two-thirds) of the loss will be assigned to Dozier and $2,000 (one-third) to Ross:

Dozier	⅔ of $(6,000) = $(4,000)
Ross	⅓ of $(6,000) = $(2,000)

These amounts represent the maximum potential reductions that could be allocated to the two remaining partners' capital accounts. These balances must therefore remain in the respective capital accounts until Holland's deficit is resolved. Therefore, a safe payment of $11,000 may be made to Dozier at the present time; this distribution reduces that partner's capital account from $15,000 to the safe capital balance of $4,000. Likewise, a safe payment of $9,000 may be made to Ross, which decreases this partner's $11,000 capital account to the $2,000 safe balance. Thus, $11,000 and $9,000 are the safe payments that can be distributed to the partners at the present time without fear of creating new deficits in the future:

Dozier, Capital	11,000	
Ross, Capital	9,000	
Cash		20,000
To record distribution of safe payments of cash to Dozier and Ross based on the assumption that Holland will not contribute further to the partnership.		

After this $20,000 cash distribution, only a few other events can occur during the remaining life of the partnership. Holland could contribute the entire $6,000 needed to offset the capital deficit. In this case, the cash contributed should be immediately distributed to Dozier ($4,000) and Ross ($2,000) based on their remaining capital balances. This final distribution effectively closes the partnership records.

A second possibility is that Dozier and Ross could be unable to recover any part of the deficit from Holland. These two remaining partners must then absorb the $6,000 loss themselves. Because adequate capital balances have been maintained, recording a complete default by Holland serves to close out the partnership books:

Dozier, Capital (⅔ of loss)	4,000	
Ross, Capital (⅓ of loss)	2,000	
Holland, Capital		6,000
To record allocation of deficit capital balance of insolvent partner.		

Partial Contribution to Partnership

One other ending to this partnership liquidation is possible. The partnership could recover a portion of the $6,000 from Holland, but the remainder could prove to be uncollectible. Holland could become bankrupt, or the other partners could simply give up trying to collect from him. The partners could also negotiate a partial settlement to avoid protracted legal actions.

To illustrate, assume that Holland manages to contribute $3,600 to the partnership but subsequently files for relief under the provisions of bankruptcy law. In a later legal arrangement, Holland makes an additional $1,000 cash payment to the partnership, but the final $1,400 will never be collected. This series of events creates the following effects within the liquidation process:

1. The $3,600 contribution made by Holland is distributed to Dozier and Ross based on a new calculation of safe payments.
2. The $1,400 default is charged against the two positive capital balances in accordance with the relative profit and loss ratio.
3. The final $1,000 contribution made by Holland is then paid to Dozier and Ross in amounts equal to their ending capital balances, a transaction that closes the partnership's financial records.

The distribution of the $3,600 contribution made by Holland depends on a recalculation of the minimum capital balances that Dozier and Ross must maintain to absorb all potential losses. At this point, the potential remaining loss is $2,400 ($6,000 deficit – $3,600 contribution). Dozier and Ross absorb this loss in a 40:20 (⅔:⅓) ratio, respectively. This approach guarantees that these two partners will continue to report sufficient capital until the liquidation is ultimately resolved.

	Current Capital		Allocation of Potential Loss		Safe Payments
Dozier	$4,000	–	⅔ of $(2,400) = $(1,600)	=	$2,400
Ross	$2,000	–	⅓ of $(2,400) = $ (800)	=	$1,200

Dozier and Ross must maintain capital balances of $1,600 and $800, respectively, to absorb a potential default by Holland on the remaining $2,400. The $3,600 in cash that is now available is distributed immediately to Dozier and Ross as safe payments. These two entries record Holland's contribution and the subsequent safe payments made to Dozier and Ross:

	Debit	Credit
Cash	3,600	
Holland, Capital		3,600
To record a cash contribution by Holland.		
Dozier, Capital	2,400	
Ross, Capital	1,200	
Cash		3,600
To record safe payments to Dozier and Ross.		

After recording this $3,600 contribution from Holland and the subsequent disbursement to Dozier and Ross, the partnership's capital accounts stay open, registering the following balances:

Holland, Capital (deficit)	$(2,400)
Dozier, Capital	1,600
Ross, Capital	800

These accounts continue to remain on the partnership books until the final resolution of Holland's deficit capital balance.

In this illustration, the $1,000 legal settlement and the remaining $1,400 loss ultimately allow the parties to close out the records:

Cash	1,000	
Dozier, Capital (⅔ of loss)	933	
Ross, Capital (⅓ of loss)	467	
Holland, Capital		2,400
To record final $1,000 cash settlement of Holland's interest and resulting $1,400 loss.		
Dozier, Capital	667	
Ross, Capital	333	
Cash		1,000
To record distribution of final cash balance based upon remaining capital account totals.		

Preliminary Distribution of Partnership Assets

LO 15-6

Prepare a proposed schedule of liquidation to determine an equitable preliminary distribution of available partnership assets.

As previously mentioned, a liquidation can take an extended time to complete. During this lengthy process, the partnership need not retain any assets that eventually will be disbursed to the partners. Partnerships often have a sufficient cash balance at the date of termination that some amount of cash can be paid out to individual partners even before noncash assets are sold. If the business is solvent (that is, cash exceeds liabilities plus estimated liquidation expenses), waiting until all affairs have been settled before transferring cash to the owners is not warranted. The partners should be allowed to receive cash to which they are entitled at the earliest possible time.

Examples presented earlier in this chapter have shown how to calculate safe payments that can be made to individual partners prior to the completion of all liquidation transactions. Indeed, in some cases, cash can be distributed to partners at the date of partnership termination before any liquidation transactions have taken place. The accountant can determine a *preliminary distribution of partnership assets* at the beginning of the liquidation process. The accountant can facilitate such an early distribution of cash by preparing a *proposed schedule of liquidation.*

The objective in making any type of preliminary distribution is to ensure that the partnership maintains enough capital to absorb all future losses. To determine safe payments that can be made to partners at any time, the accountant *assumes* that all subsequent events will result in maximum losses: No cash will be received in liquidating remaining noncash assets, and each partner is personally insolvent. Any positive capital balances that remain even after the inclusion of all potential losses can be paid to partners without delay. Although the assumption that no further funds will be generated could be unrealistic, it does ensure that negative capital balances cannot arise as a result of premature payments being made to any of the partners.

Preliminary Distribution Illustrated

Assume the partnership of Mason, Lee, and Dixon has decided to terminate operations and liquidate the business. The partnership reports the following balance sheet at the date of termination:

Cash	$ 60,000	Liabilities	$ 40,000
Noncash assets	140,000	Mason, loan	20,000
		Mason, capital (50%)	60,000
		Lee, capital (30%)	30,000
		Dixon, capital (20%)	50,000
Total assets	$200,000	Total liabilities and capital	$200,000

Assume also that the partners estimate that $6,000 will be the maximum expense incurred in carrying out this liquidation. Consequently, the partnership needs $46,000 to meet all obligations: $40,000 to satisfy partnership liabilities and $6,000 for liquidation expenses. Because the partnership holds $60,000 in cash, it can transfer the extra $14,000 to the partners immediately without fear of injuring any participants in the liquidation. However, the appropriate allocation of this money is not readily apparent; safe capital balances must be computed to guide the actual distribution of safe payments.

Before demonstrating the allocation of this $14,000, we examine the appropriate handling of a partner's loan balance. According to the balance sheet, Mason has lent $20,000 to the business at some point in the past, an amount that was considered a loan rather than additional capital. Perhaps the partnership was in desperate need of funds and Mason was willing to contribute only if the contribution was structured as a loan. Regardless of the reason, the question as to the status of this account remains: Is the $20,000 to be viewed as a liability to the partnership or as a part of the partner's capital balance? The answer becomes especially significant during the liquidation process because available funds often are limited. In this regard, the Uniform Partnership Act (UPA) (Section 807[a]) indicates that the assets of the partnership must be applied to pay obligations to creditors, including partners who are creditors; any surplus is distributed to partners based on their capital balances.

Although the UPA indicates that the debt to Mason should be repaid entirely before any distribution of capital can be made to the other partners, actual accounting practice takes a different view. "In preparing predistribution schedules, accountants typically offset partners' loans with the partners' capital accounts and then distribute funds accordingly."[2] In other words, the loan is merged with the partner's capital account balance at the beginning of liquidation. Thus, accounting practice and the UPA seem to differ in the handling of a loan from a partner. To follow common practice, this textbook accounts for a loan from a partner in liquidation as if the loan were a component of the partner's capital. By this offset, the accountant can reduce the amount accumulated as a negative capital balance for any insolvent partner. Any such loan can be transferred into the corresponding capital account at the start of the liquidation process. Similarly, any loans *due from* a partner should be shown as a reduction in the partner's capital account balance.

Proposed Schedule of Liquidation

Returning to the current illustration, the accountant needs to determine an equitable distribution of the $14,000 cash currently available. To structure this computation, a proposed schedule of liquidation is developed *based on the underlying assumption that all future events will result in total losses.* Exhibit 15.3 presents this statement for the Mason, Lee, and Dixon partnership. To expedite procedures, in accordance with common accounting practice, the $20,000 loan has already been transferred into Mason's capital account. Thus, regardless of whether this partner ends up with a positive or negative capital account balance, the loan amount already has been included.

The preparation of Exhibit 15.3 forecasts complete losses ($140,000) in connection with the disposition of all noncash assets and anticipates liquidation expenses at maximum amounts ($6,000). Following the projected payment of liabilities, any partner reporting a negative capital balance is assumed to be personally insolvent. These potential deficit balances are written off, and the losses are assigned to the remaining solvent partners based on their relative profit and loss ratio. Lee, with a negative capital balance of $13,800, is eliminated first. This allocation creates a deficit of $2,857 for Mason, an amount that Dixon alone must absorb. After this series of maximum losses is simulated, Dixon is the only partner with a positive capital balance.

Exhibit 15.3 indicates that only Dixon has a large enough capital balance at the present time to absorb all possible future losses. Thus, the entire $14,000 can be safely distributed to Dixon with no fear that this partner's capital account will ever result in a deficit balance. Based on current practice, Mason, despite having made a $20,000 loan to the partnership, is

[2] Robert E. Whitis and Jeffrey R. Pittman, "Inconsistencies between Accounting Practices and Statutory Law in Partnership Liquidations," *Accounting Educators' Journal,* Fall 1996, p. 99.

EXHIBIT 15.3

MASON, LEE, AND DIXON
Proposed Schedule of Liquidation—Initial Safe Payments

	Cash	Noncash Assets	Liabilities	Mason, Capital and Loan (50%)	Lee, Capital (30%)	Dixon, Capital (20%)
Beginning balances	$60,000	$140,000	$40,000	$80,000	$30,000	$50,000
Maximum loss on noncash assets	–0–	(140,000)	–0–	(70,000)	(42,000)	(28,000)
Maximum liquidation expenses	(6,000)	–0–	–0–	(3,000)	(1,800)	(1,200)
Payment of liabilities	(40,000)	–0–	(40,000)	–0–	–0–	–0–
Subtotal (potential balances)	14,000	–0–	–0–	7,000	(13,800)	20,800
Allocation of Lee's deficit capital balance	–0–	–0–	–0–	(9,857) (5/7)	13,800	(3,943) 2/7
Subtotal (potential balances)	14,000	–0–	–0–	(2,857)	–0–	16,857
Allocation of Mason's deficit capital balance	–0–	–0–	–0–	2,857	–0–	(2,857)
Initial safe payments	$14,000	$ –0–	$ –0–	$ –0–	$ –0–	$14,000

entitled to no part of this initial distribution. The loan is of insufficient size to prevent potential deficits from occurring in Mason's capital account.

One series of computations found in this proposed schedule of liquidation merits additional attention. The simulated losses initially create a $13,800 negative balance in Lee's capital account while the other two partners continue to report positive balances. Mason and Dixon must then absorb Lee's projected deficit according to their relative profit and loss percentages. Previously, Mason was allocated 50 percent of net income with 20 percent recorded to Dixon. These figures equate to a 50/70:20/70 or a 5/7:2/7 ratio. Based on this realigned relationship, the $13,800 potential deficit is allocated between Mason (5/7 or $9,857) and Dixon (2/7 or $3,943), reducing Mason's own capital account to a negative balance as shown in Exhibit 15.3.

Liquidation in Installments

In reality, complete losses are not likely to occur in the liquidation of any business. Thus, at various points during this process, additional cash amounts can become available as partnership property is sold. If the assets are disposed of in a piecemeal fashion, cash can actually flow into the company on a regular basis for an extended period of time. As needed, additional proposed schedules of liquidation can be developed to determine the distribution of newly available funds. Because numerous cash distributions could be required, this process is often referred to as a *liquidation made in installments.*

To illustrate, assume that the partnership of Mason, Lee, and Dixon undergoes the following *actual* events in connection with its liquidation:

- As the proposed schedule of liquidation in Exhibit 15.3 indicates, Dixon receives $14,000 in cash as a preliminary capital distribution based on the calculation of *initial* safe payments.
- Noncash assets with a book value of $50,000 are sold for $20,000.
- All $40,000 in liabilities are paid in cash.
- Liquidation expenses of $2,000 are paid; the partners now believe that only an additional $3,000 of expenses will be incurred. The original estimation of $6,000 apparently was too high.

As a result of these transactions, the partnership has an additional $21,000 in cash now available to safely distribute to the partners: $20,000 received from the sale of noncash assets and another $1,000 because of the reduced estimation of liquidation expenses. Once again, the accountant must assume maximum future losses as a means of determining the appropriate distribution of these funds. The accountant produces a second proposed schedule of liquidation to determine *subsequent* safe payments. This schedule, shown in Exhibit 15.4, indicates that $12,143 of the additional $21,000 should go to Mason with the remaining $8,857 to

EXHIBIT 15.4

MASON, LEE, AND DIXON
Proposed Schedule of Liquidation—Subsequent Safe Payments

	Cash	Noncash Assets	Liabilities	Mason, Capital and Loan (50%)	Lee, Capital (30%)	Dixon, Capital (20%)
Beginning balances	$60,000	$140,000	$40,000	$80,000	$30,000	$50,000
Cash distribution—initial safe payments*	(14,000)	–0–	–0–	–0–	–0–	(14,000)
Disposal of noncash assets	20,000	(50,000)	–0–	(15,000)	(9,000)	(6,000)
Liabilities paid	(40,000)	–0–	(40,000)	–0–	–0–	–0–
Liquidation expenses	(2,000)	–0–	–0–	(1,000)	(600)	(400)
Subtotal (actual balances)	24,000	90,000	–0–	64,000	20,400	29,600
Maximum loss on remaining noncash assets	–0–	(90,000)	–0–	(45,000)	(27,000)	(18,000)
Maximum liquidation expenses	(3,000)	–0–	–0–	(1,500)	(900)	(600)
Subtotal (potential balances)	21,000	–0–	–0–	17,500	(7,500)	11,000
Allocation of Lee's deficit capital balance	–0–	–0–	–0–	(5,357) (5/7)	7,500	(2,143) (2/7)
Subsequent safe payments	$21,000	$ –0–	$ –0–	$12,143	$ –0–	$ 8,857

*Based upon the determination of initial safe payments in Exhibit 15.3.

Dixon. To facilitate a better visual understanding, actual transactions are recorded first on this schedule, followed by the assumed losses. *A dotted line separates the real from the potential transactions.*

Predistribution Plan

LO 15-7

Develop a predistribution plan to guide the distribution of cash in a partnership liquidation.

The liquidation of a partnership can require numerous transactions occurring over a lengthy period of time. The continual production of proposed schedules of liquidation could become a burdensome chore. The previous illustration already has required two separate proposed schedules of liquidation, and the partnership still holds $90,000 in noncash assets that could be converted to cash. *Therefore, at the start of a liquidation, accountants often produce a single predistribution plan to serve as a guide for all future payments.* Thereafter, whenever cash becomes available, this plan indicates the appropriate distribution of cash without the necessity of drawing up ever-changing proposed schedules of liquidation.

A predistribution plan is developed by simulating a series of losses, each of which is just large enough to eliminate, one at a time, all of the partners' claims to partnership property. This approach recognizes that the individual capital accounts exhibit differing degrees of sensitivity to losses. Capital accounts possess varying balances and could be charged with losses at different rates. Consequently, a predistribution plan is based on calculating the losses (the "maximum loss that can be absorbed") that would eliminate each of these capital balances in a sequential pattern. This series of absorbed losses then forms the basis for the predistribution plan.

To demonstrate the creation of a predistribution plan, assume that the Rubens, Smith, and Trice Partnership is to be liquidated. The partnership's balance sheet at the date of termination follows:

Cash	$ –0–	Liabilities	$100,000
Noncash assets	221,000	Rubens, capital (50%)	30,000
		Smith, capital (20%)	40,000
		Trice, capital (30%)	51,000
Total assets	$221,000	Total liabilities and capital	$221,000

The partnership's capital totals $121,000. However, the individual partners' capital balances range from $30,000 to $51,000, and profits and losses are assigned according to three different percentages (50%, 20%, 30%). Thus, differing losses would reduce each partner's current capital balance to zero. *As a prerequisite to developing a predistribution plan, the sensitivity to losses exhibited by each of these capital accounts must be measured:*

Partner	Capital Balance/ Loss Allocation	Maximum Loss That Can Be Absorbed
Rubens	$30,000/50%	$ 60,000 ✓
Smith	40,000/20%	200,000
Trice.	51,000/30%	170,000

According to this initial computation, Rubens is the partner in the most vulnerable position at the present time. Based on a 50 percent share of profit and loss, a loss of only $60,000 would reduce this partner's capital account to a zero balance. If the partnership incurs a loss of this amount, Rubens will not receive any funds from the liquidation process. The following schedule simulates the potential effects of this loss (referred to as a *Step 1 loss*):

	Rubens, Capital	Smith, Capital	Trice, Capital
Beginning balances	$ 30,000	$ 40,000	$ 51,000
Assumed $60,000 loss	(30,000) (50%)	(12,000) (20%)	(18,000) (30%)
Step 1 balances	$ -0-	$ 28,000	$ 33,000

As previously discussed, the predistribution plan is based on describing the series of losses that would eliminate each partner's capital in turn and, thus, all claims to cash. In the previous Step 1 schedule, the $60,000 loss reduced Rubens's capital account to zero. Assuming, as a precautionary step, that Rubens is personally insolvent, all further losses would have to be allocated between Smith and Trice. Because these two partners have previously shared partnership profits and losses on a 20 percent and 30 percent basis, a 20/50:30/50 (or 40%:60%) relationship exists between them. Therefore, these realigned percentages must now be utilized in calculating a *Step 2 loss,* the amount just large enough to exclude another of the remaining partners from sharing in any future cash distributions:

Partner	Capital Balance/ Loss Allocation	Maximum Loss That Can Be Absorbed
Smith	$28,000/40%	$70,000
Trice.	33,000/60%	55,000 ✓

Because Rubens's capital balance already has been eliminated, Trice is now in the most vulnerable position: Only a $55,000 Step 2 loss is required to reduce this partner's capital balance to zero.

	Rubens, Capital	Smith, Capital	Trice, Capital
Beginning balances	$ 30,000	$ 40,000	$ 51,000
Assumed $60,000 loss	(30,000) (50%)	(12,000) (20%)	(18,000) (30%)
Step 1 balances	$-0-	$ 28,000	33,000
Assumed $55,000 loss	-0-	(22,000) (40%)	(33,000) (60%)
Step 2 balances	$ -0-	$ 6,000	$ -0-

According to this second schedule, a total loss of $115,000 ($60,000 from Step 1 plus $55,000 from Step 2) leaves capital of only $6,000, a balance attributed entirely to Smith. At this final point in the simulation, an additional loss of this amount also ends Smith's right to receive any funds from the liquidation process. Having the sole positive capital balance remaining, this partner would have to absorb the entire amount of the final loss.

	Rubens, Capital	Smith, Capital	Trice, Capital
Beginning balances	$ 30,000	$ 40,000	$ 51,000
Assumed $60,000 loss	(30,000) (50%)	(12,000) (20%)	(18,000) (30%)
Step 1 balances	$ –0–	$ 28,000	$ 33,000
Assumed $55,000 loss	–0–	(22,000) (40%)	(33,000) (60%)
Step 2 balances	–0–	6,000	–0–
Assumed $6,000 loss	–0–	(6,000) (100%)	–0–
Final balances	$ –0–	$ –0–	$ –0–

Once this series of simulated losses has reduced each partner's capital account to a zero balance, a predistribution plan for the liquidation can be devised. *This procedure requires working backward through the preceding final schedule to determine the effects that will result if the assumed losses do not occur.* Without these losses, cash becomes available for the partners; therefore, a direct relationship exists between the volume of losses and the distribution pattern. For example, Smith will entirely absorb the last $6,000 loss. Should that loss fail to materialize, Smith is left with a positive safe capital balance of this amount. Thus, as cash becomes available, the first $6,000 received (in excess of partnership obligations and anticipated liquidation expenses) should be distributed solely to Smith.

Similarly, the preceding $55,000 Step 2 loss was divided between Smith and Trice on a 4:6 basis. Again, if such losses do not occur, these balances need not be retained to protect the partners against deficit capital balances. Therefore, after Smith has received the initial $6,000, additional cash that becomes available (up to $55,000) will be split between Smith (40 percent) and Trice (60 percent). For example, if the partnership holds exactly $61,000 in cash in excess of liabilities and possible liquidation expenses, this distribution should be made:

	Rubens	Smith	Trice	Total
First $6,000	$–0–	$ 6,000	$ –0–	$ 6,000
Next $55,000	–0–	22,000 (40%)	33,000 (60%)	55,000
Cash distribution	$–0–	$28,000	$33,000	$61,000

The predistribution plan can be completed by including the Step 1 loss, an amount that was to be absorbed by the partners on a 5:2:3 basis. All cash that becomes available to the partners after the initial $61,000 should be distributed to the partners according to the original profit and loss ratio. At this point in the liquidation, enough cash would have been generated to ensure that each partner has a safe capital balance: No possibility exists that a future deficit can occur. Any additional increases in the projected capital balances will be allocated on a 5:2:3 basis. *Once all partners begin to receive a portion of the cash disbursements, any remaining funds are divided based on the original profit and loss percentages.*

To inform all parties of the pattern by which available cash will be disbursed, the predistribution plan should be formally prepared in a schedule format prior to beginning the liquidation. The following is the predistribution plan for the partnership of Rubens, Smith, and Trice. To complete this illustration, liquidation expenses of $12,000 have been estimated. Because these expenses have the same effect on the capital accounts as losses, they do not change the sequential pattern by which cash eventually will be distributed.

RUBENS, SMITH, AND TRICE PARTNERSHIP Predistribution Plan		
Available Cash		**Recipient**
First	$112,000	Creditors ($100,000) and liquidation expenses (estimated at $12,000)
Next.	6,000	Smith
Next.	55,000	Smith (40%) and Trice (60%)
All further cash		Rubens (50%), Smith (20%), and Trice (30%)

To demonstrate how this predistribution plan is used, assume that the partnership of Rubens, Smith, and Trice converts some of its noncash assets into $130,000 of cash. According to the predistribution plan, this amount would be distributed as follows:

First, $112,000 is held to pay creditors and liquidation expenses; $18,000 is available for payment to partners.
Next, $6,000 is paid to Smith.
The remaining $12,000 is paid to Smith (40% = $4,800) and Trice (60% = $7,200).

Thus, Smith would receive $10,800 and Trice would receive $7,200 from the first $130,000 of cash that becomes available.

Summary

1. Termination of a partnership's business activities and liquidation of partnership assets can take place for a number of reasons. Because of the risk that the partnership will incur large losses during liquidation, all parties usually seek frequent and timely information describing ongoing liquidation developments. The accountant is expected to furnish these data while also working to ensure the equitable treatment of all parties.
2. Liquidation procedures include (a) selling partnership assets for cash, (b) paying partnership liabilities and liquidation expenses, and (c) distributing remaining cash to the partners based on their capital account balances. As a means of reporting these transactions, a statement of partnership liquidation should be produced at periodic intervals. This statement discloses all recent transactions, the assets and liabilities still being held, and the current capital balances. Distribution of this statement on a regular basis allows the various parties involved in the liquidation to monitor the progress being made.
3. During a liquidation, negative (deficit) capital balances can arise for one or more of the partners, especially if the partnership incurs significant losses in disposing of its property. In such cases, the specific partner or partners should contribute enough cash to the partnership to offset their deficits. If a deficit partner is unable or unwilling to make such a contribution, the remaining partners absorb the deficit based on their relative profit and loss ratio.
4. Each time cash becomes available during the partnership liquidation process, the accountant can calculate the amount of safe payments that can be made to individual partners from the available cash. Safe payments are the amounts that can be distributed to partners immediately without running the risk that future losses will cause any partner to have a deficit capital balance.
5. Partnerships often have a sufficient cash balance at the date of termination that a preliminary distribution of cash can be paid to individual partners even before noncash assets are sold. A proposed schedule of liquidation can be created as a guide for such cash distributions. This schedule is based on a simulated series of transactions: sale of all noncash assets, payment of liquidation expenses, and so on. At every point, maximum losses are assumed: Noncash assets have no resale value, liquidation expenses are set at the maximum level, and all partners are personally insolvent. The proposed schedule of liquidation formally presents the calculation of safe payments that may be made to partners.
6. Because a partnership liquidation can require numerous transactions over a lengthy time period, the accountant could discover that the continual production of proposed schedules of liquidation becomes burdensome. For this reason, at the start of the liquidation process, the accountant often produces a single predistribution plan that serves as a guide for all payments to be made to the partners. To create this plan, the accountant simulates a series of losses with each loss, in turn, exactly eliminating a partner's capital balance. After these assumed losses have reduced all capital balances to zero, the accountant devises the predistribution plan by working backward through the series of simulated losses. In effect, the accountant is measuring the cash that will become available if such losses do not occur.

Comprehensive Illustration

Problem

(*Estimated Time: 30 to 40 Minutes*) For the past several years, the Andrews, Caso, Quinn, and Sheridan partnership has operated a local department store. Based on the provisions of the original articles of partnership, all profits and losses have been allocated on a 4:3:2:1 ratio, respectively. As a brick-and-mortar establishment, the store has not been profitable for the past two years. More recently, both Caso and Quinn have undergone personal financial problems and, as a result, are now personally insolvent. Caso's creditors have filed a $20,000 claim against the partnership's assets, and $22,000 of partnership assets is being sought by creditors to cover Quinn's personal debts. To satisfy these legal obligations and exit a no longer profitable enterprise, the partners have agree to terminate operations and liquidate assets. The partners estimate that they will incur $12,000 in expenses to liquidate all noncash assets.

At the time that active operations terminate and the liquidation begins, the following partnership balance sheet is produced.

Cash	$ 20,000	Liabilities	$ 140,000
Noncash assets	280,000	Caso, loan (to partnership)	10,000
		Andrews, capital (40%)	76,000
		Caso, capital (30%)	14,000
		Quinn, capital (20%)	51,000
		Sheridan, capital (10%)	9,000
Total assets	$300,000	Total liabilities and capital	$ 300,000

During the lengthy liquidation process, the following transactions take place:

- Sale of noncash assets with a book value of $190,000 for $140,000 cash.
- Payment of $14,000 liquidation expenses. No further expenses are expected.
- Distribution of safe payments to the partners.
- Payment of all business liabilities.
- Sale of the remaining noncash assets for $10,000.
- Negative capital balances of any insolvent partners written off as uncollectible.
- Cash contribution received from any solvent partner with negative capital balance.
- Distribution of ending cash balance.

Required

a. Using the information available prior to the start of the liquidation process, develop a predistribution plan for this partnership.

b. Prepare journal entries to record the actual liquidation transactions.

Solution

a. This partnership begins the liquidation process with capital totaling $160,000. This includes the $10,000 loan from Caso added to Caso's capital balance for a total of $24,000. Therefore, the predistribution plan is based on the assumption that $160,000 in losses will be incurred, entirely eliminating all partnership capital. Simulated losses are arranged in a series so that each capital balance is sequentially reduced to zero. At the start of the liquidation, Caso's capital position is the most vulnerable.

Partner	Capital Balance/Loss Allocation	Maximum Loss That Can Be Absorbed
Andrews	$76,000/40%	$190,000
Caso	24,000/30%	80,000 ✓
Quinn	51,000/20%	255,000
Sheridan	9,000/10%	90,000

As the schedule indicates, an $80,000 loss would eliminate Caso's $14,000 capital balance and $10,000 loan to the partnership. Therefore, to start the development of a predistribution plan, a loss of $80,000 is assumed to have occurred.

	Andrews, Capital	Caso, Capital and Loan	Quinn, Capital	Sheridan, Capital
Beginning balances	$ 76,000	$24,000	$ 51,000	$ 9,000
Assumed $80,000 loss	(32,000) (40%)	(24,000) (30%)	(16,000) (20%)	(8,000) (10%)
Step 1 balances	$ 44,000	$ -0-	$ 35,000	$ 1,000

With Caso's capital balance eliminated, further losses are to be split among the remaining partners in the ratio of 4:2:1 (or 4/7:2/7:1/7). Because only an additional $7,000 loss (the preceding $1,000 Step 1 capital balance divided by 1/7) is now needed to reduce Sheridan's balance to zero, this partner is in the second most vulnerable position. A simulated loss of $7,000 eliminates Sheridan's capital balance.

	Andrews	Caso	Quinn	Sheridan
Step 1 balances (above)	$44,000	$-0-	$35,000	$ 1,000
Assumed $7,000 loss	(4,000) (4/7)	-0-	(2,000) (2/7)	(1,000) (1/7)
Step 2 balances	$40,000	$-0-	$33,000	$ -0-

Following these two simulated losses, only Andrews and Quinn continue to report positive capital balances. Thus, they divide any additional losses on a 4:2 basis, or ⅔:⅓. Based on these realigned percentages, Andrews's position has become the more vulnerable. An additional loss of $60,000 ($40,000/⅔) reduces this partner's remaining capital balance to zero, whereas a $99,000 loss ($33,000/⅓) is required to eliminate Quinn's capital balance. Step 3 assumes a $60,000 loss.

	Andrews	Caso	Quinn	Sheridan
Step 2 balances	$ 40,000	$-0-	$ 33,000	$-0-
Assumed $60,000 loss	(40,000) (⅔)	-0-	(20,000) (⅓)	-0-
Step 3 balances	$ -0-	$-0-	$ 13,000	$-0-

After this simulated loss, Quinn has a capital balance of $13,000; an additional loss of this amount would reduce this partner's capital account to zero. Based on the results of this series of simulated losses, the accountant can create a predistribution plan. The first $152,000 of available cash must be held to cover the $140,000 in liabilities owed by the partnership, and $12,000 of anticipated liquidation expenses. The complete predistribution plan is as follows:

ANDREWS, CASO, QUINN, AND SHERIDAN
Predistribution Plan

Available Cash		Recipient
First	$152,000	Creditors and anticipated liquidation expenses
Next	13,000	Quinn (100%)
Next	60,000	Andrews (⅔) and Quinn (⅓)
Next	7,000	Andrews (4/7), Quinn (2/7), and Sheridan (1/7)
All further cash		Andrews (40%), Caso (30%), Quinn (20%), and Sheridan (10%)

b. Journal entries for the liquidation:

Caso, Loan	10,000	
Caso, Capital		10,000
To record offset of loan to capital balance in anticipation of liquidation.		

(continued)

(continued)

Cash	140,000	
Andrews, Capital (40%)	20,000	
Caso, Capital (30%)	15,000	
Quinn, Capital (20%)	10,000	
Sheridan, Capital (10%)	5,000	
Noncash Assets		190,000
To record sale of noncash assets and allocation of $50,000 loss.		
Andrews, Capital (40%)	5,600	
Caso, Capital (30%)	4,200	
Quinn, Capital (20%)	2,800	
Sheridan, Capital (10%)	1,400	
Cash		14,000
To record payment of liquidation expenses.		

- The partnership now holds $146,000 in cash, $6,000 more than is needed to satisfy all liabilities. According to the predistribution plan drawn up in requirement (*a*), this entire amount can be safely distributed to Quinn (or to Quinn's creditors).

Quinn, Capital	6,000	
Cash		6,000
To record distribution of safe payments of available cash.		
Liabilities	140,000	
Cash		140,000
To record extinguishment of all partnership debts.		
Cash	10,000	
Andrews, Capital (40% of loss)	32,000	
Caso, Capital (30% of loss)	24,000	
Quinn, Capital (20% of loss)	16,000	
Sheridan, Capital (10% of loss)	8,000	
Noncash Assets		90,000
To record sale of remaining noncash assets and allocation of $80,000 loss.		

- At this point in the liquidation, only the cash and the capital accounts remain open on the partnership books.

	Cash	Andrews, Capital	Caso, Capital	Quinn, Capital	Sheridan, Capital
Beginning balances	$ 20,000	$76,000	$ 14,000	$51,000	$ 9,000
Loan offset	–0–	–0–	10,000	–0–	–0–
Sale of noncash assets	140,000	(20,000)	(15,000)	(10,000)	(5,000)
Liquidation expenses	(14,000)	(5,600)	(4,200)	(2,800)	(1,400)
Cash distribution	(6,000)	–0–	–0–	(6,000)	–0–
Payment of liabilities	(140,000)	–0–	–0–	–0–	–0–
Sale of noncash assets	10,000	(32,000)	(24,000)	(16,000)	(8,000)
Current balances	$ 10,000	$18,400	$(19,200)	$16,200	$(5,400)

Because Caso is personally insolvent, the $19,200 deficit balance will not be repaid, and the remaining three partners must absorb it on a 4:2:1 basis.

Andrews, Capital (4/7 of loss)	10,971	
Quinn, Capital (2/7 of loss)	5,486	
Sheridan, Capital (1/7 of loss)	2,743	
Caso, Capital		19,200
To record write-off of deficit capital balance of insolvent partner.		

- This allocation decreases Sheridan's capital account to a negative balance of $8,143. Sheridan contributes this amount to the partnership to cover the deficit.

Cash	8,143	
Sheridan, Capital		8,143
To record contribution made to eliminate deficit capital balance.		

- Sheridan's contribution brings the final cash total for the partnership to $18,143. This amount is distributed to the two partners who continue to maintain positive capital balances: Andrews and Quinn (or Quinn's creditors).

	Andrews, Capital	Quinn, Capital
Balances above	$ 18,400	$16,200
Caso deficit	(10,971)	(5,486)
Final balances	$ 7,429	$10,714

Andrews, Capital	7,429	
Quinn, Capital	10,714	
Cash		18,143
To record distribution of remaining cash according to final capital balances.		

Questions

1. What is the difference between the termination of a partnership and the liquidation of partnership property?
2. Why would the members of a partnership elect to terminate business operations and liquidate all noncash assets?
3. Why are liquidation gains and losses usually recorded as direct adjustments to the partners' capital accounts?
4. After liquidating all property and paying partnership obligations, what is the basis for allocating remaining cash among the partners?
5. What is the purpose of a statement of partnership liquidation? What information does it convey to its readers?
6. How are safe payments to partners calculated when cash becomes available for distribution?
7. How do loans from partners affect the distribution of assets in a partnership liquidation?
8. What is the purpose of a proposed schedule of liquidation, and how is it developed?
9. How is a predistribution plan created for a partnership liquidation?

Problems

LO 15-1

1. When a partnership is liquidated, how is the final distribution of partnership cash made to the partners?
   a. Equally
   b. According to the profit and loss ratio
   c. According to the final capital account balances
   d. According to the initial investment made by each of the partners

LO 15-1

2. Which of the following statements is true concerning the accounting for a partnership going through liquidation?
   a. Gains and losses are reported directly as increases and decreases in the appropriate capital account.
   b. A separate income statement is created to measure only the profit or loss generated during liquidation.
   c. Because gains and losses rarely occur during liquidation, no special accounting treatment is warranted.
   d. Within a liquidation, all gains and losses are divided equally among the partners.

LO 15-4

3. During a liquidation, if a partner's capital account balance drops below zero, what *should* happen?
   a. The other partners file a legal suit against the partner with the deficit balance.
   b. The partner with the highest capital balance contributes sufficient assets to eliminate the deficit.
   c. The deficit balance is removed from the accounting records with only the remaining partners sharing in future gains and losses.
   d. The partner with a deficit contributes enough assets to offset the deficit balance.

LO 15-4

4. A local partnership is liquidating and is currently reporting the following capital balances:

Barley, capital (50% share of all profits and losses)	$ 44,000
Carter, capital (30%)	32,000
Desai, capital (20%)	(24,000)

   Desai has indicated that a forthcoming contribution will cover the $24,000 deficit. However, the two remaining partners have asked to receive the $52,000 in cash that is currently available. How much of this money should each of the partners receive?
   a. Barley, $22,000; Carter, $30,000
   b. Barley, $32,000; Carter, $20,000
   c. Barley, $29,000; Carter, $23,000
   d. Barley, $32,500; Carter, $19,500

LO 15-4

5. A partnership is considering possible liquidation because one of the partners (Bell) is personally insolvent. Profits and losses are divided on a 4:3:2:1 basis, respectively. Capital balances at the current time are

Bell, capital	$ 50,000
Hardy, capital	56,000
Dennard, capital	14,000
Suddath, capital	80,000

   Bell's creditors have filed a $21,000 claim against the partnership's assets. The partnership currently holds assets of $300,000 and liabilities of $100,000. If the assets can be sold for $190,000, what is the minimum amount that Bell's creditors would receive?
   a. –0–
   b. $2,000
   c. $2,800
   d. $6,000

LO 15-7

6. What is a predistribution plan?
   a. A list of the procedures to be performed during a liquidation
   b. A guide for the cash distributions to partners during a liquidation
   c. A determination of the final cash distribution to the partners on the settlement date
   d. A detailed list of the transactions that will transpire in the reorganization of a partnership

LO 15-3

7. A partnership has the following balance sheet prior to liquidation (partners' profit and loss ratios are in parentheses):

Cash	$ 33,000	Liabilities	$ 50,000
Other assets	100,000	Playa, capital (40%)	24,000
		Bahia, capital (30%)	29,000
		Arco, capital (30%)	30,000
Total	$133,000	Total	$133,000

   During liquidation, other assets are sold for $80,000, liabilities are paid in full, and $15,000 in liquidation expenses are paid. Based on the final statement of partnership liquidation, what amount of cash does each partner receive as a result of this liquidation?
   a. Playa, $6,000; Bahia, $4,500; Arco, $4,500
   b. Playa, $10,000; Bahia, $18,500; Arco, $19,500
   c. Playa, $16,000; Bahia, $23,000; Arco, $24,000
   d. Playa, $19,200; Bahia, $14,400; Arco, $14,400

LO 15-1, 15-4, 15-5

8. A partnership has the following capital balances: X (50 percent of profits and losses) = $150,000; Y (30 percent of profits and losses) = $120,000; Z (20 percent of profits and losses) = $80,000. If the partnership is to be liquidated and $30,000 becomes immediately available, who gets that money?
   a. $0 to X, $18,000 to Y, $12,000 to Z
   b. $15,000 to X, $9,000 to Y, $6,000 to Z
   c. $12,800 to X, $8,600 to Y, $8,600 to Z
   d. $24,000 to X, $6,000 to Y, $0 to Z

LO 15-7

9. A partnership is currently holding $400,000 in assets and $234,000 in liabilities. The partnership is to be liquidated, and $20,000 is the best estimation of the expenses that will be incurred during this process. The four partners share profits and losses as shown. Capital balances at the start of the liquidation follow:

Kevin, capital (40%)	$59,000
Michael, capital (30%)	39,000
Brendan, capital (10%)	34,000
Jonathan, capital (20%)	34,000

   The partners realize that Brendan will be the first partner to start receiving cash. How much cash will Brendan receive before any of the other partners collect any cash?
   a. $12,250
   b. $14,750
   c. $17,000
   d. $19,500

LO 15-7

10. Carney, Pierce, Menton, and Hoehn are partners who share profits and losses on a 4:3:2:1 basis, respectively. They are beginning to liquidate the business. At the start of this process, capital balances are

Carney, capital	$60,000
Pierce, capital	27,000
Menton, capital	43,000
Hoehn, capital	20,000

   Which of the following statements is true?
   a. The first available $2,000 will go to Hoehn.
   b. Carney will be the last partner to receive any available cash.
   c. The first available $3,000 will go to Menton.
   d. Carney will collect a portion of any available cash before Hoehn receives money.

LO 15-4, 15-5

11. A partnership has gone through liquidation and now reports the following account balances:

Cash	$16,000
Loan from Jones	3,000
Wayman, capital	(2,000) (deficit)
Jones, capital	(5,000) (deficit)
Fuller, capital	13,000
Rogers, capital	7,000

   Profits and losses are allocated on the following basis: Wayman, 30 percent; Jones, 20 percent; Fuller, 30 percent; and Rogers, 20 percent. Which of the following should occur now?
   a. Jones should receive $3,000 cash because of the loan balance.
   b. Fuller should receive $11,800 and Rogers $4,200.
   c. Fuller should receive $10,600 and Rogers $5,400.
   d. Jones should receive $3,000, Fuller $8,800, and Rogers $4,200.

LO 15-3

12. A partnership has the following account balances at the date of termination: Cash, $80,000; Noncash Assets, $660,000; Liabilities, $320,000; Bell, capital (50 percent of profits and losses), $200,000; Mann, capital (30 percent), $120,000; Scott, capital (20 percent), $100,000. The following transactions occur during liquidation:
    - Noncash assets with a book value of $500,000 are sold for $400,000 in cash.
    - A creditor reduces his claim against the partnership from $120,000 to $100,000, and this amount is paid in cash.

- The remaining noncash assets are sold for $130,000 in cash.
- The remaining liabilities of $200,000 are paid in full.
- Liquidation expenses of $24,000 are paid in cash.
- Cash remaining after the above transactions have occurred is distributed to the partners.

Prepare a statement of partnership liquidation to determine how much cash each partner receives from the liquidation of the partnership.

LO 15-1, 15-4

13. A local partnership is liquidating and has only two assets (cash of $10,000 and land with a cost of $35,000). All partnership liabilities have been paid. All partners are personally insolvent. The partners have capital balances and share profits and losses as follows.

Brown, capital (40%)	$25,000
Fish, capital (30%)	15,000
Stone, capital (30%)	5,000

a. If the land is sold for $25,000, how much cash does each partner receive in a final settlement?
b. If the land is sold for $15,000, how much cash does each partner receive in a final settlement?
c. If the land is sold for $5,000, how much cash does each partner receive in a final settlement?

LO 15-4

14. A local dental partnership has been liquidated and the final capital balances are

Atkinson, capital (40% of all profits and losses)	$ 70,000
Kaporale, capital (30%)	30,000
Dennsmore, capital (20%)	(42,000)
Rasputin, capital (10%)	(58,000)

If Rasputin contributes cash of $20,000 to the partnership, how would this amount be distributed to the other partners?

LO 15-5

15. The partnership of Ace, Ball, Eaton, and Lake currently holds three assets: Cash, $10,000; Land, $35,000; and Building, $50,000. The partnership has no liabilities. The partners anticipate that expenses required to liquidate their partnership will amount to $5,000. Capital balances are as follows:

Ace, capital	$25,000
Ball, capital	28,000
Eaton, capital	20,000
Lake, capital	22,000

The partners share profits and losses as follows: Ace (30 percent), Ball (30 percent), Eaton (20 percent), and Lake (20 percent). If a preliminary distribution of cash is to be made, what is the amount of safe payment that can be made to each partner?

LO 15-6

16. The following condensed balance sheet is for the partnership of Hardwick, Saunders, and Ferris, who share profits and losses in the ratio of 4:3:3, respectively:

Cash	$ 90,000	Accounts payable	$210,000
Other assets	820,000	Ferris, loan	40,000
Hardwick, loan	30,000	Hardwick, capital	300,000
		Saunders, capital	200,000
		Ferris, capital	190,000
Total assets	$940,000	Total liabilities and capital	$940,000

The partners decide to liquidate the partnership. Forty percent of the other assets are sold for $200,000. Prepare a proposed schedule of liquidation at this point in time.

LO 15-5

17. The following condensed balance sheet is for the partnership of Miller, Tyson, and Watson, who share profits and losses in the ratio of 6:2:2, respectively:

Cash	$ 50,000	Liabilities	$ 42,000
Other assets	150,000	Miller, capital	69,000
		Tyson, capital	69,000
		Watson, capital	20,000
Total assets	$200,000	Total liabilities and capital	$200,000

Assuming no liquidation expenses, calculate the safe payments that can be made to partners at this point in time. For how much money must the other assets be sold so that each partner receives some amount of cash in a liquidation?

LO 15-5

18. The balance sheet for the Delphine, Xavier, and Olivier partnership follows:

Cash	$ 60,000	Liabilities	$ 40,000
Noncash assets	100,000	Delphine, capital	60,000
		Xavier, capital	40,000
		Olivier, capital	20,000
Total assets	$160,000	Total liabilities and capital	$160,000

Delphine, Xavier, and Olivier share profits and losses in the ratio of 4:4:2, respectively. The partners have agreed to terminate the business and estimate that $12,000 in liquidation expenses will be incurred.

a. What is the amount of cash that safely can be paid to partners prior to liquidation of noncash assets?

b. Calculate the amount of safe payment that can be made to each partner prior to liquidation of noncash assets.

LO 15-4

19. A partnership has liquidated all assets but still reports the following account balances for its partners:

Beck, loan	$ 8,000
Cisneros, capital (40%)	5,000
Beck, capital (20%)	(12,000) (deficit)
Sadak, capital (10%)	(8,000) (deficit)
Emerson, capital (20%)	13,000
Page, capital (10%)	(6,000) (deficit)

The partners split profits and losses as follows: Cisneros, 40 percent; Beck, 20 percent; Sadak, 10 percent; Emerson, 20 percent; and Page 10 percent.

Assuming that Cisneros, Beck, and Page are personally insolvent, how much cash must Sadak now contribute to this partnership?

LO 15-6

20. The following balance sheet is for a partnership in which the partners have decided to terminate operations and liquidate assets. The partners estimate liquidation expenses will be $10,000.

Cash	$130,000	Liabilities	$ 50,000
Noncash assets	230,000	Arch, capital (40%)	120,000
		Bibb, capital (20%)	60,000
		Dao, capital (40%)	130,000
Total assets	$360,000	Total liabilities and capital	$360,000

Prepare a proposed schedule of liquidation to carry out a preliminary distribution of partnership assets at the date of termination.

LO 15-2, 15-3, 15-5

21. Alex and Bess have been in partnership for many years. The partners, who share profits and losses on a 60:40 basis, respectively, wish to retire and have agreed to liquidate the business. Liquidation expenses are estimated to be $5,000. At the date the partnership ceases operations, the balance sheet is as follows:

Cash	$ 50,000	Liabilities	$ 40,000
Noncash assets	150,000	Alex, capital	90,000
Total assets	$200,000	Bess, capital	70,000
		Total liabilities and capital	$200,000

Part A

Prepare journal entries for the following transactions that occurred in chronological order:

a. Distributed safe cash payments to the partners.

b. Paid $30,000 of the partnership's liabilities.

c. Sold noncash assets for $160,000.

d. Distributed safe cash payments to the partners.

e. Paid remaining partnership liabilities of $10,000.

f. Paid $4,000 in liquidation expenses; no further expenses will be incurred.

g. Distributed remaining cash held by the business to the partners.

Part B

Prepare a final statement of partnership liquidation.

LO 15-7

22. The partnership of Larson, Norris, Spencer, and Harrison has decided to terminate operations and liquidate all business property. During this process, the partners expect to incur $8,000 in liquidation expenses. All partners are currently solvent.

The balance sheet reported by this partnership at the time that the liquidation commenced follows. The percentages indicate the allocation of profits and losses to each of the four partners.

Cash	$ 28,250	Liabilities	$ 47,000
Accounts receivable	44,000	Larson, capital (20%)	15,000
Inventory	39,000	Norris, capital (30%)	60,000
Land and buildings	23,000	Spencer, capital (20%)	75,000
Equipment	104,000	Harrison, capital (30%)	41,250
Total assets	$238,250	Total liabilities and capital	$238,250

Based on the information provided, prepare a predistribution plan for liquidating this partnership.

LO 15-7

23. The Drysdale, Koufax, and Marichal partnership has the following balance sheet immediately prior to liquidation:

Cash	$ 36,000	Liabilities	$50,000
Noncash assets	204,000	Drysdale, loan	10,000
		Drysdale, capital (50%)	70,000
		Koufax, capital (30%)	60,000
		Marichal, capital (20%)	50,000

a. Liquidation expenses are estimated to be $15,000. Prepare a predistribution schedule to guide the distribution of cash.

b. Assume that assets costing $74,000 are sold for $60,000. How is the available cash to be divided?

LO 15-7

24. The Simpson, Hart, Bobb, and Reidel partnership has terminated operations and is undergoing liquidation. Sales commissions and other liquidation expenses are expected to total $19,000. The partnership's balance sheet prior to the commencement of liquidation is as follows:

Cash	$ 27,000	Liabilities	$ 40,000
Noncash assets	254,000	Simpson, capital (20%)	18,000
		Hart, capital (40%)	40,000
		Bobb, capital (20%)	48,000
		Reidl, capital (20%)	135,000
Total assets	$281,000	Total liabilities and capital	$281,000

Prepare a predistribution plan for this partnership.

LO 15-4

25. The partnership of Hendrick, Mitchum, and Redding has the following account balances:

Cash	$ 50,000	Liabilities	$ 30,000
Noncash assets	135,000	Hendrick, capital	100,000
		Mitchum, capital	70,000
		Redding, capital	(15,000)

This partnership is being liquidated. Hendrick and Mitchum are each entitled to 40 percent of all profits and losses with the remaining 20 percent going to Redding.

a. What is the maximum amount that Redding might have to contribute to this partnership because of the deficit capital balance?

b. How should the $20,000 cash that is presently available in excess of liabilities be distributed?

c. If the noncash assets are sold for a total of $50,000, what is the minimum amount of cash that Hendrick could receive?

LO 15-4

26. The partnership of Anderson, Berry, Hammond, and Winwood is being liquidated. It currently holds cash of $20,000 but no other assets. Liabilities amount to $30,000. The capital balances are

Anderson (40% of profits and losses)	$ 20,000
Berry (30%)	12,000
Hammond (20%)	(17,000) (deficit)
Winwood (10%)	(25,000) (deficit)

a. If both Hammond and Winwood are personally insolvent, how much money must Berry contribute to this partnership?

b. If only Winwood is personally insolvent, how much money must Hammond contribute to the partnership? How will these funds be disbursed?

c. If only Hammond is personally insolvent, how much money should Anderson receive from the liquidation?

LO 15-2

27. March, April, and May have been in partnership for a number of years. The partners allocate all profits and losses on a 2:3:1 basis, respectively. Recently, each partner has become personally insolvent and, thus, the partners have decided to liquidate the business in hopes of remedying their personal financial problems. As of September 1, the partnership's balance sheet is as follows:

Cash	$ 11,000	Liabilities	$ 61,000
Accounts receivable	84,000	March, capital	25,000
Inventory	74,000	April, capital	75,000
Land, building, and equipment (net)	38,000	May, capital	46,000
Total assets	$207,000	Total liabilities and capital	$207,000

Prepare journal entries for the following transactions:

a. Sold all inventory for $56,000 cash.

b. Paid $7,500 in liquidation expenses.

c. Paid $40,000 of the partnership's liabilities.

d. Collected $45,000 of the accounts receivable.

e. Distributed safe payments of cash; the partners anticipate no further liquidation expenses.

f. Sold remaining accounts receivable for 30 percent of face value.

g. Sold land, building, and equipment for $17,000.

h. Paid all remaining liabilities of the partnership.

i. Distributed cash held by the business to the partners.

LO 15-7

28. The partnership of Winn, Xie, Yang, and Zed has the following balance sheet:

Cash	$ 40,000	Liabilities	$ 66,000
Other assets	300,000	Winn, capital (50% of profits and losses)	100,000
		Xie, capital (30%)	84,000
		Yang, capital (10%)	50,000
		Zed, capital (10%)	40,000

Zed is personally insolvent, and one of his creditors is considering suing the partnership for the $10,000 that is currently owed. The creditor realizes that this litigation could result in partnership liquidation and does not wish to force such an extreme action unless Zed is reasonably sure of obtaining at least $10,000 from the liquidation.

Prepare a predistribution plan to determine the amount for which the partnership must sell the other assets to ensure that Zed receives $10,000 from the liquidation. Liquidation expenses are expected to be $30,000.

LO 15-6

29. On January 1, the partners of Van, Bakel, and Cox (who share profits and losses in the ratio of 5:3:2, respectively) decide to terminate operations and liquidate their partnership. The trial balance at this date follows:

	Debit	Credit
Cash	$ 28,000	
Accounts receivable	86,000	
Inventory	72,000	
Machinery and equipment, net	209,000	
Van, loan	50,000	
Accounts payable		$ 93,000
Bakel, loan		40,000
Van, capital		128,000
Bakel, capital		100,000
Cox, capital		84,000
Totals	$445,000	$445,000

The partners plan a program of piecemeal conversion of the partnership's assets to minimize liquidation losses. All available cash, less an amount retained to provide for future expenses, is to be distributed to the partners at the end of each month. A summary of the liquidation transactions follows:

January	Collected $51,000 of the accounts receivable; the balance is deemed uncollectible.
	Received $48,000 for the entire inventory.
	Paid $4,000 in liquidation expenses.
	Paid $88,000 to the outside creditors after offsetting a $5,000 credit memorandum received by the partnership on January 11.
	Retained $20,000 cash in the business at the end of January to cover liquidation expenses. The remainder is distributed to the partners.
February	Paid $5,000 in liquidation expenses.
	Retained $8,000 cash in the business at the end of the month to cover additional liquidation expenses.
March	Received $156,000 on the sale of all machinery and equipment.
	Paid $7,000 in final liquidation expenses.
	Retained no cash in the business.

Prepare proposed schedules of liquidation on January 31, February 28, and March 31 to determine the safe payments made to the partners at the end of each of these three months.

LO 15-1, 15-4

30. Following is a series of *independent cases.* In each situation, indicate the cash distribution to be made to partners at the end of the liquidation process. *Unless otherwise stated, assume that all solvent partners will reimburse the partnership for their deficit capital balances.*

Part A

The Buarque, Monte, and Vinicius partnership reports the following accounts. Vinicius is personally insolvent and can contribute only an additional $9,000 to the partnership.

Cash	$130,000
Liabilities	35,000
Monte, loan	20,000
Buarque, capital (50% of profits and losses)	50,000
Monte, capital (25%)	40,000
Vinicius, capital (25%)	(15,000) (deficit)

Part B

Drawdy, Langston, and Pearl operate a local accounting firm as a partnership. After working together for several years, they have decided to liquidate the partnership's property. The partners have prepared the following balance sheet:

Cash	$ 20,000	Liabilities	$ 40,000
Drawdy, loan	5,000	Langston, loan	8,000
Noncash assets	150,000	Drawdy, capital (40%)	65,000
		Langston, capital (30%)	50,000
		Pearl, capital (30%)	12,000
Total assets	$175,000	Total liabilities and capital	$175,000

The firm sells the noncash assets for $120,000; it will use $15,000 of this amount to pay liquidation expenses. All three of these partners are personally insolvent.

Part C

Use the same information as in Part B, but assume that the profits and losses are split 2:4:4 to Drawdy, Langston, and Pearl, respectively, and that liquidation expenses are only $6,000.

Part D

Following the liquidation of all noncash assets, the partnership of Krups, Lindau, Riedel, and Schnee has the following account balances. Krups is personally insolvent.

Liabilities	$ 9,000
Krups, loan	6,000
Krups, capital (30% of profits and losses)	(20,000) deficit
Lindau, capital (30%)	(30,000) deficit
Riedel, capital (20%)	15,000
Schnee, capital (20%)	20,000

LO 15-2, 15-3, 15-7

31. The partnership of Frick, Wilson, and Clarke has elected to cease all operations and liquidate its business property. A balance sheet drawn up at this time shows the following account balances:

Cash	$ 60,000	Liabilities	$ 40,000
Noncash assets	219,000	Frick, capital (60%)	129,000
		Wilson, capital (20%)	35,000
		Clarke, capital (20%)	75,000
Total assets	$279,000	Total liabilities and capital	$279,000

Part A

Prepare a predistribution plan for this partnership.

Part B

The following transactions occur in liquidating this business:

1. Distributed safe payments of cash immediately to the partners. Liquidation expenses of $8,000 are estimated as a basis for this computation.
2. Sold noncash assets with a book value of $94,000 for $60,000.
3. Paid all liabilities.
4. Distributed safe payments of cash again.
5. Sold remaining noncash assets for $51,000.
6. Paid actual liquidation expenses of $6,000 only.
7. Distributed remaining cash to the partners and closed the financial records of the business permanently.

Produce a final statement of liquidation for this partnership using the predistribution plan to determine payments of cash to partners.

Part C

Prepare journal entries to record the liquidation transactions reflected in the final statement of liquidation.

LO 15-2, 15-7

32. The partnership of Wingler, Norris, Rodgers, and Guthrie was formed several years ago as a local architectural firm. Several partners have recently undergone personal financial problems and have decided to terminate operations and liquidate the business. The following balance sheet is drawn up as a guideline for this process:

Cash	$ 15,000	Liabilities	$ 74,000
Accounts receivable	82,000	Rodgers, loan	35,000
Inventory	101,000	Wingler, capital (30%)	120,000
Land	85,000	Norris, capital (10%)	88,000
Building and equipment (net)	168,000	Rodgers, capital (20%)	74,000
		Guthrie, capital (40%)	60,000
Total assets	$451,000	Total liabilities and capital	$451,000

When the liquidation commenced, liquidation expenses of $16,000 were anticipated as being necessary to dispose of all property.

Part A
Prepare a predistribution plan for this partnership.

Part B
The following transactions transpire during the liquidation of the Wingler, Norris, Rodgers, and Guthrie partnership:

1. Collected 80 percent of the total accounts receivable with the rest judged to be uncollectible.
2. Sold the land, building, and equipment for $150,000.
3. Distributed safe payments of cash.
4. Learned that Guthrie, who has become personally insolvent, will make no further contributions.
5. Paid all liabilities.
6. Sold all inventory for $71,000.
7. Distributed safe payments of cash again.
8. Paid actual liquidation expenses of $11,000 only.
9. Made final cash disbursements to the partners based on the assumption that all partners other than Guthrie are personally solvent.

Prepare journal entries to record these liquidation transactions.

LO 15-2, 15-7

33. The partnership of Butler, Osman, and Ward was formed several years ago as a local tax preparation firm. Two partners have reached retirement age, and the partners have decided to terminate operations and liquidate the business. Liquidation expenses of $34,000 are expected. The partnership balance sheet at the start of liquidation is as follows:

Cash	$ 30,000	Liabilities	$170,000
Accounts receivable	60,000	Butler, loan	30,000
Office equipment (net)	50,000	Butler, capital (25%)	50,000
Building (net)	110,000	Osman, capital (25%)	30,000
Land	100,000	Ward, capital (50%)	70,000
Total assets	$350,000	Total liabilities and capital	$350,000

Part A
Prepare a predistribution plan for this partnership.

Part B
The following transactions transpire in chronological order during the liquidation of the partnership:

1. Collected 90 percent of the accounts receivable and wrote the remainder off as uncollectible.
2. Sold the office equipment for $20,000, the building for $80,000, and the land for $120,000.
3. Distributed safe payments of cash.
4. Paid all liabilities in full.
5. Paid actual liquidation expenses of $30,000 only.
6. Made final cash distributions to the partners.

Prepare journal entries to record these liquidation transactions.

Develop Your Skills

ANALYSIS CASE

CPA skills

Go to the website www.cedarfair.com and click on "Investors," then "Investor Information," "Financial Reports," and "Annual Reports." Then click on "2017 Annual Report on 10-K" to access the 2017 Form 10-K annual report for Cedar Fair, L.P.

Review the financial statements and the accompanying notes contained in the 2017 annual report, especially any that discuss the partnership form of organization.

Assume that an investor is considering investing in this partnership and has downloaded this report for analysis.

Required

1. Briefly describe Cedar Fair's business and major properties.
2. Summarize the major differences that exist between Cedar Fair's financial statements and those of a corporation.
3. Assume that the investor is not aware of the potential implications of investing in a partnership rather than a corporation. What information is available in Cedar Fair's annual report that relates to unique characteristics of investing in a partnership?

COMMUNICATION CASE 1

CPA skills

One of your colleagues has been hired by the Todd, Johnson, and Samuels partnership to guide it through the liquidation process. The partnership currently has cash in a bank account that exceeds the amount it owes creditors, and has other assets consisting of equipment, land, and a building. Each partner has a positive balance in their capital account. Your colleague has asked your opinion with respect to two questions: (1) Would it be appropriate to distribute some cash to the partners even before the other assets have been sold and creditors have been paid, and if so, (2) should each partner receive an equal amount of cash?

Required

Write a memorandum to your colleague providing your opinion with regard to questions (1) and (2).

COMMUNICATION CASE 2

CPA skills

You have been engaged to do the accounting for the termination and liquidation of the Miller, Smith, and Tavares partnership. Miller has requested an immediate distribution of cash from the partnership that is being questioned by the other partners. Although Miller currently has a positive balance in his capital account, Smith and Tavares are concerned that this might change as the liquidation process unfolds. They argue that Miller should wait before receiving a cash distribution. All of the partners would like you to explain how it is possible that they might develop a deficit in their capital account during the liquidation process.

Required

Write a memorandum to Miller, Smith, and Tavares explaining how a positive capital account balance could develop into a deficit balance during the partnership liquidation process.

chapter 16

Accounting for State and Local Governments (Part 1)

Financial statements prepared by state and local governments in conformity with generally accepted accounting principles provide citizens and taxpayers, legislative and oversight bodies, municipal bond analysts, and others with information they need to evaluate the financial health of governments, make decisions, and assess accountability. This information is intended, among other things, to assist these users of financial statements in assessing (1) whether a government's current-year revenues were sufficient to pay for current-year services (known as interperiod equity), (2) whether a government complied with finance-related legal and contractual obligations, (3) where a government's financial resources come from and how it uses them, and (4) a government's financial position and economic condition and how they have changed over time.[1]

To even a seasoned veteran of accounting, the financial statements produced by a state or local government can appear to be written in a complex foreign language.

- Financial statements for the state of North Dakota include several "other financing sources (uses)" for the state's governmental funds for the year ended June 30, 2017, that include $346 million from transfers in and $849 million for transfers out.
- The June 30, 2017, balance sheet for the governmental funds of Portland, Maine, reports total fund balances of $118.7 million. Of that amount, nonexpendable permanent funds made up of $5.9 million while another $2.9 million was committed to capital improvements.
- The 2017 comprehensive annual financial report (CAFR) for Phoenix, Arizona, contains more than 260 pages of data—including the dollar amounts of expenditures made in connection with public safety ($897.6 million), community enrichment ($216.3 million), and environmental services ($12.8 million).
- Greensboro, North Carolina, reports two complete and distinct sets of financial statements. The first discloses that the city's governmental activities owed $493.0 million in liabilities as of June 30, 2018, whereas the second indicates that, at the same point in time, the city's governmental funds owed only $20.3 million in liabilities.
- The June 30, 2017, statement of net position for the Metropolitan Government of Nashville and Davidson County, Tennessee, reports total deferred outflows of resources of $291.8 million along with total deferred inflows of resources of $1.12 billion.

[1] GASB Statement 77, *Tax Abatement Disclosures*, August 2015.

Learning Objectives

After studying this chapter, you should be able to:

- **LO 16-1** Explain the reasons for the unique characteristics of the financial statements produced by state and local governments.
- **LO 16-2** Differentiate between the two sets of financial statements produced by state and local governments.
- **LO 16-3** Understand the reason that fund accounting has traditionally been a prominent factor in the internal recording of state and local governments.
- **LO 16-4** Identify the three fund types and the individual fund categories within each.
- **LO 16-5** Understand the basic structure of government-wide financial statements and fund financial statements (as produced for the governmental funds).
- **LO 16-6** Record the passage of a budget and the subsequent recording of encumbrances and expenditures.
- **LO 16-7** Understand the reporting of capital assets, supplies, and prepaid expenses by a state or local government.
- **LO 16-8** Determine the proper timing for the recognition of revenues from various types of nonexchange transactions.
- **LO 16-9** Account for the issuance of long-term bonds.
- **LO 16-10** Account for special assessment projects.
- **LO 16-11** Record the various types of monetary transfers that occur within the funds maintained by a state or local government.

Even a quick perusal of such information points to fundamental differences between state and local government accounting and the reporting associated with financial statements created for a for-profit entity. These differences are not accidental. The financial statements produced by state and local governments are unique for many specific reasons. This chapter and the next present the principles and practices that underlie state and local government accounting and analyze the logic that forms the foundation for their application.

These chapters are designed to explain a wide variety of state and local government reporting procedures. They also introduce the evolution that has led governments to produce financial statements that are markedly different from those of for-profit entities.

LO 16-1

Explain the reasons for the unique characteristics of the financial statements produced by state and local governments.

Introduction to the Financial Reporting for State and Local Governments

In the United States, thousands of state and local governments touch the lives of the citizenry on a daily basis. In addition to the federal and 50 state governments, 90,056 local governments existed as of the most recent census of governments in 2012. Of these, 38,910 were general-purpose local governments—3,031 county governments and 35,879 subcounty governments (19,519 municipal governments and 16,360 township governments). The remainder, which comprised more than half of the total, were special purpose local governments that performed only one function or a very limited number of functions: 12,880 school districts and school system governments and 38,266 special district governments.[2]

Actions of one or more governments affect virtually every citizen each day. Nearly 14.4 million people are employed full-time by state and local governments. Income and sales taxes are collected, property taxes are assessed, schools provide education, police and fire departments maintain public safety, garbage is collected, and roads are paved.[3]

When seeking to understand the financial reporting for state and local governments, a student should first consider the question of whether a complete set of specialized accounting principles is necessary. Could the financial information of a state or local government be presented fairly by applying the same rules and procedures as a for-profit entity such as Microsoft or Coca-Cola? In response to that basic question, several major differences were identified in a study (a white paper) by the Governmental Accounting Standards Board (GASB).

> The primary purpose of governments is to enhance or maintain the well-being of citizens by providing services in accordance with public policy goals. In contrast, business enterprises focus primarily on wealth creation, interacting principally with those segments of society that fulfill their mission of generating a financial return on investment for shareholders.
>
> The white paper cites several other crucial differences that generate user demand for unique information:
>
> - Governments serve a broader group of stakeholders, including taxpayers, citizens, elected representatives, oversight groups, bondholders, and others in the financial community.
> - Most government revenues are raised through involuntary taxes rather than a willing exchange of comparable value between two parties in a typical business transaction.
> - Monitoring actual compliance with budgeted public policy priorities is central to government public accountability reporting.
> - Governments exist longer than for-profit businesses and are not typically subject to bankruptcy and dissolution.[4]

[2] Carma Hogue, U.S. Department of Commerce. United States Census Bureau. Government Organization Summary Report: 2012, released September 26, 2013. http://www2.census.gov/govs/cog/g12_org.pdf.

[3] U.S. Census Bureau, 2012 Census of Governments: Employment Summary Report. https://www2.census.gov/govs/apes/2012_summary_report.pdf.

[4] Governmental Accounting Standards Board. "Users of Governmental Financial Reports Require Substantially Different Information than Users of Business Financial Reports," News Release, March 16, 2006, http://www.gasb.org/cs/ContentServer?pagename=GASB%2FGASBContent_C%2FGASBNewsPage&cid=1176156736250.

Accounting for state and local governments is not merely the determination of when a performance obligation is satisfied and an expense incurred in order to report net income. The setting of tax rates and allocation of limited financial resources among many worthy causes such as education, police protection, welfare, healthcare, and the environment create heated debates throughout the nation. Without a profit motive, what financial reporting is appropriate for a government? Who are the potential users of the information? To enable the public to stay informed, the traditional focus of government reporting over the decades has been on identifying the sources of current financial resources and the uses made of those resources. In other words, where did the government get its money, and how did the government use that money?

Indeed, this approach is appropriate for the short-term decisions necessitated by the government's need to gather and spend current financial resources to carry out public policy. For the longer term, information to reflect the overall financial stability of the government is also essential, especially for creditors who provide funding often through the acquisition of government-issued bonds.

Hence, state and local government officials face a number of unique financial reporting challenges. Those issues are addressed by GASB, which was created in 1984 to serve as the public-sector counterpart of the Financial Accounting Standards Board (FASB). GASB holds the primary responsibility in the United States for setting authoritative accounting standards for state and local government units.[5] In the same manner as FASB, GASB is an independent body functioning under the oversight of the Financial Accounting Foundation.

"Each of the final Statements of Governmental Accounting Standards issued by the GASB since its establishment in 1984 is designed to provide taxpayers, legislators, municipal bond analysts, and others with information that is useful to their decision-making process regarding governmental entities."[6] The following pronouncements are available for download at www.gasb.org:

- Statements of Governmental Accounting Standards
- Concepts Statements
- GASB Interpretations
- GASB Technical Bulletins
- GASB Implementation Guides (Post-Statement 76)

In 1990, the Director of the Office of Management and Budget, the Secretary of the Treasury, and the Comptroller General created the Federal Accounting Standards Advisory Board (FASAB). FASAB recommends accounting principles and standards for the U.S. federal government and its agencies. Although those rules are beyond the coverage in this textbook, additional information about FASAB is available on its website at www.fasab.gov.

Governmental Accounting—User Needs

Much of this chapter and the next reflect the efforts by GASB to provide relevant information to a wide array of individuals and groups interested in assessing both resource allocation decisions and the financial health of a state or local government.

The unique aspects of any accounting and reporting system should be a direct result of the needs of the people who use the financial statements. Identifying those users and their informational requirements is a logical first step in the study of state and local government accounting.

Early in its tenure, GASB addressed this challenge by describing several distinct groups of primary users of external state and local governmental financial reports:

> The Board believes there are three groups of primary users of external state and local governmental financial reports. They are (a) those to whom government is primarily accountable

[5] The National Committee on Municipal Accounting held the authority for state and local government accounting from 1934 until 1941. The National Committee on Governmental Accounting, a quasi-independent agency of the Government Finance Officers Association, established government accounting principles from 1949 through 1954 and again from 1967 until 1983, when GASB was formed. During several time periods, no group held primary responsibility for the development of governmental accounting. For an overview of the work of GASB, see Terry K. Patton and Robert J. Freeman, "The GASB Turns 25: A Retrospective," *Government Finance Review,* April 2009.

[6] Governmental Accounting Standards Board, Standards & Guidance, https://www.gasb.org/jsp/GASB/Page/GASBLandingPage&cid=1176160042327.

> (the citizenry), (b) those who directly represent the citizens (legislative and oversight bodies), and (c) those who lend or who participate in the lending process (investors and creditors). . . . The citizenry group includes citizens (whether they are classified as taxpayers, voters, or service recipients), the media, advocate groups, and public finance researchers. The legislative and oversight officials group includes members of state legislatures, county commissions, city councils, boards of trustees, and school boards, and those executive branch officials with oversight responsibility over other levels of government. Investors and creditors include individual and institutional investors and creditors, municipal security underwriters, bond rating agencies, bond insurers, and financial institutions.[7]

Thus, the quest for useful government reporting encounters a significant obstacle. User needs are so broad that no one set of financial statements or accounting principles can satisfy all expectations. How can voters, bondholders, administrative officials, and all of the other users of the financial statements produced by state and local governments receive the information they need for decision-making purposes? How can statements that are prepared for citizens also be sufficient for the needs of creditors and investors?

LO 16-2

Differentiate between the two sets of financial statements produced by state and local governments.

Two Sets of Financial Statements

Eventually, the desire to provide information that could satisfy such broad demands led GASB to require the reporting of two separate sets of financial statements by state and local governments, each with its own unique principles and objectives. For a complete understanding of state and local government accounting, nothing is more essential than recognizing the need for creating two sets of statements.

1. **Fund financial statements** provide a picture of the ongoing activities of the various aspects of a government. At least for a portion of the government, they report current period revenues and expenditures in connection with individual government functions. These statements also focus on disclosing any restrictions that have been placed on the use of the government's financial resources. Citizens interested in the operation of the government, especially in comparison to approved budgets, are likely to study the fund financial statements.
2. **Government-wide financial statements** have a longer-term focus. They report all revenues and all costs as well as all assets and liabilities. Creditors, especially bondholders, are likely to be most interested in government-wide financial statements as they assess the likelihood of being paid when obligations come due. Citizens can also study these statements to evaluate the chance of future deficits or surpluses.

Fund Financial Statements

The preparation of fund financial statements has long been the traditional approach for state and local governments because those statements present the transactions of individual functions. They report the amount of financial resources allocated to the various activities. They report the use made of those resources. Citizens can assess the government's fiscal efficiency and accountability in raising and spending money. Fund financial statements report the amounts actually collected from various taxes and from borrowing. Fund financial statements also report amounts spent during the current year on services such as public safety, education, health, sanitation, and the construction of new roads.

Fund financial statements exhibit flexibility. As will be described in this chapter, different methods of accounting are applied to different activities. The primary measurement focus for public service activities is the amount and changes in *current financial resources*— which are assets that eventually will be spent, such as cash and receivables. For those same public service activities, the timing of recognition is based on *modified accrual accounting*. Modified accrual accounting recognizes (1) revenues when the resulting current financial resources are both measurable and available to be used and (2) expenditures when current financial resources are reduced.

In applying modified accrual accounting, identifying when financial resources are available to be used is an important decision because it influences the timing of revenue recognition.

[7] Government Accounting Standards Board, *Concepts Statement No. 1, "Objectives of Financial Reporting,"* May 1987, para. 30–31.

The term "available to be used" means that current financial resources will be received soon enough in the future so that they can be used to pay for current period expenditures. The determination of what is meant by "soon enough" is at the discretion of the reporting government.

For example, in 2017, the City of Norfolk, Virginia, disclosed that "the City generally considers revenues, except for grant revenues, to be available if collected within 45 days of the end of the fiscal year." Therefore, using modified accrual accounting, a 2017 revenue collected by the City of Norfolk within the first 45 days of 2018 is recognized in 2017 because the resulting funds are considered available to pay 2017 expenditures. In contrast, the City of Richmond, Virginia, applies a policy of two months, and the City of Raleigh, North Carolina, uses 90 days. As shown by these cities, the definition of "available to be used" often varies from one government to the next. The one exception for modified accrual accounting as designated by GASB is the recognition of property taxes, where a 60-day maximum period is mandated.

Government-Wide Financial Statements

GASB created government-wide financial statements approximately 20 years ago to provide information about a government's financial affairs as a whole. These statements provide readers with a method of assessing operational accountability, the government's ability to meet its operating objectives. This information helps users make evaluations of the financial decisions and long-term stability of the government by allowing them to

- Determine whether the government's overall financial position improved or deteriorated during the reporting period.
- Understand the cost of providing services to the citizenry.
- Gain insight into how the government finances its programs.
- Understand the extent to which the government has invested in capital assets such as roads, bridges, and other infrastructure assets.

This information has become especially relevant in recent years as a number of governments have declared bankruptcy (such as San Bernardino, CA; Stockton, CA; Central Falls, RI; Jefferson County, AL; and Detroit, MI) while others face daunting financial difficulties.[8] The need to assess the risk of overall financial instability is becoming an ever more important aspect of state and local government accounting.

To achieve these reporting goals, the government-wide financial statements' measurement focus is on all *economic resources* (not just current financial resources). These statements apply *accrual accounting* for timing purposes much like a for-profit entity. Consequently, these statements report all assets and liabilities (and deferred inflows and outflows of resources) and recognize revenues and expenses in a way that is comparable to business-type accounting.

The Benefits of Reporting Two Sets of Financial Statements

The goal of making a government and its officials accountable to the public is one aspect of financial reporting that remains constant even after many decades. Because of the essential role of democracy within U.S. society, the creators of accounting principles seek to provide a vehicle for evaluating governmental actions. Citizens should be aware of the techniques and tactics officials use to raise money and then the allocation made of those scarce financial resources.

Most citizens are both voters and taxpayers. They have a special interest in the results obtained from their involuntary contributions to the government in the form of taxes, tolls, and other fees. Because elected and appointed officials hold authority over the public's money, governmental reporting has traditionally stressed this stewardship responsibility.

> Accountability is the cornerstone of all financial reporting in government. . . . Accountability requires governments to answer to the citizenry—to justify the raising of public resources and the purposes for which they are used. *Governmental accountability is based on the belief that*

[8] A fascinating picture of a government in financial crisis can be found at http://www.npr.org/blogs/money/2012/03/23/149057880/how-a-city-goes-broke, which details the difficulties of governing Harrisburg, Pennsylvania, as it fights through a series of bad financial decisions.

the citizenry has a "right to know," a right to receive openly declared facts that may lead to public debate by the citizens and their elected representatives.[9]

To promote transparency, governmental reporting has historically been directed toward measuring and identifying the current financial resources generated and expended by the various government functions. Fund financial statements allow readers to focus on individual activities. In connection with public services, such as the police department and public library, the fund statements answer three relevant questions:

- How did a particular part of the government generate current financial resources?
- Where use was made of the current financial resources?
- What amount of the current financial resources is held presently?

The term *current financial resources* normally encompasses the monetary assets available for officials to spend to meet the government's needs during the present budget period. When accounting for current financial resources, a government is primarily monitoring cash, investments, and receivables as well as current claims to those resources. In this method of reporting, virtually no emphasis is placed on accounts such as Buildings, Equipment, and Long-Term Debts because they have no direct impact on current financial resources.

Unfortunately, stressing accountability by monitoring the inflows and outflows of current financial resources is not an approach that will meet all user needs. Prior to the creation of government-wide financial statements, many conventional reporting objectives were ignored. For example, does the government have too much debt to service? As a result, investors and creditors were frequently sharp critics of governmental accounting. "When cities get into financial trouble, few citizens know about it until the day the interest can't be met or the teachers paid. . . . Had the books been kept like any decent corporation's that could never have happened."[10]

Consequently, in 1998, GASB created a new standard to mandate that separate government-wide financial statements be included along with fund financial statements in the general-purpose financial reporting for a state or local government. This second set of statements reports all assets and other resources at the disposal of government officials. It reports all liabilities that must eventually be paid. Revenues and expenses are recognized according to accrual accounting. Consequently, government-wide statements provide a completely different perspective of a government's financial affairs.

With two sets of financial statements, each user (whether citizen, creditor, or other interested party) can select the information considered to be the most relevant. Of course, not everyone believes that this additional data will always be helpful. "One of the tougher challenges of the current information age is sorting out the information most relevant for decision making from the vast amounts of data generated by today's state-of-the-art information systems. Financial reports cannot simply keep growing in size indefinitely to encompass every new type of information that becomes available."[11]

	Fund Financial Statements*	**Government-Wide Financial Statements**
Emphasis	Individual activities (during current period).	Government as a whole.
Measurement focus	Current financial resources (cash, investments, and receivables and claims to those assets).	All economic resources (all assets, liabilities, and other resources).
General information	Inflows and outflows of current financial resources.	Overall financial health.
Timing of recognition	Modified accrual accounting.	Accrual accounting.

*The guidance provided here for fund financial statements only applies to public service activities such as public safety, infrastructure construction, and education. As will be discussed shortly, other activities in fund financial statements (business-type activities and fiduciary responsibilities) are reported more in keeping with government-wide financial statements.

[9] GASB, *Concepts Statement No. 1, "Objectives of Financial Reporting,"* May 1987, para. 56.

[10] Richard Greene, "You Can't Fight City Hall—If You Can't Understand It," *Forbes,* March 3, 1980, p. 92.

[11] Jeffrey L. Esser, "Standard Setting—How Much Is Enough?" *Government Finance Review,* April 2005, p. 3.

Continuing Evolution of Financial Reporting Model

For the past several years, GASB has been reexamining almost every element of the financial reporting of state and local governments. It is a massive project that is expected to take several additional years to complete.

In September 2018, GASB released two Preliminary Views documents, *Financial Reporting Model Improvements* and *Recognition of Elements of Financial Statements,* to describe various issues and concerns to the public and elicit as many opinions and suggestions as possible. These Preliminary Views can be found at www.gasb.org. Anyone with a serious interest in state and local government accounting and its future form should read both and consider the issues raised. The coming years are a period of possible changes that could prove beneficial, both improving the effectiveness of the financial reporting model and providing guidance to preparers and auditors when evaluating transactions for which there are no existing standards (or in implementing existing standards). In a press release, GASB Chairman David A. Vaudt said: "What the Board ultimately is trying to do through these companion projects is provide better information to financial statement users. These proposals are designed to enhance both the value and clarity of the information reported in financial statements."

All financial reporting, whether for a for-profit business, a not-for-profit entity, or a state or local government, must evolve over time as both economic reality and user needs change. Often progress in financial reporting occurs gradually with adjustments made in an almost random fashion. At other times, progress is more radical with significant changes mandated. As this reexamination still has years to complete, speculation on the final results is impossible to imagine. Nevertheless, almost everything described in this chapter and the next are currently being reconsidered by GASB with significant alterations clearly possible.

LO 16-3

Understand the reason that fund accounting has traditionally been a prominent factor in the internal recording of state and local governments.

Internal Recordkeeping—Fund Accounting

In gathering financial information, state and local governments have always faced the challenge of reporting a diverse array of activities financed from numerous sources. Accountability and control become special concerns for governments that are composed of a multitude of relatively independent departments and functions. How does a government account for its police department separately from parks and recreation? For the internal monitoring of such individual activities, most governments maintain a separate quasi-independent bookkeeping system referred to as a *fund* with its own complete set of accounts. One fund records the transactions and maintains account balances for the police department while a separate fund records them for parks and recreation. In this way, information can be accumulated and organized for every activity.

Internal information gathered in this manner serves as the foundation for fund financial statements. An underlying assumption of government reporting has long been that most statement users want to see information segregated by function in order to assess each activity individually. How much money did the fire department receive, and what was done with that money? Using fund accounting, the accounting records provide that information. The resulting figures are the basis for the fund financial statements prepared for external distribution.

Because no common profit motive exists to tie various government functions and services together, consolidated balances were historically not presented. Combining financial results from the city zoo, fire department, water system, print shop, and a wide variety of other operations provides figures of questionable utility—especially if accountability and control over the usage of current financial resources are primary goals. Fund financial reporting was designed to provide information about individual activities, not the government as a whole.

The addition of government-wide statements has no direct effect on fund accounting. Consequently, the separate funds monitored by each state and local government still serve as the foundation for internal reporting. Although a single list of identifiable functions is not possible, the following are routinely performed by many governments. As will be shown, most of these are departments, cost centers, or agencies reported within the government's general fund. Some, though, are monitored within separate funds for control purposes or because the operational nature is different from a typical government activity.

Public safety	Judicial system
Highway maintenance	Debt repayment
Sanitation	Bridge construction
Health	Water and sewer system
Welfare	Municipal swimming pool
Culture and recreation	Data processing center
Education	Endowment funds
Parks	Employee pensions

The number of funds in use depends on the extent of services that a particular government provides and the grouping of related activities. For example, separate funds might be set up to account for a high school and its athletic programs, or these activities may be combined into a single fund.

> Only the minimum number of funds consistent with legal and operating requirements should be established, however, because unnecessary funds result in inflexibility, undue complexity, and inefficient financial administration.[12]

The requirement that government-wide financial statements be reported along with fund financial statements was a radical advancement designed to better communicate the overall financial health of the government to a broader array of decision makers. One significant outcome was that governments had to track information (the total cost of roads, for example) that had never been accumulated previously because fund accounting for public service activities focuses on changes in current financial resources. As will be seen, financial statements that report all the economic resources of a government as a whole require a considerable amount of additional information.

LO 16-4

Identify the three fund types and the individual fund categories within each.

Fund Accounting Classifications

For internal recordkeeping, each individual fund (whether accounting for the police department, the municipal golf course, or some other activity) is identified within one of three distinct categories. This classification system provides clearer reporting of the government's various activities. Furthermore, dividing funds into separate groups allows unique accounting principles to be applied to each.

- *Governmental funds*—this category includes all activities a government carries out to provide citizens with services that are financed primarily through taxes and other general revenue sources. The fire department, police department, and the schools systems are a few of the many activities reported within the governmental funds.
- *Proprietary funds*—this category accounts for a government's ongoing activities that are similar to those conducted by a for-profit entity. This fund type reports operations that assess a user charge so that determining profitability or cost recovery is important. A bus system, a municipal golf course, and a toll road are all typically reported within the proprietary funds.
- *Fiduciary funds*—this category monitors monies held by the government in a trustee capacity. Such assets must be maintained for others and cannot be used by officials for government programs. One common example is the monitoring of assets held in a pension plan for government employees such as teachers, fire fighters, or sanitation workers.

Governmental Funds

In many state and municipal accounting systems, governmental funds tend to dominate because governments usually have a service orientation. The internal accounting system maintains individual funds for every distinct service function: public safety, libraries, construction of a town hall, and so on.

Each governmental fund accumulates and expends current financial resources to achieve one or more desired public goals. Modified accrual accounting is applied for timing purposes. To provide better information, governmental funds are subdivided into five fund types: the

[12] GASB, *Codification*, Sec. 1100.104.

general fund, special revenue funds, capital projects funds, debt service funds, and permanent funds. This classification system forms an overall structure for the financial reporting of the governmental funds.

The General Fund GASB's definition of the general fund appears to be somewhat understated: "to account for and report all financial resources not accounted for and reported in another fund."[13] This description seems to imply that the general fund records only miscellaneous revenues and expenditures when, in actuality, it reports many of a government's most important ongoing functions. For example, the 2017 fund financial statements for the City of Baltimore, Maryland, disclosed 12 major areas of current expenditures within its general fund:

General government	Recreation and culture
Public safety and regulations	Highways and streets
Conservation of health	Sanitation and waste removal
Social services	Public service
Education	Economic development
Public library	Debt service

Expenditures reported for these categories were in excess of $1.79 billion and comprised more than 81 percent of the total for all of Baltimore's governmental funds for the year ended June 30, 2017.

Special Revenue Funds Special revenue funds account for current financial resources restricted or committed for a specific purpose (other than debt payments or capital projects). Because of donor stipulations or legislative mandates, these government resources must be spent in a designated fashion. Saint Paul, Minnesota, for example, maintained 17 individual special revenue funds during the 2017 fiscal year. Sources of those restricted monies were as diverse as the rental use of Lowertown Ball Park, administration fees from charitable gambling, and revenues collected from solid waste and recycling programs.

The special revenue funds category records these monies because legal or donor restrictions attached to the receipt require that expenditure be limited to specific operating purposes. According to Saint Paul's comprehensive annual financial report, a special revenue fund designated for "Street Lighting Districts" accounts "for levied assessments used to operate above standard (ornamental) street lighting systems in various areas of the city, installed at the request of adjacent property owners." In the same manner, the City of Charlotte, North Carolina, maintains a special revenue fund to account for money from a room occupancy tax that must support the NASCAR Hall of Fame. Using a special revenue fund helps to ensure that money is spent as required.

Capital Projects Funds As the title implies, this fund type accounts for financial resources restricted, committed, or assigned for capital outlays such as acquiring or constructing bridges, high schools, roads, or municipal office buildings. Funding for these projects can come from a number of sources such as grants, the sale of bonds, or transfers from general revenue. The actual capital asset is not reported here. Only the money to finance construction or acquisition is monitored in a capital projects fund. For example, the Lexington-Fayette Urban County Government in Kentucky reported, as of June 30, 2017, that it held a total of more than $49.1 million of current financial resources in 14 different capital projects funds. This money had to be used in a variety of projects such as the acquisition or construction of a performing arts and exhibit facility, fire trucks, park projects, and computer equipment.

Debt Service Funds These funds record financial resources accumulated to pay long-term liabilities and interest as they come due. However, this fund type does not monitor a government's long-term debt. Debt service funds are created to account for monetary balances that are restricted, committed, or assigned to make the eventual payments needed to satisfy long-term liabilities. For example, on June 30, 2017, the city of Birmingham, Alabama, reported holding approximately $4.8 million of cash and investments in its debt service funds to pay long-term debt and interest. For the year then ended, more than $13.9 million in principal payments were made from this fund as well as $9.3 million in interest payments.

[13] GASB, *Codification,* Sec. 1300.104.

Permanent Funds The permanent funds category accounts for financial resources restricted by external donor, contract, or legislation with the stipulation that the principal can never be spent. Nevertheless, the government can use any resulting income, often for a specified public program. The City of Dallas, Texas, reported holding $10.0 million as of September 30, 2017, from private donations whose income was designated to maintain four different local parks and to help finance other municipal projects. Such gifts are frequently referred to as *endowments.*

Proprietary Funds

The proprietary funds category accounts for activities of a government, such as a bus system, toll road, or subway line, that assess a user charge. As in the business world, customers pay and receive a service in return. Because the user charge helps the government make a profit or at least recover part of its cost, the accounting process for proprietary funds resembles that of a for-profit activity in that accrual accounting is used to recognize all assets and liabilities. In contrast to governmental funds, proprietary funds are reported in much the same way on both the fund financial statements and the government-wide financial statements.

To facilitate financial reporting, proprietary funds are divided into two fund types: enterprise funds and internal service funds.

Enterprise Funds Any government operation that is open to the public and financed, at least in part, by user charges is likely to be classified as an enterprise fund. A municipality, for example, might generate revenues from the use of a public swimming pool, golf course, airport, water and sewage service, and the like. The City of Houston generated $1.6 billion in revenue during the year ending June 30, 2018, from operating three enterprise funds: the city's aviation system, combined utility system, and the convention and entertainment facilities.

The number of enterprise funds has increased rather dramatically over recent years as government officials attempt to expand services without raising taxes. Thus, citizens utilizing a particular service might have to absorb a higher percentage of its costs. "Enterprise funds have become an attractive alternative revenue source for local governments to recover all or part of the cost of goods or services from those directly benefiting from them."[14]

Enterprise fund activities that collect direct fees from customers in exchange for some type of service resemble business activities. Not surprisingly, even in fund financial statements, the accounting parallels that found in for-profit reporting. Accrual basis accounting is used with a focus on all economic resources and not just on current financial resources.

A question arises, though, as to how much revenue an activity must generate before the government should view it as an enterprise fund. For example, if a city wants to promote mass transit and charges only a nickel to ride its bus line, should that service be viewed as an enterprise fund (a business-type activity) or within the general fund (a governmental activity)?

A government may classify any activity that charges a user fee as an enterprise fund. However, this designation is *required* if the activity meets any one of the following criteria. At that point, the government should view the amount of revenue as significant to its operation.

- The activity generates revenues that provide the sole security for the debts of the activity.
- Laws or regulations require recovering the activity's costs (including depreciation and debt service) through fees or charges.
- Fees and charges are set at prices intended to recover costs including depreciation and debt service.[15]

Internal Service Funds This second proprietary fund type accounts for any operation that provides services to another department or agency within the government for a fee. As with enterprise funds, internal service funds charge for their services. Here the work is for the primary benefit of parties within the government rather than for outside users. As with enterprise funds, internal service funds are accounted for much like for-profit operations in the private sector.

[14] Jeffrey Molinari and Charlie Tyer, "Local Government Enterprise Fund Activity: Trends and Implications," *Public Administration Quarterly,* Fall 2003, p. 369.

[15] GASB, Codification, Sec. 1300.109.

The City of Lincoln, Nebraska, lists eight operations in its 2017 financial statements that are accounted for as individual internal service funds:

Information services fund—to account for the cost of operating a central data processing facility.

Engineering revolving fund—to account for the cost of operating a central engineering pool.

Insurance revolving fund—to account for the cost of providing several types of self-insurance programs.

Fleet services fund—to account for the operations of a centralized maintenance facility for city equipment.

Police garage fund—to account for the operation of a maintenance facility for police and other government vehicles.

Communication services fund—to account for the costs of providing graphic arts and telecommunications services.

Copy services fund—to account for the cost of providing copy services to the government.

Municipal services center fund—to account for the purchase, improvement, and operation of a facility to provide a location for various government functions.

Fiduciary Funds

The final classification, fiduciary funds, accounts for assets held in a trustee capacity for external parties because the money cannot be used to support the government's programs. The resources are controlled by the government but not internally derived or for the benefit of the government. Like proprietary funds, fiduciary funds use the economic resources measurement focus and accrual accounting for the timing of revenues and expenses. Because these assets are not available for the benefit of the government, fiduciary funds are omitted entirely from government-wide financial statements. Separate statements are included within the fund financial statements.

Four different fund types are identified within the fiduciary funds category.

Investment Trust Funds The first fiduciary fund type accounts for the outside portion of investment pools. This category is necessary when a government accumulates financial resources from other governments in order to have a large sum of money to invest so that a higher rate of return can be earned by all the parties. The Commonwealth of Virginia held almost $3.8 billion at June 30, 2017, in an investment trust fund that "helps local governmental entities maximize their rate of return by commingling their resources for investment purposes."

Private-Purpose Trust Funds The second fiduciary fund type accounts for monies held in a trustee capacity for the benefit of specifically designated external parties such as individuals, private organizations, or other governments. The Commonwealth of Virginia has six private-purpose trust funds including Invest529 (the Virginia College Savings Plan) and the Virginia Farm Loan Program. Notes to the government's 2017 financial statements describe this latter fund as accounting "for trust funds that are used to provide loans to individual farmers for rural rehabilitation purposes." At the end of the 2017 fiscal year, the Commonwealth of Virginia reported Invest529 as having $4.0 billion in total assets and deferred outflows of resources while the farm loan program holds $4.7 million.

Pension (and Other Postemployment Benefit) Trust Funds The third fiduciary fund type accounts for assets held to pay employee pension (and other postemployment) benefits. Because of the need to provide adequate money for retired government workers (for a period of time that might last many years), this fund type can become quite large. The City of Philadelphia, for example, reported assets of more than $5.9 billion in its pension trust fund as of June 30, 2017. As will be discussed, concern has often been expressed over the years that long-term pension responsibilities are not properly reported in a state or local government's financial statements. Consequently, GASB has now mandated the reporting of the size of any unfunded pension obligation.

Custodial (Formerly Agency) Funds This fourth fund type records any resources a government holds in a fiduciary capacity that does not fall under one of the other three categories. For example, one government could collect taxes and tolls on behalf of another. Money often passes through custodial funds quickly. To ensure safety and control, custodial funds maintain this money separately until physically transferred to the proper authority.

LO 16-5

Understand the basic structure of government-wide financial statements and fund financial statements (as produced for the governmental funds).

Overview of State and Local Government Financial Statements

Although a complete analysis of the financial statements of a state or local government is presented in the subsequent chapter, an overview of four basic financial statements will be presented at this point to help illustrate the reporting of basic events. These examples are not complete but can serve to demonstrate the presentation of various transactions and accounts.

Government-Wide Financial Statements

Only two financial statements make up the government-wide financial statements: *the statement of net position* and *the statement of activities.* The reporting is separated into (1) governmental activities (all governmental funds and most internal service funds) and (2) business-type activities (all enterprise funds and any remaining internal service funds).[16] As mentioned earlier, government-wide financial statements do not include the transactions and account balances of fiduciary funds because those resources are not available for the benefit of the reporting government. Fiduciary funds are only shown in their own separate fund financial statements.

Exhibit 16.1 outlines the basic structure of a statement of net position. Because government-wide financial statements use the economic resources measurement focus, all assets and liabilities are reported. In addition, as will be discussed later, GASB has identified several balances that relate to future periods of time but do not qualify as either assets or liabilities. As can be seen in Exhibit 16.1, these amounts are shown as deferred outflows or deferred inflows of resources.

The final section of this statement, the net position category, indicates several separate figures: (1) the amount of capital assets reported less related debt, (2) legal or external restrictions on the use of any of the reported assets or resources, and (3) the total unrestricted amount available for use by government officials. For example, in Exhibit 16.1, the Governmental Activities holds $80 that is unrestricted, whereas the Business-Type Activities has only $30. Government officials can make use of that money.

The statement of activities in Exhibit 16.2 provides details about revenues and expenses, again separated into governmental activities and business-type activities. This statement is usually read horizontally first and then vertically. Direct expenses and program revenues are shown for each government function (such as general government and public safety). Program revenues include fines, fees, grants, and the like that the specific activity generates. Thus, a single net revenue or net expense figure is determined for each function as a way of indicating the financial burden or financial benefit to the government and its citizens.

For example, at Point A, a reader can see that maintaining public safety (probably through a police department, a fire department, and maybe an ambulance service) has a net cost to the government of $8,820. Direct expenses of $9,700 are partially offset by program revenues of $880 (possibly generated by fines, fees, or other charges). A taxpayer can judge the wisdom of incurring that cost to help ensure public safety, a figure that is more than the $8,100 cost of education as shown two lines below it.

[16] Government-wide financial statements report internal service funds as governmental activities if their primary purpose is to serve the governmental funds. Conversely, internal service funds are included with business-type activities if they mainly exist to help one or more enterprise funds. For example, a print shop (an internal service fund) should be reported within the governmental activities if its work is primarily for the benefit of a governmental fund such as the public library. However, if its work is to service a bus line (or some other enterprise fund), the print shop is classified within the business-type activities.

EXHIBIT 16.1
Statement of Net Position Government-Wide Financial Statements

	Governmental Activities	Business-Type Activities	Total
Assets			
Cash	$ 100	$ 130	$ 230
Investments	900	40	940
Receivables	600	400	1,000
Internal amounts due	50	(50)	–0–
Supplies and materials	30	40	70
Capital assets (net of depreciation)	2,950	2,750	5,700
Total assets	$4,630	$3,310	$7,940
Deferred Outflows of Resources			
Unamortized cost of debt refunding	$ 200	$ 40	$ 240
Liabilities			
Accounts payable	$ 750	$ 230	$ 980
Noncurrent liabilities	2,300	920	3,220
Total liabilities	$3,050	$1,150	$4,200
Deferred Inflows of Resources			
Unavailable property tax collections	$ 100	$ –0–	$ 100
Net Position			
Net investment in capital assets	$1,410	$2,110	$3,520
Restricted for:			
Capital projects	50	–0–	50
Debt service	140	60	200
Unrestricted	80	30	110
Total net position	$1,680	$2,200	$3,880

EXHIBIT 16.2 Statement of Activities—Government-Wide Financial Statements

			Net (Expense) Revenue		
Function	**Expenses**	**Program Revenues**	**Governmental Activities**	**Business-Type Activities**	**Total**
Governmental activities					
General government	$ 3,200	$ 1,400	$ (1,800)	n/a	$ (1,800)
Public safety	9,700	880	(8,820) Ⓐ	n/a	(8,820)
Public works	2,600	600	(2,000)	n/a	(2,000)
Education	8,400	300	(8,100)	n/a	(8,100)
Total governmental activities	$23,900	$ 3,180	$(20,720)	n/a	$(20,720)
Business-type activities					
Water	$ 3,600	$ 4,030	n/a	$ 430	$ 430
Sewer	4,920	5,610	n/a	690	690
Airport	2,300	3,120	n/a	820	820
Total business-type activities	$10,820	$12,760	n/a	$1,940	$ 1,940
Total government	$34,720	$15,940	$(20,720) Ⓑ	$1,940 Ⓒ	$(18,780)
General revenues:					
Property taxes			$ 20,400 Ⓓ	$ –0–	$ 20,400
Investment earnings			420	70	490
Transfers			600	(600)	–0–
Total general revenues and transfers			$21,420	$ (530)	$ 20,890
Change in net position			$ 700 Ⓔ	$1,410 Ⓕ	$ 2,110
Beginning net position			980	790	1,770
Ending net position			$ 1,680	$2,200	$ 3,880

The net expense and net revenue for all governmental activities are then summed vertically to arrive at the total cost of operating the government, an amount that is offset by general revenues such as property taxes and sales taxes. As can be seen, governmental activities had a net cost of $20,720 (Point B), whereas the business-type activities generated a net financial benefit of $1,940 (Point C). At Point D, the statement shows that the government generated property tax revenues of $20,400 to cover virtually all of the cost of providing governmental activities. Investment earnings and transfers more than made up the difference so that the net position of the governmental activities increased by $700 this year (Point E). The net position of the business-type activities increased by $1,410 (Point F).

Fund Financial Statements

Most state or local governments produce quite a number of fund financial statements because of all the diverse functions. However, at this introductory stage, only the two fundamental statements that most parallel the two government-wide statements will be examined. Exhibit 16.3 shows *a balance sheet* for the governmental funds, and Exhibit 16.4 presents *a statement of revenues, expenditures, and changes in fund balances* for the same governmental funds. The balance sheet reports the current financial resources (assets) held by the various funds and the claims to those resources (liabilities).

As can be seen in Exhibit 16.4, three separate categories are present in this fund financial statement. They will each be discussed in detail throughout the remainder of this chapter and the next:

Revenues
Expenditures
Other Financing Sources (Uses)

EXHIBIT 16.3 Balance Sheet—Governmental Funds—Fund Financial Statements

	General Fund	Library Program	Other Governmental Funds	Total Governmental Funds
Assets				
Cash	$ 40	$ 10	$ 50	$ 100
Investments	580	120	200	900
Receivables	120	200	210	530
Supplies and materials	10	10	10	30
Total assets	$750	$340	$470	$1,560
Liabilities				
Accounts payable	$230	$170	$110	$ 510
Notes payable—current	200	–0–	100	300
Total liabilities	$430	$170	$210	$ 810
Deferred Inflows of Resources				
Unavailable property tax collections	$100	$–0–	$–0–	$ 100
Fund Balances				
Nonspendable	$ 10	$ 10	$ 10	$ 30
Restricted	100	90	60	250
Committed	30	50	100	180
Assigned	20	20	90	130
Unassigned	60	–0–	–0–	60
Total fund balances	$220	$170	$260	$ 650
Total liabilities, deferred inflows, and fund balances	$750	$340	$470	$1,560

EXHIBIT 16.4 Statement of Revenues, Expenditures, and Other Changes in Fund Balances—Governmental Funds—Fund Financial Statements

	General Fund	Library Program	Other Governmental Funds	Total Governmental Funds
Revenues				
Property taxes	$17,200	$ 900	$ 2,300	$20,400
Investment earnings	100	200	180	480
Program revenues	500	100	2,500	3,100
Total revenues	$17,800	$1,200	$ 4,980	$23,980
Expenditures				
Current:				
General government	$ 3,400	$ –0–	$ 100	$ 3,500
Public safety	5,100	–0–	400	5,500
Education	6,700	800	–0–	7,500
Debt service:				
Principal	–0–	–0–	1,000	1,000
Interest	–0–	–0–	600	600
Capital outlay	1,100	300	3,300	4,700
Total expenditures	$16,300	$1,100	$ 5,400	$22,800
Excess (deficiency) of revenues over expenditures	$ 1,500	$ 100	$ (420)	$ 1,180
Other Financing Sources (Uses)				
Bond proceeds	$ –0–	$ –0–	$ 1,000	$ 1,000
Transfers in	–0–	20	580	600
Transfers out	(1,300)	–0–	(1,000)	(2,300)
Total other financing sources and uses	$ (1,300)	$ 20	$ 580	$ (700)
Change in fund balances	$ 200	$ 120	$ 160	$ 480
Fund balances—beginning	20	50	100	170
Fund balances—ending	$ 220	$ 170	$ 260	$ 650

Note that the figures found in these fund financial statements will not be the same as those presented for the governmental activities in the government-wide statement of net position (Exhibit 16.1) and statement of activities (Exhibit 16.2). For example, the asset total reported for the governmental activities in Exhibit 16.1 is $4,630, whereas the asset total for all governmental funds in Exhibit 16.3 is only $1,560. These differences result primarily for three reasons:

1. In government-wide statements, internal service funds are grouped with the funds that they primarily benefit. Thus, they are reported with the governmental activities if they assist governmental funds and with business-type activities if they assist enterprise funds. However, fund financial statements show all internal service funds as proprietary funds, not as governmental funds. *Totals will vary between the statements because both governmental funds and some proprietary funds (in the fund statements) are classified as governmental activities (in the government-wide statements).*
2. Governmental activities apply the economic resources measurement focus. In contrast, the governmental funds, in the fund statements, use the current financial resources measurement focus. *Different assets and liabilities are being reported by the two sets of statements.*
3. Governmental activities use accrual accounting in government-wide statements, while modified accrual accounting is used in creating fund financial statements for the governmental funds. *The timing of recognition is different.*

Because of these differences, reconciliations are reported between totals presented in Exhibits 16.1 and 16.3 and between Exhibits 16.2 and 16.4. Those reconciliations are discussed in detail in the following chapter.

Major Funds

In both of the fund financial statements presented in Exhibits 16.3 and 16.4, the general fund and every other individual fund that qualifies as major is shown in a separate column. The assumption here is that the Library Program (probably one of this government's special revenue funds if financed by a designated tax levy) is the only individual fund outside the general fund that is considered major. Information for all other governmental funds is grouped into a single "nonmajor" column. Consequently, identification of a major fund is quite important for disclosure purposes. A major fund is identified as follows:

> The reporting government's main operating fund (the general fund or its equivalent) should always be reported as a major fund. Other individual governmental and enterprise funds should be reported in separate columns as major funds based on these criteria:
>
> a. The total of assets and deferred outflows of resources, the total of liabilities and deferred inflows of resources, revenues, or expenditures/expenses of that individual governmental or enterprise fund are at least 10 percent of the corresponding element(s) total (total assets and deferred outflows of resources, total liabilities and deferred inflows of resources, and so forth) for all funds of that category or type (that is, total governmental or total enterprise funds), *and*
>
> b. The same element(s) that met the 10 percent criterion in (a) is at least 5 percent of the corresponding element total for all governmental and enterprise funds combined.
>
> In addition to funds that meet the major fund criteria, any other governmental or enterprise fund that the government's officials believe is particularly important to financial statement users (for example, because of public interest or consistency) may be reported as a major fund.[17]

Fund Balances

One other unique characteristic of fund financial statements created for the governmental funds should be noted. Because state or local governments have no owners, the balance sheet does not need a stockholders' equity section to report contributed capital, retained earnings, and the like. Instead, a variety of "fund balance" accounts, as shown in Exhibit 16.3, indicate the net current financial resources being held by each fund and what use can be made of those resources.

Fund balance accounts have long been used in governmental accounting in a rather generic fashion. Official rules now standardize the reporting of fund balances within five categories discussed in this section. These designations aid financial statement readers in understanding the use that can be made of each fund's net current financial resources. Often, because of legal or external restrictions, a portion of the current financial resources cannot be used by government officials as they please. "The fund balance classifications are GASB's response to credit market participants who sought general information about the availability of reported fund balances."[18]

In Exhibit 16.3, the general fund reports assets of $750, and liabilities and deferred inflows of $430 and $100, indicating a total fund balance of $220. From a reporting perspective, the most significant question to be addressed in connection with this amount is: What use can government officials make of this $220? The purpose of the fund balance classifications is to indicate restrictions (both external and internal) that limit the ability of officials to spend these resources as they wish. For example, at June 30, 2017, the City of Las Vegas reported total fund balances for its governmental funds of $624.8 million. Its assets exceeded its liabilities and deferred inflows by that amount. What use can be made of this excess?

Fund Balance—Nonspendable As implied by the name, this amount of a fund's current financial resources cannot be spent. This restricted classification is normally necessary for

[17] GASB, *Codification,* Sec. 2200.159.

[18] Paul A. Copley, *Essentials of Accounting for Governmental and Not-for-Profit Organizations,* 13th edition, published by McGraw-Hill Education, 2018, p. 57.

one of two reasons. First, assets such as supplies and prepaid expenses are simply not in a spendable form. Second, financial resources may be received that cannot be used because of externally imposed limitations. A cash gift, for example, donated by a citizen with the stipulation that only the future income generated from this balance can be spent falls within this category. This fund balance designation indicates that assets are held but are not available for government spending. As of June 30, 2017, the City of Las Vegas, Nevada, reported that the fund balance—nonspendable within the governmental funds—totaled $19.9 million.

Fund Balance—Restricted This figure indicates the amount of net assets held by the government that must be spent as designated by an external party. For example, a grant from another government for a specified purpose such as classroom teachers or playground equipment creates an increase in this category, as does a bond covenant that requires the proceeds to be used in a particular manner. The City of Las Vegas reported a $375.6 million fund balance—restricted as of June 30, 2017. Separate disclosure information indicates the restrictions apply to a wide range of projects including economic development and assistance, public safety (fire), and parks projects.

Fund Balance—Committed Here, assets have been designated for a particular purpose, not by an outside party but rather by the highest level of decision-making authority within the government. For example, a state legislature might vote to set aside $400 million for road construction. On the government's balance sheet, that decision is disclosed by an increase in the reported amount of the "fund balance—committed." Of course, the legislature holds the power to reverse its decision so the commitment is not necessarily binding. The City of Las Vegas reports its fund balance—committed balance as $37.9 million at June 30, 2017. This amount has been committed for judicial, cultural and recreational, and several other government functions. This reporting is explained in a note to the city's financial statements as representing amounts that "can be used only for specific purposes pursuant to constraints imposed by the Mayor and City Council, the city's highest level of decision-making authority."

Fund Balance—Assigned Frequently, in the regular operations of a government, money is designated for a specific purpose without formal action by the highest level of decision-making authority. These are often larger amounts held for a particular purpose. The head of the government's finance committee might designate cash of $1 million to be used in a few months to pay the current installment of a bond. However, if necessary, that money could be switched to some other purpose in the interim. At June 30, 2017, the City of Las Vegas reports a "fund balance—assigned" of $97.1 million. Of that total, $20.7 million was assigned to parks projects.

Fund Balance—Unassigned This category is normally found only in the general fund and reflects any amount of financial resources where no use has yet been designated either externally or internally. This amount is available to government officials for any purpose viewed as appropriate. On the June 30, 2017, balance sheet for the City of Las Vegas, the "fund balance—unassigned" was $94.4 million.

To illustrate, note how each of the following affects a city government's balance sheet when reported within the fund financial statements for the governmental funds.

- Cash of $30,000 is held by the government that can be spent for any purpose. On the last day of the fiscal year, officials use the money to buy supplies for a variety of public activities. The supplies are shown as an asset with an equal amount now reported within the "fund balance—nonspendable" balance. The cash was unassigned and available for any purpose but the supplies cannot be spent.
- A citizen dies and leaves investments valued at a total of $3 million to the city with the requirement that the government expend these resources solely for park beautification. Officials have no discretion in the use. In reporting these investments, the government must also show a "fund balance—restricted" on its balance sheet.
- The highest level of decision makers for the city (perhaps the city council or the mayor, for example) officially decides to set aside $110,000 in previously unassigned cash to beautify several local parks. No asset account is affected because nothing happens to the money. Nevertheless, the amount shown on the balance sheet as "fund balance—unassigned"

drops by $110,000, and the "fund balance—committed" increases by the same amount to reflect this allocation. No one within the government can overrule the decision.

- The director of finance for the city sets aside $12,000 in previously unassigned cash to be used to buy new benches for the city's parks. Because the decision was not made at the highest level of decision making, the "fund balance—unassigned" goes down while the "fund balance—assigned" rises. The decision, as well as the authority level of the decision, is being shown in this way. Although the decision is made, it can be changed by a higher level of decision makers.
- The city government receives property tax revenues of $1.4 million. Officials might eventually choose to use some or all of this money to complete specific projects such as the beautification of local parks. However, no decision has yet been made. In the general fund, the government reports the asset along with a "fund balance—unassigned" amount. This reporting allows readers of the financial statements to see that the money is available for use by government officials.

LO 16-6

Record the passage of a budget and the subsequent recording of encumbrances and expenditures.

Accounting for Governmental Funds

The remainder of this chapter examines many of the important accounting procedures used within the five governmental funds: the general fund, special revenue funds, capital projects funds, debt service funds, and permanent funds. The distinct approach that marks governmental accounting as unique can best be seen in these individual funds. Because of the dual nature of the financial reporting model, most procedures will be demonstrated twice, once for governmental fund financial statements and a second time for the government-wide financial statements.

In contrast, the reporting applied to proprietary funds and fiduciary funds (as well as the government-wide financial statements as a whole) is more likely to resemble the accounting used by for-profit businesses. It is less unique. Thus, the emphasis here is on the accounting for the individual governmental funds.

One preliminary question to address is whether governments should establish two separate sets of internal financial records (one for fund statements and another for government-wide statements)? Or, should governments maintain only one set for fund accounting that must be adjusted rather significantly at the end of each year to create government-wide financial statements?

> Most governments have not changed their day-to-day accounting at all from basic fund accounting. They continue to record their routine transactions, like tax collections and grant reimbursements, on a cash basis. Then, at year end when government-wide statements are to be produced, the government records the full accrual amounts as required by GASB. Given the nature of control environments in most governments, they find it easier to record full accrual only at year end.[19]

From an educational perspective, this textbook could follow the lead established in practice of reporting each event based on the fund financial statement model. Then, a one-time conversion is made at the end of the year to evolve those fund financial statements into government-wide statements. Or, the textbook could examine each event and transaction from both a fund financial statement and a government-wide perspective.

The second approach is adopted here because it allows a clearer comparison of the two distinct methods of financial reporting. Therefore, this textbook analyzes individual transactions from both a fund and a government-wide perspective. Examining the two ways of reporting side by side seems to be a more understandable process than learning fund financial reporting and later converting the resulting balances into a completely different set of figures based on the government-wide model. However, students need to understand that most state and local governments make only fund financial statement journal entries for

[19] From Jack Reagan, Partner with UHY LLP, February 2, 2019.

internal reporting that are adjusted at a later time to enable the preparation of government-wide financial statements.

The Importance of Budgets and the Recording of Budgetary Entries

> Many believe the budget is the most significant financial document produced by a governmental entity. The budget has been defined as a plan for the coordination of revenues and expenditures or as the amount of money that is available for, required for, or assigned to a particular purpose.[20]

A budget is a legally approved plan for operations. In a chronological sense, the recording of budgetary entries is the first significant accounting procedure carried out by a state or locality. To enhance accountability, government officials are usually required to adopt an annual budget for each separate activity to anticipate the inflow of financial resources and establish approved expenditure levels.

The budget serves several important purposes:

1. *Expresses public policy.* If, for example, more money is budgeted for child care and less for the environment, both positive and negative consequences are likely to occur. Through the budget, citizens are made aware of government officials' decisions as to the allocation of limited financial resources.
2. *Serves as an expression of financial intent for the upcoming fiscal year.* The budget presents the government's current period financial plan.
3. *Provides control because it establishes spending limitations for each activity.* Officials typically cannot spend more for a particular activity than has been budgeted without passage of a special authorization allowing them to do so.
4. *Offers a means of evaluating performance.* The budget allows a comparison to be made between the actual financial results for the period and the authorized level that has been set and approved.
5. *Indicates whether the government anticipates having sufficient revenues to pay for all of the expenditures that have been approved.* In the current economic climate, when many governments face declining revenue totals, the amount and handling of proposed deficits should be of interest to every citizen.

GASB states that "financial reports are used primarily to compare actual financial results with the legally adopted budget."[21]

After a government enacts its budget into law, formal accounting recognition is frequently required as a means of enhancing the informational benefits. The public is given the opportunity to review the amounts of current financial resources expected to be received and expended. By entering budget figures into the accounting records at the start of each fiscal year, comparisons can be drawn between actual and budgeted amounts at any point in time. At the end of the year, because the budget entries have served their purpose, they are reversed to remove the balances from the accounting records.

In the formal reporting process, budget information must be disclosed for the general fund and each major fund that exists within the special revenue funds. For these funds, governments provide comparisons between (1) the original budget, (2) the final budget, and (3) the actual figures for the period. This information appears as required supplementary information located after the notes to the financial statements. As an allowed alternative, the government can include a separate statement within the fund financial statements to show the budget and actual figures.

To illustrate, assume that city officials enact a motel excise tax with the revenue to be spent to promote tourism and conventions. Because receipts are legally restricted for a specified purpose, the city must utilize a special revenue fund. Assume that for the 2020 fiscal year, the tax is expected to generate $490,000 in revenues.

[20] GASB, Codification, Appendix B, Concepts Statement No. 1, Objectives of Financial Reporting, para. 19.

[21] GASB, *Codification,* Appendix B, *Concepts Statement No. 1, Objectives of Financial Reporting,* Summary.

Based on this projection, the city council authorizes expenditures of $420,000 (referred to as *appropriations*) for promotional programs during the current year. Of this amount, $200,000 is designated for salaries, $30,000 for utilities, $80,000 for advertising, and $110,000 for supplies. The $70,000 difference between the anticipated revenue and the appropriation total is a budget surplus to be accumulated by the government for future use or in case actual revenue amounts prove to be too small to support budget plans.

To acknowledge the council's action, the accounting records of this fund include the following journal entry. No similar entry to record a budget is made within the government-wide financial statements.

Fund Financial Statements—Budgetary Entry

Special Revenue Fund—Tourism and Convention Promotions		
Estimated Revenues—Motel Tax Levy	490,000	
Appropriations—Salaries		200,000
Appropriations—Utilities		30,000
Appropriations—Advertising		80,000
Appropriations—Supplies		110,000
Budgetary Fund Balance		70,000
To record current annual budget for tourism and convention promotions. Funding is to come from the government's motel excise tax.		

This entry reveals the expected level of funding and its origin (the motel tax levy). It also shows the approved amount for each type of expenditure. Unless officially changed, each of these figures remains in the records of the special revenue fund for the entire year to allow for planning, disclosure, and control. The Budgetary Fund Balance account indicates an anticipated surplus (or, in some cases, a shortfall) projected for the period. Here, the current financial resources are expected to increase by $70,000 during the year.

In this way, budgetary entries reflect a government's *interperiod equity.* This term refers to the alignment of revenues and spending during a period and the possible shift of payments to future generations. If a government projects revenues as $10 million but approves expenditures of $11 million, the extra million must be financed in some manner, often by the issuance of debt to be repaid in the future. The benefits of the additional expenditures are enjoyed today, but citizens of a later time bear the cost.

The original budget is not always identical to the final appropriations figure because of later amendments formally made during the year. Government officials often vote to change appropriation levels if more or less money than anticipated becomes available or needs sudden change. For the year ended June 30, 2018, the City of Greensboro, North Carolina, reported that $28,631,161 had originally been appropriated for culture and recreation. During the year, officials increased that amount to a final budget figure of $29,417,537, but only $28,053,440 was actually spent. A perusal of the budgetary data shows how close individual functions within the culture and recreation category came to their budgeted amounts.

To continue with the earlier illustration, assume that government officials in charge of tourism make an appeal to the city council for an additional $50,000 to create a special advertising campaign. If approved, the original budgetary entry is adjusted:

Fund Financial Statements—Budget Amendment

Special Revenue Fund—Tourism and Convention Promotions		
Budgetary Fund Balance	50,000	
Appropriations—Advertising		50,000
To record an additional appropriation for advertising.		

Now assume that the city actually receives $488,000 in tax revenues during the year and spends $457,000 as follows:

Salaries	$196,000
Utilities	29,000
Advertising	125,000
Supplies	107,000

This information is disclosed as follows. The Variance column is recommended but not required:

TOURISM AND CONVENTION PROMOTIONS
Year Ended December 31, 2020
Budget Comparison Schedule

	Budgeted Amounts			Variance from Final Budget to Actual Amounts—Positive Impact on Fund Balance (negative)
	Original	Final	Actual Amounts	
Resources (inflows):				
Tax levy	$490,000	$490,000	$488,000	$ (2,000)
Charges to appropriations (outflows):				
Salaries	$200,000	$200,000	$196,000	$ 4,000
Utilities	30,000	30,000	29,000	1,000
Advertising	80,000	130,000	125,000	5,000
Supplies	110,000	110,000	107,000	3,000
Total charges	$420,000	$470,000	$457,000	$13,000
Change in fund balance	$ 70,000	$ 20,000	$ 31,000	$11,000

Encumbrances

One additional budgetary procedure that has historically played a central role in government accounting is the recording of financial commitments referred to as *encumbrances.* In contrast to for-profit accounting, purchase commitments and contracts are often recorded within governmental funds prior to any recognition of an actual liability. The recording of encumbrances provides an efficient method for monitoring financial commitments so that officials do not accidentally overspend a fund's approved appropriations. GASB states that "encumbrances should be recorded for budgetary control purposes, especially in general and special revenue funds." Information on both expended and committed amounts is then available to aid officials as they manage the government's financial resources.

To illustrate, assume that a city's police department orders $18,000 in equipment from an approved vendor. The various items will take several weeks or a month to reach the city and its police department. As an ongoing service activity, the police department is accounted for within the general fund.

Fund Financial Statements—Commitment Created by Governmental Fund Activity

General Fund—Police Department		
Encumbrances—Equipment	18,000	
Encumbrances Outstanding		18,000
To record a purchase order for equipment.		

When the equipment is received, a legal liability for payment replaces the commitment. The encumbrance is removed from the accounting records, and an Expenditures account is recognized to reflect the reduction in current financial resources. Often—because of transportation charges, discounts, or other price adjustments—actual cost will differ from the original estimate. The recorded expenditure will not necessarily agree with the corresponding encumbrance.

Because of the current financial resource focus found in the fund financial statements (for the governmental funds), no equipment account entry is recorded for this long-lived asset. Instead, the Expenditures account balance identifies the reason for the reduction in current financial resources.

Assume that the equipment has a total cost of $18,160 by the time it arrives.

Fund Financial Statements—Equipment Order Received by Governmental Fund Activity

General Fund		
Encumbrances Outstanding	18,000	
Encumbrances—Equipment		18,000
To remove encumbrance for equipment that has now been received.		
Expenditures—Equipment	18,160	
Vouchers (or Accounts) Payable		18,160
To record the receipt of equipment and the accompanying liability for its cost.		

In producing government-wide financial statements, the only entry created by this ordering and receiving of equipment is an increase in the asset and related liability when the order is filled. As in for-profit accounting, the commitment is not recorded but is disclosed in the notes to the financial statements.

At the end of the fiscal period, any commitments that remain outstanding are removed from the accounting records by reversing the original entry because no transaction has yet occurred. The recording of encumbrances is to help prevent spending more money than the amount authorized for the period.

Assuming that the commitment will still be honored in the subsequent period, is additional reporting needed on the year-end balance sheet? If the fund balance has already been reclassified as restricted, committed, or assigned in recognition of this eventual expenditure, then no further change is needed. The labeling of the fund balance reflects the decision to use that part of the fund's financial resources to meet this commitment. If no fund balance has yet been reported as restricted, committed, or assigned, then a portion of the fund balance should be reclassified as either committed (designated by the highest level of decision-making authority) or assigned (designated by a party other than the highest level of decision-making authority) for the anticipated amount to denote the expected use of the fund's current financial resources.[22]

To illustrate, assume that the general fund of the city that ordered the $18,000 in equipment reports assets and deferred outflows of $600,000 and liabilities and deferred inflows of $500,000. On the balance sheet, the fund balance accounts are shown as $40,000 assigned and $60,000 unassigned. At the end of the fiscal year, the $18,000 encumbrance is still unfulfilled, so it is removed from the records for that period. However, officials decide that the government will pay for the equipment when it arrives in the following year. Based on that decision, the reporting of the fund balance figures on the balance sheet can be affected in one of two ways.

1. If the $40,000 fund balance—assigned already includes an $18,000 amount reflecting the commitment for this equipment, no change is necessary. The appropriate amount of the fund balance is shown as assigned.
2. If the $40,000 fund balance—assigned does not include $18,000 in recognition of the amount to be spent on this equipment, then the fund balance—unassigned is reduced by

[22] The restricted designation is used to indicate that external parties or applicable laws created the restriction. A fund balance cannot be internally restricted.

that amount, and fund balance—assigned (or possibly committed depending on the level of the decision-makers who agreed to acquire the equipment) is increased. The reported assets and liabilities are not affected because the equipment has not yet been received, but the fund balance is shown as assigned (or committed) to indicate that $18,000 of the fund's resources are not freely available to government officials. "Encumbered amounts for specific purposes for which amounts have not been previously restricted, committed, or assigned should not be classified as unassigned but, rather, should be included within committed or assigned fund balance, as appropriate."[23]

LO 16-6

Record the passage of a budget and the subsequent recording of encumbrances and expenditures.

Recognition of Expenditures and Revenues

Although budgetary and encumbrance entries are unique, their impact on the accounting process is limited because they do not directly affect a fund's financial results for the period. Conversely, the method by which states and localities record the receipt and disbursement of financial resources can alter reported data significantly. Because a primary emphasis is on measuring changes in current financial resources, *neither expenses nor capital assets are recorded in the fund financial statements of the governmental funds.* Probably no more significant distinction exists between the fund statements and the government-wide statements.

As shown in the previous purchase of equipment, governmental funds report an Expenditures account in the fund statements. This balance reflects decreases in current financial resources from the acquisition of a good or service. The reduction of these resources is recorded as an expenditure, whether it is for rent, a fire truck, salaries, a computer, or the like. In each case, a good or service is acquired. The statement of revenues, expenditures, and other changes in fund balances (Exhibit 16.4) allows the reader to see the use made of an activity's current financial resources. Spending $1,000 for electricity for the past three months is an expenditure of a governmental fund's current financial resources in exactly the same way that buying a $70,000 ambulance is.

Fund Financial Statements—Expenditures for Expense and Capital Asset by Governmental Fund Activity

Expenditures—Electricity	1,000	
Vouchers (or Accounts) Payable		1,000
To record charges covering the past three months.		
Expenditures—Ambulance	70,000	
Vouchers (or Accounts) Payable		70,000
To record acquisition of ambulance.		

Within the fund financial statements for the governmental funds, the timing of the recognition of expenditures and revenues follows the *modified accrual basis of accounting.* Under modified accrual accounting, expenditures are recognized at the time that the government incurs a liability that creates a claim against current financial resources. If the claim is established in one period to be settled in the subsequent period using year-end financial resources, the expenditure and liability are recorded in the initial year. However, as discussed earlier, the maximum length of time for the change in current financial resources to occur—often 60 days into the subsequent period—should be disclosed. Thus, if equipment is received on the last day of one year and payment is to be made in a few days, the expenditure and liability are reported in the first year. In contrast, if payment will not be made until 120 days later, no recording of the expenditure is likely in the first year, depending on the recognition period established by the government.

In fund statements, a governmental fund records both operating costs such as salaries and rent and the entire cost of all buildings, machines, and other capital assets as expenditures to

[23] GASB, *Codification,* Sec. 1800.184.

show the use of current financial resources. No net income figure is calculated for these funds. Furthermore, computing and recording subsequent depreciation is not relevant to the reporting process and is omitted entirely. Depreciation has no effect on current financial resources.

For the government-wide financial statements, all economic resources are measured. Consequently, the previous two transactions are recorded in this second set of statements when the liability is created, with depreciation subsequently recorded for the ambulance as time passes.

Government-Wide Financial Statements—Recording Expense and Acquisition of Capital Asset

Utilities Expense	1,000	
Vouchers (or Accounts) Payable		1,000
To record electricity charges for the past three months.		
Ambulance	70,000	
Vouchers (or Accounts) Payable		70,000
To record acquisition of new ambulance.		

LO 16-7

Understand the reporting of capital assets, supplies, and prepaid expenses by a state or local government.

Reporting Capital Assets and Infrastructure

One result of recording only expenditures within the fund statements for the governmental funds is that virtually no assets are reported other than current financial resources such as cash, receivables, and investments. The cost of a capital asset is recorded as expenditures at the time of acquisition with that balance closed out at the end of each fiscal period. Note that the balance sheet in Exhibit 16.3 reflects no buildings, school facilities, computers, trucks, or other equipment as assets.

Prior to the development of government-wide financial statements, only a minimum amount of information was available about the capital assets controlled by state and local governments. A listing was included in the financial statements for informational purposes. Even then, the inclusion of infrastructure items was optional. Infrastructure includes roads, sidewalks, bridges, and the like that are normally stationary and can be preserved for a significant period of time. A bridge, for example, with proper care might last more than 100 years. To save time and energy, many governments simply did not maintain records of such infrastructure items after the original expenditure. The eventual requirement that government-wide financial statements include all economic resources meant that capital assets (including infrastructure items) had to be recorded and, where applicable, depreciation had to be included. As will be discussed in the following chapter, depreciation of infrastructure can still be avoided under certain circumstances.

Thus, today, the fund financial statements report the amount expended each period by the governmental funds for capital assets, while the government-wide financial statements report those capital assets as well as all infrastructure items.

Supplies and Prepaid Items

In gathering information for government-wide financial statements, the acquisition of supplies and prepaid costs such as rent or insurance is not particularly complicated. An asset is recorded at the time of acquisition and subsequently reclassified to expense as the asset's utility is consumed by use or time. The City and County of Denver, Colorado, reported $2.6 million for prepaid items and other assets in its government-wide statements as of December 31, 2017.

However, reporting prepaid costs and supplies by the governmental funds within the fund financial statements is not so straightforward. These assets have a relatively short life, but they are not current financial resources that can be spent. Should the cost incurred be reported as an asset until consumed or recorded directly as an expenditure at the time of acquisition?

Traditionally, governmental funds have used the *purchases method,* which records such costs as expenditures at the point that a claim to current financial resources is created. No asset is recorded. Thus, in 2018, the City of Kansas City, Missouri, discloses that the

Discussion Question

IS IT AN ASSET OR A LIABILITY?

During the long evolution of government accounting, many scholars have discussed its unique features. In the August 1989 issue of the *Journal of Accountancy,* R. K. Mautz described the reporting needs of governments and not-for-profit organizations (such as charities) in his essay "Not-For-Profit Financial Reporting: Another View."

To illustrate the governmental accounting challenges, Mautz examined the method by which a city should record a newly constructed high school building. Conventional business wisdom would say that such a property is an asset owned by the government. Thus, the cost should be capitalized and then depreciated over an estimated useful life. However, Mautz pointed to paragraph 26 of FASB *Concepts Statement No. 6,* which asserted that an essential characteristic of an asset is "a probable future benefit . . . to contribute directly or indirectly to future net cash inflows."

Mautz reasoned that the school building cannot be considered an asset because it provides no net contribution to cash inflows. In truth, a high school requires the government to make significant cash outflows for maintenance, repairs, utilities, salaries, and the like. Public educational facilities (as well as many of the other properties of a government, such as a fire station or municipal building) are acquired with the understanding that net cash outflows will result for years to come.

Consequently, Mautz then considered whether the construction of a high school is not actually the establishment of a liability because the government is taking on an obligation that will necessitate future cash payments. He also rejects this idea, once again based on the guidance of *Concepts Statement No. 6* (para. 36), because a probable future transfer or use of assets is not required at a "specified or determinable date, on occurrence of a specified event, or on demand."

Is a high school building an asset or is it a liability? If it is neither, how should the cost be recorded? How is a high school reported in fund financial statements? How is the same high school reported in government-wide financial statements? Which of these two approaches best portrays the decision to acquire or construct this building? Does providing two different approaches for the same building provide the information decision makers need? Can a government possibly be accounted for in the same manner as a for-profit enterprise?

"Governmental funds record an expenditure at the time of the purchase of the inventory item." For disclosure purposes, though, any remaining supplies or prepaid items (such as insurance or rent) are entered into the accounting records as assets as a step in the production of financial statements. At that time, the asset is recorded along with an offsetting amount in fund balance—nonspendable to inform the reader that assets are held that are not current financial resources available for spending.

The *purchases method* reflects modified accrual accounting because the entire cost is recognized as an expenditure when current financial resources are reduced. However, some governments have chosen an accepted alternative known as the *consumption method* for the reporting of supplies and prepaid items acquired by their governmental funds.

The consumption method parallels the process utilized in creating government-wide financial statements. Supplies or prepayments are recorded as assets when acquired. As the utility is consumed by usage or time, the governmental funds reclassify the cost into an expenditures account. As explained in 2017 by the City of Birmingham, Alabama, "Inventory consists of expendable supplies held in the General Fund for consumption. The cost is recorded as an expenditure at the time individual inventory items are used (consumption method)." Under this approach, the expenditure is recognized in the period of usage. Because these assets cannot be spent for government programs or other needs, an equal portion of the Fund Balance account should be reclassified as nonspendable as shown in the balance sheet in Exhibit 16.3.

To illustrate, assume that a municipality purchases $20,000 in supplies and prepaid items for various general fund activities. During the remainder of the fiscal period, $18,000 of this amount is consumed so that only $2,000 remains at year-end. These events could be recorded through either of the following sets of entries. Notice that, depending on the approach, the expenditures will increase by either $20,000 or $18,000 in the year of purchase. Because of budgeting limitations, that can be an important difference.

Fund Financial Statements—Supplies and Prepaid Expenses—Governmental Funds

Purchases Method		
Expenditures—Supplies and Prepayments	20,000	
Vouchers (or Accounts) Payable		20,000
To record purchase of supplies for various ongoing activities.		
Supplies and Prepayments	2,000	
Fund Balance—Nonspendable		2,000
To establish balance for supplies and prepaid items remaining at year's end.		

Consumption Method		
Supplies and Prepayments	20,000	
Vouchers (or Accounts) Payable		20,000
To record purchase of supplies and prepayments for various ongoing activities.		
Expenditures—Supplies and Prepayments	18,000	
Supplies and Prepayments		18,000
To record consumption of supplies and prepayments during period. Because an asset that cannot be spent remains on the balance sheet, a $2,000 portion of the Fund Balance is also reclassified from unassigned to nonspendable. This reclassification is normally done in creating the statements and not through a journal entry.		

LO 16-8

Determine the proper timing for the recognition of revenues from various types of nonexchange transactions.

Recognition of Revenues—Overview

The reporting of certain revenues has always posed theoretical issues in governmental accounting. Revenues such as property taxes, income taxes, and many grants do not have the same type of exchange process as is found in for-profit entities. Governments impose taxes, fines, and the like on citizens to support its operations rather than provide a specific good or service in return for payment. Consequently, these revenues are referred to as nonexchange transactions.

To assist in the timing of such revenue recognition, GASB has a comprehensive set of guidelines. These rules do not apply to revenues such as interest or rents for which a true exchange does exist. Instead, they focus on nonexchange transactions, including most taxes, fines, grants, gifts, and the like for which the government does not provide a direct and equal benefit for the amount collected.

> In a nonexchange transaction, a government (including the federal government, as a provider) either gives value (benefit) to another party without directly receiving equal value in exchange or receives value (benefit) from another party without directly giving equal value in exchange.[24]

[24] GASB, *Codification,* Sec., N50,104.

For organizational purposes, GASB separates nonexchange transactions into four distinct classifications, each with its own rules as to proper recognition:

1. *Derived tax revenues.* Some tax assessments occur when an underlying exchange takes place. Income taxes and sales taxes are common examples of derived tax revenues. A citizen earns income and a tax is incurred. A business makes a sale and a sales tax is charged. A derived tax is tied to an event.
2. *Imposed nonexchange revenues.* Property taxes, fines, and penalties are classified as imposed nonexchange revenues. The government makes an assessment, but no underlying exchange occurs. With a property tax, for example, the government taxes ownership and not a specific event or transaction.
3. *Government-mandated nonexchange transactions.* This category includes monies, such as grants conveyed from one government to another, to help cover the cost of a required program. For example, assume a state specifies that a city must create a homeless shelter and then provides a grant of $900,000 to help defray the cost. The city records this inflow of money as a government-mandated nonexchange transaction. City officials did not make the decision. The state government required construction of the shelter and provided a portion of the funding.
4. *Voluntary nonexchange transactions.* In this classification, money has been conveyed willingly to the state or local government by an individual, another government, or an organization, usually for a particular purpose. For example, a state might grant a city $1.3 million to help improve reading programs in local schools. Unless the state had mandated an enhancement in these reading programs, this grant is accounted for as a voluntary nonexchange transaction. The money will provide an important benefit, but no separate government requirement led the state to make the conveyance.

Reporting Derived Tax Revenues Such as Income Taxes and Sales Taxes

Accounting for derived tax revenues is relatively straightforward. These revenues are normally recognized in government-wide financial statements when the underlying transaction occurs. When an individual taxpayer earns income, the government records the resulting income tax revenue. Likewise, when a business makes a sale, the government should recognize the related sales tax revenue.

Assume, for example, that sales by businesses operating within a locality amount to $100 million for the current year and the government assesses a sales tax of 4 percent. In the period in which the sales are made, the following entry is required for the $4 million tax. The amount should be reported net of any estimated refunds or balances that cannot be collected.

Government-Wide Financial Statements—Derived Tax Revenues

Receivable—Sales Taxes	4,000,000	
Revenue—Sales Taxes		4,000,000
To recognize sales tax that will be collected in connection with sales during the current period.		

For fund financial statements, the preceding reporting rules also apply, except for one additional requirement. In connection with governmental funds, as mentioned previously, current financial resources must be "available" before the revenue can be recognized. That is, the amounts must be received during the present year or soon enough thereafter so that the money can be used to satisfy current claims. In that way, the essence of modified accrual accounting is applied at the fund level of reporting.

Reporting Imposed Nonexchange Revenues Such as Property Taxes and Fines

Accounting for imposed nonexchange revenues is more complicated because no underlying transaction exists to guide the timing of the revenue recognition. Interestingly, GASB set up separate rules for recognizing the asset and the related revenue. The receivable is recorded as soon as the government has an enforceable legal claim, as defined in that particular jurisdiction. Cash is recorded rather than a receivable if a prepayment is made. For the revenue side of the transaction, recognition is reported in the time period when the resulting resources are required to be used or in the first period in which use is permitted.

To illustrate, assume that on October 1, Year 1, property tax assessments to finance the government during Year 2 are mailed by the City of Alban. The total amount is $350,000. Assume that according to applicable state law, the city has no enforceable claim until January 1, Year 2 (often referred to as the *lien date*). To encourage early payment, the city offers a 5 percent discount on any amount received by December 31, Year 1.

No entry is recorded on October 1, Year 1. Although the assessments have been delivered, no enforceable legal claim yet exists, and the proceeds from the tax cannot be used until Year 2.

Assume that $30,000 of these assessments are collected from citizens during the final three months of Year 1. After reduction for the 5 percent discount, the cash collection is $28,500.

Government-Wide Financial Statements and Fund Financial Statements—Property Taxes Prepaid in Year 1 for Year 2

Year 1		
Cash	28,500	
Unavailable Property Tax Collections		28,500
To record collection of property tax prior to the start of the levy year after reduction for 5 percent discount.		

The collection of prepaid taxes does not create a liability because no type of payment or service is required. Nevertheless, because the money cannot be spent until Year 2, it is not yet reported as a revenue. As shown in Exhibit 16.1 and Exhibit 16.3, this balance represents a deferred inflow of resources on the statement of net position (government-wide statements) and the balance sheet (fund financial statements for the governmental funds). The deferred inflow is grouped with liabilities but is clearly a separate type of account. A revenue will be recognized for the amount received but not yet.

Moving into Year 2, assume that city officials expect to collect 96 percent of the remaining $500,000 in assessments, or $480,000. At the beginning of Year 2, both this receivable and the related revenue are recognized.

- The receivable is reported at that time because an enforceable claim comes into existence.
- For government-wide statements, the revenue is reported in Year 2 because that is the period in which the money can first be used.

Note here that the revenue is reduced directly by the $20,000 estimate of taxes expected to be uncollectible. In addition, the previously collected $28,500 is now recognized in Year 2 as revenue because, once again, this is the period for which use is allowed.

Government-Wide Financial Statement—Property Taxes for Year 2

January 1, Year 2		
Property Tax Receivable	500,000	
Allowance for Uncollectible Taxes		20,000
Revenues—Property Taxes		480,000
To recognize property tax assessment for Year 2.		
Unavailable Property Tax Collections	28,500	
Revenues—Property Taxes		28,500
To recognize property tax proceeds for Year 2 collected during Year 1.		

The preceding recording is the same for the fund financial statements unless some portion of the $480,000 future cash collection is viewed as not being available to be used this period. Because property taxes are such a significant source of revenue for many governments, a specific 60-day maximum period for recognition has been standardized rather than allowing a government to choose a longer period as a way of increasing the amount of revenue recognized.

To illustrate, assume that records for the past several years indicate that $400,000 of this anticipated $480,000 will be collected during Year 2, another $50,000 in the first 60 days of Year 3, and the final $30,000 in the months beyond 60 days into Year 3. For fund-based statements, this last $30,000 is not viewed as available to pay for Year 2 expenditures. For that amount, recognition is delayed until Year 3. Only $450,000 of the financial resources is expected to be available for Year 2 expenditures. Once again, the unavailable property tax collections amount ($30,000 in this case) is shown as a deferred inflow of resources for the governmental fund. The receivable is recognized but this $30,000 will not be available until Year 3.

Fund Financial Statements—Property Taxes for Year 2—Governmental Funds

January 1, Year 2		
Property Tax Receivable	500,000	
Allowance for Uncollectible Taxes		20,000
Revenues—Property Taxes		450,000
Unavailable Property Tax Collections.		30,000
To record amount of property taxes measurable and available to be used for Year 2 expenditures. Final $30,000 is not expected until after 60 days into Year 3.		
Unavailable Property Tax Collections.	28,500	
Revenues—Property Taxes		28,500
To recognize property tax proceeds for Year 2 collected during Year 1.		

Reporting Government-Mandated Nonexchange Transactions and Voluntary Nonexchange Transactions

Although these two sources of revenues are identified separately by GASB, timing of accounting recognition is the same, so they are discussed here together. Governments recognize these types of revenue (often coming in the form of a grant) when all eligibility requirements have been met. Until eligibility is established, the existence of some degree of uncertainty precludes recognition. Thus, revenue is reported at the time of eligibility even if money was received earlier.

Eligibility requirements are divided into four general classifications. Applicable requirements must all be met before revenue can be recorded for either government-mandated nonexchange transactions or voluntary nonexchange transactions.

1. *Required characteristics of the recipients.* Governments must often attain specific standards in order to qualify for the receipt of funding. To illustrate, assume that a not-for-profit foundation awards a grant to a city to finance improved reading education for all kindergarten children in the school system. Assume also that state law has been changed to mandate that all kindergarten teachers must gain proper certification within the next five years. Consequently, the foundation states that it will only convey the grant to the city when all kindergarten teachers have met the state standard. The city must conform to the law to qualify for the money. Because of this eligibility requirement, recognition of grant revenue is delayed until all kindergarten teachers are certified.
2. *Time requirements.* The parties providing the funding can specify when the money is to be used. The time becomes an eligibility requirement. For example, assume that in

April, a state government provides a grant to a city to buy milk for each child during the subsequent school year starting in September. The grant should be recognized as revenue in the period of use or in the period when the use of the funds is first permitted. Here, the money cannot be used in April so it is not yet revenue. Recognition begins in September.

3. *Reimbursement.* Many grants and other forms of similar support are designed to reimburse a state or local government for amounts spent according to specified guidelines. These arrangements are often called *expenditure-driven programs.* Assume that a state informs a locality that it will reimburse the city government for money paid to provide books to schoolchildren who could not otherwise afford them. In such cases, proper spending is the eligibility requirement. The city recognizes no revenue until it spends its own money for these books.
4. *Contingencies.* In voluntary nonexchange transactions (but not in government-mandated nonexchange transactions), funding may be withheld until a specified procurement action has been taken. A grant might be given to buy park equipment, for example, but is only available after an appropriate piece of land has been acquired on which to build the park. Until land is obtained (or other required action is taken), the revenue should not be recognized.

For most of these events, a liability is recognized in the government-wide statements if money is received before the eligibility requirements are met. The liability is necessary because the government is obligated to act in some manner. However, if only a time restriction exists, then a deferred inflow of resources is reported (rather than a liability or revenue) because no further action is required of the government—only the passage of time. In fund financial statements, if the cash is received but eligibility requirements have not yet been met, a deferred inflow of resources is reported.

LO 16-9

Account for the issuance of long-term bonds.

Issuance of Bonds

The issuance of bonds serves as a major source of financing for many, if not most, state and local governments. At the end of the second quarter of 2018, the total long-term debt outstanding for all state and local governments amounted to the almost unbelievable balance of \$3.1 trillion.[25] Money received from the issuance of these debts is used for many purposes, including general financing and a wide variety of construction projects such as roads, bridges, and airports. As of June 30, 2017, the City and County of San Francisco, California, reported approximately \$23.1 billion of noncurrent bonds, loans, and similar liabilities outstanding. Of that amount, \$8.0 billion had been incurred by governmental activities and \$15.1 billion by its business-type activities.

Because the proceeds of a long-term bond must be repaid, the government recognizes no revenues under either method of financial reporting. The reporting process for the government-wide financial statements is straightforward. Both the cash and the debt are increased to reflect the issuance just as they would be in a for-profit business.

Conversely, in the fund financial statements for governmental funds, recording is more complicated. Cash is received, but the debt is not a claim on current financial resources. From that perspective, the inflow of current financial resources creates neither a revenue nor a liability. Assume, for example, that the Town of Ruark issues \$21 million in general obligation bonds at face value to finance the construction of a new school building. Because of the intended use of the proceeds, the town establishes a capital projects fund to monitor the receipt and spending of this cash. To emphasize that the money is not derived from a revenue, Ruark will use a special designation, *Other Financing Sources.* Note in Exhibit 16.4 the placement of Other Financing Sources (Uses) at the bottom of the statement of revenues, expenditures, and other changes in fund balance to identify changes in current financial resources created by transactions other than revenues and expenditures.

[25] U.S. Federal Reserve, *Federal Reserve Statistical Release,* "Financial Accounts of the United States - Flow of Funds, Balance Sheets, and Integrated Macroeconomic Accounts," Second Quarter 2018 (Washington, D.C.: Federal Reserve, September 20, 2018), Table D.3, p. 7.

The following journal entry reflects the issuance of these bonds as recorded in the fund financial statements.

Fund Financial Statements—Issuance of Bonds—Governmental Funds

Capital Projects Fund—School Building		
Cash	21,000,000	
Other Financing Sources—Bond Proceeds		21,000,000
To record issuance of bonds to finance school construction project.		

The reporting of the governmental funds stresses accountability for the inflows and outflows of current financial resources. Although an inflow of cash has taken place, it was not generated by a revenue. The money came from a loan that will eventually have to be repaid. This increase in current financial resources is reflected by the Other Financing Sources balance, a measurement account that is closed out at each year-end. The $21 million bond liability is not reported by the capital projects fund because it is not yet a claim to current financial resources.

Recognition of long-term debts has traditionally been ignored in the reporting of governmental funds. For example, the balance sheet in Exhibit 16.3 shows no noncurrent liabilities for the governmental funds, only claims to current financial resources. A reader of the financial statements who wants to see the complete record of the government's debts must examine the statement of net position in the government-wide financial statements (see Exhibit 16.1).

Because state and local governments often issue significant amounts of debts, related costs can be quite large. To standardize reporting, GASB requires any debt issuance cost to be recognized as an expense/expenditure when incurred rather than being capitalized.

In addition, if available interest rates subsequently fall, bonds are sometimes reacquired by a government so that new financing can be arranged at a lower cost. The difference between the amount paid to retire the original debt and its net carrying amount at that time is not recorded immediately as an expense. Instead, the difference is reported on the statement of net position as a deferred outflow of resources (if more than the net carrying amount is paid) or a deferred inflow of resources (if less than the net carrying amount is paid). This deferred amount is amortized over time against interest expense. The refunding arrangement was set up in hopes of reducing the cost of interest. That justification is reflected in the subsequent handling of the difference.

Thus, the State of Florida reported at June 30, 2017, an "amount deferred on refunding of debt" as a deferred outflow of resources of $120.6 million while showing the exact same account title as a deferred inflow of resources of $101.9 million. Apparently, several debts were refunded by the state in recent years, sometimes for more than the face value of the debt and sometimes for less than the face value.

Payment of Noncurrent Liabilities

The payment of noncurrent liabilities by one of the governmental funds again demonstrates the fundamental differences between the two sets of financial statements.

- For government-wide statements, the payment of principal and interest is recorded in the same manner as that used by a for-profit organization. The liability is removed and interest expense recognized.
- On fund financial statements, an expenditure is recognized for settlement of the debt and also for the related interest. Both payments reduce current financial resources and are often made directly from a debt service fund if current financial resources have been set aside.

As an illustration, assume that a government makes a $500,000 bond payment along with three months of interest amounting to $10,000. Government officials have previously transferred sufficient cash into a debt service fund to satisfy this obligation.

Government-Wide Financial Statements—Bond and Interest Payments

Bond Payable	500,000	
Interest Expense	10,000	
Cash		510,000
To record payment of bond and related interest.		

Fund Financial Statements—Bond and Interest Payments—Governmental Funds

Debt Service Funds		
Expenditure—Bond Principal	500,000	
Expenditure—Interest	10,000	
Cash		510,000
To record payment of bond and related interest.		

Tax Anticipation Notes

Governments record one type of debt in the same manner for government-wide and fund financial statements. State and local governments often issue short-term debts to provide financing until revenue sources such as property taxes are collected. For example, if tax receipts are expected at a particular point in time, the government might need to borrow money to finance operations until that date. These short-term liabilities are often referred to as *tax anticipation notes* because they are outstanding only until a sufficient amount of taxes is collected.

As short-term liabilities, these debts are a claim on current financial resources. For fund financial statements, the issuance is not recorded as another financing source but as a liability in the same manner as in the government-wide financial statements. Amounts paid for interest, though, are still recorded as an expenditure in producing fund statements, but as an expense on the government-wide financial statements.

Assume the City of Elizabeth borrows $700,000 on a 60-day note on January 1 and agrees to pay back $712,000 on March 1. City officials expect to repay the debt with receipts from property tax assessments. In creating both sets of financial statements, cash and the related liability are both increased at the time of issuance.

At repayment, however, different entries are required.

Fund Financial Statements—Payment of Tax Anticipation Notes by Governmental Funds

General Fund		
Tax Anticipation Note Payable	700,000	
Expenditure—Interest	12,000	
Cash		712,000
To record payment of short-term debt and interest for two months.		

Government-Wide Financial Statements—Payment of Tax Anticipation Notes

Tax Anticipation Note Payable	700,000	
Interest Expense	12,000	
Cash		712,000
To record payment of short-term debt and interest for two months.		

LO 16-10

Account for special assessment projects.

Special Assessments

Governments can provide improvements or services that directly benefit a particular property and then assess the costs (in whole or in part) to the owner. In some cases, owners petition the government to initiate such projects to enhance their property values. Paving streets, installing water and sewage lines, adding street lights, and constructing curbs and sidewalks are typical examples. The government usually issues debt to finance the work and places a lien on the property being improved to ensure eventual reimbursement. The amounts are not necessarily small. The City of Fargo, North Dakota, reported special assessment receivables of more than $396 million as of December 31, 2017. This balance represents the second biggest asset listed by Fargo in its government-wide statements, with only the city's infrastructure (bridges, roads, and the like) reporting a larger balance.

Government-wide financial statements handle the debt issuance and the subsequent cost of the construction work in the same manner as for-profit enterprises. The government records the debt proceeds along with the asset's cost. Assessments are then made and collected. Receipts from the property owners are used to settle the debt.

To illustrate, assume that a sidewalk is to be built throughout a neighborhood at an approximate cost of $600,000. The city issues bonds to finance construction with repayment to be made using funds subsequently collected from the owners of the neighborhood property. Total interest of $30,000 is expected as the cost of the debt. The assessment to the owners is set at $630,000 to cover all costs, both for the construction and the interest.

Government-Wide Financial Statements—Special Assessment Project

	Debit	Credit
Cash	600,000	
Bond Payable—Special Assessment		600,000
To record debt issued to finance sidewalk construction.		
Infrastructure Asset—Sidewalk	600,000	
Cash		600,000
To record payment to contractor for the cost of building new sidewalk.		
Taxes Receivable—Special Assessment	630,000	
Revenue—Special Assessment		630,000
To record citizens' charges for special assessment project.		
Cash	630,000	
Taxes Receivable—Special Assessment		630,000
To record collection of money from assessment of citizens for sidewalk construction.		
Bond Payable—Special Assessment	600,000	
Interest Expense	30,000	
Cash		630,000
To record payment of debt on special assessment bonds.		

In the fund financial statements for government funds, this same series of transactions has a completely different appearance. Neither the infrastructure asset nor the long-term debt is recorded because the current financial resources measurement basis is used.

Fund Financial Statements—Special Assessment Project—Governmental Funds

Capital Projects Fund—Special Assessment Project	Debit	Credit
Cash	600,000	
Other Financing Sources—Bond Proceeds		600,000
To record issuance of bonds to finance sidewalk construction with payment to be made from a special assessment levy.		
Expenditures—Sidewalk	600,000	
Cash		600,000
To record payment to contractor for the cost of constructing sidewalk.		

Debt Service Fund—Special Assessment Project		
Taxes Receivable—Special Assessment	630,000	
Revenue—Special Assessment		630,000
To record assessment that will be used to pay bond principal and related interest.		
Cash	630,000	
Taxes Receivable—Special Assessment		630,000
To record collection of assessment paid by citizens to extinguish bond and interest incurred in construction of sidewalk.		
Expenditure—Special Assessment Bond	600,000	
Expenditure—Interest	30,000	
Cash		630,000
To record payment of bonds payable and interest incurred in construction of sidewalk.		

One alternative for the reporting of special assessment projects does exist. In some cases, the government may facilitate a project but accept no legal obligation. The government assumes no liability (either primary or secondary) for the debt or the construction. The money goes from the citizens to the government and then directly to the contractors. The government serves merely as a conduit.

If the government has no liability for defaults, overruns, or other related problems, the recording of special assessment assets, liabilities, revenues, expenses, other financing sources, and expenditures is not relevant to the government and its resources. In that situation, all transactions are recorded in a custodial (formerly an agency) fund as increases and decreases in (1) cash, (2) amounts due from citizens, and (3) amounts due to contractors. No other balances are needed. Because all recording is within a fiduciary fund, no dollar amounts appear in the government-wide statements.

Interfund Transactions

LO 16-11

Record the various types of monetary transfers that occur within the funds maintained by a state or local government.

Interfund transactions are common within governments as a way to direct sufficient resources to activities and functions as needed. Monetary transfers made from the general fund are prevalent because general tax revenues are initially accumulated in this fund. For example, fund financial statements for the year ended June 30, 2018, the City of Houston, Texas, indicated that $391.9 million was transferred out of the city's general fund to other funds (a significant amount went to the debt service fund) while only $73.0 million was transferred in from other funds.

Transfers into and out of a fund are not offset in the reporting of fund financial statements. The two amounts are not netted to arrive at a single transfer amount. More information is available by showing both.

In contrast, the government-wide financial statements do not report most transfers because they frequently occur solely within the governmental activities. For example, a transfer from the general fund to a debt service fund is reported in both funds on fund financial statements. Nevertheless, it creates no net impact in the government-wide financial statements because both funds are classified within the governmental activities. The increase and decrease offset.

Thus, for government-wide financial reporting, the following distinctions are drawn for transfers:

- *Intra-activity transactions* occur between two governmental funds (so that the net totals reported for governmental activities are not affected) or between two enterprise funds (so that the net totals reported for business-type activities are not affected). Transfers between governmental funds and many of the internal service funds are also included in this category because, as discussed previously, governments often identify internal service funds as governmental activities. Intra-activity transactions are not reported in government-wide financial statements. No overall change results for either the governmental activities or the business-type activities.

- *Interactivity transactions* occur between governmental funds and enterprise funds. They affect the total amount of resources reported by both governmental activities and business-type activities. One will increase as the other decreases. Thus, governments do report interactivity transactions in their government-wide financial statements. For example, in Exhibit 16.1, internal amounts due ($50) at year-end are reported as both a positive and a negative within the asset section of the statement of net position and then offset in arriving at overall totals. Likewise, in Exhibit 16.2, transfers ($600) occurring between the two classifications during the year appear at the bottom of the general revenues section. Once again, individual totals are shown and then offset so that no amount is shown for the government as a whole. Although most transfers are intra-activity, interactivity transactions are not uncommon. In its June 30, 2018, government-wide financial statements, the City of St. Louis reported (and then eliminated) internal balances of $11.0 million. These amounts appeared in the asset section of the statement of net position. On the statement of activities, the city shows offsetting transfers of $10.4 million between its governmental activities and its business-type activities.

Consequently, governments only report interfund transactions in their government-wide statements when it involves an interactivity transaction.

Monetary Transfers Illustrated

The most common interfund transactions are transfers within the governmental funds to ensure adequate financing of budgeted expenditures. For example, a city council could vote to transfer $2,000,000 from the general fund to a capital projects fund to cover a portion of the construction cost of a new school building.

Fund Financial Statements—Intra-Activity Transaction

General Fund		
Other Financing Uses—Transfers Out—Capital Projects Fund.	2,000,000	
Due to Capital Projects Fund (a payable).		2,000,000
To record authorization of transfer for school construction.		

Capital Projects Fund—School Building		
Due from General Fund (a receivable)	2,000,000	
Other Financing Sources—Transfers In—General Fund		2,000,000
To record authorization of transfer for school construction.		

The *Other Financing Uses/Sources* designations are appropriate here for the fund financial statements. Financial resources are moved into and out of these two governmental funds without either a revenue or an expenditure. As Exhibit 16.4 shows, these sources and uses are reported in the statement of revenues, expenditures, and other changes in fund balances. The figures are shown but not offset in any way. Both accounts are then closed out at the end of the current year.

In contrast, the *Due to/Due from* accounts in the preceding entries are the equivalent of interfund payable and receivable balances. They appear on the governmental funds balance sheet. Again, no elimination is made in arriving at total figures.

Because this transfer is an intra activity transaction, no reporting appears in the government-wide financial statements. Financial resources are simply shifted within the governmental activities with no net effect.

Not all monetary transfers are for normal operating purposes. Governments can also make nonrecurring or non-routine transfers. For example, officials might transfer money from the general fund to create or expand an enterprise fund such as a bus system or a toll road. To illustrate, assume a city internally transfers $20 million of previously unassigned money to help permanently finance a new subway system that will be open to the public. For convenience, this transaction is recorded as if cash is transferred immediately so that no receivable or payable is necessary. Each fund records the following.

Fund Financial Statements—Interactivity Transaction

General Fund		
Other Financing Uses—Transfers Out—Subway System	20,000,000	
Cash		20,000,000
To record transfer to help finance subway system.		

This transfer is an interactivity transaction (between governmental activities and business-type activities), so entries are also made for the government-wide financial statements. The transfer reduces the assets of the governmental activities but increases the assets held by the business-type activities. These two transfer balances are shown but will be offset in arriving at totals for the government as a whole.

Government-Wide Financial Statements—Interactivity Transaction

Governmental Activities		
Transfers Out—Subway System	20,000,000	
Cash		20,000,000
To record transfer to help finance subway system.		

Business-Type Activities		
Cash	20,000,000	
Transfers In—General Fund		20,000,000
To record receipt of transfer from unrestricted funds.		

Internal Exchange Transactions

Some payments made within a government are not transfers but are actually the same as transactions with an outside party. For example, a city will likely compensate its own print shop (or other internal service fund or enterprise fund) for services or materials acquired as if an outside vendor performed the work. To avoid confusion in reporting, such transfers are recorded as revenues and as expenditures or expenses. These transactions are not the equivalent of a transfer. Payments are made for work done or materials acquired. They are not designed to shift financial resources from one fund to another.

Fund financial statements record and report all such internal exchange transactions. However, as previously discussed, most internal service funds appear within governmental activities on the government-wide statements. Exchanges between a governmental fund and one of these internal service funds will have no net impact on the government-wide figures. The increases and decreases offset. Therefore, those balances are omitted.

To illustrate, assume that a city government pays its print shop (an internal service fund) $15,000 for work done for the police department. In addition, the government pays another $6,000 to a toll road operated as an enterprise fund to allow fire department vehicles to ride on the highway without having to make individual payments.

Fund Financial Statements—Internal Exchange Transaction

General Fund		
Expenditures—Printing	15,000	
Expenditures—Toll Road Privileges	6,000	
Cash		21,000
To record payment for printing supplies for use by police department and for use of a toll road by fire department.		

Internal Service Fund—Print Shop		
Cash	15,000	
Revenues		15,000
To record collection of money paid by the police department for printed materials.		

Enterprise Fund—Toll Road		
Cash	6,000	
Revenues		6,000
To record collection of money from government for fire department vehicular use of toll roads.		

The government-wide financial statements will not reflect the $15,000 transaction with the print shop if this internal service fund is classified within the governmental activities. In that case, the transfer is the equivalent of an intra-activity transaction. However, the $6,000 payment made by the police department (a governmental activity) to the toll road (an enterprise fund and, thus, a business-type activity) is the same as an interactivity transfer and reported through the following entries.

Government-Wide Financial Statements—Internal Exchange Transaction

Governmental Activities		
Expenses—Toll Road Privileges	6,000	
Cash		6,000
To record payment for use of toll road by fire department's vehicles.		

Business-Type Activities		
Cash	6,000	
Revenues		6,000
To record collection of money from government for fire department vehicular use of toll roads.		

Summary

1. Readers of state and local government financial statements desire a wide variety of information. No single set of financial statements is capable of meeting all those user needs, a factor that has led to the requirement that two sets of statements be reported. Accountability of government officials and control over public spending have been essential elements of traditional government accounting. By requiring two sets of financial statements, GASB is able to keep those priorities in place while also broadening the scope of the government's financial reporting.
2. A state or local government prepares fund financial statements to report the various transactions of individual funds. In this system, activities are classified into three broad categories (governmental, proprietary, and fiduciary). Governmental funds account for service activities. Proprietary funds account for activities for which a user charge is assessed. Fiduciary funds account for resources that the government holds as a trustee for an external party.
3. Governmental funds are further divided into five fund types: the general fund, special revenue funds, capital projects funds, debt service funds, and permanent funds. Proprietary funds are composed of enterprise funds and internal service funds. Fiduciary funds are composed of pension trust funds, investment trust funds, private-purpose trust funds, and custodial (formerly agency) funds.

4. Government-wide financial statements are made up of (a) a statement of net position and (b) a statement of activities. Government-wide statements separately report governmental activities (the governmental funds and most internal service funds) and business-type activities (enterprise funds and occasionally an internal service fund). These statements measure all economic resources. The timing of recognition is guided by accrual accounting. Fiduciary funds are not included because the government does not control those resources.
5. Fund financial statements include a number of financial statements. This chapter focuses mainly on (a) the balance sheet for the governmental funds and (b) the statement of revenues, expenditures, and other changes in fund balances for the governmental funds. These statements separately report the general fund and any other individual fund that qualifies as major. For the governmental funds, these statements report current financial resources (mostly cash, receivables, and investments and claims on those current financial resources). Modified accrual accounting guides the timing of recognition.
6. "Fund balance" figures reflect the net amount of resources held by a particular fund classified within the governmental funds. To indicate the government's level of control over these resources, fund financial statements classify the fund balance as nonspendable (a specific resource cannot be spent), restricted (use has been designated by a party outside the government), committed (use has been approved by the highest level of authority within the government), assigned (use has been set by the government but not by the highest level of authority), and unassigned (use has not been designated). In this way, any government official becomes aware of the amount of money over which the official might have some power.
7. To aid in control over financial resources and also to disclose government allocation decisions, the approved budgets for several of the governmental funds are recorded each year. The initial budget, a final amended budget, and actual figures for the period are reported as required supplementary information along with the financial statements (or as a separate statement within the fund financial statements).
8. Monetary commitments for purchase orders and contracts can be recorded in the individual governmental funds by recognizing encumbrances. These balances are recorded when the commitment is made, and it is removed when an actual claim to current financial resources first comes into existence. This recording helps government officials avoid spending more than the amounts properly appropriated.
9. The fund financial statements recognize expenditures for capital outlay, long-term debt payment, and expense-type costs (but only when a claim to current financial resources is created.) In contrast, government-wide financial statements capitalize capital outlay, reduce liabilities for debt payments, and record expenses.
10. Revenue recognition for nonexchange transactions such as sales taxes and property taxes is based on a classification system. The timing and method of recognition depend on whether the revenue is a derived tax revenue, imposed nonexchange revenue, government-mandated nonexchange transaction, or voluntary nonexchange transaction.
11. The issuance of long-term bonds is recorded as an "other financing source" by the governmental funds because the financial resource inflow is not a revenue. However, the same event is reported as an increase in long-term liabilities both in the proprietary funds and in the government-wide financial statements as a whole.
12. Transfers between funds are normally reported as an "other financing source" and "other financing use" within the fund financial statements. To show the impact on each fund type, these balances are not eliminated or offset. The government-wide statements do not report such transactions unless they have an effect on overall governmental activities or business-type activities. If reported, the amounts are offset in arriving at figures for the government as a whole. For internal exchange transactions in which payment is made for a good or service, the fund statements recognize a revenue and an expenditure or expense. The government-wide financial statements normally do not reflect internal exchange transfers unless they occur between an enterprise fund and a governmental fund.

Comprehensive Illustration

Problem

(*Estimated Time: 50 Minutes*). The Town of Drexel has the following financial transactions.

1. The town council adopts an annual budget for the general fund with estimated general revenues of $1.7 million, approved expenditures of $1.5 million, and approved transfers out of $120,000.
2. The town levies property taxes of $1.3 million. It expects to collect all but 3 percent of these taxes during the current year. Of the collected amount, the government will receive $40,000 next year after more than 60 days into that year.
3. The town orders two new police cars at an approximate cost of $150,000.
4. A transfer of $50,000 is made from the general fund to the debt service fund.
5. The town makes a payment on a bond payable of $40,000 along with $10,000 of interest using the money previously set aside.
6. The Town of Drexel issues a $2 million bond at face value in hopes of acquiring a building to convert into a high school.
7. The two police cars are received with an invoice price of $152,000. An official approved the voucher but the government will not pay it for three weeks.
8. The town purchases the building mentioned earlier to use as a high school for $2 million in cash and immediately begins the renovation.
9. Depreciation on the new police cars is computed as $30,000 for the period.
10. The town borrows $100,000 on a 30-day tax anticipation note.
11. The Town of Drexel begins a special assessment curbing project at the request of property owners. The government issues $800,000 in notes at face value to finance the work. The town guarantees the debt if a sufficient amount is not collected from the property owners.
12. A contractor completes the curbing project and is paid the entire $800,000 as agreed.
13. The town assesses citizens $850,000 for the completed curbing project.
14. The town collects the special assessments of $850,000 in full and repays the debt plus $50,000 in interest.
15. The town receives a $10,000 cash grant from a regional charity to beautify a local park. According to terms of the grant, the money must cover the specific costs incurred by the town.
16. The town spends the first $4,000 to beautify the park.

Required

a. Prepare journal entries in anticipation of preparing fund financial statements.

b. Prepare journal entries in anticipation of preparing government-wide financial statements.

Solution

a. ***Fund Financial Statements***

1. **General Fund**

Estimated Revenues	1,700,000	
Appropriations		1,500,000
Estimated Other Financing Uses		120,000
Budgetary Fund Balance		80,000

2. **General Fund**

Property Tax Receivable	1,300,000	
Allowance for Uncollectible Taxes		39,000
Unavailable Property Tax Revenues		40,000
Revenues—Property Taxes		1,221,000

3. **General Fund**

Encumbrances—Police Cars	150,000	
Encumbrances Outstanding		150,000

4. **General Fund**

Other Financing Uses—Transfers Out	50,000	
Cash		50,000

Debt Service Funds

Cash	50,000	
Other Financing Sources—Transfers In		50,000

5. **Debt Service Funds**

Expenditures—Principal	40,000	
Expenditures—Interest	10,000	
Cash		50,000

6. **Capital Projects Funds**

Cash	2,000,000	
Other Financing Sources—Bond Proceeds		2,000,000

7. **General Fund**

Encumbrances Outstanding	150,000	
Encumbrances—Police Cars		150,000
Expenditures—Police Cars	152,000	
Vouchers Payable		152,000

8. **Capital Projects Funds**

Expenditures—Building	2,000,000	
Cash		2,000,000

9. No entry is recorded. Expenditures rather than expenses are recorded by the governmental funds. Depreciation is not an expenditure.

10. **General Fund**

Cash	100,000	
Tax Anticipation Note Payable		100,000

11. **Capital Projects Funds**

Cash	800,000	
Other Financing Sources—Special Assessments Note		800,000

12. **Capital Projects Funds**

Expenditures—Curbing	800,000	
Cash		800,000

13. **Debt Service Funds**

Taxes Receivable—Special Assessment	850,000	
Revenues—Special Assessment		850,000

14. **Debt Service Funds**

Cash	850,000	
Taxes Receivable—Special Assessment		850,000
Expenditures—Principal	800,000	
Expenditures—Interest	50,000	
Cash		850,000

15. **Special Revenue Funds**

Cash	10,000	
Grant Collected in Advance		10,000

16. **Special Revenue Funds**

Expenditures—Park Beautification	4,000	
Cash		4,000
Grant Collected in Advance	4,000	
Revenues—Grants		4,000

*b. **Government-Wide Financial Statements***

1. Budgetary entries are not reported within the government-wide financial statements. Budgets are recorded in the individual funds and are then shown as required supplementary information or in a separate fund financial statement.

2. **Governmental Activities**

Property Tax Receivable	1,300,000	
Allowance for Uncollectible Taxes		39,000
Revenues—Property Taxes		1,261,000

3. Commitments are not reported in government-wide financial statements.
4. This transfer was entirely within the governmental funds and, therefore, creates no net effect on the governmental activities. It is an intra-activity transaction. No journal entry is needed for government-wide statements.

5. **Governmental Activities**

Bonds Payable	40,000	
Interest Expense	10,000	
Cash		50,000

6. **Governmental Activities**

Cash	2,000,000	
Bonds Payable		2,000,000

7. **Governmental Activities**

Police Cars (or Vehicles)	152,000	
Vouchers (or Accounts) Payable		152,000

8. **Governmental Activities**

Building	2,000,000	
Cash		2,000,000

9. **Governmental Activities**

Depreciation Expense	30,000	
Accumulated Depreciation		30,000

10. **Governmental Activities**

Cash	100,000	
Tax Anticipation Note Payable		100,000

11. **Governmental Activities**

Cash	800,000	
Special Assessment Notes Payable		800,000

12. **Governmental Activities**

Infrastructure Assets—Curbing	800,000	
Cash		800,000

13. **Governmental Activities**

Taxes Receivable—Special Assessment	850,000	
Revenues—Special Assessment		850,000

14. **Governmental Activities**

Cash	850,000	
Taxes Receivable—Special Assessment		850,000
Special Assessment Notes Payable	800,000	
Interest Expense	50,000	
Cash		850,000

15. **Governmental Activities**

Cash	10,000	
Grant Collected in Advance		10,000

16. **Governmental Activities**

Expenses—Park Beautification	4,000	
Cash		4,000
Grant Collected in Advance	4,000	
Revenues—Grants		4,000

Questions

1. How have users' needs impacted the development of accounting principles for the reporting of state and local government units?
2. Why have accountability and control been so important in the traditional accounting for state and local government units?
3. How has the dual system of financial statements affected the financial reporting of state and local governments?
4. What are the basic financial statements that a state or local government now produces?
5. What measurement focus is used in fund financial statements for governmental funds? What system is applied to determine the timing of revenue and expenditure recognition?
6. What measurement focus is used in government-wide financial statements? What system is applied to determine the timing of revenue and expense recognition?
7. What assets are viewed as current financial resources?
8. In applying the current financial resources measurement focus, when are liabilities recognized in fund financial statements for the governmental funds?
9. What are the three categories of funds? What funds are included in each of these three categories?
10. What are the five fund types within the governmental funds? What events do each of these five fund types report?
11. What are the two fund types within the proprietary funds? What types of events does each report?
12. What are the four fund types within the fiduciary funds? What types of events does each report?
13. What are the two major divisions reported in government-wide financial statements? What funds are *not* reported in these financial statements?
14. Fund financial statements have separate columns for each activity. Which activities are reported individually in this manner?
15. The general fund of a city reports assets of $300,000 and liabilities of $200,000 in fund financial statements. Explain what is meant by each of the following balances: fund balance—nonspendable of $40,000, fund balance—restricted of $28,000, fund balance—committed of $17,000, fund balance—assigned of $4,000, and fund balance—unassigned of $11,000.
16. Why are budgetary entries recorded in several of the individual funds of a state or local government?
17. How are budget results shown in the financial reporting of a state or local government?

18. What is an encumbrance? When is an encumbrance recorded? What happens to this balance? How are encumbrances reported in government-wide financial statements?
19. What costs necessitate the reporting of an expenditure by a governmental fund?
20. At what point does a governmental fund report an expenditure?
21. How do governmental funds report capital outlay in fund financial statements? How do government-wide financial statements report capital expenditures?
22. What are the two different ways that a state or local government can report the cost and use of supplies and prepaid items on fund financial statements for governmental funds?
23. What are the four classifications of nonexchange revenues that a state or local government can report? In each case, when are revenues normally recognized?
24. When does a government recognize a receivable for property tax assessments? When is the associated revenue recognized?
25. How is the issuance of a long-term bond reported on fund financial statements for a governmental fund? How is the issuance of a long-term bond reported on government-wide financial statements?
26. What is a special assessment project? Describe the reporting of a special assessment project.
27. How does a state or local government report interfund transfers in the fund financial statements for the governmental funds?
28. In government-wide financial statements, how do intra-activity and interactivity transactions differ? How does a state or local government report each type of transaction?
29. What is an internal exchange transaction, and how is it reported?

Problems

LO 16-4

1. Which of the following is *not* a governmental fund?
   a. Special revenue fund
   b. Internal service fund
   c. Capital projects fund
   d. Debt service fund

LO 16-4

2. What is the purpose of a special revenue fund?
   a. To account for revenues legally or externally restricted as an operating expenditure
   b. To account for ongoing activities
   c. To account for gifts when only subsequently earned income can be expended
   d. To account for the cost of long-lived assets bought with designated funds

LO 16-4

3. What is the purpose of enterprise funds?
   a. To account for operations that provide services to other departments within a government
   b. To account for asset transfers
   c. To account for ongoing activities such as the police and fire departments
   d. To account for operations financed in whole or in part by outside user charges

LO 16-4

4. Which of the following statements is true?
   a. There are three different types of proprietary funds.
   b. There are three different types of fiduciary funds.
   c. There are five different types of fiduciary funds.
   d. There are five different types of governmental funds.

LO 16-1, 16-6

5. A government expects to receive revenues of $400,000 but has approved expenditures of $430,000. The anticipated shortage will have an impact on which of the following?
   a. Interperiod equity
   b. Modified accrual accounting
   c. Consumption accounting
   d. Account groups

LO 16-4

6. A citizen donates investments valued at $22,000 to the City of Townsend. The citizen stipulates that the investments be held. Any resulting income must be used to help maintain the city's cemetery. In which fund should the city report this investment?
   a. Special revenue funds
   b. Capital projects funds
   c. Permanent funds
   d. General fund

LO 16-2

7. Which of the following statements is correct about the reporting of governmental funds?
   a. Fund financial statements measure only economic resources.
   b. Government-wide financial statements measure only current financial resources.
   c. Fund financial statements measure both economic resources and current financial resources.
   d. Government-wide financial statements measure economic resources.

LO 16-2

8. Which of the following statements is correct about the reporting of governmental funds?
   a. Fund financial statements measure revenues and expenditures based on modified accrual accounting.
   b. Government-wide financial statements measure revenues and expenses based on modified accrual accounting.
   c. Fund financial statements measure revenues and expenses based on accrual accounting.
   d. Government-wide financial statements measure revenues and expenditures based on accrual accounting.

LO 16-2, 16-7

9. During the current year, the City of Jones buys land for $80,000. Which of the following is *not* a possibility?
   a. The land could be reported as an asset by the business-type activities in the government-wide financial statements.
   b. The land could be reported as an asset by the governmental activities in the government-wide financial statements.
   c. The land could be reported as an asset by the proprietary funds in the fund financial statements.
   d. The land could be reported as an asset by the governmental funds in the fund financial statements.

LO 16-5

10. The City of Bagranoff holds $90,000 in cash that will be used to make a bond payment when the debt comes due early next year. The assistant treasurer initially made the decision to set this money aside for this purpose. Just before the end of the current year, the city council formally approved using the money in this way. The city council is the highest level of decision-making authority for this government. What impact does the council's action have on the reporting of fund financial statements?
    a. Fund balance—unassigned goes down and fund balance—restricted goes up.
    b. Fund balance—assigned goes down and fund balance—committed goes up.
    c. Fund balance—unassigned goes down and fund balance—assigned goes up.
    d. Fund balance—assigned goes down and fund balance—restricted goes up.

LO 16-6

11. Which of the following statements is true concerning the recording of a budget?
    a. At the beginning of the year, a debit is made to Appropriations.
    b. A debit to the Budgetary Fund Balance account indicates an expected surplus for the period.
    c. At the beginning of the year, a debit is made to Estimated Revenues.
    d. At the end of the year, a credit is made to Appropriations.

LO 16-1, 16-2, 16-7

12. The general fund pays rent for two months. Which of the following is *not* correct?
    a. Rent expense should be reported in the government-wide financial statements.
    b. Rent expense should be reported in the fund financial statements.
    c. An expenditure should eventually be reported in the fund financial statements.
    d. If one month of rent is in the first year with the other month in the next year, either the purchases method or the consumption method can be used in fund financial statements.

LO 16-6, 16-7

13. A purchase order for $3,000 is recorded in the general fund for the purchase of a new computer. The computer is received, but the actual cost is $3,020 because of a sales tax. Which of the following statements is correct for fund financial statements?
    a. Machinery is increased by $3,020.
    b. An encumbrance account is reduced by $3,020.
    c. An expenditure is increased by $3,020.
    d. An expenditure is recorded for the additional $20.

LO 16-5

14. At the end of the current year, a government reports $9,000 as a fund balance—assigned in connection with an encumbrance. What information does this balance convey?
    a. A donor has given the government $9,000 that must be used in a specified fashion.
    b. The government has made $9,000 in commitments in one year that will be honored in the subsequent year.

c. Encumbrances exceeded expenditures by $9,000 during the current year.

d. The government spent $9,000 less during the year than was appropriated.

LO 16-2, 16-3, 16-7

15. A government buys equipment for its police department at a cost of $54,000. Which of the following is *not* true?

    a. Equipment will increase by $54,000 in the government-wide financial statements.

    b. Depreciation in connection with this equipment will be reported in the fund financial statements.

    c. The equipment will not appear within the reported assets in the fund financial statements.

    d. An expenditure for $54,000 will be reported in the fund financial statements.

LO 16-3, 16-7

16. A city acquires supplies for its fire department and uses the consumption method of accounting. Which of the following statements is true for the fund financial statements?

    a. An expenditures account is debited at the time of receipt.

    b. An expense is recorded as the supplies are consumed.

    c. An inventory account is debited at the time of the acquisition.

    d. The supplies are recorded within the General Fixed Assets Account Group.

LO 16-8

17. An income tax is an example of which of the following?

    a. Derived tax revenue

    b. Imposed nonexchange revenue

    c. Government-mandated nonexchange revenue

    d. Voluntary nonexchange transaction

LO 16-8

18. The state government passes a law requiring all localities to upgrade their water treatment facilities. The state then awards a grant of $500,000 to the Town of Midlothian to help pay for the resulting cost. What type of revenue is this grant?

    a. Derived tax revenue

    b. Imposed nonexchange revenue

    c. Government-mandated nonexchange revenue

    d. Voluntary nonexchange transaction

LO 16-8

19. The state awards a grant of $50,000 to the Town of Glenville. The state will pay the grant money to the town but only as a reimbursement for money spent on road repair. At the time of the grant, the state pays $8,000 in advance. During the first year of this program, the town spent $14,000 and applies for reimbursement. What amount of revenue should be recognized this year?

    a. $-0-

    b. $8,000

    c. $14,000

    d. $50,000

LO 16-5, 16-9

20. A city issues a 60-day tax anticipation note to fund operations until the collection of sufficient tax money. How does the city record this liability?

    a. The liability should be reported in the government-wide financial statements, whereas an other financing source should be shown in the fund financial statements.

    b. A liability should be reported in both the government-wide financial statements and the fund financial statements.

    c. An other financing source should be shown in both the government-wide financial statements and the fund financial statements.

    d. An other financing source should be shown in the government-wide financial statements, whereas a liability is reported in the fund financial statements.

LO 16-5, 16-9

21. A city issues five-year bonds payable to finance construction of a new school. What recording should be made?

    a. Report the liability in the government-wide financial statements. Show an other financing source in the fund financial statements.

    b. Report a liability in both the government-wide financial statements and the fund financial statements.

    c. Show an other financing source in both the government-wide financial statements and the fund financial statements.

    d. Show an other financing source in the government-wide financial statements. Report a liability in the fund financial statements.

LO 16-9

22. The City of Dylan issues a 10-year bond payable of $1 million at face value on the first day of Year 1. Debt issuance costs of $10,000 are paid on that day. For government-wide financial statements, how is this debt issuance cost reported?
    a. $1,000 is recorded as an expense, and $9,000 is recorded as an asset.
    b. $1,000 is recorded as an expense, and $9,000 is recorded as a deferred outflow of resources.
    c. $10,000 is recorded as an expense.
    d. $10,000 is recorded as an asset.

LO 16-9

23. The City of Frost has a 20-year debt outstanding. On the last day of the current year, this debt has an outstanding balance of $4.8 million, and five years remain until it comes due. On the current date, the debt is paid off early for $5 million. A new debt is issued (with a lower interest rate) for $5.4 million. How is the $200,000 difference between the amount paid and the outstanding balance of $4.8 million reported on government-wide financial statements?
    a. As an expense
    b. As a reduction in liabilities
    c. As a deferred outflow of resources on the statement of net position
    d. As an asset on the statement of net position

LO 16-2, 16-9

24. A $110,000 payment is made on a long-term liability. Of this amount, $10,000 represents interest. Which of the following is *not* true for the recording of this transaction?
    a. Reduce liabilities by $100,000 in the government-wide financial statements.
    b. Record a $110,000 expenditure in the fund financial statements.
    c. Reduce liabilities by $100,000 in the fund financial statements.
    d. Recognize $10,000 interest expense in the government-wide financial statements.

LO 16-1, 16-10

25. A city constructs a special assessment project (a sidewalk) for which it is secondarily liable. The city issues bonds of $90,000. It authorizes another $10,000 transferred out of the general fund. The sidewalk is built for $100,000, and payment is made. The citizens are billed for $90,000. They pay this amount, and the debt is paid off. Where is the $100,000 expenditure for construction recorded?
    a. It is not recorded by the city.
    b. It is recorded in a custodial fund.
    c. It is recorded in the general fund.
    d. It is recorded in a capital projects fund.

LO 16-4, 16-10

26. A city constructs curbing in a new neighborhood and finances it as a special assessment. Under what condition should these transactions be recorded in a custodial fund?
    a. Never; the work is reported in a capital projects fund.
    b. Only if the city is secondarily liable for any debt incurred to finance construction costs.
    c. Only if the city is in no way liable for the costs of the construction.
    d. In all cases.

LO 16-11

27. Which of the following is an example of an interactivity transaction?
    a. A city transfers money from the general fund to a debt service fund.
    b. A city transfers money from a capital projects fund to the general fund.
    c. A city transfers money from a special revenue fund to a debt service fund.
    d. A city transfers money from the general fund to an enterprise fund.

LO 16-5, 16-11

28. A town transfers cash of $60,000 from its general fund to a debt service fund. What does the town report in its government-wide financial statements?
    a. No reporting is made.
    b. Other Financing Sources increase by $60,000. Other Financing Uses increase by $60,000.
    c. Revenues increase by $60,000. Expenditures increase by $60,000.
    d. Revenues increase by $60,000. Expenses increase by $60,000.

LO 16-5, 16-11

29. A county transfers cash of $60,000 from its general fund to a debt service fund. What is reported on the county's fund financial statements?
    a. No reporting is made.
    b. Other Financing Sources increase by $60,000. Other Financing Uses increase by $60,000.
    c. Revenues increase by $60,000. Expenditures increase by $60,000.
    d. Revenues increase by $60,000. Expenses increase by $60,000.

LO 16-5, 16-11

30. A city transfers cash of $20,000 from its general fund to an enterprise fund to pay for work performed by the enterprise fund for the school system. How does the city report this transfer on its government-wide financial statements?
    a. No reporting is made.
    b. Other Financing Sources increase by $20,000. Other Financing Uses increase by $20,000.
    c. Revenues increase by $20,000. Expenditures increase by $20,000.
    d. Revenues increase by $20,000. Expenses increase by $20,000.

LO 16-5, 16-11

31. A city transfers cash of $20,000 from its general fund to an enterprise fund to pay for work done by the enterprise fund for the school system. What is reported on the city's fund financial statements?
    a. No reporting is made.
    b. Other Financing Sources increase by $20,000. Other Financing Uses increase by $20,000.
    c. Revenues increase by $20,000. Expenditures increase by $20,000.
    d. Revenues increase by $20,000. Expenses increase by $20,000.

LO 16-3, 16-6

32. The board of commissioners of the City of Hartmoore adopts a general fund budget for the year ending June 30, 2020. It includes revenues of $1,000,000, bond proceeds of $400,000, appropriations of $900,000, and operating transfers out of $300,000. If this budget is formally integrated into the accounting records, what journal entry is required at the beginning of the year? What later entry is required?

LO 16-2, 16-6, 16-7

33. A city orders a new computer for its police department that is recorded within its general fund. The computer has an anticipated cost of $88,000. Its actual cost when received is $89,400. Payment is subsequently made. Prepare all required journal entries for both fund and government-wide financial statements. What information is found on the fund financial statements? What information is found on the government-wide financial statements?

LO 16-1, 16-2, 16-7

34. A city transfers cash of $90,000 from its general fund to start construction on a police station. The city issues a bond at its $1.8 million face value. The police station is built for a total cost of $1.89 million. Prepare all necessary journal entries for these transactions for both fund and government-wide financial statements. Assume that the city does not record the commitment for this construction. What information is found on the fund financial statements? What information is found on the government-wide financial statements?

LO 16-5

35. The governmental funds of the City of Westchester report $445,000 in assets and $140,000 in liabilities. The following are some of the assets that the government reports.

    - Prepaid items—$7,000
    - Cash from a bond issuance that must be spent within the school system according to the bond indenture—$80,000
    - Supplies—$5,000
    - Investments given by a citizen that will be sold soon with the proceeds used to beautify a public park—$33,000
    - Cash that the assistant director of finance designated for use in upgrading the local roads—$40,000
    - Cash from a state grant that must be spent to supplement the pay of local kindergarten teachers—$53,000
    - Cash that the city council (the highest level of decision-making authority in the government) voted to use in renovating a school gymnasium—$62,000

    On a balance sheet for the governmental funds, what fund balance amounts should the City of Westchester report?

LO 16-5

36. Government officials of Hampstead County ordered a computer near the end of the current fiscal year for $6,400 to be used by the police department. It failed to arrive prior to the end of the year. At its final meeting of the year, the city council (the highest decision-making authority for the government) agreed to pay for the computer when delivered in the subsequent year. In preparing a set of government-wide financial statements and a set of fund financial statements for the current year, how will this purchase be reported?

LO 16-2, 16-5, 16-11

37. A local government has the following transactions during the current fiscal period. Prepare journal entries without dollar amounts, first for fund financial statements and then for government-wide financial statements.
    a. The budget for the police department, ambulance service, and other ongoing activities is passed. Funding is from property taxes, transfers, and bond proceeds. All monetary outflows will be for expenses and fixed assets. A deficit is projected.

b. A bond is issued at face value to fund the construction of a new municipal building.

c. The government orders a computer for the tax department.

d. The computer is received.

e. The invoice for the computer is paid.

f. The city council agrees to transfer money from the general fund as partial payment for a special assessments construction project, but the funds have not yet been transferred. The city will be secondarily liable for any money borrowed to finance this construction.

g. The city council creates a motor pool to service all government vehicles. Money is transferred from the general fund to permanently finance this facility.

h. Property taxes are levied. Although officials believe that most of these taxes will be collected during the current period, they anticipate that a small percentage will be uncollectible.

i. The city collects grant money from the state that must be spent to supplement the salaries of the police force. The city has not yet made any journal entry. Appropriate payment of the supplement is viewed as an eligibility requirement.

j. A portion of the grant money in (*i*) is properly spent.

LO 16-2, 16-4, 16-7, 16-8, 16-11

38. Prepare journal entries for the City of Pudding's governmental funds to record the following transactions, first for fund financial statements and then for government-wide financial statements.

a. A new truck for the sanitation department was ordered at a cost of $94,000.

b. The city print shop did $1,200 worth of work for the school system (but has not yet been paid).

c. An $11 million bond was issued at face value to build a new road.

d. The city transfers cash of $140,000 from its general fund to provide permanent financing for a municipal swimming pool that will be maintained as an enterprise fund.

e. The truck ordered in (*a*) is received but at an actual cost of $96,000. Payment is not made at this time.

f. The city transfers cash of $32,000 from its general fund to a capital projects fund.

g. The city receives a state grant of $30,000 that must be spent to promote recycling by the citizens.

h. The first $5,000 of the state grant received in (*g*) is expended as intended.

LO 16-2, 16-5, 16-7, 16-8, 16-9, 16-11

39. Prepare journal entries for a local government to record the following transactions, first for fund financial statements and then for government-wide financial statements.

a. The government sells $900,000 in bonds at face value to finance the construction of a new warehouse.

b. A $1.1 million contract is signed for construction of the warehouse. The commitment is reported, if allowed.

c. The government transfers cash of $130,000 in unrestricted funds for the eventual payment of the debt in (*a*).

d. The government receives equipment for the fire department with a cost of $12,000. When ordered, an anticipated cost of $11,800 was recorded.

e. Supplies to be used in the schools are bought for $2,000 cash. The consumption method is used.

f. The state awards a grant of $90,000 to supplement police salaries. The money will be paid to reimburse the government but only after the supplement payments have been made.

g. The government mails property tax assessments to its citizens. The total assessment is $600,000, although officials anticipate that 4 percent will never be collected. The government holds an enforceable legal claim to this money. It can be spent immediately.

LO 16-4, 16-5, 16-6, 16-7, 16-8, 16-9, 16-10, 16-11

40. The following unadjusted trial balances are for the governmental funds of the City of Copeland.

General Fund	Debit	Credit
Cash	$ 19,000	
Taxes Receivable	202,000	
Allowance for Uncollectible Taxes		$ 2,000
Vouchers Payable		24,000
Due to Debt Service Fund		10,000
Unavailable Revenues		16,000
Encumbrances Outstanding		9,000
Fund Balance—Unassigned		103,000
Revenues		176,000

(continued)

(continued)

General Fund	Debit	Credit
Expenditures	110,000	
Encumbrances	9,000	
Estimated Revenues	190,000	
Appropriations		171,000
Budgetary Fund Balance		19,000
Totals	$530,000	$530,000

Debt Service Fund	Debit	Credit
Cash	$ 8,000	
Investments	51,000	
Taxes Receivable	11,000	
Due from General Fund	10,000	
Fund Balance—Committed		$ 45,000
Revenues		20,000
Other Financing Sources—Operating Transfers In		90,000
Expenditures	75,000	
Totals	$155,000	$155,000

Capital Projects Fund	Debit	Credit
Cash	$ 70,000	
Special Assessments Receivable	90,000	
Contracts Payable		$ 50,000
Unavailable Revenues		90,000
Encumbrances Outstanding		16,000
Fund Balance—Unassigned		–0–
Other Financing Sources		150,000
Expenditures	130,000	
Encumbrances	16,000	
Estimated Other Financing Sources	150,000	
Appropriations		150,000
Totals	$456,000	$456,000

Special Revenue Fund	Debit	Credit
Cash	$ 14,000	
Taxes Receivable	41,000	
Inventory of Supplies	4,000	
Vouchers Payable		$ 25,000
Grant Revenues Collected in Advance		3,000
Fund Balance—Nonspendable		4,000
Encumbrances Outstanding		3,000
Fund Balance—Unassigned		19,000
Revenues		56,000
Expenditures	48,000	
Encumbrances	3,000	
Estimated Revenues	75,000	
Appropriations		60,000
Budgetary Fund Balance		15,000
Totals	$185,000	$185,000

Based on the information presented for each of these governmental funds, answer the following questions:

a. How much more money can city officials expend or commit from the general fund during the remainder of the current year without amending the budget?

b. Why does the capital projects fund have no construction or capital asset accounts?

c. What does the $150,000 Appropriations balance found in the capital projects fund represent?

d. Several funds have balances for Encumbrances and Encumbrances Outstanding. How will these amounts be accounted for at the end of the fiscal year?

e. Why does the Fund Balance—Unassigned account in the capital projects fund have a zero balance?

f. What are possible explanations for the $150,000 Other Financing Sources balance found in the capital projects fund?

g. What does the $75,000 balance in the Expenditures account of the debt service fund represent?

h. What is the purpose of the Special Assessments Receivable found in the capital projects fund?

i. In the special revenue fund, what is the purpose of the Fund Balance—Nonspendable account?

j. Why does the debt service fund not have budgetary account balances?

LO 16-2, 16-3, 16-4, 16-5, 16-6, 16-7, 16-8, 16-9, 16-11

41. Following are descriptions of transactions and other financial events for the City of Tetris for the year ending December 2020. Not all transactions have been included here. Only the general fund formally records a budget. No encumbrances were carried over from 2019.

Paid salary for police officers	$ 21,000
Received government grant to pay ambulance drivers	40,000
Estimated revenues	232,000
Received invoices for rent on equipment used by fire department during last four months of the year	3,000
Paid for newly constructed city hall	1,044,000
Made commitment to acquire ambulance	111,000
Received cash from bonds sold for construction purposes	300,000
Placed order for new sanitation truck	154,000
Paid salary to ambulance drivers—money derived from state government grant given for that purpose	24,000
Paid for supplies for school system	16,000
Made transfer from General Fund to eventually pay off a long-term debt	33,000
Received but did not pay for new ambulance	120,000
Levied property tax receivables for 2020. City officials anticipate that 95% ($190,000) will be collected during the year and 5% will prove to be uncollectible	200,000
Acquired and paid for new school bus	40,000
Received cash from business licenses and parking meters (not previously accrued)	14,000
Approved appropriations	225,000

The following questions are *independent* although each is based on the preceding information. Assume that the government is preparing information for its fund financial statements.

a. What is the balance in the Budgetary Fund Balance account for the budget for the year? Is it a debit or credit?

b. Assume that 60 percent of the school supplies are used during the year so that 40 percent remain. If the consumption method is being applied, how is this recorded?

c. The sanitation truck that was ordered was not received before the end of the year. The commitment will be honored in the subsequent year when the truck arrives. What reporting is made at the end of 2020?

d. Assume that new ambulance was received on December 31, 2020. Provide all necessary journal entries on that date.

e. Prepare all journal entries that should have been made when the $33,000 transfer was made for the eventual payment of a long-term debt.

f. What amount of revenue should the city recognize for the period? Explain the composition of this total.

g. What are the total expenditures? Explain the makeup of this total. Include response to (*b*) here.

h. What journal entry or entries did the city prepare for the issuance of the bonds?

LO 16-2, 16-3, 16-4, 16-5, 16-6, 16-7, 16-8, 16-9, 16-11

42. Chesterfield County had the following transactions. Prepare the entries first for fund financial statements and then for government-wide financial statements.

    a. A budget is passed for all ongoing activities. Revenue is anticipated to be $834,000, with approved spending of $540,000 and operating transfers out of $242,000.

    b. A contract is signed with a construction company to build a new central office building for the government at a cost of $8 million. The county previously recorded the budget for this project.

    c. Bonds are issued for $8 million (face value) to finance construction of the new office building.

    d. The new building is completed. An invoice for $8 million is received by the county and paid.

    e. Previously unrestricted cash of $1 million is set aside by county officials to begin paying the bonds issued in (*c*).

    f. A portion of the bonds comes due, and $1 million is paid. Of this total, $100,000 represents interest. The interest had not been previously accrued.

    g. Property tax levies are assessed. Total billing for this tax is $800,000. On this date, the assessment is a legally enforceable claim according to the laws of the state. All money to be received is designated for the current period, and 90 percent is assumed to be collectible in this period. Receipt of an additional 6 percent is not expected until the subsequent period but in time to be available to pay current period claims. The remaining amount is viewed as uncollectible.

    h. The county collects cash of $120,000 from a toll road. The money is restricted for highway maintenance.

    i. The county receives stock investments valued at $300,000 as a donation from a grateful citizen. The investments are to be held permanently, but any income from these investments must be used to beautify local parks.

LO 16-5

eXcel

43. The following trial balance is taken from the General Fund of the City of Jennings for the year ending December 31, 2020. Prepare a condensed statement of revenues, expenditures, and other changes in fund balance. Also prepare a condensed balance sheet.

	Debit	Credit
Accounts Payable		$ 90,000
Cash	$ 30,000	
Contracts Payable		90,000
Unavailable Revenues		40,000
Due from Capital Projects Funds	60,000	
Due to Debt Service Funds		40,000
Expenditures	530,000	
Fund Balance—Unassigned		170,000
Investments	410,000	
Revenues		760,000
Other Financing Sources—Bond Proceeds		300,000
Other Financing Sources—Transfers In		50,000
Other Financing Uses—Transfers Out	470,000	
Taxes Receivable	220,000	
Vouchers Payable		180,000
Totals	$1,720,000	$1,720,000

LO 16-2, 16-5, 16-6, 16-7, 16-8, 16-9

44. A city has only one activity, its school system. The school system is accounted for within the general fund. For convenience, assume that, at the start of 2020, the school system and the city have no assets. During the year, the city assesses property taxes of $400,000. Of this amount, it collects $320,000 during the year, collects $50,000 within a few weeks after the end of the year, and expects the remainder to be collected about six months later. The city makes the following payments during 2020: salary expense, $100,000; rent expense, $70,000; equipment (received on January 1 with a five-year life and no salvage value), $50,000; land, $30,000; and maintenance expense, $20,000.

    In addition, on the last day of the year, the city purchases a $200,000 building by signing a long-term note payable. The building has a 20-year life and no salvage value, and the liability accrues interest at a 10 percent annual rate. The city also buys two computers on the last day of the year for $4,000 each. One will be paid for in 30 days and the other in 90 days. The computers should last four years and have no expected residual value. During the year, the school system charges students $3,000 for school fees and collects the entire amount. The city determines depreciation using the straight-line method.

LO 16-5, 16-7, 16-8, 16-9, 16-11

47. The following transactions relate to the general fund of the city of Lost Angels for the year ending December 31, 2020. Prepare a statement of revenues, expenditures, and other changes in fund balance for the general fund for the period to be included in the fund financial statements. Assume that the fund balance at the beginning of the year was $180,000. Assume also that the city applies the purchases method to supplies. Receipt within 60 days serves as the definition of available resources.
   a. Collects property tax revenue of $700,000. A remaining assessment of $100,000 will be collected in the subsequent period. Half of that amount should be received within 30 days, and the remainder approximately five months after the end of the year.
   b. Spends $200,000 on three new police cars with 10-year lives. The anticipated price was $207,000 when the cars were ordered. The city calculates all depreciation using the straight-line method with no expected residual value. The city applies the half-year convention.
   c. Transfers $90,000 of unrestricted cash to a debt service fund.
   d. Issues a long-term bond for its $200,000 face value on July 1. Interest at a 10 percent annual rate will be paid each year starting on June 30, 2021.
   e. Orders a new computer with a five-year life for $40,000.
   f. Pays salaries of $30,000. Another $10,000 is owed to employees at the end of the year but will not be paid for 30 days.
   g. Receives the new computer near the end of 2020. The actual cost is $41,000. Payment is to be made in 45 days.
   h. Buys supplies for $10,000 in cash.
   i. Uses $8,000 of the supplies bought in (*h*).

LO 16-7, 16-8, 16-9, 16-11

48. Use the transactions in problem (47) but prepare a statement of net position for the government-wide financial statements. Assume that the general fund held $180,000 in cash on the first day of the year and no other assets or liabilities. No amount of the cash was restricted, committed, or assigned.

LO 16-1, 16-6

49. Government officials of the City of Johnson expect to receive general fund revenues of $400,000 in 2020 but approve spending only $380,000. Later in the year, as they receive more information, they increase the revenue projection to $420,000. Officials also approve the spending of an additional $15,000. For each of the following, indicate whether the statement is true or false and, if false, explain why.
   a. In recording this budget, appropriations are credited initially for $380,000.
   b. The city must disclose this budgetary data within the required supplemental information section reported after the notes to the financial statements.
   c. When reporting budgetary information for the year, three figures should be reported: amended budget, initial budget, and actual figures.
   d. In making the budgetary entry, a debit must be made to some type of Fund Balance account to indicate the projected surplus and its effect on the future size of the fund.
   e. The reporting of the budget is presented in the government-wide financial statements.

LO 16-8

50. On December 1, 2020, a state government awards a city government a grant of $1 million to be used specifically to provide hot lunches for all schoolchildren. No money is received until June 1, 2021. For each of the following, indicate whether the statement is true or false and, if false, explain why.
   a. Because the government receives no money until June 1, 2021, no amount of revenue can be recognized in 2020 on the government-wide financial statements.
   b. If this grant has no eligibility requirements and the money is properly spent in September 2021 for the hot lunches, the revenue should be recognized during that September.
   c. Because this money came from the state government and because that government specified its use, this is a government-mandated nonexchange transaction.
   d. If the government had received the money on December 1, 2020, but eligibility reimbursement requirements had not been met, unearned revenue of $1 million would have been recognized on the government-wide financial statements.

LO 16-7, 16-8, 16-9, 16-11

51. The following are transactions of the City of Grayson. Indicate how each of the following transactions affects the fund balance of the general fund, and its classifications, for fund financial statements. Then describe the effect each transaction has on the net position balance of the Government Activities on the government-wide financial statements.
   a. Issues a five-year bond for its face value of $6 million to finance general operations.
   b. Pays cash of $149,000 for a truck to be used by the police department.

c. The city's fire department pays $17,000 to a government motor pool that services vehicles owned by the police and fire departments. Work was done on several department vehicles.

d. Levies property taxes of $75,000 for the current year that will not be collected until four months into the subsequent year.

e. Receives a grant for $7,000 from a charity that must be returned unless the money is spent according to the stipulations of the conveyance. Those actions are expected to happen in the future.

f. Local businesses make sales of $20 million during the current year. The government assesses a 5 percent sales tax. Half of this amount is to be collected 10 days after the end of the current year with the remainder to be collected 14 weeks later. "Available" has been defined by this government as 75 days.

g. Orders a computer for the school system at an anticipated cost of $23,000.

h. A cash transfer of $18,000 is approved from the general fund to a capital projects fund.

LO 16-4, 16-5, 16-11

52. Inside the City of Patience, Fund A transfers $20,000 in cash to Fund B. For each of the following, indicate whether the statement is true or false and, if false, explain why.

a. If Fund A is the general fund and Fund B is an enterprise fund, nothing is shown for this transfer on the statement of activities within the government-wide financial statements.

b. If Fund A is the general fund and Fund B is a debt service fund, nothing is shown for this transfer on the statement of activities within the government-wide financial statements.

c. If Fund A is the general fund and Fund B is an enterprise fund, a $20,000 reduction is reported on the statement of revenues, expenditures, and other changes in fund balance for the governmental funds within the fund financial statements.

d. If Fund A is the general fund and Fund B is a special revenue fund (which is not considered a major fund), no changes are shown on the statement of revenues, expenditures, and other changes in fund balance within the fund financial statements.

e. If Fund A is the general fund and Fund B is an internal service fund and this transfer is to pay for work done, the general fund will report an expense of $20,000 within the fund financial statements.

Use the following information for Problems 53–59:

Assume that the City of Coyote has produced its financial statements for December 31, 2020, and the year then ended. The city's general fund was only used to monitor education and parks. Its capital projects funds worked in connection with each of these functions at times during the current year. The city also maintained an enterprise fund to account for its art museum.

The government-wide financial statements provide the following figures:

- Education reports net expenses of $600,000.
- Parks reports net expenses of $100,000.
- Art museum reports net revenues of $50,000.
- General government revenues for the year were $800,000 with an overall increase in the city's net position of $150,000.

The fund financial statements provide the following for the entire year:

- The general fund reports a $30,000 increase in its fund balance.
- The capital projects fund reports a $40,000 increase in its fund balance.
- The enterprise fund reports a $60,000 increase in its net position.

The city asks the CPA firm of Abernethy and Chapman to examine several transactions that occurred during 2020 and indicate how to correct any erroneous reporting. Officials also want to know the effect of each error. View each of the following situations as independent.

LO 16-2, 16-5, 16-10

53. During 2020, the City of Coyote contracts to build a bus stop for schoolchildren costing $10,000 as a special assessments project. The city collects $10,000 from directly affected citizens. The government has no obligation in connection with this project. The city records both a $10,000 revenue and a $10,000 expenditure in the capital projects fund. In preparing government-wide financial statements, the city records an asset and a general revenue for $10,000.

a. In the general information, the capital projects fund reports a $40,000 increase in its fund balance for the year. What was the correct change in the capital projects fund balance during 2020?

b. In the general information, a $150,000 overall increase in the city's net position was found on the government-wide financial statements. What was the correct overall change in the city's net position on the government-wide financial statements?

LO 16-9

54. On December 30, 2020, the City of Coyote borrows $20,000 for the general fund on a 60-day note. In that fund, the city records Cash and Other Financing Sources. In the general information, this city reports a $30,000 overall increase in the fund balance of the general fund. What was the correct change in the fund balance of the general fund for 2020?

LO 16-2, 16-4, 16-5

55. The City of Coyote records an art display within its general fund. The display generates revenues of $9,000 this year as well as expenditures of $45,000 ($15,000 in expenses and $30,000 to buy land for the display). The CPA firm determines that the city should report this program as an enterprise fund activity because of its association with the city's art museum.
    a. Based on the information provided, what was the correct change in the fund balance for the general fund for 2020?
    b. What was the correct overall change in the city's net position on government-wide financial statements?
    c. What was the correct change in the net position of the enterprise fund on the fund financial statements?

LO 16-2, 16-5, 16-8

56. The City of Coyote mails property tax bills for 2021 to its citizens during August 2020. Property owners could make payments early to receive a discount. The levy becomes legally enforceable on February 15, 2021. All money received by the city must be spent during 2021 or later. The total assessment is $300,000. Of that amount, the city collects 40 percent, less a 10 percent discount, in 2020. The city expects to receive all of the remaining money during 2021 with no discount. During 2020, the government increases cash as well as revenue for the amount received. No change was made in creating government-wide financial statements.
    a. What is the correct overall change in the city's net position as should be shown on the government-wide financial statements?
    b. What is the correct change for 2020 in the fund balance reported for the city's general fund?

LO 16-2, 16-5, 16-8

57. The City of Coyote mails property tax bills for 2021 to its citizens during August 2020. Payments could be made early to receive a discount. The levy becomes legally enforceable on February 15, 2021. All money the government receives must be spent during 2021 or later. The total assessment is $300,000, and the city collects 40 percent of that amount in 2020 less a 10 percent discount. The city expects to receive all remaining money during 2021 with no discount. During 2020, the government increases cash and a revenue for the amount received. In addition, a receivable and an unavailable revenue for $180,000 are recognized.
    a. In the general information, an overall increase in the city's net position of $150,000 was found on the government-wide financial statements. What is the correct overall change in the city's net position as reported on the government-wide financial statements?
    b. In the general information, an overall increase of $30,000 is reported in the fund balance for the general fund. What was the correct change during 2020?

LO 16-2, 16-5, 16-7, 16-8

58. In 2020, the City of Coyote receives a $320,000 cash grant from the state to reduce air pollution. Although a special revenue fund could have been set up, the money remains in the general fund. The cash was received immediately but will have to be returned if the city does not lower its air pollution by 25 percent by 2024. On December 31, 2020, Coyote spends $210,000 of the money for a large machine to help begin the process of reducing air pollution. City officials expect the machine to last for five years. The city recorded the cost as an expenditure in the general fund but as an asset on the government-wide financial statements, where it was depreciated based on the straight-line method and the half-year convention. Because the city received the money, it recorded all $320,000 as a revenue on both the fund and the government-wide financial statements.
    a. What was the correct change for 2020 in the total fund balance reported by the general fund?
    b. What was the correct overall change in the net position reported on the government-wide financial statements?

LO 16-2

59. During 2020, the City of Coyote received $10,000, which was recorded as a general revenue in the general fund. It was actually a program revenue earned by the city's park program.
    a. What was the correct overall change for 2020 in the net position reported on the government-wide financial statements?
    b. In the general information, the parks program reported net expenses for the period of $100,000. What was the correct amount of net expenses that should have been reported by the parks program?

Develop Your Skills

RESEARCH CASE 1

CPA skills

The City of Hampshore is currently preparing financial statements for the past fiscal year. The city manager is concerned because the city encountered some unusual transactions during the current fiscal period and is unsure as to their handling.

Required

Locate a copy (either in hard copy or online) of GASB's *Codification of Governmental Accounting and Reporting Standards.* Either through an online search or a review of the index, answer each of the following questions.

1. For government accounting, what is the definition of an *extraordinary item?*
2. For government accounting, what is the definition of a *special item?*
3. On government-wide financial statements, how should extraordinary items and special items be reported?

RESEARCH CASE 2

CPA skills

The City of Danmark is preparing financial statements. Officials are currently working on the statement of activities within the government-wide financial statements. A question has arisen as to whether a particular revenue should be identified on government-wide statements as a program revenue or a general revenue.

Required

Locate a copy (either in hard copy or online) of GASB's *Codification of Governmental Accounting and Reporting Standards.* Either through an online search or a review of the index, answer each of the following questions.

1. How is a program revenue defined?
2. What are common examples of program revenues?
3. How is a general revenue defined?
4. What are common examples of general revenues?

ANALYSIS CASE

CPA skills

Search the Internet for the official website of one or more state or local governments. Determine whether the government's latest comprehensive annual financial report (CAFR) is available on the site. For example, the most recent comprehensive annual financial report for the City of Des Moines can be found at https://www.dmgov.org/Departments/Finance/Pages/CAFR.aspx. Use the financial statements that you locate (for Des Moines or some other government) to answer the following questions.

Required

1. How does the audit opinion rendered on the financial statements of government by its independent auditors differ from the audit opinion rendered on the financial statements for a for-profit business?
2. A reconciliation should be presented to explain the difference between the net changes in fund balances for the governmental funds (fund financial statements) and the change in net position for the governmental activities (government-wide financial statements). What were several of the largest reasons for the difference?
3. What were the city's largest sources of general revenues?
4. What was the total amount of expenditures recorded by the general fund during the period? How were those expenditures classified?
5. What assets are reported for the general fund?

6. Review the notes to the financial statements and then determine the number of days the government uses to define the end-of-year financial resources that are viewed as currently available.
7. Did the size of the general fund balance increase or decrease during the most recent year and by how much?

COMMUNICATION CASE 1

CPA skills

Go to the website www.gasb.org and click on "Projects" included in the list that runs across the top of the page. Then click on "Current Projects & Pre-Agenda Research." Click on one of the current projects that is listed. Read the sections that are titled "Project Plan" and "Recent Minutes."

Required

Write a memo to explain the reason that this issue has been chosen for study by GASB. Describe the progress that has been made to date as well as the potential impact on state and local government accounting.

COMMUNICATION CASE 2

CPA skills

Go to the website www.gasb.org and click on "About Us" included in the list that runs across the top of the page. Then click on "Mission, Vision, and Core Values." Read the information provided by GASB.

Required

Assume that a financial analyst with whom you are working is interested in knowing more about the purpose of GASB. Write a short memo explaining the work of GASB based on its vision, mission, core values, and goals.

COMMUNICATION CASE 3

CPA skills

Obtain a copy of the original version of GASB *Statement 34.* Read paragraphs 239 through 277.

Required

Write a report describing alternatives that the GASB considered when it created *Statement 34.* Indicate the alternative that you would have viewed as most appropriate, and describe why the GASB did not choose it.

COMMUNICATION CASE 4

CPA skills

Search the Internet for the official website of one or more state or local governments. On this website, determine whether the latest comprehensive annual financial report (CAFR) is available. For example, a recent comprehensive annual financial report for the City of Winston-Salem can be found at https://www.cityofws.org/Departments/Finance. Read the Managements Discussion and Analysis (MD&A) that should be located near the beginning of the annual report.

Required

Write a memo to explain four or five of the most interesting pieces of information that the Management's Discussion and Analysis provides.

EXCEL CASE

The City of Bainland has been undergoing financial difficulties because of a decrease in its tax base caused by corporations leaving the area. On January 1, 2020, the city has a fund balance of only $400,000 in its governmental funds. In 2016, the city had revenues of $1.4 million and expenditures of $1.48 million. The city's treasurer has forecast that, unless something is done, revenues will decrease at 2 percent per year while expenditures will increase at 3 percent per year.

Required

1. Create a spreadsheet to predict in what year the government will have a zero fund balance.
2. One proposal is that the city slash its expenditures by laying off government workers. That will lead to a 3 percent decrease in expenditures each year rather than a 3 percent increase. However, because of the unemployment, the city will receive less tax revenue. Thus, instead of a 2 percent decrease in revenues, the city expects a 5 percent decrease per year. Adapt the spreadsheet created in requirement (1) to predict what year the government will have a zero fund balance if this option is taken.
3. Another proposal is to increase spending to draw new businesses to the area. This action will lead to a 7 percent increase in expenditures every year, but revenues are expected to rise by 4 percent per year. Adapt the spreadsheet created in requirement (1) to predict what year the government will have a zero fund balance under this option.

chapter 17

Accounting for State and Local Governments (Part 2)

The previous chapter introduced many unique aspects of the financial reporting applicable for state and local governments. Fund accounting, budgets, encumbrances, expenditures, revenue recognition, transfers, the issuance of bonds, and the like were all described in connection with both traditional fund financial statements and government-wide financial statements. The coverage explained the rationale underlying the accounting designed for these government entities, especially the differences caused by the dual nature of the financial reporting process.

The current chapter carries this analysis further, first by delving into more complex financial situations. Many state and local government units are large and encounter numerous transactions as complicated as any faced by for-profit businesses. Tax abatements, solid waste landfills, defined benefit pension plans, donated artworks, and depreciation of infrastructure assets are discussed here to broaden the reader's understanding of state and local government accounting. The chapter also introduces new standards developed by GASB to account for leases, rules that have some interesting differences from recent rules established by FASB for business entities. A student of accounting might well want to judge whether GASB or FASB has done a better job in creating new approaches to lease reporting.

Second, the chapter discusses the overall financial reporting model for state and local governments. Within this coverage, the actual composition of a reporting entity is examined. Because of the wide variety of agencies, departments, and other activities often connected to a government, determining inclusion within the financial statements is not as easy as in a for-profit business where ownership of more than 50 percent of voting stock is the primary criterion.

Learning Objectives

After studying this chapter, you should be able to:

- **LO 17-1** Understand how the hierarchy of U.S. generally accepted accounting principles for state and local government accounting can be used to resolve financial reporting issues.
- **LO 17-2** Explain the informational benefit from required disclosure of tax abatements provided by state and local governments.
- **LO 17-3** Explain the reporting of a net pension liability resulting from a defined benefit pension plan provided to employees by a state or local government.
- **LO 17-4** Report leased assets for the government as lessee and the government as lessor.
- **LO 17-5** Recognize the liability caused by the eventual closure and postclosure costs of operating a solid waste landfill.
- **LO 17-6** Record the donation and acquisition of works of art and historical treasures.
- **LO 17-7** Explain the reporting and possible depreciation of infrastructure assets.
- **LO 17-8** Understand the composition of a state or local government's comprehensive annual financial report (CAFR).
- **LO 17-9** Explain the makeup of a primary government and its relationship to component units and related organizations as well as the combination of governments.
- **LO 17-10** Describe the physical structure of a complete set of government-wide financial statements and a complete set of fund financial statements.
- **LO 17-11** Understand the presentation of financial statements for a public college or university.

The Hierarchy of U.S. Generally Accepted Accounting Principles (GAAP) for State and Local Governments

State and local governments often face complex reporting issues. Governmental financial events can be as unusual and complex as those encountered in large for-profit entities. Officials in cities like Chicago and Boston manage billion-dollar budgets that include a wide array of monetary resources and costs. Those accounting issues rival anything companies like Coca-Cola and Proctor & Gamble have to solve.

LO 17-1

Understand how the hierarchy of U.S. generally accepted accounting principles for state and local government accounting can be used to resolve financial reporting issues.

For a vast majority of transactions, appropriate application of U.S. GAAP is not a serious question. Most events such as tax collections and bond issuances occur with regularity so that standard reporting has become widely understood and accepted. For example, the accounting procedures discussed in the previous chapter are all well established through official pronouncements or long-term practical use.

Nevertheless, events can arise that do not lend themselves to easy reporting solutions. Perhaps a new type of transaction is undertaken with an unusual nature or a particular twist that seems unique. To complicate the reporting, different rules can sometimes provide guidance that seems to be contradictory. For financial statements to be in conformity with U.S. GAAP, state and local government accountants must be able to establish the validity of the suggested reporting. The same challenge is true for independent auditors (CPAs) who are hired to examine and certify that the information is presented fairly, in all material respects, in accordance with the accounting principles generally accepted in the United States.

When faced with a new or unusual transaction, how do accountants and auditors determine what accounting is consistent with U.S. GAAP? When a variety of sources indicate different possible reporting resolutions, which guidance should be followed? For accountants, answers to these practical questions are essential.

In 2015, the Governmental Accounting Standards Board (GASB) issued its Statement No. 76, *The Hierarchy of Generally Accepted Accounting Principles for State and Local Governments.* GASB passed this pronouncement to provide reporting guidance whenever the question of establishing conformity with U.S. GAAP arises. According to this standard, all sources of authoritative U.S. GAAP for state and local governments can be divided into two categories, with Category A having more authority than Category B.

Category A: This first level of authoritative rules is composed of official GASB statements. Those statements are available on the Board's website (www.gasb.org). In addition, prior to the release of Statement No. 76, GASB occasionally issued interpretations to help clarify, explain, or provide more detailed information about various GASB statements. Over the years, the Board issued only a few interpretations and has discontinued further usage. The Board will use other methods (see Category B) to provide this type of guidance about U.S. GAAP. However, Category A does include any of the previously released interpretations that remain in effect.

Category B: The second level is made up of GASB Technical Bulletins, GASB Implementation Guides, and any literature of the American Institute of Certified Public Accountants (AICPA) that has been cleared by GASB. Again, specific listings of these resources can be found on GASB's website.

- GASB releases technical bulletins when needed to serve much the same function as the interpretations described previously. Technical bulletins outline practical guidance concerning the application of GASB statements. They can be issued in a shorter period of time to provide solutions for pressing reporting problems. Technical bulletins have not been developed frequently, but can still be used to indicate that a majority of the Board does not object to a proposed method of reporting. In this manner, GASB has an official procedure by which reporting problems can be addressed quickly. GASB released no technical bulletins between the beginning of 2015 and the end of 2018.
- Implementation guides clarify, explain, or elaborate on existing U.S. GAAP for state and local governments. In contrast to technical bulletins, they do not go beyond that function. Therefore, they do not establish the acceptability of new approaches to reporting issues. Because implementation guides tend to have a broader effect and less urgency, a period of public exposure provides a chance for feedback that can highlight potential problems before the guide is issued. Like technical bulletins, they indicate that a majority of the Board does not object to the guidance given. GASB released six implementation guides between the beginning of 2015 and the end of 2018.

To establish the validity of a proposed reporting treatment, accountants and auditors look first to Category A and then to Category B, but only if no answer is found at the first level.

What happens if no satisfactory answer can be found in either Category A or Category B? No set of generally accepted accounting principles can ever anticipate all of the wide variety of reporting issues that might be faced by a government. At that point, reasoned judgment becomes essential. "If specific guidance cannot be found in either category, financial statement preparers and auditors are to consider guidance for similar transactions or events."[1]

Is official guidance available that is similar enough to be considered applicable? For example, if a rule on the reporting of the cost of a highway is provided in a GASB statement, can the same logic be used in accounting for a parking lot? Ultimately, the reporting of complex transactions in governmental accounting (as well as that used with for-profit entities) requires accountants and auditors to have a strong understanding of the purpose of the reporting process and the principles on which it is founded.

As additional help, GASB also provides a list of nonauthoritative sources that can be considered in determining the method of reporting that is most consistent with generally accepted accounting principles: GASB Concepts Statements, pronouncements of other accounting bodies such as FASB and the IASB, practices that are prevalent in state and local governments, published literature of professional associations and regulatory agencies, and accounting textbooks and articles.

No function performed by an accountant or auditor is more significant than the determination of how a reporting entity reports a unique transaction or event to be in conformity with U.S. GAAP. That decision requires both deep knowledge and sound judgment. The nature of the event must be understood completely and then compared to rules that have been established over many decades. With Statement 76, GASB has specified which of these rules (and other sources of guidance) should be analyzed and which has the most authority.

LO 17-2

Explain the informational benefit from required disclosure of tax abatements provided by state and local governments.

Tax Abatement Disclosure

> For years, taxpayers have questioned whether the estimated $70 billion in subsidies governments shower on the free enterprise system each year are savvy investments or corporate welfare run amok. Soon, they will have more information to make that call. This month, the Governmental Accounting Standards Board—the Norwalk, Connecticut, body that oversees government accounting rules—said it will require governments to disclose how much tax revenue they are foregoing because of incentives provided to businesses. State and local governments, as well as school districts, also will have to disclose the jobs promises and other commitments businesses make in order to avoid paying taxes.[2]

Government decisions to provide tax abatements have come under increased scrutiny in recent years. Resistance to Amazon's original decision to build an additional headquarters in the New York City area focused at least in part on the size of the tax and other government benefits provided to the company. Some citizens argued that was a wise economic move for the region while others viewed it as a sign of corporate greed.

Accounting rules do not always come down to specifying the correct debits and credits that will properly reflect a transaction. Disclosure issues can be as challenging as the reporting of an actual event. One question stands at the center of any disclosure discussion: What information will create a representative financial picture for interested parties without requiring so much data that (1) readers become overwhelmed and (2) unnecessary costs are incurred? Financial statements should enlighten outside parties and not confuse them with excessive information. In any accounting debate, reporting entities usually argue for less disclosure, whereas decision makers typically call for more.

Governments often make agreements with outside organizations to forego tax revenues for a period of time in exchange for a specific action. For example, "Nevada promised to provide Tesla Motors $1.3 billion in tax incentive packages to build the Tesla Gigafactory in that state."[3] GASB recently ruled (in GASB Statement No. 77, *Tax Abatement Disclosures)* that information about such tax abatement programs is beneficial and worth the associated cost of disclosure. Disclosure becomes necessary when agreement is reached.

[1] Stephen J. Gauthier, "New Guidance on the GAAP Hierarchy," *Government Finance* Review, December 2015, pp. 47–48.

[2] Len Boselovic, "Pittsburgh Post—Gazette Len Boselovic's Heard Off the Street Column," *McClatchy Tribune Business News,* August 30, 2015.

[3] Anthony Billings, Jeanette A. Boles, and Kyungjin Kim, "Tax Abatement Under GASB Statement 77," *CPA Journal,* April 2018.

In 2014, the city of Fort Worth, Texas, listed 18 ongoing tax abatement programs provided to individual companies in exchange for commitments that were believed to benefit the city and its citizens.[4] It is a common practice. Fort Worth officials agreed to approximately one new tax abatement program per year in the decade prior to 2014. Benefiting companies were allowed to avoid either a portion or all of their real and personal property taxes for periods of up to ten years by promising to carry out specified projects such as a hotel construction, construction of a new production facility, construction of a data center, and the like. The various investments made by these companies in Fort Worth ranged from $1.5 million to $173 million and were estimated to create or retain area jobs, as few as 7 in one case and as many as 1,940 in another.

These abatement programs represent exchanged promises. The city reduces or eliminates an organization's taxes (for example, sales, income, or property taxes) for a period of time. In return, the business or other entity agrees to a defined action such as keeping operations in the city or the construction of a new facility. These tax abatements were received by companies such as Coca-Cola Enterprises, Blue Cross Blue Shield of Texas, and Omni Fort Worth.

In a traditional sense, tax abatements create no transaction to report. The choice to forego the collection of taxes is not easy to reflect in a journal entry that would be meaningful. However, the financial effect of such agreements can be quite significant. Is a company's promise to create 50 jobs and invest $1.5 million in construction worth losing real estate tax collections for 10 years? If government officials make such a decision, citizens need to be aware of the financial ramifications.

GASB has now decided that state and local governments must disclose information about tax abatements in their financial statements.

> "Tax abatement has been a common carrot that communities use to attract development. To date, however, cities and other tax-abating governments haven't shared much information about the accumulated financial consequences of those tax breaks. Now, because of an edict from the board that oversees government accounting, they will. That means that the counties, cities and public authorities in seven counties in Northeast Ohio will have to provide details about the roughly $1.4 billion in taxes that are passed up annually. . . . 'I'm going to be the happy recipient of more information,' said Tim Offtermatt, an investment banker with the Cleveland office of Stifel Financial Corp. who specializes in public finance. 'It helps us put together a comprehensive credit package for credit analysts.'"[5]

Based on the GASB statement, a state or local government must disclose significant information about abatement agreements including:

- The purpose of the tax abatement program.
- The type of tax being abated.
- Dollar amount of taxes abated.
- The type of commitments made by the tax abatement recipients.
- Any commitments made by the government (or other parties), for example, agreeing to construct infrastructure assets such as roads.

Interestingly, GASB has been criticized for not requiring governments to identify the companies receiving the abatements. Additional criticism was levied by parties who want to know about the long-term financial effect of these abatement decisions. Because of the importance of reported information, few accounting rules manage to escape some amount of criticism. "Critics disagree, arguing that governments should at least be required to disclose the names of the largest recipients. One reason for this is that many believe subsidies don't generally help small, homegrown businesses flourish."[6]

[4] http://fortworthtexas.gov/uploadedfiles/hed/business/tax-abatement-agreements-2014.pdf.

[5] Jay Miller, "GASB Ruling Will Make Tax Breaks More Transparent," *Crain's Cleveland Business,* September 7, 2015, p. 3.

[6] Liz Farmer, "3 Things the New Tax Incentive Disclosures Rules Won't Reveal," *McClatchy Business News,* November 24, 2015.

> "Policy Matters Ohio's Schiller questioned the lack of long-term cost projections—a key element in the pension fund crisis. 'It's hard to figure why (GASB) didn't approve any kind of forward-looking cost of this,' Schiller said. 'From (a municipal bond) investor's standpoint, isn't your biggest concern not what they paid last year, but what they have to pay in the future?'"[7]

LO 17-3

Explain the reporting of a net pension liability resulting from a defined benefit pension plan provided to employees by a state or local government.

Defined Benefit Pension Plans

> Sanitation workers, firefighters, teachers and other state and local government employees have performed their duties in the public sector for decades with the understanding that their often lackluster salaries were propped up by excellent benefits, including an ironclad pension. But Moody's Investors Service recently estimated that public pensions are underfunded by $4.4 trillion. That amount, which is equivalent to the economy of Germany, accounts for one-fifth of national debt. It's a significant concern for public employees who were banking on a fully funded retirement to get them through their golden years.[8]

State and local governments often provide pension plans for many of their employees. An educator in the public schools, for example, might be eligible to retire with full benefits after a specified length of service (such as 30 years). Because businesses have been moving for many years into defined contribution pension plans, government employees are more likely than for-profit business employees to have defined benefit pension plans. In 2014, 30 percent of employees in the private sector were covered by defined benefit pension plans whereas 90 percent of public-sector employees had those type of pension plans.[9]

Pension requirements create a huge financial obligation for many governments across the United States. Retirees are usually entitled to benefits based on a contractually set formula. "Future pension obligations of both companies and state governments collectively amount to trillions of dollars; obligations of numerous pension plans can be measured individually in billions of dollars. Public-sector pension obligations generally dwarf those in the private sector."[10]

Many state and local governments establish pension trust funds to (1) accumulate and invest monetary resources and (2) pay out pension benefits. Because the money is held for retirees, these pension trusts are classified as fiduciary funds and, thus, are not included in reporting government-wide financial statements. A question has long been raised as to the amount of pension obligation a government should include in its overall financial reporting, especially considering the potential size of these obligations. Historically, as long as all legal funding requirements were met in a timely manner, governments reported no pension liability. Because these requirements did not necessarily cover the expected amount of the eventual pension payments, financial analysts argued that the financial position of many state and local governments was considerably more precarious than reported.

GASB's Statement No. 68, *Accounting and Financial Reporting for Pensions,* now requires a more extensive reporting of pension liabilities. Because virtually all of these payments will take place well beyond the current period, this reporting applies almost exclusively to government-wide financial statements (and to fund financial statements for proprietary funds). GASB also created similar requirements for postemployment benefit plans other than pension plans to reflect more completely each government's total obligation to retired employees.

[7] Jay Miller, "GASB ruling will make tax breaks more transparent," *Crain's Cleveland Business,* September 7, 2015, p. 3.

[8] Olivia Mitchell and Leora Friedberg, "The Time Bomb Inside Public Pension Plans" August 23, 2018, on the Knowledge @ Wharton website, http://knowledge.wharton.upenn.edu/article/the-time-bomb-inside-public-pension-plans/.

[9] Craig Foltin, Dale L. Flesher, Gary J. Previts, and Mary S. Stone "State and Local Government Pensions at the Crossroads," *The CPA Journal,* April 2017, p. 44.

[10] Kathryn E. Easterday and Tim V. Eaton, "Defined Benefit Pension Plans," *The CPA Journal,* September 1, 2012, p. 22.

For pensions, this authoritative guidance establishes several steps in the reporting of a government's liability.

- First, an actuary estimates the total pension payments that will ultimately be required.
- Second, the government determines the portion of those payments attributable to past periods of employee service. This figure reflects the pension earned to date by employees.
- Third, the government calculates the present value of the payments relating to those past amounts to arrive at its obligation at the current time.
- Fourth, if that liability is larger than the net asset position held in the pension trust fund, the excess is shown in the government-wide financial statements as a net pension liability. It reflects the shortfall between what is owed and the amount held for that purpose. Conversely, if the net position of the pension trust fund is larger than the present value of the pension benefits earned to date, the government reports a net pension asset. This net liability or net asset appears on the statement of net position as either a governmental activity or a business-type activity, depending on the nature of the function responsible for the payments. Pensions for educators, firefighters, sanitation workers, and the like fall under governmental activities.

To illustrate, assume that a city has maintained a pension plan for several decades to cover teachers in its school system who remain employed for a minimum of three years. Years ago, the city began a pension trust fund that now holds $1 billion in cash and investments. No payments are currently due to retirees. Assume that an actuary calculates the total amount of expected pension payments to be $10 billion. To date, current and retired employees have earned only 80 percent of that amount, or $8 billion. Assume that these future cash payments to retirees have a present value of $3 billion. On government-wide financial statements, the city must report $2 billion as the net pension liability. The $1 billion held in the pension trust fund is subtracted from the $3 billion present value of the future $8 billion in payments to arrive at the $2 billion unfunded portion of the obligation. Because the school system is responsible for these specific pensions, the city reports the debt on its government-wide financial statements within the governmental activities.

Accountants must deal with a number of complex challenges in applying this reporting standard. Although many of these problems are beyond the scope of this textbook, students should be aware of several key issues.

- In any present value computation, the question of an appropriate discount rate is essential. The size of the rate is inversely related to the size of the reported liability. The higher the rate, the more interest is assigned to future cash flows, leaving a smaller liability balance to report currently. GASB specifies that, in most cases, the government should calculate the present value of the future pension obligation using the estimated long-term investment yield for the plan's assets.

The choice of this rate has proven controversial. Because the expected rate of return on investments is normally higher than other possible discount rates, the remaining pension liability to be reported is smaller. The average rate used in 2014 was 7.3 percent. Had 4 percent been used for the entire liability, "The unfunded liability would increase from $900 billion to $3.41 trillion."[11] The higher rate decreases the liability and reduces the apparent cost that taxpayers will have to bear in the future for these pension plans.[12]

> Financial economists have recommended for decades that governments calculate pension liabilities using so-called "risk-free" rates pegged to high-grade municipal bonds or long-term Treasurys. . . . However, GASB let governments stick with their desired, er, expected rate of return, which is typically about 8 percent. Public pension funds have returned 5.7 percent on average since 2000. Achieving much higher returns over the long run would require markets to perform as well as they did in the 1980s and '90s. Would that be true. Governments have resisted climbing down from Fantasyland because using lower discount rates would explode their liabilities.[13]

[11] Ibid., p. 46.

[12] "The Not-So-Great GASB," *The Economist,* Buttonwood's Notebook, May 2, 2013, www.economist.com/blogs/buttonwood/2013/05/pensions.

[13] "Pension Accounting for Dummies: New Government Reporting Rules Are No Better than the Old Ones," *The Wall Street Journal* (online), July 11, 2012.

- The government must identify the components of pension expense that are recognized immediately. GASB lists those as (1) the service cost for the current period, (2) interest expense on the total pension liability, and (3) projected earnings on plan investments. Any increases or decreases in the liability caused by changes in benefit terms are also included in pension expense immediately rather than being amortized over time as is the case with for-profit enterprises.
- Numerous assumptions (such as the life expectancy of retirees) are necessary to arrive at the total pension liability figure. The effect of periodic changes in these assumptions and differences between the assumptions and actual experience are not included immediately by the government as pension expense. Instead, those amounts are recorded as either deferred outflows of resources or deferred inflows of resources and then amortized to pension expense over the average expected remaining service lives of the employees in the pension plan. As an example, at June 30, 2017, Nashville and Davidson County, Tennessee, explains the $161 million reported deferred inflow of resources shown on its statement of net position as relating to "Certain differences between projected and actual actuarial results and certain differences between projected and actual investment earnings which are accounted for as deferred inflows of resources."

Throughout these government rules, elements of the reporting used by for-profit organizations can be seen. Nevertheless, several unique aspects have been created by GASB in the reporting of defined benefit pension plans administered by state and local government entities.

LO 17-4

Report leased assets for the government as lessee and the government as lessor.

Lease Accounting

A footnote to the 2017 financial statements for the City of Saint Paul, Minnesota, discloses, "From 1998 through 2017, the City entered into noncancelable operating leases for personal computers. Total payments made for the leases during 2017 were $1,124,409." Later, in the same statements, while discussing a new major league soccer stadium, additional information explained another lease arrangement, "The City, St. Paul Port Authority (SPPA) and Metropolitan Council negotiated a ground lease for the property known as the Bus Barn Site. The lease has a term of approximately 52 years, depending on the date the team plays its first major league game at the stadium." These two examples show how financially involved state and local governments can be in lease contracts. The monetary amounts are frequently substantial.

In February 2016, the Financial Accounting Standards Board (FASB) issued Accounting Standards Update 2016-02, *Leases.* It provided new authoritative guidance for both lessees and lessors in the financial reporting of leases. In June 2017, GASB issued Statement No. 87, *Leases,* for much the same purpose. The first pronouncement standardized the reporting for business entities and private not-for-profit entities. The second standardized the reporting for state and local government entities. A comparison of the two official approaches to these common contractual arrangements is inevitable. Although the underlying transactions are the same and these two standards provide many similar methods of reporting, fascinating differences do exist.[14]

The Lessee—According to FASB FASB ASU 2016-02 establishes five criteria to distinguish financing leases from operating leases. However, the accounting for each category is not markedly different. In either situation, the lessee records both an intangible (right-of-use) asset and liability at the present value of the payments based on the lessee's incremental borrowing rate (unless the lessee knows the implicit interest rate built into the payments by the lessor). If the contract qualifies as a financing lease, the lessee recognizes interest expense by multiplying the liability balance for the current period by the applicable rate. The lessee also reports amortization to assign the cost of the leased asset to expense over the period of its use.

For FASB, the significant difference between reporting a financing lease and an operating lease is in the computation of amortization expense. In a financing lease, the lessee applies the straight-line or some other appropriate method. In an operating lease, the lessee first calculates an expense balance for the current period as if the total of all payments was spread evenly over

[14] Extensive coverage of FASB's ASU 2016-02 can be found in any current intermediate accounting textbook. Hence, discussion is limited primarily to points of comparison with Statement No. 87.

the asset's useful life as measured by the lessee. This figure is the periodic lease expense that the lessee reports. Interest is the same calculation as earlier, the liability balance multiplied by the applicable rate. Amortization of the asset is simply the amount that brings the calculated interest number up to the lease expense figure reported by the lessee. For an operating lease, the lessee does not determine amortization based on either the reported cost of the asset or its expected life.

To illustrate an operating lease under FASB's new rules, assume that a city pays $100,000 to lease a truck over the next five years (an average of $20,000 per year). If the government computes interest for the first year as $12,000, then it automatically recognizes amortization for that period as $8,000. On the lessee's income statement, the government combines these two figures to arrive at a single lease expense of $20,000.

For any lease contract that cannot be extended beyond one year and does not contain a bargain purchase option, a short-term alternative is available. In this optional approach, the lessee merely recognizes lease expense as time passes. Other than prepaid rent, the entity reports neither an asset nor a liability.

The Lessee—According to GASB GASB takes a different approach to lease accounting. No criteria exist. Unless the maximum life is one year or less, all leases are the equivalent of financing leases. The split identified by FASB between operating and financing leases is not relevant. As the Summary to Statement No. 87 explains, GASB, "Establishes a single model for lease accounting based on the foundational principle that leases are financings of the right to use an underlying asset. Under this Statement, a lessee is required to recognize a lease liability and an intangible right-to-use lease asset."

To illustrate, assume on December 31, Year 0, that a city leases a large truck with a 20-year life for four years to use during a construction project. After the contract ends, the city must return the truck to the lessor but has not guaranteed any residual value. The lease requires four annual payments of $30,000 per year beginning immediately. Because the city does not know the implicit interest rate the lessor is charging, the lessee applies its own incremental borrowing rate of 10 percent per year. The present value of a $30,000 annuity due for four years at an annual interest rate of 10 percent is $104,604 (rounded). In government-wide financial statements, the city records the first two years of this lease contract as follows.

Government-Wide Financial Statements

	Debit	Credit
December 31, Year 0		
Right-of-Use Asset—Truck	104,604	
Lease Payable		74,604
Cash		30,000
To record city's four-year lease of truck at the present value of the payments.		
December 31, Year 1		
Interest Expense	7,460	
Lease Payable		7,460
To record interest for the year as 10 percent of the $74,604 liability.		
Amortization Expense	26,151	
Right-of-Use Asset—Truck		26,151
Cost of the leased asset is amortized over four years using straight-line method ($104,604/4 years).		
Lease Payable	30,000	
Cash		30,000
To record payment at end of Year 1.		
December 31, Year 2		
Interest Expense	5,206	
Lease Payable		5,206
To record interest as 10 percent of liability, which is now $74,604 less $30,000 plus $7,460, or $52,064.		
Amortization Expense	26,151	
Right-of-Use Asset—Truck		26,151
To record annual amortization of leased asset.		
Lease Payable	30,000	
Cash		30,000
To record payment at end of Year 2.		

If the lease had been for a maximum of one year or less, the lessee could have recorded the payment as a prepaid asset of $30,000 and then assigned that balance to rent or lease expense over the time of use.

In fund financial statements for any one of the governmental funds, the city reports neither the right-of-use asset nor the lease liability. They do not affect current financial resources. The city records expenditures and other financing sources for the present value of the payments.

Fund Financial Statements—Governmental Funds

December 31, Year 0		
Expenditure—Lease Contract	104,604	
Other Financing Sources—Lease Contract		104,604
Contract is signed that will require four annual payments of $30,000 per year with a present value of $104,604.		
Expenditure—Leased Truck	30,000	
Cash		30,000
To record first lease payment.		
December 31, Year 1		
Expenditure—Leased Truck	30,000	
Cash		30,000
To record second lease payment.		

For a short-term lease of one year or less, the entries are the same except that the initial recording is not necessary

The Lessor—According to FASB The difference between an operating lease and a financing lease becomes more significant under FASB's lease rules. If the contract meets one or more of the five criteria, the lessor records a lease receivable at its present value and removes the asset from its records. If the present value is equal to the cost of the asset, the lessor reports no immediate profit. Interest revenue constitutes the only profit. The lessor recognizes that interest over the length of the contract based on multiplying the receivable balance for each period times the implicit interest rate.

If the present value is higher than the cost of the asset, the contract is for a sales-type lease that contains a selling profit. The lessor records sales revenue for the present value of the lease (same as the initial receivable balance) and also records cost of goods sold for the cost of the asset. The difference between the revenue and cost of goods sold is an immediate increase in net income. Subsequently, the lessor recognizes interest revenue over time based on the receivable balance.

In contrast, the lease is an operating lease if the contract meets none of the five criteria. To report an operating lease, the entries are entirely different. The lessor reports the cash collected and recognizes a deferred lease revenue (a liability balance). As time passes, the lessor reclassifies the deferred lease revenue as lease revenue. For the lessor, moving between an operating lease and a financing-/sales-type lease has a dramatic effect on the reported figures.

The Lessor—According to GASB Again, for government-wide financial statements, GASB does not recognize separate categories for lease contracts. Unless the lease is for a maximum of one year or less, the lessor has only one option. Initially, the lessor records both the receivable and a deferred lease revenue at present value. This deferral is not a liability but rather a deferred inflow of resources. It appears below the government's liabilities on the statement of net position to indicate that this balance is not a debt. Regardless of the length of the contract, the asset remains within the financial records of the lessor.

The lessor reports no immediate profit. Instead, over time, the lessor reclassifies the deferred lease revenue as lease revenue in a systematic and rational manner. Concurrently, interest revenue is calculated and recognized on the receivable balance for each period. Because the asset is still present in the accounting records, the lessor also reports periodic depreciation expense.

Through this system, the lessor reports a portion of the lease revenue each period, along with interest revenue on the receivable and amortization expense on the asset. To illustrate, assume that a city holds a truck with a net book value of $120,000. The city no longer has a need for the truck and leases it to a nearby county government for eight years, the entire remaining life. Officials do not anticipate any residual value. Based on an implicit interest rate of 10 percent per year, annual payments starting on December 31, Year 0, are $20,448 (rounded). Because the lessor computes these payments based on a 10 percent annual interest rate and the asset's net book value, the initial present value is also $120,000.

The city makes the following entries.

December 31, Year 0		
Lease Receivable	120,000	
Deferred Lease Revenue		120,000
To record lease of truck for eight years with payments based on a 10 percent annual interest rate, the implicit rate built into the contract.		
Cash	20,448	
Lease Receivable		20,448
To record collection of first lease payment.		
December 31, Year 1		
Lease Receivable	9,955	
Interest Revenue		9,955
To record interest on lease receivable. Balance for Year 1 was the original balance of $120,000 less first payment of $20,448 or $99,552. Interest is 10 percent of that figure.		
Deferred Lease Revenue	15,000	
Lease Revenue		15,000
To reclassify deferred lease revenue to lease revenue. Straight-line method is used ($120,000/8 years) although GASB allows any systematic and rational approach.		
Depreciation Expense	15,000	
Accumulated Depreciation		15,000
Depreciation is recorded on remaining net book value over the asset's useful life ($120,000/8 years). City did not remove truck after signing lease contract.		

Notice here that the lease revenue and depreciation expense offset each year so that only the interest revenue affects net income. If the lease is not for the entire life of the asset or if expected residual values or bargain purchase options are present, the revenue and the depreciation expense will not necessarily be the same amounts. In that case, some amount of reported profit results each year. Furthermore, if the lease is for a maximum of one year or less, GASB simplifies the process by recognizing deferred lease revenue as the government collects payments. This deferral becomes lease revenue as time passes.

In fund financial statements for governmental funds, the entries for a lessor are virtually identical except that the asset is not present within the financial records so depreciation is not appropriate.

LO 17-5

Recognize the liability caused by the eventual closure and postclosure costs of operating a solid waste landfill.

Solid Waste Landfill

As of June 30, 2018, the City of Greensboro, North Carolina, reported a $500,000 current liability in its statement of net position as an accrued landfill liability. Within noncurrent liabilities, the city reported an additional obligation of approximately $26 million with the same account title. The city identified both balances as business-type activities.

Many communities operate landfills. These sites often create large environmental liabilities. The notes to the financial statements of the City of Greensboro, North Carolina, as of June 30, 2018, explain the reporting of its landfill debt.

> The City owns and operates a regional landfill site located in the northeast portion of the City. State and federal laws require the City to place a final cover on its White Street landfill site and to perform certain maintenance and monitoring functions at the site for thirty years after closure.

> The City reports a portion of these closure and postclosure care costs as an operating expense in each period based on landfill capacity used as of each June 30. The $26,471,656 reported as landfill closure and postclosure care liability at June 30, 2018, is based on 100% use of the estimated capacity of Phase II and Phase III, Cells 1 and 2. Phase III, Cell 3, is estimated at 56.8% of capacity. . . .
>
> The estimated liability amounts are based on what it would cost to perform all closure and postclosure care in the current year. Actual cost may be higher due to inflation, changes in technology, or changes in regulations. At June 30, 2018, the City had expended $3,876,035 to complete closure for the White Street facility, Phase II and $2,535,980 to begin closure activities at the construction and demolition site located on top of the municipal waste filled space. The balance of closure costs, estimated at $13,614,989, and an estimated $12,932,942 for postclosure care will be funded over the remaining life of the landfill estimated to be 20 to 25 years.

Similar to Greensboro, thousands of state and local governments operate solid waste landfills to provide a place for citizens and local companies to dispose of trash and other forms of refuse. Governments frequently report landfill operations within their enterprise funds if these facilities charge a user fee. Other landfills are open to the public for free so that reporting within the general fund is appropriate.

Regardless of the type of fund utilized for reporting, solid waste landfills can create huge liabilities for these governments. The U.S. Environmental Protection Agency has strict rules on closure requirements as well as groundwater monitoring and other postclosure activities. Satisfying such requirements can be costly. The operation of a landfill can ultimately necessitate large payments to ensure that the facility is closed properly and then monitored and maintained for an extended period. The relevant accounting question has always been how to report these eventual costs while the landfill is still in operation.

To illustrate, assume that a city opens a landfill in Year 1 that is expected to take 10 years to fill. To determine the annual amount to be reported, the city must estimate the current costs required to close the landfill. Such costs include the amount to be paid to cover the area and for all postclosure maintenance. As mentioned earlier by the City of Greensboro, the government uses current—rather than an estimate of future—closure and postclosure costs as a measure of the present obligation. Such amounts must then be adjusted each period for inflation, technology, and regulation changes.

Assume in this example that the current cost for closure for a landfill of this size is set at $10 million and for postclosure maintenance at $4 million for a total obligation of $14 million. Assume that during Year 1 the city makes an initial payment of $300,000 toward these closure costs. At the end of this first year, city engineers determine that 16 percent of the available space is now filled.

Landfills—Government-Wide Financial Statements

Regardless of whether the city reports this solid waste landfill as a governmental activity (within the general fund) or as a business-type activity (within an enterprise fund), closure and postclosure costs in government-wide statements must be based on accrual accounting and the economic resources measurement basis. The government anticipates that the total current cost of closure and cleanup is $14 million. Because the landfill is 16 percent filled, the city should accrue $2,240,000 at the end of the first year ($14 million × 16%). The initial $300,000 payment reduces the liability being reported:

Government-Wide Financial Statements—Estimated Landfill Closure Costs

Year 1		
Expense—Landfill Closure.	2,240,000	
Landfill Closure Liability.		2,240,000
To recognize the Year 1 portion of total costs (16 percent) for eventual closure of landfill.		
Landfill Closure Liability.	300,000	
Cash		300,000
To record first payment of costs necessitated by eventual closure of landfill.		

To complete this example, assume that the landfill is judged to be 27 percent filled at the end of Year 2 and the city makes another $300,000 payment toward future closure costs. Because of inflation and recent changes in technology, the city now believes that current closure costs are $11 million, with postclosure costs amounting to $5 million. The current cost of the total landfill obligation has thus jumped from $14 million to $16 million.

Based on this newly revised information, the city recognizes an estimated total cost of $4,320,000 at the end of Year 2 ($16 million × 27%). Because the city recognized $2,240,000 in Year 1, it accrues an additional $2,080,000 in Year 2 ($4,320,000 – $2,240,000):

Government-Wide Financial Statements—Estimated Landfill Closure Costs

Year 2		
Expense—Landfill Closure.	2,080,000	
Landfill Closure Liability.		2,080,000
To recognize Year 2 portion of costs for eventual closure of landfill.		
Landfill Closure Liability	300,000	
Cash		300,000
To record second payment necessitated by eventual closure of the landfill.		

Consequently, the city reports the following in its Year 2 government-wide financial statements, regardless of whether the landfill is part of the general fund (a governmental activity) or as an enterprise fund (a business-type activity):

Expense—Landfill closure	$2,080,000
Landfill closure liability ($2,240,000 + 2,080,000 – 300,000 – 300,000)	$3,720,000

Landfills—Fund Financial Statements

When a solid waste landfill is maintained as an enterprise fund, reporting is the same in the fund financial statements as shown for the government-wide statements. All economic resources are again measured based on accrual accounting.

If the landfill is recorded in the general fund because the facility charges little or no user fee, the city reports only the actual change in current financial resources. Despite the huge eventual liability, the reduction in current financial resources is limited to the annual payment of $300,000. The remaining liability is too far into the future to necessitate reporting. When fund financial statements are prepared, the only entry required each year is as follows:

Fund Financial Statements—Payment toward Landfill Closure Costs—Governmental Funds

Year 1 and Year 2		
General Fund		
Expenditures—Closure Costs.	300,000	
Cash		300,000
To record annual payment toward the eventual closure costs of the city's solid waste landfill.		

LO 17-6

Record the donation and acquisition of works of art and historical treasures.

Works of Art and Historical Treasures

As will be discussed in the following chapter, interested parties have long debated the proper reporting by private not-for-profit entities of artworks and other museum pieces whether bought or received by gift. State and local governments can face the same issue. How should works of art, historical artifacts, and other such treasures be reported by these governments in their financial statements? These properties have value but are they really assets in an accounting sense?

Assume, for example, that a city maintains a museum in a building formerly used as a high school. Officials created the museum to display documents, maps, paintings, and other works that depict the history of the area. Admission is free. Consequently, the museum generates no revenue.

The government bought a number of the items on display. Local citizens donated the remaining pieces. Several are quite valuable.

The basic rule in accounting for such items is clear. Other than a few specific exceptions, "governments should capitalize works of art, historical treasures, and similar assets at their historical cost or acquisition value whether they are held as individual items or in a collection."[15]

Thus, an antique map bought for $5,000 appears in the government-wide statement of net position as an asset at that cost. A similar map received as a gift is also shown as a $5,000 asset if that is the value when acquired. Such donations qualify as voluntary nonexchange transactions. In recording the gift, the city recognizes revenue for the value of the map when all eligibility requirements are met. Until that time, the government reports a liability.[16]

In preparing fund financial statements, the city might designate the museum as an enterprise fund if an entrance fee is charged. If that decision is made, the reporting of these two assets simply follows the same pattern as in government-wide statements.

In contrast, if the city views the museum as a governmental fund, it reports any such acquisition as an expenditure (rather than as an asset) to reflect the decrease in current financial resources. If obtained by gift, no entry is made within the governmental funds because the amount of current financial resources remains unchanged. The city spent no money or other resources to acquire the map.

In government-wide financial statements, a theoretical problem arises as to the recognition of such properties, regardless of whether the government acquires them by purchase or by gift. Do such items qualify as assets to be reported by the government? Owners often display historical maps, artistic paintings, and the like for the public to see but do not expect to generate any direct cash inflows or other economic benefit. Does that satisfy the characteristics of an asset?

In response to that question, GASB encourages capitalization of all artworks, historical treasures, and the like as assets. Nevertheless, if all three of the following criteria are met, the recording of such properties as an asset is optional:

1. It is held for public exhibition, education, or research in furtherance of public service rather than for financial gain.
2. It is protected, kept unencumbered, cared for, and preserved.
3. It is subject to an organizational policy that requires the proceeds from sales of collection items to be used to acquire other items for collections.[17] This last requirement ensures that the work is not held for investment purposes.

If these guidelines are met, the artwork or historical treasure provide no direct economic benefit to the government. Although recording of the transaction is necessary, recognition of an asset is not required. If this option is taken, the government records an expense in the government-wide statements rather than an asset whether the item is obtained by purchase or by gift. In government-wide statements, the artwork, museum piece, or the like is shown as either an asset or as an expense if these three requirements are met.

In its 2017 government-wide financial statements, the City of Chicago reports works of art and historical collections as assets with a reported value of $47 million although other items of this type are not capitalized. A footnote explains the reporting of these properties.

[15] Governmental Accounting Standards Board, *Codification of Governmental Accounting and Financial Reporting Standards as of December 31, 2018*, Sec. 1400.109.

[16] A deferred inflow of resources is recorded rather than a liability if all eligibility requirements have been met except for a time requirement.

[17] GASB, *Codification*, Sec. 1400.109.

> The City has a collection of artwork and historical treasures presented for public exhibition and education that are being preserved for future generations. The proceeds from sales of any pieces of the collection are used to purchase other acquisitions. A portion of this collection is not capitalized or depreciated as part of capital assets.

GASB's handling of artwork and historical treasures closely parallels rules established by FASB for private not-for-profit entities. Nevertheless, as the next chapter explains, differences do remain.

One related issue needs to be addressed: the recording of depreciation. Does the map on display in the museum actually depreciate in value over time? Does the *Mona Lisa* have a finite life? For works of art or museum artifacts reported as assets, the government records depreciation but only if it deems the asset as "exhaustible"—that is, if its utility will be consumed by display, education, or research. The recording of depreciation is not necessary if the item is judged to be inexhaustible. As long as properly maintained, many such properties can be considered as inexhaustible assets so that depreciation is allowed but not required.

LO 17-7

Explain the reporting and possible depreciation of infrastructure assets.

Infrastructure Assets and Depreciation

Many governments hold a significant number of infrastructure assets. As mentioned in the previous chapter, infrastructure is a general term for long-lived capital assets that normally are stationary in nature and can be preserved for a significantly greater number of years than most other capital assets. Common examples include roads, bridges, tunnels, lighting systems, curbing, and sidewalks.

At one time in government accounting, the recording of infrastructure items was an optional practice because these properties did not generate revenue in any traditional sense. Now, though, infrastructure costs are recorded as assets in government-wide statements. As of June 30, 2017, the City of Cincinnati, Ohio, listed infrastructure assets, net of accumulated depreciation, of $740.6 million on its government-wide statements. For governmental funds, these costs continue to be recorded as expenditures in fund financial statements because both acquisition and construction creates a reduction in current financial resources.

As discussed previously, depreciation is required for all capital assets (such as buildings) that have a finite life. Governments must also record depreciation for capitalized artworks and historical treasures that are deemed to be exhaustible. GASB debated the need for depreciating infrastructure assets in government-wide financial statements. Is depreciation appropriate for this type of asset? "The responses to the Statement's exposure draft included arguments that infrastructure assets should not be depreciated because they are intended to be preserved in perpetuity."[18]

For example, construction of the Brooklyn Bridge was finished in 1883 at a cost of about $15 million. That piece of infrastructure has operated now for more than 130 years and, with proper maintenance, might well continue to carry traffic for another 130 years. Much the same can be said of many roads, sidewalks, and the like. With appropriate repair and maintenance, such assets could have lives that are almost indefinite. What expected life should New York City use to depreciate the cost incurred in constructing a street such as Fifth Avenue?

GASB eventually determined that depreciation of infrastructure items was appropriate in government-wide financial statements. Not surprisingly, governments tend to depreciate some infrastructure items over extended periods. The City of Portland, Oregon, with approximately $4.7 billion in infrastructure, uses lives that range from 20 to 100 years. The City of Portland, Maine, with $248 million in infrastructure, depreciates this cost over periods from 30 to 67 years.

However, because of the questionable need for depreciation for such long-lived assets, GASB did provide a unique alternative to depreciating the cost of eligible infrastructure assets such as the Brooklyn Bridge or Fifth Avenue. This method, known as the *modified approach,* eliminates the need for depreciating infrastructure assets. If specified guidelines are met, a government can choose to expense all maintenance costs each year in lieu of recording depreciation. Additions and improvements must be capitalized, but the cost of maintaining

[18] Charlotte A. Pryor, "Local Governments and the Modified Approach to Reporting the Cost of Infrastructure," *Government Accountants Journal,* April 1, 2013.

the infrastructure in proper working condition is expensed. Thus, if applied, New York City would expense the amount spent on the repair and other maintenance of Fifth Avenue so that no depreciation of the street's capitalized cost need be recorded. Effectively, proper maintenance of infrastructure assets can extend their lives indefinitely.

Use of the modified approach requires the government to accumulate information about all infrastructure assets within either a network or a subsystem of a network. For example, all roads could be deemed a network while state roads, rural roads, and interstate highways might make up three separate subsystems of that network.

- For eligible assets, the government establishes a minimum acceptable condition level and then documents that this minimum level is being met.
- The government must have an asset management system in place to monitor the eligible assets. This system assesses the ongoing condition to ensure that the eligible assets are, indeed, operating at the predetermined level. The maintenance system in place keeps this network or subsystem operating adequately.

The City of Los Angeles has adopted the modified approach in reporting all of its bridges. In its comprehensive annual financial report, the system used by that government is explained as follows. This description does indicate that the city has properly followed the preceding rules.

> The modified approach is used in reporting the City's bridges infrastructure system. A comprehensive bridge database system, the Bridges and Tunnel System, enables the City to track the entire bridge inventory, the structural condition of various bridge elements, and bridge sufficiency ratings. Condition assessments of these structures are completed in a three-year cycle. The latest assessment report was as of July 1, 2016. A system of letter grades identifies the condition of each structure. Letter grades "A" through "D" represent the condition of the structure as Very Good, Good to Fair, Fair to Poor, and Very Poor. "F" rating symbolizes a failed condition where replacement of the structure is necessary. These letter grades are based on sufficiency ratings, or the overall condition of the structure based on the last inspection. It is the City's policy that at least 70% of the bridges are rated "B" or better and that no bridge shall be rated less than "D". It is also the intent of the City that at least 80% of bridges be rated "B" or better by 2020. The City performs regular inspection and maintenance of the various structural elements for any defects. Funds for annual estimated inspection, maintenance and repair costs are provided in the City's budget. *Bridges infrastructure system is excluded in the determination of depreciation provisions for capital assets, while preservation and maintenance costs are charged to expense.* [Emphasis added.]

The modified approach provides a method by which governments can avoid depreciating infrastructure assets such as the Brooklyn Bridge that have virtually an unlimited life. The issue is: How many governments will be like the City of Los Angeles and go to the trouble of creating the standards and documentation required by this approach simply to avoid recording depreciation expense? According to one expert in the field, "There are relatively few governmental entities that have adopted the modified approach. Airports, transportation authorities and large transportation departments are really the only ones that I've seen that follow the modified approach."[19]

Comprehensive Annual Financial Report

LO 17-8

Understand the composition of a state or local government's comprehensive annual financial report (CAFR).

Government-wide financial statements and fund financial statements are most often presented to the public as part of a comprehensive annual financial report (CAFR). The CAFR is not limited to financial statements. It includes an extensive amount of information about the reporting government. As an example, the 2017 CAFR for the City of Orlando, Florida, with total assets of $3.5 billion, was approximately 300 pages. In comparison, the 2017 financial statements for Walmart, with almost $200 billion in assets, was only about 50 pages (although the Form 10-K that Walmart filed with the SEC for that year was about 200 pages).

The length of the CAFR indicates an attempt to provide a broad range of information to a wide assortment of interested parties. As stated previously, bond investors and taxpayers both want information but not necessarily the same information.

[19] Jack Reagan, partner, UHY LLP, Washington, DC, February 28, 2019.

The CAFR for most state and local governments can be found quickly on the Internet through a search of the government name along with "CAFR." It is composed of three broad sections:

1. *Introductory section*—includes a letter of transmittal from appropriate government officials, an organization chart, and a list of principal officers.
2. *Financial section*—presents the general purpose external financial statements (both government-wide and fund financial statements) and reproduces the auditor's report. The CAFR also includes the management's discussion and analysis (MD&A) and other required supplementary information.
3. *Statistical section*—discloses a wide range of data about the government encompassing both financial and nonfinancial information. This statistical information can be fascinating. In its 2018 CAFR, the City of Buffalo, New York, reports the following for that year (along with considerable other information): number of police officers (762), number of firefighters (652), traffic violations (41,172), recyclables collected (65 tons per day), fire stations (20), fire hydrants (7,974), streetlights (31,935), traffic signals (669), acreage for parks (1,842), street resurfacing (378,000 square yards), and materials used to fill potholes (1,378 tons).

The financial section of the CAFR is composed of three distinct sections:

1. Management's discussion and analysis. The MD&A is required supplemental information that "should provide an objective and easily readable analysis of the government's financial activities based on currently known facts, decisions, or conditions. . . . MD&A provides financial managers with the opportunity to present both a short- and a long-term analysis of the government's activities."[20]
2. Financial statements:
   a. Government-wide financial statements.
   b. Fund financial statements.
   c. Notes to the financial statements.
3. Required supplementary information (other than the MD&A). This section includes information required by U.S. GAAP that does not fall within the financial statements or accompanying notes. For example, the City of Orlando, Florida, compares budgetary figures for the city with actual results for each major fund, although a separate statement within the fund financial statements could also have been used for this purpose. Orlando also includes required supplementary information about the pensions and postemployment benefits that it provides to former employees. The city presents a schedule of employer contributions, a schedule of investment returns, and a schedule of net pension liability. That is not required as footnote disclosure but is important to understand the government's pension obligation.

For many readers, one of the most interesting aspects of the financial section is the MD&A because it provides a relatively clear description of the past, future, and present of the government's financial situation and operations. As an illustration, the 2018 CAFR for the City of Raleigh, North Carolina, includes a 15-page management's discussion and analysis that contains information such as the following:

- "The parking facilities operations generated $16.3 million of revenues in 2017–18, an increase of 3.2% compared to 2016–17. This is the result of continued growth in the downtown area and increased demand for parking."
- "Convention Center operations including the Performing Arts venue recognized $14.7 million of operating revenues in 2017–18, a decrease of 2.6% over 2016–17. Continued management of event offerings and diversification of show types is being explored to generate increased revenue growth."
- "As of the end of the fiscal year, the City of Raleigh's governmental funds reported combined ending fund balances of $585.3 million, a decrease of $14.8 million or 2.5%, in comparison with the prior year."

[20] GASB, *Codification, as of December 31, 2014,* Sec. 2200.106.

LO 17-9

Explain the makeup of a primary government and its relationship to component units and related organizations as well as the combination of governments.

The Primary Government and Component Units

Primary Government

It always should be possible in the public sector to trace financial accountability to elected officials. Consistent with this presumption of the ultimate financial accountability of elected officials, a typical state or local government financial report is built around the core of a single government with an elected governing body, known as the primary government.[21]

Each state and local government prepares and distributes a CAFR if it qualifies as a reporting entity. However, officials must identify the exact composition of that reporting entity because it is not always easy to discern. Normally, the reporting process begins with a primary government such as a town, city, county, or state. A primary government has (1) separate legal status, (2) an elected governing board, and (3) fiscal independence. Beyond that, each reporting entity also includes all organizations, agencies, offices, and departments that are not legally separate from the primary government.

Complications arise because many of the activities that interact closely with a primary government are legally separate. For example, an agency to provide job training might have its own incorporation but still be within the purview of city officials. Should such outside functions be included by the primary government as part of the reporting entity and its financial statements? That question is less complicated in for-profit accounting. Except in unusual cases, a business enterprise such as IBM or PepsiCo consolidates all businesses over which it holds control through majority ownership. Control is not as clearly delineated in governmental accounting. Should organizations be included within a CAFR even if they are legally separate from the primary government, and if so, what reporting is appropriate?

The almost unlimited number of activities that can be connected to a primary government raises problems for officials who are attempting to outline the parameters of the entity being reported. Organizations such as turnpike commissions, port authorities, public housing boards, and downtown development commissions have become commonplace for many cities and counties. The primary government might have created many of these, but they are structured as legally separate organizations. Such operations are usually established to focus attention on specific issues or problems.

As an example, notes to the financial statements in the 2017 CAFR for the City of Boston, Massachusetts, identifies four discretely presented component units (Boston Development & Planning Agency, Economic Development Industrial Corporation, Boston Public Health Commission, and Trustees of the Boston Public Library) and three blended component units (Boston Retirement System as well as the Dudley Square Realty Corporation and Ferdinand Building Development Corporation). The city also recognizes three related organizations (Boston Housing Authority, Boston Industrial Development Finance Authority, and Boston Water and Sewer Commission). Discretely presented component units? Blended component units? Related organizations? How do all of these entities relate to the primary government (the City of Boston), and what effect do they have on the financial reporting for the city?

Identifying Component Units

In the June 30, 2017, Management's Discussion and Analysis section of its CAFR, the City of Atlanta, Georgia, describes the reporting entity:

> "The government-wide financial statements include not only the City itself (known as the primary government), but also the legally separate Atlanta Fulton County Recreation Authority and the Atlanta Development Authority (doing business as Invest Atlanta), both of which the City is financially accountable. Financial information for these component units is reported separately from the financial information presented for the primary government. The Atlanta Housing Opportunity, Inc. is presented as a component unit, however their financial statements

[21] Stephen J. Gauthier, *Governmental Accounting, Auditing, and Financial Reporting* (Chicago: Government Finance Officers Association, 2012), p. 73.

are blended with the primary government. Other blended component units of the City include Urban Design Commission, Atlanta Public Safety and Judicial Facilities Authority and Solid Waste Management Authority."

When producing a CAFR, the major requirement for inclusion as a component unit is the financial accountability of the primary government. "Financial reporting based on accountability should enable the financial statement reader to focus on the body of organizations that are related by a common thread of accountability to the constituent citizenry."[22] When elected officials of a primary government are financially accountable for an outside organization, it is labeled a component unit. Such legally separate activities are so closely connected to the primary government that omission from the financial statements cannot be justified. They are "related by a common thread of accountability."

That is the reason the CAFR for the City of Atlanta includes the Atlanta Fulton County Recreation Authority and other separate activities. They qualify as component units. They are not part of the primary government but are reported in the CAFR to reflect the City of Atlanta's financial accountability.

Because of the potential effect on the financial statements of a primary government, the determination of component units is often of significant importance. GASB established two sets of criteria to indicate the presence of financial accountability. If an activity meets either one, it qualifies as a component unit to be reported within the CAFR of the primary government. A government can also include a legally separate entity in this way, even if neither of these criteria is met if officials believe exclusion is misleading.

Criterion 1 for Financial Accountability

The separate entity (such as the Atlanta Fulton County Recreation Authority) qualifies as a component unit if it fiscally depends on the primary government (the City of Atlanta). *Fiscal dependency* means that the entity cannot do one or more of the following without approval of the primary government: adopt its own budget, levy taxes or set rates, or issue bonded debt. This criterion also requires that the primary government and the component unit must be financially interdependent (a relationship exists that creates a potential financial benefit or burden between the two).

Criterion 2 for Financial Accountability

First, officials of the primary government must appoint a voting majority of the governing board of the separate organization. Second, either the primary government must be able to impose its will on this governing board or the separate organization provides a financial benefit or imposes a financial burden on the primary government.

Because of the importance of this identification process, several aspects of these criteria need to be explained in more depth to ensure proper application.

Voting Majority of the Governing Board The primary government's authority to elect a voting majority of the separate entity must be substantive. If, for example, the primary government simply confirms the choices made by other parties, then financial accountability is not present. Likewise, financial accountability does not result when the primary government merely selects the governing board from a limited slate of candidates (such as picking three individuals from an approved slate of five). The officials of the primary government must have the actual responsibility for appointing a voting majority of the board to meet this provision of the second criterion.

Imposition of the Primary Government's Will on the Governing Board Such power is indicated if the primary government can significantly influence programs, projects, activities, or level of services the separate organization provides. This degree of influence is present if the primary government is able to remove an appointed board member at will, modify or approve budgets, override decisions of the board, modify or approve rate or fee changes, or hire or dismiss the individuals responsible for day-to-day operations. Such power shows the primary government's true level of authority.

[22] GASB, *Codification, as of December 31, 2018,* Sec. 2100.102.

Financial Benefit or Financial Burden on the Primary Government This level of financial connection exists between the primary government and the separate organization if the government is entitled to the organization's resources, the government is legally obligated to finance any deficits or provide support, or the government is responsible for the organization's debts.

Reporting Component Units

After being identified, component units are reported by a primary government in one of two ways: (1) discretely presented or (2) blended. If discretely presented, financial information about the component units is presented on the far right side of the government-wide statements. For example, as of June 30, 2017, the government-wide statements in the CAFR for the City of Detroit, Michigan, show that the primary government holds total assets and deferred outflows of resources of more than $5.9 billion. The city's discretely presented component units shown just to the right of the primary government reports similar accounts totaling $1.8 billion.

According to the notes to the Detroit's financial statements, these component unit figures were gathered from 12 separate organizations:

- Detroit Brownfield Redevelopment Authority.
- Detroit Public Library.
- Detroit Transportation Corporation.
- Detroit Housing Commission.
- Downtown Development Authority.
- Eastern Market Corporation.
- Economic Development Corporation.
- Local Development Finance Authority.
- Museum of African American History.
- Detroit Land Bank Authority.
- Eight Mile/Woodward Corridor Improvement Authority.
- Detroit Employment Solutions Corporation.

GASB allows an alternative placement of component units within the CAFR. A primary government can include a component unit as an actual part of the reporting government as if it were another fund (a process referred to as *blending*). Although legally separate, a component can be so intertwined with the primary government that inclusion is necessary to present the financial information in an appropriate fashion. The blending of a component unit is usually at the discretion of government officials but is required if the separate entity's debt will be repaid entirely, or almost entirely, from resources of the primary government. Beyond the discretely presented units previously listed, the City of Detroit blends three of its component units: Detroit Building Authority, Greater Detroit Resource Recovery Authority, and the Public Lighting Authority. This inclusion with the primary government is justified in the CAFR, "Blended component units, although legally separate entities, are, in substance, part of the City's operations."

The City of Detroit also lists several related organizations. They are not closely tied to the primary government so that less reporting is necessary. The primary government is accountable only because it appoints a voting majority of the outside organization's governing board. Fiscal dependency as defined previously is not present, and the primary government cannot impose its will on the board and does not gather financial benefits or burdens from the relationship. Consequently, the separate organization is not a component unit. For a related organization, the primary government must still identify the nature of the relationship. The City of Detroit discloses related organizations that include the Detroit Historical Society and Detroit Zoological Society.

Special-Purpose Governments

Most individuals think of primary governments in terms of general-purpose governments such as states, cities, counties, towns, and the like. Nevertheless, numerous special-purpose governments also exist around the country. As noted at the beginning of the previous chapter,

Discussion Question

IS IT PART OF THE COUNTY?

Harland County is in a financially distressed area within the state of Missouri. In hopes of enticing business to the county, the state legislature appropriates $3 million to start an industrial development commission. The federal government provides an additional $1 million. The state appoints 15 individuals to a board to oversee the operations of this commission. Harland County officials name five additional members. The commission begins operations by raising funds from local citizens and businesses. Over the past 12 months, it received $700,000 in donations and pledges. The county provides clerical assistance and allows the commission to use one wing of a county office building for its headquarters. The Harland County government must approve the commission's annual operating budget. The county will also cover any deficits that might occur.

During the current period, the commission spent $2.4 million and achieves notable success. Several large companies recently began to explore the possibility of opening manufacturing plants in the county.

Harland County is currently preparing its comprehensive annual financial report. Should the county's CAFR include the revenues, expenditures, assets, expenses, and liabilities of the industrial development commission? Is it a fund within the county's primary government, a component unit, or a related organization?

Is the industrial development commission a component unit of the State of Missouri? How should its activities be presented in the state's comprehensive annual financial report?

more than 50,000 school systems and other special-purpose districts exist across the United States. Their qualifications as primary governments can be seen in a note to the 2017 CAFR for the Atlanta Independent School System:

> The Atlanta Independent School System (School System of the District) was established by the Georgia State Legislature and is composed of nine publicly elected members serving four-year terms. The School System has the authority to approve its own budget and to provide for the levy of taxes to cover the cost of operations and maintenance and to cover debt service payments. Additionally, the School System has decision-making authority, the power to approve selection of management personnel, the ability to significantly influence operations, and primary accountability for fiscal matters. Accordingly, the School System is a primary government and consists of all the organizations that compose its legal entity.

Special-purpose governments carry out only a single function or a limited number of functions. Common examples include public school districts, colleges and universities, water utilities, hospitals, transit authorities, and library services. In deciding the appropriate method of reporting, officials must address one central question: Is such an operation truly a special-purpose government or merely a part of a larger government (such as a city or county) so that it should be reported as a fund or a component unit. Or, perhaps, it is not a government entity at all but rather a nongovernmental not-for-profit organization with accounting rules that will be explained in the subsequent chapter.

As shown by the note in the CAFR for the Atlanta Independent School System, an activity or function is deemed a special-purpose government if it meets the following criteria:

1. Has a separately elected governing body.
2. Is legally independent, which can be demonstrated by having corporate powers such as the right to sue and be sued as well as the right to buy, sell, and lease property in its own name.

3. Is fiscally independent of other state and local governments. As mentioned previously, an activity is normally considered to be fiscally independent if its leadership can determine the activity's budget without having to seek the approval of an outside party, levy taxes or set rates without having to seek outside approval, or issue bonded debt without outside approval.

A school system or other government activity that satisfies all three of these requirements is reported as a special-purpose government that produces its own CAFR. If that same activity fails to meet any one of these criteria, its financial affairs are likely to be maintained within the general fund or special revenue funds of a state or municipal government.

Acquisitions, Mergers, and Transfers of Operations

LO 17-9

Explain the makeup of a primary government and its relationship to component units and related organizations as well as the combination of governments.

With so many general-purpose governments, special-purpose governments, component units, and related organizations, combinations and realignment transactions are common.

- A city government might take over operations of a homeless shelter from a not-for-profit entity.
- A toll road operated as a special-purpose government might be acquired by a local county.
- Two independent school systems might be brought together to create more efficient operations.

> "After voters approved a ballot question last month approving the consolidation of the Atwood-Hammond and Arthur school districts, school officials, teachers and students have begun the process of merging the two districts into a single entity. Atwood-Hammond Superintendent Kenny Schwengel said the two school districts will spend the 2013–14 school year getting ready for the merger, which takes effect on July 1, 2014."[23]

GASB views a combination as a *merger* if two legally separate entities are brought together to form a new entity and no significant consideration is exchanged. The combination is still a merger even if one of these entities ceases to exist while the other continues to function. The combination of two agencies or two school systems might meet this criteria. In a merger, because of the lack of paid consideration, the net carrying values for all assets, deferred outflows of resources, liabilities, and deferred inflows of resources are simply combined. Balances are not changed. Additional accounts are neither created nor recognized as a result of this type of combination. The account balances are literally merged.

The reporting of an *acquisition* is quite different. In an acquisition, consideration is exchanged. For example, the cash purchase of a special-purpose government toll road by a county government is an acquisition if the toll road ceases to exist as a separate entity and becomes part of the county government. In government-wide financial statements, the acquiring government records all acquired assets, deferred outflows of resources, liabilities, and deferred inflows of resources at acquisition value (other than a few specific exceptions such as landfills). GASB defines acquisition value as the market-based entry price—the amount that the government would pay to acquire or discharge each separate item.

As with for-profit transactions, an acquiring entity often must pay more than the total acquisition values assigned to the various assets, liabilities, and deferrals. In for-profit accounting—as discussed in prior chapters of this textbook—any excess payment is reported as the asset "goodwill." This balance is then tested periodically for possible impairment.

On government-wide financial statements, any consideration paid in excess of acquisition value is reported initially as a deferred outflow of resources on the statement of net position. The balance is then written off to expense over a period of time determined based on factors such as the service life of capital assets, technology available, and contracts acquired.

When an acquisition takes place, fund financial statements for the governmental funds record any acquired current financial resources and the claims against those resources. That approach is in line with the usual reporting of those funds. Once again, acquisition value

[23] Tim Mitchell, "School Districts Prepare for Merger," *The News-Gazette*, May 20, 2013.

is applied to each balance. The government also records any reduction in current financial resources caused by the payment to create the acquisition. Fund balances are adjusted to reflect the net change.

To illustrate, assume cash of $4 million is paid by a large city to acquire an outside agency which holds (1) current financial resources with a total acquisition value of $1 million and (2) capital assets with a total acquisition fair value of $2 million. In the government's fund financial statements, cash is reduced by $4 million with the acquired current financial resources recorded at $1 million. The capital assets are not reported on fund statements for governmental funds. To reflect the $3 million difference, the government reduces the fund balance for the acquiring fund.

Occasionally, an entity will convey one of its activities to another entity but not the entire operation. A government might transfer the operations of a soup kitchen to a local charity. A not-for-profit entity might transfer a homeless shelter to the local city. If a government receives an operation purely by transfer, all assets, deferred outflows of resources, liabilities, and deferred inflows of resources are recorded at the previous net carrying amounts. Conversely, if a state or local government is turning over an activity to another party, a gain or loss on disposal is reported depending on whether any resources are received in return.

LO 17-10

Describe the physical structure of a complete set of government-wide financial statements and a complete set of fund financial statements.

Government-Wide and Fund Financial Statements Illustrated

At the core of a governmental reporting entity's CAFR are the general purpose financial statements. These statements are made up of government-wide financial statements and fund financial statements. Government-wide statements present financial information for both governmental activities and business-type activities (and often component units). They measure economic resources and utilize accrual accounting.

Separate fund financial statements are created for (1) the governmental funds, (2) the proprietary funds, and (3) the fiduciary funds. The measurement focus and timing of recognition depend on the fund in question. For governmental funds, the current financial resources measurement focus is used with modified accrual accounting. Both proprietary funds and fiduciary funds use accrual accounting to report all economic resources.

Four of these statements were outlined briefly in the previous chapter to introduce their basic structure. Now that a deeper understanding of government accounting has been established, government-wide and fund financial statements can be examined in more detail.[24]

Statement of Net Position—Government-Wide Financial Statements

Exhibit 17.1 presents a hypothetical version of the June 30, 2020, statement of net position for the City of Eastern South. As a government-wide financial statement, it reports the economic resources of the government as a whole (except for the fiduciary funds, which are not included because those resources must be used for a purpose outside the government).

Please note several aspects of this statement of net position:

- The measurement focus is on the economic resources controlled by the government. Thus, all assets, including capital assets, are reported. Noncurrent liabilities are presented for the same reason.
- Capital assets other than land, inexhaustible works of art, and construction in progress (and infrastructure assets if the modified approach is applied) are reported net of accumulated depreciation. Other than these exceptions, depreciation of capital assets is shown on the government-wide statements. (See Point A.)
- As discussed in the previous chapter, categories titled Deferred Outflows of Resources and Deferred Inflows of Resources are included on this statement. These sections provide

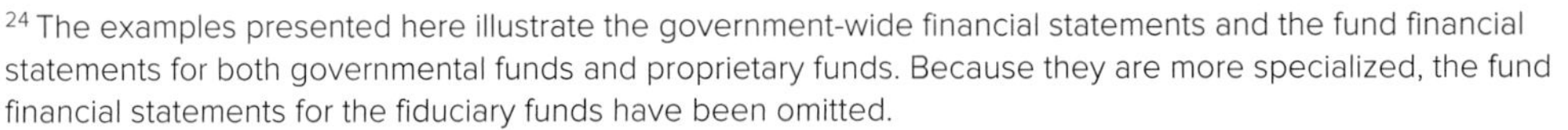
[24] The examples presented here illustrate the government-wide financial statements and the fund financial statements for both governmental funds and proprietary funds. Because they are more specialized, the fund financial statements for the fiduciary funds have been omitted.

EXHIBIT 17.1 **Government-Wide Financial Statements—Statement of Net Position**

CITY OF EASTERN SOUTH
Statement of Net Position
June 30, 2020
(in thousands)

	Primary Government			Component Unit—Eastern South Regional Art Space ©
	Governmental Activities	Business-Type Activities	Total	
Assets				
Cash and investments	$ 232,450	$ 149,333	$ 381,783	$25,735
Receivables, net	219,435	59,812	279,247	-0-
Internal balances Ⓑ	23,876	(23,876)	-0-	-0-
Inventories and supplies	11,654	12,922	24,576	2,159
Prepaid items	5,075	2,117	7,192	822
Land and other capital assets not depreciated	250,883	165,873	416,756	1,451
Other capital assets, net of depreciation Ⓐ	821,490	688,523	1,510,013	11,434
Total assets	$1,564,863	$1,054,704	$2,619,567	$41,601
Deferred outflows of resources				
Unamortized excess cost of acquisition	$ 59,447	$ -0-	$ 59,447	$ -0-
Liabilities				
Accounts payable	$ 23,775	$ 14,315	$ 38,090	$ 5,076
Other liabilities and unearned revenue	30,766	5,225	35,991	432
Bonds payable—current	87,922	12,885	100,807	3,124
Landfill closure obligation	-0-	9,078	9,078	-0-
Bonds payable—noncurrent	289,217	221,441	510,658	6,780
Net pension liability	111,000	-0-	111,000	-0-
Lease payable—noncurrent	24,548	21,669	46,217	2,277
Total liabilities	$ 567,228	$ 284,613	$ 851,841	$17,689
Deferred inflows of resources				
Unavailable property tax collections	$ 26,500	$ -0-	$ 26,500	$ -0-
Net Position				
Invested in capital assets, net of related debt	$ 811,487	$ 723,656	$1,535,143	$ 872
Restricted for:				
Capital projects	125,769	19,774	145,543	5,045
Debt service	2,355	1,056	3,411	84
Other	29,267	-0-	29,267	-0-
Unrestricted	61,704	25,605	87,309	17,911
Total net position	$1,030,582	$ 770,091	$1,800,673	$23,912

The notes to the financial statements are an integral part of this statement.

a location for balances that do not qualify as either assets or liabilities in government accounting.

- The primary government is divided into governmental activities and business-type activities. Governmental funds are reported as governmental activities, whereas enterprise funds comprise most, if not all, of the business-type activities. Even though recorded as proprietary funds, internal service funds are frequently classified as governmental activities.

That is appropriate when those services rendered are primarily for the benefit of activities within the governmental funds (for example, a print shop that works mainly for the local schools).

- The internal balances shown in the asset section (Point B) reflect receivables and payables between the governmental activities and the business-type activities. These internal balances have no financial effect outside of the government and are offset so that no change results in the totals reported for the primary government.
- Discretely presented component units are grouped and shown to the far right side of the statement (Point C) so that their reported amounts do not affect the primary government figures. In contrast, blended component units are included, as appropriate, within either the governmental activities or the business-type activities as if they were individual funds of the government. As seen in the final column of Exhibit 17.1, this city has one discretely presented component unit: the Eastern South Regional Art Space. The government could also have blended component units, but readers need to check the disclosure notes to ascertain their presence.
- As the Net Position section shows, several monetary amounts have been restricted for capital projects, debt service, and the like. Restrictions are identified in this manner only if usage of those resources has been designated (1) by external parties such as creditors, grantors, or other external party; or (2) as a result of laws that have been passed through constitutional provisions or enabling legislation.

Statement of Activities—Government-Wide Financial Statements

The statement of activities presents a wide array of information about the various functions of a state or local government. As shown in the statement for the City of Eastern South in Exhibit 17.2, the same general classification system of governmental activities, business-type activities, and component units used in Exhibit 17.1 forms the structural basis for reporting. Nevertheless, the format here is more complex and requires close analysis. It is often studied from left to right and then from top to bottom.

- The government presents its operating expenses in the first column (Point D). The balances are not classified according to individual causes such as salaries, rent, depreciation, or insurance. Instead, expenses are shown by function: general government, police, fire, general services, and the like. This approach is likely to be more relevant to the needs of the people reading the statements. "As a minimum, governments should report direct expenses for each function. Direct expenses are those that are specifically associated with a service, program, or department and, thus, are clearly identifiable to a particular function."[25] Expenses are shown in this statement for governmental activities, business-type activities, and discretely presented component units.
- Interest expense on general long-term debt is normally considered an indirect expense because borrowed money can benefit many government activities. Nevertheless, it is often a large monetary amount with significant informational value. Furthermore, it can be difficult to allocate in a logical way among different activities. For these reasons, governments can report interest expense as shown in this example (Point E) as a separate "function."
- After operating expenses have been reported in the first column, related program revenues are listed in the next three columns (Point F). Program revenues are derived by the function itself or from outsiders seeking to reduce the government's cost for providing a service or benefit. Program revenues are different from general government revenues (such as property and sales taxes) that are reported toward the bottom of the statement. As shown in Exhibit 17.2, program revenues are usually classified within three categories:

    1. *Charges for services.* For example, a monthly charge is normally assessed for water service. Therefore, this first business-type activity shows earning nearly $50.9 million in program revenues. In contrast, because of their public service nature, most government

[25] GASB, *Codification,* Sec. 2200.129.

EXHIBIT 17.2 Government-Wide Financial Statements—Statement of Activities

CITY OF EASTERN SOUTH
Statement of Activities
For the Fiscal Year Ended June 30, 2020
(in thousands)

Functions/Programs	Operating Expenses (D)	Program Revenues (F): Charge for Services	Program Revenues (F): Operating Grants and Contributions	Program Revenues (F): Capital Grants and Contributions	Net (Expenses) Revenues and Changes in Net Position — Primary Government: Governmental Activities	Business-type Activities	Total	Component Unit-Eastern South Regional Art Space
Primary government:								
Governmental activities								
General government	$ (28,055)	$ 6,554	$ 5,472	$ 2,384	$ (13,645)		$ (13,645)	
Police	(103,465)	17,980	13,256	6,747	(65,482) (H)		(65,482)	
Fire	(97,687)	5,306	19,821	23,063	(49,497)		(49,497)	
Transportation	(96,088)	31,365	355	16,984 (G)	(47,384)		(47,384)	
Economic development	(5,563)	898	143	1,875	(2,647)		(2,647)	
Parks and recreation	(64,725)	17,168	16,778	4,221	(26,558)		(26,558)	
Neighborhood services	(3,965)	649	132	2,993	(191)		(191)	
Library	(17,744)	5,365	2,784	2,257	(7,338)		(7,338)	
Interest on noncurrent debt	(23,550) (E)	–0–	–0–	–0–	(23,550)		(23,550)	
Total governmental activities	$ (440,842)	$ 85,285	$58,741	$60,524	$ (236,292) (J)		$(236,292)	
Business-type activities								
Water	$ (39,273)	$ 50,877	$ 121	$ 6,339		$18,064 (I)	$ 18,064	
Sewer	(12,868)	11,836	488	2,451		1,907	1,907	
Parking	(11,776)	25,990	1,342	844		16,400	16,400	
Others	(8,074)	795	5,434	6,009		4,164	4,164	
Total business-type activities	(71,991)	89,498	7,385	15,643		40,535 (K)	40,535	
Total primary government	$ (512,833)	$174,783	$66,126	$76,167	$(236,292)	$40,535	$(195,757)	
Component unit:								
Eastern South Regional Art Space	$ (8,128)	$ 2,896	$ 1,676	$ –0–				$(3,556) (L)

(continued)

EXHIBIT 17.2 (Continued)

CITY OF EASTERN SOUTH
Statement of Activities
For the Fiscal Year Ended June 30, 2020
(in thousands)

		Program Revenues Ⓕ			Net (Expenses) Revenues and Changes in Net Position			
					Primary Government			
Functions/Programs	**Operating Expenses Ⓓ**	**Charge for Services**	**Operating Grants and Contributions**	**Capital Grants and Contributions**	**Governmental Activities**	**Business-type Activities**	**Total**	**Component Unit-Eastern South Regional Art Space**
General revenues								
Property taxes					$ 111,762 Ⓜ	$ –0–	$ 111,762	
Income taxes					49,079	–0–	49,079	
Sales Taxes					43,809	–0–	43,809	
Unrestricted grants					17,227		17,227	
Gain on sale of capital asset					–0–	556	556	
Investment earnings					13,244	3,101	16,345	279
Transfers					18,633	(18,633)	–0– Ⓝ	
Total general revenues, transfers and others					$ 253,754	$ (14,976)	$ 238,778	$ 279
Change in net position					$ 17,462 Ⓣ	$ 25,559	$ 43,021	$ (3,277)
Net position, beginning of year					$1,013,120	$744,532	$1,757,652	$27,189
Net position, end of year					$1,030,582	$770,091	$1,800,673	$23,912

The notes to the financial statements are an integral part of this statement.

functions generate only small amounts of revenue from sources such as parking meter revenues, fines for speeding tickets, concessions at parks, and the like.

2. *Operating grants and contributions.* This column reports resources received from outside grants and similar sources designated for some type of operating purpose. For example, the police department is shown here as having gained approximately $13.3 million in operating grants and contributions during the year.
3. *Capital grants and contributions.* This column presents outside grants and similar sources designated by the donor for capital asset additions (rather than operations). As an example for the City of Eastern South, more than $16.9 million in capital grants and contributions came in to support the transportation function (Point G). Perhaps the city received grant funding to assist in developing better mass transportation.

- After operating expenses have been assigned along with related program revenues, the statement of activities shows a net (expense) or revenue for each function. This figure is an important measure of the financial cost (or benefit) of each of the various government functions. For example, in Exhibit 17.2, the police incurred $103.5 million in operating expenses but also generated enough charges, grants, and contributions so that (at Point H) taxpayers only had to bear a financial burden of roughly $65.5 million for police protection. That cost is significant information for citizens studying these statements. Are they satisfied with that level of protection? Do they wish that some of that money had been spent in other ways? In contrast, the water system reported operating expenses of $39.3 million. Because of user charges, grants, and contributions, this business-type activity generated net revenues of approximately $18.1 million (see Point I) as a financial benefit for the government.
- All of the governmental activities are combined to report net expenses of $236.3 million (Point J). In contrast, business-type activities generated total net revenues of approximately $40.5 million (Point K). The component units report net expenses of $3.6 million (Point L). The financial cost or benefit from each government function is evident. Such information enables citizens to be informed about the operations of the government.
- Reading down the statement, general revenues are reported next as additions to either the governmental activities, business-type activities, or component units. All taxes are general revenues because they do not reflect a direct charge for services. The government obtains this money from the population as a whole. At Point M, property taxes of nearly $112 million are shown as the largest revenue source. Citizens pay that money in order for the government to cover the costs of the various activities provided by the City of Eastern South. Significant amounts were also collected as income taxes and sales taxes.
- Transfers of $18.6 million between governmental activities and business-type activities are also shown within the general revenues. These inflows and outflows are offset for reporting purposes to indicate that no financial effect is created on the total figures reported for the primary government (Point N).

Balance Sheet—Governmental Funds—Fund Financial Statements

Switching now to fund financial statements, Exhibit 17.3 presents the balance sheet for the governmental funds as reported by the City of Eastern South. This statement reports only current financial resources (along with supplies and prepaid items) and claims to those current financial resources. It was prepared using modified accrual accounting for timing purposes. No proprietary funds, discretely presented component units, or fiduciary funds are included. This fund-based statement reflects just the governmental funds. Several parts of this statement should be noted:

- Separate columns are shown for the general fund and any other fund that qualifies as major. The city identifies two other funds as major. The Highway 61 Construction Fund is a major capital projects fund. The Educational Services Fund is a major special revenue fund. Remaining governmental funds that are not considered major are combined to be reported as Other Governmental Funds.
- The balance sheet reports no capital assets or long-term debts simply because they are neither current financial resources nor claims to current financial resources.

EXHIBIT 17.3 Fund Financial Statements—Balance Sheet for the Governmental Funds

CITY OF EASTERN SOUTH
Governmental Funds
Balance Sheet
June 30, 2020
(in thousands)

	General Fund	Highway 61 Construction	Educational Services	Other Governmental Funds	Total Governmental Funds
Assets:					
Cash and investments	$111,673	$87,056	$11,908	$10,905	$221,542
Receivables, net					
Taxes	53,875	–0–	17,854	–0–	71,729
Accounts	108,654	–0–	–0–	–0–	108,654
Inventory of supplies	3,222	2,076	3,112	2,175	10,585
Prepaid Items	887	1,015	1,322	556	3,780
Total assets	$278,311	$90,147	$34,196	$13,636	$416,290
Liabilities:					
Accounts payable	$ 21,659	$ 776	$ 452	$ 298	$ 23,185
Accrued liabilities	7,174	323	2,572	1,963	12,032
Other claims to financial resources	1,128	1,733	–0–	312	3,173
Bonds currently due	25,000	–0–	7,200	–0–	32,200
Total liabilities	$ 54,961	$ 2,832	$10,224	$ 2,573	$ 70,590
Deferred inflows of resources:					
Unavailable property tax collections	$ 26,500	$ –0–	$ –0–	$ –0–	$ 26,500
Total liabilities and deferred inflows of resources	$ 81,461	$ 2,832	$10,224	$ 2,573	$ 97,090
Fund balances: ⓞ					
Nonspendable	$ 11,465	$ 3,091	$ 4,434	$ 2,989	$ 21,979
Restricted	46,717	–0–	19,538	875	67,130
Committed	2,044	1,159	–0–	993	4,196
Assigned	35,009	83,065	–0–	6,206	124,280
Unassigned	101,615	–0–	–0–	–0–	101,615
Total fund balances	$196,850	$87,315	$23,972	$11,063	$319,200 ⓟ
Total liabilities, deferred inflows of resources, and fund balances	$278,311	$90,147	$34,196	$13,636	$416,290

The notes to the financial statements are an integral part of this statement.

- The Fund Balances figures (Point O) indicate the nonspendable, restricted, committed, assigned, and unassigned categories discussed in the previous chapter.
- The Total Fund Balances figure for the governmental funds of $319.2 million (Point P) is significantly different from the $1.0 billion total net position reported for governmental activities in the statement of net position (Exhibit 17.1). To explain that large disparity, the government presents a reconciliation along with the balance sheet. This reconciliation starts with the Total Fund Balance figure and shows individual differences with the total net position amount. For example, this reconciliation might look something like the following for the City of Eastern South. The inclusion of internal service funds within the governmental activities makes direct conversion from one statement to the other somewhat complicated.

Reconciliation of the Balance Sheet Governmental Funds to the Governmental Activities in the Statement of Net Position June 30, 2020 (in thousands)

Total fund balance for governmental funds, June 30, 2020, as reported on balance sheet . . .	$ 319,200
Capital assets reported by governmental activities but not reported in governmental funds. . .	1,021,800
Bonds payable reported by governmental activities but not reported in governmental funds. . .	(422,650)
Other assets and liabilities reported by governmental activities but not reported in governmental funds . . .	(43,866)
Revenues reported by governmental activities but not reported in governmental funds because they are not available . . .	32,845
Internal service funds reported by governmental activities but not reported in governmental funds . . .	123,253
Total net position, governmental activities, June 30, 2020, as reported in statement of net position. . .	$1,030,582

Statement of Revenues, Expenditures, and Other Changes in Fund Balances—Governmental Funds—Fund Financial Statements

Exhibit 17.4 presents the statement of revenues, expenditures, and other changes in fund balances for the governmental funds of the City of Eastern South. Once again, details for the general fund appear in a separate column along with each of the other major funds previously identified. Figures for all remaining nonmajor funds are accumulated and shown together.

In examining Exhibit 17.4, note the following:

- Because the government focuses here on measuring current financial resources, expenditures (Point Q) rather than expenses are reported. For example, Capital Outlay is presented as a reduction in resources rather than as the acquisition of an asset. Similarly, Debt Service—Principal is an expenditure instead of a decrease in long-term liabilities.
- Because the government applies the modified accrual method of accounting for timing purposes, reported amounts will be different than those previously shown under accrual accounting. For example, property taxes are reported here as $107.2 million but as $111.8 million in Exhibit 17.2.
- At Point R, Exhibit 17.4 presents other financing sources and uses to reflect here the financial effect of the issuance of long-term debt and transfers made between the funds. In those cases, the amount of current financial resources change but no revenues or expenditures take place. Because the fund statements focus on individual activities rather than government-wide figures, no elimination of the transfers is made. They do affect the individual funds.

Another reconciliation is needed to explain the difference that exists between the amounts reported in the statement of revenues, expenditures, and other changes in fund balances and the statement of activities. At Point S, Exhibit 17.4 indicates that the fund balances for the

EXHIBIT 17.4 Fund Financial Statements—Statement of Revenues, Expenditures, and Other Changes in Fund Balances

CITY OF EASTERN SOUTH
Governmental Funds
Statement of Revenues, Expenditures, and Other Changes in Fund Balance
For the Fiscal Year Ended June 30, 2020 (in thousands)

	General Fund	Highway 61 Construction	Educational Services	Other Governmental Funds	Total Governmental Funds
Revenues:					
Property taxes	$ 99,737	$ –0–	$ 7,500	$ –0–	$ 107,237
Income taxes	43,556	–0–	–0–	–0–	43,556
Sales taxes	38,760	5,000	–0–	–0–	43,760
Charges for services	61,223	–0–	3,327	1,196	65,746
Fines and penalties	2,657	–0–	–0–	312	2,969
Grants and contributions	87,332	17,901	9,448	1,323	116,004
Investment earnings and miscellaneous	20,775	3,989	2,887	624	28,275
Total revenues	$354,040	$26,890	$23,162	$ 3,455	$ 407,547
Expenditures: ⓠ					
Current:					
General government	$ 23,909	$ –0–	$ –0–	$ –0–	$ 23,909
Police	79,565	–0–	–0–	–0–	79,565
Fire	81,100	–0–	–0–	–0–	81,100
Transportation	76,826	8,554	–0–	–0–	85,380
Economic development	5,129	–0–	–0–	656	5,785
Parks and recreation	53,119	–0–	547	134	53,800
Neighborhood services	1,445	–0–	1,389	–0–	2,834
Library	6,022	–0–	10,083	–0–	16,105
Capital outlay	42,459	17,809	8,220	2,500	70,988
Debt service:					
Principal	5,334	–0–	2,108	–0–	7,442
Interest	3,989	–0–	434	–0–	4,423
Total expenditures	$378,897	$26,363	$22,781	$ 3,290	$ 431,331
Excess (deficiency) of revenues over (under) expenditures	$ (24,857)	$ 527	$ 381	$ 165	$ (23,784)
Other financing sources (uses): ⓡ					
Transfers in	$ 16,157	$ 442	$ 2,331	$11,090	$ 30,020
Transfers out	(30,050)	–0–	–0–	(6,552)	(36,602)
Issuance of long-term debt	45,000	8,112	2,090	–0–	55,202
Total other financing sources (uses)	$ 31,107	$ 8,554	$ 4,421	$ 4,538	$ 48,620
Net change in fund balances	$ 6,250	$ 9,081	$ 4,802	$ 4,703	$ 24,836 ⓢ
Fund balance, beginning of year	$190,600	$78,234	$19,170	$ 6,360	$ 294,364
Fund balance, end of year	$196,850	$87,315	$23,972	$11,063	$ 319,200

The notes to the financial statements are an integral part of this statement.

governmental funds increased during the period by more than $24.8 million. In Exhibit 17.2, Point T reports an increase in the net position of the governmental activities by only $17.5 million. A $7.3 million difference exists between two figures that sound alike. To avoid confusion, the government presents a reconciliation.

Although not included here, this reconciliation begins with the change in the total fund balances and makes all necessary adjustments to arrive at the reported change in net position. Those changes often include

- The acquisition of capital assets during the period that will decrease the fund balance because current financial resources are used but not the government's net position.
- The recording of depreciation that decreases the city's net position but has no effect on current financial resources.
- The recording of any revenues and expenses that do not impact current financial resources but do change the net position of the government.
- The issuance of long-term debt that increases the city's current financial resources but not its net position.

Statement of Net Position—Proprietary Funds—Fund Financial Statements

The assets and liabilities of the City of Eastern South's proprietary funds, as reported in the fund financial statements, are presented in Exhibit 17.5. This statement shows individual information about three major enterprise funds, with a single column for the summation of all other enterprise funds. The statement then provides a combined total for the enterprise funds as a whole. Because of their size, specific information is made available here for the water fund, sewer fund, and parking fund.

In examining Exhibit 17.5, please note several important features:

- This fund statement combines and exhibits all internal service funds (Point U) because they are classified as proprietary funds. However, in the government-wide financial statements, these same internal service funds are frequently reported within the governmental activities. That reporting is appropriate but only when the activity provides services primarily for functions within the governmental funds.
- Because the proprietary funds apply accrual accounting to measure economic resources, the totals for the enterprise funds in Exhibit 17.5 agree in most ways with the total figures included in Exhibit 17.1. The amount of detail, however, is more extensive in the fund financial statements. For example, the statement in Exhibit 17.1 uses only two accounts to describe capital assets, whereas Exhibit 17.5 uses five.

Statement of Revenues, Expenses, and Other Changes in Net Position—Proprietary Funds—Fund Financial Statements

Just as the statement of net position in Exhibit 17.5 provides individual information about specific enterprise funds (and totals for internal service funds), the statement of revenues, expenses, and changes in net position in Exhibit 17.6 gives the revenues, expenses, nonoperating items, and transfers for those same funds.

As an example, in Exhibit 17.2, operating expenses are listed for each of the business-type activities (water, sewer, parking, and community center). Here, in Exhibit 17.6 (Point V), operating expenses are listed based on the type of expense for each of the proprietary funds: employee services, services and supplies, depreciation and amortization, utilities, maintenance and repairs, and others. In addition, several nonoperating items are identified. Those include investment earnings and a gain on disposal of a capital asset. Finally, because this statement reflects all changes in the net position of each proprietary activity, transfers are included at the bottom. Thus, extensive information is available about the operation of each of these major enterprise funds, which is the objective of fund financial statements.

Statement of Cash Flows—Proprietary Funds—Fund Financial Statements

One of the most unique aspects of the fund financial statements is the statement of cash flows for the proprietary funds (Exhibit 17.7). Because a proprietary fund operates in a manner

EXHIBIT 17.5 **Fund Financial Statements—Statement of Net Position for Proprietary Funds**

CITY OF EASTERN SOUTH
Proprietary Funds
Statement of Net Position
June 30, 2020
(in thousands)

	Water	Sewer	Parking	Other Enterprise Funds	Total Enterprise Funds	Internal Service Funds Ⓤ
Assets						
Current assets						
Cash and equivalents	$ 18,400	$ 16,150	$ 17,100	$ 9,225	$ 60,875	$ 5,000
Investments	35,045	12,285	25,803	15,325	88,458	8,882
Receivables, net						
Accounts	22,943	9,076	7,577	3,782	43,378	2,178
Other	8,435	3,081	2,290	2,628	16,434	3,006
Due from other funds	–0–	–0–	366	43	409	9,092
Inventories and supplies	3,642	1,810	1,708	5,762	12,922	722
Prepaid items	461	226	824	606	2,117	658
Total current assets	$ 88,926	$ 42,628	$ 55,668	$ 37,371	$ 224,593	$ 29,538
Noncurrent assets						
Capital assets						
Land	$ 62,981	$ 55,773	$ 29,100	$ 18,019	$ 155,873	$ 9,817
Buildings	388,278	206,149	72,925	45,785	713,137	12,713
Leased property	3,672	8,179	10,433	7,734	30,018	2,058
Vehicles	33,012	26,567	37,007	18,633	115,219	3,118
Equipment	34,227	15,995	4,303	7,883	62,408	5,004
Less: Accumulated depreciation	(83,445)	(77,881)	(41,642)	(29,291)	(232,259)	(11,886)
Total noncurrent assets	$438,725	$234,782	$112,126	$ 68,763	$ 854,396	$ 20,824
Total assets	$527,651	$277,410	$167,794	$106,134	$1,078,989	$ 50,362

(continued)

Liabilities						
Current liabilities						
Accounts payable and other accrued expenses	$ 9,260	$ 3,065	$ 2,084	$ 1,696	$ 16,105	$ 983
Due to other funds	11,522	8,044	4,088	631	24,285	375
Unearned revenue	1,418	883	316	154	2,771	310
Lease payable, current	327	125	98	114	664	55
Bonds and notes payable, current	5,837	3,992	1,760	1,296	12,885	100
Total current liabilities	$ 28,364	$ 16,109	$ 8,346	$ 3,891	$ 56,710	$ 1,823
Noncurrent liabilities						
Liability for landfill closure	$ –0–	$ –0–	$ –0–	$ 9,078	$ 9,078	$ –0–
Capital lease payable, long-term	3,607	7,503	8,291	2,268	21,669	1,323
Bonds and notes payable, long-term	96,048	47,155	26,121	52,117	221,441	19,880
Total noncurrent liabilities	99,655	54,658	34,412	63,463	252,188	21,203
Total liabilities	$128,019	$ 70,767	$ 42,758	$ 67,354	$ 308,898	$ 23,026
Net Position						
Invested in capital assets, net of related debt	$389,145	$215,103	$ 92,771	$ 26,637	$ 723,656	$ 10,831
Restricted for:						
Capital projects	4,083	11,092	415	4,184	19,774	–0–
Debt service	227	284	432	113	1,056	–0–
Unrestricted	6,177	(19,836)	31,418	7,846	25,605	16,505
Total Net Position	$399,632	$206,643	$125,036	$ 38,780	$ 770,091	$ 27,336

The notes to the financial statements are an integral part of this statement.

EXHIBIT 17.6 Fund Financial Statements—Statement of Changes in Revenues, Expenses, and Other Changes in Net Position for the Proprietary Funds

CITY OF EASTERN SOUTH
Proprietary Funds
Statement of Revenues, Expenses, and Other Changes in Net Position
For the Fiscal Year Ended June 30, 2020
(in thousands)

	Water	Sewer	Parking	Other Enterprise Funds	Total Enterprise Funds	Internal Service Funds Ⓤ
Operating revenues:						
Charges for services	$ 50,877	$ 11,836	$ 25,990	$ 795	$ 89,498	$ 9,044
Miscellaneous	3,776	2,189	772	290	7,027	112
Total operating revenues	$ 54,653	$ 14,025	$ 26,762	$ 1,085	$ 96,525	$ 9,156
Operating expenses: Ⓥ						
Employee services	$ 16,118	$ 5,017	$ 3,982	$ 1,298	$ 26,415	$ 3,372
Services and supplies	3,109	812	971	618	5,510	611
Depreciation and amortization	6,271	1,219	1,311	294	9,095	476
Utilities	7,216	1,315	2,045	416	10,992	1,342
Maintenance and repairs	3,894	2,119	3,183	1,220	10,416	682
Others	2,665	2,386	284	4,228	9,563	525
Total operating expenses	$ 39,273	$ 12,868	$ 11,776	$ 8,074	$ 71,991	$ 7,008
Total operating income (loss)	$ 15,380	$ 1,157	$ 14,986	$ (6,989)	$ 24,534	$ 2,148
Nonoperating revenues and expenses:						
Grant revenue	$ 2,684	$ 750	$ 1,414	$ 11,153	$ 16,001	$ 447
Investment earnings	704	525	1,561	311	3,101	29
Gain on disposal of capital asset	400	–0–	156	–0–	556	–0–
Total nonoperating revenues and expenses	$ 3,788	$ 1,275	$ 3,131	$ 11,464	$ 19,658	$ 476
Income (loss) before transfers	$ 19,168	$ 2,432	$ 18,117	$ 4,475	$ 44,192	$ 2,624
Transfers to governmental and fiduciary funds	(8,703)	(454)	(9,000)	(476)	(18,633)	–0–
Change in net position	$ 10,465	$ 1,978	$ 9,117	$ 3,999	$ 25,559	$ 2,624
Net position, beginning of year	389,167	204,665	115,919	34,781	744,532	24,712
Net position, end of year	$399,632	$206,643	$125,036	$38,780	$ 770,091	$27,336

The notes to the financial statements are an integral part of this statement.

EXHIBIT 17.7 Fund Financial Statements—Statement of Cash Flows for Proprietary Funds

CITY OF EASTERN SOUTH
Proprietary Funds
Statement of Cash Flows
For the Fiscal Year Ended June 30, 2020
(in thousands)

	Water	Sewer	Parking	Other Enterprise Funds	Total Enterprise Funds	Internal Service Funds
Cash flows from operating activities: Ⓦ						
Receipts from customers	$ 49,772	$ 12,816	$ 25,045	$ 996	$ 88,629	$ 8,961
Payments to employees	(16,553)	(4,849)	(3,717)	(1,011)	(26,130)	(3,402)
Payments to suppliers	(2,816)	(785)	(963)	(580)	(5,144)	(529)
Payments on operating expenses	(13,287)	(6,612)	(5,030)	(6,016)	(30,945)	(1,873)
Receipts from operating grants	3,178	2,985	1,040	8,211	15,414	–0–
Net cash provided by operating activities	$ 20,294	$ 3,555	$ 16,375	$ 1,600	$ 41,824	$ 3,157
Cash flows from noncapital financing activities:						
Issuance of revenue anticipation notes	$ 5,000	$ –0–	$ 800	$ –0–	$ 5,800	$ –0–
Transfers	(8,703)	(454)	(9,000)	(476)	(18,633)	–0–
Net cash provided by (used for) noncapital financing activities	$ (3,703)	$ (454)	$ (8,200)	$ (476)	$ (12,833)	$ –0–
Cash flows from capital and related financing activities: ⊗						
Proceeds from bonds issued for construction	$ 27,500	$ 8,100	$ 10,500	$ –0–	$ 46,100	$ 2,316
Receipt of capital grants	2,375	–0–	1,100	–0–	3,475	–0–
Received from sale of capital assets	1,980	–0–	753	–0–	2,733	–0–
Paid to acquire capital assets	(28,900)	(17,446)	(2,545)	(5,667)	(54,558)	(1,895)
Paid on bonds issued for construction	(2,300)	(540)	(1,508)	(944)	(5,292)	(135)
Paid interest on bonds issued for construction	(1,122)	(665)	(513)	(1,029)	(3,329)	(271)
Net cash provided by (used for) capital and related financing activities	$ (467)	$ (10,551)	$ 7,787	$ (7,640)	$ (10,871)	$ 15
Cash flows from investing activities:						
Purchase of investments	$ (41,200)	$ (19,884)	$(19,936)	$ (2,415)	$ (83,435)	$(6,552)
Received from sale and maturity of investments	35,375	20,900	16,650	7,000	79,925	7,255
Received from investment earnings	704	500	1,510	300	3,014	29
Net cash provided by (usec for) investing activities:	$ (5,121)	$ 1,516	$ (1,776)	$ 4,885	$ (496)	$ 732
Net increase (decrease) in cash and cash equivalents	$ 11,003	$ (5,934)	$ 14,186	$ (1,631)	$ 17,624	$ 3,904
Cash and cash equivalents, beginning of year	7,397	22,084	2,914	10,856	43,251	1,096
Cash and cash equivalents, end of year	$ 18,400	$ 16,150	$ 17,100	$ 9,225	$ 60,875	$ 5,000

The notes to the financial statements are an integral part of this statement.

similar to a for-profit business, GASB views information about cash flows as vital as it is in a financial analysis for Intel or Coca-Cola. Nevertheless, the physical structure is not entirely the same.

One of the main differences is that the statement of cash flows shown for the proprietary funds has four sections rather than the three typically required of for-profit entities:

1. Cash flows from operating activities.
2. Cash flows from noncapital financing activities.
3. Cash flows from capital and related financing activities.
4. Cash flows from investing activities.

- The presentation of cash flows from operating activities (Point W) is similar to that prepared by a for-profit business. However, the direct method of reporting is required rather than being merely an allowed option as in for-profit accounting. The indirect method that is almost universally applied by businesses is not allowed for state and local governments.
- Cash flows from noncapital financing activities include (1) proceeds and payments on debt *not* attributable to the acquisition or construction of capital assets and (2) grants and subsidies *not* restricted for either capital purposes or operating activities.
- As the title implies, cash flows from capital and related financing activities focus on the amounts spent on capital assets and the source of that funding. Exhibit 17.7 shows typical examples (Point X): proceeds from issuance of debt, acquisition of capital assets, and proceeds from disposition of capital assets.
- Cash flows from investing activities disclose amounts paid and received from investments, which is a much narrower category than used in a for-profit business.
- The government should also provide a reconciliation of operating income to operating cash flows. That information has been omitted here because of space considerations.

LO 17-11

Understand the presentation of financial statements for a public college or university.

Reporting Public Colleges and Universities

Private not-for-profit schools such as Harvard, Duke, and Stanford follow the FASB *Accounting Standards Codification®*. Authoritative accounting literature on contributions and the proper form of financial statements provides a significant amount of official reporting guidance for these private institutions. As discussed in the following chapter, generally accepted accounting principles developed for private not-for-profit organizations have progressed greatly over the years.

In contrast, GASB has retained primary authority over the reporting of public colleges and universities. For decades the question of whether the financial statements prepared for public colleges and universities (such as The Ohio State University and the University of Kansas) should resemble those of private schools has been the subject of much theoretical discussion. Generally, the operations of public colleges and universities differ in at least two important ways from private schools.

- State and other governments directly provide a significant amount of funding, lessening the reliance on tuition and fees. For example, the statement of revenues, expenses, and changes in net position for the University of Alabama for the year ended September 30, 2018, disclosed federal grants and contracts of $44.5 million, state and local grants and contracts of $31.2 million, and local grants and contracts of $1.0 million.
- Because of the ongoing support from the government, public schools have traditionally accumulated a smaller amount of endowment funds than private colleges and universities. Private schools try to build a large endowment to help ensure financial security. This need is less urgent for public schools that are backed by the state or another government. For example, at June 30, 2017, Princeton University, a private school, held investments with a fair value of approximately $24 billion, an amount (roughly equal to $2.8 million per student) that is nearly beyond the comprehension of officials at most public colleges. On that same date, the University of Georgia reported $200 million in investments (about $5,300 per student).

Do these and other differences warrant unique financial statements for public colleges and universities? In many ways, public and private schools are much alike. They both educate students, charge tuition and other fees, conduct scholarly research, maintain libraries and sports teams, operate cafeterias and museums, and the like. What should be the measurement basis and form of the financial statements to reflect the financial activity and position of colleges and universities?

Over the years, four alternatives have been suggested for constructing the financial statements that public colleges and universities prepare and distribute:

1. Adopt FASB's requirements so that all colleges and universities (public and private) prepare comparable financial statements. As the next chapter discusses, the private school reporting model is relatively well developed. Some interested parties believe this suggestion presents potential problems. Over the decades, FASB has not had to deal with the intricacies of governmental entities and might fail to comprehend the unique aspects of public schools. Specific reporting needs associated with such institutions might not be addressed.
2. Apply a traditional model focusing on fund financial statements to highlight the wide variety of funds that such schools often have to maintain. However, both private not-for-profit organizations and governmental entities have abandoned (at least in part) the reporting of individual funds. For public schools to rely on a fund-based approach seems somewhat outdated.
3. Create an entirely new set of financial statements designed specifically to meet the unique needs of public colleges and universities. If FASB's *Accounting Standards Codification* is not to be followed, the fundamental differences between private and public schools must be significant. Identify those differences so that new statements could be developed to reflect the events and transactions of public institutions and satisfy the informational needs of users. Unfortunately, the creation of an entirely new set of financial statements would require an enormous amount of work by GASB or some other designated body. Does the benefit gained from tailor-made financial statements outweigh the cost of producing new standards for the reporting of public schools?
4. Adopt for public schools the same reporting model that has been created for state and local governments. Because a large amount of funding for public schools comes directly from governments, the financial statement format utilized by a city or county could be applicable.

GASB has selected the fourth option by specifying that public colleges and universities are special-purpose governments. "'Public universities, hospitals, utilities, and other business-type activities may operate similar to businesses but they are nonetheless governments—and therefore are accountable to the citizenry.' said GASB Chairman Robert H. Attmore."[26] This decision creates a standard reporting model for public schools such as the University of Tennessee and Michigan State University.

Nevertheless, a review of public college and university financial statements shows that many do not prepare both government-wide and fund financial statements like a city or county. Such schools can logically be viewed as large enterprise funds. They have a user charge (tuition and fees), and they are open to the public. As has been discussed, accounting for enterprise funds in both government-wide statements and fund financial statements is very similar. For such proprietary funds, financial statements report all economic resources and the use accrual accounting.

Thus, having two sets of almost identical statements was viewed by GASB as redundant. For this reason, many public schools prepare a single set of statements equivalent to those of an enterprise fund (similar to the previous examples shown in this chapter for the proprietary funds of the City of Eastern South). Consequently, Note 1 to the 2018 financial statements for Middle Tennessee State University provides a common rationale for the method by which the statements are structured.

[26] Business Wire, "GASB Publishes New User Guide on Business-Type Activities," March 12, 2013.

For financial statement purposes, Middle Tennessee University is considered a special-purpose government entity engaged *only in business-type activities.* Accordingly, the financial statements have been prepared using the economic resources measurement focus and the accrual basis of accounting. Revenues are recorded when earned and expenses are recorded when a liability is incurred, regardless of the timing of related cash flows. Grants and similar items are recognized as revenue as soon as all eligibility requirements imposed by the provider have been met. [Emphasis added.]

Exhibit 17.8 presents the financial statements for June 30, 2017, and the year then ended for James Madison University (a public school) for illustration purposes, although the accompanying notes have been omitted. The component unit that is reported here is identified as follows:

The James Madison University Foundation, Inc. is included as a component unit of the University. The Foundation is a legally separate, tax-exempt organization formed to promote the achievements and further the aims and purposes of the University.

Interestingly, James Madison University discloses that it, in turn, "Is a component unit of the Commonwealth (of Virginia) and is included in the basic financial statements of the Commonwealth."

Note, as expected, that these statements are quite similar to the fund financial statements presented in this chapter for the proprietary funds of the City of Eastern South (Exhibits 17.5, 17.6, and 17.7).

EXHIBIT 17.8

JAMES MADISON UNIVERSITY
Statement of Net Position
As of June 30, 2017

	2017	
	James Madison University	**Component Unit**
ASSETS		
Current assets:		
Cash and cash equivalents (Note 2)	$ 188,434,045	$ 3,855,387
Short-term investments (Note 2)	2,185,217	–
Accounts receivable (Net of allowance for doubtful accounts of $771,300) (Note 3)	7,313,331	75,821
Contributions receivable (Net of allowance for doubtful contributions of $54,274 (Note 3)	–	2,659,405
Due from the Commonwealth (Note 4)	6,583,908	–
Prepaid expenses	11,678,610	43,152
Prepaid expenses to component unit	360,409	–
Inventory	873,654	–
Notes receivable (Net of allowance for doubtful accounts of $54,550)	379,849	–
Total current assets	217,809,023	6,633,765
Non-current assets:		
Restricted cash and cash equivalents (Note 2)	28,613,443	–
Endowment investments (Note 2)	–	64,355,685
Other long-term investments (Note 2)	1,665,250	54,102,297
Land held for future use	–	6,264,640
Contributions receivable (Net of allowance for doubtful contributions of $202,729) (Note 3)	–	9,933,756
Prepaid expenses	362,244	–
Notes receivable (Net of allowance for doubtful accounts of $248,507)	1,729,285	3,226,647

(continued)

EXHIBIT 17.8
(Continued)

	2017	
	James Madison University	**Component Unit**
Capital assets, net: (Note 5)		
Non-depreciable	147,839,638	656,552
Depreciable	932,746,183	3,003,080
Other assets	–	2,145
Total non-current assets	1,112,956,043	141,554,802
DEFERRED OUTFLOW OF RESOURCES		
Related to debt refundings (Note 9)	10,890,597	–
Related to pensions (Note 11)	34,516,381	–
Total deferred outflow of resources	45,406,978	–
Total assets and deferred outflow of resources	$1,376,172,044	$ 148,178,567
LIABILITIES		
Current liabilities:		
Accounts payable and accrued expenses (Note 6)	$ 47,135,556	$ 192,635
Unearned revenue	19,054,651	–
Unearned revenue from James Madison University	–	360,409
Deposits held in custody for others	7,826,137	–
Long-term liabilities - current portion (Note 7)	25,343,307	251,835
Total current liabilities	99,359,651	804,879
Non-current liabilities:		
Long-term liabilities (Note 7)	334,898,377	5,519,561
Net pension liability (Note 11)	166,981,000	–
Total non-current liabilities	501,879,377	5,519,561
DEFERRED INFLOW OF RESOURCES		
Related to debt refundings (Note 9)	66,510	–
Related to pensions (Note 11)	4,529,000	–
Total deferred inflow of resources	4,595,510	–
Total liabilities and deferred inflow of resources	605,834,538	6,323,440
NET POSITION		
Net investment in capital assets	773,660,854	1,831,855
Restricted for:		
Non-expendable:		
Scholarships and fellowships	–	44,756,841
Research and public service	–	857,254
Other	–	22,592,420
Expendable:		
Scholarships and fellowships	–	15,360,477
Research and public service	1,811,692	910,730
Debt service	218,467	–
Capital projects	4,475,269	12,404,366
Loans	294,461	–
Other	–	25,785,944
Unrestricted	(10,123,237)	17,354,240
Total net position	$ 770,337,506	$ 141,854,127

The Notes to Financial Statements are an integral part of this statement.

(continued)

EXHIBIT 17.8
(Continued)

JAMES MADISON UNIVERSITY
Statement of Revenues, Expenses, and Changes in Net Position
For the Year Ended June 30, 2017

	2017	
	James Madison University	**Component Unit**
Operating revenues:		
Student tuition and fees (Net of scholarship allowances of $19,038,129)	$ 207,013,768	$ –
Gifts and contributions	–	12,289,043
Federal grants and contracts	12,818,803	–
State grants and contracts	8,514,500	–
Non-governmental grants and contracts	4,909,152	–
Auxiliary enterprises (Net of scholarship allowances of $13,620,070 (Note 13)	182,511,536	–
Sales and Services of Education and General Activities	2,051,558	–
Other operating revenues	1,848,324	863,342
Total operating revenues	419,667,641	13,152,385
Operating expenses (Note 14):		
Instruction	162,056,031	587,905
Research	3,623,976	11,586
Public service	15,632,592	153,325
Academic support	46,944,912	1,269,840
Student services	18,608,567	148,627
Institutional support	34,009,506	6,149,561
Operation and maintenance - plant	44,345,268	626,201
Depreciation	41,921,323	117,906
Student aid	9,479,895	3,510,104
Auxiliary activities (Note 13)	136,065,856	759,736
Total operating expenses	512,687,926	13,334,791
Operating loss	(93,020,285)	(182,406)
Non-operating revenues/(expenses):		
State appropriations (Note 15)	91,680,650	–
Grants and contracts (Note 1 Q.)	12,489,535	–
Pension related contribution revenue	2,552,171	–
Gifts	7,006	–
Investment income (Net of investment expense of $831 for the University and $403,766 for the Foundation respectively)	1,594,586	11,942,501
In-kind support from James Madison University	–	3,702,567
Interest on capital asset - related debt	(7,962,653)	(131,573)
Gain (Loss) on disposal of plant assets	(1,142,270)	337,757
Payment to the Commonwealth	(2,929,583)	–
Net non-operating revenues/(expenses)	96,289,442	15,851,252
Income before other revenues, expenses, gains. or losses	3,269,157	15,668,846
Capital appropriations and contributions (Note 16)	14,425,600	–
Capital gifts	4,224,690	–
Additions to permanent endowments	–	5,504,907
Net other revenues	18,650,290	5,504,907
Increase in net position	21,919,477	21,173,753
Net position - beginning of year	748,418,059	120,680,374
Net position - end of year	$ 770,337,506	$ 141,854,127

The Notes to Financial Statements are an integral part of this statement.

(continued)

EXHIBIT 17.8
(Continued)

JAMES MADISON UNIVERSITY
Statement of Cash Flows
For the Year Ended June 30, 2017

	2017
Cash flows from operating activities:	
Student tuition and fees	$ 208,302,336
Grants and contracts	26,836,094
Auxiliary enterprises	183,194,764
Other receipts	4,067,977
Payments for compensation and benefits	(282,394,454)
Payments for services, supplies and utilities	(141,599,592)
Payments for scholarships and fellowships	(9,479,895)
Payments for non-capitalized plant improvements and equipment	(30,143,063)
Loans issued to students	(399,996)
Collections of loans from students	449,288
Net cash used by operating activities	(41,166,541)
Cash flows from non-capital financing activities:	
State appropriations	91,657,608
Nonoperating grants and contracts	12,069,873
Payment to the Commonwealth	(2,929,583)
Pension related contributions	(1,551,829)
Loans issued to students and employees	(11,122)
Collections of loans from students and employees	10,872
Gifts and grants for other than capital purposes	7,006
Federal direct lending program receipts	99,042,045
Federal direct lending program disbursements	(99,042,045)
Agency receipts	13,443,222
Agency payments	(13,265,388)
Net cash provided by noncapital financing activities	99,430,659
Cash flows from capital and related financing activities:	
Capital appropriations and contributions	33,797,794
Proceeds from capital debt	59,972,584
Proceeds from sale of capital assets	52,379
Capital gifts	544,112
Purchase of capital assets	(82,699,322)
Principal paid on capital debt, leases, and installments	(17,611,632)
Interest paid on capital debt, leases, and installments	(11,955,014)
Net cash used by capital and related financing activities	(17,899,099)
Cash flows from investing activities:	
Interest on investments	320,136
Interest on cash management pools	1,327,064
Proceeds from sale of investments	146,982
Purchase of investments	1,406,101
Net cash provided by investing activities	1,388,081
Net increase in cash	40,753,100
Cash and cash equivalents - beginning of the year	176,294,388
Cash and cash equivalents - end of the year	$ 217,047,488

RECONCILIATION OF NET OPERATING LOSS TO NET CASH USED BY OPERATING ACTIVITIES:

Operating loss	$ (93,020,285)
Adjustments to reconcile net loss to net cash used by operating activities:	
Depreciation expense	41,921,323

(continued)

EXHIBIT 17.8
(Continued)

JAMES MADISON UNIVERSITY
Statement of Cash Flows
For the Year Ended June 30, 2017

Changes in assets, liabilities, deferred outflows, and deferred inflows:	
Receivables, net	(253,962)
Prepaid expenses	(1,227,092)
Inventory	26,569
Notes receivable, net	76,295
Deferred outflows of resources - pension	(12,682,259)
Accounts payable and accrued expenses	1,924,737
Unearned revenue	2,981,066
Net Pension Liability	22,377,000
Advance from Treasurer of Virginia	–
Advance compensated absences	773,542
Accrued retirement plan	2,049,986)
Federal loan programs contributions refundable	(17,461)
Deferred inflows of resources - pension	(6,096,000)
Net cash used by operating activities	$ (41,166,541)
NON-CASH INVESTING, NONCAPITAL FINANCING, AND CAPITAL AND RELATED FINANCING TRANSACTIONS:	
Gift of capital assets	$ 3,606,757
Amortization of bond premium/discount and gain/loss on debt refinancing	(2,983,708)
Capitalization of interest revenue and expense, net	(1,093,815)
Change in fair value of investments recognized as a component of interest income	33,716
Loss on disposal of capital assets	(1,194,649)
Special revenue allocation related to pensions	(4,104,000)

The Notes to Financial Statements are an integral part of this statement.

Summary

1. GASB has established a hierarchy for the generally accepted accounting principles for state and local governments. Two categories of authoritative GAAP are listed. Category A is most important and includes GASB's official statements. Category B is composed of GASB Technical Bulletins, GASB Implementation Guides, and literature of the AICPA cleared by GASB. Sources of nonauthoritative accounting literature include GASB Concepts Statements and pronouncements and other literature of the Financial Accounting Standards Board, Federal Accounting Standards Advisory Board, and International Accounting Standards Board.
2. Governments can give tax breaks to entice desired actions by businesses and other taxpayers. These abatements limit the government's ability to collect tax money. To provide citizens and other interested parties with pertinent information about the actions of government officials, disclosure is required for tax abatements. These disclosures indicate the type of commitment that was made and the benefit expected in return.
3. State and local governments determine amounts to be reported for defined benefit pension plans. Future benefits that have been earned to date are estimated and the present value calculated. If the resulting obligation is greater than the net position held by the related pension trust fund, the excess is shown in government-wide statements as the net pension liability.
4. In 2017, GASB issued authoritative guidelines for lease accounting. Both the lessee and the lessor use a single model unless the contract has a maximum life of one year or less. On government-wide financial statements, the lessee records the right-of-use asset and associated liability at the present value of the cash payments. As time passes, the lessee reports interest on the liability and amortization expense on the cost of the asset. In contrast, the lessor continues to report the asset while also recognizing a receivable and a deferred inflow of resources. The lessor then depreciates the asset and also records interest revenue on the receivable. At the same time, the deferred inflow of resources is reclassified as lease revenue on a systematic and rational basis. On fund financial statements for governmental funds, the lessee records both an expenditure and an other financing source for the present value of the payments. Subsequently, these payments are shown as additional expenditures. The lessor initially records a receivable and a deferred inflow of resources, both for

present value. Over time, collection is made to reduce and remove the receivable. The deferred inflow of resources is reclassified as lease revenue.

5. Solid waste landfills create potentially large debts for a government because of eventual closure and postclosure costs. Government-wide statements accrue a liability each period based on the latest current cost estimations and the portion of the property filled to date. Fund financial statements report no expenditures until a claim to current financial resources is made.
6. A state or local government that obtains a work of art or historical treasure normally records it as a capital asset on government-wide financial statements. If specified guidelines are met, an expense can replace recognition of the asset. Whether recorded as expense or asset, a state or local government that receives such a work of art or historical treasure as a donation must still recognize revenue according to the rules established for voluntary nonexchange transactions. Fund financial statements for the governmental funds report no capital assets and, therefore, do not recognize these items except as expenditures if purchased.
7. Depreciation must be recorded each period for works of art and historical treasures that are capitalized unless they are judged to be inexhaustible.
8. Infrastructure assets such as bridges and roads are capitalized on government-wide financial statements. Governments record depreciation over time unless they apply the modified approach. Under this method, the government must create a monitoring system to ensure that each network of infrastructure is maintained yearly at a predetermined condition. When applied, the cost of upkeep is expensed as incurred by the government in lieu of recording depreciation.
9. A state or local government must include a management's discussion and analysis (MD&A) as part of its general-purpose external financial reporting. As with for-profit businesses, this MD&A provides a verbal explanation of the government's operations and financial position.
10. A primary government produces a comprehensive annual financial report (CAFR). Both general-purpose governments (such as states, cities, towns, counties, and the like) and special-purpose governments (such as some school systems and transit systems) that meet certain provisions are viewed as primary governments. A component unit is any function that is legally separate from a primary government but where financial accountability still exists. In government-wide statements, component units are either discretely presented to the right of the primary government or blended within the actual funds of the primary government.
11. A statement of net position and a statement of activities are prepared as government-wide financial statements based on the economic resources measurement focus and accrual accounting. These statements separate governmental activities from business-type activities. Internal service funds are usually included within the governmental activities based on the activities they serve. The statement of activities reports expenses by function along with related program revenues to determine the net expense or revenue resulting from each function. The government then lists the various general revenues to indicate the method used to finance the net expenses incurred by the various functions.
12. In creating fund financial statements for governmental funds, the general fund and any other major fund are reported in separate columns. These statements are based on measuring current financial resources using modified accrual accounting. Additional statements are presented for proprietary funds and also for fiduciary funds.
13. Financial statements prepared by public colleges and universities must follow the same reporting guidelines as those created for state and local government units. As discussed in the following chapter, those statements will differ in several ways from the statements produced by private schools that follow FASB guidelines. Public schools are normally viewed as special-purpose governments. They often assume that they are engaged only in business-type activities like an enterprise fund. Thus, such schools only need to present fund financial statements as a proprietary fund.

Comprehensive Illustration

(*Estimated Time: 40 minutes*) The following is a series of transactions for a city. Indicate how the city reports each transaction within government-wide financial statements and then on fund financial statements. Assume the city follows a policy of considering resources as available if they will be received within 60 days. Incurred liabilities are assumed to be claims to current resources if they will be paid within 60 days.

Problem

1. Borrows money by issuing 20-year bonds for a total of $3 million, the face value. The city plans to use the money to construct a highway around the perimeter.
2. Transfers cash of $100,000 from the general fund to the debt service funds to make the first payment of principal and interest on the bonds in (1).

3. Pays the cash in (2) on the bonds. Of this total, $70,000 represents interest. The remainder reduces the principal of the bonds.
4. Completes construction of the highway and pays the entire $3 million construction costs.
5. The highway in (4) is expected to last 30 years. The government qualifies to use the modified approach, which it has adopted for its system of highways. The government incurs a $350,000 cost during the year to maintain the highway at an appropriate, predetermined condition. Of this amount, $290,000 was paid immediately. The other $60,000 will not be paid until the sixth month of the subsequent year.
6. Receives lights for the new highway donated from a local business. The lights are valued at $200,000 and should last 20 years. The modified approach is not used for this network of infrastructure. The city applies straight-line depreciation using the half-year convention.
7. Agrees to stop collecting property taxes from the Acme Company for eight years in exchange for the promise that the company will build a small manufacturing plant within the city to generate capital investment and new job opportunities.
8. Records cash revenues of $2 million from the local subway system. Makes salary expense payments of $300,000 to its employees.
9. At the start of the year, the city leases a new firetruck for seven years by agreeing to pay $40,000 per year starting immediately. The city does not know the implicit interest rate used by the lessor. The city has an incremental annual borrowing rate of 6 percent. The present value of an annuity due of $1 at 6 percent interest over seven years is 5.91732.
10. Opens a solid waste landfill at the beginning of the year that will be used for 20 years. This year the city fills an estimated 4 percent of the capacity. Officials anticipate closure, and postclosure requirements will be $2 million based on current cost figures although no costs have been incurred to date.

Solution

1. *Government-wide financial statements.* On the statement of net position under the governmental activities column, both cash and noncurrent liabilities increase by $3 million.

   Fund financial statements. The cash balance increases on the balance sheet by $3 million. Other financing sources increases by the same amount on the statement of revenues, expenditures, and changes in fund balances. These amounts will be shown in the other governmental funds column unless officials judge this particular capital projects fund to be major. That situation necessitates the use of a separate column.
2. *Government-wide financial statements.* No recording of this transfer is shown because the amount is an intra-activity transaction entirely carried out within the governmental activities.

   Fund financial statements. The cash balance of the general fund on the balance sheet decreases while the cash listed for the debt service fund (or the other governmental funds) increases. On the statement of revenues, expenditures, and other changes in fund balances, the general fund shows an other financing use of $100,000, whereas the debt service funds (or other governmental funds) report an other financing source. These balances will not be offset in arriving at total figures.
3. *Government-wide financial statements.* On the statement of net position, cash reported by the governmental activities decreases by $100,000 and the total reported for noncurrent liabilities drops $30,000 to reflect the principal payment. The statement of activities then recognizes $70,000 in interest expense as a governmental activity.

   Fund financial statements. First, cash decreases by $100,000 on the balance sheet under the debt service funds (or other governmental funds) column. Second, the statement of revenues, expenditures, and changes in fund balances reports a $30,000 principal expenditure and a $70,000 interest expenditure. These amounts are shown within the debt service funds (or other governmental funds).
4. *Government-wide financial statements.* Under the governmental activities on the statement of net position, cash decreases $3 million, and capital assets increases by the same amount. Governments capitalize infrastructure costs.

   Fund financial statements. On the balance sheet, cash reported for other governmental funds decreases. Again, if this particular capital projects fund qualifies as major, the effects are shown in a separate column rather than in the other governmental funds column. The statement of revenues, expenditures, and changes in fund balances reports a $3 million expenditure as a capital outlay.

5. *Government-wide financial statements.* The statement of net position reports a $290,000 decrease in cash under governmental activities and a $60,000 increase in a current liability. The statement of activities includes the $350,000 expense within an appropriate function such as public works. Because the government applies the modified approach, maintenance expense is recognized instead of depreciation expense.

   Fund financial statements. Because the $60,000 liability will not require the use of current financial resources (it will not be paid within 60 days), no recording is made at this time at the fund level. Thus, the balance sheet reports only a $290,000 drop in cash, probably under the general fund. This $290,000 expenditure appears on the statement of revenues, expenditures, and changes in fund balances for public works.

6. *Government-wide financial statements.* The lights do not qualify as works of art or historical treasures and must be reported as capital assets on the statement of net position at their $200,000 value. Based on an expected life of 20 years and use of the half-year convention, $5,000 ($200,000/20 years × 0.5 year) in accumulated depreciation reduces the reported net balance to $195,000. For the statement of activities, a $200,000 revenue is appropriate unless eligibility requirements connected to the donation have not yet been fulfilled. This revenue should be shown as a program revenue (capital grants and contributions) to offset the expenses reported for public works. Depreciation of $5,000 should also be included as an expense for public works.

   Fund financial statements. No reporting is required because current financial resources were not affected by the gift or subsequent depreciation.

7. *Government-wide financial statements and fund financial statements.* Tax abatement information should be disclosed. It includes the purpose of the tax abatement program, the tax being abated, dollar amount of taxes abated, the type of commitments made by the tax abatement recipients, and other commitments made by the government such as agreeing to build infrastructure assets like roads or sewer systems.

8. *Government-wide financial statements.* Cash reported on the statement of net position increases under the business-type activities by $1.7 million. The statement of activities reports expenses for the subway system as $300,000 while the related program revenues for charges for services increase by $2 million. The net revenue resulting from this business-type activity is $1.7 million.

   Fund financial statements. The statement of net position for the proprietary funds (see Exhibit 17.5) should include a separate column for the subway system, assuming that it qualifies as a major fund. Cash in this column increases by $1.7 million. Likewise, the statement of revenues, expenses, and changes in net position for the proprietary funds (see Exhibit 17.6) reports operating revenues of $2 million for the subway system. The operating expenses will include personnel services of $300,000. The statement of cash flows (see Exhibit 17.7) also reports both the inflow and outflow of cash under cash flows from operating activities.

9. *Government-wide financial statements.* Under the governmental activities on the statement of net position, the city reports this right-of-use asset as $236,693 (rounded). That amount is reduced by $33,813 (rounded) by the annual amortization ($236,693/7). Cash drops $40,000 because of the first payment. The lease liability begins as $236,693 but decreases immediately by the $40,000 payment to $196,693. At the end of the year, interest expense of $11,802 ($196,693 times 6 percent interest) is recognized and increases the liability balance to $208,495. On the statement of activities, the amortization and interest expenses are reported under governmental activities.

   Fund financial statements. When the city signs this agreement, it recognizes expenditures—lease contract for the present value of the obligation or $236,693 and also other financing sources—lease contract for the same amount. Both figures appear on the statement of revenues, expenditures, and other changes in fund balances for the governmental funds. When the $40,000 payment is made, then expenditures—firetruck is also shown for that amount along with a reduction in cash on the balance sheet for the governmental funds.

10. *Government-wide financial statements.* The landfill is 4 percent filled. This is its first year of operations. That portion of the overall $2 million cost ($80,000) must be recognized. The statement of net position shows this amount as a noncurrent liability. The balance is presented as either a governmental activity or a business-type activity, depending on the landfill's fund classification. Likewise, the statement of activities reports the same $80,000 figure as an expense.

    Fund financial statements. This liability does not require the use of current financial resources and is not reported if the landfill is considered a governmental fund. If the landfill is an enterprise fund, the separate statements prepared for the proprietary funds include both the $80,000 expense and liability (see Exhibits 17.5 and 17.6).

Questions

1. Authoritative U.S. GAAP for state and local governments is divided into two categories, with the first category having more authority than the second. What sources of U.S. GAAP are found in both of these categories?
2. The accountants for a city government are attempting to determine the appropriate method of reporting a series of unique financial transactions. They review all of the authoritative sources of U.S. GAAP but have not located an answer. What action should they take next?
3. Officials for the city of Winfield have agreed to forgo real estate taxes normally charged to Jamieson Corporation for the subsequent 10 years. In exchange, Jamieson agrees to build a distribution facility that is expected to hire 500 new employees. What information must the city provide in its financial statements to inform taxpayers and other interested parties about the nature of this tax abatement?
4. A teacher employed by the City of Lights qualifies for a defined benefit pension plan. The city sets up a pension trust fund to monitor the resources held for these future payments. How is the amount of net pension liability to be reported in the government-wide financial statements determined?
5. The City of Ronchester has a defined benefit pension plan for its firefighters. How is the amount of pension expense determined that the city should recognize in the current year?
6. At the start of Year 1, the City Peacock leases 30 computers for use by various officials in school administration and public safety at a total cost of $90,000 per year. The first lease payment is made immediately. The contracts are for five years, the expected life of the computers. After that period, the city will return them to the lessor. What reporting is appropriate for the city for the first year? Assume the city has an annual incremental borrowing rate of 8 percent.
7. Pittston County has an empty school building with a net book value of $700,000 and a remaining life of 10 years with no expected residual value. The building is leased to the City of Lincoln at the start of the current year for 10 years. Annual payments are set at $103,565 to reflect Pittston's implicit interest rate of 10 percent per year. This rate is known by both parties. The first payment is made immediately. What revenue and expense does Pittston report in the first year on government-wide statements? What expense does Lincoln report in the first year on government-wide statements?
8. Why does the operation of a solid waste landfill create significant reporting concerns for many local governments?
9. A city believes its new landfill will fill to capacity gradually over a 10-year period. At the end of the first year of operations, the landfill is only 7 percent filled. How much liability for closure and postclosure costs should be recognized on government-wide financial statements? How much liability should be recognized on fund financial statements, assuming that the landfill is recorded in an enterprise fund? How much liability should be recognized on fund financial statements, assuming that the landfill is recorded in the general fund?
10. The City of VanStone operates a solid waste landfill. This facility is 11 percent filled after the first year of operation and 24 percent after the second year. How much expense should be recognized on the government-wide financial statements in the second year for closure costs? Assuming that the landfill is reported in the general fund, what expenditure should be recognized in the second year on the fund financial statements?
11. A local citizen gives the City of Salem a painting by Picasso to display in city hall. Under what condition will the city *not* report this painting as a capital asset on its government-wide financial statements? If it does report the painting as a capital asset, must the city report depreciation?
12. Assume in Question 11 that the city does not choose to report the painting on the government-wide financial statements as a capital asset. Must the city report a revenue as a result of the gift?
13. Under what condition is the modified approach applied by a state or local government?
14. What effect does application of the modified approach have on reporting within the government-wide financial statements?
15. What does a state or local government normally include in its management's discussion and analysis (MD&A)? Where does a state or local government present this information?
16. What does a comprehensive annual financial report (known as the CAFR) include?
17. A primary government can be either a general-purpose government or a special-purpose government. What is the difference in these two? How does an activity qualify as a special-purpose government?
18. The Willingham Museum qualifies as a component unit of the City of Willingham. How does an activity or function meet the requirements to be deemed a component unit of a primary government?

19. What is the difference between a blended component unit and a discretely presented component unit?
20. What are the two government-wide financial statements? What does each normally present?
21. What are the two fund financial statements for governmental funds? What information does each normally present?
22. For a state or local government, what is the difference between program revenues and general revenues? Why is that distinction important?
23. Why does a government determine the net expenses or revenues for each of the functions within its statement of activities?
24. How are internal service funds reported on government-wide financial statements?
25. In governmental accounting, what is the difference between an acquisition and a merger? What differences exist between the accounting for an acquisition and for a merger?
26. A general-purpose government takes over a special-purpose government in an acquisition. The consideration is larger than the acquisition value of all assets and liabilities. How is the excess reported?
27. What are some of the major differences that exist between private colleges and universities and public colleges and universities that affect financial reporting?
28. What is the most common form used in creating the financial statements prepared by public colleges and universities?

Problems

LO 17-1

1. Which of the following has the least amount of official authority for the financial reporting of state and local governments?
   a. GASB Technical Bulletins
   b. GASB Statements of Governmental Accounting Standards
   c. GASB Concepts Statements
   d. GASB Implementation Guides

LO 17-1

2. City government officials are analyzing a complicated financial transaction. A GASB Implementation Guide seems to provide one reporting answer. A GASB Concepts Statement seems to provide a different answer. What reporting is most appropriate?
   a. The government can use either method and still be in conformity with U.S. GAAP.
   b. Government officials should follow the guidance provided by the GASB Implementation Guide.
   c. The city's financial statements must be in conformity with the GASB Concepts Statement.
   d. The city's accountants should seek some type of compromise that takes both of these pronouncements into consideration.

LO 17-1

3. The accountants for a city are attempting to determine the proper reporting for a new transaction so that financial statements will be in conformity with U.S. generally accepted accounting principles. They are unable to find any authoritative answer. What should happen next?
   a. The city will receive a qualified audit report on its financial statements.
   b. The accountants can report the transaction in the way that they believe is best.
   c. The accountants should study other nonauthoritative sources such as GASB Concepts Statements and the official standards produced by FASB.
   d. The city will separate the transaction and report it separately in such a way as to draw attention to the method of reporting that was followed.

LO 17-2

4. A city agrees to allow the Jones Company to operate within its geographical boundaries without having to pay real estate taxes for the next 10 years. In exchange, Jones agrees to continue employing at least 120 people at all times during this period. For this tax abatement, which of the following does the city not have to disclose?
   a. The party receiving the tax abatement
   b. The purpose of the tax abatement program
   c. Dollar amount of taxes abated
   d. The tax being abated

LO 17-2

5. City officials provide a tax abatement to a local business so that it can avoid paying real estate taxes for the next five years. In exchange, the business agrees to construct a new facility and hire 50 or more individuals. How does the city report this decision?
   a. Only on the government-wide financial statements
   b. Only on the fund financial statements
   c. On both the government-wide and fund financial statements
   d. Only as a footnote disclosure

LO 17-3

6. The City of Nomanchester has a defined benefit pension plan for a number of its employees. A pension trust fund has been set up that currently has a net position of $32.7 million because quite a number of investments are being held. An actuary estimates that city employees will eventually receive $99.7 million as a result of this pension. However, only $72.4 million of that amount is for work already provided. The present value of the $72.4 million in payments is $49.8 million. On its government-wide financial statements, what amount of net pension liability should be reported?
   a. $–0–
   b. $17.1 million
   c. $39.7 million
   d. $67.0 million

LO 17-3

7. The City of Huble has a defined benefit pension plan for a significant number of its employees. Which of the following does the city not include immediately in the determination of pension expense in its government-wide financial statements?
   a. Service cost
   b. Interest on total pension liability
   c. Changes in pension liability as a result of a change in benefit terms
   d. Changes in pension liability as a result of a change in economic or demographic assumptions

LO 17-4

8. Reynolds County has three large trucks with a total net book value of $600,000 and remaining lives of six years with no expected residual value. County officials lease the trucks to the City of Webster on January 1, 2020, for six years. Based on a negotiated annual implicit interest rate of 5 percent, the parties agree on annual payments of $112,581 beginning immediately and each January 1 thereafter. For both governments, the trucks relate to activities maintained with the General Fund. What is the total expense Webster reports on government-wide financial statements for 2020?
   a. $112,581
   b. $124,371
   c. $130,000
   d. $142,581

LO 17-4

9. Use the same information as in (8). What liability balance will Webster report on its government-wide financial statements on December 31, 2020?
   a. $463,048
   b. $487,419
   c. $511,790
   d. $517,419

LO 17-4

10. Use the same information as in (8). What is the total amount of expenditures that Webster will report on its fund financial statements for the governmental funds for 2020?
   a. $112,581
   b. $136,954
   c. $600,000
   d. $712,581

LO 17-4

11. Use the same information as in (8). What amount of depreciation expense will Reynolds report in its government-wide financial statements for 2020?
   a. Zero
   b. $52,581
   c. $100,000
   d. $112,581

LO 17-4

12. Use the same information as in (8). What amount of deferred lease revenue will Reynolds report on its statement of net position as of December 31, 2020, assuming that the county recognizes revenue on a straight-line method?
    a. Zero
    b. $487,419
    c. $500,000
    d. $511,790

LO 17-5

13. A city creates a solid waste landfill. It assesses a charge to every individual or company that uses the landfill based on the amount of materials added. In which of the following will the landfill probably be recorded?
    a. General fund
    b. Special revenues funds
    c. Internal service funds
    d. Enterprise fund.

Use the following information for Problems 14, 15, and 16.

A city opens a solid waste landfill that it expects to fill to capacity gradually over a 10-year period. At the end of the first year, it is 8 percent filled. At the end of the second year, it is 19 percent filled. Currently, the cost of closure and postclosure is estimated at $1 million. None of this amount will be paid until the landfill has reached 90 percent of its capacity.

LO 17-5

14. Which of the following is true for the Year 2 government-wide financial statements?
    a. Both expense and liability will be zero.
    b. Both expense and liability will be $110,000.
    c. Expense will be $110,000, and liability will be $190,000.
    d. Expense will be $100,000, and liability will be $200,000.

LO 17-5

15. If this landfill is judged to be a proprietary fund, what liability will the city report at the end of the second year on its fund financial statements?
    a. $–0–
    b. $110,000
    c. $190,000
    d. $200,000

LO 17-5

16. If this landfill is judged to be a governmental fund, what liability will the city report at the end of the second year on fund financial statements?
    a. $–0–
    b. $110,000
    c. $190,000
    d. $200,000

LO 17-6

17. The City of Wilson receives a large sculpture valued at $240,000 as a gift to be placed in front of the municipal building. Which of the following is true for reporting the gift within the government-wide financial statements?
    a. A capital asset of $240,000 must be reported.
    b. The city will not report a capital asset.
    c. If conditions are met, recording the sculpture as a capital asset is optional.
    d. The city will record the sculpture but only for the amount it had to pay.

LO 17-6

18. In problem 17, which of the following statements is true about reporting a revenue in connection with this gift?
    a. A revenue will be reported.
    b. Revenue is reported but only if the asset is reported.
    c. If the asset is not capitalized, the city recognizes no revenue.
    d. As a gift, no revenue is ever reported.

LO 17-6

19. Assume in problem 17 that the city reports the work as a capital asset. Which of the following is true?
    a. Depreciation is not recorded because the city has no cost.
    b. Depreciation is not required if the asset is viewed as inexhaustible.
    c. Depreciation must be recognized because the asset is capitalized.
    d. Because the city received the property as a gift, recognition of depreciation is optional.

LO 17-7

20. A city builds sidewalks throughout various neighborhoods at a cost of $2.1 million. Which of the following statements is *not* true?
    a. Because the sidewalks qualify as infrastructure, the asset is viewed in the same way as land so that no depreciation is recorded.
    b. Depreciation is required unless the city uses the modified approach.
    c. The modified approach recognizes maintenance expense in lieu of depreciation expense for qualifying infrastructure assets.
    d. The modified approach is allowed but only if the city maintains the network of sidewalks at least at a predetermined condition.

LO 17-7

21. Which of the following statements is true about use of the modified approach?
    a. It can be applied to all capital assets of a state or local government.
    b. It is used to adjust depreciation expense either up or down based on conditions for the period.
    c. It is required for infrastructure assets.
    d. For qualified assets, it eliminates the recording of depreciation.

LO 17-8

22. Which of the following is true about the management's discussion and analysis (MD&A)?
    a. It is an optional addition to the comprehensive annual financial report, but GASB encourages its inclusion.
    b. It adds a verbal explanation for the numbers and trends presented in the financial statements.
    c. It appears at the very end of a government's comprehensive annual financial report.
    d. It replaces a portion of the fund financial statements traditionally presented by state and local governments.

LO 17-9

23. Which of the following is *not* necessary for a special-purpose local government to be viewed as a primary government for reporting purposes?
    a. It must have a separately elected governing body.
    b. It must have specifically defined geographic boundaries.
    c. It must be fiscally independent.
    d. It must have corporate powers to prove that it is legally independent.

LO 17-9

24. An accountant is trying to determine whether the school system of the City of Abraham is fiscally independent. Which of the following is *not* a requirement for the school system to be judged as fiscally independent?
    a. Holding property in its own name
    b. Issuing bonded debt without outside approval
    c. Passing its own budget without outside approval
    d. Setting taxes or rates without outside approval

LO 17-9

25. An employment agency for individuals with disabilities works closely with the City of Hanover. The employment agency is legally separate from the city but still depends on the city for financial support. This support creates a potential financial burden for the city. How should Hanover report the employment agency in its comprehensive annual financial report?
    a. Not at all because the agency is legally separate
    b. As a part of the general fund
    c. As a component unit
    d. As a related organization

LO 17-9

26. The City of Bacon is located in the County of Pork. The city has a school system that reports buildings at a net $3.6 million although they are actually worth $4.2 million. The county has a separate school system that reports buildings at a net $5.2 million although they are actually worth $5.6 million. Both school systems qualify as special-purpose governments. If the school systems are combined in a merger, what balance should be reported for the buildings?
    a. $8.6 million
    b. $8.8 million
    c. $9.4 million
    d. $9.8 million

LO 17-9

27. For component units, what is the difference between *discrete presentation* and *blending?*
    a. A blended component unit is shown to the left of the statements; a discretely presented component unit is shown to the right.

b. A blended component unit is shown at the bottom of the statements; a discretely presented component unit is shown within the statements, like a fund.

c. A blended component unit is shown within the statements, like a fund; a discretely presented component unit is shown to the right.

d. A blended component unit is shown to the right of the statements; a discretely presented component unit is shown in completely separate statements.

LO 17-10

28. A government reports that its public safety function had expenses of $900,000 last year and program revenues of $200,000 so that its net expenses were $700,000. On which financial statement is this information presented?

a. Statement of activities

b. Statement of cash flows

c. Statement of revenues and expenditures

d. Statement of net position

LO 17-10

29. Government-wide financial statements make a distinction between program revenues and general revenues. How is that difference shown?

a. Program revenues are offset against the expenses of a specific function; general revenues are assigned to governmental activities and business-type activities in general.

b. General revenues are shown at the top of the statement of revenues and expenditures; program revenues are shown at the bottom.

c. General revenues are labeled as operating revenues; program revenues are shown as miscellaneous income.

d. General revenues are broken down by type; program revenues are reported as a single figure for the government.

LO 17-10

30. Which of the following is true about the statement of cash flows for the proprietary funds of a state or local government?

a. The indirect method of reporting cash flows from operating activities is allowed, although the direct method is recommended.

b. The structure of the statement is virtually identical to that of a for-profit business.

c. The statement is divided into four separate sections of cash flows.

d. Amounts spent on capital assets are reported in a separate section from amounts raised to finance those capital assets.

LO 17-11

31. Which of the following is most likely to be true about the financial reporting of a public college or university?

a. It resembles the financial reporting of private colleges and universities.

b. It will continue to use its own unique style of financial reporting.

c. It resembles the financial reporting made by a proprietary fund within the fund financial statements for a state or local government.

d. It will soon be reported using a financial statement format unique to the needs of public colleges and universities.

LO 17-3

32. The City of Columbus has approximately 2,000 employees. For the past three decades, the city has provided employees with a defined benefit pension plan. The plan contract calls for specific payment amounts to be made to each retiree based on a set formula. The city transfers money periodically to a pension trust fund where it is invested so that eventual payments can be made.

a. Describe how the city determines the amount (if any) of a net pension liability that should be reported within government-wide financial statements.

b. Describe how the city determines the amount (if any) of pension expense that should be reported within government-wide financial statements.

c. How is the pension reported in fund financial statements for the governmental funds?

LO 17-4

33. The City of Leonard decides to lease school desks for its school system rather than buy them because the lessor will do all scheduled maintenance. On January 1, 2020, the school system leases 5,000 school desks for four years. After that, they will be returned to the manufacturer. Payment will be $20 per desk per year with payments on January 1, beginning on January 1, 2020. The city does not know how the lessor determined the annual charge. The city has an annual incremental borrowing rate of 8 percent. The present value of an annuity due of $1 at an 8 percent annual rate for four periods is 3.5771.

a. Make the journal entries for the City of Leonard for 2020 and 2021 in preparing government-wide financial statements.

b. Make the journal entries for the City of Leonard for 2020 and 2021 in preparing fund financial statements for its governmental funds.

LO 17-4

34. The City of Raylan has a rather large warehouse that it no longer needs. The city had previously used the warehouse to store supplies and equipment for the school system, police department, and other public service functions. It has a remaining expected life of 18 years with no expected residual value. On January 1, 2020, the warehouse has a net book value of $1.4 million. On that date, city officials agree to lease the property to Acme International for its remaining life. Both parties agree to an implicit interest rate of 12 percent. The first payment is to be made immediately and on each subsequent January 1. The straight-line method is used where an allocation method is required.

    a. Assume that the present value of an annuity due of $1 at a 12 percent annual rate for 18 periods is 8.11963. Based on that assumption, what amount does the City of Raylan charge Acme each period?

    b. Assume the annual payments are properly calculated as $172,400 based on the information provided. What journal entries does the City of Raylan make for this lease for the year 2020 in preparing government-wide financial statements? Assume the city reports these transactions within the governmental activities.

    c. Assume the annual payments are properly calculated as $172,400 based on the information provided. What journal entries does the City of Raylan make for this lease for the year 2020 in preparing fund financial statements? Assume the city reports these transactions within the general fund.

LO 17-5

35. On January 1, 2020, the City of Hastings creates a solid waste landfill that it expects to reach capacity gradually over the next 20 years. If the landfill were to be closed at the current time, closure costs would be approximately $1.2 million plus an additional $700,000 for postclosure work. Of these totals, the city must pay $50,000 on December 31 of each year for preliminary closure work. At the end of 2020, the landfill reaches 3 percent of capacity. At the end of 2021, the landfill reaches 9 percent of capacity. At the end of 2021, a reassessment is made. Experts determine total closure costs will be $1.4 million rather than $1.2 million.

    a. Assume the city views the landfill as an enterprise fund. What journal entries should the city make in 2020 and 2021 in preparing government-wide financial statements?

    b. Assume the city views the landfill as being within the general fund. What journal entries should the city make in 2020 and 2021 in preparing government-wide financial statements?

    c. Assume the city views the landfill as an enterprise fund. What journal entries should the city make in 2020 and 2021 in preparing fund financial statements?

    d. Assume the city views the landfill as being within the general fund. What journal entries should the city make in 2020 and 2021 in preparing fund financial statements?

LO 17-4

36. The City of Lawrence opens a solid waste landfill in 2020 that is at 54 percent of capacity on December 31, 2020. City officials had initially anticipated closure costs of $2 million but later that year decided that closure costs would actually be $2.4 million. None of these costs will be incurred until 2024, when the landfill is scheduled to be closed.

    a. What appears on the government-wide financial statements for this landfill for the year ended December 31, 2020?

    b. Assuming that the landfill is recorded within the general fund, what appears on the fund financial statements for this landfill for the year ended December 31, 2020?

LO 17-6

37. On January 1, 2020, a rich citizen of the Town of Ristoni donates a painting valued at $300,000 to be displayed to the public in a government building. Although this painting meets the three criteria to qualify as an artwork, town officials choose to record it as an asset. The gift has no eligibility requirements. These officials judge the painting to be inexhaustible so that depreciation will not be reported.

    a. For the year ended December 31, 2020, what does the town report on its government-wide financial statements in connection with this gift?

    b. How does the answer to (*a*) change if the government decides to depreciate this asset over a 10-year period using straight-line depreciation?

    c. How does the answer to (*a*) change if the government decides not to capitalize the asset?

LO 17-6

38. On January 1, 2020, the City of Graf pays $60,000 for a work of art to display in the local library. The city will take appropriate measures to protect and preserve the piece. However, if the work is

ever sold, the money received will go into unrestricted funds. Officials view the work as inexhaustible, but they have opted to depreciate the cost over 20 years (using the straight-line method).

a. How is this work reported on government-wide financial statements for the year ended December 31, 2020?

b. How is this work reported in fund financial statements for the governmental funds for the year ended December 31, 2020?

LO 17-7

39. A city government adds streetlights within its boundaries at a total cost of $300,000. These lights should burn for at least 10 years but can last significantly longer if maintained properly. The city develops a system to monitor these lights with the goal that 97 percent will be working at any one time. During the year, the city spends $48,000 to clean and repair the lights so that they are working according to the specified conditions. The city also spends another $78,000 to construct lights for several new streets.

Describe the various ways these costs could be reported on government-wide financial statements.

LO 17-8

40. The City of Francois, Texas, is in the process of producing its current comprehensive annual financial report (CAFR). Several organizations that operate within the city are related in various ways to the primary government. Officials are attempting to determine how the city should report each of these organizations in the reporting process.

a. What is the major criterion for inclusion in a government's CAFR?

b. How does an activity or function qualify as a special-purpose government?

c. How is the legal separation of a special-purpose government evaluated?

d. How is the fiscal independence of a special-purpose government evaluated?

e. What is a component unit, and how does a government normally report it on government-wide financial statements?

f. How does a primary government prove that it can impose its will on a component unit?

g. What is meant by the blending of a component unit?

LO 17-5

41. The County of Maxnell decides to create a waste management department and offer its services to the public for a fee. As a result, county officials plan to account for this activity as an enterprise fund. Prepare journal entries for this operation for the following 2020 transactions. Also prepare any necessary adjusting entries at the end of the year. Assume the information is gathered so that the county can prepare fund financial statements. Only entries for the waste management department are required here:

January 1—Receive unrestricted funds of $160,000 from the general fund as permanent financing.

February 1—Borrow an additional $130,000 from a local bank at a 12 percent annual interest rate.

March 1—Order a truck at an expected cost of $108,000.

April 1—Receive the truck and make full payment. The actual cost including transportation was $110,000. The truck has a 10-year life and no residual value. The county uses straight-line depreciation.

May 1—Receive a $20,000 cash grant from the state to help supplement the pay of the department workers. According to the grant, the money must be used for that purpose.

June 1—Rent a garage for the truck at a cost of $1,000 per month. The county pays 12 months of rent in advance. The contract has no provisions for extensions or purchases.

July 1—Charge citizens $13,000 for services. Of this amount, $11,000 is collected.

August 1—Make a $10,000 cash payment on the 12 percent note of February 1. This payment covers both interest and principal.

September 1—Pay salaries of $18,000 using the grant money received on May 1.

October 1—Pay truck maintenance costs of $1,000.

November 1—Pay additional salaries of $10,000, first using the rest of the grant money received May 1.

December 31—Send invoices totaling $19,000 to customers for services during the past six months. Collect $3,000 of the cash immediately.

December 31—A new government landfill opened this year. At the end of the year, it is 12 percent filled. The estimated current cost for the eventual closure of this facility is $4 million, although no payments will be made for approximately nine years.

LO 17-6, 17-8, 17-10

42. The following information pertains to the City of Williamson for 2020, its first year of legal existence. For convenience, assume that all transactions are for the general fund, which has three separate functions: general government, public safety, and health and sanitation.

Receipts:	
Property taxes	$320,000
Franchise taxes	42,000
Charges for general government services	5,000
Charges for public safety services	3,000
Charges for health and sanitation services	42,000
Issued long-term note payable	200,000
Receivables at end of year:	
Property taxes (90% estimated to be collectible)	90,000
Payments:	
Salary:	
General government	66,000
Public safety	39,000
Health and sanitation	22,000
Rent:	
General government	11,000
Public safety	18,000
Health and sanitation	3,000
Maintenance:	
General government	21,000
Public safety	5,000
Health and sanitation	9,000
Insurance:	
General government	8,000
Public safety ($2,000 still prepaid at end of year)	11,000
Health and sanitation	12,000
Interest on debt	16,000
Principal payment on debt	4,000
Storage shed	120,000
Equipment	80,000
Supplies (20% still held) (public safety)	15,000
Investments	90,000
Ordered but not received:	
Equipment	12,000
Liabilities, all of which are due in one month at end of year:	
Salaries:	
General government	4,000
Public safety	7,000
Health and sanitation	8,000

Compensated absences (such as vacations and sick days) legally owed to general government workers at year-end total $13,000. These amounts will not be taken by the employees until so late in 2021 that the payment is not viewed as requiring 2020 current financial resources.

The city received a piece of art this year as a donation. It is valued at $14,000. The city plans to use it for general government purposes. The gift has no eligibility requirements. The city chose not to capitalize this property.

General government activities use the storage shed that was acquired this year. It is depreciated over a 10-year period using the straight-line method with no residual value. The city uses the equipment for health and sanitation and depreciates it using the straight-line method over five years with no residual value.

The investments are valued at $103,000 at the end of the year.

For the equipment that was ordered but not yet received, the City Council (the highest decision-making body in the government) voted to honor the commitment when the equipment eventually arrives.

a. Prepare a statement of activities and a statement of net position for governmental activities in government-wide financial statements for December 31, 2020, and the year then ended.

b. Prepare a statement of revenues, expenditures, and other changes in fund balances and a balance sheet for the general fund in fund financial statements as of December 31, 2020, and the year then ended. Assume that the city applies the consumption method.

LO 17-2, 17-3, 17-9, 17-11

43. The City of Bernard starts the year of 2020 with the following unrestricted amounts in its general fund: cash of $20,000 and investments of $70,000. In addition, it holds a small building bought on January 1, 2019, for general government purposes for $300,000 and a related long-term debt of $240,000. The building is depreciated on the straight-line method over 10 years. The annual interest rate on the debt is 10 percent. The general fund has four separate functions: general government, public safety, public works, and health and sanitation. Other information includes the following:

Receipts:	
Property taxes	$510,000
Sales taxes	99,000
Dividend income	20,000
Charges for general government services	15,000
Charges for public safety services	8,000
Charges for public works	4,000
Charges for health and sanitation services	31,000
Charges for landfill	8,000
Grant to be used for salaries for health workers (no eligibility requirements)	25,000
Issued long-term note payable	200,000
Sold investments (mentioned above)	84,000
Receivables at year-end:	
Property taxes ($10,000 is expected to be uncollectible)	130,000
Payments:	
Salary:	
General government	90,000
Public safety	94,000
Public works	69,000
Health and sanitation (all from grant)	22,000
Utilities:	
General government	9,000
Public safety	16,000
Public works	13,000
Health and sanitation	4,000
Insurance:	
General government	25,000
Public safety	12,000
Public works (all prepaid as of the end of the year)	6,000
Health and sanitation	4,000
Miscellaneous:	
General government	12,000
Public safety	10,000
Public works	9,000
Health and sanitation	7,000
Interest on previous debt	24,000
Principal payment on previous debt	10,000
Interest on new debt	18,000
Building (public works)	210,000
Equipment (public safety)	90,000
Public works supplies (30% still held)	20,000
Investments	111,000
Ordered but not received:	
Equipment	24,000
Supplies	7,000
Due at end of year:	
Salaries:	
General government	14,000
Public safety	17,000
Public works	5,000

On the last day of the year, the city borrows $64,000 from a local bank and uses the money to buy a truck. The first payment on the loan (plus interest) will be made at the end of the next year.

The city opens a landfill this year that it records within its general fund. It is a public works function. Closure costs today is estimated as $260,000 although officials do not expect the landfill to be filled for nine more years. The city has incurred no costs to date. The landfill is now 15 percent filled.

For the equipment and supplies that were ordered but not yet received, the City Council (the highest decision-making body in the government) has voted to honor the commitment when the items arrive.

The new building is depreciated over 20 years using the straight-line method and no residual value. Depreciation of the equipment is similar except that its life is only 10 years. Assume the city records a full year's depreciation in the year of acquisition.

The investments have a market value of $116,000 at year-end.

a. Prepare a statement of activities and a statement of net position for governmental activities in government-wide financial statements for December 31, 2020, and the year then ended.

b. Prepare a statement of revenues, expenditures, and other changes in fund balances and a balance sheet for the general fund in fund financial statements as of December 31, 2020, and the year then ended. Assume the purchases method is applied.

LO 17-7, 17-8, 17-9, 17-11

44. The City of Pfeiffer starts the year of 2020 with the general fund and an enterprise fund. The general fund has two activities: education and parks/recreation. For convenience, assume that the general fund holds $123,000 cash and a new school building costing $1 million. The city utilizes straight-line depreciation. The building has a 20-year life and no residual value. The enterprise fund has $62,000 cash and a new $600,000 civic auditorium with a 30-year life and no residual value. The enterprise fund monitors one activity, the rental of the civic auditorium for entertainment and other cultural affairs.

The following transactions for the city take place during 2020. Assume that the city's fiscal year ends on December 31.

a. Decides to build a municipal park and transfers cash of $70,000 into a capital projects fund. Both the creation of this fund and the transfer were made by the highest level of government authority. The city immediately expends $20,000 to acquire three acres of land.

b. Borrows $110,000 cash on a long-term bond for use in creating the new municipal park.

c. Assesses property taxes on the first day of the year. The assessment, which is immediately enforceable, totals $600,000. Of this amount, $510,000 will be collected during 2020. Officials expect another $50,000 during the first month of 2021. They anticipate the remainder halfway through 2021.

d. Constructs a covered building in the new municipal park for $80,000 cash so that local citizens can play basketball when it rains. The building is put into service on July 1. It should last 10 years with no expected residual value.

e. Builds a sidewalk through the new park for $10,000 cash and puts it into service on July 1. The sidewalk should normally last for 10 years, but the city plans to keep it fixed up to a predetermined quality level so that it can last almost indefinitely.

f. Opens the park and charges an entrance fee of only a token amount. The city reports the park within its general fund. Collections during the first year of operations total $8,000.

g. Buys a new parking deck for $200,000, paying $20,000 cash and signing a long-term note for the rest. The parking deck, which goes into operation on July 1, is across the street from the civic auditorium and is considered part of that activity. It has a 20-year life and no residual value.

h. Receives a $100,000 cash grant for the city school system that must be spent for school lunches for children in low-income families. Officials view the appropriate spending of these funds as an eligibility requirement of this grant. During the current year, $37,000 of the amount received was spent for the intended purpose.

i. Charges students in the school system a total fee of $6,000 for books and the like. Of this amount, 90 percent is collected during 2020 with the remainder expected to be collected in the first few weeks of 2021.

j. Buys school supplies for $22,000 cash and uses $17,000 of them. The general fund applies the purchases method.

k. Receives a painting by a local artist to be displayed in the local school. It qualifies as a work of art, and officials have chosen not to capitalize it. The painting has a value of $80,000. Officials have set up security precautions so that the painting will be viewed as inexhaustible.

l. Transfers $20,000 cash from the general fund to the enterprise fund as a capital contribution.

m. Orders a school bus for $99,000.

n. Receives the school bus and pays an actual cost of $102,000, including transportation and other necessary costs. The bus goes into operation on October 1. It should last for five years with no residual value.

o. Pays salaries of $240,000 to school teachers. In addition, owes and will pay $30,000 during the first two weeks of 2021. Vacations worth $23,000 have also been earned by the teachers but will not be taken until July 2021.

p. Pays salaries of $42,000 to city auditorium workers. In addition, owes and will pay $3,000 in the first two weeks of 2021. Vacations worth $5,000 have also been earned by the workers but will not be taken until July 2021.

q. Charges customers $130,000 for short-term rental of the civic auditorium. Of this balance, collects $110,000 in cash and will collect the remainder in April 2021.

r. Pays $9,000 maintenance charges for the building and sidewalk in (*d*) and (*e*).

s. Pays $14,000 on the bond in (*b*) on the last day of 2020: $5,000 principal and $9,000 interest.

t. Accrues interest of $13,000 on the note in (*g*) as of the end of 2020, an amount the city will pay in June 2021.

u. Assumes a museum operating within the city is a component unit that will be discretely presented. The museum reports to city officials that it incurred $42,000 of direct expenses this past year and earned $50,000 in revenues from admission charges. The only assets held at year-end were cash of $24,000, building (net of depreciation) of $300,000, and a long-term liability of $210,000.

Prepare the 2020 government-wide financial statements for this city. Assume the use of the modified approach.

LO 17-7, 17-8, 17-9, 17-11

45. Use the information in problem 44 to prepare the 2020 fund financial statements for (a) the governmental funds and (b) the proprietary funds. A statement of cash flows is not required. Assume the city defines "available" as within 60 days and that all funds qualify as major. Assume that major funds are labeled as "Special Revenue Fund" and "Capital Projects Fund." The general fund is used for debt repayment.

LO 17-3, 17-4, 17-6, 17-9, 17-11

46. Indicate whether each of the following statements is true or false, and include a brief explanation for your answer.

a. A pension trust fund appears in the government-wide financial statements but not in the fund financial statements.

b. Permanent funds are included as one of the governmental funds.

c. A fire department places orders of $20,000 for equipment. Later, the equipment is received but at a total cost of $20,800. In compliance with requirements for fund financial statements, an encumbrance of $20,000 was recorded when the government placed the order, and recorded an expenditure of $20,800 when the equipment arrived.

d. A city reports a landfill as an enterprise fund. At the end of Year 1, the government estimated that the landfill will cost $800,000 to clean up when it is eventually full. At that time, it was 12 percent filled. At the end of Year 2, it is 20 percent filled, and the estimated cost of the cleanup was changed to $860,000. No payments are due for several years. Fund financial statements for Year 2 should report a $76,000 expense.

e. A city reports a landfill in the general fund. At the end of Year 1, the government estimated the landfill will cost $900,000 to clean up when it is eventually full. At that time, it was 11 percent filled. At the end of Year 2, it is 20 percent filled, and the estimated cost of the cleanup was changed to $850,000. No payments are due for several years. Government-wide financial statements for Year 2 should report a $71,000 expense.

f. A custodial fund has neither revenues nor expenditures but reports expenses.

g. A city leases several ambulances to use for five years although they have an expected life of 10 years. The city must determine whether this is an operating lease or a financing lease.

h. A city has an old school building that it leases to a hospital for its entire remaining life. The city must remove the school building from its government-wide financial statements.

i. A city leases several large trucks to use by its fire department for the next eight years. Total payments will be $260,000. The present value of those payments at an appropriate interest rate is $173,000. On the date of signing, the city immediately records an expenditure and another financing source of $173,000 for its fund financial statements.

For Problems 47 through 50, use the following introductory information:

The City of Wolfe issues its financial statements for Year 4 (assume that the city uses a calendar year). The city's general fund is composed of two functions: (1) education and (2) parks. The city also utilizes capital projects funds for ongoing construction and an enterprise fund to account for an art museum. The city also has one discretely presented component unit.

The government-wide financial statements indicate the following Year 4 totals.

Education had net expenses of $710,000.

Parks had net expenses of $130,000.

Art museum had net revenues of $80,000.

General revenues were $900,000. The overall increase in net position for the city was $140,000.

The fund financial statements for Year 4 indicate the following:

The general fund had an increase of $30,000 in its fund balance.

The capital projects fund had an increase of $40,000 in its fund balance.

The enterprise fund had an increase of $60,000 in its net position balance.

Officials for the City of Wolfe define "available" as current financial resources to be paid or collected within 60 days.

LO 17-6

47. On the first day of Year 4, the city receives a painting as a gift that qualifies as a work of art. It has an expected life of 30 years, is worth $15,000, and is displayed by the city at one of the local parks. The accountant accidentally capitalizes and depreciates it although officials wanted to use the allowed alternative.

    Respond to the following questions:

    a. According to the information provided, the general fund reported a $30,000 increase in its fund balance. If the accountant had used the allowed alternative, what would the city report as the change in fund balance for the general fund for the year?

    b. According to the information provided, the parks reported net expenses of $130,000. If the accountant had used the allowed alternative, what would the city report as the correct net expense for parks for the year?

    c. Assume the same information except that the art was given to the art museum but then not recorded at all. What should have been the overall change in net position for Year 4 on government-wide financial statements, assuming that officials still preferred the allowed alternative?

LO 17-9

48. Assume that the one component unit had program revenues of $30,000 and expenses of $42,000 and spent $10,000 for land during Year 4. However, it should have been handled as a blended component unit, not as a discretely presented component unit. According to the information provided, the overall increase in net position reported was $140,000. What was the correct overall change in the net position in the government-wide financial statements?

LO 17-5

49. The city maintains a landfill and records it within its parks. The landfill generates program revenues of $4,000 in Year 4 and cash expenses of $15,000. It also pays $3,000 cash for a piece of land. These transactions were recorded as would have been anticipated, but no other recording was made this year. The city assumes that it will have to pay $200,000 to clean up the landfill when it is closed in several years. The landfill was 18 percent filled at the end of Year 3 and is 26 percent filled at the end of Year 4. No payments will be necessary for several more years. For convenience, assume that the entries in all previous years were correctly handled regardless of the situation.

    a. The city believes that the landfill was included appropriately in all previous years as one of the enterprise funds. According to the information provided, the overall increase in net position was $140,000. What is the correct overall change in the net position in the government-wide financial statements?

    b. The city believes that the landfill was included appropriately in all previous years in one of the enterprise funds. According to the information provided, the enterprise fund reports an increase in its net position of $60,000. What is the correct change in the net position of the enterprise fund in fund financial statements?

    c. The city believes that the landfill was included appropriately in all previous years within the general fund. What is the correct change in the fund balance of the general fund?

17-8, 17-10

50. On the first day of the year, the City of Wolfe buys $20,000 of equipment with a five-year life and no residual value for its school system. This cost was capitalized. No other entries were ever made. The city maintained the equipment using the modified approach.

a. Based on the information provided, what was the correct overall change in the net position in the government-wide financial statements?

b. What was the correct amount of net expenses for education in the government-wide statements?

LO 17-5

51. A city maintains a solid waste landfill that was 12 percent filled at the end of Year 1 and 26 percent filled at the end of Year 2. During those periods, the government estimated that total closure costs would be $2 million. It pays $50,000 to an environmental company on July 1 of each of these two years to begin some of the restoration process. Such payments will continue for years to come. Indicate whether each of the following *independent* statements is true or false and briefly explain each answer. The city has a December 31 year-end.

a. The government-wide financial statements will show a $230,000 expense in Year 2 but only if reported in an enterprise fund.

b. Fund financial statements will show a $50,000 liability in Year 2 if this landfill is reported in the general fund.

c. Fund financial statements will show a $50,000 liability at the end of Year 2 if this landfill is reported in an enterprise fund.

d. If the city reports this landfill in an enterprise fund, government-wide financial statements and fund financial statements will have the same basic reporting.

e. Government-wide financial statements will show a $420,000 liability at the end of Year 2.

f. Assume the city reports the landfill in the general fund. Over the landfill's entire life, the amount of expense recognized in government-wide financial statements will be the same as the amount of expenditures recognized in fund financial statements.

LO 17-5

52. Use the same information as in Problem 51, except that, by the end of Year 3, the landfill is 40 percent filled. The city now realizes that the total closure costs will be $3 million. Indicate whether each of the following *independent* statements is true or false and briefly explain each answer.

a. Assume the city reports the landfill as an enterprise fund. If the city had estimated the costs as $3 million from the beginning, the reporting on the fund financial statements would have been different in the past years.

b. Assume the city reports the landfill in the general fund. A liability will be reported for the governmental activities in the government-wide financial statements at the end of Year 3.

c. A $680,000 expense should be recognized in Year 3 in the government-wide financial statements.

d. Because the closure costs reflect a future flow of cash, any liability reported in the government-wide financial statements must be reported at present value.

LO 17-6

53. A city receives a copy of its original charter from the year 1799 as a gift from a citizen. The document is put under protective glass and displayed in the city hall for all to see. The city estimates its fair value at $10,000. Indicate whether each of the following *independent* statements is true or false, and briefly explain each answer.

a. Assume the city government does not have a policy for handling any proceeds if it ever sells the document. The city must report a $10,000 asset within its government-wide financial statements.

b. Assume this gift qualifies for optional handling and the city chooses to report it as an asset. For government-wide financial statements, depreciation is required.

c. Assume this gift qualifies for optional handling and the document is deemed to be exhaustible. The city must report an immediate expense of $10,000 in government-wide financial statements.

d. Assume this gift qualifies for optional handling. The city must make a decision as to whether to recognize a revenue of $10,000 in government-wide financial statements.

e. Assume this gift qualifies for optional handling. The city can choose to report the gift in the statement of net activities for government-wide financial statements in a way so that no overall net effect is reported.

LO 17-9

54. A city starts a public library that has separate incorporation and receives some of its operating money from the state and some from private donations. Indicate whether each of the following *independent* statements is true or false, and briefly explain each answer.

a. If the city appoints nine of the 10 directors, the city must report the library as a component unit.

b. If the library qualifies as a component unit and its financial results are shown as part of the city's governmental activities, it is a blended component unit.

c. If the library appoints its own board but the city must approve its annual budget, the city must report the library as a blended component unit.

LO 17-6, 17-7, 17-9, 17-10

55. The City of Dickens has a fiscal year ending December 31, Year 5. The city council is the highest level of decision-making authority for the government. For each of the following, indicate whether the overall statement is true or false. Assume that each situation is independent of all others.

a. On December 30, Year 5, the city spends $900,000 on a sidewalk project that is not a special assessment. On the Year 5 financial statements, a reconciliation is presented that starts with the total change in fund balances for the governmental funds and works down to end with the total change in net position for the governmental activities. As a result of this acquisition, this $900,000 must be subtracted as part of this reconciliation.

b. The city appoints all members of the board of directors for a nature museum. This fact alone qualifies this nature museum a component unit of the city.

c. The city appoints none of the governing board of a parks commission. This fact alone prohibits this parks commission from being a component unit of the city.

d. The city has a school system with a separately elected governing board (elected by the public). This fact alone makes the school system a special-purpose government with its own required financial reporting.

e. The modified approach applies only to infrastructure assets.

f. The modified approach has become widely used in state and local government accounting over the most recent few years.

g. The city's school system charges students a $10 per person fee each year. In the statement of activities, this fee should be shown as miscellaneous revenue directly under general revenues.

h. The city receives a work of art worth $100,000 as a gift and also spends $70,000 in cash to buy a second artwork. Both artworks will be exhibited publicly and properly protected and preserved. The city council passes a resolution that if either item is ever sold the proceeds must be used to buy replacement art works. Both of the artworks are viewed as inexhaustible. The city has the option to report both of these pieces of art as expenses rather than as assets in government-wide financial statements.

i. Assume that the city issues 30-day revenue anticipation notes on December 30, Year 5, to finance the government until it collects new taxes. These notes are issued at their face value of $500,000. On the Year 5 financial statements, a reconciliation is presented that starts with the total change in fund balances for the governmental funds and works down to end with the total change in the net position for the governmental activities. As a result of the note issuance, this $500,000 must be subtracted as part of this reconciliation.

Develop Your Skills

RESEARCH CASE 1

The accountant for the City of Abernethy calls the local CPA firm that audits the city's financial statements with a question.

> "At the start of the current year, city officials signed a contract to lease a new police car for seven years, its entire useful life. We drove a hard bargain. The annual payments are only $18,000 per year so the liability has a present value of $98,031. I realize the city has to report the initial liability at that amount. Nevertheless, the car has a fair value of $114,000. We know that based on its sales price. Can we report the asset at $114,000 even if we have to report the liability at $98,031?"

Required

Go to www.gasb.org. Click on "Standards & Guidance." Under "Pronouncements," click on "More." Under "View GASB Pronouncements," search for GASB Statement No. 87. Click on "Full Text." Scroll to the Table of Contents. Locate "Appendix B: Basis for Conclusions." This section explains what options GASB considered and what decisions were made. Locate and read paragraphs B47 through B50. Based on that discussion, write a memo to officials for the City of Abernethy answering the question posed by the accountant.

RESEARCH CASE 2

Officials for the City of Anderson, West Virginia, have recently formed a transit authority to create a public transportation system for the community. These same officials are now preparing the city's CAFR for the most recent year. The transit authority has already lost a considerable amount of money. Officials have become interested in its financial reporting and whether it qualifies as a component unit of the city.

Following are several articles written about the reporting of component units by a state or local government:

"Changes in Component Units," *Government Finance Review,* February 2011.

"GASB Issues Guidance on Financial Reporting Entity, Component Units," *Accounting Policy & Practice Report,* January 7, 2011.

"Financial Reporting for Affiliated Organizations," *The Journal of Government Financial Management,* Winter 2003.

"How to Implement GASB *Statement No. 34,*" *The Journal of Accountancy,* November 2001.

"GASB Issues Guidance on Blending Certain Component Units into Financial Statements," *Investment Weekly News,* February 27, 2016.

"Accounting for Affiliated Organizations," *Government Finance Review,* December 2002.

"Component Unit Reporting in the New Reporting Model," *The CPA Journal,* October 2001.

Required

Read one or more of the preceding articles and any others that you may discover about component units. Write a memo to city officials providing as much detailed information about component units and their reporting as you can to help these individuals understand the challenges and difficulties of this reporting.

ANALYSIS CASE 1

Read the following journal articles: "25 Years of State and Local Governmental Financial Reporting—An Accounting Standards Perspective," *The Government Accountants Journal,* Fall 1992, and "The GASB Turns 25: A Retrospective," *Government Finance Review,* April 2009.

Now go to http://pittsburghpa.gov/controller/cafr for the City of Pittsburgh, and pick a CAFR that is more than 25 years old. Compare it to the CAFR for Pittsburgh for the most recent year.

Required

Accounting for state and local governments has changed considerably over the years. Write a report to highlight some of the differences you noted between the process described before 2000 and the process presented in this chapter and the preceding one in this textbook.

ANALYSIS CASE 2

Go to www.phoenix.gov, and do a search for the term "CAFR." Those results should lead to the latest CAFR for the City of Phoenix, Arizona. The financial statements for a state and local government must include a Management's Discussion and Analysis of the information being reported. Read this section of the Phoenix CAFR.

Required

Write a report indicating the types of information found in this government's MD&A.

COMMUNICATION CASE 1

Read the following articles and any other papers that are available on setting governmental accounting standards:

"The Governmental Accounting Standards Board: Factors Influencing Its Operation and Initial Technical Agenda," *Government Accountants Journal,* Spring 2000.

"Governmental Accounting Standards Come of Age: Highlights from the First 20 Years," *Government Finance Review,* April 2005.

"Forward-Looking Information: What It Is and Why It Matters," *Government Accountants Journal,* December 1, 2010.

"GASB Simplifies GAAP Hierarchy for State and Local Governments," *Business Wire,* June 29, 2015.

"A Century of Governmental Accounting and Financial Reporting Leadership," *Government Finance Review,* April 2006.

"The GASB Turns 25: A Retrospective," *Government Finance Review,* April 2009.

"Proposed Changes to the Process Used to Set the GASB's Technical Agenda," *Government Finance Review,* April 1, 2013.

Required

Write a short paper discussing the evolution of financial reporting for state and local governments over the years.

COMMUNICATION CASE 2

The City of Larissa recently opened a solid waste landfill to serve the area's citizens and businesses. The city's accountant has gone to city officials for guidance as to whether to record the landfill within the general fund or as a separate enterprise fund. Officials have asked for guidance on how to make that decision and how the answer will impact the government's financial reporting.

Required

Write a memo to the government officials describing the factors that should influence the decision as to the fund in which to report the landfill. Describe the impact that this decision will have on the city's future comprehensive annual financial reports.

EXCEL CASE

Prior to the creation of government-wide financial statements, the City of Loveland did not report the cost of its infrastructure assets. Now city officials are attempting to determine reported values for major infrastructure assets that were obtained prior to the preparation of these statements. The chief concern is determining a value for the city's hundreds of miles of roads that were built at various times over the past several decades. The city assumes each road will last for 50 years (depreciation is 2 percent per year).

As of December 31, 2020, city engineers believed that one mile of new road would cost $2.3 million. For convenience, each road is assumed to have been acquired as of January 1 of the year in which it was put into operation. Officials have done some investigation and believe that the cost of constructing a mile of road has increased by 8 percent each year over the past 30 years.

Required

Build a spreadsheet to determine the value that should now be reported for each mile of road depending on the year it was put into operation. For example, what reported value should be disclosed in the government-wide financial statements for 10 miles of roads put into operation on January 1, 1999?

chapter 18

Accounting and Reporting for Private Not-for-Profit Entities

"Americans are the world's most generous contributors to philanthropic causes. Each year, we give about 2% of our GDP to nonprofit organizations, nearly twice as much as the U.K., the next closest nation, according to *The Chronicle of Philanthropy.* Some 65% of all American households with an income of less than $100,000 donate to some type of charity, according to the Center on Philanthropy at Indiana University, as does nearly every household with an income greater than $100,000. These contributions average out to about $732 a year for every man, woman, and child in America."[1]

Not-for-profit entities (NFPs) carry out their operations throughout the world. NFPs typically include nongovernmental entities such as charities, foundations, colleges and universities, health care providers, cultural institutions, religious organizations, and trade associations.[2] Many are well known for their ongoing work to achieve one or more stated missions such as the cure for a particular disease, the eradication of hunger and poverty, or the cleanup of the environment.

At the beginning of 2016, 1,571,056 tax-exempt organizations existed in the United States. That figure was made up of 1,097,689 public charities, 105,030 private foundations, and 368,337 other types of not-for-profit organizations, including chambers of commerce, fraternal organizations, and civic leagues. Nonprofits accounted for 9.2 percent of all wages and salaries paid in the United States in 2010 and 5.3 percent of gross domestic product in 2014. Public charities reported more than $1.74 trillion in total revenues in 2013. Perhaps surprisingly, only 21 percent came from contributions, gifts, and government grants. The rest was raised by program service revenues, including government grants and contracts, and other sources such as dues and rental income.[3]

Many of these organizations are huge by any standard. As of June 30, 2017, for example, The American National Red Cross reported holding $3.1 billion in assets. For the year ending June 30, 2017, Feeding America reported $2.7 billion in public support (contributions and the like) and only about $75 million as revenue from sources such as fees and conferences. For the same period, Elderhostel, Inc., (which leads educational tours under the name Road Scholar) reported $294 million in program revenues but just $2 million in contributions. Although both are NFPs, the funding models are quite different.

[1] Dan Pallotta, "Why Can't We Sell Charity Like We Sell Perfume?," *The Wall Street Journal,* September 15–16, 2012, p. C1.

[2] FASB, "Not-for-Profit Entities (Topic 958)," *Accounting Standards Update 2016-14, Presentation of Financial Statements of Not-for-Profit Entities*, August 2016.

[3] National Center for Charitable Statistics. http://nccs.urban.org/statistics/quickfacts.cfm.

Learning Objectives

After studying this chapter, you should be able to:

LO 18-1 Understand the basic composition of financial statements produced for a private not-for-profit entity.

LO 18-2 Describe the differences in net assets of a private not-for-profit entity that are without donor restrictions and those with donor restrictions.

LO 18-3 Explain the purpose and construction of a statement of functional expenses.

LO 18-4 Report the various types of contributions that a private not-for-profit entity can receive.

LO 18-5 Explain the difference between a conditional contribution and an unconditional contribution, and demonstrate the method of financial reporting for each.

LO 18-6 Account for both mergers and acquisitions of not-for-profit entities.

LO 18-7 Understand the advantages of attaining tax-exempt status.

LO 18-8 Describe the unique aspects of revenue recognition for both investor-owned and private not-for-profit health care entities.

LO 18-1

Understand the basic composition of financial statements produced for a private not-for-profit entity.

The Structure of Financial Reporting

According to the "Master Glossary" within the FASB's *Accounting Standards Codification (ASC)*, an organization is identified as a not-for-profit entity if it "possesses the following characteristics, in varying degrees, that distinguish it from a business entity:

a. Contributions of significant amounts of resources from resource providers who do not expect commensurate or proportionate pecuniary return
b. Operating purposes other than to provide goods or services at a profit
c. Absence of ownership interests like those of business entities.

Entities that clearly fall outside this definition include the following:

a. All investor-owned entities
b. Entities that provide dividends, lower costs, or other economic benefits directly and proportionately to their owners, members, or participants, such as mutual insurance entities, credit unions, farm and rural electric cooperatives, and employee benefit plans."[4]

In describing the characteristics of NFPs, the term "in varying degrees" is important because these entities clearly vary from one another in many ways. Note also that the reporting guidance here differs somewhat from the rules created by the Internal Revenue Service for achieving tax-exempt status.

Some not-for-profit entities are classified as governmental because they receive tax revenues or are controlled by a governmental unit or entity. For example, a state-operated hospital, and a public university are both governmental not-for-profit organizations. The financial reporting for these activities is established by the Governmental Accounting Standards Board (GASB) and was examined in the previous chapter. However, most not-for-profit entities are nongovernmental. The American Cancer Society and Mothers Against Drunk Driving (MADD) are just two examples of charities that do not qualify as governmental.

Private NFPs (nongovernmental) follow the rules established by the FASB in the *Accounting Standards Codification*. Topic 958 is designated specifically for not-for-profit entities. The remaining rules established in the ASC related to business entities normally also apply to NFPs, but only if a particular issue is not covered within Topic 958.

As with Elderhostel, many NFPs (such as private hospitals and universities) earn a significant amount of their resources through exchange transactions where a provider (a patient or student, for example) receives benefits of commensurate value to the amount paid. The nature of those transactions is not unique to NFPs, so the accounting is likely to fall outside of the not-for-profit accounting designation. U.S. GAAP, as established by *Accounting Standards Update* No. 2014-09, "Revenue from Contracts with Customers," is applicable for most of these exchange transactions as would be the case for a business. Nevertheless, the money and other resources freely given to NFP entities each year without an expected and direct benefit is still a staggering amount. The reporting of those contributions, grants, and the like is unique to NFP accounting so that Topic 958 of the ASC provides the official guidance.

Total estimated giving for 2017 alone totaled $410.02 billion. This generosity comes from a wide array of donors.[5]

Individuals	$286.65 billion
Foundations	66.90 billion
Bequests	35.70 billion
Corporations	20.77 billion

Recipients of these contributions represent an eclectic assortment of missions:

Religion	$127.37 billion
Education	58.90 billion

[4] FASB, "Master Glossary," *Accounting Standards Codification*, https://asc.fasb.org/glossary.

[5] "Giving USA 2018: Americans Gave $410.02 Billion to Charity in 2017, Crossing the $400 Billion Mark for the First Time." June 13, 2018: givingusa.org.

Human services	50.06 billion
Foundations	45.89 billion
Health organizations	38.27 billion
Public-society benefit organizations	29.59 billion
International affairs	22.97 billion
Arts, culture, and humanities	19.51 billion
Environment and animal organizations	11.83 billion
Other	5.63 billion

With so much money at stake, the need for not-for-profit entities to provide adequate, fairly presented financial information is understandable. Current and potential contributors as well as other interested parties want to evaluate the financial stability of these operations. They want to judge how well resources are used, especially those received from donations. "Congress, the media, watchdog agencies and funders—almost everyone wants to know how nonprofits are using their scarce resources."[6] Future gifts and grants are often based, at least in part, on an entity's ability to convince providers that available funds are spent wisely to accomplish the NFP's stated mission. Financial statements are vital for the dissemination of this information because they report the resources generated and reflect the operating decisions made by the entity's management.

At one time, private not-for-profit entities utilized a wide array of financial reporting practices. The format of these statements often varied significantly depending on the type of organization. A fund accounting approach was common because of the donor restrictions frequently attached to gifts and grants. In the early part of the 1990s, FASB standardized much of the reporting for private not-for-profit entities by creating authoritative guidance for the handling of contributions and the content and format for financial statements. During the subsequent decades, FASB mandated few additional changes for not-for-profit financial reporting. However, major improvements came about recently as a result of *Accounting Standards Update 2016-14, Presentation of Financial Statements for Not-for-Profit Entities,* (released in August 2016) and *Accounting Standards Update 2018-08, Clarifying the Scope and the Accounting Guidance for Contributions Received and Contributions Made* (released in June 2018).[7]

Over the decades, basic goals have evolved that form the framework for the generally accepted accounting principles used by private not-for-profit entities, including

1. Financial statements should focus on the entity as a whole.
2. Reporting requirements for private not-for-profit entities should be comparable to those applied by for-profit businesses unless critical differences exist in the nature of the transactions or the informational needs of financial statement users.

The first of these goals is important because it establishes that the entity's financial statements should not be structured to highlight individual funds often used by these organizations for internal recordkeeping. Although separate funds help monitor and secure restricted assets, the operations and financial position of the entire organization should be emphasized in external reporting.

The second goal is significant because it allows these organizations to apply many of the accounting techniques already available for use by for-profit businesses. Consequently, authoritative literature for many complex topics does not have to be rewritten specifically for not-for-profit entities.

[6] Karen Craig, Steps to Improve Nonprofit Functional Expense Reporting," March 9, 2018, blog.aicpa.org/2018/03/4-steps-to-improve-nonprofit-functional-expense-reporting.html.

[7] The American Institute of Certified Public Accountants (AICPA) issues an audit and accounting guide, *Not-for-Profit Entities,* to provide additional practical guidance in preparing and auditing financial statements by focusing on procedures that are unique or significant to these organizations. The AICPA also offers guidance through *Not-for-Profit Entities: Checklists and Illustrative Financial Statements* and *Not-for-Profit Entities—Best Practices in Presentation and Disclosure.* None of these are part of the FASB *Accounting Standards Codification* (ASC).

Financial Statements for Private Not-for-Profit Entities

Although many private not-for-profit entities have characteristics in common with for-profit businesses, at least three critical differences impact the financial reporting:

1. First, the donations that many private not-for-profit entities receive have no counterparts in commercial businesses. Millions of dollars can be received purely as a gift. Businesses do not face that reporting challenge.
2. Second, contributions often have donor-imposed conditions and donor-imposed restrictions that limit the availability of the resources or require the proceeds to be used for a designated purpose or only after a specified point in time.
3. Third, readers of financial statements represent a wide range of individuals and groups who often have different interests in the information.

These differences suggest the need for a somewhat unique set of financial statements. Consequently, three financial statements are required for private not-for-profit entities:

1. A *statement of financial position* reports the assets and liabilities of private not-for-profits. A net assets section replaces the reporting of owners' equity or fund balances. Until recently, NFP entities had to separate the net asset total into three classifications to reflect donor restrictions: unrestricted net assets, temporarily restricted net assets, and permanently restricted net assets. In practice, distinctions between temporarily restricted net assets and permanently restricted net assets were not always easy to delineate. Consequently, starting in fiscal years that begin after December 15, 2017, NFPs must classify the net asset figure as either without donor restrictions or with donor restrictions. This distinction is significant because it discloses the discretion that the entity's management has for spending the net assets being held.
2. A *statement of activities* reports revenues and expenses as well as other changes occurring in net assets during the period. Revenues and expenses are recognized using the accrual basis of accounting. Therefore, long-lived assets are depreciated if they have a finite life. This statement is structured to present the changes in both categories of net assets during the period. NFPs typically separate their primary operating activities (revenues, contributions, grants, and the like) from nonoperating transactions (such as investment earnings) to provide a clearer picture of the events as they relate to the mission of the organization.
3. A *statement of cash flows* presents the standard classification system: cash flows from operating activities, cash flows from investing activities, and cash flows from financing activities. As with for-profit enterprises, cash flows from operating activities may be presented by either the direct or indirect method. The new *Accounting Standards Update* (*ASU 2016-14*) makes one interesting change in the reporting of the statement of cash flows. For NFPs that choose to use the direct method, the new rule eliminates the requirement that a reconciliation must be presented between the direct and indirect methods. This added disclosure has been blamed for the reluctance that many entities have for adopting the direct method. FASB apparently wants to encourage use of the direct method. The future impact on the decision of using the direct or indirect method will be interesting to observe.

In addition to these three statements, all NFPs are now required to present information about both the nature and the function of expenses. For many decades, a *statement of functional expenses* was required of voluntary health and welfare organizations—NFP entities that promote humanitarian activities, such as public health clinics, homeless shelters, the cure of a particular disease, and the like. FASB has extended this disclosure to all NFPs, but the entity can report this information within the statement of activities, as a separate statement, or in notes to financial statements. A separate statement is shown in Exhibit 18.3, but the other methods of reporting could also have been used.

The inclusion of this additional information regarding expenses allows a critical evaluation to be made of an entity's efficient use of funds: "The cost of badly managed cancer charities isn't just wasted money. People are dying while these outfits mishandle funds that could go toward care."[8]

[8] Bill Shapiro, "Check Your Charity!," *Time*, June 13, 2011, p. 81.

LO 18-2

Describe the differences in net assets of a private not-for-profit entity that are without donor restrictions and those with donor restrictions.

Statement of Financial Position

Exhibit 18.1 presents the statement of financial position for Tenth-Avenue Hope, a fictional not-for-profit entity. The asset and liability sections resemble those reported by for-profit enterprises. Accounts such as buildings, computers, and salaries payable are not unique to NFPs; therefore, special accounting is not required. However, unlike a business, both individuals and organizations frequently provide resources to not-for-profit entities without expecting a return of commensurate value in exchange. As a result, the traditional concept of owners' equity does not apply. In place of paid-in-capital and retained earnings, the final section of this statement presents a total "net asset" figure, which is simply the excess of reported assets over liabilities (see point A in Exhibit 18.1).

As mentioned previously, the net asset total is separated into two categories—*without donor restrictions* and *with donor restrictions.* A donor (or grantor) can stipulate restrictions

EXHIBIT 18.1

TENTH-AVENUE HOPE
Statement of Financial Position
December 31, Year 2
(with comparative financial information as of December 31, Year 1)

	December 31, Year 2		December 31, Year 1
Assets			
Current assets			
Cash and cash equivalents	$ 76,000		$ 54,000
Grants and contributions receivable	804,000		589,000
Other receivables and prepaid expenses	75,000		57,000
Total current assets	955,000		700,000
Noncurrent assets			
Investments	3,623,000		3,541,000
Property and equipment, net	1,216,000		1,045,000
Intangible assets, net	360,000		420,000
Grants & contributions receivable, net current portion	2,100,000		1,785,000
Total noncurrent assets	7,299,000		6,791,000
Total assets	$8,254,000		$7,491,000
Liabilities and Net Assets			
Current liabilities			
Line-of-credit payable—Bank of Morgansville	$ 77,000		$ 110,000
Accounts payable and accrued expenses	60,000		83,000
Deferred revenue	90,000		70,000
Lease obligations	134,000		126,000
Total current liabilities	361,000		389,000
Noncurrent liabilities			
Lease obligations, net current portion	230,000		300,000
Note payable—Bank of Morgansville	3,570,000		3,566,000
Total noncurrent liabilities	3,800,000		3,866,000
Commitments and contingencies (see notes)			
Net assets (A)			
Without donor restrictions:			
Undesignated	504,000	(G)	266,000
Board-designated for building expansion	1,200,000	(F)	800,000
Subtotal without donor restrictions	1,704,000	(E)	1,066,000
With donor restrictions:			
Purpose restricted and time restricted	375,000	(B)	360,000
Perpetual in nature	2,014,000	(C)	1,810,000
Subtotal with donor restrictions	2,389,000	(D)	2,170,000
Total net assets	4,093,000		3,236,000
Total liabilities and net assets	$8,254,000		$7,491,000

See accompanying notes to these financial statements.

that establish a use for a contributed asset that is more specific and not within normal broad limits. For example, "Tenth-Avenue Hope must use this $10,000 cash donation to buy food for neighborhood children" is a donor restriction because the NFP does not have significant discretion as to actual use. In contrast, "Tenth-Avenue Hope must use this $10,000 cash donation to meet its mission" is not viewed as restricted because expenditure of the donation is not strictly limited. The charity could use this money in many different ways.

Net assets can be purpose restricted ("This donated money must be used by the charity to buy a new truck.") or time restricted ("This donated money must be used evenly over the next four years."). Other donor restrictions can be permanent. In those cases, the charity cannot spend the grant or contribution but must invest the money permanently with only the subsequent income available for use. Depending on the donor's requirements, future earnings from these endowments are classified as either without donor restrictions or with donor restrictions.

In Exhibit 18.1, as of December 31, Year 2, $375,000 of the NFP's net assets have been restricted by donors or grantors to use for a particular purpose or at a specific point in time (point B). Another $2,014,000 (point C) is permanently donor restricted, sometimes referred to as "perpetual in nature." The donor conveyed this money to the NFP so that future income will create a permanent source of funding. On December 31, Year 2, net assets with donor restrictions totals $2,389,000 (point D) as compared to $2,170,000 one year earlier. FASB now requires that "Enhanced disclosure in notes to financial statements will provide useful information about the nature, amounts, and effects of the various types of donor-imposed restrictions, which often include limits on the purposes for which the resources can be used as well as the time frame for their use."[9] Therefore, adequate information must be available so that readers of the statements will understand the donor restrictions that the NFP officials face.

The sum of all net assets that are not donor restricted is labeled as "without donor restrictions," a total of $1,704,000 (point E) as of December 31, Year 2, in Exhibit 18.1. The management and board of directors have discretion as to the use of this amount of the net assets. However, boards often set a portion of these net assets aside for particular purposes such as emergencies or construction projects. For example, Princeton University reported holding unrestricted net assets of $10.6 billion as of June 30, 2017, but identified $9.7 billion or 92 percent of the total amount as "board-designated endowment funds."

The reporting of such board designations has frequently been the subject of debate because these net assets are within the control of the NFP and can be used for any purpose and at any time. The board has simply made a decision not to use that money but, rather, let it grow for future use. In other words, that choice can be reversed. At point F, Tenth-Avenue Hope shows that the board is holding $1.2 million of the $1.704 million total of its net assets for building expansion. Nevertheless, the board is still able to spend these net assets in any way that it chooses. Critics might argue that Tenth-Avenue Hope has $1,704,000 in net assets without donor restrictions (point E) but indicates having only $504,000 in undesignated net assets (point G). The assertion is that this reporting makes the charity look as if it is in need of immediate financial assistance, a view that helps fundraising efforts. Because board-designated net assets can be misunderstood, FASB now requires that NFPs disclose the amounts and purpose of each self-imposed limitation.

FASB has also added another stipulation that relates to the reporting of the statement of financial position. Disclosures are now required to explain how the NFP expects to handle liquidity issues over the subsequent year. If cash levels fall to low levels, a for-profit can reduce prices or sell investments to meet obligations. Those remedies may not be available to an NFP, especially one that relies on contributions that might be donor restricted.

> Liquidity has also become a critical metric used by boards and stakeholders to measure the potential sustainability of an NFP. No amount of long-term investments and capital assets will keep a nonprofit operational if its finances aren't sufficiently liquid. Having the right amount of liquid and non-liquid resources available is key for an NFP to accomplish its mission. Liquidity is typically defined as how much cash and/or assets (such as short-term investments) an NFP

[9] FASB, "Not-for-Profit Entities (Topic 958)," *Accounting Standards Update 2016-14.*

> holds that can be easily converted to cash for use in the immediate or near future. An NFP is thought to be liquid if it has ready access to cash to meet its needs.[10]

Consequently, new FASB rules require disclosure of the amount of available liquid resources and the entity's plans if additional funds are needed.

> There are two requirements. The first is to disclose how a nonprofit manages its liquidity risks. That means explaining what the nonprofit does to make sure it has money to cover its ongoing operating expenses. Does it have a cash reserve? How about a line of credit? If there is a cash flow crunch, what does the nonprofit have in place to make sure it can pay the bills? Second, the new standards require the nonprofit to show the amount of financial assets available for general expenditures within one year of the balance sheet date. These changes are intended to make it easier to see, by looking at a nonprofit's financial statements, if there are liquidity issues. In other words, does the nonprofit really have the ability to pay its bills, or are the funds earmarked for other things?[11]

LO 18-2

Describe the differences in net assets of a private not-for-profit entity that are without donor restrictions and those with donor restrictions.

Statement of Activities

Exhibit 18.2 presents the statement of activities for Tenth-Avenue Hope for the years ended December 31, Year 1 and Year 2. For each year, separate columns present the increases and decreases (1) in net assets without donor restrictions, (2) in net assets with donor restrictions, and (3) in total net assets. The year-end figures at the bottom of each column agree with the ending balances shown on the statement of financial position in Exhibit 18.1.

As stated previously, many private not-for-profit entities generate revenues such as membership dues, conferences, and course fees where a performance obligation must be satisfied. An earning process exists and revenue recognition rules apply. Other NFPs receive substantial amounts from contributions and grants where the parties exchange nothing of commensurate value. In the first section of Exhibit 18.2, separate account balances serve to differentiate revenues from contributions and grants. For example, for the year ended September 30, 2017, the Girl Scouts of the United States of America reported "Girl Scout merchandise gross profit" of more than $23 million. Among other revenues, that figure reflects a lot of cookie sales.

As points H ($280,000) and I ($300,000) of the statement of activities shows, some portions of the contributions and grants accepted by Tenth-Avenue Hope came with donor restrictions attached. Those amounts appear in the second column to indicate a purpose restriction, a time restriction, or a permanent endowment restriction. As an example, for the year ended June 30, 2017, the American Heart Association reported financial contributions of $150.8 million on its statement of activities. Of that total, only $71.7 million was conveyed without any restrictions. The remaining $79.1 million in contributions had been given with some type of donor stipulation.

Expenses and the Release of Donor-Restricted Net Assets

As can be seen at point J in the statement of activities, all expenses are reported in the Without Donor Restrictions column. In this way, reported balances in the first column can be viewed as a reasonable reflection of the NFP's operating activities. When analyzing Exhibit 18.2, a reader of this financial statement can see that all Year 2 operating revenues and other support without donor restrictions totaled $2,218,000. During the same period, Tenth-Avenue Hope incurred expenses of $1,644,000 (point K). This format allows the NFP to report a single net figure titled here as "Operating revenues and other support in excess of expenses" of $574,000 (point L). Because the charity received other contributions and grants that carried donor restrictions, the $574,000 figure is not a net income balance. However, it does provide a single number as a measure of the charity's efficiency in increasing net assets without donor restrictions during the year.

Earnings generated from the NFP's investments (and other incidental gains and losses) are shown separately here as nonoperating (point M) although some charities choose to

[10] Michelle M. Cain, "Keeping Your Balance: How's the Financial Health of Your Not-for-Profit?," *Daily Record*, Rochester, NY, May 3, 2018.

[11] Jennifer Chandler, "Q & A with Rick Cole, Supervising Project Manager, FASB," Council of Nonprofits, April 5, 2018, https://www.councilofnonprofits.org/thought-leadership/what-are-the-new-significant-changes-required-fasb-nonprofit-financial-statements.

EXHIBIT 18.2

TENTH-AVENUE HOPE
Statement of Activities
For year ended December 31, Year 2
(with comparative financial information for year ended December 31, Year 1)

	Year ended December 31, Year 2			Year ended December 31, Year 1		
	Without donor restrictions	**With donor restrictions**	**Total**	**Without donor restrictions**	**With donor restrictions**	**Total**
Operating revenues and other support						
Membership dues	$ 316,000	$ —	$ 316,000	$ 340,000	$ —	$ 340,000
Conferences and course fees	145,000	—	145,000	97,000	—	97,000
Contributions	706,000	280,000 (H)	986,000	616,000	109,000	725,000
Grants	645,000	300,000 (I)	945,000	224,000	275,000	499,000
Net assets released from restrictions:						
Satisfaction of time/program restrictions (N)	406,000	(406,000)	—	218,000	(218,000)	—
Total operating revenues and other support	2,218,000	174,000	2,392,000	1,495,000	166,000	1,661,000
Expenses Program services	(J)					
Clean streets	311,000	—	311,000	89,000	—	89,000
Feed children	640,000	—	640,000	486,000	—	486,000
House homeless	377,000	—	377,000	257,000	—	257,000
Total program services	1,328,000	—	1,328,000	832,000	—	832,000
Supporting activities						
General and administrative	195,000	—	195,000	156,000	—	156,000
Fundraising	121,000	—	121,000	108,000	—	108,000
Total supporting activities	316,000	—	316,000	264,000	—	264,000
Total expenses	1,644,000 (K)	—	1,644,000	1,096,000	—	1,096,000
Operating revenues and other support in excess of expenses	574,000 (L)	174,000	748,000	399,000	166,000	565,000
Nonoperating						
Investment return, net (M)	64,000	45,000	109,000	41,000	18,000	59,000
Change in net assets	638,000	219,000	857,000	440,000	184,000	624,000
Net assets, beginning of year	1,066,000	2,170,000	3,236,000	626,000	1,986,000	2,612,000
Net assets, end of year	$1,704,000	$2,389,000	$4,093,000	$1,066,000	$2,170,000	$3,236,000

See accompanying notes to these financial statements.

report this figure within operating revenues. As shown, the amount reported is a net balance. Investment earnings are reduced by all expenses incurred, both external investment expenses and direct internal investment expenses. This netting allows the reader to see the actual profitability generated by investments as time passes year by year. For example, United Way Worldwide reported investment income (net) within operating revenues as a loss of $519,512 for the year ended December 31, 2017, and a gain of $681,453 for the year ended December 31, 2016. "Financial statement users will be better able to compare investment returns among different not-for-profits, regardless of whether investments are managed externally (for example, by an outside investment manager who charges management fees) or internally (by staff)."[12]

Recording expenses solely within the category of net assets without donor restrictions causes a practical problem. Some expenses are incurred in connection with purpose-restricted or time-restricted net assets. A cash gift, for example, could be designated by the donor to support the salaries of the organization's employees. If the contribution is reported as an increase in net assets with donor restrictions, how can the eventual salary expense be presented as a decrease in the net assets without donor restriction? How can the reporting of the support and the expense be aligned?

If a purpose or time restriction is fulfilled, that amount of net assets is reclassified. The restriction has been met and, therefore, is lifted. When an expense is incurred that meets a donor stipulation, both the expense and the related contribution revenue appear simultaneously in the Net Assets Without Donor Restrictions column of the statement of activities. As shown in Exhibit 18.2 at point N, this reclassification is reflected by a line at the bottom of the operating revenues and other support section. It increases net assets without donor restrictions by the released amount while decreasing net assets with donor restrictions by the same amount, $406,000 in this illustration. Because the appropriate expenditure has been made or a time restriction has expired, these previously restricted net assets are no longer restricted.

In its statement of activities for the year ended June 30, 2017, the American Heart Association reported that $102,988,000 of donor-restricted net assets had been released from restriction during the year because of the satisfaction of a purpose restriction, while another $81,319,000 had been released because of the expiration of a time restriction. On this NFP's statement of activities, these amounts were reclassified into the Without Donor Restrictions column, most likely for one of the following three reasons.

1. Money was appropriately expended for an expense as designated by the donor.
2. Money was appropriately expended for an asset as designated by the donor.
3. A donor restriction based on time was satisfied.

To illustrate, assume that during Year 1, a private not-for-profit entity receives three cash gifts of $10,000 each. The donor has specified that the first gift be used for employee salaries. The second gift is designated for the purchase of equipment. The third gift is to be held until Year 2 before expenditure is allowed. All three are classified initially as increases in net assets with donor restrictions. The first two were given for a particular purpose. The third was to be used only after a designated future time. When received in Year 1, cash is increased by $30,000, as is contribution revenue—with donor restrictions. The revenue appears in the appropriate column of the statement of activities.

Assume that the first two gifts are properly spent during Year 2, and the time restriction on the third gift is fulfilled, although the money has not yet been used:

- For the first gift, cash is decreased and salary expense is recorded in the Net Assets Without Donor Restrictions column. At the same time, $10,000 is reclassified on the statement of activities from the Net Assets With Donor Restrictions column to the Net Assets Without Donor Restrictions column, as was done at point N in Exhibit 18.2. The money was spent as the donor had specified. It is no longer restricted.

[12] Gillian Siemelink, "Are You Ready for the New Not-for-Profit Reporting Standard?," June 12, 2018, Briggs and Veselka Co. http://bvccpa.com/not-for-profit-reporting/.

- For the second gift, equipment (an asset) is increased and cash is decreased. In addition, the same $10,000 reclassification as before is made on the statement of activities to indicate that this restriction has also been met. The money was spent as designated.
- A $10,000 reclassification must also be made for the third gift even though it has not yet been spent. It was restricted only as to time, and the required period has passed.

In Year 2, because all restrictions have been met, the statement of activities will show a total reclassification of $30,000 as an increase in net assets without donor restrictions, with an equal decrease in net assets with donor restrictions. Until recently, an alternative was available for the reclassification in connection with the $10,000 acquisition of equipment. NFPs were allowed to defer the reclassification from net assets with donor restrictions to net assets without donor restrictions until depreciation was recorded. Under this optional approach, the reclassified amount was set equal each year to the depreciation on the acquired asset. In that way, the increase in net assets without donor restrictions and the decrease in the same column caused by the depreciation expense would exactly offset each other. FASB no longer allows this accounting unless specifically requested by the donor. Otherwise, the entire reclassification occurs at the point in time when the money is spent as specified by the donor.

Program Services and Supporting Services

Detailed information about the expenses incurred by a private not-for-profit entity is important to most current and potential contributors. A primary concern is the extent to which a charity is using financial resources to fulfill its stated mission. Is money spent, for example, to cure disease or wasted on bloated fundraising campaigns or executive salaries? That is a question that virtually all not-for-profit entities face.

For this reason, expenses are presented in two broad categories: program services and supporting services. FASB now requires all NFPs to show an analysis of expenses according to natural and functional classifications, as shown in Exhibit 18.3, Tenth-Avenue Hope presents this information as a separate statement of functional expenses, but could also provide the numbers within the statement of activities or as a note to the financial statements.

- "Program services are the activities that result in goods and services being distributed to beneficiaries, customers, or members that fulfill the purposes or mission for which the NFP exists. Those services are the major purpose for and the major output of the NFP and often relate to several major programs."[13] Tenth-Avenue Hope discloses three program service categories: clean streets, feed children, and house homeless.
- Supporting activity costs usually consist of general and administrative, fundraising, and membership development. The fundraising category might be associated with certain program services, but it is not viewed as an actual cost of providing that service.

As a means of evaluating the efficiency of an NFP, analysts often calculate the ratio of program service expenses to total expenses. A ratio of 80.8 percent can be calculated for Tenth-Avenue Hope for the year ended December 31, Year 2, ($1,328,000/$1,644,000). That is a slight improvement from the 75.9 percent ratio from the previous year ($832,000/$1,096,000). The Better Business Bureau has suggested ratios of less than 65 percent are not desirable.[14] Because this ratio is affected by the assignment of costs between program services and supporting activities, the effects, if any, of methods used for allocating such costs should be disclosed.

Not everyone agrees with the wisdom that charities should keep administrative and fundraising costs at a bare minimum. "We tend to think that policing salaries of charitable groups is an ethical imperative, but for would-be leaders, it results in a mutually exclusive choice between doing well for yourself and doing good for the world—and it causes many of the brightest kids coming out of college to march directly into the corporate world. A second area

[13] FASB, *Accounting Standards Codification 958-720-45-3, No. 2018-8*, June 2018.

[14] The Better Business Bureau provides excellent guidance at http://give.org/for-charities/How-We-Accredit-Charities/?id=236646#FINANCES to aid interested parties in assessing the efficiency and organizational structure of a charity. The 65 percent recommendation can be found in Standard 8.

EXHIBIT 18.3

TENTH-AVENUE HOPE
Statement of Functional Expenses
For year ended December 31, Year 2
(with summarized financial information for year ended December 31, Year 1)

	Program services year ended December 31, Year 2				Program services year ended December 31, Year 1 summarized totals	Supporting activities year ended December 31, Year 2			Supporting activities year ended December 31, Year 1 summarized totals	Total expenses year ended December 31, Year 2	Total expenses year ended December 31, Year 1
	(O) Clean streets	Feed children	House homeless	Total program services		(P) General and administrative	Fundraising	Total supporting services			
Salaries and wages	$ 68,000	$ 77,700	$ 51,300	$ 197,000	$140,400	$ 67,000	$ 34,700	$101,700	$ 95,100	$ 298,700	$ 235,500
Other payroll	19,000	21,700	17,900	58,600	37,200	8,100	7,200	15,300	14,400	73,900	51,600
Supplies	5,500	27,100	10,200	42,800	23,800	5,100	5,600	10,700	10,100	53,500	33,900
Professional services	26,400	40,800	29,200	96,400	55,400	16,400	19,400	35,800	30,900	132,200	86,300
Insurance	9,700	8,800	10,600	29,100	21,500	3,400	2,800	6,200	6,000	35,300	27,500
Printing and mailing	3,400	1,600	2,400	7,400	8,100	4,100	8,300	12,400	15,100	19,800	23,200
Telephone and utilities	52,600	63,000	55,800	171,400	106,600	15,700	12,000	27,700	24,000	199,100	130,600
Heating	7,100	20,800	14,400	42,300	33,700	6,200	4,900	11,100	10,100	53,400	43,800
Transportation	31,000	69,500	28,500	129,000	90,400	23,700	14,700	38,400	11,000	167,400	101,400
Rental	14,000	63,200	30,200	107,400	51,700	6,800	900	7,700	7,300	115,100	59,000
Training	30,800	71,100	27,000	128,900	74,000	1,800	2,400	4,200	3.300	133,100	77,300
Interest	15,500	49,900	25,100	90,500	73,000	10,100	2,800	12,900	15,100	103,400	88,100
Depreciation and amortization	23,800	44,300	26,000	94,100	69,300	21,000	3,700	24,700	16,800	118,800	86,100
Miscellaneous expenses	4,200	80,500	48,400	133,100	46,900	5,600	1,600	7,200	4,800	140,300	51,700
Total expenses	$311,000	$640,000	$377,000	$1,328,000	$832,000	$195,000	$121,000	$316,000	$264,000	$1,644,000	$1,096,000

See accompanying notes to these financial statements.

of discrimination is advertising and marketing. We tell the for-profit sector to spend on advertising until the last dollar no longer produces a penny of value, but we don't like to see charitable donations spent on ads. We want our money to go directly to the needy—even though money spent on advertising dramatically increases the money available for the needy."[15]

Statement of Functional Expenses

LO 18-3

Explain the purpose and construction of a statement of functional expenses.

Exhibit 18.3 presents the statement of functional expenses for Tenth-Avenue Hope. Assume entity officials have decided to present this information as a separate statement rather than within the statement of activities or as footnote disclosure. Because contributors are concerned with how their gifts are used, this statement provides a detailed analysis of expenses by both function and nature. The columns represent functions and include the three previously identified program services followed by the supporting activities of general and administrative and fundraising (points O and P). These categories are the same as reported on the statement of activities. Thus, the column totals agree with the operating expenses reported on that statement. For example, both statements show that this charity spent $311,000 to clean streets. The statement of functional expenses breaks that figure down into more detail by providing amounts incurred for salaries and wages, other payroll, supplies, and the like.

As a result of the scrutiny sometimes placed on the amount a private not-for-profit entity spends on fundraising, the allocation of those costs is quite important. At one time, the costs of monetary appeals that also contained any type of educational literature were routinely divided evenly between fundraising and program services to make operations look more effective. Direct mail solicitations were almost always accompanied by informational pamphlets and the like so that a significant portion of the printing and mailing costs could be included as a program service expense such as educating the public.

Rules now specify that a portion of the costs of fundraising campaigns can only be assigned to program services if several criteria are met.[16] Literature that is mailed or otherwise distributed must include a specific call for action that would have been made even without the fundraising request. This appeal cannot be directed purely at potential contributors, and the desired action must be specific and help accomplish the entity's overall mission. If these criteria are met, a logical percentage of the costs associated with this call-for-action campaign is reported within program services rather than as purely fundraising.

For this reason, the June 30, 2017, financial statements of the American Heart Association, Inc., included the following note:

> The Association conducts joint activities (activities benefiting multiple programs and/or supporting services) that include fundraising appeals. Those activities primarily include direct mail campaigns and special events. The costs of conducting those joint activities were allocated as follows in 2017 and 2016 (in thousands):

	2017	2016
Public health education	$145,123	$136,417
Professional education and training	2,361	2,091
Community services	1,250	950
Management and general	25,159	26,267
Fund-raising	53,221	51,651
Total joint costs	$227,114	$217,376

Statement of Cash Flows

Exhibit 18.4 presents the statement of cash flows for Tenth-Avenue Hope. The traditional classifications found in for-profit reporting are also applicable for NFPs:

- Cash flows from operating activities (cash transactions generated by the primary or central day-to-day activities of the entity).

[15] Dan Pallotta, "Why Can't We Sell Charity Like We Sell Perfume?," *Wall Street Journal,* September 15–16, 2012, p. C1.

[16] For more information on the reporting of expenses by not-for-profit entities, see FASB ASC 958-720.

EXHIBIT 18.4

TENTH-AVENUE HOPE
Statement of Cash Flows
For year ended December 31, Year 2
(with comparative financial information for year ended December 31, Year 1)

	Year ended December 31, Year 2	Year ended December 31, Year 1
Cash flows from operating activities		
Cash received as contributions (S)	$ 881,000	$731,900
Cash received as grants	740,000	526,100
Cash received as dues	306,000	343,800
Cash received from conference fees	139,000	95,400
Cash received from interest and dividends	106,000	52,700
Cash paid for personnel and professional services costs (T)	(522,800)	(374,400)
Cash paid for insurance, printing, and other operational costs	(357,100)	(263,700)
Cash paid for transportation and rental costs	(275,500)	(164,500)
Cash paid for training costs	(139,100)	(82,100)
Cash paid for interest and other miscellaneous costs	(255,700)	(140,600)
Net cash provided by operating activities	621,800	724,600
Cash flows from investing activities (Q)		
Proceeds from sales of investments (less commissions)	160,000	139,200
Paid for purchase of investments	(339,000)	(334,600)
Paid for property and equipment	(329,800)	(415,500)
Net cash used in investing activities	(508,800)	(610,900)
Cash flows from financing activities (R)		
Paid/Borrowed on line-of-credit	(23,000)	40,000
Paid on lease obligations	(72,000)	(28,500)
Paid on note payable	(70,000)	(105,000)
Proceeds from note	74,000	—
Net cash used in financing activities	(91,000)	(93,500)
Increase in cash and cash equivalents	22,000	20,200
Cash and cash equivalents, beginning of year	54,000	33,800
Cash and cash equivalents, end of year	$ 76,000	$ 54,000

See accompanying notes to these financial statements.

- Cash flows from investing activities (cash transactions that are not part of operating activities but involve an asset, see point Q).
- Cash flows from financing activities (cash transactions that are not part of operating activities but involve a liability or equity transactions although equity transactions are rare for NFPs, see point R).

Tenth-Avenue Hope presents its operating activities in Exhibit 18.4 using the direct method. Each source and use of cash is shown explicitly. For example, at point S, Tenth-Avenue Hope indicates receiving $881,000 in cash from contributions, whereas at point T, the charity discloses paying $522,800 for personnel and professional services costs. The information is clear and not likely to confuse readers. However, FASB also allows the indirect method, where net income (or an equivalent total) is reconciled to the amount of cash generated by operating activities through a rather complicated system of (1) eliminations and (2) adjustments from accrual accounting to cash accounting. FASB has long expressed a preference for the direct method because of its clarity but with no apparent effect.[17] Virtually all entities—both for-profit and not-for-profit—use the indirect method when reporting the statement of cash flows. Application of the direct method can be hard to locate in practice.

[17] Nathan H. Jeppson, John A. Ruddy, and David F. Salerno, "The Statement of Cash Flows and the Direct Method of Presentation," *Management Accounting Quarterly*, Spring 2016.

For several decades, any entity that chose to apply the direct method of reporting operating activity cash flows also had to include the same information through the reporting of the indirect method. This requirement has long been viewed as a deterrent to entities that might consider using the direct method. The extra reporting is costly and redundant. In *ASU 2016-14*, "Not-for-Profit Entities (Topic 958): Presentation of Financial Statements of Not-for-Profit Entities," FASB encourages the voluntary reporting of the direct method by allowing NFPs to elect to use the direct method for operating activity cash flow reporting without having to include a supplementary indirect method reconciliation. This easing of the reporting burden might stimulate more NFPs to apply the direct method. In the future, if a significant number of not-for-profit entities begin to switch to the direct method, FASB might consider allowing the same option in reporting for-profit businesses.

LO 18-4

Report the various types of contributions that a private not-for-profit entity can receive.

Accounting for Contributions and Exchange Transactions

Exchange Transaction or Contribution?

A not-for-profit entity receives money and other assets for many different reasons. The reporting of those funds depends on how the transaction is classified. The first decision officials must address is whether a conveyance qualifies as a contribution or an exchange transaction. To illustrate, assume a private NFP academy has provided education for individuals with disabilities for many years. At the start of the current year, a nearby county government transfers $100,000 in cash to the school to pay for the education of nine students with disabilities who reside in that county. The government's payment is a common method of providing appropriate educational services for area citizens.

For the NFP, should a donor-restricted contribution ("This money is a gift that must be used by the school to educate these nine individuals.") or an exchange transaction ("This money is paid so the school will educate these nine individuals.") be reported?

- If it is a contribution, the balance of net assets with donor restrictions increases immediately by $100,000 (see point H in Exhibit 18.2) to reflect the contribution revenue. As the NFP meets each purpose restriction, the appropriate contributed amount is reclassified from net assets with donor restrictions to net assets without donor restrictions (point N in Exhibit 18.2).
- Conversely, if the payment begins an exchange transaction, the NFP reports a deferred revenue of $100,000 within the liability section of its statement of financial position (Exhibit 18.1) when the money is received. Later, as each performance obligation is satisfied, the school reclassifies the appropriate amount from this deferred revenue to an earned operating revenue on the statement of activities. This handling is effectively the same as that made by a for-profit business. As an exchange transaction, not-for-profit accounting rules do not apply.

In an exchange transaction, the resource provider (the county government) receives a commensurate value for the money conveyed. Here, the school's work enables the government to meet its social and legal obligation to educate these nine students. The government obtains a specific value for its payment. In this example, the money is not a contribution. It compensates the NFP for work done on behalf of the government. The school records the balance received as a liability (a deferred revenue) until each performance obligation is satisfied.

However, if a local corporation conveys $100,000 to this same school with the stipulation that "the money is to be used to help educate students with disabilities," the NFP reports a contribution. FASB does not view making a donation for the general public good as an attempt to obtain commensurate value. The corporation is not paying for services rendered. The transfer is a gift and not an exchange transaction. The NFP records contribution revenue of $100,000 within its statement of activities.

In this second situation, officials must address a related reporting issue. Should the NFP classify this $100,000 contribution as an increase in net assets with donor restrictions or an increase in net assets without donor restrictions? They must consider the wording of the agreement carefully to determine the appropriate reporting. A purpose restriction normally has to be specific rather than general. According to ASC 958-605-25-2A, "An entity shall consider whether the contribution includes a donor-imposed restriction, which includes the consideration about how broad or narrow the purpose of the agreement is."

If this school is primarily for students with disabilities, officials still have significant discretion as to the ultimate use of the money. It is available for books, teachers, desks, or a wide range of other expenditures. Thus, the NFP records the gift as an increase in net assets without donor restrictions. It is simply a generous gift to the school. In contrast, if individuals with disabilities only comprise a small portion of the student body, the gift is more likely to be shown as an increase in net assets with donor restrictions until used appropriately. The NFP can still spend the money on books, teachers, desks, or the like but only if those items help the individual members of the student body who are disabled. Use is becoming more directed. Finally, if the corporation selects or names the students, the gift will be an increase in net assets with donor restriction because the terms are now quite specific. The school has to spend the money for these particular students. Because of the differences in the situation, the school's discretionary use of the money has narrowed appreciably. The ultimate reporting decision depends on evaluating the ability of the NFP officials to use the money as they choose. "Don't expect the final guidance to provide black-and-white answers in all cases. Instead, the FASB is counting on not-for-profit organizations to continue using judgment."[18]

LO 18-5

Explain the difference between a conditional contribution and an unconditional contribution, and demonstrate the method of financial reporting for each.

Contributions—Unconditional or Conditional?

In not-for-profit accounting, a contribution is an unconditional transfer of cash or other assets. This definition also extends to include unconditional promises or pledges to give. Hence, no contribution exists from an accounting perspective until it qualifies as unconditional. If a contribution pledge is conditional, the NFP makes no recording. If a donor physically conveys money or other assets but the contribution remains conditional, the NFP records a refundable liability for that amount on the statement of financial position. As long as the gift is conditional, no increase in net assets appears on the statement of activities.

For example, assume that a corporation promises to donate $300,000 to an NFP school with the stipulation that "this money must be used to hire Dr. Trevor." If the NFP views this transaction as an unconditional contribution with a donor-restriction, it records a contribution receivable on the statement of financial position as well as an increase in net assets with donor restrictions on the statement of activities. If Dr. Trevor is ever hired, the NFP reclassifies the $300,000 on the statement of activities from net assets with donor restrictions to net assets without donor restriction. In contrast, if this pledge is a conditional contribution, it remains unreported. If the NFP does receive any money or other asset, a liability is reported that remains on the statement of financial position until the condition is met or the money returned.

The next question seems obvious. How does an NFP judge if a contribution is conditional since that is the key determinant to reporting? FASB has set up two criteria.

- First, the agreement between the parties contains a donor-imposed condition. The donor stipulates that the NFP must overcome a barrier before being entitled to the promised resources.
- Second, a contribution is conditional if failure of the NFP to surmount the barrier gives the donor a right of release from making further payment and the right to demand return of any amount already paid.

Thus, a NFP views a contribution as conditional if (a) the entity must overcome a specified barrier to qualify for the gift and (b) if the NFP fails, the donor has the right to avoid making additional payments and can demand a refund of all amounts previously given. If the NFP is uncertain as to whether a contribution is unconditional, U.S. GAAP states that it is viewed as conditional. If a promise is conditional, but the chance the NFP will not meet the condition is remote, it is considered unconditional and recognized immediately as contribution revenue. In that situation, the NFP records the contribution receivable along with an increase in net assets with donor restriction.

[18] Gillian Siemelink, "Are You Ready for the New Not-for-Profit Reporting Standard?," June 12, 2018, http://bvccpa.com/not-for-profit-reporting/.

Although both of these criteria are important, identification of a barrier to be overcome is likely to be more challenging to discern in practice. FASB explains that, "indicators are used to guide the assessment of whether an agreement contains a barrier. Depending on the facts and circumstances, some indicators may be more significant than others, and no single indicator is determinative."[19] Officials should weigh the presence of these indicators to decide whether the agreement between the parties creates a barrier that the NFP must overcome.

FASB separates these indicators into three categories.

Measurable performance-related barrier or other measurable barrier. This type of indicator usually relates to a quantitative outcome, often one connected to a specified level of service. For example, a donor might tell a school that nine students must graduate from a program or might require a hospital to serve 8,000 patients each month before a $1 million promise is fulfilled. Those figures reflect measurable outcomes for the NFP to achieve to become entitled to the $1 million.

A stipulation limiting discretion by the recipient on the conduct of an activity. A requirement that an NFP assisted-living facility must hire a heart specialist in order to earn a gift leaves officials with no discretion. That is a specified barrier. If the NFP identifies and employs a qualified doctor, it collects the money. Otherwise, the donor makes no gift. However, a donor requirement that this same NFP improve its medical care provides officials with more discretion. This donor stipulation can be met in many ways.

A stipulation that ties into the agreement. For example, a cash gift of $100,000 to an NFP hospital for expansion of its emergency room seems like an unconditional contribution with a donor restriction. However, assume that the agreement also requires the hiring of four new doctors to handle the increased workload. This stipulation is made so that the growing facility will be staffed appropriately. Even though this requirement only relates indirectly to the monetary contribution for the emergency room, it does tie into the agreement and serves as a barrier for the hospital to overcome.

If an agreement has a barrier to overcome and if failure to achieve that result allows the donor to seek a release from future payment and the claim for a refund of any assets already conveyed, the contribution is conditional. The NFP reports no increase in net assets. Clearly, officials must examine agreements carefully and be alert for each of these three types of indicators before deciding whether a contribution is conditional. Both the barrier to overcome and the right of release, and possibly the right of refund, are necessary for a contribution to be deemed conditional.

Many NFPs hold fundraising campaigns that can generate huge amounts of pledges. As of June 30, 2017, Georgetown University reported contributions receivable (net) of $157.6 million. If a promise to donate has been made, no entry is recorded until the contribution is unconditional. If some or all of the payment is collected from a conditional contribution, the asset is reported along with an equal liability. When the donation is no longer conditional, the liability is reclassified as an increase in net assets on the statement of activities. On December 31, 2017, United Way Worldwide reported a contribution receivable of $10.7 million. In a footnote, that net amount is broken down into an $11.0 million total receivable less a present value discount of $54,700 and an allowance for uncollectible pledges of $195,408. Bad debt expense for 2017 was $18,735. These figures follow U.S. GAAP, as explained in the NFP's footnotes.

> Contributions receivable consist of unconditional promises to give and are recorded in the year the promise is made. Unconditional promises to give that are expected to be collected within one year are recorded at their net realizable value. Unconditional promises to give that are expected to be collected in future years are recorded at the present value of estimated future cash flows. The discounts on those amounts are computed using risk-free interest rates applicable to the years in which the promises are received. Amortization of the discount is included in contribution revenue.

Cash is not the only type of support provided to not-for-profits. Many organizations receive donations of materials intended to be used by the charity itself (such as automobiles, office

[19] FASB, "Not-for-Profit Entities (Topic 958), Clarifying the Scope and the Accounting Guidance for Contributions Received and Contributions Made," *Accounting Standards Update 2018-08*.

furniture, and computers), to be liquidated (investments or old vehicles), or to be distributed to needy groups or individuals (food, clothing, and toys). Organizations such as the Salvation Army and Goodwill Industries rely on these types of donations as essential support for the charity's mission. The term "in-kind donations" is generally used to refer to gifts of assets or services other than cash or investment securities. If fair value can be determined, it serves as the basis for recording such donations.

Because donated supplies and other materials provide important resources, these contributions are reported as support unless the not-for-profit entity cannot use or sell gifts. For example, ChildFund International, USA, includes the following note to its 2017 financial statements: "Donated or contributed property, plant and equipment, investments, services and gifts-in-kind are recorded at fair value when received. The majority of gifts-in-kind consists of TOM shoes and public service announcements. The fair value of gifts-in-kind are recorded using an exit value approach. ChildFund received approximately $12,285,545 and $8,290,714 of gifts-in-kind shoes during the years ended June 30, 2017 and 2016, respectively. ChildFund received $30,434,093 and $27,998,211 of in-kind media and broadcast time in the form of public service announcements." An exit value approach records the amount that would be received for the items under current market conditions.

To illustrate, assume that a private not-for-profit entity begins a financial campaign in Year 1. The core mission of this NFP is to fight poverty, but the campaign hopes to raise money more specifically to help children in times of natural disaster such as hurricanes and tornadoes. The program will be known as Children and Disaster Relief. The following gifts are received.

a. Cash gifts that are viewed as unconditional and not donor-restricted . . .	$20,000
b. Cash gifts that must be held until Year 2, but are not otherwise restricted as to use.	13,000
c. Cash gifts that must be used to provide food for children affected by natural disasters (the donor cannot demand return of the gift)	35,000
d. Cash gifts that must be used to buy a truck for the NFP to be used in delivering food (or the money must be returned to the donor)	40,000
e. Donated equipment (stoves and refrigerators) that will be used to help prepare food for children in need	20,000 (fair value)
f. Donated investments in the stock of a well-known corporation. These shares must be held forever with subsequent income to be spent to help pay the salary of a nurse to work with children in need.	300,000 (fair value)
g. Cash interest income is earned on the investments in f.	17,000
h. Cash in g. is spent as stipulated.	
i. Twenty pledges of $2,000 each are received from individuals who work at a local company. When received, the money can be used at the discretion of entity officials. They expect the money to be conveyed in seven months. Only one pledge is expected to prove uncollectible.	
j. The employer of the individuals in i. also pledges an equal matching amount up to the total actually contributed by the employees. The employer is under no obligation to pay more than an equal amount.	
k. The money in d. is used to buy a truck.	
l. Cash gifts from the individuals in i. start to be received. The first $8,000 is collected.	

The private NFP reports these events using the following journal entries.

a. Cash	20,000	
Contribution Revenue—Without Donor Restrictions		20,000
Money donated to entity with no restrictions or stipulations.		
b. Cash	13,000	
Contribution Revenue—With Donor Restrictions		13,000
Money donated to entity with a time restriction.		

c. Cash	35,000	
Contribution Revenue—With Donor Restrictions		35,000
Money donated to entity with a purpose restriction. Contribution is not conditional because donor does not have the right to demand a refund.		
d. Cash	40,000	
Refundable Liability—Truck Donation		40,000
This is a conditional donation. The money must be spent for one truck or be returned to the donor. Acquisition of the truck is a barrier that must be overcome for the entity to be entitled to keep the money.		
e. Equipment	20,000	
Contribution Revenue—Without Donor Restrictions		20,000
Equipment is donated to the entity. No restriction is established by the donor as to the use of this equipment. Recorded at fair value.		
f. Investment in Securities	300,000	
Contribution Revenue—With Donor Restrictions		300,000
This donation of equity securities must be held with all future earnings restricted for nursing salaries.		
g. Cash	17,000	
Interest Income—With Donor Restrictions		17,000
Income earned on donated investments with money restricted to use for nursing salaries.		
h. Salary Expense—Children and Disaster Relief	17,000	
Cash		17,000
Income from donated securities is used to pay for nursing salaries as stipulated by donor. Because money has now been spent as intended, the donor restriction is lifted. Reclassification can be recorded immediately through a second entry, although entry is more likely to be made at end of period.		
Net Assets—With Donor Restrictions	17,000	
Net Assets—Without Donor Restrictions		17,000
To reflect change in net asset totals as a result of the proper expenditure of money earned from donated securities.		
i. Contributions Receivable	40,000	
Contribution Revenue—Without Donor Restrictions		40,000
To record pledges made to NFP to be used at the discretion of the entity's officials. These donations are not conditional. They are not recorded at present value because cash is expected to be collected within one year.		
Bad Debt Expense—Fundraising	2,000	
Allowance for uncollectible receivables		2,000
To recognize that one of the 20 pledges is not expected to be collected. Receivable is reported at net realizable value.		
j. No entry is recorded for this matching pledge. The contribution is viewed as conditional because no payment will have to be made unless employees make donations. This is a barrier that has to be overcome. In addition, employer has the right to refuse to make payments if employee gifts are never made.		
k. Truck	40,000	
Cash		40,000
Donated money from d. is used as stipulated to buy truck for the NFP entity.		
Refundable Liability—Truck Donation	40,000	
Contribution Revenue—Without Donor Restrictions		40,000
Because the barrier for the gift (purchase of a truck) has been overcome, the contribution is no longer conditional and can be recognized. It is without donor restrictions because purchase of the truck has fulfilled that restriction.		(continued)

Discussion Question

IS THIS REALLY AN ASSET?

Mercy Hospital is located near Springfield, Missouri. A religious organization created the not-for-profit health care facility more than 90 years ago to meet the needs of area residents who could not otherwise afford adequate medical care. Although the hospital is open to the public, its primary mission has always been to provide needed services for the poor.

On December 23, 2019, a well-dressed individual told the hospital's chief administrative officer the following story: "My mother has been in your hospital since October 30. The doctors just told me that she will soon be well and can go home. I cannot tell you how relieved I am. The doctors, the nurses, and your entire staff have been wonderful. My mother could not have gotten better care. She owes her life to your hospital.

"I am from Idaho. Now that my mother is on the road to recovery, I must return immediately to my business. I am in the process of finding a buyer for an enormous tract of land. When this acreage is sold, I will receive approximately $30 million in cash. Because of the wonderful service that Mercy Hospital has provided my mother, I want to donate $10 million of this money." He proceeded to write this promise on a piece of personal stationery that he dated and signed.

The hospital's officials were overwhelmed by this generosity. This $10 million gift was 50 times larger than any other gift ever received. However, the controller was concerned about preparing financial statements for that year. "I have a lot of problems recording this type of donation as an asset. At present, we are having serious cash flow problems. If we show a $10 million donation in this manner, our normal donors are going to think we have become rich and don't need their support."

What problems are involved in accounting for the $10 million pledge? How should Mercy Hospital report the promised contribution?

l. Cash	8,000	
Contributions Receivable		8,000
Partial collection of pledges previously recorded in (i).		
Contributions Receivable	8,000	
Contribution Revenue—Without Donor Restrictions		8,000
First portion of the employee pledges recorded in i. are received. Thus, an equal part of the employer's matching pledge is no longer conditional. The first $8,000 of the pledge must be reported.		

One further issue should be mentioned about the donation of the investment securities. To take advantage of generous tax benefits, many taxpayers transfer the title of appreciated shares of stock to not-for-profit entities, especially near the end of each calendar year. Unless the gift is restricted by the donor, charities often have a policy in place requiring that such shares be sold immediately so that the money can be put to use. This type of conveyance is so common that a question has been raised about the reporting on the NFP's statement of cash flows. Is the sale of these shares an operating cash inflow from a contribution or an investing cash inflow from the disposal of stock? U.S. GAAP holds that this cash inflow should be reported as an operating activity if unrestricted securities are converted into cash by the entity almost immediately upon receipt.

LO 18-4

Report the various types of contributions that a private not-for-profit entity can receive.

Contributed Services

Donated services are an especially significant means of support for many not-for-profits. The number of volunteers working in some organizations can reach into the thousands. Charities rely heavily on individuals to fill administrative positions and engage in fundraising and program activities. For the year ended June 30, 2017, the American Heart Association recognized more than $17.0 million in contributed services. Notes to the NFP's financial statements disclose $9.0 million of these services as professional education and $6.6 million as research.

Not-for-profits recognize contributed services in their financial statements but only if the work being performed meets one of two criteria:

1. Creates or enhances a nonfinancial asset.
2. Requires a specialized skill possessed by the contributor that would typically need to be purchased if not donated.

Examples of work that fulfill the first standard include donated labor by carpenters, electricians, and masons. Because the work creates or enhances a nonfinancial asset, the fair value of the service is recorded as an increase in the appropriate asset with an accompanying recognition of the contributed support.

Examples of the second type of donation include legal or accounting services that are recognized as both an expense and contributed support. It is a common practice for professionals to bill a not-for-profit entity for the fair value of services rendered and then deduct an amount (or, possibly, the entire charge) from the balance as a contribution.

Contributed services (such as volunteer servers at a soup kitchen) are very common. The YMCA of the USA discloses having 600,000 volunteers working in 10,000 communities across the country. However, the value of these services is not recognized if they fail to meet both of these criteria. This exclusion is not because the services have no value, but because of the difficulty in measuring that value. For example, the American Heart Association's financial statements explain,

> The Association receives services from a large number of volunteers who give significant amounts of their time to the Association's programs, fundraising campaigns, and management. No amounts have been reflected for these types of donated services, as they do not meet the criteria for recognition.

To illustrate, assume that a certified public accountant provides accounting services to a local charity that would cost $20,000 if not donated. Assume also that a carpenter donates materials ($40,000) and labor ($75,000) to construct an addition to the charity's facilities. The not-for-profit entity records the following journal entries:

General and Administrative Expenses—Accounting Services	20,000	
Contributed Services—Without Donor Restrictions		20,000
To record contribution of professional services.		
Buildings and Improvements	115,000	
Contributed Services—Without Donor Restrictions		75,000
Contributed Materials—Without Donor Restrictions		40,000
To record contribution of professional services and materials.		

A great many not-for-profit entities are composed of numerous affiliated groups existing throughout the country or the world. At busy times, employees of one affiliate might be sent to assist in the operations of another affiliate without charge. Assuming that these workers meet either of the two criteria for recognition, should the entity receiving the work record this contributed service? Although the support is received for free, the workers are being paid by their own employer—an organization that is an affiliate of the reporting entity.

U.S. GAAP holds that the not-for-profit entity receiving the benefit of these workers should record the contribution at the cost paid by the affiliated organization. However, if that cost does not reflect the legitimate value of the services rendered, the charity has the option of reporting fair value. Once again, contributed support is recognized along with either an expense or an asset depending on whether a nonfinancial asset is created or enhanced.

LO 18-4

Report the various types of contributions that a private not-for-profit entity can receive.

Reporting Works of Art and Historical Treasures

Present-day accounting rules often came into being only after long periods of sometimes heated debate. An appreciation of that history can be necessary to understand the logic behind rules that are now used on a daily basis without incident.

In 1990, FASB issued an exposure draft of a proposed official pronouncement that would have required a recipient to record all contributions, including works of art and museum pieces, as assets with a corresponding increase in revenues. It sounds rather innocuous, but rarely has an accounting proposal created such adverse reaction. FASB was deluged with more than 1,000 letters, virtually all in opposition to the exposure draft. The argument against recognizing such contributions as assets is that works of art and historical pieces do not provide the same types of financial benefits as gifts of cash or investments. Items held for research purposes or public exhibit create little or no direct increase in cash flows. In fact, such items often require continual outflows of cash for insurance, maintenance, and other preservation costs. Thus, they are not assets in a traditional sense. Opponents of this exposure draft argued that recognizing such donations as assets and revenues would mislead potential donors into overrating the organization's financial strength. Art works and museum pieces can have enormous values that are almost impossible to determine with any degree of assurance. What is the *Mona Lisa* really worth?

This vehement opposition apparently influenced FASB because when the new principle was issued in 1993, NFPs were allowed to report works of art, historical treasures, and the like differently from other donated property. Disclosure rather than formal recognition in financial statement accounts can be selected if these art works and museum pieces meet the following criteria:

1. Added to a collection for public exhibition, education, or research.
2. Protected and preserved.
3. Covered by an organization policy whereby any proceeds generated from a future sale will be used to acquire other collection items so that these items do not function as a type of investment property. (As of this writing, FASB has proposed an expansion to this third criteria so that proceeds from a sale can also be used to support the direct care of existing collection pieces and not just the acquisition of other collection items. Insurance and maintenance costs have become so expensive that some NFPs must sell pieces of a collection in order to provide funds to maintain the remainder of that collection. If passed, this change will allow these NFPs to continue the practice of not reporting their collections despite these sales.)

A note to Georgetown University's 2017 financial statements explains the school's decision not to report art and museum pieces as assets: "The University has elected not to capitalize the cost or value of its collection of works of art, historical treasures, and similar assets on the statements of financial position. . . . The University's collections includes artifacts of historical significance and art objects that are held for education, research, scientific, and cultural purposes. Each of the items is catalogued and preserved, and the University verifies the items in its collection and assesses their condition on a regular basis."

The 2017 financial statements for Princeton University explain that school's reporting: "Art objects and rare books acquired subsequent to June 30, 1973, are recorded at cost or fair value at the date of gift. Works of art, literary works, historical treasures, and artifacts that are part of a collection are protected, preserved, and held for public exhibition, education, and research in furtherance of public service. Collections are not capitalized, and contributed collection items are not recognized as revenues in the University's financial statements."

A subtle difference exists between not-for-profit accounting for donated art and historical treasures and that utilized by state and local government units. The criteria for qualifying as a work of art or historical treasure are basically the same. However, the accounting choice for private not-for-profits is between recording both the contributed support and the asset versus no reporting, only disclosure. Governments face a different option. Under governmental accounting, contributed revenue must always be recorded for such gifts. The reporting entity then has the choice of recording either an asset or an expense when the donation is a qualifying work of art or historical treasure.

If a private not-for-profit entity does record such items as assets, the question of recording depreciation becomes relevant. The *Mona Lisa* was painted more than 500 years ago, and there is no end in sight for its ability to thrill art lovers. Consequently, private not-for-profit entities are not required to record depreciation for such assets if the lives are viewed as extraordinarily long. The assumption is that the organization has the technological and financial ability to preserve the item and that the value is such that the entity has committed to that goal.

LO 18-4

Report the various types of contributions that a private not-for-profit entity can receive.

Holding Contributions for Others

Some not-for-profit entities, such as the United Way, solicit donations that will be distributed to other designated charities. They also accept gifts that must be conveyed to specified beneficiaries. A community group might raise contributions by allowing the donor to identify the charity to be benefited. The not-for-profit entity acts as a go-between, conveying donations from one party to another.

Such conveyances raise questions as to the appropriate recording to be made by each of the parties involved: the donor, the initial recipient, and the specified beneficiary. To illustrate, assume that Donor A gives $10,000 in cash to Not-for-Profit Entity M (NFP–M) that must be conveyed to Not-for-Profit Entity Z (NFP–Z).

- Does Donor A record an expense when it initially conveys the cash to NFP–M, or must an actual transfer to NFP–Z take place before Donor A records an expense?
- Upon receipt, does NFP–M report contributed support of $10,000 or, rather, a liability to NFP–Z?
- At what point should NFP–Z recognize contributed support as a result of this gift?

For a conveyance of this type, the donor normally records an expense when the property is first conveyed to NFP–M because control over the asset has been relinquished. In this case, Donor A makes the following entry:

Donor A (Relinquishes Control)		
Expense—Charitable Contribution	10,000	
Cash		10,000

However, if the donor retains the right to redirect the use of the gift (the donor is said to have variance power) or if the donation can be revoked, Donor A continues to maintain control over the property and does not record an expense until that authority is surrendered. When this type gift is first conveyed, Donor A makes the following entry instead of the previous one:

Donor A (Retains Variance Power)		
Refundable Advance to NFP–M	10,000	
Cash		10,000

The initial recipient usually records a liability to the eventual beneficiary for such gifts (rather than reporting contribution revenue). The money is merely passing through this not-for-profit entity and does not create any direct benefit for the organization. Thus, NFP–M makes the following journal entry for the money received:

NFP–M (Donation Is Passing through to Beneficiary)		
Cash	10,000	
Liability to NFP–Z		10,000

However, other possibilities do exist. If the donor retains the right to revoke or redirect the gift, NFP–M cannot yet be certain as to whether the money will be conveyed to the beneficiary or back to the donor. Because the donor still has control over this decision, the preceding entry is replaced with the following:

NFP–M (Donor Retains Control over Gift)		
Cash	10,000	
Refundable Advance from Donor A		10,000

For a conveyed gift of this type, NFP–M does record contributed revenue and a related expense in one specific situation. Assume that the donor does not retain the right to revoke or redirect the gift but instead gives variance power to NFP-M. Thus, this first charity has the authority to change the eventual beneficiary. In this situation, NFP–M gains actual control over the asset upon receipt and records the following entry rather than either of the previous two. NFP-M views the gift as support and not a liability. When the $10,000 is conveyed to the beneficiary, NFP-M records an expense for that amount. Control is the key to recording such conveyances.

NFP–M (Holds Variance Power)		
Cash	10,000	
Contribution Revenue—With Donor Restrictions		10,000

The eventual beneficiary of such a gift must record contributed support at some point. If the donor retains the right to revoke or redirect the gift or if NFP–M is given variance power to change the recipient, the named beneficiary makes no entry until the gift is received. Too much uncertainty exists until that time. The beneficiary has no power to control the property's movement until it gains possession of the item.

However, if the donor does not keep the right to revoke or redirect the gift and NFP–M has not received variance power, the uncertainty is eliminated. In that circumstance, the eventual recipient records the contribution as soon as the donor makes the gift to the first not-for-profit entity. Assuming the gift has no restrictions, the following entry is appropriate:

NFP–Z (Gift to Be Received)		
Contribution Receivable	10,000	
Contribution Revenue—Without Donor Restrictions		10,000

Exchange Transactions

Exchange transactions are reciprocal transfers if both parties give and receive something of commensurate value. These transactions are likely to be reported based on *ASU 2014-09, Revenue from Contracts with Customers* and have little to do with basic not-for-profit accounting.

Many not-for-profit entities have regular charges. A local YMCA will assess monthly membership dues for exercise classes, locker fees, and the like. ChildFund International has monthly sponsorships to aid designated children. The reminders that arrive in the mail each month from these two organizations look similar, but should the accounting be the same? The YMCA is providing a service. ChildFund is receiving donations for its stated mission.

Dues and fees are frequently considered reciprocal transfers. A paying member typically receives benefits in the form of newsletters, journals, and use of the organization's facilities and services. These transactions do not meet the definition of a contribution. Thus, they follow normal accrual basis accounting. Revenue is recognized when each performance obligation is satisfied.

As in for-profit accounting, the entity must identify each separate performance obligation and determine its stand-alone sales value. For example, assume an NFP museum normally sells a one-year membership for $100. Each member is allowed free access to the museum throughout the year. On January 1, Year 1, as an extra incentive, a person acquiring a membership will also receive free entrance to a movie that is scheduled to play at the theater during February. The movie has an admission price of $20. On the first day of the year, the museum membership and the movie ticket are bundled together and sold for a single bargain price of $108.

The museum has two performance obligations from this transaction. The member can visit the museum for a year but is also entitled to see the movie in February. The $108 price is allocated between the two obligations based on the stand-alone sales values of $100 and $20 or a total of $120.

Museum membership	$100/$120 × $108 or $90
Movie ticket	$ 20/$120 × $108 or $18

The initial purchase is recorded by the museum based on these allocations.

January 1, Year 1	Cash	108	
	Deferred Revenue–Membership		90
	Deferred Revenue—Movie Ticket		18

Unless a reason exists for some other type of assignment, the museum reports the membership revenue at the rate of 1/12 per month ($90 × 1/12 or $7.50). In contrast, the movie ticket revenue is recognized entirely in February because that is the month that the performance obligation is satisfied.

January 31, Year 1	Deferred Revenue–Membership	7.50	
	Membership Revenue		7.50
February 28, Year 1	Deferred Revenue–Membership	7.50	
	Membership Revenue		7.50
	Deferred Revenue—Movie ticket	18.00	
	Movie Ticket Revenue		18.00

LO 18-6

Account for both mergers and acquisitions of not-for-profit entities.

Mergers and Acquisitions

> The story is the same across the country. The once-booming nonprofit sector is in the midst of a shakeout, leaving many Americans without services and culling weak groups from the strong. Hit by a drop in donations and government funding in the wake of a deep recession, nonprofits—from arts councils to food banks—are undergoing a painful restructuring, including mergers, acquisitions, collaborations, cutbacks, and closings.[20]
>
> "In 2013, United Cerebral Palsy (UCP), a $9 million nonprofit, joined with Seguin Services, a $27 million operation, creating UCP Seguin Chicago. Looking back, it's clear that the move was a good one; the combined organization has grown substantively, and it is much more effective and efficient than either pre-merger entity was on its own."[21]

Acquisitions and mergers are not limited to the world of business. Two or more not-for-profit entities might decide to join together for a number of reasons such as more efficient use of resources to achieve common goals, cost cutting, attempts to rescue charities that are

[20] Shelly, Banjo, and Mitra Kalita, "Once-Robust Charity Sector Hit with Mergers, Closings," *Wall Street Journal* (online), January 31, 2010.

[21] Donald Haider, "Nonprofit Mergers That Work," *Stanford Social Innovation Review*, https://ssir.org/articles/entry/nonprofit_mergers_that_work.

suffering financially, and expanding the scope of an organization's outreach. For example, two theater companies in Richmond, Virginia, that both specialized in the plays of William Shakespeare decided to merge to better serve a somewhat limited number of patrons.

Accounting for such combinations utilizes many of the techniques demonstrated in early chapters of this textbook in connection with the consolidation of both for-profit companies and governmental units. However, the process here takes several unique steps in creating a single set of statements when two or more not-for-profit entities come together. To begin, the resulting financial reporting depends on whether an acquisition or a merger has taken place.

Acquisitions

In not-for-profit accounting, an acquisition occurs—as might be suspected from the title—when one entity obtains control over another. As described in previous chapters, control that leads to the consolidation of for-profit businesses is normally based on gaining ownership of a majority of the voting stock. For not-for-profit entities, the U.S. GAAP definition of control is broader: "The direct or indirect ability to determine the direction of management and policies through ownership, contract, or otherwise.[22]

In many respects, accounting for a not-for-profit acquisition parallels the process demonstrated previously in consolidating two for-profit businesses. Each of the assets and liabilities of the acquired not-for-profit entity are identified and reported by the acquirer at fair value as of the acquisition date (the date on which control is achieved). If the total acquisition value of the acquired entity is greater than the total value of all identifiable assets and liabilities, the excess is reported on the balance sheet as goodwill. Those steps follow the pattern established to consolidate for-profit companies.

One important distinction in the process is made at this point. The recognition of goodwill implies the existence of an otherwise unrecorded ability to generate especially high revenues and profits in the future, higher than expected to occur based solely on the subsidiary's identifiable assets and liabilities. This reporting of goodwill is appropriate for organizations such as the YMCA and the Girl Scouts with significant sources of revenue such as the sale of goods or services or the collection of membership fees. What about acquired entities that bring in little or no revenue from exchange transactions but rather rely on donations or grants? Does the excess value of the acquired entity reflect an asset that provides economic benefit if few revenues will be generated in the future?

Consequently, in not-for-profit acquisitions, the accounting for this excess depends on the type of revenue or support that is anticipated. If the future operations of the acquired entity are expected to be predominantly supported by contributions and returns on investments (rather than fees or the sale of goods or services), any unexplained excess acquisition value is reported as a reduction in unrestricted net assets on the statement of activities rather than as the intangible asset goodwill.[23]

Mergers

All consolidated financial statements produced by for-profit businesses are created using a single set of basic rules. However, as with governmental accounting, two methods of reporting the creation of a combination exist for not-for-profit entities. If two or more not-for-profit organizations come together to form a new not-for-profit entity and control is turned over to a newly created governing board, then a merger rather than an acquisition has taken place. Two NFPs were merged to create a third. An acquirer did not gain control over an acquired entity. A different type of event took place.

In a merger, because neither entity is acquired, identifiable assets and liabilities are not updated to fair value. Instead, the carryover method is applied. The newly formed not-for-profit entity reports all previously recognized assets and liabilities at their book values as of the date of the merger. Fair-value adjustments are not made. Book value is retained for the assets and liabilities reported by both parties.

[22] FASB ASC 958-810-20.

[23] "Predominantly supported" means that significantly more of the revenues to be generated by the acquired entity will come from contributions and investment income than from all other sources combined.

Example of Acquisition and Merger

Assume that Rather Large NFP is a private not-for-profit entity that is to be joined with Small NFP, another not-for-profit. Small NFP has been struggling financially. The combination is carried out to help save this entity and the charitable work that it performs.

On the date the combination is created, Small NFP holds just one asset, a building with a net book value of $600,000 but a fair value of $700,000. It has no liabilities. Rather Large NFP has several buildings as well as many other assets. These buildings have a net book value of $3 million and a fair value of $3.9 million.

- Situation One: Assume that Rather Large NFP pays $820,000 to acquire complete control over Small NFP.

This transaction is an acquisition. Control has been gained by one entity over the other. The building owned by Small NFP is added at fair value to the net book value of Rather Large NFP's building account. The balance will now be $3.7 million ($3 million net book value of the previous buildings plus the $700,000 fair value of the new one being acquired).

If Small NFP's operations will not be predominately supported in the future by contributions and investment income, the excess acquisition value of $120,000 ($820,000 acquisition value less $700,000 fair value of the identifiable assets and liabilities) is reported as the intangible asset goodwill. In contrast, if Small NFP will be predominately supported in the future by contributions and investment income rather than sales or fees, this residual $120,000 figure is reported as a reduction in unrestricted net assets in the statement of activities rather than as goodwill.

- Situation Two: Assume that, instead of paying money to gain control, Rather Large NFP and Small NFP join together to form Huge NFP to be operated by an entirely new governing board.

LO 18-7

Understand the advantages of attaining tax-exempt status.

This event qualifies as a merger. The carryover method is applied, and book value is retained. Buildings will now be shown at $3.6 million ($3 million net book value from Rather Large NFP plus $600,000 net book value from Small NFP). No goodwill or reduction in net assets is reported. No acquisition value is determined, so an excess amount cannot result. In a merger of NFP entities, all assets and liabilities are brought together at book value.

Tax-Exempt Status

Although this is not a taxation textbook, no coverage of not-for-profit entities is complete without a short overview of tax rules. A primary reason for creating an entity as a not-for-profit is to qualify with the Internal Revenue Service for tax-exempt status. Just as there are many different types of not-for-profit entities, quite a number of tax-exempt statuses are available (more than two dozen) that establish what these entities can and cannot do. Section 501(c)(3), Section 501(c)(4), and Section 501(c)(6) are three of the most common tax-exempt statuses in the United States.

A note to the 2017 financial statements for The Museum of Modern Art explains that this not-for-profit entity is "exempt from tax under Section 501(c)(3) of the Internal Revenue Code." The same status applies to approximately 1.3 million organizations such as Duke University and the Girl Scouts of the United States of America. Section 501(c)(3) of the tax code applies to not-for-profit entities that fall within one of several categories such as charitable, educational, literary, or scientific. More than 72 percent of tax-exempt nonprofit organizations in the United States hold a Section 501(c)(3) status.[24] An organization requests this status by completing IRS Form 1023, *Application for Recognition of Exemption under Section 501(c)(3) of Internal Revenue Code.* (http://www.irs.gov/pub/irs-pdf/f1023.pdf).[25]

Not surprisingly, many well-known not-for-profit entities qualify for Section 501(c)(3) status. They are then exempt from paying federal income taxes (and likely state income taxes) on most income. However, not-for-profit entities are still subject to taxation on any unrelated

[24] *Internal Revenue Service Data Book*, 2017.

[25] The Form 1023 filed by the YMCA of the United States can be viewed at http://s3.amazonaws.com/ymca-ynet-prod/files/organizational-profile/form_1023.pdf. The form is more than 225 pages in length.

business income they generate. Because of the tax consequences, the decision as to whether income is unrelated business income is of genuine interest to these entities and their officers and can be the source of much discussion between a not-for-profit and tax officials.[26]

One of the primary benefits of Section 501(c)(3) status is that charitable donations to these organizations can reduce the donor's taxable income (but only if an individual itemizes deductions rather than takes the standard deduction). Many believe this tax benefit encourages more and larger charitable gifts. Any suggestion to reduce or eliminate this deduction is met with considerable resistance.

In addition, these entities qualify for a nonprofit postal permit that reduces mailing charges considerably. However, restrictions do exist. For example, although Section 501(c)(3) organizations may participate in a small amount of lobbying, they cannot engage in political election campaign activity.

Many other types of nonprofit entities make use of the tax laws. During 2017, there were 81,935 social welfare organizations, 44,060 fraternal beneficiary societies, 63,621 business leagues, and thousands of others.[27] For example, AARP, Inc., is a not-for-profit organization, but it is tax exempt based on Section 501(c)(4) of the Internal Revenue Code. That status is reserved for organizations that function exclusively for the promotion of social welfare. They are often referred to as *advocacy groups* because they operate primarily to further the general welfare of the people in their particular community. Again, income earned is not taxed at the federal level although it more often is at the state level. When individuals or corporations make donations to these organizations, they are not entitled to a tax deduction on their federal income tax return. Likewise, dues or membership fees paid to these groups do not qualify as tax deductible. As advocacy groups, they are allowed to lobby and engage in political election campaign activity. They do not qualify for a nonprofit postal permit unless they are also an educational organization.

As a third example of a tax-exempt status, the website for the Internal Revenue Service indicates that

> Section 501(c)(6) of the Internal Revenue Code provides for the exemption of business leagues, chambers of commerce, real estate boards, boards of trade, and professional football leagues, which are not organized for profit and no part of the net earnings of which inures to the benefit of any private shareholder or individual.[28]

Section 501(c)(6) organizations do not pay federal income taxes but are frequently required to pay state income taxes. Membership dues paid to these organizations are tax deductible so long as they are viewed as ordinary and necessary business expenses. Within certain limits, such entities can lobby and engage in political election campaign activity. As with a Section 501(c)(4), 501(c)(6) entities are allowed a nonprofit postal permit but only if they qualify as an educational organization.

Thus, although private not-for-profits are often viewed as a single group, in reality, as these three categories indicate, the tax laws and regulations include numerous distinctions among the various types of organizations.

Most tax-exempt entities are required to submit a Form 990 (*Return of Organization Exempt from Income Tax,* http://www.irs.gov/pub/irs-pdf/f990.pdf) to the Internal Revenue Service each year in order to maintain their tax-exempt status. The Form 990 requires disclosure of an extensive amount of information about operations and other activities. For many interested parties, the Form 990 is a better source of information than the entity's financial statements. Individuals and groups that study and assess charities and other not-for-profits frequently do so by gathering pertinent information from these forms.[29]

[26] A good discussion of these tax issues can be found in Travis Patton and Jocelyn Bishop, "Reporting Unrelated Business Income," *Journal of Accountancy,* February 2009.

[27] *Internal Revenue Service Data Book*, 2017.

[28] https://www.irs.gov/charities-non-profits/other-non-profits/business-leagues.

[29] The Form 990 filed by the National Kidney Foundation can be viewed at https://www.kidney.org/sites/default/files/NKF%20-FY16%20Form%20990.pdf. It is nearly 60 pages in length and contains a wide array of information about the charity.

The information disclosed in a Form 990 is extensive and available to the public even if financial statements are not issued. A few of the topics included in this document are

- Part VI—Governance, Management, and Disclosure.
- Part VII—Compensation of Officers, Directors, Trustees, Key Employees, Highest Compensated Employees, and Independent Contractors.
- Part VIII—Statement of Revenue.
- Part IX—Statement of Functional Expenses.
- Part X—Balance Sheet.

LO 18-2

Describe the differences in net assets of a private not-for-profit entity that are without donor restrictions and those with donor restrictions.

Transactions for a Private Not-for-Profit Entity Illustrated

The following transactions demonstrate typical journal entries for a private not-for-profit entity. Because financial reporting for these organizations focuses on the entity as a whole, transactions need not be recorded in separate funds. Nevertheless, not-for-profits can choose to use a fund format for internal management purposes, especially to help monitor restricted gifts.

To illustrate the external reporting of a private NFP, assume that Eastern Institute, a small private college, began the current year reporting net assets without donor restrictions of \$12,500,000 and a donor-restricted permanent endowment of \$7,000,000. During the year, the school received support from a number of alumni and friends:

Unrestricted pledges due within 12 months	\$130,000
Cash contributions to increase the permanent endowment	50,000

Based on past experience, Eastern estimates that only 85 percent of these unrestricted pledges will be received. Because officials expect to collect this money within 12 months, computation of present value is not necessary.

1. Cash	50,000	
Contributions Receivable	130,000	
Contribution Revenue—With Donor Restrictions		50,000
Contribution Revenue—Without Donor Restrictions		130,000
To record cash contributions and pledges received.		
Bad Debt Expense—Fund Raising (15% of \$130,000)	19,500	
Allowance for Uncollectible Pledges		19,500
To recognize estimated amount of uncollectible pledges.		

Before the end of the fiscal period, the school collects \$100,000 of the amount pledged and writes off \$5,000 of the remaining pledges because collection is no longer expected.

2. Cash	100,000	
Allowance for Uncollectible Pledges	5,000	
Contributions Receivable		105,000
To record pledges collected and written off.		

Because of the high costs involved in obtaining a college education, many schools distribute a significant amount of financial aid to students. At one time, schools reported scholarships and other monetary assistance as operating expenses. Now, to provide a clearer picture of the direct impact these reductions have on tuition and other fees, schools first report the amount billed, which is then reduced directly by any student aid.

With that reporting, the effect of financial assistance can be easily calculated for private colleges and universities as shown in the following table (for fiscal years ending during 2017). This required accounting allows for easier comparisons of the revenue actually generated.

School	Student Tuition and Fees	Scholarships and Other Financial Assistance	Net Amount/Percentage
Colgate	$154.1 million	$ 58.6 million	$ 95.5 million (62.0%)
Davidson	108.1 million	46.9 million	61.2 million (56.6%)
Notre Dame	607.2 million	287.4 million	319.8 million (52.6%)
Princeton	353.3 million	244.6 million	108.7 million (30.8%)
Stanford	904.6 million	286.9 million	617.7 million (68.3%)
Wake Forest	360.8 million	105.8 million	255.0 million (70.7%)

Thus, students at these six schools paid an average of 30.8 to 70.7 percent of the normal tuition and fees that their schools charged.

Returning to the current example, assume that Eastern Institute assesses its students $800,000 for tuition and fees for the current semester. For accounting purposes, the school views this charge as a performance obligation and records it as a deferred revenue until satisfied. To help offset the financial burden, the school awards $200,000 in scholarships and other assistance. At the same time, Eastern receives a $20,000 cash gift that the outside donor restricts to providing support for a series of lectures by visiting scholars. The agreement has no provision for return of the money.

The journal entries for the tuition charges and scholarships are shown first followed by recording of the restricted gift.

	Debit	Credit
3. Tuition Receivable	800,000	
Deferred Revenue—Tuition and Fees		800,000
Tuition charged for the current semester.		
Deferred Financial Aid	200,000	
Tuition Receivable		200,000
To record financial aid awards for the current semester, an amount that is reported initially as a reduction in the deferred revenue.		
Cash	20,000	
Contribution Revenue—With Donor Restrictions		20,000
Gift restricted for use in a lecture series. Because money is not refundable, this gift is not conditional.		

Next, assume that Eastern Institute incurs liabilities of $640,000 ($575,000 for operating expenses broken down as shown in the following entry and $65,000 for the acquisition of equipment). The $65,000 had been given in the previous year by a donor who designated the money for use in buying equipment. This donor did not specify that the amount remain classified as donor restricted until depreciation was recorded. Of the total liability balance, $625,000 is paid before year-end. Functional categories are included for the expenses in these journal entries.

	Debit	Credit
4. Instructional Expenses–Student Education	265,000	
Student Services Expenses–Student Education	120,000	
Laboratory Expenses—Faculty Research	75,000	
Administrative Salary Expenses–General and Administrative	115,000	
Accounts Payable		575,000
To record expenses for the year.		
5. Equipment	65,000	
Accounts Payable		65,000
To record purchases of equipment.		
6. Net assets–with donor restrictions	65,000	
Net assets–without donor restrictions		65,000
Donor-restricted money is spent for equipment as specified. Because the donor made no stipulation that reclassification should be made to correspond with depreciation, the entire amount is reclassified when the money is spent as intended.		
7. Accounts Payable	625,000	
Cash		625,000
To record partial payment of outstanding accounts payable.		

Depreciation on the school's buildings and equipment amounts to $135,000 for the year, as shown in the following journal entry:

8. Depreciation Expense—Student Education	80,000	
Depreciation Expense—Faculty Research	20,000	
Depreciation Expense—General and Administrative	35,000	
Accumulated Depreciation-Buildings and Equipment		135,000
To record depreciation on fixed assets.		

Students pay the $600,000 in tuition and fees that are due after financial assistance has been applied. Later, a few students withdraw from school and receive refunds of $18,000. All remaining students complete the semester, satisfying the school's performance obligation.

9. Cash	600,000	
Tuition Receivable		600,000
To record payment of tuition and fees after reduction for financial assistance.		
Deferred Revenue–Tuition and Fees	800,000	
Cash		18,000
Revenue from Tuition and Fees—Without Donor Restrictions		782,000
To record satisfactory completion of performance obligation as well as the refund to students who withdrew from school.		
Financial Aid	200,000	
Deferred Financial Aid		200,000
To recognize direct reduction in tuition and fees revenue when this revenue is recognized.		

The year-end reporting of the preceding transactions for this private not-for-profit entity will reflect the changes within each of the categories of net assets. As mentioned previously, these organizations must report any net assets released from restriction because the donor-designated action is taken or the stipulated time passes. On the statement of activities, this amount is reclassified by reducing net assets with donor restrictions and increasing net assets without donor restrictions.

The following table summarizes this year's changes in the net assets reported by Eastern Institute. The table does not include journal entries 2, 5, and 7 because they did not create any changes in the school's net assets.

Calculation of Change in Net Assets

Journal Entry	Net Assets without Donor Restrictions	Net Assets with Donor Restrictions
1.	$ 130,000	$50,000
	(19,500)	
3.		20,000
4.	(265,000)	
	(120,000)	
	(75,000)	
	(115,000)	
6. (reclassification)	65,000	(65,000)
8.	(80,000)	
	(20,000)	
	(35,000)	
9.	782,000	
	(200,000)	
Increase (decrease) in net assets	$ 47,500	$ 5,000

Discussion Question

ARE TWO SETS OF GAAP REALLY NEEDED FOR COLLEGES AND UNIVERSITIES?

The June 30, 2017, balance sheet for the University of Southern California—a private not-for-profit entity—reports assets of nearly $12 billion and liabilities of more than $3 billion. The school reports the $8.8 billion difference as total net assets made up of two amounts: net assets without donor restrictions of $4.2 billion and net assets with donor restrictions of $4.6 billion. The format follows that described in the current chapter. Note 1 to the statements discloses, "The consolidated financial statements have been prepared on the accrual basis of accounting, in accordance with accounting principles generally accepted in the United States of America and with the provisions of the Financial Accounting Standards Board."

The June 30, 2017, statement of net position for the University of Arizona—a public school—reports total assets of $3.8 billion, total deferred outflows of resources of $152 million, total liabilities of $2.5 billion, and total deferred inflows of resources of $305 million. Those four figures create a total net position for the university of $1.1 billion. The statement then classifies this balance according to eight different categories (all numbers in thousands):

Net investment in capital assets	$730,135
Restricted for nonexpendable:	
Endowments	118,840
Student loans	23,934
Restricted for expendable:	
Scholarships and fellowships	16,772
Academic/department uses	192,320
Capital projects	7,377
Debt service	24,611
Unrestricted	20,756

Note 1 to these statements explains that "The financial statements are presented in accordance with U.S. generally accepted accounting principles (GAAP) applicable to governmental colleges and universities engaged in business-type activities as adopted by the Governmental Accounting Standards Board (GASB)."

As this and the previous chapter have discussed, public colleges and universities follow GASB standards. These schools have been directed to use the same reporting model as state and local governments. As with the University of Arizona, such schools frequently identify themselves as special purpose governments consisting solely of business-type activities. In that way, they only need to produce fund financial statements as an enterprise fund.

In contrast, private not-for-profit colleges and universities such as the University of Southern California adhere to the FASB *Accounting Standards Codification* requirements and prepare financial statements as illustrated in this chapter. U.S. GAAP for public schools comes from GASB whereas, for private schools, it comes from FASB.

Readers of college and university financial statements might want to compare the data presented by various institutions. This information is especially important to potential donors who are attempting to evaluate each school's efficiency and effectiveness in utilizing the funding that it receives.

Are decision makers well served by the division between the financial reporting for public colleges and universities and that utilized by private colleges and universities? Are these two types of schools so different that they require two separate sets of generally accepted accounting principles created by two official bodies? Should a single set of U.S. GAAP apply to all schools? Should only one group be in charge of developing U.S. GAAP for colleges and universities?

LO 18-8

Describe the unique aspects of revenue recognition for both investor-owned and private not-for-profit entities.

Accounting for Health Care Entities—Reporting Revenues

The financial reporting for health care entities provides some especially unique challenges. Many thousands of these institutions offer a wide variety of services throughout the United States. The sheer monetary amounts are staggering.

> U.S. health care spending grew 4.3 percent in 2016, reaching $3.3 trillion or $10,348 per person. As a share of the nation's Gross Domestic Product, health spending accounted for 17.9 percent.[30]

Virtually every city or town of any size has clinics, medical group practices, emergency care facilities, surgery centers, continuing care retirement communities, home health agencies, hospitals, nursing homes, drug and alcohol rehabilitation centers, and the like. Because of society's focus on the importance of adequate health care, facilities often compete against each other in the same market. Although the infrastructure might appear similar, providing many identical services, different legal structures are common. A small sample of the hospital care available in Richmond, Virginia, demonstrates this organizational diversity.

- St. Mary's Hospital is a private not-for-profit 391-bed hospital affiliated with the Bon Secours Richmond Health System and the Sisters of Bon Secours.
- Virginia Commonwealth University Health System Authority is a political subdivision of the Commonwealth of Virginia. Several different medical centers comprise this system including the Medical College of Virginia Hospitals, an 800-bed teaching hospital in Richmond.
- Chippenham Hospital, Henrico Doctors' Hospital, and Johnston-Willis Hospital—all located in the Richmond area—are members of the HCA Healthcare network. HCA owns and operates approximately 179 hospitals and 120 freestanding surgery centers in 20 states and London, England. The ownership shares of HCA trade on the New York Stock Exchange.
- For more than 70 years, Hunter Holmes McGuire VA Medical Center in Richmond, Virginia, "Has been improving the health of the men and women who have so proudly served our nation." The U.S. Department of Veterans Affairs operates this facility. It served 60,000 different patients in 2017.

A wide array of authoritative accounting principles apply to these different organizations. Health care entities controlled by a state or local government use the rules created by GASB as covered in the previous two chapters. In contrast, a federal health care entity is likely to produce financial statements for internal oversight and budgetary purposes rather than for external reporting. Standardized rules have traditionally been of less significance, but the website for the Federal Accounting Standards Advisory Board (www.fasab.gov) does provide this information.

> The *FASAB Handbook of Accounting Standards and Other Pronouncements, as Amended (Current Handbook)*—an approximate 2,500-page PDF—is the most up-to-date, authoritative source of generally accepted accounting principles (GAAP) developed for federal entities.

Private not-for-profit entities such as St. Mary's Hospital follow Topic 958 (Not-for-Profit Entities) in FASB's *Accounting Standards Codification,* Topic 954 (Health Care Entities), and all other official rules within the *Accounting Standards Codification* that apply. As a for-profit entity, HCA Healthcare's statements must be in conformity with Topic 954 and most other official accounting rules except for Topic 958. FASB specifies the type of health care organizations that must follow its rules.

a. Investor-owned health care entities. These are owned by investors or others with a private equity interest and provide goods or services with the objective of making a profit.

b. Not-for-profit, business-oriented entities. These are characterized by no ownership interests and essentially are self-sustaining from fees charged for goods and services. The fees charged by such entities generally are intended to help the entity maintain its self-sustaining status rather than to maximize profits for the owner's benefit.[31]

[30] https://www.cms.gov/Research-Statistics-Data-and-Systems/Statistics-Trends-and-Reports/NationalHealthExpendData/NationalHealthAccountsHistorical.html.

[31] FASB, *Accounting Standards Codification 954-10-05-02.*

Whether a health care entity is investor owned (HCA affiliates) or not-for-profit (St. Mary's), revenues have long been a reporting problem. Two aspects of the recognition process are especially challenging.

- First, the customer (the patient) rarely pays a significant amount of the incurred costs. Third-party payors such as insurance companies and the government (through programs like Medicare and Medicaid) provide most of the financial remuneration. In 2017, the Mayo Clinic reported $10.1 billion in medical service revenue. Of that amount, $9.7 billion was the responsibility of various third-party payors whereas only $400 million was identified as being "self-pay" from the patient. Thus, approximately 96 percent of the revenue reported by the Mayo Clinic during that year came from insurance companies, Medicare, Medicaid, and the like rather than the person receiving treatment.
- Second, full payment of the charged amount is rarely expected. Legal contracts with third-party payors typically limit the balance to be paid. The 2017 financial statements for Duke University explains the relationship that its health care system (DUHS) has with external parties. "DUHS has agreements with third-party payors that provide for payments to DUHS at amounts that are generally less than its established rates. Payment arrangements include prospectively determined rates per discharge, reimbursed costs, discounted charges and per diem payments." These explicit price concessions serve as contractual adjustments. Third parties agree in advance to make payments based on a formula or on the average cost of a particular procedure in the local region. Furthermore, because of the high cost of medical care, noncontractual reductions are also routine. These implicit concessions often take the form of discounts for people without insurance or with only limited resources. Some health care entities make no serious attempt to collect amounts that patients (especially indigent patients) owe. In many cases, these facilities were created, at least in part, to serve the poor. A note to the financial statements of St. Jude Children's Research Hospital, Inc., states its policy, "No family ever pays the Hospital for the care their child receives. Accordingly, net patient service revenue consists only of estimated net realizable amounts from third-party payors for services rendered."

Implicit concessions occur when a health care entity plans to attempt collection from a patient but expects to receive less, often much less. In contrast for charity care, the entity makes no attempt at collection because of a definite policy. At times, the distinction between implicit concessions and charity care might be difficult to draw.

Under both the old and the new revenue rules, the reporting of charity care is omitted from the statement of financial position and the statement of activities. Neither the revenue nor the receivable are recognized although the financial effect of the decision must be disclosed because the cost of charity care can be enormous. In 2017, Cedars-Sinai Medical Center explained, "The Corporation's mission is to improve the health status of its community, regardless of the patient's ability to pay, including charity patients. The Corporation provides programs and activities that contribute to charity care, care of the poor, and community benefit." Cedars-Sinai discloses the costs associated with these programs (net of support by others) as $717.7 million.

Because of these unique industry features, health care entities have historically developed their own methods for reporting revenues. For decades, the established standard price for a service was recorded as it was provided. This amount was then offset by the estimated amount of contractual adjustments resulting from explicit concessions to third-party payors. Bad debt expense was also recorded to reflect reduced collections expected from individual patients. To illustrate, assume that three patients have appendectomies at a local not-for-profit hospital. The entity's standard charge for this particular surgery is $20,000.

- One patient has insurance. The insurance company has a contract with the hospital stating that the total allowed payment will be 70 percent of the charged amount (or $14,000).
- The second patient has no insurance, and the hospital expects to collect only about 10 percent or $2,000.
- The third patient has neither income nor insurance. The hospital has no plan to make any attempt to collect for the surgery because of its basic mission to help the poor.

The journal entries made by health care entities for these transactions have historically been as follows. Notice that no revenue entry is recorded in connection with the third patient. Health care entities do not report the financial effect of charity care although the cost is disclosed.

Previous Approach		
Accounts Receivable—Third-Party Payors	20,000	
Accounts Receivable–Patients	20,000	
Patient Service Revenues		40,000
Appendectomies performed on two patients.		
Contractual Adjustments	6,000	
Allowance for Uncollectible and Reduced Accounts		6,000
Explicit price concession to insurance company for insured patient based on contract.		
Provision for Bad Debts	18,000	
Allowance for Uncollectible and Reduced Accounts		18,000
Expense recognized for amount not expected from uninsured patient ($20,000 less $2,000).		

Under this approach, both net revenues and bad debt expense tend to be high because the entities recorded amounts despite little chance of collection. Although this hospital expects to receive $16,000 ($40,000 – $6,000 – $18,000), the statement of activities shows revenue as $34,000 with an offsetting bad debt of $18,000.

Patient service revenues (net of contractual adjustments)	$34,000	
Less provision for bad debts	(18,000)	$16,000

In 2017, Aurora Health Care, Inc. and Affiliates reported patient service revenue of $5 billion but offset that amount by $170 million in bad debts. The huge bad debt balance was necessary because the hospital likely recorded revenue that it never expected to collect.

In 2014, FASB issued *Accounting Standards Update No. 2014-09*, "Revenue from Contracts with Customers," to bring consistency to the recognition of revenue. Rather than allowing a wide-array of methods often based on industry preferences, this single approach applies to virtually all reporting entities. The new pronouncement will have a profound effect on the financial reporting of health care entities in the coming years.[32]

> "The intent of the new rules is to establish a core principle for revenue recognition across all industries."[33]

ASU No. 2014-09 requires entities to follow a five-step progression in recording revenues:

- Identify the contract with the customer.
- Identify all performance obligations in the contract.
- Determine the transaction price.
- Allocate the transaction price to the various performance obligations.
- Recognize revenue when (or as) the entity satisfies each performance obligation.

Interestingly, the establishment of the contract can be a problem at times for a health care entity. Valid contracts can be written, oral, or implied by the entity's customary business practices. For example, a person who walks into a medical examination room holding a hurt

[32] A not-for-profit entity that has issued securities (such as bonds) that are listed or traded on an exchange or over-the-counter market and public business entities must apply *ASU No. 2014-09* for fiscal years that begin after December 15, 2017. All other not-for-profit entities must apply *ASU 2014-09* for fiscal years that begin after December 15, 2018.

[33] "Trenton Fast, "New Revenue Recognition Standard Hits Health Care Entities," January 17, 2018, https://www.claconnect.com/resources/articles/new-revenue-recognition-standard-hits-health-care-entities.

hand, signs a consent form, and says aloud that treatment is needed has likely created a contract with the hospital in all three ways.

In emergency medical cases, a patient might not have the time or capacity to understand what is happening. The person could literally be unconscious, so the creation of a contract is not usually in question. Nevertheless, because of moral and legal responsibilities, health care entities treat thousands of uninsured patients who are in no condition to agree or disagree. Services—often expensive services—are rendered by the entity without a contract. Hence, no revenue is recognized unless subsequent actions establish a contract in one form or another. In such cases as these, discussions with a legal expert may prove necessary before the financial reporting is finalized.

For health care entities, the biggest problem in these five steps is the determination of a transaction price. As mentioned earlier, the standard price of a procedure is rarely collected because of contractual adjustments and other discounts and allowances. Under the new revenue rules, the key determinant is the amount that the health care entity expects to be entitled to collect. "To determine transaction price, a hospital should consider all historical, current, and forecasted information that's reasonably available, including historical cash collections from the identified payer class."[34] This estimate can be made on a contract-by-contract basis, but most health care entities will probably establish a portfolio approach, which is allowed if it provides the same basic outcomes. Under a portfolio approach, all patient debts are classified into groups with similar characteristics. One potential approach is separating balances based on who is responsible for payment: Medicare patients, Medicaid patients, patients with insurance from a specific provider, patients only owing a co-payment, Medicare-pending patients, uninsured patients, and the like. Each charge is placed within one specific portfolio.

For every group, explicit (or contractual) price concessions are taken into consideration to determine the most likely amount of cash that will be received. Perhaps, for example, a portfolio of patients who all have coverage with a particular insurance company owes $500,000, but contractual adjustments usually reduce that amount by 40 percent. Thus, the health care entity expects to be entitled to $300,000. Implicit concessions are also taken into consideration. Although no contract creates a defined reduction, the health care entity expects to collect less. For example, assume a hospital is owed $2 million by 132 patients without insurance. That is a single portfolio. Historically, the hospital has tried to collect such balances in full but only managed to receive 5 percent. The expected cash from this portfolio is $100,000.

The preceding anticipated collection examples seem exact with amounts of $300,000 and $100,000. In reality, uncertainty is ever-present for health care entities. Collection can often be determined only within a range of possible outcomes. According to the new revenue recognition rules, this uncertainty results in "variable consideration." The hospital must use the estimated numbers to determine an entitled amount for each portfolio. This process can follow an expected amount (weighted-average) approach or choose the most likely outcome—the amount with the highest chance of eventual collection.

To illustrate, assume that the private not-for-profit Thornton Medical Center (TMC) has patient service receivables of $2.9 million at the end of the current year. Each of the following categories is viewed as a separate portfolio. Of the total amount, $1.5 million is from patients covered by government programs, $1.1 million is from patients covered by insurance companies, $200,000 is for uninsured patients with income above the poverty level, and the remaining $100,000 is for uninsured patients with little or no income. TMC will make no attempt to collect this final $100,000. The charity care is not recorded through a formal journal entry.

Assume that the government programs have contracts with TMC that give explicit price concessions that the medical center estimates as $400,000. The insurance companies have contracts that give explicit concessions estimated as $300,000. The medical center expects to collect $70,000 of the $200,000 due from uninsured patients above the poverty level. The $130,000 difference is an implicit price concession.

[34] Joelle Pulver and Kate Jackson, "New Revenue Recognition Standard for Hospital," February 2017, https://www.mossadams.com/articles/2017/february/new-revenue-recognition-standard-for-hospitals.

Portfolio	Standard Charges	Explicit or Implicit Concessions	Net Amount
Government programs	$1,500,000	$400,000	$1,100,000
Insurance companies	1,100,000	300,000	800,000
Uninsured with income	200,000	130,000	70,000

Government programs and insurance companies will often make later adjustments based on their own calculations of appropriate costs. Uninsured patients typically pay far less than is due, an amount that can be difficult to assess. Based on historical, current, and forecasted data, the medical center expects payments as follows:

Government programs	80% chance of collecting 90% of net amount ($1,100,000) 20% chance of collecting 80% of net amount ($1,100,000)
Insurance companies	40% chance of collecting 100% of net amount ($800,000) 60% chance of collecting 60% of net amount ($800,000)
Uninsured with income	70% chance of collecting 50% of net amount ($70,000) 30% chance of collecting 20% of net amount ($70,000)

If TMC applies the most likely method of determining the variable consideration, it computes the transaction price as follows:

Government programs	90% of $1,100,000	$ 990,000
Insurance companies	60% of $800,000	480,000
Uninsured with income	50% of $70,000	35,000
Total		$1,505,000

The journal entry to record these transaction price amounts is as follows:

Accounts Receivable—Government Programs	990,000	
Accounts Receivable—Insurance Companies	480,000	
Accounts Receivable—Uninsured Patients	35,000	
Patient Service Revenues		1,505,000

In contrast, if the medical center chooses to determine the variable consideration by the expected amount (weighted-average) approach, the reported balances are computed as follows:

Government programs	80% x 90% = 72%	
	20% x 80% = 16%	
Expected value	88% of $1,100,000	$ 968,000
Insurance companies	40% x 100% = 40%	
	60% x 60% = 36%	
Expected value	76% of $800,000	608,000
Uninsured with income	70% x 50% = 35%	
	30% x 20% = 6%	
Expected value	41% of $70,000	28,700
Total		$1,604,700

Based on this different approach to evaluating the variable consideration, the journal entry is slightly different:

Accounts Receivable—Government Programs	968,000	
Accounts Receivable—Insurance Companies	608,000	
Accounts Receivable—Uninsured Patients	28,700	
Patient Service Revenues		1,604,700

Bad debt expense should still be considered although it will be a much lower figure now based on the transaction price computed earlier rather than the original standard price of the service. Because the receivable amounts stated earlier reflect what the health care entity expects to happen, some have argued that no bad debt expense should be necessary.

> It's the end of bad debt as we know it. A new accounting standard dramatically narrows what hospitals can report as bad debt, or payments they anticipated but never received. The majority of what used to qualify as bad debt won't be reported as such under new U.S. generally accounting principles.[35]

Nevertheless, most health care entities will probably continue to report a small amount of bad debt expense for two reasons. First, the preceding amounts are all estimates, and actual collections might fall short of reported figures. Second, unexpected events such as a recession or large local bankruptcy could alter expected collections. In the second case, TMC reports receivables of $1,608,800. Using that figure, assume that, historically, collection amounts have unexpectedly come up 1 percent short of the reported amount. Bad debt expense of $16,088 (1 percent of $1,608,800) is recognized.

Bad Debt Expense	16,088	
Allowance for Uncollectible Receivables		16,088
To recognize bad debt expense for the current year.		

Finally, because of the changes in computational methodology, this bad debt figure is no longer reported as a direct reduction to patient service revenue but rather as an operating expense.

Summary

1. Financial statements for not-for-profit entities are designed to provide users, including contributors, with an overall view of the organization's financial position, results of operations, and cash flows.
2. The required financial statements for private not-for-profit entities include a statement of financial position, statement of cash flows, and statement of activities. Expenses must also be shown by function and by the nature of the expense. This requirement can be met with a statement of functional expenses, within the statement of activities, or through disclosure.
3. The financial statements must distinguish between *net assets without donor restrictions* and *net assets with donor restrictions*. Some donor-restricted net assets are expected to be released from restriction after the passage of time or the performance of some act. The release causes an increase in net assets without donor restrictions and a decrease in net assets with donor restrictions. Other donor-restricted net assets must be held permanently so that income can be generated for the NFP entity.
4. Not-for-profit entities report expenses as reductions in net assets without donor restrictions. Program service expenses are for goods or services provided to beneficiaries or others that fulfill the organization's mission. Supporting service expenses encompass general administration and fundraising.
5. Reporting requirements have been established for contributions, which are unconditional transfers of cash or other resources to an entity in a voluntary nonreciprocal transaction. Conditional contributions are not reported. They have a barrier that must be overcome before the charity is entitled to the gift. In addition, the donor can demand return of the money or refuse to pay if not already conveyed.
6. Not-for-profit entities recognize contributions, including unconditional promises to give, as support in the period received at fair value. Pledges to be collected more than one year into the future must be reported at present value and also reduced by any expected uncollectible amounts.
7. Private not-for-profit entities recognize contributed services as support if they either create or enhance nonfinancial assets or require a specialized skill (for example, accounting, architecture, or nursing) that would be purchased if not provided by donation. Donations of works of art and historical treasures do not have to be reported if they meet three specific criteria.
8. Not-for-profit entities sometimes receive donations that must be given to a different beneficiary. While the gift is held, the asset is normally recorded along with an accompanying liability. However, if the entity is given variance power to change the beneficiary, the not-for-profit records a contribution rather than a liability.

[35] Tara Bannow, "New bad debt accounting standards likely to remake community benefit reporting," March 17, 2018, http://www.modernhealthcare.com/article/20180317/NEWS/180319904.

9. Not-for-profit organizations can be brought together by creating either an acquisition or a merger. In an acquisition, one party gains control of the other. The accounting is much like that used in the consolidation of for-profit businesses with all identifiable assets and liabilities of the acquired entity reported at fair value. As one major exception, goodwill is charged off immediately (rather than capitalized) if the acquired organization is predominantly supported by gifts and investment income. In a merger, the entities come together under the control of a newly formed not-for-profit with a different governing body. When a merger occurs, the financial information is combined using the carryover method, which retains the previous book values.
10. Private educational institutions record tuition revenue at the full amount charged. Scholarships and other financial assistance are then subtracted directly from this revenue figure on the statement of activities to better reflect the reality of the amount actually received from students.
11. Not-for-profit entities normally apply with the Internal Revenue Service for tax exemption under a specific status such as 501(c)(3). Each status has its own specific benefits. Most income is not taxed by the federal government, and for many of these statuses, individuals can take donations as itemized deductions.
12. Health care entities (whether not-for-profit or investor owned) will have to adjust to new revenue recognition rules. The standard established price is rarely collected. Explicit price concessions (contractual adjustments) are negotiated with third-party payors such as government programs and insurance companies. Amounts owed by individuals are reduced by implicit price concessions because many people cannot afford the high costs. The health care entity reports the net amount it is entitled to collect after these concessions as its revenue. Because collections can vary, the revenues are deemed variable consideration. The health care entity can report the most likely amount as its revenue or a weighted-average figure based on probability analysis. Bad debt expense may also be recognized, but it will likely be a small amount in comparison to reported balances in earlier periods.

Comprehensive Illustration

Problem

(*Estimated time: 30 to 45 minutes*) Augusta Regional Medical Center (ARMC) is a private not-for-profit hospital offering health care to patients, including some with no ability to pay for the services received. As part of its mission, the ARMC also operates several educational programs. At the start of 2020, ARMC holds net assets of $9 million. Of that amount, $1 million is without donor restrictions, $600,000 has a donor time restriction, $3.4 million has a donor purpose restriction, and $4 million is held permanently based on various donor stipulations.

Medical care and health education are the only program services according to ARMC officials. Supporting services are (1) fundraising and (2) administrative costs.

Required

During 2020, ARMC has numerous financial transactions. Prepare journal entries for each of the following:

1. Patients receive services with these standard charges:

To be paid by government	$2,000,000
To be paid by insurance companies	3,000,000
To be paid by uninsured patients	700,000
Charity care—no attempt to collect	1,600,000

The government programs will receive explicit price concessions of $900,000 based on legal requirements. The insurance companies will receive explicit price concessions of $1.2 million based on contractual agreements. Uninsured patients will receive implicit price concessions of $600,000.

Because of subsequent adjustments, officials believe ARMC has a 60 percent chance of receiving all charges from the government after the explicit price concessions but a 40 percent chance of receiving $100,000 less than that amount. They believe there is a 70 percent chance of receiving all charges from the insurance companies after the explicit price concessions but a 30 percent chance of receiving $200,000 less than that amount. The officials believe there is a 100 percent chance of receiving all charges from uninsured patients after the implicit price concessions. To reflect the expected variable consideration, ARMC applies a weighted-average approach. Historically, bad debts have amounted to $30,000 each year, and nothing at present or in the foreseeable future seems to affect that amount.

2. Local merchants donate linens and other supplies with a fair value of $200,000. Of this amount, $40,000 is used in operations before the end of the year.
3. In past years, ARMC has paid a local gardening company $36,000 each year to maintain flower beds around the hospital to improve the facility's appearance. In 2020, volunteers did this work free of charge.
4. Cash for $50,000 is given to the hospital for a new X-ray machine. The money must be returned if the machine is not acquired within three years.
5. Near the end of the year, numerous pledges of financial support totaling $120,000 are received. Of these promises, $50,000 is unconditional but cannot be spent until 2023. Another $40,000 will only be given if the hospital acquires the new X-ray machine mentioned above. The final $30,000 is unconditional and not donor-restricted. ARMC estimates that $2,000 of the unconditional pledges will prove uncollectible. Money from these pledges is expected to be received within 12 months.
6. A new X-ray machine is acquired for $90,000 in cash. Donors made no specifications about the reporting of this asset.
7. Of the three pledges in (5), $30,000 is collected by ARMC from each.
8. Doctors' salaries of $800,000 are paid. Administrators' salaries of $400,000 are paid.
9. A fundraising appeal is mailed to everyone recently associated with the ARMC at a cost of $50,000 cash. Of the total information, 90 percent relates to fundraising and the importance of giving. The remainder was designed as a health education and awareness document.
10. ARMC receives notification from the Z-Trrek Foundation that it had received a cash donation of $100,000 from Mr. and Mrs. Edwardo Nelson. The money is to be given to a local health care entity with an outstanding reputation. Z-Trrek has decided to award the money to ARMC and is waiting for final approval from the Nelsons before mailing a check for that amount.

Solutions

1. After explicit price concessions to the government programs lower the transaction price, officials believe ARMC has a 60 percent chance of collecting the remaining $1.1 million and a 40 percent chance of collecting only $1.0 million for a weighted average of $1,060,000 ($660,000 plus $400,000).

Accounts Receivable—Government Programs	1,060,000	
Patient Service Revenue		1,060,000

After explicit price concessions to the insurance companies lower the transaction price, officials believe ARMC has a 70 percent chance of collecting the remaining $1.8 million and a 30 percent chance of collecting only $1.6 million for a weighted average of $1,740,000 ($1,260,000 plus $480,000).

Accounts Receivable—Insurance Companies	1,740,000	
Patient Service Revenue		1,740,000

After implicit price concessions to the uninsured lower the transaction price, officials believe ARMC has a 100 percent chance of collecting the remaining $100,000.

Accounts Receivable—Uninsured Patients	100,000	
Patient Service Revenue		100,000

Charity care is not recorded. However, based on historical data, ARMC believes that bad debts of $30,000 will be incurred.

Bad Debt Expense—Medical Care and Health Education	30,000	
Allowance for Uncollectible Accounts		30,000

2. Linens and other supplies with a fair value of $200,000 are received by donation. Apparently, no restrictions have been placed on the use of these assets by the donors.

Supplies	200,000	
Contribution Revenue—Without Donor Restrictions		200,000
Supplies of $40,000 are used in the operation of the ARMC.		
Supplies Expense—Medical Care and Health Education	40,000	
Supplies		40,000

3. Volunteers maintain flower beds around the hospital facility. This work was done in previous years by a gardening company at a charge of $36,000. This situation shows the practical difficulty of

applying some accounting rules. Do the flowers enhance a nonfinancial asset (the building)? Is the gardening work a specialized skill? No easy answers exist for these questions. Because payment was made for the work in previous years, the assertion can be made that the volunteer work here should be recorded. Nevertheless, a health care entity could also argue that this type of contributed service does not rise to the level where recording is appropriate.

Maintenance Expense—Medical Care and Health Education	36,000	
Contributed Service Revenue—Without Donor Restrictions		36,000

4. A conditional cash donation of $50,000 is made. A new X-ray machine must be acquired or the money must be returned to the donor.

Cash	50,000	
Liability to Donor for Conditional Gift		50,000

5. An unconditional pledge of $50,000 is received that has a donor time restriction. It cannot be spent until 2023. Another $30,000 in pledges is both unconditional and unrestricted.

Contribution Receivable	80,000	
Contribution Revenue—With Donor Restrictions		50,000
Contribution Revenue—Without Donor Restrictions		30,000

Uncollectible accounts within the receivables are estimated at $2,000.

Bad Debt Expense—Fundraising	2,000	
Allowance for Uncollectible Accounts		2,000

The third pledge is conditional because the money will not be paid unless the hospital acquires a new X-ray machine. Conditional pledges are not recorded.

6. New X-ray machine is acquired.

Equipment	90,000	
Cash		90,000

The pledge in (5) that was previously conditional and not recognized is no longer conditional because an X-ray machine has been acquired as stipulated. The purchase has been made, so no donor restriction continues to exist.

Contribution Receivable	40,000	
Contribution Revenue—Without Donor Restriction		40,000

The previously received cash in (4) has now been spent as stipulated and the liability is reclassified as contribution revenue.

Liability to Donor for Conditional Gift	50,000	
Contribution Revenue—Without Donor Restriction		50,000

7. Cash of $30,000 is received from each of the pledges received in (5). The conditional pledge was not recorded until the X-ray equipment was acquired in (6).

Cash	90,000	
Contribution Receivable		90,000

8. Salaries are paid to doctors ($800,000) and administrators ($400,000).

Salary Expense—Medical Care and Health Education	800,000	
Salary Expense—Administrative	400,000	
Cash		1,200,000

9. Fundraising appeal is mailed. Of the total information, 90 percent relates to fundraising with the remainder for health education.

Printing and Postal Expenses—Fundraising	45,000	
Printing and Postal Expenses—Medical Care and Health Education	5,000	
Cash		50,000

10. Z-Trrek Foundation informs ARMC that a $100,000 gift from a donor has been awarded to the health care entity. The key here is the term "final approval from the Nelsons." Z-Trrek is waiting for approval from the original donors. That implies that the donors have the ability to say no, and, therefore, they still control the money. If that is the case, then ARMC will make no entry until this approval is received. ARMC might argue that "final approval" is simply a courtesy to the donors and does not constitute variance powers. If that is the case, the following entry is made.

Contribution Receivable	100,000	
Contribution Revenue—Without Donor Restrictions		100,000

Questions

1. Which organization is responsible for issuing reporting standards for private not-for-profit colleges and universities?
2. What information do financial statement users want to know about a not-for-profit entity?
3. What financial statements are required for private not-for-profit colleges and universities?
4. What are net assets without donor restrictions?
5. What are net assets with donor restrictions?
6. In reporting the functional expenses of a not-for-profit entity, what are the two general types of expenses? How can functional expenses be reported?
7. What ratio is frequently used to assess the efficiency of not-for-profit entities?
8. What are board-designated funds, and how are they reported?
9. What disclosure is necessary to describe the liquidity position of a not-for-profit entity? Why is this disclosure viewed as significant to readers of the financial statements?
10. Wilson Helps is a not-for-profit entity that has exchange transactions but also receives donor contributions. How can the entity's accountant differentiate the exchange transactions from the contributions?
11. A donor gives $10,000 to a not-for-profit entity to be used to pay the salary of a new administrator. Subsequently, the money is properly spent. How is the expenditure reported?
12. A donor gives $10,000 to a not-for-profit entity to be used to pay for a new piece of equipment with a 10-year life. Subsequently, the money is properly spent. How is the expenditure reported?
13. How does the reporting of a statement of cash flows by a not-for-profit entity differ from the reporting by a for-profit business?
14. A not-for-profit entity receives $20,000 as a donation. They money must be spent for a stipulated purpose. How does the reporting differ based on whether the gift is unconditional or conditional?
15. The accountant for a not-for-profit entity is trying to determine whether a gift is conditional. How is that decision made?
16. A not-for-profit entity receives a pledge for $50,000, money that must be used for a stipulated purpose. How is the pledge reported if it is judged to be unconditional? How is the pledge reported if it is judged to be conditional?
17. What is an in-kind donation? How are in-kind donations reported?
18. A not-for-profit entity reports contributed services valued at $38,000. How was the decision made to report these services?
19. A not-for-profit museum receives a painting by Monet valued at $750,000. The museum chose not to report the painting on its financial statements. What are the rules for such reporting?
20. A donor conveys a gift to a charity that is to be conveyed to a separate beneficiary. What is the normal method for each party to report this transfer?
21. A donor conveys a gift to a charity that is to be conveyed to a separate beneficiary. What is the method of reporting for each party if the donor retains the right to revoke or redirect use of the gift?
22. A donor conveys a gift to a charity that is to be conveyed to a separate beneficiary. What is the method of reporting for each party if this charity is given variance powers that enable it to change the beneficiary?
23. What are the two methods that can be used to account for the combination of two or more private not-for-profit entities into a single entity?
24. Sunshine NFP, a private not-for-profit entity, gains control over Dancing Ducks NFP, another not-for-profit entity. The acquisition price is $2.5 million although the identifiable assets and liabilities of Dancing Ducks only have a total net fair value of $2.2 million. What recording is made of the $300,000 difference?
25. Helping Hand NFP is a private not-for-profit entity that has equipment with a net book value of $1.1 million but a fair value of $1.4 million. Fancy Fingers NFP is also a private not-for-profit entity that has equipment with a net book value of $1.0 million but a fair value of $1.2 million. If these two entities combine, what are the possible amounts that can be reported for this equipment?
26. A private not-for-profit entity applies for and receives status as a 501(c)(3) organization. What is the importance of this tax-exempt status?
27. In the reporting of a private not-for-profit health care entity, officials are allowed to apply a portfolio approach. What is meant by a portfolio approach?
28. A private not-for-profit health care entity charges patients $4 million that will be covered by various government programs. These programs are entitled to $1.9 million in explicit price concessions.

a. Some part of the $22,000 should be reported as a program service cost because of the educational materials included.

b. No part of the $22,000 should be reported as a program service cost because there is no specific call to action.

c. No part of the $22,000 should be reported as a program service cost because the mailing was sent to both current and former members regardless of their donation history.

d. Some part of the $22,000 should be reported as a program service cost because more than 50 percent of the material was educational in nature.

LO 18-4

14. A private not-for-profit entity has the following activities performed by volunteers who work at no charge. In which case should *no* contribution be reported?

a. A carpenter builds a porch on the back of one building so that patients can sit outside.

b. An accountant does the organization's financial reporting.

c. A local librarian comes each day to read the newspaper to the patients.

d. A computer expert repairs the organization's computer.

LO 18-4

15. A private not-for-profit entity receives a gift of new furniture from a retail department store. The furniture has a fair value of $2,100. The entity holds the furniture for several weeks. After a flood, the entity gives the furniture to several needy families. How should the NFP entity record these conveyances?

a. No entries are required.

b. Record contribution revenue of $2,100 and community assistance expense of $2,100.

c. Record only a community assistance expense of $2,100.

d. Record only a contributed revenue of $2,100.

LO 18-4

16. George H. Ruth takes a leave of absence from his job to work full time for a charity for six months. Ruth fills the position of finance director, a position that normally pays $88,000 per year. Ruth accepts no remuneration for his work. What recording does the charity make?

a. As contribution revenue of $44,000 and salary expense of $44,000.

b. No entries should be made because no cash was paid or received.

c. As a contribution revenue of $44,000 only.

d. As a deferred revenue of $44,000.

LO 18-4

17. A group of high school seniors perform volunteer services for patients at a nearby assisted-living facility, a private not-for-profit entity. The assisted-living facility would not otherwise provide these services such as wheeling patients in the park or calling games of bingo. At a minimum-wage rate, these students would be paid $21,320, but the actual value is estimated to be $27,400. In the assisted-living facility's statement of activities, what amount should be reported as contribution revenue?

a. $27,400

b. $21,320

c. $6,080

d. $-0-

LO 18-4

18. A private not-for-profit entity receives $32,000 in cash from solicitations made in the local community. The charity receives an additional $1,500 from members in payment of their annual dues. These members receive benefits of commensurate value to the amount paid as dues. How should these receipts be reported?

a. Exchange revenues of $33,500

b. Contribution revenues of $33,500

c. Contribution revenues of $32,000 and exchange revenues of $1,500

d. Contribution revenues of $16,750 and exchange revenues of $16,750

LO 18-4

19. The Jones family lost its home in a fire during December 2020. On December 25, 2020, a philanthropist sent money to the Amer Benevolent Society, a private not-for-profit entity, specifically to be conveyed to the Jones family to help them recover. The money was conveyed in January 2021. How should Amer report the receipt of this money in its 2020 financial statements?

a. As net assets without donor restrictions

b. As net assets with donor restrictions

c. As board-designated funds

d. As a liability

LO 18-4

20. Charity A and Charity B are affiliated entities. An accountant for Charity B is paid $10,000 per month, which is equal to the fair value of the services rendered. The accountant for Charity A quits. The accountant from Charity B is sent to work with Charity A for two months. Charity A pays nothing for this service. What journal entry should Charity A record for this work?
    a. No journal entry is made.
    b. An asset is debited for $20,000 and contribution revenue (within net assets without donor restrictions) is credited.
    c. An asset is debited for $20,000 and contribution revenue (within net assets with donor restrictions) is credited.
    d. An expense is debited for $20,000 and contribution revenue (within net assets without donor restrictions) is credited.

LO 18-4

21. Pel Museum is a private not-for-profit entity. If it receives a contribution of historical artifacts, it need not report the contribution if the artifacts are to be sold and it will use the proceeds to
    a. Support general museum activities.
    b. Acquire other items for the museum's collections.
    c. Increase the size of the museum.
    d. Pay for the salaries of museum officials.

LO 18-4

22. A donor gives Charity One $50,000 in cash with the instructions to convey the money to Charity Two. According to the agreement, the donor can reconsider and revoke the gift at any time prior to its transfer to Charity Two. Which of the following statements is true?
    a. Charity One should report a contribution revenue.
    b. The donor continues to report an asset even after the money is given to Charity One.
    c. As soon as the money is conveyed to Charity One, Charity Two should recognize contribution revenue.
    d. As soon as the money is conveyed to Charity One, Charity Two should recognize an asset.

LO 18-5

23. The Peyton Corporation conveys $60,000 in cash to a private not-for-profit entity. It is viewed as a conditional contribution. Which of the following is most likely to be true about this donation?
    a. It has been restricted for use in a future period of time.
    b. The agreement requires the NFP to overcome a barrier or it must return the money to Peyton.
    c. Peyton requires the money to be held permanently with all subsequent income to be used to feed poor families.
    d. Peyton expects to receive a return from the private NFP of commensurate value.

LO 18-5

24. The Stanton Company conveys $23,000 in cash to a private not-for-profit entity. The money must be used for a designated purpose. This conveyance is viewed as a conditional contribution. Which of the following is recorded by the private not-for-profit entity?
    a. A liability
    b. No journal entry is made.
    c. Contributed revenue reported within net assets with donor restrictions
    d. Contributed revenue reported within net assets without donor restrictions

LO 18-5

25. The Houston Corporation signs a formal pledge to give $100,000 in cash to a private not-for-profit entity within the next year. The money must be spent to upgrade important equipment used by the charity. The pledge is judged to be a conditional contribution. Which of the following is recorded by the private not-for-profit entity for this pledge?
    a. A liability.
    b. No journal entry is made.
    c. Contributed revenue reported within net assets with donor restrictions.
    d. Contributed revenue reported within net assets without donor restrictions.

LO 18-5

26. A local private not-for-profit entity receives a large monetary pledge. Accountants are attempting to determine if the contribution is conditional. They are assessing the possible existence of a barrier that has to be overcome. Which of the following is not an indication of a barrier of this type?
    a. Measurable performance related barrier
    b. Stipulation limiting discretion by the recipient on the conduct of an activity
    c. Requirement preventing the money from being spent until a specific date in the future
    d. Stipulation that ties into the agreement

LO 18-6

27. AB is a private not-for-profit entity. It acquires YZ, another private not-for-profit entity. The acquisition price is $1 million. YZ has net assets with a net book value of $600,000 but a fair value of $700,000. Officials for AB expect that the primary support for YZ in the future will be contributions. After the acquisition, what amount of goodwill will be reported on the consolidated balance sheet?
   a. $-0-
   b. $100,000
   c. $300,000
   d. $400,000

LO 18-6

28. BC and OP are both private not-for-profit entities. They combine to create LM, a new private not-for-profit entity with an entirely new board of directors. BC holds land with a book value of $300,000 and a fair value of $400,000. OP holds land with a book value of $500,000 and a fair value of $550,000. After LM has been formed, what is the reported value of the land account?
   a. $800,000
   b. $850,000
   c. $900,000
   d. $950,000

LO 18-6

29. Southwest is a private not-for-profit entity. It acquires Northeast, another private not-for-profit entity. The acquisition value is $980,000. Northeast has two assets (and no liabilities): equipment with a net book value of $120,000 but a fair value of $150,000 and a building with a net book value of $500,000 but a fair value of $800,000. In the future, Northeast expects to receive some support through donations. Nonetheless, the entity is not expected to be predominantly supported by these donations and any investment income earned. After the combination, what amount should be reported for goodwill?
   a. $-0-
   b. $30,000
   c. $60,000
   d. $360,000

LO 18-7

30. Which of these forms must most tax-exempt organizations file annually with the Internal Revenue Service?
   a. 990
   b. 1203
   c. 501
   d. 501(c)(3)

LO 18-7

31. Belwood College is a private not-for-profit institution that has tax-exempt status. Which of the following is most likely to be the specific tax-exempt status that Belwood College holds?
   a. 501(c)(3)
   b. 501(c)(4)
   c. 501(c)(5)
   d. 501(c)(6)

LO 18-8

32. Which of the following are unique to the reporting of revenue by a health care entity?
   a. Charity care must be reported even if the entity does not anticipate seeking collection.
   b. The patients pay for little of the services, and significant discounts are common.
   c. Reported bad debt expenses will increase significantly under new rules.
   d. Standard charges are recorded as the revenue and receivable balances.

LO 18-8

33. A health care entity provides services to a patient. Those services have a standard charge of $76,000. The insurance company that represents the patient has a contract with the entity that leads to a $20,000 reduction in that charge. That reduction is referred to by which of the following labels?
   a. Standard legal hospital abatement amount
   b. Implicit price concession
   c. Discounted health care monitoring fee
   d. Explicit price concession

LO 18-8

34. Which of the following is *not* true about the application of new revenue recognition rules to private not-for-profit health care entities?

a. Revenues are likely to be much lower than under previous rules.
b. Bad debts will be recorded as direct reductions to revenue rather than as a separate expense.
c. A portfolio approach can be used rather than having to record on a contract-by-contract basis.
d. Variable consideration can be reported by either the expected amount method or the most likely outcome method.

LO 18-8

35. Mike Jones spends five days in a local private not-for-profit hospital. The hospital charges him $170,000 for the services. His insurance company has contracts with the hospital that will lower the amount that has to be paid. The hospital believes it has a 60 percent chance that the reduction will be $70,000 and a 40 percent chance that the reduction will be $100,000. The hospital applies the expected amount method to variable consideration. What amount of revenue should be reported?
    a. $-0-
    b. $70,000
    c. $88,000
    d. $100,000

LO 18-8

36. Shirly Ngo spends four days in a local private not-for-private hospital. The hospital charges her $140,000 for the services. Her insurance company has contracts with the hospital that will lower the amount that has to be paid. The hospital believes it has a 70 percent chance that the reduction will be $40,000 and a 30 percent chance that the reduction will be $80,000. The hospital applies the most likely outcome method to variable consideration. What amount of revenue should be reported?
    a. $-0-
    b. $60,000
    c. $88,000
    d. $100,000

LO 18-4, 18-8

37. During the year ended December 31, 2020, Andersen Hospital (operated as a private not-for-profit entity) received and incurred the following:

Fair value of donated medicines	$ 54,000
Fair value of donated services (replacing salaried employees)	38,000
Fair value of donated services (not replacing salaried employees)	11,000
Regular charges to patients (not charity care)	176,000
Charity care charges	210,000
Provision for bad debts	19,000

How should this private not-for-profit report each of these balances?

LO 18-1, 18-2, 18-4

38. A private not-for-profit entity is working to create a cure for a disease. The charity starts the year with one asset, cash of $700,000. Net assets without donor restrictions are $400,000. Net assets with donor restrictions are $300,000. Of the restricted net assets, $160,000 is to be held and used to buy equipment, $40,000 is to be used for salaries, and the remaining $100,000 must be held permanently. The permanently held amount must be invested with 70 percent of any subsequent income used to cover advertising for fundraising purposes. The rest of the income is unrestricted.

    During the current year, this health care entity has the following transactions:

    a. Receives unrestricted cash gifts of $210,000.
    b. Pays salaries of $80,000, with $20,000 of that amount coming from purpose-restricted donated funds. Of the total salaries, 40 percent is for administrative personnel. The remainder is divided evenly among individuals working on research to cure the disease and individuals employed for fundraising purposes.
    c. Buys equipment for $300,000 by signing a long-term note for $250,000 and using restricted funds for the remainder. Of this equipment, 80 percent is used in research. The remainder is split evenly between administrative activities and fundraising. The donor of the restricted funds made no stipulation about the reporting of the equipment purchase.
    d. Collects membership dues of $30,000 in cash. Members receive a reasonable amount of value in exchange for these dues including a monthly newsletter that describes research activities. By the end of the year, 1/12 of this money had been earned.
    e. Receives $10,000 in cash from a donor. The money must be conveyed to a separate charity doing work on a related disease.
    f. Receives investment income of $13,000 from the permanently restricted net assets.
    g. Pays $2,000 for advertising. The money comes from the income earned in (f).

h. Receives an unrestricted pledge of $100,000 that will be collected in three years. The entity expects to collect the entire amount. The pledge has a present value of $78,000. Related interest (considered contribution revenue) of $5,000 is earned prior to the end of the year.

i. Computes depreciation on the equipment bought in (c) as $20,000.

j. Spends $93,000 on research supplies that are used up during the year.

k. Owes salaries of $5,000 at the end of the year. None of this amount will be paid from restricted net assets. Half of the salaries are for individuals doing fundraising, and half for individuals doing research.

l. Receives a donated painting that qualifies as a museum piece being added to the entity's collection of art work that is being preserved and displayed to the public. The entity has a policy that the proceeds from any sold piece will be used to buy replacement art. Officials do not want to record this gift if possible.

a. Prepare a statement of activities for this not-for-profit entity for the current year.

b. Prepare a statement of financial position for this not-for-profit entity for the end of the current year.

LO 18-4, 18-5

39. The Willson Center is a private not-for-profit entity. During 2020, it receives pledges of $600,000 that it expects to collect during 2021. Of that amount, 10 percent is viewed as conditional. Of the rest, $300,000 must be used for automotive equipment for the NFP. In addition, $50,000 is set aside by the entity's board of directors for emergencies. The donor stipulates that another $100,000 be held permanently with all subsequent income used to buy food for hungry children. The remainder of the pledges are not restricted in any way. Of the unrestricted pledges, $5,000 is expected to prove uncollectible. In addition, a local social worker, earning $30 per hour working for the state government, contributes 600 hours of time to the Willson Center. Without these donated services, the organization would have had to hire an additional staff person. Answer the following questions.

a. What is meant by conditional pledges? How are conditional pledges reported?

b. What is the reporting of the $300,000 in pledges for automotive equipment when the pledge is received? When the money is collected? When the money is properly spent assuming the donor made no stipulation about reporting?

c. What is the reporting of the $50,000 set aside by the entity's board of directors for emergencies?

d. What is the reporting of the $100,000 to be permanently held with the income used to buy food for hungry children? What is the reporting when income is earned? What is the reporting when this income is spent as stipulated?

e. What is the reporting of the remaining pledges that are not restricted? What is the reporting of the bad debt amount?

f. Should the donated services be reported? If so, why?

g. If the donated services should be reported, what is the appropriate journal entry?

LO 18-2, 18-3, 18-4

40. The following questions concern the accounting principles and procedures applicable to a private not-for-profit entity. Write answers to each question.

a. What is the difference between exchange revenue and contributed revenue?

b. What is the significance of the statement of functional expenses?

c. What accounting is made when a private not-for-profit entity receives in-kind contributions?

d. What is the difference in net assets without donor restrictions and net assets with donor restrictions?

e. Under what conditions should a private not-for-profit entity record donated services?

f. What makes a contribution or a pledge conditional? How are conditional contributions and conditional pledges reported?

g. What reporting is appropriate for costs associated with direct mail and other solicitations that also contain educational materials?

h. A private not-for-profit entity received a gift of an art object. What are the two ways that this can be reported? How is the decision made as to the proper reporting?

LO 18-1, 18-2, 18-4, 18-5

41. The University of Danville is a private not-for-profit university that starts the current year with $700,000 in net assets: $400,000 without donor restrictions and $300,000 with donor restrictions. The $300,000 is composed of $200,000 with purpose restrictions and $100,000 that must be held permanently.

The following transactions occurred during the year. Prepare journal entries for each transaction. Then determine the end-of-year balances for net assets without donor restrictions and net assets with donor restrictions by creating a statement of activities for the period. The school has two program services: education and research. It also has two supporting services: fundraising and administration.

a. Charged students $1.2 million for tuition and fees.

b. Received a donation of equity investments that had cost the owner $100,000 but is worth $300,000 currently. According to the terms of the gift, the university must hold the investments forever but can spend the dividends for any purpose. Any changes in the value of these securities must be held forever and cannot be spent.

c. Received a cash donation of $700,000 that must be spent to acquire laboratory equipment.

d. Awarded scholarships to students in the amount of $100,000.

e. Paid salary expenses of $140,000 (teaching), $80,000 (research), $50,000 (administrative), and $40,000 (fundraising).

f. Learned that a tenured faculty member is contributing his services for this year and will not accept his $80,000 salary. His time is 70 percent teaching and 30 percent research.

g. Spent $200,000 of the money in (c) on laboratory equipment. The donor had made no specifications about the recording of the acquisition. The equipment is used 80 percent of the time for research and 20 percent of the time for teaching.

h. Learned that the investments in (b) are worth $330,000 at the end of the year.

i. Received cash dividends of $9,000 on the investments in (b).

j. Computed depreciation expense for the year on the equipment in (g) as $32,000.

k. The school's board of trustees votes to set aside $100,000 of previously unrestricted cash for the future purchase of library books.

l. Received an unconditional promise of $10,000 halfway through the year. The school expects to collect the money in three years. The $10,000 future payment has a present value of $7,513 based on a reasonable annual interest rate of 10 percent.

m. Received an art object as a gift. It is worth $70,000. For financial reporting, it qualifies as work of art/museum piece. The school prefers not to record such gifts unless required.

n. Paid utilities and other general expenses of $74,000 (teaching), $45,000 (research), $43,000 (fundraising), and $50,000 (administrative).

o. Received free services from alumni who come to campus each week and put books on the shelves in the library. Over the course of the year, the school would have paid $103,000 to have this work done.

p. Near the end of the year, the school received a pledge of $40,000 to be collected in two years. It is judged to be conditional and has a present value of $31,200.

LO 18-2, 18-4

42. The College of Central North (a small private not-for-profit entity) has the following events and transactions.

a. On January 1, Year 1, the board of trustees votes to restrict $1.9 million of previously unrestricted investments to construct a new football stadium at some future point in time.

b. On April 1, Year 1, Dr. Johnson, a graduate of the college, gives the school $4 million in investments that must be held forever. All subsequent cash income is to be used to help pay for construction of the football stadium. After that, the money must be used for maintenance of the stadium.

c. On December 31, Year 1, the investments in (b) generate $500,000 in cash interest revenue. In addition, the investments went up in value by $44,000.

d. On January 1, Year 2, the school builds the new football stadium with the restricted $2.4 million. Cash is paid. The stadium has an expected life of 20 years and no anticipated residual value.

e. On January 2, Year 2, Dr. Johnson buys a seat for the current year on the 50-yard line of the stadium for cash of $30,000. The seat's fair value for that year is $12,000.

f. On January 3, Year 2, Dr. Johnson provides free medical services to the school. These services have a fair value of $14,000. A specialized skill was needed and the school would have bought the services if not donated.

g. On January 4, Year 2, Dr. Johnson donates a small painting by Picasso to be displayed in the school library. It is appraised as having a value of $30,000. The donors had made no stipulations about the financial reporting in connection with their gifts.

For each of the following independent situations, indicate whether the statement is true or false. Briefly explain the reason for your answer.

(1) On January 1, Year 1, net assets without donor restrictions reported by the school will be reduced.

(2) As of December 31, Year 1, net assets with donor restrictions will have increased by $500,000 during the year because of purpose restrictions stipulated by donors.

(3) On December 31, Year 1, the amount of net assets that must be permanently held according to donor specifications went up by $44,000.

(4) On January 1, Year 2, net assets without donor restrictions increased by $500,000.

(5) Based on the information provided, depreciation expense will not be recorded in connection with the football stadium in Year 2.

(6) Based on the information provided, depreciation expense will not be recorded in connection with the football stadium in Year 3.

(7) For financial reporting purposes, net assets without donor restrictions increased by $30,000 on January 2, Year 2.

(8) For financial reporting purposes, contributed revenue increased by $18,000 on January 2, Year 2.

(9) On January 3, Year 2, net assets without donor restrictions went up and down at the same time.

(10) On January 3, Year 2, net assets without donor restrictions might be reported as going up and down at the same time.

(11) On January 3, Year 2, net assets without donor restrictions will go down and might go up.

(12) On January 4, Year 2, contributed revenue of $30,000 must be reported.

(13) On January 4, Year 2, contributed revenue of $30,000 must not be reported.

LO 18-1, 18-2, 18-4

43. You are preparing a statement of activities for the University of Richland, a private not-for-profit entity. The following questions should be viewed as independent of each other.

Part I

During the current year, a donor gives $400,000 cash to the school and stipulates that the money must be held forever. Any investment income earned on this money must be used to supplement faculty salaries. By the end of the current year, $31,000 has been earned and, of that amount, the school has expended $22,000 appropriately. At the end of the current year, the board of trustees also set aside $150,000 in unrestricted cash that must be held with income going to faculty salaries. What was the overall change in each of the following for the year?

a. Net assets without donor restrictions

b. Net assets with donor restrictions

Part II

At the beginning of the current year, Ms. Landis made several contributions to the school: a cash gift of $90,000 that must be spent for listening rooms for the music department, a cash gift of $50,000 that must be invested and spent in the following year, a cash gift of $70,000 that must be returned unless the football team wins 10 games in a single season (over the next three years), and a pledge of $300,000 that will be be paid early in the following year if the school manages to raise the average SAT score of its students by 10 points. What was the overall change in each of the following for the year?

a. Net assets without donor restrictions

b. Net assets with donor restrictions

Part III

Several years ago, a donor presented the school with $400,000 in cash to help fund its financial aid program. This year, the school charges students $2 million in tuition but granted $700,000 in financial aid. The donor's gift offsets $300,000 of the financial aid. Collections to date from the students have totaled $1.1 million. What was the overall change in each of the following for the year?

a. Net assets without donor restrictions

b. Net assets with donor restrictions

LO 18-1, 18-2, 18-4, 18-5

44. The Watson Foundation, a private not-for-profit entity, starts 2020 with cash of $100,000, contributions receivable (net) of $200,000, investments of $300,000, and land, buildings, and equipment (net) of $200,000. Net assets without donor restrictions were reported as $400,000, the same figure as the net

assets with donor restrictions. Of the restricted net assets, $300,000 was purpose restricted whereas the other $100,000 had to be held permanently, although the subsequently earned income is without restriction. Fifty percent of the purpose restricted net assets had to be used to help pay for a new building. The remainder was restricted to the payment of officer salaries. Donors made no stipulations about the eventual reporting of buildings and other long-lived assets when acquired. Watson has one program service (health care) and two supporting services (fundraising and administrative).

During the current year, Watson Foundation has the following transactions.

(1) Computed interest of $20,000 on the unrestricted contribution receivable.

(2) Received cash of $100,000 from the contributions receivable and wrote off another $4,000 as uncollectible.

(3) Received unrestricted cash donations of $180,000.

(4) Received $23,000 in cash that must be spent for a particular type of office machine within the next year or the money must be returned.

(5) Paid salaries of $90,000. Of that amount, $15,000 came from restricted funds. The payment was made to individuals doing health care work.

(6) Spent the $23,000 in (4) for the appropriate office machine.

(7) Received a cash gift of $12,000 that Watson must convey to another specified charity. However, Watson has the right to give this money to a different organization if officials so choose.

(8) Bought a building for $500,000 by signing a long-term note for $450,000 and using restricted funds for the remainder.

(9) Collected annual membership dues of $30,000. Individuals receive substantial benefits from their memberships. By the end of the year, two-thirds of the time for the average membership has passed.

(10) Received unrestricted income of $40,000 generated by net assets that must be held permanently.

(11) The board of directors of the Watson Foundation vote to set aside $9,000 of its investments for emergency purposes.

(12) Paid rent of $12,000 for the past month, advertising of $15,000, and utilities of $16,000. These were half for the program service and one-fourth each for the two supporting services.

(13) Received an unrestricted pledge of $200,000. Watson will collect the money in five years and does not expect any part to be uncollectible. Present value at inception is $149,000, but interest for the year to date is $6,000.

(14) Computed depreciation of $40,000, 60 percent for health care, 30 percent for administrative, and 10 percent for fundraising.

(15) Paid $15,000 in interest on the note signed in (8). All of this cost is assumed to be related to health care.

a. Prepare a statement of activities for the Watson Foundation for this year.

b. Prepare a statement of financial position for the Watson Foundation at the end of this year.

LO 18-1, 18-2, 18-4, 18-5, 18-8

45. For a number of years, a private not-for-profit entity has been preparing financial statements that do not necessarily conform to U.S. generally accepted accounting principles. At the end of the most recent year (Year 2), those financial statements show total assets of $900,000, total liabilities of $100,000, net assets without donor restriction of $400,000, and net assets with donor restrictions of $400,000. This last category is composed of $300,000 in net assets with purpose restrictions and $100,000 in net assets that must be permanently held. At the end of Year 1, financial statements show total assets of $700,000, total liabilities of $60,000, net assets without donor restriction of $340,000, and net assets with donor restrictions of $300,000. This last category is composed of $220,000 in net assets with purpose restrictions and $80,000 in net assets that must be permanently held. Total expenses for Year 2 were $500,000 and reported under net assets without donor restrictions. Each part that follows should be viewed as an independent situation.

Part One

Assume that this entity is a private college that charged its students $600,000 for tuition in Year 2 but then provided $140,000 in financial aid. The $600,000 was reported as revenue. The $140,000 was reported as an expense. Both of these amounts were included in the net assets without donor restrictions.

a. What is the appropriate amount that should be reported as net assets without donor restrictions at the end of Year 2?

b. What is the appropriate amount that should be reported as expenses for Year 2?

Part Two

Assume that during Year 1, the entity receives a cash gift of $80,000. The donor specified that this money be invested in U.S. government bonds with the income to be used to help pay the salaries of the entity's employees. The gift was recorded as an increase in net assets with donor restrictions. The investments earned $5,000 during Year 1 and $7,000 during Year 2. The entity reported these amounts on the statement of activities as increases in net assets without donor restrictions. In both cases, the money was immediately expended for salaries, amounts that were recorded as expenses within net assets without donor restrictions. No other journal entries were made in connection with this income and the income earned.

a. What was the appropriate amount of net assets without donor restrictions to be reported at the end of Year 2?

b. What was the appropriate amount of expenses to be reported under net assets without donor restrictions for the year ending December 31, Year 2?

c. What was the appropriate amount of net assets with donor restrictions to be reported at the end of Year 2?

Part Three

Assume that, at the beginning of Year 1, the entity received $50,000 in cash as a donation with the stipulation that the money be used to buy a bus or be returned to the donor. At that time, the entity increased cash and increased contributed revenue under net assets with donor restrictions. On the first day of Year 2, the $50,000 was spent on the bus. The entity reclassified $50,000 from net assets with donor restrictions to net assets without donor restrictions. At the end of Year 2, the entity recorded $5,000 as depreciation expense, a figure that was shown as a reduction under net assets without donor restrictions.

a. What was the appropriate amount of net assets with donor restrictions to be reported at the end of Year 1?

b. What was the appropriate amount of net assets without donor restrictions to be reported at the end of Year 2?

c. What was the appropriate amount of expenses to be reported under net assets without donor restrictions for the year ending December 31, Year 2?

d. What was the appropriate amount of net assets with donor restrictions to be reported at the end of Year 2?

Part Four

Assume that this entity charges its members $100,000 each year (Year 1 and Year 2). The members get nothing in return for their dues. The entity has consistently recorded the cash collections as an increase in cash and an increase in exchange revenues under net assets without donor restrictions. The board of trustees has had a policy for several years that 10 percent of the money collected be set aside and invested with the money held for emergency purposes. Cash is decreased and "investments held for emergencies" are increased with each purchase.

a. What was the appropriate amount of net assets without donor restrictions at the end of Year 1?

b. What was the appropriate amount of net assets without donor restrictions at the end of Year 2?

c. What was the appropriate amount of net assets with donor restrictions at the end of Year 2?

Part Five

Assume that on January 1, Year 2, several supporters of the entity spent their own time and money to construct a garage for the entity's vehicles. It was donated for free. The labor had a fair value of $20,000, and the materials had a fair value of $50,000. It was expected to last for 10 years and have no residual value. On that day, the entity increased its contributed support under net assets without donor restrictions by $70,000 and increased its expenses under net assets without donor restrictions by the same amount. No further entry has ever been made.

a. What was the appropriate amount of net assets without donor restrictions at the end of Year 2?

b. What was the appropriate amount of total assets at the end of Year 2?

c. What was the appropriate amount of expenses for Year 2?

Part Six

Assume that the entity is a private not-for-profit hospital. During Year 2, the hospital has two portfolios: patients with insurance and patients without insurance. Work with a standard charge of $2 million is done for the first group and work with a standard charge of $1 million is done for the second group. Insurance companies have contracts that create explicit price concessions. The hospital believes it has a 60 percent chance of collecting $1.5 million and a 40 percent chance of collecting $1.3 million. Because of the high cost of health care, uninsured patients receive a variety of implicit price concessions. The hospital believes it has a 70 percent chance of collecting $300,000 and a 30 percent chance of collecting $200,000. The hospital reported exchange revenue of $3 million and a provision for bad debt (a contra revenue account) of $1.2 million to drop the reported balance to the expected collection amount. Assume the hospital wants to use the most likely amount where possible even though the hospital historically collects 5 percent less than that figure.

a. What was the appropriate amount of net assets without donor restrictions at the end of Year 2?

b. How much should total revenue for Year 2 be increased or decreased to arrive at the appropriate balance?

LO 18-6

46. Help & Save is a private not-for-profit entity that operates in Kansas. Swim For Safety is a private not-for-profit entity that operates in Missouri. The leaders of these two organizations have decided to combine forces on January 1, 2020, in order to have a bigger impact from their work. They are currently discussing ways by which this combination can be created. The following are statements of financial position for both charities at that date.

HELP & SAVE
Statement of Financial Position
January 1, 2020

Assets	
Cash	$1,600,000
Contributions receivable (net)	70,000
Investments	300,000
Buildings & equipment (net)	700,000
Total assets	$2,670,000
Liabilities	
Accounts payable and accrued liabilities	$ 110,000
Notes payable	1,100,000
Total liabilities	$1,210,000
Net Assets	
Net assets without donor restrictions	$1,100,000
Net assets with donor restrictions	360,000
Total net assets	$1,460,000
Total liabilities and net assets	$2,670,000

SWIM FOR SAFETY
Statement of Financial Position
January 1, 2020

Assets	
Cash	$ 500,000
Contributions receivable (net)	210,000
Investments	170,000
Buildings & equipment (net)	590,000
Total assets	$1,470,000
Liabilities	
Accounts payable and accrued liabilities	$ 70,000
Notes payable	620,000
Total liabilities	$ 690,000
Net Assets	
Net assets without donor restrictions	$ 420,000
Net assets with donor restrictions	360,000
Total net assets	$ 780,000
Total liabilities and net assets	$1,470,000

The buildings and equipment reported by Help & Save have a fair value of $900,000. The buildings and equipment reported by Swim For Safety have a fair value of $730,000.

a. Assume Help & Save pays $1 million in cash from its net assets without donor restrictions to gain complete control over Swim For Safety. If it is not assumed that Swim For Safety will be predominantly supported by contributions and investment income in the future, what balances will appear on the statement of financial position immediately after control is gained?

b. Assume Help & Save pays $990,000 in cash from its net assets without donor restrictions to gain complete control over Swim For Safety. It is assumed that Swim For Safety will be predominantly supported by contributions and investment income in the future. What balances will appear on the statement of financial position immediately after control is gained?

c. Assume that these two organizations are combined into a new private not-for-profit entity to be known as Help–Swim–Save. A new governing body will be formed to manage and operate this new organization. What balances will appear on the statement of financial position immediately after control is gained?

LO 18-4, 18-6

47. Assume that Charity A and Charity B are alike in every possible way except as described next. Assume that each question is independent of the other questions.

a. Each charity suffers significant damage from a hailstorm this year. Each hires a person to repair this damage. Each of these workers donates the labor to the charity. Charity A examines the repair work and decides that it required a specialized skill that it would have had to buy. Charity B examines the repair work and decides that it did not require a specialized skill. After recording these events, which entity will report the larger amount of net assets? Explain why.

b. Each charity receives a large investment in shares of a publicly traded company. The investment must be held forever. Charity A can spend the resulting income as it sees fit. Charity B must spend the resulting income to supplement salaries. Both charities receive the same amount of income this year. Both charities immediately spend the income to supplement salaries. After recording these events, which charity will report the larger amount of net assets without donor restrictions?

c. At the beginning of the current year, each charity combines with another similar charity. In both cases, the similar charity has assets worth $780,000, but with a net book value of $700,000. It has no liabilities. Both Charity A and Charity B paid $800,000 in cash to make this acquisition. Charity A is acquiring a charity that gets most of its resources through exchange transactions (it sells cookies and popcorn). Charity B is acquiring a charity that gets most of its resources through donations. After those events, which charity will report the larger amount of net assets without donor restrictions?

d. Assume that these two charities are both private not-for-profit hospitals. During the year, each does an appendectomy on one of its patients. The cost of the operation is $76,000, but the normal charge to the patient is $100,000. Because the patient was not insured, Charity A gave implicit price concessions and hoped to collect $30,000. Despite efforts to collect, by the end of the year, hospital officials realized that nothing could be collected. Charity B assumed from the beginning that collection of any amount was impossible and made no efforts to collect. After that, which charity will report the larger amount of earned revenue?

e. Both Charity A and Charity B have volunteers make 1,000 cakes to sell to their donors. The cost of the material for these cakes is $20 each, but they will be sold for $50 apiece. Officials for Charity A believed that $50 was a reasonable fair value for a cake. Officials for Charity B believed that the fair value of the cakes was actually only $30 apiece. After the cakes are sold to the donors, which charity will report the larger amount of net assets without donor restrictions?

LO 18-8

48. The following questions concern the appropriate accounting for a private not-for-profit health care entity. Write complete answers for each of these independent questions.

a. What is a third-party payor, and how does the presence of third-party payors impact the financial reporting of a health care entity?

b. Jones Hospital and Smith Hospital operate within three miles of each other. Jones is a for-profit business. Smith is a private not-for-profit hospital. In general, how do the accounting rules differ for these two similar organizations?

c. A private not-for-profit health care entity charges a group of patients $7 million for various services. They have health coverage through a government program. The program has contracts with the health care entity that provides explicit cost concessions. For that reason, the health care entity thinks it has a 40 percent chance of collecting $5 million, a 30 percent chance of collecting $4 million, and a 30 percent chance of collecting $3 million. Describe the financial reporting the health care entity should make for these revenues.

d. A private health care entity charges a group of patients $5 million for various services. They are uninsured. The health care entity has implicit price concessions that it applies to this portfolio of patients. For that reason, the health care entity thinks it has a 50 percent chance of collecting $1 million, a 30 percent chance of collecting $700,000, and a 20 percent chance of collecting $400,000. Describe the financial reporting the health care entity should make for these revenues.

e. In connection with the financial reporting of a private not-for-profit entity, what is charity care? Describe the financial reporting for charity care.

LO 18-4, 18-5, 18-8

49. Under Lennon Hospital's standard rate structure, it earned $9 million in revenues for the year ended December 31, 2020. However, Lennon did not expect to collect this entire amount because officials deemed $1.5 million to be charity care. Of the remainder, 90 percent was for patients who had insurance, and the rest was for patients who did not have insurance. For the insured parties, the hospital gave explicit price concessions of $2.2 million. For the uninsured, the hospital gave implicit price concessions of $300,000. Even after the explicit price concessions, officials believe the hospital only has a 40 percent chance of collecting the net amount from the insurance companies, with a 60 percent chance of collecting $200,000 less than that. Even after the implicit price concessions, officials believe the hospital only has a 10 percent chance of collecting the net amount from the patients, with a 90 percent chance of collecting $100,000 less than that. The hospital reports variable consideration using a weighted-average approach.

During 2020, Lennon purchased medical supplies from Harrison Supply Company at a retail price of $4,000. Harrison notified Lennon that it was donating the supplies to the hospital.

Late in 2020, Lennon received a $400,000 pledge from Starr, Inc. The money would be given if Lennon acquired a new magnetic resonance imaging (MRI) machine within the next nine months. The pledge will not be paid if the MRI machine is not obtained.

How does Lennon report each of these three separate set of events?

LO 18-2, 18-8

50. A local private not-for-profit health care entity (Rochester Medical) incurred the following transactions during the current year. Record each of these transactions in appropriate journal entry form. Prepare a schedule calculating the change in net assets without donor restrictions and net assets with donor restrictions. The entity has one program service (health care) and two supporting services (fundraising and administrative).

a. The board of governors for Rochester Medical (RM) announces that $160,000 in previously unrestricted cash will be used in the near future to acquire equipment. These funds are invested until the purchase eventually occurs.

b. RM receives a donation of $80,000 in cash with the stipulation that the money be invested in U.S. government bonds. All subsequent income derived from this investment must be paid to supplement nursing salaries.

c. RM spends $25,000 in cash to acquire medicines. RM had received this money during the previous year. The donor had specified that it had to be used for medicines.

d. RM charges patients $2 million. These amounts are the responsibility of government programs and insurance companies. These third-party payors will receive explicit price concessions because of long standing contracts. Officials believe RM has an 80 percent chance of receiving $1.5 million and a 20 percent chance of receiving $1.0 million. RM has a policy of reporting the most likely outcome.

e. RM charges patients $1 million. These patients are not insured. RM sets implicit price concessions because of the high cost of health care. Officials believe RM has a 70 percent chance of collecting $250,000 and a 30 percent chance of receiving $100,000. As stated before, RM has a policy of reporting the most likely outcome.

f. RM charges patients $600,000. These patients have little or no income. The hospital administration chooses to view this work as charity care and make no attempt at collection.

g. Depreciation expense for the year is $110,000. Of that amount, 70 percent relates to health care, 20 percent to administrative, and 10 percent to fundraising.

h. RM receives interest income of $15,000 on the investments acquired in (a).

i. Based on past history, officials estimate that $50,000 of the reported receivable amount from third-party payors will never be collected. Of the amount reported by uninsured patients who are expected to pay a portion of their debt, officials estimate that $20,000 of the reported receivable amount will not be collected.

j. The medicines in (c) are consumed through daily patient care.

k. RM sells the investments in (a) for $172,000 in cash. RM used that money plus the previously recorded interest income (along with $25,000 in cash given last year to RM with the donor stipulation that the money be used for equipment) to buy new equipment.

l. RM receives pledges near the end of the year totaling $200,000. Of that amount, $38,000 is judged to be conditional. The remaining $162,000 has a donor-stipulated purpose restriction. The present value of the $162,000 is calculated as $131,000.

Develop Your Skills

RESEARCH CASE 1

CPA skills

The law firm of Hackney and Walton has decided to start supporting a worthy charity. The partners want to select an organization that makes good use of its resources to meet its stated mission.

Go to the website www.give.org. Click on "For Donors." Find a search box titled "Find a Charity Report." Above the box is a link to "Our 20 Standards." First, read those standards. Then, enter the names of two or more charities that are well known into the search box. Read the information that is available about each charity on this website.

Required

Write a report to the partners of Hackney and Walton. Describe the charities you selected and recommend which of these charities they should support. Give adequate justification for this recommendation.

RESEARCH CASE 2

CPA skills

Go to www.charitynavigator.org and scroll down until you find "Rating Methodology." Read the information that is provided and write a short memo to explain how this organization rates charities.

RESEARCH CASE 3

CPA skills

Go to the website www.guidestar.org and enter the name of a private not-for-profit organization. Considerable information will be available about the entity. By registering, it should be possible to find a link to the Form 990 (Return of Organization Exempt from Income Tax) filed with the Internal Revenue Service for informational purposes. Scan through this document and answer the following questions:

Required

1. On line I near the top of the first page, determine the organization's specific type of Section 501(c) designation.
2. At Part VII, there is a list of officers, directors, trustees, and key employees. List the three individuals with the highest level of compensation.
3. In Part IX, there is a statement of functional expenses. For this organization, what percentage of its total expenses is labeled as program service expenses?
4. Scan the entire Form 990 for information that would not otherwise be available about this organization.

RESEARCH CASE 4

CPA skills

Go to the following URL for Georgetown University: https://financialaffairs.georgetown.edu/management/financial-statements. Review the most recent set of financial statements for the university. You will also have access to the 1987 financial statements; review those as well.

Required

Prepare a list of three or four of the most obvious structural differences between the 1987 financial statements and the current financial statements.

ANALYSIS CASE 1

Go to the website of a private voluntary health and welfare entity such as United Cerebral Palsy (www.ucp.org), the American Heart Association (www.heart.org), or the American Cancer Society (www.cancer.org). Find the charity's latest financial statements, which usually can be found by clicking on a button such as "About Our Charity" and then clicking on "Financial Information" or "Audited Financial Statements." Some financial statements are easy to find while others seem well hidden. Some entities simply do not include financial statements on their websites.

Required

After examining these financial statements, answer the following questions about the private not-for-profit entities:

1. How many different program services were listed? Name each.
2. What percentage of total expenses went to supporting services?
3. Were any contributed services recognized and, if so, for how much?
4. What dollar amount was spent on fundraising?

ANALYSIS CASE 2

CPA skills

Go to https://about.usc.edu/files/2017/12/USC-Financial-Report-2017.pdf to find the 2017 financial statements for the University of Southern California.

Required

The financial statements for the University begin on page 11. Use those financial statements and the accompanying notes to answer each of the following questions.

1. What amount of pledges receivable is shown on the balance sheet?
2. At the end of 2017, what is the amount of net assets without donor restrictions and the amount of net assets with donor restrictions that is reported?
3. What amount of revenues is recognized for student tuition and fees?
4. By how much (in dollars and as a percentage) does financial aid reduce the amount of student tuition and fees?
5. How much of the revenue for the year came from contributions?
6. Note 1 attached to the financial statements describes net assets without donor restrictions and net assets with donor restrictions. Read this material and describe the information that is conveyed.
7. Note 14 attached to the financial statements describes the functional expenses. Read this material and describe the information that is conveyed.

COMMUNICATION CASE

CPA skills

Go to https://independentsector.org/resource/principles/. Click on "Principles Guide for Good Governance and Ethical Practice." Read through the 33 Principles to be followed. Focus on the explanation for the six principles under the heading of Strong Financial Oversight. Write a short report on the types of policies, actions, and procedures that a private not-for-profit entity should take to help ensure proper financial transparency and accountability.

chapter 19

Accounting for Estates and Trusts

Trillions of dollars of assets will soon pass from one generation to another as baby boomers age and pass.

Individuals labor throughout their lives in part to accumulate property that they eventually can convey for the benefit of spouses, children, relatives, friends, charities, and the like. After amassing wealth, donors typically seek to achieve two goals:

- To minimize the amount of these assets that must be surrendered to the government.
- To ensure that the ultimate disposition of all property is consistent with the donor's wishes.

Therefore, accountants (as well as attorneys and financial planners) often assist individuals who are developing estate plans or creating trust funds to accomplish these goals. At a later date, the accountant may also serve in the actual administration of the estate or trust. In either estate or trust planning, the person's intentions must be spelled out in clear detail so that no misunderstanding arises. All available techniques also should be considered to limit the impact of taxes. To carry out these varied responsibilities properly, it is of paramount importance that the persons doing so have a knowledge of the legal and reporting aspects of estates and trusts.

Although many of the complex legal rules and regulations in these areas are beyond the scope of an accounting textbook, an overview of both estates and trusts can introduce the issues that members of the accounting profession frequently encounter.

Learning Objectives

After studying this chapter, you should be able to:

LO 19-1 Understand the proper methods of accounting for and administering an estate and the corresponding legal terminology.

LO 19-2 Describe the types of estate distributions and identify the process of asset allocations and distributions from an estate.

LO 19-3 Understand the federal estate tax and state inheritance tax systems, the corresponding exemptions, and tax planning opportunities.

LO 19-4 Understand and account for the distinction between principal and income in the context of estate and trust accounting.

LO 19-5 Describe the financial statements and journal entries utilized to account for estate and trust transactions.

LO 19-6 Describe various trusts, their proper use, and accounting for activities.

Accounting for an Estate

> While none of us want to contemplate our death, or that of our spouse, we all need an estate plan. If you need motivation to reach this decision, remember that every dollar you keep from the folks in Washington or your state capital goes to someone you like a heck of a lot better—such as your kids, your younger sister, or your alma mater.[1]

The term *estate* simply refers to the property (assets) owned by an individual. However, in this chapter, *estate* is more specifically defined as a separate legal entity holding title to the real and personal assets of a deceased person. *Thus, estate accounting refers to the recording and reporting of financial events from the time of a person's death until the ultimate distribution of all property the estate holds.* To ensure that this disposition is as intended and to avoid disputes, each individual should prepare a *will,* "a

[1] Ellen P. Gunn, "How to Leave the Tax Man Nothing," *Fortune,* March 18, 1996, p. 94.

LO 19-1

Understand the proper methods of accounting for and administering an estate and the corresponding legal terminology.

person's declaration of how he desires his property to be disposed of after his death."[2] If an individual dies *testate* (having written a valid will), this document serves as the blueprint for settling the estate, disbursing all remaining assets, making various tax elections, and appointing fiduciaries to accomplish these tasks.

When a person dies *intestate* (without a legal will), state laws control the administration of his or her estate. Although these legal rules vary from state to state, they normally correspond with the most common patterns of distribution. When intestacy laws rather than a will apply, real property is conveyed based on the *laws of descent,* whereas personal property transfers are made according to the *laws of distribution.*

Each individual state establishes laws governing wills and estates known as *probate laws. The National Conference of Commissioners on Uniform State Laws* developed the Uniform Probate Code in hopes of creating consistent treatment in this area. To date, about half of the states have officially adopted the Uniform Probate Code.[3] In many of the other states, the rules and regulations applied are similar to those of the Uniform Probate Code. In practice, however, an accountant must become familiar with the specific laws of the state having jurisdiction over the estate of the specific decedent.

Administration of the Estate

Regardless of the locale, probate laws generally are designed to achieve three goals:

1. Gather, preserve, and account for all of the decedent's property.
2. Administer an orderly and fair settlement of all debts.
3. Discover and implement the decedent's intent for the remaining property held at death.

This process usually begins by filing a will with the probate court or indicating that no will has been discovered. If a will is presented, the probate court must rule on the document's validity. A will must meet specific legal requirements to be accepted. These requirements vary from state to state. For example, would the following signed and dated statement constitute a valid will?

"I want my children to have my money."

Because the writer is dead, the intention of this statement cannot be verified. Was this an idle wish made without thought, or did the decedent truly intend for this one sentence to constitute a will conveying all money to these specified individuals upon death? Did the decedent mean for all noncash assets to be liquidated with the proceeds being split among the children? Or did the writer strictly mean that just the cash on hand at the time of death should be transferred to them? Obviously, in some cases, a will's validity (and the decedent's intention) is not easily proven.

If deemed to be both authentic and valid, a will is admitted to probate, and the decedent's specific intentions will be carried to conclusion. All of the decedent's property must be located, debts paid, and distributions appropriately conveyed. Whether a will is present or not, an estate administrator must be chosen to serve in a stewardship capacity. This individual serves in a fiduciary position and is responsible for (1) satisfying all applicable laws and (2) making certain that the decedent's wishes are achieved (if known and if possible).

If a specific person is named in the will to hold this position, the individual is referred to as the *executor* (*executrix* if female; this text will generically use the term *executor*) *of the estate.* If the will does not designate an executor or if the named person is unwilling or unable to serve in this capacity (or if the decedent dies without a will), the courts must select a representative. A court-appointed representative is known legally as the *administrator* (female: *administratrix*) *of the estate.* An executor/administrator is not forced to serve in this role for free; that person is legally entitled to reasonable compensation for all services rendered.[4]

[2] *Barron's Law Dictionary,* 4th ed. (New York: Barron's Educational Services, Inc. 1996), p. 553.

[3] To see your state's version of the Uniform Probate Code, review the following link: www.law.cornell.edu/uniform/probate.html.

[4] To avoid using convoluted terminology, the term *executor* is generally used throughout this chapter to indicate both executors and administrators.

The executor is normally responsible for fulfilling several tasks:

- Taking possession of all of the decedent's assets and inventorying this property.
- Discovering all claims against the decedent and settling these obligations.
- Filing federal and state estate income tax returns, federal estate tax returns, and state inheritance or estate tax returns.
- Distributing property according to the provisions of the will (according to state laws if a valid will is not available) or according to court order if necessary.
- Making a full accounting to the probate court to demonstrate that the executor has properly fulfilled the fiduciary responsibility.

Property Included in the Estate

The basis for all estate accounting is the property the decedent held at death. These assets are used to settle claims and pay taxes. Any property that remains is distributed according to the decedent's will (or applicable state intestacy laws). For estate-reporting purposes, all items are shown at fair value; except for unique situations involving decedents passing in calendar year 2010 (which we explain below), the historical cost paid by the deceased individual is no longer relevant. Fair value is especially important because the sale of some or all properties may be required to obtain enough cash to satisfy claims against the estate. If valuation problems arise, hiring an appraiser could become necessary.

Normally, an estate includes assets such as these:

- Cash.
- Investments in stocks and bonds.
- Interest accrued to the date of death.
- Dividends declared prior to death.
- Investments in businesses.
- Unpaid wages.
- Accrued rents and royalties.
- Valuables such as paintings and jewelry.

At the time of death, the decedent legally owned a certain amount of assets. The executor's task is to locate and value each item belonging to the estate as of that date.

Some state laws specify that real property such as land and buildings (and possibly certain types of personal property) be conveyed directly to the beneficiary or co-owner at the time of death, depending on the type of ownership held. Therefore, in these states, the inventory of the estate property that the executor develops for probate purposes does not include these assets. However, such items must still be listed in the filing of estate and inheritance tax returns because a legal transfer has occurred.

Discovery of Claims against the Decedent

An adequate opportunity should be given to the decedent's creditors to allow them to file claims against the estate. Usually, a public notice must be printed in an appropriate newspaper once a week for three weeks.[5] In many states, all claims must be presented within four months of the first of these notices. The executor must verify the validity of these claims and place them in order of priority. If insufficient funds are available, this ordering becomes quite important in establishing which parties receive payment. Consequently, claims in category 4 of the following list, most of which are paid before a beneficiary receives any assets, have the greatest chance of remaining unpaid.

[5] Although many states require three weeks, *Ind. Code* §29-1-7-7(b) requires publication of notice for only two consecutive weeks. The CPA must understand the particular state's requirement(s) because this is a typical statutory variance from state to state.

Typical Order of Priority

1. Expenses of administering the estate. Without this preferential treatment, the appointment of an acceptable executor and the hiring of lawyers, accountants, and/or appraisers could become a difficult task in estates with limited funds.
2. Funeral expenses and the medical expenses of any last illness.
3. Debts and taxes given preference under federal and state laws.
4. All other claims, such as unsecured obligations, credit card debts, and the like.

Protection for Remaining Family Members

As indicated, a number of states have adopted the Uniform Probate Code. However, other states have passed a wide variety of individual probate laws that differ in many distinct ways. Thus, no absolute rules about probate laws can be listed. Normally, they provide some amount of protection for a surviving spouse and/or the decedent's minor and dependent children. Small monetary allowances are conveyed to these parties prior to the payment of legal claims. For example, a *homestead allowance* is provided to a surviving spouse[6] and/or minor and dependent children. Even an estate heavily in debt would furnish some amount of financial relief for the members of the decedent's immediate family.

In addition, these same individuals frequently receive a small *family allowance* during a limited period of time while the estate is being administered. Family members are also typically entitled to a limited amount of exempt property such as automobiles, furniture, and jewelry. All other property is included in the estate to pay claims and be distributed according to the decedent's will or state inheritance laws.

LO 19-2

Describe the types of estate distributions and identify the process of asset allocations and distributions from an estate.

Estate Distributions

If a will has been located and probated, property remaining after all claims are settled is conveyed according to that document's specifications.[7] A gift of real property such as land or a building is referred to as a *devise;* a gift of personal property such as stocks or furniture is a *legacy* or a *bequest.* A devise is frequently specific: "I leave 3 acres of land in Henrico County to my son," or "I leave the apartment building on Monument Avenue to my niece." Unless the estate is unable to pay all claims, a devise is simply conveyed to the intended party. However, if claims cannot be otherwise satisfied, the executor could be forced to sell or otherwise encumber the property despite the will's intention.

In contrast, a legacy may take one of several forms. The identification of the type of legacy becomes especially important if the estate has insufficient resources to meet the specifications of the will.

A *specific legacy* is a gift of personal property that is directly identified. "I leave my collection of pocket watches to my son" is an example of a specific legacy because the property is named.

A *demonstrative legacy* is a cash gift made from a particular source. The statement "I leave $10,000 from my savings account in the First National Bank to my sister" is a demonstrative legacy because the source is identified. If the savings account does not hold $10,000 at the time of death, the beneficiary will receive the amount available. In addition, the decedent may specify alternative sources if sufficient funds are not available. Ultimately, any shortfall usually is considered a general legacy.

A *general legacy* is a cash gift whose source is undesignated. "I leave $8,000 in cash to my nephew" is a gift viewed as a general legacy.

A *residual legacy* is a gift of any remaining estate property. Thus, it includes assets left after all claims, taxes, and other distributions are conveyed according to the residual provisions of the will. "The balance of my estate is to be divided evenly between my brother and the University of Notre Dame" is an example of a residual legacy.

[6] Many states provide a $25,000 protective allowance for a surviving spouse. See *Ind. Code* §29-1-4-1.

[7] An exception, however, is that property legally held in joint tenancy with one or more individuals will pass to the surviving joint tenants at death and not be subject to the provisions of a will or intestate distribution.

An obvious problem arises if there are not enough assets in the estate to satisfy all legacies the will specified. The necessary reduction of the various gifts is referred to as the *process of abatement*. For illustration purposes, assume that a will lists the following provisions:

I leave 1,000 shares of AT&T to my brother (a specific legacy).

I leave my savings account at Chase Bank of $20,000 to my sister (a demonstrative legacy).

I leave $40,000 cash to my son (a general legacy).

I leave all remaining property to my daughter (a residual legacy).

Example 1

Assume that after paying all claims, the estate holds the shares of AT&T stock, the $20,000 Chase Bank savings account, and $75,000 in other cash. The first three parties (the brother, sister, and son) receive the specific assets stated in the will, and the residual legacy (to the daughter) would be the $35,000 cash balance left after the $40,000 general legacy is paid.

Example 2

Assume that after paying all claims, the estate holds the shares of AT&T stock, the Chase Bank savings account, and only $35,000 in other cash. The first two individuals (the brother and sister) receive the specified assets, but the son can claim only the remaining $35,000 cash rather than the promised $40,000. Based on the process of abatement, the daughter receives nothing; no amount is left as a residual legacy after the other legacies have been distributed.

Example 3

Assume that after paying all claims, the estate holds the shares of AT&T stock, but the Chase Bank savings account has a balance of only $12,000 rather than the promised $20,000. Other cash held by the estate totals $51,000. The stock is distributed to the brother, but the sister gets just the $12,000 cash in the Chase Bank savings account. In most states, the remaining $8,000 is treated as a general legacy. Consequently, in those states, the sister receives the additional $8,000 in this manner and the son receives the specified $40,000. The daughter is then left with only the $3,000 in cash that remains. If the decedent resided in a state that did not treat the $8,000 shortfall as a general legacy, then the sister would receive only the $12,000 in the Chase Bank account, and the daughter would receive the $11,000 in cash that remains. Remember that general legacies are paid prior to residual legacies.

Example 4

Assume that the decedent sold the shares of AT&T stock before death and that after paying all claims, the Chase Bank savings account holds $23,000. Other cash amounts to $30,000. The brother receives nothing from the estate because the specific legacy did not exist at death.[8] The sister collects the promised $20,000 from the Chase Bank savings account, and the remaining $3,000 is added to the general legacy. Therefore, the son receives a total of $33,000 from the two cash sources. Because the general legacy was not fulfilled, no remainder exists as a residual legacy; thus, the daughter collects nothing from the estate.

Insufficient Funds

The debts and expenses of the administration are paid first in settling an estate. If the estate has insufficient available resources to satisfy these claims, the process of abatement is again

[8] The legal term *ademption* refers to a situation in which a specific bequest or devise fails because the property is not available for distribution. As a different possibility, a bequest or devise is said to *lapse* if the beneficiary cannot be located or dies before the decedent. This property then becomes part of the residual estate. For instance, if the singer Prince's last will and testament leaves his purple motorcycle to his sister, Apollonia, but his sister predeceased Prince, his attempted transfer to Apollonia likely lapses.

utilized. Each of the following categories is exhausted completely to pay all debts and expenses before money is taken from the next category:

Residual legacies (first to suffer abatement is the last to receive inheritance).
General legacies.
Demonstrative legacies.
Specific legacies and devises (last to suffer abatement).

LO 19-3

Understand the federal estate tax and state inheritance tax systems, the corresponding exemptions, and tax planning opportunities.

Estate and Inheritance Taxes

Taxes incurred after death can be quite costly. For example, Helen Walton received $5.1 billion in stock at the death of her husband Sam Walton (founder of Walmart Inc.). At this value, these shares could eventually have cost her heirs as much as *$2.8 billion* in taxes at her death: $2.2 billion to the U.S. government and $640 million to the State of Arkansas.[9]

Historically, estate taxes have been used as a method for redistributing wealth and raising revenues. According to tax experts, in 2017, estate taxes raised approximately $20.8 billion in net revenue.[10] This total amounted to less than 1 percent of all tax money generated by the federal government in that year.

The budget surpluses that appeared in the latter part of the 1990s began to cast doubts on the continued need for a federal estate tax. Many arguments can be made both for this tax (to some, there is a perceived limit to the amount that a beneficiary should receive without work or effort) and against it (income that has been taxed once when earned should not be taxed again when the resulting assets are conveyed at death).

In 1999 (and again in 2000), the U.S. Congress voted a phased-in repeal of the estate tax, a measure that then-President Bill Clinton vetoed as being too costly. However, in 2001, Congress passed the Economic Growth and Tax Relief Reconciliation Act of 2001, which included provisions to gradually reduce and then abolish this tax by 2010. President George W. Bush signed the measure into law.

Incredibly, Congress failed to reinstate any estate tax for calendar year 2010 until December 2010. The result of this inaction was that taxpayers passing during 2010 did so potentially without the burden of the federal estate tax. Several extremely wealthy individuals managed to transfer hundreds of millions of dollars of additional inheritance to loved ones rather than paying Uncle Sam.[11] Without the federal estate tax scheme, the blanket basis increase at death was also limited—the result being that many wealthy beneficiaries will encounter a sizeable capital gain tax, albeit at a lower rate.

Congress enacted a significant revision to the estate tax in December 2010 that provided limited certitude for planning 2011 and 2012.[12] The provisions were to sunset at the end of 2012, leaving the potential for reversion to the exemption and rates in effect in 2001. However, on January 2, 2013, Congress passed and President Obama signed the American Taxpayer Relief Act (ATRA), which provided long-term answers for estate planners, CPAs, and attorneys.

In December 2017, Congress enacted the Tax Cuts and Jobs Act (TCJA), which included a substantial increase to the estate tax exemption. The increased exemption amounts are set to expire at the end of 2025, reverting back to the 2017 provisions unless legislative action is taken. The top estate tax rate remained unchanged at 40 percent.

Federal Estate Taxes

The federal estate tax is an excise tax assessed on the right to convey property. The computation begins by determining the fair value of all property held at death. Therefore, even if real

[9] Warren Midgett, "Mrs. Walton's Options," *Forbes,* October 19, 1992, pp. 22–23. Helen Walton passed away in April 2007 with a fortune estimated to exceed $16 billion. This dramatic increase in Mrs. Walton's net worth reflects the need for, and value of, estate planning. Walmart stock has continued to appreciate over the past decade, thus resulting in Mrs. Walton's beneficiaries receiving the economic benefit of her insightful estate planning.

[10] *IRS Data Book,* 2017, www.irs.gov/pub/irs-soi/17databk.pdf.

[11] The Probate Lawyer, July 14, 2010, at www.probatelawyerblog.com/2010/07/george-steinbrenners-heirs-avoid-estate-tax-or-do-they.html.

[12] Tax Relief, Unemployment Insurance Reauthorization, and Job Creation Act of 2010, P.L. 111–312, December 17, 2010.

property is transferred immediately to the beneficiary and is not subject to probate, the value must still be included for federal estate tax purposes.[13] In establishing fair value, the executor may choose an alternate valuation date if that tax election will reduce the amount of estate taxes to be paid. This date is six months after death (or the date of disposition for any property disposed of within six months after death). Thus, the federal estate tax process starts by determining all asset values at death or this alternate date. Note that a piecemeal valuation cannot be made; one of these dates must be used for all properties.

Several items then reduce the gross estate figure to arrive at the taxable value of the estate:

- Funeral expenses.
- Estate administration expenses (including fees paid to accountants and attorneys).
- Liabilities.
- Casualties and thefts during the administration of estate.
- Charitable bequests.
- Marital deduction for property conveyed to spouse.
- State inheritance taxes.

Individuals are allowed to deduct a specified amount from the value of the estate in arriving at the federal estate tax. Recent tax legislation has escalated the portion of an estate that is exempted. Any remaining amount is taxed at graduated rates based on the year of death. However, the tax legislation that provided escalating exemptions expired at the end of 2010,[14] as shown in the following chart. The new 2010 legislation renewed an increased exemption, the 2013 legislation indexed the exemption while raising the tax rate, and the 2017 legislation significantly increased the exemption while leaving the tax rate unchanged.

Date of Death	Estate Tax Exemption at Death	Highest Estate Tax Rate
2009	$ 3.5 million	45%
2010	Tax is repealed	N/A
2011	5.0 million	35%
2012	5.12 million	35%
2013	5.25 million	40%
2014	5.34 million	40%
2015	5.43 million	40%
2016	5.45 million	40%
2017	5.49 million	40%
2018	11.18 million	40%
2019	11.4 million	40%
Beyond 2020	Indexed for inflation	40%

In the past, individuals have often sought to decrease the size of their estates to reduce estate taxes by making gifts during their lifetimes. Annual gifts of $15,000 per person (an amount that is indexed to change with inflation) can be made tax-free to an unlimited number of donees.[15] The federal gift tax has not been eliminated by tax legislation, but an $11.4 (2019) million lifetime tax-free exclusion (also indexed at the same rate as the estate tax exemption) has been established over and above the $15,000 exclusion per person per year. The maximum gift tax rate remains at 40 percent.

[13] Life insurance policies with named beneficiaries are also included in the value of the estate as long as the decedent had the right to change the beneficiary. This rule may result in decedents of modest means having taxable estates. This rule is also one that all estate planning and administration professionals must understand and consider.

[14] 26 U.S.C. §2001 (c) as amended. The 2010 Tax Relief Act permitted estates to elect to apply the "new" provisions to estates for decedents passing in 2010. The 2010 Tax Relief Act also provided "portability" for a spouse's exemption, permitting a surviving spouse to increase her $5.0 million ($5.12 million for 2012) exemption by her deceased husband's remaining or unused exemption up to a total combined amount of $10.0 million.

[15] This amount increased from $11,000 to $12,000 in 2006 and to $13,000 in 2009 due to the indexing; Rev. Proc. 2008–66. An IRS announcement, Rev. Proc. 2012–41 increased the annual exemption to $14,000 in 2013. IRS announcement Rev. Proc. 2017-58 increased the annual exemption to $15,000.

What is the impact of all these changes? Prognosticators more than a decade ago were correct.

> The death of the estate tax is at best premature, and any planner thinking of abandoning an estate planning practice is missing a large opportunity. In fact, the estate planning provisions within the Economic Growth and Tax Relief Reconciliation Act of 2001 should be a boon for most planners, not a death toll.[16]

Federal Estate Taxes—Example 1

The determination of the taxable estate is obviously an important step in calculating estate taxes. Assume for illustration purposes that a person dies holding assets valued at $20 million and has total debts of $500,000 at death. Funeral expenses cost $100,000, and estate administration expenses amount to $200,000. This person's will left $5,200,000 to charitable organizations, and the remaining $14,000,000 (after debts and expenses) goes to the surviving spouse.[17] Under this set of circumstances, no taxable estate exists:

Gross estate (fair value)		$ 20,000,000
Funeral expenses	$ 100,000	
Administration expenses	200,000	
Debts	500,000	
Charity bequests	5,200,000	
Marital deduction	$14,000,000	(20,000,000)
Taxable estate		$ –0–
Estate tax		$ –0–

Federal Estate Taxes—Example 2

Because of the current exemptions, estate property ($11.4 million in 2019) can be conveyed tax-free to a beneficiary other than a spouse. The ability to shelter this amount of assets from tax has an important impact on estate planning. For example, in the preceding case, if the couple has already identified the recipient of the estate at the eventual death of the second spouse (their children, for example) and the first spouse does not use the exemption, then the portability election of the unused estate tax exemption allows for conveyance to the surviving spouse. The American Taxpayer Relief Act also provides this "portability," thus permitting the unused portion of a decedent's exemption to be utilized by the surviving spouse. The Tax Cuts and Jobs Act of 2017 preserves this portability. The second estate will then be smaller for subsequent taxation purposes if it exceeds the then-applicable exemption amount. Frequently, individuals establish a trust fund for the exemption amount, ensuring its proper distribution at the surviving spouse's eventual passing.

To illustrate, assume that the first spouse died in 2019. Assume also that the will that is written is identical to the preceding example except that only $2,600,000 is conveyed to the surviving spouse and the remaining $11.4 million is placed in a trust fund for the couple's children (a nondeductible amount for estate tax purposes). The estate tax return must now be adjusted to appear as follows:

Gross estate		$ 20,000,000
Funeral expenses	$ 100,000	
Administration expenses	200,000	
Debts	500,000	
Charity bequests	5,200,000	
Marital deduction	2,600,000	(8,600,000)
Taxable estate (conveyed to trust for surviving spouse)		11,400,000
Tax-free amount ($11,400,000 exemption)		(11,400,000)
Taxable estate		$ –0–

[16] Thomas J. Brzezenski, "New Era for Estate Planning," *Financial Planning,* July 1, 2001. The "death" was indeed short-lived as Congress acted in December 2010.

[17] Although not applicable in this case, surviving spouses have the right in many states to renounce the provisions of a will and take an established percentage (normally one-third or one-half) of the decedent's estate. Such laws protect surviving spouses from being disinherited and are referred to as *elective forced share provisions.*

Again, the estate pays no taxes, but only $2,600,000 is added to the surviving spouse's taxable estate rather than $14,000,000 as in the previous example. Thus, an eventual decrease in the couple's *total* estate has been accomplished. This is a particularly important consideration because, while the first spouse's exemption amount of $11.4 million is portable to the surviving spouse, such planning options are subject to the legislative whims of Congress.

To facilitate the necessity of planning, accountants and estate planners must understand the implications of how assets are titled as well. Legally, if a couple holds property as joint tenants or tenants by the entirety, the property passes automatically to the survivor at the death of the other party. Thus, if all property were held in one of these ways, the decedent would have no estate. However, if property is held by the couple as tenants in common, the portion the decedent owned is included in that person's estate and, up to the set limit, can be conveyed tax-free to a nonspouse beneficiary.

Other Approaches to Reducing Estate Taxes

One technique previously used by families with large fortunes to reduce estate taxes was to transfer assets to grandchildren and even great-grandchildren. This manner reduced the number of separate conveyances (each of which would have been subject to taxation at the top rate) from parent to child to grandchild. However, the government effectively eliminated the appeal of this option by establishing a generation-skipping transfer tax. Under this law, after an exemption, a flat tax was assessed on transfers by gift, bequest, or trust distribution to individuals two or more generations younger than the donors or decedents. (However, the exemption was unlimited for a transfer to a grandchild when the grandchild's parent was deceased and she was a lineal descendent of the transferor.)

With its passage of the Tax Relief, Unemployment Insurance Reauthorization, and Jobs Creation Act of 2010, Congress implemented a $5 million exemption per donor from the generation-skipping transfer tax (increased to $5.12 million for 2012 and $5.25 million for 2013). The American Taxpayer Relief Act of 2012 further indexed this amount to track the gift tax exemption prospectively. The Tax Cuts and Jobs Act of 2017 increased the exemption to $11.18 million in 2018, with the amount to increase each year until the end of 2025. The exemption is $11.4 million for 2019.

State Inheritance Taxes

States assess inheritance taxes on the right to receive property with the levy and all other regulations varying, as discussed earlier, based on state laws. However, the specifications of a will determine the actual impact on the individual beneficiaries. Many wills dictate that all inheritance tax payments are to be made from any residual cash amounts that the estate holds. Consequently, individuals receiving residual legacies are forced to bear the entire burden of this tax—although, presumably, that was the testator's desire.

If the will makes no provisions for state inheritance taxes (or if the decedent dies intestate), the amounts conveyed to each party must be reduced proportionately based on the fair value received. Thus, the recipient of land valued at $200,000 would have to contribute twice as much for inheritance taxes as a beneficiary collecting cash of $100,000. Decreasing a cash legacy to cover the cost of inheritance taxes creates little problem for the executor. However, a direct reduction of an estate asset such as land, buildings, or corporate stocks might be virtually impossible. Normally, the beneficiary in such cases is required to pay enough cash to satisfy the applicable inheritance tax. The estate planning process often establishes life insurance policies to provide cash for such payments. However, the ownership of such insurance may in turn result in the proceeds being subjected to the federal estate tax. Thus, the need for estate professionals such as CPAs is essential for planning.

Estate and Trust Income Taxes

Although all estates require time to be settled, the period can become quite lengthy if complex matters arise. From the date of death until ultimate resolution, an estate is viewed legally as a taxable entity and must file a federal tax return if gross income is $600 or more. The return is due by the 15th day of the fourth month following the close of the estate's taxable year. The calendar year or any other fiscal year may be chosen as the taxable year. In 2017, the Internal Revenue Service collected $29 billion of income taxes from estates and trusts.[18]

Applicable income tax rules for estates and trusts are generally the same as for individual taxpayers. Therefore, dividend, rental, interest, and other income earned by an estate in the period following death is taxable to the estate unless the income is of a type that is specifically nontaxable (such as municipal bond interest).

A $600 personal exemption is provided as a decrease to the taxable balance. In addition, a reduction is allowed for (1) any taxable income donated to charity and (2) any taxable income for the year distributed to a beneficiary. In 2019, federal tax rates are 10 percent on the first $2,600 of taxable income per year with various rates levied on any excess income earned up to $12,750. At a taxable income level more than $12,750, a 37 percent rate is incurred.

As an illustration, assume that, in 2019, an estate earned net rental income of $30,000 and dividend income of $10,000. The dividend income was distributed immediately to a beneficiary and was taxable income for that individual, and $7,400 of the rental income was given to charity. Estate income taxes for the year would be computed as follows:[19]

Rental income	$ 30,000
Dividend income	10,000
Total revenue	40,000
Exemption	(600)
Gift to charity	(7,400)
Distributed to beneficiary	(10,000)
Taxable income	$ 22,000
Income tax:	
10% of first $2,600	$ 260.00
24% of next $6,700 ($9,300 – $2,600)	1,608.00
35% of next $3,450 ($12,750 – $9,300)	1,207.50
37% of excess over $12,750 ($22,000 – $12,750)	3,422.50
	$6,498.00

LO 19-4

Understand and account for the distinction between principal and income in the context of estate and trust accounting.

The Distinction between Income and Principal

In many estates, the executor faces the problem of differentiating between income and principal transactions. For example, a will might state, "all income earned on my estate for five years after death is to go to my sister, with the estate then being conveyed to my children." The recipient of the income is known as an *income beneficiary,* whereas the party who ultimately receives the principal (also known as the *corpus*) is called a *remainderman.* As the fiduciary for the estate, the executor must ensure that all parties are treated fairly. Thus, if amounts are distributed incorrectly, the court can hold the executor legally liable.

The definitional difference between principal and income appears to pose little problem. The *estate* principal encompasses all of the decedent's assets at death; *income* is the earnings on these assets after death. However, some transactions are not easily categorized as either principal or income. As examples, consider these:

- Are funeral expenses charged to principal or income?
- Is the executor's fee charged to principal or income?
- Are dividends that are declared before death but received after death viewed as principal or income?
- If stocks are sold for a gain, is this gain viewed as income or an increase in principal?
- Are repairs to rental property considered a reduction of principal or of income?

[18] *IRS Data Book,* 2017, p. 14.

[19] As fiduciary entities, estates and trusts are taxed at the same income tax rates. Note that their top rate of 37 percent becomes applicable at a taxable income level of only $12,750. In comparison, for 2019, this same top income tax rate of 37 percent was not assessed for a single taxpayer, head of household, or married filing joint return until taxable income reached a much greater threshold ($612,350 for joint returns).

Clearly, the distinction between principal and income is not always obvious. For this reason, in writing a will, an individual may choose (and should be advised) to spell out the procedure by which principal and income are to be calculated. If defined in this manner, the executor merely has to follow these instructions.

In certain cases, the decedent will have provided no guidance as to the method by which transactions are to be classified. The executor must apply state laws to determine these principal and income figures. Many states have adopted the Revised Uniform Principal and Income Act as a standard for this purpose. However, some states have adopted modified versions of the Revised Uniform Principal and Income Act, and still others have created their own distinct laws. Generally accepted accounting principles are not applicable; the distinction between principal and income is defined solely by the decedent's intentions or by state laws.

Although differences exist because of unique state laws or the provisions of a will, the following transactions are normally viewed as adjustments (either increases or decreases) to the *principal of the estate:*

- Life insurance proceeds if the estate is named as the beneficiary.
- Dividends declared prior to death and any other income earned prior to death.
- Liquidating dividends even if declared after death.
- Debts incurred prior to death.
- Gains and losses on the sale of corporate securities or rental property.
- Major repairs (improvements) to rental property.
- Investment commissions and other costs.
- Funeral expenses.
- Homestead and family allowances.

The *income of the estate* includes all revenues and expenses recognized after the date of death. Within this calculation, the following items are normally included as reductions to income:

- Recurring taxes such as real and personal property taxes.
- Ordinary repair expenses.
- Water and other utility expenses.
- Insurance expenses.
- Other ordinary expenses necessary for the management and preservation of the estate.

Several costs such as the executor's fee, court costs, and attorneys' and accountants' charges must be apportioned between principal and interest as required by state law or in some fair manner, if such allocation has not been specified in the decedent's last will and testament.

Recording of the Transactions of an Estate

The accounting process that the executor of an estate uses is quite unique. *Because the probate court has given this individual responsibility over the assets of the estate, the accounting system is designed to demonstrate the proper management and distribution of these properties.* Thus, several features of estate accounting should be noted:

- All estate assets are recorded at fair value to indicate the amount and extent of the executor's accountability. Any assets subsequently discovered are disclosed separately so that these adjustments to the original estate value can be noted when reporting to the probate court. The ultimate disposition of all properties must be recorded to provide evidence that the executor's fiduciary responsibility has been fulfilled.
- Debts, taxes, and other obligations are recorded only at the date of payment. In effect, the system is designed to monitor the disposition of assets. Thus, claims are relevant to the accounting process only at the time that the assets are disbursed. Likewise, distributions of legacies are not entered into the records until actually conveyed. As mentioned earlier, devises of real property are often transferred by operation of law at death so that no accounting is necessary.

- Because of the importance of separately identifying income and principal transactions in many estates, the accounting system must always note whether income or principal is being affected. Quite frequently, the executor maintains two cash balances to assist in this process.

To illustrate, assume that James T. Wilson dies on April 1, 2019. The following valid will has these provisions:

I name Tim Hernly as executor of my estate.
I leave my house, furnishings, and artwork to my aunt, Ann Wilson.
I leave my investments in stocks to my uncle, Jack E. Wilson.
I leave my automobile and personal effects to my grandmother, Nancy Wilson.
I leave $38,000 in cash to my brother, Brian Wilson.
I leave any income earned on my estate to my niece, Karen Wilson.
All remaining property is to be placed in trust for my children.

Tim Hernly must (1) perform a search to discover all estate assets and (2) allow an adequate opportunity for every possible claim to be filed. The assets should be recorded immediately at fair value with the creation of the Estate Principal account. This total represents the amount of assets for which the executor is initially accountable. The following journal entry establishes the values for the assets owned by James T. Wilson at his death that have been found to date:

Cash—Principal	11,000	
Interest Receivable on Bonds	3,000	
Dividends Receivable on Stocks	4,000	
Life Insurance—Payable to Estate	40,000	
Residence	90,000	
Household Furnishings and Artwork	24,000	
Automobile	4,000	
Personal Effects	2,000	
Investment in Bonds	240,000	
Investment in Stocks	50,000	
Estate Principal		468,000

The following is a list of subsequent transactions incurred by this estate with each appropriate journal entry. Because estate income is to be conveyed to one party (Karen Wilson) but the remaining principal is to be placed in trust, careful distinction between these two elements is necessary.

Transaction 1

The executor paid funeral expenses of $4,000.

Funeral and Administrative Expenses	4,000	
Cash—Principal		4,000

Transaction 2

The life insurance policy payable to the estate (shown in the initial entry) is collected.

Cash—Principal	40,000	
Life Insurance—Payable to Estate		40,000

Transaction 3

The title to 4.0 acres of land is discovered in a safe deposit box. This asset was not included in the original inventory of estate property. An appraiser sets the value of the land at $22,000.

Land	22,000	
Assets Subsequently Discovered (Estate Principal)		22,000

Transaction 4

The executor receives claims totaling $24,000 for debts the decedent incurred *prior to death.* This amount includes medical expenses covering the decedent's last illness ($11,000), property taxes ($4,000), utilities ($1,000), personal income taxes ($5,000), and other miscellaneous expenses ($3,000). The executor pays all of these claims.

Debts of the Decedent	24,000	
Cash—Principal		24,000

Transaction 5

Interest of $8,000 is collected on the bonds held by the estate. Of this amount, $3,000 was earned prior to the decedent's death and was included as a receivable in the initial recording of the estate assets.

Cash—Principal	3,000	
Cash—Income	5,000	
Interest Receivable on Bonds		3,000
Estate Income		5,000

Transaction 6

Dividends of $6,000 are collected from the stocks held by the estate. Of this amount, $4,000 was declared prior to the decedent's death and was included as a receivable in the initial recording of the estate assets.

Cash—Principal	4,000	
Cash—Income	2,000	
Dividends Receivable on Stocks		4,000
Estate Income		2,000

Transaction 7

The executor now has a problem. The Cash—Principal balance is currently $30,000:

Beginning balance	$11,000
Funeral expenses	(4,000)
Life insurance	40,000
Payment of debts	(24,000)
Interest income	3,000
Dividends	4,000
Current balance	$30,000

However, the decedent bequeathed his brother, Brian Wilson, $38,000 in cash. This general legacy cannot be fulfilled without selling some property. Most assets have been promised as specific legacies and cannot, therefore, be used to satisfy a general legacy.

Discussion Question

IS THIS REALLY AN ASSET?

Robert Sweingart died during July 2019 at the age of 101. He had outlived many of his relatives, including the person named in his will as executor of his estate. Thus, the probate court selected the decedent's nephew, Timothy J. Lee, as administrator. Lee promptly began his duties including reading the will and taking an inventory of Sweingart's properties. Although the will had been written in 1984, Lee could see that most of the provisions would be easy to follow. Sweingart had made a number of specific and demonstrative legacies that could simply be conveyed to the beneficiaries. The will also included a $20,000 general legacy to a local church with a residual legacy to a well-known charity. Unfortunately, after all other legacies were distributed, the estate would have only about $14,000 cash.

One item in the will concerned the administrator. Sweingart had made the following specific legacy: "I leave my collection of my grandfather's letters which are priceless to me, to my cousin, William." Lee discovered the letters in a wall safe in Sweingart's home. About 40 letters existed, all in excellent condition. They were written by Sweingart's grandfather during the Civil War and described in vivid detail the Second Battle of Bull Run and the Battle of Gettysburg. Unfortunately, Lee could find no trace of a cousin named William. He apparently had died or vanished during the 35-year period since the will was written.

Lee took the letters to two different antique dealers. One stated, "A museum that maintains a Civil War collection would love to have these. They do a wonderful job of explaining history. But a museum would not pay for them. They have no real value since many letters written during this period still exist. I would recommend donating them to a museum."

The second dealer took a different position: "I think if you can find individuals who specialize in collecting Civil War memorabilia, they might be willing to pay a handsome price, especially if these letters help to fill out their collections. A lot of people in this country are fascinated by the Civil War. The number seems to grow each day. The letters are in great condition. It would take some investigation on your part, but they could be worth a small fortune."

Lee now has to prepare an inventory of his uncle's property for probate purposes. How should he report these letters? What should Lee do next with the letters in order to meet his fiduciary obligation(s) to the estate and the beneficiaries?

Two assets, though, are residual: the investment in bonds and the land that was discovered. The executor must sell enough of these properties to generate the remaining funding needed for the $38,000 conveyance. In this illustration, assume that the executor chooses to dispose of the land and negotiates a price of $24,000. Because a principal asset is being sold, the extra $2,000 received above the recorded value is considered an adjustment to principal rather than an increase in income. Similarly, if the asset sold at an amount below the appraised value of $22,000, this transaction would result in a reduction to principal.

Cash—Principal	24,000	
Land		22,000
Gain on Realization—Principal		2,000

Transaction 8

Fees of $1,000 charged for administering the affairs of the estate are paid. Of this amount, we assume that $200 is considered to be applicable to estate income.

Funeral and Administrative Expenses—Principal	800	
Expenses—Income	200	
Cash—Principal		800
Cash—Income		200

Transaction 9

On October 13, 2019, the house, furnishings, and artwork are given to the decedent's aunt (Ann); the stocks are transferred to the uncle (Jack); and the grandmother (Nancy) receives the decedent's automobile and personal effects.

Legacy—Ann Wilson (residence, furnishings, and artwork)	114,000	
Legacy—Jack E. Wilson (stocks)	50,000	
Legacy—Nancy Wilson (automobile and personal effects)	6,000	
Residence		90,000
Household Furnishings and Artwork		24,000
Investment in Stocks		50,000
Automobile		4,000
Personal Effects		2,000

LO 19-5

Describe the financial statements and journal entries utilized to account for estate and trust transactions.

Charge and Discharge Statement

As necessary, the executor files periodic reports with the probate court to disclose the progress being made in settling the estate. This report, which may vary from state to state, is generally referred to as a *charge and discharge statement.* If income and principal must be accounted for separately, the statement is prepared in two parts. For both principal and income, the statement should indicate the following:

1. The assets under the executor's control.
2. Disbursements made to date.
3. Any property still remaining.

Thus, the executor of James T. Wilson's estate can produce Exhibit 19.1 immediately after Transaction 9. (Transaction numbers are included in parentheses for clarification purposes.)

At this point in the illustration, only three transactions remain: distribution of the $38,000 cash to the decedent's brother, conveyance of the $6,800 cash generated as income since death to the niece, and establishment of the trust fund with the remaining principal. The trust fund will receive the $240,000 in bonds and the $15,200 in cash that is left in principal ($53,200 total less $38,000 paid to the brother).

Legacy—Brian Wilson	38,000	
Cash Principal		38,000
Distribution to Income Beneficiary—Karen Wilson	6,800	
Cash—Income		6,800
Principal Assets Transferred to Trustee	255,200	
Cash—Principal		15,200
Investment in Bonds		240,000

The executor would then prepare a final charge and discharge statement and then closing entries to signal the conclusion of the estate as a reporting entity.

EXHIBIT 19.1 Executor's Charge and Discharge Statement

ESTATE OF JAMES T. WILSON
Charge and Discharge Statement
April 1, 2019–October 13, 2019
Tim Hernly, Executor

As to Principal			
I charge myself with:			
Assets per original inventory			$468,000
Assets subsequently discovered: land (Trans. 3)			22,000
Gain on sale of land (Trans. 7)			2,000
Total charges			492,000
I credit myself with:			
Debts of decedent (Trans. 4):			
Medical expenses	$ 11,000		
Property taxes	4,000		
Utilities	1,000		
Personal income taxes	5,000		
Others	3,000	$ 24,000	
Funeral and administrative expenses (Trans. 1 and 8)		4,800	
Legacies distributed (Trans. 9):			
Ann Wilson (house, furnishings, and artwork)	114,000		
Jack E. Wilson (stocks)	50,000		
Nancy Wilson (automobile and personal effects)	6,000	170,000	
Total credits			198,800
Estate principal			$293,200
Estate principal:			
Cash			$ 53,200
Investment in bonds			240,000
Estate principal			$293,200
As to Income			
I charge myself with:			
Interest income (Trans. 5)			$ 5,000
Dividend income (Trans. 6)			2,000
Total charges			7,000
I credit myself with:			
Administrative expenses charged to income (Trans. 8)			200
Balance as to income			$ 6,800
Balance as to income:			
Cash			$ 6,800

LO 19-6

Describe various trusts, their proper use, and accounting for activities.

Accounting for a Trust

A trust is created by the conveyance of assets to a fiduciary (or trustee) who manages the assets and ultimately disposes of them to one or more beneficiaries. The trustee may be an individual or an organization such as a bank or other financial institution. Over the years, trust funds have become quite popular in this country for a number of reasons. Often they are established to reduce the size of a person's taxable estate and, thus, the amount of estate taxes that must eventually be paid. As one financial adviser has stated, "Who needs to establish a trust? You do, and so does your spouse. There may be several good reasons, but start with this: If you don't set up trusts, your heirs may pay hundreds of thousands of dollars in unnecessary estate taxes."[20]

[20] Jeff Burger, "Which Trust Is Best for Your Family?" *Medical Economics,* August 1, 1988, p. 141.

Estate taxes are not the only reason for establishing a trust. People form trust funds to protect assets and ensure that the eventual use of these assets is as intended. Trusts can also result from the provisions of a will, specified by the decedent as a means of guiding the distribution of estate property. In legal terms, an *inter vivos trust* is one started by a living individual, whereas a *testamentary trust* is created by a will.

Frequently, the *trustor* or *settlor* or *grantor* (the person who funds the trust) will believe that a chosen trustee is simply better suited to manage complicated investments than is the beneficiary. A young child, for example, is not capable of directing the use of a large sum of money. The trustor may have the same opinion of an individual who possesses little business expertise. Likewise, the creation of a trust for the benefit of a person with a mental or severe physical handicap might be considered a wise decision.

During recent years, one specific type of trust, a *revocable living trust,* has become especially popular and controversial. The trustor usually manages the fund and receives most, if not all, of the income until death. After that time, future income and possibly principal payments are made to one or more previously named beneficiaries. Because the trust is revocable, the trustor can change these beneficiaries or other terms of the trust at any time.

> You want to leave knowing your loved ones have the best financial breaks possible. That's why the idea of a revocable living trust may sound so promising. During your lifetime, you turn over all assets to a trust. But you act as your own trustee, so you determine how the assets will be managed and distributed. Then, happy in the knowledge that you can change the trust at any time, you have the joy of knowing you're setting up a financial plan for your life and after death.[21]

Revocable living trusts offer several significant advantages that appeal to certain individuals. First, this type of trust avoids the delay and expense of probate. At the trustor's death, the trust continues and makes future payments as defined in the trust agreement. In some states, this advantage can be quite important, but in others, the cost of establishing the trust may be more expensive than the potential probate costs. The taxable income of the revocable living trust is included in the grantor's individual income tax return while that person remains alive. It is not taxed within a fiduciary income tax return until after the grantor's death.

Second, conveyance of assets through a trust can be made without publicity, whereas a will is a public document. Thus, anyone who values privacy may want to consider the revocable living trust. The entertainer Bing Crosby, for example, set up such a trust so that no outsider would know how his estate was distributed.[22]

Although the number of other types of trusts is quite large,[23] several of the more common trusts that have been utilized and that clients are likely to have established include the following:

- *Credit shelter trust* (also known as a *bypass trust* or *family trust*). This trust is designed for couples. Each spouse agrees to transfer at death an amount of up to the tax-free exclusion ($11.4 million in 2019) to a trust fund for the benefit of the other. Thus, the income that these funds generate goes to the surviving spouse, but at the time of this second individual's subsequent death, the principal is conveyed to a different beneficiary. As discussed in the previous section, this arrangement can be used to reduce the estate of the surviving spouse and, therefore, the amount of estate taxes paid by the couple. With portability of the $11.4 million exemption, the use of credit shelter trusts will be significantly reduced.

  > If your estate is large enough to be threatened by the federal estate tax, you can incorporate provisions to soften the blow. This year [2003], federal law permits each person to leave $1 million in assets tax-free—in addition to the unlimited amount that can go to a surviving spouse. But leaving everything to a spouse can be a costly mistake if it inflates the survivor's estate to the level at which it may be hit by the tax. To avoid this, couples

[21] Estelle Jackson, "Living Trust May Sound Promising," *Richmond Times–Dispatch,* October 13, 1991, p. C1.

[22] Ibid., p. C5.

[23] The cost of establishing and maintaining trusts can be significant. Therefore, use of these trusts may be limited to taxpayers of substantial means.

> should make sure each owns enough individually to take advantage of the $1 million tax-free allowance, even if it means splitting jointly owned assets. Then, both husband and wife could include in their wills a trust (called a bypass or credit shelter trust) to hold $1 million, from which the survivor would get all the income and possibly some principal during his or her lifetime, with the balance going to the children upon the spouse's death. That $1 million would go to the kids tax-free, rather than being included—and possibly taxed—in the surviving spouse's estate.[24]

- *Qualified terminable interest property trust* (known as a *QTIP trust*). Individuals frequently create a QTIP trust to serve as a credit shelter trust. They convey property to the trust and specify that the income, and possibly a portion of the principal, be paid to the surviving spouse (or other beneficiary). At a specified time, the trust conveys the remainder to a designated party. Such trusts are popular because they provide the spouse a steady income, but the trustee can guard the principal and then convey it at a later date to the individual's children or other designated parties. However, no trust exists without some potential problems:

> During the spouse's lifetime, no one else—not even the children—can benefit from the QTIP trust. However, this can mean years of potential conflict as the children wait for their inheritance. To minimize this potential problem, it often makes sense to set up another trust for the benefit of the children. This is particularly so if a new spouse (stepparent) is close in age to your children.[25]

- *Charitable remainder trust.* All income is paid to one or more beneficiaries identified by the trustor. After a period of time (or at the death of the beneficiaries), the principal is given to a stated charity. Thus, the trustor is guaranteeing a steady income to the intended parties while still making a gift to a charitable organization. These trusts are especially popular if a taxpayer holds property that has appreciated greatly (such as real estate or stocks) that is to be liquidated. By conveying it to the trust prior to liquidation, the sale is viewed as that of the charity and is, hence, nontaxable. Thus, tax on the gain is avoided, and significantly more money remains available to generate future income for the beneficiaries (possibly the original donor). "This trust lets you leave assets to your favored charity, get a tax break, but retain income for life."[26]
- *Charitable lead trust.* This trust is the reverse of a charitable remainder trust. Income from the trust fund goes to benefit a charity for a specified time with the remaining principal then going to a different beneficiary. For example, a charity might receive the income from trust assets until the donor's children reach their 21st birthdays.

> Jacqueline Kennedy Onassis used this technique and ended up sheltering roughly 90 percent of the trust assets from estate taxes. Setup and operating costs, however, preclude the use of this type of trust unless the assets involved are substantial. As such this is a vehicle for the very wealthy, allowing them to keep an asset in the family but greatly reducing the cost of passing it on.[27]

- *Grantor retained annuity trusts* (known as *GRATs*). The trustor maintains the right to collect fixed payments from the trust fund while giving the principal to a beneficiary after a stated time or at the trustor's death. For example, the trustor might retain the right to receive an amount equal to 7 percent of the initial investment annually with any remaining balance of the trust fund to go to his or her children at death. Because the beneficiary will not receive the residual amount for years, a current value is computed for gift tax purposes. Depending on (1) the length of time before final distribution to the beneficiary, (2) the assumed rate of income, and (3) the amounts to be distributed periodically to the trustor,

[24] Josephine Rossi, "Your Will Be Done," *Kiplinger's Personal Finance,* January 2003. By 2009, this $1 million amount had grown to $3.5 million and increased to $11.4 million in 2019. With portability of the exemptions, this planning strategy is significant.

[25] Philip Maynard, "A QTIP Protects the Family," *CreativeLiving Magazine,* Autumn 2001.

[26] Lynn Asinof, "Estate-Planning Techniques for the Rich," *The Wall Street Journal,* January 11, 1995, p. C1.

[27] Ibid., p. C15.

this value is often quite small so that the gift tax is reduced or eliminated entirely. However, GRATs can have certain risks.

> When setting up a GRAT, remember that the annuity you establish at its outset could drain the trust if the expected growth doesn't materialize. Then you will have paid taxes and legal costs . . . and will have left little to your heirs. Equally important, the grantor must outlive the trust. If you die before the GRAT ends, the assets will revert to your estate.[28]

- *Minor's Section 2503(c) trust.* Established for a minor, this trust fund usually is designed to receive a tax-free gift of up to $15,000 each year ($30,000 if the transfer is made by a married couple). Over a period of time, especially if enough beneficiaries are available, this trust can remove a significant amount of assets from a person's estate. The change in the gift tax laws and the expansion of the estate exemption may make this trust less attractive.
- *Spendthrift trust.* This trust is established so that the beneficiary cannot transfer or assign any unreceived payments. The purpose of such trusts is to prevent the beneficiary from squandering the assets the trust fund is holding or the beneficiary's creditors from reaching the assets. This type of trust is particularly useful to protect irresponsible beneficiaries: for example, children, and beneficiaries whose former spouses maintain legal actions against them.
- *Irrevocable life insurance trust.* With this trust, the donor contributes money to buy life insurance on the donor. If a married couple is creating the trust, usually the life insurance policy is designed to pay the proceeds only after the second spouse dies. The proceeds are not part of the estate, and the beneficiary can use the cash to pay estate and inheritance taxes.
- *Qualified personal resident trust (QPRT).* The donor gives his or her home to the trust but retains the right to live in the house for a period of time rent-free. This removes what is often an individual's most valuable asset from the estate. This type of trust has characteristics similar to a GRAT.

> The term of the trust can be as short or as long as desired. The longer the term the lower the value of the gift. If the grantor dies before the term of the trust expires, however, the property will revert back to the estate of the deceased and be subject to estate taxes at its current value. Therefore, a term should be picked that the grantor believes he or she will outlive for the benefits of the QPRT to be effective.[29]

As these examples indicate, many trust funds generate income for one or more beneficiaries (known as *life tenants* if the income is to be conveyed until the person dies). At death or the end of a specified period, the remaining principal is transferred to a different beneficiary (a *remainderman*). Therefore, as with estates, differentiating between principal and income is ultimately important in accounting for trust funds. This distinction is especially significant because trusts frequently exist for decades and can control and generate enormous amounts of assets.

The reporting function is also important because of the trustee's legal responsibilities. This fiduciary is charged with the wise use of all funds and may be sued by the beneficiaries if actions are considered to be unnecessarily risky or in contradiction to the terms of the trust arrangement. To avoid potential legal problems, the trustee is normally called on to exercise reasonable and prudent care in managing the assets of the fund.

Recordkeeping for a Trust Fund

Trust accounting is quite similar to the procedures demonstrated previously for an estate. However, because many different types of trusts can be created and an extended time period might be involved, the accounting process may become more complex than that for an estate.

[28] Pam Black, "A GRAT Can Be Great for Saving Your Kids a Bundle," *BusinessWeek*, March 1, 1999, p. 116.

[29] Michael Mingione, "Trust Your House," *The CPA Journal*, September 1996, p. 40.

As an example, an apartment house or a significant portion of a business could be placed in a trust for 20 years or longer. Thus, the possible range of transactions to be recorded becomes quite broad. In such cases, the fiduciary often establishes two separate sets of accounts, one for principal and one for income. As an alternative, the fiduciary could utilize a single set of records with the individual accounts identified as to income or principal.

In the same manner as an estate, the trust agreement should specify the distinction between transactions to be recorded as income and those to be recorded as principal. If the agreement is silent or if a transaction that is not covered by the agreement is incurred, state laws apply to delineate the accounting. Generally accepted accounting principles usually are not considered appropriate. For example, trusts utilize the cash method rather than accrual accounting in recording most transactions. Although a definitive set of rules is not possible, the following list indicates the typical division of principal and income transactions:

Adjustments to the Trust's Principal

Investment costs and commissions.
Income taxes on gains added to the principal.
Costs of preparing property for rent or sale.
Extraordinary repairs (improvements).

Adjustments to the Trust's Income

Rent expense.
Lease cancellation fees.
Interest expense.
Insurance expense.
Income taxes on trust income.
Property taxes.

Trustee fees and the cost of periodic reporting (accountant and legal fees) must be allocated between trust income and principal. This allocation is often based on the value of assets within each (principal/income) category.

Accounting for the Activities of a Trust

An *inter vivos* trust reports on an annual basis (often more frequently) to all income and principal beneficiaries. However, testamentary trusts come under the jurisdiction of the courts so that additional reporting regularly becomes necessary. Normally, a statement resembling the charge and discharge statement of an estate is adequate for these purposes. Two accounts, Trust Principal and Trust Income, monitor changes that occur. For a testamentary trust, the opening principal balance is the fair value used by the executor for estate tax purposes.

To illustrate, assume that the following events occur in connection with the creation of a charitable remainder trust. The will of Samuel Statler created a trust with the income earned each year to go to his niece for 10 years and the principal then conveyed to a local university (the charity).

1. Cash of $80,000 and stocks (that originally cost $39,000 but are now worth $47,000) are transferred from the estate to the First National Bank of Michigan because this organization has agreed to serve as trustee for these funds.
2. The trustee invested cash of $76,000 in bonds paying 11 percent annual cash interest.
3. Dividends of $6,000 on the stocks are collected, and interest of $7,000 is received on the bonds. No receivables had been included in the estate for these amounts.
4. At the end of the year, an additional $3,000 in interest is due on the bonds.
5. As trustee, the bank charges $2,000 for services rendered for the year. Statler's will provided that such fees should be allocated equally between principal and income.
6. The niece is paid the appropriate amount of money from the trust fund.

As the trustee, the bank should record these transactions as follows:

1. Cash—Principal	80,000	
Investment in Stocks	47,000	
Trust Principal		127,000
To record trust assets at the fair market value figure used for estate tax purposes.		
2. Investment in Bonds	76,000	
Cash—Principal		76,000
To record acquisition of bonds using cash in trust fund.		
3. Cash—Income	13,000	
Trust—Income		13,000
To record dividends and interest collected.		
4. No entry is recorded. These earnings cannot be paid to the income beneficiary until collected so that accrual provides no benefit. Therefore, the trustee uses a cash basis system rather than accrual accounting.		
5. Trustee Expense—Income	1,000	
Trustee Expense—Principal	1,000	
Cash—Income		1,000
Cash—Principal		1,000
To allocate the trustee's fees evenly between principal and income.		
6. Equity in Income: Beneficiary	12,000	
Cash—Income		12,000
To record yearly payment made to income beneficiary. Amount is computed as the total of the dividends and interest of $13,000 less expenses of $1,000.		

Summary

1. An *estate* is the legal entity that holds title to a decedent's property until a final settlement and distribution can be made. State laws, known as *probate laws,* govern this process. These laws become particularly significant if the decedent has died intestate (without a will).
2. A decedent's will should name an executor to oversee the estate. If it does not, the probate court selects an administrator. The executor or administrator takes possession of all properties, settles valid claims, files tax returns, pays taxes due, and distributes any remaining assets according to the provisions of the decedent's will or state inheritance laws. The executor must issue a public notice so that all creditors have adequate opportunity to file a claim against the estate. Prior to paying these claims, a homestead allowance and a family allowance are provided to the members of the decedent's immediate family. Claims are then ranked in order of priority to indicate the payment schedule if existing funds prove to be insufficient. For example, administrative expenses and funeral expenses are at the top of this priority listing.
3. *Devises* are gifts of real property; *legacies* (or *bequests*) are gifts of personal property. Legacies can be classified legally as specific, demonstrative, general, or residual, depending on the type of property and the identity of the source. If available funds are insufficient to fulfill all legacies, the process of abatement is applied to determine the final allocations. After residual legacies have been reduced to zero, general legacies are decreased if necessary. Demonstrative legacies are reduced next, followed by specific legacies.
4. Federal estate taxes are assessed on the value of nonexempt estate property. Reductions in the total value of an estate are allowed for funeral and administrative expenses as well as for liabilities, charitable gifts, and all property conveyed to a spouse. For estate tax purposes, the tax code provides a tax-free exemption amount of $5.0 million in 2011, $5.12 million in 2012, $5.25 million in 2013, $5.34 million in 2014, $5.43 million in 2015, $5.45 million in 2016, $5.49 million in 2017, $11.18 million in 2018, and $11.4 million in 2019. Any unused exemption may be utilized by a surviving spouse, thus making the exemption portable. The same exemption amount applies to the generation-skipping tax. Individuals in 2019 have an $11.4 million lifetime gift exclusion, in addition to a $15,000 per donee annual exclusion.
5. The distinction between income and principal for both estates and trusts is frequently an important issue. Income may be assigned to one party with the principal eventually going to a different beneficiary. Such arrangements are especially common in trust funds such as charitable remainder trusts. The decedent (for an estate) or the trustor (for a trust) should have identified the method of

classification to be used for complicated transactions. If no guidance is provided, state laws apply. For example, major repairs and investment costs usually are considered reductions in principal, whereas expenses such as property taxes and ordinary repairs are charged to income. The bookkeeping procedures for estates and trusts are designed to separate and then reflect the transactions affecting principal and income.

6. To provide evidence of the proper handling of an estate or trust, the fiduciary produces a charge and discharge statement. This statement reports the assets over which the representative has been given responsibility. The statement also indicates all disbursements of assets and the property remaining at the current time. Separate reports are prepared for income and principal.

Comprehensive Illustration

Problem

(*Estimated Time: 1 Hour*)

Part A

Upon her death, Marie Peterson's will contained the following provisions:

1. I leave my home, personal effects, and stock investments to my husband, Erik.
2. I leave my savings account at State Bank, up to a total of $20,000, to my oldest son, Zach.
3. I leave $5,000 to my niece, Nikki.
4. I leave all remaining assets, including my valuable coin collection, to be placed in trust and managed by Kevin Leahy, if he is willing and able to do so. If not, then I request that a financial institution be engaged to manage such assets. The income from these assets shall be utilized for the benefit of my husband, Erik. At his death, the principal of this trust shall be distributed to St. Patrick's Church, Elkhorn, Wisconsin.
5. In the event that it is necessary for a custodian or guardian to be appointed for any of my children, I request that Mary Breese be appointed in this capacity.
6. I appoint my sister Jodie to manage my estate.

Jodie has now paid all taxes and other claims, and the following assets remain; their fair value(s) follow:

Home	$400,000
Personal effects	100,000
Stock investments	50,000
Bond investments	75,000
State Bank savings account	10,000
Cash	60,000
Coin collection	Disposed of prior to death

Required

a. Identify the following:

1. Testatrix
2. Trustor
3. Life tenant
4. Remainderman
5. Beneficiaries
6. Devise
7. General legacy
8. Demonstrative legacy
9. Trustee
10. Executrix

b. Answer the following questions:

1. Is this trust an *inter vivos* trust or a testamentary trust?
2. What specific type of trust has been created?
3. How will Marie Peterson's assets be distributed?

Part B

Upon his death on July 4, 2019, Brian Ulvog's will contained the following provisions:

1. I leave my home and personal effects to my wife, Linny.
2. I leave $20,000 cash to my son, Jake.
3. I leave all my investments to Marquette University.
4. I leave all income earned on my investments but not collected prior to death, and all income earned subsequent to death, to Marquette University.
5. I leave the remainder of my estate to Jamie O'Brien.
6. I appoint Jodie Reichel to be the executrix of my estate.

The executrix, Jodie Reichel, prepares an inventory and identifies the assets. Each asset's fair value, as determined by a qualified appraiser, follows:

Cash	$400,000
Home	500,000
Personal effects	75,000
Stock investments	50,000
Bond investments	70,000
Rental building	200,000
Coin collection	90,000
Dividends receivable	1,000
Interest receivable	2,000
Rent receivable	4,000

The executrix paid the following claims against the estate:

Funeral expenses	$ 20,000
Appraisal expenses	15,000
Executor fees	25,000
Medical expenses	10,000
Debts	125,000

The estate received the following cash payments:

Dividends	$ 2,000
Interest	3,000
Rent	7,000
Sale of coin collection	92,000

Assume that today is December 31, 2019, and that the executrix has completed the distributions to Linny and Jake but not to any other beneficiary.

Required

Prepare a charge and discharge statement for Brian's estate.

Solution

Part A

Prepare a charge and discharge statement for Brian's estate.

a. 1. The testatrix, a female dying with a valid will, is Marie Peterson.

2. The trustor is also Marie Peterson, the person creating the trust.
3. The life tenant is Erik (the testatrix's husband), the person possessing an interest in assets, or their income, during a measuring life.
4. The remainderman is St. Patrick's Church, the legal person receiving the *remainder* of assets after the life tenant's interest terminates.
5. The beneficiaries include all persons receiving *benefits* from the testatrix via her testamentary documents: Erik, Zach, Nikki, and St. Patrick's Church.

6. The devise includes Ms. Peterson's home (real estate), which the executrix will transfer to her husband, Erik.
7. The general legacy, the transfer not originating from a designated fund, includes the transfer of $5,000 to Nikki.
8. The demonstrative legacy, the testamentary transfer derived from a specific source, includes Zach's interest in his mother's savings account.
9. The trustee, Kevin Leahy, is the person or entity managing trust assets for the benefit of the trust beneficiaries. If Kevin is unable or unwilling to serve as the trustee, a court may appoint a financial institution as an alternate or successor trustee.
10. The executrix is Jodie, the female handling the testatrix's estate.

b. 1. Because she created the trust through the provisions of her will, Marie Peterson's trust is a *testamentary trust.*

2. Marie Peterson's trust is an example of a *charitable remainder trust.* This type of trust provides earnings for a specific period of time to a specific income beneficiary, the life tenant (Erik). After the specific time, the remainder is transferred to a charitable organization (St. Patrick's Church).
3. Jodie, the executrix, should distribute the estate assets as follows:
   - Erik—Home ($400,000); personal effects ($100,000); and stock investments ($50,000).
   - Zach—State Bank savings account ($10,000). Note that because the account is not large enough to satisfy the upper limit of this demonstrative legacy, Zach will not receive the maximum amount specified by his mother.
   - Nikki—Cash ($5,000).
   - Trustee—Bond Investments ($75,000); and balance of cash ($55,000).

Part B

ESTATE OF BRIAN ULVOG
Charge and Discharge Statement
July 4, 2019–December 31, 2019
Jodie Reichel, Executrix

As to Principal

I charge myself with:			
Assets per original inventory			$1,392,000
Gain on sale of coin collection			2,000
Total charges			1,394,000
I credit myself with:			
Decedent's debts:			
Medical expenses	$ 10,000		
Other debts	125,000	$135,000	
Funeral and administrative expenses (20,000 + 15,000 + 25,000)		60,000	
Devises and legacies distributed:			
Linny (home and personal effects)	575,000		
Jake	20,000	595,000	
Total credits			790,000
Estate principal			$ 604,000
Estate principal:			
Cash			$ 284,000
Investments:			
Stocks			50,000
Bonds			70,000
Rental building			200,000
Estate principal			$ 604,000
Cash balance analysis:			
Beginning cash			$ 400,000

(Continued)

(Continued)

Sale of coin collection	92,000
Collection of interest	2,000
Collection of dividend	1,000
Collection of rent.	4,000
Payment of funeral expense	(20,000)
Payment of appraisal expense	(15,000)
Payment of executor fees	(25,000)
Payment of medical expenses	(10,000)
Payment of other debts	(125,000)
Legacy distribution to Jake	(20,000)
Cash balance	$ 284,000

As to Income

I charge myself with:	
Dividend income (gross less receivable amount at date of death)	$ 1,000
Interest income (gross less receivable amount at date of death)	1,000
Rent income (gross less receivable amount at date of death)	3,000
Balance as to income	$ 5,000
Balance as to income	
Cash	$ 5,000

Questions

1. Distinguish between *testate* and *intestate*.
2. If a person dies without leaving a valid will, how is the distribution of property regulated?
3. What are probate laws?
4. What are the objectives of probate laws?
5. What are the responsibilities of the executor of an estate?
6. At what value are the assets within an estate reported?
7. If an asset of an estate has no readily ascertainable fair value, how should it be presented/valued on the charge/discharge statement?
8. How does an executor discover the claims against an estate?
9. What claims against an estate have priority?
10. What are homestead and family allowances?
11. What are the differences between a devise, a legacy, and a bequest?
12. Describe the four types of legacies, and give examples of each.
13. What is the purpose of the process of abatement? How does the executor of an estate utilize this process?
14. How is the federal estate tax computed?
15. What was the impact of the Tax Cuts and Jobs Act of 2017 on the conveyance of property?
16. What is a taxable gift?
17. Why is the establishment of a credit shelter trust fund considered a good estate planning technique?
18. What deductions are allowed in computing estate income taxes?
19. Other than financial considerations, why should individuals consider preparing a valid will?
20. In accounting for an estate or trust, how is the distinction between principal and income determined?
21. What transactions are normally viewed as changes in the principal of an estate? What transactions are normally viewed as changes in the income of an estate?
22. What is the alternate date for valuing the assets of an estate? When should this alternate date be used?
23. In the initial accounting for an estate, why does the executor record only the assets?
24. What is the purpose of the charge and discharge statement that the executor of an estate issues?
25. What is a trust fund?
26. Why have trust funds become especially popular in recent years?

27. What is an *inter vivos* trust?
28. What is a testamentary trust?
29. What are QTIP trusts, GRATs, and charitable remainder trusts?
30. Why is the distinction between principal and income so important in accounting for most trusts?

Problems

LO 19-1

1. Which of the following is *not* a true statement?
   a. *Testate* refers to a person having a valid will.
   b. The laws of descent convey personal property if an individual dies without a valid will.
   c. *Intestate* refers to a person having no valid will.
   d. A specific legacy is a gift of personal property that is specifically identified.

LO 19-1

2. Why might real estate be omitted from an inventory of estate property?
   a. Real estate is subject to a separate inheritance tax.
   b. State laws prohibit real property from being conveyed by an estate.
   c. State laws require a separate listing of all real estate.
   d. In some states, depending on the ownership, real estate is considered to be conveyed directly to a beneficiary at the time of death.

LO 19-1

3. What is the purpose of the laws of distribution?
   a. To guide the distribution of personal property when an individual dies without a will.
   b. To verify the legality of a will, especially an oral will.
   c. To guide the distribution of real property when an individual dies without a will.
   d. To outline the functions of the executor of an estate.

LO 19-4

4. A deceased individual owned a bond. Which of the following is included in the estate principal?
   a. All interest collected prior to distributing the bonds to a beneficiary is considered part of the estate principal.
   b. Only the first cash payment after death is included in the estate principal.
   c. Interest that was not collected prior to death is excluded from the estate principal.
   d. Interest earned prior to death is considered part of the estate principal even if received after death.

LO 19-1

5. Which of the following is *not* a goal of probate laws?
   a. To gather and preserve all of the decedent's property.
   b. To ensure that each individual produces a valid will.
   c. To discover the decedent's intent for property held at death and then to follow those wishes.
   d. To carry out an orderly and fair settlement of all debts and distribution of property.

LO 19-1

6. How are claims against a decedent's estate discovered by an executor?
   a. Public notice must be printed in an appropriate newspaper to alert all possible claimants.
   b. The executor waits for nine months until all possible bills have been received.
   c. The executor directly contacts all companies that the decedent did business with.
   d. Claims the estate is to pay are limited to all of the bills received but not paid prior to the date of death.

LO 19-1

7. Why are claims against an estate put into an order of priority?
   a. To help the executor determine the due date for each claim
   b. To determine which claims are to be paid if funds are insufficient to pay all claims
   c. To assist in determining which specific assets are to be used to satisfy these claims
   d. To list the claims in order of age so that the oldest can be paid first

LO 19-1

8. Which of the following claims against an estate does *not* have priority?
   a. Funeral expenses because the amounts incurred are usually at the discretion of family members
   b. Medical expenses associated with the decedent's last illness
   c. The costs of administering the estate
   d. Unpaid rent on the decedent's home if not paid for the three months immediately prior to death

LO 19-2

9. How does a devise differ from a legacy?
   a. A devise is a gift of money, and a legacy is a nonmonetary gift.
   b. A devise is a gift to an individual, and a legacy is a gift to a charity or other organization.

c. A devise is a gift of real property, and a legacy is a gift of personal property.
d. A devise is a gift made prior to death, and a legacy is a gift made at death.

LO 19-1

10. What is the homestead allowance?
 a. A reduction of $20,000 in estate assets prior to computing the amount of federal estate taxes
 b. The amount of property conveyed in a will to a surviving spouse
 c. An allotment from an estate to a surviving spouse and/or minor and dependent children before any claims are paid
 d. A decrease in the value of property on which state inheritance taxes are assessed, with the reduction is equal to the value of property conveyed to a surviving spouse

LO 19-2

11. Which of the following is a specific legacy?
 a. The gift of all remaining estate property to a charity
 b. The gift of $44,000 cash from a specified source
 c. The gift of $44,000 cash
 d. The gift of 1,000 shares of stock in IBM

LO 19-2

12. A will has the following statement: "I leave $20,000 cash from my savings account in the Central Fidelity Bank to my sister, Angela." This gift is an example of
 a. A residual legacy.
 b. A general legacy.
 c. A demonstrative legacy.
 d. A specific legacy.

LO 19-2

13. What is the objective of the process of abatement?
 a. To give legal structure to the reductions that must be made if an estate has insufficient assets to satisfy all legacies
 b. To ensure that all property distributions take place in a timely manner
 c. To provide adequate compensation for the estate executor and any appraisers or other experts that must be hired
 d. To ensure that all legacies are distributed to the appropriate party as specified by the decedent's will or state laws

LO 19-3

14. For estate tax purposes, what date is used for valuation purposes?
 a. Property is always valued at the date of death.
 b. Property is always valued at the date of distribution.
 c. Property is valued at the date of death unless the alternate date, which is the date of distribution or six months after death—whichever comes first—is selected.
 d. Property is valued at the date of death, although a reduction is allowed if the value declines within one year of death.

LO 19-3

15. Which of the following is true concerning the Tax Cuts and Jobs Act of 2017?
 a. This tax law leads to the immediate elimination of the federal estate tax.
 b. This tax law leads to the immediate elimination of the federal gift tax.
 c. This tax law provides for an $11.4 million tax-free exemption, as a result of indexing, for estates created in 2019.
 d. This tax law leads to the immediate elimination of the generation-skipping tax.

LO 19-3

16. In computing federal estate taxes, deductions from an estate's value are allowed for all of the following *except*
 a. Charitable bequests.
 b. Losses on the disposal of investments.
 c. Funeral expenses.
 d. Debts of the decedent.

LO 19-3

17. The following unmarried individuals died in 2019. The estate of John Lexington has a taxable value of $4,590,000. The estate of Dorothy Alexander has a taxable value of $6.9 million. The estate of Scotty Fitzgerald has a taxable value of $11.6 million. None of these individuals made any taxable gifts during their lifetimes. Which of the following statements is true?
 a. Only Fitzgerald's estate will have to pay federal estate taxes.
 b. All three of the estates will have to pay federal estate taxes.

c. None of these estates are large enough to necessitate the payment of estate taxes.

d. Only the estates of Alexander and Fitzgerald are large enough to necessitate the payment of estate taxes.

LO 19-3

18. Sally Anne Williams died on January 1, 2019. All of her property was conveyed to several relatives on April 1, 2019. For federal estate tax purposes, the executor chose the alternate valuation date. On what date was the value of the property determined?

a. January 1, 2019

b. April 1, 2019

c. July 1, 2019

d. December 31, 2019

LO 19-3

19. M. Wilson Waltman died on January 1, 2019. All of his property was conveyed to beneficiaries on October 1, 2019. For federal estate tax purposes, the executor chose the alternate valuation date. On what date was the value of the property determined?

a. January 1, 2019

b. July 1, 2019

c. October 1, 2019

d. December 31, 2019

LO 19-3

20. Which of the following is *not* true concerning gift taxes?

a. Gift taxes are not abolished but a lifetime exclusion of $11.4 million is available in 2019.

b. The Tax Cuts and Jobs Act of 2017 will eventually eliminate the federal gift tax.

c. Historically, gift taxes and estate taxes have been linked through a unified transfer credit.

d. Gift taxes are different from generation-skipping taxes.

LO 19-6

21. A married couple have written a will that leaves part of their money to a trust fund. The income from this trust will benefit the surviving spouse until death, with the principal then going to their children. Why was the trust fund created?

a. To reduce the estate of the surviving spouse and, thus, decrease the total amount of estate taxes to be paid by the couple

b. To ensure that the surviving spouse is protected from lawsuits filed by the couple's children

c. To give the surviving spouse discretion over the ultimate use of these funds

d. To maximize the earning potential of the money because trust funds generate more income than other investments

LO 19-3

22. The executor of an estate is filing an income tax return for the current period. Revenues of $25,000 have been earned. Which of the following is *not* a deduction allowed in computing taxable income?

a. Income distributed to a beneficiary

b. Funeral expenses

c. A personal exemption

d. Charitable donations

LO 19-4

23. What is a remainderman?

a. A beneficiary that receives the principal left in an estate or trust after a specified time

b. The beneficiary of the decedent's life insurance policy

c. An executor or administrator after an estate has been completely settled

d. If a legacy is given to a group of people, the remainderman is the last of the individuals to die

LO 19-4

24. In an estate, which of the following is charged to income rather than to principal?

a. Funeral expenses

b. Investment costs

c. Property taxes

d. Losses on the sale of investments

LO 19-5

25. In recording the transactions of an estate, when are liabilities recorded?

a. When incurred

b. At the date of death

c. When the executor takes responsibility for the estate

d. When paid

LO 19-6

26. What is the difference between a testamentary trust and an *inter vivos* trust?

a. A testamentary trust conveys money to a charity; an *inter vivos* trust conveys money to individuals.

b. A testamentary trust is created by a will; an *inter vivos* trust is created by a living individual.

c. A testamentary trust conveys income to one party and the principal to another; an *inter vivos* trust conveys all monies to the same party.

d. A testamentary trust ceases after a specified period of time; an *inter vivos* trust is assumed to be permanent.

LO 19-6

27. Which of the following is a charitable lead trust?

a. The income of the trust fund goes to an individual until death, at which time the principal is conveyed to a charitable organization.

b. Charitable gifts are placed into the trust until a certain dollar amount is achieved and is then transferred to a specified charitable organization.

c. The income of a trust fund goes to a charitable organization for a specified time, with the principal then being conveyed to a different beneficiary.

d. A charity conveys money to a trust that generates income for the charity's use in its various projects.

LO 19-3

28. The estate of Nancy Hanks reports the following information:

Value of estate assets	$8,400,000
Conveyed to spouse	700,000
Conveyed to children	100,000
Conveyed to charities	420,000
Funeral expenses	50,000
Administrative expenses	20,000
Debts	110,000

What is the taxable estate value?

a. $7,070,000

b. $7,100,000

c. $7,180,000

d. $7,420,000

LO 19-3

29. An estate has the following income:

Rental income	$5,000
Interest income	3,000
Dividend income	1,000

The interest income was immediately conveyed to the appropriate beneficiary. The dividends were given to charity as per the decedent's will. What is the taxable income of the estate?

a. $4,400

b. $5,000

c. $8,000

d. $8,400

LO 19-1, 19-4, 19-6

30. Define each of the following terms:

a. Will

b. Estate

c. Intestate

d. Probate laws

e. Trust

f. *Inter vivos* trust

g. Charitable remainder trust

h. Remainderman

i. Executor

j. Homestead allowance

LO 19-1

31. Answer each of the following questions:

a. What are the objectives of probate laws?

b. What tasks does the executor of an estate perform?

c. What assets are normally included as estate properties?

d. What claims have priority to the distributions made by an estate?

LO 19-1, 19-2, 19-4, 19-6

32. The will of Josh O'Brien has the following stipulations:

Antique collection goes to Ilsa Lunn.

All money in the First Savings Bank goes to Richard Blaine.

Cash of $9,000 goes to Nelson Tucker.

All remaining assets are put into a trust fund with the income going to Lucy Van Jones. At her death, the principal is to be conveyed to Howard Amadeus.

Identify the following:

a. Remainderman
b. Trustor
c. Demonstrative legacy
d. General legacy
e. Specific legacy
f. Life tenant
g. Testator

LO 19-2

33. Marie Hardy's will has the following provisions:

"I leave the cash balance deposited in the First National Bank (up to a total of $50,000) to Jack Abrams. I leave $18,000 cash to Suzanne Benton. I leave 1,000 shares of Coca-Cola Company stock to Cindy Cheng. I leave my house to Dennis Davis. I leave all of my other assets and properties to Wilbur N. Ed."

a. Assume that the estate has the following assets: $41,000 cash in the First National Bank, $16,000 cash in the New Hampshire Savings and Loan, 800 shares of Coca-Cola stock, 1,100 shares of Xerox stock, a house, and other property valued at $13,000. What distributions will be made from this estate?

b. Assume that the estate has the following assets: $55,000 cash in the First National Bank, $6,000 cash in the New Hampshire Savings and Loan, 1,200 shares of Coca-Cola stock, 600 shares of Xerox stock, and other property valued at $22,000. What distributions will be made from this estate?

LO 19-3

34. Zac Peterson's estate reports the following information:

Value of estate assets	$2,300,000
Conveyed to spouse	1,000,000
Conveyed to children	230,000
Conveyed to trust fund for benefit of cousin	500,000
Conveyed to charities	260,000
Funeral expenses	23,000
Administrative expenses	41,000
Debts	246,000

What is the taxable estate value?

LO 19-3

35. Donna Stober's estate has the following assets (all figures approximate fair value):

Investments in stocks and bonds	$1,400,000
House	700,000
Cash	70,000
Investment land	60,000
Automobiles (three rare vehicles)	51,000
Other assets	100,000

The house, cash, and other assets are left to the decedent's spouse. The investment land is contributed to a charitable organization. The automobiles are to be given to the decedent's brother. The investments in stocks and bonds are to be put into a trust fund. The income generated by this trust will go to the decedent's spouse annually until all of the couple's children have reached the age of 25. At that time, the trust will be divided evenly among the children.

The following amounts are paid prior to distribution and settlement of the estate: funeral expenses of $20,000 and estate administration expenses of $10,000.

What value is to be reported as the taxable estate for federal estate tax purposes?

LO 19-3

36. During 2019, an estate generated income of $20,000:

Rental income	$9,000
Interest income	6,000
Dividend income	5,000

The interest income is conveyed immediately to the beneficiary stated in the decedent's will. The dividends are given to the decedent's church.

What is the taxable income of the estate?

LO 19-4, 19-5

37. The executor of Rose Shield's estate listed the following properties (at fair value):

Cash	$300,000
Life insurance receivable	200,000
Investments in stocks and bonds	100,000
Rental property	90,000
Personal property	130,000

a. Prepare journal entries to record the property held by Ms. Shield's estate and then each of the following transactions that occur in the months following the decedent's death:

(1) Claims of $80,000 are made against the estate for various debts incurred before the decedent's death.

(2) Interest of $12,000 is received from bonds held by the estate. Of this amount, $5,000 had been earned prior to death.

(3) Ordinary repairs costing $6,000 are made to the rental property.

(4) All debts ($80,000) are paid.

(5) Stocks recorded in the estate at $16,000 are sold for $19,000 cash.

(6) Rental income of $14,000 is collected. Of this amount, $2,000 had been earned prior to the decedent's death.

(7) Cash of $6,000 is distributed to Jim Arness, an income beneficiary.

(8) The proceeds from the life insurance policy are collected and the money is immediately distributed to Amanda Blake as specified in the decedent's will.

(9) Funeral expenses of $10,000 are paid.

b. Prepare in proper form a charge and discharge statement.

LO 19-4, 19-5

38. The executor of Gina Purcell's estate has recorded the following information:

Assets discovered at death (at fair value):	
Cash	$600,000
Life insurance receivable	200,000
Investments:	
Walt Disney Company	11,000
Polaroid Corporation	27,000
Ford Motor Company	34,000
Dell Inc.	32,000
Rental property	300,000
Cash outflows:	
Funeral expenses	$ 21,000
Executor fees	12,000
Ordinary repairs of rental property	2,000
Debts	81,000
Distribution of income to income beneficiary	4,000
Distribution to charitable remainder trust	300,000
Cash inflows:	
Sale of Polaroid stock	$ 30,000
Rental income ($4,000 earned prior to death)	11,000
Dividend income ($2,000 declared prior to death)	12,000
Life insurance proceeds	200,000

Debts of $17,000 still remain to be paid. The Dell shares have been conveyed to the appropriate beneficiary. Assume that Ms. Purcell's will stated that all executor fees are to be paid from principal.

Prepare an interim charge and discharge statement for this estate.

LO 19-4, 19-5

39. Jerry Tasch's will has the following provisions:
    - $150,000 in cash goes to Thomas Thorne.
    - All shares of Coca-Cola go to Cindy Phillips.
    - Residence goes to Kevin Simmons.
    - All other estate assets are to be liquidated with the resulting cash going to the First Church of Freedom, Missouri.

    Prepare journal entries for the following transactions:

    a. Discovered the following assets (at fair value):

Cash	$ 80,000
Interest receivable	6,000
Life insurance policy	300,000
Residence	200,000
Shares of Coca-Cola Company	50,000
Shares of Polaroid Corporation	110,000
Shares of Ford Motor Company	140,000

    b. Collected interest of $7,000.
    c. Paid funeral expenses of $20,000.
    d. Discovered debts of $40,000.
    e. Located an additional savings account of $12,000.
    f. Conveyed title to the residence to Kevin Simmons.
    g. Collected life insurance policy.
    h. Discovered additional debts of $60,000. Paid debts totaling $100,000.
    i. Conveyed cash of $150,000 to appropriate beneficiary.
    j. Sold the shares of Polaroid for $112,000.
    k. Paid administrative expenses of $10,000.

LO 19-4, 19-5

40. After the death of Lennie Pope, his will was read. It contained the following provisions:
    - $110,000 in cash goes to decedent's brother, Ned Pope.
    - Residence and other personal property go to his sister, Sue Pope.
    - Proceeds from the sale of Ford stock go to uncle, Harwood Pope.
    - $300,000 goes into a charitable remainder trust.
    - All other estate assets are to be liquidated with the cash going to Victoria Jones.

    a. Prepare journal entries for the following transactions that subsequently occur:
    (1) Discovered the following assets (at fair value):

Cash	$ 19,000
Certificates of deposit	90,000
Dividends receivable	3,000
Life insurance policy	450,000
Residence and personal effects	470,000
Shares of Ford Motor Company	72,000
Shares of Xerox Corporation	97,000

    (2) Collected life insurance policy.
    (3) Collected dividends of $4,000.
    (4) Discovered debts of $71,000.
    (5) Conveyed title to the residence to Sue Pope along with the decedent's personal effects.
    (6) Discovered title to land valued at $15,000.
    (7) Discovered additional debts of $37,000. Paid all of the debts totaling $108,000.
    (8) Paid funeral expenses of $31,000.
    (9) Conveyed cash of $110,000 to Ned Pope.

(10) Sold the shares of Ford for $81,000.

(11) Paid administrative expenses of $16,000.

(12) Made the appropriate payment to Harwood Pope.

b. Prepare a charge and discharge statement.

LO 19-4, 19-5

41. James Albemarle created a trust fund at the beginning of 2019. The income from this fund will go to his son Edward. When Edward reaches the age of 25, the principal of the fund will be conveyed to United Charities of Cleveland. Mr. Albemarle specified that 75 percent of trustee fees are to be paid from principal. Terry Jones, CPA, is the trustee.

    Prepare all necessary journal entries for the trust to record the following transactions:

    a. James Albemarle transferred cash of $300,000, stocks worth $200,000, and rental property valued at $150,000 to the trustee of this fund.

    b. Immediately invested cash of $260,000 in bonds issued by the U.S. government. Commissions of $3,000 are paid on this transaction.

    c. Incurred permanent repairs of $7,000 so that the property can be rented. Payment is made immediately.

    d. Received dividends of $4,000. Of this amount, $1,000 had been declared prior to the creation of the trust fund.

    e. Paid insurance expense of $2,000 on the rental property.

    f. Received rental income of $8,000.

    g. Paid $4,000 from the trust for trustee services rendered.

    h. Conveyed cash of $5,000 to Edward Albemarle.

LO 19-4, 19-5

42. Henry O'Donnell created an *inter vivos* trust fund. He owns a large department store in Higgins, Utah. He also owns a tract of land adjacent to the store used as an extra parking lot when the store is having a sale and during the Christmas season. O'Donnell expects the land to appreciate in value and eventually be sold for an office complex or additional stores.

    O'Donnell places this land into a charitable lead trust, which will hold the land for 10 years, until O'Donnell's son is 21. At that time, title will transfer to the son. The store will pay rent to use the land during the interim. The income generated each year from this usage will be given to a local church. The land is currently valued at $320,000.

    During the first year of this arrangement, the trustee records the following cash transactions:

Cash inflows:	
Rental income	$60,000
Cash outflows:	
Insurance	$ 4,000
Property taxes	6,000
Paving (considered an extraordinary repair)	4,000
Maintenance	8,000
Distribution to income beneficiary	30,000

    Prepare all journal entries for this trust fund including the entry to create the trust.

Develop Your Skills

RESEARCH CASE 1

CPA skills

The CPA firm of Simon, Winslow, and Tate has been approached by a client who is interested in information about the possibility of establishing a minor's Section 2503(c) trust.

Go to the website www.finaid.org/savings/2503ctrust.phtml. Alternatively, use an Internet search engine to find other analyses of a Section 2503(c) trust.

Required

Based on the results of this search, write a memo for the client outlining the requirements, design, advantages, and disadvantages of a minor's Section 2503(c) trust so the client can make an informed decision.

RESEARCH CASE 2

A staff employee for the CPA firm of O'Brien, Leahy, and Sweeney is currently preparing Form 1041 as an income tax return for an estate. The staff employee knows that the estate is allowed a deduction for income distributions to beneficiaries up to the amount of the estate's distributable net income (DNI) for the period. However, the employee is not certain how to compute the exact amount of this deduction.

Go to the website www.irs.gov. Do a search for "Instruction 1041" to get the instruction information for estate and trust income taxes published by the IRS.

Required

Read the information provided, and write a memo to the employee explaining (in general terms) how to calculate this deduction.

RESEARCH CASE 3

A client, Beth Voga, asks for advice. She tells you that her grandmother, a widowed resident of Montana, has no will. She asks whether any portion of her grandmother's estate will pass to her (Beth's) cousins, whom her grandmother despises.

Required

Use an Internet search engine to locate the Montana version of the Uniform Probate Code. Then briefly advise Ms. Voga, answering her specific question. Also advise her on the necessity of a will for her grandmother.

ANALYSIS CASE 1

Use an Internet search engine to locate an explanation of the benefits of a grantor retained annuity trust.

Required

Write a memo describing the circumstances that would make this type of trust most advantageous.

ANALYSIS CASE 2

A law firm is preparing to file a federal estate tax return (Form 706). The estate's executor has elected to use the alternate valuation date. The partner in charge of filing this return is not certain about all of the ramifications of having chosen to use this alternate date.

Go to the website www.irs.gov. Do a search for "Instruction 706" to get the instruction information published by the IRS for federal estate taxes.

Required

Read the information provided, and write a memo to the partner outlining the information the IRS provides as to the significance of the alternate valuation date.

Index

G

J

Q

R

W

Y

Z